WALLER & WIL[illegible] Criminal La[illegible]

CW01590148

Text and Cases

Twelfth Edition

The previous editions of this book were published as:

First edition: *Cases and Materials in Criminal Law* (1962)
P Brett and P L Waller

Second edition: *Cases and Materials in Criminal Law* (1965)
P Brett and P L Waller

Third edition: *Criminal Law Cases and Text* (1971)
P Brett and P L Waller

Fourth edition: *Criminal Law Text and Cases* (1978)
P Brett and P L Waller

Fifth edition: *Brett and Waller's Criminal Law Text and Cases* (1983)
C R Williams

Sixth edition: *Brett, Waller and Williams Criminal Law Text and Cases* (1989)
L Waller and C R Williams

Seventh edition: *Brett, Waller and Williams Criminal Law Text and Cases* (1993)
L Waller and C R Williams

Eighth edition: *Brett, Waller and Williams Criminal Law Text and Cases* (1997)
L Waller and C R Williams

Ninth edition: *Criminal Law Text and Cases* (2001)
L Waller and C R Williams

Tenth edition: *Criminal Law Text and Cases* (2005)
L Waller and C R Williams

Eleventh edition: *Waller & Williams Criminal Law Text and Cases* (2009)
L Waller and C R Williams

WALLER & WILLIAMS
Criminal Law

Text and Cases

Twelfth Edition

Thalia Anthony

BA (Hons), LLB (Hons), MCrim, PhD (Syd)
Senior Lecturer, Faculty of Law, University of Technology, Sydney

Penny Crofts

BEc, LLB (Hons), LLM (Syd), MPhil (Cantab), PhD (Griffith)
Senior Lecturer, Faculty of Law, University of Technology, Sydney

Thomas Crofts

LLB (Hons) (Lond), LLM (Würzburg), Dr.iur. (Frankfurt/O)
Associate Professor and Director, Sydney Institute of Criminology, Faculty of Law, University of Sydney

Stephen Gray

BA (Hons), LLB (Hons), LLM (Melb), PhD (Monash)
Senior Lecturer, Faculty of Law, Monash University
Barrister and Solicitor, Supreme Court, Northern Territory

Arlie Loughnan

BA (Hons), LLB (Hons), LLM (NYU), PhD (Lond)
ARC Postdoctoral Research Fellow, Faculty of Law, University of Sydney

Bronwyn Naylor

BA (Hons), LLB (Hons), LLM (Monash), MPhil (Crim), PhD (Cantab)
Associate Professor, Faculty of Law, Monash University

LexisNexis Butterworths
Australia
2013

LexisNexis

AUSTRALIA	LexisNexis Butterworths 475–495 Victoria Avenue, Chatswood NSW 2067 On the internet at: www.lexisnexis.com.au
ARGENTINA	LexisNexis Argentina, Buenos Aires
AUSTRIA	LexisNexis Verlag ARD Orac GmbH & Co KG, Vienna
BRAZIL	LexisNexis Latin America, Sao Paulo
CANADA	LexisNexis Canada, Markham, Ontario
CHILE	LexisNexis Chile, Santiago
CHINA	LexisNexis China, Beijing, Shanghai
CZECH REPUBLIC	Nakladatelství Orac sro, Prague
FRANCE	LexisNexis SA, Paris
GERMANY	LexisNexis Germany, Frankfurt
HONG KONG	LexisNexis Hong Kong, Hong Kong
HUNGARY	HVG-Orac, Budapest
INDIA	LexisNexis, New Delhi
ITALY	Dott A Giuffrè Editore SpA, Milan
JAPAN	LexisNexis Japan KK, Tokyo
KOREA	LexisNexis, Seoul
MALAYSIA	LexisNexis Malaysia Sdn Bhd, Petaling Jaya, Selangor
NEW ZEALAND	LexisNexis, Wellington
POLAND	Wydawnictwo Prawnicze LexisNexis, Warsaw
SINGAPORE	LexisNexis, Singapore
SOUTH AFRICA	LexisNexis Butterworths, Durban
SWITZERLAND	Staempfli Verlag AG, Berne
TAIWAN	LexisNexis, Taiwan
UNITED KINGDOM	LexisNexis UK, London, Edinburgh
USA	LexisNexis Group, New York, New York LexisNexis, Miamisburg, Ohio

National Library of Australia Cataloguing-in-Publication entry

Author:	Anthony, Thalia.
Title:	Waller & Williams Criminal Law: Text and Cases.
Edition:	12th edition.
ISBN:	9780409333961 (pbk). 9780409333978 (ebk).
Notes:	Includes index.
Subjects:	Criminal law — Australia.
Other Authors/Contributors:	Crofts, Penny; Crofts, Thomas (Wayne Thomas); Gray, Stephen; Loughnan, Arlie; Naylor, Bronwyn Glynis.
Dewey Number:	345.94.

1st ed, 1962; 2nd ed, 1965; 3rd ed, 1971; 4th ed, 1978; 5th ed, 1983; 6th ed, 1989; 7th ed, 1993; 8th ed, 1997; 9th ed, 2001; 10th ed, 2005; 11th ed, 2009.

Typeset in Adobe Caslon Pro and Trade Gothic.

Printed in Australia.

Visit LexisNexis Butterworths at www.lexisnexis.com.au

Contents

Detailed Contents

Preface

This is the twelfth edition and fiftieth anniversary of this book. The first edition was published in 1962, entitled Brett and Waller's *Cases and Materials in Criminal Law*. It was the product of an experiment by Peter Brett and Louis Waller to teach criminal law in problem-based classes in the Law School of the University of Melbourne, where the subject was one of four core units in the second year of the LLB. The course and the book were elements in the development of criminal law as an esteemed discipline in legal teaching and scholarship, and in the practice of law.

After Peter Brett's untimely death in 1975, the fourth edition, published in 1978, was prepared by Louis Waller. He invited Bob Williams, the second-named author, to join him in preparing the fifth edition. That edition, published in 1983, was prepared and edited by Bob Williams alone. The sixth, seventh, eighth, ninth, tenth and eleventh editions were written and edited by both authors. Professor Waller is particularly well known for his work in medical and criminal law. He was Professor of Law at Monash University from 1965 until 2000, and Dean of the Law Faculty from 1968 to 1970, and he continues to contribute to the life of the faculty as Emeritus Professor. Professor Waller was appointed an Officer in the Order of Australia in 1989. Professor Williams is a member of the Victorian Bar, and a Fellow of the Academy of the Social Sciences in Australia. He was a Professor of Law at Monash University from 1987 to 2010 and Dean of the Law Faculty from 1988 to 1998. Professional appointments have included Member, Mental Health Review Board; Member, Victorian Civil and Administrative Tribunal, Guardianship List; and Assistant Editor (Criminal Cases), Victorian Reports. Professors Waller and Williams have now retired, with recognition from students, academics, members of the legal profession and the community for their services to legal scholarship and justice.

We were honoured to be invited to update this book for the 50-year anniversary edition. Many of us used the text when we were undergraduate law students. We all now prescribe the text for our Criminal Law classes. In preparing this edition, we have drawn upon our experiences teaching criminal law and the comments and criticisms of colleagues in law schools, and students who have used the book in their classes. We have included new leading cases from the principal appellate courts in Australia, and legislative provisions which have effected most significant changes to the fabric of the criminal law. We have revised some comments on, and evaluations of, developed and developing jurisprudence in this vital part of the law, and we have deleted some cases which, in our judgment, no longer figure in the modern law. We have drawn upon our own research interests in criminal law and legal theory to enrich the commentary and analysis and to highlight the social, political and historical context within which the criminal law operates.

This book was the first of its kind published in Australia. After 50 years, it has kept its place in current scholarship and in the hands of those whose legal education is progressing in the law schools in Australia. We consider that is the case because this book unites the principal authoritative sources of the criminal law and a critical appraisal and evaluation of its doctrines. We are pleased that the book continues to be used by teachers of law and by their students.

Our publishers have given us their stalwart support. We value it highly. In particular, Serena Cubie, Commissioning Editor at LexisNexis Butterworths, has provided every assistance and encouragement to ensure the timely completion of the highest quality book. We have also appreciated the support of our colleagues. What we have done has been made possible by the confidence and the affection shown to us, always, by our families.

The law stated in this book takes account of materials available to us on 30 August 2013.

Thalia Anthony, University of Technology, Sydney
Penny Crofts, University of Technology, Sydney
Thomas Crofts, University of Sydney
Stephen Gray, Monash University
Arlie Loughnan, University of Sydney
Bronwyn Naylor, Monash University

30 August 2013

Acknowledgments

The authors and publishers are grateful to the holders of copyright in material from which extracts appear in this work. While every care has been taken to establish and acknowledge copyright, the publishers tender their apologies for any accidental infringement. The publishers would be pleased to come to a suitable arrangement with the rightful owners in each case.

About the Authors

Dr Thalia Anthony is a Senior Lecturer at the Faculty of Law, University of Technology, Sydney. She is a specialist in criminal justice, particularly as it relates to Indigenous people. She has published widely on criminal justice, criminology, legal history and Indigenous legal issues, and has recently published *Indigenous People, Crime and Punishment* (Routledge). She contributes to public debates, senate inquires and United Nations committees on these issues. Thalia works closely with Aboriginal legal services, the Jumbunna Indigenous legal clinic at the University of Technology, Sydney, and conducts ongoing fieldwork in Northern Territory Indigenous communities. Thalia has produced a number of textbooks that critically engage students, such as the *Critical Criminology Companion* (Hawkins Press), *Indigenous Legal Issues* (Thomson) and *Connecting with Law* (Oxford University Press).

Dr Penny Crofts is a Senior Lecturer at the Faculty of Law, University of Technology, Sydney. She lectures in criminal law, criminology, jurisprudence and wickedness and vice. Penny researches criminal law theory, particularly legal constructions of wickedness, and has recently published *Wickedness and Crime: Laws of Homicide and Malice* (Routledge). She is also the author of *Criminal Law Elements* (LexisNexis) and has published extensively on the regulation of the sex industry. Photo by Cath Muscat.

Dr Thomas Crofts is Associate Professor and Director of the Sydney Institute of Criminology in the Faculty of Law at the University of Sydney. His research in criminal law, criminology and criminal justice centres on criminalisation and criminal responsibility with a particular focus on the criminal responsibility of, and for, children, comparative criminal law, criminal law reform and the role of labelling. Thomas has published in English and German in these fields in national and international journals. He is the co-author of *Principles of Criminal Law in Queensland and Western*

Australia (LBC, 2011) and *The Criminal Codes: Commentary and Materials* (LBC, 6th ed, 2009), and author of *Criminal Law in Queensland and Western Australia* (LexisNexis, 2009). In 2011 he was awarded the Australian and New Zealand Society of Criminology's inaugural Adam Sutton Crime Prevention Award. Currently, he is conducting research funded by the Australian Institute of Criminology into young people's perceptions of 'sexting'.

Dr Stephen Gray is a Senior Lecturer in the Law Faculty at Monash University. His research interests include criminal law, Indigenous people and the law, Malaysian law and politics, and intellectual property and Indigenous art. His PhD concerned the 'stolen wages' issue in the Northern Territory. Stephen lived and worked in Darwin for 16 years, and was a member of the Northern Territory Law Reform Committee from 1994 until 2005. His published books include *Criminal Laws Northern Territory* (Federation Press, 2nd ed, 2012), as well as a novel, *The Artist is a Thief* (Allen & Unwin, 2001) and a non-fiction work on Aboriginal 'protection' entitled *The Protectors* (Allen & Unwin, 2011).

Dr Arlie Loughnan is an ARC Postdoctoral Research Fellow in the Law Faculty, University of Sydney. Her research project is entitled *Responsibility in Criminal Law* (No DE130100418). She is the author of *Manifest Madness: Mental Incapacity in Criminal Law* (OUP, 2012). Arlie is co-editor (with Dr Shae McCrystal) of *Sydney Law Review* and the Sydney Institute of Criminology's journal, *Current Issues in Criminal Justice* (with Dr Murray Lee). She has been a member of the New South Wales Law Society's Criminal Law Committee since 2009.

Dr Bronwyn Naylor is an Associate Professor in the Law Faculty at Monash University. She has been teaching, researching and publishing in criminal law, corrections, regulation, and criminal justice and gender for over 20 years and is a Chair of the Monash University Human Research Ethics Committee. She has research grants on defences to homicide, criminal records, human rights in places of detention, and aspects of imprisonment, has consulted to the Victorian Law Reform Commission on law reforms on defences to homicide, sexual assault, and abortion law, and is co-author (with Bernadette McSherry) of *Australian Criminal Laws: Critical Perspectives* (OUP, 2004).

Table of Cases

References are to paragraph numbers
Case extracts are in **bold**

B

H

N

O

P

Q

R

Table of Statutes

Those provisions reprinted in whole or at length are distinguished by E
References are to paragraphs

AUSTRALIAN CAPITAL TERRITORY

NEW SOUTH WALES

NORTHERN TERRITORY

QUEENSLAND

SOUTH AUSTRALIA

TASMANIA

VICTORIA

WESTERN AUSTRALIA

ENGLAND

CANADA

INDIA

INTERNATIONAL

ISRAEL

ITALY

NEW ZEALAND

UNITED STATES OF AMERICA

Abbreviations

A	Atlantic Reporter (USA)
AC	Appeal Cases (UK)
A Crim R	Australian Criminal Reports
All ER	All England Law Reports (UK)
All ER Rep	All England Law Reports, Reprint
All ER Rep Ext	All England Law Reports, Reprint, Extension Volumes
ALJR	Australian Law Journal Reports
ALR	Australian Law Reports
ALJ	Australian Law Journal
Am Dec	American Decisions (1760–1870) (USA)
Ann Dig Pub Int Law Cas	Annual Digest and Reports of Public International Law Cases (UK)
Aust and NZ Journal of Criminology	Australian and New Zealand Journal of Criminology
Aust Bar Rev	Australian Bar Review
B & Ad	Barnewell & Adolphus' King's Bench Reports (UK)
Bl Comm W	Blackstone, *Commentaries on the Laws of England* (1765–69)*
c	Chapter (of Parliament) (UK)
Camb LJ	Cambridge Law Journal (UK)
Canb LR	Canberra Law Review
Car & P	Carrington & Payne's Nisi Prius Reports (1823–1841) (UK)
CCC	Canadian Criminal Cases (Canada)
CCC (2d)	Canadian Criminal Cases (2nd Series)
Cl & F, Cl & Fin	Clark and Finnelly's Reports (UK)
C & K	Carrington and Kirwan's Reports (UK)
CLR	Commonwealth Law Reports

CLJ	Criminal Law Journal
Cmnd	Command Paper (UK)
Coke, Co Inst	Sir Edward Coke CJ, *Coke's Institutes of the Lawes of England* (1628–44)*
Colum L Rev	Columbia Law Review
Cowp	Cowper's King's Bench Reports (UK)
Cox CC	Cox's Criminal Cases (UK)
CR (3d)	Criminal Reports, 3rd Series (Canada)
Cr App Rep	Criminal Appeal Reports (UK)
Crim LJ	Criminal Law Journal
Crim LR	Criminal Law Review (UK)
Dears & Bell	Dearsley and Bell's Crown Cases Reserved (UK)
Dears CC	Dearsley's Crown Cases Reserved (UK)
DCR (NSW)	District Court Reports (New South Wales)
DLR	Dominion Law Reports (Canada)
ER	English Reports UK)
East, East PC	Sir Edward Hyde East, *A Treatise of the Pleas of the Crown* (1803)*
Fed 2d	Federal Reporter (2nd Series) (USA)
Fed Cas	Federal Cases (USA)
F & F	Foster & Finlayson's Reports (UK)
Foster, Crown Law	Sir Michael Foster, *Crown Cases and Discourse on A Few Branches of the Crown Law*, 3rd ed, M Dodson (ed) (1792)*
Geo II	English statute passed during reign of King George II (followed by chapter reference)
Geo 3, Geo III	English statute passed during reign of King George III
Geo IV	English statute passed during reign of King George IV
Geo 5, Geo V	English statute passed during reign of King George V
Hale, Hale PC	Sir Mathew Hale, *History of the Pleas of the Crown* (1736)*
Hare, Const Law	J I Clark Hare, *American Constitutional Law* (1889)*
Harv LR	Harvard Law Review (USA)
Hawkins, Pleas of the Crown	William Hawkins, *A Treatise of the Pleas of the Crown* (1716–21)*

Hist Crim Law	Sir James Fitzjames Stephen, *The History of the Criminal Law of England* (1883)*
HL	House of Lords (UK)
How St Tr	State Trials (1163–1820) (UK)
JLM, Jo Law Med	Journal of Law and Medicine
J L & Soc	Journal of Law and Society (UK)
KB	King's Bench (UK)
L & C	Leigh & Cave's Crown Cases Reserved (1861–1865) (UK)
Ld Raym	Lord Raymond's King's Bench and Common Pleas Reports (UK)
Lew CC	Lewin's Crown Cases Reserved (UK)
LQR	Law Quarterly Review (UK)
LR CCR	Law Reports, Crown Cases Reserved (UK)
MLR, Mod LR	Modern Law Review (UK)
Mo	Missouri Reports, Missouri Supreme Court (USA)
Mon LR	Monash University Law Review
MULR	Melbourne University Law Review
M & W	Meeson and Welsby's Exchequer Reports (UK)
NC	North Carolina Reports (USA)
N Mex	New Mexico Reports (USA)
NZLJ	New Zealand Law Journal (NZ)
NSWLR	New South Wales Law Reports
NYS 2d	New York Supplement (2nd Series, 1938) (USA)
NZLR	New Zealand Law Reports (NZ)
P 2d	Pacific Reporter, Second Series (USA)
Pa, Pa St	Pennsylvania State Reports (USA)
Pac	Pacific Reporter (USA)
PC	Privy Council (UK)
Proc Med-Leg Soc Vic	Proceedings of the Medico-Legal Society of Victoria
QB	Queen's Bench (UK)
OR	Ontario Reports (Canada)
QBD	Queen's Bench Division (UK)
Qd R	Queensland Reports

Rhod & Nyas LR	Rhodesia and Nyasaland Law Reports (Southern Rhodesia 1956–1964)
SA	South African Law Reports (SA)
SASR	South Australian State Reports
SCR	Canada: Supreme Court Reports
	South Africa: Juta's Supreme Court Reports, Cape of Good Hope
SE	South Eastern Reporter (USA)
St Tr	State Trials and Proceedings (UK)
St R Qd	State Reports, Queensland
Syd LR	Sydney Law Review
Tas SR	Tasmanian State Reports
Univ Tas LR	University of Tasmania Law Review
Vict	English statute passed during reign of Queen Victoria
VLR	Victorian Law Reports
VR	Victorian Reports
WLR	Weekly Law Reports (UK)
WN (NSW)	Weekly Notes, New South Wales
Wigmore, Treatise on Evidence	*Treatise on the Anglo-American System of Evidence in Trials at Common Law* (1940)*
Yale LJ	Yale Law Journal (USA)

* See Bibliography for full publication details.

PART 1

Introduction

Foundations

CHAPTER 1

THE CRIMINAL LAW

1.1 Everyone knows something about crime and the criminal law. It is impossible to live in today's Australia and not hear, see and read about these subjects every day. Both in fact and in fiction, the commission of offences, the apprehension of their perpetrators, their prosecutions and their punishments are constantly put before us. Apprehensiveness about crimes affects the community. Some of us know what it is to be a victim of crime, either personally or via our families, or among our friends and acquaintances. The criminal law is that division of the law which comes most readily to mind when a lay person is asked what she or he knows about law and the legal system. It is, of course, the case that the criminal law is only part of the law. As an American jurist put it: 'The criminal law represents the pathology of civilization': M R Cohen, (1940) 149 *Yale LJ* 987 at 1025.

Nonetheless, the remark made much earlier by an English jurist, Sir James Fitzjames Stephen, in the introduction to his magisterial work, *The History of the Criminal Law of England* (1883), continues to have great force, both for lay persons and for students of the law (at I.ix):

> No department of law can claim greater moral importance than that which, with the detail and precision necessary for legal purposes, stigmatises certain kinds of conduct as crimes, the commission of which involves, if detected, indelible infamy and the loss, as the case may be, of life, property or personal liberty.

This book sets out to examine these ideas and to introduce students to the now complex body of laws that fall into the category of criminal law.

WHAT IS A CRIME?

Introduction

1.2 Professor Glanville Williams defines a crime in the following terms: 'A crime (or offence) is a legal wrong that can be followed by criminal proceedings which may result in punishment': *Textbook of Criminal Law*, 2nd ed, Stevens & Sons, 1983, p 27. Professor Williams considers and rejects the charge that this definition is circular. In the Australian legal system, and in other legal systems based upon the English model, it is possible to identify and describe criminal proceedings and to distinguish them from civil proceedings. This is a 'positivist' definition of criminal law, where the focus is on the form of a law — whether it has been correctly made — rather than its substance. This positivist definition of crime appears clear and straightforward. However, there are shortcomings.

Underlying Williams' proposed definition of 'crime' is an assumption of a clear distinction between civil and criminal law:

> One way of distinguishing criminal cases from civil is generally, and subject to exceptions and various hybrids, by reference to the procedure adopted — public prosecutor, conviction and sentence — rather than by reference to the content of the law itself [A Ashworth, 'Is the Criminal Law and Lost Cause?' (2000) *Law Quarterly Review* 225 at 232].

As this indicates, it is not the nature of the prohibited conduct that distinguishes prohibitions on that conduct from other legal prohibitions (such as torts, or civil wrongs). Rather, it is criminal procedure (with, for instance, its distinctive standard of proof) that is crucial to the scope of the criminal law.

Williams' definition also points to 'punishment' as a means of distinguishing crime from civil wrongs. Many laws prohibit conduct, but only the criminal law has the power to impose punishment in the name of the State following a verdict of guilt. 'Punishment' (which typically follows from conviction of a crime) is different from other unpleasant consequences (such as being required to pay compensation) which may follow as a result of civil law proceedings. Professor Herbert Hart, a famous positivist, in 'Prolegomenon to the Principles of Punishment' (in H L A Hart, *Punishment and Responsibility*, Oxford University Press, 1968, pp 4–5) defines the standard or central case of punishment in terms of five elements:

> (i) It must involve pain or other consequences normally considered unpleasant.
> (ii) It must be for an offence against legal rules.
> (iii) It must be of an actual or supposed offender for his offence.
> (iv) It must be intentionally administered by human beings other than the offender.
> (v) It must be imposed and administered by an authority constituted by a legal system against which the offence is committed.

Though civil remedies such as exemplary damages and injunctions have coercive aspects, from the viewpoint of legal classification they are not criminal proceedings as they do not flow from a determination of guilt following criminal proceedings. The Customs Act 1901 (Cth) and Trade Practices Act 1974 (Cth) contain a range of similar civil penalties but they are not regarded as criminal offences.

The positivist definition of crime is problematic in part because it rests on an assumption of a clear distinction between civil and criminal law, and this distinction is blurred. In a High Court decision, Hayne J observed that the distinction is 'at best unstable' (*CEO Customs v Labrador Liquor Wholesale Pty Ltd* (2003) 216 CLR 161 at 198):

> It seeks to divide the litigious world into only two parts when, in truth, that world is more complex and varied than such a classification acknowledges. There are proceedings with both civil and criminal characteristics: for example, proceedings for a civil penalty under companies and trade practices legislation. The purposes of these proceedings include purposes of deterrence, and the consequences can be large and punishing [footnotes omitted].

Moreover, the definition focuses on *formal* aspects of law, particularly procedures, rather than the *substance* of a law; that is, Williams' definition is *descriptive* rather than *normative*. It does not consider the question of why certain behaviour is criminalised, and how this can be justified by the State. The positivist definition of crime conceals the deeply contested normative character of criminal law. This is in accordance with positivist assertions that law and morality should be separate. However, as argued below, the relationship between law and morality is more complex than that proposed by positivists.

Justifications for criminalisation or 'the aims of the criminal law'

1.3 At this point it is useful to consider briefly what are often termed 'the aims of the criminal law'. The phrase is a convenient one but it is apt to be misleading. Particular criminal offences have either developed gradually as part of the common law or have been created by statute. The present criminal law, with its myriad offences, is not a coherent body of law seeking to achieve one particular aim. Nevertheless, there are some general considerations which have swayed both judges and legislators in arriving at a decision whether a particular type of transaction will or will not be made criminally punishable.

Fitzjames Stephen thought that the real aim of the criminal law was to provide an organised means for controlling the passion of revenge. Indeed, he compared the role played by the criminal law, in relation to this passion, to that played by the institution of marriage relative to the sexual appetite. His theme was thus a simple one — that unless a community provides for the punishment of offenders, the people injured by offences would take matters into their own hands to the general detriment of the community. In short, blood feuds would run riot. This view, which has achieved a great deal of popularity, is based in part upon the notion that the criminal law developed from a primitive means of dealing with homicide. It was said that as a community became organised, it replaced the institution of the blood feud by an organised system under which the killer was forced to compensate the relatives of the deceased; and that this system of enforced monetary compensation in turn gave rise to a system of punishment imposed by the state. A similar argument was advanced to account for the development of the lesser assaults and of theft. More recent research, however, has shown that homicide was not the 'original' crime and that all primitive communities have had some system of providing for community punishment of those who commit incest or witchcraft. In any event, this theory is not of great assistance in determining how to deal with the concrete problems raised by specific offences.

1.4 It is for the lawmaker (the legislature and the courts) to determine within any given legal system what acts should be classified as criminal: see the comments of Lord Atkin in *Proprietary Articles Trade Association v Attorney-General (Canada)* [1931] AC 310 at 324. Theoretically, there is no limit on what kind of conduct can be made criminal. There are three major justifications for criminalisation in classic accounts of criminal law. These justifications are at times in conflict with each other.

The prevention of harm

1.5 The prevention of harm forms the basis for the reach and limits of criminal law. This idea was espoused by the liberal philosopher John Stuart Mill in *On Liberty* (1859), Penguin, Harmondsworth, United Kingdom, 1974. Articulated as the 'harm principle', restrictions on individual liberty must be curtailed and are justifiable only in order to prevent harm to others (p 68):

> [T]he only purpose for which power can be rightfully exercised over any member of a civilized community, against his [or her] own will, is to prevent harm to others. His [or her] own good, either physical or moral, is not a sufficient warrant. He [or she] cannot rightfully be compelled to do or forbear because it will be better for him [or her] to do so, because it will make him [or her] happier, because, in the opinion of others, to do so would be wise or even right.

According to this account, the criminal law should not be used to prohibit non-harmful behaviour, or even to prevent individuals from harming themselves. The harm principle is a way of balancing the interests of the State while protecting the freedom and autonomy of the individual. The harm principle has played a highly influential role in modern criminal law, particularly in the liberalisation or decriminalisation of offences classed as 'victimless crimes'. These are acts which are treated by our law as crimes because, when they were first created as such, the view was taken that they were morally wrong or injurious to the public and could thus be properly so treated. It has been urged that if two people of full age and understanding (wherever the age of majority happens to be fixed) wish to engage in certain conduct which will not cause injury to themselves or to others, their conduct should not be prohibited by the law merely because a majority of the community may consider it to be morally wrong. While the list of consensual activities still treated as criminal has shrunk in recent years, many still remain. In all Australian jurisdictions, homosexuality is no longer criminal. Bestiality, however, remains a crime, as does incest, including cases where the participants are adults. In England, a majority of the House of Lords has held that consensual sado-masochistic activities performed on private premises constitute unlawful assaults: *R v Brown* [1994] 1 AC 212 (at 2.36). Strong arguments have been advanced for removing from such conduct the stigma of criminality, informed by drawing on the tenets of the harm principle.

1.6 One of the major difficulties of the harm principle is uncertainty about what constitutes 'harm to others'. Is insulting or offensive behaviour 'harm to others'? Must the harm be direct or can it be indirect? Does harm focus only on physical harm or does it include psychological and emotional harm? How does one assess harm suffered by those who cannot articulate their reactions in readily comprehensible ways, such as young children, severely disabled or ill people, or animals?

1.7 The harm principle has also formed the basis for the expansion of criminal law. Modern political debates about the criminalisation of conduct frequently revolve around the harmfulness of conduct. Offences such as drink driving are based on explicit harm narratives.

The public interest

1.8 A primary justification for criminalisation is the 'publicness' of the conduct. On this account, an act will only be labelled a crime if it is thought to be more than an offence against one or more individuals. It must be injurious to the public in general. Of course all private injuries, if they become sufficiently widespread, become detrimental to the public. Nonetheless, the element of publicness seems to be an important aspect of any justification for treating conduct as criminal. This account rests on and reinforces the criminal/civil distinction — public wrongs will be the subject of criminal law, while private wrongs can be addressed through civil law.

The principle of privacy protects citizens from the arbitrary intrusion by the State into their homes and private lives, and particularly from intervention by the state in moral interests. Privacy is a fundamental human right protected by Art 17 of the International Covenant on Civil and Political Rights (ICCPR):

> 1. No one shall be subjected to arbitrary or unlawful interference with his [or her] privacy, family, home or correspondence, nor to unlawful attacks on his [or her] honour and reputation.
> 2. Everyone has the right to the protection of the law against such interference or attacks.

Australia is a signatory to the First Optional Protocol of the ICCPR which allows individuals to make claims to the International Court of Human Rights if Australia is in breach of its obligations. In *Toonen v Australia*, Communication No 488/1992, UN Doc CCPR/C/50/D/488/1992 (1994), Toonen successfully argued that Australia was in breach of its international obligations under the ICCPR due to Tasmanian legislation criminalising a range of sexual activity in private between adult men, and anal sex (both heterosexual and homosexual). As a consequence of the United Nations Human Rights Committee's finding, the Commonwealth Government passed the Human Rights (Sexual Conduct) Act 1994 (Cth), overriding the Tasmanian legislation.

1.9 The idea that there exists a 'private' sphere of activity that cannot be subject to State intervention has been influential in the decriminalisation or liberalisation of laws governing homosexuality and prostitution. The concept of privacy has, however, been the subject of extensive feminist critique. Feminists have noted that the legal division of public and private plays a significant role in veiling and legitimating the subordination of certain groups in society. Historically, the 'family' was a site for female subordination — a man could not be prosecuted for raping his wife under the doctrine of marital immunity, and 'domestic' violence was not viewed as a proper matter for State regulation. Although the doctrine of marital immunity has been removed from the substantive law, and there have been a raft of domestic violence offences created, there is still a lingering reluctance to intervene in violence within the family.

The boundaries between the spheres of public and private life are subject to change:

> The public/private dichotomy of liberal thought, far from constituting two analytically discrete realms, is a malleable creation of the public realm [M Thornton, 'The Public/Private Dichotomy: Gendered and Discriminatory' (1991) 18 *Journal of Law and Society* 448 at 459].

The concept of privacy is important in protecting individuals in positive ways from the arbitrary exercise of power by the State into one's private life. However, the concept of privacy has also been used in negative ways to structure certain oppressive and harmful behaviour as beyond the reach of criminal law.

Morality

1.10 The third justification for criminalisation is that of moral wrongdoing. On this argument, for conduct to warrant classification as criminal, it must involve moral wrongdoing. Many people argue that certain crimes, even serious crimes, are not morally wrongful. An example is euthanasia which, in all Australian jurisdictions, is murder, although frequently prosecuted as manslaughter: see further **4.6**. People who argue that certain crimes are not morally wrongful, however, are not arguing against a connection between crime and moral wrongdoing. Rather, they are asserting that the particular conduct under consideration should not be criminal.

1.11 Broadly speaking, invasions of a person's right to life, liberty or property constitute the crimes most commonly dealt with by the courts. The invasions may either be direct, as in the case of assaults and thefts, or indirect, as in the case of various driving offences which are designed as such to protect the liberties of all users of the road.

Of course, not every transaction that can be considered morally wrong or injurious to the public interest is treated by our law as a crime. It was long ago pointed out by St Thomas Aquinas that it is necessary to tolerate certain evils lest worse evils should rise from the effort to repress them. The 'noble experiment', the American attempt to outlaw the consumption of alcoholic liquor between 1919 and 1933, provides an excellent example of the truth of this statement and, at the present time, a large number of people would urge that the statement applies with equal truth to efforts to repress the use of certain illicit drugs.

1.12 In debates, the relation between law and morality tends to be presented in starkly opposing terms. On one account, the immorality of conduct supplies a sufficient reason for criminalisation. For example, in *The Enforcement of Morals* (Oxford University Press, 1965), Lord Patrick Devlin argued that the criminal law ought to enforce morality. He believed that there existed a positive morality that binds members of society together and that society may use the law to preserve morality in the same way as it uses it to safeguard anything else that is essential to its existence. The opposing account asserts that morality is a private matter that should not be the subject of criminal law unless it harms others. Thus H L A Hart in *Law, Liberty and Morality* argued against Devlin on specific grounds, including that changes in morality do not mean that society will be destroyed, and concerns that using criminal law to enforce common morality would undermine individual freedom significantly. Many modern theorists have expressed distaste for the influence of some moral and religious precepts upon law historically and in the present, and a concern that a morally informed criminal law may support enactment of repressive and discriminatory offences. (See, for example, N Bamforth, *Sexuality, Morals and Justice*, Continuum Press, 1997).

1.13 Yet the relationship between law and morality is more complex than suggested by the framing of the oppositional question of whether or not the law should regulate morality. This debate assumes that morality is a prior state of affairs to which the law responds. However, morality is not a natural concept that exists out there awaiting discovery. Positive morality changes from time to time and place to place. Moreover, the law will affect, reflect and reinforce perceptions of the morality of a particular practice and behaviour. For example, in *From Mr Sin to Mr Big* (Oxford University Press, 1993), Desmond Manderson undertook an analysis of drug laws in Australia and argued that a change in the legal status of drug laws leads people to think of an activity as immoral even through they had not thought so previously. Immoral connotations in relation to illicit drugs developed through a process of social stigmatisation of drug users, by shifting from regulation by the free market to doctors and then to police and criminal justice agencies.

1.14 In *Wickedness and Crime* (Routledge, 2013), Penny Crofts argues that not only does criminal law shape our understandings of particular behaviours as right or wrong, but it also reflects and reinforces our understanding of what it means to be wicked. Laws communicate a system and order, separating, classifying and organising actions. The structure and general principles of criminal law can be analysed in terms of how law explores, expresses and organises wickedness. Crofts argues that a central narrative of blameworthiness in contemporary criminal law is that a person is not 'wicked' unless they intended or adverted to the prohibited consequences of their behaviour. This is an account of subjective culpability, whereby a person is not sufficiently blameworthy to justify punishment unless they had mens rea; that is, a guilty mind. This reflects and reinforces contemporary understandings of wickedness in society generally, where we are reluctant to hold people responsible for 'accidents' or harmful consequences over which they had no control. On this account, offences in which subjective blameworthiness is established are at the centre of criminal law, while offences which lack this subjective element are regarded as exceptional or tangential. Offences such as 'attempt' demonstrate the ascendancy of subjective criminality (G Fletcher, *Rethinking Criminal Law*, Oxford University Press, 1978), whereby a person can be subjected to the same punishment as if they had succeeded in committing the offence, purely on the basis of their wrongful intent. Offences such as strict and absolute liability offences, manslaughter by criminal negligence and constructive murder constitute exceptions to the general principle that an accused ought not to be convicted of an offence where his or her conduct did not involve an element of moral culpability. However, Crofts argues that there are alternative models of wickedness, such as the classic model of wickedness as an absence of goodness, which underlies negligence and so-called regulatory offences (see **Chapter 6**).

SOURCES OF THE CRIMINAL LAW

1.15 In the early days of English law, criminal cases were dealt with largely by local courts and, except for spasmodic interventions by parliament, much of the law was traditional and expounded by the judges from case to case. As the central government of England grew to its full power, the local courts fell into disuse and their place was taken by the King's courts. In these courts, judicial activity continued to be a main source of the criminal law, with parliament intervening increasingly frequently to remedy deficiencies which resulted from problems which emerged in the case law, or to further policy objectives.

For a long period of time, there was no system of appeals in criminal cases. It was occasionally possible to bring a conviction by the criminal court before a higher court for review by way of writ of error. That procedure, however, was limited to a review of the written record of proceedings in the case and, as the record did not include either the evidence or the directions given by the judge to the jury, the appeal was largely confined to formal matters; for example, whether the correct form of words had been used in specifying the charge against the defendant.

An informal system of appeal in the more serious criminal cases came to be used during the eighteenth century. If the trial judge had some doubts about the correctness of the conviction, he would suspend the execution of the sentence and consult with his brother judges of the three common law courts who would give him their opinion (all judges at the time were men). If they thought that the case had been correctly handled, the suspension of sentence would be lifted by the trial judge and the sentence would be executed; but if they thought that something amiss had occurred then the trial judge would recommend that the Crown should grant the accused a free pardon, which had the effect of wiping out the conviction. These rulings of the 12 judges of these courts (whose number grew slightly in the nineteenth century) came to be reported and formed a source from which criminal law doctrine could be deduced. At the beginning of the nineteenth century, the practice grew up of reporting the proceedings at trials which, again, provided more detailed records of judicial decisions. Eventually, with the introduction of a regularised system of appeals, reports of criminal cases and of judicial rulings therein came to be on a similar footing to reports of civil cases.

1.16 Although we now have records of criminal trials from the sixteenth and seventeenth centuries, and quite detailed records from the eighteenth century onwards, historically, a considerable reliance was placed in criminal law upon the works of writers of authority. Among the best known of these are Coke, Hale, Hawkins, Foster, Blackstone and East, and their works are often referred to even today in judicial decisions. In the first half of the nineteenth century, a Royal Commission on the criminal law produced a valuable series of reports which are also a useful source for ascertaining the criminal law as it existed at that time. In the 1870s, a draft Criminal Code, which was intended to restate the criminal law in statutory form, was produced in the United Kingdom by Sir James Fitzjames Stephen, a distinguished jurist and judge of that period and himself the author of an authoritative history of the criminal law. It was referred to a Royal Commission which made some amendments to it, but otherwise reported upon it favourably. Political developments, however, prevented its enactment by the parliament of the day.

1.17 In speaking of sources of criminal law, it is also important to understand the significance of the fact that Australian history did not begin in 1788, when the first British convict settlement was established in New South Wales: Australia began as, and in many senses still is, Aboriginal and Torres Strait Islander land. On their land, Indigenous people practise their own customs and laws, including criminal law. It is beyond the scope of this book to describe Indigenous systems of criminal law, then or now. Nevertheless, the continuing presence of Australia's Indigenous peoples, as well as Australia's history of invasion, massacre and dispossession, remains a fundamental moral and legal challenge for all Australians, not least for the Australian criminal law.

European colonisation of Australia was accompanied by armed conflict with Aboriginal people, dispossession of their land, and the introduction of disease. Massacres were commonplace. Their scale is little understood by most Australians, even today. In Victoria and New South Wales, the main 'killing times' occurred prior to 1850, when guns were single-shot and muzzle-loading, with the result that most recorded killings were of one to three people. In Queensland, however, recent research suggests that an Aboriginal population of approximately 250,000 was reduced by over 90%, with many of those people being massacred with the aid of the more effective breech-loading Snider carbines: see T Bottoms, *Conspiracy of Silence: Queensland's Frontier Killing Times*, Allen & Unwin, 2013. Nor were such deeds the exclusive actions of isolated settlers: they were official policy, with many murders being committed by the Queensland Native Police force, which operated from 1848 to around 1910. While it is questionable whether the crime of genocide existed at this time under international law, it is certainly an appropriate label for the scale and quality of what occurred. Murder is another appropriate term, although it is important to understand that prosecutions were rarely brought, and when brought were rarely successful. In part this was because of legal prohibitions on Aboriginal people giving evidence. It was also because of the reluctance of judges and juries to accept Aboriginal evidence over that of non-Aboriginal evidence.

1.18 One result of this history is the continuing over-representation of Indigenous people in the criminal justice system. The issue of Aboriginal deaths in custody first received broad public attention in 1991, when the Royal Commission into Aboriginal Deaths in Custody published its Final Report. This report highlighted the fact that the high levels of deaths in custody were primarily the result of the fact that Aboriginal people were 27 times more likely than non-Aboriginal people to be in police custody, and 15 times more likely to be in gaol. The Royal Commission made 339 recommendations designed primarily to reduce this rate of over-representation. Following the Royal Commission, all Australian governments, including those in Victoria and New South Wales, published reports claiming either to have implemented or to be in the process of implementing the Royal Commission's recommendations. More than 20 years later, however, Indigenous imprisonment rates in most parts of Australia continue to rise, and the vast majority of recommendations remain unimplemented.

1.19 Other results have included significant challenges by Indigenous people to various aspects of the operation of the criminal justice system. In one case, *Walker v New South Wales* (1994) 182 CLR 45, the High Court rejected the proposition that Aboriginal customary criminal laws could continue to exist (see also *Director of Public Prosecutions Reference No 1 of 1999* (1999) 8 NTLR 148). In another case, a challenge to the low representation of Aboriginal people on juries was rejected by the Northern Territory Supreme Court: see *R v Woods* (2010) 246 FLR 4. Indigenous people have also argued that Aboriginal customary law and background should be taken into account in various ways, including as part of the sentencing process: see, for example, *R v Minor* (1992) 59 A Crim R 227 and *R v Fernando* (1992) 76 A Crim R 58. In a case before the High Court at the time of writing, an Aboriginal man was challenging the weight attributed to the seriousness of the offence over Indigenous social disadvantage: see *Bugmy v The Queen* [2013] HCA Trans 111 (10 May 2013), and T Anthony, 'Indigenising Sentencing? *Bugmy v The Queen*' (2013) 35 *Sydney Law Review* 451. It is certain that challenges posed to the operation of the criminal justice system by Indigenous people will continue to arise.

1.20 Despite these significant issues, the English common law of the colonial period formed the basis of criminal law in the various colonial courts, which became jurisdictions. In three of the states — New South Wales, South Australia and Victoria — it has continued to be the chief source of the criminal law, so that, in those states, the prevailing law is that which was originally introduced from England and later modified by statutes of the respective state legislatures, and by subsequent judicial law-making. In Queensland, however, Sir Samuel Griffith, who was Chief Justice of Queensland at the time and who subsequently became the first Chief Justice of Australia, produced a draft Criminal Code which was based largely on that prepared by Fitzjames Stephen and the subsequent Royal Commission, the New York Penal Code of 1881 and the Italian Penal Code of 1899. This Code was enacted in 1899 and came into force on 1 January 1901. A new Criminal Code Act was passed in that state in 1995 but it was not proclaimed and, in 1997, it was itself repealed. Western Australia adopted the same Queensland Code, enacted first in 1902 and repealed and re-enacted in 1913. In 1924, Tasmania adopted a modified version of the Queensland and Western Australian Codes. Decisions in these three states, therefore, are not always of great value as a source of criminal law in the other three states, which derive their law from that of English common law. In 1983 the Northern Territory became the fourth jurisdiction to adopt a criminal code.

1.21 A more significant recent development has been the enactment of the Commonwealth Criminal Code Act 1995. In its practical effect, it is not yet a comprehensive Code, but rather the first part of such an enactment, designed to affect the interpretation and application of all federal statutes dealing with the criminal law, of which the most important is the Crimes Act 1914 (Cth). As time passes, however, the Commonwealth Criminal Code may come to have a far more substantial operation than merely the interpretation of federal statutes. Parts of the Code were adopted in the Australian Capital Territory in 2002, and the Crimes Act 1900 (ACT) currently operates in tandem with a gradually expanding Criminal Code. In the Northern Territory, Pt IIAA of the Criminal Code (NT) now substantially adopts the provisions of the Criminal Code Act 1995 (Cth). These provisions, which were passed in 2006, apply to many of the most serious offences, including murder, manslaughter, and sexual assault: see S Gray and J Blokland, *Criminal Laws Northern Territory*, 2nd ed, Federation Press, 2012, p 5. Uniformity in the criminal law across the different Australian states and territories is certainly a desirable goal in principle, and it is possible that the Commonwealth Criminal Code may one day form the basis for a uniform Australian criminal law.

In each of the three common law states, the statutory provisions amending the inherited law were scattered among several different statutes. In each state, the major amendments relating to the more serious offences have now been collected into a single statute: Crimes Act 1900 (NSW); Criminal Law Consolidation Act 1935 (SA); Crimes Act 1958 (Vic). Each of these consolidating statutes has been substantially amended, by additions and subtractions, since its enactment. The law of two of these states — New South Wales and Victoria — forms the subject matter of this textbook. In common law states such as New South Wales and Victoria, offences and defences can exist at common law as well as under legislation. Fundamental elements of criminal responsibility are drawn from the common law. It is advisable to refer to statute first to ascertain whether or not an offence is specified under legislation. Cases will then provide definitions or applications of the law. Alternatively, some offences and defences exist only at common law, and cases will provide statements of law and their application.

1.22 Further reading

T Anthony, *Indigenous People, Crime and Punishment*, Routledge, 2013

S Gray and J Blokland, *Criminal Laws Northern Territory*, Federation Press, 2012

THE DEFINITION OF CRIMES

Subjective blameworthiness

1.23 As has been noted, it is generally accepted that punishment is justified only if the person to be punished is morally blameworthy. Accounts of what it means to be morally blameworthy are constructed and contingent. The dominant account in contemporary criminal law requires subjective blameworthiness; that is, knowledge and/or intention of wrongfulness. This requirement of subjective blameworthiness (while sometimes breached, as we discuss below) marks out the criminal law of the current era from that of early modern criminal law.

The maxim

1.24 The common law accepted this idea of subjective blameworthiness and enshrined it in the maxim *actus non facit reum nisi mens sit rea*, or, in Blackstone's words (4 *Bl Comm* 21), 'as a vicious will without a vicious act is no civil crime, so on the other hand, an unwarrantable act without a vicious will is no crime at all'. This notion has been traced back at least as far as St Augustine, and it runs through the works on criminal law of the great writers of authority mentioned in 1.16 as well as those of yet earlier writers such as Bracton and Staundforde. However, in *Wickedness and Crime* (2013), Crofts traces a long history of alternative accounts of moral blameworthiness in criminal law and philosophy that present a negative conception of wickedness as an absence of goodness.

Despite its deep roots in the criminal law, this idea of a 'vicious will' is not an unchanging concept. The classic writers on criminal law used the maxim as a basis for justifying all those excuses which have traditionally been recognised as defences to a criminal charge — infancy, duress, coercion, insanity or mental impairment, and so on. In all these cases, they explained that, although an unwarrantable act had been committed and harm done, there was no vicious will accompanying it and, hence, there was no crime. In this way of dealing with the matter, 'vicious will' is simply an abstract and imprecise concept used to give an underlying unity to several different ideas, which would now fall across the boundary between offences and defences. Crofts (2013) has argued that the contemporary emphasis on the 'vicious will' in historical accounts of criminal law is a misreading. Instead, treatise writers up to the eighteenth century were focused on establishing the wickedness of an accused. This included, but was not limited to, intentional wrongdoing, causing harm, manifest criminality, and an emotional account of wickedness. Thus, an accused might not be guilty of murder despite acting with intention, because he or she had not *wanted* to kill: he or she had been compelled by circumstances and had killed with a sadness of heart. Crofts (2013) argues that this emotional account of wickedness continues to underlie contemporary compulsion defence structures (see **Chapter 12**).

1.25 Up to the eighteenth century, the notion of mens rea was a loose and convenient expression for describing the absence of a number of defences which were recognised as available to charges of crime. The idea that criminal conduct should be committed with a particular mental state (mens rea) in order to ground criminal liability was still emerging at this time. At the beginning of the nineteenth century, however, a change of approach took place. By that time, the theory expounded by the philosopher Descartes, that the human body may be regarded as a complex piece of mechanism directed in some mysterious manner by a non-material mind (the exact nature of which he did not make clear), had become widely and uncritically accepted. This idea of the mind/body distinction was adopted by the legal reformer Jeremy Bentham, and subsequently by the legal philosopher John Austin. Austin expressed it in a form which has been repeated by successive writers on jurisprudence so often that the theory sometimes appears to be regarded as scientifically-established fact rather than what it is, a highly dubious philosophical proposition: see J Austin, *The Province of Jurisprudence Determined* (1832), Weidenfeld and Nicolson, 1954. Of course, this was a development that took place on an intellectual level. For a mens rea requirement to take hold on the criminal law, a number of developments had to take place on organisational, institutional and evidentiary levels. These changes, including what has been called the 'factualisation' of mens rea (N Lacey, 'Responsibility and Modernity in Criminal Law' (2001) 9(3) *Journal of Political Philosophy* 249–76) (whereby it came to be generally accepted that it was possible to prove mental states as a question of fact), made it possible for intellectual ideas about individual mental states to have 'life' in the law. Crofts (2013) has argued that the contemporary focus on whether or not the accused has the necessary intent or knowledge was one way of deferring or submerging the normative element of the law. Instead of being asked whether or not the accused was 'wicked', juries instead considered the factual question of whether the accused had knowledge or intent.

A theory of human action

1.26 According to the Austinian doctrine, a human act is muscular contraction resulting from the operation of the mind or will. Such an 'act' is to be sharply distinguished from its surrounding circumstances (which may include past facts) and equally sharply from its consequences. Therefore, what an ordinary person would consider, and describe as, 'my act of shooting my enemy' is analysed as a muscular contraction of 'my finger', operating in surrounding circumstances (the fact that 'my finger' is touching the trigger of a gun, the fact that the gun is pointing at 'my enemy', and so on) and having certain consequences as a result of the inexorable operation of physical and chemical principles (the explosion of the primer of the cartridge in the gun, the resulting propulsion of the bullet from the gun-barrel into 'my enemy's body', and so on).

Such an analysis requires me to think of 'myself' (perhaps equivalent to 'my mind' or 'my will') as continually using 'my body' or some part thereof as an instrument. But we do not normally think of our bodies as instruments. Even if I am speaking of shooting my enemy, I think of the gun — not of my trigger-finger — as my instrument. I may sometimes ascribe a deed to a part of my body rather than to myself, but in such a case it will be found that I am seeking some special benefit, such as an evasion of responsibility for what I appear to have done ('it was my hand — not me — that struck the blow').

The changing concept of mens rea

1.27 To pursue these matters further would take us into the more remote realms of philosophy. It is, accordingly, enough to note that the sharp distinctions drawn by the Austinian theory of human action led to a change in the concept of mens rea. It came to be thought that blameworthiness rested in the existence, in every instance, of a specific 'state of mind' prompting the muscular contraction in question. It was and is argued that one cannot properly be blamed for some transaction (and hence be regarded as possessing a mens rea in regard to it) unless, at the time when one willed the muscular contraction that produced the particular consequences, one's mind at least correctly appreciated the existence of the surrounding circumstances and realised or foresaw the consequences that, in fact, resulted from the muscular contraction. Such a blameworthy mental state is normally termed in modern writing 'recklessness'; if there is added to it a desire to produce the consequences, the resultant blameworthy mental state is often termed in modern writing as 'intention'.

This is not the only way in which these two words may be used. The word 'reckless' may also properly be used to describe the gross negligence or carelessness of a person who neither intended nor foresaw the consequences of his or her actions. Nonetheless, the reader needs to be aware that modern writers and judges normally use the words in the way indicated, and, on occasion, insist this is the only correct 'legal' usage of them. 'Recklessness' is a term of legal art, and caution must be exercised whenever the word is used. In *Crime, Reason and History* (Weidenfeld and Nicolson, 1993), Alan Norrie highlights the policy choices that were made in the legal construction of 'recklessness' as requiring advertance, rather than the broader standard of non-advertant recklessness which might equally have been chosen.

The problem of negligence

1.28 The problem of negligent behaviour has loomed large in modern discussions of mens rea. Negligent behavior increasingly forms an element of the the mens rea of criminal offences in Australian common law jurisdictions. Negligence may be defined as a failure to comply, in a given activity, with the standard of care that a reasonable person engaging in that activity would adopt. For the purpose of those crimes which may be committed negligently (manslaughter, for example), the criminal law insists upon a higher degree of negligence than does the civil law: see, generally, *Nydam v R* [1977] VR 430; *R v Shields* [1981] VR 717.

1.29 It is sometimes argued that since negligence involves a negative state of mind — that is, a failure to advert to possible consequences — the notion of degrees of negligence is nonsensical because there can be no degrees of inadvertence. Professor Hart has shown that the fallacy in this argument lies in assuming that to say that a person was negligent is equivalent to saying that he or she did not advert to the possibility of harm. In 'Negligence, *Mens Rea* and Criminal Responsibility' in *Punishment and Responsibility*, above, he writes (pp 147–8):

> When harm has resulted from someone's negligence, if we say of that person that he has acted negligently we are not thereby *merely* describing the frame of mind in which he acted … [W]e are referring to the fact that the agent failed to comply with a standard of conduct with which any ordinary reasonable man *could* and *would* have complied: a standard requiring him to take precautions against harm.

When negligence is analysed in this way, it becomes clear that there can be degrees of negligence. Professor Hart states (at p 149) that negligence can be said to be gross 'if the precautions to be taken against harm are very simple, such as persons who are but poorly endowed with physical and mental capacities can easily take'.

1.30 This analysis also meets the objection that there is necessarily something unjust about punishing an accused in cases where his or her mind was a blank as to the possible consequences of his or her actions. Professor Hart states that this view seems to be based upon the belief that possession of knowledge of consequences is a necessary and sufficient basis for the imputation of moral responsibility. Yet, plainly, this is not so. In the case of a signaller who has a duty to signal trains, and who causes a collision by going off to play a game of cards without thinking about a coming train, moral responsibility is imputed although his or her mind was blank as to specific possible consequences. Professor Hart concludes (at pp 151–2):

> A hundred times a day persons are blamed outside the law courts for not being more careful, for being inattentive and not stopping to think … [I]f anyone is ever responsible for anything, there is no general reason why men should not be responsible for such omissions to think, or to consider the situation and its dangers before acting.

1.31 In *Wickedness and Crime* (2013), Crofts has argued in favour of the doctrine of negligence. Crofts argues that there are certain things or values that we as a society (should) care about, and the failure to think or care about these values can and should be constructed as culpable and wicked. Accordingly, there is an objective parameter around this evaluation of failure to care. What values do we as a society protect, and thus with what values should we expect to care? We do not expect care all the time. A failure to care about a television show is not culpable; however, the failure to care about a person's life or bodily integrity does matter, and could be organised as wicked. This is a blending of subjective and objective evaluations; of the individual and the social.

Strict liability

1.32 Although it has traditionally been held that mens rea is an essential feature of crime, the judges have, during the past 150 years, been faced with the task of implementing a host of statutory offences in which parliament has said simply that anyone who does X shall suffer penalty Y (in many instances, a fine). Were the judges to require a showing of mens rea, despite parliament's failure to say, in express words, that it was needed? As time went on, they became more and more disposed to say that parliament had decided not to require such a showing on the basis that if parliament had wanted mens rea to be an element of the offence, it would have said so. And so we often find that, under modern statutes, people are punished (admittedly not, as a rule, very severely) for doing something which, in a very real sense, they might perceive as lacking moral blameworthiness, or that they could not help doing. The crimes created by such statutes are called crimes of strict (or, sometimes now, absolute) liability. So-called 'regulatory offences' provide an example of one of the ways in which the law has shaped our perceptions of immoral and moral behaviour. Thus drink driving is a class of strict liability offence — the law does not care whether or not a driver *knew* they were over the limit, but only whether they *were* over the limit. Past generations did not take drink driving seriously, whereas in contemporary society, through an emphasis upon the harmful consequences of drink driving, people now view drink driving with opprobrium. There is much debate about regulatory offences, but we shall postpone further discussion of the topic until **Chapter 13**.

Fitzjames Stephen's view

1.33 Sir James Fitzjames Stephen argued in his judgment in *Tolson* (1889) 23 QBD 168, that the expression 'mens rea' was unhelpful and misleading. He pointed out that it encompasses several very different states of mind, depending on the crime under consideration. For instance, in some crimes it is necessary to show the presence of intention to bring about a specific result, while in others mere inattention will suffice. Furthermore, as we have seen, the presence of any one of certain well-recognised excuses, such as infancy and insanity, will be taken as demonstrating an absence of mens rea. In Stephen's opinion, the use of one phrase to describe so many different matters was likely to lead to misunderstanding. He therefore preferred to say that each crime has its own particular mens rea, some parts of which may be expressed in the words either of a statutory provision or of a received common law definition (for example, Coke's definition of murder: see **Chapter 4**) and some parts of which are always understood to be implied (for example, that a person must be above a certain age and of sane mind in order to be capable of committing that crime).

Stephen's view, it is submitted, represents the practice of the courts and, for this reason (to say nothing of its inherent attractiveness) we shall follow it in substance.

Actus reus

1.34 In whatever sense the phrase may be used, mens rea denotes the 'mental' element in the definition of any given crime. The other elements of that crime have come to be known as the 'actus reus'. The phrase 'actus reus', if accurately translated into English, is nonsensical; an act cannot be guilty — only human beings can be. However, despite this criticism, the phrase is constantly used and is, in fact, a convenient way of distinguishing the 'non-mental' or external elements of a given crime from the mental (or internal) element thereof.

This separation of mental and non-mental elements of a crime raises the question: how does one distinguish them? Almost all expositions of criminal law theory accept, without discussion, the Cartesian theory of mind and body referred to at 1.25. That is to say, they treat mental operations as being related to physical activity as cause is related to effect. Later philosophers (notably Professor Gilbert Ryle in his book *The Concept of Mind*, Hutchinson's University Library, 1949) have argued strongly for a different view: that to analyse a particular transaction into its mental and non-mental elements is merely to analyse it from two different standpoints. In other words, when we speak of the non-mental elements we are concentrating on a different aspect of the transaction or act; but the one does not cause the other. For most purposes, it is not necessary to choose between these two philosophies.

Evidence of the mental element

1.35 How can the existence of the mental (or internal) element be proved in a court of law? We shall turn this question aside by pointing out that, in practice, we do not have any difficulty in attributing a particular mental state to another person if we know enough, by our observation or the observations of others reported to us, about his or her conduct. Thus where a person fires a pistol at another from point blank range, there is normally little difficulty in deciding that he or she intended harm to that other. Equally, where a person picks a wallet from another's pocket and runs off with it, it will usually be easy to draw the inference that she or he intended permanently to deprive that other of that property.

Subjective and objective standards

1.36 Often, it is uncertain what the accused's state of mind may have been. One solution to the difficulty is to reason along the following lines. When I see another person behaving in a particular way, I may reason that if I performed the same bodily actions as that other is performing, I would do so only as a result of a particular thought or wish. I therefore assume that the other person must be doing what has been done as the result of a similar thought or wish.

The theory seems to have been accepted in many of the writings and judgments in the criminal law. It has, however, been given a gloss by substituting 'me', in the above account, with a hypothetical 'reasonable person'. As a result, judges sometimes speak as though there are only two ways of determining what were a person's thoughts or desires on a given occasion, which are:

(a) by asking that person; and

(b) by considering what a reasonable person, behaving as that person was seen to behave on that occasion, would have thought or desired in order to produce such behaviour.

They have gone on to choose (b) rather than (a). This has been partly because, until the beginning of the twentieth century, an accused person could not give evidence on oath and be tested about it by cross-examination, so that method (a) was generally not available; and partly, it would seem, because when method (a) became available they feared that if it were adopted the accused would be presented with a simple means of controlling the outcome of the trial. In this connection, it must be remembered that an accused person does not have to do more in most trials than raise a reasonable doubt of his or her guilt in the minds of the jury; and if the accused gives evidence that he or she had not at the particular time had a particular thought or wish, how could this evidence fail to raise that reasonable doubt? One answer to this question is that the jurors might have no difficulty, when considering the whole of the evidence, in concluding that the accused was lying to serve his or her own ends. However, this answer does not seem often to have been thought very persuasive.

There has thus arisen a debate whether 'subjective' or 'objective' standards should be used for ascertaining the mental element of a given crime. In this context, a 'subjective' standard involves asking what was the actual mental state of the accused person, while an 'objective' standard asks what would have been the supposed mental state of a hypothetical 'reasonable person' behaving in the way in which the accused behaved.

For the reasons outlined above, there has been, during the past century or so, a strong pressure for the adoption of objective tests for determining a mens rea. As well as the reasons already given, the use of objective tests is argued for on the basis that it makes for the consistent application of the criminal law from case to case. Objectivity is seen as providing for each case a measure which everyone can use in the same way, whereas subjectivity is seen as leading to each case being governed by personal and, perhaps, emotional considerations. Such an argument is fallacious, for each of us has his or her own idea of what in any given situation is reasonable. The spurious objectivity involved in applying a 'reasonable person' test is utterly different from the true objectivity involved in, say, determining the speed at which a person is driving by using an amphometer. The real effect of adopting objective tests to determine the intentions or wishes to be imputed to an accused has often been, in practice, to transfer the power of making the decision from the jury to the judge. It has been said that the question whether there is any evidence on which a jury might find that a reasonable person would behave in a particular way is a question of law, to be decided by the judge; and if the judge, using his or her own notions of reasonableness, decides that there is no such evidence, then the jury is prevented from ever considering the matter, though, if they were allowed to do so, they might apply a very different notion of reasonableness in the situation being considered.

In recent years, there has been a swing back to the adoption of subjective standards of intentions and desires, so that juries are left to decide what the accused actually intended or wished, using whatever means they think appropriate to make the decision. This tendency has resulted from an increasing acceptance of the view that people should not be punished for things that they did not mean to do, with the result that what they actually meant to do becomes a matter of paramount importance. See M Weinberg, 'Moral Blameworthiness — The "Objective Test" Dilemma' (2003) 24 *Aust Bar Rev* 173.

Crofts (2013) has argued that the distinction between subjective and objective standards is fallacious. There is no such thing as purely subjective standards. All subjective standards in criminal law have objective parameters. It is not 'intention' that is criminalised; it is the intention to act or cause a prohibited consequence that is culpable. For example, it is not the 'intention to *smile*' that is culpable, but the 'intention to *kill*'. There are objective parameters around *all* subjective standards in law. The law does not propose a pure, autonomous individualistic account of culpability. It necessarily draws upon social expression of values and preferences, which can include values such as human integrity, human life and the protection of property. Crofts (2013) argues that the contemporary emphasis upon subjectivism fails to adequately enunciate and protect social values, and precludes debates about social values. The dominance of subjectivism reflects and reinforces a lack of confidence in the capacity of law to articulate values. Taken to its logical conclusions it is a highly individualistic account of culpability that lacks social content.

This discussion about the definition of crimes allows us to draw an important distinction — the distinction between criminal liability and criminal responsibility. These terms are often confused, or used interchangeably by lawyers and scholars alike, but, properly understood, they refer to different things. Criminal liability refers to the outcome of a criminal trial — the judgment that an individual has (or has not) committed the actus reus of an offence with the requisite mens rea. Actus reus and mens rea (and defences) form the architecture of criminal liability. But this architecture is built on a particular foundation which is usually obscured in any trial process. This foundation is the assumption of criminal responsibility — the assumption that, as subjects of the criminal law, all individuals have certain cognitive, moral and volitional capacities. These capacities mean that they can be judged as autonomous individuals when alleged to have committed criminal offences. As Lacey (2001) puts it, the conditions of criminal responsibility are thought to 'reside in fundamental aspects of human agency'. Some individuals, such as those with particular mental conditions or those who are very young, may not be criminally responsible. These individuals are carved out from the reach of the criminal law, as they are generally not considered able to conform their behavior to the standards of the criminal law and thus to be appropriately subject to criminal punishment. The issue of criminal responsibility is discussed further in relation to the insanity defence in **Chapter 14**.

WHO CAN COMMIT CRIMES?

Infancy

1.37 It follows from the foregoing principles that crimes can be committed by only those 'legal persons' who can perform mental and physical acts in the exercise of a choice to do or refrain from doing them. It is, for example, obvious that a babe in arms cannot have a mens rea or perform an actus reus.

The common law accordingly held that a child under seven years of age was incapable of committing a crime (such a child could, of course, perform in some cases the actus reus, for example an administration of poison, as an innocent agent of a capable adult). This means that whatever proof is available, a child under this age cannot be convicted of a crime, though child welfare legislation may enable care and control proceedings to be instituted. In all jurisdictions the minimum age of criminal responsibility has been raised to 10 years; Criminal Code Act 1995 (Cth) Sch, s 7.1; Criminal Code 2002 (ACT) s 25; Criminal Code (NT) s 38(1); Children (Criminal Proceedings) Act 1987 (NSW) s 5; Criminal Code (Qld) s 29(1); Young Offenders Act 1993 (SA) s 5; Criminal Code (Tas) s 18(1); Children, Youth and Families Act 2005 (Vic) s 344; Criminal Code (WA) s 29, para 1.

On attaining the age of 10 years, a child becomes, in theory, capable of committing a crime, but the common law continues to require that until he or she attains the age of 14 years, it is necessary to show that, as well as possessing the appropriate state of mind for the crime in question (for example, dishonesty in the case of theft), the defendant knew that the act was wrong. This is called the presumption of doli incapax (incapable of wrongdoing) and as well as proving all elements of the offence the prosecution must bring evidence to rebut this presumption before a child can be convicted of any offence. In some jurisdictions this presumption is anchored in legislation; for example, the Criminal Code Act 1995 (Cth) Sch, s 7.2 provides: 'A child aged 10 years but under 14 years old can only be criminally responsible for an offence if the child knows that his or her conduct is wrong'. In *R v M* (1977) 16 SASR 589 it was established that this requires proof that the child understood that the act or omission was wrong according to the ordinary standards of reasonable people. As such, the required understanding means wrongness according to the reasons which govern the conduct of ordinary persons, as it does in the context of the rules relating to the defence of insanity or mental impairment: see **Chapter 14**. Thus, establishing that a child understood that the act or omission was disapproved of by adults would not be sufficient evidence, because '[a]dults frequently disapprove of breaches of decorum and good manners on the part of children ... without regarding the acts or omissions in question as wrong in the relevant sense': *R v M* (1977) 16 SASR 589 at 591. For consideration of the doli incapax rule, see *R v ALH* (2003) 6 VR 276.

In practice, the rule requiring proof of knowledge of wrongness is observed with strictness only where a serious charge, such as homicide, is involved. More commonly, the rule is regarded as satisfied when a police officer gives evidence that the accused admitted that he or she knew that his or her action was wrong: see *R v M* (1977) 16 SASR 589; see also *R (a child) v Whitty* (1993) 66 A Crim R 462. In *C (a minor) v DPP* [1996] 1 AC 1, the House of Lords decided that the doli incapax rule was still part of the common law and could only be removed or altered by the parliament. It was abolished by the Crime and Disorder Act 1998 (UK) s 34. The Australian Law Reform Commission noted in its report *Seen and Heard: Priority for Children in the Legal Process* (1997) that the presumption of doli incapax had been controversial for a number of years in both Australia and the United Kingdom. However, it concluded that the presumption is 'a practical way of acknowledging young people's developing capacities'. It therefore recommended that all Australian jurisdictions establish the presumption in legislation (rec 195).

1.38 A further protection for the young is provided by the existence of Children's Courts, which have been set up in all of the Australian states: Children's Court Act 1987 (NSW); Children, Youth and Families Act 2005 (Vic). In Victoria, for example, these courts have exclusive jurisdiction to deal with all crimes committed by persons aged under 17 years, except homicide. If, however, the offence is an indictable one, the accused may elect to be tried by a judge and jury in the normal way. Conviction by a Children's Court, even for a serious crime, does not expose the offender to the same consequences as does conviction in an ordinary criminal court. Special measures are available and are used; they are designed to emphasise the achievement of rehabilitation rather than the imposition of punishment.

Corporations

1.39 A corporation is a legal person and, as such, may be convicted of crime. Since a corporation may act only through its officers or employees, the question becomes which acts of a corporation's officers or employees may be attributed to the corporation. The present rule is that the corporation will be liable for the criminal acts of its officers or employees if it can be shown that those acts were, in reality, the acts of the corporation. Whether this can be shown will depend on the nature of the charge, the position, powers and responsibilities of the officer or employee concerned, and other relevant circumstances. See, generally, *Director of Public Prosecutions v Kent and Sussex Contractors Ltd* [1944] KB 146; *R v ICR Haulage Ltd* [1944] KB 551; *R v Blamires Transport Services Ltd* [1964] 1 QB 278; *R v McDonnell* [1966] 1 QB 233; *Tesco Supermarkets Ltd v Nattrass* [1971]

2 All ER 127; *R v Andrews-Weatherfoil Ltd* [1972] 1 All ER 65. Part 2.5 of the Criminal Code Act 1995 (Cth) introduces a statutory regime for the prosecution of corporations under federal law.

1.40 A corporation cannot be imprisoned. If the offence is one for which a licence may be revoked or some other restriction imposed, then a corporation may be punished accordingly. A corporation may be fined, and fined at levels beyond those set for individuals: see, for example, Crimes Act 1914 (Cth) s 4B(3); Crimes Act 1900 (NSW) s 360A. These two enactments provide that a fine may be imposed on a corporation where imprisonment is the only punishment provided for an offence. It remains most doubtful, however, whether this would permit a corporation to be prosecuted for murder, where a mandatory prison sentence is prescribed in all Australian jurisdictions. See, generally, J Clough and C Mulhern, *The Prosecution of Corporations*, Oxford University Press, 2002.

Immunities — The Sovereign, etc

1.41 From its earliest times, the common law held that 'the King is the fountain of justice' and 'the King can do no wrong'. Neither of these statements can be taken at face value today, but it is clear, nevertheless, that the reigning Sovereign cannot be put on trial in the courts for a crime. The same rule also applies to his or her representative in the Commonwealth (the Governor-General) and the states (the Governors). The latter, however, can be brought to trial after they have ceased to hold office for criminal acts performed while in office (subject, no doubt, to the constitutional conventions relieving the Sovereign of responsibility for acts done on the advice of Ministers). An illustration of the principle was seen in 1974 in the United States, when a grand jury named the then President Richard M Nixon as a conspirator in the Watergate 'cover-up', but indicted only the other conspirators. On his resignation, Mr Nixon became open to indictment, but President Ford's award of a pardon precluded this. The process of impeachment available for the removal of a President, Cabinet officer or federal judge is quite distinct from ordinary criminal prosecution in the United States.

Aliens who commit criminal acts within the jurisdiction may be arrested and brought to trial in the same way as may citizens. If they have left the jurisdiction in the meantime, it may be possible to secure their enforced return for the purpose of being brought to trial, by means of extradition; this may depend on whether there is an appropriate treaty between Australia and the country where they are living at the time in question. On grounds of comity, however, it was thought that a foreign sovereign or head of state is immune from our criminal process, and from extradition, but see now *Ex parte Pinochet Ugarte (No 3)* [2002] AC 61. So, too, are all those persons who possess diplomatic privileges. It must be noted that these immunities do not render their possessors incapable of committing a crime, and therefore citizens who act as their accomplices in a criminal transaction may be proceeded against in the normal way, as may an accomplice of the Sovereign who commits a crime.

THE AIMS OF PUNISHMENT

1.42 As mentioned above, one of the ways of distinguishing what constitutes criminal offences is that conviction of them exposes an individual to punishment by the State. Modern treatments of the subject usually list the three competing aims of punishment as those of retribution, deterrence and rehabilitation. We briefly comment on each of these.

Retribution

1.43 The retributive theory views a crime as a wrong which, of its very nature, justifies the infliction upon the criminal of a certain amount of punishment. Many ethical philosophers have supported this theory, sometimes on a somewhat mystical basis, as in the case of Hegel's argument that the crime is a negation and the punishment a negation of that negation. Other ethical philosophers have urged cogent arguments against the theory. We need not, however, consider these rival arguments. On a more practical level, it has often been pointed out that it is impossible for human beings to assess with any degree of accuracy the relative *degree* of wrongness involved in different crimes. For example, is it more wrong for an adult to assault another adult who has insulted her or him, than it is for another person to steal $50 from a millionaire? Nevertheless, however much force there may be in criticisms of this kind, it is obvious that most people regard the infliction of punishment as justifiable only if there has been a prior wrong, and that most people can see that some offences are much more wrong than others. Would you doubt, for example, that it is more wrong for a person to murder a parent in order to inherit the parent's money than it is for that person to exceed the speed limit on a clear road? The idea that punishment should reflect the level of seriousness of the harm is embodied in the expression from Hebrew Law, 'an eye for an eye', which specified that any punishment must be equal to, and not more onerous than, the crime.

Strictly speaking, the retributive theory of punishment requires that punishment be inflicted even though it would serve no apparently useful purpose. Thus the philosopher Kant urged that, even if we knew the world would end tomorrow, it would be our moral duty to hang a convicted murderer today. Some modern writers on punishment shrink from such a conclusion, or regard it as insupportable; they prefer to adopt a theory of 'desert'. This, like the retributive theory, sets a maximum on the amount of punishment which may be inflicted, and increases or decreases that maximum according to the degree of wrong involved in the particular crime. However, the theory does not require the infliction of any punishment at all; it merely limits the *amount* which may be inflicted if a decision to punish has been made. For a particularly strong argument taking this line, see Professor Hart's 'Prolegomenon to the Principles of Punishment' in H L A Hart, *Punishment and Responsibility*, Oxford University Press, 1968. 'Desert theory' is elaborated in the text by A von Hirsch, *Past or Future Crimes*, Rutgers University Press, 1985.

Deterrence

1.44 The deterrent theory is probably the one which receives the greatest amount of articulate popular support. Its most clear expression in modern times has been provided by the great philosopher-jurist Jeremy Bentham, who expounded its philosophical basis and drew up a scheme for a Criminal Code based almost entirely upon the theory.

According to Bentham, every human being has as his or her twin objects in life the achievement of pleasure and the avoidance of pain. It follows, accordingly, that you can deter the person from committing an act which will bring him or her a certain degree of pleasure by holding out as a prospect the infliction upon that person of a slightly greater degree of pain if he or she should commit the act. Such deterrence was thus the purpose of the criminal law, and Bentham graded offences according to the probable degree of pleasure that they would normally afford to those indulging in the prohibited behaviour, and suggested that punishments should be graded accordingly. See J Bentham, *An Introduction to the Principles of Morals and Legislation* (1789), J H Burns and H L A Hart (eds), Athlone Press, 1970.

1.45 There are a number of grave difficulties with this theory. Modern philosophers have dissected the notions of pleasure and pain as they were used by Bentham, and by careful analysis have shown that they are the cause of hopeless confusion. Once more, we need not pursue here the deeper philosophical problems. It is sufficient to note some practical difficulties of Bentham's theory. In the first place, the theory would appear to dispense altogether with the notion of wrong. If parliament wishes to stop a particular type of conduct, it can threaten the imposition of a sufficiently severe punishment and thereby produce the desired result. However, this would surely offend the normal person's sense of justice. Bentham himself did not wish to press the theory thus far, and he recognised that the notion of punishment is inextricably mixed up with the notion of wrong.

Another severe difficulty with the theory is that it is apt to conflict in certain cases with the deep-rooted human instinct for justice. For example, it would require a far more severe prospect of punishment to deter a starving person from stealing a loaf of bread than it would to deter a comparatively wealthy criminal from committing fraud in order to buy a second yacht; yet most people would regard the rich rogue as the more deserving of punishment. Again, since Bentham recognised that punishment should not be inflicted unless it was likely to prove useful for deterrent purposes, it can be argued that no punishment should be inflicted when there is no prospect of it having any useful effect.

1.46 This brings us to a further difficulty. Unless great care is taken, there is likely to be extraordinary confusion between the effect of inflicting punishment on that person in deterring others from committing similar acts (general deterrence), and the effect of prospective punishment on *this* person either to deter him or her from committing this act, or to deter him or her from committing similar acts in the future (special deterrence). Bentham himself produces some of this confusion in discussing what he calls 'cases unmeet for punishment'.

Among these he refers to the case of the lunatic, and says that he would be excused on the ground that the prospect of punishment could not have a deterrent effect upon him — but it is obvious, is it not, that the hanging of a lunatic murderer might well deter other would-be murderers from carrying out their plans?

1.47 Although the deterrent theory may not be of great value in dealing with particular cases, it should not be overlooked in considering the purposes of the criminal law. Its particular force lies in the fact that it is almost impossible to imagine what it would be like to live in a community where nothing was punishable. Experience has shown that when the official law and order machinery breaks down (for example, if the police force goes on strike) there is likely to be an immediate and unwelcome increase in crime, and citizens have to form themselves into vigilante groups to get some measure of protection for their lives, persons and property. (The Melbourne police strike of 1923 was accompanied by outbursts of riotous destruction, and looting in the city.) Similarly, a severe reduction in punishment for a particular type of offence may produce odd results. For example, it is recorded that in the Middle Ages the punishment for rape was reduced from hanging to two years' imprisonment, but that within a very short space of time parliament restored the former punishment of hanging. The reasons for this may be left to the reader's conjecture.

Rehabilitation

1.48 The rehabilitative theory sees crimes as a social disease for which steps can and should be taken to cure. The punishment, according to this theory, is inflicted for the purpose of reforming the criminal and inducing him or her to lead a non-criminal life in the future. While it is true that deterrent punishment has the same general object, the difference is that rehabilitative punishment is designed to change an evil person into a good person, while deterrent punishment is not intended to change the criminal's general outlook but merely to stop him or her from pursuing evil ways and putting this outlook into practice in the future.

The objections to the rehabilitative theory may be stated in a very short compass. Ideally, a cure should be based on an understanding of the disease. Applying that analogy, it may be said that while many theories have been advanced as to the causes of crime, all these are speculative and none has been validated in a scientific manner. Furthermore, although many theories have been advanced as to what types of punishment may be regarded as curative, again no theory has, as yet, been demonstrated as working in practice. It would seem that it is idealistic to talk of reforming the criminal as the aim if no-one can state how this can effectively be done. Some reformers have contemplated the compulsory incarceration of convicted criminals for as long as they remain unreformed. Others have proposed surgical operations or medical treatments such as 'chemical castration' for criminals as an avenue to reformation. How does that square with our general feeling of 'just deserts'? In these examples, rehabilitation remains an imperfect and under-developed punishment paradigm.

1.49 Two other theories as to the aims of the criminal law are occasionally put forward. The first regards punishment as a measure of 'warehousing' which protects society by removing the criminal from it, either permanently or for a set period. While appropriate forms of punishment can provide for these ends, crime cannot be completely eradicated from a community by punishing on this basis unless the punishments are made so severe that they conflict with our notions of justice. In that event, the system will break down because people will be unwilling to prosecute and juries unwilling to convict.

The second theory points to the criminal law as an educative force in the community; when people are constantly presented with the spectacle of punishment being inflicted for a certain type of conduct, they will come to realise that such conduct is wrong. This theory undoubtedly has a measure of truth in it and should be borne in mind by legislators. However, education of this kind can only be a side effect of the practical operation of the criminal law.

Deterrence and certainty

1.50 We have seen in the foregoing brief discussion what an important part is played by general deterrence in the operation of the criminal law: see **1.44–1.47**. Realisation of this has led many eminent jurists to stress the desirability of making the criminal law certain. For instance, in 1966 Lord Gardiner LC, in issuing the Practice Statement wherein it was announced that the House of Lords would no longer regard itself as bound to follow its previous decisions, said that, in carrying out its new practice, the House would bear in mind 'the especial need for certainty in the criminal law'.

The theoretical link between certainty and general deterrence is quite plain. If one wishes to deter people from engaging in various activities by holding out to them a threat of punishment, it seems essential to state quite clearly and precisely what the forbidden activity is; it would seem the threat cannot have any effect on the mind of the prospective criminal unless he or she can associate it easily with a particular proposed activity on his or her part.

1.51 It will be seen that this argument, in order to have validity, requires at least two assumptions. One is that members of the community order their behaviour by reference to the commands and prohibitions of the criminal law. This, however, is most unlikely to be the case. The ordinary citizen who wishes to be a law-abiding member of this community orders his or her behaviour by reference to the accepted practices of the community. It is, broadly speaking, only the person who is bent on transgressing the spirit of the criminal law while conforming to its letter — sailing as close to the wind as he or she possibly can — who will seek to know the precise ambit of its commands. It may well be asked whether one should strive to encourage such a person.

The second assumption made by those who demand certainty in the criminal law is that it can be achieved. This, however, is open to the gravest doubt. There are certain notions, on which we necessarily rely in formulating statements of law, which are inherently imprecise and take on meaning only when given a specific context. Among them are such concepts as those of relevance, importance and reasonableness, to name only three. There is simply no way of ensuring that each person's understanding of the meaning to be given to such terms, even in a specific context, is the same as that of another. Terms of this kind import the making of value judgments, and the ranking of value is inevitably a personal matter. Attempts are often made to give precision to certain areas of the criminal law by using concepts of this kind, but the only effect that this has is to change the question being asked without solving the basic problem. For instance, we shall later encounter the troublesome problem of deciding when a course of conduct ceases to be 'preparation' for a particular transaction and becomes an 'attempt' to carry it out. The courts have, in specific decisions, provided illustrations giving a general idea of where the line is to be drawn between these two stages, but it is not possible to express it precisely. An effort, for example, to do so by saying that the person whose conduct is in question must have taken a substantial step towards the completion of the transaction, changes the question to one of the meaning of 'substantial', but this change does not remove the basic indeterminacy as to the position of the line.

Certainty and codification

1.52 The desire for certainty lies behind the pressures for stating the criminal law in the form of a complete Code. For the reasons just given, however, a Code is bound to fail in achieving complete certainty. There is also the further problem, inherent in codification, that the Code encapsulates the understanding of a particular period as to the desirable form and limits of the criminal law. The original Queensland Criminal Code, for example, sets out the ideas current at the end of the nineteenth century and, at the same time, inhibits further development of the kind which can take place under the common law system. Once the Code is enacted, the law must, so to speak, stand still until parliament decides to vary it. In 1995 a new Criminal Code was enacted in Queensland, which incorporated the many legislative changes made in the period from 1899 onwards. It was not proclaimed and, in 1997, it was repealed, so the original Code remains in force. It is a matter of experience that parliament can usually more readily be induced to rectify what it regards as an error in the course of common law development than to modify the provisions of a Code to which it has given birth after much effort.

Codification has been on the agenda of those concerned about the revision and reform of the criminal law, not in the common law states alone but as a part of a move for uniform criminal law throughout Australia. In 1990 the Standing Committee of Attorneys-General decided to establish the Criminal Law Officers Committee, which would prepare an Australian model Criminal Code. This followed extensive reviews in both the common law and Code states of their criminal law statutes, and the publication of the Gibbs Committee Report on *Principles of Criminal Responsibility* (in the context of the Commonwealth's criminal legislation). In 1995, the Commonwealth Parliament enacted the Criminal Code Act which deals with those most important general matters, including the elements of an offence, the limits of criminal responsibility and extensions of criminal liability, discussed at 1.21 above.

Some practical realities

1.53 The cry for certainty gets whatever plausibility it may have from the focusing of attention solely upon those aspects of the criminal law which are discussed in judicial decisions. Those decisions, however, form a comparatively small part of the administration of the criminal law in practice. Moreover, the majority of them are decisions of appellate courts. An appreciation of the workings of the criminal law based wholly or mainly on a study of appellate decisions will have more than a tinge of unreality. The appellate court deals with a situation in which it is generally assumed, as a starting point, that the facts of the transaction have been ascertained. The only matter with which the court concerns itself is whether the legal rules were correctly stated and applied during the course of the trial, though this inquiry may include an examination of whether or not the facts were appropriately re-created at the trial. Attention is thus focused on questions of the admissibility of certain evidence and of the correctness or otherwise of the terms in which the trial judge formulated his or her directions to the jury. If, in either of these matters, the trial judge made some error the normal result would be that the conviction must be quashed. Thus, in the appellate court the trial judge's behaviour is subjected to the most detailed scrutiny, but the rest of the process which occurred before or during the trial is, usually, almost entirely neglected. There are some significant exceptions to this, especially under the rubric of 'abuse of process' which was used by the High Court of Australia in deciding criminal appeals in some leading cases in the last decade of the twentieth century. It is difficult, on occasion, to escape the feeling that the appellate court is debating and determining a problem which in truth had little more than a marginal effect on the whole transaction. In practice, Magistrates' Courts deal with most of the criminal trials that take place and, because the penalties imposed by them are usually relatively light and the costs of pursuing an appeal may be relatively large, the decisions of those courts, for the most part, are not subjected to appeal. Magistrates work under heavy pressures of time in order to clear their lists and it is not to be expected that the fine distinctions drawn from time to time by appellate courts will always be given by magistrates the weight to which they are theoretically entitled. This is not to say that Magistrates' Courts do not loyally implement the requirements of the law. The point is that the conditions under which they have to work, and the realities of the daily practice of the justice system, force them sometimes to neglect some of the niceties.

DISCRETION, THE PREROGATIVE OF MERCY AND THE ROLE OF THE JURY

The role of discretion

1.54 If one examines closely the actual operation of the criminal law, it becomes obvious that, at almost every stage, discretions arise and must be exercised. Police officers in their daily work must continually decide which of the many transgressions occurring within their view they will officially notice. If an officer decides to notice a particular one, that officer must also then decide how far he or she will go. When the officer intervenes, it will sometimes be appropriate for the offender to be let off with a caution. At other times, the officer will want either to make an arrest or perhaps to report the matter to superior officers who will then themselves decide on the next step.

Since it is only the rare case in which offending provides a single breach of the law, a decision to prosecute involves a further decision as to what and how many charges will be laid. In some cases, it will be thought appropriate to lay a single, comparatively minor charge. In others, the police will 'throw the book' at the offender. When the case comes to court, it may be that the offender will offer to plead guilty to some of the charges if the remainder of them are dropped. The making and subsequent discussion of such an offer is known as 'plea bargaining'. Plea bargaining is a practice which obviously carries dangers. Police and prosecutors may overcharge accused persons in order to establish an advantageous position from which to negotiate. An accused may fail to appreciate the nature of the arrangement being proposed, or may be unwilling to take the chance of going to trial notwithstanding that she or he in reality has a good defence to the charges. Despite the dangers involved in any form of plea bargaining, some use of the practice now seems to be established as part of our system of the administration of criminal justice. It must be remembered that, in practice, the vast majority of those who are prosecuted in the courts plead guilty to the charges against them. Indeed, if only a small percentage of those who at present plead guilty decided to contest the charges, our courts would break down under the pressure of cases for trial, and not simply for sentence. In these circumstances, it is hypocritical to condemn the practice of plea bargaining outright. Recognition of the practice is found, for example, in statutory provisions such as those in the Criminal Procedure Act 2009 (Vic) s 219. The practices of state and federal Directors of Public Prosecutions on plea negotiations are now published and provide clear criteria by which to examine, and where appropriate to criticise, particular arrangements.

1.55 A second form of plea bargaining involves the obtaining of a private indication from the trial judge of the likely penalty to be imposed following a plea of guilty. In England, the Court of Appeal in *R v Turner* [1970] 2 All ER 281 recognised the existence of such a practice, and laid down guidelines to govern it. The High Court, however, in *Bruce v R* (HCA, 21 May 1976, unreported) strongly condemned the practice as 'carrying on the administration of justice behind closed doors'. Since guilty pleas are accepted as a proper basis for mitigation of sentence (*R v Webb* [1971] VR 147), it would seem that the English approach of seeking to regulate this form of plea bargaining is to be preferred to the High Court's moralistic denunciation of it. The enactment in Victoria of ss 5(2)(e) and 6AAA of the Sentencing Act 1991 announces a contrary legislative view on this practice.

1.56 Where a trial results in a verdict of guilty then the judge has a wide discretion as to the penalty which he or she will impose. Appeal courts from time to time lay down general guidelines as to sentencing when cases come before them. However, they are on the whole reluctant to overrule a trial judge except in those instances where they think he or she has stepped outside any reasonable boundaries on judicial discretion.

The prerogative of mercy

1.57 A brief word must be said about the Crown's discretion in regard to the enforcement of sentences imposed by courts. The power of the Crown to pardon an offender has been recognised as part of the Royal prerogative since ancient times; it is known technically as the prerogative of mercy. From time to time the power is exercised outright. For instance, if it is demonstrated at some time after a trial that an accused was not, in fact, guilty, the Crown will issue what is known as a free pardon which has the effect of wiping out the conviction.

It is also open to the Crown, in the exercise of its prerogative of mercy, to require a lesser penalty than that imposed by the court. An offender can be released from imprisonment before the sentence has expired, or payment of only part of a fine can be required. One commonly recurring situation in which the prerogative of mercy came to be exercised was in relation to the death penalty. The abolition of capital punishment for murder in all Australian jurisdictions has consigned this to the realm of the historical. In New South Wales, Victoria and South Australia, the death penalty was abolished in 1955, 1975 and 1976 respectively. Prior to the abolition of the death penalty in these states, however, it was carried out only rarely. In Victoria, for example, of 88 persons convicted of murder between 1951 and 1972 only four were hanged. In New South Wales and Victoria, murder now carries a maximum penalty of life imprisonment: Crimes Act 1900 (NSW) s 19A; Crimes Act 1958 (Vic) s 3.

Motive

1.58 Among the many factors which make the exercise of discretion a necessity is the refusal of the criminal law to recognise the importance of motive. For present purposes, a 'motive' may be loosely defined as the circumstances leading a person to take certain action. It is commonly stated that the criminal law pays no attention to motive. In one sense, this is undoubtedly correct. The common law principle, *actus non facit reum nisi mens sit rea* includes no reference to motive. Robin Hood may steal from the rich in order to give the proceeds of the theft to the poor but, if he appears before a court charged with stealing, his benevolent motive will be disregarded in determining whether he has committed that crime. If he is convicted, his motive may be taken into account in fixing sentence. In other senses, however, the proposition is anything but correct. Many of the general defences, such as provocation and duress, involve the acceptance of motive as bearing on criminal liability. Where the law is steadfast in its refusal to take account of motive, unsatisfactory results may follow; thus mercy killing (euthanasia) is classified as murder in all Australian jurisdictions despite the fact that the benevolent motive of the killer may be regarded by most people as greatly lessening, if not completely removing, his or her moral culpability. (See the discussion at 4.6.) In such situations, the discretion of prosecutors to charge the lesser crime of manslaughter is of great significance. The power of the judge in New South Wales and Victoria to impose a lesser penalty than life imprisonment for murder (see 1.57) constitutes a further important discretion enabling the strictness of the law to be tempered by regard for the accused's motive.

The role of the jury

1.59 Our discussion of the exercise of discretion in the criminal process would be incomplete without some consideration of the part played by the jury at the criminal trial. It is commonly stated that, where a trial takes place before a judge and jury, the task of the jury is to act as a fact-finding body. When they have found the facts, so it is said, they must apply to them the principles of law expounded to them by the judge in the charge. This analysis leads to the proposition that, if the facts appear clearly enough from the evidence, the judge can direct the jury as to the verdict which they ought to return.

Whatever may be the case where civil trials are concerned, in the criminal sphere this analysis misconceives the role of the jury. The law places in their hands the power of giving the ultimate decision on the general issue of whether the accused is guilty or not guilty and thus affords them an opportunity to exercise discretion. A person who intentionally kills a loved one to save them from the agony of a terminal illness is guilty of murder. Nonetheless, it may be proper for a jury — which supposedly represents a cross-section of the community and thus of its values — to return a verdict of manslaughter only, or even of acquittal. Such results have been reached by juries in Australia.

In the long history of the jury as part of our legal institutions, it has been the case that, until very recently, its task of exercising discretion has been recognised, although the basis on which this recognition has been afforded has, from time to time, changed. It is fashionable nowadays, however, to describe the jury as a fact-finding body and thus, by implication, to deny them the power to exercise discretion. This, in turn, inevitably leads to a question of their efficiency as a fact-finding body which, we may concede, is not very great. Therefore, there has been an increasing tendency to remove the jury from various types of trial and to commit those types of trial to the hands of a judge or magistrate sitting alone. This tendency has gone very far in the civil law, and, from time to time, there are moves towards restricting the role of the jury in the criminal process. It is our belief that these steps proceed in a wrong direction. They are part of an effort to introduce precision into an area where, as we have endeavoured to show, precision cannot be expected and would be undesirable if it could be obtained.

CRIMINAL PROCEDURE AND EVIDENCE — PRELIMINARY

1.60 There are long-established rules and standards which apply only to criminal prosecutions. These are conveniently described as 'criminal procedure'. The study and evaluation of that body of law is an important part of the education of a student of the law, and there are readily accessible resources to which reference should be made: see, for example, in Victoria, R G Fox, *Victorian Criminal Procedure: State and Federal Law*, 13th ed, Monash Law Book Co-operative, Legibook, 2010.

1.61 A few of the most salient elements of criminal procedure and evidence must be described and considered here as a necessary prologue to the examination of the substance of the criminal law. The first is double jeopardy, which reflects a central principle of justice in the administration of the criminal law and which is currently under critical review. The second is the burden and standard of proof in criminal prosecutions. The third is appeals in criminal cases.

DOUBLE JEOPARDY

Special pleas

1.62 In *Green v United States* (1957) 355 US 184, Black J (at 187–9) explained the rationale of the principle of double jeopardy as follows:

> The State with all its resources and power should not be allowed to make repeated attempts to convict an individual for an alleged offence, thereby subjecting him to embarrassment, expense and ordeal and compelling him to live in a continuing state of anxiety and insecurity, as well as enhancing the possibility that even though innocent he may be found guilty.

At common law, the principle of double jeopardy found expression in the special pleas of autrefois convict (previously convicted) and autrefois acquit (previously acquitted). These pleas operated as a bar to the further prosecution of an indictment for a criminal offence. The pleas differ from a plea to the general issue (guilty or not guilty) in that, by them, the accused is asserting that the court cannot proceed to try the charges laid in the indictment.

The previous jeopardy

1.63 It is immaterial whether the first acquittal or conviction was on indictment or in summary proceedings: see, for example, *R v Gamble; Ex parte Cleary* [1947] VLR 491 where the first trial was before a magistrate sitting alone. If it is established that the court before which the defendant was previously tried was for some reason without jurisdiction, then that plea in bar will not succeed, since the accused was never truly in jeopardy on the earlier occasion: *Hackwill v Kay* [1960] VR 632. See also *Island Maritime Ltd v Filipowski* (2006) 228 ALR 1.

What constitutes jeopardy?

1.64 It is clear that the previous trial must have proceeded to a verdict if the defendant is to plead its results in bar of the present prosecution. In this connection, a conviction quashed by an appellate tribunal, on such grounds as do not impugn the original trial as a nullity, is regarded as an acquittal, and the defendant may plead autrefois acquit should she or he be subsequently indicted for the same offence: see *R v Barron* [1914] 2 KB 570.

The original proceedings may terminate because the prosecution files a nolle prosequi (a formal statement to the court that it does not wish to proceed further with the indictment) or withdraws a charge by leave of the court, or because the presiding judge discharges the jury without receiving their verdict (as he or she may do for a variety of reasons, of which a common one is the inadvertent reception of inadmissible but highly prejudicial evidence). In such an event, the defendant cannot plead this result as an acquittal should he or she be subsequently presented in respect of the same charge. It should also be remembered that where a magistrates' court declines to commit a defendant at the conclusion of a preliminary investigation of an indictable offence, this does not constitute an acquittal since the proceedings are really not judicial but investigatory. The prosecution may thereafter present the defendant directly in a superior court, or institute further committal proceedings, as it chooses: see *Grassby v R* (1989) 87 ALR 618 per Dawson J.

Abuse of process

1.65 The pleas of autrefois acquit and autrefois convict are not sufficient to cover all cases in which an accused might, in substance, be placed in jeopardy more than once in respect of the same matter. For example, the driver of a train causes an accident in which 100 people are killed. The Crown believes the accident was due to the gross negligence of the accused and prosecutes the driver for manslaughter of one passenger. If the accused were to be acquitted, the plea of autrefois acquit would not prevent a further prosecution of the driver for the manslaughter of another passenger. Since the victim is different, the offence is not the same and, accordingly, the plea of autrefois acquit is not available to the accused.

In seeking to remedy the limitations of the pleas of autrefois acquit and autrefois convict, the courts have held that it is an abuse of process for the prosecution to seek to rely on evidence which is only relevant on the assumption that the accused was guilty of an offence of which he or she was previously acquitted.

1.66 In *R v Storey* (1978) 22 ALR 47 the two accused were charged with abduction and rape. It was alleged that they forcibly took the complainant from a railway station and conveyed her to a pavilion in a nearby park where they raped her. They were acquitted by the jury on the charge of abduction, but the jury was unable to agree on the counts of rape. The accused were tried again on two counts of rape. At the second trial, it was submitted that the Crown could not lead evidence that the prosecutrix was forcibly taken from the railway station on the ground that the acquittal on the abduction charge concluded that matter against the Crown. The trial judge rejected this submission, and the jury found the accused guilty. They appealed to the Court of Criminal Appeal of Victoria which held that the Crown was precluded from leading evidence in the second trial that was inconsistent with the acquittal on the count of abduction. The court set the convictions aside and ordered a new trial. The Crown was granted special leave to appeal to the High Court.

By a majority of four to three (Mason, Jacobs, Aickin and Stephen JJ; Barwick CJ, Gibbs and Murphy JJ dissenting), the High Court dismissed the Crown's appeal. Both the majority and the minority affirmed the principle that a verdict of acquittal must not be challenged at a subsequent trial, and that an accused must be given the full benefit of such a verdict. Barwick CJ stated (at 51–2):

> The accused in the hearing of a subsequent charge must be given the full benefit of his acquittal on the earlier occasion. Evidence which was admissible to establish the earlier offence is, in my opinion, not inadmissible merely because it was tendered in the earlier proceedings: but it may not be used for the purpose of challenging, or diminishing the benefits to the accused of, the acquittal. Such evidence will be admissible, provided it is relevant to the subsequent charge, or to a defence to it, but must only be allowed to be used to support that charge or negative a defence.
>
> But the citizen must not be twice put in jeopardy, that is to say, as relevant to the present discussion, must not be placed at the risk of being thought guilty of an offence of which he has been acquitted, or of in any sense being treated as guilty. It is the use of the evidence given on the prior occasion to canvass the acquittal which, if allowed, would offend the rule against double jeopardy, giving that rule a generous application. The principle that the accused in the subsequent trial must be given the full benefit of the acquittal thus might be regarded as akin to, but not a mere extrapolation of, the principle of autrefois acquit, both being grounded upon the protection of the law against double jeopardy. But, to my mind, they are distinct principles.

With the exception of Jacobs J, all members of the court held the evidence of the circumstances of the taking of the victim from the railway station to have been admissible. The case turned on whether the trial judge had adequately instructed the jury that they were bound to accept the verdict of acquittal given by the first jury, and to treat the two accused as entirely innocent of the offences of abduction. Three members of the court (Barwick CJ, Gibbs and Murphy JJ) held that the trial judge's direction had been adequate, and three (Mason and Aickin JJ, Stephen J agreeing with Aickin J) held that it had not. Jacobs J held the evidence itself to be inadmissible. Accordingly, by a majority of four to three, the appeal by the Crown was dismissed.

Perjury

1.67 Where an accused has been acquitted of an offence, he or she may not be convicted of perjury in respect of evidence given by him or her at that earlier trial. In *R v Carroll* (2002) 194 ALR 1, the High Court held that it is an abuse of process for the prosecution to seek to go behind the earlier verdict of acquittal notwithstanding that that verdict was obtained, in part at least, as a consequence of fraud. In *R v Carroll*, the accused was charged with the murder of a 17-month-old child. The prosecution case included forensic odontology evidence that bite marks on the victim's thigh were caused by the accused. The accused gave evidence under oath at his trial that he did not kill the deceased. Notwithstanding the denial, the jury returned a verdict of guilty. On appeal, the Court of Criminal Appeal of Queensland concluded that, on the evidence led at the trial, it could not be concluded beyond reasonable doubt that the accused was guilty. A verdict of acquittal was entered. Fourteen years later, the accused was indicted for perjury in relation to his sworn evidence at his murder trial. Additional evidence of the guilt of the accused was presented by the prosecution, including new and different expert evidence which purported to demonstrate that the bite marks on the victim's thigh matched the bite mark of the accused. The jury returned a verdict of guilty. On appeal, the Court of Criminal Appeal of Queensland concluded that the trial should have been stayed as an abuse of process in that the principle of double jeopardy had been substantially breached. The conviction of the accused for perjury was quashed and a verdict of acquittal was entered. The prosecution appealed to the High Court. The High Court upheld the decision of the Court of Criminal Appeal of Queensland. Gleeson CJ and Hayne J stated (at 13):

> The inconsistency between the charge of perjury and the acquittal of murder was direct and plain. The laying of the charge of perjury, solely on the basis of the respondent's sworn denial of guilt, for the evident purpose of establishing his guilt of murder, was an abuse of process regardless of the cogency and weight of the further evidence that was said to be available.

McHugh J stated (at 28):

> It is an abuse of process for the Crown to charge a person with an offence of perjury when proof of the charge necessarily contradicts or tends to undermine an acquittal of the accused in respect of another criminal charge. A perjury charge that has that effect is an abuse of process even if the evidence supporting the charge is different from the evidence that supported the prosecution case in respect of the charge on which the accused was acquitted. The long established policy of the law is that an acquittal is not to be contradicted or undermined by a subsequent charge that raises the same ultimate issue or issues as was or were involved in the acquittal. That is so even though the evidence proving perjury is unanswerable.

Proposals for change

1.68 The decision of the High Court in *R v Carroll*, involving the escape from punishment of an accused twice found by a jury to have committed murder, gave impetus for review of the scope of the principle of double jeopardy in Australia. Review had independently taken place in England. This resulted in the enactment of the Criminal Justice Act 2003 (UK). Part 10 of the Act provides new prosecution rights of appeal against acquittal. It provides that, where a person has been acquitted of a 'qualifying offence', a prosecutor can, with written authorisation of the Director for Public Prosecutions, apply to the Court of Appeal for an order quashing the acquittal and an order for a retrial in respect of the qualifying offence: s 75. Thirty-one serious offences are listed by the Act as qualifying offences, including murder, manslaughter, kidnapping, sexual offences, robbery, arson, terrorist offences and serious drug offences. The Court of Appeal can make such an order if satisfied there is 'new and compelling' evidence that the acquitted person is guilty of the qualifying offence. 'Compelling' is defined as reliable, substantial, and indicating that it is highly probable that the person is guilty of the qualifying offence. The Court of Appeal must also be satisfied that a retrial would be in the interests of justice. An appeal to the House of Lords is permitted for either the prosecution or the defence.

1.69 Following the decision in *R v Carroll*, the New South Wales Government announced its intention to formulate legislation to enable the retrial of an acquitted person where new evidence of guilt emerges. Reform of the law of double jeopardy is canvassed in the discussion paper of the Model Criminal Code Officer's Committee, *Issue Estoppel, Double Jeopardy and Prosecution Appeals Against Acquittals* (November 2003). In 2007 the Council of Australian Governments (COAG) recommended reforms to the rule against double jeopardy, allowing further prosecution after acquittal in cases such as where there is fresh and compelling evidence (such as DNA evidence); where the acquittal is 'tainted'— for instance, the person acquitted subsequently admits to the crime; or where it becomes clear that a juror or court official has been bribed or that key witnesses have given false evidence. Procedural safeguards were to include only permitting the Director of Public Prosecutions (DPP) to make one application for a retrial in relation to any particular acquittal, and requiring police to obtain written authorisation from the DPP before they reinvestigate a person for an offence of which the person has previously been acquitted (unless there is an urgent need to preserve evidence). A court hearing an application for retrial was only to order a retrial if 'in all the circumstances it is in the interests of justice' to do so. In considering whether the interests of justice would be served by a retrial, the court was to consider the length of time since the offence allegedly occurred, and whether the police or prosecution had failed to act with reasonable diligence in applying for the retrial.

1.70 Legislation along these lines has now been passed in New South Wales, Queensland, Tasmania, South Australia and Western Australia. Victoria and the Australian Capital Territory did not support the original COAG recommendation. Both these jurisdictions have passed human rights legislation reflecting international human rights principles, including the rule against double jeopardy. The Charter of Human Rights and Responsibilities Act 2006 (Vic) provides in s 26: 'A person must not be tried or punished more than once for an offence in respect of which he or she has already been finally convicted or acquitted in accordance with law'. (See also Human Rights Act 2004 (ACT) s 24.) However, the human rights legislation in Victoria leaves parliament free to override its provisions (Charter s 31). The Victorian Parliament did so in 2011 with the Criminal Procedure Amendment (Double Jeopardy and Other Matters) Act 2011 (Vic). The Australian Capital Territory continues to debate the issue.

THE BURDEN AND STANDARD OF PROOF

Law and fact

1.71 Traditionally, lawyers have regarded all cases which may demand a solution at their hands as being separable into two main constituents — the facts and the law. It is said that the resolution of every case depends on ascertaining the facts and then applying to them the appropriate rule of law.

1.72 In law schools and elsewhere, when the law is being studied, there is a strong tendency to think in terms of 'rules of law' and to look to the facts only when factual differences lead to a modification of the rule of law which is prima facie applicable. One unfortunate result of this is that the law student gets the facts of the cases he or she studies in an already-established form; the facts are given and the student then discusses the law. One may thus come to think that the establishment of the facts is a fairly simple task. However, every practitioner of the law knows that, in most cases, the real problem lies in establishing the facts. Witnesses differ, not because some of them are lying (they may be, but you should not assume this) but because their recollections are hazy. Moreover, if a witness' motives for some past action are being investigated, that person will tend to portray them in the most favourable light.

Most criminal cases thus turn, in practice, on the view which is ultimately taken of the facts. In more serious cases, the judge decides the question of law and the jury decides questions of fact. In those cases where there is no jury, the judge or magistrate decides questions of law and fact. Decisions on the facts must be made. Usually, it is a difficult decision. Commonly, the person who has the task of making the decision feels some doubt. Thus rules are needed, in both criminal and civil cases, to tell the decision-maker what to do when he or she is in doubt. The criminal rules differ from those in civil cases because a criminal conviction carries with it a moral stigma which is usually, though not always, absent in civil cases. In both civil and criminal law, however, the rules are known as rules regulating the burden (onus) of proof.

The two burdens

1.73 In the cases which raise problems about the burden of proof, there appears to be a deep-rooted conflict of opinion. In some cases, it is stressed that the burden of proof never shifts. In others, the judge will remark that at a certain stage of the case the burden of proof shifted from one party to the other and perhaps that it shifted back again at a still later stage.

What is the source of these apparent contradictions? The pioneering work on this matter was carried out by Professor J B Thayer of the Harvard Law School, which he published as *A Preliminary Treatise on the Law of Evidence* (1898). Thayer's views were further developed by Dean J H Wigmore in his great *Treatise on Evidence* (3rd ed, 1940). These two writers pointed out that the single phrase 'burden of proof' has two quite separate meanings and that much confusion arises from the failure to distinguish adequately in the cases between the two very different principles which may be involved. For an analysis of the concept of burden of proof, see C R Williams, 'Placing the Burden of Proof' in E Campbell and L Waller (eds), *Well and Truly Tried: Essays on Evidence in Honour of Sir Richard Eggleston*, Law Book Co, 1982, p 271.

The legal burden

1.74 The first sense in which the term 'burden of proof' is used is as referring to the rules directing the trier of fact, the jury or, in cases tried without a jury, the judge, what to do if they are unable to determine where the truth lies. In this sense, the burden of proof has been defined as 'the peculiar duty of him who has the risk of any given proposition on which the parties are at issue — who will lose the case if he does not make this proposition out, when all has been said and done': Thayer (1898), p 355. In criminal cases, the risk of failure to persuade the trier of fact lies normally on the prosecutor, not on the accused. This 'risk of failure to persuade' is one meaning of the phrase 'burden of proof'. It is often distinguished from the other meaning of the phrase by being termed the 'legal burden'. The normal situation in criminal cases is thus summarised by saying that the legal burden of proof lies on the prosecutor.

The evidential burden

1.75 The second sense in which the phrase 'burden of proof' is used is bound up with the common law mode of trial by judge and jury. The long process by which the modern jury has evolved from its somewhat obscure origin may be studied in the pages of Thayer's *Preliminary Treatise*. Here it is enough to say that, although the jury remains as the body which decides questions of fact, the judges have managed to assert a considerable measure of control over the process of decision-making.

Why is such control needed? One reason is that, without some degree of control, we would be unable to ensure that all defendants were judged by the same principles. The jury speak only through their decision; they are neither compelled nor empowered to give their reasons for arriving at the decision. It is not possible, generally speaking, to find fault with a decision which is not supported by reasons. If, therefore, we wish to ensure that jury decisions are made within the framework of our principles of law, steps to that end must be taken before the decision is made.

1.76 Consider, for example, the question of provocation in a murder case. In New South Wales, but not Victoria, provocation may operate as a partial defence reducing murder to manslaughter. Suppose that we are dealing with a man who has killed his girlfriend on finding her in bed with a rival. It is quite probable that during the course of his trial his motives for the killing will have come to light. It is also possible that the jury might be tempted to sympathise with him and to show their sympathy by finding him guilty of manslaughter rather than of murder. However, the sight of one's girlfriend having intercourse with another has not been generally, and without more evidence, regarded by the law as sufficient provocation to reduce a charge of murder to manslaughter, and the judge will accordingly control the jury by directing it that there is no evidence before it on which it can properly find provocation.

1.77 The rule has accordingly been evolved that on every issue which may arise in a case, the appropriate party to the case must satisfy the judge that he or she has presented sufficient evidence in support of that party's stand on that issue for a jury to consider. If the party fails to satisfy the judge, then the judge will not allow that issue to be considered by the jury but will instead direct them to disregard it (with the appropriate legal consequences). It follows, therefore, that at various stages in a case, a party to the case may be placed by the judge under a duty of producing some (though not very much) evidence sufficient for the jury to consider on a particular issue, on penalty of having a verdict directed against him or her on that issue if he or she fails to discharge this duty. To take a simple example, if, on a charge of theft, the prosecution offers only evidence to the effect that the defendant was found in possession of the stolen goods some 10 years after they were stolen, the judge will rule this evidence is too thin to allow a conviction and will direct the jury to return a verdict of 'not guilty'. This duty of producing or going forward with evidence in a particular issue is also described by the phrase 'burden of proof'. It is often distinguished from the legal burden by being termed the 'evidential burden'.

It will be seen that the two burdens of proof perform quite different functions. The evidential burden operates on a party to the case, by placing upon that party a duty. The legal burden, in outward form, operates by allocating a risk on a party, but its real function in the case is to operate on the trier of fact by telling him or her what to do when the decision-maker cannot make up his or her mind.

In strict theory, there is no need to have a rule about the duty of producing evidence unless the court is a composite tribunal of judge and jury. A judge or magistrate sitting to hear a case without a jury needs only a rule for allocating the risk of non-persuasion. However, as with many other procedural rules originally devised for jury trials, our law does not distinguish between the two types of trial in dealing with burden of proof, and so the rules as to the burden of producing evidence are applied in non-jury trials.

1.78 The above discussion has, however, so far failed to provide the complete answer to a vital question: upon whom does the burden of proof in a criminal trial rest? This is a question which is asked only too often, but it is ambiguous. We ought rather to ask:

1. Upon whom does the duty of producing evidence (the evidential burden) lie?
2. Upon whom does the risk of non-persuasion as to the issues (the legal burden) lie?

The answers to these questions will not necessarily be the same.

Incidence of the evidential burden

1.79 In relation to the evidential burden, a distinction is drawn between the elements which go to constitute the particular crime charged and the general defences. So far as the constituent elements of the crime charged are concerned then, apart from statute, the prosecution always bears the evidential burden. In a murder case, for example, the prosecution bears the evidential burden of showing that the accused killed the deceased and did so with the requisite intent. The prosecution must prove the guilt of the accused regardless of whether or not the accused has raised a defence or chosen to exercise his or her right to silence. However, in relation to what are termed the 'general defences' (self-defence, provocation, duress, necessity, honest and reasonable mistake of fact, etc), the evidential burden is placed upon the accused. The reason for placing the evidential burden upon the accused in respect of the general defences is that it would be impractical to require the prosecution to rebut, as part of its case, each and every defence theoretically open to the accused. Since the evidential burden is not a heavy one, convenience justifies placing this burden upon the accused.

Incidence of the legal burden

1.80 Let us now turn to the rules which govern the allocation of the risk of non-persuasion. Here, the general rule is that the person who makes a claim must establish it. Accordingly, the rule is that, in a criminal case, the prosecution must bear the risk both of failing to establish all or any of the various elements which make up the crime, and of failing to rebut any defence raised by the accused. In other words, if the trier of fact cannot make up his or her mind that a particular element of the crime charged occurred or that the requirements of a particular defence are not met, the prosecution must fail and the accused be acquitted. Such a rule is of course essential if the citizen's liberties are to be respected, and it is followed by every civilised country in the world, although folklore persists in regarding it as peculiar to the common law countries.

Standard of proof

1.81 A quite separate matter from the *burden* of proof is the *standard* of proof. What does it mean to say that the trier of fact cannot make up his or her mind? What standard or degree of certainty must the adjudicator reach in order to be able to say: 'I have decided that so-and-so occurred'? At this point, we have to remember the basic difference between criminal and civil cases. A criminal conviction carries with it a moral stigma; an adverse judgment in a civil case normally does not. Therefore, in a civil case, it is safe for a court to take action against a defendant when the trier of fact thinks it more likely than not that the alleged facts occurred. In technical language, this is expressed by the rule that a party having the legal burden in a civil action must establish the case 'on the balance of probabilities'.

It would, however, be unsafe to label a person a criminal on such a basis. Before the label is pinned on, one ought to be sure that it is deserved; in our world of uncertainties, it is difficult to come by exact, certain knowledge about the past, but one must be as sure as is possible, bearing in mind the impossibility of being absolutely certain. Hence the rule has been laid down that, in a criminal case, the prosecution must establish the guilt of the accused 'beyond a reasonable doubt'. This is the criminal 'standard of proof'.

The golden thread

1.82 The classical discussion of the legal burden of proof in criminal cases is to be found in *Woolmington v Director of Public Prosecutions* [1935] AC 462. Woolmington killed his wife, who had left him, and was charged with her murder. There was evidence to suggest that the killing was deliberate but Woolmington claimed that it had occurred by accident. At his first trial, the jury disagreed and he was retried before Swift J. The judge told the jury that once they were satisfied that Woolmington had killed his wife, the killing was presumed to be murder unless Woolmington satisfied them that it was something less; that is, manslaughter or excusable homicide. Woolmington was convicted and the Court of Criminal Appeal dismissed his appeal, pointing out that there was authority to support the judge's direction extending at least as far back as the writings of Sir Michael Foster.

Woolmington then obtained the Attorney-General's fiat to appeal to the House of Lords, where his conviction was quashed. Viscount Sankey LC, speaking for the whole House, reviewed the authorities; he doubted whether they supported the judge's direction and suggested that they could bear a different interpretation. Then, in an oft-quoted passage, he laid down the rule in these words (at 481–2):

> Throughout the web of the English Criminal Law one golden thread is always to be seen, that it is the duty of the prosecution to prove the prisoner's guilt subject to what I have already said as to the defence of insanity and subject also to any statutory exception. If, at the end of and on the whole of the case, there is a reasonable doubt, created by the evidence given by either the prosecution or the prisoner as to whether the prisoner killed the deceased with a malicious intention, the prosecution has not made out the case and the prisoner is entitled to an acquittal. No matter what the charge or where the trial, the principle that the prosecution must prove the guilt of the prisoner is part of the common law of England and no attempt to whittle it down can be entertained.

It seems likely that *Woolmington* represented an alteration rather than a restatement of the law as it then was: see further, G P Fletcher, 'Two Kinds of Legal Rules: A Comparative Study of Burden-of-Persuasion Practices in Criminal Cases' (1968) *Yale Law Journal* 77, 880–935. Nonetheless, it set the standard for the burden of proof in criminal cases.

The insanity exception

1.83 In the passage above, the Lord Chancellor mentioned two 'exceptions' to the general rule — the defence of insanity, and special provisions made by statute. We must glance at these, bearing in mind that neither of them were issues in *Woolmington* and that, accordingly, Viscount Sankey's remarks about them may properly be treated as obiter dicta, not as binding authority.

The defence of insanity raises interesting challenges, which will be discussed later: see Chapter 14. It is clear that if an accused was insane at the time of committing the act or omission that comprises the external element of the offence, that person could not have committed an offence. It is also plain that the prosecutor does not have to prove, in every case, that the accused was sane at the time of the alleged crime. The evidential burden of proving insanity clearly lies on the accused.

It is difficult, however, to see any adequate justification for placing the legal rather than the evidential burden with respect to insanity upon the accused. It is sometimes said that every person is presumed to be sane, but this is another way of stating the effect of the rule rather than a justification for it. In *Davis v United States* (1895) 160 US 469, the United States Supreme Court held the burden to rest upon the prosecution. Harlan J asked rhetorically (at 488):

> How, then, upon principle or consistently with humanity, can a verdict of guilty be properly returned if the jury entertain a reasonable doubt as to the existence of a fact which is essential to guilt, namely, the capacity in law of the accused to commit the crime?

It is sometimes said that the difficulty of disproving insanity constitutes a justification for placing the burden upon the accused. However, it is equally difficult to disprove other defences in respect of which the burden is clearly not upon the accused. For a critical discussion of the burden of proof in insanity, see A Loughnan, *Manifest Madness: Mental Incapacity in Criminal Law*, Oxford, 2012.

In spite of the difficulty of finding any adequate justification for the insanity exception to the *Woolmington* principle, the exception has been accepted and applied in numerous Australian cases, and must be taken as representing settled law. See, for example, *R v Porter* (1933) 55 CLR 182, *Sodeman v R* (1936) 55 CLR 192, *Thomas v R* (1960) 102 CLR 584; *Mizzi v R* (1960) 105 CLR 659; *Taylor v R* (1978) 22 ALR 599. The burden placed on the accused, however, is only on the balance of probabilities: *Woolmington v Director of Public Prosecutions* [1935] AC 462 at 475. See also *R v Ayoub* (1984) 10 A Crim R 312 at 316. Statutory provisions in each jurisdiction now embody this rule: see **14.21–14.25**.

Statutory exceptions

1.84 Some statutes distinctly place a legal burden of proof upon the accused. An example is s 233B of the Customs Act 1901 (Cth) (now repealed) which cast the burden of proving reasonable excuse as a defence to a charge of possession of prohibited drugs upon the accused. Other examples in Victoria concern the sexual offences against children contained in ss 45–50 of the Crimes Act 1958 (Vic), to which the defence may be raised that the defendant honestly and reasonably believed the victim was of age. Where this is done, the burden placed upon the accused is, as with insanity, on the standard of the balance of probabilities.

On occasion, some courts have shown a willingness to interpret ambiguous statutes as casting a legal burden upon the accused. See, for example, *R v Edwards* [1975] QB 27; *Johnson v R* (1976) 11 ALR 23. The decision in the latter case was, incidentally, reversed by a subsequent amendment to the relevant statute. The tendency is unfortunate. The 'golden thread' of the *Woolmington* case is properly regarded as central to our concepts of fairness in a criminal trial, and it is submitted that the provisions of a statute should be treated as breaking that thread only where that intention is expressly spelt out in the statute.

Beyond reasonable doubt

1.85 In the early 1950s the attempt was made in England, largely as a result of the influence of Lord Goddard CJ, to move away from the traditional formula of instructing the jury that the prosecution must prove its case beyond a reasonable doubt: *R v Kritz* [1950] 1 KB 82; *R v Summers* [1952] 1 All ER 1059; *R v Hepworth and Fearnley* [1955] 2 QB 600; and note also *Ferguson v R* [1979] 1 All ER 877.

Such attempts to alter the standard of proof in criminal law were never made in Australia, the High Court always insisting that the traditional direction be given. The view maintained in this country has been that it is for the jury to determine what is meant by a reasonable doubt, and the trial judge should attempt neither to define the term nor elaborate its meaning. In *Dawson v R* (1961) 106 CLR 1 at 18, Dixon CJ stated:

> [I]n my view it is a mistake to depart from the time-honoured formula. It is, I think, used by ordinary people and is understood well enough by the average man in the community. The attempts to substitute other expressions, of which there have been many examples not only here but in England, have never prospered. It is wise as well as proper to avoid such expressions.

See also *Thomas v R* (1960) 102 CLR 584; *Green v R* (1971) 126 CLR 28; *La Fontaine v R* (1976) 136 CLR 62.

APPEALS

1.86 At common law, appeals in criminal cases were comparatively rare. A convicted prisoner could appeal against the conviction only by way of a writ of error which was confined to inquiries into the sufficiency of the formal written record that embodied neither the details of the evidence nor the directions given by the judge to the jury as discussed above at 1.15. The practice developed, however, of the judges of the common law courts meeting informally as a body to consider the propriety of rulings given by the trial judge of which the judge felt some doubt. The decisions taken at these judges' meetings became available to the legal profession and began to be embodied in reports. Ultimately, in 1848 the matter was put on a regular footing by the establishment of the Court for Crown Cases Reserved. This court dealt with points reserved for its consideration by the trial judge and, pending its decision, the judge would not pass judgment but would wait until its direction was received and then take the appropriate action. Since, however, the reservation of a point for discussion by the court depended on the trial judge, the process was not altogether satisfactory and, in 1908, a Court of Criminal Appeal was established in England. This court was given power to hear appeals by the accused, provided that, if the convicted person wished to appeal on any matter other than a pure point of law, he or she obtained the leave either of the trial judge or of the Court of Criminal Appeal itself. At the same time, a further appeal to the House of Lords was provided in exceptional cases. Since then, the Court of Criminal Appeal has been abolished and its former jurisdiction transferred to the Criminal Division of the Court of Appeal. The opportunities for appealing to the Supreme Court (formerly the House of Lords) have also been widened.

1.87 Similar developments have followed in the various Australian jurisdictions. In each state, the first appeal lies from the trial court to the Full Court of the Supreme Court, or to the Court of Appeal where established. Following that, an appeal may be taken to the High Court of Australia, but only if that court gives its 'special leave' (which it will do only if there is some special feature in the case which it regards as warranting its intervention). Appeals from the High Court to the Privy Council were abolished by the Privy Council (Appeals from the High Court) Act 1975 (Cth). Appeals from state Supreme Courts to the Privy Council were finally abolished by s 11 of the Australia Act 1986 (Cth).

Powers of appellate courts

1.88 The powers of the Supreme Court in relation to appeals are spelt out by statute: Crimes Act 1958 (Vic) ss 568–569; Criminal Appeal Act 1912 (NSW) ss 6, 7, 8. In Victoria, a separate Court of Appeal has been established, with jurisdiction in both criminal and civil matters: Constitution (Court of Appeal) Act 1994. There was one important difference between the powers of the English Court of Appeal (Criminal Division) and its predecessor and those of the corresponding appellate courts in the Australian states. Both sets of courts have power to dismiss an appeal if they are satisfied that no substantial miscarriage of justice has occurred. This power, however, is treated as being exercisable only if the court is satisfied that a jury which was not acting perversely would inevitably have convicted the accused if it had received correct instructions from the trial judge: see *R v Anderson* [1972] 1 QB 304. It is comparatively rarely that this high test can be satisfied and, in many instances, the court has no option but to allow the appeal. In so doing, its only power in England (apart from some exceptional cases which do not have any effect upon the general pattern) used to be to quash the conviction and order the release of the prisoner, who, because of the double jeopardy rule, could not be put on trial again. In the Australian states, however, the appellate court has an express statutory authority, when it allows an appeal, either to order a retrial of the accused or to quash the conviction and order immediate release. The English Court of Appeal was given a general power to order a retrial after a successful appeal: Criminal Justice Act 1988 s 43(2). In practice, retrials are not ordered unless there is a fairly strong probability that the accused would have been convicted if the trial had not been defective. Furthermore, a retrial cannot be ordered in respect of a charge upon which the accused has been acquitted by a jury (but see 1.70). Thus, if at the trial for murder the prisoner was found not guilty of murder but guilty of manslaughter, and successfully appeals against the conviction on the latter charge, the court will either order a retrial on the charge of manslaughter or quash the conviction and order the defendant's release; but it will not order a retrial on the charge of murder, because the prisoner has been acquitted by the jury on that charge.

Rather than order a retrial, the appellate tribunal may, when quashing a conviction on one charge, substitute for it a conviction on some other charge if the jury could have exercised a similar power at the trial. Thus, the court might quash a conviction for murder and substitute for it a conviction for manslaughter; and again, it might quash a conviction for an offence and substitute for it a conviction for attempting to commit that offence. As with the more general power, these special powers are exercised only if the appellate court is satisfied that the jury must, in reaching the decision which is being quashed, have been satisfied as to the facts necessary to constitute the offence which is being substituted. For discussion of this power, see *Pemble v R* (1971) 124 CLR 107; *Johnson v R* (1976) 11 ALR 23.

Appeals against acquittal

1.89 At present, the Crown has no general right of appeal against a jury's verdict of acquittal. If, however, the accused is convicted by a jury and the conviction is reversed by an appellate court, then it is open to the Crown to seek an appeal against that decision to the High Court of Australia.

Where a case results in an acquittal, the Crown may, in each of the common law states, refer any point of law which arose in the case to the Full Court or Court of Appeal for its opinion: Crimes Act 1958 (Vic) s 450A; Criminal Appeal Act 1912 (NSW) s 5A. The 'appeal' is heard in the normal way, but if the Court of Appeal decides in favour of the Crown, the decision, although being a precedent for future cases, has no effect upon the accused's acquittal. For this reason, these appeals are sometimes referred to as 'academic appeals'.

Appeals against sentence

1.90 In each state there are provisions which enable a prisoner to appeal against the sentence passed on him or her, subject to obtaining leave from the appellate court: Crimes Act 1958 (Vic) s 567; Criminal Appeal Act 1912 (NSW) s 5. Where a sentence is thought to have been too lenient, the Attorney-General has the right to appeal against sentence: Crimes Act 1958 (Vic) s 567A; Criminal Appeal Act 1912 (NSW) s 5D. In Victoria and New South Wales, the appellate court has power to increase the sentence even in cases where the appeal has been brought by the prisoner: Crimes Act 1958 (Vic) ss 567A(4), 568(4); Criminal Appeal Act 1912 (NSW) ss 5D, 6(3). This power is attended with a number of qualifications due to the obvious risks attached to the defendant.

1.91 Further reading

D Brown et al, *Criminal Laws: Materials and Commentary on Criminal Law and Process of New South Wales*, 5th ed, The Federation Press, Sydney, 2011

P Crofts, *Wickedness and Crime*, Routledge, 2013

T Crofts, *The Criminal Responsibility of Children and Young Persons: A Comparison of English and German Law*, Ashgate, 2002

R A Duff, *Answering for Crime: Responsibility and Liability in the Criminal Law*, Hart Publishing, 2007

G P Fletcher, 'Two Kinds of Legal Rules: A Comparative Study of Burden-of-Persuasion Practices in Criminal Cases' (1968) *Yale Law Journal* 77, 880–935

N Lacey, 'Responsibility and Modernity in Criminal Law' (2001) 9(3) *Journal of Political Philosophy* 249–76

A Loughnan, *Manifest Madness: Mental Incapacity in Criminal Law*, Oxford University Press, 2012

A Norrie, *Crime, Reason and History: A Critical Introduction to Criminal Law*, Cambridge University Press, 2001

V Tadros, *Criminal Responsibility*, Oxford University Press, 2005

PART 2

Offences

Assault and Related Offences

CHAPTER 2

INTRODUCTION

2.1 East states the basic principles of the law as follows (Sir Edward Hyde East, *A Treatise of Pleas of the Crown*, Vol I, Butterworth, London, 1803, p 406):

> An assault is any attempt or offer with force and violence to do a corporal hurt to another, whether from malice or wantonness; as by striking at him, or even by holding up one's fist at him in a threatening or insulting manner, or with such other circumstances as denote at the time an intention, coupled with a present ability of using actual violence against his person; as by pointing a weapon at him within the reach of it. Where the injury is actually inflicted, it amounts to a battery, (which includes an assault) and this, however small it may be; as by spitting in a man's face, or any way touching him in anger without any lawful occasion. But if the occasion were merely accidental and undesigned, or if it were lawful …; it is no assault or battery in the law …

2.2 In the modern criminal law, largely as a result of the disappearance of the technicalities of criminal pleading, the term 'battery' has become almost obsolete. Statutes and cases use the term 'assault' to cover both a (psychological) assault and a battery: *R v Lynsey* [1995] 3 All ER 654. This practice will be adopted in the present work, save for cases in which the context requires a greater precision.

In New South Wales, there is a new regime of aggravated assault offences that negate the need to prove common assault. In Victoria far-reaching changes in the law of assault and related offences have rendered the common law offences less significant. The common law crimes do, however, remain and the principles underlying those crimes continue to be important. The Victorian and New South Wales statutory provisions are considered at **2.16E** and **2.17E**.

COMMON ASSAULT

The elements of unlawfulness

2.3 Clearly, not every putting of another in fear of bodily hurt or touching of another is an assault. Although the slightest touching can ground an assault (*Collins v Wilcock* [1984] 3 All ER 374), something more is needed to establish the offence of common assault. It would be absurd to treat the pointing of a gun at a criminal who is being arrested, or the touching of a person's shoulder to warn that person of danger, as criminal. There must be an element of unlawfulness in the transaction, but it does not seem possible to provide a single definition of that element which would cover all possible cases.

Some have suggested that, as regards battery, the absence of the victim's consent to the touching supplies that element. However, that would require the positing of an implied consent in a variety of situations so wide as to make the concept virtually devoid of meaning.

2.4 The solution of the problem seems to lie in considering whether, having regard to all the circumstances of the given case, the touching was within the limits of what is socially accepted or at least tolerated. This would explain the warning of danger. Section 20(2)(a) of the Criminal Law Consolidation Act 1935 (SA) provides 'conduct that lies within limits of what would be generally accepted in the community as normal incidents of social interaction or community life cannot amount to an assault'. Section 182(3) of the Tasmanian Code excludes from an 'assault' any 'act which is reasonably necessary for the common intercourse of life if done only for the purpose of such intercourse, and which is not disproportionate to the occasion'. This provision would appear to state the position at common law: see *Boughey v R* (1986) 60 ALJR 422.

Intention and recklessness

2.5 At common law it is well established that either intention or recklessness is required in order for there to be an assault: *Fagan v Metropolitan Police Commissioner* [1969] 1 QB 439 (at **2.23C**); *R v Venna* [1976] QB 421; [1975] 3 All ER 788 (at **2.27C**).

2.6 The early writers leave it an open question whether an assault can be committed by grossly negligent conduct. Of course, Parliament can make it an offence thus to cause another injury and, in the case of grievous bodily harm, the Victorian and New South Wales Parliaments have done so: Crimes Act 1958 (Vic) s 24; Crimes Act 1900 (NSW) s 54. To constitute these crimes, the degree of negligence which must be established is the criminal standard appropriate to the crime of negligent manslaughter: *R v O* [1984] 3 NSWLR 29.

The victim's mental state

2.7 The nature of a battery is such that (questions of consent being set aside) it does not matter whether the victim was or was not conscious of what was being done. However, it is an essential feature of (psychological) assault that the accused's show of violence should put the victim in fear of hurt. Therefore, it was held in *State v Barry* (1912) 45 Mont 598 that to point a rifle from behind at a victim who was unaware of what was going on was not an assault. In *Pemble v R* (1971) 124 CLR 107, the facts were similar, save that the rifle discharged and the victim was killed. The accused claimed the rifle had discharged accidentally, and the point arose in the High Court whether, if his story were accepted, he was nonetheless necessarily guilty of manslaughter on the basis of the doctrine of manslaughter by an unlawful and dangerous act; on this aspect of the case, see **6.5, note 1(b)**. The court held that, since the victim was unaware that the accused was threatening her with the rifle, an assault was not committed. The accused was, however, convicted of manslaughter on other grounds, Barwick CJ and Windeyer J holding that the accused had committed the crime of attempted assault.

2.8 What if the victim is aware of the threat, but unmoved by it? This occurred in *Brady v Schatzel* [1911] St R Qd 206 where the victim testified that, when the accused pointed a gun at him, he did not try to protect himself because he did not think she would fire it. Chubb J held the accused guilty of assault on the grounds that otherwise an accused's liability would vary according to whether his or her chosen victim was timid or courageous. But why should it not vary? The offence is one which depends on the creation of fear and the expectation of hurt. Moreover, in other contexts, the courts say again and again that an accused must take the victim as he or she finds the victim. Thus, if an exceptionally fragile victim dies as a result of an injury that would not have killed a normally built person, the accused is responsible for the death: see **Chapter 4**. This well-settled principle should surely be available to exculpate as well as to inculpate. This would appear to have been the view adopted by McGarvie J in *Ryan v Kuhl* [1979] VR 315. The accused and the victim were in neighbouring cubicles in a public toilet. The accused thrust a carving knife through a hole in the partition between the cubicles in order, he said, to stop the victim from annoying him. The victim testified that the sight of the knife had not frightened him, since he realised that the accused could not harm him with the knife while he remained in his cubicle. In these circumstances, the accused's conduct not having created a fear of violence in the victim, McGarvie J held there was no case to answer on a charge of assault. The accused could, of course, have been charged with attempted assault. See also *R v Mostyn* [2004] NSWCCA 97.

Unloaded guns

2.9 Where the accused has brandished a gun at the victim, the prosecution may fail to establish that the gun was loaded. Thus the fact must be taken in favour of the accused, that is, it must be assumed that it was not. Or the accused may produce evidence that the gun was, in fact, unloaded. In either case, it is to be assumed that the victim supposed that it was, or at any rate might be, loaded; for if the victim supposed otherwise, he or she could not be put in fear and there could be no assault (unless the two were close enough for the gun to be used as a club).

It is now established that it is an assault to point an unloaded gun if apprehension is thereby created: *R v St George* (1840) 9 Car & P 483; 173 ER 921; *R v Everingham* (1949) 66 WN (NSW) 122; *Logdon v Director of Public Prosecutions* [1976] Crim LR 121.

AGGRAVATED ASSAULT

2.10 The above paragraphs have been concerned with what are termed 'common assaults'. The penalty for common assault is spelt out for New South Wales in Crimes Act 1900 (NSW) s 61 and for Victoria in the Summary Offences Act 1966 (Vic) s 23. In addition, a wide variety of statutory offences commonly termed 'aggravated assaults' are punishable more severely than common assault: Crimes Act 1900 (NSW) ss 27–30, 32–60E; Summary Offences Act 1966 (Vic) s 24. Speaking broadly, aggravated assaults fall into three classes:

(1) assaults which are accompanied by an intention of a particular kind or are performed in a particular manner;

(2) assaults committed on particular classes of person; and

(3) assaults which result in harm of a particular kind.

Strictly speaking, these statutory offences are not all assaults. Poisoning, for example, does not technically constitute an assault: *R v Sherriff* [1969] Crim LR 260. The malicious infliction of grievous bodily harm normally involves an assault, but may be committed in circumstances in which there is no assault: see *R v Salisbury* [1976] VR 452 (at **2.31C**). Nevertheless, the expression 'aggravated assault' is a commonly used generic term for these offences which have as their common element a non-fatal infliction or potential infliction of physical harm upon the victim.

Assaults accompanied by particular intentions or performed in a particular way

2.11 The most important form of aggravated assault involving a particular intention is assault with intent to commit murder: Crimes Act 1900 (NSW) s 27; in Victoria, there is no precisely equivalent provision, although assault with intent to commit an indictable offence is a crime: Crimes Act (Vic) s 31(1). With intent to commit murder means 'with intent to kill'. It is not sufficient that the accused acted with an intention to inflict grievous bodily harm even though that would be sufficient to render the accused guilty of murder if death resulted (*R v Whybrow* (1951) 35 Cr App R 141; *R v Grimwood* [1962] 2 QB 621; *R v Bozikis* [1981] VR 587 at 591), nor is it sufficient that the accused acted with recklessness as to the possibility of death: *R v Belfon* [1976] 3 All ER 46.

Various forms of aggravated assault performed in particular ways include poisoning (Crimes Act 1900 (NSW) ss 39, 41, 41A), the use of stupefying drugs (Crimes Act 1900 (NSW) ss 38, 38A) and the use of explosives: Crimes Act 1900 (NSW) ss 46–48.

Assaults on persons of a particular class

2.12 Although other classes of person receive special protection (for example, clergymen and sailors), the most important offence of this type is assaulting a police officer in the execution of his or her duty: Crimes Act 1900 (NSW) s 60; Crimes Act 1958 (Vic) s 31. In *R v Reynhoudt* (1962) 107 CLR 381, the High Court held, by a majority of three to two, that it is not necessary that the accused be aware that the victim is a police officer. Taylor J, with whom Menzies and Owen JJ agreed, held (at 395) that the offence extended:

> … to assaults on members of the police force committed in ignorance of the victim's membership of that force but recklessly or indifferently and without regard to whether the victim was a member of the police force or not.

See also *McBride v Turnock* [1964] Crim LR 456. It is submitted, however, that the following statement of Dixon CJ (dissenting, at 387), with whom Kitto J agreed, accords more with principle:

> The offence is an aggravated assault, aggravated by the fact that the person assaulted is a policeman and is in the execution of his duty. That is a compound offence and I think that the guilty mind should go to the elements of which it is composed.

The court further stated that the idea of acting in the execution of a police officer's duty should be construed broadly to protect the performance of all police duties and to apply whenever the police officer is doing something which can fairly and reasonably be regarded, given the existing circumstances, as a carrying out of her or his duty.

Section 60 of the Crimes Act 1900 (NSW) is not limited in its operation to assaults. Section 60(1) covers a person who 'assaults, throws a missile at, stalks, harasses or intimidates a police officer while in the execution of the officer's duty, although no actual bodily harm is occasioned to the officer'. Section 60(2) contains the offence of assaulting a police officer in the execution of the officer's duty, and by the assault occasioning actual bodily harm. Section 60(3) contains the offence of maliciously wounding or inflicting grievous bodily harm on a police officer while in the execution of the officer's duty. Issues as to when an officer is acting in the execution of his or her duty are avoided by s 60(4) which provides:

> For the purposes of this section, an action is taken to be carried out in relation to a police officer while in the execution of the officer's duty, even though the police officer is not on duty at the time, if it is carried out:

(a) as a consequence of, or in retaliation for, actions undertaken by that police officer in the execution of the officer's duty; or
(b) because the officer is a police officer.

In addition, under s 60(1A), (2A) and (3A) there are additional offences, with higher penalties, for assaulting a police officer during a public disorder.

Assaults resulting in harm of a particular kind: New South Wales

2.13 The most important of these forms of aggravated assault are assault occasioning actual bodily harm (Crimes Act 1900 (NSW) s 59) and wounding or inflicting grievous bodily harm: Crimes Act 1900 (NSW) ss 33, 35, 54. These offences are set out at **2.16E**.

A number of terms used in these provisions require explanation:

(1) 'Actual bodily harm' covers any hurt or injury calculated to interfere with the health or comfort of the victim, provided it is something more than merely transient and trifling: *R v Donovan* [1934] 2 KB 498 at 509; *R v Miller* [1954] 2 QB 282 at 292; note *R v Percali* (1986) 42 SASR 46; *Coulter v R* (1987) 62 ALJR 74. Examples include cutting a person's hair (*DPP v Smith* [2006] EWHC 94) or psychiatric injury (*R v Chan-Fook* [1994] 2 All ER 552 (see **2.34, note 6**)).

(2) 'Grievous bodily harm' means bodily harm of a really serious kind: *Director of Public Prosecutions v Smith* [1961] AC 290 at 334–5; *R v Saunders* [1985] Crim LR 230; *R v Perks* (1986) 41 SASR 335; *R v Blevins* (1988) 48 SASR 65. This can include chronic psychiatric injuries: *R v Ireland; R v Burstow* [1997] 4 All ER 225 (see **2.34, note 7**). Section 4 of the Crimes Act 1900 (NSW) defines grievous bodily harm as:

   (a) the destruction (other than in the course of a medical procedure) of the foetus of a pregnant woman, whether or not the woman suffers any other harm, and
   (b) any permanent or serious disfiguring of the person, and
   (c) any grievous bodily disease (in which case a reference to the infliction of grievous bodily harm includes a reference to causing a person to contract a grievous bodily disease).

(3) 'Wound' is an injury which breaks the skin and penetrates below the epidermis (exterior layer) into the dermis (interior layer): *Vallance v R* (1961) 108 CLR 56. Penetration of the dermis will cause bleeding, and consequently evidence of free bleeding will suffice to prove a wound was inflicted: *R v Devine* (1982) 8 A Crim R 45.

2.14 The statutory offences relating to particular forms of harm have varying levels of mens rea. Some are directly relevant to the type of harm. For example, s 33 of the Crimes Act 1900 (NSW) provides for the offence of wounding or grievous bodily harm with intent. Here, the mens rea is directed to the intention to cause grievous bodily harm. However, the mens rea need not be directed to the harm and can be in relation to a lesser form of harm. For example, in s 35 of the Crimes Act the mens rea for the offence of reckless grievous bodily harm is recklessness as to causing actual bodily harm. In s 59, the mens rea for the offence of assault occasioning actual bodily harm is the mens rea for common assault. In addition, s 54 provides an offence for causing grievous bodily harm by any unlawful act or omission.

2.15 In order to occasion or cause a particular harm, the act or omission must substantially cause the victim to suffer the injury. For example, the offence of assault occasioning actual bodily harm under s 59 of the Crimes Act 1900 (NSW) requires that the defendant's actions were a substantial and operating cause of the actual bodily harm (*Zanker v Vartzokas* (1988) 34 A Crim R 11).

2.16E Crimes Act 1900 (NSW)

33 Wounding or grievous bodily harm with intent

(1) Intent to cause grievous bodily harm A person who:

(a) wounds any person, or

(b) causes grievous bodily harm to any person,

with intent to cause grievous bodily harm to that or any other person is guilty of an offence.

Maximum penalty: Imprisonment for 25 years.

(2) Intent to resist arrest A person who:

(a) wounds any person, or

(b) causes grievous bodily harm to any person,

with intent to resist or prevent his or her (or another person's) lawful arrest or detention is guilty of an offence.

Maximum penalty: Imprisonment for 25 years.

35 Reckless grievous bodily harm or wounding

(1) Reckless grievous bodily harm-in company A person who, in the company of another person or persons:

(a) causes grievous bodily harm to any person, and

(b) is reckless as to causing actual bodily harm to that or any other person,

is guilty of an offence.

Maximum penalty: Imprisonment for 14 years.

(2) Reckless grievous bodily harm A person who:

(a) causes grievous bodily harm to any person, and

(b) is reckless as to causing actual bodily harm to that or any other person,

is guilty of an offence.

Maximum penalty: Imprisonment for 10 years.

(3) Reckless wounding-in company A person who, in the company of another person or persons:

(a) wounds any person, and

(b) is reckless as to causing actual bodily harm to that or any other person,

is guilty of an offence.

Maximum penalty: Imprisonment for 10 years.

(4) Reckless wounding A person who:

(a) wounds any person, and

(b) is reckless as to causing actual bodily harm to that or any other person,

is guilty of an offence.

Maximum penalty: Imprisonment for 7 years.

54 Causing grievous bodily harm

Whosoever by any unlawful or negligent act, or omission, causes grievous bodily harm to any person, shall be liable to imprisonment for two years.

59 Assault occasioning actual bodily harm

(1) Whosoever assaults any person, and thereby occasions actual bodily harm, shall be liable to imprisonment for five years.

(2) A person is guilty of an offence under this subsection if the person commits an offence under subsection (1) in the company of another person or persons. A person convicted of an offence under this subsection is liable to imprisonment for 7 years.

Victorian assault legislation

2.17E Crimes Act 1958 (Vic)

Subdivision (4) — Offences Against the Person

15 Definitions

'injury' means —

(a) physical injury; or

(b) harm to mental health — whether temporary or permanent;

'serious injury' means —

(a) an injury (including the cumulative effect of more than one injury) that —

(i) endangers life; or

(ii) is substantial and protracted; or

(b) the destruction, other than in the course of a medical procedure, of the foetus of a pregnant woman, whether or not the woman suffers any other harm;

'harm to mental health' includes psychological harm but does not include an emotional reaction such as distress, grief, fear or anger unless it results in psychological harm;

'physical injury' includes unconsciousness, disfigurement, substantial pain, infection with a disease and an impairment of bodily function;

15A Causing serious injury intentionally in circumstances of gross violence

(1) A person must not, without lawful excuse, intentionally cause serious injury to another person in circumstances of gross violence.

Penalty: Level 3 imprisonment (20 years maximum).

(2) For the purposes of subsection (1), any one of the following constitutes circumstances of gross violence —

(a) the offender planned in advance to engage in conduct and at the time of planning —
   (i) the offender intended that the conduct would cause a serious injury; or
   (ii) the offender was reckless as to whether the conduct would cause a serious injury; or
   (iii) a reasonable person would have foreseen that the conduct would be likely to result in a serious injury;

(b) the offender in company with 2 or more other persons caused the serious injury;

(c) the offender participated in a joint criminal enterprise with 2 or more other persons in causing the serious injury;

(d) the offender planned in advance to have with him or her and to use an offensive weapon, firearm or imitation firearm and in fact used the offensive weapon, firearm or imitation firearm to cause the serious injury;

(e) the offender continued to cause injury to the other person after the other person was incapacitated;

(f) the offender caused the serious injury to the other person while the other person was incapacitated.

15B Causing serious injury recklessly in circumstances of gross violence

(1) A person must not, without lawful excuse, recklessly cause serious injury to another person in circumstances of gross violence.

Penalty: Level 4 imprisonment (15 years maximum).

(2) For the purposes of subsection (1), any one of the following constitutes circumstances of gross violence —

(a) the offender planned in advance to engage in conduct and at the time of planning —
   (i) the offender intended that the conduct would cause a serious injury; or
   (ii) the offender was reckless as to whether the conduct would cause a serious injury; or
   (iii) a reasonable person would have foreseen that the conduct would be likely to result in a serious injury;

(b) the offender in company with 2 or more other persons caused the serious injury;

(c) the offender participated in a joint criminal enterprise with 2 or more other persons in causing the serious injury;

(d) the offender planned in advance to have with him or her and to use an offensive weapon, firearm or imitation firearm and in fact used the offensive weapon, firearm or imitation firearm to cause the serious injury;

(e) the offender continued to cause injury to the other person after the other person was incapacitated;

(f) the offender caused the serious injury to the other person while the other person was incapacitated.

16 Causing serious injury intentionally

A person who, without lawful excuse, intentionally causes serious injury to another person is guilty of an indictable offence. Penalty: Level 3 imprisonment (20 years maximum).

17 Causing serious injury recklessly

A person who, without lawful excuse, recklessly causes serious injury to another person is guilty of an indictable offence.

Penalty: Level 4 imprisonment (15 years maximum).

18 Causing injury intentionally or recklessly

A person who, without lawful excuse, intentionally or recklessly causes injury to another person is guilty of an indictable offence.

Penalty: If the injury was caused intentionally — level 5 imprisonment (10 years maximum). If the injury was caused recklessly — level 6 imprisonment (5 years maximum).

19 Offence to administer certain substances

(1) A person who —

(a) without lawful excuse, administers to or causes to be taken by another person any substance which is capable, and which the first person knows is capable, in the circumstances, of interfering substantially with the bodily functions of the other person; and

(b) knows that the other person has not consented to the administration or taking of the substance or is reckless as to whether or not the other person has so consented —

is guilty of an indictable offence.

Penalty: Level 6 imprisonment (5 years maximum).

(2) For the purposes of subsection (1) —

(a) a person is not to be taken to have consented to the administration or taking of a substance if, had the person known the likely consequences, the person would not be likely to have consented to the administration or taking; and

(b) a substance shall be taken to interfere substantially with bodily functions if the substance is capable of inducing unconsciousness or sleep.

19A Intentionally causing a very serious disease

(1) A person who, without lawful excuse, intentionally causes another person to be infected with a very serious disease is guilty of an indictable offence. Penalty: Level 2 imprisonment (25 years maximum).

(2) In subsection (1) ***very serious disease*** means HIV within the meaning of the *Health Act 1958*.

20 Threats to kill

A person who, without lawful excuse, makes to another person a threat to kill that other person or any other person —

(a) intending that that other person would fear the threat would be carried out; or

(b) being reckless as to whether or not that other person would fear the threat would be carried out —

is guilty of an indictable offence.

Penalty: Level 5 imprisonment (10 years maximum).

21 Threats to inflict serious injury

A person who, without lawful excuse, makes to another person a threat to inflict serious injury on that other person or any other person —

(a) intending that that other person would fear the threat would be carried out; or

(b) being reckless as to whether or not that other person would fear the threat would be carried out —

is guilty of an indictable offence.

Penalty: Level 6 imprisonment (5 years maximum).

22 Conduct endangering life

A person who, without lawful excuse, recklessly engages in conduct that places or may place another person in danger of death is guilty of an indictable offence.

Penalty: Level 5 imprisonment (10 years maximum).

23 Conduct endangering persons

A person who, without lawful excuse, recklessly engages in conduct that places or may place another person in danger of serious injury is guilty of an indictable offence.

Penalty: Level 6 imprisonment (5 years maximum).

24 Negligently causing serious injury

A person who by negligently doing or omitting to do an act causes serious injury to another person is guilty of an indictable offence.

Penalty: Level 6 imprisonment (5 years maximum).

2.18 The Crimes (Amendment) Act 1985 (Vic) abolished the existing assault provisions contained in ss 11–43 inclusive of the Crimes Act 1958 (Vic), and replaced those sections with wholly new provisions. The more important of these provisions are set out at **2.17E**.

The common law relating to assault and battery was not, however, swept away. First, although s 37 of the Crimes Act 1958 (Vic) containing the penalty for assault occasioning actual bodily harm (battery) and common assault was repealed, the common law offences of assault and battery were not abolished. Thus they continue to exist as common law crimes, triable on indictment and carrying a maximum penalty of five years' imprisonment: *R v Patton* [1998] 1 VR 7 (at **2.26C**); Crimes Act 1958 (Vic) s 320. Second, assault and battery remain significant in relation to the doctrine of unlawful act manslaughter: see **Chapter 6**. Third, the Summary Offences Act 1966 (Vic) ss 23 and 24 establishes offences of 'assault' for which no statutory definition is provided. Finally, other provisions of the Crimes Act 1958 (Vic), such as indecent assault (s 39), piracy (s 70A) and burglary (s 76), continue to use the common law concept of assault in defining the offences they create. While the new legislation has certainly achieved simplification of the law, it remains the case that practitioners and students must continue to be familiar with the old common law concepts.

The statutory provisions may conveniently be divided into five classes of offences against the person:

(1) *Offences involving the infliction of harm:* Section 16 contains the offence of causing serious injury intentionally, s 17 the offence of causing serious injury recklessly, s 18 the offence of causing injury intentionally or recklessly, and s 19 the offence of administering a substance known to be capable of interfering substantially with the bodily functions of another person. 'Injury' and 'serious injury' are defined in s 15. Section 19A creates the offence of intentionally causing a very serious disease (specifically HIV). Amendments passed in 2013 have introduced two new offences with significantly heavier penalties: intentionally (s 15A) or recklessly (s 15B) causing serious injury in circumstances of gross violence.

(2) *Offences involving a threat:* Section 20 contains the offence of threatening to kill, and s 21 the offence of threatening to inflict serious injury. Section 21A (discussed at 2.21) creates the offence of stalking.

(3) *Offences involving endangerment:* Section 22 contains the offence of recklessly engaging in conduct that may endanger life, and s 23 the offence of recklessly engaging in conduct that may cause serious injury: note *R v Nuri* [1990] VR 641; *Mutemeri v Cheesman* [1998] VR 484 (at 2.34, note 8). Note also D Lanham, 'Danger Down Under' [1999] *Crim LR* 960; CMV Clarkson, 'General Endangerment Offences: The Way Forward' (2005) 32(2) *University of Western Australia Law Review* 131.

(4) *Negligent infliction of serious harm:* Section 24 contains the offence of negligently causing serious injury.

(5) *Miscellaneous offences:* The statutory provisions also cover setting traps with intent to kill (s 25) or cause serious injury (s 26), extortion (ss 27, 28), using firearms to resist arrest (s 29), threatening injury to prevent arrest (s 30) and assault with intent to commit an indictable offence or resist arrest: s 31.

Although these new provisions appear logical and simple, this apparent simplicity is deceptive. Section 15 was amended in 2013 to provide a detailed definition of injury and serious injury. 'Injury' is defined to mean 'physical injury' or 'harm to mental health'. Physical injury is defined to include 'unconsciousness, disfigurement, substantial pain, infection with a disease and an impairment of bodily function', and 'harm to mental health' is defined to include 'psychological harm but does not include an emotional reaction such as distress, grief, fear or anger unless it results in psychological harm'. 'Serious injury' is defined to mean '(a) an injury (including the cumulative effect of more than one injury) that (i) endangers life; or (ii) is substantial and protracted; or (b) the destruction, other than in the course of a medical procedure, of the foetus of a pregnant woman, whether or not the woman suffers any other harm'. If further elaboration is needed, it appears that injury may be regarded as equating with actual bodily harm at common law (see 2.13), and cover any hurt or injury calculated to interfere with the health or comfort of the victim, provided it is something more than merely transient and trifling. Serious injury may be regarded as equating with grievous bodily harm at common law and meaning bodily harm of a really serious kind: see Hedigan J in *Director of Public Prosecutions v Williams* [1993] VR 15. Other constituent elements of the various crimes are left undefined. The legislation does not define many of the key words comprising the various crimes, including, inter alia, 'intentionally', 'recklessly', 'negligently' and 'without lawful excuse'. Far from making the law clear and simple, the new provisions leave many of the problems which existed under the old law lurking within these undefined expressions. In *R v Campbell* [1997] 2 VR 585 (at **2.29C**) the Court of Appeal held that the word 'recklessly' in the sections was used in its subjective sense as referring to the state of mind of a person who foresees a result of her or his actions as being likely or probable.

Domestic violence: partners and children

2.19 Centuries ago, it was accepted practice for wives (and domestic servants) to be punished corporally in the home; the emancipation of wives in this regard was put beyond doubt by the Court of Appeal in *R v Jackson* [1891] 1 QB 671, and firmly restated in *R v Reid* [1973] QB 299. Prohibitions on violence against women have been embodied in international instruments, including the United Nations *Declaration on the Elimination of Violence Against Women*, UNGA, 85th plen mtg, UN Doc A/RES/48/104 (20 December 1993).

2.20 It was also established at common law that a parent (or person in the position of a parent; for example, a guardian) may inflict reasonable and moderate punishment on a child: see *R v Terry* [1955] VLR 114 adopting the United Kingdom decision of *R v Hopley* (1860) 175 ER 1204. On attaining full age, a person ceases to be liable to domestic corporal punishment. Australia has been criticised on numerous occasions in recent years for retaining the defence, by United Nations Committees overseeing Australia's compliance with the Convention on the Rights of the Child, and the Convention Against Torture. See further, B Naylor and B Saunders, 'Parental Discipline, Criminal Laws and Responsive Regulation' in M Freeman (ed), *Law and Childhood Studies: Current Legal Issues*, Vol 14, Oxford University Press, 2012, pp 506–29. In New South Wales, the chastisement of children by corporal punishment was given a statutory basis in 2002. Section 61AA of the Crimes Act 1900 (NSW) limits the extent to which a child can be physically disciplined. It provides that, in criminal proceedings brought against a person arising out of the application of physical force to a child, it is a defence that the force was applied for the purpose of the punishment of the child, but only if:

(a) the physical force was applied by the parent of the child or by a person acting for a parent of the child, and
(b) the application of that physical force was reasonable having regard to the age, health, maturity or other characteristics of the child, the nature of the alleged misbehaviour or other circumstances.

Numerous studies have shown that the home is the most common context in which acts of serious personal violence occur: see, for a comprehensive recent analysis, Australian Law Reform Commission, *Family Violence — A National Legal Response*

(2010), Report No 114. The problem of domestic violence is compounded by the fact that the police are frequently unwilling to become involved, the fact that the victim may be unwilling or afraid to support a prosecution, and that some jurors may still adopt the view that acts of violence by a man upon members of his family are not the business of the law. The inability or unwillingness of the authorities to intervene at an early stage in what may be a continuing and escalating situation of domestic violence may have tragic and often fatal consequences. For this reason, in each jurisdiction legislation has been enacted empowering courts to make 'intervention orders', or 'apprehended violence orders', following application by police officers, the affected family member and others. In some cases, courts can issue an intervention order independently, and police can also issue an order to protect the safety of family members. Such orders require potential offenders not to approach or otherwise contact members of their family thought to be at risk. Failure to comply with such an order constitutes a specific offence: Crimes (Domestic and Personal Violence) Act 2007 (NSW) s 14(1); Family Violence Protection Act 2008 (Vic) s 123.

Stalking

2.21 The practice of stalking (that is, following or otherwise showing repeated unwanted attention to another, often a woman), in circumstances which arouse reasonable fear or apprehension in the person being stalked, represents a twofold danger. First, there is the fear caused by the practice itself. Second, the practice of stalking is not infrequently a precursor to serious violence. The activities of a stalker usually fall short of constituting an assault or an attempt to commit a crime, the underlying element of a threat normally being implicit only. In each of the common law jurisdictions, anti-stalking legislation has been enacted. In Victoria, the Crimes (Amendment) Act 1994 introduced a new s 21A into the Crimes Act 1958. The section makes it an offence to act in a range of ways in relation to the victim or any other person, including following, telephoning, sending emails, publishing on the internet, loitering, keeping under surveillance or 'otherwise act[ing] in a way that could reasonably be expected to arouse apprehension or fear in the victim for his or her own safety or that of any other person'.

It is a requirement of the offence that the accused acted with the intention of causing physical or mental harm to the victim, or of arousing apprehension or fear in the victim for his or her safety or that of any other person. Section 21A(3) extends the scope of the offence by providing that an offender also has the intention to cause physical or mental harm to the victim or to arouse apprehension or fear in the victim for his or her own safety or that of any other person if that offender knows, or in all the particular circumstances that offender ought to have understood, that engaging in a course of conduct of that kind would be likely to cause such harm or arouse such apprehension or fear and it actually did have that result. Section 21A(3) imports an objective element into the offence, with the result that the required state of mind is not the actual state of mind of the offender, but what that offender in those circumstances ought to have understood: *R v Hoang* [2007] VSCA 117.

The equivalent stalking or intimidation provision in New South Wales is Crimes (Domestic and Personal Violence) Act 2007 (NSW) s 13. Section 13(3) requires that the accused actually 'knows that the conduct is likely to cause fear in the other person' (that is, a subjective standard). However, s 13(4) does not require the prosecution to prove that the victim actually feared physical or mental harm.

See, generally, M Goode, 'Stalking: Crime of the Nineties?' (1995) 19 *Crim LJ* 21; M Pathe, R Mackenzie and P Mullen, 'Stalking by Law: Damaging Victims and Rewarding Offenders' (2004) 12 *JLM* 103.

Ritual circumcision

2.22 In many countries, circumcision of young males is a traditional religious practice. Forms of circumcision of young girls are also practised in some religious traditions. Female circumcision, now widely referred to as 'female genital mutilation', has been challenged in recent years as a form of violence and an unlawful assault, and has been criminalised in many jurisdictions: see Crimes Act 1958 (Vic) ss 32–34A; Crimes Act 1900 (NSW) s 45. Ritual male circumcision appears to be lawful on the basis of community acceptance (see 2.4). There is some suggestion that male circumcision has health benefits, but this has also been challenged. See L Haberfield, 'The Law and Male Circumcision in Australia: Medical, Legal and Cultural Issues' (1997) 23(1) *Monash University Law Review* 92; Tasmania Law Reform Institute, *Non-Therapeutic Male Circumcision* (2012), Report No 17. Its legality has been challenged as a possible breach of the United Nations *Convention on the Rights of the Child*, which requires States Parties (of which Australia is one) to 'take all effective and appropriate measures with a view to abolishing traditional practices prejudicial to the health of children' (Art 24(3)). Criticism of circumcision has also arisen recently in countries that do not have a religious tradition of circumcising infant males: see H Askola, 'Cut-Off Point: Regulating Male Circumcision in Finland' (2011) 25(1) *International Journal of Law, Policy and the Family* 100. It appears, however, to continue to be acceptable as a customary practice.

ELEMENTS OF ASSAULT

2.23C Fagan v Metropolitan Commissioner of Police

[1969] 1 QB 439; [1968] 3 All ER 422
Queen's Bench Divisional Court

...

Lord Parker CJ: I will ask James J to read the judgment which he has prepared, and with which I entirely agree.

James J: The appellant, Vincent Martel Fagan, was convicted by the Willesden magistrates of assaulting David Morris, a police constable, in the execution of his duty on August 31, 1967. He appealed to quarter sessions. On October 25, 1967, his appeal was heard by

Middlesex Quarter Sessions and was dismissed. This matter now comes before the court on appeal by way of case stated from that decision of quarter sessions.

The sole question is whether the prosecution proved facts which in law amounted to an assault.

On August 31, 1967, the appellant was reversing a motor car in Fortunegate Road, London, NW10, when Police Constable Morris directed him to drive the car forwards to the kerbside and standing in front of the car pointed out a suitable place in which to park. At first the appellant stopped the car too far from the kerb for the officer's liking. Morris asked him to park closer and indicated a precise spot. The appellant drove forward towards him and stopped it with the offside wheel on Morris's left foot. 'Get off, you are on my foot', said the officer. 'Fuck you, you can wait', said the appellant. The engine of the car stopped running. Morris repeated several times 'Get off my foot'. The appellant said reluctantly 'Okay man, okay', and then slowly turned on the ignition of the vehicle and reversed it off the officer's foot. The appellant had either turned the ignition off to stop the engine or turned it off after the engine had stopped running.

The justices at quarter sessions on those facts were left in doubt as to whether the mounting of the wheel on to the officer's foot was deliberate or accidental. They were satisfied, however, beyond all reasonable doubt that the appellant 'knowingly, provocatively and unnecessarily allowed the wheel to remain on the foot after the officer said "Get off, you are on my foot"'. They found that on those facts an assault was proved.

Mr Abbas for the appellant relied upon the passage in Stone's Justices' Manual, 1968, vol 1, p 651, where assault is defined. He contends that on the finding of the justices the initial mounting of the wheel could not be an assault and that the act of the wheel mounting the foot came to an end without there being any *mens rea*. It is argued that thereafter there was no act on the part of the appellant which could constitute an *actus reus* but only the omission or failure to remove the wheel as soon as he was asked. That failure, it is said, could not in law be an assault, nor could it in law provide the necessary *mens rea* to convert the original act of mounting the foot into an assault.

Mr Rant for the respondent argues that the first mounting of the foot was an *actus reus* which act continued until the moment of time at which the wheel was removed. During that continuing act, it is said, the appellant formed the necessary intention to constitute the element of *mens rea* and once that element was added to the continuing act, an assault took place. In the alternative, Mr Rant argues that there can be situations in which there is a duty to act and that in such situations an omission to act in breach of duty would in law amount to an assault. It is unnecessary to formulate any concluded views on this alternative.

In our judgment the question arising, which has been argued on general principles, falls to be decided on the facts of the particular case. An assault is any act which intentionally — or possibly recklessly — causes another person to apprehend immediate and unlawful personal violence. Although 'assault' is an independent crime and is to be treated as such, for practical purposes today 'assault' is generally synonymous with the term 'battery' and is a term used to mean the actual intended use of unlawful force to another person without his consent. On the facts of the present case the 'assault' alleged involved a 'battery'. Where an assault involves a battery, it matters not, in our judgment, whether the battery is inflicted directly by the body of the offender or through the medium of some weapon or instrument controlled by the action of the offender. An assault may be committed by the laying of a hand upon another, and the action does not cease to be an assault if it is a stick held in the hand and not the hand itself which is laid on the person of the victim. So for our part we see no difference in principle between the action of stepping on to a person's toe and maintaining that position and the action of driving a car on to a person's foot and sitting in the car whilst its position on the foot is maintained.

To constitute the offence of assault some intentional act must have been performed: a mere omission to act cannot amount to an assault. Without going into the question whether words alone can constitute an assault, it is clear that the words spoken by the appellant could not alone amount to an assault; they can only shed a light on the appellant's action. For our part we think the crucial question is whether in this case the act of the appellant can be said to be complete and spent at the moment of time when the car wheel came to rest on the foot or whether his act is to be regarded as a continuing act operating until the wheel was removed. In our judgment a distinction is to be drawn between acts which are complete — though results may continue to flow — and those acts which are continuing. Once the act is complete it cannot thereafter be said to be a threat to inflict unlawful force upon the victim. If the act, as distinct from the results thereof, is a continuing act there is a continuing threat to inflict unlawful force. If the assault involves a battery and that battery continues there is a continuing act of assault.

For an assault to be committed both the elements of *actus reus* and *mens rea* must be present at the same time. The *actus reus* is the action causing the effect on the victim's mind (see the observations of Park B in *R v St George* (1840) 9 C & P 483, 490, 493). The *mens rea* is the intention to cause that effect. It is not necessary that *mens rea* should be present at the inception of the *actus reus*; it can be superimposed upon an existing act. On the other hand the subsequent inception of *mens rea* cannot convert an act which has been completed without *mens rea* into an assault.

In our judgment the Willesden magistrates and quarter sessions were right in law. On the facts found the action of the appellant may have been initially unintentional, but the time came when knowing that the wheel was on the officer's foot the appellant (1) remained seated in the car so that his body through the medium of the car was in contact with the officer, (2) switched off the ignition of the car, (3) maintained the wheel of the car on the foot and (4) used words indicating the intention of keeping the wheel in that position. For our part we cannot regard such conduct as mere omission or inactivity.

There was an act constituting a battery which at its inception was not criminal because there was no element of intention but which became criminal from the moment the intention was formed to produce the apprehension which was fl owing from the continuing act. The fallacy of the appellant's argument is that it seeks to equate the facts of this case with such a case as where a motorist has accidentally run over a person and, that action having been completed, fails to assist the victim with the intent that the victim should suffer.

We would dismiss this appeal.

Bridge J: I fully agree with my Lords as to the relevant principles to be applied. No mere omission to act can amount to an assault. Both the elements of *actus reus* and *mens rea* must be present at the same time, but the one may be superimposed on the other. It is in the application of these principles to the highly unusual facts of this case that I have, with regret, reached a different conclusion from the majority of the Court. I have no sympathy at all for the appellant, who behaved disgracefully. But I have been unable to find any way of regarding the facts which satisfies me that they amounted to the crime of assault. This has not been for want of trying. But at every attempt I have encountered the inescapable question: after the wheel of the appellant's car had accidentally come to rest on the constable's foot, what was it that the appellant did which constituted the act of assault? However the question is approached, the answer I feel obliged to give is: precisely nothing. The car rested on the foot by its own weight and remained stationary by its own inertia. The appellant's fault was that he omitted to manipulate the controls to set it in motion again.

Neither the fact that the appellant remained in the driver's seat nor that he switched off the ignition seem to me to be of any relevance. The constable's plight would have been no better, but might well have been worse, if the appellant had alighted from the car leaving the ignition switched on. Similarly I can get no help from the suggested analogies. If one man accidentally treads on another's toe or touches him with a stick, but deliberately maintains pressure with foot or stick after the victim protests, there is clearly an assault. But there is no true parallel between such cases and the present case. It is not, to my mind, a legitimate use of language to speak of the appellant 'holding' or 'maintaining' the car wheel on the constable's foot. The expression which corresponds to the reality is that used by the justices in the case stated. They say, quite rightly, that he 'allowed' the wheel to remain.

With a reluctantly dissenting voice I would allow this appeal and quash the appellant's conviction.

[Appeal dismissed.]

[See also *R v Miller* [1983] 2 AC 161; 1 All ER 978.]

2.24 The case below is included for its discussion of mens rea. Note that arson in Victoria is an offence under s 197 of the Crimes Act 1958 (Vic), and arson causing death is an offence under s 197A, and under ss 195–197 of the Crimes Act 1900 (NSW).

2.25C R v Miller

[1983] 2 AC 161; 1 All ER 978
House of Lords (on appeal from the Court of Appeal (Criminal Division))

[The accused had been charged with arson under the Criminal Damage Act 1971 (UK) in that he 'without lawful excuse damaged by fire a house … intending to do damage to such property or recklessly as to whether such property would be damaged'. Mr Miller said in his statement to police:

> Last night I went out for a few drinks and at closing time I went back to the house where I have been kipping for a couple of weeks. I went upstairs into the back bedroom where I've been sleeping. I lay on my mattress and lit a cigarette. I must have fell to sleep because I woke up to find the mattress on fire. I just got up and went into the next room

> and went back to sleep. Then the next thing I remember was the police and fire people arriving. I hadn't got anything to put the fire out with so I just left it.

He was convicted at the Leicester Crown Court and appealed to the Court of Appeal on the ground that his actions did not disclose any offence. His appeal was dismissed but the Court of Appeal granted leave to appeal to the House of Lords to decide the following question: 'Whether the actus reus of the offence of Arson is present when a Defendant accidentally starts a fire and thereafter, intending to destroy or damage property belonging to another or being reckless as to whether any such property would be destroyed or damaged, fails to take any steps to extinguish the fire or prevent damage to such property by that fire?'.]

Diplock LJ: The first question to be answered where a completed crime of arson is charged is: 'Did a physical act of the accused start the fire which spread and damaged property belonging to another (or did his act cause an existing fire, which he had not started but which would otherwise have burnt itself out harmlessly, to spread and damage property belonging to another)?' I have added the words in brackets for completeness. They do not arise in the instant case; in cases where they do, the accused, for the purposes of the analysis which follows, may be regarded as having started a fresh fire.

The first question is a pure question of causation; it is one of fact to be decided by the jury in a trial upon indictment. It should be answered 'No' if, in relation to the fire during the period starting immediately before its ignition and ending with its extinction, the role of the accused was at no time more than that of a passive bystander. In such a case the subsequent questions to which I shall be turning would not arise. …

If on the other hand the question, which I now confine to: 'Did a physical act' of the accused start the fire which spread and damaged property belonging to 'another?', is answered 'Yes', as it was by the jury in the instant case, then for the purpose of the further questions the answers to which are determinative of his guilt of the offence of arson, the conduct of the accused, throughout the period from immediately before the moment of ignition to the completion of the damage to the property by the fire, is relevant; so is his state of mind throughout that period.

Since arson is a result-crime the period may be considerable, and during it the conduct of the accused that is causative of the result may consist not only of his doing physical acts which cause the fire to start or spread but also of his failing to take measures that lie within his power to counteract the danger that he has himself created. And if his conduct, active or passive, varies in the course of the period, so may his state of mind at the time of each piece of conduct. If at the time of any particular piece of conduct by the accused that is causative of the result, the state of mind that actuates his conduct falls within the description of one or other of the states of mind that are made a necessary ingredient of the offence of arson by section 1(1) of the Criminal Damage Act 1971, (i.e. intending to damage property belonging to another or being reckless as to whether such property would be damaged) I know of no principle of English criminal law that would prevent his being guilty of the offence created by that subsection. Likewise I see no rational ground for excluding from conductcapable of giving rise to criminal liability, conduct which consists of failing to take measures that lie within one's power to counteract a danger that one has oneself created, if at the time of such conduct one's state of mind is such as constitutes a necessary ingredient of the offence. I venture to think that the habit of lawyers to talk of '*actus reus*', suggestive as it is of action rather than inaction, is responsible for any erroneous notion that failure to act cannot give rise to criminal liability in English law.

No one has been bold enough to suggest that if, in the instant case, the accused had been aware at the time that he dropped the cigarette that it would probably set fire to his mattress and yet had taken no steps to extinguish it he would not have been guilty of the offence of arson, since he would have damaged property of another being reckless as to whether any such property would be damaged.

I cannot see any good reason why, so far as liability under criminal law is concerned, it should matter at what point of time before the resultant damage is complete a person becomes aware that he has done a physical act which, whether or not he appreciated that it would at the time when he did it, does in fact create a risk that property of another will be damaged; provided that, at the moment of awareness, it lies within his power to take steps, either himself or by calling for the assistance of the fire brigade if this be necessary, to prevent or minimise the damage to the property at risk.

[**Lord Diplock** concluded (with the concurrence of the remaining four Law Lords) that the certified question be answered 'yes' and the appeal dismissed.]

2.26C R v Patton

[1998] 1 VR 7

Court of Appeal, Supreme Court of Victoria

[The accused was convicted of a number of offences including burglary arising from a spate of criminal activity over the course of an afternoon. The Crown alleged the accused had entered a building as a trespasser with 'intent to assault and injure a person (in the premises)'. On appeal it was argued that the accused should not have been convicted of burglary because the intent relied on was an intent to commit a common assault, and that crime had been abolished in Victoria when the former s 37 of the Crimes Act 1958 (Vic) was repealed in 1985.]

Phillips CJ, **Winneke P** and **Southwell AJA**: ... The proposition that common assault no longer persists as an indictable common law offence in this State has more than academic interest. Since the former s 37 of the Crimes Act was repealed in 1985 it has been commonly assumed that the offence has remained as an indictable common law offence for which the penalty is at large. During the past 10 years the Crown has continued to present accused persons, on indictment, for the offence of common assault. Indeed the applicant Robinson was so presented in this case. The forms and precedents which are annexed to the Presentment Rules in the current reprint of the Crimes Act still contain, in form 16, a precedent for the presentment of an accused on the charge of common assault. Furthermore, during the past few years, the courts in this State have readily accepted (no doubt because it has not been contended to the contrary) that the offence of common assault still persists as an indictable common law offence: see, for example, *R v Johnson* (unreported, Court of Criminal Appeal, 8 December 1994); *R v Coulston* (unreported,

Court of Criminal Appeal, 12 April 1995); *R v Bailey* (unreported, Court of Appeal, 9 November 1995); *R v Gillingham* (unreported, Court of Appeal, 5 December 1995).

Mr Holdenson contends that, notwithstanding the practice to which we have referred, common assault is no longer an indictable offence in Victoria. He derives some support for his contention from the 5th edition of *Howard's Criminal Law* where the author states at p 141:

> In Victoria, common assault is no longer an indictable offence, and has been replaced under the Crimes Act by the offence of intentionally or recklessly causing injury.

In a footnote at p 137 the author further stated:

> In Victoria, indictable common assault has been abolished, by implication: See *Crimes Act* (Vic) s 37 (repealed by *Crimes (Amendment) Act 1985* (Vic); *Interpretation of Legislation Act* (Vic) s 14; *R v Harrow Justices; Ex parte Osaseri* [1985] 3 WLR 819 at 824 per May LJ. The closest equivalent is now the offence of intentionally or recklessly causing injury: *Crimes Act* (Vic) s 18. Common assault is also a summary offence in all jurisdictions, including Victoria ...

Mr Just has submitted that these statements are wrong and that the indictable offence of common assault has never been abolished in this State, by implication or otherwise. He concedes that the offence remains one triable summarily (see s 23 of the *Summary Offences Act 1966*) but, he says, the fact that a statute provides for the trial of the offence in a summary fashion, as it always has, cannot preclude the Crown from presenting an accused person for an indictable common law offence. ...

For our own part we believe that the former s 37 of the Crimes Act did no more than prescribe a maximum penalty for the offence of common assault which was, and always had been, a common law indictable offence. Nor do we believe that the repeal of s 37 has resulted, by implication, in the abolition of that common law offence. In normal circumstances, it is to be presumed that if Parliament had intended to abolish an existing common law offence it would make its intention clear: see Pearce and Geddes, *Statutory Interpretation in Australia*, 3rd ed, p 104. The *Crimes (Amendment) Act 1985* purported, in Pt 2, to codify the law relating to the offence of 'attempt', and in Pt 3, to 'reform the law relating to certain offences against the person'. In that Part of the Act relating to 'Attempts' it was specifically provided (s 321(s)) that, 'The offence of attempt at common law is abolished'. No such provision was stipulated in Pt 3 with respect to the common law offence of common assault.

Consistently with our view that the former s 37 had done no more than prescribe a penalty for the common law offence of common assault, we are satisfied that the Parliament did not intend, when it repealed s 37, to do more than remove the penalty which had been so prescribed. The effect of the repeal was, we believe, to leave the offence of common assault as a common law offence capable of being tried on indictment and for which the penalty was at large.

...

[Appeal dismissed.]

2.27C R v Venna

[1976] QB 421; [1975] 3 All ER 788
Court of Appeal (Criminal Division) (UK)

[The appellant was involved in a struggle with police officers who were attempting to arrest him. The appellant fell to the ground and then proceeded to lash out wildly with his legs. In doing so, he kicked the hand of one of the police officers, fracturing a bone. The appellant claimed that he was kicking out in an attempt to get up off the ground, and that he did not intend his foot to strike the police officer. The appellant was charged, inter alia, with assault occasioning actual bodily harm. The trial judge directed the jury that they could find the appellant guilty if they found that he had lashed out with his feet 'reckless as to who was there, not caring one iota as to whether he kicked somebody'. The appellant was convicted and appealed.]

James LJ: … Counsel for the appellant argued that the direction [given by the trial judge] is wrong in law because it states that the mental element of recklessness is enough, when coupled with the *actus reus* of physical contact, to constitute the battery involved in assault occasioning actual bodily harm. Recklessness, it is argued, is not enough; there must be intention to do the physical act the subject matter of the charge. Counsel relied on *R v Lamb* [1967] 2 All ER 1282, [1967] 2 QB 981 and argued that an assault is not established by proof of a deliberate act which gives rise to consequences which are not intended.

In *Fagan v Metropolitan Police Commissioner*, it was said ([1968] 3 All ER 442, [1969] 1 QB 439 at 440): 'An assault is any act which intentionally or possibly recklessly causes another person to apprehend immediate and unlawful personal violence'. In *Fagan* it was not necessary to decide the question whether proof of recklessness is sufficient to establish the *mens rea* ingredient of assault. That question falls for decision in the present case. Why it was considered necessary for the Crown to put the case forward on the alternative bases of 'intention' and 'recklessness' is not clear to us. This resulted in the direction given in the summing up.

On the evidence of the appellant himself, one would have thought that the inescapable inference was that the appellant intended to make physical contact with whoever might try to restrain him. Be that as it may, in the light of the direction given, the verdict may have been arrived at on the basis of 'recklessness'. Counsel for the appellant cited *Ackroyd v Barrett* (1894) 11 TLR 115 in support of his argument that recklessness, which falls short of intention, is not enough to support a charge of battery, and argued that, there being no authority to the contrary, it is now too late to extend the law by a decision of the courts and that any extension must be by the decision of Parliament.

Counsel for the appellant sought support from the distinction between the offences which are assaults and offences which by statute include the element contained in the word 'maliciously', eg unlawful and malicious wounding contrary to s 20 of the Offences against the Person Act 1861, in which recklessness will suffice to support the charge: see *R v Cunningham* [1957] 2 All ER 412; [1957] 2 QB 396. Insofar as the editors of textbooks commit themselves to an opinion on this branch of the law, they are favourable to the view that recklessness is or should logically be sufficient to support the charge of assault or battery: see Glanville Williams, *Criminal Law* (2nd ed, 1961), p 65, para 27; *Kenny's Outlines of Criminal Law* (19th ed, 1964), vol 1, p 164; Russell, *Russell on Crime* (12th ed, 1964), vol 1, p 656 and Smith and Hogan, *Criminal Law* (3rd ed, 1973), pp 284 at 286.

We think that the decision in *Ackroyd v Barrett* is explicable on the basis that the facts of the case did not support a finding of recklessness. The case was not argued for both sides. *R v Bradshaw* (1878) 14 Cox CC 83 can be read as supporting the view that unlawful physical force applied recklessly constitutes a criminal assault. In our view the element of *mens rea* in the offence of battery is satisfied by proof that the defendant intentionally or recklessly applied force to the person of another. If it were otherwise, the strange consequence would be that an offence of unlawful wounding contrary to s 20 of the Offences Against the Person Act 1861 could be established by proof that the defendant wounded the victim either intentionally or recklessly, but if the victim's skin was not broken and the offence was therefore laid as an assault occasioning actual bodily harm contrary to s 47 of the 1861 Act, it would be necessary to prove that the physical force was intentionally applied.

We see no reason in logic or in law why a person who recklessly applies physical force to the person of another should be outside the criminal law of assault. In many cases the dividing line between intention and recklessness is barely distinguishable. This is such a case. In our judgment the direction was right in law; this ground of appeal fails.

[Appeal dismissed.]

[See also *Vallance v R* (1961) 108 CLR 56; *MacPherson v Brown* (1975) 12 SASR 184; *R v Spratt* [1990] 1 WLR 1073.]

2.28C R v Coleman

(1990) 19 NSWLR 467

Court of Criminal Appeal, Supreme Court of New South Wales

[In relation to a charge of maliciously inflicting actual bodily harm with intent to have sexual intercourse, the trial judge directed the jury that an act was done recklessly if the accused realised the possibility that injury might result but nevertheless proceeded to act. On appeal, it was argued that the realisation of such a possibility of injury is insufficient; the realisation should be of the probability (or likelihood) of injury.]

Hunt J: … As the High Court made it clear in *R v Crabbe* (1985) 156 CLR 464, although there had previously been some difference of opinion in that court as to the appropriate test for murder, the balance of opinion had been in favour of 'probable' which had been stated to be the law as long ago as 1877 in *Stephen's Digest of Criminal Law* (art 223). There was no change in the law intended by the High Court when it stated (at 469) that such should now be regarded as settled law in Australia.

At the time of that decision, it was also generally accepted law in Australia that, in statutory offences other than murder, the degree of recklessness required in order to establish that an act was done maliciously was a realisation on the part of the accused that the particular kind of harm in fact done (that is, some physical harm — but not necessarily the degree of harm in fact so done) *might* be inflicted (that is, may possibly be inflicted) yet he went ahead and acted. That general acceptance in Australia appears to have fl owed from the decision of the English Court of Criminal Appeal in *R v Cunningham*, as explained by that court in *R v Mowatt* [1968] 1 QB 421 at 426.

That there was no conflict seen between the 'probable' test for murder and the 'possible' test for other statutory offences is demonstrated by a series of decisions in Victoria. *R v Cunningham* [1957] 2 QB 396 was followed in relation to statutory offences involving malicious acts (such as malicious wounding) with full recognition of the lower standard of 'possibility' which that decision permitted: *R v Smyth* [1963] VR 737 at 738–9; *R v Kane* [1974] VR 759 at 760 and *R v Lovett* [1975] VR 488 at 493–4. Over the same period, however, the Victorian courts also accepted the view that knowledge of a possibility was not enough for the crime of murder: *R v Sergi* [1974] VR 1 at 9–10; *Nydam v R* [1977] VR 430 at 437 and *R v Windsor* [1982] VR 89 at 93; (1980) 4 A Crim R 197 at 201.

In this State, the decision in *R v Crabbe* was made the basis of an argument that the recklessness by which the Crown may establish that an accused knows that a victim does not consent to sexual intercourse (s 61D) should be a realisation of the probability (and not merely the possibility) that she is not consenting but proceeding with that sexual intercourse notwithstanding; the argument was unsuccessful: *R v Hemsley* (1988) 36 A Crim R 334 at 336–8. The possibility test was always accepted for the common law crime of rape: *R v Daly* [1968] VR 257 at 258–9; *R v Sperotto* (1970) 71 SR (NSW) 334 at 337; 92 WN (NSW) 223 at 226 and *Director of Public Prosecutions v Morgan* [1976] AC 182 at 203, 209, 213–14, 215. In *R v Hemsley*, this court said (at 337) that the concepts involved in murder and in rape or sexual intercourse without consent (s 61D) are entirely different.

I do not accept the appellant's argument that the decision of the High Court in *R v Crabbe* should be interpreted as requiring a change in what I have described as the generally accepted law in Australia as to the meaning of 'maliciously' in statutory crimes other than murder, following *R v Cunningham* (as explained in *R v Mowatt*). The degree of reckless indifference required for the crime of murder, amounting to an act done 'of malice' (or malice aforethought) is altogether of a different order to that required for lesser crimes. The contemplation by the accused of the probable consequence of death is required for murder because it has to be comparable with an intention to kill or to do grievous bodily harm. Such a test of probable consequences is by no means required in relation to lesser crimes as a matter of law, of logic or of commonsense.

…

[**Finlay** and **Allen JJ** concurred. Appeal dismissed.]

[See also *R v Savage* [1992] 1 AC 699; *Filmer v Barclay* [1994] 2 VR 269.]

2.29C

R v Campbell

[1997] 2 VR 585
Court of Appeal, Supreme Court of Victoria

[The accused was arguing with his female companion while drunk in the carpark of a block of flats. Three men, who were nearby, became involved and a gun belonging to the accused was discharged, seriously injuring one of the three. The accused was charged with attempted murder, intentionally causing serious injury and recklessly causing serious injury. Early in his charge, the trial judge directed the jury that, to be guilty of recklessly causing serious injury, the accused must have fired the gun knowing that serious injury would probably occur. Near the end of his charge, the judge said that, if the accused fired the gun, for guilt to be established, he must be shown to have done so knowing that serious injury might occur and taking the risk of doing so. The accused was convicted of recklessly causing serious injury and acquitted of the other two charges. The accused appealed.]

...

Hayne JA and **Crockett AJA**: ... In our view there is little doubt that the trial judge misdirected the jury. We have no doubt that the appropriate test to apply is that it is possession of foresight that injury probably will result that must be proved. As said by the High Court in its joint judgment in *R v Crabbe* (1985) 156 CLR 464 at 469–70:

> It should now be regarded as settled law in Australia, if no statutory provision affects the position, that a person who, without lawful justification or excuse, does an act knowing that it is probable that death or grievous bodily harm will result, is guilty of murder ... It is not enough that he does the act knowing that it is possible but not likely that death or grievous bodily harm might result.

Whilst that citation is from a case specifically regarding murder, the same principles are relevant. Indeed the Court of Criminal Appeal in *R v Nuri* [1990] VR 641 said at 643:

> Presumably conduct is relevantly reckless if there is foresight on the part of the accused of the probable consequences of his actions and he displays indifference as to whether or not those consequences occur.

In that case the court was considering s 22 of the *Crimes Act 1958* which involves conduct endangering life. *Crabbe's* case was referred to by the Court of Criminal Appeal.

The offence of which the applicant was found guilty was laid under s 17 of the Crimes Act. That section is one of a group of sections which include s 22. It cannot be supposed that the legislature intended that there be, or that the courts would interpret the relevant sections so as to produce, a different requirement concerning the extent of 'the intent' with regard to each of those sections.

It should also be said that the Crown cited a number of cases that favour the test of 'might' or 'possibility' over the 'probability' test for intent: see *R v Smyth* [1963] VR 737; *R v Kane* [1974] VR 759; *R v Lovett* [1975] VR 488. These are relatively old cases and concerning the now repealed offences of unlawful and malicious wounding or unlawful and malicious infliction of grievous bodily harm. The spirit of the decision in *Crabbe* indicates that such cases should not be applied to the offence of recklessly causing injury. Nuri used a test of 'probability' in a kindred section to this case and it must be the case that all relevant sections in the group bear the same interpretation.

...

[**Phillips CJ** dissented. Appeal allowed and a new trial ordered.]

[Approved by the Victorian Court of Appeal in *Paton v The Queen* [2011] VSCA 72. Rejected by the New South Wales Court of Appeal in *Blackwell v The Queen* (2011) 81 NSWLR 119 such that *R v Campbell* (1990) 19 NSWLR 467 is still the authority on reckless assault.]

2.30C Rozsa v Samuels

[1969] SASR 205

Supreme Court of South Australia

[The appellant, a taxi driver, placed his taxi at the head of a queue of taxis in front of a taxi driven by one Drummond. Drummond got out of his taxi and remonstrated with the appellant who replied 'I am here and I am staying here'. Drummond replied that he would punch the appellant in the head, whereupon the appellant reached under the dashboard of his taxi and produced a table knife which he held in his hand, saying 'I will cut you to bits if you try it'. The appellant made a movement to get out of the taxi, which was frustrated by Drummond slamming the door of the taxi. The appellant was convicted of assault and appealed.]

Hogarth J: ... The first question arising in these circumstances is whether, putting aside for the moment the consideration of whether the appellant was acting in reasonable self-defence, his actions constituted an assault.

A person is guilty of an assault if he unlawfully displays force against another in such a way that he creates in the mind of that other the belief that force is about to be used against him, provided he intended to create such belief. The gist of the offence is the creation of a fear in the mind of the person assailed that unlawful force is about to be used against him. On the facts of the present case this raises the question whether a threat to use force, accompanied by words which indicate that the threat is conditional upon an unlawful act of the man threatened, Drummond, can constitute an assault in the eyes of the law. It is well established that a gesture which could otherwise constitute an assault will not be an assault if it is accompanied by words which clearly indicate that, notwithstanding the gesture, the man making the apparent threat does not in fact intend to use force. Thus in the old case of *Tuberville v Savage* (1669) 1 Mod 3 (86 ER 684), the defendant attempted to justify an assault upon the plaintiff as being in self-defence when it was proved that the plaintiff had placed his hand upon his sword saying, 'Were it not assize time I would not take such language from you.' It was held that these words clearly indicated that, in spite of this gesture, the plaintiff did not intend to use his sword for the purpose of attacking the defendant and consequently the defendant was unable to rely upon the defence of self-defence. What is to be said, however, of a gesture which of itself would amount to a threat of violence, accompanied by words which indicate that the violence will only be offered in fact if the person threatened does or fails to do some act? Or where the assailant does some act which of itself is equivocal, but which is accompanied by words indicating an intention to use violence if the person threatened does or fails to do some particular thing? Where a threat was made to apply force if a police constable approached the assailant in order to do his duty, it was held by the Court of Appeal of New Zealand that the mere fact that the threat was conditional did not prevent its constituting one of the elements necessary for establishing the assault (*Police v Greaves* [1964] NZLR 295); and similarly, if a threat is made to apply force unless the person assailed complies with some unlawful demand eg as pointed out in *Police v Greaves*, the threat of a highwayman, 'Your money or your life'. In such a case, if a pistol is pointed at the victim it would be idle to say that there was not a threat to apply force to the person of another in circumstances in which the person making the threat had, or at least had caused the other to believe on reasonable grounds that he had, present ability to effect this purpose; and therefore an assault had been committed. But what of the case where a threat is made to apply force unless the person threatened desists from some unlawful course of action which he proposes? The problem was discussed by Dr Glanville Williams in his article 'Assault and Words' [1957] *Crim LR* 219, where at pp 222–3 he discusses some American authorities.

In *State v Myerfield* (1867) 61 NC 108, Pearson CJ explained the law of conditional threat as follows: when the threat to strike is explained by words showing that it is not the intention of the party to strike, this is not an assault. (This is consistent with *Tuberville v Savage* (1669) 1 Mod 3 (86 ER 684).) On the other hand, when the threat is made with a condition precedent showing that it is not the intention to strike provided that the condition is performed by the other, a distinction is taken. If the condition is one which the party has a right to impose, the threat to strike unless the condition is complied with is not an assault; so that where a man, being forbidden, is about to enter my house and I raise a stick and say, 'If you attempt to enter I will knock you down', there is no assault even though it would be battery for me to carry out my threat (Dr Williams points out that this dictum is inconsistent with the English case of *Read v Coker* (1853) 13 CB 850 (138 ER 1437)). But if the condition is one that the party has no right to impose, the threat to strike is an assault notwithstanding the condition. Pearson CJ went on to say that there is an exception to the general rule when the threat to strike is made with a deadly weapon, in which case the law does not allow the case to be qualified by the imposition of a condition even though it is one that the party had the right to impose. Dr Williams pointed out that in English law there is no authority for distinguishing between threatening with a deadly weapon and other threats of extreme force. He takes the view that a threat of extreme force is unlawful if the use of the force would be unlawful. He is supported in this view by another American case, *Hairston v The State* (1877) 54 Miss 689. In that case the defendant pointed a pistol at another and said, 'I will shoot any man who attempts to stop my mules'. It was held that the defendant could not on these facts be convicted of an assault with intent to murder, because the intent in such an assault must be absolute and not conditional; but the court intimated that he could have been convicted of an assault simply because he had threatened more force than he could lawfully have used. If the mules had been stopped he could have used moderate force, as by striking with the hand or threatening to do so. But since he could not have justified actual shooting to prevent the mules being stopped, he could not justify threatening to do so. Dr Williams points out that this general line of argument accords with that implicit in *Read v Coker* (1853) 13 CB 850, (138 ER 1437).

I have come to the conclusion that the views expressed by Dr Williams correctly state the law as it is to be applied in this State. In the present case it seems to me that the proper test to determine whether or not there was an assault is to ask, if Drummond had attempted to strike the appellant in the manner which he threatened, would the appellant have been justified in defending himself by using the table knife? If he would have been justified in doing so, then he was entitled to make the conditional threat, and there was no assault.

As the matter was argued in the court below the case presented for the appellant was that the defendant did no more than offer reasonable force in self-defence, and that for that reason the force offered was not unlawfully offered. In this connection it seems to me that it would be dangerous to take the appellant at his word when he threatened to cut Drummond 'to bits'; but I have no doubt that the threat was intended to convey the meaning that he would use the knife to stab Drummond, or at least to stab at him if he attacked the appellant. This problem poses the same question as that which I raised earlier in considering whether a conditional threat of violence could constitute an assault. On this, the Special Magistrate said: 'The defendant in the case before me had a knife in his car, and I feel that what he did was beyond the ordinary bounds of self-defence.' It follows that, on his finding, the appellant's conditional threat to use violence was a threat to use more force than the Special Magistrate would have considered reasonable in the circumstances.

[Appeal dismissed.]

[See also *Director of Public Prosecutions Reference (No 1 of 1991)* (1992) 60 A Crim R 43; *R v Lean and Aland* (1993) 66 A Crim R 296; *Branson v South Australian Police Force* (1993) 60 SASR 325; and *R v Hawes* (1994) 35 NSWLR 294.]

2.31C R v Salisbury

[1976] VR 452

Full Court of the Supreme Court of Victoria

[The accused had hit another man in the eye, causing the victim to lose most of the sight of that eye. He was convicted of maliciously inflicting grievous bodily harm: Crimes Act 1958 (Vic) s 19A (now repealed). On appeal it was argued that the trial judge had erred in not directing the jury that they were entitled to find the accused guilty of one of the lesser offences of assault occasioning actual bodily harm or common assault. The accused had not been charged with these offences; thus the question whether the trial judge should have given such a direction could only arise if an assault constituted an essential ingredient of the offence contained in s 19A.]

Young CJ, **Nelson** and **Harris JJ**: ... Section 19A was introduced into the *Crimes Act 1958* by s 4 of the *Crimes (Amendment) Act 1972* and, by s 3(a) of the same Act, s 19 was amended to restrict its operation to wounding. Before that amendment, s 19 has been in the same terms as s 20 of the English Offences against the Person Act 1861 (24 and 25 Vict c 100), except that the English section includes the words 'either with or without any weapon or instrument'. There is a substantial body of authority on s 20 of the English Act, but the cases fall into two classes.

In one class the question considered was whether or not a verdict of assault was open as an alternative verdict on a charge of inflicting grievous bodily harm. It has been held that inflicting grievous bodily harm necessarily involves an assault so that the alternative verdict was open. In the other class the question considered was whether or not an offence under s 20 was disclosed. Some of the facts considered in this class of case were such that grievous bodily harm was inflicted without any assault having taken place unless the concept of assault is extended beyond its generally accepted meaning. There has been no attempt to reconcile the two classes of case. The authorities extend from 1869 to 1973 and it is now necessary to turn to them.

[Their Honours considered a number of authorities and continued:]

We began our consideration of s 19A by pointing out that the question whether an assault is an essential element of inflicting grievous bodily harm is a matter of construing the words of the section. From the examination of the cases on s 20 of the English Act, it appears that the English Courts, from at least 1881 (when *R v Martin* (1881) 8 QBD 54 was decided) to 1973 (when *Cartledge v Allen* [1973] Crim LR 530 was decided), in one line of cases have held facts to disclose the offence of inflicting grievous bodily harm without being concerned to make any inquiry whether those facts also constituted an assault. In these cases, the courts have held that grievous bodily harm has been 'inflicted', where they were satisfied that an intentional act of the accused had resulted in serious physical harm to the victim, by force being violently applied to his body, even though the accused had not applied such force directly to the body of the victim by an assault, but had done something which directly resulted in the application of that force. At the same time, during this period, the English Courts have continued to maintain the proposition enunciated in *R v Taylor* (1869) LR 1 CCR 194, that assault is an alternative verdict to inflicting grievous bodily harm: see *R v Snewing* [1972] Crim LR 267.

None of the cases in the two lines of English authorities are binding on us, though all are of considerable persuasive power. Having examined the cases for the purpose of obtaining assistance with the construction of s 19A, we have found the reasoning in the line of authority which includes *R v Martin*, supra, the judgment of Wills J in *R v Clarence* (1888) 22 QBD 23 and *R v Halliday* (1889) 61 LT 701 more persuasive and of more assistance in construing s 19A than the line which has continued to maintain that assault is an alternative verdict on a charge of inflicting grievous bodily harm.

It may be that the somewhat different wording of s 20 of the English Act has played a part in bringing about the existence of the two lines of authority in England, but, be that as it may, we have come to the conclusion that, although the word 'inflicts' in s 19A does not have as wide a meaning as the word 'causes' in s 17, the word 'inflicts' does have a wider meaning than it would have if it were construed so that inflicting grievous bodily harm always involved assaulting the victim.

In our opinion, grievous bodily harm may be inflicted, contrary to s 19A, either where the accused has directly and violently 'inflicted' it by assaulting the victim, or where the accused has 'inflicted' it by doing something, intentionally, which, though it is not itself a direct application of force to the body of the victim, does directly result in force being applied violently to the body of the victim, so that he suffers grievous bodily harm. Hence, the lesser misdemeanours of assault occasioning actual bodily harm and common assault, contrary to s 37, are not necessarily included in the misdemeanour of inflicting grievous bodily harm, contrary to s 19A.

It follows from what has been said that, in our opinion, the learned trial judge acted correctly in not leaving the charge of assault to the jury as an alternative to the charge of inflicting grievous bodily harm and that the ground of the application for leave to appeal which was based on his failure to do so is not made out.

This is sufficient to dispose of the application for leave to appeal against conviction, but another point was fully argued at the hearing and, in the circumstances, we consider we should indicate our view upon this point. The point arose in this way. The applicant was faced with the fact that the jury had found him guilty of an offence under s 19A, which was a more serious offence than either of the offences under s 37, and that therefore it could be said that the verdict of the jury ruled out the possibility of the applicant only having been guilty of an offence under s 37. The decision of the Full Court in *R v Evans & Lewis* [1969] VR 858 (O'Brien and Little JJ, Smith J, dissenting) was referred to. It was submitted by counsel for the applicant that we should not follow the decision of the majority of the court in that case, but we are bound by that decision (which has been applied by this court in *R v Salika* [1973] VR 272 and, as we were informed, in other unreported cases also) and, furthermore, we are of the view that *R v Evans & Lewis*, supra, was correctly decided.

The result is that this application for leave to appeal against conviction must be dismissed.

[Appeal dismissed.]

[A similar view was taken by the House of Lords in *R v Wilson (Clarence)* [1984] AC 242. See also *R v Cameron* [1983] 2 NSWLR 66; *R v Caple* (1984) 14 A Crim R 106; *R v Savage* [1992] 1 AC 699; *R v Mandair* [1994] 2 All ER 715; *R v Ireland*; *R v Burstow* [1997] 4 All ER 225.

The problem considered by the court in *R v Salisbury* no longer arises as an issue in Victoria and South Australia, although it does in New South Wales. The offence of causing injury intentionally (Crimes Act 1958 (Vic) s 18; Criminal Law Consolidation Act 1935 (SA) s 24) is necessarily included in the offence of causing serious injury intentionally: Crimes Act 1958 (Vic) s 16; Criminal Law Consolidation Act 1935 (SA) s 23.]

2.32C

R v Westaway

(1991) 52 A Crim R 336
Court of Criminal Appeal, Supreme Court of Victoria

[The applicant appealed against his conviction under s 16 of the Crimes Act 1958 (Vic) for intentionally causing serious injury to a child.]

Brooking J: … In the present case, the learned trial judge told the jury that the requirement that serious injury be intentionally caused was met if the accused intended to do the act which in fact caused serious injury. It was not necessary that the accused should have intended to cause serious injury. If the accused intended to do an act, meant to do that act, and that act in fact caused serious injury, the offence was committed. There was on the presentment an alternative charge of recklessly causing serious injury. His Honour told the jury that serious injury was recklessly caused if the accused caused serious injury and at the time of the act causing serious injury he was aware that the act involved the risk of causing serious injury and was indifferent as to whether the act caused serious injury.

At the trial exception was taken by the applicant's counsel to that part of the charge which dealt with the requirement of intention in the more serious offence, it being put that a specific intent to cause serious injury was an ingredient of the crime. His Honour declined to redirect. It is clear that in this respect the learned judge fell into error. When s 16 refers to a person who 'intentionally causes serious injury', what it requires to have been intentionally done is the causing of serious injury. The section does not speak of intentionally doing an act which causes serious injury. It speaks of intentionally causing serious injury. The intention required is an intention to do that.

The word 'intentionally' in s 16 is superfluous on the view taken by his Honour, for if the section simply made it an offence to cause serious injury an Australian court would be bound to hold that the act causing serious injury must have been intentionally done for an offence to have been committed: *R v O'Connor* (1980) 146 CLR 64.

If the requirement of intention in s 16 is attached not to the causing of serious injury but merely to the doing of the act which in fact causes serious injury, then the requirement of recklessness in s 17 is presumably attached not to the causing of serious injury but merely to the doing of the act which in fact causes serious injury. But the learned judge's approach was not consistent here, for his Honour directed the jury that 'recklessly' in s 17 required that the accused should have been aware that his act involved the risk of causing serious injury and have been indifferent as to whether the act caused serious injury. Consistency of approach would have required his Honour to tell the jury that 'recklessly' in s 17 required not recklessness as to the causing of serious injury but recklessness as to the mere doing of the act which in fact caused serious injury.

It would be extraordinary if s 16 made it an offence punishable by up to 15 years imprisonment to do an act intentionally wherever that act in fact caused serious injury, even though the serious injury was unintended and was indeed improbable and even not reasonably foreseeable.

…

[**Young CJ** and **Marks J** agreed with **Brooking J**. Appeal allowed and a new trial ordered.]

2.33C R v Abdul-Rasool

(2008) 180 A Crim R 556
Court of Appeal, Supreme Court of Victoria

[The applicant was convicted of reckless conduct endangering life. In the course of an altercation in the office of the deputy principal of the school attended by the daughter of the applicant, the applicant poured petrol over herself, some of which splashed on to the deputy principal and an interpreter who was present. At trial the Crown submitted that, in the applicant's highly agitated state, she may have lit the petrol by striking a lighter or matches she was carrying and setting fire to herself. On appeal against conviction.]

[Footnotes to the extract appear at the end of the extract.]

Redlich JA: ... Though relatively new offences, the general endangerment offences in Australian jurisdictions have received either judicial,[1] legislative[2] or scholarly[3] criticism of some sort. The reason for this criticism has generally arisen because of the complexities involved in the overarching structure of the offences. In *R v Nuri*[4] Young CJ, Crockett and Nathan JJ said in relation to the offence created by s 22:

> Its enactment was designed to create a general endangerment offence to replace a large number of offences that previously were to be found in the Crimes Act. Sections repealed were ss 17, 21, 22, 29, 32, 197(2) and 197(5). The problem is that, in an endeavour to subsume all life-endangering behaviour in one offence, the very generality of that offence has given rise to difficulties of construction and interpretation.[5]

The elements of the offence under s 22 as discussed in *Nuri* and as further refined and developed by subsequent case law[6] leaving aside the element of lawful excuse, are:

(1) The accused engaged in conduct; and
(2) That conduct placed a person in danger (ie conduct that carried with it an appreciable risk) of death; (*the actus reus*)
(3) The accused engaged in that conduct voluntarily;
(4) A reasonable person in the position of the accused, engaging in the very conduct in which the accused engaged and in the same circumstances, would have realised that they had placed another in danger of death; (*the objective mental element*) and
(5) The accused engaged in that conduct recklessly in that they foresaw that placing another in danger of death was a probable consequence of their conduct in the surrounding circumstances (*the subjective mental element*). [Emphasis added]

...

It will be apparent from the foregoing that in my opinion the future conduct of the applicant is not conduct that can be considered. It has no place in an evaluation of the *actus reus* of the crime. To take contemplated but unperformed acts into account would undermine the fundamental principle that as a general rule, an evil mindset must be translated into some voluntary bodily action for it to attract criminal sanction. Nor can it be said that the future conduct shares a sufficient temporal and causal proximity with the conduct actually engaged in for it to be characterised as part of that conduct. Finally, since it did not in fact occur, the voluntariness of any such anticipated action can not be imputed to the accused via principles of voluntariness.

Such future conduct can form no part of the objective element. The danger of death encompassed by s 22 is not a hypothetical construct. It does not facilitate speculation as to the future conduct of the accused. To objectively ascertain danger of an appreciable risk of death, that risk must be 'included in' or 'carried by' the very same conduct performed by the applicant and not by some anticipated future conduct. The applicant's emotional state of mind does not provide a basis for evaluating the dangerousness of any conduct the applicant is likely to perform. The applicant's future actions have no legal relevance to the subjective element. The subjective element cannot be established without presupposing the satisfaction of the objective element. The *mens rea* of recklessness required the accused to have adverted to the probability of an appreciable risk of death from her conduct. That does not include future conduct which may have given rise to such a risk, even if it could be established that the applicant foresaw the prospect of that risk.

As a matter of law no account was to be taken of the future conduct of the applicant — whether it be likely or not. The jury verdict may have rested on this impermissible foundation. Moreover, even if the jury could have taken into account the applicant's future conduct, the evidence could not sustain the conclusion that the applicant foresaw the probability of that conduct or the consequential appreciable risk of death.

[**Chernov JA** and **King AJA** agreed with **Redlich JA**. Conviction quashed.]

Notes:

1. See *Bedi v R* (1993) 61 SASR 269, 274 (Duggan J, with Bollen and Mullighan JJ agreeing); *R v D* (Unreported, Supreme Court of Victoria, Hampel, 1 May 1996): BC9607711, 5–6.
2. Northern Territory, Parliamentary Debates, Ninth Assembly: First Session, 5 May 2005, Parliamentary Record No 26 (Dr Toyne, Justice and Attorney-General).
3. Blokland, 'Dangerous Acts: A Critical Appraisal of Section 154 of the Northern Territory Criminal Code' (1995) 9 *Criminal Law Journal* 74; Lanham, 'Danger Down Under' [1999] *Criminal Law Review* 960; Clarkson, 'General Endangerment Offences: The Way Forward?' (2005) 32 *University of Western Australia Law Review* 131. See also the extra-judicial comments made by Scott J of the Western Australian Supreme Court (Model Criminal Code Officers Committee, *Model Criminal Code: Chapter 5; Non-Fatal Offences Against the Person*, Final Report 1998, 69) and Nader J of the Northern Territory Supreme Court (Nader J 'The Criminal Code in the Northern Territory', paper presented to the Australian Bar Association Conference, 1990, 28–30 see Blockland ftn 7).
4. [1990] VR 641.
5. Ibid 643.
6. *R v McCarthy* (Unreported, Supreme Court of Victoria: Court of Criminal Appeal, Brooking, Teague and Coldrey JJ, 4 November 1993): BC9300908; *Filmer v Barclay* [1994] 2 VR 269; *R v B* (Unreported, Supreme Court of Victoria, Teague J, 19 July 1995): BC9507977;

R v Anderson (Unreported, Supreme Court of Victoria, Hampel J, 5 December 1997); *Mutemeri v Cheesman* [1998] 4 VR 484; *R v Bekhazi* (2001) 3 VR 321, 329; *R v Wilson* [2005] VSCA 78, [17]; *R v Khien Lam* [2006] VSCA 162, [11]–[16]. Cf *R v D* (Unreported, Supreme Court of Victoria, Hampel J, 1 May 1996): BC9607711; *R v Adams* (Unreported, Supreme Court of Victoria: Court of Appeal, Winneke P, Callaway JA and Hampel AJA, 15 February 1996).

2.34 Illustrations

1. D was convicted of assault under s 61 of the Crimes Act 1900 (NSW), following threatening and abusive telephone calls to a police officer, a magistrate and a judge. Apart from the telephone calls, which were traced to D at a considerable distance from the targets, there was no evidence in relation to the assault charges. Held, convictions quashed. There was no evidence that the threats made were of immediate violence. In given circumstances, a threat of violence made over the phone could be a threat of immediate violence: *R v Knight* (1988) 35 A Crim R 314. It has also been held that threats made by a driver (the D) in a moving vehicle, where the V is a passenger, can create an apprehension of imminent harm for the purpose of (psychological) assault: *Zanker v Vartzokas* (1988) 34 A Crim R 11. In that case it was stated (at 16) that 'there was no escape, no reasonable possibility of a *novus actus interveniens* to break the causal link between the threat and the expected infliction of harm'.
2. D was convicted of assault. He entered the grounds of a private house at night and looked through the window of a bed-sitting room occupied by Ms M, who was in her nightclothes. Ms M saw D staring at her for about three or four seconds. She was frightened, screamed and called the police. On appeal, held, conviction affirmed. It was open to the justices to find that the intention of D was to frighten Ms M so as to cause her to fear some act of immediate violence: *Smith v Chief Superintendent, Woking Police Station* (1983) 76 Cr App R 234.
3. D was convicted of maliciously inflicting grievous bodily harm. D put out the gaslights in a theatre and placed an iron bar across the doorway of an exit. In the resulting panic, several people were seriously injured. On appeal, held, conviction affirmed. It is not necessary to constitute the offence that D directly inflict injury upon V: *R v Martin* (1881) 8 QBD 54 (CCR). Could D have been charged with assault? See *R v Salisbury* [1976] VR 452 (at **2.31C**).
4. D, who was very drunk, ordered his wife and their daughter to bed. A few moments later, on learning his wife was not yet in bed, he called, 'I'll make you so that you can't go to bed' and staggered towards the bedroom. The wife

ran to the window but was held at the sill by the daughter. Both of them were very frightened. D entered the bedroom and when he was within reach of them he ordered his daughter to 'Let the bugger go'. The daughter did so, and the wife fell to the pavement and sustained injuries. D was convicted of assault occasioning actual bodily harm and maliciously inflicting grievous bodily harm. On appeal, held, conviction affirmed. Lord Coleridge CJ stated *(R v Halliday* [1886–90] All ER Rep 1028 (CCR 1889)):

> If a man creates in another man's mind an immediate sense of danger which causes such person to try to escape, and in so doing he injures himself, the person who creates such a state of mind is responsible for the injuries which result. I think that in this case there was abundant evidence that there was a sense of immediate danger in the mind of the woman caused by the acts of the prisoner, and that her injuries resulted from what such sense of danger caused her to do.

Accord *R v Roberts* (1971) 56 Cr App R 95; *Zanker v Vartzokas* (1988) 34 A Crim R 11. In both these cases V was travelling in D's car and jumped out of the car in order to avoid threats made by D. One issue was whether D caused the injuries. In both cases a causal link was found between the threat of the defendant and the injuries sustained by the victim. See also *Royall v R* (1991) 172 CLR 378 (at **4.30C**).

5. D punched a woman in the face while she was holding her 12-month-old child. As a result, the child fell from her arms and hit his head on the floor. D was convicted of battery upon the child. On appeal it was argued that a person could not be convicted of battery unless he or she had direct physical contact with the victim, either through the offender's body (for example, a punch) or through a medium controlled by the actions of the offender, for example, a weapon. Held, conviction affirmed. Although most batteries were directly inflicted (for example, through one person striking another with their fist or an instrument, or through a missile thrown by the assailant), it was not essential that the violence should be so directly inflicted. Even if D's submission on the meaning of battery was correct, however, the test was made out on the facts. The movement by which the woman lost hold of the child was entirely and immediately the result of D's action in punching her. There was no difference between the facts of the case and one in which D might have used a weapon to fell the child to the floor, save only that the instant case was one of reckless rather than intentional battery: *Heystead v Chief Constable of Derbyshire* [2000] 3 All ER 890. Also note that spitting, which does not involve any touching, can constitute an assault: *DPP v JWH* (SC(NSW), 17 October 1997, unreported).
6. D was told by his fiancée that she suspected that C, a foreign student lodging with her family, had stolen her engagement ring. D and other

members of the family questioned C about the disappearance of the ring, and D then dragged C upstairs and locked him in a second floor room. C tried to escape through the window but was injured when he fell to the ground below. D was charged with assault occasioning actual bodily harm. The Crown alleged that even if C had not suffered any physical injury as a result of the assault upon him by D, he had nevertheless been reduced to a mental state which in itself amounted to actual bodily harm. There was no medical evidence to support that allegation, the only evidence being that of C that he had felt abused, humiliated and frightened. The trial judge directed the jury that an assault which caused a hysterical or nervous condition was capable of being an assault occasioning actual bodily harm. D was convicted. On appeal, held, conviction quashed. The phrase 'actual bodily harm' was capable of including psychiatric injury but did not include mere emotions such as fear, distress, panic or a hysterical or nervous condition, nor did it include states of mind that were not themselves evidence of some identifiable clinical condition. Where psychiatric injury was relied on as the basis for an allegation of bodily harm which was disputed by the defence, the Crown should call expert evidence and, in the absence of such expert evidence, the question whether psychiatric injury had been occasioned by an assault should not be left to the jury: *R v Chan-Fook* [1994] 2 All ER 552.

7. In two separate appeals to the House of Lords, questions arose as to the ambit of assault occasioning actual bodily harm and unlawfully and maliciously inflicting grievous bodily harm: Offences Against the Person Act 1861 (UK) ss 20, 47. In the first appeal, D made repeated silent telephone calls, mostly at night, to three women, as a result of which they suffered psychiatric illness. D was convicted on three counts of assault occasioning actual bodily harm. In the second appeal, D had conducted an eight-month campaign of harassment against a woman which included making both silent and abusive telephone calls to her, distributing offensive cards in the street where she lived, visiting her place of work and her home, taking photographs of her and of her family, and sending her a note which was intended, and was understood to be, menacing. The woman was so badly affected by the campaign of harassment that she suffered from a severe depressive illness. D was convicted of unlawfully and maliciously inflicting grievous bodily harm. Held, convictions affirmed. The words 'bodily harm' were capable of covering recognised psychiatric illnesses, such as an anxiety disorder or a depressive disorder, which affected the central nervous system of the body. However, those neuroses had to be distinguished from simple states of fear, or problems in coping with everyday life, which did not amount to psychiatric illnesses. Since the victims had developed anxiety and depressive disorders, it followed that they had suffered 'bodily harm'. The making of

silent telephone calls which caused psychiatric injury to the victim was capable of amounting to an assault occasioning actual bodily harm where the calls caused the victim to apprehend an immediate application of force. Furthermore, the offence of inflicting grievous bodily harm could be committed even though no physical violence was applied directly or indirectly to the body of the victim: *R v Ireland; R v Burstow* [1997] 4 All ER 225.

8. D engaged in acts of unprotected sexual intercourse with V while D knew himself to be HIV positive. D was convicted in the Magistrates' Court of recklessly engaging in conduct that placed another in danger of death, contrary to s 22 of the Crimes Act 1958 (Vic). Expert evidence was given that the risk of transmission of the HIV virus by unprotected sex in the case of an infected male and an uninfected female was between one in 667 and one in 2000. The magistrate took judicial notice of the fact that HIV is a life-endangering disease. On appeal, held, conviction quashed. Section 22 does not require that D foresaw as a probable consequence of her or his conduct that V would die, but only the danger of V's death. Danger of death means an 'appreciable risk' of death. The magistrate was justified in taking judicial notice of the fact that HIV was a life-endangering disease. It was not, however, open to the magistrate to find beyond reasonable doubt, without evidence, that D's conduct placed V in danger of death (that is, that it exposed V to an 'appreciable risk' of death), something more than a 'mere possibility'. The evidence established only the risk of V's contracting the HIV virus; there was no evidence as to the degree of risk of V's dying if she had contracted HIV: *Mutemeri v Cheesman* [1998] 4 VR 484. How should the prosecution have conducted its case in order to secure a conviction? If V were to contract HIV, then could D be charged with the offence of intentionally causing another person to be infected with a very serious disease contrary to s 19A of the Crimes Act 1958 (see 2.38)? Where V contracts the disease, are there other offences D might be charged with? Consider this question after you have read the next section, 'Consent'. See further, *R v Neal* [2011] VSCA 172; and the discussion below at 2.38.

9. In New South Wales the definition of grievous bodily harm encompasses 'any grievous bodily disease' (Crimes Act 1900 (NSW) s 4). Grievous bodily harm can be inflicted intentionally (s 33), recklessly (s 35) or negligently (s 54). In addition, the Public Health Act 2010 (NSW) criminalises persons who do not inform a person with whom they are proposing to have sexual intercourse that they have a sexually transmitted infection. The duties of persons in relation to sexually transmitted infections are set out in s 79 of the Public Health Act 2010 (NSW):

(1) A person who knows that he or she suffers from a sexually transmitted infection is guilty of an offence if he or she has sexual intercourse with another person unless, before the intercourse takes place, the other person:
(a) has been informed of the risk of contracting a sexually transmitted infection from the person with whom intercourse is proposed, and
(b) has voluntarily agreed to accept the risk.

…

(4) It is a defence to any proceedings for an offence under this section if the court is satisfied that the defendant took reasonable precautions to prevent the transmission of the sexually transmitted infection.

CONSENT

Limits of consent

2.35C **R v Brown**
[1994] 1 AC 212; [1993] 2 All ER 75
House of Lords

[The appellants belonged to a group of sado-masochistic homosexuals who, over a 10-year period from 1978, willingly participated in the commission of acts of violence against each other, including genital torture, for the sexual pleasure which it engendered in the giving and receiving of pain. The passive partner or victim in each case consented to the acts being committed and suffered no permanent injury. The activities took place in private at a number of different locations, including rooms equipped as torture chambers at the homes of three of the appellants. Video cameras were used to record the activities and the resulting tapes were then copied and distributed amongst members of the group. The appellants were tried on charges of assault occasioning actual bodily harm, and unlawful wounding. Following a ruling by the trial judge that the consent of the victim afforded no defence to the charges, the appellants pleaded guilty and were sentenced to terms of imprisonment. The appellants appealed against their convictions, contending that a person could not be guilty of assault occasioning actual bodily harm or unlawful wounding in respect of acts carried out in private with the consent of the victim. The Court of Appeal dismissed their appeals. The court certified the following point of law of general public importance:

> Where A wounds or assaults B occasioning him actual bodily harm in the course of a sadomasochistic encounter, does the prosecution have to prove lack of consent on the part of B before they can establish A's guilt under s 20 and s 47 of the 1861, Offences against the Person Act?

The appellants appealed to the House of Lords.]

Lord Templeman: … In the present case each of the appellants intentionally inflicted violence upon another (to whom I shall refer as 'the victim') with the consent of the victim and thereby occasioned actual bodily harm or in some cases wounding or grievous bodily harm. Each appellant was therefore guilty of an offence under s 47 or s 20 of the 1861 Act unless the consent of the victim was effective to prevent the commission of the offence or effective to constitute a defence to the charge.

In some circumstances violence is not punishable under the criminal law. When no actual bodily harm is caused, the consent of the person affected precludes him from complaining. There can be no conviction for the summary offence of common assault if the victim has consented to the assault. Even when violence is intentionally inflicted and results in actual bodily harm, wounding or serious bodily harm the accused is entitled to be acquitted if the injury was a foreseeable incident of a lawful activity in which the person injured was participating. Surgery involves intentional violence resulting in actual or sometimes serious bodily harm but surgery is a lawful activity. Other activities carried on with consent by or on behalf of the injured person have been accepted as lawful notwithstanding that they involve actual bodily harm or may cause serious bodily harm. Ritual circumcision, tattooing, earpiercing and violent sports including boxing are lawful activities.

In earlier days some other forms of violence were lawful and when they ceased to be lawful they were tolerated until well into the nineteenth century. Duelling and fighting were at first lawful and then tolerated provided the protagonists were voluntary participants. But, where the results of these activities was the maiming of one of the participants, the defence of consent never availed the aggressor: see *Hawkins' Pleas of the Crown*, 8th ed (1824) vol 1, ch 15. A maim was bodily harm whereby a man was deprived of the use of any member of his body which he needed to use in order to fight but a bodily injury was not a maim merely because it was a disfigurement. The act of maim was unlawful because the King was deprived of the services of an able-bodied citizen for the defence of the realm. Violence which maimed was unlawful despite consent to the activity which produced the maiming. In these days there is no difference between maiming on the one hand and wounding or causing grievous bodily harm on the other hand except with regard to sentence.

When duelling became unlawful, juries remained unwilling to convict but the judges insisted that persons guilty of causing death or bodily injury should be convicted despite the consent of the victim.

Similarly, in the old days, fighting was lawful provided the protagonists consented because it was thought that fighting inculcated bravery and skill and physical fitness. The brutality of knuckle fighting however caused the courts to declare that such fights were unlawful even if the protagonists consented. Rightly or wrongly the courts accepted that boxing is a lawful activity.

In *R v Coney* (1882) 8 QBD 534 the court held that a prize-fight in public was unlawful. Cave J said, at p 539:

> The true view is, I think, that a blow struck in anger, or which is likely or is intended to do corporal hurt, is an assault, but that a blow struck in sport, and not likely,

nor intended to cause bodily harm, is not an assault, and that an assault being a breach of the peace and unlawful, the consent of the person struck is immaterial.

Stephen J said, at p 549:

> When one person is indicted for inflicting personal injury upon another, the consent of the person who sustains the injury is no defence to the person who inflicts the injury, if the injury is of such a nature, or is inflicted under such circumstances, that its infliction is injurious to the public as well as to the person injured. But the injuries given and received in prize-fights are injurious to the public, both because it is against the public interest that the lives and the health of the combatants should be endangered by blows, and because prize-fights are disorderly exhibitions, mischievous on many obvious grounds. Therefore the consent of the parties to the blows which they mutually receive does not prevent those blows from being assaults ... In cases where life and limb are exposed to no serious danger in the common course of things, I think that consent is a defence to a charge of assault, even when considerable force is used, as, for instance, in cases of wrestling, single-stick, sparring with gloves, football and the like; but in all cases the question whether consent does or does not take from the application of force to another its illegal character, is a question of degree depending upon circumstances.

Hawkins J said, at p 553:

> ... whatever may be the effect of a consent in a suit between party and party, it is not in the power of any man to give an effectual consent to that which amounts to, or has a direct tendency to create, a breach of the peace; so as to bar a criminal prosecution. In other words, though a man may by consent debar himself from his right to maintain a civil action, he cannot thereby defeat proceedings instituted by the Crown in the interest of the public for the maintenance of good order ... He may compromise his own civil rights, but he cannot compromise the public interest.

Lord Coleridge CJ said, at p 567:

> ... I conceive it to be established, beyond the power of any argument however ingenious to raise a doubt, that as the combatants in a duel cannot give consent to one another to take away life, so neither can the combatants in a prize-fight give consent to one another to commit that which the law has repeatedly held to be a breach of the peace. An individual cannot by such consent destroy the right of the Crown to protect the public and keep the peace.

The conclusion is that, a prize-fight being unlawful, actual bodily harm or serious bodily harm inflicted in the course of a prize-fight is unlawful notwithstanding the consent of the protagonists.

In *R v Donovan* [1934] 2 KB 498; [1934] All ER Rep 207 the appellant in private beat a girl of 17 for purposes of sexual gratification, it was said with her consent. Swift J said at [KB 507; All ER Rep 210]:

> ... it is an unlawful act to beat another person with such a degree of violence that the infliction of bodily harm is a probable consequence, and when such an act is proved, consent is immaterial.

In *A-G's Reference (No 6 of 1980)* [1981] QB 715; [1981] 2 All ER 1057 where two men quarreled and fought with bare fists Lord Lane CJ, delivering the judgment of the Court of Appeal, said at [QB 719; All ER 1059]:

> ... it is not in the public interest that people should try to cause, or should cause, each other bodily harm for no good reason. Minor struggles are another matter. So, in our judgment, it is immaterial whether the act occurs in private or in public; it is an assault if actual bodily harm is intended and/caused. This means that most fights will be unlawful regardless of consent. Nothing which we have said is intended to cast doubt on the accepted legality of properly conducted games and sports, lawful chastisement or correction, reasonable surgical interference, dangerous exhibitions etc. These apparent exceptions can be justified as involving the exercise of a legal right, in the case of chastisement or correction, or as needed in the public interest, in the other cases.

Duelling and fighting are both unlawful and the consent of the protagonists affords no defence to charges of causing actual bodily harm, wounding or grievous bodily harm in the course of an unlawful activity.

The appellants and their victims in the present case were engaged in consensual homosexual activities. The attitude of the public towards homosexual practices changed in the second half of this century. Change in public attitudes led to a change in the law.

The Wolfenden Report (*Report of the Committee on Homosexual Offences and Prostitution* (1957) (Cmnd 247)), declared that the function of the criminal law in relation to homosexual behaviour 'is to preserve public order and decency, to protect the citizen from what is offensive or injurious, and to provide sufficient safeguards against exploitation and corruption of others, particularly those who are especially vulnerable because they are young, weak in body or mind, inexperienced, or in a state of special, physical, official or economic dependence': paragraph 13 of chapter 2.

In response to the Wolfenden Report and consistently with its recommendations, Parliament enacted s 1 of the Sexual Offences Act 1967 ...

[His Lordship set out the terms of the section and continued:]

By the Act of 1967, Parliament recognised and accepted the practice of homosexuality. Subject to exceptions not here relevant, sexual activities conducted in private between not more than two consenting adults of the same sex or different sexes are now lawful. Homosexual activities performed in circumstances which do not fall within section 1(1) of the 1967 Act remain unlawful. Subject to the respect for private life embodied in the Act of 1967, Parliament has retained criminal sanctions against the practice, dissemination and encouragement of homosexual activities.

My Lords, the authorities dealing with the intentional infliction of bodily harm do not establish that consent is a defence to a charge under the Act of 1861. They establish that the courts have accepted that consent is a defence to the infliction of bodily harm in the course of some lawful activities. The question is whether the defence should be extended to the infliction of bodily harm in the course of sado-masochistic encounters. The Wolfenden Committee did not make any recommendations about sado-masochism and Parliament did not deal with violence in 1967. The Act of 1967 is of no assistance for present purposes because the present problem was not under consideration.

The question whether the defence of consent should be extended to the consequences of sado-masochistic encounters can only be decided by consideration of policy and public interest. Parliament can call on the advice of doctors, psychiatrists, criminologists, sociologists and other experts and can also sound and take into account public opinion. But the question must at this stage be decided by this House in its judicial capacity in order to determine whether the convictions of the appellants should be upheld or quashed.

Counsel for some of the appellants argued that the defence of consent should be extended to the offence of occasioning actual bodily harm under section 47 of the Act of 1861 but should not be available to charges of serious wounding and the infliction of serious bodily harm under section 20. I do not consider that this solution is practicable. Sado-masochistic participants have no way of foretelling the degree of bodily harm which will result from their encounters. The differences between actual bodily harm and serious bodily harm cannot be satisfactorily applied by a jury in order to determine acquittal or conviction.

Counsel for the appellants argued that consent should provide a defence to charges under both section 20 and section 47 because, it was said, every person has a right to deal with his body as he pleases. I do not consider that this slogan provides a sufficient guide to the policy decision which must now be made. It is an offence for a person to abuse his own body and mind by taking drugs. Although the law is often broken, the criminal law restrains a practice which is regarded as dangerous and injurious to individuals and which if allowed and extended is harmful to society generally. In any event the appellants in this case did not mutilate their own bodies. They inflicted bodily harm on willing victims. Suicide is no longer an offence but a person who assists another to commit suicide is guilty of murder or manslaughter.

The assertion was made on behalf of the appellants that the sexual appetites of sadists and masochists can only be satisfied by the infliction of bodily harm and that the law should not punish the consensual achievement of sexual satisfaction. There was no evidence to support the assertion that sado-masochist activities are essential to the happiness of the appellants or any other participants but the argument would be acceptable if sado-masochism were only concerned with sex, as the appellants contend. In my opinion sado-masochism is not only concerned with sex. Sado-masochism is also concerned with violence. The evidence discloses that the practices of the appellants were unpredictably dangerous and degrading to body and mind and were developed with increasing barbarity and taught to persons whose consents were dubious or worthless.

A sadist draws pleasure from inflicting or watching cruelty. A masochist derives pleasure from his own pain or humiliation. The appellants are middle-aged men. The victims were youths some of whom were introduced to sado-masochism before they attained the age of 21. In his judgment in the Court of Appeal, Lord Lane CJ said that two members of the group of which the appellants formed part, namely one Cadman and the appellant Laskey:

> were responsible in part for the corruption of a youth 'K' ... It is some comfort at least to be told, as we were, that 'K' has now it seems settled into a normal heterosexual relationship. Cadman had befriended 'K' when the boy was 15 years old. He met him in a cafeteria and, so he says, found out that the boy was interested in homosexual activities. He introduced and encouraged 'K' in 'bondage' affairs. He was interested in viewing and recording on video tape 'K' and other teenage boys in homosexual scenes ... One cannot overlook the danger that the gravity of the assaults and injuries in this type of case may escalate to even more unacceptable heights. [See 94 Cr App R 302 at 310.]

The evidence disclosed that drink and drugs were employed to obtain consent and increase enthusiasm. The victim was usually manacled so that the sadist could enjoy the thrill of power and the victim could enjoy the thrill of helplessness. The victim had no control over the harm which the sadist, also stimulated by drink and drugs, might inflict. In one case a victim was branded twice on the thigh and there was some doubt as to whether he consented to or protested against the second branding. The dangers involved in administering violence must have been appreciated by the appellants because, so it was said by their counsel, each victim was given a code word which he could pronounce when excessive harm or pain was caused. The efficiency of this precaution, when taken, depends on the circumstances and on the personalities involved. No one can feel the pain of another. The charges against the appellants were based on genital torture and violence to the buttocks, anus, penis, testicles and nipples. The victims were degraded and humiliated, sometimes beaten, sometimes wounded with instruments and sometimes branded. Bloodletting and the smearing of human blood produced excitement. There were obvious dangers of serious personal injury and blood infection. Prosecuting counsel informed the trial judge against the protests of defence counsel that, although the appellants had not contracted AIDS, two members of the group had died from AIDS and one other had contracted an HIV infection although not necessarily from the practices of the group. Some activities involved excrement. The assertion that the instruments employed by the sadists were clean and sterilised could not have removed the danger of infection, and the assertion that care was taken demonstrates the possibility of infection. Cruelty to human beings was on occasions supplemented by cruelty to animals in the form of bestiality. It is fortunate that there were no permanent injuries to a victim though no one knows the extent of harm inflicted in other cases. It is not surprising that a victim does not complain to the police when the complaint would involve him in giving details of acts in which he participated. Doctors of course are subject to a code of confidentiality.

In principle there is a difference between violence which is incidental and violence which is inflicted for the indulgence of cruelty. The violence of sado-masochistic encounters involves the indulgence of cruelty by sadists and the degradation of victims. Such violence is injurious to the participants and unpredictably dangerous. I am not prepared to invent a defence of consent for sado-masochistic encounters which breed and glorify cruelty and result in offences under sections 47 and 20 of the Act of 1861.

...

Society is entitled and bound to protect itself against a cult of violence. Pleasure derived from the infliction of pain is an evil thing. Cruelty is uncivilised. I would answer the certified question in the negative and dismiss the appeals of the appellants against conviction.

...

Lord Mustill [dissenting]:

...

The purpose of this long discussion has been to suggest that the decks are clear for the House to tackle completely anew the question whether the public interest requires section 47 of the Act of 1861 to be interpreted as penalising an infliction of harm which is at the level of actual bodily harm, but not grievous bodily harm: which is inflicted in private (by which I mean that it is exposed to the view only of those who have chosen to view it); which takes place not only with the consent of the recipient but with his willing and glad cooperation; which is inflicted for the gratification of sexual desire, and not in a spirit of animosity or rage; and which is not engaged in for profit.

My Lords, I have stated the issue in these terms to stress two considerations of cardinal importance. Lawyers will need no reminding of the first, but since this prosecution has been widely noticed it must be emphasised that the issue before the House is not whether the appellants' conduct is morally right, but whether it is properly charged under the Act of 1861. When proposing that the conduct is not rightly so charged I do not invite your Lordships' House to indorse it as morally acceptable. Nor do I pronounce in favour of a libertarian doctrine specifically related to sexual matters. Nor in the least do I suggest that ethical pronouncements are meaningless, that there is no difference between right and wrong, that sadism is praiseworthy, or that new opinions on sexual morality are necessarily superior to the old, or anything else of the same kind. What I do say is that these are questions of private morality; that the standards by which they fall to be judged are not those of the criminal law; and that if these standards are to be upheld the individual must enforce them upon himself according to his own moral standards, or have them enforced against him by moral pressures exerted by whatever religious or other community to whose ethical ideals he responds. The point from which I invite your Lordships to depart is simply this, that the state should interfere with the rights of an individual to live his or her life as he or she may choose no more than is necessary to ensure a proper balance between the special interests of the individual and the general interests of the individuals who together comprise the populace at large. Thus, whilst acknowledging that very many people, if asked whether the appellants' conduct was wrong, would reply 'Yes, repulsively wrong', I would at the same time assert that this does not in itself mean that the prosecution of the appellants under sections 20 and 47 of the Offences against the Person Act 1861 is well founded.

This point leads directly to the second. As I have ventured to formulate the crucial question, it asks whether there is good reason to impress upon section 47 an interpretation which penalises the relevant level of harm irrespective of consent, ie, to recognise sadomasochistic activities as falling into a special category of acts, such as duelling and prizefighting, which 'the law says shall not be done'. This is very important, for if the question were differently stated it might well yield a different answer. In particular, if it were to be held that as a matter of law all infliction of bodily harm above the level of common assault is incapable of being legitimated by consent, except in special circumstances, then we would have to consider whether the public interest required the recognition of private sexual activities as being in a specially exempt category. This would be an altogether more difficult question and one which I would not be prepared to answer in favour of the appellants, not because I do not have my own opinions upon it but because I regard the task as one which the courts are not suited to perform, and which should be carried out, if at all, by Parliament after a thorough review of all the medical, social, moral and political issues, such as was performed by the Wolfenden Committee [see *Report of the Committee on Homosexual Offences and Prostitution* (Cmnd 247, 1957)]. Thus, if I had begun from the same point of departure as my noble and learned friend Lord Jauncey of Tullichettle I would have arrived at a similar conclusion; but differing from him on the present state of the law, I venture to differ.

Let it be assumed however that we should embark upon this question. I ask myself, not whether as a result of the decision in this appeal, activities such as those of the appellants should cease to be criminal, but rather whether the Act of 1861 (a statute which I venture to repeat once again was clearly intended to penalise conduct of a quite different nature) should in this new situation be interpreted so as to make it criminal. Why should this step be taken? Leaving aside repugnance and moral objection, both of which are entirely natural but neither of which are in my opinion grounds upon which the court could properly create a new crime, I can visualise only the following reasons:

(1) Some of the practices obviously created a risk of genito-urinary infection, and others of septicaemia. These might indeed have been grave in former times, but the risk of serious harm must surely have been greatly reduced by modern medical science.

(2) The possibility that matters might get out of hand, with grave results. It has been acknowledged throughout the present proceedings that the appellants' activities were performed as a prearranged ritual, which at the same time enhanced their excitement and minimised the risk that the infliction of injury would go too far. Of course things might go wrong and really serious injury or death might ensue. If this happened, those responsible would be punished according to the ordinary law, in the same way as those who kill or injure in the course of more ordinary sexual activities are regularly punished. But to penalise the appellants' conduct even if the extreme consequences do not ensue, just because they might have done so, would require an assessment of the degree of risk, and the balancing of this risk against the interests of individual freedom. Such a balancing is in my opinion for Parliament, not the courts; and even

if your Lordships' House were to embark upon it the attempt must in my opinion fail at the outset for there is no evidence at all of the seriousness of the hazards to which sado-masochistic conduct of this kind gives rise. This is not surprising, since the impressive argument of Mr Purnell QC for the Crown did not seek to persuade your Lordships to bring the matter within the Act of 1861 on the ground of special risks, but rather to establish that the appellants are liable under the general law because the level of harm exceeded the critical level marking off criminal from non-criminal consensual violence which he invited your Lordships to indorse.

(3) I would give the same answer to the suggestion that these activities involved a risk of accelerating the spread of auto-immune deficiency syndrome [AIDS], and that they should be brought within the Act of 1861 in the interests of public health. The consequence would be strange, since what is currently the principal cause for the transmission of this scourge, namely consenting buggery between males, is now legal. Nevertheless, I would have been compelled to give this proposition the most anxious consideration if there had been any evidence to support it. But there is none, since the case for the Crown was advanced on an entirely different ground.

(4) There remains an argument to which I have given much greater weight. As the evidence in the present case has shown, there is a risk that strangers (and especially young strangers) may be drawn into these activities at an early age and will then become established in them for life. This is indeed a disturbing prospect, but I have come to the conclusion that it is not a sufficient ground for declaring these activities to be criminal under the Act of 1861. The element of the corruption of youth is already catered for by the existing legislation; and if there is a gap in it which needs to be filled the remedy surely lies in the hands of Parliament, not in the application of a statute which is aimed at other forms of wrongdoing. As regards proselytisation for adult sado-masochism the argument appears to me circular. For if the activity is not itself so much against the public interest that it ought to be declared criminal under the Act of 1861 then the risk that others will be induced to join in cannot be a ground for making it criminal.

Leaving aside the logic of this answer, which seems to me impregnable, plain humanity demands that a court addressing the criminality of conduct such as that of the present should recognise and respond to the profound dismay which all members of the community share about the apparent increase of cruel and senseless crimes against the defenceless. Whilst doing so I must repeat for the last time that in the answer which I propose I do not advocate the decriminalisation of conduct which has hitherto been a crime; nor do I rebut a submission that a new crime should be created, penalising this conduct, for Mr Purnell has rightly not invited the House to take this course. The only question is whether these consensual private acts are offences against the existing law of violence. To this question I return a negative response.

[**Lord Jauncey** and **Lord Lowry** delivered separate judgments agreeing with **Lord Templeman**. **Lord Slynn** delivered a separate judgment agreeing with **Lord Mustill**. Appeals dismissed.]

2.36 Notes and questions

1. Which of the approaches taken above do you agree with? Was Lord Mustill correct in categorising the behaviour of the appellants as a matter of personal morality with which the criminal law should not be concerned? Are there circumstances in which a degree of paternalism in the criminal law may be warranted? Do you agree with Lord Templeman's view that society is entitled to protect itself against a cult of violence, including consensual violence? Kell points out that the majority and one of the minority judges (Mustill LJ) began from diametrically opposed starting points, with the majority assuming that the behaviour was unlawful and then considering whether a defence should be recognised, and the minority assuming that the behaviour was lawful and then considering whether there was a justification for criminalisation: D Kell, 'Social Disutility and the Law of Consent' (1994) 14 *OJLS* 121. For further consideration of these issues, see I Freckleton, 'Masochism, Self-mutilation and the Limits of Consent' (1994) 2 *JLM* 48; S Bronitt, 'The Right to Sexual Privacy, Sado-Masochism and the Human Rights (Sexual Conduct) Act 1994 (Cth)' (1995) 2 *AJHR* 59; A Houlihan, 'When "No" Means "Yes" and "Yes" Means Harm: HIV Risk, Consent and Sadomasochism Case Law' (2011) 20 *Law and Sexuality* 31.
2. *R v Brown* has been accepted as correct law in Victoria. In *R v Stein* [2007] VSCA 300, the accused and his partner, a prostitute, agreed with the deceased to engage in a bondage session. The partner dressed the deceased in women's clothing and tied him up using leather restraints and left the deceased spread-eagled on his back on the bed. The accused then entered the room and tied two handkerchiefs, knotted to form a gag, around the head and mouth of the deceased. The deceased showed signs of distress, and the partner left the room. The accused remained in the room and the deceased died. The accused was charged with murder and convicted of manslaughter. The Court of Appeal upheld the conviction on application of the doctrine of unlawful act of manslaughter. The relevant unlawful act was assault. The court held that there was no evidence of consent to the application of the gag, and certainly no evidence that the deceased had consented to not having it removed when he suffered distress. The court further held, following *R v Brown*, that there could not be valid consent to the level of risk of harm involved. Kellam JA, with whom Vincent and Neave JJA agreed, stated (at [19], [22]):

> In any event, any consent by the deceased to the application of the gag cannot be regarded as being consent to the risk of the infliction upon him of actual bodily harm by reason thereof … [It] cannot be said that the general activity in which the applicant and the deceased were engaged was unlawful for the purposes of the application of the unlawful and dangerous

act formulation of the crime of manslaughter. Nevertheless, even though it might be accepted that the deceased had consented to bondage activity, the application of a gag to his mouth, whether or not he had consented, involved exposure to the risk of serious physical injury to him ... There was a foreseeable risk of serious injury.

See also *R v Emmett* (EWCA, 18 June 1999, unreported); *R v Mcintosh* [1999] VSC 358; *R v Neal* [2011] VSCA 172.

Sexual diseases

2.37 In *R v Brown*, the House of Lords was considering the question of the limits the criminal law places on that to which a person may consent. In *R v Clarence* (1889) 22 QBD 23; [1886–90] All ER Rep 133, the Court for Crown Cases Reserved had considered the question of whether an apparent consent to sexual relations could be negated by the fact that, unbeknown to the person consenting, the other party was infected with a life-threatening sexually transmitted disease. The accused was convicted of assault occasioning actual bodily harm and malicious infliction of grievous bodily harm upon his wife. The accused was, to his knowledge, infected with gonorrhoea — in the nineteenth century, a life-endangering disease. He had intercourse with his wife without informing her of the fact and infected her. The case was reserved for the opinion of the Court for Crown Cases Reserved. It was heard before 13 judges of whom nine held the conviction should be quashed. Wills J stated (at 34,139):

> I cannot help saying that to me it seems a strange misapplication of language to call such a deed as that under consideration either a rape or an assault. The essence of rape is, to my mind, the penetration of the woman's person without her consent. ... Of course the thing done in the present case is wicked and cruel enough. No one wishes to say a word in palliation of it. But that seems to me to be no reason for describing it as something else than it is, in order to bring within the criminal law an act which up to a very recent time no one ever thought was within it.

Hawkins J, dissenting, stated (at 51–5, 148–51):

> In my judgment wilfully to place his diseased person in contact with hers without her express consent amounts to an assault. It has been argued that to hold this would be to hold that a man who suffering from gonorrhoea has communion with his wife might be guilty of the crime of rape. I do not think this would be so. ...
>
> I have arrived at the conclusion that this conviction is right and in accordance with the law, and I cannot, therefore, be a party to a judgment which in effect would proclaim to the world that by the law of England in this year 1888 a man might deliberately, knowingly, and maliciously perpetrate upon the body of his wife the abominable outrage charged against the prisoner, and yet not be punishable criminally for such atrocious barbarity.

2.38 It is submitted that the opinion of the minority in *R v Clarence* is to be preferred. The wife consented to the sexual intercourse that occurred and, for that reason, her husband could not be guilty of raping her (apart from the consideration that, at that time, a husband could not be guilty of raping his wife). The wife did not, however, consent to the infliction of serious injury upon herself in the form of a potentially fatal disease. If it is accepted that infecting a spouse or other sexual partner in such a manner should constitute an offence, how far should this principle be extended? Should a person who communicates gonorrhoea to someone whom he or she casually picks up in a bar be guilty of assault? Should a person who knowingly or recklessly communicates influenza to someone he or she kisses be guilty of assault? How do you think a court should now decide if confronted with a case similar to *R v Clarence* involving AIDS?

Note that, in Victoria, the issue of the knowing transmission of HIV has been dealt with by the creation of separate statutory offences. Section 19A of the Crimes Act 1958 (Vic) creates the offence of intentionally causing another person to be infected with a very serious disease, with 'very serious disease' being defined as meaning 'HIV within the meaning of the *Health Act 1958* [Vic]'. No specific provision is made to cover the case of the intentional infliction of diseases other than HIV. The requirement that the infecting of another be intentional, however, would seem to place a significant limitation on the section. In the absence of a positive desire to bring about infection, the risk of transmission from a single act of unprotected sex would not seem to be sufficiently high to amount to intention. D may, however, in such cases be charged with recklessly engaging in conduct that places another in danger of death contrary to s 22 of the Crimes Act 1958 (Vic). Why do you think s 19A was drafted so narrowly? Note, generally, S Bronitt, 'Criminal Liability for the Transmission of HIV/AIDS' (1992) 16 *Crim LJ* 85.

Consent and the transmission of sexually transmitted diseases has been considered in Victoria in the case of *Neal v The Queen* [2011] VSCA 172. In that case, the defendant was charged with various offences, including s 19A of the Crimes Act 1958 (Vic) (intentional infliction of a 'very serious disease') and reckless endangerment under s 22 of that Act. The defence argued that the victim had given informed consent to the risk. The Victorian Court of Appeal distinguished the decisions in *Brown* and *Stein* in so far as they addressed the intentional infliction of harm, and concluded that valid consent could be given to taking a risk of serious injury in a sexual relationship, following the United Kingdom case of *R v Dica* [2004] EWCA Crim 1101. See further, M Weait, 'Criminal Law and the Sexual Transmission of HIV: *R v Dica*' (2005) 68 *Modern Law Review* 121. The Victorian Court of Appeal in *Neal* stated (at [72]):

> In our view, informed consent is capable of providing a defence to a charge of recklessly endangering a person with HIV through unprotected sexual intercourse, so long as the consent is communicated to the offender. It follows that, in order for the Crown to succeed in a prosecution for an offence of reckless conduct endangering a person with HIV through unprotected sexual intercourse, if the accused puts consent in issue, the Crown must prove beyond reasonable doubt that

the complainant did not give informed consent to the risk or that the accused did not honestly believe that the complainant had given informed consent to the risk.

In relation to New South Wales, see 2.34 on the criminalisation of the transmission of sexually transmitted diseases in the Crimes Act 1900 (NSW) and those who engage in sexual intercourse and fail to warn the person with whom intercourse is proposed that they are suffering from a sexually transmitted infection in the Public Health Act 2010 (NSW).

Boxing and other contact sports

2.39 Prize fights (bare knuckle contests of indefinite duration, ending only when one contestant was unable to continue) have been illegal since the nineteenth century: see *R v Coney* (1882) 8 QBD 534. In *Pallante v Stadiums Pty Ltd (No 1)* [1976] VR 331, McInerney J considered the legality of modern boxing contests. The plaintiff brought an action for damages in respect of injuries suffered to his eyesight in the course of a professional boxing contest organised by the first defendant, Stadiums Pty Ltd. The first defendant raised the argument that professional boxing contests were, at common law, unlawful, and that since the plaintiff had been engaged in an unlawful fight he could maintain no action for damages in respect of those injuries. It may be noted that it would seem surprising that the first defendant should have raised this argument for, if successful, the result would have been that they could no longer have continued with their major business enterprise. The argument was, however, rejected. McInerney J stated (at 343):

> [B]oxing is not an unlawful and criminal activity so long as, whether for reward or not, it is engaged in by a contestant as a boxing sport or contest, not from motive of personal animosity, or at all events not predominantly from that motive, but predominantly as an exercise of boxing skill and physical condition in accordance with rules and in conditions the object of which is to ensure that the infliction of bodily injury is kept within reasonable bounds, so as to preclude or reduce, so far as is practicable, the risk of either contestant incurring serious bodily injury, and to ensure that victory shall be achieved in accordance with the rules by the person demonstrating the greater skill as a boxer.

In *R v Brown* [1994] 1 AC 212; [1993] 2 All ER 75 at 109, Lord Mustill, dissenting, commented on the decision in *Pallante v Stadiums Pty Ltd (No 1)* as follows:

> I intend no disrespect to the valuable judgment of McInerney J in *Pallante v Stadiums Pty Ltd (No 1)* [1976] VR 331 when I say that the heroic efforts of that learned judge to arrive at an intellectually satisfying account of the apparent immunity of professional boxing from criminal process have convinced me that the task is impossible. It is in my judgment best to regard this as another special situation which for the time being stands outside the ordinary law of violence because society chooses to tolerate it.

On consent to the infliction of injury during sporting contests, see C Davies, 'Criminal Law and Assaults in Sport: An Australian and Canadian Perspective' (2006) 30 *Crim LJ* 151. It is clear that an application of force during a sporting contest is legal where it is not in contravention of the rules of the game. There seems also to be a strong argument that players of such sports accept that the rules will be breached on a regular basis, and that not every infringement will amount to a criminal act: see *McAvaney v Quigley* (1992) 58 A Crim R 457 at 459–60. Beyond this, and particularly where a player is 'king-hit' from behind, the imposition of criminal liability seems to depend on the willingness of the victim to bring the matter to court, as well as the cultural attitudes embedded in the relevant sporting code. For further examples, see *R v Matthews* (Magistrates Court, Victoria, 1985, unreported); *Abbott v The Queen* (1996) 16 WAR 313; *R v Bertuzzi* [2004] BCPC 474.

Surgery and body modifications

2.40 Surgical operations are lawful when performed with the patient's consent, even though the operation may be dangerous to life. An operation to terminate a pregnancy must here be noted as an exception since it is covered by special legislation: see **4.15**. Surgery must not ordinarily be carried out unless the patient freely consents to it. A surgeon who operates on an unwilling patient commits an assault, no matter how selfless the surgeon's motives might be or how great her or his concern for the patient's well-being. However, this applies only to those cases where the patient's consent could be obtained. If the patient is unconscious, then the surgeon, exercising a proper medical judgment, would be able to proceed without risk of criminal conviction. In situations of emergency, surgical procedures may be carried out without the patient's consent. In such cases, the defence of necessity (see **Chapter 12**) precludes liability for what would otherwise be an assault: see generally, P Skegg, 'A Justification for Medical Procedures Performed Without Consent' (1974) 90 *LQR* 512. In Victoria, the issue of emergency surgical procedures is covered by a combination of common law and legislation: see **2.42**.

2.41 The requisite consent is that of the patient, in the usual case. The consent of his or her spouse, even when the patient is unconscious, adds nothing (though it may relieve the surgeon of some potential civil liability to which he or she might otherwise become subject). If the patient is a child too young to make an informed judgment, then the parent or guardian may give consent in those cases where it is necessary; so, also, on attaining the age of 16, a person is ordinarily capable of deciding whether to accept surgery and that from that age onwards the consent of the parent or guardian is unnecessary. The matter of consent in surgery is well discussed in paras 474–84 of the English *Report of the Committee on the Age of Majority* (Cmnd 3342, 1967); and see New South Wales Law Reform Commission, *Young People and Consent to Health Care* (2008), Report No 119, at [6.1].

2.42 There are special provisions in relation to human tissue transplants and a child for this purpose is deemed to be a person under 18 years and who is not married (Human Tissue Act 1983 (NSW) s 4). In New South Wales, s 7 of the Human Tissue Act 1983 (NSW) allows an adult to give consent in writing to the removal from the person's body of regenerative tissues for the purposes of transplantation to another person for therapeutic, medical or scientific purposes. Section 8 allows consent to be given for removal of non-regenerative tissue for the purposes of transplants to another person. Section 10 provides that a parent of a child may give consent in writing to the removal from the child's body of regenerative tissue for the purpose of transplantation to the body of a parent, brother or sister of the child.

In Victoria, s 24 of the Human Tissue Act 1982 (Vic) empowers a medical practitioner to give a blood transfusion to a person under 18 years of age, if the consent of the person legally entitled to give it is refused or not obtained and, in the opinion of the practitioner, the transfusion is a reasonable and proper treatment for the condition from which the person is suffering, and that without the transfusion the person is likely to die. A second opinion must be obtained before the transfusion is administered. The provision is not applicable to surgical procedures other than the giving of blood transfusions. In cases not covered by the provision, where the parents or guardian cannot be located or, if located, refuse to give consent to surgery necessary to preserve the life of the child or to prevent serious injury to the child's health, it is submitted that a doctor would be justified at common law in performing such emergency surgery. The doctor's defence to a charge of assault in such a case would rest upon the principles of the general defence of necessity: see **Chapter 12**. In Victoria, a medical enduring power of attorney can be executed under the Medical Treatment Act 1988 (Vic) by which the donor appoints an agent to make medical decisions for the donor should illness or accident prevent the donor from making such decisions for himself or herself. In the case of adult persons suffering from a permanent or long-term disability who have not executed a medical enduring power of attorney, decisions regarding proposed medical treatment can be made by one of a variety of classes of person specified in Pt 4A of the Guardianship and Administration Act 1986 (Vic). Section 42A provides for the giving of treatment without consent in cases of emergency.

In New South Wales, the Children and Young Persons (Care and Protection) Act 1998 s 174 provides that for emergency medical treatment, a medical practitioner or dentist may carry out medical or dental treatment on a child (under 16 years) or young person (16 or 17 years) without the consent of the child/young person or his or her parent if the medical practitioner or dentist 'is of the opinion that it is necessary, as a matter of urgency, to carry out the treatment on the child or young person in order to save his or her life or to prevent serious damage to his or her health'. This abrogates the need for consent where the assault is inflicted to protect the health of the minor.

2.43 Elective procedures, such as liposuction and cosmetic surgery, can also be validly consented to. Gender reassignment surgery is also now socially accepted. But what about genital modification or mutilation? What about healthy limb amputation, sometimes referred to as 'body dysmorphia disorder', in which a healthy and apparently sane person earnestly desires the removal of what they feel to be a superfluous limb? In the end, such questions seem best decided by reference to prevailing social attitudes towards the procedure concerned. See also the discussion on ritual circumcision at 2.22, and the scope of the prohibition on 'genital mutilation' in the relevant criminal legislation.

Surgical or bodily procedures carried out by non-medical practitioners present somewhat different problems. It is socially accepted that tattooing and piercing is a form of body modification to which a 'victim' can consent. So too, in one English case, with branding: see *R v Wilson* [1996] 3 WLR 125, although the result in that case might not be applied in present-day Australia, particularly given the questionable nature of the victim's 'consent'.

OTHER OFFENCES AGAINST THE PERSON

Affray

2.44 Thus far, assaults have been considered from the standpoint of the participants. The law has, however, long recognised that when a fight takes place in the presence of others the spectators may be frightened by it. Accordingly, the common law knew an offence of affray. Affray consists of using or threatening unlawful violence towards another in circumstances where third persons of reasonable firmness, present at the scene, would fear for their own personal safety. In England and in New South Wales, the offence has been put upon a statutory footing: Public Order Act 1986 (Eng); Crimes Act 1900 (NSW) s 93C. It remains a common law offence in Victoria. However, the offence appears to be aimed at upholding public order rather than protecting spectators of threatened violence. In New South Wales, an offence of affray can be proven even where no persons are present, or likely to be present, at the scene of the threatened unlawful violence (Crimes Act 1900 (NSW) s 93C(4)). Other public order crimes, including riot, are discussed at 11.39–11.42.

The offence of affray was considered by the House of Lords in *I v Director of Public Prosecutions* [2001] 2 All ER 583. In response to an anonymous telephone call, a number of police officers were dispatched to a block of flats in a marked police carrier. On arrival, the police saw a group of 40–50 youths outside the block. Eight or nine of them were carrying petrol bombs, but none of the fuses had been lit. When the carrier came into view, the group immediately dispersed and no violence was shown or threatened towards the police officers. Nobody else was present at the scene. The police pursued some of the group and arrested the three accused who, before capture, had thrown away the petrol bombs they had been carrying. The accused were charged with affray. They were convicted in the Magistrates' Court and their appeals to the Divisional Court dismissed. On appeal to the House of Lords, two issues arose: (1) whether the overt possession of a weapon could constitute a threat of violence for the purpose of affray when it was not used or brandished in a violent manner, and

(2) whether the threat of unlawful violence had to be towards a person or persons present at the scene. In answer to the first question, the House of Lords held that the carrying of dangerous weapons, such as a petrol bomb, by a group of persons could, in some circumstances, constitute a threat of violence without those weapons being waved or brandished. The mere possession of a weapon, without threatening circumstances, was not enough to constitute a threat of unlawful violence, nor could the carrying of a concealed weapon itself be such a threat. In the instant case, the visible carrying in public of primed petrol bombs by a large number of what was obviously a 'gang out for no good' was clearly capable of constituting a threat of unlawful violence. In answer to the second question, the House of Lords held the threat of unlawful violence had to be directed towards a person or persons present at the scene. The offence of affray is not committed by a person whose conduct constitutes a threat of violence to persons who were not present. In the instant case, there was no-one present at the scene apart from the police officers and no threat was made towards them. Accordingly, the appeals of the accused were allowed.

The requirement that the threat must be directed to persons who are actually present may have been modified in Victoria in a decision of the Court of Appeal. The court specified only that the violence must be *capable* of terrifying a bystander of reasonable firmness and courage: 'In order to convict the applicant of affray, the jury would need to have been satisfied beyond reasonable doubt not only that the applicant intentionally joined the unlawful fighting or violence but also that the fighting or violence was such that a bystander of reasonable firmness and courage might reasonably be terrified': *Paisley v The Queen* [2012] VSCA 79 at [46] per Nettle and Neave JJA (with whom Maxwell P agreed)

The offence of affray may be committed by an individual who is acting alone in using or threatening unlawful violence towards another. If two or more persons use or threaten unlawful violence, the conduct of those persons may be taken together and considered for the purposes of determining whether an offence of affray has been committed: Crimes Act 1900 (NSW) s 93C(2). However, the offence does not require a group of persons to be so acting for an offence to be committed: *Colosimo v Director of Public Prosecutions (NSW)* (2005) 64 NSWLR 645.

False imprisonment: kidnapping

2.45 Every unlawful restraint of the liberty of a person, by confining her or him in custody, is a false imprisonment and a common law crime. This is so even if the restraint occurs solely in a public street. However, the mere blocking of a person's path, so that he or she cannot go in a particular direction, is no offence. It is false imprisonment where a person is detained in consequence of threats whether those threats relate to the person detained or to another: *R v Garrett* (1988) 30 SASR 392.

2.46 Kidnapping, also a common law crime, is an aggravated species of false imprisonment, and is committed by unlawfully taking and carrying away a person against her or his will. In *R v D* [1984] 2 All ER 449, Lord Brandon stated the elements of the crime as follows (at 453):

> First, the nature of the offence is an attack on, and infringement of, the personal liberty of the individual. Secondly, the offence contains four ingredients as follows: (1) the taking or carrying away of one person by another; (2) by force or by fraud; (3) without the consent of the person so taken or carried away; and (4) without lawful excuse.

In *R v Reid* [1973] 1 QB 299, the Court of Appeal held that a husband could be guilty of kidnapping his wife, even if at the time they were still to be regarded as cohabiting. In *R v D* [1984] 2 All ER 449, the House of Lords held that a parent could be guilty of kidnapping her or his child. Where a person consents to being taken, but that consent is obtained by deception, the crime may be committed. Thus, in *R v Cort* [2003] 3 WLR 1300, the Court of Appeal held the accused could be guilty of kidnapping where he induced women to enter his car by falsely telling them the bus for which they were waiting had broken down and offering them a lift to their destination.

Similar justifications apply to these offences as to other forms of assault; for example, the execution of power of arrest, and so on. In *R v Henman* [1987] Crim LR 333, the Court of Appeal held that attempting to save a person from moral and spiritual danger from a religious sect to which she belonged did not constitute a lawful excuse.

2.47 In Victoria and New South Wales, kidnapping and abduction of children have now been made specific statutory offences: Crimes Act 1958 (Vic) ss 63, 63A; Crimes Act 1900 (NSW) ss 86, 87. Note *R v Hudson* (1985) 63 ALR 257.

Sexual Offences

CHAPTER 3

INTRODUCTION

3.1 At common law the most important sexual offence was rape. Common law rape involved non-consensual penetration, however slight, of the vagina by the penis. Neither complete penetration nor ejaculation were necessary: *Holland v R* (1993) 67 ALJR 946. Non-consent meant that the offence could be committed through conscious refusal or where a woman was unconscious; for example, as a result of a beating by the perpetrator or where the perpetrator spiked the victim's drink. In the ordinary case, however, where the woman was fully conscious and her mental capacity was not in doubt, it was important that the jury be made aware that rape was only committed where the act of penetration was against her will: *R v Wilkes and Briant* [1965] VR 475: see **3.15C**. The common law definition of rape as requiring penetration of a vagina by a penis meant that a woman could not be guilty of rape nor a man guilty of raping another man. A woman could, however, be convicted as an accomplice to an act of rape performed by a man: *R v Ram and Ram* (1893) 17 Cox CC 609.

3.2 Over recent decades in each of the common law states, the law relating to rape and other sexual offences has been amended in the most fundamental fashion. In Victoria, the crime of rape has been greatly increased in scope. This reform was first achieved by the Crimes (Sexual Offences) Act 1980 (Vic). The Victorian legislation was further amended by the Crimes (Sexual Offences) Act 1991 and then by the Crimes (Rape) Act 1991, which introduced a purely statutory crime of rape and abolished the common law offence (s 6) and, most recently, by the Crimes Amendment (Rape) Act 2007. In New South Wales, the Crimes (Sexual Assault) Amendment Act 1981 abolished the crime of rape, replacing it with categories of sexual assault. This legislation was itself abolished by the Crimes (Amendment) Act 1989 (NSW), introducing offences of sexual assault, aggravated sexual assault, assault with intent to have sexual intercourse, indecent assault, aggravated indecent assault, acts of indecency and aggravated acts of indecency. Most recently, the Crimes Act 1900 (NSW) was amended by the Crimes Amendment (Consent — Sexual Assault Offences) Act 2007. These provisions are set out at **3.12E**. To understand these statutes, it is necessary to have some appreciation of the scope of the crime of rape at common law, and the criticisms of it that led to the enactment of the present provisions.

3.3 At common law, acts of sodomy performed upon a non-consenting woman were not rape, although they constituted the equally serious statutory crime of buggery: Crimes Act 1958 (Vic) s 68, now repealed; Crimes Act 1900 (NSW) s 79, now repealed. Equally, forcible acts of oral intercourse, the forcible insertion of physical objects into the vagina or anus or the forcible insertion of the penis into the anus were not classified as rape. In such cases, however, the accused would be guilty of indecent assault (see **3.40–3.44**) and, in some cases, assault occasioning actual bodily harm or even some more serious forms of aggravated assault: see **2.10**.

3.4 It was argued that forcible acts of anal sex, oral sex or sexual assaults involving vaginal or anal penetration with a physical object should equally constitute rape. The argument was not solely that the penalties for such acts were inadequate, although some were inadequate. For example, a forcible act of oral sex not involving serious bodily injury to the victim would constitute no more serious a crime than indecent assault, carrying a maximum penalty of five years' imprisonment. However, it would have been a simple matter to have increased the maximum penalty for indecent assault. The argument was rather that the victim in these cases would feel violated in such a way as to amount to rape, and that it was important that the law respond to this feeling by branding the offender as a rapist. It was further argued that all such acts of non-consensual penetration should constitute rape not just when performed by a man upon a woman, but equally when performed by a man upon another man, or, much more rarely, by a woman upon a man or upon another woman.

3.5 A variation of this argument for equality in respect of sexual offences was that the crime of rape should be not extended, but abolished and replaced by one or more assault provisions which would apply whatever the sex of the attacker or victim, and whatever form the act of sexual connection took.

3.6 At common law, there were previously a number of irrebuttable presumption to the law of rape. First, a boy under the age of 14 years was incapable of rape: *R v Waite* [1892] 2 QB 600. Second, a husband could not be guilty of raping his wife: Hale's *The History of the Pleas of the Crown*, vol 1, p 629. He could, however, be guilty as an accomplice to an act of rape performed upon his wife by another: *R v Cogan and Leak* [1976] 1 QB 217; *Director of Public Prosecutions v Morgan* [1976] AC 182 (at **3.19C**). It was established also that a husband could be guilty of raping his wife where they were living apart pursuant to a court order: *R v Clarke* [1949] 2 All ER 448; *R v McMinn* [1982] VR 53. For this purpose, an undertaking given by the husband to a court not to molest his wife was treated as equivalent to a court order: *R v Steele* (1976) 65 Cr App R 22.

However, a husband could not be guilty where he was merely living separately to his wife: *R v Miller* [1954] 2 QB 282. Although the husband could not be guilty of rape in such circumstances, he could, however, be convicted of assault if he used force or violence for the purpose of achieving intercourse: *R v Miller* [1954] 2 QB 282; *R v Caswell* [1984] Crim LR 111.

3.7 The purported justification for a husband's immunity at common law to a charge of raping his wife was the view that by entering into the marriage the wife impliedly and irrevocably consented to all further acts of intercourse by the husband with her: Hale's *The History of the Pleas of the Crown*, vol 1, p 629; see also *R v Clarence* (1888) 22 QBD 23 (at 2.37). The policy argument urged in support of the rule was that if the law were otherwise, a wife on bad terms with her husband would be in a position to make an allegation of rape against her husband which it would be extremely difficult for him to disprove. As the institution of marriage has evolved, women are no longer treated by the law as the subject of their husbands. Further, critics of the law of spousal immunity have asserted that the law has a primary responsibility to protect women from acts of rape committed within marriage. This view has now been adopted both legislatively and in the common law: *R v L* (1991) 174 CLR 379; 103 ALR 577; *R v R* [1991] 2 WLR 1065.

3.8 Criticism and amendment of the law of rape have not been limited to the substantive law. In each of the Australian jurisdictions, significant reforms of the rules of evidence and procedure in relation to rape trials have also been enacted. A detailed consideration of these reforms is beyond the scope of this book: see, generally, J D Heydon, *Cross on Evidence*, 9th Aust ed, LexisNexis Butterworths, Sydney, 2013, pp 641–5.

3.9 One change in the rules of evidence worthy of particular note, however, is the modification of the common law rule that the victim in a rape case may be cross-examined about her sexual relations with men other than the accused. The justification for this rule was that such cross-examination was said to be relevant to credibility; a woman who was prepared to engage in extra-marital sexual relations would be more likely to commit perjury than a woman who led a sexually blameless life. This is obviously an absurd proposition, and the practical effect of the rule was that a woman who proceeded with a rape complaint could expect to have the whole of her sexual life ripped open and exposed to public view at the trial. Of course, in some cases, the fact that the victim has had sexual relations with men other than the accused may be relevant to an issue in the case: see *Gregory v R* (1983) 48 ALR 427. For example, if the accused's defence was that he had not had sexual intercourse with the complainant, and that her allegation of rape was fabricated in order to explain an unwanted pregnancy, the fact of her sexual relations with men other than the accused at times which could account for that pregnancy would be relevant, not to the complainant's credibility but to an issue in the case. Reforming legislation in each of the common law jurisdictions has had the effect of prohibiting cross-examination of a complainant about sexual activities where such cross-examination is essentially intended to suggest that the complainant is the type of person who is likely to have consented to the sexual activity the subject of the charge: see, for example, Criminal Procedure Act 2009 (Vic) s 343; Criminal Procedure Act 1986 (NSW) s 293. Such evidence continues to be admissible in Victoria, only with the leave of the court, where the court is persuaded that it has 'substantial relevance to facts in issue' or that it is a 'proper matter for cross-examination as to credit': see Criminal Procedure Act 2009 (Vic) ss 342, 346(2)(c). The equivalent New South Wales provision, Criminal Procedure Act 1986 (NSW) s 293, provides that evidence relating to the sexual reputation of the complainant is inadmissible except where it is connected to the offence or the relationship between the accused and the complainant, or is relevant to the complaint's sexually transmitted disease or pregnancy.

3.10 Procedural and substantive reform of the law of rape has led to positive changes to the handling of sexual assault cases. However, levels of reporting, prosecutions and convictions remain low. Approximately 30 per cent of adult sexual assaults are reported to the police (Australian Bureau of Statistics, *Crime Victimisation 2011–12*, Cat. No. 4530.0, 2013, Table 5). Of those, only a small proportion proceed to trial and an even smaller percentage result in a conviction. Some of the reasons for the low levels of conviction include the attrition of sexual assault cases at various stages of the justice system, treatment of complainants throughout the trial, distrust of complainants by the criminal justice system, difficulty in obtaining sufficient evidence, and belief in sexual assault myths and stereotypes (R Fileborn, 'Sexual Assault Laws in Australia', *Australian Centre for the Study of Sexual Assault Resource Sheet*, February 2011, pp 1–2).

THE STATUTORY PROVISIONS

3.11E Crimes Act 1958 (Vic)

(8) Sexual Offences (General Provisions)

35 Definitions

(1) In Subdivisions (8A) to (8G) —

De facto spouse means a person who is living with a person of the opposite sex as if they were married although they are not.

Sexual penetration means —

(a) the introduction (to any extent) by a person of his penis into the vagina, anus or mouth of another person, whether or not there is emission of semen; or

(b) the introduction (to any extent) by a person of an object or a part of his or her body (other than the penis) into the vagina or anus of another person, other than in the course of a procedure carried out in good faith for medical or hygienic purposes.

Vagina includes —

(a) the external genitalia; and

(b) a surgically constructed vagina.

[1.A ...]

(2) For the purposes of Subdivisions (8B) to (8E) both the person who sexually penetrates another person and the other person are taking part in an act of sexual penetration.

36 Meaning of consent

For the purposes of Subdivisions (8A) to (8D) 'consent' means free agreement. Circumstances in which a person does not freely agree to an act include the following:

(a) the person submits because of force or the fear of force to that person or someone else;

(b) the person submits because of the fear of harm of any type to that person or someone else;

(c) the person submits because she or he is unlawfully detained;

(d) the person is asleep, unconscious, or so affected by alcohol or another drug as to be incapable of freely agreeing;

(e) the person is incapable of understanding the sexual nature of the act;

(f) the person is mistaken about the sexual nature of the act or the identity of the person;

(g) the person mistakenly believes that the act is for medical or hygienic purposes.

37 Jury directions

(1) If relevant to the facts in issue in a proceeding the judge must direct the jury on the matters set out in sections 37AAA and 37AA.

(2) A judge must not give to a jury a direction of a kind referred to in section 37AAA or 37AA if the direction is not relevant to the facts in issue in the proceeding.

(3) A judge must relate any direction given to the jury of a kind referred to in section 37AAA or 37AA to —

(a) the facts in issue in the proceeding; and

(b) the elements of the offence being tried in respect of which the direction is given —

so as to aid the jury's comprehension of the direction.

37AAA Jury directions on consent

For the purposes of section 37, the matters relating to consent on which the judge must direct the jury are —

(a) the meaning of consent set out in section 36;

(b) that the law deems a circumstance specified in section 36 to be a circumstance in which the complainant did not consent;

(c) that if the jury is satisfied beyond reasonable doubt that a circumstance specified in section 36 exists in relation to the complainant, the jury must find that the complainant was not consenting;

(d) that the fact that a person did not say or do anything to indicate free agreement to a sexual act at the time at which the act took place is enough to show that the act took place without that person's free agreement;

(e) that the jury is not to regard a person as having freely agreed to a sexual act just because —

(i) she or he did not protest or physically resist; or

(ii) she or he did not sustain physical injury; or

(iii) on that or an earlier occasion, she or he freely agreed to engage in another sexual act (whether or not of the same type) with that person, or a sexual act with another person.

37AA Jury directions on the accused's awareness

For the purposes of section 37, if evidence is led or an assertion is made that the accused believed that the complainant was consenting to the sexual act, the judge must direct the jury that in considering whether the prosecution has proved beyond reasonable doubt that the accused was aware that the complainant was not consenting or might not have been consenting, the jury must consider —

(a) any evidence of that belief; and

(b) whether that belief was reasonable in all the relevant circumstances having regard to —

(i) in the case of a proceeding in which the jury finds that a circumstance specified in section 36 exists in relation to the complainant, whether the accused was aware that that circumstance existed in relation to the complainant; and

(ii) whether the accused took any steps to ascertain whether the complainant was consenting or might not be consenting, and if so, the nature of those steps; and

(iii) any other relevant matters.

37A Objectives of Subdivisions 8A to 8G

The objectives of Subdivisions (8A) to (8G) are:

(a) to uphold the fundamental right of every person to make decisions about his or her sexual behaviour and to choose not to engage in sexual activity;

(b) to protect children and persons with a cognitive impairment from sexual exploitation.

37B Guiding principles

It is the intention of Parliament that in interpreting and applying Subdivisions (8A) to (8G), courts are to have regard to the fact that:

(a) there is a high incidence of sexual violence within society; and

(b) sexual offences are significantly under-reported; and

(c) a significant number of sexual offences are committed against women, children and other vulnerable persons including persons with a cognitive impairment; and

(d) sexual offenders are commonly known to their victims; and

(e) sexual offences often occur in circumstances where there is unlikely to be any physical signs of an offence having occurred.

(8A) Rape and Indecent Assault

38 Rape

(1) A person must not commit rape.

Penalty: Level 2 imprisonment (25 years maximum).

(2) A person commits rape if —

(a) he or she intentionally sexually penetrates another person without that person's consent —

(i) while being aware that the person is not consenting or might not be consenting; or

(ii) while not giving any thought to whether the person is not consenting or might not be consenting; or

(b) after sexual penetration he or she does not withdraw from a person who is not consenting on becoming aware that the person is not consenting or might not be consenting.

(3) A person (the offender) also commits rape if he or she compels a person —

(a) to sexually penetrate the offender or another person irrespective of whether the person being sexually penetrated consents to the act; or

(b) who has sexually penetrated the offender or another person not to cease sexually penetrating the offender or that other person, irrespective of whether the person who has been sexually penetrated consents to the act.

(4) For the purposes of subsection (3), a person compels another person (the victim) to engage in a sexual act if the person compels the victim (by force or otherwise) to engage in that act —

(a) without the victim's consent; and

(b) while —

(i) being aware that the victim is not consenting or might not be consenting; or

(ii) not giving any thought to whether the victim is not consenting or might not be consenting.

38A Compelling sexual penetration

(1) A person must not compel another person to take part in an act of sexual penetration.
Penalty: Level 2 imprisonment (25 years maximum).

(2) A person (the offender) compels another person (the victim) to take part in an act of sexual penetration if —

(a) the offender compels the victim to introduce (to any extent) an object or a part of his or her body into his or her own anus or, in the case of a female victim, her own vagina, other than in the course of a procedure carried out in good faith for medical or hygienic purposes; or

(b) the offender compels the victim to take part in an act of bestiality within the meaning of section 59.

(3) For the purposes of subsection (2), a person compels another person (the victim) to take part in an act of sexual penetration if the person compels the victim (by force or otherwise) to engage in that act:

(a) without the victim's consent; and

(b) while —

(i) being aware that the victim is not consenting or might not be consenting; or

(ii) not giving any thought to whether the victim is not consenting or might not be consenting.

39 Indecent Assault

(1) A person must not commit indecent assault.
Penalty: Level 5 imprisonment (10 years maximum).

(2) A person commits indecent assault if he or she assaults another person in indecent circumstances —
   (a) while being aware that the person is not consenting or might not be consenting; or
   (b) while not giving any thought to whether the person is not consenting or might not be consenting.

...

62 Abrogation of obsolete rules of law

(1) The rule of law whereby a male person under the age of fourteen years is conclusively presumed to be impotent is hereby abrogated.

(2) The existence of a marriage does not constitute, or raise any presumption of, consent by a person to an act of sexual penetration with another person or to an indecent assault (with or without aggravating circumstances) by another person.

3.12E Crimes Act 1900 (NSW)

61H Definition of 'sexual intercourse' and other terms

(1) For the purposes of this Division, ***sexual intercourse*** means:
   (a) sexual connection occasioned by the penetration to any extent of the genitalia (including a surgically constructed vagina) of a female person or the anus of any person by:
      (i) any part of the body of another person, or
      (ii) any object manipulated by another person except where the penetration is carried out for proper medical purposes, or
   (b) sexual connection occasioned by the introduction of any part of the penis of a person into the mouth of another person, or
   (c) cunnilingus, or
   (d) the continuation of sexual intercourse as defined in paragraph (a), (b) or (c).

(1A) For the purposes of this Division, a person has a **'cognitive impairment'** if the person has:
   (a) an intellectual disability, or
   (b) a developmental disorder (including an autistic spectrum disorder), or
   (c) a neurological disorder, or
   (d) dementia, or
   (e) a severe mental illness, or
   (f) a brain injury,

   that results in the person requiring supervision or social habilitation in connection with daily life activities.

(2) For the purposes of this Division, a person is under the authority of another person if the person is in the care, or under the supervision or authority, of the other person.

(3) For the purposes of this Act, a person who incites another person to an act of indecency, as referred to in section 61N or 61O, is taken to commit an offence on the other person.

61HA Consent in relation to sexual assault offences

(1) **Offences to which section applies** This section applies for the purposes of the offences under sections 61I, 61J and 61JA.

(2) **Meaning of consent** A person **consents** to sexual intercourse if the person freely and voluntarily agrees to the sexual intercourse.

(3) **Knowledge about consent** A person who has sexual intercourse with another person without the consent of the other person knows that the other person does not consent to the sexual intercourse if:

- (a) the person knows that the other person does not consent to the sexual intercourse, or
- (b) the person is reckless as to whether the other person consents to the sexual intercourse, or
- (c) the person has no reasonable grounds for believing that the other person consents to the sexual intercourse.

For the purpose of making any such finding, the trier of fact must have regard to all the circumstances of the case:

- (d) Including any steps taken by the person to ascertain whether the other person consents to the sexual intercourse, but
- (e) not including any self-induced intoxication of the person.

(4) **Negation of consent** A person does not consent to sexual intercourse:

- (a) If the person does not have the capacity to consent to the sexual intercourse, including because of age or cognitive incapacity, or
- (b) If the person does not have the opportunity to consent to the sexual intercourse because the person is unconscious or asleep, or
- (c) If the person consents to the sexual intercourse because of threats of force or terror (whether the threats are against, or the terror is instilled in, that person or any other person), or
- (d) If the person consents to the sexual intercourse because the person is unlawfully detained.

(5) A person who consents to sexual intercourse with another person:

- (a) under a mistaken belief as to the identity of the other person, or
- (b) under a mistaken belief that the other person is married to the person, or
- (c) under a mistaken belief that the sexual intercourse is for medical or hygienic purposes (or under any other mistaken belief about the nature of the act induced by fraudulent means),

does not consent to the sexual intercourse. For the purposes of subsection (3), the other person knows that the person does not consent to sexual intercourse if the other person knows the person consents to sexual intercourse under such a mistaken belief.

(6) The grounds on which it may be established that a person does not consent to sexual intercourse include:

- (a) If the person has sexual intercourse while substantially intoxicated by alcohol or any drug, or

(b) If the person has sexual intercourse because of intimidatory or coercive conduct, or other threat, that does not involve a threat of force, or

(c) If the person has sexual intercourse because of the abuse of a position of authority or trust.

(7) A person who does not offer actual physical resistance to sexual intercourse is not, by reason only of that fact, to be regarded as consenting to the sexual intercourse.

(8) This section does not limit the grounds on which it may be established that a person does not consent to sexual intercourse.

61I Sexual assault

Any person who has sexual intercourse with another person without the consent of the other person and who knows that the other person does not consent to the sexual intercourse is liable to imprisonment for 14 years.

61J Aggravated sexual assault

(1) Any person who has sexual intercourse with another person without the consent of the other person and in circumstances of aggravation and who knows that the other person does not consent to the sexual intercourse is liable to imprisonment for 20 years.

(2) In this section, **circumstances of aggravation** means circumstances in which:

(a) at the time of, or immediately before or after, the commission of the offence, the alleged offender intentionally or recklessly inflicts actual bodily harm on the alleged victim or any other person who is present or nearby, or

(b) at the time of, or immediately before or after, the commission of the offence, the alleged offender threatens to inflict actual bodily harm on the alleged victim or any other person who is present or nearby by means of an offensive weapon or instrument, or

(c) the alleged offender is in the company of another person or persons, or

(d) the alleged victim is under the age of 16 years, or

(e) the alleged victim is (whether generally or at the time of the commission of the offence) under the authority of the alleged offender, or

(f) the alleged victim has a serious physical disability, or

(g) the alleged victim has a cognitive impairment, or.

(h) the alleged offender breaks and enters into any dwelling-house or other building with the intention of committing the offence or any other serious indictable offence, or

(i) the alleged offender deprives the alleged victim of his or her liberty for a period before or after the commission of the offence.

61JA Aggravated sexual assault in company

(1) A person:

(a) who has sexual intercourse with another person without the consent of the other person and who knows that the other person does not consent to the sexual intercourse, and

(b) who is in the company of another person or persons, and

(c) who:
   (i) at the time of, or immediately before or after, the commission of the offence, intentionally or recklessly inflicts actual bodily harm on the alleged victim or any other person who is present or nearby, or
   (ii) at the time of, or immediately before or after, the commission of the offence, threatens to inflict actual bodily harm on the alleged victim or any other person who is present or nearby by means of an offensive weapon or instrument, or
   (iii) deprives the alleged victim of his or her liberty for a period before or after the commission of the offence,

is liable to imprisonment for life.

(2) A person sentenced to imprisonment for life for an offence under this section is to serve that sentence for the term of the person's natural life.

(3) Nothing in this section affects the operation of section 21 of the *Crimes (Sentencing Procedure) Act 1999* (which authorises the passing of a lesser sentence than imprisonment for life).

(4) Nothing in this section affects the prerogative of mercy.

61K Assault with intent to have sexual intercourse

Any person who, with intent to have sexual intercourse with another person:

(a) Intentionally or recklessly inflicts actual bodily harm on the other person or a third person who is present or nearby, or

(b) threatens to inflict actual bodily harm on the other person or a third person who is present or nearby by means of an offensive weapon or instrument,

is liable to imprisonment for 20 years.

61L Indecent assault

Any person who assaults another person and, at the time of, or immediately before or after, the assault, commits an act of indecency on or in the presence of the other person, is liable to imprisonment for 5 years.

61M Aggravated indecent assault

(1) Any person who assaults another person in circumstances of aggravation, and, at the time of, or immediately before or after, the assault, commits an act of indecency on or in the presence of the other person, is liable to imprisonment for 7 years.

(2) Any person who assaults another person, and, at the time of, or immediately before or after, the assault, commits an act of indecency on or in the presence of the other person, is liable to imprisonment for 10 years, if the other person is under the age of 16 years.

(3) In this section, ***circumstances of aggravation*** means circumstances in which:

   (a) the alleged offender is in the company of another person or persons, or
   (b) the alleged victim is under the age of 16 years, or
   (c) the alleged victim is (whether generally or at the time of the commission of the offence) under the authority of the alleged offender, or
   (d) the alleged victim has a serious physical disability, or
   (e) the alleged victim has a cognitive impairment.

61N Act of indecency

(1) Any person who commits an act of indecency with or towards a person under the age of 16 years, or incites a person under that age to an act of indecency with or towards that or another person, is liable to imprisonment for 2 years.

(2) Any person who commits an act of indecency with or towards a person of the age of 16 years or above, or incites a person of the age of 16 years or above to an act of indecency with or towards that or another person, is liable to imprisonment for 18 months.

61O Aggravated act of indecency

(1) Any person who commits an act of indecency with or towards a person under the age of 16 years, or incites a person under that age to an act of indecency with or towards that or another person, in either case in circumstances of aggravation, is liable to imprisonment for 5 years.

(1A) Any person who commits an act of indecency with or towards a person of the age of 16 years or above, or incites a person of the age of 16 years or above to an act of indecency with or towards that or another person, in either case in circumstances of aggravation, is liable to imprisonment for 3 years.

(2) Any person who commits an act of indecency with or towards a person under the age of 10 years, or incites a person under that age to an act of indecency with or towards that or another person, is liable to imprisonment for 7 years.

(2A) A person:

- (a) who commits an act of indecency with or towards a person under the age of 16 years, or incites a person under the age of 16 years to an act of indecency with or towards that person or another person, and
- (b) who knows that the act of indecency is being filmed for the purposes of the production of child abuse material, is guilty of an offence.

Maximum penalty: imprisonment for 10 years.

(3) In this section, ***circumstances of aggravation*** means circumstances in which:

- (a) the alleged offender is in the company of another person or persons, or
- (b) the alleged victim is (whether generally or at the time of the commission of the offence) under the authority of the alleged offender, or
- (c) the alleged victim has a serious physical disability, or
- (d) the alleged victim has a cognitive impairment.

61P Attempt to commit offence under sections 61I–61O

Any person who attempts to commit an offence under section 61I, 61J, 61JA, 61K, 61L, 61M, 61N or 61O is liable to the penalty provided for the commission of the offence.

61Q Alternative verdicts

(1) **Question of aggravation** If on the trial of a person for an offence under section 61J, 61M or 61O the jury is not satisfied that the accused is guilty of the offence charged, but is satisfied on the evidence that the accused is guilty of an offence under section 61I, 61L or 61N, it may find the accused not guilty of the offence charged but guilty of the latter offence, and the accused is liable to punishment accordingly.

(1A) **Question of aggravation in company** If on the trial of a person for an offence under section 61JA the jury is not satisfied that the accused is guilty of the offence charged, but is satisfied on the evidence that the accused is guilty of an offence under section 61I or 61J, it may find the person not guilty of the offence charged but guilty of the latter offence, and the accused is liable to punishment accordingly.

(2) **Question of consent regarding alleged victim under 16** If on the trial of a person for an offence under section 61I the jury is not satisfied that the accused is guilty of the offence charged, but is satisfied on the evidence that the accused is guilty of an offence under section 66C (3) or 66C (4), it may find the accused not guilty of the offence charged but guilty of the latter offence, and the accused is liable to punishment accordingly.

(3) **Question of consent or authority regarding alleged victim under 16** If on the trial of a person for an offence under section 61J or 61JA the jury is not satisfied that the accused is guilty of the offence charged, but is satisfied on the evidence that the accused is guilty of an offence under section 66A or 66C, it may find the accused not guilty of the offence charged but guilty of the latter offence, and the accused is liable to punishment accordingly.

(4) **Question of consent regarding incest** If on the trial of a person for an offence under section 61I or 61J the jury is not satisfied that the accused is guilty of the offence charged, but is satisfied on the evidence that the accused is guilty of an offence under section 78A or 78B, it may find the accused not guilty of the offence charged but guilty of the latter offence, and the accused is liable to punishment accordingly.

(5) **Question of consent regarding cognitive impairment** If on the trial of a person for an offence under section 61I, 61J or 61JA, the jury is not satisfied that the accused is guilty of the offence charged, but is satisfied on the evidence that the accused is guilty of an offence under section 66F, it may find the accused not guilty of the offence charged but guilty of the latter offence, and the accused is liable to punishment accordingly.

(6) **Question of whether offence committed for purposes of production of child abuse material** If on the trial of a person for an offence under section 61O(2A) the jury is not satisfied that the accused is guilty of the offence charged, but is satisfied on the evidence that the accused is guilty of an offence under section 61O(2) or 61N, it may find the accused not guilty of the offence charged but guilty of the latter offence, and the accused is liable to punishment accordingly.

61S Offenders who are minors

(1) For the purposes of any offence, a person is not, by reason only of age, to be presumed incapable of having sexual intercourse with another person or of having an intent to have sexual intercourse with another person.

(2) Subsection (1) does not affect the operation of any law relating to the age at which a child can be convicted of an offence.

61T Offender married to victim

The fact that a person is married to a person:

(a) upon whom an offence under section 61I, 61J, 61JA or 61K is alleged to have been committed is no bar to the firstmentioned person being convicted of the offence, or

(b) upon whom an offence under any of those sections is alleged to have been attempted is no bar to the firstmentioned person being convicted of the attempt.

61U Circumstances of certain sexual offences to be considered in passing sentence

Where a person is convicted of:

(a) both an offence under section 61I and an offence under section 61K, or

(b) both an offence under section 61J and an offence under section 61K, or

(c) both an offence under section 61JA and an offence under section 61K,

whether at the same time or at different times, the Judge passing sentence on the person in respect of the two convictions or the later of the two convictions is required, if it appears that the two offences arose substantially out of the one set of circumstances, to take that fact into account in passing sentence.

[**62** Repealed]

63 Common law offences of rape and attempted rape abolished

(1) The common law offences of rape and attempted rape are abolished.

(2) Parts 1A, 1 and 19 of Schedule 11 make provision with respect to rape and other former sexual offences.

3.13 Notes

1. Victorian and New South Wales statutes cover the insertion of physical objects into the vagina or anus, and render such acts rape whether committed by a woman or a man. Under both statutes it is rape where the penis is inserted into the mouth of another (fellatio), whether the unwilling party is a male or a female: note *R v Preval* [1984] 3 NSWLR 647 in which it was held that the touching of the penis in between the lips is sufficient for the act of sexual intercourse even where it does not enter the mouth. In New South Wales and Victoria, it is rape where a part of the body other than the penis is inserted into the vagina. Thus stimulation of the vagina with the tongue (cunnilingus) becomes rape. The wording of the Victorian and New South Wales statutes is such that actual penetration is required for cunnilingus.
2. It is also an offence to continue to engage in sexual intercourse when, during the intercourse, the victim withdraws her or his consent and the accused does not desist: Crimes Act 1900 (NSW) s 61H(1)(d); Crimes Act 1958 (Vic) s 38(2)(b); *Ibbs v R* (1987) 163 CLR 447. The legislation enforces the Privy Council decision in *Kaitamaki v R* [1984] 2 All ER 435. That case, which involved an appeal from the New Zealand Court of Appeal, rejected

the appellant's argument that once penetration is complete the act of sexual intercourse is concluded. The appellant submitted that it is immaterial if the victim withdraws consent after the penetration has commenced because the act of penetration has been completed. In dismissing the appeal, the Privy Council held that 'sexual intercourse is a continuing act which only ends with withdrawal'. See also *R v Murphy* (1988) 37 A Crim R 405.

3. The statutes in each of the common law jurisdictions abolish the immunity possessed by a spouse at common law. Further, the old common law rule has now been judicially rejected as a correct statement of the modern common law: *R v L* (1991) 103 ALR 577; *R v R* [1991] 2 WLR 1065. It is submitted that the abolition, both statutory and judicial, of the old rule is clearly correct. The possibility that malicious wives may seek to punish or blackmail husbands by unfounded charges of rape no doubt exists. It is submitted, however, that this risk may be met by the careful and proper use of prosecutorial discretion, and by reliance upon the principle that the prosecution must ultimately prove its case beyond a reasonable doubt. It is difficult to believe that a jury would convict a husband of raping his wife in the absence of considerable evidence supporting the wife's allegation. Rape within marriage is a well-documented phenomenon, and it was never proper to deny wives the protection of the criminal law because of the possibility that some women might seek to misuse the law for their own ends.

3.14 Further reading

I Cunliffe, 'Consent and Sexual Offences Law Reform in New South Wales' (1984) 8 *Crim LJ* 271

R Fileborn, 'Sexual Assault Laws in Australia', *Australian Centre for the Study of Sexual Assault Resource Sheet*, February 2011: <http://www.aifs.gov.au/acssa/pubs/sheets/rs1/rs1.pdf>

Law Reform Commission of Victoria, *Sexual Offences: Law and Procedure — Final Report* (2004)

B McSherry and B Naylor, *Australian Criminal Laws: Critical Perspectives*, OUP, Melbourne, 2004, Ch 5

N Naffine, 'Possession: Erotic Love in the Law of Rape' (1994) 57 *Mod LR* 10

J Temkin, *Rape and the Legal Process*, Sweet and Maxwell, London, 1987

L Townsley and I Dobinson, 'Sexual Assault Law Reform in New South Wales: Issues of Consent and Objective Fault' (2008) 32(3) *Criminal Law Journal* 152

V Waye, 'Rape and the Unconscionable Bargain' (1992) 16 *Crim LJ* 94

THE SCOPE OF CONSENT

3.15C R v Wilkes and Briant

[1965] VR 475

Full Court of the Supreme Court of Victoria

[At a trial of a charge of rape the only issue was whether the girl consented. Her denial of consent was supported by other evidence, but there was also substantial evidence of consent by conduct. In instructing the jury, the trial judge defined the crime of rape as being carnal knowledge of a female without her consent, and he defined the expression 'without her consent' as meaning 'without her free and conscious permission'. After retiring for several hours, the jury returned and, through the foreman, asked 'whether permission has to be absolutely verbal as to whether intercourse may take place'. The trial judge replied: 'No, it does not have to be absolutely verbal, but there has to be a free and conscious permission.' The accused were convicted and appealed.]

Smith J: The trial judge, it seems clear from his charge, was concerned to prevent the jury from falling into the error of supposing that a cessation of resistance by a woman if due to her having been overpowered, or an absence of resistance if due to intimidating conduct which has frightened her into believing resistance to be useless and dangerous, can amount in law to consent. To that end he told them four times within a very short space that 'without her consent' meant 'without her free and conscious permission'. He told them further that mere submission is not consent; and that if non-resistance proceeds merely from being overpowered or intimidated the crime is complete. And he concluded this part of his charge with a statement that 'her physical acquiescence is not consent nor is her mental submission consent if she is too frightened to do otherwise'.

In the same part of his charge he told the jury that in the definition of rape the words are 'without her consent', and that they are not 'against her will'. This is a form of charge which is appropriate and necessary where the woman in question is mentally deficient, or is not fully conscious when the act is done. But it can be dangerous in cases such as the present in which she is under no such disability. For it may convey to the jury that even if they believe she desired the intercourse, nevertheless they may quite well hold that she did not consent; whereas in truth if it once appears that she desired the intercourse, the conclusion would ordinarily be irresistible that any evidence that she expressed her desire by words or by conduct is truthful and should be accepted.

His Honour's concern to prevent an error of the kind already mentioned would seem to have led him to assume that the jury would be aware that consent might be given by conduct. For at no stage did he tell them that this was so. Yet the whole issue was whether, by certain specific acts or by a repetitive pattern of conduct consisting of token resistance followed by cooperation, she had expressed her consent to what was done.

The charge as to consent having taken the form that it did, it is, to my mind, not surprising that the jury felt difficulty and asked for a further direction.

What they said was: 'We wish to have your direction as to whether permission has to be absolutely verbal as to whether intercourse may take place.' And this, I understand as meaning that they wanted to know whether what they were to look for was words alone, and words amounting to a statement in advance that intercourse might take place. The answer given to the jury was as follows: 'Well the answer to your question, Mr Foreman, is "No". The charge you will remember is "without her consent", so that there must be a free and conscious permission for the act of intercourse to take place. Free and conscious permission. The answer to your question as to "Has permission to be absolutely verbal as to whether intercourse can taken place?", — the answer to that question is "No". It does not have to be absolutely verbal but there has to be a free and conscious permission.'

This answer, in my view was inadequate to deal with the situation that had arisen. The repetition, once again, of the expression 'free and conscious permission' was likely to convey to the jury that though they need not look to words alone, something must be found in words before it could be held that consent had been given; or at least that some particular act equivalent to words was necessary. But apart altogether from the possibility of such a specific misunderstanding, the situation revealed by the question was that the judge's attempt in his charge to convey the meaning of 'consent' had failed to give the jury any real understanding of the concept. And 'consent or no consent' being the only matter in issue it was essential, I consider, that the judge, instead of giving the somewhat ambiguous answer that he did, should have restated the law as to consent in such a way as to make it clear that consent might be given by an act or by a course of conduct.

[**Winneke CJ** delivered a separate judgment agreeing with **Smith J**. **Little J** dissented. Appeal allowed and a new trial ordered.]

3.16C Question of Law (No 1 of 1993)

(1993) 59 SASR 214

Supreme Court of South Australia

[The accused was acquitted on charges of rape and attempted rape of his wife. The Director of Public Prosecutions reserved two questions of law for the consideration and determination of the court. One of these questions concerned the correctness of a direction to the jury that a husband may attempt to persuade a wife to freely consent to intercourse by 'a measure of rougher than usual handling'.]

Perry J: It was perfectly correct for the learned trial judge to state, as he did, 'submission is not consent'. The law is clear that consent must be freely given, and acquiescence to intercourse by reason of any threat or duress may properly be regarded as negativing consent for the purposes of the law of rape. Whether or not consent has been freely given is a question of fact for the jury to determine, having regard to all the circumstances. The question is not concluded against the accused simply by reason of the fact that there was an initial refusal to consent to intercourse. Even following such a refusal there may be a freely given consent after further dealings between the parties. True it is that the difference between submission and consent can be a fine line. But the distinction at law is clear, it is well supported by a long line of judicial authority, and it is for juries, properly instructed, to deal with the matter.

Returning to the passage in question from the learned trial judge's summing up, if the words: 'There is nothing wrong with a husband faced with his wife's initial refusal to engage in intercourse in attempting, in an acceptable way, to persuade her to change her mind', had stopped there, there would have been no error of law, or any other reason to doubt the propriety of the direction. However, the problem arises because of the following words:

> ... and that may involve a measure of rougher than usual handling. It may be that in the end, handling and persuasion will persuade the wife to agree.

The difficulty which that passage poses is that it suggests to the jury that a consent born of 'rougher than usual handling' may be a valid consent. For the matter to be put in that way was apt to lead the jury into error.

Of course, consensual 'rougher than usual handling' would not vitiate consent for the purposes of the law of rape. No doubt in some relationships a degree of rough handling or horseplay might be regarded by both parties as an acceptable prelude to intercourse. Consensual sexual behaviour between humans and the preliminaries to it can take a variety of forms.

But there was no evidence in this case on either side of consensual 'rougher than usual handling'. A direction in the terms in question was apt to convey the impression that consent might be induced by force, against the will of the victim. That has never been the law. It seems to me that the sentence, which includes the words 'measure of rougher than usual handling' is so close to the earlier passage where his Honour defines the word 'consent' that it may well have been understood by the jury as part and parcel of that definition.

Looking at the matter in that way, in my opinion, that direction also involved an error of law.

[**Duggan J** delivered a separate judgment agreeing with **Perry J**. **King CJ** dissented.]

3.17C Papadimitropoulos v R

(1957) 98 CLR 249; [1958] ALR 21
High Court of Australia

Dixon CJ, **McTiernan**, **Webb**, **Kitto** and **Taylor JJ**: The applicant for special leave to appeal in this case was convicted before Gavan Duffy J, on 17 April 1958 of rape ... and sentenced to four years' imprisonment. The case made against him was that he had obtained the actual consent of the woman to his having carnal knowledge of her by a fraudulent pretence which made it no consent at all. The presentment contained two counts. The first count stated that at Fitzroy in Victoria between 13 June and 19 June 1956 the applicant had carnal knowledge of Dina (probably a misspelling of Dena) Karnezi without her consent. The second count contained a charge that at that same place between the same dates the applicant stole certain money the property of Dina Karnezi.

It appears that since the events upon which the charge depends Dina Karnezi has married, and at the trial she was Dena Arvaniti. She is described as a Greek girl who has not learned to speak English. For some three months she had been employed at a factory in Fitzroy. On the morning of 14 June 1956, accompanied by the applicant, who is also a Greek but who speaks English intelligibly, she saw the manager. They requested that she should have a week off saying that they had been married that morning. Mrs Arvaniti's story was that she met the applicant in Australia and that four or five days later he asked her to marry him. He bought her a ring and got her to wear it in the street. On the morning of 14 June 1956 he asked her to go to the registry office and get married … Mrs Arvaniti said that on the morning of 14 June 1956, which was in fact a Thursday, in compliance with the applicant's request she went with him accompanied by her two cousins and an aunt, none of whom spoke English, to the registry office in Queen Street, Melbourne. There she and the applicant signed a card and a form which had been filled in by the officer on information supplied in English by the applicant. The two documents were produced at the trial and identified by her and were respectively a notice of intention that the marriage would be celebrated and an information paper giving the particulars for registration and for the filling in of the marriage certificate. Mrs Arvaniti said that then the applicant, speaking to her of course in Greek, told her that they were married. Next they went to her employer, as already stated, to obtain leave, and after that to his employer for the like purpose. Having done that they went to obtain a room at what is presumably a lodging house. It was in Brunswick Street, Fitzroy and was conducted by a Mrs Fatouris. According to Mrs Fatouris, the applicant had already bespoken the room for himself and his intended wife, and on this occasion the applicant introduced the girl as his wife and said that they had been married that morning at the registry. That night they went into occupation of the room. They lived there together for the next four days, during which, according to the evidence of Mrs Arvaniti, they had sexual intercourse two or three times. On the Sunday morning he told her that they had to go to the registry again at 3 pm on the following day to collect a paper, a document. Early on Monday morning he left and did not return. She then discovered that there had not been a marriage ceremony. She said that when she came to live with him in the room she brought £400 with her in her handbag. She placed it in the wardrobe. From a drawer she had given the applicant twenty or thirty pounds but he knew she had the money. After his departure on the Monday she found that the money had gone. She received two letters from him dated 19 June and 21 June, which she produced, and he telephoned to her from Sydney. In both letters he professed his love for her. In the first he signed himself 'your husband', and in the second he addressed her as his 'beloved little wife Dena'. He gave no reasons for leaving her but asked forgiveness and reiterated that it would be all right. In the second letter he wrote that he had obtained employment stating his wages and saying in effect that as soon as he could obtain accommodation for them both in Sydney, he would send or come for her. She remained in Mrs Fatouris's room until, according to the latter, she turned her out on discovering that she was a 'bad girl'.

The applicant gave evidence on his own behalf. His story was that he had arranged with Dena Karnezi some time in 1955 that they should marry and that about a fortnight before they went to the registry they had arranged that the marriage should then take place. He had explained to her what had to be done and that they must go to the registry office twice. When they attended on Thursday 14 June 1956 they were accompanied by Dena's two uncles and her aunt. One of her uncles, Stelios by name, knew English and did the translating to the registrar and to Dena. He told her that she was not yet married and that she would be married on Monday. They told Mrs Fatouris they were married because otherwise they would not have obtained the room. The applicant said that he sought to have intercourse with Dena but she refused until Sunday, when she sought it and it took place. He left her next morning because as he said in effect, he had been told stories about her earlier conduct and character and because he considered that she had had intercourse with some other man before him. However he did intend to return to her until he heard a worse account of her in Sydney. He had not stolen £400 from her and did not know that she possessed such a sum.

Gavan Duffy J directed the jury that rape consisted in having carnal knowledge of a woman without her consent; but, in law, if the girl did believe that the accused had become her husband by marriage and acquiesced in sexual intercourse with him on that basis and would not have so acquiesced otherwise, and that belief of hers had been brought about by the accused representing to her that they were married, he knowing they were not, and with the intention of persuading her to consent to sexual intercourse with him as her husband, then there would be no consent at all.

The acquittal of the applicant on the charge of larceny may have been due to a failure to satisfy the jury that Mrs Arvaniti ever had the money in her bag in the cupboard. Perhaps, however, the jury may have thought that someone else was possibly the thief, or yet again that perhaps the truth was that Mrs Arvaniti did not lose her money. …

On application to the Full Court of the Supreme Court sitting as a Court of Criminal Appeal for leave to appeal that court was divided in opinion. Lowe and O'Bryan JJ were of opinion that the direction to the jury was correct and that it was open to the jury to find that the woman's consent was vitiated by fraud and amounted to no consent. Monahan J adopted a contrary conclusion. In the elaborate reasons which were given in the joint judgment of Lowe and O'Bryan JJ on the one hand and by Monahan J on the other hand the distinction was accepted between a consent given under a deception or mistake as to the thing itself, that is to say as to the act of intercourse, and a consent to that act itself induced by a deception or mistake as to a matter antecedent or collateral thereto. Under the first heading come the cases in which the woman is deluded into supposing that she is undergoing medical treatment, and the cases where in the dark she is induced to assume that her husband is the man with whom she is having intercourse. Under the second heading comes consent induced by fraudulent representations made by the man as to his wealth, position and freedom to marry the woman. Consent obtained by frauds of the latter character is nevertheless a consent. But Lowe and O'Bryan JJ were of the opinion that a misrepresentation as to the performance of the marriage ceremony fell under the former head. Their Honours said:

> A mistake of such a kind in our opinion makes the act which took place essentially different from that to which she supposed she was consenting. What she was

> consenting to was a marital act, an act to which in her mistaken belief she was in duty bound to submit. What she got was an act of fornication — an act wholly different in moral character. On principle it seems to us that the consent relied on is no real consent at all and should afford no help to the applicant.

On the other hand Monahan J speaking of the two classes of cases given above as examples of the first heading, said:

> I have no more difficulty in understanding the essential differences between the act consented to and the act done in the personation cases than I have in understanding the same essential differences in the acts which have been considered in the medical cases. My difficulty arises when I am asked to say that there is the same essential difference between the act consented to and the act done in this case; the sexual act was the act to which the prosecutrix intended to consent and the prisoner was the person with whom she consented to perform that act.

The modern history of the crime of rape shows a tendency to extend the application of the constituent elements of the offence. The *violenter et felonice rapuit* of the old Latin indictment is now satisfied although there be no use of force: *R v Bourke* [1915] VLR 289; (1915) 21 ALR 197. The *contra voluntatem suam* requires only a negative absence of consent (as to the need of the man's being aware of the absence of consent, see *R v Lambert* [1919] VLR 205 at 213; (1919) 25 ALR 100 at 101). The *violenter et felonice carnaliter cognovit* is established if there has been some degree of penetration although slight, and no more force has been used than is required to effect it: *R v Bourke,* supra; *R v Burles* [1947] VLR 392; [1947] ALR 460.

There has been some judicial resistance to the idea that an actual consent to an act of sexual intercourse can be no consent because it is vitiated by fraud or mistake. The key to the difficulty may perhaps be found in a brief sentence of Cussen J in *R v Lambert* [1919] VLR 205 at 212; (1919) 25 ALR at 101:

> Now, carnal knowledge is merely the physical fact of penetration, though, of course, there cannot be consent even to that without some perception of what is about to take place.

In 1822 Bayley J reserved for the consideration of the twelve judges the case of one Jackson who had been convicted before him of burglary with intent to commit rape. Jackson had entered a dwelling house by night in the absence of the householder with the intention of impersonating him and deceiving his wife into submitting to sexual intercourse with him. As he was proceeding to his purpose she discovered the deception and he made off.

> Four judges thought, that having carnal knowledge of a woman whilst she was under the belief of it being her husband would be a rape, but the other eight judges thought it would not: and Dallas CJ pointed out forcibly the difference between compelling a woman against her will, when the abhorrence which would

> naturally arise in her mind was called into action, and beguiling her into consent and cooperation; but several of the eight judges intimated that if the case should occur again they would advise the jury to find a special verdict: *R v Jackson* (1822) R & R 487; 168 ER 911.

The case did occur again. In *R v Saunders* (1938) 8 C & P 265; 173 ER 488 (Stafford Assizes, 1838), it appeared that the person had got into a married woman's bed and by impersonating her husband had connection with her. Bayley J directed the jury that he was bound to tell them that the charge of rape was not made out 'as the crime was not committed against the will of the prosecutrix, as she consented believing it to be her husband'. Alderson B applied the same law in a similar case in the same year: *R v Williams* (1838) 8 C & P 286; 173 ER 497 (Monmouth Assizes, 1838). Twelve years later a case arose for the consideration of the judges in which a prisoner who was a medical man had been convicted of assault on evidence that he had induced a girl of fourteen years of age to submit to his having connection with her by leading her to believe that it was but 'medical treatment for the ailment under which she laboured'; the conviction was affirmed: *R v Case* (1850) 1 Den 580; 169 ER 381 (CCR 1850). In 1854 another case was reserved for the judges in which a prisoner had been convicted of rape on evidence that he impersonated the woman's husband and so obtained her assent to sexual intercourse. The judges declined to permit the question to be re-opened and followed *Jackson's* case: *R v Clarke* (1854) Dears 397; 169 ER 779 (CCR 1854).

In 1868 the Court of Crown Cases Reserved quashed a conviction of rape based on a similar impersonation. 'It falls', said Bovill CJ, for the judges, 'within the class of cases which decide that, when consent is obtained by fraud, the act does not amount to rape': *R v Barrow* (1868) LR 1 CCR 156. In *R v Young* (1878) 14 Cox CC 114, the court upheld a conviction of a man who had connection with a sleeping woman who, when she first awoke, thought the man was her husband, and then discovering it was not threw him off. In the course of the reasons doubts were raised about the decisions beginning with *Jackson's* case. In Ireland the court refused to follow the reasoning: *R v Dee* (1884) 15 Cox CC 579. In the meantime the Court of Crown Cases Reserved in *R v Flattery* (1877) 2 QBD 410, had questioned the decision in *Barrow's* case, supra. The facts resembled those in *R v Case,* supra, except that the prisoner was not a medical man but a quack, and the representations about his giving some form of treatment were put to the mother as well as the girl, and in a form which might well have excited the mother's suspicions. Field J said: 'The question is one of consent, or not consent; but the consent must be to sexual connection. There was no such consent.'

This decision was strongly criticised by Sir James Fitzjames Stephen in his *Digest of the Criminal Law* (3rd ed, 1883), p 185, on the ground that it almost overruled the principle 'that where consent is obtained by fraud the act does not amount to rape'. At this point a declaration of the law was made by statute. Section 4 of the Criminal Law Amendment Act 1885 (Eng), after reciting that doubts had been entertained whether a man who induces a married woman to permit him to have connection with her by personating her husband is or is not guilty of rape, enacted and declared that every such offender should be deemed to be guilty of rape (cf now *Sexual Offences Act* 1956 s 1).

The next judicial step was taken in the case of *R v Clarence* (1888) 22 QBD 23. The decision was simply that a husband who infects his wife with venereal disease is not thereby guilty of inflicting grievous bodily harm. But this led to the judges' giving much consideration to what was involved in the wife's consent, ignorant as she was of her husband's condition. The judgments contain many observations which are pertinent to the distinction upon which this case turns. For example, in the judgment of Wills J there is to be found, to say the least of it, a dyslogistic description of a fraud that will afford no basis for treating the woman's consent as a nullity and the act of intercourse as rape.

Take, for example, [said his Lordship] the case of a man without a single good quality, a gaol-bird, heartless, mean and cruel, without the smallest intention of doing anything but possessing himself of the person of his victim, but successfully representing himself as a man of good family and connections prevented by some temporary obstacle from contracting an immediate marriage, and with conscious hypocrisy acting the part of a devoted lover, and in this fashion, or perhaps under the guise of affected religious fervour, effecting the ruin of his victim: (1888) 22 QBD at 29, 30.

The conception which Wills J had of what sufficed to vitiate consent is expressed as follows:

> The essence of rape is, to my mind, the penetration of the woman's person without her consent. In other words it is, roughly speaking, where the woman does not intend that the sexual act shall be done upon her either at all, or, what is pretty much the same thing, by the particular individual doing it, and an assault which includes penetration does not seem to me under such circumstances to be anything but rape: (1888) 22 QBD at 34.

Stephen J (22 QBD at 43) refers to the conflict between the decision in *R v Barrow*, supra, and the Irish decision in *R v Dee*, supra, and remarks that the decisions were examined minutely in the latter case. Stephen J proceeded:

> I think they justify the observation that the only sort of fraud which so far destroy the effect of a woman's consent as to convert a connection consented to in fact into a rape are frauds as to the nature of the act itself, or as to the identity of the person who does the act: (1888) 22 QBD at 44.

Field J speaks of the woman's consenting to the act of intercourse yet not consenting to it in its actual nature and conditions, and he again says that a consent obtained to one act is not a consent to an act of a different nature: (1888) 22 QBD at 60–61.

In *R v Williams* [1923] 1 KB 340; [1922] All ER Rep 433, a new version of the 'medical treatment' cases was dealt with by the Court of Criminal Appeal. This time it was a singing master and the pretence was that the treatment was for breathing. Possibly the case went a little further than *R v Case,* supra, and *R v Flattery,* supra, but, if so, that is only with reference to the complexion the facts were given. The materiality of the case lies in a broad statement which Lord Hewart CJ quoted from a textbook. 'A consent or submission obtained by fraud is, it would seem, not a defence to rape or cognate offences': [1923] 1 KB at 347; [1922] All ER Rep at 435. It is interesting to notice that this statement is the contradictory of that of Sir James Fitzjames Stephen in the note in his *Digest* quoted above, in which he describes the principle to be 'that where consent is obtained by fraud the act does not amount to rape'. It is the contradictory too of that made by Bovill CJ in *R v Barrow* also quoted above. From what has been said already, however, it should be clear enough that the truth lies between the two opposing generalisations.

In the language of a note to the Canadian decision of *R v Harms* [1944] 2 DLR 61 (Sask, 1943), fraud in the inducement does not destroy the reality of the apparent consent; fraud in the factum does. The note distinguishes 'between the type of fraud which induces a consent that would not otherwise have been obtained but which is none the less a valid consent and the type of fraud which prevents any real consent from existing'. The same distinction exists in relation to fraud inducing marriage itself ...

In Canada there are three decisions which are of assistance in applying the distinction. In *State of California v Skinner* (1924) 33 Brit Colum Rep 555, extradition to California was refused by the Court of British Columbia in a case of rape where the charge was based upon the view that consent was vitiated by fraud consisting of a feigned marriage. A form of marriage had been gone through by the woman in 1919 believing it was genuine, but no licence to marry had been obtained and the supposed clergyman performing the ceremony had no authority to celebrate marriages and was not a minister of religion. About four years later the woman discovered the fraud. The decision turned not so much on the law of California as upon that of Canada, by which rape was defined as follows:

> Rape is the act of a man having carnal knowledge of a woman who is not his wife without her consent, or with consent which has been extorted by threats or fear of bodily harm, or obtained by personating the woman's husband, or by false and fraudulent representations as to the nature and quality of the act: s 298 of the Canadian Criminal Code.

It was held that the definition did not cover deception of the kind under consideration. The learned County Judge, Cayley J, repeated the language of Stephen J ((1888) 22 QBD at 44): 'cases of fraud as to the nature of the act done' and said: 'This before me is not that kind of fraud at all. The woman here knew the nature of the act' ((1924) 33 Brit Colum Rep at 558).

In *R v Harms* ([1944] 2 DLR 61), the Court of Appeal in Saskatchewan sustained a conviction for rape based on the 'medical treatment' cases. One may perhaps think that the facts went outside the limits of those cases. For, when all the humbug of treatment had been gone through and 'Dr Harms' proceeded to the sexual act, the woman, who understood what he was doing, resisted, but later was persuaded to submit. The editorial note makes the comments:

> In the present case the complainant appreciated the nature of the act but submitted because she thought that it was a necessary part of a medical treatment. Is there not in such circumstances a real consent?: [1944] 2 DLR at 62.

In *R v Arnold* [1947] 2 DLR 438 (Ont), although there seems to have been sufficient evidence of rape overcoming resistance, there was also evidence that the man had a little earlier held out some false promises or representations to induce consent. The defence was consent. As to this the jury were directed as follows:

> And the consent, if it be a consent, given by the woman, must be obtained without threats, inducements or anything of the kind, and must be freely and voluntarily given by the woman: [1947] 2 DLR at 440.

This was held a clear misdirection.

It must be noted that in considering whether an apparent consent is unreal it is the mistake or misapprehension that makes it so. It is not the fraud producing the mistake which is material so much as the mistake itself. But if the mistake or misapprehension is not produced by the fraud of the man, there is logically room for the possibility that he was unaware of the woman's mistake so that a question of his *mens rea* may arise. So in *R v Lambert* [1919] VLR 205 at 213; (1919) 25 ALR 100 at 101, Cussen J says:

> It is plain that, though in these cases the question of consent or non-consent is primarily referable to the mind of the woman, if she has really a mind, yet the mind of the man is also affected by the facts which indicate want of consent or possible want of capacity to consent.

For that reason it is easy to understand why the stress has been on the fraud. But that stress tends to distract the attention from the essential inquiry, namely, whether the consent is no consent because it is not directed to the nature and character of the act. The identity of the man and the character of the physical act that is done or proposed seem now clearly to be regarded as forming part of the nature and character of the act to which the woman's consent is directed. That accords with the principles governing mistake vitiating apparent manifestations of will in other chapters of the law.

In the present case the decision of the majority of the Full Court extends this conception beyond the identity of the physical act and the immediate conditions affecting its nature to an antecedent inducing cause — the existence of a valid marriage. In the history of bigamy that has never been done. The most heartless bigamist has not been considered guilty of rape. Mock marriages are no new thing. Before the Hardwicke Marriage Act it was a fraud easily devised and readily carried out. But there is no reported instance of an indictment of rape based on the fraudulent character of the ceremony. No indictment of rape was founded on such a fraud. Rape, as a capital felony, was defined with exactness, and although there has been some extension over the centuries in the ambit of the crime, it is quite wrong to bring within its operation forms of evil conduct because they wear some analogy to aspects of the crime and deserve punishment. The judgment of the majority of the Full Court of the Supreme Court goes upon the moral differences between marital intercourse and sexual relations without marriage. The difference is indeed so radical that it is apt to draw the mind away from the real question which is carnal knowledge without consent. It may well be true that the woman in the present case never intended to consent to the latter relationship. But, as was said before, the key to such a case as the present lies in remembering that it is the penetration of the woman's body without her consent to such penetration that makes the felony. The capital felony was not directed to fraudulent conduct inducing her consent. Frauds of that kind must be punished under other heads of the criminal law or not at all: they are not rape. To say that in the present case the facts which the jury must be taken to have found amount to wicked and heartless conduct on the part of the applicant is not enough to establish that he committed rape. To say that in having intercourse with him she supposed that she was concerned in a perfectly moral act is not to say that the intercourse was without her consent. To return to the central point; rape is carnal knowledge of a woman without her consent: carnal knowledge is the physical fact of penetration; it is the consent to that which is in question; such a consent demands a perception as to what is about to take place, as to the identity of the man and the character of what he is doing. But once the consent is comprehending and actual the inducing causes cannot destroy its reality and leave the man guilty of rape.

The application for special leave should be granted. The hearing of the application should be treated as the hearing of the appeal. The appeal should be allowed and the conviction quashed.

3.18 Notes and illustrations

1. The statutory reforms in Victoria and New South Wales reject the common law definition of rape as an act which was 'against the victim's will' in favour of a definition focused on whether there was 'lack of consent'. Consent in each jurisdiction is defined in terms of 'free agreement', and factors which demonstrate the lack of free agreement are spelt out in the legislation. These reforms reflect a shift from a 'penetrative/coercive' model of sexuality to a 'positive communicative' model of sexuality based on mutuality and sexual pleasure during a sexual encounter: see B McSherry and B Naylor, *Australian Criminal Laws: Critical Perspectives*, OUP, Melbourne, 2004, pp 215–16.
2. Note that the effect of s 61HA(5)(b) of the Crimes Act 1900 (NSW), as amended, is to bring *Papadimitropoulos v R* within the scope of sexual assault and aggravated sexual assault. Section s 61HA(5) also clarifies the mens rea for those who commit sexual assault knowing the victim is under a mistaken belief in relation to marriage or to the identity of the accused, or that the act is for a medical or hygienic purpose. It provides that the accused has knowledge that there is no consent if the accused knows the victim 'consents to sexual intercourse under such a mistaken belief.'
3. D entered V's bed in the dark, while V was asleep, and commenced to have intercourse with her. When she awoke she permitted him to continue, being under the impression that he was her husband. D was convicted of rape. Affirmed on appeal: *R v Gallienne* [1964] NSWR 919.

4. V was taken by her mother to consult D, who pretended to practise as a doctor, for advice concerning her fits. D said that 'nature's string wanted breaking' and with the mother's consent had intercourse with the girl. Both the mother and the girl thought D was performing a surgical operation. Held, rape: *R v Flattery* (1877) 2 QBD 410 (CCR 1877). Accord, where D, a choirmaster, had intercourse with V under the pretence that he was opening an air passage to improve her breathing, and she did not realise what he was doing: *R v Williams* [1923] 1 KB 340; [1922] All ER Rep 433.
5. V, believing (wrongly) that D was a doctor, consulted him in his lodgings about a pain in her chest. He asked her about her periods, which she said were irregular. He said he would cure this, and at his request she returned the same evening. He then gave her a drink which made her feel a little dizzy, and told her to lie down. He removed her underwear, and inserted into her vagina two pills (later ascertained to be contraceptives), telling her that they would effect the 'cure'. He then attempted to have intercourse with her in order to 'make the pills effective', but she resisted for some time. Ultimately, when he threatened that she must take the consequences if she refused treatment, she consented and had intercourse with him. Held, rape: 'a man shall be deemed guilty of rape if he had succeeded by fraud no less than by force in overcoming her permanent will to virtue': *R v Harms* [1944] 2 DLR 61 (Sask).
6. D was convicted, following a plea of guilty, of causing alcohol to be taken by V with intent to render her incapable of resistance to enable him to have sexual intercourse with her: Crimes Act 1958 (Vic) s 53. On appeal, held, conviction quashed. With intent to render the person incapable of resistance means intent to render that person incapable of physical resistance, not merely lack of emotional resistance. It appeared that D's plea of guilty was based on him being misled into believing that he had the necessary criminal intent if his aim had been to render V amenable to agreeing, or persuading her, to engage in sexual intercourse: *R v O'Connor* (1992) 59 A Crim R 278. In New South Wales, the Crimes Act 1900 (NSW) s 61HA(6)(a) provides that a person does not consent to sexual intercourse if that person is substantially intoxicated. This means that the person is so intoxicated that he or she is not capable of consenting. In Victoria, under Crimes Act 1958 s 36(d), a person is deemed not be consenting if they were 'asleep, unconscious, or so affected by alcohol or another drug as to be incapable of freely agreeing'.
7. D was convicted on three counts of rape. The counts related to acts performed by D during the course of his employment as a radiographer. The case for the Crown was that on each occasion D had introduced an ultrasound transducer or probe manipulated by him into the vagina of a young woman without her consent, thereby committing an act of rape. Each

of the women had given her apparent consent expressly or by her conduct. It was contended for the Crown that the apparent consents were vitiated and not real consents because each woman consented to the introduction of the transducer only for medical diagnostic purposes. On appeal, held, convictions quashed. In each case the woman's consent to the proposed act which she knew to be of the nature and character of the act which was done, was not deprived of reality if she believed D proposed to do the act solely for a medical diagnostic purpose and if he actually did it solely for his own sexual gratification. D did no act which was essentially different from the act which the women knew he proposed to do, and to which they consented: *R v Mobilio* [1991] 1 VR 339. In Victoria and New South Wales, the effect of the decision in *R v Mobilio* has now been overturned by statute: Crimes Act 1900 (NSW) s 61HA(5)(c); Crimes Act 1958 (Vic) s 36(g). Note J Morgan, 'Rape in Medical Treatment: The Patient as Victim' (1991) 18 *MULR* 403.

8. In Victoria, the issue of 'fraud' is now addressed as a 'mistake' which negates the existence of free agreement under Crimes Act 1958 s 36(f). This provision states that there is no free agreement where 'the person is mistaken about the sexual nature of the act or the identity of the person'. Read with the case law discussed in this section, this appears to mean that a mistake as to the 'sexual nature' of an act will vitiate any consent, but mistake as to a 'collateral matter' (such as whether one is married, or arguably whether one is having 'safe sex': see also *R v Clarence* (1888) 22 QBD 23 (at 2.37)) will not vitiate consent. Note that in Victoria there is a statutory offence of procuring intercourse by fraud which adequately covers those cases that cannot properly be treated as rape: Crimes Act 1958 (Vic) s 57(2).

9. D agreed to have sexual intercourse with a prostitute for the sum of £25. D did not have £25 on him at the time and, after intercourse had taken place, he made off without paying. The prostitute claimed that she had been raped and D was arrested and charged with rape. The trial judge directed the jury that if they found either that D had forced himself upon the prostitute or tricked her inasmuch as he obtained her consent to intercourse by falsely pretending that he intended to pay, he was guilty of rape. D was convicted of rape and appealed. Held, conviction quashed. Where there was fraud either as to the nature of the act itself or as to the identity of the person who did the act, there was no consent and the perpetrator was guilty of rape, but where the victim consented to sexual intercourse in return for a promise that he or she would be paid, when in fact the perpetrator did not intend to fulfil that promise, the existence of fraud on the perpetrator's part did not mean that there was lack of consent and, therefore, the perpetrator was not guilty

of rape: *R v Linekar* [1995] 3 All ER 69. What offence might D have been convicted of?

10. D was present in a store when he observed V stealing goods. D approached V and threatened to inform security unless she commit sexual acts with him. V accompanied D to a nearby location where she performed various sexual acts upon him. D also took money from V. D was convicted of sexual intercourse without consent (Crimes Act 1900 (NSW) s 61I), assault with indecency (Crimes Act 1900 (NSW) s 61L), and stealing. On appeal against conviction in respect of the sexual offences, held, convictions quashed. A non-violent threat, such as that made by D, did not vitiate consent for the purpose of either s 61I or 61L: *R v Aiken* (2005) 63 NSWLR 719. The New South Wales Act has since been amended. Section 61HA(6)(b) now provides that the grounds on which it may be established that a person does not consent to sexual intercourse include 'if the person has sexual intercourse because of intimidatory or coercive conduct, or other threat, that does not involve a threat of force'.

THE MENTAL ELEMENT IN RAPE

3.19C Director of Public Prosecutions v Morgan

[1976] AC 182

House of Lords

Lord Hailsham of St Marylebone: My Lords, in *R v Hyam* [1975] AC 55 this House discussed the mental element in murder. This appeal is concerned with the mental element in rape. It involves two questions at vastly different levels of importance but each strangely illustrative of the other, which were argued before us. The first is a question of great academic importance in the theory of English criminal law, certified for this House by the Court of Appeal, which also gave leave to appeal. The second, which arises only if the first is answered favourably to the appellants, is whether the House can be satisfied that no miscarriage of justice has taken place so as to compel them to apply the proviso to s 2(1) of the Criminal Appeal Act 1968. As I propose to answer these two questions, as to the first favourably, and as the second, unfavourably to the appellants, and thus dismiss the appeals, I will begin this opinion with the facts.

The four appellants were all convicted at the Stafford Crown Court of various offences connected with alleged rapes upon the person of Daphne Ethel Morgan of whom the first appellant is, or, at the material time was, the husband. The second, third and fourth appellants were convicted each of a principal offence against Mrs Morgan, and each of aiding and abetting the principal offences alleged to have been committed by each of the other two. The appellant Morgan, who also had connection with his wife allegedly without her consent as part of the same series of events, was not charged with rape, the prosecution evidently accepting and applying the ancient common law doctrine that a husband cannot be guilty of raping his own wife. Morgan was therefore charged with and convicted of aiding and abetting the rapes alleged to have been committed by the other three.

Although each appellant was originally separately represented, their appeals raise the same point, and they were accorded single representation before this House. The question certified as being of general public importance by the Court of Appeal, and the only point of principle raised on their behalf is: Whether in rape the defendant can properly be convicted, notwithstanding that he in fact believed that the woman consented, if such belief was not based on reasonable grounds.

The question arises, in the following way. The appellant Morgan and his three co-defendants, who were all members of the RAF, spent the evening of 15 August 1973, in one another's company. The appellant Morgan was significantly older than the other three, and considerably senior to them in rank. He was, as I have said, married to the alleged victim, but not, it seems at the time habitually sleeping in the same bed. At this time, Mrs Morgan occupied a single bed in the same room as her younger son aged about 11 years, and by the time the appellants arrived at Morgan's house, Mrs Morgan was already in bed and asleep, until she was awoken by their presence.

According to the version of the facts which she gave in evidence, and which was evidently accepted by the jury, she was aroused from her sleep, frog-marched into another room where there was a double bed, held by each of her limbs, arms and legs apart, by the four appellants, while each of the three young appellants in turn had intercourse with her in the presence of the others, during which time the other two committed various lewd acts upon various parts of her body. When each had finished and had left the room, the appellant Morgan completed the series of incidents by having intercourse with her himself.

According to Mrs Morgan she consented to none of this and made her opposition to what was being done very plain indeed. In her evidence to the court, she said that her husband was the first to seize her and pull her out of bed. She then 'yelled' to the little boy who was sleeping with her to call the police, and later, when the elder boy came out on the landing, she called to him also to get the police and 'screamed'. Her assailants, however, covered her face and pinched her nose, until she begged them to let her breathe. She was held, wrists and feet, 'dragged' to the neighbouring room, put on the bed where the various incidents occurred. At this stage she was overcome by fear of 'being hit'. There was never a time when her body was free from being held. When it was all over she grabbed her coat, ran out of the house, drove straight to the hospital and immediately complained to the staff of having been raped. This last fact was fully borne out by evidence from the hospital.

In their evidence in court, the appellants made various damaging admissions which certainly amounted to some corroboration of all this. They admitted that some degree of struggle took place in the bedroom, that Mrs Morgan made some noise which was forcibly suppressed, and that she was carried out forcibly into the other bedroom, and that her arms and legs were separately held. In addition to this, Mrs Morgan's evidence was far more fully corroborated by a number of statements (each, of course, admissible only against the maker) which virtually repeated Mrs Morgan's own story but in far greater and more lurid detail. Of course, the appellants repudiated their statements in the witness box, saying that the words were put into their mouths by the police, even though at least one was written out in the hands of the makers of the statement. I think it likely to the extent of moral certainty that the jury accepted that these statements were made as alleged and contained the truth. But I need not rest my opinion upon this, since the undeniable fact is that the jury accepted, after an impeccable summing up and adequate corroboration, that Mrs Morgan was telling the truth in her evidence. I mention all these details simply to show that if, as I think plain, the jury accepted Mrs Morgan's statement in *substance* there was no possibility whatever of any of the appellants holding any belief whatever, reasonable or otherwise, in their victim's consent to what was being done.

The primary 'defence' was consent. I use the word 'defence' in inverted commas, because, of course, in establishing the crime of rape, the prosecution must exclude consent in order to establish the essential ingredients of the crime. There is no burden at the outset on the accused to raise the issue. Nevertheless, at the close of the prosecution case the accused had a formidable case to answer, and they answered by going into the witness box and swearing to facts which, if accepted, would have meant, not merely that they reasonably believed that Mrs Morgan had consented, but that, after she entered the bedroom where the acts of intercourse took place, she not merely consented but took an active and enthusiastic part in a sexual orgy which might have excited unfavourable comment in the court of Caligula or Nero.

All four defendants explained in the witness box that they had spent the evening together in Wolverhampton, and by the time of the alleged offences had had a good deal to drink. Their original intention had been to find some women in the town, but when this failed, Morgan made the surprising suggestion to the others that they should all return to his home and have sexual intercourse with his wife. According to the three younger appellants (but not according to Morgan who described this part of their story as 'lying') Morgan told them that they must not be surprised if his wife struggled a bit, since she was 'kinky' and that was the only way in which she could get 'turned on'.

However this may be it is clear that Morgan did invite his three companions home in order that they might have sexual intercourse with his wife, and, no doubt, he may well have led them in one way or another to believe that she would consent to their doing so. This however, would only be matter predisposing them to believe that Mrs Morgan consented, and would not in any way establish that, at the time, they believed she did consent whilst they were having intercourse.

I need not enter into the details of what the defendants said happened after they had arrived at the house. As I have said they admitted that some degree of struggle took place in the wife's bedroom. But all asserted that after she got into the double bedroom she not merely consented but actively cooperated with and enjoyed what was being done. She caressed and masturbated their private parts, she licked their private parts, she made noises and 'moans' of pleasure. When it was all over she said, 'Have you all had a go?', but not in a sarcastic sense. In other words she was actively participating in a sexual orgy, and was anxious to see that each of the participants had enjoyed himself as much as she.

The choice before the jury was thus between two stories each wholly incompatible with the other, and in my opinion it would have been quite sufficient for the judge, after suitable warnings about the burden of proof, corroboration, separate verdicts and the admissibility of the statements only against the makers, to tell the jury that they must really choose between the two versions the one of a violent and unmistakable rape of a singularly unpleasant kind, and the other of active cooperation in a sexual orgy, always remembering that if in reasonable doubt as to which was true they must give the defendants the benefit of it. In spite of the valiant attempts of counsel to suggest some way in which the stories could be taken apart in sections and give rise in some way to a situation which might conceivably have been acceptable to a reasonable jury in which, while the victim was found not to have consented, the appellants, or any of them could conceivably either reasonably or unreasonably have thought she did consent, I am utterly unable to see any conceivable half-way house. The very material which could have introduced doubt into matter of consent goes equally to belief and vice versa. As the judge's summing up, so far as relevant to this point, was wholly impeccable, and as the jury obviously accepted the victim's story in its substance there is in my view no conceivable way in which a miscarriage of justice can have taken place and therefore no possibility of quashing these convictions, even though, as I shall show, the substantial question of principle should be answered in favour of the appellants' contention.

The certified question arises because counsel for the appellants raised the question whether, even if the victim had not consented, the appellants may not have honestly believed that she did. As I have pointed out, the question was wholly unreal, because if there was reasonable doubt about belief, the same material must have given rise to reasonable doubt about consent, and vice versa. But, presumably because, at that stage, the jury's view of the matter had not been sought, the matter was left to them, as the appellants complain, in a form which implied that they could only acquit if the mistaken belief in consent was reasonable, and it was not enough that it should be honest. This ruling was originally made at the close of the case for the prosecution, but, as it was subsequently embodied in the summing up, it is sufficient to refer to this.

I will quote the principle passage *in extenso* from the record. The learned judge said:

> First of all, let me deal with the crime of rape. What are its ingredients? What have the prosecution to prove to your satisfaction before you can find a defendant guilty of rape? The crime of rape consists in having unlawful sexual intercourse with a woman without her consent and by force. By force. Those words mean exactly what they say. It does not mean there has to be a fight or blows have to be inflicted. It means that there has to be some violence used against the woman to overbear her will or that there has to be a threat of violence as a result of which her will is overborne. You will bear in mind that force or the threat of force carries greater weight when there are four men involved than when there is one man involved. In other words, measure the force in deciding whether force is used. One of the elements to which you will have regard is the number of men involved in the incident.
>
> Further, the prosecution have to prove that each defendant intended to have sexual intercourse with this woman without her consent, not merely that he intended to have intercourse with her but that he intended to have intercourse

> without her consent. Therefore if the defendant believed or may have believed that Mrs Morgan consented to him having sexual intercourse with her, then there would be no such intent in his mind and he would be not guilty of the offence of rape, but such a belief must be honestly held by the defendant in the first place. He must really believe that. And, secondly, his belief must be a reasonable belief; such a belief as a reasonable man would entertain if he applied his mind and thought about the matter. It is not enough for a defendant to rely upon a belief, even though he honestly held it, if it was completely fanciful; contrary to every indication which could be given which would carry some weight with a reasonable man. And, of course, the belief must be not a belief that the woman would consent at some time in the future, but a belief that at the time when intercourse was taking place or when it began that she was then consenting to it.

No complaint was made of the first paragraph where the learned judge is describing what, to use the common and convenient solecism, is meant by the *actus reus* in rape. Nor is there any complaint by the appellants of the judge's first proposition describing the mental element.

It is upon the second proposition about the mental element that the appellants concentrate their criticism. An honest belief in consent, they contend, is enough. It matters not whether it be also reasonable. No doubt a defendant will wish to raise argument or lead evidence to show that his belief was reasonable, since this will support its honesty. No doubt the prosecution will seek to cross examine or raise arguments or adduce evidence to undermine the contention that the belief is reasonable, because, in the nature of the case, the fact that a belief cannot reasonably be held is a strong ground for saying that it was not in fact held honestly at all. Nonetheless, the appellants contend, the crux of the matter, the *factum probandum*, or rather the fact to be refuted by the prosecution, is honesty and not honesty plus reasonableness. In making reasonableness as well as honesty an ingredient in this 'defence' the judge, say the appellants, was guilty of a misdirection.

My first comment upon this direction is that the propositions described 'in the first place' and 'secondly' in the above direction as to the mental ingredient in rape are wholly irreconcilable. In practice this was accepted by both counsel for the appellants and for the respondent, counsel for the appellants embracing that described as 'in the first place' and counsel for the respondent embracing the 'secondly', and each rejecting the other as not being a correct statement of the law. In this, in my view, they had no alternative.

If it be true, as the learned judge says 'in the first place', that the prosecution have to prove that '... each defendant intended to have sexual intercourse without her consent, not merely that he intended to have intercourse with her but that he intended to have intercourse without her consent', the defendant must be entitled to an acquittal if the prosecution fail to prove just that. The necessary mental ingredient will be lacking and the only possible verdict is 'not guilty'. If, on the other hand, as is asserted in the passage beginning 'secondly', it is necessary for any belief in the woman's consent to be 'a reasonable belief' before the defendant is entitled to an acquittal, it must either be because the mental ingredient in rape is not 'to have intercourse and to have it without her consent' but simply 'to have intercourse' subject to a special defence of 'honest and reasonable belief', or alternatively to have intercourse without a reasonable belief in her consent. Counsel for the Crown argued for each of these alternatives, but in my view each is open to insuperable objections of principle. No doubt it would be possible, by statute, to devise a law by which intercourse, voluntarily entered into, was an absolute offence, subject to a 'defence' of belief whether honest or honest and reasonable, of which the 'evidential' burden is primarily on the defence and the 'probative' burden on the prosecution. But in my opinion such is not the crime of rape as it has hitherto been understood. The prohibited act in rape is to have intercourse without the victim's consent. The minimum *mens rea* or guilty mind in most common law offences, including rape, is the intention to do the prohibited act, and that is correctly stated in the proposition stated 'in the first place' of the judge's direction. In murder the situation is different, because the murder is only complete when the victim dies, and an intention to do really serious bodily harm has been held to be enough if such be the case.

The only qualification I would make to the direction of the learned judge's 'in the first place' is the refinement for which, as I shall show, there is both Australian and English authority, that if the intention of the accused is to have intercourse *nolens volens*, that is recklessly and not caring whether the victim be a consenting party or not, that is equivalent on ordinary principles to an intent to do the prohibited act without the consent of the victim.

The alternative version of the learned judge's direction would read that the accused must do the prohibited act with the intention of doing it without an honest and reasonable belief in the victim's consent. This in effect is the version which took up most of the time in argument, and although I find the Court of Appeal's judgment difficult to understand, I think it the version which ultimately commended itself to that court. At all events I think it the more plausible way in which to state the learned judge's 'secondly'. In principle, however, I find it unacceptable. I believe that '*mens rea*' means 'guilty or criminal mind', and if it be the case, as seems to be accepted here, the mental element in rape is not knowledge but intent, to insist that a belief must be reasonable to excuse is to insist that either the accused is to be found guilty of intending to do that which in truth he did not intend to do, or that his state of mind, though innocent of evil intent, can convict him if it be honest but not rational. Even if full value is to be given to the 'probative' burden as defined in *Woolmington v Director of Public Prosecutions* [1935] AC 462, this is to insist on an objective element in the definition of intent, and this is a course which I am extremely reluctant to adopt, especially after the unhappy experience of the House after the decision in *Director of Public Prosecutions v Smith* [1961] AC 290, a case which is full of warnings for us all, and which I fully discussed in *R v Hyam* [1975] AC 55.

So far from my being constrained to adopt this objective element in the mental element in rape, the prosecution had to travel to New South Wales for direct authority in their favour: see *R v Flaherty* (1968) 89 WN Pt 1 (NSW) 141 and *R v Sperotto and Salvietti* (1970) 71 SR (NSW) 334. In place of direct authority they relied on the very wide range of bigamy cases in England and Australia from *R v Tolson* (1889) 23 QBD 168 to *Thomas v R* (1937) 59 CLR 279, *R v King* [1964] 1 QB 285 and *R v Gould*

[1968] 2 QBD 65, on the abduction case of *R v Prince* (1875) LR 2 CCR 154, on the analogies of the 'defences' of 'self-defence' and 'provocation' in murder and assault, and on the remarks of Lord Diplock in *Sweet v Parsley* [1970] AC 132 at 164, 165.

By contrast, the appellants' counsel had a fairly impressive list of authorities directly applying to the crime of rape and saying that the prohibited act is sexual intercourse without consent, and the intention is to do the prohibited act, that is to have sexual intercourse without consent or irrespective of whether the victim consents or not. First amongst these authorities I would cite the traditional definition of rape as enshrined in the current Archbold, *Criminal Pleadings, Evidence & Practice* (38th ed, 1973), para 2871: 'Rape consists in having unlawful sexual intercourse with a woman without her consent by force, fear or fraud' for which are cited as authorities 1 *East's Pleas of the Crown*, p 434 and 1 *Hale's Pleas of the Crown*, p 627.

It is true that this definition contains no express explicit reference to a mental element, and the model indictment displayed some paragraphs later observes the same reticence. But this is misleading. Not only would it be repugnant for any common law crime of this gravity to lack a mental element, but as Lord Diplock pointed out in *Sweet v Parsley* [1970] AC 132 at 162, both statutory and common law offences employ habitually in their definitions words which impliedly import into the definition of the crime an implication of an intent or state of mind in the accused. I regard the words 'force, fear or fraud' as of this sort. It was suggested in arguments that these simply described ways of disproving consent. I do not agree.

There is also a series of direct statements by successive judges charging juries speaking of rape which bear out the appellants' contention. Thus in *R v Wright* (1866) 4 F & F 967 at 968 Channell B, who had to deal with charges of rape and assault with intent to commit rape, charged a jury: 'both charges required an intent ... to commit the act by force against her [the victim's] will.' The note to the case also contains reference to a similar and earlier charge by Coleridge J in the case of *R v Stanton* (1844) 1 Car & K 415. In *R v Tolson* (1889) 23 QBD 168 Stephen J in talking of the mental element in crime said at 185, '*Mens rea* means ... in the case of rape, an intention to have forcible connection with a woman without her consent'. He had made a similar statement in *Roscoe's Criminal Evidence* (7th Edn, 1868). A similar charge in cases of assault with intent to commit rape was given by Patteson J in *R v Lloyd* (1836) 7 C & P 318.

In contrast to the New South Wales cases, in four Victorian cases, the court took a view directly in support of the appellants' contention: see *R v Hornbuckle* [1945] VLR 281; *R v Daly* [1968] VR 257; *R v Flannery and Prendergast* [1969] VR 31 and *R v Burles* [1947] VLR 392. In passing I may say that although on the whole case that court favoured the 'objective' test, even the Court of Criminal Appeal of New South Wales expressly approved this view of the mental ingredient of the crime in *R v Sperotto and Salvietti* (1970) 71 SR (NSW) 334 at 337 where they said:

> In all crimes at common law a guilty intention is a necessary element and with the crime of rape this intention is to have carnal knowledge of the woman without her consent. In order to convict the accused of the crime of rape and, subject to what is hereinafter said, to establish this intention on his part the Crown must

> prove beyond reasonable doubt that when the accused had intercourse with the woman either (i) he was aware that she had not consented, or (ii) he realised that she might not be consenting and was determined to have intercourse with her whether she was consenting or not. The intent and the act must both concur to constitute the crime.

They then cited *Thomas v The King* (1937) 59 CLR 279 at 287.

How then can one explain the apparently analogous cases relied on by the respondents which seem to establish that the defence of mistake of fact, in order to be a 'defence' to a criminal charge must depend on an 'evidential' burden to be discharged by the defence before the 'probative' burden reverts to the Crown, to introduce material on which the jury could find a belief on the part of the accused which is not only honest, but reasonable?

Bridge J, giving the judgment of the Court of Appeal, attempted to do so by three propositions which, again, I quote *in extenso*. He said [ante, pp 190F–191E]:

> The relevant principles can perhaps be re-stated in the following propositions:
>
> 1. In all crimes the Crown has both the evidential and the probative burden of showing that the accused did the prohibited act, and where that act, according to the definition of the offence, is an act of volition, of showing that the act of the accused was voluntary. An obvious example of a crime where the evidential burden on the Crown is limited to these two elements is common assault.
> 2. Wherever the definition of a crime includes as one of its express ingredients a specific mental element both the evidential and the probative burden lie upon the Crown with respect to that element. Typical examples are dishonesty in theft and knowledge or belief in handling. In seeking to rebut the Crown's case against him in reference to his state of mind the accused may and frequently does assert his mistaken belief in non-existent facts. Of course it is right that in this context the question whether there were reasonable grounds for the belief is only a factor for the jury's consideration in deciding whether the Crown has established the necessary mental element of the crime. This is because the issue is already before the jury and no evidential burden rests upon the accused. The decision of the Divisional Court in *Wilson v Inyang* [1951] 2 KB 799 is to be understood in the light of this principle. The court there rejected the argument that an acquittal by a magistrate of a defendant charged with an offence under s 40 of the Medical Act 1858, should be reversed on appeal by case stated on the ground that the defendant had no reasonable ground for his belief that he was entitled to call himself a 'physician'. Lord Goddard CJ said at 830: 'If he has acted without any reasonable ground, and has refrained from making any proper inquiry, that is generally very good evidence that he is not acting honestly. But it is only evidence, …' The statute, however, under which that prosecution was brought required the prosecution to prove that the defendant acted 'wilfully and falsely'. Inevitably, therefore, if this subjective mental element was not proved the prosecution failed.

3. But where the definition of the crime includes no specific mental element beyond the intention to do the prohibited act, the accused may show that though he did the prohibited act intentionally he lacked *mens rea* because he mistakenly, but honestly and reasonably, believed facts which, if true, would have made his act innocent. Here the evidential burden lies upon the accused but once evidence sufficient to raise the issue is before the jury the probative burden lies upon the Crown to negative the mistaken belief. The rationale of requiring reasonable grounds for the mistaken belief must lie in the law's consideration that a bald assertion of belief for which the accused can indicate no reasonable ground is evidence of insufficient substance to raise any issue requiring the jury's consideration. Thus, for example, a person charged with assault upon a victim shown to have been entirely passive throughout who said he had believed himself to be under imminent threat of attack by the victim but could indicate to no circumstance giving cause for such a belief would not discharge the evidential burden of showing a mistaken belief that he was acting lawfully in self-defence.

In the event Bridge J then went on to subsume rape under the third and not the second heading and so to reach the conclusion, ante, pp 191H–192B:

> The correct view, we think, is that on proof of the fact of absence of consent from circumstances which in the nature of the case must have come to the notice of the defendant he may be presumed to have appreciated their significance, and it is this presumption which casts upon the defendant the evidential burden of showing an honest and reasonable belief in consent before any issue as to his state of mind can arise for the jury's consideration.

He goes on to say that, once the 'evidential' burden is discharged the 'probative' burden is cast once more on the Crown.

With due respect, though with one qualification there is something to be said for the premises of this statement, I do not believe the conclusion follows. The qualification I make to the premise is that I can see no reason why the class of case to which his second proposition applies should be limited to cases where the mental ingredient is limited to a 'specific mental element' if, as appears to be the case, by that is meant an 'ulterior' intent within Smith and Hogan's [*Criminal Law* (3rd ed, 1973), p 47] definition of that term.

I believe the law on this point to have been correctly stated by Lord Goddard CJ in *R v Steane* [1947] KB 997 at 1004, when he said:

> … if, on the totality of the evidence, there is room for more than one view as to the intent of the prisoner, the jury should be directed that it is for the prosecution to prove the intent to the jury's satisfaction, and if, on a review of the whole evidence, they either think that the intent did not exist or they are left in doubt as to the intent, the prisoner is entitled to be acquitted.

That was indeed, a case which involved a count where a specific, or, as Professor Smith has called it, an ulterior intent was, and was required to be, charged in the indictment.

But, once it be accepted that an intent of whatever description is an ingredient essential to the guilt of the accused I cannot myself see that any other direction can be logically acceptable. Otherwise a jury would in effect be told to find an intent where none existed or where none was proved to have existed. I cannot myself reconcile it with my conscience to sanction as part of the English law what I regard as logical impossibility, and, if there were any authority which, if accepted would compel me to do so, I would feel constrained to declare that it was not to be followed. However, for reasons which I will give, I do not see any need in the instant case for such desperate remedies.

The beginning of wisdom in all the '*mens rea*' cases to which our attention was called is, as was pointed out by Stephen J in *R v Tolson* (1889) 23 QBD 168 at 185, that '*mens rea*' means a number of quite different things in relation to different crimes. Sometimes it means an intention, eg, in murder, 'to kill or to inflict really serious injury'. Sometimes it means a state of mind or knowledge, eg, in receiving or handling goods 'knowing them to be stolen'. Sometimes it means both an intention and a state of mind, eg, 'dishonestly and without a claim of right made in good faith with intent permanently to deprive the owner thereof'. Sometimes it forms part of the essential ingredients of the crime without proof of which the prosecution, as it were, withers on the bough. Sometimes it is a matter, of which, though the 'probative' burden may be on the Crown, normally the 'evidential' burden may usually (though not always) rest on the defence, eg, 'self-defence' and 'provocation' in murder, though it must be noted that if there is material making the issue a live one, the matter must be left to the jury even if the defence do not raise it. In statutory offences the range is even wider since, owing to the difficulty of proving a negative, Parliament quite often expressly puts the burden on the defendant to negative a guilty state (see per Lord Reid in *Sweet v Parsley* [1970] AC 132 at 150), or inserts words like 'fraudulently', 'negligently', 'knowingly', 'wilfully', 'maliciously' which import special types of guilty mind, or even imports them by implication by importing such words as 'permit' (cf per Lord Diplock in the same case at 162) or, as in *R v Warner* [1969] 2 AC 256, prohibit the 'possession' of a particular substance, or as, in *Sweet v Parsley* itself, leaves the courts to decide whether a particular prohibition makes a new 'absolute' offence or provides an escape by means of an honest, or an honest and reasonable belief. Moreover, of course, a statute can, and often does, create an absolute offence without any degree of *mens rea* at all. It follows from this, surely, that it is logically impermissible, as the Crown sought to do in this case, to draw a necessary inference from decisions in relation to offences where *mens rea* means one thing, and cases where it means another, and in particular from decisions on the construction of statutes, whether these be related to bigamy, abduction or the possession of drugs, and decisions in relation to common law offences. It is equally impermissible to draw direct or necessary inferences from decisions where the *mens rea* is, or includes, a state of opinion, and cases where it is limited to intention (a distinction I referred to in *R v Hyam* [1975] AC 55) or between cases where there is a special 'defence', like self-defence or provocation and cases where the issue relates to the primary intention which the prosecution has to prove.

Once one has accepted, what seems to me abundantly clear, that the prohibited act in rape is non-consensual sexual intercourse, and that the guilty state of mind is an intention to commit it, it seems to me to follow as a matter of inexorable logic that there is no room either for a 'defence' of honest belief or mistake, or of a defence of honest and reasonable belief or mistake. Either the prosecution proves that the accused had the requisite intent, or it does not. In the former case it succeeds, and in the latter it fails. Since honest belief clearly negatives intent, the reasonableness or otherwise of that belief can only be evidence for or against the view that the belief and therefore the intent was actually held, and it matters not whether, to quote Bridge J in the passage cited above, 'the definition of a crime includes no specific element beyond the prohibited act'. If the mental element be primarily an intention and not a state of belief it comes within his second proposition and not his third. Any other view, as for insertion of the word 'reasonable' can only have the effect of saying that a man intends something which he does not.

By contrast, the appellants invited us to overrule the bigamy cases from *R v Tolson* (1889) 23 QBD 168 onwards and perhaps also *R v Prince* (1875) LR 2 CCR 154 (the abduction case) as wrongly decided at least in so far as they purport to insist that a mistaken belief must be reasonable. The arguments for this view are assembled, and enthusiastically argued, by Professor Glanville Williams in his treatise on *Criminal Law,* 2nd Edn (1961), pp 176–205, and by Smith and Hogan, *Criminal Law* (3rd Edn, 1973), pp 148, 149.

Although it is undoubtedly open to this House to reconsider *R v Tolson* and the bigamy cases, and perhaps *R v Prince* which may stand or fall with them, I must respectfully decline to do so in the present case. Nor is it necessary that I should. I am not prepared to assume that the statutory offences of bigamy or abduction are necessarily on all fours with rape, and before I was prepared to undermine a whole line of cases which have been accepted as law for so long, I would need argument in the context of a case expressly relating to the relevant offences. I am content to rest my view of the instant case on the crime of rape by saying that it is my opinion that the prohibited act is and always has been intercourse without consent of the victim and the mental element is and always has been the intention to commit that act, or the equivalent intention of having intercourse willy-nilly not caring whether the victim consents or not. A failure to prove this involves an acquittal because the intent, an essential ingredient, is lacking. It matters not why it is lacking if only it is not there, and in particular it matters not that the intention is lacking only because of a belief not based on reasonable grounds. I should add that I myself am inclined to view *R v Tolson* as a narrow decision based on the construction of a statute, which prima facie seemed to make an absolute statutory offence, with a proviso, related to the seven year period of absence, which created a statutory defence. The judges in *R v Tolson* decided that this was not reasonable, and, on general jurisprudential principles, imported into the statutory offence words which created a special 'defence' of honest and reasonable belief of which the 'evidential' but not the probative burden lay on the defence. I do not think it is necessary to decide this conclusively in the present case. But if this is the true view there is a complete distinction between *Tolson* and the other cases based in statute and the present.

I may also add that I am not impressed with the analogy based on the decision in *Wilson v Inyang* [1951] 2 KB 799 at 803 which has attracted the attention of some academic authors. That clearly depends on the construction of the words 'wilfully and falsely' where they are used in the relevant statute. Also, though I get some support for what I have been saying from the reasoning of the decision in *R v Smith (David)* [1974] QB 354, I nevertheless regard that case as a decision on the Criminal Damage Act 1971, rather than a decision covering the whole law of criminal liability.

For the above reasons I would answer the question certified in the negative, but would apply the proviso to the Criminal Appeal Act on the ground that no miscarriage of justice has or conceivably could have occurred. In my view, therefore, these appeals should be dismissed.

Lord Simon of Glaisdale [Dissenting. His Lordship considered a number of authorities and continued]:

It remains to consider why the law requires, in such circumstances, that the belief in a state of affairs whereby the *actus* would not be *reus* must be held on reasonable grounds. One reason was given by Bridge J in the Court of Appeal, ante, 191D–E:

> The rationale of requiring reasonable grounds for the mistaken belief must lie in the law's consideration that a bald assertion of belief for which the accused can indicate no reasonable ground is evidence of insufficient substance to raise any issue requiring the jury's consideration.

I agree; but I think there is also another reason. The policy of the law in this regard could well derive from its concern to hold a fair balance between victim and accused. It would hardly seem just to fob off a victim of a savage assault with such comfort as he could derive from knowing that his injury was caused by a belief, however absurd, that he was about to attack the accused. A respectable woman who has been ravished would hardly feel that she was vindicated by being told that her assailant must go unpunished because he believed, quite unreasonably, that she was consenting to sexual intercourse with him. The policy behind s 6 of the Sexual Offences Act is presumably that Parliament considered that a girl under 16 is generally unlikely to be sufficiently mature to realise the full implications of sexual intercourse; so that her protection demands that a belief by a man under the age of 24 that she herself was over the age of 16 should not only be an honest but also a reasonable belief.

All the foregoing accords, I trust and believe, with the passage in the speech of my noble and learned friend, Lord Diplock, in *Sweet v Parsley* [1970] AC 132 at 164E–G which was cited by Bridge J.

I would therefore answer the question certified for your Lordships' consideration, Yes. But, even did I consider that it should be answered No, I would, for the reasons given by my noble and learned friends, think this a suitable case to apply the proviso.

I would therefore dismiss the appeal.

[While all five members of the House of Lords agreed that the appeals should be dismissed, **Lord Edmund-Davies** agreed with the view of **Lord Simon of Glaisdale**, delivering a separate judgment to that effect. **Lord Cross of Chelsea** and **Lord Fraser of Tullybelton** both agreed with the views of **Lord Hailsham of St Marylebone**. Each of them delivered concurring judgments. See also *R v Brown* (1975) 10 SASR 139; *R v Wozniak and Pedry* (1977) 16 SASR 67; *R v McEwan* [1979] 2 NSWLR 926.]

[Note that in England the decision in *Director of Public Prosecutions v Morgan* has been overturned by statute: Sexual Offences Act 2003 (UK).]

3.20 Notes and questions

1. In *Director of Public Prosecutions v Morgan*, the majority of the House of Lords adopted a view, that if the accused honestly believed the victim was consenting, even if this belief was held unreasonably, the accused lacks the mens rea for sexual assault, which had been accepted by the Victorian Supreme Court in a series of cases stretching back over 60 years: *R v Burles* [1947] VLR 392; *R v McCready* [1967] VR 325; *R v Daly* [1968] VR 257; *R v Flannery and Prendergast* [1969] VR 31; *R v Maes* [1975] VR 541. This view was affirmed by the Full Court of the Supreme Court of Victoria in *R v Saragozza* [1984] VR 187. In a joint judgment Starke, Kaye and Brooking JJ stated (at 193):

   > Once it is accepted that it is an element of the crime of rape that the accused either was aware that the woman was not consenting, or else realised that she might not be and determined to have intercourse whether she was consenting or not, the conclusion is inescapable that a man who believes that the woman is consenting cannot be guilty of the offence; for the existence of this belief is inconsistent with the presence of the mental element of the crime. Logic then insists that the reasonableness of the belief bears only on whether the accused in fact held it.

   The principle laid down in *Director of Public Prosecutions v Morgan* is reflected in legislation in Victoria: Crimes Act 1958 (Vic) s 38(2)(a)(i). In response to *Morgan's* case, however, a jury direction is required where the accused claims belief in consent, specifying that the jury consider whether the asserted belief is reasonable in all the circumstances, having regard to whether the accused was aware of the existence of any of the factors negativing consent in s 36, and 'whether the accused took any reasonable steps to ascertain whether the complainant was consenting … and if so, the nature of those steps': Crimes Act 1958 (Vic) s 37AA. In New South Wales, however, the minority view in *Morgan* has been adopted by legislation. Section 61HA(3) of the Crimes Act 1900 (NSW) includes among the situations in which a person is regarded as knowing that the other person does not consent to sexual intercourse, those instances where '(c) the person has no reasonable grounds for believing that the other person consents to the sexual intercourse.' The effect of the New South Wales provision is that the accused must have taken reasonable steps to ascertain consent if he or she is to rely on a claim of honest belief to negate mens rea: s 61HA(3)(d)).

2. Is there merit in the argument adopted by Lord Simon in *Director of Public Prosecutions v Morgan* and incorporated in the New South Wales Act that the rule laid down by the majority gives insufficient protection to potential victims? Do you think that a jury, having satisfied itself beyond reasonable doubt that the victim did not consent, is likely to believe an assertion made

by the accused that the accused believed the victim was consenting? Bear in mind that in Victoria, where the law has been as laid down in *Director of Public Prosecutions v Morgan* for some 60 years, there is no evidence to suggest that accused persons have been able to use such a defence to secure unjustified acquittals.

3.21 In Victoria, the mental element for rape includes not only awareness of the victim's lack of consent, but, as an alternative, awareness that the victim 'might not be consenting' and (more controversially), 'not giving any thought to whether the person is not consenting or might not be consenting' (Crimes Act 1958 s 38(2)(a)(ii)). This provision represents a form of negligent liability: see also *R v Kitchener* (1993) 29 NSWLR 696 (at **3.25C**).

3.22 The meaning of these Victorian provisions has been further examined by the High Court in a decision which has effectively overturned the decision in *Morgan*'s case, in *R v Getachew* [2012] HCA 10; (2012) 286 ALR 196. The decision has been applied in *NT* v *The Queen* [2012] VSCA 213.

3.23C

R v Getachew

[2012] HCA 10; (2012) 286 ALR 196
High Court of Australia

[G and V went to a house to sleep, after a night out with two others. G and V slept on a mattress while the other two slept on a bed in the same room. V told G several times not to touch her or she would sleep in the car. Later in the night, V woke to find G sexually penetrating her from behind. At his trial for rape, G gave no evidence and denied penetrating V. The trial judge directed the jury that if they were satisfied that G was 'aware that V was asleep, or unconscious, or so affected by alcohol as to be incapable of freely agreeing, or aware that she might be in one of these states', the mens rea for rape would be proven. G was convicted and appealed. The Court of Appeal ordered a new trial (by a majority of 2:1) and held that the jury should have been directed that 'the prosecution might fail to prove the mental element of the offence of rape even though a belief [in the] consent [of the complainant] on the part of the accused was unreasonable because the accused was aware that the complainant might be asleep' (*Getachew v The Queen* [2011] VSCA 164). The prosecution then appealed to the High Court from this decision. The High Court allowed the appeal and made the order that the appeal to the Court of Appeal be dismissed.]

French CJ, **Hayne**, **Crennan**, **Kiefel** and **Bell JJ**:

17 The 2007 Act made other important changes to the law which took account of the recommendations made by the 2004 Victorian Law Reform Commission report. But not all of the recommendations made by that report were reflected in amendments made after the report was published. In particular, neither the 2007 Act nor any of the earlier amendments gave effect to the recommendation[1] that what was called '[t]he defence of honest belief in consent' not be available 'where … one or more of the circumstances listed in section 36(a)–(g) existed and the accused was aware of the existence of such circumstances'. Instead, the accused's awareness of the existence of such a circumstance was treated, in the amendments made by the 2007 Act, as a matter about which a trial judge was required to direct the jury. The required direction was that the jury should consider the accused's awareness of the s 36 circumstance in deciding whether the prosecution established beyond reasonable doubt that the accused was aware that the complainant was not or might not be consenting to the sexual act.

…

Section 37AA application and effect

21 For present purposes, there are two critical observations to make about s 37AA. First, the directions about awareness for which the section provided were to be given 'if evidence is led or an assertion is made' at the trial that the accused *believed* that the complainant was consenting. Second, s 37AA was expressed to be '[f]or the purposes of section 37'. Thus, s 37(1) *required* the giving of the directions s 37AA set out '[i]f relevant to the facts in issue in a proceeding' — that is, if evidence was led or an assertion made of the identified kind — and s 37(2) *prohibited* the giving of a direction of the kind referred to in s 37AA 'if the direction is not relevant to the facts in issue in the proceeding' — that is, the criterion for engaging s 37AA was *not* met.

22 It follows that an accused's *belief* in consent is relevant at a trial for rape only 'if evidence is led or an assertion is made' that the accused did believe that the complainant was consenting to the sexual act. The reference to 'an assertion' being made is important. It would encompass the case in which an accused's out of court statement (commonly in a record of interview with police) is tendered in evidence and contains an assertion that the accused believed that the complainant was consenting. And of course there are other ways in which the issue may be enlivened at trial, whether by evidence or by assertion.

23 In considering any question about an accused's asserted belief in consent it is necessary to keep at the forefront of consideration that s 38(2) prescribed the relevant mental element for the offence of rape as awareness that the complainant was not or might not be consenting or, after the 2007 Act, not giving any thought to whether the complainant was not or might not be consenting. Belief in consent is not the controlling concept. It is relevant only so far as it sheds light on the accused's awareness that the complainant was not or might not be consenting.

24 If evidence is led or an assertion is made that the accused believed that the complainant was consenting, the directions required by s 37AA would oblige the jury to consider whether the belief was reasonable (and any evidence of that belief). But neither s 37AA nor any other relevant provision of the Crimes Act provided that an accused *must* be taken to be aware that the complainant might not be consenting unless the accused *reasonably* believed that the complainant was consenting. Rather, consideration of whether an accused's belief in consent was reasonable would bear upon whether the accused in fact held the belief.[2]

25 It by no means follows from this last observation, however, that the relevant provisions of the Crimes Act are to be read as requiring the judge (in a case where no evidence has been led and no assertion made that the accused believed the complainant was consenting) to direct the jury that the prosecution must prove beyond reasonable doubt that the accused had no belief in consent. Rather, when s 37AA is read in the light of s 37, it is apparent that a jury is to be given directions about an accused's belief in consent (and the bearing that this belief may have on awareness of the lack of consent) *only* if the possibility that the accused held such a belief has been raised at the trial (whether because evidence was led that the accused had such a belief or an assertion was made that the accused had such a belief).

Belief and awareness

26 Reference to an accused holding the belief that the complainant was consenting invites close attention to what was the accused's state of mind. It was said[3] in the Explanatory Memorandum accompanying the Bill for the 2007 Act that 'belief in consent and awareness of the possibility of an absence of consent are not mutually exclusive'. So much may be accepted if 'belief in consent' is treated as encompassing a state of mind where the accused accepts that it is possible that the complainant might not be consenting. Whether such a state of mind is properly described as a 'belief in consent' need not be explored. On the face of it, evidence of a state of mind that did *not* exclude the possibility that the complainant might not be consenting appears not to engage at all with, let alone negate, the central statutory requirement that the accused was aware that the complainant was not or might not be consenting.

27 For present purposes, it is enough to notice that, if an accused asserted, or gave evidence at trial, that he or she thought or 'believed' the complainant was consenting, the prosecution may yet demonstrate to the requisite standard either that the accused was aware that the complainant might not be consenting or that the asserted belief was not held. It is to be recalled that, since the 2007 Act, the fault element of rape has been identified as the accused being aware that the complainant was not or might not be consenting or the accused not giving any thought to whether the complainant was not or might not be consenting. The reference to an accused's awareness that the complainant *might not be* consenting is, of course, important. An accused's belief that the complainant *may* have been consenting, even *probably was* consenting, is no answer to a charge of rape. It is no answer because each of those forms of belief demonstrates that the accused was aware that the complainant might not be consenting or, at least, did not turn his or her mind to whether the complainant might not be consenting.

28 One further and important observation must be made about s 37AA. Section 37AA(b)(i) dealt with the case of a proceeding in which the jury find that a circumstance specified in s 36 (such as the complainant being asleep) existed in relation to the complainant.

Section 37AA required the judge to direct the jury to consider whether the accused's asserted belief that the complainant was consenting was reasonable having regard to 'whether the accused was aware that that circumstance existed in relation to the complainant',[4] 'whether the accused took any steps to ascertain whether the complainant was consenting or might not be consenting, and if so, the nature of those steps'[5] and 'any other relevant matters'.[6] But neither s 37AA nor any other relevant provision of the Crimes Act required that an accused who asserted a belief in consent nonetheless *must* be taken to have been aware that the complainant was not or might not be consenting if the accused was aware that the relevant s 36 circumstance — here, the complainant being asleep — did exist or might exist. If evidence was led or an assertion was made that the accused *believed* that the complainant was consenting, demonstration that the accused knew that the complainant was or might be asleep did not require the conclusion that the accused was aware that the complainant was not or might not be consenting. In such a case, s 37AA required the judge to direct the jury to take account of the asserted belief of the accused in deciding whether the accused was aware that the complainant was not or might not be consenting.

...

34 In the present case the complainant did not consent to the sexual act if, as she asserted, she was asleep when penetrated. Because there was no evidence led at trial and no assertion made that the accused believed that the complainant was consenting, demonstration beyond reasonable doubt (1) that the complainant was asleep at the time of penetration and (2) that the accused was aware that the complainant was then asleep or might then have been asleep would, without more, demonstrate in this case that the accused was aware that the complainant was not or might not be consenting to the sexual act.

...

36 There was therefore no occasion to give a direction of the kind which the Court of Appeal held should have been given about the accused's state of mind.

37 The appeal to this Court should be allowed. Orders 2, 3 and 4 of the orders of the Court of Appeal made on 2 June 2011 should be set aside. In their place there should be an order that the appeal to the Court of Appeal is dismissed.

Notes:

1. Victoria, Victorian Law Reform Commission, *Sexual Offences: Final Report*, Report No 5 (2004), at 422 (Recommendation 174).
2. cf *Director of Public Prosecutions v Morgan* [1976] AC 182; *R v Flannery* [1969] VR 31 at 33–34; *R v Saragozza* [1984] VR 187 at 193–196.
3. Victoria, Legislative Assembly, Crimes Amendment (Rape) Bill 2007, Explanatory Memorandum at 4.
4. s 37AA(b)(i).
5. s 37AA(b)(ii).
6. s 37AA(b)(iii).

3.24 Further reading

K Arenson, '*The Queen v Getachew*: Rethinking *DPP v Morgan*' (2013) 77 *Journal of Criminal Law* 151

J Faulkner, 'Mens Rea in Rape: *Morgan* and the Inadequacy of Subjectivism' (1991) 18 *MULR* 60

M Goode, 'The Mental Element of Rape, the Naffin Report and Other Questions: A Defence of the Common Law' (1985) 9 *Crim LJ* 17

W Larcombe, '*Worsnop v The Queen*: Subjective Belief in Consent Prevails (Again) in Victoria's Rape Law (2011) 35 *Melbourne University Law Review* 697

D Smith, 'Reckless Rape in Victoria' (2008) 32 *Melbourne University Law Review* 1007

K Warner, 'The Mental Element and Consent Under the New "Rape" Laws' (1983) 7 *Crim LJ* 245

3.25C R v Kitchener

(1993) 29 NSWLR 696

Court of Criminal Appeal, Supreme Court of New South Wales

[The appellant was convicted on three counts of sexual intercourse without consent and one count of indecent assault. The appellant was the president of the Life and Death Motorcycle Club, Penrith Division. He took the complainant for a ride on his motorcycle and rode to a deserted area where, according to the complainant, he forcibly performed various sexual acts upon her. The appellant's defence at his trial was that the complainant consented to the acts which occurred. On appeal.]

Carruthers J: ... The first ground of appeal is expressed in the following terms: 'The learned trial judge erred in directions he gave concerning *mens rea*.'

This ground focuses upon the following passage in his Honour's summing-up (at 10):

> The Crown has to prove beyond reasonable doubt that the accused at the relevant time of the intercourse foresaw at least the possibility that the girl was not consenting, but went ahead regardless, *or he failed to avert (sic) at all to the question of whether she was consenting and just went ahead.* In other words, he treated consent, as far as he was concerned, as entirely irrelevant. So there are two aspects I have just told you of in relation to that deemed knowledge coming from recklessness. It is foreseeing that leads to a possibility that she is not consenting, but going ahead regardless, *or failing to even avert (sic) to the question in the situation in which he was and which he wanted.* (Emphasis added.)

Thus the trial judge put the issue of consent to the jury on three bases: namely, that the appellant knew that the complainant was not consenting; that the appellant adverted to the possibility that the complainant was not consenting, but that he went ahead regardless of this possibility; and that the appellant failed to advert to the question of consent at all. The appellant submitted that the directions on the third basis, which are quoted in italics above, constituted a misdirection. It was submitted that where an accused does not advert to the question of consent at all, then the requisite *mens rea* has not been made out. When counsel for the appellant was pressed to illustrate such a situation he could only cite cases of intoxication or lack of intellect.

It was, in effect, conceded by counsel for the appellant that the instant case was not one which called for a direction on recklessness as the defence case was that at all times the complainant, to the knowledge of the appellant, consented. However, it was submitted that as the judge elected to direct the jury on recklessness, it was necessary that the direction be in accordance with the law, because the jury may have acted on it. Thus there may have been a miscarriage of justice: see *Domican v R* (1992) 173 CLR 555 at 568–70.

It was submitted that recklessness within the meaning of s 61D(2) necessarily involves an advertence by the accused to the possibility that the complainant was not consenting. The direction of the trial judge was therefore bad in that it did not direct the jury to the need for the Crown to prove that the appellant had adverted to the possibility of non-consent. It was submitted that the requirement in relation to *mens rea* in cases under s 61D(2) is the same as that at common law in relation to rape: namely, that the Crown must establish beyond reasonable doubt, either that the accused was aware that the complainant was not consenting, or else realised she might not be consenting and yet determined to have intercourse whether she were consenting or not.

[His Honour referred to a number of authorities, and continued:]

The coup de grace to the appellant's submission, however, is that it has been specifically rejected by this court in the appeal of *R v Henning* (Court of Criminal Appeal, 11 May 1990, unreported), where the court said in a joint judgment (at 31):

> We do not think it follows that a conscious advertence to the possibility of non-consent is necessary to a finding of recklessness under s 61D(2). A failure to advert at all to the question of consent, in other words, treating it as an entirely irrelevant factor, would almost certainly amount to either knowledge or recklessness if consent was in fact withheld.

Counsel for the appellant submitted, however, that the above statement constitutes a departure from the law as laid down by this court over many years both at common law and under the Crimes Act, and that this departure was made without reference to authority and without the benefit of full argument. Reliance was also placed upon the fact that no real question of recklessness arose on the facts in *R v Henning* and the statement therefore amounted to obiter dicta.

However (if I may respectfully say so) nothing has been put before this court which leads me to conclude that the above-quoted statement from *R v Henning* is erroneous.

The following general observations may be made. First, the word 'reckless' is not defined in the Crimes Act; secondly, while the concept of recklessness is one well-known to the criminal law, the concept in the present context should be read in conjunction with the body of law relating to sexual assaults. It is true that *Gillies* (1985) at 467, discusses the appropriate *mens rea* for the common law concept of rape in a way favourable to the appellant's contention. However, the learned author then states as follows:

> Alternative conceptions of recklessness in this context are that D penetrates V 'not caring' whether she has consented, or that he penetrates her with 'reckless indifference' as to whether she has consented.

[His Honour referred to *Director of Public Prosecutions v Morgan* (at **3.19C**), and continued:]

The question of recklessness was also considered by the English Court of Appeal in *R v Kimber* [1983] 1 WLR 1118 at 1121; [1983] 3 All ER 316 at 320. In that case, (cited with approval in *R v Satnam* (1983) 78 Cr App R 149 at 154) Lawton LJ stated in relation to a defendant who had said that at the time of the alleged rape of a mentally defective woman, he 'was not really interested in [the victim's] feelings at all' (at 1121; 320):

> … His own evidence showed that his attitude to her was one of indifference to her feelings and wishes. This state of mind is aptly described in the colloquial expression, 'couldn't care less'. In law this is recklessness.

The *Shorter Oxford English Dictionary* definition of 'reckless' also makes clear that non- advertence to a possibility would be capable of being 'reckless' as to that possibility. That definition is in the following terms:

> 1. Of persons: Careless of the consequences of one's actions; heedless (of something); lacking in prudence or caution.

Leaving aside those cases where the accused may be incapable of forming the requisite intent, I consider that where consent is withheld, a failure to advert at all to the possibility that the complainant is not consenting, necessarily means that the accused is 'reckless as to whether the other person consents' within the meaning of s 61D(2). Such a conclusion is, in my view, consistent with both logical and legal principle.

Thus the directions which the trial judge gave to the jury on recklessness, were, in my view, correct in law. …

Kirby P: I agree with the judgment of Carruthers J.

In addition to the plain meaning of s 61D(2) of the *Crimes Act 1900* and the authority of this court in *R v Henning* (Court of Criminal Appeal, 11 May 1990, unreported) there are sound reasons of policy which support the instruction given by the trial judge (Ward DCJ) to the jury on the meaning of what is 'reckless' which the appellant contests.

To criminalise conscious advertence to the possibility of non-consent, but to excuse the reckless failure of the accused to give a moment's thought to that possibility, is self-evidently unacceptable. In the hierarchy of wrong-doing, such total indifference to the consent of a person to have sexual intercourse is plainly reckless, at least in our society today. Every individual has a right to the human dignity of his or her own person. Having sexual intercourse with another, without the consent of that other, amounts to an affront to that other's human dignity and an invasion of the privacy of that person's body and personality. It would be unacceptable to construe a provision such as s 61D(2) so as to put outside the ambit of what is 'reckless' a complete failure to advert to whether or not the subject of the proposed sexual intercourse consented to it or declined consent. Such a law would simply reaffirm the view that our criminal law, at crucial moments, fails to provide principled protection to the victims of unwanted sexual intercourse, most of whom are women. Our law is not unprincipled or inadequate in this regard.

[**Smart J** agreed with **Carruthers J**. Appeal dismissed.]

3.26C Banditt v R

(2005) 224 CLR 262; [2005] HCA 80
High Court of Australia

[The accused was convicted in the New South Wales District Court of breaking and entering a dwelling house and committing sexual intercourse without consent. The victim was asleep when the accused began the intercourse and when the victim realised that it was her cousin, she reprimanded him and told him to get off, which he did. The accused submitted that he thought the victim liked him and did not realise otherwise until she resisted. At the point at which the victim resisted, the accused desisted from the act. He argued before the New South Wales Court of Criminal Appeal that the trial judge had misdirected the jury on the concept of recklessness. The court dismissed the appeal. On appeal to the High Court.]

[Footnotes to the extract appear at the end of the extract.]

Gummow, **Hayne** and **Heydon JJ**: … [I]n this appeal the question remains as to what degree or extent of advertence in the state of mind of the complainant will answer the statutory criterion of recklessness found in s 61R(1) of the Act. That sub-section is a deeming provision which extends what otherwise might be the limited denotation of the phrase 'does not consent' in s 61I. A person who is reckless as to whether the other person consents to the sexual intercourse 'is to be taken to know' of a critical matter for s 61I, namely, that the other person does not consent to the sexual intercourse.

A starting point for further analysis of the legislation is that it was strongly influenced by developments in England, including *Morgan* and s 1 of the 1976 UK Act, and that those developments were not at odds with what was previously understood in Australian common law jurisdictions, as exemplified in *R v Daly*.[1] Different considerations may apply in the Code jurisdictions.[2]

Secondly, it may be possible, as is the case elsewhere in the law, to construe the term 'reckless' as involving measurement against an objective criterion. But, it is evident from the formulations in *Morgan* that there is a need here to accommodate the term to the requisite mental element. This, as stated in s 61I, is knowledge of absence of consent and s 61R(1) is appendant, albeit explanatory, of s 61I.

Thirdly, as Gibbs J emphasised in *La Fontaine*:[3]

> The purpose of a summing up is not to endeavour to apprise the jury of fine legal distinctions but to explain to them as simply as possible so much of the law as they need to know in order to decide the case before them.

Fourthly, the following words of Professor Sir John Smith respecting s 1 of the 1976 UK Act are in point in construing s 61R(1):[4]

> If D is aware that there is any possibility that P is not consenting and proceeds to have intercourse, he does so recklessly. Lord Hailsham in *Morgan* required an 'intention of having intercourse, willy-nilly, not caring whether the victim consents or [no]'.[5] Another way of putting it is to ask, 'Was D's attitude one of 'I could not care less whether she is consenting or not, I am going to have intercourse with her regardless."[6] What, however, of the man who knows that the woman may not be consenting but hopes, desperately, that she is? He could care much less; but is he not reckless?

It may well be said that 'reckless' is an ordinary term and one the meaning of which is not necessarily controlled by particular legal doctrines. However, in its ordinary use, 'reckless' may indicate conduct which is negligent or careless, as well as that which is rash or incautious as to consequences; the former has an 'objective', the latter a 'subjective', hue. These considerations make it inappropriate for charges to juries to do no more than invite the application of an ordinary understanding of 'reckless' when applying s 61R(1).

A direction that 'reckless' has the meaning to be given by the jury in the particular circumstances of the case would be erroneous, and the respondent does not contend otherwise.[7] In the present case, the trial judge properly emphasised that it was not the reaction of some notional reasonable man but the state of mind of the appellant which the jury was obliged to consider and that this was to be undertaken with regard to the surrounding circumstances, including the past relationship of the parties.

The respondent's submission, recorded earlier in these reasons, is to the effect that in a particular case one or more of the expressions used in Morgan and by Professor Smith, as well as those recorded in the respondent's submission, may properly be used in explaining what is required by s 61R(1). That submission, as explained below, should be accepted.

The appellant's submission that proceeding with an awareness of a risk of non-consent cannot suffice without the 'discrete mental state' described as 'Even if I know, I would continue. It does not matter to me', should not be accepted.

The present case illustrates the point. The evidence of the complainant was that she was asleep and woke to find the appellant on top of her and then, for a few moments, 'being half asleep', she was not sure who it was until she felt the appellant's head, realised who it was and pushed him off. The appellant's case was that the complainant was awake, she consented to intercourse and the appellant thought she was consenting.

With respect to the past relationship of the parties, the trial judge directed the jury:

> The Crown is entitled to argue as it does, that even if there had been some earlier act of sexual intercourse, although [the complainant] denies that there had been any such act and the accused said there had, but even if there had, the Crown is entitled to argue, the last time there was any attempted intimacy between the two of them was this attempted kiss a few weeks before and she had rebuffed him. That, he says, the accused says in evidence, 'Well that doesn't mean that she was rejecting me for all time', but you might think, so the Crown is entitled to put, that it at least put him on notice that she might not be willing to have intercourse with him on 6 October. And that is important from this point of view, the Crown suggested to you late in the piece in his closing address, that even on the accused's point of view, you might find that he knew she was not consenting, because he was reckless.

In this setting, as it will be in many other cases, it was proper for the trial judge to have gone on to direct the jury in the terms which the appellant challenges.

The Court of Criminal Appeal did not err in dismissing the appeal and the further appeal to this Court should be dismissed.

[**Callinan J** delivered a separate judgment agreeing that the appeal should be dismissed. Appeal dismissed.]

[See also *R v Zilm* [2006] VSCA 72.]

Notes:

1. [1968] VR 257.
2. See *Director of Public Prosecutions (NT) v WJI* [2004] HCA 47; (2004) 219 CLR 43.
3. [1976] HCA 52; (1976) 136 CLR 62 at 77. See also *Green v The Queen* [1971] HCA 55; (1971) 126 CLR 28 at 32–33 per Barwick CJ, McTiernan and Owen JJ.
4. Smith and Hogan, *Criminal Law*, 10th ed (2002) at 471.
5. [1975] UKHL 3; [1976] AC 182 at 215.
6. *Taylor* (1984) 80 Cr App Rep 327; *Haughian* (1985) 80 Cr App Rep 334.
7. cf *Green v The Queen* [1971] HCA 55; (1971) 126 CLR 28 at 32–33.

The issue of sexual identity

3.27 In two cases, the Supreme Court of Victoria and the Court of Criminal Appeal of New South Wales considered the legal status of transsexuals for the purposes of the criminal law. In both cases, the court rejected a view adopted in earlier English decisions that sexual identity is established at birth and remains fixed for the remainder of an individual's life: *Corbett v Corbett* [1971] P 83; *R v Tan* [1983] QB 1053. Although decided six months earlier, the New South Wales decision, *R v Harris and McGuiness* (1988) 17 NSWLR 158, had not been reported at the time of the Victorian case, *R v Cogley* [1989] VR 799, and was not cited to the Victorian Supreme Court. There is a significant difference in the approach by the two courts, and it is submitted that the New South Wales decision is to be preferred.

3.28 It will be convenient first to focus on the Victorian decision. In *R v Cogley* [1989] VR 799, the court was concerned with the question of whether a male-to-female transsexual is a woman for the purposes of the law of rape. The accused was charged with assault with intent to commit rape with aggravating circumstances and detaining a person with intent to take part in an act of sexual penetration. The victim was a transsexual who had been born a male but had undergone male-to-female sex reassignment surgery and lived her life as a female. As the Victorian Act was then drafted, the insertion of a penis into a surgically created vagina was not dealt with and accordingly the question of whether such an act amounted to rape depended for its resolution upon the common law definition of rape as 'the carnal knowledge of any woman ... against her will'.

Quite clearly, penetration of the surgically created vagina of a transsexual should be regarded as amounting to rape. The purpose of the extension to the definition of rape in the Victorian Act was to extend the protection of the law of rape to other parts of the anatomy which may be penetrated sexually, and to have the law's protection apply to persons of both sexes. The reason why the section applied to the anus and mouth of a person, whether male or female, and not to the vagina of a person formerly a male is almost certainly that the individual drafting the legislation neglected to consider the situation of a person classified by the law as male, and therefore beyond the protection of the common law of rape, having a vagina.

The trial judge, Cummins J, ruled the victim was properly regarded as a woman. He held that a male-to-female transsexual should be regarded by the law as a woman where female core identity is established and where sexual reassignment surgery has taken place. The combination of these two elements was, in his Honour's view, essential. Core identity is a necessary but not sufficient condition in the finding that a male-to-female transsexual is a woman.

The accused was convicted and appealed unsuccessfully to the Full Court. The Full Court held that to establish the crime of assault with intent to commit rape, it was not necessary for the prosecution to establish the victim was, in fact, a woman. The criminality of the offence comes from the assault and the intent to commit the crime of rape. Whether the victim was a man or a woman, or a person who had the physical appearance or physical attributes of a man or a woman, are not, the court held, relevant to determining whether in the circumstances the crime has been committed. Likewise, the criminality of the offence of detaining with intent to take part in an act of sexual penetration is the detention of another person against her or his will with the intent to take part in an act of sexual penetration. It is not to the point whether or not the intended act of sexual penetration was capable of being effected.

While upholding the conviction, however, the court rejected the reasoning of Cummins J. The court held that if a finding as to whether the victim was a woman with a vagina capable of being penetrated was essential to establish guilt on the count of assault with intent to rape or the count of detaining with intent to take part in an act of sexual penetration, the trial judge should have left the question to the jury. The question 'what constitutes a person a woman for the purposes of the criminal law' thus becomes an issue to be defined and determined by the jury.

The question 'what constitutes a woman' is an unusual one to leave to the jury. The significance of the question in the present context is, of course, that it determines the scope of the crime of rape. Yet a decision as to the scope of a crime is usually regarded as a matter of law to be determined by the judge. On a more basic level, however, there simply appears to be no sound reason for possibly denying to the transsexual the protection of the law of rape. No sensible reason exists for regarding anal or oral penetration of a transsexual as rape, yet not so regarding vaginal penetration of such a person.

The view of the Full Court was overturned by amendments introduced by the Crimes (Sexual Offences) Act 1991 (Vic). Section 35 of the Crimes Act 1958 (Vic) now provides that for the purposes of the law of rape and related offences, 'vagina' includes a surgically created vagina.

3.29 A more satisfactory approach to that adopted by the Victorian Full Court was taken by the Court of Criminal Appeal of New South Wales in *R v Harris and McGuiness* (1988) 17 NSWLR 158. The appellants, H and M, were charged with offences under the Crimes Act 1900 (NSW) s 81A (now repealed). That section made it an offence for a male person to procure or attempt to procure another male person to commit an act of indecency. Each of the appellants had made sexual approaches to men who were, in fact, police officers. The only issue at the hearing before the magistrates was whether the appellants themselves were 'male persons'. The appellant H was a transsexual who lived and appeared as a woman, and had undergone sex reassignment surgery involving the removal of the male genitalia and the creation of a vaginal cavity. The appellant M likewise lived and appeared as woman but had not had any sex reassignment surgery.

On a case stated, the majority of the court (Street CJ and Mathews J, Carruthers J dissenting) held that whether a person is to be regarded as a male or female is to be determined by a combination of psychological sex identification and physical attributes existing at the time of the commission of the alleged offence, and not by reference to a classification based on chromosomal features which are immutable from the time of birth. Relevant criteria are whether, through medical intervention or otherwise, the person has assumed the external features of the opposite sex, thereby bringing those genital features into conformity with the person's psychological sex. Psychological sex identification alone is not, the court held, sufficient to warrant a change of classification. The majority concluded, applying these criteria, that the appellant H should be regarded as female and the appellant M should be regarded as male.

All members of the court proceeded upon the basis that the test for determining the sex of a person was one to be laid down by the court as a matter of law and not to be transferred to the jury. Carruthers J, dissenting, chose to follow the decisions in *Corbett v Corbett* and *R v Tan.* Street CJ delivered a short judgment in which he agreed with Matthews J. Matthews J undertook a detailed and careful analysis of the authorities and both the scientific and the legal literature, expressing his conclusion as follows (at 192):

> The fundamental purpose of the law, as Ormrod J himself said [in *Corbett v Corbett*], is the regulation of the relations between persons, and between persons and the state or community. Within this context, the criminal law is concerned with the regulation of behaviour. It is the relevant circumstances at the time of the behaviour to which we must have regard. And I cannot see that the state of a person's chromosomes can or should be a relevant circumstance in the determination of his or her criminal liability. It is equally unrealistic, in my view, to treat as relevant the fact that the person has acquired his or her external attributes as a result of operative procedure. After all, sexual offences — with which we are particularly concerned here — frequently involve the use of the external genitalia. How can the law sensibly ignore the state of those genitalia at the time of the alleged offence, simply because they were artificially created or were not the same at birth?
>
> The time, then, has come when we must, for the purposes of the criminal law, give proper legal effect to successful reassignment surgery undertaken by transsexuals. Thus I consider that the conviction of Harris cannot stand, as she was not at the relevant time a 'male person' within the meaning of s 81A.

OTHER SEXUAL OFFENCES

Child sexual assault

3.30 Sex with a minor who, under statute, is deemed incapable of consenting, is sometimes referred to as 'statutory rape'. In legislation in Victoria and New South Wales, a child under the age of 10 is incapable of consenting to a sexual transaction, so that sexual penetration is a statutory offence: Crimes Act 1958 (Vic) s 45; Crimes Act 1900 (NSW) ss 66A–66B. It is also unlawful in both jurisdictions to have sexual intercourse with a minor above the age of 10 and under the age of 16: Crimes Act 1958 (Vic) s 45; Crimes Act 1900 (NSW) ss 66C–66D.

In Victoria, consent is a defence only if the child was aged 12 or older *and* the accused satisfies the court on the balance of probabilities that he or she believed on reasonable grounds that the child was aged 16 or older, or the accused was not more than two years older than the child, or the accused satisfies the court on the balance of probabilities that he or she believed on reasonable grounds that he or she was married to the child: Crimes Act 1958 (Vic) s 45(4). In New South Wales, consent is no defence to statutory rape charges under s 77 of the Crimes Act 1900 and no other defences are listed in relation to ss 66A–66D. However, for the specific offence of procuring or grooming child under 16 for unlawful sexual activity (s 66EB), it is a defence if the accused reasonably believed that the other person was not a child (s 66EB(7)).

3.31 Section 48 of the Crimes Act 1958 (Vic) makes it an offence for a person to take part in an act of sexual penetration with a 16- or 17-year-old child to whom the person is not married and who is under her or his care, supervision or authority. Consent is only a defence if the person believed on reasonable grounds (a) that the child was aged 18 or older, or (b) that he or she was married to the child. Section 48(4) provides that a child is under the care, supervision or authority of a person if the person is the child's teacher, foster parent, legal guardian, minister of religion with pastoral responsibility for the child, employer, youth worker, sports coach, counsellor, health professional, member of the police force acting in the course of duty in respect of the child or prison or related worker acting in the course of duty in respect of the child. In New South Wales, this offence is stipulated in s 73 of the Crimes Act 1900 (NSW) and includes the above categories of care. Consent is no defence to this offence (s 77).

3.32 Section 47A of the Crimes Act 1958 (Vic) and s 66EA of the Crimes Act 1900 (NSW) contain the offence of persistent sexual abuse of a child. The crime consists of a course of conduct involving the commission of a sexual offence against a child on at least three separate occasions. The offence carries a maximum penalty of 25 years' imprisonment in Victoria and New South Wales.

3.33 Various statutory offences cover permitting or being a party to acts of indecency with young persons not involving penetration: for example, Crimes Act 1958 (Vic) ss 47, 49; Crimes Act 1900 (NSW) ss 61N, 61O. Other than in the case of s 49 of the Crimes Act 1958 (Vic), a young person in these provisions means a person under the age of 16 years. Section 49 of the Crimes Act 1958 (Vic) applies in the case of 16- and 17-year-olds who are under the care, supervision or authority of the accused. The Victorian sections provide that a belief on the part of the accused that the young person was of the age of 16 years or above (or, in the case of s 49, of the age of 18 years or above) shall be a defence only if that belief was held on reasonable grounds. The New South Wales provisions make no allowance for a defence of mistake. The common law defence of honest and reasonable mistake, however, would apply to similar effect as the Victorian statutory provision: *CTM v R* (2008) 247 ALR 1; [2008] HCA 25 (at 13.3C).

3.34 In Victoria it is an offence to make travel arrangements or otherwise facilitate or contribute to the commission by another person of an offence against a child whether that offence is to be committed in Victoria or outside Victoria: Crimes Act 1958 (Vic) s 49A. There are offences relating to child pornography: Crimes Act 1958 (Vic) ss 67A–70; Crimes Act 1900 (NSW) s 91G.

3.35 In each jurisdiction, the various offences relating to young persons apply equally whether the perpetrator or the victim is male or female.

3.36 For further reading, see B McSherry and B Naylor, *Australian Criminal Laws: Critical Perspectives*, OUP, Melbourne, 2004, pp 228–38.

Sexual assault of persons with cognitive impairment

3.37 Sexual relations with a person of cognitive impairment may, despite apparent acquiescence, constitute rape if the accused realised that the victim might lack the capacity to understand the nature of the act being performed. To obtain a conviction, the prosecution must establish that the victim had not sufficient knowledge or understanding to comprehend (a) that what was proposed to be done was the physical penetration of their body or, if that is not proved, (b) that the proposed act of penetration was one of sexual connection as distinct from an act of a totally different character: *R v Morgan* [1970] VR 337. The jury may see and hear the victim in order to determine this matter (see *R v Lambert* [1919] VLR 205) and, where appropriate, they may hear expert evidence as to the victim's mental condition.

3.38 Recall that in New South Wales, the Crimes Act 1900 s 61HA(4)(a) provides that a person does not consent to sexual intercourse if the person does not have the capacity to consent because of cognitive incapacity (see **3.12E**). In Victoria, the only reference to capacity to consent in the general definition of rape is the provision that there will be no 'free agreement' where the person is 'incapable of understanding the sexual nature of the act': Crimes Act 1958 s 36(e).

3.39 In addition, there exist statutory offences relating to engaging in sexual acts with persons of cognitive impairment: Crimes Act 1958 (Vic) ss 50–52; Crimes Act 1900 (NSW) ss 66F. Reforms have taken place in recent years aimed at recognising the autonomy of people with cognitive impairments to engage in sexual relationships, while protecting them from abuse from particular therapeutic or caring contexts. In Victoria, an offence is committed only where the accused provides medical or therapeutic services to the person concerned, or where the accused is a worker and the victim a resident in a residential facility. In New South Wales, an offence is committed where the accused provides care to the victim at a facility that treats persons with cognitive impairment or at the home of the victim in the course of a care program. The care of a person with a cognitive impairment includes 'voluntary care, health professional care, education, home care and supervision' (s 66F(1)). In these circumstances, consent is not a defence for sexual intercourse or acts of indecency with a person who has a cognitive impairment (s 66F(5)–(6)). However, it is a defence if the accused did not know the victim had a cognitive impairment or was married to the person or a de facto partner of the person with a cognitive impairment, or carried out the act for a proper medical or hygienic purpose (s 66F(7)).

Indecent assault

3.40 Indecent assault exists as a form of aggravated assault in each jurisdiction: Crimes Act 1958 (Vic) s 39; Crimes Act 1900 (NSW) ss 61L–61O.

3.41 To constitute an indecent assault, there must first be an assault (*Fitzgerald v Kennard* (1995) 38 NSWLR 184). Mere inactivity on the part of the accused cannot constitute an assault. Thus, where the accused invited a child to touch his penis (*Fairclough v Whipp* (1951) 35 Cr App R 138) or to masturbate him (*Director of Public Prosecutions v Rogers* [1953] 2 All ER 644), an indecent assault was not committed. In such cases, the accused could, however, be convicted of being a party to an act of indecency with a young person: see 3.33. See also *R v Speck* [1977] 2 All ER 859, where a man did not move a child's hand that the child voluntary placed on his penis, outside his trousers, while sitting in his lap, and left it there for about five minutes while the man had an erection.

If, however, the accused physically interferes with a child who is too young to give an effective consent (as opposed to allowing or encouraging the child to interfere with the accused), then an indecent assault is committed notwithstanding that the child acquiesces in the actions of the accused. Therefore, where the accused takes the penis of a young boy in her or his hand (*Faulkner v Talbot* [1981] 3 All ER 468), an indecent assault is committed notwithstanding the child's willingness for the accused to act in this way. The test for determining whether a child is capable of giving an effective consent is whether the child understands the nature and character of the act being performed. See, generally, M Goode, 'The Politics of Child Sexual Abuse and the Role of the Criminal Law' (1989) 13 *Crim LJ* 31; R K Oates, 'The Effects of Child Sexual Abuse' (1992) 66 *ALJ* 186.

3.42 Where the object of the actions of the accused is capable of consenting and does consent, then, provided no actual bodily harm is inflicted, no assault and hence no indecent assault is committed, however reprehensible the conduct of the accused might be thought to be. In the case of acts performed with young persons who are capable of giving an effective consent and who in fact consent, the accused may, however, be guilty of statutory rape if penetration is effected or, if not, of being a party to an act of indecency with a young person: see 3.30–3.36.

3.43 Even a child may give an effective consent to acts which are not themselves indecent, and such consent will prevent an assault, and hence an indecent assault, from being committed. In *R v Sutton* [1977] 3 All ER 476, the accused was the coach and manager of a boy's football club. He took three boys, who were aged 11 to 12 and who played for the club, to his home for the purpose of photographing them and selling the photographs to magazines. The boys were photographed partly unclothed or in the nude, and the photographs were so taken as to draw attention to their genitals. The boys all consented to so posing. The accused remained fully clothed throughout and did not invite any of the boys to touch him; nor did he touch any of the boys except on the arms, legs or torso, and then only for the purpose of indicating how he wished them to pose. The Court of Appeal held that, in these circumstances, the accused was not guilty of indecent assault. Since the touching of the boys was not itself indecent, their consent operated to prevent it being an assault and, therefore, an indecent assault. The court added that, in a case such as this, the correct course is to prosecute not for indecent assault, but for the offence of being a party to an act of indecency with a young person: see 3.33.

3.44 Assuming there is an assault, what renders it an indecent one? What must be shown is an assault which is accompanied by circumstances of indecency on the part of the accused towards the person assaulted. It is not necessary that the acts constituting the assault itself should be of an indecent kind. Therefore, in *R v Leeson* (1968) 52 Cr App R 185 it was held that to kiss a girl against her will, and to accompany the kiss by indecent suggestions, was an indecent assault notwithstanding that there was nothing indecent in the kiss itself. See also *R v Pratt* [1984] Crim LR 41; cf *R v Thomas* [1985] Crim LR 677. In *R v Salmon* [1969] SASR 76, the accused, in answer to a charge of rape, claimed that intercourse had commenced with the consent of the prosecutrix, that during the intercourse she screamed, and that he then hit her twice while continuing with the sexual act. The court held that, in these circumstances, the accused was properly convicted of indecent assault notwithstanding that the blows were not themselves indecent. The accused must have intended an act that was indecent, and this will usually mean an act that has obviously sexual connotations: *R v Court* [1989] AC 28 at 42–3. The test for indecency is the ordinary standards of morality of 'respectable people' within the community rather than simply the standards of an 'ordinary person': *R v Harkin* (1989) 38 A Crim R 296.

Sodomy and bestiality

3.45 Buggery, formerly described in the Crimes Act 1958 (Vic) s 68 as the 'abominable crime', is the penetration by the penis of the anus of a man, woman or animal. If committed with a human being it is also known as sodomy, and when committed with an animal is also known as bestiality. Sir Edward Coke spoke of it as the 'crime which is not to be named among Christians' (3 *Co Inst* 58, 59) and in many of the older writings it is referred to as a 'crime against nature': 4 *Bl Comm* 216.

3.46 Values and attitudes have changed greatly since Coke's time. Sodomy between consenting adults in private has been abolished as a crime: Crimes (Sexual Offences) Act 1980 (Vic) s 5; Crimes (Amendment) Act 1984 (NSW). Bestiality, however, continues to be a crime in each jurisdiction: Crimes Act 1958 (Vic) s 59; Crimes Act 1900 (NSW) ss 79–80.

Incest

3.47 It was not until the early twentieth century that incest became a crime: see, generally, V Bailey and S Blackburn, 'The Punishment of Incest Act 1908: A Case Study of Law Creation' [1979] *Crim LR* 708. In New South Wales, the offence was created as late as 1924. Cases in which parents and other relations exploit young people are, of course, covered by other offences: see **3.30–3.36**. The risk of such exploitation therefore does not constitute a valid argument for rendering incest a crime. The two arguments traditionally urged in favour of retaining incest as a separate crime are, first, the danger incest poses to the family unit, and, second, the eugenic argument that incest intensifies the risk of defective recessive traits being passed on to the children. Based on these reasons, however dubious, incest remains a crime: Crimes Act 1900 (NSW) ss 78A–78B; Crimes Act 1958 (Vic) s 44.

3.48 In New South Wales, the offence covers 'close family members', which is defined as a parent, son, daughter, sibling (including a half-brother or half-sister), grandparent or grandchild, being such a family member from birth.

3.49 In Victoria, the offence covers acts of sexual penetration performed with children and other lineal descendants as well as step-children, parents and other lineal ancestors including step-parents, siblings and half-siblings. Illegitimate as well as legitimate relationships are covered. For the purpose of the offence, an adopted child's relationship with his or her adoptive parents is treated in the same way as the child's relationship with his or her natural parents: Adoption Act 1984 (Vic) s 53.

Offences associated with prostitution

3.50 Prostitution per se is not a criminal offence in any of the Australian jurisdictions. However, a number of activities associated with prostitution are. In Victoria, the majority of these offences are contained in the Sex Work Act 1994 (Vic), and include inducing a child to take part in sex work (s 5), forcing a person into or to remain in sex work (s 8), forcing a person to provide financial support out of sex work (s 9), living on the earnings of sex work (s 10), allowing a child to take part in sex work (s 11), street sex work (offences by clients) (s 12), street sex work (offences by prostitutes) (s 13) and particular forms of advertising sex work services (s 17).

In New South Wales, the majority of offences are contained in the Summary Offences Act 1988 (NSW) and include living on the earnings of prostitution (s 15), causing or inducing prostitution (s 15A), prostitution or soliciting in massage parlours (s 16), allowing premises to be used for prostitution (s 17), advertising premises for prostitution (s 18), advertising for prostitutes (s 18A), soliciting clients by prostitutes (s 19) (note *Coleman v Director of Public Prosecutions* (2000) 49 NSWLR 371), soliciting prostitutions by clients (s 19A) and public acts of prostitution (s 20).

In New South Wales and Victoria, there are offences dealing with child prostitution, child pornography and related offences: Crimes Act 1900 (NSW) ss 91C–91H; Crimes Act 1958 (Vic) ss 67A–70AC.

3.51 In Victoria, sex work is a regulated occupation: Sex Work Act 1994 (Vic). Sex work service providers, meaning people who carry on the business of brothels and escort agencies providing sexual services, are required to be licensed, with exemption for small owner-operated businesses: ss 22, 23. It is an offence to carry on business as a sex work service provider without a licence or exemption. The Business Licensing Authority, within Consumer Affairs Victoria, determines licence applications and monitors the operation of sex work service providers. Brothels are also subject to planning controls.

Abduction

3.52 In Victoria, there are crimes specifically relating to the abduction of persons or children for the purposes of possible marriage or of sexual intercourse (Crimes Act 1958 (Vic) ss 55–56), in addition to the general offences of child stealing and kidnapping: Crimes Act 1958 (Vic) ss 63, 63A. In New South Wales, the kidnapping and child abduction prohibitions are more general: Crimes Act 1900 (NSW) ss 86–87.

Sexual servitude

3.53 Each jurisdiction contains offences of sexual servitude: Crimes Act 1958 (Vic) ss 60AB–60AE; Crimes Act 1900 (NSW) ss 80B–80E. In Victoria, s 60AB of the Crimes Act 1958 (Vic) contains the offence of sexual servitude, which is committed by a person who by the use of force, a threat, unlawful detention, fraud or misrepresentation or a manifestly excessive debt causes another person to provide, or to continue providing, commercial sexual services. Section 60AD contains an offence of deceptive recruiting for commercial sexual services. Section 60AC and s 60AE respectively contain offences of aggravated sexual servitude and aggravated deceptive recruiting for commercial sexual services where the person concerned is under the age of 18 years. In New South Wales, the provisions have similar effect. Section 80D of the Crimes Act 1900 (NSW) contains the offence of knowingly or recklessly causing sexual servitude, and s 80E contains the offence of knowingly or recklessly conducting a business that involves the sexual servitude of another person. 'Sexual servitude' is defined by s 80B as the condition of a person who provides sexual services and who, because of the use of force or threats (a) is not free to cease providing sexual services, or (b) is not free to leave the place or area where the person provides sexual services.

3.54 The Criminal Code Act 1995 (Cth) also contains a detailed scheme of offences regarding slavery and human trafficking: Div 270 — Slavery and Slavery-like Conditions; and Div 271 — Trafficking in Persons and Debt Bondage. The offences cover both sexual and non-sexual slavery and trafficking. The provisions of Div 270 were considered by the High Court of Australia in *R v Tang* (2008) 249 ALR 200, extracted below. See further, J Joudo Larsen et al, *Trafficking in Persons Monitoring Report: January 2009–June 2011*, Australian Institute of Criminology, Canberra, June 2012.

3.55C

R v Tang

(2008) 249 ALR 200
High Court of Australia

[The accused was charged on five counts of possessing a slave contrary to s 270.3(1)(a) of the Criminal Code Act 1995 (Cth) (the Code) and five counts of using a slave contrary to the same provision. The prosecution alleged that, at various times, the accused possessed as slaves five women of Thai nationality who came to Australia pursuant to agreements entered in Thailand for them to work as prostitutes in the sex industry in Australia. Each of the women voluntarily entered an agreement, through a broker, whereby she incurred a substantial debt which she was required to pay off by having sex with men in Australia. The accused was convicted on all counts and sentenced to a total effective sentence of 10 years' imprisonment with a single non-parole period of six years. The accused appealed to the Court of Appeal (Vic) against conviction and sentence. The court allowed the appeal against conviction and ordered a re-trial. The Crown appealed to the High Court, and the accused cross-appealed against the order for re-trial.]

[Footnotes to the extract appear at the end of the extract.]

Gleeson CJ: ... The Court of Appeal quashed the respondent's convictions, and ordered a new trial, substantially upon a single ground of criticism of the primary judge's directions to the jury. The point on which the Court of Appeal differed from the primary judge comes down to a question of the application of the provisions of Ch 2 of the Code to charges of breaches of s 270.3(1)(a). Before turning to those provisions, it is convenient to set out what was said in the Court of Appeal by Eames JA, with whom Maxwell P and Buchanan JA agreed.

Eames JA described as 'the critical issue' one that 'concerns the character of the exercise of power by the accused over the victim.' He said that the prosecutor's argument and the trial judge's directions 'did not, in terms, [invite or] direct the jury to consider the subjective intention of the [respondent] — her state of mind — when dealing with the complainants.' This, he said, 'was a critical element of the offence that had to be established if the [respondent] was to be convicted.' The jurors, Eames JA held, 'were not alerted as to the relevance, when considering the question of intention, of the belief which the [respondent] may have held as to the basis on which she was dealing with each of the complainants.' What his Honour understood to be the relevance of that belief was made clear in his reasons. The primary judge had told the jury that, in order to convict, they had to find that the complainants were slaves in accordance with the statutory definition as he explained it to them, that the respondent knew the facts that brought the complainants within that definition (although not that she was aware of the legislation, or the legal definition of slavery) and that she intended to possess or use persons in the condition disclosed by those facts. (It may be noted that the elements of the offence as explained by the primary judge in his directions were somewhat similar to what the Trial Chamber in *Kunarac* identified as the *actus reus* and the *mens rea* for the crime of enslavement.)

Eames JA said that the critical element of the offence of possessing a slave, missing from the primary judge's directions, was '[the respondent's] *appreciation* of the character of her own actions' (emphasis added). He described the element as follows (references omitted):

> Fourthly, the accused must have possessed the worker in the intentional exercise of what constitutes a power attaching to a right of ownership, namely, the power of possession. For that to be the case the accused must be shown to have regarded the worker as though she was mere property, a thing, thereby intending to deal

> with her not as a human being who had free will and a right to liberty, but as though she was mere property. However harsh or oppressive her conduct was towards the worker it would not be sufficient for a conviction if, rather than having possessed the worker with the knowledge, intention, or in the belief that she was dealing with her as though she was mere property, the accused possessed her in the knowledge or belief that she was exercising some different right or entitlement to do so, falling short of what would amount to ownership, such as that of an employer, contractor, or manager.

In a footnote to his reasons on this point, Eames JA said that it was not necessary to prove that an offender knew that the power to possess or use property was an incident of the right of ownership. That is correct, but it is not easy to relate that to the concluding words of the paragraph just quoted, which seem to postulate, as exculpatory, a knowledge or belief that the offender was exercising some other right or entitlement. If it were not necessary to prove that the respondent knew what rights of ownership were, it would be curious if it were relevant to consider what she knew or believed about other rights or entitlements. One would have expected that a person could be convicted of the offence of possessing a slave without knowing, or caring, anything about possible alternative sources of rights or entitlements.

In a further footnote, Eames JA supported the above paragraph by references to ss 5.2(2) and 5.2(3) of the Code, which, he said, were both relevant. This is a matter to which it will be necessary to return.

Later, Eames JA said (in a passage that also is difficult to reconcile with the first of the footnotes mentioned above):

> What the judge omitted to state was that the Crown had to prove intention to exercise power over the slave in the knowledge or belief that the power that was being exercised was one attaching to ownership. That is, the power must have been intentionally exercised as an owner of property would exercise power over that property, acting in the knowledge or belief that the victim could be dealt with as no more than a chattel. It would not suffice for the power to have been exercised by the accused in the belief that she was dealing with the victim as her employee, albeit one in a subservient position and being grossly exploited.

These passages, notwithstanding the footnote, indicate that Eames JA had in mind that it was necessary for the prosecution to establish a certain state of knowledge or belief on the part of the respondent as to the source of the powers she was exercising, in addition to an intention to exercise those powers. They appear to require advertence by the respondent to the different capacities (owner or employer) by virtue of which she might have been able to exercise powers. This was made even clearer by the form of an answer which his Honour said should have been given to a question asked by the jury:

> You must be satisfied that the accused was intentionally exercising a power that an owner would have over property *and was doing so with the knowledge or in the belief that the complainant was no more than mere property.*

> If it is reasonably possible that the accused acted to possess or to use the complainant with the knowledge or in the belief that she was exercising her rights and entitlements as her employer or contractor and not in the belief that the complainant had no rights or free will, but was property, a thing, over whom she could exercise power as though she owned her then, however exploitative and unfair you may think her treatment of the complainant was, it would not constitute the offences of intentionally possessing or using a slave. [Emphasis added.]

This cannot be accepted. What the respondent knew or believed about her rights and entitlements as an employer or contractor, as distinct from rights of property, in the perhaps unlikely event that she knew or believed anything on that subject, was not something that the prosecutor had to establish or that the jury had to consider.

It seems likely that the Court of Appeal was, with good reason, concerned about a problem presented by s 270.3(1)(a), at least in a borderline case: how is a jury to distinguish between slavery, on the one hand, and harsh and exploitative conditions of labour, on the other? The answer to that, in a given case, may be found in the nature and extent of the powers exercised over a complainant. In particular, a capacity to deal with a complainant as a commodity, an object of sale and purchase, may be a powerful indication that a case falls on one side of the line. So also may the exercise of powers of control over movement which extend well beyond powers exercised even in the most exploitative of employment circumstances, and absence or extreme inadequacy of payment for services. The answer, however, is not to be found in the need for reflection by an accused person upon the source of the powers that are being exercised. Indeed, it is probably only in a rare case that there would be any evidence of such consideration.

It should also be noted that the concluding words of the definition of slavery in s 270.1 of the Code show that the existence of a contract between an alleged offender and a complainant is not inconsistent with the commission of an offence. The legislation, in terms, accepts that a condition of slavery may result from a contract. The above reasoning appears to construct a false dichotomy between employment and effective ownership, in addition to importing a requirement of rights analysis by the offender which is unnecessary.

Chapter 2 of the Code does not provide support for the Court of Appeal's reasoning. In the case of both of the offences alleged in relation to each complainant, the physical element of the offence was conduct, which is defined to include both an act and a state of affairs. It was not suggested by the Court of Appeal that recklessness, as the default element in relation to circumstances, had a role to play.[1] As Brennan J pointed out in *He Kaw Teh v The Queen*,[2] having something in possession is more easily seen as a state of affairs that exists because of what the person who has possession does in relation to the thing possessed. Both possessing a slave and using a slave are conduct, and the prosecution had to establish the existence of the conduct and *one* of the fault elements specified in s 5.1(1). The prosecution case was conducted on the basis that the relevant fault element was intention. In a footnote earlier mentioned, Eames JA said that all of sub-ss (1), (2) and (3) of s 5.2 were relevant. This is not easy to understand: sub-s (1) applies where the physical element is conduct; sub-s (2) applies where the physical element is a circumstance; sub-s (3) applies where the physical element is a result. Section 4.1 says a physical element may be conduct *or* a result of conduct *or* a circumstance in which conduct or a result of conduct occurs.

The physical element was conduct (which includes a state of affairs); the fault element was intention. It was, therefore, s 5.2(1) that was relevant. A person has intention with respect to conduct if he or she means to engage in that conduct. Knowledge or belief is often relevant to intention.[3] If, for example, it is the existence of a state of affairs that gives an act its criminal character, then proof of knowledge of that state of affairs ordinarily will be the best method of proving that an accused meant to engage in the proscribed conduct.

The terms of s 270.3(1) reinforce the conclusion that intention is the relevant fault element. The offences in question were of intentionally possessing a slave or intentionally exercising over a slave another power (here, using) attaching to the right of ownership. It is agreed on all sides that it was unnecessary for the prosecution to prove that the respondent knew or believed that the complainant was a slave, or even that she knew what a slave was. Thus, Eames JA said that the respondent 'does not have to have known the definition of a slave, nor even that there was an offence of slavery'. So much is uncontroversial. If a person is known by an accused to possess the qualities that, by virtue of s 270.1, go to make that person a slave, then the state of knowledge relevant to intention, and therefore intention itself, may be established regardless of whether the accused appreciates the legal significance of those qualities. An accused does not have to know anything about the law in order to contravene s 270.3(1)(a).

Insofar as a state of knowledge or belief is factually relevant to intention as the fault element of the offence, it is knowledge or belief about the facts relevant to possession or using, and knowledge or belief about the facts which determine the existence of the condition described in s 270.1. This is a condition that results from the exercise of certain powers. Whether the powers that are exercised over a person are 'any or all of the powers attaching to the right of ownership' is for a jury to decide in the light of a judge's directions as to the nature and extent of the powers that are capable of satisfying that description. This is not to ignore the word 'intentionally' in s 270.3(1). Rather, it involves no more than the common exercise of relating the fault element to the physical elements of the offence.[4]

In this case, the critical powers the exercise of which was disclosed (or the exercise of which a jury reasonably might find disclosed) by the evidence were the power to make the complainants an object of purchase, the capacity, for the duration of the contracts, to use the complainants and their labour in a substantially unrestricted manner, the power to control and restrict their movements, and the power to use their services without commensurate compensation. As to the last three powers, their extent, as well as their nature, was relevant. As to the first, it was capable of being regarded by a jury as the key to an understanding of the condition of the complainants. The evidence could be understood as showing that they had been bought and paid for, and that their commodification explained the conditions of control and exploitation under which they were living and working.

It was not necessary for the prosecution to establish that the respondent had any knowledge or belief concerning the source of the powers exercised over the complainants, although it is interesting to note that, in deciding to order a new trial, the Court of Appeal evidently took the view that the evidence was capable of satisfying a jury, beyond reasonable doubt, of the existence of the knowledge or belief that the Court of Appeal considered necessary.

The ground on which the Court of Appeal regarded the primary judge's directions as inadequate has not been sustained.

[**Hayne J** delivered a separate judgment agreeing with **Gleeson CJ**. **Gummow, Heydon, Crennan** and **Kiefel JJ** concurred. **Kirby J** dissented. Appeal allowed and conviction restored. Matter remitted to Court of Appeal for consideration of application for leave to appeal against sentence.]

Notes:

* Case No IT-96-23 & It-96-23/1-A, 12 June 2002.

1. Cf *R v Saengsai-Or* (2004) 61 NSWLR 135.
2. (1985) 157 CLR 523 at 564; [1985] HCA 43.
3. *He Kaw Teh v The Queen* (1985) 157 CLR 523 at 570.
4. Cf *He Kaw Teh v The Queen* (1985) 157 CLR 523 at 568.

Murder

CHAPTER 4

SOME GENERAL PROPOSITIONS ABOUT CRIMINAL HOMICIDE

4.1 The institutional writers divide homicide, the killing of one person by another, into three categories: justifiable, excusable and felonious. Blackstone, as usual basing himself on Coke, wrote that '[t]he first has no share of guilt at all; the second very little; but the third is the highest crime against the law of nature, that a man is capable of committing': 4 *Bl Comm* 177–8. Excusable and justifiable homicides are those killings committed in necessary self-defence and similar situations: see 4.58 and Chapter 12. Felonious homicides, in Coke and Blackstone's taxonomies, comprised suicide (see 4.5), murder and manslaughter.

4.2 Sir Edward Coke (3 *Co Inst* 47) described murder as:

> … when a man of sound memory and of the age of discretion unlawfully kills any reasonable creature in being, and under the King's peace, with malice aforethought, either express or implied by the law, the death taking place within a year and a day.

The later institutional writers reiterated his description without any alteration, and it is accepted at the present day in those common law jurisdictions (Victoria and South Australia) where there has been no significant statutory intervention. In New South Wales, a partial definition of murder is contained in s 18 of the Crimes Act 1900: see 4.36.

Let us briefly examine the elements in Coke's description. With the exception of 'malice aforethought', they are all applicable to *both* murder and manslaughter.

'Of sound memory and of the age of discretion'

4.3 Only a person of sound memory and the age of discretion can be guilty of murder. 'Sound memory' merely means 'sane' or 'not mentally impaired'. Questions of mental impairment and related defences, such as diminished responsibility or substantial impairment by abnormality of mind, are considered in Chapter 14. Reference to the 'age of discretion' means the age at which a child can be held criminally responsible, which is briefly discussed at 1.37.

'Unlawfully'

4.4 A person can only be liable for murder where the killing was unlawful. The old common law distinguished two forms of lawful homicide — justifiable and excusable. Justifiable homicide was regarded as springing from the killer's right or duty to kill in the situation in which that person was placed, and resulted in a complete acquittal of all wrongdoing. Excusable homicide was regarded as morally blameworthy, but not deserving of criminal punishment; the killer's goods were, however, forfeited to the Crown. The practice of forfeiture has long since been abolished, and some argue that there is no longer any significance to the distinction between the two forms of lawful homicide. These matters are examined extensively in **Chapter 12**.

Suicide

4.5 The common law regarded a person who committed suicide as a self-murderer or *felo de se* (felon against himself). Anyone who instigated or aided him or her to commit suicide was guilty of murder as an accomplice; this included the survivor of a suicide pact. A person who unsuccessfully attempted to commit suicide was guilty of a crime of attempt.

In the Criminal Codes of Queensland (s 311), Western Australia (s 288) and Tasmania (s 163), suicide is not treated as a form of murder, but there are specific crimes created of aiding or instigating the suicide of another.

Victoria and New South Wales have now enacted provisions similar to those of the Suicide Act 1961 (Eng): see Crimes Act 1958 (Vic) s 6A; Crimes Act 1900 (NSW) s 31A. Suicide and attempted suicide are therefore no longer criminal offences. It is an offence, however, for a person to incite, counsel, aid or abet another to commit suicide or attempt to commit suicide: Crimes Act 1958 (Vic) s 6B(2); Crimes Act 1900 (NSW) s 31C. Provision is made for a lower maximum sentence if such acts were performed pursuant to a suicide pact: Crimes Act 1958 (Vic) s 6B(1); Crimes Act 1900 (NSW) s 31B. The survivor of a suicide pact is to be found guilty of manslaughter rather than murder. A defendant cannot rely on a mistaken belief that such a pact was concluded with the victim: see the decision of the Full Court of the Supreme Court of Victoria in *R v Jannazzone* [1983] 1 VR 649. The legal burden of proving the existence of a suicide pact is placed on the accused: see the ruling of Kaye J in *R v Sciretta* [1977] VR 139. These provisions are very much in point in current debates on 'active' as opposed to 'passive' euthanasia measures.

The statutes provide a justification for any person who uses force that is reasonably necessary to prevent a suicide or for what is reasonably believed to be a suicide: Crimes Act 1958 (Vic) s 463B; Crimes Act 1900 (NSW) s 574B. Victoria's pioneering Medical Treatment Act 1988 (amended in 1990 and 1992) permits competent adults to make refusal of treatment decisions, and to empower an agent or agents to make them when they cease to be competent. The legislation expressly preserves the operation of ss 6B(2) and 463B of the Crimes Act 1958 (Vic).

Euthanasia — assisting certain suicides

4.6 In 1995, the Northern Territory enacted the Rights of the Terminally Ill Act, which provided for a patient who was terminally ill, and who was experiencing pain, suffering and/or distress to an extent that patient found unacceptable, to ask that patient's doctor to help to end her or his life. A terminal illness was defined as one which will, in the course of normal medical treatment, 'without the application of extra ordinary measures or of treatment unacceptable to the patient result in death of the patient'. The legislation thus provided for medically-assisted suicide in specified circumstances, which not only confined its lawful availability to the terminally ill, but also further restricted its lawful availability in order to avoid abuse. The Act provided, in s 16, that any action taken by a doctor in accordance with its provisions could not be counted as homicide of, or any level of assault against, the patient who died as a result, but was taken to be medical treatment.

The legislation came into operation in July 1996, but its lifespan was quickly curtailed. The Federal Parliament, exercising its constitutional power to 'make laws for the government of any territory surrendered by any State', enacted the Euthanasia Laws Act 1997 (Cth) which came into effect on 25 March 1997. That Act, in effect, abrogated the Northern Territory statute. During its brief existence, four persons were helped to die under its provisions. In 2008 the Rights of the Terminally Ill (Euthanasia Laws Repeal) Bill was introduced by Senator Bob Brown into the Federal Parliament. This bill, which was not passed, was designed to repeal the Euthanasia Laws Act 1997 and reinstate the Rights of the Terminally Ill Act 1997 (Cth). Other Australian jurisdictions have also debated bills to legalise active voluntarily euthanasia. However, to date no such bills have been enacted, and active voluntary euthanasia remains illegal throughout Australia.

Given that surveys over the last two decades show that around three-quarters of Australians support the concept of active voluntary euthanasia (as noted by Senator Bob Brown in his Second Reading speech on the Rights of the Terminally Ill (Euthanasia Laws Repeal) Bill 2008), it is no surprise that there continues to be much debate in Australia about the legalisation of active voluntary euthanasia. This is a controversial issue, because the contention that adult autonomy should prevail where the patient perceives her or his life as not worth living is met by the contention that doctors should never kill their patients, but should strive to alleviate or palliate their suffering. There is also the more general argument about the impact such a legislative measure may have on the community's respect for the sanctity of human life.

The organised medical profession, as represented by the Australian Medical Association, publicly expressed its strong opposition to the Northern Territory legislation. There is a fine line between, on the one hand, pain alleviation and palliation, even though these may accelerate or advance the death of a patient, and, on the other hand, actively causing death. Nevertheless the courts have distinguished between killing or assisting to kill someone who is near the end of life and not continuing, or not beginning, certain procedures as a result of which decisions death will ensue: see the House of Lords in the now famous case of *Airedale NHS Trust v Bland* [1993]

AC 789 (discussed at 6.17, note 3) in connection with manslaughter by omission to act. The provisions on palliative care in the Victorian statute were carefully reviewed in *Gardner; Re BWV* [2003] VSC 173 by Morris J. His interpretation of the language of the Act of 1988 is in line with the reasoning of the House of Lords in *Bland.* See A Rothschild, '*Gardner; Re BWV:* Resolved and Unresolved Issues at End of Life' (2004) 11 *Jo Law Med* 292.

It is safe to predict that there will be further legislative, and judicial, episodes in the development of the law on euthanasia.

Infanticide

4.7 The offence (or in some instances partial defence) of infanticide is discussed at 5.3.

ACTUS REUS

4.8 The actus reus (physical elements) of murder and manslaughter are the same. They are that a person kills. 'Kills' means that a person causes the death of a person.

'Kills'

4.9 In many cases of homicide, D's responsibility for killing V is so obvious that it is taken for granted. However, in some cases the collocation of circumstances, or the several contributions of persons involved in an incident or series of incidents in which someone dies, do raise problems in determining whether an accused, or several accused, has or have killed the victim. The several cases which are reproduced (see 4.28C–4.31) illustrate these difficulties.

4.10 Before this issue is addressed, consider the rule that the behaviour of the accused which is in issue must be voluntary. Another way to express this is that the accused's act must be willed. An involuntary (or unwilled) act is one committed by a person whose actions have been committed independently of the exercise of their will. Most cases in which this issue is raised are today characterised as cases of automatism: see 14.6; and *R v Falconer* (1990) 171 CLR 30 (at 14.12C), an important decision of the High Court.

In two recent cases, the High Court of Australia has reinforced the fundamental rule, even where the defence of automatism is not raised: *Ugle v R* (2002) 211 CLR 171; *Murray v R* (2002) 211 CLR 193; 189 ALR 40: see 4.25C. These decisions follow *Ryan v R* (1967) 121 CLR 205. In all three cases, the accused claimed that the gun or knife he held was not voluntarily fired or wielded by him. In *Ryan's* case, Barwick CJ clearly stated that the prosecution must prove the accused voluntarily pulled the trigger, even though there was evidence he had presented the loaded gun in the course of robbery. However, Windeyer J warned against too specific an analysis of the act in question.

The appeal was dismissed. In the two recent cases, the High Court held that both trial judges had failed to direct juries adequately on this issue, and ordered new trials.

4.11 The common law did evolve one very simple rule of causation; the rule that a charge of criminal homicide will not lie unless the death occurred within a year and a day from the act whereby the accused inflicted the injury. The same rule was adopted by the Criminal Codes of Queensland (s 299) (now repealed), Tasmania (s 155) (now repealed) and Western Australia (s 276) (now repealed), and it presumably applied also to those types of criminal homicide which are the creation of modern statutes, for example, culpable driving causing death: see 6.19.

Coke, in his 3 *Co Inst* 53, gives as the reason for the rule the difficulty of determining the cause of death after a long lapse of time. It might be thought that the advances made by medical science in the centuries since Coke wrote would have led to the disappearance of the rule, but in *R v Dyson* [1908] 2 KB 454 the Court of Criminal Appeal declined to depart from it. A different stance was taken by the majority of the Supreme Court of Pennsylvania in *Commonwealth v Ladd* 166 A 2d 501 (1960) in holding that each case should be decided in light of the medical evidence, regardless of the time which had elapsed between the injury and the death. But Musmanno J vigorously dissented, expressing the view that it is too dangerous in cases of this kind to let the accused's fate rest in the hands of medical experts whose opinions may well be open to doubt. The Full Court of the Supreme Court of Victoria clearly accepted the rule as in force in Victoria in *R v Evans and Gardiner (No 2)* [1976] VR 523.

The rule has now been abolished by statute in Victoria and New South Wales, as elsewhere in Australia: Crimes (Injuries) Amendment Act 1990 (NSW), inserting a new s 17A into the Crimes Act 1900; Crimes (Year and a Day Rule) Act 1991 (Vic), inserting a new s 9AA. The justifications for this course are set out in the Law Reform Commission of Victoria's Report No 40, *Homicide* (1991), pp 119–21. The chief reason of principle is that it is unjust that a person who intentionally communicates a disease like AIDS, or who negligently creates a situation where another contracts asbestosis, should escape criminal responsibility for murder or manslaughter because the victim dies several years, or many years, after the injurious act is perpetrated. Any concerns about very long passages of time 'can be dealt with by prosecutorial discretion, the power of the court to prevent abuse of process, or by adjustments to length of sentence': p 120.

'Any reasonable creature in being'

4.12 The word 'reasonable' here means 'human'. See, on this, L Waller, 'Any Reasonable Creature in Being' (1987) 13 *Mon LR* 37 at 54–5.

4.13 It is well settled that a child *en ventre sa mere* (in the womb) is not 'in being'. For practical purposes, however, a test must be provided to use in borderline cases. In *R v Hutty* [1953] VLR 338 at 339, Barry J explained the test by saying that:

> Legally a person is not in being until he or she is fully born in a living state. A baby is fully and completely born when it is completely delivered from the body of its mother and it has a separate and independent existence in the sense that it does not derive its power of living from its mother. It is not material that the child may still be attached to the mother by the umbilical cord; that does not prevent it from having a separate existence. But it is required … that the child should have an existence separate from and independent of its mother, and that occurs when the child is fully extruded from its mother's body and is living by virtue of the functioning of its own organs.

In the older cases, the fact of independent existence was usually proved by calling evidence that after fully emerging from the body of the mother, the baby had breathed, coughed or sneezed. Such evidence would still be sufficient but, even if it is not available, evidence of a medical examination after death may be given to show that the child had had an independent existence, however brief. Once a baby is born alive it is capable of being the victim of murder or manslaughter, even if it is too weak to survive: *R v West* [1848] ER 78; *R v Iby* [2005] NSWCCA 178.

Statutory definitions to the same effect have been provided by the Criminal Codes of Queensland, Western Australia and Tasmania. In New South Wales, s 20 of the Crimes Act 1900 provides an identical statutory definition, applicable only, however, to trials for the murder of a child.

4.14 If a child is injured whilst in the womb or during the course of birth, and is born alive but thereafter dies of the injuries received, homicide has been committed, and, in appropriate circumstances, the person who caused the injuries may be convicted in the same manner as if the injury had been inflicted on a living child: see *R v West* (1848) 2 Cox CC 500. Further examples of the application of this approach are *Kwok Ming v R (No 1)* [1963] HKLR 349 (manslaughter), and *McCluskey v HM Advocate* 1989 SLT 175 (causing death by reckless driving).

One of the more recent considerations of the matter has been by the House of Lords in *Attorney-General's Reference (No 3 of 1994)* [1998] AC 245. In that case, D stabbed his girlfriend V, who was, as he knew, about 23 weeks pregnant with their child W. V recovered well from her wound, but gave birth prematurely to W, who died four months later. D was acquitted of W's murder when the trial judge accepted the submission of D's counsel that, on the facts, D could not be found guilty of murder or the manslaughter of the baby. The judge had previously held that on the evidence the jury could conclude that D had caused W's death. The Court of Appeal held that D could be criminally responsible for the murder or manslaughter of W. If D intended to kill or cause grievous bodily harm to V when he stabbed her then the doctrine of transferred malice (discussed at **4.38**) operated to make him guilty of the murder of W, it being proved that he had killed her. There was no legal requirement that the victim W had to be a person in being when the act which caused her death was perpetrated. She was, of course, in being when she died: see [1996] QB 581; and see further, *Martin* (1995) 85 A Crim R 587, on appeal in *Martin (No 2)* (1996) 86 A Crim R 133, for Australian authority in support of this view.

Such was the significance of the issues that, at the request of D, a further reference to the House of Lords was authorised.

The House of Lords held that the mother and the foetus, W, were two distinct human organisms living symbiotically. W, the foetus, was neither a distinct person nor simply an adjunct to her mother. Accordingly, D could not be guilty of the murder of W; there was no evidence of an intention to kill or to injure the foetus, or the child who would be born. The doctrine of transferred malice was not applicable here. D could, however, be guilty of the manslaughter of W, on the basis that he committed an unlawful and dangerous act likely to cause injury to another. On public policy grounds, said the House of Lords, W could be regarded as that person: see 6.2.

It is difficult to understand why their Lordships condemned the doctrine of transferred malice, and yet they were prepared to conclude that D might be guilty of manslaughter on the basis of 'an act likely to cause injury to another'. It is suggested that an attack upon the foetus is an attack upon the mother and the foetus, and if the mother gives birth to a child who dies as a consequence of the attack then, if the mens rea of murder exists in relation to either, the crime of murder may be committed. The necessary connection between the two is illustrated by the decision of the New South Wales Court of Criminal Appeal in *R v King* [2003] NSWCCA 399. The defendant kicked and stomped on the stomach of V who had refused to have an abortion, she having become pregnant after a single act of intercourse with him. As a result, the foetus was delivered stillborn several days later. The defendant was charged, under s 33 of the Crimes Act 1900 (NSW), with 'maliciously … [inflicting] bodily harm to any person'. The defendant argued that the foetus, the victim of his attack, was not 'a person'. The court held that 'the foetus is part of the mother': at [97]. The court emphasised the close physical bond between the mother and the foetus. Accordingly, the mother was a person maliciously injured by the defendant.

Abortion

4.15 The old offence of abortion was committed if the mother, or another person, destroyed the foetus in the womb. In such cases, that person could be guilty of the offence of procuring an abortion; and if unsuccessful, of attempting to procure an abortion: Crimes Act 1958 (Vic) s 65 (now repealed and replaced); Crimes Act 1900 (NSW) ss 82–83. The law relating to abortion now differs between New South Wales and Victoria. This old law is still applicable in New South Wales. However, in Victoria the Crimes Act 1958 (Vic) s 65 has been repealed and replaced with a new statutory regime incorporating a new s 65, discussed below.

4.16 In New South Wales, the sections speak of 'unlawfully' administering, or causing to be taken, any noxious thing or 'unlawfully' using any instrument to cause a miscarriage. Hence acts done by medical practitioners for the purpose only of preserving the life or good health of the mother do not come within the ambit of the provisions; for such acts are not unlawfully done.

The landmark decision in Australia is the judgment of Menhennitt J in *R v Davidson* [1969] VR 667 (see **12.12C**). This was a ruling by a trial judge in which he reviewed the earlier law, drew heavily upon analogies from other branches of the criminal law, and concluded that the relevant questions to be considered in deciding the matter of unlawfulness are those of necessity and proportion. Specifically a person who performs a prohibited act upon a woman with intent to procure her miscarriage does so lawfully if that person honestly believes on reasonable grounds that the act was:

(a) necessary to preserve the woman from a serious danger to her life or her physical or mental health (not being merely the normal dangers of pregnancy and childbirth) which the continuance of the pregnancy would entail; and

(b) in the circumstances, not out of proportion to the danger to be averted.

It follows from this that the Crown can secure a conviction only if it proves beyond reasonable doubt that the accused did not hold one or other of these beliefs honestly and on reasonable grounds.

R v Davidson was followed by the New South Wales District Court in *R v Wald* (1971) 3 DCR (NSW) 25. In that case, Levine Ch QS extended the matters to be taken into account to include economic, social or medical grounds which could result in serious danger to the woman's physical or mental health.

The *Davidson* ruling has not come under the scrutiny of an appellate court. It cast a heavy burden of proof on the Crown, and accordingly acquittals are more likely to result than convictions, save in the case of 'backyard operators'.

4.17 It affords some protection to the properly-qualified doctor who directs his or her mind to the relevant matters (the different risks to the mother that are involved), considers them honestly, and reaches a decision. There is no issue as to whether that decision was 'right', in a sense of being one which a majority, even a large majority, of doctors would have made; the issue is solely whether it was honestly made on the basis of the relevant considerations. On the other hand, those who operate without possessing proper qualifications, or in unhygienic conditions, or using dangerous methods, are in serious danger of conviction, for they will find it hard to satisfy the requirement of proportion. See, for instance, *R v Salika* [1973] VR 272, where the defendant's conviction for murder, after the death of a woman upon whom he had operated unlawfully, was upheld by the Full Court.

4.18 There have been no effective prosecutions in either New South Wales or Victoria for nearly 30 years. Thousands of terminations have been performed over that period, yet still in New South Wales the law remained unamended on the statute book. In recent years there have been movements in various jurisdictions to reconceptualise abortion as a medical procedure regulated under health laws. For example, in the Northern Territory, abortion is regulated by s 11 of the Medical Services Act (NT). This legislation, passed in this form in 2006, allows a medical practitioner to terminate the pregnancy of a woman reasonably believed to have been pregnant for not more than 14 weeks, and in emergencies, not more than 23 weeks, if the termination is necessary to prevent serious harm occurring to the woman's physical or mental health.

4.19 In Victoria, the Abortion Law Reform Act 2008, foreshadowed by a report from the Victorian Law Reform Commission (Final Report No 15, *Law of Abortion* (2008)), has amended ss 65 and 66 of the Crimes Act 1958 and introduced a new statutory regime. Abortions no longer fall within the criminal law if carried out by medical practitioners. Abortions may be lawfully performed by registered medical practitioners upon a woman who is 'not more than 24 weeks pregnant': s 4. There are supplementary provisions authorising registered nurses and pharmacists to administer and supply appropriate drugs in such cases: s 6. Abortions may be performed on women who are more than 24 weeks pregnant where the doctor 'reasonably believes that the abortion is appropriate in all the circumstances', and has consulted one other doctor who is of the same belief: s 5. In considering the appropriateness of the post-24 week termination, s 5(2) states that the doctor:

> … must have regard to —
>
> (a) all relevant medical circumstances; and
> (b) the woman's current and future physical, psychological and social circumstances.

The performance of an abortion by an unqualified person remains a serious crime, carrying a maximum sentence of 10 years imprisonment: new s 65 of the Crimes Act 1958. The Abortion Law Reform Act 2008 provides that a doctor who has a conscientious objection to performing an abortion is not obliged to do so, except in an emergency situation: s 8. The doctor must, however, tell the woman of her or his belief, and must refer her to another doctor who does not share that belief: s 8(1)(b).

The legislation was the subject of a conscience vote. Members of the several political parties in both Houses were free to vote as they chose. Various provisions, particularly s 8(1)(b), aroused public controversy, but the legislation passed in both Houses with clear majorities. Its administration will allow some conclusions to be drawn about its real impact on the operation of this long-debated area of medical practice and the criminal law.

Child destruction

4.20 If a child is in the process of being born, but is not yet alive and separate from its mother, then to destroy it is neither abortion nor murder. A statutory offence of child destruction was introduced in Victoria to meet this contingency. Section 10 of the Crimes Act 1958 (Vic) provided as follows:

> Any person who, with intent to destroy the life of a child capable of being born alive, by any wilful act unlawfully causes such child to die before it has an existence independent of its mother, shall be guilty of an indictable offence, to wit of child destruction, and shall be liable on conviction thereof to be imprisoned for a term of not more than 20 years.

The Victorian offence of child destruction has now been repealed. Instead, the definition of 'serious injury' in s 15 of the Crimes Act 1958 (Vic) has been expanded to encompass the destruction of the foetus of a pregnant woman, other than in the course of a medical procedure and whether or not the woman suffers any other harm. New South Wales did not have an equivalent offence of child destruction, but similar to Victoria, the definition of 'grievous bodily harm' in s 4 Crimes Act 1900 (NSW) was amended to include the destruction of a foetus of a pregnant woman, other than in the course of a medical procedure and whether or not the woman suffers any other harm. Thus, in both jurisdictions where a person causes the death of an unborn foetus, whether or not it could have survived if it had been born at that time, they can be charged with a serious injury offence (Vic) or a grievous bodily harm offence (NSW).

Death

4.21 At the other extreme of the continuum of life and death is the obvious rule that a corpse cannot be the victim of a homicide. Until recently, it was thought that the end of life presented no problems of demarcation in the criminal law; death came clearly and distinctly. However, advances in medicine, especially in the field of resuscitation, have displaced this simple view. The dead have been brought back to life, in the sense that persons whose hearts have stopped beating and whose breathing has ceased, sometimes for a considerable period, have been revived. Furthermore there are people whose natural respiratory and cardiac functions have been assumed by machines. In some cases respiration and circulation have been maintained for long periods by these heart-lung machines, though it has been apparent to the doctors that all brain activity has ceased permanently. Can a body kept alive in this fashion be a victim of homicide? If yes, does the doctor who disconnects the machine bring life to an end and so commit murder of a reasonable creature in being? How may transplants of vital single organs such as hearts, livers or even complex systems such as hearts and lungs, be lawfully performed where these must be removed from brain-dead but breathing donors?

It used to be common for lawyers to say that the meaning of death was a medical matter, and that it was for doctors alone to determine when a person had died: see M Ewing and R H Fullagar, 'The Lore and Law of Tissue Homotransplantation', 10 *Proc Med-Leg Soc Vic* 161, 162 (1966). But now it has been recognised that a legal formula must be devised to be applied to the medical facts ascertained by doctors, as has been done for life. Section 41 of the Human Tissue Act 1982 (Vic) provides the following general definition of death:

> For the purposes of the law of Victoria, a person has died when there has occurred —
> (a) irreversible cessation of circulation of blood in the body of the person; or
> (b) irreversible cessation of all function of the brain of the person.

The same definition is contained in s 33 of the Human Tissue Act 1983 (NSW). Note that these definitions are not confined in operation to the transplantation legislation.

An extensive literature has developed on the subject of the meaning of death. See, in particular, P D G Skegg, 'Irreversible Comatose Individuals: "Alive" or "Dead"?' [1974] *Camb LJ* 130; Australian Law Reform Commission, Report No 7, *Human Tissue Transplants* (1977).

'Under the King's peace'

4.22 The concept of the King's (or, at present, the Queen's) peace extends to everyone within the territorial bounds of the relevant jurisdiction. Difficult problems may arise where the act or acts leading to death are performed in one state, but death in fact results in another. In such a case, which state law has jurisdiction to deal with the homicide?

This difficult problem has been resolved in various ways, by the legislation of the several states. In Victoria (Crimes Act 1958 s 9), there is jurisdiction if either the act of killing or the death occurs within the state. In New South Wales, there is now jurisdiction where there is 'a territorial nexus' between the state and the offence: s 10C of the Crimes Act 1900 (NSW), inserted by the Crimes (Application of Criminal Law) Amendment Act 1992. A geographical nexus exists if the whole or part of the offence is committed in the state, or the offence is committed outside the state but has an effect in the state.

Exceptionally, the question of what constitutes the boundaries of a state may give rise to difficulties. In *Ward v R* (1980) 29 ALR 175, the accused, standing at the top of a steep bank of the River Murray, on the Victorian side of the river, shot and killed the deceased who was fishing by the river's edge, some 30 feet below. The accused was tried and convicted of murder in the Supreme Court of Victoria. On appeal the High Court held that the Victorian court did not have jurisdiction, the killing having taken place in New South Wales. The court took the view that it is not where the physical act of the accused is performed, but where that act takes effect upon its victim which determines the locus of a homicide. The court held that the boundary of Victoria and New South Wales comprises a line drawn along the top of the south bank of the Murray, and, hence, that both the act of killing and the death had occurred in New South Wales. See also *R v Graham* [1984] VR 649.

'The death taking place within a year and a day'

4.23 The removal of this requirement has been considered at 4.9–4.11

Act and causation

4.24 For a case of murder or manslaughter it must be established that the accused's act (or omission, where the accused had a duty to act) caused the death of the victim. As *Ugle v R* illustrates, the act which causes death must be willed by the accused.

4.25C Ugle v R

(2002) 211 CLR 171; 189 ALR 22
High Court of Australia

[The appellant was tried for wilful murder in the Supreme Court of Western Australia. The deceased died from a knife wound to the chest. The appellant was holding the knife when the wound was sustained. The appellant claimed the deceased was attacking him with a cricket bat, and that he was trying to fend off the deceased at the time the deceased was stabbed. The appellant stated that he had been acting in self-defence and that he had not realised the deceased had been stabbed. Section 23 of the Criminal Code (WA) provides:

> Subject to the express provisions of this Code relating to negligent acts and omissions, a person is not criminally responsible for an act or omission which occurs independently of the exercise of his will, or for an event which occurs by accident.

The trial judge did not give the jury a direction about unwilled acts. The appellant was convicted of murder and appealed unsuccessfully to the Supreme Court of Western Australia. On appeal to the High Court.]

Gummow and **Hayne JJ**: ... It appears not to have been disputed in the Court of Criminal Appeal, or in this court, that in the present case the relevant 'event' against which the accident limb of s 23 had to be considered was the death of the deceased. There was, however, no issue raised at the trial about whether the consequences of the knife entering the body of the deceased were unlikely or unforeseen. That being so, the accident limb of s 23 was not engaged. What was in issue, however, was whether the insertion of the knife in the body of the deceased was a voluntary act — an act willed by the appellant. One view of the evidence that the jury might have taken was that the prosecution had not proved that it was. And that was a question for the jury, not a question to be decided by the judge. It follows that the jury should have been directed to consider this issue.

In this court, the respondent did not dispute that the jury should have been directed to consider whether the act of inserting the knife in the body of the deceased was an act willed by the appellant. It was submitted that, nonetheless, there had been no miscarriage of justice or, if there had been a miscarriage, the proviso to s 689(1) applied, no substantial miscarriage of justice having actually occurred.

As Parker J pointed out (in the Supreme Court of Western Australia), the trial judge told the jury, in effect, that if they were not persuaded beyond reasonable doubt that the appellant's version of events (that he 'did not use the knife as a weapon') was false, they should return a verdict of acquittal. This direction, however, did not cure the difficulty presented by there being no direction about whether the act of inserting the knife was an act that occurred independently of the exercise of the appellant's will.

Similarly, in the circumstances of this case, requiring the jury to consider what was the intention with which the 'fatal blow was struck' did not cure the difficulty. Lying behind both the question of use of the knife 'as a weapon', and the question of a fatal blow being 'struck', was the logically prior question whether the knife had entered the body of the deceased independently of the exercise of the will of the appellant. Did the appellant put the knife in the body of the deceased, or did the deceased impale himself on the knife the appellant was holding? Once it is recognised that the evidence at trial could have been understood by the jury as not proving the former beyond reasonable doubt, that was an issue to which the jury's attention should have been, but was not, directed. Both the direction about using the knife as a weapon and the direction about the intention with which the fatal blow was struck assumed that the act had been done in the exercise of the appellant's will.

[**Gaudron, Kirby** and **Callinan JJ** each delivered separate judgments holding that the jury should have been directed regarding unwilled acts. Appeal allowed and a new trial ordered.]

[See also *Murray v R* (2002) 211 CLR 193; 189 ALR 40, heard immediately after *Ugle's* case. In *Murray*, **Gaudron J** said (at ALR 44–5):

> The question whether a reflex or automatic motor action is an involuntary or unwilled act is a question for the jury. … [T]here is much to be said for the view expressed by Windeyer J in Ryan (1967) that the pressing of a trigger in response to a sudden threat or apprehension of danger is a probable and foreseeable consequence of presenting a loaded gun and a jury might, on that account, find it to be a voluntary act.]

4.26 Notes

Although *Ugle v R* was a case decided under the Western Australia Criminal Code, it is equally a requirement at common law that the death of the deceased be caused by a willed act or omission on the part of the accused. In determining issues of causation, below, it is necessary to determine what the relevant willed act or omission which is said to have caused the death of the deceased is. The nature of a willed act is considered further in relation to the defence of automatism in **Chapter 14**.

4.27 It is well established that there are two steps to determining whether the act (or omission where there is a duty to act) of the accused caused the death of the victim. First, factual causation (or causal connection) must be established using the 'but for' test. This asks whether the victim would be dead but for the behaviour of the accused. If the victim would not be dead but for the act or omission of the accused then he or she is a factual cause of death: *Royall v R* (1991) 172 CLR 378; 100 ALR 669 per McHugh J at [99]. This can be a very wide test, and therefore the second stage is to determine legal causation (or causal responsibility). This requires a judgment to be made about whether the 'but for' act or omission of the accused was 'causally responsible' for death. Various tests have been developed through case law to help determine whether the accused is legally responsible for the death of the victim (see cases below). It is also possible that a causal link could be established but other events may occur which might break the chain of causation. In such instances it must be determined whether the causal chain has been broken by a new intervening act (novus actus interveniens), such as a natural event (*R v Hallett* [1969] SASR 141); actions of the accused trying to escape (*RIK* [2004] NSWCCA 282; *Royall v R* (1991) 172 CLR 378); lack of care on the part of the accused (*R v Bingapore* (1975) 11 SASR 469); actions of a third party (*R v Pagett* (1983) Cr App R 279); or medical treatment (*R v Blaue* [1975] 1 WLR 1411).

4.28C R v Hallett

[1969] SASR 141
Supreme Court of South Australia

[The appellant was convicted of the murder of Whiting. It was common ground that the appellant had beaten Whiting unconscious, and left him in that condition on the beach; the pathologist's conclusion was that he drowned in shallow water. The appellant argued that he did not drown Whiting and, therefore, did not cause his death. He had hit Whiting because he made homosexual advances to him; both had been drinking.

Whiting's body was discovered buried in the sand. His penis and testicles had been removed, and his small intestine extracted from a wound in his abdomen. These injuries had been inflicted after death. The appellant stated that he left Whiting near the water's edge.]

Bray CJ, **Bright** and **Mitchell JJ**: If the evidence of Dr Dwyer is accepted, and Mr Elliott did not challenge it, the deceased died from drowning. On the story just related the appellant did not drown him directly but left him as he thought in a position of apparent safety while he was lying on the beach with his ankles in a few inches of water. If the jury accepted that story or had a reasonable doubt about it and also accepted the evidence of Dr Dwyer, could they have found that the appellant caused the death of the deceased?

The learned judge told the jury that it was enough on the question of causation if the accused was the substantial cause of Whiting's death. It is desirable we think to quote some extracts from the summing up on this topic which was lengthy.

> But what in law is the position where a n accused person inflicts injury on a man and afterwards some other act or event intervenes before his death? I raise this because on the account of the accused he left Whiting unconscious, but moving, his limbs moving, lying on his back, with his feet in the water, his body at an angle to the water's edge, and his head and the upper part of the body, or the body itself, and the upper part of his lower limbs as I understand it, out of the water. This type of thing has been considered, and I am now basing my remarks on Smith and Hogan, *Criminal Law* (1st ed, 1965) p 172.

His Honour for reasons which he gives slightly adapted the language of the learned authors. He then quoted from them as follows:

> The victim dies as the result of some act or event which would not have occurred but for the infliction of the injury by the accused. This can be a more difficult case and you have got to distinguish between different situations. First you have cases

> where death from the subsequent act or event was the natural consequence of the act of the accused. That is, it was foreseeable as likely to occur in the normal course of events. Here the accused may be held to have caused the death. On the other hand, cases may occur where death from the act or event was not the natural consequence of the accused's act; and here the accused is not to be held liable for homicide ... If one man knocks down another and goes away, leaving his victim unconscious on the floor of a building in which the assault occurred, and before the victim recovers consciousness he is killed in the fall of the building which is shaken down by a sudden earthquake, this is not homicide. The law attributes such a death to the act of God and not to the assault. *[Then his Honour explained the meaning of the phrase 'act of God'.]* The law attributes such a death to the act of God and not to the assault, even if it may be certain that the deceased would not have been in the building at the time of the earthquake had he not been rendered unconscious. The blow was the reason that the man was there, but the blow was not the cause of the earthquake nor was the deceased left in the position of obvious danger. On the other hand, if the blow had been struck on the seashore, and the assailant had left his victim in imminent peril of an incoming tide which drowned him before consciousness returned, it would be homicide ...
>
> The victim's being drowned in the latter example was a natural consequence of the action of the accused. That is, a consequence which might be expected to occur in the normal course of events. The victim's being killed by the falling building in the former example was an abnormal and unforeseeable consequence.

His Honour told the jury that the statement from Smith and Hogan was a correct statement of the law.

His Honour then proceeded as quoted hereunder. The passage is a long one, but we think it advisable to set it out in full since Mr Elliott complained, as we understand him, both that the direction was erroneous in law and that it was not properly related to the facts of the case. The witness Stewart referred to is a hydrographic surveyor who gave evidence about the state of the tides:

> Now one of the examples is getting close, remarkably close, to the facts of this case, and that is the example of a man being struck on the seashore and the assailant leaving his victim in imminent peril of an incoming tide. Now here I draw your attention to what Mr Elliott has said about the nature of the tide. He said in effect that it was not an incoming tide, and that the evidence of Stewart proves this. We have Dr Dwyer's evidence, which I think is accepted by both sides, to the effect that Whiting died from drowning, and what is more, died from drowning in shallow water. This was the sand in the trachea. And he said that it might have been drowning in only a few inches of water. Of course it is a question for you, if that is what happened. What has to be proved is how he came to be in the position to be drowned like that. The injuries to the head could have resulted in his losing unconsciousness. Similarly, choking. It is for you to say, but whichever it was, the condition must have resulted, I think you will agree, from force applied by the accused.

The accused has given two accounts — that to Detective Thomas, and that before the court — which suggests that he choked the deceased into a state of unconsciousness. Now if you believe that, it still does not necessarily follow that you will find it proved that he has been shown in law to have caused the death by drowning. The accused suggests that the deceased may have committed suicide. He may have come to after having been rendered unconscious, and he may have gone out and drowned himself. The accused points to the fact, on his statement both prior to coming to court and in court, that the deceased did run out into the sea, and that he went out, in effect, to save him. You must ask yourself is it really a possible view, in view of the injuries described by Dr Dwyer? And is it likely in view of the evidence of the death having taken place in shallow water? I think you will probably come to the conclusion, although it is for you to say, that if the deceased had wanted to drown himself, he would have done what the accused described in the first instance; that is to say, go out to the deeper water; and not just put his face into a few inches of water, breathing in sand with the water. However, that is for you to say.

On the account given by the accused, I suggest that it is more probable either that the tide came in, or that the deceased rolled down the slope, or that both happened. We do know this, that if we accept as reasonably possible the account given by the accused, the deceased's head was not in the water when the accused went around to the car. And later on the whole body was floating. So it speaks for itself, either the deceased went to meet the water, or the water came to meet him, or they went to meet each other. It may be that the slope of the beach and the movements while unconscious by the deceased, let him roll down into the water. It is for you to say, if you believe this to be established, and, of course, beyond reasonable doubt. But however that may be, the basic question I think that you must ask yourself is whether the deceased was rendered unconscious by the unlawful act of the accused, and left in a hazardous position, hazardous either because he was so close to the edge of the water that he might roll in, or because the tide might be coming in.

Now on this question of tides, on Mr Stewart's evidence, the high tide on mid-day Sunday was considerably lower than the high tide the previous night. And on statements which he has given, and which there is no reason to doubt, because I think he is supported by photographs showing the seaweed line, it is pretty clear that the tide the night before came up to the off-side front wheel of the station wagon. So whatever else may be said of the actions of the accused, he was at least in a position to know that tides on that beach, or the previous tide on that beach, had come in to a position which, as I understand the evidence, was further up the beach than the position where the body of the deceased was left lying.

Ultimately it is for you to say whether you are satisfied that the drowning, which I think you will believe without any hesitation was the immediate cause of death, was caused by the accused leaving the deceased in a position of obvious danger on the beach. If so, you are entitled as a matter of law to come to the conclusion that the application of force which rendered him unconscious was the cause of death.

Mr Elliott contended that the jury should have been told that unless they were satisfied that the deceased's death ensued as a result of the injury which the appellant inflicted on him and the leaving of the deceased at the edge of the sea, they could not be satisfied that the appellant had caused the death of the deceased and that they had to be satisfied that it was not the involuntary intervention of sleep on the part of the appellant which altered the situation from one of a safe situation so far as the deceased was concerned to a hazardous.

We disagree with this argument. Some confusion has sometimes arisen, particularly in the older cases, between the factors relevant when considering causation and those relevant when considering the necessary mental state required to constitute the crime of murder. Compare 1 *Russell on Crime* (12th ed, 1964), p 413. The learned judge in a passage not quoted was at pains to point out to the jury the necessity to separate the two questions. Foresight by the accused of the possibility or probability of death or grievous bodily harm from his act, though very relevant to the question of malice aforethought, has nothing to do with the question of causation. The death of the deceased is the material event. The question to be asked is whether an act or series of acts (in exceptional cases an omission or series of omissions) consciously performed by the accused is or are so connected with the event that it or they must be regarded as having a sufficiently substantial causal effect which subsisted *up* to the happening of the event, without being spent or without being in the eyes of the law sufficiently interrupted by some other act or event. It does not matter on the question of causation whether or not the accused after the commission of his act fails to appreciate or takes unavailing steps to avoid its probable consequences or mistakenly thinks he has taken such steps or fails to take such steps through some supervening factor unless that supervening factor so interrupts the effect of the original act as to prevent that original act from being in the eyes of the law the cause of death. In this case if the deceased was drowned and violent acts consciously performed by the accused had a causal effect which continued up to the moment of drowning, it does not matter, so far as causation is concerned, whether he lay unconscious on the beach until the tide covered him or whether while unconscious he rolled down the slope into the water or even whether in a state of insufficient consciousness he staggered further into the water. Only if he consciously entered the water would it in our view be even arguable that the chain of causation had been broken. (Compare the American cases cited in Howard, *Australian Criminal Law* (1965), p 32.) And his Honour expressly left this possibility to the jury. In our view, it is irrelevant on the question of causation, assuming the appellant's story to be true, whether or not he thought he had placed Whiting in a position of safety, whether or not it was reasonable for him to think so, whether or not he foresaw or ought to have foreseen that the deceased might be reached by the tide and drowned, whether or not the appellant was to blame for going to sleep, or whether or not he could or would have saved the life of the deceased if he had not gone to sleep. We say this because it was the act of the appellant in reducing the deceased to unconsciousness which, on his own story, originated the chain of events which led to drowning.

The only question, it seems to us, which can be raised in this connection is whether the action of the sea on the deceased can be regarded as breaking the chain of causation. We do not think it can. In the exposure cases the ordinary operation of natural causes has never been regarded as preventing the death from being caused by the accused. Such are the cases mentioned by Hale, Hawkins and East (1 *Hale PC* 431; 1 *Hawkins PC*, c 13, s 6; 1 *East PC* 226), of the infant being placed in the orchard and being killed by a kite, or the infant being placed in a pig sty and eaten by the pigs. ... In these cases, of course, the *actus reus* was the exposure of the helpless victim by itself; in the instant case the *actus reus* on the appellant's story is one stage further removed and consists of the violence exercised by him on the deceased in the water. Hence the questions raised by Mr Elliott's argument as to whether the situation in which the appellant left the unconscious Whiting on the water's edge was a safe one or a hazardous one, or was only turned from a safe one to a hazardous one by the involuntary intervention of sleep are irrelevant when considering causation ...

We are not concerned to deny that there may be cases where the extraordinary as opposed to the ordinary operation of natural forces might be regarded as breaking the chain of causation, as in the case of the earthquake referred to in the passage from Smith and Hogan cited by the learned judge. So here if the deceased had been placed in a situation safe from the ordinary operations of the sea and had been engulfed by an extraordinary tidal wave as the result of an earthquake in the sea it may be that the earthquake and not the act of the appellant would be regarded as the cause of death. But we cannot regard the ordinary operations of the tides at Tumby Bay, whether known to the appellant or not, as being such a supervening cause.

For these reasons the direction of the learned judge on this topic was not such as to call for the intervention of this court. His Honour might have directed the jury in terms of the passage from *R v Bristow* [1960] SASR 210, citing *R v Smith* [1959] 2 QB 36; [1959] 2 All ER 193 (C-MAC), that if at the time of death the original wound (here the original violence in the water referred to in the accused's story) was still an operating cause and a substantial cause the death could be said to be the result of this, even if some other cause, such as the action of the water, was still operating and that only if it could be said that the original violence was merely the setting in which the action of the sea operated could it be said that the death did not result from that violence. *Bristow's* case is after all binding upon the judges of this court unless the Full Court for some reason sees fit to depart from it. His Honour did in substance, though not in precise words, so direct. He told the jury specifically that the act of the accused must be a substantial cause. He did not use the word operational; but his remarks about the death by drowning postulate that the accused was still unconscious from the violence used by the appellant when he was involved with the sea, either by the action of the tide or by rolling down the slope or by both. If this was so, clearly the violence which preceded the unconsciousness was still operational. His Honour, by clear inference if not expressly, told the jury that if the deceased had remained conscious and gone out and drowned himself the violence of the accused would not have been the cause of death. If his Honour erred in referring to the question of foreseeability in this context that could only operate in favour of the appellant ...

If the deceased was unconscious as a result of the assault and drowned by the sea in any of the circumstances mentioned by his Honour then we do not think it matters whether the appellant left him in a position of mortal peril or not, or whether subsequent drowning was a consequence which might or might not have been expected to occur in the normal course, apart of course from extraordinary events like the tidal wave we mentioned previously. But all this could only operate in the accused's favour …

Accordingly the appeal on the question of causation fails. The argument for the appellant is fallacious in two ways: firstly, in that it assumes that the relevant act of the appellant was the leaving of the deceased on the beach and not the violence in the water reducing him to unconsciousness, and secondly, because the chain of causation could not be broken by the appellant's omissions to take further measures for the safety of the deceased, even if such omissions were contrary to his original intention and were excused by his inadvertently falling asleep …

4.29 Illustrations

1. D, a United States airman, stabbed V in the abdomen in the course of a cafe brawl. V was admitted to hospital where his wound was treated. In the course of the treatment, an antibiotic, terramycin, was administered; it was found that V was intolerant to it, and its use was discontinued for a day, but unfortunately its use thereafter was resumed. V died, and D was convicted of murdering him. On appeal, fresh evidence was admitted from experts. They testified that the treatment given to V was palpably wrong, and that the wound inflicted by D had almost completely healed by the time of V's death. The Court of Criminal Appeal quashed the conviction: *R v Jordan* (1956) 40 Cr App R 152.
2. D, a private in the King's Regiment, was convicted of the murder of V, a soldier in the Gloucestershire Regiment. During a fight in barracks D stabbed V with a bayonet, once in the arm and once in the back; the latter blow pierced V's lung and caused a haemorrhage, though this was not known to anyone. V was dropped twice by accident while he was being carried to a dressing station, and at the station an unsuccessful attempt was made to give him a saline transfusion. He was also given oxygen and subjected to artificial respiration treatment when his breathing seemed impaired. V died two-and-a-half hours after the original stabbing. There was medical evidence to show that, had V been given a blood transfusion, he would have had a 75 per cent chance of recovery. There was also evidence that, in the light of V's injuries, the treatment he did receive was thoroughly bad. D was convicted of murder. On appeal, held, conviction affirmed: *R v Smith* [1959] 2 QB 36.
3. D1, D2 and V were all prisoners in Pentridge. D1 stabbed V in the stomach, while D2 was present aiding and abetting the commission of the crime. A bowel resection operation was performed successfully and V resumed an apparently healthy life. Eleven months after the stabbing, V began to suffer from abdominal pains and vomiting. His condition worsened during the course of the following week, at the expiration of which he died. An autopsy

showed that the cause of death was a fibrous ring which had formed, causing a stricture in the small bowel at the site of the resection operation. At the trial of D1 and D2 for murder, medical evidence was given that such a stricture was not an uncommon complication following a bowel resection operation. Although V was examined by a number of doctors in the week prior to his death, none of them had correctly diagnosed his condition. It was open to the jury on the evidence to find that the doctors should have diagnosed the condition, and that operative treatment would have rectified it. D1 and D2 were found not guilty of murder but guilty of manslaughter. On appeal to the Full Court of the Supreme Court of Victoria, held, convictions affirmed. The court stated in *R v Evans and Gardiner (No 2)* [1976] VR 523 at 528:

> As an event intervening between an act alleged to be felonious and to have resulted in death, and the actual death, a positive act of commission or an act of omission will serve to break the chain of causation only if it can be shown that that act or omission accelerated the death, so that it can be said to have caused the death and thus to have prevented the felonious act which would have caused death from actually doing so. … However we have seen no criminal case in which an omission to give or undergo treatment has been held to break the chain of causation between the felonious act and the death.

See also *R v Bingapore* (1975) 11 SASR 469.

4. D shot V, but medical evidence was given that the wound so inflicted was 'neither necessarily nor probably mortal' and that death ensued from scarlet fever negligently communicated by V's doctor when he came to attend the wound. Conviction of murder reversed: *Bush v Commonwealth* 78 Ky 268 (1880).

4.30C Royall v R

(1991) 172 CLR 378; 100 ALR 669
High Court of Australia

Mason CJ: The deceased, Kelly Louise Healey, died in the early hours of 16 November 1986 when she fell from the bathroom window of the sixth floor flat in which she and the applicant had lived for the previous four months. How the deceased came to fall and just what part the applicant played in the events which precipitated the deceased's fall were central to the issues which the jury were called upon to determine at the trial.

The relationship between the applicant and the deceased in the days immediately preceding her death had been far from serene … The deceased's body was naked when found in the street and her hair was wet. This, it was said, was consistent with the hypothesis that the deceased had undressed and taken a shower.

There was evidence of a forcible entry into the bathroom, which was extremely confined, and of a struggle there. The deceased's blood was found splashed in the bathroom and throughout the flat. There was a chipped glass ashtray in the washbasin as well as hair and glass chips, evidently from the ashtray, on the bathroom floor. There were gouge marks in the bathroom wall which, according to evidence, were consistent with an arc created by someone swinging his or her right arm while holding an object such as the ashtray. The location of these marks on the wall was said to support an inference that the deceased may have involuntarily jumped backwards to avoid a swinging arm, whether it was clutching an object or not. There were no marks on the deceased's scalp to indicate that she had been struck by the ashtray. There were neither bloodstains nor fingerprints on the ashtray, though the ashtray was wet and, on that account, might not have yielded fingerprints.

The Crown case was that the applicant murdered the deceased in one of three ways:

(1) that the applicant pushed or forced the deceased out of the window;
(2) that the applicant physically attacked the deceased in the bathroom and that, in retreating from or avoiding that attack, she fell from the window; or
(3) that, immediately before her fall from the window, the deceased had a well-founded and reasonable apprehension that, if she remained in the bathroom, she would be subjected to life-threatening violence from the applicant and, in order to escape from the violence, she jumped out the window.

The applicant's case at the trial, as expressed in his unsworn statement, was that, after the deceased had entered the bathroom to take a shower, he had become concerned for her. He had heard a thump on the wall. He said that he knew that the deceased had used amphetamines over a long time and that she suffered from epilepsy which caused her to faint or become unconscious. This knowledge, it was suggested, was the foundation of his concern for the deceased and of the claim that she took her own life by voluntarily jumping out the window. The applicant forced the lock with a knife and banged against the door until it opened. He said: 'When I finally got it open she was going out the window.' There was evidence that, in his record of interview, he said that, when the bathroom door opened, 'I just saw the back of Kelly going out the window. She just jumped out.' The applicant denied that any violence was done to the deceased or that he touched her in the bathroom. Moreover, his case was that he did not cause her death or intend to injure her.

The case was left to the jury on the footing that it was for them to determine whether the applicant had caused the deceased's death in any of the three ways suggested by the Crown. The trial judge instructed them that, if they were satisfied that the applicant caused the deceased's death, they should consider whether he had the requisite intent. His Honour stated that the requisite intent would be satisfied by an intent to kill, an intent to inflict grievous bodily harm or reckless indifference to human life. In making this statement his Honour did not differentiate between the three ways in which the Crown suggested that the applicant had caused the deceased's death; in other words, the jury was left with the impression that, if they were satisfied on the issue of causation in any one of the three suggested ways, the requisite intention would then be satisfied by an intent to kill or an intent to inflict grievous bodily harm or reckless indifference to human life ...

Causation

It is convenient to deal initially with the question of causation. The applicant submits that neither the trial judge nor the Court of Criminal Appeal defined adequately the act done by the applicant which was alleged to have caused the death of the deceased, thereby creating difficulties in determining the issues of causation and intent, in particular the coincidence of act and intent. Ordinarily there is not occasion for a trial judge to spend much time on the identification of the act causing death, but there is a 'logical and practical necessity to isolate that act, for it is of it, and it alone, that one or more of the several specified conditions or concomitants must be predicated if the terms of s 18 are to be satisfied', to repeat the words of Barwick CJ in *Ryan v R* (1967) 121 CLR 205 at 217–18. In *Ryan* the trial judge's directions were deficient in that they failed to isolate the particular act or acts which the jury might identify as the cause of death. In that case there was room for argument about what was the act which caused death. Different considerations arose for determination in ascertaining whether Ryan's state of mind satisfied the requirements of s 18, depending upon which act was identified as the cause of death. The Crown case was that Ryan went to rob a service station. While he had his finger on the trigger of a loaded, cocked gun pointed at the deceased's back, with his other hand he tried to find a cord in his pocket. The deceased made a sudden movement, Ryan stepped back and the gun discharged, killing the deceased. If pressing the trigger was identified as the act causing death, the question was whether Ryan willed that act and intended to kill or inflict grievous bodily harm or whether it was an unwilled reflex movement. If, however, presentation of the gun was identified as the act causing death, the question was whether Ryan knew that in the circumstances the involuntary discharge of the gun was probable. See per Barwick CJ at 219; and note *R v Crabbe* (1985) 156 CLR 464; 58 ALR 417 (where the test applied by Barwick CJ in *Ryan* was discarded in favour of that just stated).

Thus the case was one in which identification of the act causing death required 'specific and close consideration'. Yet the directions given to the jury 'appeared at times to treat the whole conduct of the applicant from the inception of his exploit as the act causing death', without descending to particularity: see, generally, per Barwick CJ at 218–20.

In *Ryan*, the Chief Justice pointed out (at 218) that 'the choice of the act causing death is not for the presiding judge or for the Court of Criminal Appeal: it is essentially a matter for the jury under proper direction'. So the question on this aspect of the present case is whether the trial judge adequately directed the jury as to the particular acts any one of which they might regard as the cause of the deceased's death. In this respect there was, in my view, just as there was in *Ryan,* a need for the trial judge to give specific and close attention to the identification of the various acts which, on the Crown case, might have been the cause of death. It is not to the point to say that in the present case the requirement of intent under s 18 was the same, no matter which of the acts identified by the Crown was selected by the jury as the cause of death. The point is that, in ascertaining whether there was the requisite intent, different matters may need to be taken into account, depending upon which act is identified as the act which caused death. As Stephen J said in *White v Ridley* (1978) 140 CLR 342 at 359; 21 ALR 661 at 675:

> It is always necessary, if there is said to be any lack of temporal coincidence between act and intent, accurately to identify the relevant act. It was to this need that Barwick CJ drew attention in *Ryan v R* [at 219].

Aickin J agreed with Stephen J: CLR at 363. The relationship of act to intent is a matter to which I shall return later. At this stage it is sufficient to say that, if the jury concluded that the applicant pushed the deceased out the window, it would have been easy to find that the applicant intended to kill or inflict grievous bodily harm. If, however, the jury concluded that the deceased met her death in one of the two other ways suggested by the Crown, the drawing of such an inference would not be quite as straightforward.

However, accepting the necessity in this case for the trial judge to isolate the various acts which the jury might regard as the act which caused death, I would reject the applicant's submission that the summing up was deficient in this respect. The trial judge clearly identified the three acts alleged to have been done by the applicant which may have led to the deceased's death. In so far as the applicant submits that the trial judge did not correctly instruct the jury as to the intent which must accompany the act in order to constitute the offence of murder, that is another question which can be considered apart from causation.

Indeed, I did not understand the applicant to contend, apart from the submission that there must be an interaction between act and intent, that any of the three possibilities put forward by the Crown could not amount to an act which was causative of the deceased's death, if the jury accepted that the act took place. The issue of causation was left to the jury to decide as one of fact. In this respect I agree with the statement made by Burt CJ in *Campbell v R* [1981] WAR 286 at 290; (1980) 2 A Crim R 157 at 161, that it is 'enough if juries [are] told that the question of cause for them to decide is not a philosophical or a scientific question, but a question to be determined by them applying their common sense to the facts as they find them, they appreciating that the purpose of the inquiry is to attribute legal responsibility in a criminal matter': see also *Timbu Kolian v R* (1968) 119 CLR 47, per Windeyer J at 69. That is the test that has been applied in negligence cases by this court: see *March v E & MH Stramare Pty Ltd* (1991) 65 ALJR 334; 99 ALR 423. Although the trial judge's direction was not so explicit, the jury would have plainly understood it in the sense expressed in the statement just quoted.

Of the three ways in which the Crown case was left to the jury on the issue of causation, only the third calls for comment. His Honour put it this way:

> The third allegation is that Kelly Healey at the time immediately before her fall from the window, had a well-founded and reasonable apprehension that if she remained in the bathroom she would be subjected to such further violence as would endanger her life and if in those circumstances she sought to escape by jumping out the window thinking that by so doing she had a better chance of saving her life than by staying inside, and was killed in that fall, the causal link between the acts of the accused and the death are established.

No exception was taken to this direction at the trial.

Generally speaking, an act done by a person in the interests of self-preservation, in the face of violence or threats of violence on the part of another, which results in the death of the first person, does not negative causal connection between the violence or threats of violence and the death. The intervening act of the deceased does not break the chain of causation. But the governing principle has been expressed in a variety of different ways. The trial judge's direction was based on that approved by the Full Court of the Supreme Court of New South Wales in *R v Grimes and Lee* (1894) 15 NSWR 209 (where the deceased jumped to his death from the window of a railway carriage in order to escape from the accused who had assaulted and robbed him). The key element in the chain of causation, as contemplated by the direction, is that an accused's conduct creates in the mind of the victim a well-founded and reasonable apprehension of danger as a result of which the victim takes steps to escape leading to his or her death. According to this view, it is enough that the victim's apprehension of danger is well-founded and reasonable; there is no requirement that the steps taken to escape should be reasonable. However, in England, formulations have been applied from time to time which pay more attention to the mode of escape chosen by the victim which results in death, no doubt with a view to emphasising the causative link between the accused's conduct and the death of the victim. Thus, it has been held that a reasonable act performed for the purpose of self-preservation in attempting to escape the violence of the accused does not destroy the causative connection with the accused's violence: *R v Pitts* (1842) Car & M 284; 174 ER 509; *R v Pagett* (1983) 76 Cr App R 279, per Robert Goff LJ at 289. In this context, 'reasonable' means reasonable in the light of the accused's conduct and the apprehension of danger which is induced in the mind of the victim. A variant on this formulation is to say that the victim's act which results in death is caused by the accused's violence if the act is 'the natural consequence' of that violence, something that is very likely to happen: *R v Beech* (1912) 7 Cr App R 197, per Darling J (where the victim was injured after jumping out of a window to escape from a man whom she had reason to fear). The natural consequence test has been explained as a test which poses the question whether the victim's act 'was something that could reasonably have been foreseen as the consequence of what [the accused] was saying or doing': *R v Roberts* (1971) 56 Cr App R 95, per Stephenson LJ at 102. So if an act is so unexpected that no reasonable person could be expected to foresee it, then it is a voluntary act on the part of the victim which breaks the chain of causation between the accused's conduct and the ultimate injury: *Roberts* at 102.

In *Director of Public Prosecutions v Daley* [1980] AC 237, the Judicial Committee appears to have endorsed the approach adopted in *Roberts.* In so doing, their Lordships pointed out that the fear of physical harm induced by the accused's conduct must be 'reasonable' and such that it caused the victim to try to escape: per Lord Keith of Kinkel at 245–6. It is important to note that in *Daley* their Lordships were dealing with the elements of 'constructive manslaughter'; they were not isolating the issue of causation for examination on its own. Moreover, the case was one in which the victim sought to escape by running away rather than engaging in a hazardous act such as jumping out of a window or from a speeding train. So the mode of escape did not call for separate attention.

It seems to me that, in the context of causation, the principle is best formulated as follows: where the conduct of the accused induces in the victim a well-founded apprehension of physical harm such as to make it a natural consequence (or reasonable) that the victim would seek to escape and the victim is injured in the course of escaping, the injury is caused by the accused's conduct. Whether it is necessary for the prosecution to establish also that the mode of escape adopted is a natural consequence of the victim's apprehension for his or her safety does not arise here for the deceased had no means of escape other than jumping out of the window in the situation posited. The question could arise only in circumstances where the victim does something irrational or unexpected, in which event it might be more difficult to establish that the injury sustained was a consequence of the accused's act and not the product of the victim's voluntary act. In such a situation much may turn on the nature and extent of the well-founded apprehension of the victim; and it is to be expected that persons fearful for their own safety forced to react on the spur of the moment will not always make a sound or sensible judgment and may act irrationally.

In the English cases the natural consequence test has been linked to the concept of foreseeability. Because the natural consequence test inevitably invites conjecture about the likelihood of an occurrence, it is impossible to divorce completely the application of the test from the concept of foreseeability. However, in my view, to invite the jury to consider foreseeability would be more likely, at least in the majority of cases, to confuse than to clarify the issue of causation. In many cases, for much the same reason, I see no point in linking that issue to the accused's state of mind. On the other hand, in some situations, the accused's state of mind will be relevant to that issue as, for example, where there is evidence that the accused intended that injury should result in the way in which it did and where, in the absence of evidence of intention, the facts would raise a doubt about causation.

McHugh J:

Causation in criminal cases

Causation is a question of fact: *R v Evans and Gardiner (No 2)* [1976] VR 523 at 527; *R v Pagett* (1983) 76 Cr App R 279 at 290–1. To constitute a cause for the purposes of the criminal law, it is not necessary that an act or omission be the sole or main cause of a wrong: *Pagett* at 290. But, as I have indicated, the purpose of the legal doctrine of causation is to attribute legal responsibility, not to determine the factors which played a part in the happening of an event or occurrence. It is for this reason that the common law doctrine of causation has not accepted that a person is criminally responsible for an event or occurrence simply because his or her act or omission was a *causa sine qua non* of that event or occurrence. If, as a matter of common sense, an ordinary person would not hold an accused's act or omission to be a cause of the event or occurrence, it is irrelevant that it was a *causa sine qua non* of that event or occurrence: cf *Campbell v R* [1981] WAR 286 at 290.

In most criminal cases, the issue of causation is not controversial. If an accused's act or omission is causally linked with the event or occurrence, it is always only one of the conditions which were jointly necessary to produce the event or occurrence.

Ordinarily, however, the application of the common sense test of causation is enough to determine whether the accused's act or omission was sufficiently significant to make him or her 'causally responsible' for the event or occurrence in question. But there are two cases where the invocation of common sense principles of causation often provides little assistance to the jury. The first is the case where an accused's act would not have brought about the event or occurrence without the intervention of a subsequent act of the victim or a third party. The second is the case where, notwithstanding the accused's act or omission, the event or occurrence could have been prevented if the victim or a third person had taken action to avoid the consequences of the act or omission. In these cases, common law judges have sought to use more specific tests for determining whether 'but for' acts or omissions of the accused were 'causally responsible' for the event or occurrence. The common law judges have used at least four tests for this purpose. They are: (1) the operating and substantial cause test; (2) the natural consequence test; (3) the reasonable foresight of the consequences test; and (4) the *novus actus interveniens* test, which is used sometimes in conjunction with and sometimes independently of one of the other three tests. Unfortunately, the cases show no consistent pattern in applying these tests. Frequently, one test has been used to the exclusion of the others without any express recognition of the existence of the other tests: see Colvin, at 259.

In *R v Smith* [1959] 2 QB 36, where the appellant had been convicted of murder, Lord Parker CJ said (at 42–3):

> It seems to the court that if at the time of death the original wound is still an operating cause and a substantial cause, then the death can properly be said to be the result of the wound, albeit that some other cause of death is also operating. Only if it can be said that the original wounding is merely the setting in which another cause operates can it be said that the death does not result from the wound. Putting it in another way, only if the second cause is so overwhelming as to make the original wound merely part of the history can it be said that the death does not flow from the wound.

In this context, 'substantial cause' has been said to be 'a convenient word to use to indicate to the jury that it must be something more than *de minimis*': *R v Hennigan* [1971] 3 All ER 133, per Lord Parker CJ at 135.

In *Smith*, there was medical evidence that, if the deceased had received proper treatment after he was stabbed, there was a 75 per cent chance he would have recovered. Yet Lord Parker CJ said (at 44) that, although the treatment given was harmful, no reasonable jury, properly directed, could come to any conclusion except that death resulted from the original wound caused two hours earlier.

The principle laid down in *Smith* was followed in *Evans and Gardiner (No. 2)*, where the deceased had died almost one year after being stabbed by the applicants. After the stabbing, a bowel resection operation was performed successfully. The deceased resumed an apparently healthy life. But he died about 11 months after the stabbing. The immediate cause of death was a fibrous ring causing a stricture in the small bowel at the site of the resection operation. The medical evidence established that such a stricture was not an uncommon sequel to that particular operation. There was evidence upon which the jury could have found that the deceased's condition should have been diagnosed and that operative treatment would have rectified it. The Full Court of the Supreme Court of Victoria upheld the applicant's convictions for murder. The court said (at 529) that the passage from *Smith* which I have quoted was 'the most satisfactory expression of the law to be found in the authorities'.

In *Evans and Gardiner (No 2),* the Full Court distinguished *R v Jordan* (1956) 40 Cr App R 152, where a stabbing wound was stitched up but the victim died a week later. In that case, fresh evidence was called on the appeal to establish that death had not been caused by the stab wound but by the introduction of terramycin after the deceased had shown that he was intolerant of it and by the intravenous introduction of abnormal quantities of liquid which led to broncho-pneumonia from which the victim died. The Court of Criminal Appeal in *Jordan* held (at 158) that, if the jury had heard this evidence, they 'would have felt precluded from saying that they were satisfied that death was caused by the stab wound'. The court thought that abnormal treatment could be regarded as a supervening event which broke the causal chain. In distinguishing *Jordan,* the Full Court in *Evans and Gardiner (No. 2)* (at 531) agreed with Lord Parker's opinion in *Smith* 'that *R v Jordan* should be regarded as a case decided on its own special facts and not as an authority relaxing the common law approach to causation'.

The judgment of the Full Court of the Supreme Court of South Australia in *R v Hallett* [1969] SASR 141 also adopted the substantial, operating cause doctrine of causation in a case where the deceased drowned after an assault by the accused. The court said (at 149):

> The death of the deceased is the material event. The question to be asked is whether an act or series of acts (in exceptional cases an omission or series of omissions) consciously performed by the accused is or are so connected with the event that it or they must be regarded as having a sufficiently substantial causal effect which subsisted up to the happening of the event, without being spent or without being in the eyes of the law sufficiently interrupted by some other act or event. It does not matter on the question of causation whether or not the accused after the commission of his act fails to appreciate or takes unavailing steps to avoid its probable consequences or mistakenly thinks he has taken such steps or fails to take such steps through some supervening factor unless that supervening factor so interrupts the effect of the original act as to prevent the original act from being in the eyes of the law the cause of death.

There was evidence that the accused had violently assaulted the deceased on a beach, knocked him unconscious and left him lying at the edge of the water with his feet in the sea. The deceased died from drowning, probably in shallow water whilst unconscious. The Full Court said (at 149):

> The only question, it seems to us, which can be raised in this connection is whether the action of the sea on the deceased can be regarded as breaking the chain of causation. We do not think it can. In the exposure cases the ordinary

operation of natural causes has never been regarded as preventing the death from being caused by the accused.

The principle that an act or omission of an accused is a legal cause of a wrongful act if it is 'an operating cause and a substantial cause' of that act seems to have been referred to infrequently, however, in cases where the harm to the injured person would never have occurred but for a subsequent act of the victim or a third person. One test which has been used in this class of case is to ask whether the intervening act was a voluntary act or abnormal occurrence which amounted to a *novus actus interveniens* which broke 'the chain of causation'. In *Pagett* (1983) 76 Cr App R 279, the Court of Appeal upheld a conviction of manslaughter where a girl, whom the accused was holding as a shield in front of him, was shot dead by police who were returning shots fired by the accused at the police. The Court of Appeal said (at 288):

> ... although an act of the accused constitutes a *causa sine qua non* of (or necessary condition for) the death of the victim, nevertheless the intervention of a third person may be regarded as the sole cause of the victim's death, thereby relieving the accused of criminal responsibility. Such intervention, if it has such an effect, has often been described by lawyers as a *novus actus interveniens.*

Their Lordships thought (at 289) that it was broadly correct to say that the intervention of a third person, not acting in concert with the accused, had the effect of relieving the accused of criminal responsibility if the intervention was voluntary in the sense that it was 'free, deliberate and informed'. Their Lordships said, however, that there was no doubt that a reasonable act performed for the purpose of self-preservation does not operate as a *novus actus interveniens* if that act is caused by the accused's act. Consequently, the act of the police officers did not constitute a *novus actus interveniens* severing the chain of causation between the accused's unlawful act in using the girl as a shield and her death.

In *R v Blaue* [1975] 1 WLR 1411; [1975] 3 All ER 446, the Court of Appeal held that the chain of causation was not broken because the victim of a stabbing, who was a Jehovah's Witness, had refused to have a blood transfusion which would probably have saved her life. The court said (at [WLR] 1415; [All ER] 450):

> It has long been the policy of the law that those who use violence on other people must take their victims as they find them. This in our judgment means the whole man, not just the physical man. It does not lie in the mouth of the assailant to say that his victim's religious beliefs which inhibited him from accepting certain kinds of treatment were unreasonable. The question for decision is what caused her death. The answer is the stab wound. The fact that the victim refused to stop this end coming about did not break the causal connection between the act and death.

On the other hand in *R v Dalby* [1982] 1 WLR 425; [1982] 1 All ER 916, the Court of Appeal set aside a conviction of manslaughter where the appellant had supplied drugs to a person who subsequently died of an overdose. The trial judge had directed the jury to ask themselves whether supplying the drugs 'was a substantial cause of the victim's death'. The court said (at [WLR] 428–9; [All ER] 919) that supplying the drugs was not an act which caused direct harm and would have caused no harm 'unless the deceased had subsequently used the drugs in a form and quantity which was dangerous'. Ingestion of the drugs by the victim was seen as a *novus actus interveniens.*

A quite different test of causation was applied in the earlier case of *R v Beech* (1912) 7 Cr App R 197, where the accused was convicted of inflicting grievous bodily harm after the complainant had jumped out of a window to escape his threatened attack and injured herself. The Court of Criminal Appeal upheld the conviction and said (at 200) that no one could say 'that if she jumped through the window it was not the natural consequence of the prisoner's conduct. It was a very likely thing for a woman to do as the result of the threats of a man who was conducting himself as this man indisputably was.'

The 'natural consequence' test applied in *Beech* was formulated in different terms in *R v Roberts* (1971) 56 Cr App R 95, where a young woman who was a passenger in the appellant's car injured herself by jumping out of it while the car was in motion. She alleged that she had jumped because of what the appellant had said he would do to her. The Court of Appeal rejected a submission that the accused must foresee the actions of a victim which result in the grievous bodily harm or the actual bodily harm. Their Lordships said (at 102):

> The test is: Was it the natural result of what the alleged assailant said and did, in the sense that it was something that could reasonably have been foreseen as the consequence of what he was saying or doing? As it was put in one of the old cases, it had got to be shown to be his act, and if of course the victim does something so 'daft', in the words of the appellant in this case, or so unexpected, not that this particular assailant did not actually foresee it but that no reasonable man could be expected to foresee it, then it is only in a very remote and unreal sense a consequence of his assault, it is really occasioned by a voluntary act on the part of the victim which could not reasonably be foreseen and which breaks the chain of causation between the assault and the harm of injury.

The foresight principle laid down in *Roberts* was approved in *R v Mackie* (1973) 57 Cr App R 453, where the appellant was convicted of the manslaughter of a small boy who fell down stairs when running away in fear of being ill-treated by the appellant who had ill-treated the boy in the past. The Court of Appeal said (at 459–60):

> Where the injuries are not fatal, the attempt to escape must be the natural consequence of the assault charged, not something which could not be expected, but something which any reasonable and responsible man in the assailant's shoes would have foreseen. Where the injuries are fatal, the attempt must be the natural consequence of an unlawful act and that unlawful act 'must be such as all sober and reasonable people would inevitably recognise must subject the other person to, at least, the risk of some harm resulting therefrom, albeit not serious harm'.

The Judicial Committee of the Privy Council approved the law concerning manslaughter as laid down in *Mackie* in *Director of Public Prosecutions v Daley* [1980] AC 237, where the defendants had quarrelled with the deceased and had thrown stones at him. The deceased tripped and fell while running away. He was later found to be dead. Death could have been caused by a blow from one of the stones or by the impact of the fall. Their Lordships said (at 245–6):

> It is sufficient to paraphrase what in their Lordships' view were there [that is, in *Mackie*] held to constitute the essential ingredients of the prosecution's proof of a charge of manslaughter, laid upon the basis that a person has sustained fatal injuries while trying to escape from assault by the defendant. These are: (1) that the victim immediately before he sustained the injuries was in fear of being hurt physically; (2) that his fear was such that it caused him to try to escape; (3) that whilst he was trying to escape, and because he was trying to escape, he met his death; (4) that his fear of being hurt there and then was reasonable and was caused by the conduct of the defendant; (5) that the defendant's conduct which caused the fear was unlawful; and (6) that his conduct was such as any sober and reasonable person would recognise as likely to subject the victim to at least the risk of some harm resulting from it, albeit not serious harm.

The law as to causation laid down in *Mackie* and *Daley* — where the victims were seeking to escape the violence of the accused — is different from the direction as to causation which Cole J gave the jury in the present case. The direction of his Honour was based on a direction approved by the Full Court of the Supreme Court of New South Wales in *R v Grimes and Lee* (1894) 15 NSWR 209. There, the defendants and the victim were travelling in the same compartment in a railway carriage. After being robbed and assaulted by the defendants, the victim, thinking that his life was in danger, jumped out of the train and was killed. The Full Court approved the direction of the trial judge that the defendants were guilty of murder if immediately after the robbery and wounding had taken place the victim jumped through the window because of 'a well-founded and reasonable fear of apprehension that if he stayed in the carriage he would be subjected to such further violence as would endanger his life, and if he left the carriage thinking that by doing so he had a better chance of saving his life than by staying in, and was killed in the fall'.

The direction in *Grimes and Lee* concentrated on the state of mind of the victim and required a finding of causal connection if the objective facts made the fear well-founded and reasonable. Thus, on a *Grimes and Lee* direction, it is not enough that the conduct of an accused person has induced the victim to take a course of action which resulted in injury or was a substantial, operating cause. The fear of the victim must be both 'well-founded and reasonable'. It is, however, not easy to understand what is meant by a well-founded and reasonable fear. If the fear was well-founded, it is difficult to see how any question of reasonableness could arise. Further, the direction in *Grimes and Lee* did not take into account whether the conduct of the victim was reasonably foreseeable; nor did it take into account whether what the victim did was the natural consequence of the defendants' conduct. Consequently, the law as laid down in *Grimes and Lee* is difficult to reconcile with the law as laid down in many of the cases decided in this century.

The purpose of this extended discussion of the case has been to demonstrate that the rules concerning causation are in an inconsistent and unsatisfactory state in cases where harm to the victim has occurred because of the subsequent acts or omissions of the victim or a third party. This branch of the law is in evident need of rationalisation. When such a situation exists, it is the duty of this court, as the ultimate appellate tribunal of the nation, to seek to achieve that object by recourse to the underlying principles of the common law.

Judicial and academic efforts to achieve a coherent theory of common law causation have not met with significant success. Perhaps the nature of the subject matter when combined with the lawyer's need to couple issues of factual causation with culpability make achievement of a coherent theory virtually impossible. But there is little hope of obtaining a coherent theory of causation if the principles of causation in criminal cases are significantly different from those in the civil law. No doubt the object of the civil law is not the same as the object of the criminal law. But both areas of law use principles of causal responsibility to limit liability for the consequences of wrongful acts. Tort and contract law do so, inter alia, by rules of remoteness of damage which are based on notions of justice and morality: cf *Overseas Tankship (UK) Ltd v Morts Dock & Engineering Co Ltd (The Wagon Mound (No 1))* [1961] AC 388 at 422–3. Criminal law does so by reference to rules which are based on notions of moral culpability. Speaking generally, the broad principles of causation applicable in civil cases should be equally applicable in criminal cases. The law of negligence, where issues of causation have arisen frequently, has used the doctrines of reasonable foreseeability and *novus actus interveniens* to limit responsibility for negligent acts and omissions which are causally connected with injury suffered: *Mahony v J Kruschich (Demolitions) Pty Ltd* (1985) 156 CLR 522 at 529; 59 ALR 722. Reasonable foreseeability has been used to limit the liability of a tortfeasor because 'it does not seem consonant with current ideas of justice or morality that for an act of negligence, however slight or venial, which results in some trivial foreseeable damage the actor should be liable for all consequences however unforeseeable and however grave, so long as they can be said to be 'direct"; *The Wagon Mound (No 1)* at 422. The *novus actus interveniens* doctrine has been used to limit the liability of a tortfeasor because he or she is perceived as having no moral responsibility for damage when a fully-informed actor, not acting under a constraint or pressure flowing from the tortfeasor's actions, has intervened and produced that damage even though it would not have occurred but for the tortfeasor's act or omission. For the same reasons, in a criminal case, a person should not be held liable for a wrongful act or omission which has caused harm in a 'but for' sense if that harm was the product of a *novus actus interveniens* or was not a reasonably foreseeable consequence of the act or omission. It goes almost without saying, however, that a person should be held liable for harm which is causally linked with his or her conduct and which he or she intended should be brought about by that conduct: cf Hart and Honore, *Causation in the Law*, 2nd ed (1985), p 79.

The test of reasonable foresight is to be preferred to the 'natural consequence' test and the 'operating cause and … substantial cause' test. The balance of authority favours the reasonable foresight test over the 'natural consequence' test. Moreover, the word 'natural' is ambiguous. In *Overseas Tankship (UK) Ltd v The Miller Steamship Co Pty*

(The Wagon Mound (No 2)) [1967] 1 AC 617, Lord Reid said (at 634), 'the word "natural" is found very often and is peculiarly ambiguous'. In *Beech,* Darling J, in using the term 'natural consequence', seemed to mean that the consequence was one which 'was a very likely thing'. But the expression can also mean a consequence that might be expected to occur. In *Roberts* (at 102), Stephenson LJ approved the test in *Beech.* Yet his Lordship said that the test was: 'Was it the natural result of what the alleged assailant said and did, in the sense that it was something that could reasonably have been foreseen as the consequence of what he was saying or doing?' Furthermore, despite the enthusiasm which some courts and writers have shown for the 'operating cause and ... substantial cause' test, I do not think that it is a satisfactory formula. The adjective 'operating' adds nothing. Either an accused's act is a cause or it is not a cause. The word 'substantial' means no more than not de minimis. The result of the application of the 'operating cause and ... substantial cause' test in most cases is that the 'but for' test has been applied under another label.

In *Hallett,* however, the Full Court said (at 149):

> Foresight by the accused of the possibility or probability of death or grievous bodily harm from his act, though very relevant to the question of malice aforethought, has nothing to do with the question of causation.

As I have already pointed out, however, for the purposes of the criminal law, causation cannot be separated from questions of moral culpability. And a person should not be regarded as morally culpable in respect of harm which he or she did not intend and which no reasonable person could foresee.

However, notwithstanding what was said in *Daley* and *Grimes and Lee,* I do not think that either principle or policy requires the conclusion that an accused is not causally responsible for the harm suffered by the victim simply because the accused's act or omission has caused the victim to act unreasonably. One of the basic objects of the criminal law is the preservation of the Queen's peace. If the conduct of the accused in fact induces the victim to do something which 'causes' harm to him or her, the act of the victim ought not to be regarded as a *novus actus interveniens* merely because it was unreasonable. Persons subjected to violence or the threat of violence do not always think rationally or act reasonably. The instinct of self-preservation often causes them to flee or to take action which, while avoiding the immediate danger, places them in greater peril. Indeed, in some cases, the suicide of the victim should not be regarded as breaking the causal chain of responsibility. If a person suicided to avoid further torture and eventual death, I do not see why the causal chain should be taken as broken: cf *People v Lewis* (1899) 57 Pac 470. The unreasonable failure of a victim to receive medical attention will not constitute a *novus actus interveniens: Blaue.* How then can unreasonable conduct on the part of a victim in escaping an attack automatically constitute a *novus actus interveniens?* It is true that in the first case the victim has refused to take action which would prevent his or her death, while in the second case the victim has taken action which causes his or her death. But in each case, the death occurs only because of conduct on the part of the victim which is unreasonable by objective standards. It is not easy to see any distinction in principle between the two cases. It is even more difficult to see why the conduct of the victim should absolve the accused in one case and not the other.

The fact that the victim's act is unreasonable in seeking to escape from the violent conduct of the accused, therefore, does not seem enough by itself as a matter of either principle or policy to enable the accused to escape causal responsibility for the harm which ensues. On the other hand, even though the victim's act is not a *novus actus interveniens,* to hold that the accused was criminally responsible for harm which was not intended and which no reasonable person could have foreseen was likely to result from his or her conduct would be an onerous imposition of the criminal law.

Consequently, in a case such as the present, an accused should not be held to be guilty unless his or her conduct induced the victim to take action which resulted in harm to him or her and that harm was either intended by the accused or was of a type which a reasonable person could have foreseen as a consequence of the accused's conduct. In determining whether a reasonable person could have foreseen the harm suffered by the victim, any irrational or unreasonable conduct of the victim will be a variable factor to be weighed according to all the circumstances of the case.

The verdict on the third alternative was not unsafe or unsatisfactory

When the evidence relied on by the Crown in this case is examined in the light of the principles of causation to which I have referred, a reasonable jury were entitled to find the applicant guilty of murder on the basis of the third alternative. If the deceased jumped out of the window to avoid his attack, a causal link existed between the applicant's attack and her death and the applicant should be held to be causally responsible for her death unless her death was not a reasonably foreseeable consequence of the attack. The conduct of the applicant in relation to the deceased makes it impossible to regard her act in jumping (if it occurred) as a *novus actus interveniens* for which the applicant has no responsibility. So the question is: was the death of the deceased a reasonably foreseeable consequence of the applicant's conduct?

Unfortunately, the learned trial judge did not instruct the jury of the need to isolate a particular act as the cause of the deceased jumping out of the window. If the jury found that the deceased jumped, it was open to them to find that she did so because of what occurred in the bathroom or because of the applicant's act in forcing the door open. The causal act most favourable to the applicant is that she jumped as the result of his forcing the door open. But, having regard to the ferocity of the attack which had taken place in the living room, the arguing which continued after the deceased locked herself in the bathroom, and the banging on the door, I think that a reasonable jury were entitled to hold that the deceased's death was a reasonably foreseeable consequence of the breaking down of the door. It was reasonably foreseeable because the conduct of the applicant up to and including that time was capable of inducing such fear in the deceased that she would take any step to avoid his violence even if it meant going out the window. The irrational act of a person in the deceased's position, having regard to the circumstances, was not beyond the limits of reasonable foresight.

Moreover, I think that a reasonable jury were entitled to find that even at the time of the breaking open of the door the applicant had the intention to kill her or cause her grievous bodily harm or was recklessly indifferent to her life. A reasonable jury were entitled to find that, having regard to the violence which had taken place at the earlier stage, the applicant broke open the door with intent to kill the deceased or to inflict grievous bodily harm upon her or realised that his actions would probably cause death to the deceased and was recklessly indifferent to that occurring. It is beside the point that the applicant may not have intended to kill the deceased or inflict grievous bodily harm on her, or may not have foreseen the probability of the deceased dying, by jumping or falling out of the window. As McGarvie and O'Bryan JJ said in *R v Demirian* [1989] VR 97 at 113:

> If a person creates a situation intended to kill and it does kill it is no answer to a charge of murder that it caused death at a time or in a way that was to some extent unexpected.

For these reasons, I am of the opinion that a reasonable jury were entitled to find on the third alternative that the applicant was causally responsible for the death of the deceased and that, whichever of the three states of mind was selected as the relevant one, it was a state of mind which a reasonable jury were entitled to find. Accordingly, the verdict of the jury, based on the third alternative, was not unsafe or unsatisfactory.

The important principles of law which had to be discussed in reaching the conclusion that the verdict was not unsafe or unsatisfactory make the case one for the grant of special leave to appeal. But the appeal on this ground must be dismissed.

Direction on the third alternative

I have already set out the judge's direction on the third alternative. It was clearly based on *Grimes and Lee.* It departs from the reasonable foresight model of causation in two respects. First, it required that the deceased should have had a well founded and reasonable apprehension that she would be subjected to violence which would endanger her life. This was an unduly favourable direction from the point of view of the applicant. Persons do not always and cannot always be expected to act rationally. Secondly, the judge did not direct the jury as to the need for reasonable foresight of the consequences of the applicant's act. In this respect, however, the trial judge's direction was unfavourable to the applicant and amounted to a misdirection.

Further, the trial judge failed to direct the jury as to the need to identify the act which caused the death of the deceased. In *Ryan v R* (1967) 121 CLR 205 at 217–18, Barwick CJ drew attention to the 'logical and practical necessity to isolate that act, for it is of it, and it alone, that one or more of the several specified conditions or concomitants must be predicated if the terms of s 18 are to be satisfied'. I have already said that the verdict was not unsafe or unsatisfactory irrespective of which of the acts of the applicant was the act which caused death. But, of course, it was still open to the jury in the present case to find that the death of the deceased was not a reasonably foreseeable consequence of whatever was the relevant causal act of the applicant.

In my opinion, however, the direction of the trial judge on causation did not constitute any miscarriage of justice. I do not think that there is a real possibility that the failure of the trial judge to instruct the jury as to the need to identify the precise act which caused death or his failure to direct the jury in terms of reasonable foreseeability affected the result. Having regard to the evidence of the attack in the bathroom, I do not think that there is a significant possibility that the jury accepted that the deceased jumped out of the window because the door was forced open. The evidence strongly favours the view that the deceased did not jump out of the window. The only evidence that she did so is the assertion of the applicant. His assertion seems quite inconsistent with the abrasions on the back of the legs of the deceased. Moreover, if the jury rejected the applicant's account that there was no violence in the bathroom, his story about the deceased jumping out of the window as the door was forced open lost its credibility. The evidence is overwhelming that, despite the applicant's denials, a violent struggle took place in the bathroom. Consequently, I do not think that there is any significant possibility that the jury found that she jumped out of the window as the result of the door being forced open. If the jury found that a struggle took place in the bathroom, as I think they certainly did, and that the deceased jumped out of the window to avoid that attack, there is no doubt in my mind that the jury would have come to the conclusion that death was a reasonably foreseeable consequence of the applicant's attack. It is not necessary that the reasonable person could foresee the precise manner in which the act caused death.

In the circumstances, I am not persuaded that the trial judge's directions on the third alternative constituted a miscarriage of justice.

The time at which the relevant state of mind was held

Early in his summing up, when the learned trial judge was directing the jury as to the elements of the offence of murder, he instructed them that there must be an act of the accused which caused death and 'at the time of the doing of the act the act must have been accompanied by an attitude of mind on the part of the accused, which here would be either intent to kill or to do grievous bodily harm or was an act done with reckless indifference to human life'. When his Honour went on to deal with the question of the accused's mental state, however, he erroneously directed the jury that the accused's mental state must exist at the time when the deceased fell from the building. His Honour said:

> The first question is whether, at the time of the act bringing about the death, that being the time when the deceased left the building and fell to the ground below, there was present in the accused an intent to kill; and if you are satisfied that there was such an intent to kill you would not need to consider the next two matters, namely whether there was an intent to do grievous bodily harm or whether the act of the accused, done at that time, was done with a reckless indifference to her life. If you are not so satisfied of an intent to kill then you must consider whether the accused had the intent, at the relevant time, to inflict grievous bodily harm.

Later, after directing the jury concerning the meaning of reckless indifference to human life, his Honour said that their 'task would be to consider the accused's actual state of mind at the relevant time which, as I have said, is the time when the deceased fell from the building to the ground below'. When dealing with the question of manslaughter, the trial judge also directed the jury that they must consider the unlawful acts, if they found any, at the time when the deceased went out the window.

All the foregoing directions were substantially repeated towards the end of the summing up.

After a request by the Crown, the learned judge repeated his direction concerning reckless indifference to human life. He then went on to say:

> Your task, therefore, is to consider the accused's actual state of mind at the relevant time, which I have said to you on a number of occasions is the time when the deceased fell to her death.

Against this background, there is little doubt that the jury must have had the impression that the applicant had to have the relevant state of mind at the time the deceased went out the window. If the jury did retire under the impression that this was the time at which they had to consider the applicant's state of mind, they were acting under a legal error. It is trite law that the relevant state of mind and the harm-causing act 'must both concur to constitute the crime': *Fowler v Padget* (1798) 7 TR 509 at 514; 101 ER 1103 at 1106. Section 18 of the Crimes Act gives effect to this common law principle. All that s 18 requires is that the act of an accused causing death be accompanied by one of the relevant states of mind. This means that the state of mind of an accused does not have to coincide with the time of the deceased's death. In those cases of murder where death follows instantaneously from the act of the accused, there will be no practical difference between the time of the accused's act and the time of death. But in other cases, a considerable time lapse may occur between the act of the accused and the death of the deceased. Section 18(1)(a) requires that the relevant state of mind accompany the relevant act or omission causing death. It is irrelevant that, at the time of death, an accused no longer had the state of mind or acquired it after the occurrence of his or her act or omission. The directions of the learned trial judge on this matter were erroneous.

However, the misdirections could not have affected the results. No matter which act of the applicant caused the death of the deceased, the interval between that act and her fall from the window was too short for the jury to have thought that, although he had an innocent state of mind at the time of the act, he had a guilty state of mind at the time of the fall.

The challenge to the trial judge's directions on this issue also warrants the grant of special leave to appeal, but the appeal on this ground should be dismissed. Appeal dismissed.

[**Brennan J** and **Deane** and **Dawson JJ** delivered separate judgments granting special leave to appeal but dismissing the appeal. **Toohey** and **Gaudron JJ** delivered a dissenting judgment.]

4.31 Notes and illustrations

1. In *Arulthilakan v The Queen* (2003) 189 ALR 40, the High Court of Australia endorsed the language of 'substantial cause' and applied the decision in *Royall's* case. Kirby J, dissenting in the result, applied the same formulation, and approved the reasoning of McHugh J in *Royall's* case.
2. On a trial for murder, the Crown case was that D1 and D2 who were acting in concert chased V1 and V2 who, in order to escape, jumped into the Yarra River where they both drowned. The Crown submitted that it should be permitted to put its case to the jury on the basis that it was not necessary that the accused chased the deceased to the river. The prosecution submitted that if the jury found that the accused chased the deceased to a bus stop some hundreds of metres from the river and there attacked a third victim, it was open to the jury to find that the accused caused the deceased to flee to the river to escape even if it was other individuals who chased the deceased to the river bank from the bus stop. Held, ruling the accused would not be responsible for the deaths in such circumstances. In all of the reported self-defence cases, the victim, confronted and threatened by the accused, generally in a confined space and faced with the risk of impending further violence, took immediate life threatening action in an attempt to escape. Causal responsibility cannot be assigned to D1 and D2 if the jury found that the conduct of neither accused extended beyond the area in the immediate vicinity of the bus stop. In those circumstances, it would be the conduct of third parties who are not said by the prosecution to be acting in concert with D1 and D2 and the acts of the deceased that caused the deaths of the deceased: *R v Cuong Quoc Lam* (2005) 15 VR 574.
3. D raped V in extremely brutal circumstances, biting her all over the body. V managed to procure some mercury bichloride tablets and took a large dose. D refused to procure medical aid for V and kept her in an hotel for some hours, before dumping her on the doorstep of her home. V died a month later, partly from bichloride poisoning and partly (perhaps) from a breast abscess clearly caused by D's bites. D appealed from a conviction of murder, on the ground that V's death was caused by the intervening act of a responsible person, V, in taking the poison. The jury's verdict showed that they had found V to have been 'distracted with the pain and shame' inflicted on her by D at the time that she took the poison. Held, conviction affirmed: *Stephenson v State* 179 NE 633 (Ind 1932).
4. D determined to kill her baby son, V, by poisoning him with laudanum. She gave the poison to S, V's nurse, whom she told that it was medicine. S decided that V did not need any medicine, and accordingly put the bottle of laudanum on a shelf. During S's absence, her five year-old son 'T' took the bottle from the shelf and gave a large dose of its contents to V, who

died. At D's trial for murder, the judge told the jury that if the poison was administered by an unconscious agent, and D's original intention was still continuing at the time, they might convict her of murder. They did so. The judgment was respited so that the opinion of the judges might be taken. They were unanimous in holding that the conviction was right: *R v Michael* (1840) 169 ER 48.

5. In the first case, D stabbed his wife causing a deep wound in her abdomen which made hospital treatment necessary. After treatment the wife appeared to be recovering but several days later she collapsed in hospital and, shortly afterwards, her heart stopped beating. Surgery was performed to remove a blood clot from the pulmonary artery and thereafter the heart, after not beating for 30 minutes, started to beat again. Because of the danger of brain damage resulting from the period when the heart was not beating, the wife was put on a life-support machine. She appeared to have suffered irretrievable brain damage. After tests were carried out to confirm that that was the position, it was decided to disconnect the life-support machine and shortly afterwards the wife was declared to be dead. In the second case, A attacked a girl causing her grave head injuries. On the same day, she was taken to hospital and put on a life-support machine. Two days later, the doctors concluded that her brain had ceased to function and the machine was disconnected. Shortly afterwards she was declared to be dead. In each case, the medical treatment given to the victim was normal and conventional. D and A were each charged with murder. At each trial, the judge, after hearing submissions from counsel, decided to withdraw from the jury the issue of the cause of the victim's death on the ground that, at the time of death, the original injuries inflicted on the victim were an operating cause of death and that it was not open to the jury to conclude that the accused had not caused the death of his victim. D and A were each convicted of murder. They appealed on the ground that the judge had been wrong to withdraw the issue of causation from the jury because there was evidence that the cause of death in each case was the switching off of the life-support machine and the jury in each case should have been allowed to consider that evidence. Held, appeals dismissed. Where competent and careful medical treatment given to a victim for an injury inflicted by an assailant included putting the victim on a life-support machine, the decision by the medical practitioners concerned — to disconnect the machine because, by generally accepted medical criteria, the victim was dead — could not exonerate the assailant from responsibility for the death if, at the time of death, the original injury was a continuing or operating cause of the death; for then the disconnection of the machine did not break the chain of causation between the infliction of the original injury and the death. Since there was no evidence that the original injury inflicted on each

victim had ceased to be a continuing or operating cause of death at the time of the victim's death following a disconnection of the life-support machine, it followed that the issue of causation was, in each case, properly withdrawn from the jury: *R v Malcherek; R v Steel* [1981] 2 All ER 422.

MALICE AFORETHOUGHT (MENS REA)

Introduction

4.32 The sole feature which distinguished murder from manslaughter was the concept traditionally called 'malice aforethought'. Perhaps the only clear thing about this concept is that it need not involve 'malice' in the modern sense of that word — spite or ill-will — and, equally, it does not require any premeditation or 'afore-thinking'. This concept is now usually referred to as 'mens rea', or as the mental or fault element.

It was not until Sir Michael Foster wrote his *Discourse on Homicide* in the eighteenth century that any writer of authority attempted to give a concise description of the matters comprehended by the phrase. Before that time, judges and writers had contented themselves with giving examples, culled from the cases, of what did or did not constitute malice aforethought.

4.33 Foster, and East following him, described malice aforethought as meaning that the fact (the killing):

> … hath been attended with such circumstances as are the ordinary symptoms of a wicked, depraved, malignant spirit, … such circumstances as carry in them the plain indications of an heart regardless of social duty and fatally bent on mischief.

This description still finds favour in some United States courts. However, from the early part of the nineteenth century, English judges, and Australian judges following them, have sought for greater precision.

This is not to disagree with the argument that Foster's formulation lacks precision. The point rather is that its defects in that regard are offset to a considerable extent by the fact that it explains certain aspects of the law of homicide that become very puzzling if a precise analytical approach is used. Why, for example, does a surgeon, whose patient dies following an operation involving a high risk of death, of which the surgeon (and in many instances the patient) is well aware, not stand in peril of prosecution for murder? Why can a killing upon provocation be treated as manslaughter in New South Wales (but not in Victoria) notwithstanding the killer's plain intention to kill? Suggested answers to these questions will be offered presently, but a glance at Foster's formulation will show that one answer to them might be that, in each case, what he described as the 'plain indications' of malice aforethought are conspicuously lacking. In *La Fontaine v R* (1976) 11 ALR 507, Jacobs J expressed some approval for the old language as still the most appropriate means of announcing 'the element of moral culpability' which he said was firmly entrenched in the definition of murder.

4.34 The modern view of malice aforethought can be summarised by saying that it may be found to have existed in any of the following situations:

(1) where D's act was accompanied by an intention to kill;

(2) where D's act was accompanied by an intention to cause grievous bodily harm; that is, really serious injury;

(3) where D's act was accompanied by knowledge or belief that death would probably result from it;

(4) in Victoria, but not New South Wales, where D's act was accompanied by knowledge or belief that grievous bodily harm would probably result from it;

(5) where D's act was one of intentional violence and was:

   (a) in Victoria, committed in the course or furtherance of a crime, the necessary elements of which include violence for which a person upon first conviction may be sentenced to death or to life imprisonment or to imprisonment for a term of 10 years or more;

   (b) in New South Wales, committed in an attempt to commit, or during or immediately after the commission of, a crime punishable by imprisonment for life or for 25 years; and

(6) in Victoria, where D's act was one of violence committed in the course of resisting a lawful arrest, or escaping from lawful custody.

It should be stressed that this is only a starting point; it is not and does not purport to be a complete description of the concept.

4.35 As a matter of terminology, types (1), (2), (3) and (4) are normally referred to as cases of express malice, and types (5) and (6) as cases of implied or constructive malice. Types (3) and (4) are commonly referred to as 'murder by recklessness', although it is clear since *La Fontaine v R* that this expression should not be used in directing a jury.

4.36 The difference between the law in New South Wales and that in Victoria, referred to in (4) above, is a consequence of the fact that in New South Wales the mens rea of murder is spelt out in s 18(1)(a) of the Crimes Act 1900. That subsection provides:

> Murder shall be taken to have been committed where the act of the accused, or thing by him or her omitted to be done, causing the death charged, was done or omitted with reckless indifference to human life, or with intent to kill or inflict grievous bodily harm upon some person, or done in an attempt to commit, or during or immediately after the commission, by the accused, or some accomplice with him or her, of a crime punishable by imprisonment for life or for 25 years.

In *R v Solomon* [1980] 1 NSWLR 321, the New South Wales Court of Criminal Appeal held that the effect of this provision is to give recklessness a more limited operation in relation to murder than is the case in the common law jurisdictions. In that case, the trial judge had instructed the jury that they might convict of murder if 'satisfied beyond reasonable doubt that there was a recklessness that involved actual foresight of the probability of causing death or grievous bodily harm and an indifference to that risk'. By a majority, the court quashed the accused's conviction for murder and submitted a manslaughter conviction. Begg J, with whom Street CJ agreed, stated (at 377):

> I am of the opinion that there must be evidence which, on a practical basis, justified the jury being invited to consider murder based on 'reckless indifference to human life', not merely reckless indifference to whether serious harm might be caused.

Grievous bodily harm

4.37 It is settled law that 'intention to cause grievous bodily harm' means, in the law of murder, intention to cause bodily injury of a really serious kind: *Director of Public Prosecutions v Smith* [1961] AC 290. While in most of its other aspects *Director of Public Prosecutions v Smith* has been subjected to strong criticism, and expressly dissented from by the High Court in *Parker v R* (at **4.46**), its status as an authority on this point has never been in doubt, and was clearly affirmed by the House of Lords in *Hyam v Director of Public Prosecutions* [1975] AC 55. See also *R v Rhodes* (1984) 14 A Crim R 124. The intention may, of course, be inferred from the range of injuries inflicted on the victim, and their circumstances: *Meyers v R* (1997) 147 ALR 440. In New South Wales, the definition of 'grievous bodily harm' is extended in s 4 of the Crimes Act 1900 to include inflicting a grievous bodily disease.

Transferred malice

4.38 It is settled law that if D shoots at V, and hits and kills W instead, D is guilty of the murder of W (and of the attempted murder of V). The doctrine which so provides is called the doctrine of transferred malice, and is of ancient origin: 'If he strike at one and missing him kills another, whom he did not intend, this is felony and homicide, and not casualty or *per infortunium*: 1 *Hale PC* 38.

4.39 A particularly vivid application of the doctrine of transferred malice occurred in *R v Saunders and Archer* (1577) 2 Plowd 473; 75 ER 706, reported by Foster (*Crown Law* 371) as follows:

> Saunders with intention to destroy his wife, by the advice of one Archer mixed poison in a roasted apple, and gave it to her to eat. She having eaten a small part of it gave the remainder to their child. Saunders at this dreadful moment made a faint attempt to save the child; but conscious of the horrid purpose of his own heart, and unwilling to make his wife a witness of it, desisted; and stood by and saw the infant he dearly loved eat the poison, of which it soon afterwards died. It was ruled without much difficulty that Saunders was guilty of murder of the child.

See now *Attorney-General's Reference (No 3 of 1994)* [1998] AC 245, discussed at 4.14. The refusal of the House of Lords to apply the doctrine in the circumstances of that case may reveal only judicial conservatism. D's intention to kill V has always been held sufficient to sheet home guilt if D kills W by mischance. In relation to responsibility for manslaughter, the House of Lords seems to have been happy to use the rejected doctrine.

The doctrine of transferred intention applies equally to crimes other than murder: see, for example, *R v Latimer* (1886) 17 QBD 359, a case of malicious wounding.

Express malice

4.40C R v Crabbe

(1985) 156 CLR 464; 58 ALR 417
High Court of Australia

Gibbs CJ, **Wilson**, **Brennan**, **Deane** and **Dawson JJ**: This is an application by the Crown for special leave to appeal from a decision of the Full Court of the Federal Court which, by a majority, quashed the conviction of the respondent on five counts of murder and ordered a new trial (*Crabbe v R* (1984) 56 ALR 733).

The alleged offences occurred in the early hours of the morning of 18 August 1983 in a motel near Ayers Rock. The respondent had driven a road train, consisting of a prime mover and three trailers, to Ayers Rock on 17 August. He there uncoupled one trailer and went about his work of delivering, loading and unloading. Later during the evening, after he had consumed a substantial amount of alcohol, he visited the Inland Motel and drank in a crowded bar. His behaviour in the bar caused nuisance and annoyance and he was physically ejected from the bar. In the early hours of the morning following this incident he returned to the motel at the controls of his prime mover, to which one trailer was now attached. He drove the vehicle through the wall and into the bar; as a result five persons died and many were injured. The respondent did nothing to assist the injured but left the motel. He was apprehended on the following day.

The respondent was tried by the learned Chief Justice of the Northern Territory and a jury. After a summing up to which no objection was or could have been taken, the jury retired but shortly afterwards was recalled by the learned Chief Justice who, at the request of the Crown Prosecutor, gave a short redirection which included the following passage:

> It is this, I said to you, you will recall, that you had to be satisfied beyond reasonable doubt, on the question of recklessness, that he knew that there would be people in the bar.
>
> It is also a matter of law, of which I have been reminded, that if he thought there might have been, but chose to blind himself, chose not to avail himself of any opportunity of finding out. In other words, if he swept round the corner and his state of mind then was that there might be people in there, but he just went straight ahead blinding himself, not giving himself the opportunity of finding

out if there were going to be any people in there. So that he cannot — if he deliberately stops himself being able to see whether or not there were people in there, as a deliberate choice. If he says, 'Well, I'm going to go ahead anyway. I think there might be people in there, but I'm not going to have a look, so no one can say I know, because I didn't look'.

Is that clear to you, that if he blinds himself to the possibility, so to speak, well, then he cannot hide behind that. He cannot say that hiding behind his lack of actual knowledge. The jury again retired, but about two and a half hours later returned seeking a 'full definition' of murder and manslaughter. The learned Chief Justice then gave them a second redirection. Amongst other things, he said:

> A man commits murder if he kills somebody, having at the time that he did the action which caused the death, an intention to kill, or an intention to do really serious bodily injury; or, if when he kills someone, his state of mind is such that he knows what he's about to do is likely to kill someone, but nevertheless goes ahead and does that act with reckless indifference to the consequences; or, and this is the final alternative, if, when he does an act, he foresees the possibility that when he does an act, he foresees the possibility that what he does might cause death, or really serious bodily injury, nevertheless takes no reasonable available step to ascertain whether or not it will.
>
> Now, I'll apply those things that I've told you to the case in hand. There appears, as I said to you earlier, to be no dispute that Crabbe killed these people, in the sense that he drove the prime mover and semi-trailer into the bar of this motel at Ayers Rock, and that thereby he caused the deaths of these five people, so that, when you're considering whether or not he is guilty of murder, you have to consider the state of his mind at the time that he did it. If you're satisfied beyond reasonable doubt that, when he drove the truck into the motel, he intended to cause death or really serious bodily harm to whoever might be in there, then he's guilty of murder. If you're satisfied beyond reasonable doubt that his state of mind was that he knew that it was likely that if he drove the truck into the motel bar, that he would cause death or really serious bodily injury, then he is guilty of murder. He's further guilty of murder if you're satisfied beyond reasonable doubt that he foresaw the possibility that there might be some people in the bar, but didn't take any step that might have been available to him to find out whether there were any people there or not, before he went ahead and drove the vehicle in

The majority of the Full Court held that the jury was misdirected by these passages. Assuming that the doctrine of 'wilful blindness', to which the learned Chief Justice alluded in his first redirection, is applicable to a case such as the present, their Honours considered that it was erroneous to refer to foresight of a possibility, rather than of a probability, that people might be in the bar and that death or grievous bodily harm might result from the actions of the respondent. Further, the second redirection fails to mention any element of deliberation — it suggests that a person should be treated as having knowledge of facts if he neglects to take reasonable steps (or perhaps any available steps) to find out the truth, even though he does not deliberately refrain from taking such steps because he prefers to remain in ignorance.

The *Criminal Code Act 1983* (NT) had not been passed at the times material to this case and the rules of the common law governed the question what mental element is necessary to constitute the crime of murder, or, to use the traditional terminology, what is meant by malice aforethought. That question was answered in *Stephen's Digest of Criminal Law* (1st ed, 1877), in art 223 which, so far as is relevant, is as follows:

> ... Murder is unlawful homicide with malice aforethought. Malice aforethought means ... (a) An intention to cause the death of, or grievous bodily harm to, any person, whether such person is the person actually killed or not; (b) Knowledge that the act which causes death will probably cause the death of, or grievous bodily harm to, some person, whether such person is the person actually killed or not, although such knowledge is accompanied by indifference whether death or grievous bodily harm is caused or not, or by a wish that it may not be caused ...

There has been in this court some difference of opinion as to whether the knowledge which an accused person must possess in order to render him guilty of murder when he lacks an actual intent to kill or to do grievous bodily harm must be a knowledge of the probability that his acts will cause death or grievous bodily harm (as *Stephen's Digest of Criminal Law* holds) or whether knowledge of a possibility is enough. In *Pemble v R* (1971) 124 CLR 107; [1971] ALR 762, Barwick CJ thought it sufficient that death or grievous bodily harm should be foreseen as possible (see 124 CLR at 118–21), but McTiernan and Menzies JJ were of the opinion that it was necessary that the accused should have foreseen or known (the words are used without any apparent distinction) that death or grievous bodily harm would be a probable or likely (both expressions are used) consequence of the act: see at 127, 135. The matter was considered again in *La Fontaine v R* (1976) 136 CLR 62; 11 ALR 507. In that case Stephen J agreed (at (CLR) 85–6) with the opinion expressed by Barwick CJ in *Pemble v R* that it was enough that the accused foresaw the possible consequences of his acts, but Barwick CJ himself appeared now to think that it is an open question whether it is sufficient if the accused appreciated a possibility rather than the probability of serious harm (see CLR at 69). Gibbs and Jacobs JJ held that in a case of this kind an accused would not be guilty of murder unless he foresaw that death or grievous bodily harm was a probable consequence of his behaviour (see at 75–7 and 94-100) and although Mason J left the question open he noted (at 91) that the suggestion made by Barwick CJ in *Pemble v R* was not a view shared by McTiernan and Menzies JJ in that case and that it was at odds with the speeches of the members of the House of Lords in *R v Hyam* [1975] AC 55. Clearly the balance of opinion in this court has been in favour of the view that the mental state necessary to constitute murder in a case of this kind is knowledge by the accused that his acts will probably cause death or grievous bodily harm. The view that knowledge of a possibility is not enough has been accepted by the Full Court of the Supreme Court of Victoria (*R v Jakac* [1961] VR 367; *R v Sergi* [1974] VR 1; *Nydam v R* [1977] VR 430; *R v Windsor* [1982] VR 89) and by the Full Court of the Supreme Court of South Australia (*R v Hallett* [1969] SASR 141).

The conclusion that a person is guilty of murder if he commits a fatal act knowing that it will probably cause death or grievous bodily harm but (absent an intention to kill or do grievous bodily harm) is not guilty of murder if he knew only that his act might possibly cause death or grievous bodily harm is not only supported by a preponderance of authority but is sound in principle. The conduct of a person who does an act, knowing that death or grievous bodily harm is a probable consequence, can naturally be regarded for the purposes of the criminal law as just as blameworthy as the conduct of one who does an act intended to kill or to do grievous bodily harm. Indeed, on one view, a person who does an act knowing its probable consequences may be regarded as having intended those consequences to occur. That view was expressed in *R v Hyam* by Viscount Dilhorne ([1975] AC at 82), Lord Diplock (at 86) and possibly by Lord Cross of Chelsea (at 96), although Lord Hailsham of St Marylebone LC denied its correctness (at 74–5). There is other authority in favour of the view, including some of the cases mentioned in *Archbolds Criminal Pleading, Evidence and Practice* (41st ed), pp 995–1001 and the passage from Kenny: *Outlines of Criminal Law* cited by Dixon CJ in *Vallance v R* (1961) 108 CLR 56 at 59. It is, however, unnecessary to enter upon that controversy. If an accused knows when he does an act that death or grievous bodily harm is a probable consequence, he does the act expecting that death or grievous bodily harm will be the likely result, for the word 'probable' means likely to happen. That state of mind is comparable with an intention to kill or to do grievous bodily harm. There is a difference between the case in which a person acts knowing that death or serious injury is only a possible consequence and where he knows that it is a likely result. The former is not a case of murder even if death ensues, unless death or grievous bodily harm is intended (or, perhaps — and it is unnecessary to consider this proposition — unless the act is done with the intention and for the sole purpose of creating a risk of death or grievous bodily harm).

It should now be regarded as settled law in Australia, if no statutory provision affects the position, that a person who, without lawful justification or excuse, does an act knowing that it is probable that death or grievous bodily harm will result, is guilty of murder if death in fact results. It is not enough that he does the act knowing that it is possible but not likely that death or grievous bodily harm might result.

A person who does an act causing death knowing that it is probable that the act will cause death or grievous bodily harm is, as *Stephen's Digest* states, guilty of murder, although such knowledge is accompanied by indifference whether death or grievous bodily harm is caused or not, or even by a wish that death or grievous bodily harm might not be caused. That does not mean that reckless indifference is an element of the mental state necessary to constitute the crime of murder. It is not the offender's indifference to the consequences of his act but his knowledge that those consequences will probably occur that is the relevant element. Of course, not every fatal act done with the knowledge that death or grievous bodily harm will probably result is murder. The act may be lawful, that is, justified or excused by law. A surgeon who competently performs a hazardous but necessary operation is not criminally liable if the patient dies, even if the surgeon foresaw that his death was probable. Academic writers have pointed out that in deciding whether an act is justifiable its social purpose or social utility is important: see, for example, Howard: *Criminal Law* (4th ed, 1982), pp 54–5 and 357–9. That question need not be discussed in the present case where there was no possible justification or excuse for the actions of the applicant. It should, however, be made clear that lack of social purpose is not an element of the mental state with which we are here concerned, though it may bear on the question whether the act is justifiable.

It was submitted on behalf of the Crown that a distinction can be drawn between foresight of the consequences of an act — ie what harm it would do if persons were in a position to be affected by it when it occurred — and a foresight of circumstances — ie of the fact that persons were in a position to be affected. There is no justification in logic or principle for drawing a distinction of this kind. The test simply is whether the accused person knew that his actions would probably cause death or grievous bodily harm.

Finally, there is the question whether the jury should have been directed on the question of wilful blindness. When a person deliberately refrains from making inquiries because he prefers not to have the result, when he wilfully shuts his eyes for fear that he may learn the truth, he may for some purposes be treated as having the knowledge which he deliberately abstained from acquiring. According to Professor Glanville Williams, *Criminal Law: The General Part* (2nd ed, 1961), p 159: 'A court can properly find wilful blindness only where it can almost be said that the defendant actually knew. He suspected the fact; he realised its probability; but he refrained from obtaining the final confirmation because he wanted in the event to be able to deny knowledge. This, and this alone, is wilful blindness. It requires in effect a finding that the defendant intended to cheat the administration of justice.'

Again, in his *Textbook of Criminal Law,* 1978, p 79, Professor Glanville Williams said, in a passage cited by Lord Edmund-Davies in *R v Caldwell* [1982] AC 341 at 358: 'A person cannot, in any intelligible meaning of the words, close his mind to a risk unless he first realises that there is a risk; and if he realises that there is a risk, that is the end of the matter.'

These statements support the view that it cannot be said that an accused was wilfully blind to the consequences of his acts unless he knew that those consequences were probable; if that is so, the doctrine has no part to play in cases of murder.

Professor Howard, on the other hand, considers that an accused may be convicted of murder even though he foresaw only the bare possibility that someone might be killed if, having foreseen that possibility, he deliberately took no steps to ascertain the magnitude of the risk: op cit, p 54. However, it seems to us that to state the proposition in that manner is likely to mislead. The question is whether the accused knew or foresaw that his actions would probably cause death or grievous bodily harm and actual knowledge or foresight is necessary; imputed knowledge is not enough. Deliberate abstention from inquiry might, of course, be evidence of the actual knowledge or foresight of the accused.

In the present case, there was no evidence that the respondent deliberately refrained from finding out whether there was anyone in the bar and it was unnecessary to advert to the matter. Moreover, it was misleading to speak in terms which suggest that the respondent may have foreseen the possibility that there may have been some people in the bar. This passage, which is contained in the trial judge's second redirection, was likely to confuse in the jury's mind the mental state which the respondent was required to have had before he could be found guilty of murder. It amounts to a material misdirection.

For these reasons the majority of the Full Court of the Federal Court was correct in setting aside the conviction and ordering a new trial. Having regard to the importance of the matter, special leave to appeal will be granted but the appeal must be dismissed.

4.41 Notes and questions

1. At the retrial, the defendant was found guilty of murder and sentenced to imprisonment for life: *R v Crabbe* (SC(NT), Rice J, 4 October 1985, unreported).
2. In *La Fontaine v R* (1976) 11 ALR 507, the High Court of Australia held that the issue of murder by recklessness ought only to be left to the jury when it arises as a real possibility on the facts of the case, and held that the word 'reckless' should not be used in directing a jury as to murder. Why? Does the court's judgment in *Crabbe* clarify this issue? Consider this question further after you have read **Chapters 5** and **6**. Do you consider that the state of mind of a person who foresees the probability of death or grievous bodily harm as a result of his or her actions, and who performs those actions without wishing to bring them about, is sufficiently culpable to be guilty of the crime of murder? If so, would you go further and adopt the view of Barwick CJ in *La Fontaine* that it is sufficient that the accused foresaw the *possibility* of death or grievous bodily harm? The High Court considered the issue of 'wilful blindness', in *Crabbe's* case, as irrelevant where the question is one of murder by recklessness. Was the court right?
3. In *R v TY* (2006) 12 VR 557, D, who was 14-years-old, was a member of a group which became involved in an altercation with another group. D struck a member of the other group twice in the head with the steel tip of an umbrella. The umbrella tip penetrated V's skull and his brain, and V died two days later. The judge directed the jury on reckless murder and manslaughter by unlawful dangerous act. D was convicted of murder. On appeal, held, appeal allowed and a re-trial ordered. The directions of the judge were deficient in that the judge failed to distinguish expressly between the mental elements of reckless murder and manslaughter by unlawful and dangerous act. Warren CJ stated that a jury in the circumstances of reckless murder should be directed that they must be satisfied beyond reasonable doubt that:
   (a) The accused caused the death of the deceased.
   (b) The accused ought and must have foreseen the consequences of the act contemplated; and further, that,
   (c) In assessing foresight, what a reasonable person might have foreseen is relevant but the accused's *actual* state of mind is critically important and they should not treat what they think a reasonable person's reaction would be in the circumstances as decisive of the accused's state of mind.
   (d) In assessing the accused's state of mind the accused's circumstances are relevant (such as age, background, educational and social circumstances, emotional state and state of sobriety)

   See also *R v Barrett* (2007) 16 VR 240.

4. The House of Lords has rejected the version of malice aforethought accepted, and refined, in *Crabbe's* case. In *R v Moloney* [1985] AC 905, D was convicted of the murder of V, his stepfather. After a family celebration in which both had been drinking heavily, they challenged each other as to who could fire a shotgun, after loading, more quickly. D shot V, who died immediately. The House of Lords held that D's foresight of the probable occurrence of death or grievous bodily harm is not the equivalent of or an alternative to an intention to kill or to cause grievous bodily harm. D's conviction was quashed, and a verdict of manslaughter was substituted. (D had been ready to plead guilty to manslaughter at his trial, but the Crown refused to accept that plea.) Lord Bridge, who spoke for the House of Lords, stated that there may be 'extremely rare' cases in which the trial judge will need to refer to foresight of consequences, as bearing on intention in murder. He identified that foresight, however, as an element affecting the law of evidence, not the law of murder.
5. In *R v Hancock and Shankland* [1986] 1 AC 455, the defendants, coal miners on strike, were convicted of the murder of a taxi driver, who was driving a miner to work. They had pushed a concrete block from a bridge above the road on which the taxi was travelling; it struck the taxi and the driver died in the ensuing wreck. The defendants denied that they intended to hurt anyone. While the House of Lords criticised part of Lord Bridge's speech in *Moloney*, it maintained its holding in *Moloney* that recklessness is not a separate category of malice aforethought in murder. Juries should be directed, their Lordships stated, that only where there is evidence that the defendant foresaw as a virtual certainty that the victim would die or suffer grievous bodily harm, may they infer an intention to bring about the proscribed result.
6. However, the Australian position is now firmly and unequivocally different. There remains, however, an ambiguity as to the meaning of the word 'probable'. For most purposes, a consequence is foreseen as probable when it is perceived that it is more likely than not to occur. Judges are not, however, to direct juries in terms of 'an odds on chance' or 'a more than 50 per cent chance': *La Fontaine v R* (1976) 136 CLR 62 at 99 per Jacobs J; *Boughey v R* (1986) 161 CLR 10 at 15 per Gibbs CJ, at 19–22 per Mason, Wilson and Deane JJ. In some cases, foresight of a less than even chance of death or grievous bodily harm may be regarded as sufficient to render the accused guilty of murder if death results. If D places two bullets in a six-chamber revolver, twirls the cylinder, points the gun at V and pulls the trigger once, the chances of V being shot are one in three. It would, however, seem that D could be said to be acting with knowledge that death or grievous bodily harm was a probable outcome of his conduct.

In *R v Faure* [1999] 2 VR 537, D shot and killed V and was convicted of murder. D's defence was that he and V had played Russian roulette after they had both been drinking. D claimed that the game had been played with a six-shot revolver containing one round of ammunition and that he and V had, by agreement, twice pulled the trigger while pointing the gun at the other. On appeal to the Victorian Court of Appeal, D's conviction was quashed on the ground of inadequate direction as to intoxication. This aspect of the case is considered at **15.24**. The court ordered a retrial. In the course of discussing murder by recklessness, Brooking J stated (at 549): 'In my own view it is dangerous in the necessary sense to fire once with one round in a six-round chamber'. His Honour continued (at 551):

> When text writers describe a game like Russian roulette as dangerous, they are not gainsaying the role of the jury. They are seeking to convey that a reasonable jury, properly instructed, should find that the necessary element of danger existed in such a case. To make the process of reasoning more explicit, they are asserting a proposition of law, namely, that 'probable' as contrasted with 'possible but not likely' (*R v Crabbe* (1985) 156 CLR 464 at 469–70) means a substantial, or real and not remote, chance, whether or not it is more than 50 per cent (*Boughey* at 21 per Mason, Wilson and Deane JJ) and saying that accordingly in the case put a reasonable jury should regard the chance as substantial.

Contemporaneity

4.42 The act or omission causing the death of a person (the actus reus of murder) must coincide with the mens rea of murder.

4.43C **Thabo Meli v R**
[1954] 1 All ER 373
Privy Council

[The appellants, in accordance with a preconceived plan, took a man to a hut, gave him beer so that he was partially intoxicated, and then struck him over the head. Believing him to be dead, they then took his body and rolled it over a low cliff, dressing up the scene to make it look like an accident. In fact, the man was not then dead, it being established from medical evidence that the final cause of his death was exposure when he was left unconscious at the foot of the cliff. The accused were convicted of murder in the High Court of Basutoland, and appealed to the Privy Council.]

Lord Reid [reading the judgment of the court]: The point of law which was raised in this case can be simply stated. It is said that two acts were done: — first, the attack in the hut; and, secondly, the placing of the body outside afterwards — and that they were separate acts. It is said that, while the first act was accomplished by *mens rea*, it was not the cause of death; but that the second act, while it was the cause of death, was not accomplished by *mens rea*; and on that ground, it is said that the accused are not guilty of murder, though they may have been guilty of culpable homicide. It is said that the *mens rea* necessary to establish murder is an intention to kill, and that there could be no intention to kill when the accused thought that the man was already dead, so their original intention to kill had ceased before they did the act which caused the man's death. It appears to their Lordships impossible to divide up what was really one series of acts in this way. There is no doubt that the accused set out to do all these acts in order to achieve their plan, and as parts of their plan; and it is much too refined a ground of judgment to say that, because they were under a misapprehension at one stage and thought that their guilty purpose had been achieved before, in fact, it was achieved, therefore they are to escape the penalties of the law. Their Lordships do not think that this is a matter which is susceptible of elaboration. There appears to be no case, either in South Africa or England, or for that matter elsewhere, which resembles the present. Their Lordships can find no difference relevant to the present case between the law of South Africa and the law of England; and they are of opinion that by both laws there can be no separation such as that for which the accused contend. Their crime is not reduced from murder to a lesser crime merely because the accused were under some misapprehension for a time during the completion of their criminal plot.

Their Lordships must, therefore, humbly advise Her Majesty that this appeal should be dismissed.

[Appeal dismissed.]

4.44 Notes and illustrations

1. The problem raised by *Thabo Meli* — that of the relationship which must exist in point of time between the wrongful act performed by the accused and his or her wrongful intention — is one of general application. For an example in relation to the crime of assault, see again *Fagan v Metropolitan Police Commissioner* (at **2.23C**).

   Had the basic facts in *Thabo Meli* been the same but the interval of time between rendering the victim unconscious and rolling his body over the cliff been greater, might the decision in that case have been different? If the answer is yes, is there any reason of principle why this should be so? See the discussion by Professor G Williams, *Textbook of Criminal Law,* 2nd ed, Stevens & Sons, London, 1983, p 256. If the accused had not been guilty of murder, of what crimes might they have been convicted? Note *Attorney General's Reference (No 4 of 1980)* [1981] 2 All ER 617.

2. D was charged with the murder of a woman whose badly injured body was found in the river Ouse. The cause of death was drowning. D's defence was that he had taken the woman to his van for sexual purposes, was mocked

by her for failing to satisfy her, and, a fight ensuing, he had knocked her unconscious. He tried to rouse her for about half an hour then, thinking she was dead, panicked and threw her into the river. The accused was convicted of manslaughter and appealed to the Court of Criminal Appeal. Held, D's conduct in inflicting the initial injuries and later throwing the body into the river constituted a single series of acts, and that therefore a verdict of guilty of manslaughter at least was inevitable: *R v Church* [1966] 1 QB 59. See now *Royall v R* (at **4.30C**). The High Court, while maintaining that causation and intention are separate questions, now clearly recognises their interdependence. This is particularly emphasised in the judgment of McHugh J in *Royall.*

3. In *R v Taber* (2002) 56 NSWLR 443, V was attacked in her home and left bound and gagged by the three accused. Shortly after abandoning her, one of the accused made a call to emergency services and supplied some information concerning the situation of V. The phone call was not acted upon by the emergency services. After the telephone call, no further attempt was made to have V rescued. V died of dehydration between 9 and 11 days later. At trial, an application was made for a directed verdict of not guilty of murder. The judge, Barr J, refused the application. His Honour stated (at 451):

> It seems to me that it is legitimate to describe what caused the death of the deceased as a single continuous act, commencing when she was attacked and ending when she died or, as an act, commencing when she was attacked and ending when she was abandoned, and an omission, commencing then and ending when she died. On the authorities which I have cited I think that the jury are entitled to find any accused guilty of murder who had the relevant state of mind during the continuous act. If that be so, it seems to me impossible reasonably to argue that the same result may not follow if the same state of mind arises at any time after the commencement of the act as secondly defined and during the period of the omission. However the cause of death is categorised it seems accurately to be able to be described as a single transaction. If the Crown can prove it and if it can also prove that during its continuance any accused had the necessary state of mind, then that accused ought to be found guilty of murder.

Proof of express malice

4.45 Before concluding discussion of the four forms of express malice aforethought listed as (1), (2), (3) and (4) at **4.34**, mention must be made of the problem of how the existence of any of the four is to be ascertained. Only rarely will there be any unequivocal statement by D that, at the time of the fatal act, he or she possessed one or other of these states of mind. In most instances, the jury will have to determine from all the circumstances whether or not the defendant did. Thus the question may be asked, are they to do so by use of a subjective test or by use of an objective one?: see 1.36.

There is no doubt about the answer to this question. It is now beyond dispute that in this context — and, indeed, in any context in the criminal law where responsibility turns on a person's intentions, realisations, beliefs, or other similar mental states — a subjective test is to be used. There was a brief period in England when, as a result of the decision of the House of Lords in *Director of Public Prosecutions v Smith* [1961] AC 290 (approving that of the Court of Criminal Appeal in *R v Ward* [1956] 1 QB 351), a different view prevailed. During this period, the accused's state of mind was ignored by the English courts, attention being focused instead on the hypothetical mental state of a hypothetical reasonable person placed in the accused's position. However, the decision drew a storm of criticism and was on this matter eradicated by the Criminal Justice Act 1967 (Eng) s 8. In *R v Frankland* [1987] AC 576, the Privy Council decided that the rule in Smith was wrong.

4.46 In Australia, it has long been recognised that intentions and other mental states are 'subjective' matters which must be ascertained 'subjectively'. The High Court had spoken strongly on the matter on more than one occasion, and it was not to be expected that the decision in *Smith* would be welcomed by the court. In the event, in *Parker v R* (1963) 111 CLR 610 at 632, Dixon CJ, in the final paragraph of his judgment, condemned it. He said:

> There are propositions laid down in the judgment which I believe to be misconceived and wrong. They are fundamental and they are propositions which I could never bring myself to accept. I shall not discuss the case … I wish there to be no misunderstanding on the subject. I shall not depart from the law on the matter as we had long since laid it down in this court and I think *Smith's* case should not be used as authority at all.

The Chief Justice added that in saying this he spoke for the entire High Court. Since that statement, there has been no need for further discussion of the matter.

It should not be thought, however, that the statement in *Parker* removed all 'objective' tests from the criminal law, or was intended to do so. It dealt only with those instances (of which there are many) where the common law or statute requires proof of the possession of a particular state of mind as a condition of criminal responsibility. However, it leaves untouched those areas of criminal responsibility which are not so linked, such as the question of dangerousness or negligence in manslaughter (see 6.7–6.19) and reasonable necessity for the use of force in self-defence: see Chapter 12. Thus, to take one example, whether a particular activity was dangerous will turn on how it would be regarded by the ordinary person, not whether the accused thought it to be dangerous.

4.47 The reader will find in many of the cases a reference to the 'presumption that a man intends the natural or probable consequences of his acts'. The phrase made its appearance at the beginning of the nineteenth century, and it was used over and over again in directing juries thereafter. It has, indeed, an important substratum of truth. In determining someone's intentions at a given moment, you look at what that person is doing and saying, and take account of the fact that people usually do intend to bring about the results of their physical acts. A person who aims a loaded gun at someone else and pulls the trigger usually intends to injure them.

But the phrase also contains the seeds of serious error. As Lord Reid explained in *Gollins v Gollins* [1964] AC 644 at 664:

> In fact people often intend something quite different from what they know to be the natural and probable result of what they are doing. To take a trivial example, if I say I intend to reach the green, people will believe me although we all know that the odds are ten to one against my succeeding; and no one but a lawyer would say that I must be presumed to have intended to put my ball in the bunker because that was the natural and probable result of my shot.

4.48 If this were always explained clearly to a jury no problems would arise, but in practice this is not always done. Judges have used the phrase without explanation and thus left juries with the impression that they are bound to attribute to an accused an intention which that person probably, perhaps obviously, did not have. The evidence in each case must be considered; that means all the evidence.

To overcome the difficulty, the High Court has said, in a series of cases culminating in *Smyth v R* (1957) 98 CLR 163, that the phrase is not to be used in directing juries. The House of Lords has now reached the same position: see particularly *R v Moloney* [1985] AC 905 (at **4.41**).

Constructive malice

4.49 At common law it was murder to cause death in the course of committing a felony or while resisting lawful arrest: Foster, *Crown Law,* 3rd ed, 1809; *R v Serne* (1887) 16 Cox CC 311. In *Director of Public Prosecutions v Beard* [1920] AC 479, the House of Lords restricted the doctrine of felony-murder to cases of killing by an act of violence done in the course of, or in the furtherance of, a felony involving violence.

4.50 In Victoria, it was decided as a matter of policy that the felony-murder rule be stated in statutory form when it was decided to abolish the classification of crimes into felonies and misdemeanours. The Crimes (Classification of Offences) Act 1981 (Vic) inserted a new s 3A into the Crimes Act 1958 (Vic):

> (1) A person who unintentionally causes the death of another person by an act of violence done in the course or furtherance of a *crime the necessary elements of which include violence* for which a person upon first conviction may, under or by virtue of any enactment, be sentenced to level 1 imprisonment (life) or to imprisonment for a term of 10 years or more shall be liable to be convicted of murder as though he had killed that person intentionally.

(2) The rule of law known as the felony-murder rule (whereby a person who unintentionally causes the death of another by an act of violence done in the course or furtherance of a felony of violence is liable to be convicted of murder as though he had killed that person intentionally) is hereby abrogated.

The words in italics were inserted by way of amendment to the bill during its passage through Parliament. They were inserted to replace the words 'crime of violence' because that expression was said to be 'ambiguous'. The significance of the amendment is that it makes it clear that a crime does not count for the purposes of the new constructive-murder rule merely because it is committed in circumstances involving violence. For a crime to attract the operation of the rule, it must be one 'the necessary elements of which include violence'.

4.51 It appears from the parliamentary debates that the intention of this provision was to preserve the existing common law position as spelt out in *R v Ryan and Walker* [1966] VR 553 (at **4.55C**). The Full Court adopted that view of the provision in *R v Butcher* [1986] VR 43, and this view was affirmed by the Court of Appeal in *R v Galas; R v Mikhael* (2007) 18 VR 205 (**4.56C**). The expression 'crime the necessary elements of which include violence' is an unfortunate way of seeking to achieve this outcome since, as a matter of strict logic, there are few crimes which have violence as one of their 'necessary' elements. Even crimes such as rape can arguably be committed without violence as in the case of rape by impersonation. Likewise kidnapping — Crimes Act 1958 (Vic) s 63A can occur without violence as in the case where the victim is, without violence, enticed or detained by deception. Such a restrictive interpretation of the expression was rejected by the Full Court in *R v Butcher* and by the Court of Appeal in *R v Galas; R v Mikhael*. Nonetheless, the list of crimes which may attract the operation of the constructive-murder rule is short, being limited to those crimes which at common law were regarded as crimes of violence. The only ones of general significance would seem to be rape, robbery, armed robbery, piracy with violence and piracy, and aggravated burglary: Crimes Act 1958 (Vic) ss 38, 75, 75A, 70A, 70B and 77, respectively. In *R v Butcher* [1986] VR 43 and *R v Galas; R v Mikhael* (2007) 18 VR 205 (**4.56C**), the crime was armed robbery.

4.52 The present status of the resisting arrest-murder rule must be regarded as uncertain. It is suggested that the view the courts are likely to adopt is that it is unaffected by the new legislation. In *R v Ryan and Walker*, the resisting arrest-murder rule was treated as quite distinct from the felony-murder rule. Thus it is probable that a Victorian court will hold that the felony-murder rule only was abolished by s 3A(2).

4.53 In New South Wales also, the rule has been cast into statutory form. Section 18(1)(a) of the Crimes Act 1900 (NSW) defines murder as including the case where death was caused by an act 'done in an attempt to commit, or during or immediately after the commission, by the accused, or some accomplice with him or her, of a crime punishable by imprisonment for life or for 25 years'. This provision is quite limited in that it applies only in respect of crimes punishable by imprisonment for life or for 25 years. Therefore, it does not, for example, apply to any of the categories of sexual assault set out: see **3.12E**. In New South Wales, there exists no separate resisting arrest-murder rule: see *R v Foster* (1995) 78 A Crim R 517.

4.54 Three of the Criminal Codes have their own form of the felony-murder rule: see Criminal Code (Qld) s 94; Criminal Code (WA) s 279; Criminal Code (Tas) s 157. In the Northern Territory, the statutory form of the felony-murder rule was abolished in 2006: see S Gray and J Blokland, *Criminal Laws Northern Territory*, 2nd ed, Federation Press, 2012, p 216.

4.55C

R v Ryan and Walker

[1966] VR 553

Full Court of the Supreme Court of Victoria

[The applicants were prisoners at Pentridge Gaol. On the day in question, Ryan seized a rifle and overpowered a warder whom he forced to open the gate which led into a public street outside the gaol. As the applicants were making their way out of the gaol, they were pursued by three warders. Evidence was given that as Walker was being chased by a warder named Hodson, Ryan shot and killed Hodson. The applicants subsequently eluded the warders and were not recaptured until several weeks later. At the trial of the applicants for murder, Ryan's defence was that he had not fired the fatal shot. The trial judge directed the jury that if it had a reasonable doubt as to whether Ryan had fired the shot which killed Hodson, it should acquit both accused. The jury convicted Ryan of murder and Walker of manslaughter. They applied for leave to appeal against their respective convictions.]

Winneke CJ, **Hudson** and **McInerney JJ**: Section 35 of the *Gaols Act 1958* provides:

> Every male person lawfully imprisoned for any crime misdemeanour or offence by the sentence of any Court of competent jurisdiction, or employed at labour as a criminal on the roads or other public works of Victoria, who escapes or attempts to escape from any gaol or from the custody of any member of the police force gaoler or other officer in whose custody he may be, shall be guilty of felony; and being lawfully convicted thereof shall be liable to imprisonment with or without hard labour for a term of not more than five years.

The learned judge at the trial took the view that upon the proper construction of this section the offence created by the words 'who escapes … from any gaol' may be established by proof of conduct on the part of the prisoner which takes place even after he has succeeded in getting outside the confines of the gaol in which he is incarcerated; that the offence of escaping from gaol involves as one of its essential elements the regaining by the prisoner of his liberty: that this element is not satisfied the moment a prisoner sets foot outside the walls of his gaol if he is followed immediately by his gaolers in pursuit of him who have not lost sight of him and are hot on his heels.

Having taken this view, the learned judge considered that it was beyond doubt that in the circumstances disclosed by the evidence the applicants were still in the course of escaping and committing the felony created by s 35 of the *Gaols Act 1958* when Hodson was killed.

It was on the basis of this view that the learned judge directed the jury as to what the Crown had to prove to establish murder — the crime charged. He said:

> To establish murder the Crown must prove beyond reasonable doubt these things: First, that a person, in this case Hodson, was killed. Well, gentlemen, it is a matter for you but there would not appear to be much doubt about that. Secondly, that the accused caused his death whilst the accused was of sound mind. Well, there seems to be no dispute that the accused were both of sound mind although it remains a matter for you. Of course, that the accused Ryan caused his death is probably the great issue in this case. Thirdly, you have to be satisfied beyond reasonable doubt that the act which brought about his death was intentional, voluntary, conscious and deliberate. In other words not accidental, or not done in a blackout or something of that nature. Again, although it remains a matter for you, it seems, if it were done at all, to be no real question of that element. Fourthly, that at the time the act was done it was done either with the intention of killing Hodson or with the intention of doing him grievous bodily harm. Now grievous bodily harm means, gentlemen, really serious bodily harm. Gentlemen, you see there are two intents here that have to be established. The act has to be done intentionally, that is one, and with the intention of killing the other person, that is two.

The learned judge then gave an example of a deliberate act of shooting resulting in the death of a man which would not amount to murder because it was not done with the intention of causing harm. He then proceeded:

> The last two elements, I think, need not concern you in this case but they remain strictly of course a matter for you. First, provided that there is no lawful justification or excuse for the killing — that means such things as self-defence, there are some circumstances where you can kill a man lawfully in self-defence; there seems to be no question of self-defence here although it remains a matter for you; and provided there is nothing in the circumstances which is sufficient in law to reduce the killing from murder to manslaughter. That refers to such things as provocation, gentlemen, and again there seems to be no question of that here, although it remains a matter for you. That is a general definition of murder but there is one qualification, gentlemen. In certain circumstances the crime of murder may be established even though the accused had no actual intention of killing and that is so in these circumstances. If a killing occurs by an act of violence *in the course of a commission of a felony involving violence or in the furtherance of the purpose of such felony* the accused is guilty of murder even though there is no actual intention of killing. This is known to lawyers as felony-murder. The intention is imputed to the accused by law; it is what is called constructive intention or constructive malice. Now what has the Crown got to establish in order to establish

what I might for convenience call felony-murder? First, it has got to establish that there was a felony being committed.

Then the learned judge referred to s 35 of the Gaols Act and the admissions that had been made by counsel for both the applicants that they were in Pentridge serving sentences of long terms of imprisonment as a result of convictions. He then proceeded:

> The next thing is, it has got to be by an act of violence. Now, what is an act of violence in this connection? This may be said in definition, when the actor did the act *if he must have contemplated or as a reasonable man should have contemplated that death or grievous bodily harm was likely to result, then this portion of the definition is satisfied.* Next, in the commission of a felony involving violence: commission means while he is doing it and before it is over. Once it is complete, of course, there can be no question of felony-murder. Furtherance: in the furtherance of the purpose of such felony. Furtherance means the promotion or advancement of the purpose or helping forward of the purpose.

The learned judge then gave an example of an act which would and one which would not amount to the furtherance of the purpose of a felony and proceeded:

> Now gentlemen, in the case of an escape from gaol, it is a matter for you, of course, but it may be that the accused hoped very much that they would get away with it without anyone seeing them at all and there would not be any violence. But it is open to you to find that this is just the sort of crime that if detection occurred it is very likely indeed to lead to violence of one kind or another. Now, gentlemen, if you are satisfied of those things, satisfied beyond reasonable doubt *you would be entitled to return a verdict of murder on this basis.* It seems to me, but it is a matter for you, that as far as Ryan is concerned this is not very important. The entire fight in this case has been as to whether beyond reasonable doubt Ryan fired the shot. If he did not, of course, he is not guilty of anything. If he did, no argument has been addressed to you by Mr Opas [counsel for Ryan] as to why you should not find that all the other elements of murder were present. Evidence seems to disclose, and again I repeat it is a matter for you, that if he did fire the shot he stopped dead in his tracks and fired deliberately at Hodson and killed him. If that were so that would be murder without any resort to the doctrine of felony-murder at all, so you may think … However, the question of felony-murder may be important when we come to Walker's case. Gentlemen, that is the law so far as it applies to Ryan and of course both definitions also apply to Walker. As far as Walker is concerned, no one has suggested he fired the fatal shot, or ever had a gun; and if you acquit Ryan I direct you in point of law that you must acquit Walker. However, gentlemen, the Crown presents its case against Walker in this way.

The learned judge then proceeded to state the law which he directed the jury was applicable to the case of Walker …

[The court here discussed a contention that the felony of escaping from a gaol was completed before the shot was fired. They held that a prisoner who has completely emerged from the gaol has incurred the penalty imposed by s 35, but that the felony created by s 35 was, in this case, still being committed when Ryan and Walker were endeavouring to elude pursuit outside and in the immediate vicinity of the gaol.]

As appears from his charge, the learned judge directed the jury that a verdict of murder might be found on either of two bases.

If the jury founded its verdict on the first basis of express malice — an intention by Ryan to kill or do grievous bodily harm — clearly no exception could be, or in fact was taken, to it. But if, as was possible, it reached its verdict on the second basis, this is of felony-murder, it becomes necessary to consider the seventh and final ground of Ryan's application, namely, that the learned judge misdirected the jury that in the case of felony-murder the intention of the accused either to kill or do grievous bodily harm was irrelevant in the circumstances of the case. Such a direction was in fact given and the learned judge did tell the jury that it was sufficient in such a case if the killing was brought about by an act of violence which the actor must have contemplated or as a reasonable man should have contemplated was likely to result in death or grievous bodily harm. It was contended for the applicant that this brought into the definition of felony-murder an objective element which was inconsistent with the ruling of the High Court in *Parker v R* (1963) 111 CLR 610 at 632; [1963] ALR 524 at 537.

As to this there are, in our opinion, two answers.

In the first place, we think that the Solicitor-General was right in his submission that the principle stated in *Parker v R,* supra, was expressed in relation to cases of express malice, and is not applicable to cases of constructive murder. In the latter, once the intentional act of violence is found, the malice is imputed by law, and if the principle referred to were to be applied, the effect would be to abolish the rule of felony-murder.

Second, we think that the question whether the act by which the death is brought about is an act of violence is, if abortion cases are put on one side, one ordinarily to be determined by the character of the particular act itself rather than by the intent of the actor. To that extent the learned trial judge's direction at this point introduced an unnecessary element, for it is apparent that he was adopting the language of directions given in the case of deaths following abortion or an attempted abortion: see *R v Lumley* (1911) 22 Cox CC 635 (CCC); *R v Brown and Brian* [1949] VLR 177 at 181, [1949] ALR at 466, per Lowe J. In such cases the direction is given as a guide in the determination of whether the killing is murder or manslaughter. But such cases stand in a special category, no doubt for the reason pointed out by the Court of Criminal Appeal, in *R v Stone* (1937) 53 TLR 1046 at 1047, [1937] 3 All ER 920 at 921, namely, that 'In those cases, although an illegal act was being done, there was no intention to do any harm or anything against the wish of the person hurt. Indeed the desire was to help or assist that person ...'.

In *Stone's* case the direction complained of was the affirmative answer given by the trial judge to the jury's question: 'If as a result of an intention to commit rape a girl is killed, although there was no intention to kill her, is the man guilty of murder?' Answer: 'Yes, undoubtedly.'

In dismissing the appeal, the Court of Criminal Appeal rejected the appellant's argument that 'The same steady growth of a current of mercy which had appeared in recent years in constructive murder arising out of the crime of abortion should apply to constructive murder arising out of the crime of rape'.

The position is, therefore, that in *R v Stone,* supra, the court rejected the view that in felony-murder not only must the act which caused death be one done in the course of committing a felony, but also that the act must be one which, in the contemplation of a reasonable man, must be capable at least of causing grievous bodily harm.

The direction of Sholl J, in the case of *R v Parmenter* [1956] VLR 312 at 313; [1956] ALR 717 at 718 (1955), in which *R v Stone*, supra, was not cited, is quite inconsistent with that decision, and with the direction explicitly approved in *Ross v R* (1922) 30 CLR 246; 28 ALR 138 per Knox CJ, Gavan Duffy and Starke JJ, 30 CLR at 252; 28 ALR at 42, and per Higgins J, 30 CLR at 271; 28 ALR at 150. It is also inconsistent with the direction approved in *Director of Public Prosecutions v Beard* [1920] AC 479 at 493; [1920] All ER Rep 21 at 24 (HL), and with the decision in *R v Betts and Ridley* (1930) 22 Cr App Rep 148 at 152–3; 144 LT 526 at 528.

In these circumstances, the introduction of the unnecessary element could not have operated to the prejudice of the applicant.

But even if, contrary to our view, the interpretation placed upon s 35 of the *Gaols Act 1958* by the learned judge was wrong so that his direction as to felony-murder constituted a misdirection, we are none the less of opinion for the following reasons that no substantial miscarriage of justice has actually occurred.

In our opinion, it is clear law that the killing of a person by the intentional use of force, knowingly to prevent such person from making an arrest which he is authorised by common law to make, is murder even if the person using the force did not intend to kill or do grievous bodily harm, and even if he did not foresee that he was likely to do so. See 1 *East PC* 295; *Stephen's Digest of the Criminal Law* (9th ed, 1950), p 213; 10 *Halsbury, Laws of England* (Simonds ed), p 707; *R v Woolmer* (1832) 1 Mood 334, 168 ER 1293 (CCR); *R v Williams* (1833) 1 Mood 387, 168 ER 1314 (CCR); *Archbold, Criminal Pleading, Evidence and Practice* (35th ed, 1962), pp 973–4, 1077 [sic]; *R v Howarth* (1828) 1 Mood 207, 168 ER 1243 (CCR); *Russell on Crime* (10th ed, 1950), pp 503–4, 544–51; *R v Porter* (1873) 12 Cox CC 444 (Hertford Assizes); *R v Appleby* (1940) 28 Cr App Rep 1; *R v Vickers* [1957] 2 QB 664 at 670; [1957] 2 All ER 741 at 743 (CCA), and *R v Scriva (No 2)* [1951] VLR 298 at 304–5; [1951] ALR 733 at 738 (1950), and the authorities there referred to per Smith J; and *R v Tommy Ryan* (1890) 11 NSWLR 171.

Whether the jury's verdict against Ryan was based on express malice or felony-murder it must by that verdict, having regard to the direction of the learned judge, be taken to have found that Ryan intentionally fired the shot which killed Hodson. On the evidence, a jury properly directed could not, in our opinion, reasonably have failed to draw the inference that, at the time when Ryan intentionally fired that shot

(a) Walker had committed the felony of escaping from gaol;
(b) Hodson had reasonable grounds for believing that Walker had committed that felony;

(c) Hodson was attempting to apprehend Walker following the commission of that felony;
(d) Ryan knew that Walker had committed that felony;
(e) Ryan knew that Hodson was attempting to apprehend Walker following the commission of that felony;
(f) Ryan fired that shot to prevent the apprehension of Walker by Hodson.

The result is that in law the case was one of constructive-murder by Ryan, because that finding and those inferences mean that Ryan, knowing that Walker had committed the felony created by s 35 of the *Gaols Act 1958* and knowing that Hodson was attempting to arrest Walker therefore, intentionally used force, which resulted in Hodson's death, to prevent him from making that arrest. That, coupled with the fact that Hodson was, in the above circumstances, lawfully authorised by common law to make the arrest of Walker (see *Christie v Leachinsky* [1947] AC 573, [1947] 1 All ER 567 (HL), and *R v Hunt* (1825) 1 Mood 93, 168 ER 1198 (CCR)), constituted Ryan's action in killing Hodson, murder.

In any event, on the evidence and having regard to the closeness of the range at which Ryan fired the shot, we are of opinion that a jury properly directed could not reasonably have failed to draw the inference that Ryan did in fact contemplate that death or at least grievous bodily harm was likely to result to Hodson: see *Smyth v R* (1957) 98 CLR 163; [1957] ALR 441, and *Parker v R* (1963) 111 CLR 610 at 648–9, [1963] ALR 524 at 548–9, per Windeyer J.

As there was no suggestion that the firing was done in self-defence or provocation, the only verdicts reasonably open in such circumstances were murder, or manslaughter, on the basis of the learned judge's charge of the jury's common law right to return such a verdict which it must be taken to have rejected.

For these reasons, we are of opinion that the application on behalf of Ryan cannot succeed …

[The court dismissed Walker's appeal for reasons not material here. Ryan's application for special leave to appeal to the High Court of Australia was refused: *Ryan v R* (1966) 40 ALJR 326.]

4.56C

R v Galas; R v Mikhael

(2007) 18 VR 205

Court of Appeal, Supreme Court of Victoria

[The first accused was convicted of one count of murder, one count of aggravated burglary and one count of armed robbery. The second accused was convicted of one count of manslaughter, one count of aggravated burglary and one count of attempted armed robbery. They, together with two co-offenders, entered premises which they believed were being used to grow cannabis, armed and with the intention of stealing the cannabis from the occupants. One of the occupants was fatally shot by the first accused. The defence of the first accused was that the gun he was carrying discharged accidentally while he was tying up the deceased. The prosecution case against the first accused was that he had shot and killed the deceased with an intention to kill or to cause really serious injury (common law murder) or in circumstances attracting the operation of s 3A of the Crimes Act 1958 (Vic) (the Act) (constructive or statutory murder). The prosecution put its case on statutory murder on the basis that the act of violence was committed in the course of an attempted armed robbery. The prosecution case against the second accused was that he was an abettor to the first accused. The first accused sought leave to appeal against his conviction for murder and the second accused sought leave to appeal against his conviction for manslaughter.]

[Footnotes to the extract appear at the end of the extract.]

Kellam JA: … In these circumstances, I do not consider that the jury could have been satisfied beyond reasonable doubt that the discharge of the firearm was in consequence of a voluntary and deliberate act on the part of the first applicant. It was not possible to exclude the possibility that the discharge of the firearm was an unintentional consequence of the first applicant holding the firearm in one hand as he endeavoured to tape together the two hands of the deceased. The evidence before the jury was not such that it was possible to exclude the possibility that as the first applicant was engaged in this activity he placed pressure unintentionally on the trigger of the firearm causing it to discharge. In such circumstances, I conclude that it was not open to the jury to convict the first applicant of common law murder. Since one or more of the members of the jury may have convicted on the basis of common law murder, the conviction of the first applicant cannot stand. …

The question now arises as to whether or not the convictions should be quashed and verdicts of acquittal entered or whether retrial should be directed in each case, and if so, upon what charge. Counsel for the first applicant submits that a verdict of acquittal should be entered on the count of murder, as it was not open to the jury to convict the first applicant of statutory murder pursuant to s 3A of the *Crimes Act 1958* (Vic).

[His Honour set out s 3A, and continued:]

In the course of the trial, the 'act of violence' relied upon by the prosecution and left to the jury for the purposes of statutory murder was 'the presenting of a loaded firearm to Mr D'Amico and while tying him up and subduing him the firearm discharges'. Statutory murder was left to the jury on the basis that the intentional act of violence causing death occurred in the course or furtherance of either an attempted armed robbery or an armed robbery. …

… counsel for the first applicant submits that statutory murder should not have been left to the jury on either basis. He argues that neither the crime of armed robbery nor the crime of attempted armed robbery is a crime, the necessary elements of which include violence for the purposes of s 3A. It is argued that whilst the crime of armed robbery may well involve the use of violence, the offence may be committed without violence. This submission, as is conceded by counsel for the first applicant, is a submission which faces considerable difficulty because the Full Court of this Court in *R v Butcher*[1] held that armed robbery is a crime the necessary elements of which include violence for the purposes of s 3A.[2]

It is submitted by counsel for the first applicant that *R v Butcher* is decided wrongly in that regard. As is conceded by counsel for the first applicant however, it is not for this Court to so determine. The trial judge was bound by the decision of *R v Butcher*, as are we.

Counsel for the first applicant argues that even if *R v Butcher* is authority for the proposition that armed robbery is a crime of violence for the purposes of s 3A of the Act, the question of whether or not attempted armed robbery is such a crime was not considered in that case. Counsel for the first applicant submits that attempted armed robbery may be committed without any violence at all and thus it is not a crime, the necessary elements of which include violence for the purposes of s 3A. By way of example, counsel for the first applicant argues that if a person with a weapon concealed on his person, hands a note on which he mistakenly believes is written a demand for money and contains a threat of menace with the weapon, but in fact the note contains no such demand or threat, he has nevertheless attempted an armed robbery. In this example, as postulated by counsel, if the perplexed would-be victim hands back the blank note and the would be robber walks away in silent embarrassment, there is an attempted armed robbery, but there is no violence.

This submission assumes that in the circumstances of this case the crime which is appropriately under consideration for the purposes of s 3A is the crime of attempted armed robbery. However, there is no reason to make such an assumption. The fact that the only crime which was complete at the time of the death of the deceased was that of attempted armed robbery does not make that crime the relevant crime for the purposes of s 3A. The elements which must be proven in order to establish statutory murder are:

(a) the deceased was killed unintentionally,

(b) the death was caused by,

- an act of violence,
- which act was conscious, voluntary and deliberate,
- done in the course of or furtherance of a crime — the necessary elements of which include violence — which carries a penalty of life imprisonment or a maximum penalty of not less than ten years' imprisonment.

The background to the introduction of s 3A of the Act was examined by the Court in *R v Butcher* in the following terms:[3]

> For some time prior to 1981 numerous criticisms of what was loosely called the felony murder rule had been made. The Law Reform Commissioner, Mr T W Smith QC in his first report to the Victorian Government of August 1974 on the law of murder stated that the felony murder rule offended against 'basic concepts of justice' and he instanced in his Report the apparent width of its application and recommended that it be abolished: *Report No 1 Law of Murder*, August 1974 pp 10–15.
>
> Upon the second reading of the Crimes (Classification of Offences) Bill in the House by the Minister, s 3 was amended by omitting the words 'crime of violence'

appearing in the original Bill and substituting in their stead the present words 'crime the necessary elements of which include violence': *Hansard* Vol 358, 6 May 1981, p 8688.

We gather from reading *Hansard* that the intent of the amendment was to make it abundantly clear that the crimes in the commission of which the felony murder rule as defined in s.3(2) was to continue in force in the State of Victoria were to be of a class having 'violence as one of its ingredients' (see *Hansard, supra)* and that the rule was not to apply simply because the particular crime committed was in fact one which was committed violently.

Accordingly the prosecution must prove that the death was caused by 'an act of violence done in the course or furtherance of a crime' of the stated class, which carries the penalties stipulated.

The meaning of the phrase 'act of violence' was likewise considered in detail in *R v Butcher.* The Court said:[4]

In our opinion, the word 'violence' where it is used in s 3A is not to be understood to refer only to physical force but rather to include those aspects of intimidation and seeking to intimidate by the exhibition of physical force or menaces as in the past have been considered to constitute violence.

When the words 'act of violence' and 'crime the necessary elements of which include violence' are used in s 3A, violence is used in a descriptive sense. 'Act of violence' means an act of a violent kind, for there is no legal definition of violence as such inside or outside which any particular act or threats may be said to fall. Nor is there any common law crime in which violence is by definition an element.

This view is also consistent with violence as understood during the development of the English language. As a matter of etymology, violence is a word having its origin in the Latin *violentia,* often connoting vehemence or impetuosity. It is not synonymous with the use of physical force, although physical force falls within its meaning. It is a word of wider significance in the law, as the cases show. Smith and Hall in their *English-Latin Dictionary* give as their first meaning of violence: 'inherent overpowering force, whether physical or mental.' In the *Oxford English Dictionary* violence is defined as follows: '(Law) unlawful exercise of physical force, intimidation by the exhibition of this'.

...

However, it seems to us that if the word violence in the phrase 'act of violence' is understood to be used in its etymological sense and in the descriptive way that it has been used in the cases, and to embrace actual force used to overcome or nullify resistance and as well, threats or menaces to induce fear and terror or to intimidate in order to remove or nullify resistance, the phrase is apt to express the type of act which is required to call into play the felony murder rule under s 3A.

...

The Court said further:[5]

> ... violence must be interpreted to include threats such as in common experience would be expected or likely to take away resistance, which has always been considered to be an element, necessary to prove, in the crime of robbery.
>
> Without attempting to deal exhaustively with what other acts may or may not be considered to be acts of violence, we are satisfied from our reading of the cases that holding out a knife towards another person whilst he is three to four feet away and at the same time demanding money from him, is capable of being found to be an act of violence within the meaning of s 3A(1).
>
> Likewise, I am satisfied that the act of holding a loaded handgun in one hand and at the same time attempting to restrain a person by tying his hands behind his back is capable of being found to be an act of violence within the meaning of s 3A(1) of the Act. The question then arises as to whether the act of violence is capable of being found to be an act of violence 'done in the course or furtherance of a crime the necessary elements of which include violence'.

The word 'course' is described in the *Oxford English Dictionary* as: 'The continuous process (of time), succession (of events); progress through successive stages' and 'a line of conduct, a person's method of proceeding'. The word 'furtherance' is defined as being: 'The fact of being helped forward; the action of helping forward; advancement, aid, assistance'.

It appears to me to be clear that the relevant crime, the necessary elements of which include violence, need not be complete at the time of the act of violence which causes death. Accordingly any act of violence which is undertaken in the course of or the furtherance of the crime of armed robbery is capable of being found to be an act of violence within the meaning of s 3A(1). It is not to the point that each of the applicants was charged with attempted armed robbery and not armed robbery. In my view it would be open to a jury to be satisfied beyond reasonable doubt that an act of violence which caused the death of the deceased was done 'in the course of or furtherance' of the crime of armed robbery.

[**Chernov** and **Vincent JJA** agreed. Appeals against conviction allowed and order that first accused be re-tried on the count of murder and second accused be re-tried on the count of manslaughter.]

Notes:

1. [1986] VR 43.
2. At 46–51.
3. At 51.
4. At 53.
5. At 54.

4.57 Notes and questions

1. In *R v Maurangi and Rivett* (2000) 80 SASR 295, Matheson AJ considered and followed *R v Butcher*. The two accused were charged with murder when the deceased died from a single gunshot wound during an attempted robbery. The prosecution case was that the two accused went to a pool hall intending to steal money and alcohol, the accused Rivett being armed with a sawn-off shotgun supplied by Maurangi. The defence of the accused, Rivett, was that he had not intended to fire the gun; that it discharged accidentally when he passed it to Maurangi. Counsel for Rivett submitted that the words 'an intentional act of violence' in s 12A of the Criminal Law Consolidation Act 1935 (SA) meant that it had to be shown that Rivett had intentionally shot the deceased. Matheson AJ rejected the submission, holding that the presentation of a loaded firearm at another in a menacing manner is an 'act of violence'. His Honour directed the jury that it was open to them to conclude that the intentional pointing of a loaded and cocked shotgun at a person at close range in a menacing manner constituted an 'act of violence' and to find that such an act caused the death of the deceased in the course of the armed robbery. Both accused were found not guilty of murder and guilty of manslaughter.
2. The High Court of Australia has approved the decision in *R v Butcher*. In *Arulthilakan v The Queen* (2003) 189 ALR 40, the appellant and two co-accused were convicted of the murder of V, in the course of robbing him of his mobile telephone. V died as the result of a stab wound inflicted by one co-accused, who pleaded guilty to the murder of V. Both the appellant and the second co-accused, who also appealed, knew that the first co-accused was armed with a knife. The High Court dismissed the appeal. The court held that whether the presentation of a knife during an armed robbery was capable of being an 'act of violence' for the purpose of s 12A of the Criminal Law Consolidation Act 1935 (SA) may be a question of law, but it is the jury which must decide as a matter of fact whether the behaviour constitutes an act of violence. Kirby J, who would have allowed the appeal on the grounds that the trial judge misdirected the jury, came to the same conclusion as the majority on this issue. This case also raises issues of causation (see **4.31**, **note 1**) and complicity.
3. Do you agree with the following statement of the English Royal Commission on Capital Punishment (1953) at p 34 of their Report (Cmnd 8932)?

   > The main objection to the doctrine can be briefly stated. It is a fundamental principle of our law, embodied in the traditional maxim *actus non facit reum nisi mens sit rea*, that no person is liable to be punished at common law for an act which he has done unless it is also proved that he had a wrongful intention. It is not inconsistent with this principle to hold that, if a man foresaw the consequences of his act, he cannot be heard to say that he did

not intend to bring them about, even though he may not have desired to do so. There is nothing 'constructive' about this rule, since 'the only possible way of discovering a man's intention is by looking at what he actually did, and by considering what must have appeared to him at the time the natural consequence of his act' (Stephen, 2 *History of the Criminal Law* (1883), p 111). A person may therefore properly be convicted of murder if he has caused death either by an act intended to kill or do grievous bodily harm or by an act likely to cause death or grievous bodily harm and committed with reckless disregard to the consequences. But it is quite inconsistent with the general principle of criminal liability to say that, if a person kills another inadvertently while committing a felony or resisting arrest, malice is implied and he is guilty of murder, although he neither intended to cause death or grievous bodily harm nor foresaw that he was likely to do so. Moreover, it is argued, not only is it unjust to punish a man for an effect which he neither foresaw nor intended, but to exact such a penalty would in practice seldom be effective as a deterrent to others.

4. A similar view was taken by the Criminal Law and Penal Methods Reform Committee of South Australia at pp 15–16 of their Fourth Report.

6.5 In the course or furtherance of a felony of violence. The felony-murder rule does not require that the defendant advert to even the mere possibility of death. In the cases to which it applies it is sufficient if the defendant caused death by an act which at the most is likely to cause death or grievous bodily harm to someone other than himself. As far as murder is concerned, therefore, felony-murder requires no mental element at all beyond the mere capacity to act voluntarily. The mental element required is that of the incidental felony, a quite other crime which may well be rape *DPP v Beard* [1920] AC 479 or arson, cf *Serne* (1887) 16 Cox 311 or escaping from gaol *Ryan* [1966] VR 553. Reprehensible though these activities are, they are punishable as serious crimes in themselves and do not necessarily entail any danger to life. On no rational principle do they become murder, as that term is otherwise understood, if in the course of their commission someone's death is caused by a defendant who neither intended nor foresaw such an occurrence. Even if the scope of the rule is understood as nowadays being confined to deaths caused negligently in the course of the felonious activity, which may be the case, no sufficient reason appears why this should be murder when negligent killing is otherwise regarded as the province, at most, of manslaughter. The rule requires that the incidental activity be legally classified as a felony, an obsolete distinction the abandonment of which we recommend in the course of this report, and that its commission involve some element of violence, which may be only technically the case. These details do not justify so great a departure from principle. If the death was significantly more than negligent on the part of the defendant, the rest of the law of murder, both as it stands and as we recommend that it should become, is more than adequate to cover the case. We therefore recommend abolition of the felony-murder rule.

> **6.6 Arrest.** Similarly we do not regard the mere fact that the defendant was in an arrest situation as a distinction sufficient to justify extending the law of murder beyond what he intended or foresaw as probable. The fact that under this rule he must have been acting violently is neither here nor there. If the object is to discourage resistance to arrest, it is immaterial how that resistance is manifested. If the object is to discourage violence causing death, we have indicated already what we believe are the proper limits of the law of murder. If the object is to give additional protection to enforcers of the law, who will normally be police, we are unable to see how this rule furthers the purpose, for by definition death is not what the defendant had in mind. We therefore recommend abolition of this head of murder also.

The Victorian Law Reform Commissioner recommended complete abolition of the felony-murder and resisting-arrest murder doctrines in his Working Paper No 8, *Murder: Mental Element and Punishment* (1984). That recommendation is firmly reiterated in the Victorian Law Reform Commission's Report No 40, *Homicide* (1991).

5. In England, both the felony-murder and resisting arrest-murder rules were entirely abolished by the Homicide Act 1957. The Act provided, in s 1, that:

> (1) Where a person kills another in the course or furtherance of some other offence, the killing shall not amount to murder unless done with the same malice aforethought (express or implied) as is required for a killing to amount to murder when not done in the course or furtherance of another offence.
>
> (2) For the purposes of the foregoing subsection, a killing done in the course or for the purpose of resisting an officer of justice, or of resisting or avoiding or preventing a lawful arrest, or of effecting or assisting an escape or rescue from legal custody, shall be treated as a killing in the course or furtherance of an offence.

The experience of administering the law of murder in England since 1957 has not resulted in any suggestion that constructive murder be re-introduced.

6. Despite the fact that most Australian jurisdictions provide for felony murder, its existence remains relatively controversial. The Model Criminal Code Officers Committee recommended the abolition of constructive murder in Australia in 1998, on the basis that it is inappropriate to allow a murder conviction in the absence of an intention or other culpable state of mind related to the killing: *Fatal Offences Against the Person*, Discussion Paper 1998, Ch 5, p 63.

LAWFUL HOMICIDE

4.58 A person may not be liable for murder even where the actus reus and mens rea requirements are satisfied, if the killing is not unlawful. This may be because the person has a full defence, such as self-defence, or a partial defence which reduces a murder charge to manslaughter in New South Wales (for example, provocation, substantial impairment by reason of abnormality of mind, surviving a suicide pact or excessive self-defence) or defensive homicide in Victoria.

Voluntary Manslaughter

CHAPTER 5

INTRODUCTION

5.1 Manslaughter is traditionally divided into two forms: voluntary manslaughter and involuntary manslaughter. Both voluntary and involuntary manslaughter require that the accused cause the death of a person; in other words, the actus reus for manslaughter is the same as for murder.

The legislation on manslaughter is not prescriptive. In New South Wales, s 18(1) of the Crimes Act 1900 provides that 'every other punishable homicide [other than murder] shall be taken to be manslaughter'. The punishment is stipulated in s 24. In Victoria, s 5 of the Crimes Act 1958 merely provides that 'whosoever is convicted of manslaughter shall be liable to level 3 imprisonment (20 years maximum)', leaving further clarification of the scope of the crime to the common law.

This chapter will consider the law of voluntary manslaughter.

5.2 Voluntary manslaughter covers those unlawful homicides in which the accused possessed the malice aforethought required for the crime of murder, but liability is reduced to manslaughter because of some mitigating circumstance. Mitigating circumstances include provocation (in New South Wales, but not in Victoria), excessive self-defence (known in Victoria as 'defensive homicide') and substantial impairment of the mind (in New South Wales, but not in Victoria). Killing pursuant to a suicide pact is regarded as manslaughter in both Victoria and New South Wales (see **Chapter 4**). Also, in New South Wales, infanticide (where a biological mother kills her child due to mental disturbance) is dealt with and punished as if the defendant were guilty of the offence of manslaughter. In Victoria, infanticide is a separate offence with a lesser penalty (see 5.3).

The partial defences discussed in this chapter are only available for homicide, and not for other crimes. In relation to other crimes (such as assault), provocation and excessive self-defence may also operate in sentencing. The same is true of substantial mental impairment by abnormality of mind (see 5.7 and 14.28). By contrast, defences such as self-defence and mental impairment (see 12.2 and 14.1, respectively) operate as complete defences to murder and other offences such as assault. Duress and necessity (see 12.16 and 12.6, respectively) are complete defences to offences other than murder.

Infanticide

5.3 The offence (or on occasions, partial defence) of infanticide is governed by s 6 of the Crimes Act 1958 (Vic) and by s 22A of the Crimes Act 1900 (NSW). The Victorian section provides that a woman is guilty of infanticide, and not murder, where she kills her child at a time when the balance of her mind was disturbed because of not having fully recovered from the effect of giving birth to that child within the previous two years; or a disorder consequent to her giving birth to that child within the preceding two years. The maximum penalty is less than that for manslaughter, being five years maximum imprisonment. Infanticide is an alternative verdict to murder. The provision does not affect the power of the jury to return a verdict of not guilty because of mental impairment.

5.4 In New South Wales, a woman who causes the death of her child under the age of 12 months is liable for infanticide rather than murder if at the time of the act or omission the balance of her mind was disturbed due to not having fully recovered from the effects of childbirth or due to the effects of lactation. Where a verdict of infanticide is reached, the woman will be dealt with and punished as if she had been guilty of manslaughter. The provision does not affect the power of the jury to return a verdict of not guilty on the ground of insanity or a verdict of concealment of birth.

5.5 Where a woman is charged with infanticide, the prosecution has the onus of proving the offence beyond reasonable doubt (*R v Hutty* [1953] CLR 338 at 339; see New South Wales Law Reform Commission (NSWLRC), *People with Cognitive and Mental Health Impairments in the Criminal Justice System: Criminal Responsibility and Consequences*, Consultation Paper 6, 2010, [5.9]). By contrast, where the defence raises infanticide, neither s 22A of the Crimes Act 1900 (NSW) nor s 6(1) of the Crimes Act 1958 (Vic) clarify whether the prosecution or defence has the burden of proof. Arguably it operates in the same way as the partial defence of substantial impairment by abnormality of the mind (see 5.7 and 14.28), where the defendant has to establish mental impairment on the balance of probabilities (Crimes Act 1900 (NSW) s 23A(4)). This is based on a presumption of mental soundness. Alternatively, it may operate like the defence of provocation (see 5.19), in which the defendant is merely required to raise evidence of provocation which the Crown then has to negative beyond reasonable doubt. Given that in both New South Wales and Victoria the focus of the legislation is on the defendant's disturbed mind, it seems likely that, in conformity with other mental impairment defences, the defendant would be required to prove the defence on the balance of probabilities.

5.6 Although the laws of infanticide provide distinctive recognition of women who experience post-natal depression, they are controversial because they are restricted both in terms of defendant (biological mother) and victim (biological child), as well as the age of the child. This ignores broader stresses of child-rearing that apply to both parents. These stresses can be socially and psychologically, as much as biologically, induced (see B McSherry, 'The Return of the Raging Hormones Theory: Premenstrual Syndrome, Postpartum Disorders and Criminal Responsibility' (1993) 15 *Sydney Law Review* 292). Furthermore, given that infanticide is concerned with the disturbed mind of the mother, it may overlap with the New South Wales defence of substantial impairment by abnormality of mind (see 5.7). However, the partial defence of substantial impairment by abnormality of mind may not be available in all cases of post-natal depression, and may neglect the woman's broader social and economic context (NSWLRC, *People with Cognitive and Mental Health Impairments in the Criminal Justice System: Criminal Responsibility and Consequences*, Consultation Paper 6, 2010, [5.20]). Historically, the partial defence of substantial impairment by abnormality of mind has not been associated with the same sort of lenient penalties that have followed the few infanticide convictions (Law Commission for England and Wales, *Murder, Manslaughter and Infanticide*, 2006, p 200).

Substantial impairment by abnormality of mind

5.7 The partial defence to murder of substantial impairment by abnormality of mind is dealt with comprehensively at 14.28. It is only available in New South Wales. The rationale is that, in some instances, culpability is reduced, but not abrogated, where the accused has a mental impairment that affects him or her in a particular way at the time of the offence. The elements of proof for substantial impairment by abnormality of mind are set out in s 23A of the Crimes Act 1900 (NSW). It requires that at the time of the killing, the accused was suffering from an abnormality of the mind that arose from an underlying condition with a legally recognised cause. The abnormality must have affected the accused's capacity to understand events or judge whether the actions were right or wrong (s 23A(1)(a)). Further, the impairment must have been so substantial as to warrant liability for murder being reduced to manslaughter (s 23A(1)(b)).

Excessive self-defence (defensive homicide)

5.8 Unlike self-defence (see 12.2), the partial defence of excessive self-defence is premised on the idea that the killing in defence was not a reasonable response in the circumstances. Nonetheless, the accused must have believed, at the time of the killing, that the conduct was necessary to defend himself or herself, or another.

5.9 The High Court of Australia abolished the common law doctrine of excessive self-defence in *Zecevic v DPP (Vic)* (1987) 162 CLR 645. New South Wales reintroduced excessive self-defence in s 421 of the Crimes Act 1900 (NSW). This defence reduces murder to manslaughter. Section 421 states:

> (1) This section applies if:
> (a) the person uses force that involves the intentional or reckless infliction of death, and
> (b) the conduct is not a reasonable response in the circumstances as he or she perceives them,
>
> but the person believes the conduct is necessary:
> (c) to defend himself or herself or another person, or
> (d) to prevent or terminate the unlawful deprivation of his or her liberty or the liberty of another person.
>
> (2) The person is not criminally responsible for murder but, on a trial for murder, the person is to be found guilty of manslaughter if the person is otherwise criminally responsible for manslaughter.

In Victoria, a defence broadly equivalent to excessive self-defence has been reintroduced by the creation of a new offence of defensive homicide: Crimes Act 1958 (Vic) ss 9AC, 9AD. These provisions, together with the special evidentiary provisions in s 9AH applicable to circumstances where family violence is alleged, were introduced in 2005, at the same time as the defence of provocation was abolished. They will be further discussed at **12.5**.

In New South Wales, there are differing views about whether the partial defence of excessive self-defence assists or hinders women who have killed their abusive partners. On the one hand, it provides some defence to women who cannot satisfy all of the elements of self-defence. One the other hand, it may prevent women from being acquitted on the basis of self-defence because excessive self-defence provides an easier middle ground that does not require careful assessment of reasonableness in the circumstances. Indeed, a Judicial Commission of New South Wales study found that when the partial defence of excessive self-defence was successfully used by women who had killed their male partners, those women were under attack at the time of the killing. These would appear to be cases where the response was reasonable (see L Roth and L Blayden, *Provocation and Self-defence in Intimate Partner and Sexual Advance Homicides*, Briefing Paper 5/2012, New South Wales Parliamentary Research Service, 2012, [10.4]). Similarly, in Victoria concern has been expressed with the way that defensive homicide has been operating. A key rationale for the enactment of defensive homicide was to provides a safety net for women who kill in response to abuse but who may fail to have their actions recognised as self-defence, and be acquitted. Much of the criticism has been in response to the number of men who have been convicted of defensive homicide. These concerns prompted a review of defensive homicide by the Department of Justice: *Review of the Offence of Defensive Homicide Discussion Paper*, August 2010.

PROVOCATION

Introduction: rationales and reforms

> The brain may devise laws for the blood, But a hot temper leaps o'er a cold decree.
>
> *The Merchant of Venice*, Shakespeare

5.10 In New South Wales, a killing under provocation provides a partial defence for murder, resulting in a conviction of manslaughter (Crimes Act 1900 (NSW) s 23(1)). The policy justification for this is that a person who kills after having lost their self-control as a result of sufficiently provocative conduct on the part of the victim is not as morally culpable as an 'ordinary' killer. It is important to distinguish the loss of self-control necessary for the defence of provocation from the requirement of 'malice aforethought' which forms the mental element for murder. Nevertheless, it is sometimes stated that a perpetrator who kills in response to the deceased's provocation is not entirely in control of his or her faculties to commit a crime, because the perpetrator often acts under the influence of passion or frustration (New South Wales Parliamentary Select Committee on the Partial Defence of Provocation, *The Partial Defence of Provocation*, Final Report, 2013, [2.6]).

5.11 Obviously, such a concession to human frailty could have no place in a case where the accused already possessed malice aforethought but worked himself or herself up into a rage, or seized upon some trifling act of provocation to provide an apparent excuse. In other words, we are speaking of cases of genuine action under provocation — of those cases where there is no mere pretence. Another way of putting the point is to say that provocation cannot operate in a case where the defendant's intention to kill or to injure was premeditated, in the sense of having been formed before the occurrence of the provocative incident: see *Parker v R* (1963) 111 CLR 610; [1963] ALR 524 (at 5.28C) and *Johnson v R* (1976) 11 ALR 23. Equally, if the person is truly no longer in control of their actions this would be a case of automatism rather than provocation. For a provocation claim, it must still have been possible for the defendant, while acting in the heat of passion, to control his or her actions.

5.12 A classic instance of provocation involves a man killing in response to the infidelity of his female partner (see D Tyson, *Sex, Culpability and the Defence of Provocation*, Routledge, 2013, p 17). The justification for reducing the offence of murder in these circumstances is that killing in hot blood, and having lost control, is less culpable than a cold-blooded crime that is calculated and controlled. It is embedded in a historical idea, articulated by Chief Justice Lord Holt, that 'jealousy is the rage of man, and adultery is the highest invasion of property' (*R v Mawgridge* (1707) 84 ER 1107 at 1114–15). Women who kill in retaliation to their partner's long-term abuse, by contrast, have not been as successful in relying on provocation. Juries may perceive them as killing in circumstances that are cold and calculated; for example, while their partner is asleep or otherwise less able than usual to defend themselves. This includes where the defence submits evidence of battered women's syndrome to adduce that the accused actually lost self-control and it was within the minimum limits of self-control that must be attributed to the ordinary person (see **12.5**, **12.19C** and **12.20** on Battered Women's Syndrome); *Osland v R* (1998) 197 CLR 316 (at **11.13C**); cf *R v Muy Ky Chhay* (1994) 72 A Crim R 1). Feminists argue that the partial defence of provocation has operated 'as a profoundly sexed excuse for male anger and violence towards women that allows [these men] to avoid a conviction for murder' (Tyson at 17).

5.13 The operation of provocation has also been criticised for gender bias in homosexual advance cases. This is explained by the New South Wales Parliamentary Select Committee on the Partial Defence of Provocation, *The Partial Defence of Provocation*, Final Report, 2013, [4.3]: 'The threat of being "hit on" by a man perceived by the defendant to be homosexual (whether they are or not) challenges the male defendant's masculinity [and heterosexual identity] because the advance indicates that he is also perceived to be homosexual, or at least open to an offer of male on male intimacy'. In the trial, the perpetrator is presented as '"regularly masculine" and even sexually naïve or vulnerable men and boys with goodwill pushed to the limit in being physically humiliated by homosexual desire' (S Tomsen and T Crofts, 'Social and Cultural Meanings of Legal Responses to Homicide Among Men: Masculine Honour, Sexual Advances and Accidents' (2012) 45(3) *Australian & New Zealand Journal of Criminology* 423 at 426). According to these arguments, the operation of provocation enforces heterosexual stereotypes and legitimises the response of killing to homosexual advances.

5.14 The defence of provocation developed when the death penalty was mandatory for murder. In this context, the 'concession to human frailty' argument in support of the defence carried far more force than it does now, given the abolition of the death penalty and the introduction of judicial discretion in determining the sentence for murder. However, the defence of provocation is not simply about reducing a sentence, but providing an appropriate offence label (that is, manslaughter) that reflects the lesser culpability of the offender (see T Crofts and A Loughnan, 'Provocation: The Good, the Bad and the Ugly' (2013) 37 *Criminal Law Journal* 23–37).

5.15 With changing social expectations, higher standards have been set for self-control. Viscount Simon, in *Holmes v DPP* [1946] AC 588 at 601, stated: '[A]s society advances it ought to call for a higher measure of self-control in all cases … [T]he law has to reconcile respect for the sanctity of human life with recognition of the effect of provocation on human frailty'. In *R v Kumar* (2002) 5 VR 193, the Court of Appeal upheld the decision of the trial judge not to leave the defence to the jury where the accused had stabbed his former de facto wife to death after she had allegedly insulted him and his family. O'Bryan J stated (at [176]–[177]):

> I regard provocation as anachronistic in the law of murder since the abolition of capital punishment and would support its abolition (by Parliament) as a so-called defence. I adopt the view of Kirby J in *Green v R*, which is repeated in … Eames JA's judgement [in this case]. I have experienced, as I believe have other judges who have presided over murder trials, unjustified jury verdicts which could only be explained in terms of provocation … It is important and necessary to maintain objective standards of behaviour for the protection of human life. Judges' views will differ, as they have in the present case, as to how an ordinary person will react to particular conduct or words [footnote omitted] …

5.16 The Victorian Law Reform Commission recommended abolition of the defence in *Defences to Homicide: Final Report* (2004). The commission adopted the general position that 'an intentional killing only justifies a partial or complete defence to murder in circumstances in which a person honestly believes that his or her actions were necessary to protect himself, herself or another person from injury': at p 55. The commission stated (at p 56):

> The continued existence of provocation as a separate partial defence to murder partly legitimates killings committed in anger. It suggests there are circumstances in which we, as a community, do not expect a person to control their impulses to kill or to seriously injure a person. This is of particular concern when this behaviour is in response to a person who is exercising his or her personal rights, for instance to leave a relationship or to start a new relationship with another person. In our view, anger and a loss of self-control, regardless of whether such anger may be understandable, is no longer a legitimate excuse for the use of lethal violence.

The recommendation of the commission was accepted by the Victorian Government, and the Crimes (Amendment) Act 2005 (Vic) introduced a new s 3B into the Crimes Act 1958 (Vic) abolishing the defence of provocation. For further insight into the arguments leading up to the abolition of provocation in Victoria, see *R v Ramage* [2004] VSC 508.

5.17 In 2013, the New South Wales Parliamentary Select Committee on the Partial Defence of Provocation handed down a number of recommendations to amend the provocation partial defence in the Crimes Act 1900 (NSW) s 23. The key recommendations are that:

- a specific guideline be included in the Guidelines of the Office of the Director of Public Prosecutions in relation to laying charges for homicide occurring in a domestic context, particularly where there is a history of violence towards the defendant;
- an amendment be introduced similar to s 9AH of the Crimes Act 1958 (Vic) (see 12.5) in relation to adducing family violence evidence;
- s 23 be renamed as 'the partial defence of gross provocation' and this be reflected in the wording of the section;

- s 23 be amended to ensure that the partial defence is not available for self-induced provocation (see 5.33), or in response to non-violent sexual advances, or where self-induced intoxication leads to a sense of the defendant being seriously wronged or a mistaken belief; and
- s 23 be amended to ensure provocation is not available, except in the most extreme and exceptional circumstances, to defendants in a domestic relationship where the defendant kills the deceased based on the decision of the deceased to end the relationship, or to change the nature of the relationship, or where the deceased taunts the defendant about sexual inadequacy, or where the defendant knows or believes their partner or ex-partner is having another relationship, or where the defendant discovers their partner or ex-partner in flagrante delicto, or where they are in conflict about parenting arrangements for children.

These recommendations reflect a broadening of the partial defence of provocation for defendants who kill in circumstances of ongoing family violence. At the time of writing, the New South Wales Parliament is yet to respond to these recommendations.

5.18 Further reading

For further insight into the arguments leading up to the abolition of provocation in Victoria, see:

G Coss, 'Provocative Reforms: A Comparative Critique' (2006) 30 *Criminal Law Journal* 138

T Crofts and A Loughnan, 'Provocation: The Good, the Bad and the Ugly' (2013) 37 *Criminal Law Journal* 23–37

On the various arguments in relation to the abolition or retention of the partial defence in the Crimes Act 1900 (NSW), refer to various submissions of the New South Wales Parliamentary Select Committee on the Partial Defence of Provocation (2013): <http://www.parliament.nsw.gov.au/prod/parlment/committee.nsf/0/78B96853E8FC1F2DCA257A22001D0442>.

Principles

5.19 The accused bears the evidential burden of ensuring that there is material, on the issue of provocation, for the jury to consider, but the prosecution, here as elsewhere, bears the legal burden of proof. That is to say, once there is an issue for them to consider, the prosecution must persuade the jury, beyond reasonable doubt, that provocation in either or both of its aspects did not exist: Crimes Act 1900 (NSW) s 23(4) (at 5.22).

5.20 Provocation has two distinct aspects. First and foremost, there must be some evidence that the accused was, in fact, acting under provocation and in the heat of passion. The accused cannot assert that the situation would have aroused the ire of another, although it, in fact, left him or her unmoved. From this point of view, provocation is tested subjectively. Second, the issue is also tested objectively. The provocation must be such as could or might have moved an ordinary person, standing in the accused's shoes, to act as the accused did.

5.21 The objective or ordinary person limb of the test has a twofold operation. Obviously, it means that the accused must raise a reasonable doubt in the mind of the jury to the effect that an ordinary person might have been provoked to act as the accused did. However, prior to this point being reached, the ordinary person test empowers the judge to withdraw the issue of provocation from the jury if the judge considers the evidence does not support the view that an ordinary person might have reacted as the accused did.

5.22 The substantive law for provocation in New South Wales is set out in the Crimes Act 1900 (NSW) s 23:

23 Trial for murder — provocation

(1) Where, on the trial of a person for murder, it appears that the act or omission causing death was an act done or omitted under provocation and, but for this subsection and the provocation, the jury would have found the accused guilty of murder, the jury shall acquit the accused of murder and find the accused guilty of manslaughter.

(2) For the purposes of subsection (1), an act or omission causing death is an act done or omitted under provocation where:

(a) the act or omission is the result of a loss of self-control on the part of the accused that was induced by any conduct of the deceased (including grossly insulting words or gestures) towards or affecting the accused, and

(b) that conduct of the deceased was such as could have induced an ordinary person in the position of the accused to have so far lost self-control as to have formed an intent to kill, or to inflict grievous bodily harm upon, the deceased,

whether that conduct of the deceased occurred immediately before the act or omission causing death or at any previous time.

(3) For the purpose of determining whether an act or omission causing death was an act done or omitted under provocation as provided by subsection (2), there is no rule of law that provocation is negatived if:

(a) there was not a reasonable proportion between the act or omission causing death and the conduct of the deceased that induced the act or omission,

(b) the act or omission causing death was not an act done or omitted suddenly, or

(c) the act or omission causing death was an act done or omitted with any intent to take life or inflict grievous bodily harm.

(4) Where, on the trial of a person for murder, there is any evidence that the act causing death was an act done or omitted under provocation as provided

by subsection (2), the onus is on the prosecution to prove beyond reasonable doubt that the act or omission causing death was not an act done or omitted under provocation.

(5) This section does not exclude or limit any defence to a charge of murder.

5.23 From this section it is clear that there must be provocative conduct induced by the deceased and that the killing must be done as a result of the accused's loss of self-control. This is the subjective test enshrined in ss 23(2)(a). The objective test enshrined in s 23(2)(b) requires that the conduct of the deceased be such as could have induced an ordinary person in the position of the accused to have so far lost self-control as to have formed the requisite mens rea for murder. However, there is no further guidance on the formulation of the objective test. Accordingly, the case law continues to be relevant to its interpretation.

5.24 A series of cases, beginning with the decision of the High Court and the Privy Council in *Parker v R* (at **5.28C**), have defined the modern explication of the objective test. In *Stingel v R* (1990) 171 CLR 312, the High Court of Australia held that for the objective test, the court needs to first determine the gravity of the provocation. In so doing, it may take into account the personal attributes of the accused. Having determined this question, the court must then ask whether an ordinary person could have lost self-control to such an extent as to form the intention to kill or inflict grievous bodily harm and to act upon that intention as the accused did. It unanimously decided that the expression 'ordinary person', employed in s 160 of the Tasmanian Criminal Code, which deals with the defence of provocation, means (at 11):

> … [a] truly hypothetical 'ordinary person'. Subject to a qualification in relation to age … the extent of the power of self-control of that hypothetical ordinary person is unaffected by the personal characteristics or attributes of the particular accused. It will, however, be affected by contemporary conditions and attitudes …

The court went on to say (at 327–9):

> No doubt, there are classes or groups within the community whose average powers of self-control may be higher or lower than the community average. Indeed, it may be that the average power of self-control of the members of one sex is higher or lower than the average power of self-control of members of the other sex. The principle of equality before the law requires, however, that the differences between different classes or groups be reflected only in the limits within which a particular level of self-control can be characterised as ordinary. The lowest level of self-control which falls within those limits or that range is required of all members of the community. There is, however, one qualification which should be made to that general approach.

> It is that considerations of fairness and commonsense dictate that, in at least some circumstances, the age of the accused should be attributed to the ordinary person of the objective test. It has generally been accepted that it would be unduly harsh to require of an immature accused the minimum standard of self-control possessed by an ordinary adult. True it is that there are those who would see this qualification as a departure from an entirely objective standard of self-control ... But the approach may be justified on grounds other than compassion, since the process of development from childhood to maturity is something which, being common to us all, is an aspect of ordinariness ...

5.25 In *R v Enright* [1961] VR 663, the Victorian Full Court clarified that the jury should be told to consider an 'ordinary' rather than a 'reasonable' person. Barwick CJ also adopted this view in *Johnson v R* (1976) 11 ALR 23. This distinction has the effect of preventing the jury from supposing that they should consider how a 'reasonable' person might behave. After all, a person acting in hot blood under provocation might well be 'ordinary' or 'average' but could scarcely be termed 'reasonable'.

5.26 Earlier judicial decisions placed a number of restrictions on the application of provocation: precluding provocative conduct amounting to 'mere words' (*Holmes v DPP* [1946] AC 588 at 600); not allowing the partial defence where a period of time existed between the provocation and retaliation (*R v Duffy* [1967] 1 QB 63); and restricting the defence where there was a significant disproportion between the provocation received and the retaliation given in answer to it (*Mancini v DPP* [1942] AC 1). However, as a consequence of a number of Australian higher court decisions (see *Parker v R* (at **5.28C**), *Moffa v R* (1977) 138 CLR 601; 13 ALR 225 (at **5.30C**) and *R v R* (1981) 28 SASR 321 (at **5.32C**)), it is now clear that the objective ordinary person test is far less restrictive in scope, and far more flexible in operation, than was previously the case. Section 23 of the Crimes Act 1900 (NSW) also broadens the scope of the traditional defence by stating that the provocative conduct need not have occurred immediately before the killing (s 23(2)(b)), and that provocation is not necessarily negatived if the killing was disproportionate to the provocative conduct (s 23(3)(a)).

5.27 The decision of the High Court in *Masciantonio v R* (1995) 183 CLR 58; 129 ALR 575 (at **5.34C**) deals with the common law doctrine, and enunciates some limited measure of flexibility, but emphasises the firmly established nature of the objective or ordinary person test, which only the enactment of legislation can affect. The principles and rules expounded in *Masciantonio* have again been considered by the High Court in *Green v R* (1997) 191 CLR 334; 148 ALR 659 (at **5.35C**). In *Green v R*, the provisions of s 23 of the Crimes Act 1900 (NSW) formed the legislative setting for the court's intensive exploration of the doctrine.

Leading cases

5.28C **Parker v R**

(1963) 111 CLR 610; [1963] ALR 524
High Court of Australia

Dixon CJ: This is an application for special leave to appeal from an order made on 24 November 1961 by the Full Court of the Supreme Court of New South Wales sitting as a Court of Criminal Appeal, whereby an appeal by the appellant from a conviction of murder was dismissed. The application for special leave to appeal was of course made long out of time, but the Solicitor-General who, as it seemed, was fully apprised of the circumstances, made no objection to the enlarging of the time and it was extended accordingly. The appellant no doubt has been serving his sentence in the meantime but inasmuch as the most serious question arising upon the application is whether the jury should have been directed that they might, if they thought fit, find that the prisoner acted upon provocation reducing the homicide to manslaughter, his imprisonment under sentence may not be as important as might otherwise appear. The sentence for murder, however, is penal servitude for life: *Crimes Act 1900–1962* (NSW) ss 18 and 453.

The case is a curious one and at the trial, although on the proofs no doubt could exist that the appellant, by the injuries which he inflicted upon the deceased, had killed him, yet there was never any admission on his behalf that it was out of the question for the jury to find a simple verdict of not guilty and thereby acquit him completely. Part of the complaint of the applicant against his conviction is that a question of provocation was not submitted to the jury and therefore was not considered by the tribunal of fact.

It goes without saying that a distinction must be maintained between the manner in which the court examines the evidence for the purpose of ascertaining whether a question of provocation should have been submitted to the jury and the manner in which the court examines the evidence in considering whether there is material sufficient to support the jury's conclusion that the applicant was guilty of homicide amounting, if considered independently of any possible extenuation such as provocation, to murder. Compare the statement of Lord Devlin for the Privy Council in *Lee Chun-Chuen v R* [1963] AC 220 at 229–30, [1963] 1 All ER 73 at 77–8 (1962). It was for the jury to decide what weight they would give to the evidence before them as it affected this primary question and since they have decided it against the applicant it is enough to sustain their conclusion so considered if contained in the evidence there is enough reasonably to lead to that conclusion, even if another view might be formed of this or that part of the evidentiary material. But on the question of provocation there has been no decision of the jury and the question is whether they ought to have been allowed to decide it. Perhaps it may be said that the question is to be considered just as if the jury had decided it in favour of the prisoner and, by some freak of procedure, the question arose whether that decision could be sustained. The point is that the issue before the Court of Criminal Appeal was whether by any possibility the jury might not unreasonably discover in the material before them enough to enable them to find a case of provocation. The selection and evaluation of the facts and factors upon which that conclusion would be based would be for the jury and it would not matter what qualifying or opposing considerations the court might see: they would not matter because the question was, *ex hypothesi*, one for the jury and not for the court.

The facts material to the homicide may be stated very shortly. The indictment alleged the murder of one Daniel Christopher Bingham, known as Daniel Kelly, at Jerilderie on 16 October 1960. Jerilderie is in the plain country in the Southern Riverina about 40 miles north of the Victorian border. There was an outstation in the district called New Camp, consisting of a two-roomed dwelling probably of galvanised iron. There a stationhand named Noel Craig and his wife and children had been living for some weeks. Some distance away at New Camp there were shearer's quarters and a shearing shed and there some four months earlier Craig had found that Dan Kelly, as it is convenient to call the deceased, had taken up his quarters. Some time in the earlier part of September, as it would seem from Craig's evidence, the prisoner, his wife and six children arrived in a car at New Camp. The prisoner's wife was Craig's sister and was of Maori extraction. They had been married for 10 years but Craig had not seen them for the last seven years before they drove up to the outstation with their six children in their car. Parker said he wished to look around for a job and asked could they stay. He and his wife and their youngest child slept in the car and the other five children slept in the Craigs' house. Shortly after the Parkers came Craig went in search of a sheep to kill and met Dan Kelly. Craig was accompanied by Parker and his wife and a nephew of Craig. Dan Kelly asked them to have a cup of tea at the shearers' huts and they all took tea in the kitchen. In the ensuing week Dan Kelly visited the house at New Camp on five or six evenings and once or twice in the daytime. There were various purposes for the visits by day and in the evenings cards were played. The play went on so late on one night during the week that Dan Kelly was given a stretcher in the kitchen and slept there. On Friday (which was 13 October 1960) [sic] Dan Kelly came over early in the afternoon during the hours he might have been expected to be at work. Some comment was made and Parker said to Craig that he was only coming over to hang about Joan, Parker's wife, and asked if Craig had noticed. A little later Parker again said that Dan Kelly was only 'hanging around Joan'. Craig says he made no answer. On Sunday morning (16 October) about 10.30, Craig and Parker were about to set out for a neighbouring station to borrow some tools. Dan Kelly was to go with them but after getting in the car he got out of the car to stay behind. Perhaps Kelly had come over that morning. Perhaps he had slept the night there. Parker commented to Craig that Kelly was still hanging around Joan. He called his wife Joan over to the car, according to Craig, and told her to go inside and do some work so that Dan Kelly would not hang around. Craig said that he and Parker were absent until about 1.05 pm. They found Mrs Craig and her children, Mrs Parker and her children and Dan Kelly on their way to a dam about 300 yards distant to swim. Parker whistled to his wife and called out to her, speaking Maori. What he said was not translated, though no reason appears for thinking that her brother, Craig, did not understand it. However, she turned round and stood while Parker drove over to her to talk to her. Craig told his wife to come and get his meal and began to use the tools he had obtained and to do some work. Kelly came to see what he was doing and then went into the house. About a quarter of an hour later Craig himself returned to the house and there he heard Parker say to Dan Kelly: 'Why can't you find a single girl? Have you no principles?' Kelly replied: 'I lost my principles years ago.' According to the prisoner, during this conversation he referred to his wife being part Maori and thereupon Kelly made a response implying the worst intentions and of a kind most insulting to her. Parker returned too from talking to his wife in order to speak to Craig. She apparently had gone to the dam to swim, whence with the rest of the party with her she returned an hour later. Parker said to Craig: 'I think there is something on between Joan and Dan Kelly', and asked Craig: 'Don't you think so?' Craig replied: 'It appears so.' An hour and twenty minutes later Parker called Craig from the job he had returned to do. Craig went to him at his car and Parker said to him: 'She is leaving with Dan and if she does I will get him. There are a lot of dark nights and one of these dark nights I will be waiting for him.' Parker was a very small man and Kelly a big one and it seems that there had been some talk already of the futility of Parker attempting to deal with Kelly with his hands. A few minutes later he called Craig over to speak to him with his wife and children. He told them that he had got a job at Albury. Would she go with them there? The children said that they would like to go there. Craig says that Mrs Parker said, 'It's no good, Frank', and walked away. Craig said that Parker already asked him to put Kelly off the place. Craig said that he would tell Kelly to go and in fact he did tell him to go. Parker got out of his car and told Kelly to get going while he was lucky: he said that if his, Parker's, wife was going with him he had better go up to the gate and wait for her; he (Parker) would escort her to the gate. Next Craig saw Parker take a broken rod from the old Ford at which Craig had been working to his, Parker's, car, get out his tool box and cut the end off. He, Craig, saw him proceed to file it: his evidence is that he asked him what he was doing, that Parker answered, 'Nothing': he wrenched it from Parker saying, 'You had better give that to me', and that he had better pull himself together, he had gone off the deep end, and that he had the children to think of. Parker, he said, replied: 'I won't be here to look after the kids — Joan will — and that other bastard will not be either.' He then seemed to quieten down a little but went down to some trees and there wept and sobbed. He came back for a jacket and returned to the trees sobbing. Somewhere in this colloquy Parker said to Craig: 'It is no good me fighting him, he would beat me by hand, he is too big, he fights too well.'

In the meantime, Mrs Parker went off, with Craig's niece and nephew, in the direction of the road, where Kelly had already gone. They helped with three bags. It was the opposite direction that Parker took to weep in the trees or bushes. According to Craig's evidence it was after the three had gone in the same direction as Dan Kelly that Parker went down to the trees or bushes and cried. After about 15 or 20 minutes Parker came back and asked for help in starting the car. It would seem that a track starting in the opposite direction from the vicinity of the shed or hut came out on the same road, which was called the Goolgumbla Road. The prisoner may have taken that track or road. Jerilderie lay to the south along Goolgumbla Road and the couple on the bicycle went south. The evidence seemed to show, in any case, that the prisoner left in the car about five minutes later and followed them. In a more general description of Parker's conduct before his wife left Craig said that he seemed dazed, that he followed her about and seemed to be begging her (scil. to stay). Craig said that Parker was emotionally very upset, that he was deeply in love with his wife and children and took great pride in them. There was a 'knuckle duster' in Parker's car and both Parker and Dan Kelly habitually carried sheath knives. According to the evidence of a niece and nephew the three cases or pieces of luggage were carried up towards but not quite to the gate to the road. Then Joan Parker and Dan Kelly got on his bicycle and left. She sat in front of him, sideways, on the bar between the seat and the handle bars. She faced left. The prisoner overtook them. They dismounted. In a statement which the police took from the prisoner at the Jerilderie Police Station on the night of 16 October 1960 and which the notation says he signed at 11.30 pm, the following account appears of what occurred from this point:

> I started the car up and drove up the road: getting up the road I seen Kelly doubling my wife on his push bike and as I got up closer they both got off the bike then stood alongside the road, he was standing on the gravel and the wife was standing on the grass. I aimed the front left hand mudguard at him and the bike after I hit him I swerved and put my foot down onto the accelerator as I was going off the road and I went through a greasy boggy patch and then swerved up over the wrong side of the road with the nose of my car facing towards the table drain. I got out of the car and I looked for the wife and at first I couldn't see her and when I first seen her she was laying in the table drain face down and I thought that I had killed her. I done my block, lost my temper and walked to where Kelly was and started hitting him, then I heard the wife moan and struggling in the water. I left Kelly and pulled the wife out of the table drain and she was in agony then. It flashed through my mind that if it had not been for Kelly I wouldn't have injured the wife, I pulled out my knife that I had in my belt and went back and stabbed him in the throat. After I done that the wife struggled and tried to sit herself up on the bank. I pulled her up further and told her to lay still and from there I went over to Johnny Littles' through the paddock and when I got to Johnny Littles' he was not there.

The statement goes on to describe how he, the prisoner, broke into the empty dwelling in order to obtain the use of the telephone, how he telephoned to the police at Jerilderie to obtain medical aid as well as to bring them to the scene. The statement concluded by a brief account of what he himself next did.

The prisoner gave evidence on his own behalf and gave an account of what he did to Kelly and there was medical evidence on the wounds and the cause of death. It is upon that evidence and the evidence already recounted that a detailed knowledge of the steps taken by the prisoner in the actual commission of the homicide depends. Perhaps some inference might be drawn or supported by the additional evidence of marks seen on the ground. Mrs Joan Parker was put in the witness box but declined to give evidence.

[His Honour quoted a passage from the transcript of the prisoner's evidence in chief, and continued:]

The medical evidence is to the effect that the Government Medical Officer who, with the police, reached the scene of the homicide about 4 pm on 16 October 1960, found Dan Kelly lying dead on his right side on the western side of the roadway across a table drain. Both his legs were broken below the knees. He had numerous wounds on the face, throat and neck on the exposed part of the body. He was attired in a singlet and blue jeans. The body was warm but the man was dead. There were a great number of wounds on the face (the 'knuckle duster' might have been responsible) but the only two of significance were one on each side of the neck. On the right side there was an incised wound about half an inch long made by a sharp instrument which had penetrated the larynx but had missed large blood vessels. There was a wound on the left side of the neck which had penetrated at a different angle and had severed the internal jugular vein. There was a great deal of blood. The knife had penetrated further into the muscles at the base of the tongue, deeply. There was a lot of blood. The 'knuckle duster' and the prisoner's knife were produced. Both bones of the legs were broken at about 14 inches above the ground. All this was borne out by the evidence of a post-mortem. Death might be attributed to the combined wounds or to the wounds in the neck, particularly the last one, and the loss of blood.

Mrs Joan Parker's injuries were of course very severe but they were not of the same character as Kelly's and she lived. ...

Inasmuch as the evidence was that the prisoner had forced the knife into Kelly's neck and through his jugular vein, no question of intent to do grievous bodily harm arose, so far as I can see. He actually did it by the very act he consciously performed: that is to say, in itself it amounted to grievous bodily harm. It may be desirable to return to this question because counsel for the prisoner in supporting this application attacked the charge to the jury in respect of the intent to inflict bodily harm. But as I regard the manner in which it was treated as misconceived once the killing by the prisoner was made out to the complete satisfaction of the tribunal of fact, as clearly it was, I pass to what appears to me to be the crux of the case. The question upon which the fate of this application depends is, I think, whether it was right to withdraw from the jury the possibility of holding the homicide by the prisoner to be manslaughter and not murder because done under provocation of a kind which in the circumstances reduced, or might be regarded as reducing, what otherwise might be murder to manslaughter. It appears to have been treated as established, ie as proved, that the prisoner drove his car at the deceased, although perhaps he did not drive then or earlier at such a very high pace as the language of the judge's report might suggest. It seems to have been taken as proved, if not admitted, that he attacked Dan Kelly while lying on the ground and that after using the knuckle duster he drove his knife into each side of his neck or throat, death being the result, on the footing he killed him so that he committed the crime of murder, unless by something exterior to the killing or leading up to it the homicide was justified or reduced to manslaughter. Nothing seems to me to have been of more importance at the stage when the case was in the Court of Criminal Appeal than a consideration of the possibility of a jury finding manslaughter on the ground of provocation. On the application before this court the Solicitor-General for New South Wales appeared for the Crown and he informed us that he conceded that there were substantial arguments that could be put for the applicant that provocation should have been left to the jury and that he would not oppose special leave being granted limited to that ground. When the learned Solicitor-General came to argue the application for the Crown he went somewhat further. After saying that he understood that before the Court of Criminal Appeal the prosecutor argued that the learned judge was right in withdrawing the issue from the jury, he went on to say that so far he (the Solicitor-General) had not said more than that there are substantial arguments that could be put for the appellant. The learned Solicitor-General proceeded:

> If the court was asking me what I would submit, I would be inclined to say that on the whole I would submit that the issue ought to have been left to the jury, but there are some difficult questions, and that is a rather hesitant reply.

In dealing with any question of the law of homicide which is affected by its history there is more than one matter in its bygone history that must not be forgotten. There was of course the view that an act causing death must expose the man who did it to some prejudicial legal consequences and it was for the jury to find the circumstances and the court to give judgment as to the consequences. ... The definition of murder was developed from the exclusion by statute of benefit of clergy and thus 'malice aforethought' or *malitia praecogitata* came to look like the test of the capital nature of the homicide. The prevalance [sic] of duelling made this of daily importance ...

But it had long been recognised that a homicide might be 'reduced', that is extenuated, to manslaughter if it was the result of a provocation which the law would accept as sufficient extenuation to warrant the crime being treated as manslaughter.

[His Honour referred to a number of works of authority and continued:]

Had Parker found Dan Kelly and his wife in adultery and then and there killed Kelly with his knife it seems clear enough that the jury might have held that he acted on sufficient provocation and that the crime was manslaughter only. There would in such a case be no delay in which the blood might cool and cease 'his safer guides to rule'. In the present case Parker had been engaged in an emotional attempt to prevent Kelly taking his wife away with him: it did not cease, the pursuit was but part of it. He had been insulted, taunted, he had listened to his children's prayers to his wife not to depart with his adulterous rival. He drove after them as they left. So far from there being an interval for cooling, time was occupied in events, speech on the part of Dan Kelly and also of his wife, and the mounting certainty that Kelly would take his wife from him. It is not for the court to find the facts but for the jury, and certainly on the evidence the inference was open to them that after a persistent emotional effort to prevent the success of Kelly's attempt to deprive him of his wife and his children of her care, and after passionate appeals to Kelly and Joan Parker, met by Kelly with insults, the prisoner armed himself and followed them with no intermission or interval and in a completely distraught condition. We are not living in the conditions of the sixteenth, seventeenth or eighteenth century. According to the standards governing our society in the later nineteenth century and the twentieth century the succession of events and the conduct of Dan Kelly brought a very strong provocation to an emotional nature, a provocation still in actual operation when Parker came upon Dan Kelly with his wife. That at all events is a view which the jury were entitled to adopt. They might, if properly directed, have considered that (again to use Othello's words) 'passion having [his] best judgment collied assayed to lead the way'. See further *Lee Chun-Chuen v R* [1963] AC 220; [1963] 1 All ER 73 (PC, 1962).

Much difficulty about provocation appears to have arisen from the dicta contained in the speech of Viscount Simon in *Holmes v Director of Public Prosecutions* [1946] AC 588, particularly at 598, [1946] 2 All ER 124 at 127 (HL), upon which much of the obiter dicta in *R v Scriva (No 2)* [1951] VLR 298; [1951] ALR 733, appears to rest. When Viscount Simon says: '... where the provocation inspires an actual intention to kill, ... or to inflict grievous bodily harm, the doctrine that provocation may reduce murder to manslaughter seldom applies', I should have thought that the use of the word 'seldom' implied that sometimes the doctrine nevertheless did apply.

[His Honour referred to *Lee Chun-Chuen v R* [1963] AC 220 and *Attorney-General for Ceylon v Perera* [1953] AC 200, and continued:]

There has been an ever-recurring tendency to treat 'provocation' as merely something inconsistent with and therefore negativing malice aforethought, and no doubt that can be seen in the discussion of the reference by Viscount Simon to intention. In the constant use in definitions or descriptions of 'provocation' of the word 'sudden' the same desire appears to exclude cases of premeditation. On the facts of the present case a jury might readily have taken the view that no premeditated intention had actuated the homicide, that the prisoner had responded to the sustained mental torture by the deceased and his own wife until all self-control broke. In the view of Lord Devlin (for the Privy Council):

> If there was some material on which a jury acting reasonably could have found manslaughter, it cannot be said with certainty that they would have found murder. It is not, of course, for the defence to make out a prima facie case of provocation. It is for the prosecution to prove that the killing was unprovoked. All that the defence need do is to point to material which could induce a reasonable doubt (ibid [1963] AC at 229; [1963] 1 All ER at 77).

I do not think that the criteria of 'provocation' should nowadays be expressed in terms directed to duels and personal quarrels among men who ordinarily bear arms or to violence produced by violence. But however that may be, the jury might find all the elements of suddenness in the unalleviated pressure and the breaking down of control as the prisoner came to the end of his pursuit of the man taking away his wife. Unless the special provisions of the statute law of New South Wales require a different conclusion, I would treat the case as one in which the prisoner was entitled to a direction authorising the jury, if they so chose, to find manslaughter and not murder.

In *Holmes v Director of Public Prosecutions* [1946] AC 588; [1946] 2 All ER 124 (HL), it was held that provocative words without action did not afford sufficient provocation to reduce to manslaughter a homicide that otherwise amounted to murder. This was not laid down absolutely, but subject to an explanation of what was meant by 'mere words' and an allowance of the exclusion of cases where there are circumstances of a most extreme and exceptional character: apparently what was in contemplation were words of a 'violently provocative' nature. It seems that considered as a general or abstract question, there had been varying views of dicta expressed. In New South Wales an attempt to settle the question by statute was made and, by the *Criminal Law Amendment Act 1883* s 370, a provision was enacted in the following terms:

> Where on the trial of a person for murder it appears that the act causing death was induced by the use of grossly insulting language or gestures on the part of the deceased the jury may consider the provocation offered as in the case of provocation by a blow. And where on any such trial it appears that the act or omission causing death does not amount to murder but does amount to manslaughter the jury may acquit the accused of murder and find him guilty of manslaughter and he shall be liable to punishment accordingly. Provided always that in no case shall the crime be reduced from murder to manslaughter by reason of provocation unless the jury find that (a) such provocation was not intentionally caused by any word or act on the part of the accused (b) that it was reasonably calculated to deprive an ordinary person of the power of self-control and did in fact deprive the accused of such power (c) and that the act causing death was done suddenly in the heat of passion caused by such provocation without intent to take life.

It will be seen that the provision includes a statement of what one would suppose to have been the long-accepted rule that a prisoner might upon an indictment of murder be convicted of manslaughter: 1 *Chitty's Criminal Law* (1816), p 638. Apart from a desire to clear up the doubt as to mere words as provocation it is not easy to see why it was framed. In the *Crimes Act 1900* s 23 represents the material parts of s 370. The great importance of the provision in the present case lies in the concluding words 'without intent to take life'. When the prisoner thrust his knife into each side of Dan Kelly's throat the absence of all intention of every kind to take life might be too hard to credit. But having regard to the observations by Lord Devlin already quoted and upon general principles of interpretation it seems proper to understand the words in question as limited to premeditated intention. Further, the following account of the 'modern law' of the 'burden of proof' in relation to the subject, given by Lord Devlin in *Lee Chun-Chuen's* case [1963] AC 220 at 229, [1963] 1 All ER 73 at 77 (1962), must be kept in mind:

> It is not, of course, for the defence to make out a prima facie case of provocation. It is for the prosecution to prove that the killing was unprovoked. All that the defence need do is to point to material which could induce reasonable doubt.

This of course is qualified in application by the quotation from Lord Simon which follows. But it leaves it as a matter for the jury: cf the discussion in *Vallance v R* (1961) 108 CLR 56; [1963] ALR 461.

In my opinion, the prisoner's case on provocation should have been left to the jury and the conviction of murder cannot stand ...

I think that Parker should be tried again: that is unless it were thought better in all the circumstances to substitute a conviction of manslaughter for that of murder.

Taylor and **Owen JJ** [After reiterating facts in **Dixon CJ's** judgment, the judges added]: [Parker's wife] informed [Parker] that she was in love with Kelly. She added, 'Three days ago we made arrangements to run away together'. But she said that they did not want to tell him as they did not want to hurt him. The applicant, as he says, tried to make her see reason and asked her to stay 'for the kiddies' sake'. However, she was resolved to go, saying, 'It's no use Frank, I couldn't stop with a man I don't love. I am in love with Kelly', and, in spite of the applicant's protestations and pleas, she remained adamant. Shortly afterwards the applicant asked Craig to tell Kelly to leave the place and this Craig then did. There can be no doubt that right up to the time that Kelly left the applicant was in a highly emotional state and shortly before he left he obtained a brake rod from an old Ford motor-car and commenced to sharpen the rod. Craig took the rod from him and told him to 'Pull himself together, that he had gone off the deep end and had the children to think of'. The applicant was then alleged to have said 'It will be no good me fighting him, he would beat me by hand, he is too big, he fights too well'. According to Craig the applicant seemed to quieten down a little at this stage and Craig went back to his work. Before Kelly left the applicant told him that if his wife was going with him he had better get up to the gate and wait there and, shortly afterwards, the applicant's wife left in the direction of the road with her bags, assisted by her niece and nephew. There is evidence that after this event the applicant went off in the opposite direction and was weeping. Very shortly afterwards he came back to the house then went to his car and proceeded in it towards the gateway of the property which opened on to the main road. His wife and Kelly appear to have proceeded down this road on Kelly's cycle with the applicant's wife, so we are told, seated on the handle bars. According to the applicant's evidence at the trial he followed his wife because he wanted to bring her back. When he came within sight of them he saw that Kelly and his wife had dismounted and were standing beside the road. In the course of a statement made to the police the applicant said that he 'aimed the front left-hand mudguard at Kelly and the bicycle and then swerved back on to the other side of the road'. In his evidence, however, the applicant said that as he saw Kelly and his wife 'Just standing there … everything seemed to just go black'. Up to that point of time, he asserted in his evidence, the only purpose which he had in mind when he left in his car was to bring his wife back to their children and to stop her from running away. When Kelly was struck by the motor-car both of his legs were broken whilst the impact, apparently, threw the applicant's wife into the tabledrain at the side of the road where he saw her lying face downwards. In his statement to the police the applicant said that he thought that he had killed her and he said 'I done my block, lost my temper and walked to where Kelly was and started hitting him'. Then he heard his wife moan and struggling in the water. He left Kelly and 'pulled his wife out of the table-drain and she was in agony then'. He then said 'It flashed through my mind if it had not been for Kelly I would not have injured the wife, I pulled out my knife that I had in my belt and went back and stabbed him in the throat'. Having done that he endeavoured to make his wife a little more comfortable, then went to a nearby homestead, forced his way in and telephoned the police and informed them of what had happened. (at p 636)

… [W]e are unable to perceive any reason why we should strain to give to the proviso [to s 23] any meaning other than that which upon its face it so clearly bears.

On this view of the section the learned trial judge, in our opinion, acted correctly in withdrawing the issue of provocation from the jury. The reason why we hold this opinion may be stated shortly. The applicant followed Kelly and his wife either with the intention of killing the former or with no such intent. If he did follow them with that intent that is the end of the matter. It is, we think, not unfair to say the evidence that he did follow with such an intent is almost overwhelming. Indeed, the evidence is that the applicant so declared on more than one occasion and this evidence, so far as we can see, was not disputed. But in evidence at the trial he said that when he followed them he merely did so in order to bring his wife back and that he had no intention of killing Kelly at that time. If the jury were at liberty so to find then, whatever may have been the applicant's condition earlier in the day, he was not, when he set out to follow them, deprived of the power of self-control in any relevant sense. It may, perhaps, be said that the sight of his wife and Kelly together on the road was just another circumstance in the sequence of events relied upon as provocation and that this was the final event which caused him to lose his self-control. But no such case was made and, in any case, it was not the running down of Kelly which caused his death. On the applicant's evidence at the trial it was the sight of his injured wife, whom he, at first, thought had been killed, that determined him to kill Kelly. This is the alternative view which emerges from his evidence at the trial and on neither view was there a case of provocation to go to the jury.

There is, we think, a further reason why it was proper that this issue should not have been left for the jury's consideration. It has been said that the proviso is silent upon the question whether there must be some reasonable relationship between the provocation and the act or acts causing death. This is so in the sense that no express mention is made of this factor. But, surely, when the proviso requires that the provocation must be such that it was reasonably calculated to deprive an ordinary person of the power of self-control, and did in fact deprive the accused of such power, it is speaking of loss of the power of self-control in relation to the act or acts causing death. In other words, the question is not whether there was some loss of the power of self-control, but whether the loss of self-control was of such extent and degree as to provide an explanation for, or to constitute, in some measure, an excuse for the acts causing death. And, of course, the provocation must have been of such a character as was calculated to deprive an ordinary person of the power of self-control to that extent. In our view, the sequence and nature of the acts which caused Kelly's death were such that it was not open to a jury to find for the applicant on either of these matters … Accordingly the application for special leave should, in our opinion, be refused.

[**Menzies J** delivered a separate judgment agreeing, in general, with the views expressed in the joint judgment of **Taylor** and **Owen JJ** and with their conclusion that special leave to appeal should be refused. **Windeyer J** delivered a separate dissenting judgment agreeing in substance with the views of **Dixon CJ**. Special leave to appeal refused. The accused then sought special leave to appeal to the Privy Council. (The opinion of the Privy Council appears at **5.29C**.) In allowing the appeal, the Privy Council agreed with **Dixon CJ**'s dissenting judgment.]

5.29C Parker v R

(1964) 111 CLR 665; [1964] ALR 1153
Judicial Committee of the Privy Council

Lord Morris of Borth-Y-Gest [(speaking for a board consisting of himself, **Viscount Radcliffe** and **Lords Evershed, Hodson** and **Pearce**.) Their Lordships considered the background to the enactment of s 23 of the Crimes Act 1900 (NSW) and continued]:

If the most limited and most literal construction of the words of the proviso to s 23 is adopted it seems to their Lordships that even on that basis the issue of provocation ought not in the present case to have been withdrawn from the jury. On that basis it was open to the jury to say that though the act causing death was done with intent to cause grievous bodily harm it was not done with intent to take life. Their Lordships have referred to the evidence which was given. It was for the jury to determine what was the 'act causing death': it was for them to determine whether it was done suddenly in the heat of passion caused by provocation and without intent to take life. It was for them to consider the nature and duration of the provocation and whether it was reasonably calculated to deprive an ordinary person of the power of self-control and whether the appellant was so deprived and whether he continued to be so deprived at the time that he committed the act causing the death of the deceased. The jury might well have taken the view that the appellant was tormented beyond endurance. His wife whom he loved was being lured away from him and from their children despite protests, appeals and remonstrances. In open defiance of his grief and his anguish his wife was being taken by one who had jeered at his (the appellant's) lesser strength and who had spoken with unashamed relish of his lascivious intents. Though there was an interval of time between the moment when the appellant's wife and the deceased went away and the moment when the appellant overtook them and then caused the death of the deceased a jury might well consider and would be entitled to consider that the deceased's whole conduct was such as might 'heat the blood to a proportionable degree of resentment and keep it boiling to the moment of the fact': see 1 East PC 238.

Something which is done 'suddenly' and 'in the heat of passion' caused by provocation is, as it were, something done automatically or impulsively and at a time when there is a temporary suspension of the reason: an act so done is not controlled or planned or preconceived or deliberate. It would seem therefore that the concluding words in para (c) were designed to cover an intent which in whole or in part does not arise from the passion and which is unrelated to the provocation and is not caused by it. As already indicated it has long been recognised that the defence of provocation may apply even where an intent to kill has been created. When in delivering the judgment of the Board in *Attorney-General for Ceylon v Perera* [1953] AC 200 at 206, Lord Goddard said: '... the defence of provocation may arise where a person does intend to kill or inflict grievous bodily harm but his intention to do so arises from sudden passion involving loss of self-control by reason of provocation' new doctrine was not being proclaimed. (See also *Lee Chun-Chuen v R* [1963] AC 220, [1963] 1 All ER 73 (PC).) It would seem most unlikely that the words now being considered were designed to change the law so as to take away much of the substance of the conception of provocation as a reason for reducing a crime from murder to manslaughter. Their Lordships would therefore accept the adjective used by Dixon, CJ, namely 'premeditated'[,] understanding that what is thereby meant is that the homicidal act was the result of the passionate impetus caused by the provocation (assuming always that the conditions of paras (a) and (b) are satisfied) and that it was not done pursuant to an 'intent' to take life which was either formed previously to or was formed independently of the provocation. Just as under para (a) the provocation must not be intentionally caused by the accused so under para (c) some provocative act must not be seized upon by an accused (who does not as a result act suddenly and in the heat of passion) as providing an appropriate moment and a convenient excuse for carrying out some previously existing purpose or acting upon an old grudge.

If the evidence given in a case contains some reasonable evidence of provocation ie some evidence fit for the consideration of the jury then the issue of provocation must be left to the jury even though the issue has not been specifically raised by the defence ... Whether in any case there is evidence fit for consideration by a jury on a particular matter is a question of law. A judge may therefore in some cases properly withdraw any question of provocation from the jury ... but for the reasons which they have given their Lordships consider that in the present case the issue should have been left to the jury.

[Appeal allowed.]

5.30C Moffa v R

(1977) 138 CLR 601; 13 ALR 225
High Court of Australia

[Moffa was convicted of the murder of his wife. He did not deny that he killed her by striking her on the head and neck with a piece of iron piping. His defence was that he was gravely provoked at the time and that accordingly the proper verdict was guilty of manslaughter. Moffa said that in 1975 when he returned from a trip to Italy, he found that his wife had become indifferent to him, and she had afterwards refused to have sexual relations with him. Subsequently, she said that she was going to leave him and their children. On the night before the killing, Moffa pleaded with his wife and begged her not to leave. The next morning, according to M, he resumed his conversation with her, and the following took place:

> I then went to caress her.
>
> As I went near her she said: 'Don't come near me — I'll scratch your eyes out.' She grabbed at me and I pushed her away.
>
> She said: 'Don't you understand. I don't love you any more, I don't want to look at your face any more. Don't you understand I've been enjoying myself screwing with everybody on the street. You fucking bastard. You understand that all right?'
>
> At this point she took the photographs from her drawer and said: 'If you want to look at me, look at pictures', and threw them at me. She was very angry.
>
> When she said these things I became very mad.

I said: 'Why have you done this? You promised you would never do it.'

I said: 'Kay, why have you done this to me?' and I started to cry.

When I was crying she was laughing at me and said: 'Get out you black bastard.'

She then threw the telephone at me.

I then lost control and I remember going out to the back of the house. I went outside on the back porch. I picked up a piece of pipe. It was bent.

I went back inside the house. I went back into the room. I had the pipe in my hand. She was seated on the bed.

I came in and I said: 'Is this what you want? You force me to do it.' When she saw me she said: 'I'm not scared of you, you fucking bastard.' I then hit her.

I lost control and hit her again.

I didn't grab her by the neck or anything.

I can't remember grabbing her chain.

I can't remember how many times I hit her.

It was more than once.

I picked up the photographs from the floor.

I pulled the door shut but I don't remember locking it.

I got into the car and went to Lenzi's place.

Somewhere between leaving the house and arriving at Lenzi's I threw the pipe away.

I went to Lenzi's first because I wanted him to look after the children.

After I spoke to Lenzi I went to the police.

The judgment of the High Court follows.]

Barwick CJ: I feel bound to agree with my brother Gibbs' conclusion that if nothing more had been established by the applicant by way of provocation than mere words and if those words were not, to use the language of Viscount Simon in *Holmes v Director of Public Prosecutions* [1946] AC 588; [1946] 2 All ER 124, of a violently provocative character, the onus upon the Crown of establishing beyond any reasonable doubt that the killing of the applicant's wife was unprovoked did not specifically arise. In that situation, the trial judge would have been in error in leaving to the jury a case of provocation and, consequently, errors made in the summing up in relation to that issue, had there been occasion to place a case of provocation before the jury, would not have required the quashing of the applicant's conviction. Accordingly, on that footing, special leave should be refused.

But I am unable to agree that the statement of the applicant at his trial disclosed no more than a case of mere words by way of provocation or, if there were no provocation but by mere words, that those words could not be said to be of a violently provocative character. Whilst I agree that it has long been accepted that a confession of adultery, even if unexpected and suddenly made, can never afford ground for the conclusion that an ordinary man would thereby be led to lose his self-control to the point of forming an intent to murder or to do grievous bodily harm, I must say that circumstances do alter cases and that such an unqualified rule is hardly consonant with the 'benignity of the law' in its concession to 'human infirmity': Foster, *Discourse II on Homicide*, 2nd ed, p 255.

Before setting out my reasons for thinking that the situation described by the applicant to the jury an account which they would be entitled to accept — provided a basis for placing on the Crown the onus of establishing beyond reasonable doubt that the killing of the deceased was unprovoked, I ought to observe that it was not suggested by the Crown that that killing was premeditated. The intent to kill or to do grievous bodily harm to the deceased was formed on the morning of her death. Indeed, it could well be concluded that it was formed after and consequential upon the exchanges between the deceased and the applicant on that morning. There was therefore material upon which it could be concluded that the applicant had lost his self-control at the time he formed the intent to kill or grievously wound the deceased: and that that was due to what the deceased had said and done immediately before that loss occurred. There is nothing suggested about the applicant, his disposition or mental balance, which could be called in human terms extraordinary. That he was emotionally disturbed by his wife's disclosed attitude to him did not make him, in my view, other than an ordinary man: and, in particular, other than an ordinary man of his ethnic derivation. If the use of the word 'reasonable', in the statement of what is called the objective test in relation to provocation, would exclude from consideration such emotional reactions, I have even greater reason for preferring the description 'ordinary man' in the formulation of that test.

The applicant's account of the critical events of the morning of 21 August, the day of the death of the deceased, is set out in the reasons for judgment to which I have referred. The totality of the deceased's conduct on that occasion, according to that account, was that there was vituperative and scornful rejection of the applicant's connubial advances, a contemptuous denial of any continuing affection, a proclamation of finality in the termination of their relationship coupled with an expression of pleasure in having had intercourse promiscuously with neighbouring men. This statement of enjoyment in that course of conduct might reasonably be thought, particularly if coupled with the manner of her rejection of the applicant, to contain an assertion, contemptuously expressed by the deceased, of sexual inadequacy on the part of the applicant. Whilst in themselves small matters, the threat of physical violence to reinforce her rejection of him, the throwing of the telephone as an expression of contempt and the use made of the nude photographs, form part of the whole situation. To describe that situation as consisting merely of words is not, in my opinion, to reflect the reality of the total scene. I am of opinion that a jury would be entitled to view the situation in its entirety as I have briefly described it, including the implied taunt of the applicant's incapacity sexually to satisfy the deceased as she had found other men could. If they took that view, it was open to them to conclude that an ordinary man, placed as was the applicant, would so far lose his self-control as to form an intention at least to do grievous bodily harm to his wife. Whether they would or would not take such a view of the situation would essentially be a matter for them. They are credited with a knowledge of how the ordinary man would react in such a situation. Many might think that they should not draw any such conclusion. But there are limits to the control of such a factual situation which the court can exercise. If, as I think, the situation was not composed of mere words of a not violently provocative character, the court cannot refuse to allow the tribunal of fact to decide the matter unless it is quite clear that no reasonable person could possibly conclude that, in the situation most favourably viewed from the standpoint of the accused, an ordinary man could have so far lost his self-control as to form an intent at least to do grievous bodily harm to his wife. With every respect to those of a different opinion, I cannot think that the trial judge would have been justified in this case, in refusing to leave to the jury the question of provocation. In particular, and with due respect to the views expressed in the Supreme Court of South Australia, I do not think that it can properly be said that it was not reasonably possible to conclude that, in the total situation described by the applicant, an ordinary man might so far lose his self-control as to form at least an intent to do his wife grievous bodily harm. As I have said, whether it should be concluded that an ordinary man would do so is a question exclusively for the jury, however much a court may be inclined to think that a jury should not do so. Accordingly, it was not an error to place that matter before them.

It therefore becomes necessary for me to consider the submissions made on behalf of the applicant as to the propriety and sufficiency of the summing-up in relation to provocation. These submissions are recounted in the reasons of my brother Gibbs; I have no need to repeat them. I shall deal, first, with the submission that the learned trial judge did not tell the jury that, if they thought the accused's account of the events of the fatal morning was reasonably possible and further thought that it was reasonably possible that such a situation would cause an ordinary man to lose his self-control so far as to form an intent to kill or do grievous bodily harm, the onus lay on the Crown to establish beyond reasonable doubt that the killing was unprovoked. I have expressed the submission in this expanded form in order to bring out the essential elements. As I have said, the state of South Australia has not by statute varied the relevant common law. The question of onus is therefore governed by *Woolmington v Director of Public Prosecutions* [1935] AC 462; [1935] All ER Rep 1. The difficulties which that decision places in the path of the Crown in its endeavour to establish an unlawful killing are obvious: and the difficulty a jury must have in applying the onus in a case where the provocation may be marginal in some or all of its necessary ingredients is equally obvious. Thus extreme care is called for in the instruction of a jury where provocation is open to them if a proper balance is to be maintained between Crown and accused. In my reasons for judgment in *Johnson v R* (1976) 11 ALR 23, I indicated that a claim to the reduction of murder to manslaughter by reason of provocation is not really a matter of defence which the Crown should be required to negative beyond reasonable doubt: and that it would not be unjust or unfair to place upon the accused the satisfaction of the jury on a balance of probabilities of all the elements necessary to warrant a refusal to find murder and a finding of manslaughter. The administration of criminal justice would, in my opinion, be aided and not impaired by the production by statute of such a position.

But, as the law stands in South Australia, if there is room for a finding of provocation, it is for the Crown to establish beyond reasonable doubt that the killing was unprovoked. It is essential that the jury be so instructed in plain and direct terms. There is no doubt the trial judge did not do so in this case. Indeed, the impression I get from reading and rereading the summing-up is that the jury would, by its terms, be led to believe that the onus was on the accused. I take the following extracts from the summing-up, which, though extracted, do present a fair picture of the summing-up as a whole.

Though the judge correctly instructed the jury that it was for the Crown 'to prove beyond reasonable doubt ... that the killing was unlawful, without lawful excuse', it is plain from the illustration immediately given by the judge, an illustration related to self-defence, that this direction was not in any way related to the matter of provocation.

[His Honour then dealt with the summing up of the judge, and continued:]

In making these observations upon the summing-up, I am not unmindful of the considerable difficulty faced by a trial judge in ensuring, on the one hand, that the onus is properly expressed and, on the other hand, that the jury are assisted in their difficult task of examining the facts in relation to each necessary ingredient of operative provocation. But, allowing for the difficulty, I am clearly of opinion that this summing-up failed properly to instruct the jury as to the onus of proof, if the possibility of provocation reasonably appeared. For this reason, being of the view that provocation was open upon the facts of the case, the conviction for murder cannot stand.

Having reached that conclusion, it is unnecessary for me to deal with the other submissions. No doubt for the future, having regard to this court's decision in *Johnson v R,* supra, the place of proportionality in provocation will be clearly left to a jury. It might not be out of place, however, for me to remark that the antithesis of 'provocation' and 'retaliation' does not seem apt in explaining the legal situation to a jury. It may be correct on an occasion when there is a long interval of time between the acts said to be provocative and the killing that the latter wears the aspect of cold-blooded retaliation rather than hot-blooded response. But in a case such as the present the antithesis and, indeed, the emphasis on a cooling-off period — would seem to me more to confuse than to enlighten.

There remains the question whether there should be a new trial or whether we should adopt the course taken in *Johnson v R*, supra. The Crown was asked to indicate whether, in the event that the court was of opinion that the conviction for murder could not stand, it would insist upon a new trial. We have been informed that, in the circumstances of the case, the Crown does not do so. Accordingly, in my opinion, the conviction for murder should be set aside and a conviction for manslaughter substituted, there being no basis on which the accused could be acquitted.

Mason J [in the course of a judgment agreeing that special leave to appeal should be allowed and a conviction of manslaughter substituted]:

There is no absolute rule against words founding a case of provocation. The existence of such an absolute rule would draw an arbitrary distinction between words and conduct which is insupportable in logic. No doubt provocative acts justifying the reduction of murder to manslaughter are more readily imagined and more frequently encountered than provocative words which justify the same result. Violent acts, rather than violent words, are more likely to induce an ordinary person to lose his self-control. And a case of provocation by words may be more easily invented than a case of provocation by conduct, particularly when the victim was the wife of the accused. There is, therefore, an element of public policy as well as common sense in requiring the close scrutiny of claims of provocation founded in words, rather than conduct.

The observations of Blackburn J and Viscount Simon to which I have referred are salutary warnings against a too ready acceptance of claims of provocation based on words alone. They emphasise the necessity of compliance with the demanding requirements which underlie the concept of provocation.

[His Honour referred to *Parker v R*, above, and continued.]

The questions for the jury here, then, were whether the acts relied upon by the applicant were reasonably calculated to deprive an ordinary man of the power of self-control, whether they in fact did so deprive the applicant and whether he continued to be so deprived at the time he struck the deceased with the pipe. The question for us is whether it can be said that no reasonable man could answer these questions favourably to the applicant in light of the account of the relevant events given by him at the trial. For my part, I feel some diffidence in predicting with assurance how an ordinary man placed in the applicant's situation might react if he were confronted with the occurrences on which the applicant relied. I am not prepared to say that no reasonable man could conclude that an ordinary man would be so deprived of his power of self-control by what occurred as to form an intention to kill or do grievous bodily harm to his wife.

[**Murphy J** delivered a separate judgment allowing the appeal. **Stephen J** delivered a brief concurring judgment. **Gibbs J** dissented.]

5.31 The cases of *Parker* and *Moffa* are classic provocation cases where a male kills due to infidelity. The following case of *R v R* demonstrates how a background of ongoing domestic violence on a female, triggered by a specific incident, can amount to provocative conduct that allows the female to rely on the partial defence.

5.32C

R v R

(1981) 28 SASR 321

Supreme Court of South Australia

[The accused killed her husband by attacking him with an axe while he was sleeping. Through the course of a long marriage, the deceased had been violent and domineering towards both the accused and the children of the marriage. He had, without apparent knowledge of the accused, committed incest with each of the five daughters of the marriage. Two of the daughters had left home some years before and, several days before the killing, two of the remaining daughters announced their intention of leaving. A series of violent quarrels took place, with the deceased taking one of the girls, D, off in the car, raping her and inflicting minor injuries with a knife. The morning before the killing, the accused obtained a rifle and purchased some bullets. Later that morning, the daughter, D, told the accused of the history of sexual abuse of all the girls. The accused then went to work and returned in the evening.

The deceased and D arrived home about midnight, and D told the accused that the deceased had again tried to rape her. The deceased attempted to effect reconciliation with the accused which she repulsed, and the two went to bed. After further overtures by the deceased, he went to sleep. The accused sat on the edge of the bed smoking for a time, then went outside and got an axe. She returned and struck the deceased a number of blows, killing him.

The trial judge withdrew the defence of provocation from the jury, and the accused was convicted of murder. She appealed to the Supreme Court of South Australia.]

King CJ: In the light of that recital of the version of the facts most favourable to the appellant, it is desirable to make some observations as to what does not constitute provocation in law. The loss of self-control which is essential, is not to be confused with the emotions of hatred, resentment, fear or revenge. If the appellant, when in control of her mind and will, decided to kill the appellant because those emotions or any of them had been produced in her by the enormity of the deceased's past behaviour and threatened future behaviour or because she considered that that was the only way in which she or her children could be protected from the deceased's molestations in the future, the crime would nevertheless be murder. The law of a well ordered and civilised society cannot countenance deliberate killing, even to the extent of treating it as extenuated, as a response to the conduct of another however abhorrent that conduct might be. Nor can society countenance killing a person as a means of averting some apprehended harm in the future. The law of course permits the use by a person of force, even to the extent of inflicting death, if that is necessary to defend that person against immediately threatened harm. But the law has always and must always set its face against killing by way of prevention of harm which is merely feared for the future. Other measures which are peaceful and lawful must be resorted to in order to deal with threats of future harm. Self-defence is therefore not in question in this case. Moreover, the history of incest occurring in the absence of the appellant cannot of itself amount to provocation, even though recounted to her later. Words or conduct cannot amount to provocation unless they are spoken or done to or in the presence of the killer (*R v Fisher* (1837) 8 C & P 182 (173 ER 452); *R v Mouers* (1921) 57 DLR 569; *R v Terry* [1964] VR 248; *R v Arden* [1975] VR 449), although, of course, such words or conduct may be important as part of the background against which what is said or done by the deceased to the killer is to be assessed.

In determining whether the deceased's actions and words on the fatal night could amount to provocation in law, it is necessary to consider them against the background of family violence and sexual abuse. I have reached the conclusion that, at least on the version of the facts most favourable to the appellant, it was open to a reasonable jury to take the view that an ordinary person possessing those characteristics of the appellant which rendered her susceptible, might suffer, in consequence of the deceased's words and actions on the fatal night, a loss of self-control to the extent of doing what the appellant did. The deceased's words and actions in the presence of the appellant on the fatal night might appear innocuous enough on the face of them. They must, however, be viewed against the background of brutality, sexual assault, intimidation and manipulation. When stroking the appellant's arm and cuddling up to her in bed, and when telling her that they could be one happy family and that the girls would not be leaving, the deceased was not only aware of his own infamous conduct but must also have at least suspected that the appellant knew or strongly suspected that, in addition to the long history of cruelty, he had habitually engaged in sexual abuse of her daughters. The implication of the words was therefore that this horror would continue and that the girls would be prevented from leaving by forms of intimidation and manipulation which were only too familiar to the appellant. In this context it was, in my opinion, open to the jury to treat the words themselves and the caressing actions which accompanied them as highly provocative and quite capable of producing in an ordinary mother endowed with the natural instincts of love and protection of her daughters, such a loss of self-control as might lead to killing. A jury might find, to adopt the words of Dixon J in *Parker v R* (1963) 111 CLR 610 at 630, 'all the elements of suddenness in the unalleviated pressure and the breaking down of control' as the night's events reached their climax in the bed. There was the effect of a sustained course of cruelty over the years: *R v Jeffrey* [1967] VR 467 at 484. There was, moreover, the progressive build-up of tension and horror from the time the girls returned on the previous Friday. There was an intensification of the tension on the Wednesday night. The effect of the final actions and words are to be gauged in this context. There was, it is true, some interval of time between the provocative conduct and the killing, but in the words of Windeyer J in *Parker v R* (1963) 111 CLR at 663, 'passion and emotion were mounting not declining'. …

I think also that it was open to a reasonable jury to conclude that this appellant did lose her self-control and that she killed while in that state. The ferocity of the attack and the words and actions which accompanied it, as described by the appellant, are suggestive of loss of control. The appellant in her evidence did not expressly describe her state of mind in terms of loss of self-control, but that is not necessary: *Lee Chun-Chuen v R* [1963] AC 220 at 232. Loss of self-control can be shown by inference instead of direct evidence: *Lee Chun-Chuen v R* at 233; *R v Hopper* [1915] 2 KB 431; *Kwaku Mensah v R* [1946] AC 83; *Sreckovic v R* [1973] WAR 85. There is sufficient, in my opinion, in the circumstances of the killing and the account given by the appellant to enable the jury, if it thought proper, to infer that the appellant killed at a time when she had lost her self-control.

There is, I am bound to say, a substantial body of evidence which tends to indicate that the appellant killed the deceased, not in consequence of any loss of self-control, but in consequence of a decision made while in command of her mind and will, and motivated by hatred and by a desire to ensure that he never again molested her daughters. There is, indeed, much evidence to suggest that the decision to kill was made many hours before the fatal incident occurred. It is unnecessary to refer in detail to this evidence. It would require the careful consideration of a jury at a new trial. To say that there is an issue fit for the consideration of a jury is to say nothing as to whether that issue ought to be resolved in favour of the prosecution or the defence. Whatever might be thought of the cogency of the evidence suggestive of the formation of an intention to kill quite independently of any provocation offered by the words or conduct of the deceased on the Wednesday night, there is, in my opinion, material on the issue of provocation which ought to have been left to the jury.

[**Jacobs J** delivered a separate judgment agreeing with **King CJ**. **Zelling J** dissented. Appeal allowed and a new trial ordered.]

5.33 Notes and illustrations

1. D killed V by knocking him down and beating his head on a rough and stony road, fracturing his skull in several places. At his trial for murder, D alleged in his defence that V assaulted him and invited him to commit a homosexual offence, and that he was the worse for drink when he attacked V. The trial judge directed the jury that, in considering the question of provocation, they were not entitled to take into account the fact that D was the worse for drink and might be more excitable and liable to lose his self-control if provoked. D was convicted of murder and appealed to the Court of Criminal Appeal. Held, unless a man was in such a complete state of intoxication as to make him incapable of forming the intent to cause death or grievous bodily harm, drunkenness which might lead him to attack another in a manner which no reasonable sober man would do could not be pleaded as an excuse reducing the crime from murder to manslaughter if death resulted: *R v McCarthy* [1954] 2 QB 105. Note also *R v Newell* (1980) 71 Cr App R 331.
2. D consumed a good deal of alcohol in the company of a woman, V. They returned to her house where they attempted sexual intercourse. D, however, was unable to achieve climax. D then stabbed V to death when she taunted him with his impotence. The trial judge instructed the jury that in applying the ordinary man test they must have regard to an ordinary man unaffected by alcohol. On appeal to the Full Court of the Supreme Court of Victoria, the trial judge's direction was affirmed. Starke ACJ (*R v O'Neill* [1982] VR 150) quoted with approval the following passage from the judgment of the Court of Criminal Appeal of New South Wales in *R v Croft* [1981] 1 NSWLR 126 at 158:

   > [T]he intoxication of the accused is not, and never has been, at common law or under any of the legislation which has modified it in those jurisdictions which have derived the doctrine to provocation from the common law, a matter to be taken into account in the application of the objective test in provocation.

3. In *Director of Public Prosecutions v Shaw* (SC(Vic), 20 May 1991, unreported), Teague J ruled that he was bound to follow the law as stated in the decisions of the Victorian Court of Criminal Appeal in *Dincer* [1983] 1 VR 460 and *Voukelatos* [1990] VR 1; that is, that the jury in applying the objective test must take into its consideration those physical and mental characteristics of the accused considered in those and earlier cases. He concluded that he was not bound to direct the jury to consider only the age of the accused person, attributed to the ordinary person. He decided that *Stingel's* case was confined to the provisions of the Tasmanian Criminal Code, but stated:

> The analysis made by the High Court in *Stingel* is such that I would certainly apply it if it were not for the position adopted by the Victorian Courts of Criminal Appeal in *Voukelatos* and in the other cases which I have listed.

After his conviction for murder, Shaw applied for special leave to appeal to the Court of Criminal Appeal, but the issue of the direction given on provocation was not pursued as a ground of appeal. In *R v Baraghith* (1991) 54 A Crim R 240, a majority of the New South Wales Court of Criminal Appeal followed *Stingel's* case.

4. A had lived with a woman and her three-year-old daughter, whom A regarded as a step-daughter. The girl told A that the deceased had sexually assaulted her, and the girl's mother told A that a medical examination suggested that the girl had been sexually assaulted. A also learned that the deceased had indecently assaulted his five-year-old niece. Both matters were reported to the police and they were under investigation. Some days after A became aware of the deceased's conduct, A killed the deceased while the deceased was sleeping. Held, dismissing A's appeal, provocation should not be left to the jury where the claimed provocative conduct does not occur in the hearing or presence of the defendant: *Davis v R* (1998) 100 A Crim R 573. *Davis* upheld *R v Quartly* (1986) 11 NSWLR 332, in which it was held that hearsay provocation does not amount to provocative conduct within the meaning of the Crimes Act 1900 (NSW) s 23, which requires provocative 'conduct by the deceased towards or affecting the accused'. However, Simpson J provided plausible dissenting observations concerning the operation of s 23; namely, that the section does not import a requirement of presence: it is sufficient that the victim was actually responsible for the provocative conduct.
5. A cannot rely on self-induced provocation. This includes where A commits a crime or threatens V and V retaliates proportionately: *Edwards v R* [1973] AC 648; cf *R v Johnson* [1989] 2 All ER 839.

5.34C Masciantonio v R

(1995) 183 CLR 58; 129 ALR 575
High Court of Australia

[The appellant killed his son-in-law by stabbing him a number of times. He had confronted the victim at his workplace in relation to his ill-treatment of his wife, the appellant's daughter. There was a brief struggle, which followed an altercation in which the victim insulted the appellant orally and physically. The appellant then took a knife from his car and attacked the victim, the final knife blows being delivered when he lay on the ground.

The appellant came from Italy, and had had little formal education. He had suffered a head injury some time before the killing, and had some predisposition to fall into a dissociative state when under stress.

The appellant was convicted of murder after the trial judge, following the decision of the High Court of Australia in Stingel's case (at **4.99**), did not instruct the jury that they could take his background and life experience into account in determining whether an ordinary person in his position would have been provoked. The appellant's appeal to the Court of Criminal Appeal was dismissed.]

[Footnotes to the extract appear at the end of the extract.]

Brennan, **Deane**, **Dawson** and **Gaudron JJ**: The appellant raised the defences of accident, automatism, self-defence and provocation. The trial judge clearly intended to leave provocation to the jury and he probably intended to do so both in relation to the events which occurred at the side of the deceased's Fiat motor car and the events which occurred when the deceased was lying on the footpath. However, the trial judge directed the jury as follows:

> The dispute between the pathologists is obviously an important matter in terms of the defences relied upon, because, if the deceased received a fatal injury near the Fiat, the defences of accident and automatism and lack of intent, self-defence *and provocation* would all be very relevant and open. But, if the fatal injury occurred when the deceased had collapsed on the footpath and was still being attacked by the accused, defences of accident, lack of intent, self-defence *and provocation*, would appear not to be open and to have no relevance whatsoever in this trial. Only automatism would then remain [emphasis added].

[Their Honours dealt in more detail with the direction of the trial judge, and continued:]

Having regard to the absence of any mention of provocation in the last passage cited from the trial judge's charge, it was perhaps merely a slip on his part when he said that, if the fatal wound was inflicted whilst the deceased was on the footpath, provocation as well as the defences of accident, lack of intent and self-defence 'would appear not to be open and to have no relevance whatever in this trial'. Be that as it may, the effect of that direction was to withdraw provocation from the jury's consideration in relation to the second stage of events, or at least that is how the jury may well have interpreted it. Thus, if provocation ought to have been left to the jury in relation to the second stage of events, then there was a misdirection of a fundamental kind which was not subsequently corrected.

In the Court of Criminal Appeal Crockett and Marks JJ concluded that, in relation to the second stage of events, there was no evidence of provocation fit to be left to the jury. They were of the view that, accepting the version of the facts most favourable to the appellant, 'no jury could have been other than satisfied that an ordinary person would not have continued as the applicant … did namely, to attack the deceased when he was lying helpless on the ground from the stab wounds inflicted at the side of the Fiat motor car'. The remaining member of the court, Ormiston J, concluded that provocation ought not to have been left to the jury in relation to either stage of events. The court was, therefore, unanimous in concluding that the alleged misdirection upon provocation could not have occasioned any miscarriage of justice.[1]

This court recently re-examined the law of provocation in *Stingel v R*.[2] The re-examination was in the context of s 160 of the *Criminal Code* (Tas) and the attention of the court was focused upon that section, particularly the phrase 'wrongful act or insult' which appear in it. However, as the court observed, there is a large degree of conformity in the law of provocation whether it be common law or statutory. No doubt that is because the codes and various statutory provisions either attempt to declare or to build upon the common law, but it means that almost invariably in any exposition of the law in statutory form, the common law is also expounded. Thus, the court said in *Stingel*[3] that it shared the perception 'that, in this particular field of criminal law, the common law, the Codes and other statutory provisions, and judicial decisions about them, have tended to interact and to reflect a degree of unity of underlying notions'. It is common law provocation which applies in Victoria, but much of the reasoning in *Stingel* is that of the common law and it is therefore appropriate to set out the basic concepts recognised by that decision which are applicable in this case.

Homicide, which would otherwise be murder, is reduced to manslaughter if the accused causes death whilst acting under provocation. The provocation must be such that it is capable of causing an ordinary person to lose self-control and to act in the way in which the accused did. The provocation must actually cause the accused to lose self-control and the accused must act whilst deprived of self-control before he has had the opportunity to regain his composure.

It follows that the accused must form an intention to kill or to do grievous bodily harm (putting recklessness to one side) before any question of provocation arises. Provocation only operates to reduce what would otherwise be murder to manslaughter. Since the provocation must be such as could cause an ordinary person to lose self-control and act in a manner which would encompass the accused's actions, it must be such as could cause an ordinary person to form an intention to inflict grievous bodily harm or even death.[4]

The test involving the hypothetical ordinary person is an objective test which lays down the minimum standard of self-control required by the law. Since it is an objective test, the characteristics of the ordinary person are merely those of a person with ordinary powers of self-control. They are not the characteristics of the accused, although when it is appropriate to do so because of the accused's immaturity, the ordinary person may be taken to be of the accused's age.

However, the gravity of the conduct said to constitute the provocation must be assessed by reference to relevant characteristics of the accused. Conduct which might not be insulting or hurtful to one person might be extremely so to another because of that person's age, sex, race, ethnicity, physical features, personal attributes, personal relationships or past history. The provocation must be put into context and it is only by having regard to the attributes or characteristics of the accused that this can be done. But having assessed the gravity of the provocation in this way, it is then necessary to ask the question whether provocation of that degree of gravity could cause an ordinary person to lose self-control and act in a manner which would encompass the accused's actions.

It has been said on a number of occasions that it is an element of provocation that the retaliation should be proportionate to the provocative incident. For example, in

Mancini v Director of Public Prosecutions,[5] Viscount Simon LC said: 'In short, the mode of resentment must bear a reasonable relationship to the provocation if the offence is to be reduced to manslaughter.' However, it is now well established[6] that the question of proportionality is absorbed in the application of the test of the effect of the provocation upon the ordinary person. As Lord Diplock said in *Phillips v R*[7] Viscount Simon's remark was 'an elliptic way of saying that the reaction of the defendant to the provocation must not exceed what would have been the reaction of a reasonable man'. And as Barwick CJ pointed out in *Johnson v R*[8] in considering whether an ordinary person could have reacted in the way in which the accused did, it is the formation of an intent to kill or do grievous bodily harm which is the important consideration rather than the precise form of physical reaction.

The answer to the question whether the trial judge should have left provocation to the jury at either stage of events in this case depends upon whether there was evidence which was capable of constituting provocation. However, because the onus of disproving provocation rests upon the prosecution once there is evidence to raise the question, the actual test must be expressed somewhat more precisely. It is 'whether, on the version of events most favourable to the accused which is suggested by material in the evidence, a jury acting reasonably might fail to be satisfied beyond reasonable doubt that the killing was unprovoked in the relevant sense'.[9] The question is the same when a trial judge is considering whether or not to leave provocation to the jury as it is when an appellate court is considering whether it ought to have been left, but as a matter of practicality a trial judge is likely to lean towards leaving provocation if he or she can. As was observed by the Privy Council in *Lee Chun-Chuen v R*:[10]

> ... there is a practical difference between the approach of a trial judge and that of an appellate court. A judge is naturally very reluctant to withdraw from a jury any issue that should properly be left to them and he is therefore likely to tilt the balance in favour of the defence. An appellate court must apply the test with as much exactitude as the circumstances permit.

There was clear evidence of provocation in this case. Upon the version most favourable to the appellant, the deceased told the appellant to 'piss off' and attempted to kick him. The deceased also pushed the appellant so that he fell to the ground injuring his elbow. The gravity of this provocation must be seen against the appellant's long-standing concern over the deceased's treatment of his daughter and his emotional response to the situation. His concern might be inferred from the fact that he sought out the deceased to speak with him about the matter notwithstanding the failure of previous approaches to the deceased. In those circumstances, it is possible that a reasonable jury might regard as highly provocative to the appellant the unequivocal rejection by his son-in-law of his approach to him. That rejection was in the form of conduct which was both physically and verbally insulting. Moreover, there was evidence that the appellant, an older man, experienced both fear and anger at the actions of the deceased. Whilst anger is primarily a feature of provocation and fear a feature of self-defence, loss of self-control may be due to a mixture of fear and anger.[11]

There was ample evidence from which a jury might conclude that the appellant lost self-control as a result of the deceased's conduct. Apart from his statement to the police that he lost self-control, the very ferocity of his actions in stabbing the deceased repeatedly in the presence of a number of onlookers suggests a loss of self-control.[12] Nor, in our view, is it possible to draw a distinction in this regard between the two stages of events, the one when the deceased was beside the Fiat motor car and the other when he was lying on the footpath. Indeed, the continuation of the attack by the appellant whilst the deceased was on the footpath, despite the attempted intervention of bystanders, would point to a continuing loss of self-control. Moreover, the whole altercation occurred within a short space of time such that a jury might conclude that there was insufficient time for the appellant to regain his composure and that he acted from loss of self-control at both stages of events.

Whether an ordinary person could have reacted in the way in which the appellant did would pose a more difficult question for a jury. However, if a jury were to conclude, as it might, that the provocation offered by the deceased was, in the circumstances in which the appellant found himself, of a high degree (and there was some evidence to support such a conclusion) then it is possible that a reasonable jury might also conclude that an ordinary person could, out of fear and anger as a result of that provocation, form an intention to inflict at least grievous bodily harm and act accordingly.

In *Stingel*[13] this court quoted with approval an observation by Viscount Simon in *Holmes v Director of Public Prosecutions*[14] that the wrongful act or insult must have been capable of provoking an ordinary person not merely to some retaliation but 'to the degree and method and continuance of violence which produces the death'. Reliance was placed by the respondent upon the use of the word 'continuance', it being suggested that an ordinary man would not have continued to stab the deceased repeatedly as the appellant did. But this, we think, is to place a wrong interpretation upon the word 'continuance' in the particular context. In that context, the word was not, in our view, intended to indicate more than that the conduct in question must have been capable of provoking an ordinary person to retaliation of the like nature and extent as that of the accused. The question is not whether an ordinary person, having lost his self-control, would have regained his composure sooner than the accused nor is it whether he would have inflicted a lesser number of wounds. It is whether an ordinary person could have lost self-control to the extent that the accused did.[15] That is to say, the question is whether the provocation, measured in gravity by reference to the personal situation of the accused, could have caused an ordinary person to form an intention to kill or do grievous bodily harm and to act upon that intention, as the accused did, so as to give effect to it. The associated question whether, in the sequence of events, an accused, having lost his self-control, had regained it so that the continued infliction of injury was in fact no longer provoked, is not a question to be answered by reference to the ordinary person. It is to be answered by reference to the conduct of the accused himself and to common experience of human affairs. It is the nature and extent — the kind and degree — of the reaction which could be caused in an ordinary person by the provocation which is significant, rather than the duration of the reaction or the precise physical form which that reaction might take. And in considering that matter, the question whether an ordinary person could form an intention to kill or do grievous bodily harm is of greater significance than the question whether an ordinary person could adopt the means adopted by the accused to carry out the intention.

In reaching our opinion that a reasonable jury could conclude that the appellant was acting under provocation in the legal sense when he killed the deceased, or at least have a reasonable doubt about it, we are, of course, not expressing any view that a jury should or would reach such a conclusion. Indeed, there are weaknesses in the evidence which are readily apparent. We are merely expressing the view that upon the evidence it was open to a jury, properly directed as to the law, to reach that conclusion.

Since the trial judge, whether inadvertently or not, effectively withdrew from the jury's consideration the issue of provocation at the second stage of events and since the appellant's loss of self-control may have continued to that stage, there cannot be said to be no substantial miscarriage of justice. We would allow the appeal and order a retrial.

McHugh J: Giovanni Masciantonio (the accused) was convicted by a jury in the Supreme Court of Victoria of the murder of his son-in-law, Maurizio Femia. The Court of Criminal Appeal of that state unanimously dismissed an appeal against his conviction. Pursuant to the grant of special leave, he now appeals to this court. The principal question in the appeal is whether it was open to the jury to find manslaughter on the ground of provocation if the jury found that the deceased had died as the result of a stab wound inflicted after he had broken away from an altercation with the accused and had collapsed on a nearby footpath. The other question in the appeal is whether the trial judge did in fact take this aspect of provocation away from the jury.

Although parts of the learned judge's directions indicate that he intended to leave provocation to the jury as an answer to the whole of the Crown case, his comments on the facts make it likely that the jury would have understood that a finding of provocation was not open if they found that the fatal wound was inflicted while the deceased was lying on the footpath. It would be unsafe to proceed upon the basis that the jury thought otherwise. The appeal must be determined, therefore, on the basis that the learned judge's directions took away the issue of provocation if death was caused by a wound inflicted while the deceased lay on the footpath.

Provocation

At common law a jury is entitled to return a verdict of manslaughter instead of murder if it finds that the death of the deceased was the result of a sudden and temporary loss of self-control on the part of the accused that was caused by provocative conduct on the part of the deceased. The issue can be left to the jury although the loss of self-control did not follow immediately upon, or as the result of a specific incident of, provocative conduct.[16] Moreover, the issue of provocation is predicated on a finding that the jury has found that the elements of murder have been established and that the accused had acted with reckless indifference to human life or had an intention to kill or cause grievous bodily harm to the deceased.[17] However, before the provocation of the deceased can reduce a verdict from murder to manslaughter there must be evidence which could induce the jury to find that the Crown had not proved beyond reasonable doubt that an ordinary person would not have lost self-control as the result of the provocation to 'the extent and degree' that the accused did.[18] In *Stingel v R*,[19] this court unanimously held that the provocative conduct 'must have been capable of provoking an ordinary person not merely to some retaliation, but to retaliation 'to the degree and method and continuance of violence which produces the death'. *Stingel* was decided on the provisions of the Tasmanian *Criminal Code*, but the court saw no significant difference between the objective self-control requirement of the Code and the objective self- control requirement of s 23(2)(b) of the *Crimes Act 1900* (NSW) considered by the court in *Johnson v R*[20] and the common law doctrine on the point. In *Stingel*,[21] the court noted that, 'in this particular field of criminal law, the common law, the Codes and other statutory provisions, and judicial decisions about them, have tended to interact and to reflect a degree of unity of underlying notions'.

The characteristics of the ordinary person

In determining the extent to which the conduct of the deceased would have provoked an ordinary person, the jury is entitled to consider all 'the attributes or characteristics' of the accused[22] and 'the totality of the deceased's conduct'.[23] The accused's age, sex, ethnicity, personal characteristics and physical features are only some of the matters that the jury can consider in determining the nature, extent and gravity of the provocative conduct of the deceased. Because the doctrine of provocation is the product of 'the mercy of the law [interposing] in pity to human frailty',[24] it is natural that the law should regard as relevant any circumstance that throws light on the effect of the deceased's conduct on the accused. Such a circumstance may arise from the personal history of the accused or his or her relationship with the deceased or otherwise. The rationale of the doctrine is the frailty of human nature and the consequent need to make concessions to that frailty. However, neither the common law nor any of the Codes or statutory substitutions has been able to accept all the implications of this rationale of the doctrine of provocation.

The requirement that the conduct of the deceased must have been capable of provoking an ordinary person to 'retaliation 'to the degree and method and continuance of violence which produces the death" departs from the rationale of the doctrine of provocation.[25] It does so by ignoring the personal idiosyncrasies of the accused and substituting the objective standard of the ordinary person's reaction to the provocation. In *Stingel*,[26] the court accepted that 'the rationale underlying the objective test' was that identified by Wilson J in *R v Hill*[27] where the learned judge said:

> The objective standard, therefore, may be said to exist in order to ensure that in the evaluation of the provocation defence there is no fluctuating standard of self-control against which accuseds are measured. The governing principles are those of equality and individual responsibility, so that all persons are held to the same standard notwithstanding their distinctive personality traits and varying capacities to achieve the standard.

As a result, the court held in *Stingel* that the age of the accused is the only personal characteristic of that person that can be attributed to the hypothetical person whose capacity of self-control is the criterion of the objective standard of provocation.

Thus, a curious dichotomy exists. The personal characteristics and attributes of the accused are relevant in determining the effect of the provocative conduct but they are not relevant in determining the issue of the self-control. The distinction has been strongly criticised on the ground that 'it runs counter to human reality'.[28] It has been argued that the dichotomy is 'inconsistent with the opinion of behavioural scientists that the accused's personality must be taken as a whole and cannot be dissected into the way he or she would view some provocative conduct on the one hand and the way he or she would respond emotionally to that conduct on the other'.[29] No doubt there is inconsistency between taking the personal characteristics and attributes of the accused into account on the issue of provocation but not on the issue of self-control. But it is an inconsistency that could be abolished only by abolishing the 'ordinary person' test itself.[30]

The 'ordinary person' standard would become meaningless if it incorporated the personal characteristics or attributes of the accused on both the issue of provocation and the issue of self-control. In so far as the courts have incorporated those characteristics and attributes in respect of the issue of provocation, they have acted inconsistently with the rationale of the objective test. To go further and incorporate them in the self-control issue would require the abolition of the objective test, and that test is too deeply entrenched in the common law to be excised by judicial decision. Besides, the Codes and statutory substitutions for the common law of provocation contain objective tests of self-control. It would defeat the considerable unity that exists between the common law and statutory regimes of provocation if the common law rejected its own doctrine and became inconsistent with the statutory regimes.

Ethnic or cultural characteristics

The ordinary person standard would not become meaningless, however, if it incorporated the general characteristics of an ordinary person of the same age, race, culture and background as the accused on the self-control issue. Without incorporating those characteristics, the law of provocation is likely to result in discrimination and injustice. In a multicultural society such as Australia, the notion of an ordinary person is pure fiction.[31] Worse still, its invocation in cases heard by juries of predominantly Anglo-Saxon-Celtic origin almost certainly results in the accused being judged by the standard of self-control attributed to a middle class Australian of Anglo-Saxon-Celtic heritage, that being the stereotype of the ordinary person with which the jurors are most familiar.

I was a party to the joint judgment of the court in *Stingel*. At the time, I thought that the principle of equality before the law, which is the rationale of the objective standard,[32] justified rejecting any attribute of the accused to the 'ordinary person' except that of age. But after reading Mr Stanley Yeo's criticism[33] of this aspect of *Stingel* and further reflection on the matter, I have concluded that, unless the ethnic or cultural background of the accused is attributed to the ordinary person, the objective test of self-control results in inequality before the law. Real equality before the law cannot exist when ethnic or cultural minorities are convicted or acquitted of murder according to a standard that reflects the values of the dominant class but does not reflect the values of those minorities.

If it is objected that this will result in one law of provocation for one class of persons and another law for a different class, I would answer that that must be the natural consequence of true equality before the law in a multicultural society when the criterion of criminal liability is made to depend upon objective standards of personhood. Moreover, to a large extent a regime of different laws already exists because the personal characteristics of the accused including attributes of race and culture are already taken into account in determining the effect of the provocative conduct of the deceased on the ordinary person. In any event, it would be much better to abolish the objective test of self-control in the law of provocation than to perpetuate the injustice of an 'ordinary person' test that did not take into account the ethnic or cultural background of the accused.

Neither the ethnicity nor the cultural background of the accused was an issue in *Stingel*. Prior to the decision in that case, there were statements in the cases[34] to the effect that the ethnic or cultural background of the accused was to be taken into account on the issue of the ordinary person's self-control. Nothing said in *Stingel* expressly overruled those statements, although they can hardly stand with the general formulation of principle in that case. However, it is open to this court to reconsider the issue, and I think that it should. Consequently, for the reasons that I have given, I would hold that relevant matters arising from the ethnic or cultural background of the accused can be taken into account in determining whether an ordinary person would have lost his or her self-control as the result of the deceased's provocation.

The central idea of the law of provocation has always been that of a sudden and temporary loss of control that results from the provocative conduct of the deceased. When that loss of control results in an intention to kill or cause grievous bodily harm to the provoker and the intention is accompanied by action that causes the death of that person, the law has been prepared to forgo the ultimate penalty for the taking of a human life that is done with the requisite intent. But the doctrine of provocation was never intended as a general licence to kill or wreak havoc. The concept of suddenness negatived any question of premeditation. The concept of temporariness ensured that an intentional killing would be excused as manslaughter only when it was committed while the killer's capacity for self-control had been overwhelmed by the desire for retribution that often arises when an interest or relationship that a person values is harmed or threatened by the conduct of another person.[35] The concept of the ordinary person incorporated the notions of suddenness and temporariness and ensured equality of treatment for offenders by insisting that the mode of retaliation be objectively proportionate to the provocation and continue for no longer than the period that would elapse if an ordinary individual had received that provocation. To what extent, if any, and for how long would the ordinary person have lost self-control if he or she had been provoked in the circumstances that confronted the accused are key questions if society is 'to maintain objective standards of behaviour for the protection of human life'.[36]

A jury might reasonably think that the provocation in this case was not trivial. But it was by no means extreme. In my opinion it was not reasonably open to the jury to have a reasonable doubt as to whether the deceased's conduct was 'capable of provoking an ordinary person not merely to some retaliation, but to retaliation "to the degree and method and continuance of violence which produce[d] the death"'[37] of the deceased. No jury in my view could reasonably hold that the alleged provocation of the deceased might cause an ordinary person to lose self-control to the extent and for such a period that that person would plunge a knife into a helpless person at the time and in the circumstances that the accused did.

The appeal should be dismissed.

[Appeal allowed.]

[The defendant was retried in October 1995. He was acquitted of murder and convicted of manslaughter, receiving a sentence of five years' imprisonment, with a minimum term of two years.]

Notes:

1. *Lee Chun-Chuen v R* [1963] AC 220 at 235; *Moffa v R* (1977) 138 CLR 601 at 617; 13 ALR 225.
2. (1990) 171 CLR 312; 97 ALR 1.
3. ibid at CLR 320.
4. *Johnson v R* (1976) 136 CLR 619 at 639; 11 ALR 23 per Barwick CJ.
5. [1942] AC 1 at 9; see also *Da Costa v R* (1968) 118 CLR 186 at 215.
6. See *Johnson v R* (1976) 136 CLR at 639, 640, 659.
7. [1969] 2 AC 130 at 137.
8. (1976) 136 CLR at 639.
9. *Stingel v R* (1990) 171 CLR at 334.
10. [1963] AC at 230, see also *Moffa v R* (1977) 138 CLR at 617.
11. *Van Den Hoek v R* (1986) 161 CLR 158 at 167; 69 ALR 1.
12. *The Queen v R* (1981) 28 SASR 321 at 327 per King CJ.
13. (1990) 171 CLR at 325.
14. [1946] AC 588 at 597.
15. *Moffa v R* (1977) 138 CLR at 613 per Gibbs J and *Stingel v R* (1990) 171 CLR at 325.
16. *Chhay v R* (1994) 72 A Crim R 1 at 13.
17. *Johnson v R* (1976) 136 CLR 619 at 633–4; 11 ALR 23; *Stingel v R* (1990) 171 CLR 312 at 328; 97 ALR 1.
18. *Parker v R* (1963) 111 CLR 610 at 641; *Johnson* (1976) 136 CLR at 637–8, 658, 666; *Stingel* (1990) 171 CLR at 325.
19. (1990) 171 CLR at 325 citing *Holmes v Director of Public Prosecutions* [1946] AC 588 at 597.
20. (1976) 136 CLR 619.
21. (1990) 171 CLR at 320.
22. ibid at CLR 326.
23. *Moffa v R* (1977) 138 CLR 601 at 606; 13 ALR 225; *Stingel* (1990) 171 CLR at 326.
24. *East's Pleas of the Crown* (1803), vol 1, p 239.
25. Yeo, 'Power of Self-Control in Provocation and Automatism' (1992) 14 *Sydney Law Review* 3 at 6.
26. (1990) 171 CLR at 324.
27. [1986] 1 SCR 313 at 343.
28. Yeo, op cit at 6.
29. ibid at 7.
30. Elsse, *Howard's Criminal Law*, 5th ed (1990), p 89; Yeo, op cit at 8.
31. In *R v Jeffrey* [1967] VR 467 at 478, Sir John Barry described the ordinary person as 'a mythical person'.

32. *Hill* [1986] 1 SCR at 343.
33. Yeo, op cit at 12–13.
34. *Kwaku Mensah v R* [1946] AC 83 at 93: 'the ordinary West African villager'; *Moffa* (1977) 138 CLR at 606; 'an ordinary man of his ethnic derivation'; *Saliba v R* (1986) 10 Crim LJ 420 at 421: 'the same social and ethnic background as the accused'.
35. cf Posner, *The Federal Courts: Crisis and Reform* (1985), pp 5–6: 'Part of our biological inheritance is the sense of indignation, and its complement the desire for retribution (by violent means if necessary), that is aroused when someone invades an interest that we value highly.'
36. *Johnson* (1976) 136 CLR at 656.
37. *Stingel* (1990) 171 CLR at 325.

5.35C Green v R

(1997) 191 CLR 334; 148 ALR 659
High Court of Australia

[The accused was charged with murder and raised a defence that he had been so provoked by the conduct of the deceased in making advances of a homosexual character that he lost control of himself and killed the deceased. Evidence of the accused's special sensitivity to sexual interference and evidence of a history of sexual abuse within his family, involving the accused's father and his sisters, was ruled not to be admissible on the issue presented by s 23(2)(a) of the Crimes Act 1900 (NSW), and the trial judge directed the jury that whether or not the accused was particularly sensitive to matters of sexual abuse, the family history was not relevant on the issue of provocation. Under s 23(2)(b), the New South Wales Court of Criminal Appeal held that evidence of both matters was not inadmissible and that the direction upon relevancy was wrong, but held that the proviso to s 6(1) of the Criminal Appeal Act 1912 (NSW) applied and that no substantial miscarriage of justice had occurred.]

[Footnotes to the extract appear at the end of the extract.]

Brennan CJ: On appeal to this court, the question whether this court should interfere with the view of a Court of Criminal Appeal was submitted by the Solicitor-General for New South Wales to be subject to the principle of review of discretionary or evaluative judgments contained in *House v R.*[1] That is an entirely erroneous approach. Once there is an unqualified grant of special leave to appeal, the function of this court is to dismiss the appeal or to make the order which the Court of Criminal Appeal ought to have made. For that purpose, this court must step into the shoes of the Court of Criminal Appeal. Thus, in *Parker v R*[2] Windeyer J said:

> If the case is one for special leave then, in considering whether the appeal should be allowed, we must approach the matter as if we were a court of criminal appeal. It then becomes of little importance that on the facts the verdict may seem to have been right, if the jury were not properly directed on a material issue and this misdirection might have affected their decision.

Parker was a case in which provocation was wrongly withdrawn from the jury's consideration. However the observation of Dixon CJ as to an appeal court's assessment of the sufficiency of the evidence to raise provocation indicates the approach to be taken when an appellate court must determine whether the jury could have resolved an element of provocation in favour of an accused. ...

If a reasonable jury, properly directed, could have had a reasonable doubt as to whether the appellant was provoked to such a degree that an ordinary person experiencing provocation to that degree could have formed an intention to kill or to inflict grievous bodily harm to the deceased, this appeal must be allowed. In determining that question, regard must be had to all the relevant evidence including evidence of the sexual abuse factor. If the view formed by the Court of Criminal Appeal was correct, no reasonable jury properly directed could have entertained a reasonable doubt on that question and the trial judge was in error in allowing the issue of provocation to go to the jury.

In my opinion, the trial judge was right to allow the issue of provocation to go to the jury. On the appellant's evidence and on the statements he made to the police, he was grievously incensed and insulted by the conduct of the deceased. The Court of Criminal Appeal appears to have placed some emphasis on the absence of evidence on the part of the deceased — 'the touching was amorous, not forceful', Priestley JA said in speaking for the majority. That led the majority to the view that:

> ... the basis for the jury's decision was that they were satisfied beyond reasonable doubt that the sexual advances of Mr Gillies up to the point where the appellant lost his self-control were not such as could have induced an ordinary person in the position of the appellant to have so far lost self-control as to have formed an intent to kill or inflict grievous bodily harm upon Mr Gillies.

And that view, imputed to a jury that had been directed to ignore the sexual abuse factor in considering the 'ordinary person in the position of the accused' test, was confirmed by the majority having taken that factor into consideration. Priestley JA said:

> It is easy to see that many an ordinary person in the position in which the appellant was when Mr Gillies was making his amorous physical advances would have reacted indignantly, with a physical throwing off of the deceased, and perhaps with blows. I do not think however that the ordinary person could have been induced by the deceased's conduct so far to lose self-control as to have formed an intent to kill or inflict grievous bodily harm upon Mr Gillies.

With respect, the conclusion arrived at by the majority was a finding of fact that might not have been arrived at by a jury. A jury would be entitled to evaluate the circumstances in a different way.[3] The real sting of the provocation could have been found not in the force used by the deceased but in his attempt to violate the sexual integrity of a man who had trusted him as a friend and father figure, in the deceased's persistent homosexual advances after the appellant had said 'I'm not like this' and in the evoking of the appellant's recollection of the abuse of trust on the part of his father. These were matters for the jury to evaluate in determining the decree of provocation experienced by the appellant. Smart J in dissent described the deceased's actions, as narrated by the appellant, as revolting. He added:

> All this was bad enough but there were further factors, namely, the deceased's betrayal of the relationship of trust, dependency, friendship and his abuse of his hospitality. He was trying to coerce the appellant into providing him (the deceased) with sexual gratification.
>
> The past history of the accused, including the family history of the father's sexual assaults, must not be overlooked.
>
> The provocation was of a very grave kind. It must have been a terrifying experience for the appellant when the deceased persisted. The grabbing and the persistence are critical.
>
> Some ordinary men would feel great revulsion at the homosexual advances being persisted with in the circumstances and could be induced to so far lose their self-control as to form the intention to and inflict grievous bodily harm. They would regard it as a serious and gross violation of their body and their person. I am not saying that most men would so react or that such a reaction would be reasonable. However, some ordinary men could become enraged and feel that a strong physical reaction was called for. The deceased's actions had to be stopped.

In the last paragraph, Smart J speaks of the reaction of 'some ordinary men' to the deceased's conduct. With respect, the relevant question was the reaction of the appellant. The 'ordinary person' in para (b) of s 23(2), like the ordinary person considered in *Stingel*,[4] does not refer to a person having precisely the appellant's powers of self-control but refers 'to a person with powers of self-control within the range or limits of what is "ordinary" for a person of the relevant age'.

A reasonable jury might have come to the conclusion that an ordinary person, who was provoked to the degree that the appellant was provoked, could have formed an intent to kill or to inflict grievous bodily harm upon the deceased. It was essentially a jury question, a question the answer to which depended on the jury's evaluation of the degree of outrage which the appellant might have experienced. It was not for the court to determine questions of that kind, especially when reaction to sexual advances are critical to the evaluation. A juryman or woman would not be unreasonable because he or she might accept that the appellant found the deceased's conduct 'revolting' rather than 'amorous'. The case is not like *Stingel*. In that case, Stingel sought out and allegedly came upon a scene of consensual sexual activity between the deceased and Stingel's erstwhile girlfriend — a scene which inflamed his jealousy. Here, the deceased was the sexual aggressor of the appellant.

As the trial judge was in error in ruling that the sexual abuse factor was irrelevant to the issue of provocation, and as it was open to the jury not to be satisfied beyond reasonable doubt that s 23(1) did not apply, the accused lost a chance of acquittal of murder. Accordingly, the proviso did not apply.[5]

The appeal must be allowed, the order of the Court of Criminal Appeal set aside and in lieu thereof the appeal to that court should be allowed, the conviction quashed and a new trial ordered.

McHugh J: This court's examination of the defence of provocation in *Stingel v R*[6] and *Masciantonio v R*[7] provides assistance on the meaning of s 23(2). That examination took place in the context of s 160 of the *Criminal Code* (Tas) and the common law as applied in Victoria, respectively. Nevertheless, as the court said in *Stingel*,[8] 'in this particular field of criminal law, the common law, the Codes and other statutory provisions, and judicial decisions about them, have tended to interact and to reflect a degree of unity of underlying notions'.

[His Honour quoted at length from the judgment of **Brennan**, **Deane**, **Dawson** and **Gaudron JJ** in *Masciantonio v R*, above, and continued:]

The only qualification I would make to this statement is to add considerations of 'ethnic or cultural background of the accused' to age and maturity as relevant to any inquiry into the objective standard by which the self-control of an accused is measured.[9]

The accused contended that the language of s 23(2)(b), and in particular the phrase 'an ordinary person in the position of the accused', has modified the law of provocation in New South Wales. That is, he contended that in New South Wales the jury must consider the accused's subjective experience when measuring the level of self-control required of him or her. If this is so, s 23 significantly departs from the law of provocation as stated in *Masciantonio*. The validity of this argument depends on whether the words 'in the position of the accused' in s 23(2)(b) require an approach different from that expounded in *Masciantonio* and allow the accused's subjective characteristics to be imputed to the 'ordinary person' in considering the loss of self-control issue.

It is clear that the personal attributes of the accused are relevant to the issue posed by s 23(2)(a). Thus, the Crown correctly conceded that the trial judge had erred in ruling that evidence of the accused's special sensitivity to sexual interference, and of his family history which explained that sensitivity, was inadmissible under para (a). What, however, do the words 'in the position of the accused' in para (b) mean? Do they mean, as the accused contended, that the 'ordinary person' must effectively be given all the characteristics of the accused?

The legislative history of s 23 offers little by way of explanation. However, in the second reading speech of the legislation inserting the provision into the Act, the Attorney-General stated that '[t]he formula of words used does not introduce an entirely subjective test of provocation'.[10] This must be so given the retention of the words an 'ordinary person' at the beginning of the phrase.

In my opinion, the phrase 'an ordinary person in the position of the accused' means an ordinary person who suffered the provocation which the accused suffered as the result of the conduct of the deceased. The standard against which the loss of self-control is judged is that of a hypothetical ordinary person. That person is unaffected by the accused's idiosyncrasies, personal attributes or past history, save and except that the words 'in the position of the accused' require that the hypothetical person be an ordinary person who has been provoked to the same decree of severity and for the same reasons as the accused. In the present case, this translates to a person with the minimum powers of self-control of an ordinary person who is subjected to a sexual advance that is aggravated because of the accused's special sensitivity to a history of violence and sexual assault within his family.

All of the accused's attendant circumstances and sensitivities are relevant in determining the effect of the provocation on 'an ordinary person in the position of the accused'. Indeed, '[w]ere it otherwise, it would be quite impossible to identify the gravity of the particular provocation'.[11] As the court said in *Stingel*:[12]

> [N]one of the attributes or characteristics of a particular accused will be necessarily irrelevant to an assessment of the content and extent of the provocation involved in the relevant conduct. For example, any one or more of the accused's age, sex, race, physical features, personal attributes, personal relationships and *past history* may be relevant [emphasis added].

The fact that an accused is especially sensitive to the conduct constituting the provocation, or that he or she takes the conduct as being aimed at a particular sensitivity when in fact it is not, will not preclude a finding of provocation, nor prevent it from being attributed to the hypothetical ordinary person. For example, in *Luc Thiet Thuan v R*,[13] the Privy Council held that the accused's impaired mental condition which made him prone to respond explosively even to minor provocation was a factor which could properly be taken into account when assessing the gravity of the conduct by the deceased. Similarly, the fact that the accused in the present appeal had a special sensitivity to sexual assault because of what he believed had occurred to his sisters was relevant to the issue of provocation under s 23(2)(a) and the extent of his provocation must be attributed to the ordinary person for the purpose of s 23(2)(b).

The Crown attempted to distinguish the present case from *Luc Thiet Thuan* on the ground that the conduct of the deceased was unrelated to the sensitivity of the accused. The Crown contended that the deceased made a non-violent homosexual advance which was unconnected with the accused's beliefs. Those beliefs related to incidents of heterosexual sexual assault by his father upon his sisters, not homosexual activity. There are two answers to this contention. First, as demonstrated by the passages quoted earlier in the judgment, the advance, although initiated in a non-violent manner, soon became quite rough and aggressive. To the extent that Priestley JA suggests otherwise,[14] his remarks cannot be reconciled with the accused's evidence or record of interview. Thus, in the record of interview, the accused said: 'He started grabbing me harder. I tried and forced him to the lower side of me. He still tried to grab me.' In evidence, the accused said: '[H]e grabbed me by both arms and pulled me towards him till there was no room in between us. Then he moved his hand down to my backside, arse. I pushed it away then he slowly touched my groin area that's when I got aggressive and hit him.'

Second, the fact that the advance was of a homosexual nature was only one factor in the case. What was more important from the accused's point of view was that a sexual advance, accompanied with some force, was made by a person whom the accused looked up to and trusted. The sexual, rather than homosexual, nature of the assault filtered through the memory of what the accused believed his father had done to his sisters, was the trigger that provoked the accused's violent response. Viewed in this light, the conduct of the deceased was directly related to the accused's sensitivity. Indeed, any unwanted sexual advance is a basis for 'justifiable indignation', especially when it is coupled with aggression.[15] Such an unwanted advance may lay the foundation for a successful defence of provocation.

Kirby J [dissenting]:

Legal context: insistence upon the 'ordinary person' test

Throughout the long line of cases in this court in which the law of provocation has been examined, there has been a steady insistence upon the application of an objective standard to the self-control which may be expected of the accused, provoked as he (and all of them have been male) was. This principle was taken from the common law and from the development of the availability of provocation in the English courts. The principle has been criticised as based upon the socially unacceptable assumption that provocation to uncontrolled anger and rage should sometimes be exculpatory.[16] However, in the light of legal history and the statutory provisions applicable to this case, which accept that assumption, this debate can safely be ignored.

In 1803 *East's Pleas of the Crown*[17] explained that the doctrine of provocation was the product of 'the mercy of the law interposes in pity to human frailty'. It was thus a doctrine fashioned to relieve from the ultimate punishment those accused who, according to society's changing assessments, were not 'morally speaking' murderers and who, if solely so presented, might be acquitted out of the jury's sympathy on the ground of a lack of the relevant malice aforethought.

However, the common law always set its face against extending its mercy to extreme loss of self-control on the part of an accused person, however unwarranted the provocation described.[18] In certain circumstances to give way to sudden and temporary loss of self-control might be understandable. But a basic measure of self-control, according to what might be expected of a reasonable person or ordinary person, has run through the case law for more than 150 years.[19]

In 1837, Coleridge J[20] observed:

> ... [t]hough the law condescends to human frailty, it will not indulge human ferocity. It considers man to be a rational being, and requires that he should exercise a reasonable control over his passions.

The test was formulated in its modern version in 1869, thus:[21]

> ... [t]here must exist such an amount of provocation as would be excited by the circumstances in the mind of a reasonable man, and so as to lead the jury to ascribe the act to the influence of that passion.

Because a person hates or fears Jews or Roman Catholics or women, the law would not, for that reason, diminish a murderous attack on a Jew or Roman Catholic or woman. Because an accused is a member of the criminal mafia and is deeply insulted by an affront to a leader of that organisation the law will not ordinarily afford a basis for diminishing the homicide 'provoked' by such an affront. The gravity of the affront may help to explain whether the accused was *in fact* provoked. But provocation in law has conventionally required a second element which is measured against the objective standard of the self-control of the ordinary person.[22]

[His Honour reviewed the case law, and continued:]

What is the result of this unbroken line of decisions? The law of provocation in Australia is clearly established as requiring an objective criterion for the measurement of the measure of self-control that the law presumes. This is so by principle having its roots in legal history. History is reinforced by a reflection on the rationale of this provision of the law. In the face of some academic criticism and two dissenting voices within this court, the objective standard has been consistently applied. Despite the critics, that standard certainly has its supporters.[23] The psychological difficulties inherent in dividing the attribution of subjective personal responses to some aspects of the consideration of provocation, but not to others, has been noted both in this court[24] and by other Australian courts.[25] The desirability of simplifying this area of the law has been suggested, including by some who favour persistence with an objective standard because of the perceived absurdities and injustices that a purely subjective test would produce.[26] Where there is a code or (as in this case) a general criminal statute which expressly refers to the 'ordinary person', meaning must obviously be given to that expression. This court, in the series of decisions which I have reviewed, has repeatedly called attention to the basic similarity of the principle applicable in the several Australian jurisdictions. Wherever possible, commonality of such bedrock legal doctrine should be upheld, whether the case is governed by the common law, by statute or by a code.[27]

In the end, the answer to the arguments in the present appeal must be found not in such generalities but in the meaning of s 23 of the Act and the application of the proviso to the conceded errors. Nevertheless, the language of the Act should itself be read against the background of the history and purposes of the law of provocation which we do well to remember and which it would be wrong to ignore.

Factual context — homosexual advance defence

...

For the law to accept that a non-violent sexual advance, without more, by a man to a man could induce in an ordinary person such a reduction in self-control as to occasion the formation of an intent to kill, or to inflict grievous bodily harm, would sit ill with contemporary legal, educative, and policing efforts designed to remove such violent responses from society, grounded as they are in irrational hatred and fear.[28]

In my view, the 'ordinary person' in Australian society today is not so homophobic as to respond to a non-violent sexual advance by a homosexual person as to form an intent to kill or to inflict grievous bodily harm. He or she might, depending on the circumstances, be embarrassed; treat it at first as a bad joke; be hurt; insulted. He or she might react with the strong language of protest; might use as much physical force as was necessary to effect an escape; and where absolutely necessary assault the persistent perpetrator to secure escape.[29] But the notion that the ordinary 22-year-old male (the age of the accused) in Australia today would so lose self-control as to form an intent to kill or grievously injure the deceased because of a non-violent sexual advance by a homosexual person is unconvincing. It should not be accepted by this court as an objective standard applicable in contemporary Australia.

'Ordinary person in the position of the accused'

...

The killing of an individual is still of profound concern to the community in which it occurs. The law in Australia has not yet surrendered the standard of provocation to the wholly subjective responses of the most vulnerable to hurt, rage or affront. With all respect to those of a different opinion, I align myself with nearly all of the justices of this court who have considered provocation in the past. I would sustain the wisdom of the law's insistence that the relevant standard of self-control to be expected of a person subject to an alleged provocation is the objective standard of an ordinary person. In New South Wales, by statute, that is an 'ordinary person in the position of the accused'. Save in the respect explained in *Stingel*, the additional words cannot expel the 'ordinary person' who survives into the New South Wales Act, as amended. Further support for this view may be found in the fact that, in several decisions of justices of this court, long before the amendments to the New South Wales Act, similar phrases appear in describing the hypothetical 'ordinary person' or 'reasonable man' against whose measure of self-control the accused's intentions must be judged.[30]

The appellant's attempt, on the ground of the amendment, to import into the meaning of s 23(2)(b) of the Act, as relevant to the measure of self-control to be expected of him, all of the subjective features of his past, was misconceived. It was rightly rejected. ...

Conclusion: no miscarriage of justice

The accused was faced with, what for him in his situation, may be accepted to have been a provocation. It may be allowed that it was provocation of a sexual kind affecting deep feelings and affronting him. It intruded into his privacy in a way most unwelcome to him. It may even have suggested to him assumptions about his own sexuality which he found confronting or offensive. But he was a 22-year-old adult male living in contemporary Australia. He was at all times wearing at least his tracksuit pants and underwear. At no time were these garments removed or displaced. He was awake. He was aware of what the deceased was doing. He was also aware that the deceased was highly intoxicated. He was younger. He was physically fit. He was very soon able to achieve physical superiority over the deceased. His great physical power is indicated by the course which his violence took. He had relatives close at hand. He knew that they would answer a telephone call and come at once to collect him. His sister's home was within short walking distance. He could not explain in his evidence why he did not simply say 'I am going'. He agreed that there was nothing at all to prevent him from leaving. Following the killing of the deceased he was readily able to summon a motor vehicle and coolly to direct that he be taken to the police station there to assert that the deceased had done 'worse' to him than he had done to the deceased.

No jury acting reasonably, could fail to be satisfied beyond reasonable doubt of the relevant matters. These were that the conduct of the deceased, however unwanted and offensive to the appellant, was not of such a nature as to be sufficient, objectively, to deprive a hypothetical ordinary 22-year-old Australian male in the position of the appellant of the power of self-control imputed to him by law to the extent of inducing him to form an intent to kill or to inflict grievous bodily harm on the deceased. Adapting what was said unanimously by this court in *Stingel*, no jury, acting reasonably, could fail to be satisfied beyond reasonable doubt that the appellant's reaction to the conduct of the deceased fell far below the minimum limits of the range of powers of self-control which must be attributed to the hypothetical ordinary 22-year-old Australian male in the position of the appellant.[31]

That standard of self-control remains, in this country, objective. Both Mr Stingel and the appellant stated that they were provoked more than they could bear by a confronting sexual challenge. No lesser standard of self-control is demanded by our society in the case of the appellant than of Mr Stingel, simply because sexual conduct of the deceased was homosexual in character. To condone a lesser standard is to accept an inequality before the law which this court has previously, repeatedly and rightly rejected. The ultimate foundation of adherence to the objective test was explained in *Stingel*,[32] in the terms of Wilson J's reasons, in the Supreme Court of Canada, in *R v Hill*:[33]

> The objective standard ... may be said to exist in order to ensure that in the evaluation of the provocation defence there is no fluctuating standard of self-control against which accuseds are measured. The governing principles are those of equality and individual responsibility, so that all persons are held to the same standard notwithstanding their distinctive personality traits and varying capacities to achieve the standard.

If every woman who was the subject of a 'gentle', 'non-aggressive' although persistent sexual advance, in a comparable situation to that described in the evidence in this case could respond with brutal violence rising to an intention to kill or inflict grievous bodily harm on the male importuning her, and then claim provocation after a homicide, the law of provocation would be sorely tested and undesirably extended. A neutral and equal response to the meaning of the section requires the application of the same objective standard to the measure of self-control which the law assumes, and enforces, in an unwanted sexual approach by a man to a man. Such an approach may be 'revolting' to some.[34] Any unwanted sexual advance, heterosexual or homosexual, can be offensive. It may intrude on sexual integrity in an objectionable way. But this court should not send the message that, in Australia today, such conduct is objectively capable of being found by a jury to be sufficient to provoke the intent to kill or inflict grievous bodily harm. Such a message unacceptably condones serious violence by people who take the law into their own hands. Even allowing for the appellant's alleged memories of his father's sexual conduct many years earlier directed to his sisters, there is no way that this could have induced an ordinary person in his position to have so far lost self-control as to have formed the intention to kill or inflict grievous bodily harm on the deceased.

[**Toohey J** delivered a separate judgment agreeing with **Brennan CJ**. **Gummow J** delivered a dissenting judgment. Appeal allowed and a new trial ordered.]

Notes:

1. (1936) 55 CLR 499.
2. (1963) 111 CLR 610 at 647.
3. See *Stingel v R* (1990) 171 CLR 312 at 332–4; 97 ALR 1.
4. (1990) 171 CLR at 331–2.
5. *Mraz v R* (1955) 93 CLR 493 at 514.

6. (1990) 171 CLR 312; 97 ALR 1.
7. (1995) 183 CLR 58; 129 ALR 575.
8. (1990) 171 CLR at 320. Quoted with approval in *Masciantonio* (1995) 183 CLR 58 at 66 per Brennan, Deane, Dawson and Gaudron JJ, at 71 per McHugh J.
9. See generally my comments in *Masciantonio* (1995) 183 CLR at 72–4: cf Yeo, 'Sex, Ethnicity, Power of Self-Control and Provocation Revisited' 18 *Sydney Law Review* 304 (1996).
10. New South Wales, Legislative Assembly, *Parliamentary Debates (Hansard)*, 11 March 1982, p 2486. Section 23 was introduced into the Act by the *Crimes (Homicide) Amendment Act 1982* (NSW).
11. *Stingel* (1990) 171 CLR at 326; 97 ALR at 10.
12. (1990) 171 CLR at 326; 97 ALR at 10.
13. [1997] AC 131 at 146.
14. Priestley JA said that 'the touching was amorous, not forceful'.
15. Dressler, 'When 'Heterosexual' Men Kill 'Homosexual' Men: Reflections on Provocation Law, Sexual Advances, and the 'Reasonable Man' Standard' (1995) 85 *Journal of Criminal Law and Criminology* 726 at 754.
16. cf Coss, 'Lethal Violence by Men' (1996) 20 *Criminal Law Journal* 305.
17. (1803) vol 1 at 239 cited in *Masciantonio* (1995) 183 CLR 58 at 72 per McHugh J; see also Dixon CJ in *Parker v R* (1963) 111 CLR 610 at 627.
18. Leader-Elliott, 'Sex, Race and Provocation; In Defence of *Stingel*', (1996) 20 *Criminal Law Journal* 72 at 84.
19. cf *Masciantonio* (1995) 183 CLR 58 at 71; 129 ALR 575; *R v Chhay* (1994) 72 A Crim R 1 at 13.
20. *R v Kirkham* (1837) 8 Car & P 115 at 119; 173 ER 422 at 424.
21. *R v Welsh* (1869) 11 Cox CC 336 at 338.
22. cf Leader-Elliott, 'Sex, Race and Provocation: In Defence of *Stingel*' at 79.
23. Eg, Leader-Elliott, 'Sex, Race and Provocation: In Defence of *Stingel*' (1996) 20 *Criminal Law Journal* 72; Berman, 'Provocation: Difficulties in the Application of the Subjective Test' (1995) 2 *Criminal Law News* 1 at 7. See also Fairall, 'The Objective Test in Provocation' (1983) 7 *Criminal Law Journal* 142.
24. McHugh J called it a 'curious dichotomy' in *Masciantonio* at 72.
25. Eg, *R v Voukelatos* [1990] VR 1 at 27.
26. Leader-Elliott, 'Sex, Race and Provocation: In Defence of *Stingel*' at 96; Detmold; 'Provocation to Murder: Sovereignty and Multiculture' (1997) 19 *Sydney Law Review* 5; The Review of Commonwealth Criminal Law in *Principles of Criminal Responsibility and Other Matters* (1990) has proposed the abolition of provocation such that it should be a consideration relevant only in mitigation of punishment. This proposal has been criticised (1990) 14 *Criminal Law Journal* 383 at 386) on the ground that the 'powerful stigmatising label of 'murderer' should be confined' to killing in cold blood. Compare earlier Victorian proposals noted in Dixon, 'A Blueprint for Heroism or a Rational and Humane Code?' (1983) 7 *Criminal Law Journal* 132 at 138–9. The 1982 legislation in New South Wales itself followed the abolition of the mandatory life sentence for murder: see (1983) 7 *Criminal Law Journal* 132 at 140.
27. Eg, *Stingel* (1990) 171 CLR 312 at 320; *Masciantonio* (1995) 183 CLR 58 at 71. As to the position in New Zealand the provisions of the Crimes Act 1961 (NZ) s 169(4)

have been said to fuse 'two discordant notions' giving rise to a 'minor growth industry of scholarship': see Brookbanks, 'Provocation — Defining the Limits of Characteristics' (1986) 10 *Criminal Law Journal* 411. See Mason and Tomsen, *Homophobic Violence* (1997) 132 at 133.

28. See Mason and Tomsen, *Homophobic Violence* (1997) 132 at 133.
29. Homosexual advance defences were raised in the 1950s in England. See, eg, *R v Cunningham* [1959] 1 QB 288 and *R v McCarthy* [1954] 2 QB 105 at 109–10. Lord Goddard CJ said in *McCarthy* 'this provocation would no doubt have excused ... a blow, perhaps more than one'. Viscount Simon in *Holmes v Director of Public Prosecutions* [1946] AC 588 at 601 said: '[A]s society advances, it ought to call for a higher measure of self-control in all cases ... [T]he law has to reconcile respect for the sanctity of human life with recognition of the effect of provocation on human frailty.' Compare the Australian decisions in *Pritchard v R* (1990) 49 A Crim R 67; *Stiles v R* (1990) 50 A Crim R 13; *R v Grmusa* (1990) 50 A Crim R 358; *R v Preston* (1992) 58 A Crim R 328; *Whittaker v R* (1993) 68 A Crim R 476.
30. See, eg, Dixon J in *Packett v R* (1937) 58 CLR 190 at 217–18 ('At common law the test of provocation is ... whether it would suffice to deprive a reasonable man *in his situation* of self-control'): Windeyer J in *Parker* (1963) 111 CLR 610 at 655 ('[T]he matter must be considered from the standpoint of the mind of an ordinary man *in the circumstances*') and Brennan, Deane, Dawson and Gaudron JJ in *Masciantonio* (1995) 183 CLR 58 at 69 ('Whether an ordinary person could have reacted in the way in which the appellant did [might depend on whether] the provocation offered by the deceased was, *in the circumstances in which the appellant found himself*, of a high degree') (emphasis added in each case).
31. (1990) 171 CLR 312 at 324.
32. [1986] 1 SCR 313 at 343.
33. cf Howe, 'More Folk Provoke Their Own Demise' (1997) 19 *Sydney Law Review* 336 at 355.
34. *Stingel* (1990) 171 CLR 312 at 336–7.

5.36 Illustrations

1. D was convicted of the murder by stabbing of his ex-wife's lover. D and V were Ethiopian and D's ex-wife was Eritrean. D gave evidence that the behaviour of his ex-wife and V was contrary to Ethiopian customs, that there were rumours about their relationship circulating in the Ethiopian community and that this had upset him and made him ashamed. He said that shortly before he attacked V his ex-wife had said to him, in the presence of V, that she and V were lovers and were going to live together, and V had then smiled at him in an arrogant or condescending manner. The prosecution agreed that provocation should be left to the jury. In directing the jury on provocation, the judge said the jury could consider D's personal characteristics in considering the degree of provocation and referred, by way of example, to a person with a physical defect. On appeal, held, appeal allowed and a retrial ordered. The judge misdirected the jury by failing to explain to them that, in the consideration of the gravity of the allegedly provocative conduct, D was entitled to have brought into consideration his ethnicity, that is, the fact that he and all the others involved were Ethiopian or Eritrean and, to the extent that the jury accepted it, the evidence of what was occurring between D's ex-wife and V, of the rumours in the Ethiopian community as to their relationship and of D's shame and humiliation by reference to Ethiopian cultural values and mores: *R v Abebe* (2000) 1 VR 429.

2. D was party to a hearing before the Family Court in which V, his estranged de facto wife, sought maintenance. This was part of a longstanding and bitter dispute between them, which included access rights to their children. During an adjournment of the hearing, D attacked V with a long-bladed kitchen knife and stabbed her 48 times, killing her. D was charged with murder. Defence counsel, in his opening statement, said V had said to D immediately before the attack: 'We have got you now, you bastard' and that she could now do what she liked with the children. There was no corroboration of this from bystanders. The defence also relied on the stress caused by the family law proceedings. The judge ruled that the evidence did not raise any issue of provocation. D was convicted of murder and appealed. Held, conviction affirmed. The judge was right to withdraw provocation from the jury. Even assuming V had behaved as D alleged, no reasonable jury could have failed to be satisfied beyond reasonable doubt that D's reaction fell a long way below the minimum limits of self-control that must be attributed to the ordinary person. To hold that provocation arose in this case would be to encourage savagery at the expense of civilised behaviour: *R v Parsons* (2000) 1 VR 161. Contrast this finding with the following case.

3. D was tried for the murder of his estranged wife. D had stabbed V many times with a kitchen knife, having confronted her in a shopping centre. D claimed V had spat at him prior to his stabbing her. Prior to the fatal incident, V had left D, and he believed her to be having an affair with another man. According to D, V had refused to return a gold necklace to him, taken his British passport, taken and used his MasterCard, obtained an intervention order against him, and withdrawn sponsorship of him which would result in his expulsion from the country. The trial judge, Coldrey J, ruled that provocation not be left to the jury. The accused was convicted of murder. On appeal, held, appeal allowed and a new trial ordered, by Charles and Batt JJA, Vincent J dissenting. On the version of the facts most favourable to D, it would have been open to a jury acting reasonably to fail to be satisfied beyond reasonable doubt that the killing was unprovoked in the relevant sense. Accordingly, provocation should have been put to the jury: *R v Yasso* [2004] VSCA 127. See also *R v Kumar* (2002) 5 VR 193.

5.37 Further reading

S De Pasquale, 'Provocation and the Homosexual Advance Defence: The Deployment of Culture as a Defence Strategy' (2002) 26 *MULR* 110

M J Detmold, 'Provocation to Murder: Sovereignty and Multiculture' (1997) 18 *Syd LR* 5

I Leader-Elliott, 'Sex, Race and Provocation: In Defence of *Stingel*' (1996) 20 *Crim LJ* 72

J Morgan, 'Provocation Law and Facts: Dead Women Tell No Tales, Tales Are Told About Them' (1997) 21 *MULR* 237

New South Wales Parliamentary Select Committee on the Partial Defence of Provocation, *The Partial Defence of Provocation: Final Report* (2013)

D Tyson, *Sex, Culpability and the Defence of Provocation*, Routledge, Oxford, 2013

Victorian Law Reform Commission, *Defences to Homicide: Final Report* (2004)

M Weinberg, 'Moral Blameworthiness — The "Objective Test" Dilemma' (2003) 24 *Aust Bar Rev* 173

S Yeo, 'Power of Self-Control in Provocation and Automatism' (1992) 14 *Syd LR* 3

CHAPTER 6

Involuntary Manslaughter

INTRODUCTION

6.1 As noted in Chapter 5, manslaughter is traditionally divided into two forms: voluntary manslaughter and involuntary manslaughter. This chapter focuses on involuntary manslaughter. Involuntary manslaughter is the category of unlawful homicide where an accused lacks the mens rea for murder, but is regarded by the law as sufficiently culpable that he or she should still be held responsible for the death. Since the decisions of the High Court in *Wilson v R* (1992) 174 CLR 313; 107 ALR 257 (at 6.4C) and *R v Lavender* (2005) 22 CLR 67 (at 6.10C), common law involuntary manslaughter may be divided into two types:

(1) unlawful and dangerous act manslaughter; and

(2) negligent manslaughter.

Manslaughter by omission, is best referred to as an example of negligent manslaughter.

6.2 Until the latter part of the nineteenth century, the law was that if the accused, in the course of committing any unlawful act, brought about the death of another, that person was necessarily guilty of manslaughter. Such a rule was obviously unduly harsh, and the modern history of the doctrine has largely been one of attempts to place limitations upon it. The first step was to confine the concept of 'unlawful act' to those acts which are subject to criminal punishment and not simply to civil liability; and that restriction of the doctrine has been accepted ever since *R v Franklin* (1883) 15 Cox CC 163. In *R v Larkin* [1943] 1 All ER 217 at 219, the Court of Criminal Appeal stated that the unlawful act must also be 'dangerous', and defined a dangerous act as one 'likely to injure another person'. In *R v Church* [1966] 1 QB 59 at 70, that court went even further in stating that the 'unlawful act must be such as all sober and reasonable people would inevitably recognise must subject the other person to, at least, the risk of some harm resulting therefrom, albeit not serious harm'.

Prior to the decision in *Wilson v R*, there had been authority supporting the existence of a category of manslaughter by the intentional infliction of bodily harm, or battery manslaughter, distinct from the doctrine of unlawful and dangerous act manslaughter. Thus in *Mamote-Kulang v R* (1964) 111 CLR 62, D hit V, who had a weak spleen. D was unaware of the weak spleen and the assault unexpectedly caused V's death. D was found guilty of battery manslaughter. In *Wilson v R*, the High Court rejected this view, holding that unlawful and dangerous act manslaughter is the only true common law manslaughter in cases where no question of criminal negligence is present.

A further modification of the rule was developed in Victoria. In *R v Holzer* [1968] VR 481, Smith J held that, for the doctrine to apply, 'the circumstances must be such that a reasonable man in the accused's position, performing the very act which the accused performed, would have realised that he was exposing another or others to an appreciable risk of really serious injury'. He went on to state (at 482): 'It is not sufficient, as it was held to be in *R v Church*, to show there was a risk of some harm resulting, albeit not serious harm'. The High Court has now embraced that approach in *Wilson v R* (at **6.4C**).

6.3 If a person kills another with either an act or omission with a very high degree of carelessness, that person can be guilty of manslaughter. There is, of course, a recognised civil wrong or tort termed 'negligence'. The doctrine of tort law cannot be applied to the crime of manslaughter. Many of the tort cases have treated quite trivial acts of carelessness as sufficient to found liability in damages. However, the crime of manslaughter, which may attract a very heavy sentence of imprisonment, requires evidence of carelessness of a very high degree.

The courts have used various adjectives to stress the very high degree of negligence which must have been present for the accused to be guilty of manslaughter: see **6.11**. In *Andrews v DPP* [1937] AC 576 at 583, Lord Atkin suggested 'reckless' was the most suitable adjective. Using 'recklessness' in these circumstances can invite confusion with the subjective standard applied in murder. Accordingly, the standard enunciated in *Nydam v R* [1977] VR 430 is to be preferred of 'criminal negligence' or stated by the High Court in *R v Lavender* (2005) 222 CLR 67 as 'wicked negligence'.

Most instances of criminal negligence encountered in practice involve careless action. However, responsibility for manslaughter may also result from a failure to take steps needed to preserve life in situations in which the accused was under a legal duty to take such steps. This type of manslaughter by omission is a sub-category of manslaughter by criminal negligence.

Most people would agree that a person always has a moral duty to assist another whose life is in danger. However, it is clear that not every case of moral duty will give rise to a legal duty so as to ground a manslaughter charge. Legal duties have been held to exist only where there is something over and above the moral obligation. Broadly speaking, they are cases either of obligations to helpless persons springing from the natural ties of marriage, parenthood, or some other close relationship, or of obligations which arise because the accused has by his or her conduct entitled the deceased to expect aid from that person in particular, as opposed to citizens in general. The law has also recognised a legal duty to act in cases where a person has created a dangerous situation. The law here is clearly developing and the categories of duty situations are not closed.

UNLAWFUL AND DANGEROUS ACT MANSLAUGHTER

6.4C Wilson v R

(1992) 174 CLR 313; 107 ALR 257
High Court of Australia

[Footnotes to the extract appear at the end of the extract.]

Mason CJ, **Toohey**, **Gaudron** and **McHugh JJ**: The appellant was charged with the murder of Warren George Forsythe Ormsby. He was acquitted of that charge but was convicted of manslaughter. He stood trial jointly with Wayne Dennis Cumming who was found not guilty of murder and manslaughter. Both offences are dealt with in the *Criminal Law Consolidation Act 1935* (SA) (the Act) but neither is defined in the Act. Their elements are to be found in the common law.

The facts

The events giving rise to the charge against the appellant were as follows. On the evening of 15 September 1989 the appellant, his girlfriend Kerri Ann Bennier and Cumming were at the home occupied by Cumming's step-father and the appellant's mother. The appellant and Bennier walked to a hotel nearby to collect some alcohol from the appellant's mother who was at the hotel with Cumming's step-father. On the way they met the deceased, a middle-aged man, who was under the influence of liquor. The deceased exchanged words with the appellant and Bennier. The appellant thought that the deceased was 'strange, a bit weird'. The thrust of the appellant's evidence was that the deceased was rambling on and making it hard for him to pass. The appellant then told Bennier to go back home to get Cumming so, he said, that Cumming might go to the hotel and collect the alcohol. When Cumming arrived at the scene with Bennier, the appellant and the deceased were still there. The appellant claimed that the deceased had earlier pushed him and that, after Cumming arrived, the deceased 'put his arm on the back of my neck and tried to kiss me'. The deceased then 'shouldered me'. The appellant tried to walk away, saw that the deceased's fists were clenched at his side and thought that the deceased was going to hit him. This evidence followed:

Q — So what did you do. A — That's when I hit him.
Q — How hard did you hit him. A — It wasn't really — I didn't think it was really that very hard.
Q — It wasn't soft either. A — No. Q — Only the one time. A — Yes, I only hit him the once.

The blow was to the deceased's face, causing him to fall to the ground where his head 'landed in the dirt part near the hedge'. The appellant then walked off with Bennier. As he did, Cumming rolled the deceased on to his stomach, went through his pockets, rolled him on to his back and 'smashed his head on the concrete … twice'. The cause of the deceased's death was brain damage, his injuries being consistent with one impact. The Crown's case, as presented in final address, suggested the fall from the appellant's punch as the more likely cause of death. The trial judge's direction seems to have left the fall from the appellant's punch or Cumming's later actions as likely to have caused the death. This aspect is not crucial to the questions now before this court.

The case against the appellant

The case against both accused was one of felony murder, it being alleged that they assaulted the deceased in the course of robbing him. In answer to this charge the appellant denied any participation in the robbery and any intention of causing serious harm to the deceased; he also relied on self-defence. This court is not directly concerned with the trial judge's directions as to murder. But it may be noted that his Honour directed the jury that if the deceased was killed in the course of a joint enterprise between Cumming and the appellant or, if one aided or abetted the other in the killing, they should find both guilty of murder. The trial judge also directed the jury to consider whether either man, acting on his own, was guilty of murder. Since both were found not guilty of murder, it must be taken that the jury rejected an intention to kill or to do grievous bodily harm on the part of either.

On the alternative verdict of manslaughter, his Honour directed the jury in the following terms:

> In this case if you have not found murder proved, but had gone on to consider manslaughter it would be manslaughter by an unlawful and dangerous act. The killing of a man in the course of committing a crime is manslaughter. The crime must be an act in serious breach of the criminal law. A serious assault — you may think the punch by Wilson or the hitting of the head on the concrete by Cumming to be serious assaults — would be an unlawful act for this purpose. Whether the particular act you are considering is a dangerous act is a matter for your judgment.

In the case of the appellant, the trial judge also left to the jury provocation as a possible basis for manslaughter. But, as King CJ pointed out ((1991) 53 A Crim R 281 at 282):

> [T]here was no suggestion of an intent to cause death or grievous bodily harm and as the only available basis of a verdict of murder was felony murder, provocation could have played no part in the jury's deliberations.

While the appellant's main attack on the direction to the jury focused on the passage quoted above, he also complained that the direction on self-defence related only to the charge of murder and failed to relate self-defence to the requirement of unlawfulness, where manslaughter was open to the jury on the basis of death caused by an unlawful and dangerous act. King CJ (with whom Cox J agreed) rejected this complaint (supra, at 283) on the ground that:

> [while] the directions on self-defence were primarily concerned with murder and did not expressly relate self-defence to the assault which was alleged to be the unlawful act which could lead to a verdict of manslaughter[,] [t]he judge twice told the jury ... that if the appellant was acting in lawful self-defence he would not be 'guilty of anything'.

Although the complaint regarding self-defence and manslaughter is part of the grounds of appeal to this court, it is hard to see how self-defence could have been a real issue at the trial. The appellant was free to walk away from the deceased at any time and the deceased could not have been thought by the appellant to represent a threat to him, particularly as Cumming was with him. The appellant's real complaint, to which we now turn, is the direction as to 'an unlawful and dangerous act' as an element of manslaughter.

The question of manslaughter arising from an unlawful and dangerous act is an uncertain area of the law, reflecting a divergence between Australian and English authorities as to the degree of danger which must exist. It is useful to approach the question on an historical footing with a view to determining whether it is possible to spell out any clear principle from the relevant authorities. This involves looking first at the development of the law relating to culpable homicide.

Culpable homicide

The common law of homicide began with the principle that all who cause death, whether intentionally or accidentally, are liable to conviction for murder.[1] Its history reflects a continuing effort to limit that liability.[2] Fletcher observes:

> The historic point of departure is the principle that unless a killing is justified ... the party causing death is always accountable ... It was causing death, not the manner and culpability of acting, that determined liability. When the law of homicide came under the King's jurisdiction in the twelfth century and became a crime punished by death, the general principle of liability began to admit of exceptions.[3]

By the time of Bracton[4] and following the abolition of the distinction between *botless* or unemendable homicide and other homicides during the reign of Henry II, homicide was culpable if the death occurred during the commission of an unlawful act. However, it is important to note the basis of this liability.

By the thirteenth century, a charge of homicide arising from an accidental death could be met by the plea of *per infortunium* or misadventure.[5] Death occurring in the course of an unlawful act was culpable by reason of the unavailability of the *per infortunium* or misadventure plea; W Hawkins,[6] M Hale[7] and E Coke[8] consider the matter in that context. The excuses of accident, self-preservation and insanity marked the beginning of the move to bring homicide back to the category of cases in which the offender had a fair opportunity of avoiding the death of the victim.[9]

Even as late as the sixteenth century, culpable homicide was thought of as a single undivided offence and the judges were more concerned with distinguishing between:

> what was culpable [homicide] and what was covered by such defences as self-defence and misadventure, than with making distinctions based on differing degrees of culpability.[10]

However, in that century manslaughter was used from time to time as a term mitigating murder in cases in which the killing had been accidental or unintended or, though deliberate, involved an element of provocation or self-defence.[11] But the distinction between murder and manslaughter was not precisely formulated. The earliest reported verdict of manslaughter was recorded in *Salisbury's* case (1553) 1 Plowd 100; 75 ER 158 where co-conspirators, intending to ambush and kill Ellis, by mistake killed his servant. John Salisbury, a servant of one of the conspirators, having no part in the conspiracy, joined the affray and wounded the deceased.

The emergence of manslaughter as a separate and lesser offence than murder marks the beginning of an approach that causing death is innocent unless additional factors (such as an intent to kill or the taking of an excessive risk) are present. The grounds for rejecting an excuse become the grounds for liability, and killing in the course of an unlawful act, in the absence of the requisite intent for murder, is recognised as constituting manslaughter.

Even after the emergence of manslaughter as a separate and lesser offence, Coke[12] maintained that the unavailability of the plea *per infortunium* meant that the killing was murder. Logically this was so. The fact that Coke's view was not adopted indicates how attractive was the culpability/dangerousness approach. Hale did not follow Coke's view. Unlike Coke, he classified the killing of a boy when shooting at a deer in another's park as manslaughter, evidently treating the shooting in the park as unlawful.[13]

In the early eighteenth century, Hawkins, in his chapter on *per infortunium*, appears to place the unavailability of the plea not so much on the fact of the unlawfulness of the act as on the level of risk involved:

> Sect 9. But if a person kill another by shooting at a deer, &c in a third person's park, in the doing whereof he is a trespasser; or by shooting off a gun, or throwing stones in a city or highway, or other place where men usually resort; or by throwing stones at another wantonly in play, which is a dangerous sport, and has not the least appearance of any good intent; or by *doing any other such idle action as cannot but endanger the bodily hurt of some one or other*; or by tilting or playing at handsword without the king's command; or by parrying with naked swords covered with buttons at the points, or with swords in the scabbards, or such like rash sports, which cannot be used without the manifest hazard of life, he is guilty of manslaughter.
>
> Sect 10. And if a man happen to kill another in the execution of a malicious and deliberate purpose to do him a personal hurt, by wounding or beating him; or *in the wilful commission of any unlawful act, which necessarily tends to raise tumults and quarrels, and consequently cannot but be attended with the danger of personal hurt to some one or other*; as by committing a riot, robbing a park, &c he shall be adjudged guilty of murder.
>
> …
>
> Sect 12. Neither shall he be adjudged guilty of a less crime, who kills another, *in doing such a wilful act, as shews him to be as dangerous as a wild beast, and an enemy to mankind in general*; as by going deliberately with a horse used to strike, or discharging a gun, among a multitude of people, or throwing a great stone or piece of timber from a house into a street, through which he knows that many are passing; and it is no excuse that he intended no harm to anyone in particular, or

> that he meant to do it only for sport, or to frighten the people, &c (in each case, emphasis added).[14]

Thus, an unlawful and dangerous act was not a rationale or basis for liability, but a factor negativing a defence which otherwise was available to cut down what approached strict liability for causing death. Though expressed in that way, the grounds for negativing the defence were easily transformed into grounds of liability.[15]

This transformation began to occur with the publication of Foster's *Discourse of Homicide* in 1762.[16] Beginning with *per infortunium* as a concept of excuse, Foster then discussed the unlawful act as a standard for gauging the gravity of the killing. However, he adopted the felony murder rule so that a killing in the course of an act with intent to commit a felony amounted to murder. The rule ascribes malice aforethought to the accused when he kills in the perpetration of a felony. The doctrine of transferred felonious intent and its analytical consequence, the crime of felony murder, not only were regarded by Stephen[17] as the only blot on Foster's work, but also marked the end of the possibility of matching moral culpability to legal liability in homicide. Liability contingent on such a felony as the lawfulness of the accused's intended act, with only limited relation to its foreseeable consequences, is precisely the kind of rule that 'erodes the relation between criminal liability and moral culpability'.[18]

The felony murder rule was kept within confined bounds by insisting that the felonious act be 'known to be dangerous to life, and likely in itself to cause death': *R v Serné* (1887) 16 Cox CC 311 at 313.

By the mid-eighteenth century, Blackstone[19] was able to say that killing another 'amounts to murder, unless where *justified* ...; *excused* on the account of accident or self-preservation; or *alleviated* into manslaughter'.

In the nineteenth century the English courts applied the rule that, if a death occurred in the course of an unlawful act not amounting to a felony, the killing should be treated as manslaughter. Stephen, in *A Digest of The Criminal Law* (1887) Arts 222–3, states it as the common law rule. As thus expressed, the rule was harsh because it involved liability for manslaughter in the case of an unlawful act which was not dangerous. In other words, causing death in the course of performing a mere unlawful act does not supply the level of culpability appropriate to manslaughter as an instance of culpable homicide.

Manslaughter by an unlawful and dangerous act

The rigour of the common law was softened by a number of decisions. In *R v Franklin* (1883) 15 Cox CC 163 at 165 Field J spoke of his 'great abhorrence of constructive crime' and held that the requirement of unlawfulness was not met by the act in question being no more than a civil wrong.[20] In *R v Larkin*[21] the Court of Criminal Appeal required that the unlawful act be dangerous and that it be 'likely to injure'.[22] In *R v Church* [1966] 1 QB 59 at 69 the Court of Criminal Appeal rejected as erroneous a direction that:

> ... amounted to telling the jury that, whenever any unlawful act is committed in relation to a human being which resulted in death there must be, at least, a conviction for manslaughter.

In the view of the court (at 70):

> For such a verdict inexorably to follow, the unlawful act must be such as all sober and reasonable people would inevitably recognise must subject the other person to, at least, the risk of some harm resulting therefrom, albeit not serious harm.

In *DPP v Newbury* [1977] AC 500 the House of Lords examined the matter afresh. It affirmed the test adopted in *Larkin* and *Church*. It held that an accused was guilty of manslaughter if he intentionally did an act that was unlawful and dangerous and the act inadvertently caused death; that it was unnecessary to prove that the accused knew that the act was unlawful or dangerous; and that the test was still the objective test, namely whether all sober and reasonable people would recognise that the act was dangerous in the sense of carrying with it the risk of some harm, not whether the accused recognised its danger. As King CJ observed in the present case (at 284):

> In the course of a discussion of the judgment of Lord Denning MR in *Gray v Barr* [1971] 2 QB 554, Lord Salmon, who delivered the leading judgment, appears to imply that the test is also met if there is an actual intention to cause harm or an actual realisation that harm is likely, although that is not necessary if the act is objectively dangerous.

And, as King CJ pointed out, *Larkin*, *Church* and *Newbury* were not cases of intentional infliction of harm. There are however decisions of English courts which suggest that the intentional infliction of harm by means of an unlawful act may be sufficient to constitute manslaughter.[23] The question of battery manslaughter is considered later in this judgment.

The Australian decisions

A convenient starting point for a review of the Australian authorities is the decision of this court in *Mamote-Kulang v R* (1964) 111 CLR 62. It will be necessary to refer to that case again in the context of battery manslaughter. The appellant struck the deceased a blow with the back of his hand to the side of her abdomen, intending to hurt her and to cause her pain but not further injury. He was convicted of manslaughter. The judgments were concerned mainly with the meaning of the term 'accident' in the relevant legislation of Papua New Guinea but it seems that, in the view of Taylor, Owen and Windeyer JJ, death resulting from the intentional infliction of pain by an unlawful blow would constitute manslaughter at common law.[24]

R v Holzer [1968] VR 481 required consideration of a question which had not arisen in *Mamote-Kulang* but which was at the heart of some of the English decisions to which reference has been made. The question was as to the application in Australia of the notion that, in the case of manslaughter by an unlawful and dangerous act, the test of recognition of danger was objective. In dealing with that aspect Smith J said (at 482):

> The better view, however, is I think that the circumstances must be such that a reasonable man in the accused's position, performing the very act which the accused performed, would have realised that he was exposing another or others to an appreciable risk of really serious injury … [I]t is not sufficient, as it was held

> to be in *R v Church* ... to show there was a risk of some harm resulting, albeit not serious harm.

As can be seen from this passage, Smith J imposed a stricter test than had been applied in *Church* and in some other decisions, by requiring that the Crown establish an appreciable risk of 'really serious injury'. There is a respectable body of later authority which tends to support the approach taken by Smith J in *Holzer*. That approach was expressly approved by the Court of Criminal Appeal of Victoria in *R v Wills* [1983] 2 VR 201 at 211–13, though the court was concerned primarily with the objective nature of the test to be applied. In *Crusius v R* (1982) 5 A Crim R 427 at 428 the Court of Criminal Appeal of Victoria referred to *Holzer* with apparent approval though the court was concerned only with 'one limb' of that case, namely, 'specific intent to commit a battery'. It may be that *Holzer* was tacitly approved by the Court of Criminal Appeal of New South Wales in *Coomer*,[25] by the Court of Criminal Appeal of Western Australia in *Ward v R* [1972] WAR 36 at 40 and by judges at first instance in *R v McCallum* [1969] Tas SR 73 at 87–8, *R v Brown* (1984) 58 ACTR 33 at 35 and *R v Jones* (1988) 144 LSJS 58 at 61–2.

Finally, there is the decision of this court in *Pemble* but, as King CJ pointed out in the present case:

> In that case ... the unlawful act, namely the brandishing or pointing of a rifle was so obviously capable of causing grievous bodily harm that the question of the degree of potential harm required to render an act dangerous, did not arise for consideration.[26]

Faced with this conflict of authority, King CJ concluded (at 286) that the Court of Criminal Appeal of South Australia 'should adopt the *Holzer* test'. In the event, King CJ, while holding that there had been a defect in the trial judge's summing up, concluded that there had been no miscarriage of justice (at 288). Cox J considered that the English authorities, in particular *Larkin* and *Church*, should be followed in preference to *Holzer* (at 304–5). Matheson J also favoured the English approach. His Honour was influenced by the fact that *Newbury* was decided at a time when appeals lay from Australia to the Privy Council and that therefore a decision of the House of Lords was 'very persuasive' (at 307). This, with respect, is a tenuous basis on which to resolve the conflict of authority.

Unlawful and dangerous act

The jury must be taken to have convicted the appellant of manslaughter by reason of an unlawful and dangerous act causing death. This was not a case of death resulting from criminal negligence and, for reasons already given, provocation afforded no basis for a verdict of manslaughter. The question is whether the trial judge's direction relevantly erred and, if it did, whether the proviso may properly operate so as to sustain the conviction.[27]

Whether the 'act' in question was the punch by the appellant to the deceased's face or the hitting of the deceased's head on the concrete by Cumming, it was an unlawful act. In view of Cumming's acquittal, only the punch arises for consideration. In view of what has been said about self-defence, the punch must be treated as an unlawful act. Before the Court of Criminal Appeal the appeal was conducted as if only the punch was in issue so far as the appellant was concerned. And that is how the appeal was conducted before this court. Whatever may be said of the consequences of that act, there was no suggestion that it was accidental.[28]

Thus the area of inquiry narrows further and, in the end, focuses on the question: was the act of the appellant in punching the deceased dangerous? That question in turn gives rise to another: was it enough that the appellant (that is, a reasonable person in his position) appreciated the risk of some injury to the deceased from the act or did the jury have to be satisfied that he appreciated the risk of really serious injury?

Resolving the authorities

There are good reasons why the test in *Holzer* should be preferred to that in *Newbury*; the reasons are those advanced by King CJ in the present case. One is the development of the law 'towards a closer correlation between moral culpability and legal responsibility': (1991) 53 A Crim R 281 at 286. Another is that the scope of constructive crime 'should be confined to what is truly unavoidable' (at 286). A further reason advanced by King CJ is that the persuasive authority of a decision of the Full Supreme Court of an Australian state in this area of the law is greater than decisions of courts of other countries 'which may reflect different community attitudes and standards' (at 287). The decision to which his Honour referred was, no doubt, a reference to *Wills*.

It is not possible to resolve this conflict of authority and assert a proposition in general terms without first considering another category of manslaughter envisaged by Smith J in his direction to the jury in *Holzer*. He said ([1968] VR 481 at 483):

> [T]he blow, the assault and battery, was given or committed by the accused with the intention of doing Harvey some physical injury, not merely of a trivial or negligible character. The intended injury need not be a serious injury. Indeed, if it were a serious injury that was intended we would be in the field of murder, not manslaughter. The injury intended may be of a minor character but it must not be merely trivial or negligible.

Battery manslaughter

Although Smith J did not use the term, effectively he was speaking of battery manslaughter. This additional category of manslaughter (if it exists) involves a subjective test of intention and a low degree of harm. Because of the low degree of requisite harm, it has been suggested that there is significant congruity between the English test for unlawful and dangerous act manslaughter and Smith J's identification of a third category of manslaughter, although the latter imports a subjective intention.[29]

The idea of such a category as battery manslaughter does nothing to advance the law in what is, in any event, a somewhat clouded area. In particular, it tends to confuse intent with a willed act. The *actus reus* here is the unlawful and dangerous act which causes the death. Questions of causation will of course arise but they do not arise here. The *mens rea* required relates to the unlawful and dangerous act; that act must be willed and not accidental. At common law (and, indeed, under the Criminal Codes) manslaughter is not generally an offence requiring a particular intention; in that respect it is sharply distinguishable from the offence of murder.

In two decisions of this court Windeyer J lent some support to the idea of manslaughter resulting from a blow intended to hurt. He did so in *Mamote-Kulang* (1964) 111 CLR 62 at 79 when he said, in the passage quoted earlier:

> There is, however, no doubt that at common law a man is guilty of manslaughter if he kills another by an unlawful blow, intended to hurt, although not intended to be fatal or to cause grievous bodily harm.

This statement has been criticised[30] because the only authority offered by Windeyer J for the proposition was Hale's *History of the Pleas of the Crown*. Again, the criticism continues, it is not clear if Windeyer J was in truth referring to manslaughter by an unlawful and dangerous act, whether he had in mind reckless negligence, or whether the assertion 'was a vestige of the old common law principle that all killings caused by any unlawful act were at the least manslaughter'. Later, in *Timbu Kolian v R* (1968) 119 CLR 47 at 59–60, 67–8, Windeyer J spoke somewhat obliquely in terms which might be thought to affirm what he had said in *Mamote-Kulang*.

There is nothing in the earlier cases, and only Stephen among the text-writers, to provide explicit support for the intentional harm category. In *Mamote-Kulang* (at 79) Windeyer J relied on Hale's *History of the Pleas of the Crown*[31] which reads:

> Regularly he that voluntarily and knowingly intends hurt to the person of a man, tho he intend not death, yet if death ensues, it excuseth not from the guilt of murder, or manslaughter at least; as if A intends to beat B but not to kill him, yet if death ensues, this is not per infortunium, but murder or manslaughter, as the circumstances of the case happen.

The passage is equivocal because it does not seek to distinguish between an intent to cause grievous bodily harm and an intent to inflict a lesser degree of harm. Section 10 of the passage quoted from Hawkins earlier in this judgment is inconsistent with the concept of battery manslaughter. According to Hawkins, the intention to cause some hurt would result in murder. It may be thought that s 9 of the passage provides justification for what was said in *Mamote-Kulang* but only on the footing that the doctrine of transferred malice does not apply. That doctrine achieved recognition subsequently in consequence of Foster's work.

However, Stephen provides support for Windeyer J's view. He gives the following illustrations.

(1) A, knowing that B is suffering from disease of the heart, and intending to kill B, gives B a slight push, and thereby kills B. A commits murder.

(2) A in the last illustration pushes B unlawfully, but without knowledge of his state of health or intention to kill him, or do him grievous bodily harm. A commits manslaughter. If A laid his hand gently on B to attract his attention, and by doing so startled and killed him, A's act would be no offence at all.[32]

These illustrations obviously cover the factual situation faced by Windeyer J in *Mamote-Kulang*. It should, however, be noted that Stephen footnotes each illustration with the comment: 'I know of no direct authority for these illustrations, but they follow directly from the principles stated in the note.'

…

Two further illustrations by Stephen are apposite:

(4) A waylays B, intending to beat, but not intending to kill him or do him grievous bodily harm. A beats B and does kill him. This is manslaughter at least, and may be murder if the beating were so violent as to be likely, according to common knowledge, to cause death.

(5) A strikes at B with a small stick, not intending either to kill or to do him grievous bodily harm. The blow kills B. A commits manslaughter.

This time Stephen cites authority.[33]

An examination of Foster does not bear out Stephen's examples. Foster first distinguishes different types of unlawful acts.[34] If death results from an act which is *malum in se* (inherently wrong, or wrong in itself), it may be murder or manslaughter, 'as circumstances may vary the nature of it'.[35] If death results from an act which is merely *malum prohibitum* (wrong under the law), it will be manslaughter. Foster then sets out Hale's statement that if A intends to beat B, but not to kill him, and death ensues, it is murder or manslaughter depending on the circumstances. Foster interprets this to mean that if A intends to beat B '*in anger or from preconceived malice*' and death ensues, it will be murder, because his act was *malum in se*.[36] Foster, therefore, provides no reason for drawing a distinction between intent to do grievous bodily harm and intent to do some lesser harm.

Likewise, *Rowley's* case, relied upon by Stephen for his illustration (5), fails to make the distinction clear.[37] Two boys were fighting and one, bloodied, ran home to his father. The father, on seeing his son, ran three-quarters of a mile and struck the other boy on the head with a small cudgel, of which blow the boy died. The father was convicted of manslaughter. Foster interprets the verdict as arising from the fact that a stroke with 'a cudgel' was 'not likely to kill'.[38]

Rowley's case does not state that the nature of the father's intention was to hurt the boy to an extent less than grievous bodily harm. It may have been to do grievous bodily harm or a lesser hurt. The decisive factor leading to a manslaughter verdict was that the blow was 'not likely to kill', that is, an objective test rather than an inquiry into subjective intent.

Another early case, similar to *Rowley's* case, is *Turner's* case.[39] There, a master struck a servant with a clog and the boy died. The master was convicted of manslaughter on the basis that:

> … because the clog was so small, there could be no design to do any great harm to the boy, much less to kill him; and a master may correct a servant in a reasonable manner for a fault.[40]

In the same category is *R v Wiggs* (1784) 1 Leach 378; 168 ER 291. The victim was a shepherd boy who negligently allowed some sheep to escape. His employer, seeing this, picked up a stake that was lying on the ground and threw it at the boy. The stake, which hit the boy on the head, fractured his skull, causing his death soon after. The report is short, and is a mixture of references to provocation, the right of a master to correct his servant and the degree of dangerousness of the act. As to the latter factor, the judge's direction to the jury is reported (at Leach 378; ER 292) as:

> For the using a weapon from which death is likely to ensue, imports a mischievous disposition, and the law implies that a degree of malice attended the act, which, if death actually happen, will be murder. Therefore if you should think the stake was an improper instrument, you will further consider whether it is probable that it was used with an intent to kill. If you think it was, you must find the prisoner guilty of murder. But on the contrary, if you are persuaded that it was not done with an intent to kill, the crime will then amount at most to manslaughter.

The verdict was manslaughter.

Lastly, in this regard, there is *R v Oneby* (1727) 2 Ld Raym 1485; 92 ER 465. The accused was convicted of murder when he killed the deceased in a fight. The court found that the accused had malice towards the deceased for some time before the fight, thus negating the defence of provocation. In its deliberations, the court discussed murder and manslaughter, saying (at Ld Raym 1488–9; ER 467–8) murder is the proper verdict where the accused:

> ... strikes at him [B, the deceased] with any dangerous weapon, as a pistol, hammer, large stone, &c which in probability might kill B or do him some great bodily hurt ... this will be murder ... since in all probability it might have occasioned B's death, or done him some great bodily harm, the law implies malice prepense.

And, further (at Ld Raym 1489; ER 468):

> Malice express, is a design formed of taking away another man's life, or of doing some mischief to another, in the execution of which design death ensues.

Rowley's case, *Turner's* case and *Wiggs* are all consistent with the Stephen/Windeyer J battery manslaughter doctrine. But the three cases are also consistent with reasoning directed to the doing of an unlawful and dangerous act resulting in death. If anything, that seems to be the more likely explanation since the distinction between the degrees of intent to cause harm was not mentioned in the judgments. In these circumstances, there is no authority which should constrain this court to accept the correctness of the battery manslaughter doctrine.

Conclusion

The notion of manslaughter by the intentional infliction of some harm carries with it the consequence that a person may be convicted of manslaughter for an act which was neither intended nor likely to cause death. In this context we do not think it is helpful to speak in terms of reasonable foreseeability; the concept is one likely to cause confusion.[41] But it is appropriate to observe that in such a case a person may be held guilty of manslaughter for a death that was quite unexpected, whether the test applied in that respect is subjective or objective. It may be said that the same is true of unlawful and dangerous act manslaughter. But the criticism loses its force if the test in *Holzer* is applied so that, before a conviction may ensue, a reasonable person would have realised that he or she was exposing another to an appreciable risk of really serious injury.

However, the utility of a qualifier such as 'really' is very questionable. 'Serious' and 'really serious' may have quite different connotations in some situations.[42] While the *Holzer* direction does not seem to have given rise to difficulties in this regard, the emphasis on really serious injury brings manslaughter perilously close to murder in this respect. The distinction between the two may easily be blurred in the minds of the jury. It is better to speak of an unlawful and dangerous act carrying with it an appreciable risk of serious injury. A direction in those terms gives adequate recognition to the seriousness of manslaughter and to respect for human life, while preserving a clear distinction from murder. The approach in *Holzer* takes away the idea of unexpectedness to a large extent. It does not remove it entirely but then we are not in the area of murder (and its relevant intent) but in the area of manslaughter.

Manslaughter by an unlawful and dangerous act (in the *Holzer* sense) is a relevant and appropriate category of manslaughter. Manslaughter by the intentional infliction of some harm answers neither description. It continues the rigour of the early common law and ought to play no part in contemporary law. This approach leaves two categories of involuntary manslaughter at common law: manslaughter by an unlawful and dangerous act carrying with it an appreciable risk of serious injury and manslaughter by criminal negligence. There have been suggestion[s] that these two categories should be replaced by one.[43] But, as the law stands, there are differences between them. In the case of manslaughter by criminal negligence, it is unnecessary to prove that the accused's act was unlawful: *Andrews v DPP* [1937] AC 576. And the tests of dangerousness are different. An appreciable risk of serious injury is required in the case of manslaughter by an unlawful and dangerous act. For manslaughter by criminal negligence, the test is 'a high risk that death or grievous bodily harm would follow': *Nydam v R* [1977] VR 430 at 445. As the question of criminal negligence was not relied on in the present appeal, we need say no more as to the appropriateness of the distinctions that presently exist between this category of manslaughter and manslaughter by an unlawful and dangerous act.[44]

Adoption of the test in *Holzer* as to the level of danger applying to manslaughter by an unlawful and dangerous act and abolition of battery manslaughter do not create a gap in the law. Cases of death resulting from a serious assault, which would have fallen within battery manslaughter, will be covered by manslaughter by an unlawful and dangerous act. Cases of death resulting unexpectedly from a comparatively minor assault, which also would have fallen within battery manslaughter, will be covered by the law as to assault.[45] A conviction or manslaughter in such a situation does not reflect the principle that there should be a close correlation between moral culpability and legal responsibility, and is therefore inappropriate.

The direction and the proviso

In the present case the trial judge's direction to the jury fell short of what is required by *Holzer* in two respects.

First, the jury were not invited directly to resolve for themselves whether the punch administered by the appellant constituted an assault and therefore an unlawful act. But, as suggested earlier in this judgment, it is hard to conceive of the punch as being other than an assault in the circumstances. As King CJ pointed out in *Wilson v R* (1991) 53 A Crim R 281 at 287:

> The only suggested justification, however, was self-defence and that was negatived by the verdict of the jury.

There remains the further question: were the jury sufficiently directed to assess whether a reasonable person, in the appellant's position, would have realised that, in punching the deceased, he was exposing him to an appreciable risk of serious injury? The trial judge spoke of a 'dangerous act' without identifying what that meant. The jury might well have thought that if the punch carried a risk of injury to the deceased, not necessarily an appreciable risk of serious injury, that was enough to constitute manslaughter. In applying the proviso, King CJ said (at 288):

> A deliberate blow to the face of the kind described by the appellant gives rise to an inescapable inference that he intended to cause some harm. If that issue had been left to the jury the answer would have been inevitable.

The first sentence in the passage is logically supportable, though it has overtones of battery manslaughter. It is the second sentence that causes problems. In the end the jury had to determine whether the appellant's act in punching the deceased was, from the standpoint of a reasonable person, an act carrying with it an appreciable risk of serious injury to the deceased. They were not so directed; they were told to consider whether it was a dangerous act. The distinction is not merely semantic. An act may be dangerous without carrying with it an appreciable risk of serious injury and, unless the two elements are brought to the minds of the jury, there is a real danger that they may wrongly convict of manslaughter. The answer the jury may have reached in the present case, had they been adequately directed, cannot be assumed.

It is not possible to conclude that no substantial miscarriage of justice occurred and it is therefore not appropriate to apply the proviso in s 353(1) of the Act. The appeal should be allowed, the conviction for manslaughter quashed and a new trial on that charge ordered.

Brennan, **Deane** and **Dawson JJ**: Once it is accepted that the test in a case of manslaughter by an unlawful and dangerous act is that of the existence, objectively determined, of a likelihood or risk of injury such that it can be said that the act in question was dangerous, there is no function for the so-called battery manslaughter doctrine. If the test were to be set at the higher level suggested by Smith J in *Holzer*, then there would be a gap in the law which could be filled only by some such doctrine. One principle which stands higher than all others in the criminal law is the sanctity of human life. If manslaughter by an unlawful and dangerous act were limited to cases where the act in question exposed another or others to grievous bodily harm, there would be a need for the law to hold at the same time that, where a person deliberately and without lawful justification or excuse causes injury to another which is not trivial or negligible and that other dies as a result, the crime of manslaughter is committed. There would be a need because the law does and should regard death in those circumstances with gravity. In *Giorgianni v R* (1985) 156 CLR 473 at 503; 58 ALR 641, Wilson, Deane and Dawson JJ cited as an accurate statement of the law a passage from the judgment of the Court of Criminal Appeal in *R v Creamer* [1966] 1 QB 72 at 82 that included the following:

> A man is guilty of involuntary manslaughter when he intends an unlawful act and one likely to do harm to the person and death results which was neither foreseen nor intended. It is the accident of death resulting which makes him guilty of manslaughter as opposed to some lesser offence such as assault, or, in the present case, abortion. This can no doubt be said to be illogical, since the culpability is the same, but nevertheless, it is an illogicality which runs throughout the whole of our law, both the common law and the statute law.

Of course, not every case of manslaughter is of the same gravity. As Lord Salmon pointed out in *Newbury* [1977] AC 500 at 507 cases of manslaughter vary infinitely in this respect. That is the utility of the offence. It enables the law to express forcefully its regard for human life, at the same time allowing the particular circumstances to be reflected in the penalty imposed.

And if, as we think is the law, the test for a dangerous act is no more than whether there is a sufficient likelihood of risk of sufficient injury to enable the act to be characterised as dangerous, then any offence of battery manslaughter, if it emerged at some time in the diverse history of the crime of manslaughter, has been subsumed in the crime of manslaughter by an unlawful and dangerous act. A battery is always unlawful and the only question now is whether the act involved is at the same time dangerous.

In this case the appellant, on his own evidence, struck the deceased in the face with sufficient force to cause him to fall to the ground. He described the blow as not 'really that very hard' but not soft. The trial judge directed the jury:

> A serious assault — you may think the punch by Wilson or the hitting of the head on the concrete by Cumming to be serious assaults — would be an unlawful act for this purpose. Whether the particular act you are considering is a dangerous act is a matter for your judgment.

While that direction was less helpful than it might have been, it was not, in the circumstances, inadequate. Clearly the act in question exposed the deceased to injury and it was open to the jury to find that it was dangerous.

The appellant relied on two further grounds of appeal with which it is necessary to deal briefly. In his summing up the trial judge told the jury that the verdicts which were open to them in relation to both the appellant and his co-accused (Cumming) were murder, manslaughter or acquittal. He continued: '[t]here are now two matters of law relevant only to Wilson arising out of those possible verdicts.' The first of these matters was provocation about which the trial judge gave a lengthy direction and as to which no question arises on this appeal. The second of these matters was self-defence, as to which his Honour gave a somewhat briefer direction, saying:

> If you think there is a reasonable possibility that the accused, Wilson, believed on reasonable grounds that it was necessary in his own defence to hit Ormsby [the deceased] as he did, in other words, that he acted in self-defence and in so doing did not use more force to defend himself than was necessary, even though you think the blow caused Ormsby's death, then your verdict will be that Wilson was not guilty of murder, for self-defence is a complete answer to a charge of murder. In that case too Cumming would not be guilty of anything.

At the request of the jury, his Honour later repeated his direction to the jury on self-defence and repeated the passage we have set out above, although on this occasion his Honour omitted the words: 'for self defence is a complete answer to a charge of murder. In that case too Cumming would not be guilty of anything.'

In a memorandum of possible verdicts which was given to the jury by his Honour, he stated that they could:

> 7. … find Wilson guilty of murder because he killed Ormsby with the intention of inflicting grievous bodily harm on him, and that he [Wilson] was not acting … in self-defence …
>
> 9. … find Wilson guilty of manslaughter because he was engaged in an unlawful and dangerous act — the punch — but without the intention to cause grievous bodily harm, and not acting in self defence, and as a result of which Ormsby was killed …
>
> 10. … find Wilson not guilty of either murder or manslaughter because although he caused the death of Ormsby by his punch, and did so with either intention to inflict grievous bodily harm or by an otherwise unlawful and dangerous act, he was acting in self defence …

The appellant submitted that in his summing up the trial judge did not put self-defence to the jury as a defence to manslaughter. He also contended that the trial judge failed to relate the plea of self-defence to the evidence.

Although the trial judge's first direction to the jury on the question of self-defence as a defence to manslaughter might have been more clearly put, it was in our view adequate to convey to the jury that both the appellant and his co-accused were to be acquitted on all counts if they found that the appellant acted in self-defence. Any ambiguity in the further direction would, we think, have been removed by the memorandum with which the trial judge provided the jury. We would observe that no objection was taken at the trial to this aspect of the trial judge's directions.

Nor do we think that there was any failure on the part of the trial judge to relate the plea of self-defence to the evidence. The relevant facts were, as we have indicated, few and not complex. In the circumstances of this case it was, in our view, sufficient for the trial judge to deal with them as he did.

For these reasons, we would dismiss the appeal.

[Appeal allowed.]

[See also *R v Bednikov* (1997) 95 A Crim R 200; and *R v Chai* (2002) 187 ALR 436.]

Notes:

1. See, generally, Green, 'The Jury and the English Law of Homicide, 1200–1600' (1976) 74 *Michigan Law Review* 413; Kaye, 'The Early History of Murder and Manslaughter: Part II', (1967) 83 *Law Quarterly Review* 569.
2. Speaking of the growth of the English law of homicide, Sir Owen Dixon said: 'For eight centuries the course of its very gradual evolution has been from an almost exclusive concern with the external act which occasioned death to a primary concern with the mind of the man who did the act.' 'The Development of the Law of Homicide', (1935) 9 *ALJ* Supp 64, at 64.
3. *Rethinking* Criminal *Law*, 1978, p 237.
4. *De Legibus et Consuetudinibus Angliae*, (c1256).
5. Together *with* homicide committed in self-defence, this formed the category of excusable homicide. A finding of excusable homicide did not result in acquittal. Rather, the defendant could seek a royal pardon (subject to the possibility of the victim's relatives bringing a private prosecution), which issued as a matter of course in cases of misadventure. By the late fourteenth century, the judges frequently entered an acquittal without requiring that a royal pardon be secured, a trend reversed in the sixteenth and seventeenth centuries. See Green, op cit, at 444 et seq.
6. *A Treatise of the Pleas of the Crown*, 6th ed, vol 1, 1777, ch 29, pp 111–13 (first published in 1716).
7. *History of the Pleas of the Crown*, vol 1, 1800, p 475 (first published in 1736).
8. *The Third Part of the Institutes of the Laws of England*, 1797, p 56 (first published in 1644).
9. Fletcher, op cit, p 237.
10. *Kaye*, op cit, pp 571–2.
11. Ibid, pp 574–5.
12. op cit, p 56.
13. op cit, p 474.
14. op cit, pp 112–13.
15. See Fletcher, op cit, p 240.
16. *Report and Discourses*, 1st ed, 1762, p 258.
17. *A History of the Criminal Law of England*, vol III, 1883, pp 74–6.
18. Ibid, p 283.
19. *Commentaries on the Laws of England*, 17th ed, vol IV, 1830, pp 200–1 (first published in 1765).
20. See also *R v Lamb* [1967] 2 QB 981 at 988; *R v Bush* [1970] 3 NSWR 500 at 503; *Boughey v R* (1986) 161 CLR 10 at 35; 65 ALR 609.
21. [1943] 1 All ER 217 at 219; (1943) 29 Cr App R 18 at 23. This aspect of the judgment does not appear in [1943] KB 174, or in [1943] WN 13.
22. See also *Hall* (1961) 45 Cr App R 366 at 372; *Pemble v R* (1971) 124 CLR 107 at 122.
23. *R v Garforth* [1954] Crim LR 936; *R v Sharmpal Singh* [1962] AC 188; see also *Smith and Hogan*, Criminal Law, 6th ed, 1988, p 350.
24. See ibid, per Taylor and Owen JJ at 64 and in particular per Windeyer J at 79: 'There is, however, no doubt that at common law a man is guilty of manslaughter if he kills another by an unlawful blow, intended to hurt, although not intended to be fatal or to cause grievous bodily harm.'

25. (1989) 40 A Crim R 417 at 423. This was not the view taken by Cox J in the instant case, his Honour being of the opinion that a 'passing reference' to Holzer in Coomer did not signify approval of that decision: *R v Wilson* (1991) 53 A Crim R 281 at 297.
26. (1991) 53 A Crim R 281 at 286. Again, Cox J declined to regard a 'passing reference' to *Holzer* as significant: *R v Wilson* (1991) 53 A Crim R 281 at 298.
27. Section 353(1) of the Criminal Law Consolidation Act 1935 empowers the Full Court, notwithstanding that it is of the opinion that the point raised in the appeal might be decided in favour of the appellant, to dismiss the appeal 'if it considers that no substantial miscarriage of justice has actually occurred'.
28. cf *Mamote-Kulang*. The references by Lord Salmon in *Newbury* to intention as an element of manslaughter were severely criticised by Glanville Williams in *Textbook of Criminal Law*, 2nd ed, 1983, pp 272–4. This aspect is discussed later in this judgment.
29. See Willis, 'Manslaughter by the Intentional Infliction of Some Harm: A Category that Should be Closed' (1985) 9 *CLJ* 109.
30. Willis, op cit, p 117.
31. op cit, p 472.
32. *A Digest of the Criminal Law*, op cit, p 145.
33. Foster, *Report and Discourses*, 2nd ed, 1776, p 259 for illustration (4); *Rowley's Case*, discussed in (1611) 12 Co Rep 87; 77 ER 1364 and in (1727) 2 Ld Raym 1485 at 1498; 92 ER 465 at 473 and in Foster, ibid, pp 294–5, for illustration (5).
34. Foster, ibid, pp 258–9.
35. Ibid, p 258.
36. Ibid, p 259.
37. *A Digest of the Criminal Law*, op cit, p 145.
38. Ibid, p 295. Other reports of the case cite provocation as the reason for the manslaughter verdict, which Foster doubts: p 294. The report in (1727) 2 Ld Raym 1485 at 1498; 92 ER465 at 473 gives both reasons.
39. (1727) 2 Ld Raym 1485 at 1498; 92 ER 465 at 473. The case also appears at (1697) *Comberbach* 406 at 407; 90 ER 557 at 558.
40. Ibid, at 1499; 473 of ER.
41. See, in a different context, *Royall v R* (1991) 172 CLR 378 at 390, 412–13, 424–5; 100 ALR 669.
42. See *R v Perks* (1986) 41 SASR 335 at 337, as to the use of 'serious bodily harm' instead of' grievous bodily harm' in directions as to murder.
43. See, for example, Law Reform Commission, Victoria, Discussion Paper No 13, *Homicide* (1988), p 68.
44. The approach taken in this judgment does not necessarily conflict with the concept of manslaughter under the Criminal Codes. Notwithstanding the existence of an unlawful and dangerous act, the 'accident' provision of the Codes may operate to relieve an accused of responsibility for a consequential death: *R v Martyr* [1962] Qd R 398. But, it would still be open to an accused, charged with manslaughter at common law, to argue that his or her unlawful and dangerous act did not cause the death.
45. See Willis, op cit, at pp 120, 124.

6.5 Notes and questions

Based on *Wilson v R* (1992) 174 CLR 313, the prosecution must prove:

1. an unlawful act;
2. caused the death of the victim; and
3. a reasonable person would realise that the unlawful act was exposing others to an appreciable risk of serious injury.

1. *Unlawful act: Wilson* requires that the act breach criminal law. Even a minor breach of the criminal law can satisfy this requirement. The objective element of unlawful and dangerous act manslaughter arises in the requirement of considering whether or not the accused's act was dangerous. The most common breach of criminal law for the purposes of manslaughter by unlawful and dangerous act is assault. The prosecution must prove all elements of the foundational offence. An act performed in self-defence is not an unlawful act: *R v Cornelissen* [2004] NSWCCA 449. An unlawful omission is not an unlawful act and thus will not provide the foundation for this head of manslaughter. As demonstrated below, at times, it can be difficult for the prosecution to establish a foundational unlawful act:

(a) D pointed a partly-loaded revolver at his friend, V. Two chambers of the revolver's cylinder contained bullets, but neither bullet was in the chamber opposite the barrel. Because D and V did not understand the way in which a revolver works, both thought there was no danger and treated the matter as a joke. D pulled the trigger, the revolver's cylinder rotated, placing a bullet opposite the barrel, and the gun discharged, killing V. Three expert witnesses gave evidence that many people would suppose, as D did, that the revolver could not discharge because there was no bullet in the chamber opposite the barrel. D was convicted and appealed to the Court of Appeal. Held, conviction quashed. D believed that a bullet would not be discharged, and thus lacked the mens rea for battery assault. In addition, as V was treating the matter as a joke, there was no assault by causing apprehension, as V did not apprehend imminent unlawful contact. Therefore, there was no foundational unlawful act, thus unlawful and dangerous act manslaughter doctrine did not apply: *R v Lamb* [1967] 2 QB 981.

(b) D had been jilted by his girlfriend, V. V was sitting on the bonnet of a car outside a hotel when D approached her from behind carrying a sawn-off rifle. The rifle discharged, and the bullet entered the back of V's head, killing her. D's story was that he only intended to frighten V, and that the rifle had discharged accidentally when he stumbled. D was convicted of murder in the Supreme Court of the Northern Territory and appealed to the High Court. Held, the trial judge's summing-up had been defective and the conviction must be quashed;

by a majority of 3:2, a verdict of manslaughter substituted. It is to be noted that V had been facing the other way when D approached her, so there had not been the putting in fear necessary to constitute a technical assault. The judges offered different arguments as to how to justify D's culpability. Per Barwick CJ, D was guilty of manslaughter, his actions being dangerous and amounting to an attempted assault. Per McTiernan J, D had committed the unlawful act of discharging a firearm in a public place, and it was 'obvious' that such an act was dangerous. Per Windeyer J, a jury obedient to their oaths would have had to have found D guilty of manslaughter by gross negligence. Menzies and Owen JJ dissented, holding that a new trial should be ordered: *Pemble v R* (1971) 124 CLR 107.

2. *Causation:* The unlawful act must cause the death of the victim:

   (a) After drinking at a public house, D returned with a friend, V, to the house that they shared. V produced a bag of white powder, which he said was heroin, and some syringes. He invited D to have a 'fix' with him. They injected each other a number of times, following a procedure whereby each prepared a mixture of heroin and water in the syringe to his own liking and for his own consumption, and then gave it to the other to administer by injection. They continued to give each other injections right through the night. By the following morning, they were both gravely ill. D's life was saved but V died. D was charged with the manslaughter of V and with unlawfully and maliciously administering a noxious thing to V. The trial judge directed the jury, inter alia, that they could convict D of manslaughter on the basis of the unlawful and dangerous act doctrine. D was convicted and appealed to the Court of Appeal. It is to be noted that in England, and in most of the Australian jurisdictions, while the possession of heroin and the supply of heroin are criminal offences, the actual use of heroin is not itself a crime. (For Australia, see generally Customs Act 1901 (Cth); Narcotic Drugs Act 1967 (Cth); Drug Misuse and Trafficking Act 1985 (NSW). Note, however, that self-administration of a drug of addiction is a separate offence in Victoria (Drugs, Poisons and Controlled Substances Act 1981 s 75) (previously dealt with under the terms of s 23 of Poisons Act 1962). These matters are considered more extensively in **Chapter 9**.)

   Held, heroin is a noxious substance and the direct and deliberate insertion of the syringe into V's body, knowing that it contained a noxious substance, was unlawful and malicious. D had therefore committed an unlawful act, and was thus properly convicted of unlawful act manslaughter. Held further, even if the administration of heroin did not constitute the crime of unlawfully and maliciously administering a noxious substance, there was nevertheless an unlawful act on the part of D which could found a conviction of manslaughter. The unlawful act could be described by injecting V with a mixture of heroin and water which at the time of the injection and for the purposes of the injection D had unlawfully taken into his possession: *R v Cato* [1976] 1 All ER 260.

Do you think that the court was correct in holding that the offence of unlawfully and maliciously administering a noxious thing was committed, in spite of the fact that V consented to its being administered? Can it be said that the use of heroin on a single occasion involves such risk of serious bodily injury as to preclude consent to its being administered operating as a defence to a charge of aggravated assault? If the answer to this question is no, can the court's decision be justified on the further ground that the use of a substance unlawfully in one's possession is itself an unlawful act? Was the court not here committing the fallacy of inferring an unlawful act from the general social undesirability of D's conduct?

Note that if V had injected himself with drugs supplied by D, then D would not be guilty of manslaughter by unlawful and dangerous act. This is because although D had unlawfully supplied a drug to V, V broke the chain of causation with a voluntary act: *R v Dalby* [1982] 1 All ER 916.

(b) D1 and D2 were convicted of the manslaughter of V, a woman who died as a result of an unlawful abortion performed on her by them. On appeal to the Court of Appeal, Edmund-Davies J stated: 'In my judgment, where death flows directly from a felony of the kind here charged the offence must, at the very least, be manslaughter … It is an offence which involves a considerable risk to the person, no matter with what care it may be committed': *R v Buck and Buck* (1960) 44 Cr App R 213. Accord *R v Creamer* [1966] 1 QB 72.

Note that the justification for the decision in *R v Buck and Buck* is factually incorrect. Abortion is very dangerous in unskilled hands, but as safe as many other operations in skilled hands. In *R v Salika* [1973] VR 272, the Full Court of the Supreme Court of Victoria referred to and left open the question of whether *R v Buck and Buck* and *R v Creamer* represent good law in Victoria.

Since the abolition of abortion as a criminal offence in Victoria in 2008, the question of whether abortion causing death can give rise to a conviction for unlawful and dangerous act manslaughter will only arise in the case of an 'unauthorised' abortion, or an abortion performed by an unqualified person: see s 65 of the Crimes Act 1958 (Vic).

3. *Appreciable risk of serious injury:* In *Wilson v R* (at **6.4C**), the High Court approved the formulation that a jury must assess whether the act was such that a 'reasonable person would realize that it was exposing others to an appreciable risk of serious injury'.

Under this formulation, the hypothetical reasonable person is not attributed 'anything personal to [D] which … may affect his reasoning and his judgment on the question of whether the act is dangerous or not': *R v Wills* [1983] 2 VR 201 at 214 per Fullagar J. This would preclude consideration of D's intoxication. Lush J stated (at 212):

> … It is sufficient for the present case to say that the circumstances relevant to the question whether a reasonable man would appreciate the danger include the physical features of the situation and the action of the accused man involved. I would not, for my part, include the idiosyncrasies of the accused man or his ephemeral emotional or mental state. They are matters peculiar to him which would affect his judgment of danger but the relevant judgment must be, by definition, the judgment of a reasonable man.

Fullagar J said (at 214):

> … the reasonable man for the purposes of this particular rule of law is a man who judges with unclouded reasoning power of a healthy and reasonable mind.

6.6 Further reading

Law Reform Commission of Victoria, Report No 40, *Homicide* (1991), pp 106–17

J Willis, 'Manslaughter by the Intentional Infliction of Some Harm: A Category that Should be Closed' (1985) 9 *Crim LJ* 109

NEGLIGENT MANSLAUGHTER

6.7 In all jurisdictions, it is manslaughter for D to kill V by an act or omission done with a very high degree of negligence. Liability for negligent manslaughter is based on causing death by an act or omission that falls so far short of the standard of care required of a reasonable person that it is worthy of criminal punishment: *Nydam v R* [1977] VR 430; *R v Lavender* (2005) 222 CLR 67.

6.8 The law differs slightly, depending on whether death has been caused by an act or omission. Where negligent manslaughter is due to an act, the elements of the offence are specified in *Nydam v R* [1977] VR 430. The prosecution must establish that:

- D's acts were voluntary;
- D's acts caused V's death;
- the standard of care required of a reasonable person; and
- there has been a gross departure from the standard of care amounting to criminal negligence.

The test of negligent manslaughter by omission, articulated by the High Court in *R v Lavender* (2005) 222 CLR 67, is that:

- D must be under a legally recognised duty to act;
- D must have omitted to fulfil this duty in a way which exhibited a great degree of negligence, as required by the doctrine of negligent manslaughter; and
- as a result of this omission, V died.

Defining negligence

6.9C **Nydam v R**
[1977] VR 430
Full Court of the Supreme Court of Victoria

[N was tried for the murder of two women who died as a result of burns they suffered when a bottle of petrol, which N had ignited, was thrown into a hairdressing salon, where one of the women was a customer and the other an employee. N and the customer had been acquainted for some time, but the relationship had deteriorated. N bought a quantity of petrol from a service station, followed the customer to the salon and, shortly afterwards, threw the petrol towards her and then lit it. He later told police that '… my intention was to take my own life, no-one else's'.

The trial judge left the issue of 'murder by recklessness' and manslaughter by criminal negligence to the jury. The jury found N guilty of murder. The following extract from the judgment in N's appeal deals only with the issue of manslaughter.]

Young CJ, **McInerney** and **Crockett JJ**: What then is the appropriate test to be applied for manslaughter by criminal negligence? In Victoria a dictum of Smith J, in *R v Holzer*, supra, has been accepted as a correct statement of the law. In that case his Honour said, at 482: '… we are not here concerned with the doctrine of manslaughter by criminal negligence, under which, as I understand the law founded upon the House of Lords' decision in *Andrews v Director of Public Prosecutions* [1937] AC 576; [1937] 2 All ER 552, the accused must be shown to have acted not only in gross breach of a duty of care but recklessly, in the sense that he realised that he was creating an appreciable risk of really serious bodily injury to another or others and that nevertheless he chose to run the risk.'

Any dictum of Smith J, a very learned judge and a most distinguished lawyer, is entitled to the greatest respect. Yet we have come to the conclusion that it ought not to be accepted as correctly propounding the test to be applied in cases of manslaughter by criminal negligence. We have reached this conclusion for substantially three reasons, which may be summarised as follows:

1. Although the dictum of Smith J, in *Holzer's* case has not been expressly criticised in the High Court, it appears to be inconsistent with such guidance on the point as can be extracted from the judgments of that court in *Pemble's* case and *La Fontaine's* case;
2. The dictum may in any event represent a misreading of Lord Atkin's speech in *Andrews v Director of Public Prosecutions*, supra, which has been much criticised and which has been said to leave the position far from clear: cf Smith and Hogan, *Criminal Law* (2nd ed, 1969), p 225.
3. The weight of authority appears to favour an objective rather than a subjective test. We shall develop each of these reasons in turn.

In *Pemble v R* (1971) 124 CLR 107, counsel for the accused had invited the jury to convict the accused of manslaughter on the basis that the death had been caused by an unlawful and dangerous act which was done without any intention of killing or inflicting grievous bodily harm (see 111–12). In his charge to the jury the trial judge had, inter alia, left murder by recklessness as one of the ways open to the jury to convict the accused of murder: see 113. No question of manslaughter by criminal negligence was left to the jury, although as in many cases of manslaughter by an unlawful and dangerous act it is not clear that it would not have been open on the facts (see 110–11). Barwick CJ mentioned, at 122, the concept that 'culpable or criminal negligence resulting though by accident in a killing will make that killing manslaughter', but found no need to consider it. His Honour and McTiernan J, who did not mention criminal negligence, treated the case as one of manslaughter by an unlawful and dangerous act.

Menzies J, however, considered that specific direction was necessary as to manslaughter by an unlawful and dangerous act and as to manslaughter by criminal negligence: see 133. His Honour cited the observations of Smith J in *R v Longley* [1962] VR 137 at 148. He also quoted, at 134, the very dictum of Smith J, in *R v Holzer*, supra, which is here under discussion, and did so without any indication of disapproval. Indeed, his Honour preceded the reference by the observation: 'It is no longer sufficient to sustain a verdict of manslaughter to establish merely that the homicide occurred in the course of the commission of an unlawful act …'. In spite, however, of this apparent approval of Smith J's dictum in *Holzer's* case, Menzies J proceeded, at 135, to define the difference between murder and recklessness and manslaughter by criminal negligence in a way that may be said, with the greatest respect, to be inconsistent with an acceptance of Smith J's dictum. We shall quote the passage in full because in addition to containing his Honour's definition of the difference, it gives useful examples, as Crockett J pointed out in *Allwood's* case of the cases which the doctrine of murder by recklessness was developed to meet.

After saying that the trial judge in *Pemble's* case was in error because he directed the jury that the killing occurred in the course of doing an unlawful act likely to harm, rather than submitting that matter to the decision of the jury with a proper direction of law, his Honour said:

> The conclusion which I have just expressed is sufficient to determine this case, but I should add, that I do not think that his Honour succeeded in the very difficult task of distinguishing clearly between what may be described as a reckless killing constituting murder and a negligent killing constituting manslaughter. The difference, as I apprehend it, is that to do an unjustifiable act causing death, knowing that it is likely to cause death or grievous bodily harm is murder, whereas to do a careless act causing death, without any conscious acceptance of the risk which its doing involves is manslaughter, if the negligence is of so high a degree as to show a disregard for life deserving punishment. An instance of the former might be to kill a person in a street by intentionally dropping a large block of stone from a high building into the crowded street below; an instance of the latter might be to kill a person in a street by carelessly letting fall a large block of stone from a high building into a crowded street below. It would not be a misuse of language to use the word 'reckless' both in relation to dropping and to letting fall the stone, but that word without more in relation to the first would not, of itself, bring out the essential difference between the first and the second. The use of the words 'recklessness' or 'reckless indifference' of itself would not bring home to the jury that it is only a recklessness that involves actual foresight of the probability of causing death or grievous bodily harm and indifference to that risk which does constitute the mental element that must be found to support a conviction for murder. The difference between murder and manslaughter is not to be found in the degree of carelessness exhibited; the critical difference relates to the state of mind with which the fatal act is done.

That passage may, with great respect, be said to contain some suggestion that negligence is a state of mind rather than conduct, a view criticised by Smith and Hogan, supra, at 222, but the examples which his Honour gave seem clearly enough to involve the proposition that the test for manslaughter by criminal negligence is an objective and not a subjective test.

Windeyer J appears to have considered the case as one possibly involving manslaughter by criminal negligence, but his Honour did not in any way define the difference between that crime and murder by recklessness. Similarly, Owen J did not discuss the distinction.

In *La Fontaine's* case only Gibbs J adverted to the problem. After saying that 'recklessness' or 'reckless indifference' should not be used by a judge when summing up to a jury, because to do so is to invite confusion between murder and manslaughter resulting from criminal negligence, his Honour pointed out that in many, if not most, cases where the Crown alleges murder by recklessness, it will also allege in the alternative that the accused was guilty of manslaughter by criminal negligence. His Honour also said:

> It is enough to tell them that it is only if the accused actually knows that his act will probably cause death or grievous bodily harm that he can be convicted of murder. The extreme gravity of his offence lies in the fact that he fully realised the probable consequences of his act and was prepared to take the chance that they would ensue. If he did not in fact foresee that death or grievous bodily harm would probably be caused by his act, he would not be guilty of murder even though a

> reasonable man would have foreseen that such a result was probable; in those circumstances he might however be guilty of manslaughter.

This passage suggests that his Honour had an objective test in mind in the case of manslaughter by criminal negligence.

We turn next to *Andrews'* case itself. Lord Atkin's speech has been subjected to much comment and discussion, but with all respect to those who think otherwise (eg, Russell on Crime (12th ed, 1964), vol 1 by J W C Turner, p 591, and see Kenny's Outlines of Criminal Law (19th ed, 1966), by J W C Turner, p 189 where the learned editor says that Lord Atkin oscillated between the adoption of an objective and a subjective test), we do not think that his Lordship was intending to lay down a subjective test. We shall not quote extensively from the speech. It is sufficient to refer to the passage, at 583, where his Lordship said: 'Simple lack of care such as will constitute civil liability is not enough: for purposes of the criminal law there are degrees of negligence: and a very high degree of negligence is required to be proved before the felony is established.'

This formulation is entirely consistent with an objective standard and it is to be noted that a little earlier Lord Atkin said that he did not find the connotations of mens rea (a reference to what was said in *R v Bateman* (1925) 19 Cr App R 8 at 11 by Lord Hewart CJ) helpful in distinguishing degrees of negligence. Much of the difficulty in understanding the test being propounded has stemmed from Lord Atkin's use of the word 'reckless' as being the epithet that most nearly covers the case. That word might be said to connote a subjective element, but there is a later indication in the speech that Lord Atkin may not have intended it to do so. His Lordship said: '... but it is probably not all-embracing, for "reckless" suggests an indifference to risk whereas the accused may have appreciated the risk and intended to avoid it and yet shown such a high degree of negligence in the means adopted to avoid the risk as would justify a conviction.' This passage suggests that the negligence involved may be conduct only, the intention being to avoid the risk, and Starke J certainly seems to have regarded the case as establishing an objective test: see *R v Coventry* (1938) 59 CLR 633 at 639–40.

So far as other authorities are concerned, there are undoubtedly cases of manslaughter by negligence in which a subjective test has been applied by most eminent judges ... On the other hand, there are cases where the direction was given that where death followed from an intentional act done without lawful justification or excuse the killing was manslaughter if the death was fairly and reasonably to be considered as a consequence of the wrongful act, even though the act was done out of mere 'wantonness and sport' ...

A modern statement of the test for manslaughter by criminal negligence may be found in the reasons of the Court of Criminal Appeal for allowing the appeal in *R v Bateman* (1925) 19 Cr App R 8 which were delivered by Lord Hewart CJ. It was there pointed out, at 11, that in a civil case, if there has been a falling short of the standard of reasonable care required by law, it matters not how far from the standard the falling short is; the extent of the liability depends not on the degree of liability but on the amount of damage done. In the Criminal Court, on the other hand, the amount and the degree of negligence are the determining factors. Lord Hewart added: 'There must be mens rea.' The passage was quoted by Lord Atkin in *Andrews'* case, supra, and save that his Lordship said that he did not find the connotations of mens rea helpful in distinguishing between degrees of negligence, he expressed no disapproval of the test thus propounded. On the contrary, as we have already suggested, he approved it. The problem has rather been to enunciate a test which enables a jury to decide whether there has been such a falling short of the standard of care that a crime has been committed.

The Irish Court of Criminal Appeal clearly preferred the objective test in *People v Dunleavy* [1948] IR 95 in which the court said, at 101:

> To say that a person is driving with a reckless disregard for life means that he does not care whether he kills anybody or not. Such a state of mind will ordinarily, but perhaps not universally, amount to general malice sufficient to justify a conviction for murder. To say that a person is driving with a reckless disregard for the safety of others, may mean no more than that he does not care whether or not he puts them in danger. This may amount to no more than dangerous driving. To associate these two ideas is not to achieve the desired mean, but possibly to import an ambiguity. On the other hand, if the reference to recklessness is merely omitted, the jury are hardly given all the assistance which they are entitled to expect.
>
> This court is of the opinion that a more satisfactory way of indicating to a jury the high degree of negligence necessary to justify a conviction for manslaughter, is to relate it to the risk or likelihood of substantial personal injury resulting from it, rather than to attach any qualification to the word 'negligence' or to the driver's disregard for the life or safety of others. In this connection the American case of *Commonwealth v Welansky*, 55 North Eastern Reporter, 2nd Series, 902, a decision of the Supreme Court of Massachusetts, is of very considerable interest.
>
> If the negligence proved is of a very high degree and of such a character that any reasonable driver, endowed with ordinary road sense and in full possession of his faculties, would realise, if he thought at all, that by driving in the manner which occasioned the fatality he was without lawful excuse, incurring, in a high degree, the risk of causing substantial personal injury to others, the crime of manslaughter appears clearly to be established.

The court concluded that the jury should be clearly told, inter alia: 'That before they can convict of manslaughter, which is a felony and a very serious crime, they must be satisfied that the fatal negligence was of a very high degree; and was such as to involve, in a high degree, the risk or likelihood of substantial personal injury to others.' In laying down that test the court clearly did not think that it was departing in any way from *Andrews'* case, to which it had expressly referred. ...

In several cases the Crown allegations have been left to the jury upon the basis that they might constitute manslaughter by criminal negligence or manslaughter by an unlawful and dangerous act. *R v Church*, supra, was such a case. In it an objective test of what constituted a dangerous act was adopted. This test was applied by Smith J in *R v Holzer*, supra, and it was approved by the House of Lords in *DPP v Newbury* [1976] 2 WLR 918 at 921–2 and 924; [1976] 2 All ER 365. It has been said that *R v Lamb* [1967] 2 QB 981 at 989–90; [1967] 2 All ER 1282 adopted a subjective test, but in *DPP v Newbury* Lord Salmon made it clear (WLR at 923) that he did not regard it as doing so.

No doubt manslaughter does involve mens rea. But to use the language of Lord Salmon in *Newbury's* case (WLR at 923), the necessary intent is no more than an intent to do the acts which constitute the crime. The problem is to formulate the requirement in terms which will enable the jury to determine whether the case is one of murder by recklessness or manslaughter by criminal negligence. The requisite mens rea in the latter crime does not involve a consciousness on the part of the accused of the likelihood of his act's causing death or serious bodily harm to the victim or persons placed in similar relationship as the victim was to the accused. The requisite mens rea is, rather, an intent to do the act which, in fact, caused the death of the victim, but to do that act in circumstances where the doing of it involves a great falling short of the standard of care required of a reasonable man in the circumstances and a high degree of risk or likelihood of the occurrence of death or serious bodily harm if that standard of care was not observed, that is to say, such a falling short and such a risk as to warrant punishment under the criminal law. This formulation proceeds on the footing that the accused man did not in fact advert (although a reasonable man would have adverted) to the probability that death or grievous bodily harm would ensue. It adopts the view of Menzies J in *Pemble v R*, supra, and of Lord Hailsham in *Hyam v Director of Public Prosecutions*, supra, (AC at 79) that if the accused knows that the act is likely to cause death or grievous bodily harm, and consciously accepts the risk, it is murder. The formulation is consistent with the objective test of manslaughter by an unlawful and dangerous act approved by the House of Lords in *DPP v Newbury*, supra.

An alternative formulation would have to be along lines suggested by Turner in the 19th edition of *Kenny's Outlines of Criminal Law,* (1966), p 191, viz that involuntary manslaughter is constituted when a person has caused the death of another in the course of conduct which he realised would or might cause someone a physical harm falling short of grievous bodily harm but not being of a trivial or negligible character, provided that he had no lawful justification or excuse for inflicting or for risking the infliction of the physical harm which he foresaw.

Either of these formulations would offer an intelligible distinction between murder by recklessness and manslaughter by criminal negligence. The former, however, appears to us to be the only formulation consistent with the weight of authority.

Finally, we would draw support from the decision of the High Court in *Callaghan v R* (1952) 87 CLR 115. We have not referred to it earlier for it is a case which was concerned with the degree of negligence required to establish manslaughter under the Criminal Code of Western Australia. Its significance for present purposes is that the court decided that the standard set by the Code for the degree of negligence punishable as manslaughter should be regarded as that set by the common law in cases where negligence amounts to manslaughter. The court discussed many of the cases, including *Andrews'* case, supra, in which manslaughter by negligence was involved, and nowhere suggested that the standard of negligence set by the common law was to be measured by a subjective test.

In order to establish manslaughter by criminal negligence, it is sufficient if the prosecution shows that the act which caused the death was done by the accused consciously and voluntarily, without any intention of causing death or grievous bodily harm but in circumstances which involved such a great falling short of the standard of care which a reasonable man would have exercised and which involved such a high risk that death or grievous bodily harm would follow that the doing of the act merited criminal punishment. A direction to that effect was not given in the instant case and the direction which was in fact given by the learned trial judge was not in accordance with the test as we have formulated it. This consideration provides an additional reason for quashing the verdict and ordering a new trial, although the ground was not taken in the notice of appeal or argued before us.

[See also *R v Adomako* [1995] 1 AC 171.]

6.10C R v Lavender

(2005) 218 ALR 521
High Court of Australia

[Lavender was employed to drive a front-end loader at a sand mine. The machine weighed 25 tonnes and was much higher and longer than a car, and travelled at four kilometres per hour. The driver's vision was restricted by a bucket at the front of the loader. On the day in question, four boys aged between 11 and 13 years had gone to play on the mine site. Although the mine site was unfenced, the boys should not have been there, and Lavender decided to chase them away. He drove the loader towards the boys. The boys ran away, and Lavender could see two of them in the distance, but not the other two. Unfortunately, the boys had hidden in shrub. Lavender drove over the shrub, causing injuries that resulted in the death of one of the boys. Lavender was convicted of manslaughter.

The New South Wales Court of Criminal Appeal allowed Lavender's appeal on the grounds that the judge had failed to direct the jury that the prosecution needed to prove a vital element of manslaughter; that is, malice.

The prosecution appealed to the High Court, which unanimously held that it was not necessary for the prosecution to prove 'malice' as a constituent element of manslaughter by criminal negligence. The High Court held that the reference in s 18(2)(a) to acts or omissions being 'within this section' if they were malicious, referred only to the provisions in s 18 that dealt with murder. Section 18 defined murder; s 18(1)(b) left manslaughter to be defined by common law.]
[Footnotes omitted.]

Gleeson CJ, **McHugh**, **Gummow** and **Hayne JJ**:

13 The trial judge told the jury that, relevantly to this case, there were five elements in the offence of involuntary manslaughter. The first was that the respondent had a duty of care to the victim. The second was that he was in breach of that duty. The third was that his actions were deliberate in the sense that he was in control of the vehicle. The fourth was that the actions of the respondent in driving the vehicle caused the death of the victim. The trial judge explained those four elements, but that explanation is not presently relevant. It is what he said about the fifth element that is now important.

14 The trial judge said:

> And finally, the Crown has to prove that that action of driving into the bush in the circumstances that the Crown says obtained fell so far short of the standard of care which a reasonable person would have exercised in the circumstances and involved such a high risk that death or really serious bodily harm would follow, that the actions merit criminal punishment.
>
> Members of the jury can I say this here and now that the degree of negligence required to constitute the crime of manslaughter is very high indeed. It has been described in the past as having to be wicked. In other words, a person has to be wickedly negligent before they can be convicted of the crime of manslaughter.
>
> The Crown in this case says that you would be satisfied beyond reasonable doubt that the actions of the accused did amount to such a high degree of negligence. The Crown says that you would be satisfied beyond reasonable doubt that the accused intentionally drove the loader into an area of bush where he knew there were four boys. In circumstances where he had lost sight of the boys, he continued to drive his loader in that area where the Crown says the evidence would satisfy you that the topography and the vegetation combined with the nature and structure of the loader, necessitated an inability on the part of the accused to see and hear adequately and to proceed with safety. And the Crown says in those circumstances you would be satisfied that his actions fell so far short of the standard of care which a reasonable person would have exercised in the circumstances, and involved such a high risk that death or really serious bodily harm would follow, that they merit criminal punishment.
>
> …
>
> Now members of the jury, they are matters for you to determine. A determination of this question of negligence and the degree of negligence is an objective test. You have to decide whether — you have to compare the conduct of the accused as you find it to have been with the conduct of a reasonable person who possesses the same personal attributes as the accused, that is to say a person of the same age, having the same experience and knowledge as the accused and the circumstances in which he found himself, and having the ordinary fortitude and strength of mind which a reasonable person would have, and determine on that basis whether the Crown has made out its case. In other words, it is an objective test. The Crown does not have to prove that the accused appreciated that he was being negligent or that he was being negligent to such a high degree. It is your task to determine whether having decided on the conduct of the accused, whether his actions amounted to negligence based upon, as I say, what you think a reasonable person in the position of the accused would have done.
>
> The Crown says that when you look at it on that basis, you would be satisfied beyond reasonable doubt that a reasonable person in the position of the accused, that is to say, of his age and experience and with the knowledge that he had of the circumstances at the time and being a person of normal fortitude and strength of mind would never have done what he did. A reasonable person in that situation would have realised that there was a very high risk of death or serious injury by

proceeding into the bush in circumstances, the Crown says, where he knew that he could not see properly, his vision was obscured by the vegetation and by the loader itself to some extent, where he knew that there were young boys, the Crown says, behaviour was always going to be unpredictable [sic], and the Crown says that when you compare the actions of the accused with what you might expect a reasonable person in his position to have done, you would be satisfied beyond reasonable doubt that those actions were negligent, they were deliberate and that they caused the death of Michael Milne and that they were so negligent, that is to say they fell so far short of the standard of care which a reasonable person would have exercised in the circumstances and involved such a high risk that death or really serious bodily harm would follow, that they merit criminal punishment.

If you are so satisfied members of the jury, then your verdict in respect of that count will be guilty, and you need not proceed any further. If you are not so satisfied as to all of those elements, then your verdict in relation to that count will be not guilty and you would go on to consider count 2.

Can I just reiterate members of the jury, it is immaterial in this case both in relation to count 1 and count 2 what the accused believed to be the case at the time. The test is an objective one, that is to say you must try to put yourself in a position of a reasonable person in the position of the accused, same age, knowing what he knows and a person of ordinary fortitude and strength of mind, and ask yourselves would that person have done what the accused did. Was it reasonable for him to have done that? If not, were his actions negligent, were they deliberate, and I do not mean deliberate in the sense of intending to hurt Michael Milne, no one has suggested that, but deliberate in the sense that he had control over his vehicle. Were the actions the cause of Michael Milne's death and were the actions so far short of the standard of care which a reasonable person would have exercised, and did they involve such a high risk of death or really serious bodily injury that [it] would follow that they merit criminal punishment?

15 For the purposes of one of the subsidiary issues, it is to be noted that, although the trial judge described the test as 'objective' he told the jury, repeatedly, to have regard to the circumstances in which the respondent found himself and 'the knowledge that he had of the circumstances at the time'. The jury were told to put themselves in the position of the respondent 'knowing what he knows'. Indeed, some aspects of what the respondent knew were relied upon by the prosecution, but the jury were invited to consider everything he knew. The reference to the immateriality of 'what the accused believed to be the case at the time', in the context in which that was said, was plainly a reference to, and a reiteration of, the earlier statement that '[t]he Crown does not have to prove that the accused appreciated that he was being negligent'. That the statement was so understood by those at the trial is evident from the fact that no objection was taken by trial counsel to that aspect of the directions …

17 The trial judge's directions on what he called the fifth element of the offence were based on the judgment of the Full Court of the Supreme Court of Victoria in *Nydam v R*, a judgment which was approved by four members of this court in *Wilson v R* …

The subsidiary issues

56 On each of these issues, the conclusion of Giles JA in the Court of Criminal Appeal was correct.

57 The first issue concerns a point that was taken at trial by counsel for the respondent. In considering the issue, it is necessary to note the precise terms of counsel's submission to the trial judge. Reference has earlier been made to the five elements of manslaughter identified by the judge. Counsel said: 'I would invite your Honour to add, in relation to the manslaughter, a sixth element, being that the accused did not hold an honest and reasonable belief that it was safe to proceed.' The invitation was declined.

58 There are two reasons why it would have been erroneous and inappropriate to give the jury such a direction. The first reason is that, as the trial judge pointed out, the supposed sixth element of the offence was subsumed by the fifth element (as to which counsel made no objection). In order to satisfy the fifth element, the prosecution had to persuade the jury beyond reasonable doubt that the conduct of the respondent was not only unreasonable, but that it was 'wickedly negligent'. If the jury were not satisfied of that, the charge of manslaughter failed. If the jury were satisfied of that, how could they entertain the possibility that the respondent held an honest *and reasonable* belief that it was safe to proceed?

59 The second reason is that the principle on which counsel based his argument, which applies in other contexts, is a principle relating to honest and reasonable mistake of fact. The principle was recently discussed in this court in *Ostrowski v Palmer*. As the decision in that case illustrates, the principle concerns mistakes of fact. The belief concerning which counsel sought a direction was a (supposed) 'belief that it was safe to proceed'. Such a state of mind involves an opinion. It might be based upon certain factual inferences or hypotheses (the respondent did not give evidence, so the jury were not told by him exactly what facts or circumstances were operating in his mind), but it necessarily involves an element of judgment. Indeed, it involves a conclusion by the respondent that his conduct was reasonable. The direction sought would be inconsistent with what has been described as the objectivity of the test for involuntary manslaughter. The respondent's opinion that it was safe to act as he did was not a relevant matter. If there had been some particular fact or circumstance which the respondent knew, or thought he knew and which contributed to that opinion, and the jury had been informed of that, and counsel had asked for a direction about it, then it may have been appropriate to invite the jury to take that into account.

60 Counsel for the respondent in this court attempted to persuade the court that *Nydam v R* should not be followed, and that manslaughter by criminal negligence requires a subjective appreciation by the offender that the conduct engaged in is unsafe. This would bring this form of involuntary manslaughter into disconformity with the other form of involuntary manslaughter dealt with in *Wilson v R*. Furthermore, it is erroneous in principle. This branch of the criminal law reflects the value placed by the law upon human life. Giles JA was right to say, in the present case, that 'appreciation of risk is not necessary for a sufficiently great falling short of the objective standard of care, and … the law would be deficient if grossly negligent conduct causing death could not bring criminal punishment unless the accused foresaw the danger'.

61 The second issue concerns a point not taken at trial. The fact that it was not taken is significant, because it involves giving the trial judge's directions a strained interpretation, an interpretation inconsistent with what he had previously said, an interpretation that was clearly unintended, and an interpretation that did not occur to trial counsel at the time.

62 The relevant directions are set out earlier in these reasons. As has been noted, the trial judge repeatedly told the jury to take account of the facts and circumstances known to the respondent when he was driving the front end loader near the boys. The judge also told the jury that it was not necessary for the prosecution to prove that the respondent appreciated that he was acting negligently. In the course of saying those things (both of which were orthodox) he 'reiterate[d]' that it was immaterial what the accused believed to be the case at the time. That is now said to be an error. In the next sentence the judge again directed the jury to take account of what was within the knowledge of the accused. Plainly, the reiteration was not intended, as is now submitted, to contradict what was said earlier, and what was said again in the very next sentence. In the context of what went before and after, the judge was reiterating that the respondent's view, at the time, as to whether his conduct was negligent, was immaterial. The jury were told to make their own judgment of the reasonableness of the respondent's conduct, taking account of what he knew at the time. They were told that his opinion, at the time that his conduct was safe, and therefore reasonable, was irrelevant. Those propositions are not contradictory. The reiteration of the second did not involve a withdrawal of the first, especially when the first proposition was repeated in the next sentence.

63 The appellant succeeds on the subsidiary issues ... The appeal should be allowed.

6.11 Notes and illustrations

1. *Gross criminal negligence:* Whether the death has been caused by an act and/ or omission, the criminal law requires a high degree of negligence before criminal sanctions are applied. This is an objective test, with the standard being that of a reasonable person in the same position as D: *Nydam* (1977) and *Lavender* (2005). *Nydam* defined the standard as 'circumstances which involved such a great falling short of the standard of care which a reasonable man would have exercised and which involved such a high risk of death or grievous bodily harm would follow, that the doing of the act merited criminal punishment'. The jury must be satisfied that D's act or omission was 'grossly negligent' or 'wicked': *Lavender* (2005). In the English case *Bateman* (1925) 19 Cr App R 8, Lord Hewart CJ at 11 directed the jury that it must be the case that 'in the opinion of the jury, the negligence of the accused went beyond a mere matter of compensation between subjects and showed such disregard for the life and safety of others, as to amount to a crime against the state and conduct deserving of punishment'. This is an explicitly normative question for the jury — was D so negligent that he or she merits criminal punishment?

(a) D was deer hunting in a forest and shot at a target which he said he believed to be a deer, however it was V who was walking his dog. V was killed. D was convicted of negligent manslaughter. The judge in his charge to the jury described the element of criminal or gross negligence as satisfied by 'circumstances which involve such a great falling short of the standard of care which a reasonable person would have exercised, and which involve such a high risk that death or bodily injury would follow, that the doing of the act or acts merits criminal punishment'. On appeal to the Court of Appeal, it was argued that the judge should additionally have directed the jury on the defence of honest and reasonable mistake. Held, appeal dismissed. The 'defence' of honest and reasonable mistake is subsumed in the direction on gross negligence required in cases of negligent manslaughter. The jury could not have been satisfied beyond reasonable doubt that the act or acts of the accused was or were performed by him 'in circumstances which involved such a great falling short of the standard of care which a reasonable person would have exercised' without concluding that any belief which D had that his target was a deer was not a reasonable belief: *R v Osip* (2000) 2 VR 595.

2. *Negligent manslaughter by omission:* Negligent manslaughter by omission is essentially a subcategory of negligent manslaughter. While there is a general duty imposed on all of us not to cause death by a positive act, the duty is more complex in relation to allegations of gross negligence by D's omissions rather than actions. In cases of omission, the prosecution must establish a legal duty to act. A moral duty will not be sufficient.

3. *Legal duty to act:* The prosecution must identify a legal duty to act. At common law, legal duties to act have been found in parent/child relationships (*R v Russell* [1933] VLR 59); voluntary employment in an occupation that bears upon public safety (*R v Lowe* (1850) 175 ER 489); voluntary assumption of care for helpless persons (*R v Taktak* (1988) 14 NSWLR 226; *R v Stone and Dobinson* [1977] QB 354); and situations where D has created a situation of danger by dealing with dangerous things or doing dangerous acts (*R v Styman; R v Taber* [2004] NSWCCA 245). Once a legal duty to act has been identified it will be necessary to identify that a duty of care was owed to V, although this will usually follow inexorably from the duty to act:

(a) D drove a lorry from Rotterdam to Zeebrugge and embarked on a vehicle ferry to Dover. The lorry had been loaded with a container in which 60 illegal immigrants were concealed. The ventilation of the container was by means of a small vent. Those inside the container had been told that for part of the journey the vent would be shut and that while it was shut, to assist in avoiding detection, they had to remain silent. The vent was shut several kilometres before the lorry arrived at Zeebrugge and remained closed for over five hours. Fifty-eight of the people hidden in the container died from lack of air. D's fingerprints were later found on the outside covering of the vent. D was convicted of 58 offences of manslaughter. On appeal to the Court of Appeal, it was argued that no duty of care could be said to have been owed by D to the illegal immigrants because they shared with him the same joint illegal purpose. Held, appeal dismissed. There was no justification for concluding that the criminal law should decline to hold a person as criminally responsible for the death of another simply because the two were engaged in some joint unlawful activity at the time or because there might have been an element of acceptance of a degree of risk by the victim in order to further the joint unlawful enterprise: *R v Wacker* [2003] 4 All ER 295.

4. *Breach of duty of care:* The prosecution must prove that D breached this duty of care according to the standard for manslaughter by criminal negligence in *Nydam* (1977) and *Lavender* (2005), discussed at note 1, above. The application of this objective standard was demonstrated in *R v Stone and Dobinson* [1977] QB 354, extracted at **6.14C**:

    (a) D was charged with the manslaughter of her infant grandchild, V. D was a penniless old woman, and V had been left in her care. She failed to supply sufficient food and proper care, and V died. Brett J directed the jury that:

    > [I]f a grown-up person chooses to undertake the charge of a human creature, helpless either from infancy, simplicity, lunacy, or other infirmity, he is bound to execute that charge without (at all events) wicked negligence, and if a person who has chosen to take charge of a helpless creature lets it die by wicked negligence, that person is guilty of manslaughter.

    Verdict, not guilty: *R v Nicholls* (1874) 13 Cox CC 75 (Stafford Assizes).

    (b) D was convicted of the manslaughter of her daughter, V, an unmarried girl of 18. V had been in service, but had returned to live with D after quitting that service. V was pregnant and when she went into labour, D did not call a midwife. V died in childbirth. On appeal, the conviction was quashed on the ground that D was under no duty to call in aid for V, who was entirely emancipated: *R v Shepherd* (1862) 169 ER 1340.

    (c) D was charged with the murder of his wife and their two young children, who met their deaths by drowning late one evening in a public swimming pool. The Crown case was that he had deliberately drowned each of them. D's defence was that his wife had first drowned the children and then herself, he being unable to prevent her. The jury asked to be directed as to the responsibility of D on the assumption that his wife took the children into the water without his assistance, while he stood by 'conniving to' the act. The trial judge directed the jury that in such event, D would be guilty of manslaughter. The jury found D guilty of manslaughter of his wife and children. On appeal to the Full Court of the Supreme Court of Victoria: held, the verdicts of manslaughter of the children should stand, and, by Cussen ACJ and Mann J (McArthur J dissenting), the verdict of manslaughter of the wife should also stand: *R v Russell* [1933] VLR 59. See also *R v Russell and Russell* [1987] Crim LR 494.

EXAMPLES OF NEGLIGENT MANSLAUGHTER

6.12C

R v Instan

[1893] 1 QB 450

Court for Crown Cases Reserved

[Miss Instan was a spinster living with and maintained by her aunt, who was 73 years old. Until a few weeks before her death, the aunt was healthy and able to look after herself. Shortly before her death, the aunt suffered from gangrene in the leg, which rendered her unable to attend to herself or to move about. No-one knew of her condition but the accused, who continued to live in the house and take in the food supplied by tradesmen, but did not procure medical or nursing attendance, or notify the neighbours of the aunt's illness. The aunt died after 10 days, the cause of death being exhaustion from the gangrene, but substantially accelerated by want of food, nursing and medical care. These wants could have been supplied if the accused had notified any of the neighbours, or the aunt's relations who lived within a few miles.

The accused was indicted for manslaughter of the aunt, and the judge left it to the jury to say whether, in the circumstances, the accused did not impliedly undertake either to provide care for the aunt herself or to notify others of her helpless condition; and that if the jury found such an implied undertaking and that death was substantially accelerated by failure to carry it out, the charge of manslaughter was made out. The jury found her guilty, and the judge stated a case.]

Lord Coleridge CJ: It would not be correct to say that every moral obligation involves a legal duty; but every legal duty is founded on a moral obligation. A legal common law duty is nothing else than the enforcing by law of that which is a moral obligation without legal enforcement. There can be no question in this case that it was the clear duty of the prisoner to impart to the deceased so much as was necessary to sustain life of the food which she from time to time took in, and which was paid for by the deceased's own money for the purpose of the maintenance of herself and the prisoner; it was only through the instrumentality of the prisoner that the deceased could get the food. There was, therefore, a common law duty imposed upon the prisoner which she did not discharge.

Nor can there be any question that the failure of the prisoner to discharge her legal duty at least accelerated the death of the deceased, if it did not actually cause it. There is no case directly in point; but it would be a slur upon and a discredit to the administration of justice in this country if there were any doubt as to the legal principle, or as to the present case being within it. The prisoner was under a moral obligation to the deceased from which arose a legal duty towards her; that legal duty the prisoner has wilfully and deliberately left unperformed, with the consequence that there has been an acceleration of the death of the deceased owing to the non-performance of that legal duty. it is unnecessary to say more than that upon the evidence this conviction was most properly arrived at.

[**Hawkins**, **Cave**, **Day** and **Collins JJ** concurred. Conviction upheld.]

6.13 Questions

What do you think the court would have decided if:

1. the defendant had adequately fed the deceased, but had failed to provide nursing or medical care, which failure accelerated the death; or
2. the food supplied to the household had not been paid for by the deceased?

6.14C R v Stone; R v Dobinson

[1977] 1 QB 354
Court of Appeal (UK)

[The two accused, a partially deaf and almost blind man of low average intelligence, with no appreciable sense of smell, and his mistress, described as 'ineffectual and inadequate', lived together in his house with his mentally-subnormal son. The man's sister came to live at the house as a lodger. She occupied a small room without ventilation, toilet or washing facilities except a polythene bucket. She was morbidly anxious not to put on weight, denied herself proper meals, spent days at a time in her room and became helplessly infirm within three years so that she did not leave her bed. She did not, however, complain. The mistress, who took the sister such food as she required, attempted to wash her with the aid of a neighbour, who advised the mistress to go to the social services. The licensee of a public house which the accused used to visit advised her to obtain a doctor. The sister refused to give the accused the name of her doctor, whom they tried unsuccessfully to find. An attempt by the man to obtain his own doctor for her was unsuccessful, but the accused did no more to enlist outside professional help although aware of the poor condition of her health. Some three weeks after the attempt to wash the sister, she died from toxaemia spreading from infected bed sores, prolonged immobilisation and lack of food. Had she received medical care in the intervening period she would probably have survived.

The accused were charged with her manslaughter. The jury were directed to determine whether the prosecution had established a gross neglect of duty of care amounting to reckless disregard of the sister's health and well-being. The two accused were convicted and appealed to the Court of Appeal.]

Geoffrey-Lane LJ, **Nield** and **Croom-Johnson JJ**: There is no dispute, broadly speaking, as to the matters on which the jury must be satisfied before they can convict of manslaughter in circumstances such as the present. They are (1) that the defendant undertook the care of a person who by reason of age or infirmity was unable to care for himself; (2) that the defendant was grossly negligent in regard to his duty of care; (3) that by reason of such negligence the person died. It is submitted on behalf of the appellants that the judge's direction to the jury with regard to the first two items was incorrect.

At the close of the prosecution case submissions were made to the judge that there was no, or no sufficient evidence that the appellants, or either of them, had chosen to undertake the care of Fanny.

That contention was advanced by Mr Coles before this court as his first ground of appeal. He amplified the ground somewhat by submitting that the evidence which the judge had suggested to the jury might support the assumption of a duty by the appellants does not, when examined, succeed in doing so. He suggests that the situation here is unlike any reported case. Fanny came to this house as a lodger. Largely, if not entirely due to her own eccentricity and failure to look after herself or feed herself properly, she became increasingly infirm and immobile and eventually unable to look after herself. Is it to be said, asks Mr Coles rhetorically, that by the mere fact of becoming infirm and helpless in these circumstances she casts a duty on her brother and the appellant Dobinson to take steps to have her looked after or taken to hospital? The suggestion is that, heartless though it may seem, this is one of those situations where the appellants were entitled to do nothing; where no duty was cast upon them to help, any more than it is cast upon a man to rescue a stranger from drowning, however easy such a rescue might be.

This court rejects that proposition. Whether Fanny was a lodger or not she was a blood relation of the appellant Stone; she was occupying a room in his house; the appellant Dobinson had undertaken the duty of trying to wash her, of taking such food to her as she required. There was ample evidence that each appellant was aware of the poor condition she was in by mid-July. It was not disputed that no effort was made to summon an ambulance or the social services or the police despite the entreaties of Mrs Wilson and Mrs West. A social worker used to visit Cyril. No word was spoken to him. All these were matters which the jury was entitled to take into account when considering whether the necessary assumption of a duty to care for Fanny had been proved.

This was not a situation analogous to the drowning stranger. They did make efforts to care. They tried to get a doctor; they tried to discover the previous doctor. The appellant Dobinson helped with the washing and the provision of food. All these matters were put before the jury in terms which we find it impossible to fault. The jury were entitled to find that the duty had been assumed. They were entitled to conclude that once Fanny became helplessly infirm, as she had by 19 July, the appellants were, in the circumstances, obliged either to summon help or else to care for Fanny themselves.

Mr Cole's second submission presents greater difficulty. It is that the judge's direction on the nature of the negligence or recklessness required was wrongly stated.

[The court quoted extracts from the trial judge's direction to the jury, and continued:]

Mr Coles submits that … there must be an appreciation by the defendant of the risk of death or serious injury before a conviction for manslaughter in these circumstances can result. We disagree … It is to *Andrews v Director of Public Prosecutions* [1937] AC 576, that one must turn to discover the definition of the requisite degree of negligence. Lord Atkin, at 582, cites with approval the words of Lord Hewart CJ in *Rex v Bateman* (1925) 19 Cr App R 8, and goes on to say, at 583:

> Simple lack of care such as will constitute civil liability is not enough; for purposes of the criminal law there are degrees of negligence: and a very high degree of negligence is required to be proved before the felony is established. Probably of all the epithets that can be applied 'reckless' most nearly covers the case. It is difficult to visualise a case of death by reckless driving in the connotation of that term in ordinary speech which would not justify a conviction for manslaughter: but it is probably not all-embracing for 'reckless' suggests an indifference to risk whereas the accused may have appreciated the risk and intended to avoid it and yet have shown such a high degree of negligence in the means adopted to avoid the risk as would justify a conviction.

It is clear from that passage that indifference to an obvious risk and appreciation of such risk, coupled with a determination nevertheless to run it, are both examples of recklessness.

The duty which a defendant has undertaken is a duty of caring for the health and welfare of the infirm person. What the prosecution have to prove is a breach of that duty in such circumstances that the jury feel convinced that the defendant's conduct can properly be described as reckless, that is to say a reckless disregard of danger to the health and welfare of the infirm person. Mere inadvertence is not enough. The defendant must be proved to have been indifferent to an obvious risk of injury to health, or actually to have foreseen the risk but to have determined nevertheless to run it.

The direction given by the judge was wholly in accord with those principles. If any criticism is to be made it would be that the direction was unduly favourable to the defence. The appeals against conviction therefore fail.

6.15 Questions

Had the accused in *R v Stone; R v Dobinson* simply ignored the deceased from the moment of her arrival, would the court have held them to have been under a duty of care for her? If the answer to this question is no, how can inadequate attempts to help someone properly be used as a basis for imputing criminal responsibility for not making further, more satisfactory, attempts? Do you think the correct result was reached in *R v Stone; R v Dobinson*? In what ways does the case differ from *R v Instan*?

6.16C **R v Styman; R v Taber**

[2004] NSWCCA 245
Court of Criminal Appeal, Supreme Court of New South Wales

[The defendants broke into V's house, bound and gagged her, robbed her of over $23,000 and abandoned her. The defendants made a 000 telephone call from a pay phone on Greenwell Point Road, Nowra East, reporting a break and enter in Spies Avenue. This call was not acted upon. V died as a consequence of smothering and dehydration some days after the burglary.

At first instance, the defendants were found guilty of murder by omission, on the basis that the defendants' omission to rescue caused V's death, and at the time of the omission the defendants recognised the probability, that is, were recklessly indifferent under the requirements of s 18 of the Crimes Act (NSW), that the omission would probably cause V's death. On appeal, the appellants submitted that the trial judge erred in law in not directing verdicts of acquittal on all counts at the close of the Crown case, on the basis that there was no evidence that the conduct of the appellants caused the death of V. It was also contended that his Honour erred in law in misdirecting and/or failing to direct the jury adequately or properly in respect of murder, manslaughter, the legal duty to rescue, causation and joint enterprise.

On appeal to the Court of Criminal Appeal of New South Wales, it was held that V's death would not have occurred but for the omission on the part of the defendants to remove her from danger after the 000 call. Had the operator passed on the call as she should have, V would have been rescued and would not have died. However, it was clear that no jury would fail to find that the omission to remove her from danger was a 'substantial and operating cause' of her death. Accordingly, the chain of causation was not broken.

In order to convict the defendants for murder, the jury had at least to be satisfied beyond reasonable doubt that, in the time that passed after the 000 call was made and before V died, they became aware that she had not been, and would not be, rescued and thereby fully realised that she would probably die. Given that they believed that the 000 call would be acted upon, this meant that there was a reasonable doubt that they lacked the necessary mens rea for murder. Accordingly, the convictions of the defendants for murder were quashed. The extract begins with an analysis of whether or not the defendants had a legal duty to act.

Barr J referred to several cases in which were listed what his Honour described as well-recognised categories of circumstances which gave rise to a legal duty in one person to act in a particular way towards another, a failure to perform which would render the obligated person liable to be dealt with criminally. Among these were *R v Taktak* (1988) 14 NSWLR 226 at 236–45. His Honour quoted from the judgment of **McAlvay CJ** in *People v Beardsley* (1907) 113 NW 1128 at 1129–30. There the Chief Justice said:

> The law recognizes that under some circumstances the omission of a duty owed by one individual to another, where such omission results in the death of the one to whom the duty is owing, will make the other chargeable with manslaughter … This rule of law is always based upon the proposition that the duty neglected must be a legal duty, and not a mere moral obligation. It must be a duty imposed by law or by contract, and the omission to perform the duty must be the immediate and direct cause of death.]

Sheller JA, **Sperling** and **Adams JJ**:

124 So stated, the principle has ready application to relationships giving rise to such a duty. Reference was made to the legal relation of protector, as husband to wife, parent to child, master to seaman, knowing such person to be in peril and to proper efforts to rescue without jeopardising the life of the person owing the duty or the lives of others. Failure to make such reasonable and proper efforts could result in the person being guilty of manslaughter 'at least' if by reason of the omission of duty the person to whom it was owed died. Barr J referred to four situations, identified by Yeldham J in *Taktak* where failure to act might constitute a breach of legal duty. These were the statutory duty to care for another, a certain status relationship to another, assumption of a contractual duty of care to another and a voluntary assumption of care to another.

125 With more particular relevance to the present case, in *Lawford* at 547–8, the South Australian Full Court said that a duty not to leave a person in danger might arise where the defendant had put that person in danger by a wrongful act.

126 Barr J referred to *R v Miller* [1980] 2 QB 532 (Court of Appeal) [1983] 2 AC 176 (House of Lords). In that case the appellant, a house squatter, fell asleep on a mattress with a lighted cigarette and the mattress caught fire. The appellant awoke and realised that the mattress was smouldering. He did nothing about it but moved to another room in the premises. The house caught fire. The appellant was charged with arson. He was convicted and appealed. The question of law involved ([1983] 2 AC at 174) was whether the actus reus of the offence of arson was present when a defendant accidentally started a fire and thereafter, intending to destroy or damage property belonging to another or being reckless as to whether any such property would be destroyed or damaged, failed to take any steps to extinguish the fire or to prevent damage to such property by that fire. Lord Diplock at 174 preferred to speak in terms of the conduct of the accused and his state of mind at the time of that conduct instead of speaking of actus reus and mens rea. He also preferred to speak in terms of 'responsibility' rather than 'duty'.

127 Like arson in the classification referred to by Lord Diplock, murder is a 'result crime' not complete unless, and until, the conduct of the accused has caused death. So the period from that immediately before the act and the death may be considerable and the conduct of the accused causative of the result may consist not only of the physical acts but also of the failure to take measures that lie within the accused's power to counteract the danger the accused has created. As the accused's conduct, active or passive, varies during this period so too may the accused's state of mind at the time of each piece of conduct (175).

128 At 175–6 Lord Diplock said:

> If at the time of any particular piece of conduct by the accused that is causative of the result, the state of mind that actuates his conduct falls within the description of one or other of the states of mind that are made a necessary ingredient of the offence ... I know of no principle of English criminal law that would prevent his

> being guilty of the offence … Likewise I see no rational ground for excluding from conduct capable of giving rise to criminal liability, conduct which consists of failing to take measures that lie within one's power to counteract a danger that one has oneself created, if at the time of such conduct one's state of mind is such as constitutes a necessary ingredient of the offence … I cannot see any good reason why, so far as liability under criminal law is concerned, it should matter at what point of time before the resultant damage is complete a person becomes aware that he has done a physical act which, whether or not he appreciated that it would at the time when he did it, does in fact create a risk that property of another will be damaged, provided that, at the moment of awareness, it lies within his power to take steps, either himself or by calling for the assistance of the fire brigade if this be necessary, to prevent or minimise the damage to the property at risk.

129 In *Royall v R* (1991) 172 CLR 378 at 390–391, Mason CJ referred to the necessity for coincidence between act and intent and the way in which the deceased met her death. At 458 McHugh J said:

> It is trite law that the relevant state of mind and the harm-causing act 'must both concur to constitute the crime' … [but] the state of mind of an accused does not have to coincide with the time of the deceased's death.

130 These statements apply, of course, as much to omissions as to acts.

131 Thus the case against each accused was necessarily one where the Crown had to prove acts by the accused imposing upon him a duty or responsibility to take all reasonable and practicable steps to release Mrs Alchin and his omission after the 000 call to perform that duty accompanied by a realisation that as a result Mrs Alchin would probably die.

…

259 It was submitted that once the language of 'duty' is employed in homicide, one is immediately in the realm of manslaughter by criminal negligence: *Taktak v R* (1988) 34 A Crim R 334. It was said that the reason why objection was made to the trial Judge leaving murder for the consideration of the jury was that the jury would not be able to effectively differentiate between the 'duty' in murder by omission and the 'duty' in manslaughter by criminal negligence and this confusion was capable of creating a miscarriage of justice. Again, reference to the summing up, the written direction and the written questions for the jury denied the possibility of such confusion.

260 What this passage made clear was that before any accused could be found guilty of the murder of Mrs Alchin the jury must be satisfied that the accused fully realised at the time that the probable consequence would be death. The written direction took the form: Murder is committed when —

— the act of the accused or for which he is responsible or the omission of the accused causes the death of the deceased, and

— at the time of the act or omission the accused fully realises that the deceased will probably die but goes on and takes the risk.

Notes

1. The accused does not have to desire the death of the deceased.
2. An omission may consist of a failure to fulfil a duty imposed by the law.
3. If a person deliberately puts another in danger the law imposes a duty on that person to remove the danger.

261 A separate written direction for manslaughter by criminal negligence was:
Manslaughter is committed when —

— the accused has a duty of care towards the deceased,
— he is negligent because his act or omission amounted to a breach of his duty of care,
— his negligent act or omission falls so far short of the standard of care that a reasonable person would exercise in the circumstances and involves such a high risk of death or really serious injury that it merits criminal punishment, and
— his negligent act or omission causes the death of the deceased.

The eight notes that follow are omitted.

262 The written direction for manslaughter by unlawful and dangerous act was:
Manslaughter is committed where —

— the accused does an act which causes death,
— the act is unlawful, and
— the act is dangerous.

Notes

1. It is unlawful to apply force or restraint to a person without permission.
2. An act may include or consist of an omission.
3. An act is dangerous if a reasonable person in the position of the accused would realise that it exposed somebody to an appreciable risk of serious injury.
4. The accused does not have to realise that the act is dangerous.

263 The Crown submitted that it was difficult to envisage why the use of the term 'duty' would have created confusion. It was made clear to the jury that the omission to act, ie to remove the danger, was not by itself sufficient to constitute murder. There had to be an accompanying relevant mental state. The necessary mental state was only established if the jury was satisfied beyond reasonable doubt that the appellant, in omitting to act, realised that the victim would probably die. His Honour's direction to the jury on manslaughter by criminal negligence accorded with the written direction. It was submitted that the murder verdict indicated that the jury was satisfied that the appellant not only did the act or omission causing death but did so with a mental state by which he adverted to the probability that the victim would die as a consequence of his conduct. The latter was not relevant to manslaughter by criminal negligence and the distinction between the two was made clear to the jury. It was said that the same observation could be made about the directions about manslaughter by unlawful and dangerous act. The distinctions between the relevant physical acts constituting the offence and the different mental elements were clearly stated. In our opinion, these grounds of appeal fail.

[The appeal against the murder convictions was successful. The court permitted the Crown to apply for orders substituting verdicts of guilty of manslaughter.]

6.17 Notes

1. D, at R's request, procured a 15-year-old prostitute, V, for a party. He brought her to R's shop at 9 pm, at which time V 'was OK for a normal street girl'. R telephoned D at 3 am; he asked D to collect V. D found V unconscious in the lobby of a city building; she was clearly under the influence of drugs. D took V to his home, and tried to awaken her. He called a doctor at about 10 am. After some delay, the doctor accompanied D to his flat, but found V dead. D was convicted of the manslaughter of V and sentenced to 13 years' imprisonment. On appeal to the Court of Criminal Appeal of New South Wales. Held, the conviction of manslaughter must be quashed, and a verdict of acquittal entered: *R v Taktak* (1988) 34 A Crim R 334. Yeldham J (with whom Loveday J agreed), stated that D had assumed a duty of care for 'a helpless human being' and 'had so secluded the helpless person as to prevent others from rendering aid'. However, D's behaviour did not amount to a failure to obtain medical treatment or assistance which could be characterised as that high degree of negligence (which he also described as 'recklessness') the law required for the crime of manslaughter.

   Carruthers J, in his separate concurring judgment, said (at 358):

   > The complexity of modern society is such that the duty of care cannot be confined to specific categories of legal relationships such as husband and wife, parent and child; the duty will also arise where one person has voluntarily assumed the care of another who is helpless, through whatever cause …

   See also *Jones v US* (1962) 307 F 2d 397.

   Does this decision indicate a judicial move towards a general duty of care imposed on adults whose relationship with the victim of alleged neglect is transient and slight? In its Report No 40, *Homicide* (1991), the Law Reform Commission of Victoria considered (at p 109) the well-known 'moral duty' example of several people who stand by on a beach and watch while a child drowns: 'Unless there is a special relationship between one of these people and the child, the law does not impose a duty on any of them to assist the child'. Today, would an adult, casually asked by the child's parent to 'keep an eye on the kid while I go to the toilet', be held to be under a duty of rescue? Remember that the duty decision does not necessarily result in a conviction of manslaughter: there must also be a gross failure to help. The duty is to take only reasonable steps to rescue. This formulation leaves uncertain the position of people, such as those in *R v Stone; R v Dobinson* (at **6.14C**), who seem to be incapable of taking reasonable steps, because of low intelligence or other causes or circumstances. In 1991, the Law Reform Commission of Victoria recommended (at p 116) that inability to meet reasonable standards, arising from either physical or mental deficiency, should be a specific defence in this case. This recommendation has still not been adopted.

2. Despite recommendations by different medical practitioners, the parents of Gloria Sam did not seek medical treatment for a bad skin condition. Instead, the parents gave her homeopathic treatments. Over several weeks the condition worsened, and Gloria became malnourished, as she was in too much distress to eat. Gloria died at the age of nine months, from septicaemia. The infection entered her blood stream either through her infected skin or an infected eye. The court accepted that the neglect that was criminally negligent was not confined to the hours, or even the limited number of days, before her death. The accused omitted to obtain medical care in the period from 27 April 2002 to 5 May 2002 being the time after which the appellants returned from India. The evidence made it entirely inappropriate, when considering the possible criminal liability of the parents, to separate the last hours of Gloria's life when she became critically ill from the earlier period when her physical condition deteriorated, making her vulnerable to an ultimate critical infection. The evidence of causation was clear. Gloria's condition had been neglected, and conventional medicine ignored until her body could no longer resist the infection which led to her death. Her parents, Thomas Sam and Manju Sam, were found guilty of her unlawful killing by criminal negligence: *Thomas Sam v R; Manju Sam v R* [2011] NSWCCA 36.
3. In 1993, the House of Lords gave judgment in a case involving a victim of the Hillsborough football stadium disaster, in Sheffield, Yorkshire. As a result of the injuries Tony Bland received in the crowd crush, he had been in a persistent vegetative state (PVS) for almost four years. His brain cortex had been destroyed, so that he could not see, hear, communicate or feel. His brain stem continued to function, so that his breathing, heartbeat and digestion persisted. He was being fed by nasogastric tube. Bland's doctors and his parents believed that this feeding, and other supportive medical measures, should be stopped. The National Health Service (NHS) Trust managing the hospital in which Bland was being nursed applied to the Family Division of the High Court of Justice for a ruling that feeding and other measures might be lawfully discontinued. Sir Stephen Brown P so decided; the Court of Appeal upheld his decision, and the House of Lords confirmed that conclusion: *Airedale NHS Trust v Bland* [1993] AC 789.

   Lord Keith stated that it would be manslaughter if a person having charge of a child, or of an adult too frail to care for herself or himself, failed to feed that child or adult (at 858–9):

   > It is, of course, true that in general it would not be lawful for a medical practitioner who assumed responsibility for the care of an unconscious patient simply to give up treatment in circumstances where continuance of it would confer some benefit on the patient. On the other hand a medical practitioner is under no duty to continue to treat such a patient where a large body of informed and responsible medical opinion is to the effect that no

> benefit at all would be conferred by continuance. Existence in a vegetative state with no prospect of recovery is by that opinion regarded as not being a benefit, and that, if not unarguably correct, at least forms a proper basis for the decision to discontinue treatment and care: *Bolam v Friern Hospital Management Committee* [1957] 1 WLR 582.
>
> Given that existence in the persistent vegetative state is not a benefit to the patient, it remains to consider whether the principle of the sanctity of life, which it is the concern of the state, and the judiciary as one of the arms of the state, to maintain, requires this House to hold that the judgment of the Court of Appeal was incorrect. In my opinion it does not. The principle is not an absolute one. It does not compel a medical practitioner on pain of criminal sanctions to treat a patient, who will die if he does not, contrary to the express wishes of the patient. It does not authorise forcible feeding of prisoners on hunger strike. It does not compel the temporary keeping alive of patients who are terminally ill where to do so would merely prolong their suffering. On the other hand it forbids the taking of active measures to cut short the life of a terminally ill patient. In my judgment it does no violence to the principle to hold that it is lawful to cease to give medical treatment and care to a PVS patient who has been in that state for over three years, considering that to do so involves invasive manipulation of the patient's body to which he has not consented and which confers no benefit upon him.

The United States Supreme Court has taken a different approach to a similar fact situation. In 1993, Nancy Beth Curzon was involved in a car accident that left her in a PVS. A gastronomy tube had been implanted to allow for artificial feeding. After five years, the Curzon family requested that the feeding tube be removed, but the doctors refused to do so in the absence of a court order. At first instance, the Missouri trial court held that Nancy Curzon had a right to have the 'death prolonging' procedures removed. On appeal, the Supreme Court of Missouri reversed the decision, stating that permission for discontinuance of artificial feeding would only be given if there was convincing evidence that Curzon would have wanted to be allowed to die. The United States Supreme Court upheld the approach of the Supreme Court of Missouri: 497 S 261; 110 S Cr 2841 (1990). The majority held that medical treatment and artificial hydration and nutrition must be continued unless there is clear evidence the patient would not have wished to have been kept alive in those circumstances. Accordingly, the focus was on advance directives as to withdrawal of treatment, rather than the best interests of the patient. Six months after the decision, new witnesses testified as to Curzon's prior wishes that treatment should cease if she were in such circumstances, and the Missouri court then allowed her to die.

In Victoria, a similar approach to the House of Lords decision in *Bland* was adopted by Morris J in interpreting the provisions of the Medical Treatment Act 1988 (Vic); *Gardner; Re BWV* [2003] VSC 173. Morris J approved the removal of nutrition and hydration tubes as a removal of medical treatment of a patient who had not had any cortical activity and showed only reflex actions for the past three years. This decision views the supply of fluid and nutrition via tubes as medical treatment that is subject to the same process of consent or refusal as any other form of treatment. Rothschild describes the process of withdrawing artificial hydration and nutrition as 'passive, non-voluntary euthanasia' because in reality the patient dies from dehydration rather than the disease. See A Rothschild, '*Gardner; Re BWV*: Resolved and Unresolved Issues at End of Life' (2004) 11 JLM 292; D Mendelson and M Ashby, 'The Medical Provision of Hydration and Nutrition: Two Very Different Outcomes in Victoria and Florida' (2004) 11(3) *Journal of Law and Medicine* 282; I Freckelton, 'Withdrawal of Life Support: The Persistent Vegetative State Conundrum' (1993) 1(1) *Journal of Law and Medicine* 35; and E Geraghty 'What Price Uncertainty? The Persistent Vegetative State in New South Wales' (2002) 2 *Macquarie Law Journal* 185.

In the Criminal Codes of Queensland and Western Australia, specific provision is made to exempt from criminal responsibility those who act as the doctors in Bland's case acted: see s 282 of the Criminal Code (Qld), and s 259 of the Criminal Code (WA).

4. Commentators have queried the distinction in *Bland's* case between an omission to treat and active forms of non-voluntary euthanasia: see, for example, C Favour, 'Puzzling Cases about Killing and Letting Die' (1996) 1 *Res Publica: A Journal of Legal and Social Philosophy* 18; J Finnis, '*Bland*: Crossing the Rubicon?' (1993) 109 *Law Quarterly Review* 329. Lord Goff (at 865) pointed out that an omission was not the same as taking some positive step to bring life to an end, because 'the law does not feel able to authorize [active] euthanasia, even in circumstances such as these; for once euthanasia is recognized as lawful in these circumstances, it is difficult to see any logical basis for excluding it in others'. Lord Brown Wilkinson (at 879) posed the ethical question arising from *Bland's* case as follows:

   > Should society draw a distinction (which some would see as artificial) between adopting a course designed to produce certain death, on the one hand through lack of food, and on the other from a fatal injection, the former being permissible and the latter (euthanasia) prohibited?

5. The Consent to Medical Treatment and Palliative Care Act 1995 (SA) contains a novel section, as set out below:

   > **17 The care of people who are dying**
   >
   > (1) A medical practitioner responsible for the treatment or care of a patient in the terminal phase of a terminal illness, or a person participating in the treatment or care of the patient under the medical practitioner's supervision, incurs no civil or criminal liability by administering medical treatment with the intention of relieving pain or distress —

(a) with the consent of the patient or the patient's representative; and
(b) in good faith and without negligence; and
(c) in accordance with proper professional standards of palliative care, even though an incidental effect of the treatment is to hasten the death of the patient.

(2) A medical practitioner responsible for the treatment or care of a patient in the terminal phase of a terminal illness, or a person participating in the treatment or care of the patient under the medical practitioner's supervision, is, in the absence of an express direction by the patient or the patient's representative to the contrary, under no duty to use, or to continue to use, life sustaining measures in treating the patient if the effect of doing so would be merely to prolong life in a moribund state without any real prospect of recovery or in a persistent vegetative state.

(3) For the purposes of the law of the State —
(a) the administration of medical treatment for the relief of pain or distress in accordance with subsection (1) does not constitute an intervening cause of death; and
(a) the non-application or discontinuance of life sustaining measures in accordance with subsection (2) does not constitute an intervening cause of death.

Consider the application of this provision in a case such as *Bland.*

6.18 Further reading

H Biggs, 'Euthanasia and Death with Dignity: Still Poised on the Fulcrum of Homicide' [1996] *Crim LR* 878

P Crofts, *Wickedness and Crime*, 2013, Routledge, London, Ch 6

H Gamble, 'Manslaughter by Neglect' (1977) 1 *Crim LJ* 247

Culpable driving causing death

6.19 Experience has shown that juries are often reluctant to convict drivers of motor vehicles of manslaughter when they have caused a fatal accident, even though the case may appear plain. For this reason, the Victorian and New South Wales Parliaments have created statutory offences to cover driving that causes death. Section 318 of the Crimes Act 1958 (Vic) (as amended by the Crimes (Culpable Driving) Act 1992 (Vic)) provides:

(1) Any person who by the culpable driving of a motor vehicle causes the death of another person shall be guilty of an indictable offence and shall be liable to level 3 imprisonment (20 years maximum) or a level 3 fine or both.

(2) For the purposes of subsection (1) a person drives a motor vehicle culpably if he drives the motor vehicle —

(a) recklessly, that is to say, if he consciously and unjustifiably disregards a substantial risk that the death of another person or the infliction of grievous bodily harm upon another person may result from his driving; or

(b) negligently, that is to say, if he fails unjustifiably and to a gross degree to observe the standard of care which a reasonable man would have observed in all the circumstances of the case; or

(c) whilst under the influence of alcohol to such an extent as to be incapable of having proper control of the motor vehicle; or

(d) whilst under the influence of a drug to such an extent as to be incapable of having proper control of the motor vehicle.

(3) Without limiting subsection (2)(b), negligence within the meaning of that subsection may be established by proving that —

(a) a person drove a motor vehicle when fatigued to such an extent that he or she knew, or ought to have known, that there was an appreciable risk of him or her falling asleep while driving or of losing control of the vehicle; and

(b) by so driving the motor vehicle the person failed unjustifiably and to a gross degree to observe the standard of care which a reasonable person would have observed in all the circumstances of the case.

Note that the Victorian provision certainly covers nothing that would not at common law be manslaughter. Indeed, an accused who fell within s 318(2)(a) of the Victorian Act might, in theory at least, be liable to be convicted of murder. See generally, *Callaghan v R* (1952) 87 CLR 115. In *R v De' Zilwa* (2002) 5 VR 408 the Victorian Court of Appeal held that where a person is charged with culpable driving under s 318(2)(b), the judge should direct the jury that, in order to convict, the jury are required to find that the driving of the accused involved such a great falling short of the standard of care which a reasonable person would have exercised in the circumstances, and which involved such a high risk that death or 'serious injury would follow, that the driving causing death merits criminal punishment. The assimilation of the statutory provision in the common law of manslaughter may be said to be complete.

Cases where a lesser degree of culpability in driving leads to death, or where serious injury not resulting in death is caused, are covered by a lesser offence, of dangerous driving causing death or serious injury, introduced in 2008. Section 319 of the Crimes Act 1958 (Vic) provides:

(1) A person who, by driving a motor vehicle at a speed or in a manner that is dangerous to the public having regard to all the circumstances of the case, causes the death of another person is guilty of an indictable offence and liable to level 5 imprisonment (10 years maximum).

(1A)A person who, by driving a motor vehicle at a speed or in a manner that is dangerous to the public having regard to all the circumstances of the case, causes serious injury to another person is guilty of an indictable offence and liable to level 6 imprisonment (5 years maximum).

(2) In this section serious injury has the meaning given by section 15.

The equivalent provision in New South Wales is s 52A of the Crimes Act 1900 (NSW). Section 52A creates offences of dangerous driving occasioning death (10 years' imprisonment); aggravated dangerous driving occasioning death (14 years' imprisonment); dangerous driving occasioning grievous bodily harm (7 years' imprisonment); and aggravated dangerous driving occasioning grievous bodily harm (11 years' imprisonment).

The New South Wales offence under s 52A is a strict liability offence that does not require that the accused knowingly or intended to drive dangerously. The question of dangerousness is an objective question for the jury. Thus, in *R v Gillett* [2006] NSWCCA 370, the Court of Criminal Appeal held that when considering this issue it was irrelevant that the accused did not know that he was suffering from sleep apnoea, a condition that increased the risk of epileptic seizure which resulted in the fatal collision. This was an issue of mens rea, not actus reus. See generally, *McBride v R* (1966) 115 CLR 44; *R v Wilson* [1965] QWN 42; *R v Hain* (1966) 85 WN (Pt 1) (NSW) 7. In *Jiminez v R* (1992) 106 ALR 162 (discussed at 13.3C) the High Court held that the excuse of honest and reasonable mistake of fact is available. Accordingly, if a jury had decided that the driving was, in fact, dangerous, they had to go on to consider whether D might have honestly believed on reasonable grounds that it was safe for him to drive. There was little evidence to support a finding that Jiminez had felt sleepy or that he had reason to believe he was tired. He had not been driving for an excessive period before the accident, was not intoxicated, and had slept before starting on the trip. Thus, if a jury found that there was no warning of the onset of sleep, this would have been evidence that Jiminez honestly and reasonably believed that it was safe for him to drive. See J R Spencer, 'Motor Vehicles as Weapons of Offence' [1985] *Criminal Law Review* 29.

Industrial manslaughter

6.20 In *Power, Crime and Mystification*, Box (1983) estimates that, adjusting for the population at risk, seven times as many people die from occupational accidents or disease than from homicide. Very few of those deaths result in any form of prosecution, and if any charges are brought these are most likely to be pursued as health and safety offences, rather than the more serious manslaughter offence. It is difficult to obtain a clear picture of work related injuries and deaths. This is because, first, accidents at work are not always reported; second, those that are reported are not always subject to formal investigation and enforcement; third, it is not always suspected that ill health is a result of exposure to hazards at work; and fourth, it is not always to prove ill health is a result of exposure of hazards at work even if it is recognised as a probable cause. Work-related injuries and deaths are under-reported and differentially enforced in comparison with other offences.

6.21 There have been major industrial incidents in which employees of corporations carrying on their relevant enterprises have been killed. The Longford gas plant explosion in Victoria in 1998 resulted in the deaths of several workers. This led to the establishment of a Royal Commission and the successful prosecution of the corporation involved, on occupational safety charges.

One issue emerging from these incidents has been whether the corporation in question may be charged with manslaughter in respect of the deaths of employees, contractors, or members of the public. This would be in addition to, or in substitution for, charges which may be laid under occupational health and safety, environmental and local government legislation.

Corporations may be charged with manslaughter, and some have been successfully prosecuted in the United Kingdom and Australia: see J Clough and C Mulhern, *The Prosecution of Corporations*, Oxford University Press, Melbourne, 2002, pp 175–7. The cases have turned on the question of whether the acts and the omissions to act of the corporation's officers and employees may be attributed to the corporation: see **1.39**. There has been a judicial reluctance to countenance attribution to the corporation of that degree of negligence that merits criminal conviction and punishment. The corporation's employees, including senior officers, may be, and some have been, properly charged and convicted as a consequence of an incident. As with death by negligent driving, some legislatures have sought to respond to what has been identified as a social evil, by the enactment of specific legislation. The evil so identified has been the erosion of protection to the employees of corporations, through the most effective general and specific deterrence provided by the criminal law, because of the immunity of corporations in this connection.

6.22 In Victoria, the government introduced the Crimes (Workplace Deaths and Serious Injuries) Bill 2001, which failed to pass the Upper House. Clause 13 provides that a corporation that 'by negligence kills' an employee in the course of employment is guilty of manslaughter. The punishment is a fine not exceeding 50,000 penalty units, or $5,000,000. Clause 14 creates the new offence of the corporate infliction of serious injury through negligence; the maximum fine is 20,000 penalty units.

The novel aspect of the legislation is in cl 14A(2), which provides that 'the conduct of an employee, agent or senior officer of a body corporate acting within the actual scope of their employment, or within their actual authority, must be attributed to the body corporate'. 'Negligence' is defined in cl 14B, in terms derived from the leading cases: see **6.9–6.10** and **6.12–6.16**.

6.23 The Occupational Health and Safety Amendment (Workplace Safety) Act 2005 (NSW) creates the offence of reckless conduct causing death in a workplace by a person with occupational health and safety duties. The maximum penalty for a corporation is 15,000 penalty units, while an individual may be sentenced to five years' imprisonment or a fine of 1500 penalty units. Prosecutions under the Act may only be dealt with summarily before the Industrial Relations Commission.

6.24 Further reading

A Hopkins, 'A Culture of Denial: Sociological Similarities between the Moura and Gretley Mine Disasters' (2000) 16 *Journal of Occupational Health and Safety, Australia and New Zealand* 29

A Hopkins, H Easson and J Harrison, 'The Legal Response to Work-related Fatalities in NSW in 1984' (1992) *ANZ Journal of Criminology* 135

S Pemberton, 'A Theory of Moral Indifference: Understanding the Production of Harm by Capitalist Society' in P Hillyard et al, *Beyond Criminology: Taking Harm Seriously*, Pluto Press, 2004, Ch 5

INVOLUNTARY MANSLAUGHTER — A CRITIQUE

6.25 Where a person causes the death of another by the intentional infliction of bodily injury of a serious nature, he or she would be regarded as morally responsible for that death. It seems clearly correct that legal responsibility should follow. Now that battery manslaughter has been expunged as a category by the High Court's decision in *Wilson v R* (at **6.4C**), unlawful and dangerous act manslaughter alone remains, recognised and reconfirmed in that same landmark decision.

6.26 Now that it has been finally settled that negligent manslaughter is an objective head of liability, a question arises as to the relationship between unlawful and dangerous act manslaughter and negligent manslaughter. The quantum of harm which must have been at risk is different. In order to establish manslaughter by unlawful and dangerous act, the prosecution must prove a reasonable person would have recognised 'an appreciable risk of serious injury' (*Wilson*). In contrast, for manslaughter by criminal negligence, the prosecution must prove a 'high risk of death or grievous bodily harm' (*Nydam*). The question is whether this difference is sufficient to justify the two categories of manslaughter, or whether they should be merged. It is carefully considered in the Law Reform Commission of Victoria's Report No 40, *Homicide* (1991) at pp 112–17. The commission's recommendation is that the two categories be replaced by one, where the test of criminal responsibility will be: Did the defendant do an act in a gross breach of the duty of care, which a reasonable person in the circumstances would have realised exposed another to a substantial and unjustifiable risk of a life-endangering injury? This would remove the category of unlawful and dangerous act, based on the idea that whether or not an accused was committing an unlawful act may be unconnected with his or her blameworthiness. However, the objective standard specified in *Wilson*, that an accused's act was dangerous, provides a parameter that justifies criminalisation. What then of negligent manslaughter? Does negligence constitute an acceptable basis for the imputation of serious criminal responsibility? The doctrine of negligent manslaughter is now firmly established as objective in nature (*R v Lavender* (at **6.10C**)). In this form it has been strongly criticised by some commentators. One of its earliest and most influential critics was Dr J W C Turner, who was for many years the editor of *Russell on Crime* and *Kenny's Outlines of Criminal Law*: see, in particular, 'The Mental Element in Crimes at Common Law' in L Radzinowicz and J W C Turner, *The Modern Approach to Criminal Law*, Macmillan and Co, London, 1945, p 195.

6.27 Dr Turner argued that it was unjust to punish an accused for consequences which he or she neither intended nor foresaw. Dr Turner further argued that the concept of degrees of negligence, which was the basis of the House of Lords decision in *Andrews v DPP*, was nonsensical. Negligence is, argued Dr Turner, a negative state of mind that is a failure to advert possible consequences. There logically cannot, the argument proceeded, be degrees of inadvertence.

6.28 Some commentators have also criticised the doctrine: note, in particular, G Williams, *Textbook of Criminal Law*, 2nd ed, Stevens and Sons, London, 1983, Ch 12. In its Fourth Report, *The Substantive Criminal Law*, the Criminal Law and Penal Methods Reform Committee of South Australia recommended abolition of the doctrine. The committee stated (at para 18):

> [W]e have emphasised throughout our adherence to the principle that the defendant should be judged on the facts as the jury believe that he saw them. It is a logical consequence of this line of thought that no-one should be convicted of criminal homicide for a death which he did not foresee. By contrast, the present law of involuntary manslaughter justifies conviction on the basis that a reasonable man in the position of the defendant would have foreseen death, or alternatively that the defendant possessed an intention to inflict some lesser degree of harm, or committed an unlawful and dangerous act. It may be that such an approach to criminal liability is justifiable by reference to practical factors where relatively minor offences are concerned. A burden of proof upon the prosecution of intention or recklessness may be out of proportion to the gravity of the offence charged. Such an argument has no application to so serious an offence as manslaughter. … We therefore recommend abolition of the law relating to involuntary manslaughter.

6.29 In spite of the eminence of these critics of the doctrine of negligent manslaughter, it is submitted that negligence of a sufficiently high degree does constitute an acceptable basis for the imputation of serious criminal liability. The concept of negligence in the criminal law was analysed at 1.28–1.31. It was there argued that the fallacy in the line of argument adopted by Dr Turner is its assumption that to say that a person was negligent is equivalent to saying that he or she did not advert to the possibility of harm. To say that a person was negligent in reality involves a statement that that person failed to measure up to a standard of conduct which any ordinary reasonable person could and would have complied with. There can thus be degrees of negligence. Negligence can be said to be gross 'if the precautions to be taken against harm are very simple, such as persons who are but poorly endowed with physical and mental capacities can easily take': see 1.29.

6.30 This analysis also meets the objection that there is necessarily something unjust about punishing an accused in cases where his or her mind was a blank as to the possible consequences of the actions in question. We commonly in everyday life impute moral responsibility to people who have failed to foresee consequences which they could have foreseen and avoided. There is no good reason why such form of blameworthiness should not constitute a basis for the imputation of criminal responsibility. This is clearly the view of the Law Reform Commission of Victoria in its Report No 40, *Homicide* (1991), pp 115–16.

6.31 Negligent manslaughter is thus seen as an objective head of liability, but of such a nature that it does not operate unjustly against an accused. The courts have used various adjectives to stress the very high degree of negligence which must have been present for the accused to be guilty of manslaughter. In *R v Bateman* (1925) 19 Cr App R 8, Lord Hewart CJ listed 'culpable', 'criminal', 'gross', 'wicked', 'clear' and 'complete', but attached no particular importance to any of them. In *Andrews v DPP* Lord Atkin suggested 'reckless' was the most suitable adjective. Whatever the adjective used, the substance of the distinction between this degree of negligence and ordinary civil negligence appears to be that, for a person to be guilty of negligent manslaughter, the conduct in question must have fallen so far below an acceptable standard of care as to amount to moral culpability on his or her part. In *R v Bateman* Lord Hewart CJ stated (at 11–12):

> To support an indictment for manslaughter the prosecution must prove the matters necessary to establish civil liability (except pecuniary loss), and, in addition, must satisfy the jury that the negligence or incompetence of the accused went beyond a mere matter of compensation and showed such disregard for the life and safety of others as to amount to a crime against the state and conduct deserving punishment.

In *Nydam v R* (at 6.9C) the Full Court of the Supreme Court of Victoria used similar language. The court stated:

> In order to establish manslaughter by criminal negligence, it is sufficient if the prosecution shows that the act which caused the death was done by the accused consciously and voluntarily, without any intention of causing death or grievous bodily harm but in circumstances which involved such a great falling short of the standard of care which a reasonable man would have exercised and which involved such a high risk that death or grievous bodily harm would follow that the doing of the act merited criminal punishment.

The effect of these judgments is clearly to limit the scope of negligent manslaughter to cases in which the accused's negligence has been of such a degree as to render that person morally culpable in respect of the deceased's death. When limited in this way, there seems no sound reason of principle why negligence cannot properly serve as a basis of criminal liability, even in respect of a crime as serious as manslaughter.

6.32 Dr Crofts has recently argued in favour of the offence of manslaughter by criminal negligence: *Wickedness and Crime*, Routledge, London, 2013. Crofts argues that the criminal justice system is one of many social discourses that organises and expresses morality, in particular, what it means to be sufficiently bad to be worthy of criminal sanctions. Her book focuses on how the law communicates what it means to be blameworthy. Crofts argues that contemporary criminal law presents itself as focused on subjective blameworthiness; that is, whether or not the accused had the necessary mens rea for an offence. However, by drawing on philosophies of wickedness and historical legal doctrine, Crofts argues that negligence can and should be regarded as a legitimate basis for legal culpability. This is based on a classic account of wickedness as a lack or dearth of goodness, balance or care. In criminal negligence, it is the failure to care for a thing or value that society states we (should) care about that is wicked. This is a combination of a subjective evaluation (whether or not the accused cared) and an objective evaluation (what we should care about). Criminal law is an important public discourse for the organisation and expression of social values and emotions; for making choices between different goods and values. It offers an opportunity and a responsibility for the expression of what we do and should care about. On this account, the relationship of law and morality is not that of enforcement or mutual exclusivity, but is more complex. Law and morality are mutually constitutive. Attributions of blameworthiness in criminal law communicate, shape and reflect moral values. It is appropriate and necessary that the law requires that we exercise care for human life.

Property Offences: New South Wales

CHAPTER 7

INTRODUCTION

7.1 In Australia, three quite different sets of legal rules govern offences against property. New South Wales retains the common law. Queensland, Western Australia and Tasmania have Codes which were enacted in the period from 1899 to 1924. Victoria, South Australia and the Australian Capital Territory have provisions based upon the English Theft Act 1968. Similar provisions are contained in the Northern Territory Code.

7.2 In this chapter, the law as it exists in New South Wales will be dealt with. In Chapter 8, the legislation in force in Victoria will be considered. The Code jurisdictions are beyond the scope of the present work. The law relating to property offences in New South Wales is complex and highly technical. New South Wales retains a combination of very old common law offences overlaid with more recent common law and statutory offences created piecemeal to cover gaps that older offences were not filling. New South Wales is the only Australia jurisdiction to still rely on larceny.

7.3 The core offence of property offences, larceny, is a common law offence with elements based on Australian and English case law some of which date back to the Middle Ages. It is important to see these offences in their historical context as this has an impact on the shape of contemporary property offences.

A BRIEF HISTORY

7.4 The history of property offences can be understood as starting with the simple needs of feudal societies to expanding to respond to the needs of more complex industrial societies. George Fletcher has provided a lovely explanation for the shape and complexity of property offences. In *Rethinking Criminal Law* (1978), Fletcher asserts that criminal liability can be understood as shaped and guided by patterns of blameworthiness. He articulates three major patterns of blameworthiness: manifest criminality, subjective culpability and harmful consequences. Manifest criminality is based on the notion that an act that threatens the peace and order of community life should be penalised. A central aspect of the concept of this pattern of blameworthiness is that criminality is manifest; that is, it can be seen. The pattern of subjective culpability focuses on the state of mind of the accused — in terms of criminal law, whether or not the accused has the necessary mens rea. This pattern of blameworthiness is dominant in contemporary criminal law. The third pattern, that of harmful consequences, criminalises behaviour on the basis of the harm done. A classic example of offences informed by this pattern of blameworthiness is homicide.

Fletcher argues that the early offence of larceny was based on the pattern of blameworthiness of manifest criminality. Criminalisation was informed by the collective image of acting like a thief. Early understandings of theft were based upon a single image of the thief coming at night, endangering the security of the home. A characteristic form of conduct came to be associated with the act of thieving: thieves could be seen thieving; they could be caught in the act. In addition, manifest criminality in the offence of larceny required the thief to tread on a significant boundary and enter a forbidden area. However, with the industrial revolution, this pattern of blameworthiness no longer served the needs of the community. People no longer knew everyone in their community. They traded with strangers who they might never see again. While these strangers may look trustworthy, they could use trickery and fraud to take advantage of them. In order to be successful in taking property away, these strangers could not look like thieves; that is, they were not manifestly criminal — their conduct might be criminal even though they appeared to be innocent. In response, property offences gradually transformed away from manifest criminality to subjective culpability. Attributions of blameworthiness were no longer to be based on how the accused acted or appeared, but upon the accused's culpable intent. Rather than overturn older cases that had been based on manifest criminality, judges reinterpreted them, asserting that they had been decided on the basis of a focus on felonious intent. This reinterpretation of older cases accounts in part for the complexity of contemporary property law. This theoretical analysis provides a frame to the legal history and contemporary structure of property offences.

7.5 The basic property offence at common law was larceny. The crime of larceny developed in the Middle Ages and was, accordingly, in origin a simple crime designed to meet the needs of a primarily agricultural society. It consisted of the felonious taking and carrying away of the personal goods of another. It was a crime against possession, and thus one of its elements was a 'trespass'; that is, a taking without the consent of the person in possession. Therefore, if a person was given goods by another, however fraudulent the intent of the receiver, that person could not be guilty of larceny.

7.6 The first major change in the law was made by *Carrier's Case* (1473) Y B Pash, 13 Edw IV, f 9, pl 5. The accused was hired to carry certain bales to Southampton. Instead of fulfilling his obligation, he carried the goods to another place, broke open the bales and took the contents. He was apprehended and charged with felony. On the then existing state of the law, the accused clearly was not guilty of larceny. The goods had been delivered to him and thus there was no trespassory taking. However, the position was complicated by virtue of the fact that the King (Edward IV) possessed a twofold interest in the case. First, the owner of the goods was a foreign merchant who had come to England with the King's safe conduct; and, second, the goods, if stolen, were possibly waif and therefore forfeited to the King. The case was considered by the judges on two occasions, first in the Star Chamber and later in the Exchequer Chamber. The accused was finally held guilty of felony by a majority of the judges. The King's right to waif, however, was denied. Although the majority could not concur on a rationale for holding the accused guilty, Choke J's reasoning came to be accepted as the ratio of the case. Choke J argued that although the bales had been given to the accused, their contents had not. Therefore, when the accused broke open the bales and abstracted their contents he became guilty of larceny. *Carrier's Case* came to be taken as settling the rule that a bailee who 'broke bulk' and abstracted the contents of a package bailed to him was guilty of larceny. This form of larceny became known as 'larceny as a bailee'. In cases in which there was no breaking of bulk, there remained no larceny. This latter rule endured until 1857 when it was changed by statute: 20 and 21 Vic c 54.

7.7 In the fourteenth and fifteenth centuries, there was considerable controversy as to whether servants could be guilty of larceny where they misappropriated property placed in their care by their masters. The rule requiring a trespassory taking appeared to preclude liability in such cases. However, after some vacillation, the argument was accepted that servants entrusted with their masters' goods did not obtain possession of the goods but merely custody, possession remaining in the masters: Y B Hil 21 H 7, f 14, pl 21. Thus when servants appropriated their masters' goods, they could be guilty of larceny. The matter was settled in 1529 when Parliament intervened with a statute declaring that it was felony for a servant, to whom goods had been entrusted by the master to keep, to make off with them with intent to steal or 'imbezil' them or otherwise convert them to the servant's own use, if the goods were of a value of 40 shillings or more: 21 Hen VIII, c 7.

7.8 Throughout the sixteenth, seventeenth and early eighteenth centuries, the criminal law continued its failure to respond to the conduct of cheats and confidence tricksters who induced their victims to part with money or goods by means of deception and false pretences. Such conduct may have been tortious but, except in the rarest of circumstances, it was not criminal. If the owners gave over their money or goods voluntarily, the fact that they had been induced to do so by the deceit of the other could not alter the fact of delivery. There was no trespass and hence no felony. The policy of the criminal law during this period may be summed up as embodying the principle that while the law ought to protect people against forcible deprivations of their property, they ought to protect themselves against breaches of trust and deception. In 1703, when quashing a novel indictment, Holt CJ felt able to ask rhetorically: 'Shall we indict one man for making a fool of another?': *R v Jones* (1703) 2 Ld Raym 1013; 92 ER 174.

7.9 It was in the second-half of the eighteenth century that the common law came to assume its modern form. By this time England had been transformed into a busy commercial society in relation to which older notions concerning the proper scope of the law relating to property offences were clearly no longer adequate. In 1757, Parliament enacted legislation (30 Geo II, c 24) which provided that:

> … all persons who knowingly or designedly, by false pretence or pretences, shall obtain from any person or persons, money, goods, wares or merchandises, with intent to cheat or defraud any person or persons of the same … shall be deemed offenders …

However, this seemingly comprehensive false pretences provision was narrowly construed by the courts for a considerable period after the date of its enactment. Not until 1789 was this approach reversed, and full effect given to the plain words of the statute, a process discussed in detail in the following paragraphs.

7.10 In 1779, a new form of larceny ('larceny by a trick' as it came to be known) was established as a result of the decision of the Court for Crown Cases Reserved in *R v Pear* (1779) 2 East *PC* 685. The accused was indicted for stealing a horse. He had hired the horse from a man in London, telling him that he wanted to go to Sutton for the day and would return the same evening. In fact, he sold the horse in London. The jury found that the proposed journey had been a pretence by the accused who intended to sell the horse all along. The question referred to the judges was whether, in the circumstances, the accused had committed larceny, or whether his conduct was a mere 'breach of trust' attracting no criminal sanction. The judges differed among themselves, seven holding the accused to be guilty of larceny, two holding to the contrary, and two delivering judgments which were equivocal. The reasoning of the majority was that the accused's secret fraudulent intention had negatived any bona fide contract of bailment. Thus the accused's taking had been trespassory and, because of his fraudulent intention, had amounted to larceny.

7.11 The decision in *Pear's* case was also significant in terms of the construction it caused to be placed on the false pretences statute of 1757. Counsel for the accused had submitted that the whole transaction fell within the ambit of the 1757 Act, and thus constituted a statutory misdemeanour rather than the felony of larceny. Had the court accepted this submission, the result would have been complete acquittal for the accused, as at this time there was no provision for an alternative verdict. The court, however, chose to construe the 1757 Act narrowly, as though it merely reiterated the terms of an earlier Act of 1541, holding that it was 'confined to cases where credit was obtained in the name of the third person; and did not extend to cases where a man on his own account got goods with an intention to steal them': 2 East *PC* 689. The 1757 Act was construed as being wider in scope than the 1541 Act only to the extent that it permitted the means of deception to be other than by 'token or counterfeit letter'. In other words, any type of false pretence would be adequate, provided however that the goods or money were obtained in the name of another person.

7.12 This aspect of the reasoning in *Pear's* case did not long survive. In *Young v R* (1789) 3 TR 98; 100 ER 475, the accused falsely represented to the prosecutor that a race was to be run on which they had placed bets. They persuaded him to hand them money to be used for betting, and then made off with it. The Court of King's Bench held that this was a misdemeanour within the 1757 Act, although the accused had obtained the money on their own account. It followed that *Pear's* case could no longer be held to lie outside the false pretences statute on the ground that the horse had been obtained by the accused purely on his own account. Some other basis had to be found for distinguishing between larceny by a trick and obtaining by false pretences.

7.13 Two cases decided shortly after *Pear's* case provided the criterion for distinguishing larceny by a trick from obtaining by false pretences which was eventually adopted. In *R v Patch* (1782) 2 East *PC* 678, the accused and two others joined the prosecutor in a street in London and, after walking a short way, one of them pretended to find a valuable diamond ring. In fact the ring was worthless, but the prosecutor was persuaded by the accused to keep it on all their behalfs, and to give them his watch and money as security. At his trial for larceny, it was submitted that the conduct of the accused and his accomplices was mere fraud, but he was convicted of the felony because 'the possession was obtained by fraud, and the property was not altered; for the prosecutor was to have it again': at 679. In *R v Moore* (1784) 2 East *PC* 679 an accused was convicted of larceny on the authority of *Pear's* case because the money in question was delivered as security only 'so that though the possession was parted with, the property was not': at 680.

7.14 These judicial statements appear to stem from certain dicta of Baron Eyre in *Pear's* case, who alone of all the judges in that case suggested a wider view of the 1757 statute, and distinguished it from larceny by a trick by the device of considering whether the accused obtained title or mere possession of the goods in question. *Pear's* case is inadequately reported, and certainly cannot be said to have created the distinction between larceny by a trick and obtaining by false pretences. However, by 1803, East was able to write that it had become clear that the distinction between obtaining by false pretences and larceny by a trick was 'whether or not the owner deceived by appearances intended to part with the absolute *property*, and not barely with the *possession* or *temporary use* of the thing at the time of the delivery': 2 East *PC* 816.

7.15 Ten years after *Young's* case, the decision in *R v Bazely* (1799) 2 Leach 835; 168 ER 517 drew attention to another defect in the law. The accused was a cashier in a bank. A customer paid him £137 for deposit in his account, the money including a £100 note. The accused put the £137 in the appropriate drawers, but immediately appropriated the £100 note. It was held by the Court for Crown Cases Reserved that the accused could not be convicted of larceny of the £100 note. He had not stolen from the customer, since the customer had voluntarily parted with possession of the note. Nor had he stolen from his employers since, because he had immediately placed the note in his pocket, the money never came into their possession. Arguably, the accused was a bailee for the note. However, at that time larceny as a bailee could only be committed where there was a breaking of bulk. In response to *Bazely's* case, the English legislature enacted the first general embezzlement statute (39 Geo III, c 85), which provided:

> … if any servant or clerk, or any person employed for the purpose in the capacity of a servant or clerk, to any person or persons whomsoever, or to any body corporate or politick, shall, by virtue of such employment, receive or take into his possession any money, goods, bond, bill, note, bankers draft, or other valuable security, or effects, for or in the name or on the account of his master or masters, or employer or employers, and shall fraudulently embezzle, secrete, or make away with the same, or any part thereof, every such offender shall be deemed to have feloniously stolen the same.

This statute was soon shown to be inadequate in that it applied only to servants and clerks. Accordingly, throughout the nineteenth century, a series of embezzlement statutes were passed dealing with persons in special positions such as factors, bankers and stockbrokers.

7.16 Throughout the period under consideration, the crimes of robbery and burglary co-existed with those offences already discussed. The crime of robbery, consisting of larceny accompanied by the use or threatened use of violence, is of ancient origin dating back at least to the reign of Henry II. Burglary is also a crime of ancient origin. The requirement that burglary be committed at night, however, and the development of the independent misdemeanour of housebreaking in relation to breakings committed during the day, appear to date only from the sixteenth century.

7.17 Other crimes related to larceny received their modern form in the period from the mid-eighteenth to the mid-nineteenth century. The earliest statutory offence of blackmail is contained in the Waltham Black Act of 1722. That Act was of comparatively limited operation, however, applying only to demands made in writing and containing threats of violence to the person or to property. Offences of extortion were further dealt with in statutes passed between 1757 and 1827.

7.18 Statutes penalising receivers of stolen property date back to 1692, when Parliament enacted that any person receiving goods feloniously taken or stolen from another person, knowing the same to be stolen, shall be taken and deemed an accessory to such felony after the fact: 3 and 4 W & M, c 9, s 4. This legislation was defective in that its effect was to deem a receiver to be an accessory to the thief. This meant that the prosecution of the receiver was dependent upon the prior conviction of the thief. By a series of eighteenth century statutes, efforts were made to extend the reach of the law in relation to receivers. Not until the consolidating Act of 1827, however, was receiving stolen property made a felony in its own right, as distinct from the statutory misdemeanour it had been since 1692.

7.19 In the course of the nineteenth century, the ambit of the crime of larceny was extended somewhat by judicial decision. A series of four decisions of the Court for

Crown Cases Reserved marked the last major judicial extension of the law in this field. In *R v Thurborn* (1849) 1 Den 387; 169 ER 293 (at 6.36), the court held that a finder of lost property could, despite the apparent absence of a trespass, be guilty of larceny if, at the time of taking possession of the property, the finder believed that the true owner could be found and the finder at that time possessed a fraudulent intent to appropriate the property. In *R v Riley* (1853) 1 Dears CC 149; 169 ER 674 (at 7.78), the court held that a taking without fraudulent intent followed by a fraudulent appropriation could constitute larceny, provided the original taking was trespassory. This decision involved a departure from the normal rule that, for larceny to be committed, the accused must possess a fraudulent intent at the time of the taking. In *R v Middleton* (1873) LR 2 CCR 38 (at 7.57) and *R v Ashwell* (1885) 16 QBD 190 (at 7.58), the court held that an accused who dishonestly converts property given to her or him as a result of a mistake on the part of the owner might, in certain cases, be guilty of larceny notwithstanding that, in such situations, there is clearly no taking which could be described as trespassory.

7.20 The statutes relating to larceny and allied crimes were consolidated and amended by the Acts of 1827 (7 and 8 Geo IV, c 29) and 1861 (24 and 25 Vict, c 96). A new statutory misdemeanour, fraudulent conversion, was added to the 1861 Act by s 1 of the Larceny Act 1901 (UK). This new crime consisted of the fraudulent conversion of property entrusted to the accused, or received by the accused for, or on account of, any other person. All the offences considered thus far could be committed only where the accused took or converted property the legal title to which was in some person other than the accused. The misdemeanour of fraudulent conversion, however, could be committed where the accused obtained legal title to the property received, but converted that property in circumstances which involved breach of a fiduciary obligation.

7.21 In 1916, the then existing law of larceny and related offences was codified by the Larceny Act of that year. That Act introduced, for the first time, a statutory definition of larceny. The Act did not purport to make any change in the then existing law of larceny and related offences. It was, rather, a consolidation of the existing common law and statute law. The Larceny Act 1916 (UK) remained in force until the coming into operation of the Theft Act 1968 (UK).

7.22 No codification of the law similar to the Larceny Act 1916 (UK) was carried out in New South Wales. The position is similar to that which existed in England prior to the passing of that Act. The basic offence of larceny remains undefined by statute. Nonetheless, there are a great number of statutory provisions relating to larceny and allied crimes. These provisions are to be found in Pt IV of the Crimes Act 1900 (NSW) (as amended) ss 93J–249J. In 2010, the law relating to offences of dishonest acquisition involving deception was replaced with a general fraud offence (s 192E), with key terms defined in ss 192BB–192D.

7.23 Further reading

G Fletcher, *Rethinking Criminal Law*, Little, Brown and Company, Boston, 1978, pp 1–113

—, 'The Metamorphosis of Larceny' (1976) 89(3) *Harvard Law Review* 469

J Hall, *Theft, Law and Society*, 2nd ed, Bobbs-Merrill, Indianapolis, 1952, pp 3–152

C R Williams, *Property Offences*, 3rd ed, Law Book Co, Sydney, 1999

SIMPLE LARCENY AND LARCENY AS A BAILEE

Introduction

7.24E Crimes Act 1900 (NSW)

117 Punishment for larceny

Whosoever commits larceny, or any indictable offence by this Act made punishable like larceny, shall, except in the cases hereinafter otherwise provided for, be liable to imprisonment for five years.

125 Larceny by bailee

Whosoever, being a bailee of any property, fraudulently takes, or converts, the same, or any part thereof, or any property into or for which it has been converted, or exchanged, to his or her own use, or the use of any person other than the owner thereof, although he or she does not break bulk, or otherwise determine the bailment, shall be deemed to be guilty of larceny and liable to be indicted for that offence.

The accused shall be taken to be a bailee within the meaning of this section, although he or she may not have contracted to restore, or deliver, the specific property received by him or her, or may only have contracted to restore, or deliver, the property specifically.

7.25 The Crimes Act 1900 (NSW) contains no definition of simple larceny. A definition was, however, contained in the Larceny Act 1916 (UK), now repealed by the Theft Act 1968 (UK). That Act was intended as a codification of the then existent law, and the definition of larceny contained in it may be accepted as an adequate description of common law larceny. Section 1(1) provided:

> A person steals who, without the consent of the owner, fraudulently and without a claim of right made in good faith, takes and carries away anything capable of being stolen with intent, at the time of such taking, permanently to deprive the owner thereof.

In *Ilich v R* (1987) 162 CLR 110 at 123, Wilson and Dawson JJ summarised the elements of larceny:

> At common law, larceny is committed by a person who, without the consent of the owner, fraudulently and without a claim of right made in good faith, takes and carries away anything capable of being stolen with intent, at the time of such taking, permanently to deprive the owner thereof … Because larceny at common law requires a trespass — it is sometimes described as an offence against possession — a person lawfully in possession of something cannot be guilty of larceny of it.

Elements of the crime

7.26 According to *Ilich v R* (1987) 162 CLR 110, the elements of larceny are:

(1) *Actus reus:* That the accused:

- (a) took and carried away;
- (b) property capable of being stolen;
- (c) in the possession of another; and
- (d) without the consent of the owner.

(2) *Mens rea:* That, at the time of taking, D acted:

- (a) with the intention of permanently depriving the owner;
- (b) without a claim of right; and
- (c) fraudulently.

7.27 Note that the protection of s 125 extends not only to the property originally bailed, but also to any property into or for which it has been converted or exchanged. For discussion of the significance of this extension, see *Slattery v R* (1905) 2 CLR 546; *R v Wall* (1932) 32 SR (NSW) 171.

7.28 Bailment is defined by Pollock and Wright in *Possession in the Common Law*, Clarendon Press, Oxford, 1888, p 163, as follows:

> [I]n general any person is to be considered as a bailee who otherwise than as a servant either receives possession of a thing from another or consents to receive or hold possession of a thing for another upon an undertaking with the other person either to keep and return or deliver to him the specific thing or to (convey and) apply the specific thing according to the directions antecedent or future of the other person.

7.29 The concept of bailment covers a wide variety of transactions, both commercial and non-commercial. A bailment will exist in the following circumstances:

(1) where goods are lent to another for that other's benefit;

(2) where goods are delivered to another who is to hold them or deal with them for the benefit of the bailor;

(3) where goods are delivered to another for carriage, either for reward or gratuitously;

(4) where goods are leased, either by way of simple lease or hire–purchase; and

(5) where goods are pawned or pledged.

7.30 These examples are not exhaustive, but merely illustrations of the more common forms of bailment. The essential element common to all forms of bailment is that possession of the bailed goods is transferred to the bailee while property or ownership remains in the bailor.

7.31 Note that a servant who fraudulently appropriates the master's property is guilty not of larceny as a bailee but of simple larceny. This is because the servant is not a bailee of the master's property as he or she does not have possession but merely custody: see **7.7**. Note Crimes Act 1900 (NSW) ss 156, 159.

Actus reus

The requirement of a taking and carrying away

7.32 The prosecution must prove that the accused took and carried away the property. This requirement is also known as asportation. There must be some physical movement of the property. The slightest movement will satisfy the requirement of 'carrying away', but there must be some movement. In *R v Lapier* (1784) 168 ER 263; [1784] Eng R 69, the offender tried to steal an earring, and moved it to the point where the earring became entangled in the owner's hair. It was held that this was sufficient asportation.

7.33 The issue of asportation was also considered in *Wallis v Lane* [1964] VR 293. The accused was making deliveries of boxes to one of his employer's clients. One of the boxes, which contained bicycle toe clips, was opened. The accused moved two pairs of toe clips from the box and left them on the tray of the truck while he delivered the rest of the boxes to the client. The accused was caught whilst in the midst of the delivery. His conviction was upheld by Herring CJ who noted (at 295):

> It would appear that any movement of goods with an intent to steal them is sufficient to constitute asportation ... it is sufficient asportation if there is a removal of the property from the spot where it was originally placed with an intent to steal.

Property capable of being stolen

7.34 The prosecution must prove that the property was capable of being stolen. The forms of property that can be stolen have developed over time. Property is defined in s 4 of the Crimes Act 1900 (NSW):

> 'Property' includes every description of real and personal property; money, valuable securities, debts and legacies; and all deeds and instruments relating to, or evidencing the title or right to any property, or giving a right to recover or receive any money or goods; and includes not only property originally in the possession or under control of any person, but also any property into or for which the same may have been converted or exchanged, and everything acquired by such conversion or exchange, whether immediately or otherwise.

Larceny can be committed against real and tangible property. The property must be of some value; even the slightest value will be sufficient: *R v Perry* (1845) 174 ER 1008. A piece of paper is of sufficient value: *R v Daley* (1879) 12 SCR (NSW).

There are complexities with regard to some types of property, some of which will be considered below.

7.35 Land Misappropriation of land cannot be the subject of larceny (but it can be, and often is, the subject of fraud). Ostensibly, land cannot be the subject of larceny because it cannot be taken and carried away. Historically, other reasons were given for not regarding land as capable of being stolen. William Blackstone stated that taking another's field was a civil injury, not a crime (*Commentaries on the Laws of England*, 1st ed, Book IV, Dawsons of Pall Mall Reprint, 1966, p 5). In New South Wales, those who removed fences, dispossessed those with title, or squatted on land could not be charged with larceny. Indeed, in the 1830s, much of New South Wales was originally occupied by graziers who 'squatted' illegally, extending beyond the 'Limits of Location' established by Governor Darling. The squatters were later legitimated by the issue of grazing licences and leases (C J King, *An Outline of Closer Settlement in New South Wales*, 1957, Vol 1).

The issue of land 'theft' is particularly important in Australia, given that British colonisation of the continent involved the forced taking of land from Indigenous peoples. In *Mabo v Queensland (No 2)* (1992) 175 CLR 1, the High Court held that the fiction of terra nullius could not be used to justify the dispossession of Indigenous peoples of their lands. Nevertheless, the common law concept of native title recognised in *Mabo* is a legal validation of the 'theft'. This has been explained by Luke McNamara and Scott Grattan in 'The Recognition of Indigenous Land Rights As "Native Title": Continuity and Transformation' (1999) 3 *Flinders Journal of Law Reform* 137 at 149:

> Native title is both the product of the High Court's moral condemnation of the racism of colonial land theft across Australia's history, and a key component (along with the unshakeable bedrock of Crown sovereignty) in the legal technology for legitimating much of that very same practice … Native title is defined by its contradictory attributes because it the product of a judicial (and more recently, legislative) attempt to achieve two incompatible objectives: one, a 'makeover' for Australia's colonial legal history with respect to the denial of Indigenous land rights; and, two, the perpetuation of the colonial project, including the protection of the political institutions and the economic interests which this project has produced. The result of the simultaneous pursuit of these two objectives is the concept of native title.

7.36 Tangible property The property must be tangible, so it has been held not to include information: *R v Lloyd* [1985] 3 WLR 30, but does include gas: *R v White* (1853) 169 ER 696. Choses in action cannot be stolen. While it is possible to steal paper money, it is not possible to be guilty of the offence of larceny for illegally removing money from a bank account. This is because the money in that bank does not exist as a physical possession, but is merely a chose in action; that is, a debt owed by the bank to the original owner of that account. This issue was considered by the High Court in the case of *Croton v R* (1967) 117 CLR 326 (extracted at 7.49C).

7.37 Fungibles Fungibles are objects that are interchangeable; for example, money, eggs, sugar etc. In everyday life, we treat these goods as interchangeable. Thus if someone borrows some money, we would not expect to see the same notes back. We are happy to receive the equivalent in value in return and accept this. However, the law does not treat fungibles in the same way. The law focuses on the particular notes, coins, sugar, chairs etc as unique. The focus is on the specific object, rather than any objective equivalence.

This has implications in terms of the mens rea and actus reus of larceny. In relation to mens rea, if D borrows $20 from V, with the intention of repaying V later in the week the equivalent of $20 in different notes, the law would characterise this as an intention to permanently deprive V of that specific $20 note: *Cockburn* [1968] 1 All ER 466.

In terms of the actus reus, if V has handed over a fungible it is highly unlikely that D intended to hand over physical possession and ownership. Historically, the common law has not protected victims who handed over ownership of property with consent, even if that consent was due to trickery: *R v Ilich* (1987) 162 CLR 110. This means that D could not be guilty of larceny by trick or larceny by a bailee, but can be guilty under new statutory fraud offences.

In the possession of another

7.38 Larceny was historically conceived as an offence against possession, but has extended to ownership and control. Property may simultaneously belong to more than one person, as ownership, possession and control are not mutually exclusive: *Anic v R* (1993) 68 A Crim R 313. Thus property can be stolen from more than one person, even if the person is in possession or control. The concept of possession will be outlined first, followed by control and ownership.

7.39 Possession The ordinary meaning of possession is 'one has in one's possession whatever it is, to one's knowledge, physically in one's custody or under one's physical control': *DPP v Brooks* [1974] 2 WLR 899; AC 862 at 866.

Actual possession is where one person has physical custody of the property or has it in such a place that he or she has the right or power to place his or her hands upon it and take custody of it: *R v Dib* (1991) 52 A Crim R 64.

7.40 There is no requirement that the person in possession is aware of the property. In *Hibbert v McKiernan* [1948] 2 KB 142; 1 All ER 860, D trespassed on the links of a private golf club and took a number of 'lost' balls, and, when questioned, stated that he knew he had no right to them. Held, larceny, despite the justices' finding that the original owners had abandoned the balls:

> … every householder or occupier of land means or intends to exclude thieves and wrongdoers from the property occupied by him, and this confers on him a special property in goods found on his land sufficient to support an indictment if the goods are taken therefrom, not under a claim of right, but with a felonious intent.

7.41 A person may be in possession not withstanding that their possession is unlawful. In *R v Davies* [1970] VR 27, D purchased a stolen car, unaware that it had been stolen. Subsequently, he learnt it had been stolen but kept it, changing the number plates and making other alterations. The trial judge directed the jury that these facts amounted to stealing. The accused was convicted and appealed to the Full Court of the Supreme Court of Victoria which quashed the conviction. The court held that, because the car had been obtained with the consent of the person in possession, there had been no trespassory taking, and a subsequent dishonest conversion could not render the accused guilty of larceny. This decision has been reversed by s 93J of the Crimes Act 1900 (NSW) which provides:

> Where on the trial of a person for any offence which includes the stealing of any property it appears that the property was, at the time when it was taken by the accused, already out of the possession of the owner by reason of its having been previously stolen, the accused may be convicted of the offence charged notwithstanding that it is not proved that the taking by him or her amounted to an interference with the right to possession of, or a trespass against, the owner.

7.42 **Constructive possession** Constructive possession is where the person does not have actual possession, but has the legal right to assume possession whenever that person wishes to do so. For example, in employer–employee situations, even if an employee has physical custody over the property, the employer is regarded as being in possession by law. This was considered in *Ellis v Lawson* (1987) 33 A Crim R 69. D took a radio from a shelf in a shop with the consent of the shop assistant, whom she knew, knowing that the owner did not consent to this and in the absence of payment. Held, D was guilty of larceny. The facts disclosed a trespass against the possession of the owner, notwithstanding that unauthorised consent to the removal of the goods was given by the shop assistant. This was because constructive possession remained in the owner, and the latter's failure to consent to the removal of the radio was decisive.

7.43 Control Property can be stolen from someone who is merely in control of the property, rather than having possession. This is so even in cases where the person is not aware of the existence of the property: *Hibbert v McKiernan* [1948] 2 KB 142; 1 All ER 860.

7.44 For the purposes of larceny, control not amounting to possession may be sufficient. In *Anic, Stylianou and Suleyman v R* (1993) 68 A Crim R 313 the accused were charged with housebreaking with intent to steal and rob when they broke into a house in the mistaken belief that it contained cannabis. They appealed on the grounds that it was not possible to steal property from a person who had it unlawfully in their possession. It was held that a person can be convicted for stealing prohibited drugs from another person. Bollen J stated (at 229–33):

> Despite the fact that she had no right in law to have these supposed drugs, [the occupier of the house] Mrs Hollis did have possession of them. The drugs were tangible personal property having some value. The *Controlled Substances Act* does not make such drugs incapable of being the subject of property rights. That Act makes it an offence for anyone to have prohibited drugs or drugs of dependence in their possession. But that does not, in my opinion, mean that the drugs cannot in law be subject to some proprietary rights by the holder of them. I think so much was decided by the Full Court of New South Wales and by the High Court in *R v Waterhouse* (1911) XI SR (NSW) 217 and (1911) 13 CLR 228 at 230 [a case dealing with stolen opium] … The decision in *R v Waterhouse* recognises that there was some right of property invested in the opium despite the fact that it was prohibited. So, I think, by parity of reasoning we can, and should, here say that Mrs Hollis had some proprietary rights in the drugs of which she had possession. For my part, too, I think that possession was sufficient to found the charges (see again by parity of reasoning *Russell v Wilson* (1923) 33 CLR 538.
>
> I do not think that the law sees no offence in the taking of drugs, illegally held by one person, by another who intends to permanently deprive the one of those drugs. I do not think that the cry 'He has no right to have had them' amounts to an exculpatory answer for the culprit.
>
> In the nineteenth edition (1966) of *Kenny's Outlines of Criminal Law* the author Mr JWC Turner wrote (p 267, paragraph 227):
>
> > Larceny was always conceived as an offence against possession, and naturally so, since the English law has never recognised in a subject of the realm any absolute right of ownership of chattels, our 'owner' being merely the person who has the best right to possess the thing. It follows therefore that a man can be guilty of larceny by stealing a thing from another who had himself stolen that thing from someone else, for a thief holds possession (albeit mala fide) of what he has stolen…
>
> For these reasons I think that the appeals based on the suggestion that a person cannot be convicted for stealing prohibited drugs from another person must fail.

7.45 Ownership Property can be stolen from an owner who is not in possession or control of property. This is demonstrated in larceny by finding cases: *R v Flood* (1869) 8 NSW 299.

7.46 A person lawfully in possession cannot commit larceny: *Ilich v R* (1986) 162 CLR 110. An owner of property can be guilty of larceny if he or she takes property from the person in lawful possession of it. Thus in *Rose v Matt* [1951] 1 KB 810; 1 All ER 361 D bought a model aircraft engine from S. S gave him credit for the purchase price and accepted D's clock as security for payment. It was agreed that if D did not pay the purchase price within a month, S could sell the clock and take the price of the engine from the proceeds of sale. Some days later, D came to S's shop and, seeing the clock on a shelf, took it away without S's knowledge or permission. The justices dismissed an information against D for stealing the clock; but on appeal their decision was reversed, on the ground that S had a special property in the clock and that D had intended permanently to deprive him of that property. See also *R v Cameron* (1924) 24 SR (NSW) 302.

7.47 Abandonment Property which is abandoned cannot be the subject of larceny. Abandonment is narrowly defined as the intentional giving up of ownership and possession: *Hibbert v McKiernan* [1948] 2 KB 142. Abandonment will not lightly be inferred: *Donaghue v Coombe* (1987) 45 SASR 330.

7.48 The issue of possession and property capable of being stolen was considered by the High Court in the case of *Croton v R*, extracted below.

7.49C

Croton v R

(1967) 117 CLR 326

High Court of Australia

[The accused, a married man, and a divorced woman formed an association. By arrangement, they lived on his wages and banked her wages into an account in their joint names upon which either could operate. The accused withdrew certain moneys from this account without the authority or knowledge of the woman and deposited these in two accounts in his own name. The accused was convicted of larceny of these moneys in the Supreme Court of the Australian Capital Territory. On appeal to the High Court.]

Barwick CJ: The terms of s 117 of the *Crimes Act 1900* of the state of New South Wales are applicable in the Australian Capital Territory so that simple larceny as at common law is an offence in that Territory. At common law, larceny is taking and carrying away the personal goods of another from any place with the felonious intent to convert them to the taker's own use, and to make them permanently his own property without the consent of the true owner. Statutory extensions of the common law effected by the Crimes Act of New South Wales and operative in the Australian Capital Territory include in the property which is susceptible of larceny any valuable security, which by definition includes a cheque (see s 134, *Crimes Act 1900*). By virtue of s 162 of the Crimes

Act also operative in the Territory, one of the joint owners who steals or embezzles any property belonging to the joint owners may be convicted of larceny as if he were not a joint owner of the property stolen. Section 3 of the *Crimes Ordinance 1931* of the Australian Capital Territory provides that whosoever having received any money upon terms requiring him to account for the whole or any part of such money, fraudulently misappropriates to his own use the whole or any part of such money, commits an offence. Provision is made in s 120 of the New South Wales Act operative in the Territory for an alternative verdict of fraudulent misappropriation upon an indictment of larceny if that offence is found to be proved.

The counts in the indictment of the applicant were that as one of two joint owners he stole the three several amounts of dollars withdrawn by him from the Commonwealth Savings Bank, Ainslie, in April 1967, the property in the 'money' being laid in each charge in the joint owners.

The learned trial judge in his charge to the jury said: 'Now, so far as this charge of stealing is concerned, gentlemen, the law provides that although two people may own property jointly, such as money in the bank, as in this case, nevertheless, it is possible for one joint owner to steal the money of another joint owner and that is the charge in this case. Now, a charge of stealing means this, in this particular case, that the accused without the consent of the co-owner, Mrs Webster, wrongfully and without any claim of right made in good faith, took possession of these joint moneys in the bank, with intent to deprive Mrs Webster, the other joint owner, permanently of such moneys and when you say he did this wrongfully, in this case the wrongful act consists — or the wrongful intent consists in this intending to appropriate the moneys to his own use, of course, without her consent.' Later, his Honour said: 'But it is the expression, "without a claim of right, made in good faith", that may need some little further explanation. The fact, gentlemen, that the accused person had a right to draw the moneys from the bank, or perhaps I should say, rather than a right to draw the moneys, an authority to draw the moneys from the bank, does not mean that he was entitled to deprive her of her savings, of her share in these joint moneys, unless, of course, he had her consent; and it is quite erroneous to suggest that because he was authorised to sign cheques and her signature was not necessary that that gave him a right to the moneys that were in the bank to her exclusion entirely. She had just as much right to these moneys as he had.' A number of objections were made to the summing up by counsel for the applicant but none called in question the appropriateness of the charges of larceny to the facts of the case.

The appellant was convicted on each charge and sentenced to 12 months' imprisonment in respect of each conviction, such sentences to be served concurrently. On this application, counsel for the applicant has submitted that the evidence led by the prosecution did not support the charges of larceny and that for that reason the convictions should be set aside.

...

This case, in my opinion, is in somewhat the same situation as that dealt with by Lord Goddard in *R v Davenport* [1954] 1 WLR 569, [1954] 1 All ER 602. His Lordship said, as I would respectfully repeat of this case, 'For some reason or another the indictment charged the appellant with stealing all this money. That could only have been done, I think, because throughout this case there was a misapprehension, under which everyone seems to have been, with regard to the more or less elementary principles of the law of banking and the law of larceny' [1954] 1 WLR at 570; [1954] 1 All ER at 603.

As I have indicated, larceny consists in the taking and carrying away of the property of another without his consent, and without colour of right, intending at the time of the taking permanently to deprive the owner of that property. It follows that there must be what is called an asportation. Therefore, apart from any special statutory provision, larceny can only be committed of property which is capable of physical possession and removal. It also follows that to constitute larceny, the property must be removed, except in the case of larceny by a bailee, from the possession of some other person against the will of that person. The special doctrine relating to larceny by a bailee was made to conform to these requirements by treating the larcenous bailee as converting the nature of his possession at the moment he formed the intention to steal.

The subject matter of the instant charges was money, in each case expressed as a number of dollars, that is, paper money, or coin to the stated face value. That can be asported and be the subject of larceny. But, though in a popular sense it may be said that a depositor with a bank has 'money in the bank', in law he has but a chose in action, a right to recover from the bank the balance standing to his credit in account with the bank at the date of his demand, or the commencement of action. That recovery will be effected by an action for debt. But the money deposited becomes an asset of the bank which may use it as it pleases: see generally Nussbaum, *Money in the Law*: s 8, p 103. Neither the balance standing to the credit of the joint account in this case, nor any part of it, as it constituted no more than a chose in action in contradistinction to a chose in possession, was susceptible of larceny, though it might be the subject of misappropriation: see also on this point the judgment of Lord Goddard in *R v Davenport* [1954] 1 WLR 569, [1954] I All ER 602 with which I respectfully agree.

The receipt of the paper money or coins by the applicant from the bank could not have been larcenous for several reasons. In the first place, the transference of possession of that paper money or coin was voluntary on the part of the bank: it was not a taking of that paper money or coins out of the possession of the bank against the will of the bank. Secondly, if it matters, that paper money or coins was not taken out of the possession of the joint owner of the bank credit, Mrs Webster; for she never did have possession of that paper money or coins: nor did the bank at any time hold possession of that money as in any sense her agent. Further, the property in that paper money or coins was in the bank immediately before it was handed over to the applicant, and not in Mrs Webster, or Mrs Webster and the applicant jointly. And, lastly, as I see the evidence of the suggested arrangement between the applicant and Mrs Webster, the property in and possession of the money or coins, in my opinion, passed to the applicant solely, even if on receipt of them he came under an obligation to account to Mrs Webster for all or some part of the 'money' they represented. No critical attention was paid in the summing up to the question of what was the actual arrangement between the applicant and Mrs Webster. It was assumed in the passages which I have quoted that the 'moneys' in the bank were the joint property of the two, in the sense that each owned half, or at any rate that each had a definable share. But that conclusion does not necessarily flow from what was proved.

The precise arrangement would in the first place be a matter of fact for the jury under proper direction. But, in my opinion, there was no evidence at all upon which it could be found that the paper money or coins withdrawn by either the applicant or Mrs Webster, were themselves to be held on behalf of both, pending the use of the specific coinage for the stated purpose. The most that could be drawn, in my opinion, from that evidence was that if either withdrew any of the credit of the account, he or she would be accountable. In deciding what the arrangement really was, a jury would no doubt be reminded that it should not overlook the fact that the pair had been living on the earnings of the applicant, which may well have been much in excess of the salary of Mrs Webster. However, I shall later return to the significance of the absence of any consideration of, or direction upon, the nature of the actual arrangement which was made in connection with the bank account. It would, therefore, seem to me that the radical elements of larceny were missing in this case. Of course, s 162 was material in the case but it was not the source of liability. It does no more than remove the objection that one joint owner could not at common law be guilty of larceny of the property jointly owned. It simply requires that he be treated as if he were not a joint owner. It does not remove the necessity for all the elements of larceny to be present: see, for example, in *R v Neat* (1899) 69 LJQB 118 at 120 per Wills J and per Wright J (1899) 69 LJQB at 121. But it does allow a part owner to be a bailee for his co-owner where otherwise he would be a bailee for both of property susceptible of larceny.

But it was submitted for the Crown in opposition to the grant of leave that the convictions for larceny were maintainable because when the applicant received the money he came under an obligation to apply 'it' for the purposes of the joint owners, and that it was larceny to form and carry out an intention to apply 'it' to his own purposes exclusively. But, in my opinion, this proposition is unacceptable. It confuses the senses in which the word money is used in the law and fails to observe a fundamental distinction between larceny and fraudulent misappropriation: see in this connection the analysis of Jordan CJ in *R v Ward* (1938) 38 SR (NSW) 308 at 315 *et seq*.

If the arrangement between the parties was that, whilst each might, neither would, withdraw the money without the particular consent of the other, the withdrawal of money by the applicant would not be criminal unless attended with a fraudulent intention to misappropriate the money: in which event it would not be larceny but, if anything, fraudulent misappropriation.

If the arrangement was that, although either might withdraw the credit standing in the account, and so reduce the 'fund' — to use a neutral term — into his own possession, but so that, none the less, the fund would be held for use exclusively in furtherance of agreed purposes, it would be fraudulent misappropriation at the time when a fraudulent intention was formed not to apply the 'fund' to the stated purposes, but to employ it for the sole purposes of the party withdrawing it from the bank; but again it would not, in my opinion, be larceny.

But, if the arrangement was that the party withdrawing the fund would hold the specie, the actual paper money or coins received from the bank, and apply that only for the stated purposes, it might be argued that the applicant by withdrawing the credit in the account, and accepting the specie from the bank, agreed with his co-owner or mutually consented that he would hold the specie, presumably as bailee, until it was paid over in pursuit of the agreed purpose. For my part, such an argument should fail, even if the agreement in that sense was made out. For, in my opinion, even so, as I shall later mention, he would not be a bailee of the specie, so as to be in a position to commit the offence of larceny as a bailee. Of course, none of these possible arrangements were put before the jury: and, in my opinion, there was no evidence upon which either the first or third possibilities could have been found to have existed in fact.

It seems to me that the submission of the Crown in respect of the convictions for larceny really amounts to an assertion that the applicant became a bailee of the paper money or coin for the joint owners, and that he committed larceny as a bailee when he formed the intention to take the paper money and coin to deposit it to his own credit with his bank. But, other considerations apart, as I have indicated, I do not think he could be such a bailee. It is settled beyond dispute that to constitute a bailment there must be a delivery, actual or constructive, by the bailor, whether owner or possessor, or by his duly authorised agent, ie, authorised to create the bailment, to the bailee, so that something which requires the physical possession of the chattel bailed, be done with, or to it, or that it be kept against its return to the bailor. This is so, though by the second paragraph of s 125 of the New South Wales Crimes Act there is no need for any agreement by the bailee to restore or deliver the specific property delivered to him.

Here the suggested subject of the bailment was the paper money or coins. Mrs Webster did not pass possession of it to the applicant; nor was the bank an agent of Mrs Webster to bail the paper money or coins to the applicant for, in my opinion, neither the nature of the bank account, nor the ability of either of the depositors to withdraw the whole or part of the money, constituted the bank such an agent. Finally, on any view of the evidence, in my opinion, it could not be held that the applicant was required, either to do some particular thing or act with the paper money or coins or to return it or them to the bailor. This is so, in my opinion, even if it be correct to say that, upon Mrs Webster's account of the matter, the applicant was bound to account for the 'money' withdrawn. The actual paper money or coins was, in my opinion, even in that case his own and he was under no obligation not to use it for his own purposes. He was not, in my opinion, a bailee of it.

I have indicated my doubt that it was established that he came under an obligation to account to Mrs Webster, or to apply the money in any particular way, at the time he received from the bank the amount withdrawn from the bank account. It was a joint account with a right in each to withdraw. Whether or not there was evidence of a legally binding arrangement as to the ultimate use of the money standing in it may be doubted: and in default of such an arrangement it may be that either could withdraw the whole or any part without coming under any obligation to account. Whether or not the proceeds of the account were joint property is not answered merely by the fact that, in the circumstances, the account was in the joint names. Further, even supposing such an agreement as to the use of the proceeds of the joint account, it does not follow that it extended to require the amount to be kept in that account: the ability of either to withdraw from the account might be thought to tend against such a construction of these arrangements. These considerations are not of critical importance in connection with my treatment of the submission with which I am presently dealing. But they indicate that, on any view, the summing up was not adequate; also they are of importance in connection with the suggestion that an alternative verdict of fraudulent misappropriation might have been returned by the jury.

If the correct conclusion of fact is that there was a binding arrangement of a kind to be legally enforceable that the credit in the account should only be used for a sufficiently defined purpose, and that the withdrawal of the balance in the account by the applicant, itself evidenced his intention to use the proceeds for some purpose unconnected with the agreed purpose (which I doubt), the applicant none the less, in my opinion, would not commit larceny, but might be found guilty of misappropriation.

For these reasons, in my opinion, the convictions should be set aside on the ground that there was no evidence to support them.

[**McTiernan J** concurred with **Barwick CJ. Menzies J** dissented. Convictions quashed.]

Without the consent of the person in possession

7.50 The taking of the property must be without the consent of the possessor; that is, it must be a trespassory taking. A trespass is defined as unprivileged interference with a possession of another. A trespassory taking will occur where the property is taken against the will of the person in possession: *Davies v R* [1970] VR 27. It is clear that consent due to threats or intimidation may be vitiated: *R v Lovell* [1881] 8 QBD 185. Where consent has been obtained by fraud or trickery the accused can be charged with fraud offences.

Two major issues have arisen with regard to the requirement of a taking without consent:

(1) Has the victim consented to, or merely facilitated, the taking?

(2) Where an accused has received property due to mistaken consent by the owner, is this consent real, or is the consent vitiated due to the mistake?

Each of these issues will be considered in turn.

7.51 Facilitation and consent Where an owner facilitates or allows property to be taken away, this will not necessarily amount to consent. The distinction between facilitation and consent will be a question of fact for the jury, and appears to have little relation to the blameworthiness of an accused, as shown by the following examples.

7.52C

Kennison v Daire

(1986) 160 CLR 129; 64 ALR 17
High Court of Australia

[The accused opened an Easybank account and obtained a card to operate the Automated Teller Machine (ATM) together with a Personal Identification Number (PIN). The accused subsequently closed the account but retained the card. He then used the card to operate an ATM which paid out $200. He was convicted of larceny of that sum, and that conviction was upheld by the Supreme Court of South Australia. On appeal to the High Court.]

Gibbs CJ, **Mason**, **Wilson**, **Deane** and **Dawson JJ**: It is not in doubt that the appellant acted fraudulently with intent permanently to deprive the bank of $200. The appellant's submission is that the bank consented to the taking. It is submitted that the bank intended that the machine should operate within the terms of its program, and that when it did so it gave effect to the intention of the bank.

In the course of an interesting argument, Mr Tilmouth pointed out that if a teller, having the general authority of the bank, pays out money on a cheque when the drawer's account is overdrawn, or on a forged order, the correct conclusion is that the bank intends that the property in the money should pass, and that the case is not one of larceny: see for example, *Chambers v Miller* (1862) 13 CB (NS) 125, 143 ER 50 and *R v Prince* [1868] 1 CCR 150. He submitted that, in effect, the machine was invested with a similar authority and that if, within the instructions in its program, it handed over the money, it should be held that the property in the money passed to the card-holder with the consent of the bank.

With all respect, we find it impossible to accept these arguments. The fact that the bank programmed the machine in a way that facilitated the commission of a fraud by a person holding a card did not mean that the bank consented to the withdrawal of money by a person who had no account with the bank. It is not suggested that any person, having the authority of the bank to consent to the particular transaction, did so. The machine could not give the bank's consent in fact and there is no principle of law that requires it to be treated as though it were a person with authority to decide and consent. The proper inference to be drawn from the facts is that the bank consented to the withdrawal of up to $200 by a card-holder who presented his card and supplied his personal identification number, only if the card-holder had an account which was current. It would be quite unreal to infer that the bank consented to the withdrawal by a card-holder whose account had been closed. The conditions of use of the card supplied by the bank to its customers support the conclusion that no such inference can be drawn. It is unnecessary to consider what the position might have been if the account had remained current but had insufficient funds to its credit. The decision in *R v Hands* (1887) 16 Cox CC 188 is consistent with the view that no inference of consent can be drawn although, as Mr Tilmouth submitted, there are points of distinction between that case and this.

For these reasons, which are substantially those expressed by King CJ in the Full Court of the Supreme Court of South Australia, the appeal should be dismissed.

[Appeal dismissed.]

7.53 Notes and illustrations

1. D approached W in an attempt to persuade him to steal certain property from his employer. W informed his employer, who instructed him to hand the property over to D in order to trap him. W did so. Held, D was not guilty of larceny. Lord Goddard LCJ stated: '[T]here was no evidence here of what, to use a technical expression, is termed asportation. He did not carry away the goods against the will of the owner but because the owner was willing that he should have the goods and gave them to him': *R v Turvey* [1946] 2 All ER 60. Cf *Martin v Puttick* [1968] 1 QB 82.
2. D came into P's shop and asked her to show him some linen. When she delivered it into his hands, he ran out of the shop with it. Held, larceny, for P retained possession of the linen: *R v Chisser* (1678) T Raym 275; 83 ER 142.
3. X left a video camera and a bag in a taxi. The taxi driver was unaware that the items were in the back of his taxi until D, a subsequent passenger, alighted. The taxi driver then noticed the items and, assuming they belonged to D, gave them to him. D took them. Held, D was guilty of larceny. Legal possession of the video camera and other items never left the owner. Nothing the taxi driver said or did altered the legal situation: *Hayes v Fries* (1988) 49 SASR 184.

7.54 Consent due to mistake The present section deals with the problem of the accused who converts property given to her or him as the result of a mistake on the part of the owner. Does an accused who converts property in such circumstances commit larceny? As a matter of logic, the answer should be no. In such a case, no trespass is committed and the property is handed over with the consent of the owner. Thus, two essential elements of the offence of larceny are absent. However, while logic suggests the answer should be no, historically it has been argued on policy grounds that the answer should be yes. This is because it is argued that a person who receives property as the result of another's mistake and converts that property acts fraudulently and ought not to be able to argue successfully that no offence has been committed. The cases on this difficult subject are characterised by a continuing and still unresolved conflict between the dictates of logic and the dictates of this historical policy. It is submitted that the best solution is dictated by logic. A person who receives property due to a mistaken consent that was not caused by any trickery or fraud should not be liable for larceny.

7.55 The problem of the accused who receives property as the result of another's mistake arises in two forms. First, there is the case where the accused realises, at the time the property is handed over, that this is being done as the result of a mistake. In this type of case, the difficulty in saying that the accused commits larceny is that the taking is not trespassory; that is, the property is taken with the consent of the owner. To the extent that an accused can be guilty of larceny where he or she obtains property by another's mistake, the mistake cases must be regarded as an exception to the general rule that, for larceny to be committed, the taking must be trespassory.

The second type of case is where the accused receives the property without realising that it has been given to her or him, subsequently becomes aware of its existence, and converts it knowing that it was given to her or him by mistake. Here there is an additional difficulty in saying that the accused commits larceny, arising from the general requirement that the wrongful taking and the fraudulent intent must coincide in point of time.

7.56 Historical approach to mistaken consent cases The historical approach to mistaken consent was to find an accused guilty of larceny on the basis that consent was vitiated due to mistake.

7.57 In *R v Middleton* (1873) LR 2 CCR 38 the accused had 11 shillings standing to his credit in a post office savings account. He gave written notice of his intention to withdraw 10 shillings and, in due course, a letter of advice authorising the withdrawal of 10 shillings was sent to the local branch office. Middleton went to the branch office to withdraw the 10 shillings. By mistake, the post office clerk referred to a letter of advice authorising payment of £8/16/10 to another depositor, and put down coins and notes amounting to that larger sum. Middleton took up the money and went away. He was charged with stealing £8/16/10. At his trial, the jury found that he intended to steal when he took up the money from the counter, and he was convicted. The case was reserved for the Court for Crown Cases Reserved. It was heard first by a court of five judges who failed to agree, and then by a full court of 15 judges.

Bovill CJ reading the judgment for the majority held that Middleton was found guilty of larceny because he was aware of the mistake at the time of taking and thus had the necessary mens rea and the consent was vitiated because of the mistake. Pigott B held Middleton guilty on the ground that the clerk had put the money on the counter and Middleton had picked it up. He stated that he would not have favoured conviction if the clerk had put the money into Middleton's hand. Bovill CJ, Kelly CB and Keating J held Middleton guilty on the ground that the clerk did not have authority to part with the money to Middleton. Martin, Bramwell, Cleasby BB and Brett J dissented, holding that Middleton could not be guilty of larceny because he had received the money with the consent of the clerk. Conviction affirmed by a majority of eleven to four.

7.58 In *R v Ashwell* (1885) 16 QBD 190, Ashwell asked Keogh to lend him a shilling. Keogh agreed and handed Ashwell a coin which both parties believed to be a shilling. It was, in fact, a sovereign. Ashwell subsequently realised the mistake and appropriated the coin. At Ashwell's trial for stealing the sovereign, the jury found a verdict setting out the facts, and saying that if the law allowed they would find Ashwell guilty. The trial judge entered a verdict of guilty but stated a case for the Court for Crown Cases Reserved. The case was argued before 14 judges. Ashwell was found guilty on the basis that mistake vitiated consent. To circumvent the problem that Ashwell did not have mens rea at the time of taking, the court held that D was not in possession of the coin until he knew what it was.

One particularly unsatisfactory aspect of *R v Ashwell* is that the trial judge (Denman J) was one of the 14 judges who heard the appeal. Thus Denman J effectively had two votes, and it was his second vote which resulted in Ashwell's conviction.

7.59 Notes

1. In subsequent English cases it was generally assumed that *Middleton's* case was rightly decided. The matter was settled in England by s 1(2)(i)(d) of the Larceny Act 1916 (UK) (now repealed) which provided that an accused steals where he or she takes 'under a mistake on the part of the taker that possession has been so obtained'.
2. In cases where the accused obtained property by another's mistake, but did not realise the mistake until some time after receiving the property, *R v Ashwell* was sometimes distinguished and sometimes followed. In *R v Flowers* (1886) 16 QBD 643, where an employee was given a wages bag intended for another employee and appropriated the contents of the bag, *R v Ashwell* was not followed and the conviction quashed. In *R v Hudson* [1943] 1 KB 458, however, where the accused appropriated a cheque delivered to him by mistake, the conviction was upheld. In *Moynes v Coopper* [1956] 1 QB 439, where the accused appropriated an overpayment of wages in his pay packet, the conviction was quashed. In *Russell v Smith* [1958] 1 QB 27, where the accused, a lorry driver, appropriated an excess number of sacks of pig meal mistakenly loaded onto his lorry, the conviction was upheld.

7.60 Contemporary approach to mistaken consent Two cases, *R v Potisk* (1973) 6 SASR 389 and *R v Ilich* (1987) 162 CLR 110; [1987] HCA 1, have looked at the issue of mistaken consent. Both cases are extracted below.

7.61C R v Potisk

(1973) 6 SASR 389
Supreme Court of South Australia

[The accused took traveller's cheques worth US$1480 to a bank to exchange them for Australian currency. At the prevailing rate of exchange, the teller should have paid him A$1233 but, by mistake, the teller applied the wrong conversion rate and paid him $2985. The accused took the money away. When interviewed by the police two days later, the accused said he did not realise that a mistake had been made until he counted the money after he got home. The accused was charged with larceny of a sum of money representing the difference between what he was paid and what he should have been paid. The trial judge reserved for the consideration of the Supreme Court the question of the direction that should be given to the jury. The Supreme Court considered the case on the basis of two possible assumptions: (a) that the accused was aware of the mistake at the time he received the money; and (b) that the accused only became aware of the mistake subsequently.]

Bray CJ: These questions raise acutely and directly for our solution some of the most notorious controversies of the law of larceny and, in particular, the proper construction and the force in South Australia at the present time of the two famous cases of *Middleton* (*R v Middleton* (1873) LR 2 CCR 38) and *Ashwell* (*R v Ashwell* (1885) 16 QBD 190). It may be optimistic to think that our decision will set those controversies to rest. ...

It is desirable at this stage to look at some of the earlier definitions before the complications of the mid-nineteenth century cases. It is not, however, I think, necessary to go further back than *East's Pleas of the Crown* (1803) where in vol 2, p 553 the learned author defines the crime as: 'the wrongful or fraudulent taking and carrying away by any person of the mere personal goods of another, from any place, with a felonious intent to convert them to his (the taker's) own use, and make them his own property, without the consent of the owner.' That definition is an adaptation of the definition in Coke 3 Inst c 47, expanding it in some places and curtailing it in others by omitting any reference to the differentiating characteristics of graver crimes. In later passages it is made clear that the felonious intention must exist at the time of the taking; see pp 655 and 665.

Already, however, by the date of *Middleton's* case (1873) LR 2 CCR 38 the simplicity of this definition had been qualified in several respects.

1. The common law had developed the conceptions of larceny by a servant and larceny by a bailee who breaks bulk. In these cases the formation of the felonious intention and the subsequent appropriation of the thing constituted larceny, notwithstanding that the thing had come into the physical custody of the accused lawfully and with the owner's consent before the formation of the intention. This has no application here. The accused was not the servant or the bailee of the bank.
2. In certain cases where the owner had parted with the possession, as opposed to the ownership, of the thing as a result of the fraud of the accused, he was held to be guilty of larceny by a trick. This does not arise here either. The mistake of the bank was in no way induced by anything done by the accused.
3. In *Riley's* case (*R v Riley* (1853) Dears 149, 169 ER 674) in 1853 it was held that if the accused acquired possession by trespass, even though without any felonious intention, and subsequently formed that intention and appropriated the thing, he was guilty of larceny. This distinction was novel at the time and it is difficult to justify historically, since, as Stephen J points out in *Ashwell's* case (1885) 16 QBD 190 at 209, at common law every larceny involved a trespass, or, in other words, trespass was a necessary though not a sufficient condition of the crime, and hence, if *Riley's* case is right, there would seem to be little room at common law for the requirement that the taking and the *animus furandi* must be contemporaneous. But, as I said in *Minigall v McCammon* [1970] SASR 82 at 84, I think we now have to take *Riley's* case as establishing the law. It has been followed on several occasions

> since, both in England and in Australia (see, for example, besides the cases cited in *Minigall v McCammon, R v O'Brien* (1921) 21 SR (NSW) 136, 38 WN 10). However, I think there can be no question of the accused here being a trespasser when the teller handed him the money. It is indeed suggested by the learned authors of Pollock and Wright's *Possession in the Common Law* (1888) that in the case of things handed over by the owner under a mistake, as in *Ashwell's* case (1885) 16 QBD 190, the possession is from the start trespassory, though innocent in the absence of the *animus furandi*; see pp 110 and 210. I am perhaps anticipating when I say that, with respect, I disagree. If the accused on the facts assumed in this case was a trespasser when he received the money from the teller, it would follow that even if he had discovered the mistake when he got home and immediately returned the money to the bank, he could still have been sued for nominal damages for trespass for his handling and custody of it in the meantime. That cannot be right.

I have mentioned these qualifications of the common law definition simply in order to dismiss them. I revert to that definition. If the facts in the case submitted to us were submitted to any intelligent layman unversed in the subtleties of the law of larceny, he would unhesitatingly say that the accused took the money when the teller handed it to him and that he took it with the teller's consent. I have finally come to the conclusion that that is not only common sense but good law. But *Middleton's* case and *Ashwell's* case need detailed consideration.

Mr Duggan, for the Crown, founded on these two cases. On the authority of *Middleton's* case he says that there was no consent of the owner within the meaning of the definition. On the authority of *Ashwell's* case he says that there was no taking until the accused realized the mistake. If *Middleton's* case was wrongly decided and is not binding on us, we should, I think, answer both questions in the negative. If it was rightly decided, or if, though not rightly decided, it is binding on us, then, unless it can be distinguished, the first question should be answered in the affirmative. If *Ashwell's* case was wrongly decided and is not binding on us, the second question should be answered in the negative, even if the first question is answered in the affirmative. If it was rightly decided, or if, though not rightly decided, it is binding on us, then, unless it can be distinguished, the second question should be answered in the affirmative, if the first one is.

I find it more convenient to deal with the points in reverse order and first with the question of taking and the authority of *Ashwell's* case, since the authority of *Ashwell's* case is more obviously vulnerable than that of *Middleton's* case.

[His Honour discussed a number of authorities and continued:]

Running through the judgments in favour of the conviction is the notion that somehow or other there was no delivery of the coin by Keogh to Ashwell and no receipt of it by him while the parties were under the mistake as to its value, and no possession of it by Ashwell until he found out that it was a sovereign. I can only say that I cannot understand all this. Let us suppose that someone had taken the coin off Ashwell, whether before or after he found out the mistake. Can there be any doubt that he would have been entitled to all normal civil possessory remedies? There can be no question that Keogh did not hand over the coin merely for some limited or temporary purpose. He did not expect to get the identical coin back. He expected to be repaid a shilling, not the same shilling. In fact, as I see it, he parted with not only the possession, but also the ownership of the coin. The transaction was *mutuum*, not *commodatum*, if I may employ Roman law terms. The case is nothing like the handing over of a coin to a goldsmith to be tested, or the entrusting of money to a clerk or servant to be taken somewhere in specie and not spent, or to the use of a plate or a glass by a customer in a restaurant. ...

For these reasons I think that *Ashwell's* case ((1885) 16 QBD 190) was wrongly decided, that it is not binding on us, and that where something more valuable is handed over by the owner in mistake for something less valuable of the same general nature and the recipient takes it in good faith and in ignorance of the mistake, he is not guilty of larceny because he forms the intention to appropriate it and does appropriate it later on after he has found out the mistake. By the word 'something' in that proposition I mean some tangible physical object or objects. But, as I have said, here there was no mistake at all about the identity or the value of the notes. I think, therefore, the second question should be answered 'No'.

...

I turn now to the first question. *Middleton's* case (1873) LR 2 CCR 38 is a harder nut to crack. It appears from what I have said that I think that in this case there was a taking when the teller handed over the money, and if the accused realised the mistake at that time and formed the intention to appropriate it or the surplus, then the offence would be complete apart from the question of the owner's consent. But can it really be said that he received the money without the teller's consent or that the teller's consent is not equivalent to that of the owner, the bank?

In *Middleton's* case the majority for sustaining the conviction was eleven to four. But the learned judges in the majority did not all come to their conclusion for the same reasons.

[His Honour discussed the minority judgments of **Pigott B**, **Bovill CJ**, **Kelly CB** and **Keating J**, and continued:]

There remains the ground on which Cockburn CJ, Blackburn, Mellor, Lush, Grove, Denman and Archibald JJ decided in favour of the conviction.

Those learned judges held that, though the clerk intended to pass the possession of the money, the case was like the cases of larceny by a trick because Middleton had the *animus furandi* at the time (see at 43) and that, though the clerk intended to pass the ownership, it did not really pass because of the mistake (see at 42–3) and that the intention to pass the ownership without its actual passage was not enough (see at 43).

I can only say, with respect, first, as I have said before, that in the cases of larceny by a trick the mistake was induced by the fraud of the accused (see *Russell*, vol 2, p 971), and that in *Middleton's* case (1873) LR 2 CCR 38 as here, the accused did nothing to induce the mistake; second, that cases where ownership has been held not to pass, despite delivery, because of a mistake are cases relating to the title to specific chattels, and I doubt whether they can apply to delivery of money in circumstances like these;

and thirdly, that when the question is whether the money was handed over without the consent of the clerk (treating his consent as equivalent to that of the Postmaster-General for the present purpose), it is his intention which counts. I agree, with respect with what Bramwell B said at 65, that even if the clerk did not intend to give to Middleton what did not belong to him yet he intended to do the act he did, and with the remarks of Brett J, as he then was, at 62:

> Consent or non-consent is an action of the mind; it consists exclusively of the intention of the mind. These propositions, therefore, are treating of a question of intention. If it be said that a man intends to part with the property in a thing which he delivers to another, the meaning of the words is that he intends that the other should take the thing and keep it as his own; and it seems a contradiction in sense to say that the thing so delivered is taken from him without his consent.

[His Honour referred to a number of earlier cases and continued:]

It appears from this analysis that in *Middleton's* case (1873) LR 2 CCR 38 only seven judges out of 15 were in favour of the proposition that money handed over in the circumstances of the present case is handed over without the consent of the owner, leaving aside the question of any limitation of the teller's authority. With respect I disagree with the reasoning of those seven judges and I prefer the reasoning of Martin, Bramwell and Cleasby BB and Brett J. I cannot find that the views of the seven judges have ever been expressly considered and affirmed by a court of higher authority in England between 1873 and 1916. Between 1916 and 1968 the question was set at rest there by the provisions of the English Larceny Act of 1916, which provided that the expression 'takes' in the definition of larceny included obtaining of possession 'under a mistake on the part of the owner with knowledge on the part of the taker that possession has been so obtained' (s 1(2)(c)). It is true that that Act has been superseded by the English Theft Act 1968 and *Middleton's* case made a curious reappearance in a recent case under that Act (*R v Gilks* [1972] 3 All ER 280 at 282–3), but there was no independent examination of it there and lack of the owner's consent is not an essential element of the new crime created by the Theft Act (*Lawrence v Commissioner of Police for the Metropolis* [1971] 2 All ER 1253).

No legislation corresponding to either English Act is in force in South Australia. Nor can I find that *Middleton's* case has ever been confirmed and adopted by any court in Australia whose decisions are binding on us, and it is clearly contrary to the decision of the Full Court of Tasmania in *R v Goodrick* (1922) 18 Tas LR 36. …

In my opinion, the views of the seven judges are not binding on us and they are erroneous. It follows that I think that both questions should be answered 'No'.

[**Mitchell J** agreed with **Bray CJ**. **Wells J** dissented. Directions to acquit.]

7.62C

R v Ilich

(1987) 162 CLR 110; 69 ALR 231; [1987] HCA 1
High Court of Australia

[D was overpaid by an employer for work. D had not returned the excess, but had put it aside while deciding what to do with it. D was found guilty at first instance, but the High Court quashed his conviction.

Under s 371(1) of the Criminal Code (WA) stealing was defined to include both fraudulent taking and fraudulent conversion. Under s 371(2) a taking or conversion was deemed to be fraudulent when done with: '(a) An intent to permanently deprive the owner of the thing or property of it or any part of it;' or '(f) In the case of money, an intent to use it at the will of the person who takes or converts it although he may intend to afterwards repay the amount to the owner'. Section 371(4) provided that: 'In the case of conversion, it is immaterial whether the property converted is taken for the purpose of conversion or whether it is at the time of the conversion in the possession, control or management of the person who converts it.']

Wilson and **Dawson JJ**: … At common law, larceny is committed by a person who, without the consent of the owner, fraudulently and without a claim of right made in good faith, takes and carries away anything capable of being stolen with intent, at the time of such taking, permanently to deprive the owner thereof. This is the definition, which was intended to be declaratory of the common law, given in s 1(1) of the Larceny Act 1916 (UK) which has, of course, now been repealed by the Theft Act 1968 (UK). What we wish to draw attention to is the fact that at common law larceny involves the taking of something without the consent of the owner who may, for this purpose, include the person in possession of the thing. For this reason it is said that there is no larceny if the circumstances would not sustain an action for trespass. Under the Code, on the other hand, a person who fraudulently takes anything capable of being stolen is said to steal that thing. Absence of consent on the part of the owner is not required and there is, for that reason, no necessary element of trespass. Of course, if the taking is to be fraudulent, there must be the requisite intent but, given that intent, there may be a fraudulent taking of something under the Code even if the owner intentionally delivers the thing to the person said to take it.

Because larceny at common law requires a trespass — it is sometimes described as an offence against possession — a person lawfully in possession of something cannot be guilty of larceny of it. 'Hence, even if consent to the mere taking of possession was obtained by fraud, but there was then no *animus furandi*, it is not larceny at common law if the chattel is subsequently permanently misappropriated. A bailee could not be guilty of larceny at common law of the goods bailed, so long as the bailment continued': *R v Ward* (1938) 38 SR (NSW) 308 at 314 per Jordan CJ; *Slattery v R* (1905) 2 CLR 546. Under the Code, however, stealing contains no trespassory element although there must be a taking …

With these differences between the common law and the Code in mind, it is possible to look at those cases dealing with mistake in relation to larceny to see what assistance might be gained from them. Mistake is relevant in this case because, upon one version of events, an overpayment was made by Brighton by mistake. Because of the differences between the Code and the common law the exercise can only be helpful in a general way and it is unnecessary to go into great detail. Moreover, we should say at the beginning that the decisions to which we are about to refer are far from having received universal approbation.

The cases fall into two categories. First there are those, of which *R v Middleton* (1873) LR 2 CCR 38 is the principal decision, in which the person handling over the thing said to be stolen did so under a mistake which was known at the time by the person to whom the thing was handed. Cases in the second category, of which *R v Ashwell* (1885) 16 QBD 190 is the leading authority, occur where the thing said to be stolen was handed over under a mistake which was unknown at the time by the person to whom the thing was handed and was learnt by him only subsequently.

In *Middleton* the accused was handed by a post office clerk by way of withdrawal from a savings account an amount which was more than was standing to the accused's credit in that account. At the time the clerk made the payment, he mistakenly referred to a letter which authorised the payment, but to another depositor. The accused was convicted upon trial, the case being reserved for the Court of Crown Cases Reserved where it was eventually heard by a Full Court of 15 judges. By a majority of 11 to 4 the conviction was upheld.

In *Ashwell* the accused asked for a loan of a shilling and was handed by mistake, in the dark, a sovereign. The accused did not at first realise the mistake, but when he did some time later, he appropriated the sovereign. He was convicted upon trial but again a case was stated for the Court of Crown Cases Reserved. The 14 judges (who included the trial judge) were equally divided and accordingly the conviction stood.

Many analyses of the judgments in these cases have been made, but it is sufficient for present purposes to observe that the decision in *Middleton* can only be explained upon the basis (somewhat of a fiction upon any view) that there was a taking against the consent of the owner at the time the accused received the money and that he acquired neither the right to possession nor ownership of it. The apparent consent of the clerk who paid the money was vitiated by his mistake. It may also be observed that it was the whole of the money which was held to be stolen, not just the amount by which the payment exceeded the money which was in the accused's account.

The decision in *Ashwell* must, we think, rest upon the proposition (difficult to accept as it is) that the mistake on the part of the person handing over the coin and on the part of the accused, meant that the accused, although he obtained physical possession of the coin, did not obtain possession of the sovereign until he realised that the coin was a sovereign. At that point he formed an intention to keep it and was held to have taken it without consent.

The cases of *Middleton* and *Ashwell* have received a measure of acceptance in England, although they have been the subject of considerable criticism: see M R E Kerr, 'The Time of Criminal Intent in Larceny' (1950) 66 *Law Quarterly Review*, at 174; R Cross, 'Larceny De Lege Lata' (1950) 66 *Law Quarterly Review*, at 497; *R v Hudson* [1943] KB 458; *Russell v Smith* [1958] 1 QB 27; *R v Gilks* [1972] 1 WLR 1341; [1972] 3 All ER 280 cf *R v Flowers* (1886) 16 QBD 643; *Moynes v Coopper* [1956] 1 QB 439. In Australia they have never been confirmed or adopted and the decision in *R v Goodrick* (1922) 18 Tas LR 36 is clearly contrary to *Middleton:* see also *R v Wauchope* (1957) 2 FLR 191.

In *R v Potisk* (1973) 6 SASR 389 the accused changed some travellers' cheques into Australian currency at a bank. The teller applied the wrong exchange rate and gave the accused too much. The accused did not realise this until he got home and counted the money. He then decided to keep it. In the Full Court of the Supreme Court of South Australia, Bray CJ, with whom Mitchell J agreed, found both *Middleton* and *Ashwell* distinguishable but would have declined to follow them in any event. The reasons which the Chief Justice gave for regarding both of those decisions as unsatisfactory are cogent and we should be inclined to agree with his view that they should not be followed. However, in this case, as in *Potisk*, there are important differences which make the English decisions clearly distinguishable and which render unnecessary any detailed discussion of the reasons in those cases.

Both *Middleton* and *Ashwell* have been treated, and in our view must be treated, as cases in which the mistake which was made was of a sufficiently fundamental kind to negate the apparent consent and to prevent ownership from passing. A mistake will be of that kind if it is as to the identity of the transferee or as to the identity of the thing delivered or as to the quantity of the thing delivered: see Glanville Williams, *Textbook of Criminal Law* (1978), at 779; Williams and Weinberg, *Property Offences*, 2nd ed (1986), at 44; *Russell on Crime*, vol 2, 12th ed (1964), at 1553; JC Smith, (1972) *Criminal Law Review*, at 586–8. In those circumstances, and perhaps only in those circumstances, can it be said that the mistake is such that the transferor never really intended to deliver the thing transferred and so never gave consent to the transfer. *Middleton* may be regarded as a case of mistake as to the identity of the transferee: the clerk thought that the accused was the person referred to in the letter authorising the payment. Less plausibly, *Middleton* may be regarded as a case of mistake as to the identity of the deposit: see (1972) *Criminal Law Review*, at 587. *Ashwell* may be regarded as a case of mistake as to the identity of the thing delivered: both the lender and the accused thought it was a shilling whereas it was in fact a sovereign. The third category — mistake as to the quantity of the thing delivered — requires in our view some qualification where the thing is money but may be illustrated by *Russell v Smith* where eight sacks too many of pig meal were mistakenly delivered to the accused who appropriated them. He was convicted of theft.

Where there is a mistake which is not of a fundamental character it will not vitiate consent so that possession and ownership will pass in accordance with the apparent intention of the owner. Thus in *R v Prince* (1868) LR 1 CCR 150, where the cashier of a bank handed over money, intending to do so although deceived by a forged order, there was held to be no larceny. In *Lacis v Cashmarts* [1969] 2 QB 400 where the accused took goods from a self service store and paid the amount which the manager read from the cash register, which was less than the price, there was held to be no larceny. Upon this view the decision in *R v Gilks*, which was made in reliance upon *Middleton*, was wrong and it has been criticised accordingly: (1972) *Criminal Law Review*, at 585 *et seq*, GF Orchard, 'The Borderland of Theft Revisited' (1973) *New Zealand Law Journal*, at 110.

In the present case there was no mistake as to the identity of the person to whom the money was delivered. There was no mistake as to the identity of the thing delivered, which was money. If there was any mistake it was as to the quantity of money delivered and it is therefore necessary to turn to the qualification of that category of fundamental mistake which we think must be made in the case of money.

In *Potisk* there was no mistake as to the quantity of money handed to the accused. The teller made a mistake in applying the wrong exchange rate but he intended to hand over the amount which he did. The case might have been decided simply upon the basis that there was no fundamental mistake to prevent possession and ownership passing, but Bray CJ at 401 adverts to the qualification which we have suggested saying that '... cases where ownership has been held not to pass, despite delivery, because of a mistake are cases relating to the title to specific chattels, and I doubt whether they can apply to delivery of money in circumstances like these'. And at 404 he refers to the 'curious question' which would have arisen in *Potisk* if the accused had been guilty of larceny, namely, whether he stole the whole of the money delivered to him or only the amount which was in excess of the sum to which he was entitled in exchange for his travellers' cheques.

It is an error, as Lord Mansfield pointed out as long ago as 1758 in *Miller v Race* (1758) 1 Burr 452 at 457; 97 ER 398 at 401, to treat money in the form of cash in the same way as other goods. Money in most circumstances cannot be followed, which is to say that property, or ownership, generally passes with possession. 'It has been quaintly said, "that the reason why money can not be followed is, because it has no ear-mark:" but this is not true. The true reason is, upon account of the currency of it: it can not be recovered after it has passed in currency': ibid. Money is, of course, capable of being stolen and if it is stolen, property in the notes or coins does not pass to the thief. But if the thief passes the money into currency, which he may do by making payment with it, ownership will pass with possession notwithstanding the thief's lack of title providing the transaction was bona fide and for valuable consideration: *Moss v Hancock* [1899] 2 QB 111; *Banque Belge v Hambrouck* [1921] 1 KB 321; *Clarke v Shee and Johnson* (1774) 1 Cowp 197; 98 ER 1041. That is because of the doctrine of negotiability—and negotiability was first attributed to chattels in the form of money — which constitutes an exception to the common law rule that a man who has no title himself cannot pass title to another; *nemo potest dare quod non habet: Banque Belge v Hambrouck*, at 329.

In the circumstances of this case this aspect of negotiability is of less importance — since Brighton had title in the money — than the rule that when money passes into currency property goes with possession. Whether money only passes in currency when it is negotiated, that is, when it is used for payment bona fide and for value, or whether money may pass in currency in other circumstances when it is not delivered in specie, is something which it is unnecessary to examine here. Definitions of currency tend to speak in terms of it being a medium of exchange, but this nevertheless imports the notion of payment: see *Moss v Hancock* at 116 Mann, *The Legal Aspect of Money*, 4th ed (1982), at 8. Upon any view money passes into currency when it is negotiated and in this case, upon the applicant's version of the facts, the transaction in which the money changed hands was both bona fide and for value. He was unaware of the overpayment when it was made and consequently there was no reason to doubt the bona fide character of the transaction. Thus the notes or coins ceased to be the subject of specific title as chattels and passed as currency, that is to say, passed 'from hand to hand in point, not merely of possession, but of property': *Sinclair v Brougham* [1914] AC 398 at 418 per Viscount Haldane LC. We do not think that it is possible to say that only the correct amount was paid for valuable consideration and that the amount of the overpayment passed hands for no consideration and hence as mere chattels rather than currency. Apart from the insuperable difficulty of identifying the notes or coins which constituted the overpayment, it is the transaction itself which characterises the payment. The transaction between the applicant and Brighton was bona fide and for value. The payment, which was part of that transaction, was also of that character. It is not possible, in our view, to apportion the consideration to some of the chattels comprising the notes or coins transferred and not to others.

With goods other than currency, property does not pass with possession unless it is the owner's intention that it should and it has been held (not without some difficulty) that it is possible to conclude in cases of overdelivery that appropriation of the whole of the goods involves the theft of the excess goods without any need to identify them: see *R v Tideswell* [1905] 2 KB 273; *Pilgram v Rice-Smith* [1977] 1 WLR 671; [1977] 2 All ER 658; cf *Lacis v Cashmarts* at 411. However where property passes with possession, as with currency, no such conclusion is possible in relation to an amount overpaid. There is, we should add, a civil action to recover money paid under a mistake of fact and equitable rights may arise: see *Chase Manhattan Bank v Israel-British Bank* [1981] Ch 105.

The result is that in this case, even without rejecting *Middleton* and *Ashwell*, there was no mistake of a fundamental kind which would have operated to prevent ownership in the money passing at the time at which, upon the applicant's evidence, it was handed by Brighton to the applicant. There was no mistake as to the identity of the transferee, there was no mistake as to the identity of the money and any overpayment, being in currency, did not prevent property in the whole amount being transferred to the applicant.

If in this case Brighton intentionally handed the money to the applicant, including the amount of the overpayment, and the applicant took the money without being aware of any mistake on the part of Brighton, property in the money passed with possession and there was neither a fraudulent taking within the meaning of s 371 of the Code nor a subsequent conversion when the applicant realised Brighton's mistake. To the extent that the prosecution alleged that the applicant fraudulently took an amount of money, the applicant was entitled to rely upon s 24 of the Code. That section gave to the applicant the benefit of an honest and reasonable mistake of fact which, upon his version of events, arose on his part when he took the money believing it to be the amount to which he was entitled. That section in this case, however, seems to add little in terms of practical result to the law as we have endeavoured to explain it. Nor upon the evidence did a bona fide claim of right arise as a separate defence requiring reliance upon s 22 of the Code.

Clearly the directions given by the learned trial judge to the jury were defective. As we have said, the question asked by the jury after they had retired indicates that they had not rejected the applicant's version of events. The applicant was entitled to a direction that if the jury was satisfied — or if it was left with a reasonable doubt about it — that Brighton delivered the money to the applicant who took it unaware of any overpayment, then the applicant should be acquitted of stealing, notwithstanding that he subsequently realised Brighton's mistake and retained the money. No such direction was given.

It remains to consider whether the applicant should be exposed to a new trial. His story is not inherently improbable and, had the jury been adequately directed, it is likely that he would have been acquitted. It is not an invariable rule that a new trial should be ordered where there is evidence upon which a jury could have convicted on an adequate direction: see *Clemesha v R* [1978] WAR 193 at 201, per Wickham J. Justice having once miscarried in this case, we think that it would be better served in the end if there were no order for a retrial. We would grant special leave, allow the appeal, quash the conviction and direct a verdict and judgment of acquittal be entered.

[The conviction was quashed.]

7.63 Notes

1. The law with regard to mistaken consent is not settled. It should be noted that in *Ilich* the High Court was focusing on the offence of stealing under s 371 of the Criminal Code (WA). This section does not require an absence of consent on the part of the owner. Despite the differences in law, the decision provides an indication of how the High Court may decide a case based on the common law offence of larceny. This is particularly persuasive given that the High Court considered mistaken consent cases at common law. Wilson and Dawson JJ approved of the decision of Bray CJ in *Potisk*. Both authorities, *Ilich* and *Potisk*, must be considered.
2. In summary, *Potisk* (1973), which was decided before *Ilich* (1987), criticised the existing authorities in relation to larceny by mistake. *Potisk* goes further than *Ilich* and proposes that where the victim has handed over property due to a mistake, this will not amount to larceny because the handing over was with consent.
3. In *Ilich* the High Court came to a similar conclusion as the decision in *Potisk*, subject to some qualifications. The High Court held that where an accused has obtained property due to a mistake, and the accused is aware of the mistake at the time or subsequently becomes aware of the mistake and then converts the property, the accused can be charged with larceny only where the mistake is so fundamental as to prevent ownership from passing. The High Court held that there were three types of mistake that were sufficiently fundamental as to negate consent and prevent ownership from passing:
   (a) mistake as to the identity of the person;
   (b) mistake as to the identity of the thing that has been handed over; and
   (c) where an excess quantity of goods is delivered, ownership of the excess has not passed to the receiver.

The High Court did not overturn *Ashwell* and *Middleton*, but stated that the reasoning in these cases only applies where there has been a fundamental mistake. The High Court expressly excluded excess money from the concept of fundamental mistake; that is, if an accused received too much money due to the victim's mistaken consent, the accused cannot be guilty of larceny. This is because ownership of money in the form of currency passes when the person in possession hands it to another intending him or her to be the owner. A mistake merely as to the amount was not a fundamental mistake.

4. The High Court was clear that fundamental mistake could not apply to mistakes involving money. When an intention to pass possession and ownership of money is attributable to a payer and he mistakes merely the amount he intends to pay, a payee who has not induced the mistake is not criminally liable, though he may be civilly liable, for failing to refund any excess paid by mistake. This is because ownership of money in the form of currency passes when the person in possession hands it to another intending him to be the owner. A mistake merely as to amount was not a fundamental mistake (*Ilich* at 254):

> If it were otherwise, the customer who counts the change after coming home from the supermarket would be guilty of stealing any excess received if, on discovering the excess, the customer resolves to spend that money and to refund the excess when shopping next week.

5. Where there is a mutual error and the accused lacks mens rea at the time of taking, different results are yielded depending on whether *Ilich* or *Potisk* applies. If *Potisk* is applied, not only will the prosecution be unable to establish a taking without consent, but D will also lack mens rea at the time of taking. However, if *Ilich* is applied and a fundamental mistake has been made and an accused only subsequently becomes aware of the error but decides to keep the property, then the *Riley* principle (considered at 7.77) can be applied to overcome the difficulty of an absence of mens rea at the time of taking; that is, once a fundamental error has been established, so that consent is vitiated (according to *Ilich*), the original taking will be trespassory. Under the *Riley* principle, this original trespassory taking will extend unless and until the accused forms the necessary mens rea. D can thus be guilty of larceny in cases of mutual and unilateral (fundamental) mistakes under *Ilich*.

Mens rea

7.64 The definition of larceny contained in s 1(1) of the Larceny Act 1916 (UK) requires:

(a) an intent to permanently deprive the owner of her or his property;

(b) the absence of a claim of right made in good faith; and

(c) an element of fraud.

Intention to permanently deprive

7.65 Larceny is not committed unless, at the time of taking, an accused intends to deprive the owner of the property permanently: *R v Foster* (1967) 118 CLR 117. Difficulties can arise when a person takes property but claims that they had an intention to return it.

7.66C R v Holloway

(1849) 1 Den 370; 169 ER 285
Court for Crown Cases Reserved

[Holloway was a workman, employed at the tannery of Barton to dress skins of leather. He was paid according to the number of skins dressed. The dressed skins were handed to a foreman, who stored them in a warehouse adjoining the workroom. Holloway got access to the warehouse and removed from it skins dressed by other workmen; he did not remove them from the tannery. The next day he was detected and later indicted for stealing the skins. The jury found that he intended to deliver the skins to the foreman as his own work and receive payment accordingly. Judgment was postponed for the opinion of the judges as to whether Holloway was guilty of larceny. The case was argued before **Lord Denman CJ**, **Parke** and **Alderson BB**, and **Coltman** and **Coleridge JJ**.]

Parke B: The difficulty here is that it is essential to larceny, that there should be a taking with intent wholly to deprive the owner of his property; a mere temporary appropriation is not enough to constitute a felonious taking. Here the intent was to return them to the master.

Lord Denman CJ: … in giving judgment against the conviction, … said that if this case could be considered open upon the authorities, there seemed great reason to hold that it was a larceny, but that as the court had so lately determined that the intention of the taker must be to deprive the owner wholly of his property, the conviction could not be supported.

Parke B: We are bound to say that this is no larceny… All the cases shew that if the intention were not to take the entire dominion over the property that is no larceny … Therefore the essential element of larceny is here wanting, viz, the intention to deprive the owner wholly of his property.

[**Anderson B** and **Coltman** and **Coleridge JJ** agreed.]

7.67 Notes, questions and illustrations

1. If Holloway had put his plan into effect, what crime could he have been charged with?
2. What of the person who takes property and pawns it on a Wednesday, intending, at the time, to redeem the pawn and replace the property the following Friday on being paid her or his weekly wage? Historically, under

common law, D would be entitled to an acquittal where D had a reasonable chance of fulfilling the intention return the property: *R v Medland* (1851) 5 Cox CC 292. If D had taken the property with the intention of returning it when D was paid later that week, the D would not have the necessary mens rea for larceny. If however D 'borrowed' the property to pawn it with the intention of returning it when D won the lottery, then D would have the necessary mens rea, as D would not have a reasonable chance of winning.

3. Section 118 of the Crimes Act 1900 (NSW) has altered the common law position:

> Where, on the trial of a person for larceny, it appears that the accused appropriated the property in question to the accused's own use, or for the accused's own benefit, or that of another, but intended eventually to restore the same, or in the case of money to return an equivalent amount, such person shall not by reason only thereof be entitled to acquittal.

Thus, where D takes property, an intention to return the property is not a defence to the charge of larceny if D has appropriated the property for D's own use or benefit, or for another's benefit. This is despite the reasonableness of D's intention to reclaim the property and return it to its owner.

4. The operation of s 118, and its relationship to the element of intention to permanently deprive is explained by Barwick CJ in *Foster v R* (1967) 118 CLR 117. D had been staying in Goulburn at the home of V, who was a night watchman. V had a pistol for the purposes of his job. D went to Canberra to visit his parents, having told V's wife that this was his intention. He took with him the pistol (which he removed from its holster when it was lying in the hallway of V's home) and showed it to his parents. When V arrived home that evening, he found the pistol missing and at once notified the police. The same day, D was questioned and arrested in Canberra. Subsequently, he was convicted in Canberra on a charge of having had in his possession, without lawful excuse, a gun stolen in New South Wales, knowing it had been stolen. However, when first questioned in Canberra and at his trial, he claimed that at all times he had intended to return the same evening to Goulburn and to replace the pistol in its holster. On appeal, held, the conviction must be quashed, as the trial judge had directed the jury in to convict if there had been a borrowing without permission:

> Larceny ... being undefined, is as under the common law. It involved an intention on the part of [D] to assume ownership of the gun, to deprive [V] permanently of it, to deprive him of the property in it. I use these three expressions, which are several ways of establishing the same essential element of larceny, namely, the intention to appropriate the goods to himself. To intend to deprive the true owner permanently of the possession of the

goods is one form of the requisite intention. An intention to deprive him of his property in the goods is another, that is, an intention to appropriate the goods as distinct from merely to assume possession of them. Thus, if the intention is to deprive the true owner of possession for a limited time, larceny is not made out. But if the intention of the taker is to exercise ownership of the goods, to deal with them as his own, an intention later to restore the property in the goods will not prevent the original taking being larcenous. [*Foster v R* (1967) 118 CLR 117 at 121 per Barwick CJ.]

5. One context in which the rule that a taking of property for a temporary purpose is not larceny raises particular difficulties is that of what is popularly known as 'joyriding'; that is, the unauthorised use of another's car with the intention of returning it or abandoning it. In New South Wales, illegal use of a motor vehicle or other conveyance is deemed to be larceny: Crimes Act 1900 (NSW) s 154A.
6. Where a person intends to return the property to the owner, but in a substantially altered condition or with reduced value, larceny can be charged: *R v Duru* (1973) 58 Cr App R 151; *Weatherstone v R* (1987) 8 Petty Sessions Review 3729.

Claim of right

7.68 Belief in a claim of legal right to the property taken is inconsistent with the commission of larceny. The claim of right may arise from a mistake of fact or of law. Although mistake of law is, in general, no defence (see **Chapter 13**) it will be a defence where, as in the present context, that mistake prevents the formation of an essential part of the mens rea of the crime charged: see *R v Bernhard* [1938] 2 KB 264 (at **7.126C**); *R v Lopatta* (1983) 35 SASR 101; *R v Sanders* (1991) 57 SASR 102; *Lenard v R* (1992) 57 SASR 164.

7.69 Nor need the mistake be 'reasonable'. In *R v Nundah* (1916) 16 SR (NSW) 482, the accused was charged with larceny of two heifers. His defence was that he believed the heifers were his, and the trial judge directed the jury that they must consider whether he had 'reasonable grounds' for this belief. It was held by the Supreme Court of New South Wales that this constituted a misdirection. Cullen CJ stated (at 489–90):

> [I]n the case of larceny where the question is between honesty and dishonesty, the guilt or innocence of a man cannot, as I understand the principles applicable to that branch of the criminal law, be his belief. The question whether he honestly believed the property to be his is that which is material.

Although the question is whether the accused believed he or she had a bona fide claim of right to the property taken, the reasonableness of such a belief will, of course, be relevant in determining whether the accused held that belief.

7.70C R v Fuge

(2001) 123 A Crim R 310; [2001] NSWCCA 208
Court of Criminal Appeal, Supreme Court of New South Wales

[Fuge had been convicted of being an accessory to an attempted armed robbery at a Hungry Jack's restaurant. One of the principals, Baker-Vollmer, had previously worked at the restaurant but had been dismissed for lateness. When planning the robbery, Baker-Vollmer had mentioned that this was the only way in which she would get money she was owed, but this was not mentioned in the summing up or directions. It was suggested that her statement was a joke. On appeal, the issue of claim of right was raised for the first time. The argument was that the jury should have been directed that Fuge may have believed that Baker-Vollmer had a claim of right to unpaid wages, and this was why Fuge had become involved in the robbery.]

Wood CJ: In an appropriate case, the existence of a claim of right is relevant to the commission of the foundational offence. In the present case, had Pohl and Baker-Vollmer held a bona fide belief that Hungry Jack's owed her a sum of money, then the taking of that sum of money from the restaurant, in circumstances which otherwise would have involved robbery would not have constituted an offence on their part. The reason for that lies in the absence of the mens rea which is an essential element of the offence: *Walden v Hensler* (1987) 163 CLR 561 at 569, 603 and 608.

The same principle applies to any crime of which larceny is an element, and it extends to any person who takes the property on behalf of another, or in collaboration with another, whom he believes to have a bona fide claim of right to the money or property in question: *Sanders* 57 SASR 102 at 105, per King CJ.

A review of the authorities shows that:

(a) the claim of right must be one that involves a belief as to the right to property or money in the hands of another: *Langham* (1984) 36 SASR 48.

(b) the claim must be genuinely, ie honestly held, it not being to the point whether it was well founded in fact or law or not: *Nundah* (1916) 16 SR (NSW) 482, *Bernhard* (1938) 2 QB 264; *Lopatta* (1983) 35 SASR 101 at 107; *Walden v Hensler*; and *Langham* at 52–53.

(c) while the belief does not have to be reasonable: *Nundah* at 485–490; *Langham* at 49; and *Kastratovic* (1985) 19 A Crim R 28, a colourable pretence is insufficient: *Dillon* (1878) 1 SCR NS (NSW) 159 and *Wade* (1869) 11 Cox CC 549.

(d) the belief must be one of a legal entitlement to the property and not simply a moral entitlement: *Bernhard and Harris v Harrison* (1963) Crim LR 497.

(e) the existence of such a claim when genuinely held, may constitute an answer to a crime in which the means used to take the property involved an assault, or the use of arms; the relevant issue being whether the accused had a genuine belief in the legal right to the property rather than a belief in a legal right to employ the means in question to recover it: *Love* (1989) 17 NSWLR 608 at 615–616; *Salvo* (1980) VR 401; *Langham* at 58; *Kastratovic* at 66; *Barker*

(1983) 153 CLR 338; *Williams* (1986) 21 A Crim R 460; and see also *Boden* (1844) 1 C & K 395.

(f) the claim of right is not confined to the specific property or banknotes which were once held by the claimant, but can also extend to cases where what is taken is their equivalent in value, of which *Langham* and *Lopatta* provide examples; although that may be qualified when, for example, the property is taken ostensibly under a claim of right to hold them by way of safekeeping, or as security for a loan, yet the actual intention was to sell them: *Lenard* (1992) 58 A Crim R 123.

(g) the claim of right must, however, extend to the entirety of the property or money taken. Such a claim does not provide any answer where the property or money taken intentionally goes beyond that to which the bona fide claim attaches: *Astor v Hayes* (1988) 38 A Crim R 219 at 222.

(h) In the case of an offender charged as an accessory, what is relevant is the existence of a bona fide claim in the principal offender or offenders, since there can be no accessorial liability unless there has in fact been a foundational offence: *Gregory* LR 1 CCR 77 at 79; see *Lun* (1932) 32 SR (NSW) 363; *Richards* (1974) QB 776 and *Howe* (1987) AC 417, and unless the person charged as an accessory, knowing of the essential facts which made what was done a crime, intentionally aided, abetted, counselled or procured those acts: *Giorgianni* (1985) 156 CLR 473; *Stokes & Difford* (1990) 51 A Crim R 25 and *Buckett* 79 A Crim R 303.

(i) It is for the Crown to negative a claim of right where it is sufficiently raised on the evidence, to the satisfaction of the jury: *Lopatta* at 108, *Astor v Hayes* (1998) 38 A Crim R 219, *Lenard and Williams* at 475.

In applying these principles to the present case, it is correct that a direction would have been required had there been an issue sufficiently raised by the evidence, as to whether Baker-Vollmer had a bona fide belief as to a claim of right to moneys owing to her by Hungry Jack's.

The obligation of the trial Judge to have given such a direction would have continued even though counsel had overlooked requesting it, or had deliberately refrained from seeking it out of concern that it may disadvantage a case of outright denial of any knowledge of, or complicity in a planned robbery: *Pemble* (1971) 124 CLR 118 at 130; and *Stokes v Difford* at 32.

I am not, however, persuaded that the issue was sufficiently raised by the evidence, in circumstances where:

(a) the possibility of a motive in Baker-Vollmer was mentioned only in passing by Pohl, and was dismissed by him as a joke;

(b) counsel for the appellant put to McFaddyen in positive terms, in cross examination, that everybody thought that what Baker-Vollmer had said about Hungry Jack's was a joke;

(c) Baker-Vollmer made no mention of having any belief to a claim of right, or of having mentioned it to anyone else;

(d) the appellant made no mention of ever hearing any such claim being made, or of any particular reason for robbing Hungry Jack's being discussed;
(e) no mention was made by any witness of any consideration being given to a particular sum being taken from the safe to discharge any perceived indebtedness to Baker-Vollmer;
(f) there was no attempt by trial counsel to explore the issue, or to request a direction;
(g) the case was fought on the single issue whether the appellant had participated, to any extent, in providing assistance or encouragement to Pohl and Baker-Vollmer;
(h) both Baker-Vollmer and Pohl pleaded guilty to the robbery, the intention to commit which was an essential ingredient of the offence of which they were convicted, and of the offence for which the appellant stood trial.
(i) the possibility that those who set out to commit the robbery intended to take only a limited sum from the safe, rather than whatever cash they could take, was so remote as not to raise any possibility of the jury having a reasonable doubt on such an issue.

In all of these circumstances, I am not persuaded that there was any risk of a miscarriage of justice going to the root of the proceedings, by reason of the absence of the direction which, it is now submitted, should have been given: *Tripodina* (1988) 35 A Crim R 183. Rather, the case is one where it appears to me, not only from the affidavit of counsel, but from the entirety of the evidence, that the point now sought to be taken was of no importance, and should not be permitted to be ventilated. I would, accordingly, refuse leave under r 4 of the Criminal Appeal Rules 1952 to argue this ground.

7.71 Notes

D entered V's dwelling and took away a television and other items. D claimed that V owed him money to the value of the items taken and had agreed that, if she failed to pay by a due date, he could enter her premises and take her television as collateral. While D alleged he took the goods as 'collateral', he made little effort to have V redeem the goods, and sold the television the next day. D was convicted of housebreaking and larceny. On appeal to the Supreme Court of South Australia, held, conviction affirmed. White J stated in *R v Lenard* (1992) 57 SASR 164 at 168:

> If the appellant also had a second intention, a secret intention, when he carried the television from her house, that he would sell it as quickly as he could and get his money back, regardless of her right of redemption of the goods, then he would necessarily be acting fraudulently without claim of right because the second intention would cut across, taint and destroy the claim of right.

Fraudulently

7.72 The common law offence of larceny requires that the accused took the property 'fraudulently'. The case of *R v Glenister* [1980] 2 NSWLR 597 at 604 asserted that 'fraudulently' has 'a meaning interchangeable with "dishonestly"'. For whether or not these terms are interchangeable, see Steel, 'The Meaning of Dishonesty in Theft' (2009) 38 *Common Law World Review* 103.

7.73 There is wide variation between jurisdictions over what fraudulence means. This involves questions about whether or not fraudulence has a moral basis or not, and what this might be. In England there was some dispute as to the term 'fraudulently', with some authorities suggesting it required a degree of moral blameworthiness, and others arguing that it meant no more than a lack of any belief in a right to the property. The term 'fraudulently' was replaced with 'dishonesty', and a series of English cases culminating in *R v Feely* [1973] 1 QB 530 defined 'dishonesty' as having:

(1) an ordinary everyday meaning that did not need to be explained to the jury; and

(2) a moral basis.

Lord Justice Lawton expressed this in *Feely* at 541 as:

> Jurors, when deciding whether an appropriation was dishonest can be reasonably expected to, and should, apply the current standards of ordinary decent people. In their own lives they have to decide what is and is not honest …
>
> We find it impossible to accept that a conviction for stealing, whether it be called larceny or theft, can reveal no moral obloquy. A man so convicted would have difficulty in persuading his friends and neighbours that his reputation had not been gravely damaged. He would be bound to be lowered in the estimation of right thinking people.

7.74 In Australia, the High Court in *Peters v R* (1998) 192 CLR 493; 151 ALR 51 has held that the approach in *Feely* represents the Australian common law meaning of dishonesty.

7.75C **Peters v R**

(1998) 192 CLR 493; 151 ALR 51

High Court of Australia

[The accused, a solicitor, was convicted of conspiracy to defraud the Commonwealth contrary to s 86(1)(e) of the Crimes Act 1914 (Cth). The accused had been retained by a client to act in certain mortgage transactions. The accused knew that the mortgage transactions were a sham and that their effect was to deprive the Commissioner of Taxation of tax payable as income. In summing up, the judge instructed the jury that it was necessary for the prosecution to prove that the accused had acted dishonestly. The judge further instructed the jury that they had to be satisfied that what the accused agreed to do was dishonest according to the standard of ordinary and reasonable people and, if it was, that the accused realised it was dishonest by those standards. On appeal to the High Court.]

[Footnotes to the extract appear at the end of the extract.]

Toohey and Gaudron JJ:

The argument on appeal

The appellant contends in this court, as he did in the Court of Appeal, that the trial judge misdirected the jury as to the test of dishonesty. In this regard, it is put that the jury should have been instructed to apply a subjective test in accordance with the decision of the Full Court of the Supreme Court of Victoria in *R v Salvo*[1] and not the test adopted in *Ghosh*.[2] More precisely, it is put that the jury should have been instructed that the prosecution had to prove 'an absence of belief [on the appellant's part] that he had a legal right to do what he did'. However, the appellant's belief in that regard was not in issue at the trial. His case was simply that he was not a party to the conspiracy alleged, rather than that he did not act 'dishonestly'.

To understand the appellant's argument, it is necessary to say something of the offence of conspiracy to defraud the Commonwealth. It is a statutory offence created by the Act which, at relevant times, provided, firstly in s 86(1)(e)[3] and later in s 86A,[4] that a person who conspired with another 'to defraud the Commonwealth or a public authority under the Commonwealth' was guilty of an indictable offence.[5] There being no express provision as to the elements of that offence, it is to be taken that s 86(1)(e) and, later, s 86A enacted the substance of the common law offence of conspiracy to defraud in its application to fraudulent agreements the intended victim of which was the Commonwealth or one or more of its public authorities.

The appellant's argument assumes that dishonesty is an element of the common law offence of conspiracy to defraud and, thus, of the offence of conspiracy to defraud the Commonwealth. As will later appear, that assumption is correct in the sense that dishonesty is a characteristic of the means agreed to be employed to effect the fraud and is also descriptive of what is involved in fraud. However, the assumption is not correct in the sense that dishonesty is a separate element of the offence. The difficulty which emerges in this case is partly due to the failure to appreciate that dishonesty is not a separate element and partly due to the different tests of dishonesty which have been adopted in the decided cases.

The tests of dishonesty in *Ghosh* and in *Salvo*

The issue in *Ghosh*[6] was the test of dishonesty for the offence of dishonest appropriation by deception contrary to s 1 of the Theft Act 1968 (UK) (the Theft Act). In that case, a number of earlier cases, including *R v Scott*[7] and *R v Landy*,[8] were referred to in support of the proposition that 'the test for dishonesty ... should be the same whether the offence charged be theft or conspiracy to defraud.'[9] The Court of Appeal declined to apply the subjective test which had been applied in some earlier cases under the Theft Act,[10] namely, whether the accused believed his or her actions to be honest, and adopted, instead, the test which formed the basis of the trial judge's direction in this case.

The test adopted in *Ghosh*, namely, whether the acts in question were dishonest according to current standards of ordinary decent people and, if so, whether the accused must have realised that they were dishonest by those standards[11] has its origins in *R v Feely*.[12] That, too, was a case of dishonest appropriation contrary to s 1 of the Theft Act. It was held in *Feely* that the question of dishonesty was for the jury and, as 'dishonesty' was a word in ordinary use, it was unnecessary for the trial judge to explain what it meant. Further, it was said that it was for the jury to decide whether the act involved was dishonest by application of 'the current standards of ordinary decent people'.[13]

The test of dishonesty adopted in *Salvo*[14] was whether the accused believed he had a legal right to the property in question. In that case, the accused was charged with dishonestly obtaining a motor vehicle by deception contrary to s 81(1) of the *Crimes Act 1958* (Vic) (the Crimes Act), one of a number of provisions in that Act based on the Theft Act. In his defence, the accused asserted his belief that he had a legal right to possession of the vehicle concerned.

In *Salvo*, Murphy J expressed the view that 'the word "dishonestly" is clearly used in a special sense in s 81(1) of the *Crimes Act 1914*'[15] and that '*R v Feely*[16]... ought not to be applied ... if it means that the judge should not tell the jury anything about the word 'dishonestly'.[17] Fullager J likewise thought that dishonesty was used in a special sense and expressed the view that it 'imports that the accused person must obtain the property [in question] ... without any belief that he has in law the right to deprive the other of [it]'.[18] His Honour also described the interpretation of 'dishonestly' in *R v Feely* as 'unworkable'.[19]

The approach adopted in *Salvo* was followed in Victoria in *R v Brow*[20] and *R v Bonollo*,[21] both cases involving charges of dishonestly obtaining by deception under s 81(1) of the *Crimes Act*. It was followed in New South Wales in *R v Love*,[22] another case involving a charge of dishonestly obtaining by deception,[23] and in *Condon*,[24] a case involving a charge of defrauding the Commonwealth under s 29D of the Act. In each of the two last mentioned cases, the accused asserted a belief that he was legally entitled to the property or money in question.

In the present case, the Court of Appeal held that, notwithstanding the decision of the New South Wales Court of Appeal in *Condon*,[25] the subjective test adopted in *R v Salvo* has no application to Commonwealth offences involving fraudulent conduct.[26] It did so on the basis that the application of a subjective test would be inconsistent with its earlier decision in *R v Lawrence*,[27] with dicta in other cases decided in Victoria[28] and with the course of authority in Queensland,[29] South Australia[30] and Western Australia.[31]

Dishonesty

There is a degree of incongruity in the notion that dishonesty is to be determined by reference to the current standards of ordinary, honest persons and the requirement that it be determined by asking whether the act in question was dishonest by those standards and, if so, whether the accused must have known that that was so. That incongruity comes about because ordinary, honest persons determine whether a person's act is dishonest by reference to that person's knowledge or belief as to some fact relevant to the act in question or the intention with which the act was done. They do not ask whether he or she must be taken to have realised that the act was dishonest by the standards of ordinary, honest persons. Thus, for example, the ordinary person considers it dishonest to assert as true something that is known to be false. And the ordinary person does so simply because the person making the statement knows it to be false, not because he or she must be taken to have realised that it was dishonest by the current standards of ordinary, honest persons.

There are also practical difficulties involved in the *Ghosh* test. Those difficulties arise because, in most cases where honesty is in issue, the real question is whether an act was done with knowledge or belief of some specific thing or with some specific intent, not whether it is properly characterised as dishonest. To take a simple example: there is ordinarily no question whether the making of a false statement with intent to deprive another of his property is dishonest. Rather, the question is usually whether the statement was made with knowledge of its falsity and with intent to deprive. Of course, there may be unusual cases in which there is a question whether an act done with knowledge of some matter or with some particular intention is dishonest. Thus, for example, there may be a real question whether it is dishonest, in the ordinary sense, for a person to make a false statement with intent to obtain stolen property from a thief and return it to its true owner.

The practical difficulties with the *Ghosh* test arise both in the ordinary case where the question is whether an act was done with knowledge or belief of some specific matter or with some specific intent and in the unusual case where the question is whether an act done with some particular knowledge, belief or intent is to be characterised as dishonest. In the ordinary case, the *Ghosh* test distracts from the true factual issue to be determined; in the unusual case, it conflates what really are two separate questions, namely, whether they are satisfied beyond reasonable doubt that the accused had the knowledge, belief or intention which the prosecution alleges and, if so, whether, on that account, the act is to be characterised as dishonest. In either case, the test is likely to confuse rather than assist in deciding whether an act was or was not done dishonestly.

In a case in which it is necessary for a jury to decide whether an act is dishonest, the proper course is for the trial judge to identify the knowledge, belief or intent which is said to render that act dishonest and to instruct the jury to decide whether the accused had that knowledge, belief or intent and, if so, to determine whether, on that account, the act was dishonest. Necessarily, the test to be applied in deciding whether the act done is properly characterised as dishonest will differ depending on whether the question is whether it was dishonest according to ordinary notions or dishonest in some special sense. If the question is whether the act was dishonest according to ordinary notions, it is sufficient that the jury be instructed that that is to be decided by the standards of ordinary, decent people. However, if 'dishonest' is used in some special sense in legislation creating an offence, it will ordinarily be necessary for the jury to be told what is or, perhaps, more usually, what is not meant by that word. Certainly, it will be necessary for the jury to be instructed as to that special meaning if there is an issue whether the act in question is properly characterised as dishonest.[32]

The question whether any and, if so, what direction should have been given to the jury with respect to dishonesty in this case must be answered by reference to the elements of the offence of conspiracy to defraud and the issues which arose in the trial. However, it follows from what has been said that it was not appropriate for the jury to be instructed in accordance with the test adopted in *Ghosh*. It also follows that it was not appropriate for it to be instructed in accordance with the test in *Salvo*, a case concerned with an offence against a statutory provision in which, as earlier noted, the word 'dishonest' was held to have been used in a special sense. ...

We have earlier dealt with dishonesty in a general way. It is now necessary to indicate what is involved in dishonest means for the purposes of conspiracy to defraud.

As in other contexts, the question whether the agreed means are dishonest is, at least in the first instance, a question of knowledge, belief or intent and, clearly, that is a question of fact for the jury. On the other hand, the question whether, given some particular knowledge, belief or intent, those means are dishonest is simply a question of characterisation. And as in other contexts, the question whether an act done with some particular knowledge, belief or intent is properly characterised as dishonest is usually not in issue. Thus, putting to one side the exceptional case where it is in issue, it is sufficient for a trial judge simply to instruct the jury that they must be satisfied beyond reasonable doubt as to the knowledge, belief or intent alleged by the prosecution before they can convict. Alternatively, the trial judge may instruct the jury that, if satisfied as to the knowledge, belief or intent alleged, the means in question are properly characterised as dishonest and they should so find.

Because of the view expressed by McHugh J and Gummow J in this case, we should indicate that we incline to the view that should an issue arise whether the agreed means are properly characterised as dishonest, that issue should be left to the jury. At least, that is so if the means are capable of being so characterised. And the jury should be instructed that the question whether they are to be characterised as dishonest is to be determined by application of the standards of ordinary, decent people. However, these issues need not be pursued in this case.

As already explained, 'dishonesty' does not appear in the statute establishing the offence of conspiracy to defraud the Commonwealth. But when properly analysed, the offence of conspiracy to defraud involves dishonesty at two levels. First, it involves an agreement to use dishonest means. Ordinarily, the means will be dishonest if they assert as true something which is false and which is known to be false or not believed to be true or if they are means which the conspirators know they have no right to use or do not believe that they have any right to use the means in question. And quite apart from the use of dishonest means, the offence involves an agreement to bring about a situation prejudicing or imperilling existing legal rights or interests of others. That, too, is dishonest by ordinary standards. If those matters are properly explained to a jury, further direction that the accused must have acted dishonestly is superfluous. Conversely, if those matters are not properly explained, a direction that the jury must be satisfied that the conspirators were dishonest is unlikely to cure the defect.

It need hardly be said again that a statute establishing an offence may use the term 'dishonestly' in its ordinary meaning[33] or use it in a special sense.[34] In either case it will ordinarily be necessary for the trial judge to explain precisely what the legislation requires. In the case of conspiracy to defraud, it will ordinarily be sufficient to instruct the jury as to the facts they must find if the agreed means are to be characterised as dishonest. Alternatively, it will be sufficient to instruct them that, if satisfied as to those facts, they will be satisfied that the agreed means were dishonest. Only in the borderline case will it be necessary for the question whether the means are to be so characterised to be left to the jury. In this area, but only in this area, we differ from the approach taken by McHugh J and Gummow J. …

The appeal must be dismissed.

[**McHugh J**, with whom **Gummow J** agreed, held that it is for the judge to determine whether the facts alleged constitute the offence of conspiracy to defraud and, if the judge finds that they do, for the jury to determine whether the relevant facts have been proved so as to make the accused guilty of the offence. His Honour held that the facts alleged by the prosecution amounted to conspiracy to defraud and that the judge's direction had unduly favoured the accused. **Kirby J**, dissenting, took the view that dishonesty imports a subjective test, and that the judge should have focused the minds of the jury on what the accused personally believed as to the honesty of the means chosen to achieve the agreement entered into. Since the jury had not received such a direction, **Kirby J** would have allowed the appeal. His Honour accepted that his approach to dishonesty was in conflict with the opinion of **McHugh J**, with whom **Gummow J** agreed, and with the opinion of **Toohey** and **Gaudron JJ**. Having regard to the desirability of providing clear instruction for future cases, his Honour withdrew his own preferred opinion and concurred with the opinions expressed by **Toohey** and **Gaudron JJ**. Appeal dismissed.]

Notes:

1. [1980] VR 401.
2. [1982] QB 1053.
3. Until 24 October 1984. By s 3 and Sch 1 of the *Statute Law (Miscellaneous Provisions) Act (No 2)* (Cth), s 86(1)(e) was omitted and replaced by s 86A.
4. Until 14 September 1995. By s 8 of the *Crimes Amendment Act 1995* (Cth), s 86A together with s 86 were repealed and replaced by a new s 86.
5. Note that the offence of conspiracy to defraud the Commonwealth now derives from the combined operation of ss 86 and 29D of the Act. Section 86(1) provides that '[a] person who conspires with another person to commit an offence against a law of the Commonwealth punishable by imprisonment for more than 12 months, or by a fine of 200 penalty units or more, is guilty of the offence of conspiracy to commit that offence'. And by s 29D, a person who defrauds the Commonwealth or a public authority under the Commonwealth is guilty of an indictable offence punishable by 1,000 penalty units or imprisonment for 10 years, or both.
6. [1982] QB 1053.
7. [1975] AC 819.
8. [1981] 1 WLR 355.
9. [1982] QB 1053 at 1059. Cf *R v McIvor* [1982] 1 WLR 409 in which it was held that a subjective test was to be applied for conspiracy to defraud and an objective test for theft.
10. See, for example, *R v Greenstein* [1975] 1 WLR 1353 and *R v Waterfall* [1970] 1 QB 148. See also *R v Royle* [1971] 1 WLR 1764.
11. [1982] QB 1053 at 1064.
12. [1973] QB 530.
13. [1973] QB 530 at 538.
14. [1980] VR 401.

15. [1980] VR 401 at 422.
16. [1973] QB 530.
17. [1980] VR 401 at 423.
18. [1980] VR 401 at 440.
19. [1980] VR 401 at 439.
20. [1981] VR 783.
21. [1981] VR 633.
22. (1989) 17 NSWLR 608.
23. See s 178BA of the *Crimes Act 1900* (NSW).
24. (1995) 83 A Crim R 335.
25. (1995) 83 A Crim R 335.
26. Note that in *R v Harris* (unreported, Court of Appeal of Victoria, 13 February 1997), the Court of Appeal again held that the subjective test in *Salvo* did not apply to a fraud offence, this offence charged pursuant to s 29D of the *Crimes Act 1914* (Cth).
27. [1997] 1 VR 459.
28. See *R v Smart* [1983] 1 VR 265 at 294–5; *R v Walsh and Harney* [1984] VR 474 at 478 per Young CJ (with whom Murray J agreed); *R v Edwards* [1988] VR 481 at 489 per Young CJ.
29. See *R v Maher* [1987] 1 Qd R 171.
30. See *R v Aston and Burnell* (1987) 44 SASR 436.
31. See *Cornelius & Briggs* (1988) 34 A Crim R 49. See also *Turner v Campbell* (1987) 88 FLR 410.
32. As in *Salvo*.
33. As in *Ghosh*.
34. As in *Salvo*.

7.76 Notes

1. Although *Peters v R* was a case of conspiracy to defraud, the reasoning adopted by Toohey and Gaudron JJ should be seen as equally applicable to common law larceny. The approach adopted by their Honours is, in principle, correct. The older definitions of larceny all stressed the necessity for a taking which was morally wrongful. In the great majority of cases, it is clear that if the accused acted without a bona fide claim of legal right and with the intention of permanently depriving the owner of her or his property, the accused acted fraudulently. In the exceptional case, however, it is suggested that the accused should be regarded as having a possible defence based on the residual meaning of the word 'fraudulently'. In such exceptional cases, it is for the jury to determine by application of the standards of ordinary, decent people whether the conduct of the accused should be characterised as dishonest.
2. It should be noted that s 4B of the Crimes Act has provided a definition of 'dishonest' that is applicable where the word 'dishonest' is used in the statute:

> *Dishonest* means dishonest according to the standards of ordinary people and known by the defendant to be dishonest according to the standards of ordinary people.

This definition of dishonesty mirrors the English test of dishonesty articulated in *Ghosh* [1982] QB 1053 and rejects the test propounded by the High Court in *Peters*. At this stage it is uncertain whether s 4B will apply to s117, but it seems logical that it will.

3. In most cases, the word 'fraudulent' adds little to the definition of larceny. Clearly, there will be few cases where an accused who takes something without a claim of right and with the intention of permanently depriving the owner of it can claim he or she was not acting fraudulently.
4. One class of case giving rise to this question involves fungibles; that is, items one specimen of which is as good as another or those where weight or quantity are the common measure. In the course of daily living, people speak of borrowing, say, an egg in just the same way as of borrowing a book. However, their expectations differ in the two cases. If someone borrows my book, I expect that person to return the identical book, but if I 'lend' someone an egg, I expect that person to use it and to give me an egg of similar quality in return. So, also, if I lend someone money. On principle, there seems no good reason why a person who takes something intending to return that very thing should not be guilty of larceny, while a person who takes a fungible such as money, intending to and reasonably expecting to be able to return a precise equivalent of that which was taken, should be guilty of larceny. In such a case, it is suggested that the accused should have a defence on the ground that her or his conduct is not properly classified as fraudulent. The same arguments can be made in relation to section 118, which foregoes the requirement that D intends to deprive V of the property permanently.
5. *Critical analysis of 'fraudulently' and 'dishonestly'*: Under *Feely* and *Peters* the question of whether or not the jury was dishonest was asked with little guidance given to the jury. The test proposed in *Ghosh* and in s 4 of the Crimes Act NSW imposes a two-part test for the jury:
   (a) dishonest according to the standards of ordinary people; and
   (b) known by the defendant to be dishonest according to the standards of ordinary people.

   The first part of this test is objective, while the second part is subjective.
6. The implications of the two-stage test were articulated in *Ghosh* [1982] QB 1053. The first part means that the test is not purely subjective. An accused is not entitled to rely on his or her own views about whether his or her conduct is honest:

> For example, Robin Hood or those ardent anti-vivisectionists who remove animals from vivisection laboratories are acting dishonestly, even though they may consider themselves to be morally justified in doing what they do, because they know that ordinary people would consider those actions to be dishonest [per Lord Lane at 1063].

Nor is the test purely objective:

> Take the man who comes from a country where public transport is free. On his first day here he travels on a bus. He gets off without paying. He never has any intention of paying. His mind is clearly honest; but his conduct, judged objectively by what he has done, is dishonest [per Lord Lane at 1063].

7. All the proposed tests of dishonesty and fraudulence have attracted criticism. Tests that call on the ordinary person and impose an objective test assume that juries are heterogenous and have consistent values. However, it is unlikely that this is the case. Values in this country vary widely, across cultural and socio-economic divides. There is no reason to suppose that such variations will not extend to dishonesty. Do we all agree, per Lord Lane, that Robin Hood was dishonest, or that openly using force to release animals from vivisection laboratories is dishonest? If there are reasonably held different views on these matters, then there is a risk of different verdicts, on the same facts, from different juries. This undermines the rule of law, that a citizen should be able to predict whether or not his or her behaviour will contravene the law.

   However, a purely subjective test, focusing on an accused's beliefs regarding honesty is also undesirable. Defendants cannot be permitted entirely to supplant their own values for the law. Law works by preventing people from doing what they want, through imposing a standard of acceptable behaviour and demanding they conform to that standard. If law could be displaced by the beliefs of a particular defendant, then there would be no standard for the law to impose. Individuals cannot be allowed to conduct themselves outside the law merely because they have different moral values.

   The line between dishonest and honest behaviour is not always clear and/or uncontroversial. For further analysis, see A Halpin, 'The Test for Dishonesty' [1996] *Crim LR* 283.

8. *Larceny by finding cases and fraudulence:* The element of fraudulence is also important in larceny by finding cases. These are cases where an accused finds property that is lost. The rules of simple larceny apply, but there is an emphasis upon fraudulence in the mens rea requirements.

   The actus reus of larceny by finding are that D:

   (a) took and carried away;

   (b) property capable of being stolen;

(c) which belonged to another (abandonment may be an issue here: see 7.47);

(d) without the consent of the owner: if D picks up property with the intention of finding the owner, then the owner's consent is assumed and the taking is not trespassory (*R v MacDonald* [1983] 1 NSWLR 729). If D picks up property without any intention of finding the owner, or not knowing what D will do with it, then this is a taking without the consent of the owner.

The mens rea of larceny by finding is that at the time of taking, D:

(a) had an intention to permanently deprive;

(b) without a claim of right; and

(c) fraudulently: if D honestly believes that the property has been abandoned, or that the owner cannot be found, then D will not be guilty of larceny because D has not acted fraudulently.

9. D found a banknote on the highway. There was nothing in the circumstances to suggest who the owner of the note was. D took the note with the intention of appropriating it to his own use. The following day, D was informed who the owner of the note was but he nevertheless kept the note. Held, D was not guilty of larceny of the note. At the time of taking possession of the note, he was acting innocently since he believed the owner of the note could not be discovered. When D learned the identity of the owner of the note and decided to keep it, he was already its lawful possessor and he could not, therefore, commit larceny at that point of time. Delivering the judgment of the Court for Crown Cases Reserved, Parke B in *R v Thurborn* (1849) 1 Den 387; 169 ER 293 laid down the following rule:

> [I]f a man finds goods that have been actually lost, or are reasonably supposed by him to have been lost, and appropriates them, with intent to take the entire dominion over them, really believing when he takes them, that the owner cannot be found, it is not larceny. But if he takes them with the like intent, though lost, or reasonably supposed to be lost, but reasonably believing that the owner can be found, it is larceny.

10. D found a camera hanging on a fence post. He asked a man next door if the camera was his; upon a negative reply, D took the camera and kept it. It was held that his failure to make any inquiries, or contact the owner of the house or the police, demonstrated a fraudulent intention to keep the property despite a belief that the owner could be found. The New South Wales Court of Criminal Appeal stated (at 732): '[W]hat the finder does in relation to the goods but also what he does not do that might reasonably be regarded as consistent with the actions of an honest man finding goods': *R v McDonald* [1983] 1 NSWLR 729. See also *Donaghue v Coombe* (1987) 45 SASR 330.

Temporal coincidence

7.77 There is a general requirement that an accused has a guilty mind at the time of committing the external act. However, an honest but trespassory taking and the development of a subsequent fraudulent intent may amount to larceny, under the *Riley* principle.

The *Riley* principle, or the doctrine of 'continuing trespass', was developed to cover situations where D innocently acquires property, and later forms the intention to permanently deprive the owner of the property. Under the *Riley* principle, where an original taking is trespassory, a subsequent fraudulent intent will ground a charge of larceny.

7.78 D placed 29 black-faced lambs in a field belonging to a neighbour. The prosecutor had earlier placed 10 white-faced lambs in the same field. The following morning, D returned and drove off with his black-faced lambs, together with one of the white-faced lambs. Because the morning was misty, D was not aware of the additional lamb. He drove the lambs to a farm, and agreed to sell the 29 lambs to the farmer. The farmer counted the flock and informed D that there were 30 lambs instead of 29 lambs. At that time, D became aware that he had an additional lamb, but nevertheless he sold all 30 to the farmer. D was convicted of larceny, but the case was reserved for the Court for Crown Cases Reserved. The court held that the conviction was correct. The court affirmed the general rule that where a person rightfully gets possession of an article without any intention of stealing it, a subsequent dishonest appropriation will not render that person guilty of larceny. It held, however, that where the original taking amounts to a trespass a subsequent intention to appropriate will render the taker guilty of larceny. Parke B in *R v Riley* (1853) 1 Dears CC 149; 169 ER 674 stated:

> The original taking was not lawful. The prisoner being originally a trespasser, he continued a trespasser all along. and, being a trespasser, the moment he took the lamb with a felonious intent, he became a thief. He at first simply commits a trespass; but as soon as he entertains a felonious intent that becomes a felonious trespass.

Note also *Ruse v Read* [1949] 1 KB 377; *R v Kindon* (1957) 41 Cr App R 208; *R v Buttle* (1959) 60 SR (NSW) 320.

7.79 The *Riley* principle is particularly important in larceny by finding cases, where D picks up property belonging to another without any specific intention regarding the property. In these cases, the original taking is trespassory, because D has not picked up the property with the intention of finding the owner. If D later decides to permanently deprive the owner of the property then D may be guilty of larceny.

7.80 The *Riley* principle may also apply in cases of mistaken consent if *Ilich* is applied and if there has been a fundamental mistake. If there has been a fundamental mistake then the taking was trespassory, and if D later forms the intention to keep or use the property, then the *Riley* principle will apply to ground a charge in larceny.

OFFENCE OF FRAUD

Introduction

7.81 Until 2010, New South Wales law relating to dishonest acquisition of property involving deception was a complex mix of common law and statutory offences introduced across time, including larceny by trick and obtaining by false pretences. As a result of legislative reforms in 2010, there is now one general fraud offence in s 192E of the Crimes Act 1900 (NSW), with definitions in ss 192B–192D. Although larceny by trick continues to exist as a sub-category of the offence of larceny, the specificity and limitations of larceny by trick mean that any offence involving trickery or fraud is now better covered by the new fraud offence.

7.82E **Crimes Act 1900 (NSW)**

192E Fraud

(1) A person who, by any deception, dishonestly:
  (a) obtains property belonging to another, or
  (b) obtains any financial advantage or causes any financial disadvantage,
  is guilty of the offence of fraud.

Maximum penalty: Imprisonment for 10 years.

(2) A person's obtaining of property belonging to another may be dishonest even if the person is willing to pay for the property.

(3) A person may be convicted of the offence of fraud involving all or any part of a general deficiency in money or other property even though the deficiency is made up of any number of particular sums of money or items of other property that were obtained over a period of time.

(4) A conviction for the offence of fraud is an alternative verdict to a charge for the offence of larceny, or any offence that includes larceny, and a conviction for the offence of larceny, or any offence that includes larceny, is an alternative verdict to a charge for the offence of fraud.

7.83 Under s 192E, there are three different forms of the offence based on consequences. These are:

(1) obtaining property;

(2) obtaining financial advantage; or

(3) causing a financial disadvantage.

All three consequences of the offence must be caused by deception. The mens rea of the offence requires that the accused was either reckless as to deception or intentionally deceptive, and obtained or caused the consequences dishonestly.

Elements

7.84 In order to establish fraud, the prosecution must prove:

(1) Actus reus:

  (a) deception; and

  (b) this deception caused an obtaining of property, financial advantage or disadvantage.

(2) Mens rea:

  (a) the actions of the accused were intentionally or recklessly deceptive; and

  (b) it was dishonest to cause that consequence. If an accused had a claim of right, then they will not be dishonest.

  The prosecution is required to prove an additional mens rea requirement of an intention to permanently deprive if the accused has been charged with the prohibited consequence of obtaining property.

(3) Temporal coincidence: at the time of the actus reus, D must have the necessary mens rea.

Actus reus

Deception

7.85 All forms of fraud in s 192E must be committed by an accused engaging in deception. Section 192B(1) defines the actus reus element of deception.

7.86E **Crimes Act 1900 (NSW)**

192B Deception

(1) In this Part, **deception** means any deception, by words or other conduct, as to fact or as to law, including:

  (a) a deception as to the intentions of the person using the deception or any other person, or

  (b) conduct by a person that causes a computer, a machine or any electronic device to make a response that the person is not authorised to cause it to make.

7.87 Although there are yet to be any cases exploring the new statutory concept, it is possible to draw upon earlier common law that has since been replaced by the new fraud offence, to give some indication of the reach of s 192B. The broad definition of deception at least incorporates earlier common law deceptions. Section 192B is clear that, in accordance with common law, a deception can be as to fact or law.

7.88 False statement The most common form of deception is making a false statement; that is, telling a lie. These statements might be completely or partially false. For example, in *M* [1980] 2 NSWLR 195 the New South Wales Court of Appeal held (at 204):

> It is now well established that the falsity of a statement may arise, not only because a fact therein alleged is falsely alleged, but because the statement, by omitting material facts, creates a false impression.

7.89 At common law, exaggeration will not amount to a deception. It will be a question of fact for the jury to determine the distinction: *R v John Bryan* [1857] 169 ER 1002. In that case it was held that claiming a spoon was made of the 'best material' and 'had as much silver on them as Elkington's' was mere exaggeration or puffery. In contrast, stating that a diamond was 7½ carats, when it was actually only four carats, was held to be a deception: *Patmoy* (1944) 62 WN (NSW) 1.

7.90 Deception under s 192B will include deceptions as to the past, present and future. In *R v Freeman* [1981] 2 NSWLR 686, D appealed against conviction for a range of offences that included the now repealed offence of obtaining by false pretence or promise (s 179). D had falsely presented profits as actual profits earned by a franchise, when in fact they were based on assumptions regarding profits. D also promised franchisees they would earn that level of profit. Both accused were found guilty of offences under s 179. Glass J stated (at 60–1):

> The submission put for the appellants was that a promise that a franchisee will earn not less than a stipulated amount per week depends for its performance on many factors outside the control of the promisor, such as the patronage of the motoring public, and that a promise which the promisor is unable to perform is not a promise within the meaning of the section …
>
> I am of the opinion that a promise, the fulfilment of which lies outside the power of the promisor, is within the statutory description. The evidence must, of course, establish that the promise was a wilfully false one when made. The evidence here that the appellants had compiled a document based upon mere speculation and were representing both that it showed the profits being made by existing franchisees and also the profits that would be made by intending franchisees was capable of supporting a conclusion that they were not only making a false promise as to the past which was to their knowledge false, but also a promise for the future which was wilfully false.

7.91 Deception by conduct and silence Conduct without words, that is, implied representations, can amount to a deception: this has been termed an implied representation. In accordance with recommendations by the Model Criminal Code Officers Committee in *Chapter 3: Theft, Fraud, Bribery and Related Offences, Final Report* (1995), s 192B(1)(b) extends the scope of deception to deceiving machines. This contrasts with dicta in *Kennison v Daire* (1985) 16 A Crim R 338, that suggested that a machine cannot be deceived in relation to the common law offence of larceny.

Section 192B(1)(b) would include many forms of ATM fraud. The deception is that the customer has the authority to use the card and is operating the account in accordance with the terms and conditions of use (which include the condition that a cardholder has sufficient balance in their account to cover the amount requested). Similarly, using another person's ATM card and PIN would constitute a deception.

7.92 English cases demonstrate the minimal actus reus requirement of 'deception'. The primary focus in evaluations of deception is upon the mens rea of the accused. For example, in *DPP v Ray* [1974] AC 370, D had ordered a meal in a restaurant with the intention of borrowing money from one of his companions to pay for it. However, at the end of the meal he and his companions decided to run away from the restaurant without paying. D was charged with dishonestly obtaining a pecuniary advantage by deception. D was not charged with obtaining property or services by deception presumably because the prosecution accepted that at the time the meal was obtained, there was no deception being practised by the accused. The House of Lords held that in ordering the meal the accused had, by his conduct, represented that he would pay for it. Although that was an honest representation at the time, by sitting at the table some time after making his decision not to pay, his conduct created the dishonest deception that he was an ordinary customer still intending to pay. Lord Morris held (at 386):

> By ordering his meal and by his conduct in assuming the role of an ordinary customer the respondent had shown that it was his intention to pay. By continuing in the same role and behaving just as before he was representing that his previous intention continued. That was a deception because his intention, unknown to the waiter had become quite otherwise. The dishonest cause of intention was not likely to produce the result that the waiter would be told of it. The essence of the deception was that the waiter should not know of it or be given any sort of clue that it (the change of intention) had come about. Had the waiter suspected that by a change of intention a secret exodus was being planned, it is obvious that he would have taken action to prevent its being achieved.

Lord MacDermott stated (at 382) that the representation covered 'the whole transaction up to and including payment and must therefore be covered … as continuing and still active at the time of the change of mind.'

In dissent, Lord Reid stated (at 379–80):

> So the respondent, after he changed his mind, must have done something intended to induce the waiter to believe that he still intended to pay before he left. Deception, to my mind, implies something positive. It is quite true that a man intending to deceive can build up a situation in which his silence is as eloquent as an express statement. But what did the accused do here to create such a situation? He merely sat still.

The concept of an implied deception was also applied in *R v Benli* [1998] 2 VR 149. In that case, D, a driving instructor, had had his licence to drive and therefore instruct suspended. He continued to provide lessons and obtain fees. He was charged with obtaining property by deception. At trial, students gave evidence that they had believed he was a licensed instructor and would not have continued to use his services if they had known he was not licensed. It was held that although there was no express representation that he was a licensed instructor, this was implied by his conduct.

In *Barnard* [1837] 7 C & P 784; 173 ER 342, deception was found where D obtained credit from a tradesman by entering his shop dressed in an Oxford cap and gown.

See also *Rai* [2000] 1 Cr App R 242; *Firth* (1991) Cr App R 217.

Causation

7.93 The prosecution must prove that the accused 'obtained by deception'; that is, that the deception caused that victim to part with their property or services. The deception need not be the only cause for the victim handing over their property, but must be a factor that substantially contributed to V's decision. If the deception does not have its intended effect on the mind of the person to whom it is addressed because the person does not believe the deception, the offence is not committed, even if property is handed over. However, there will have been an attempt to obtain by deception.

7.94 D falsely represented to V (who, unbeknown to him, was a detective) that he had the power to communicate with the spirits of the dead. V encouraged D to make these claims in order to entrap him and, in fact, paid over a sum of money to him in supposed exchange for these 'valuable revelations'. D could not be found guilty of obtaining by false pretences, but only attempting to obtain money by false pretences:

> In order to satisfy a presentment for obtaining money by false pretences, there should be a pretence false in fact, and there should have been money obtained, and the money should have been obtained in consequence of that false pretence. That denotes that the person who parts with the money believes the falsehood to be the truth, otherwise he would not have parted with his money. But where the person who parts with his money knows that the pretence is false, the falsehood is known to him. He parts with his money, not because he is deceived by the statement, but for another reason — viz, because he wants to detect the imposter, and although he has not been deceived, the prisoner has attempted to deceive him [*R v Perera* [1907] VLR 240 at 244 per Madden CJ].

See also *Kassis v Katsantonis* [1984] 3 NSWLR 330.

7.95 D, who was a good runner and had won a race at Frith, entered two races at Lincoln. On the entry forms, he used the name of X, a moderate runner. The handicapper, using X's record of performance, gave D a good start in each race, and D won both easily. Before he could claim the prizes (which were £10/10/- each), the handicapper became suspicious. D was convicted of attempting to obtain the prize money by false pretences, the handicapper having testified that he would not have given him such good starts had he known his true name and record. On case reserved, held, affirmed: *R v Button* [1900] 2 QB 597 (CCR). Accord *R v Lambassi* [1927] VLR 349.

7.96 D wished to place a large sum of money on a horse but knew that, because he had been in the habit of collecting on winning bets and defaulting on losing bets, he could not get a bookmaker to accept his bet. He placed a bet by falsely representing his name and that the sum wagered was the aggregate of a number of small amounts bet by workmen for whom he was commission agent. The horse won and D was paid. Held, not guilty of obtaining money by false pretences. The effective cause of D's obtaining the money was not his representations as to his agency, but the fact that the horse won: *R v Clucas* [1949] 2 KB 226; 2 All ER 40.

7.97 D worked for a business that bought and sold futures contracts through a broker at the Sydney Futures Exchange. D deceived their clients into believing the contracts were being traded on the Futures Exchange, when they were actually being traded within the business itself. Both accused were found not guilty as their deceptions were not the effective cause of payment; there was no nexus between the deception of D upon the member and the obtaining of that money from the association for him: *R v Ho and Szeto* (1989) 39 A Crim R 145.

The consequence of the fraud

7.98 The prosecution must prove one of three consequences of the fraud:

(1) obtaining property from another;

(2) obtaining a financial advantage; or

(3) causing a financial disadvantage.

7.99 **Obtaining property from another** The first limb of the offence is based on the wording used in the Theft Act 1968 (UK). Property is defined to include both tangible and intangible property (s 4 of the Crimes Act 1900 (NSW)). The definition includes not only possession but also control of property. This has led, in England, to a series of appeal cases. Given the availability of the simpler financial advantage limb, it is likely that s 192E(a) will be used primarily in instances of simple tangible property frauds.

7.100 Section 192C(1) defines the obtaining of property to require only that the accused or a third party gain control or possession of the property. This means that the fraud covers those situations where a victim has been tricked into handing over possession or control, but does not hand over the property permanently.

7.101E **Crimes Act 1900 (NSW)**

192C Obtaining property belonging to another

(1) For the purposes of this Part, a person **obtains property** if:

(a) the person obtains ownership, possession or control of the property for himself or herself or for another person, or

(b) the person enables ownership, possession or control of the property to be retained by himself or herself or by another person, or

(c) the person induces a third person to do something that results in the person or another person obtaining or retaining ownership, possession or control of the property.

(2) A person does not commit an offence under this Part by obtaining or intending to obtain property belonging to another unless the person intends to permanently deprive the other of the property.

(3) For the purposes of this Part, **property belongs** to a person if:

(a) the person has possession or control of the property, or

(b) the person has a proprietary right or interest in the property (not being an equitable interest arising only from an agreement to transfer or grant an interest or from a constructive trust).

If property is subject to a trust, the persons to whom it belongs include any person having a right to enforce the trust.

(4) A person obtaining property belonging to another without meaning the other permanently to lose the thing itself has, nevertheless, the intention of permanently depriving the other of it if the person's intention is to treat the thing as his or her own to dispose of regardless of the other's rights. A borrowing or lending of the property may amount to so treating it if, but only if, the borrowing or lending is for a period and in circumstances making it equivalent to an outright taking or disposal.

(5) Without limiting the generality of subsection (4), if:

(a) a person has possession or control (lawfully or not) of property belonging to another, and

(b) the person parts with the property under a condition as to its return that the person may not be able to perform, and

(c) the parting is done for the purposes of his or her own and without the other's authority,

the parting amounts to treating the property as his or her own to dispose of regardless of the other's rights.

7.102 **Obtaining financial advantage** This limb of the offence is substantially based upon the now repealed s 178BA, thus case law on that offence is likely to be applicable. Financial advantage is defined broadly in s 192D.

7.103E	Crimes Act 1900 (NSW)

192D Obtaining financial advantage or causing financial disadvantage

(1) In this Part, **obtain** a financial advantage includes:

- (a) obtain a financial advantage for oneself or for another person, and
- (b) induce a third person to do something that results in oneself or another person obtaining a financial advantage, and
- (c) keep a financial advantage that one has,

whether the financial advantage is permanent or temporary.

7.104 Similar offences exist in Victoria. It has been held that the term 'financial advantage' should be given its plain meaning and not narrowly construed so as to allow it to have the broadest scope possible: *R v Vasic* (2005) 11 VR 380. Thus in *Matthews v Fountain* [1982] VR 1045 it was held that a financial advantage was obtained by the use of a valueless cheque given to an employee, even though the accused could not pay the money owed, on the basis that the accused obtained the benefit of further time to pay and did not have to pay the value of the cheque. However, there was no financial advantage where the accused merely secured the deferral or repayment of money owed by giving a valueless cheque: *Fisher v Bennett* (1987) 85 FLR 469. A financial advantage can be obtained even though there is no financial disadvantage to be suffered by the victim: *R v Walsh* (1990) 52 A Crim R 80.

7.105 **Causing a financial disadvantage** Historically, one issue that has caused difficulty for the interpretation of financial advantage offences is where the accused attempts to evade a debt. It has been questioned whether this amounts to gaining a financial advantage for the accused or whether there is no advantage. Section 192D(2) overcomes these difficulties.

7.106E	Crimes Act 1900 (NSW)

192D Obtaining financial advantage or causing financial disadvantage

(2) In this Part, **cause** a financial disadvantage means:

- (a) cause a financial disadvantage to another person, or
- (b) induce a third person to do something that results in another person suffering a financial disadvantage,

whether the financial disadvantage is permanent or temporary.

7.107 In cases where an accused seeks to evade a debt, the question of liability will now turn on the disadvantage caused to the creditor by dishonest failure to repay, rather than whether the debtor accrues an advantage. Section 192D(2) will also cover situations where an accused receives no advantage but is aiming to cause harm to the victim; for example, by withdrawing money from an account. It might be easier in some cases for the prosecution to prove financial disadvantage than advantage.

Mens rea

Intentional or reckless deception

7.108 Section 192B(2) requires that the deception is intentional or reckless:

> (2) A person does not commit an offence under this Part by a deception unless the deception was intentional or reckless.

7.109 Historically, a false pretence had to be intentional. Section 192B(2) therefore extends the common law position to include recklessness. Accordingly, the prosecution must prove either that the accused intended to deceive, or that the accused was reckless as to the truthfulness of their statements. At this stage it is uncertain what the definition of recklessness will be, but it is likely that the applicable test will be if an accused recognised the possibility that the behaviour is deceptive: *Stokes and Difford* (1990) 51 A Crim R 25 at 40. An example of reckless deception would include a situation where an accused exposes another to a risk of loss. If D borrows $100 from V promising to pay it back on Friday, but D knows that there is a risk that D will not be able to repay the debt on Friday and then fails to do so, D could be charged with reckless deception dishonestly causing financial disadvantage, even if the loss is only temporary.

Dishonestly

7.110E **Crimes Act 1900 (NSW)**

192E Fraud

(1) A person who, by any deception, dishonestly:

(a) obtains property belonging to another, or

(b) obtains any financial advantage or causes any financial disadvantage,

is guilty of the offence of fraud.

7.111 Dishonesty is defined in s 4B:

> (1) In this Act:
>
> ***Dishonest*** means dishonest according to the standards of ordinary people and known by the defendant to be dishonest according to the standards of ordinary people.

This definition of dishonesty mirrors the English test of dishonesty articulated in *Ghosh* [1982] QB 1053 and rejects the test propounded by the High Court in *Peters*.

The issue of dishonesty is considered in more detail at 7.72.

7.112 It is likely that the common law defence of claim of right will be implied as an element of the new fraud offences. Under the now repealed offences, it was held that where D has a bona fide belief in a claim of legal right, this will negative an intention to defraud: *R v Kastratovic* (1985) 42 SASR 59; 19 A Crim R 28. This is because an intention to defraud (at 62–3 per King CJ):

> … connotes the intention to produce a consequence that is in some sense detrimental to a lawful right, interest, opportunity or advantage of the person to be defrauded, and is an intention distinct from and additional to the intention to use the forbidden means.

As a consequence (at 65 per King CJ):

> … an intent to do no more than procure payment of a debt which is presently due and payable to the accused, or which the accused believes to be presently due and payable by the alleged victim, is not an intent to defraud, and is not converted into an intent to defraud by the employment of dishonest means.

In the Discussion Paper on the new fraud offences, it was stated that New South Wales would continue to rely on the common law defence of claim of right under the proposed bill.

Intention to permanently deprive

7.113 If the prohibited consequence of the offence is the first limb of obtaining property, s 192C(2) requires an additional mens rea element of intention to permanently deprive:

> (2) A person does not commit an offence under this Part by obtaining or intending to obtain property belonging to another unless the person intends to permanently deprive the other of the property.

This mirrors the common law requirement of mens rea for the offence of larceny. The meaning of 'intention to permanently deprive' is complicated by s 192C(4):

> (4) A person obtaining property belonging to another without meaning the other permanently to lose the thing itself has, nevertheless, the intention of permanently depriving the other of it if the person's intention is to treat the thing as his or her own to dispose of regardless of the other's rights. A borrowing or lending of the property may amount to so treating it if, but only if, the borrowing or lending is for a period and in circumstances making it equivalent to an outright taking or disposal.

This subsection appears to mirror the common law interpretation of section 118.

Temporal coincidence

7.114 The requirement that the deception is either intentional or reckless imports a requirement that the accused had the necessary mens rea at the time of the deception. This is also considered in *DPP v Ray* [1974] AC 370 which imports a requirement of temporal coincidence.

ROBBERY, BURGLARY, BLACKMAIL AND RECEIVING

Robbery

7.115E Crimes Act 1900 (NSW)

94 Robbery or stealing from the person

Whosoever:

> robs or assaults with intent to rob any person, or steals any chattel, money, or valuable security from the person of another,

shall, except where a greater punishment is provided by this Act, be liable to imprisonment or fourteen years.

7.116 Additionally, the Act contains a number of offences of aggravated robbery. These are robbery with violence (s 95), robbery with wounding (s 96) and armed robbery and robbery in company (s 97). Note *R v Brougham* (1986) 43 SASR 187.

7.117C Smith v Desmond

[1965] AC 960

House of Lords

[The two respondents had been convicted of robbery with violence. There was evidence that, together with two other men, they had broken into a bakery and stolen a large sum in cash from a safe. At 11.50 pm on the night in question, a maintenance engineer had been in the bakery workshop with a night watchman. The latter went out to get some sandwiches but was assaulted and brought back to the workshop where both men were tied up and blind folded. They were then taken to a lavatory and their feet tied as well. They were left there while the respondents went off and broke into the cash office through a window. The respondents were then separated from the two men by a distance of 33 yards. There were two doors, at least one of which was locked, between them. The victims could hear the sounds of the safe being burned open from where they lay.

At the trial, the Recorder instructed the jury that they could find that the stealing had occurred 'in the presence of' the victims since at all times they were aware of what was going on in the room where the safe was kept. The Court of Criminal Appeal, while conceding that the offence of robbery could be committed where the stealing took place 'in the presence of' the victim rather than from his person, took the view that the Recorder's statement of the law was too broad and quashed the conviction. The Crown appealed to the House of Lords.]

Lord Pearce: Robbery is an aggravated form of theft. It adds an offence against the person to the offence of stealing since the theft is carried out by using violence to the person from whose possession the goods are stolen or by putting him in fear of violence. Blackstone (*Commentary*, vol 4, p 242) says: 'This previous violence, or putting in fear, is the criterion that distinguishes robbery from other larcenies ... it is enough that so much force, or threatening by word or gesture, be used, as might create an apprehension of danger, or induce a man to part with his property without or against his consent.'

The simplest case of robbery is that where the property is stolen, by violence or putting in fear, from the actual person of the victim. Sir Edward Coke (probably erroneously) derived the word robbery from robe 'because in ancient times (as sometimes yet is done) they bereave the true man of some of his robes or garments, and also for that his money or other goods are taken from his person, that is, from or out of some part of his garment, or robe about his person. And is ranked in this place, for that it concerneth not only the goods, but the person of the owner'. Owing to the essentially personal nature of the crime the indictment always used to allege that the goods were stolen 'à persona'.

Nevertheless from early times the crime was constructively extended to cover cases where the goods were not actually stolen from the victim's person. The real nature of the crime, stealing by violence, was the same whether the goods were on the victim's person or in his presence. This extension is admitted invariably and without doubt in many writings. For instance: 'If any one takes any of my chattels in such place as I am present and against my will this is robbery whether it is taken from my person or not' (Sir William Staunford, *Les Plees del Coron*, 1574 ed, p 27). Again: 'As if in my presence a felon taketh away my goods openly against my will; this is robbery, though he neither taketh them from my person, nor assaulteth me: for the loss is the same, and the fear alike, as though it had been from my person.' (Dalton, *Country Justice*, 1697 ed, p 492.)

But how far was this constructive extension to be carried, and what were the implications of the phrase 'in his presence'?

[His Lordship referred to a number of early authorities and continued:]

The essence of the offence is that violence is done or threatened to the person of the custodian who stands between the robber and the property in order to prevent or over come his resistance and oblige him to part with the property and submit to the thief stealing it. Thus the offence against the person and the theft are combined.

Where the sequence of events is not planned, but there is an assault which happens to be followed by a theft, there may be room for niceties of argument. But where the whole sequence appears to be one planned transaction one must regard the events as a whole to see if together they amount to robbery. A thief cannot escape the charge of robbery by merely planning his crime in two stages, namely, first violently removing the owner or custodian of the property from its vicinity to a distance at which he cannot see or hear the actual stealing of the property and then, secondly, stealing the property. For that reason, I do not think that it is of any relevance how great the distance to which the custodian of the property is removed (if he is removed by force or fear for the purpose of the theft) whether he be forcibly transported or driven away or rendered insensible. It has no relevance whether in such circumstances he is aware of the actual act of stealing if his lack of awareness has been forcibly produced by the thieves for the purpose of the theft.

Although in the old cases there constantly appears the limitation that it must be 'in his presence' yet it was accepted that robbery may consist in the driving off of sheep or cattle. This shows that some latitude was given to the words 'in his presence'. For one would not expect a man who is robbed of his cattle to be standing within 50 yards of them. I do not find it possible to accept the limit of individual perception as the test. It would be absurd that the same acts would constitute a robbery in the case of a young victim in full possession of his faculties who could perceive the driving off of his cattle and yet would not constitute a robbery if the victim were an old man who is too short-sighted and hard of hearing to perceive it though he may know that it is going on.

The only relevance of the victim's awareness is this. Is he aware of the theft or intended theft and is he compelled by force or fear to submit to it? Or has he been prevented by violence or threat from becoming aware of the theft and has that enabled the thieves to steal? If the answer to either of these questions is yes, the offence against the person and the theft are combined and the offence of robbery is constituted.

But the offence can only exist where the victim has sufficient care or personal possession of the goods to allow the court to say that constructively the goods were taken 'in his presence'. Were the night watchman or the maintenance engineer sufficiently the custodians of the safe and its contents to render the rifling of it a robbery 'in their presence'? The Court of Criminal Appeal in view of some of the old cases felt a difficulty which I can well understand. They would have preferred to hold this a robbery but they felt that to do so would be an extension which they were not justified in making. With all respect to that view I think that your Lordships should take a contrary view.

If the night watchman had been carrying out the duty of sitting by the safe to guard its contents with his hand upon it, no one would have felt any difficulty about this case. This forcible abduction from the property which he was guarding and touching would clearly have constituted robbery with violence. He was not, however, in fact in the room where the safe was kept. It was locked and he was some distance away from it when he was set upon. But it was within the area of his vigilance. He had a duty to go his rounds every half-hour and see that all was secure. And he had a telephone at hand for summoning the police if any unlawful attempt was made on the property that he was guarding. Had he not been overpowered no doubt he would have done so. He was the temporary custodian who stood between the thieves and the money which they intended to steal. And it was in that capacity and because of it that he was overpowered and bound.

It is a question of degree for the jury to decide whether the victim of the violence was sufficiently the custodian of the property stolen, whether he had sufficient possession and care of it, to constitute the stealing as being in his presence.

The fact that the thieves thought it necessary or desirable to overpower the night watchman and his companion is cogent evidence that their possession and control stood between the thieves and their objective. There might be cases where that consideration is not cogent, where for instance, a night watchman is overpowered because he has strayed on to a portion of premises which he was not intended to guard, and his unauthorised and unexpected presence has led to their attacking him. But here he was performing his duty within the proper sphere of his vigilance and part of his duty was to see that the office and the safe were not broken into. There was, therefore, ample evidence on which the jury should have found a verdict of guilty on the charge of robbery with violence.

[**Lord Morris** and **Lord Hodson** delivered judgments agreeing in substance with **Lord Pearce**. **Lord Reid** and **Lord Donovan** concurred. Appeal allowed and conviction restored.]

7.118C R v Langham

(1984) 36 SASR 48

Supreme Court of South Australia

[The accused was convicted of armed robbery. He had purchased a crossbow for $675 from a sports store. The crossbow did not suit his needs and he returned it to the store on13 April. He was told it was not the policy of the store to give cash in exchange for returned goods but that he would be given a credit note instead. Subsequently, the accused informed the store manager that he wanted to have the amount of his credit back in cash, but this request was refused. On 10 June, he went to the store and purchased a shotgun using part of his credit for that purpose, leaving a balance owing of $301. Later that day, he returned to the store carrying the shotgun and menaced the store manager. He demanded and received the sum of $301 in cash.

The accused gave sworn evidence at his trial. He asserted that he had believed that he had been legally entitled to have the money which he had taken, that he had needed cash urgently, and that he had decided to frighten the manager into paying him what he considered was owing to him.

In the course of his summing up to the jury, the trial judge told them that the issue of claim of right required not merely that the accused believed that he had a legal right to the $301, but also that he believed that he had a legal right to take it. On appeal to the Supreme Court.]

King CJ: The question of law for consideration is, therefore, whether it is sufficient, in order to be an answer to the charge, that the accused believe that he has a right to the property taken or whether his belief must extend to a right to take the property. In *R v Skivington* (1967) 51 Cr App R 167 a direction, apparently based on a passage in *Russell on Crime*, 12th ed, vol 2, p 855, that the jury 'must be satisfied that he had no honest belief that he was entitled to take the money in the way in which he did' was held to be erroneous. Lord Chief Justice Parker expressed the view of the court as to the correct principle (at 171):

> In the opinion of this court this matter is plain, namely that a claim of right is a defence to robbery or any aggravated form of robbery, and that it is unnecessary to show that the defendant must have had an honest belief also that he was entitled to take the money in the way in which he did.

Although the words 'in the way in which he did' possibly introduce some ambiguity into the proposition enunciated in *Skivington's* case, supra, I think that properly understood it is authority for the proposition that what is required is simply a genuine belief in the accused's legal entitlement to the property taken and not necessarily to his right to take it, either in the particular way in which he has taken it or in any other way. I think that the older authorities referred to in *Skivington* confirm that view.

...

Stealing, which is an integral part of robbery, is in the eyes of the common law the fraudulent or dishonest taking and carrying away of personal property without the consent of the owner and with the intention of depriving him permanently of that property. A claim of right, in order to negative fraud and dishonesty, must be genuine, but it need have no foundation in law or fact. Fraud and dishonesty are negatived by a genuine belief in a legal entitlement to the property taken. *R v George* (1890) 11 LR (NSW) (L) 373 shows that even when there is no belief as to entitlement to the property taken, dishonesty may nevertheless be negatived by a genuine belief in a legal right to take the property. In my opinion, however, the cases cited above show that where there is a genuine belief in a legal entitlement to the property taken, it is not necessary that the belief should extend to a legal right then and there to take the property either by the means adopted or at all. It is neither necessary nor desirable for the law to be specific as to the nature of the right or legal entitlement of which there must be a bona fide claim. The essential notion is that the claim of right must be of such a nature as to negative fraud or dishonesty in the taking of the property. Whatever criminal offence or civil wrong may be committed by taking property to which one believes oneself to be entitled, it is not the crime of larceny nor any crime of which larceny is a necessary ingredient.

I think therefore that the final directions given to the jury in answer to their request for a full direction on claim of right were wrong in law. ...

I have grave doubts whether a jury, properly directed, would convict the appellant of a crime involving dishonesty. The gravamen of his criminal wrongdoing lay in the methods which he adopted to obtain what he thought he was entitled to. I would not order a new trial on the information.

[**Johnston J** delivered a separate judgment agreeing with **King CJ**. **Mohr J** dissented. Appeal allowed.]

[See also *R v Tucker* (1984) 36 SASR 135.]

Burglary

7.119 At common law, the felony of burglary was defined as the breaking and entering of the dwelling-house of another at night with intent to commit a felony. The accused was guilty of burglary whether the intended felony was actually committed or not. To do in the daytime what would be burglary at night was, at common law, a misdemeanour known as housebreaking. These and other related crimes are now the subject of statutory definition: Crimes Act 1900 (NSW) ss 109–113.

7.120 At common law and under most, though not all, of the statutory provisions referred to above, both a breaking and entering are required. Each of these elements is of a somewhat technical nature. There is a breaking whenever an opening is made in a part of the building which is closed. Thus, plainly, the removal of a pane of glass from a window is a breaking. However, so also is the opening of a closed door by turning the key in the lock, or by lifting a latch. Again, if a window is unlatched and is lifted up, or, being slightly open, is further opened to permit entry, there is a breaking. Entering through an open space does not normally constitute a breaking, but, at common law, it is counted as breaking if one enters a house down a chimney.

7.121 There may also be a constructive breaking where an accused gains admission to a building without the use of force, but by a trick or by intimidation. In *R v Boyle* [1954] 2 QB 293, the accused gained admission to a house from which he stole a handbag by means of false representation that he was an employee of the BBC sent to examine a wireless set. This was held by the Court of Criminal Appeal to be constructive breaking.

7.122 At common law, an entry was accomplished when any part of the breaker's body, or any part of any instrument held by her or him, projected into the building. If, however, the instrument was being used for the breaking and projected into the building during the breaking process, this was not regarded as an entry, for the entry has to be a separate and distinct transaction.

7.123 Most of the statutory provisions referred to above apply only in respect of dwelling-houses, although a number extend to other types of building. A definition of 'dwelling-house' is contained in the Crimes Act 1900 (NSW).

7.124 It is also an offence to be in possession of implements of housebreaking and the like: Crimes Act 1900 (NSW) ss 114, 115.

Blackmail

7.125E **Crimes Act 1900 (NSW)**

99 Demanding property with intent to steal

(1) Whosoever, with menaces, or by force, demands any property from any person, with intent to steal the same, shall be liable to imprisonment for ten years.

(2) A person is guilty of an offence under this subsection if the person commits an offence under subsection (1) in the company of another person or persons. A person convicted of an offence under this subsection is liable to imprisonment for 14 years.

7.126C **R v Bernhard**

[1938] 2 KB 264; 2 All ER 140

Court of Criminal Appeal

[Bernhard, a Hungarian divorcee, met the prosecutor, a married man, in Europe, and became his mistress for a short while in France. She told him before they parted that she had lost all her money and that, unless he could help her, she would have to go on the streets or commit suicide. At the time they parted, he agreed to pay her £20 a month for one year; she asked for a lump sum payment, and he gave her £80 to cover the first four months. He returned to England and paid her no more money. She thereupon followed him to England and sought him out; at an interview she threatened to expose him to his wife and in the public newspapers unless he paid her £160 forthwith. There was evidence on which the jury might find that the agreement was for the payment of the remainder (after the first £80) in a single lump sum.

Bernhard was indicted for demanding money with menaces with intent to steal. At her trial, the **Lord Chief Justice** (**Lord Hewart**) directed the jury that the bargain was one arising out of an immoral consideration and that it could not give rise to a claim of right. He further told the jury that it was irrelevant whether Bernhard did or did not honestly believe that she was entitled to the immediate payment of £160. Bernhard was convicted and appealed to the Court of Criminal Appeal.]

Charles J: ... After hearing the questions arising on the appeal fully argued, and upon consideration of the relevant authorities, we were of opinion that Lord He wart CJ's direction to the jury was erroneous in point of law, and that the conviction could not be allowed to stand. We now proceed to state our reasons for this conclusion.

We agree with the view which is implicit in Lord He wart CJ's direction to the jury that the words 'with intent to steal' in s 30 must be construed with reference to the definition contained in s 1 of the Act. The test is whether, if the money had been obtained, it would have been obtained in such circumstances that it could properly be said to have been stolen: see *R v Walton* (1863) 9 Cox CC 268 (CCR). It is as to the true construction of the words 'fraudulently and without a claim of right made in good faith' that we differ from the opinion of Lord Hewart CJ. If the matter were *res integra* there would no doubt be much to be said for the view which found favour with Lord Hewart CJ, that the words 'claim of right' cannot be read as including a claim which is unfounded in law. We are, however, bound by a long series of decisions, many before and one at least subsequently to the Larceny Act 1916, to hold that this view is incorrect, and that a person has a claim of right, within the meaning of the section, if he is honestly asserting what he believes to be a lawful claim, even though it may be unfounded in law or in fact. The material words in s 1 of the Larceny Act 1916are declaratory of the common law, and a long and unbroken chain of authority supports this proposition. ...

It follows in our judgment that the proper answer to the question which troubled at least one of the jury would have been that if the prisoner honestly thought that she had a claim, she was entitled to be acquitted, even though she was wrong in so thinking.

Further, we are of opinion that neither the nature of the consideration for the alleged bargain nor the evidence given as to the terms of that bargain, justified or supported the view which Lord Hewart CJ so clearly expressed to the jury that the appellant's defence of a claim of right could not be maintained.

In our opinion, the agreement sworn to by the prosecutor was not made for an immoral consideration, inasmuch as illicit relations between the parties had ceased, and their renewal was not contemplated, at the time when it was made. It was unenforceable only because of want of consideration. The law is succinctly and correctly stated in *Leake on Contracts* (8th ed, 1931), p 585:

> A promise made in consideration of the cessation of an illicit cohabitation, or in consideration of past illicit cohabitation, or by way of compensation for seduction, is void simply for want of consideration; so that if made in the form of a bond or a covenant under seal, there is prima facie a valid contract. ...

It is, we think, plainly impossible to found any argument against the existence in the appellant's mind of an honest belief in the justice and legality of her claim upon her failure to appreciate the distinction which an English lawyer would have drawn between the legal results of a parol agreement and an agreement under seal. It is indeed by no means clear that the validity of the agreement, which was made in France, should be held to depend on the law of England, but, as no evidence was called as to the French law applicable in such a case, it is impossible (as indeed it is unnecessary) for us to inquire whether according to French law the appellant might have maintained an action against the prosecutor. ...

The appeal is therefore allowed, and the conviction quashed.

7.127 Notes and illustrations

1. The word 'menaces' is widely interpreted. In *Thorne v Motor Trade Association* [1937] AC 797 at 817, Lord Wright defined the word as follows:

   > I think the word 'menace' is to be liberally construed and not as limited to threats of violence but as including threats of any action detrimental to or

unpleasant to the person addressed. It may also include a warning that in certain events such action is intended. This has generally been accepted as a correct definition.

See *R v Tomlinson* [1895] 1 QB 706; *R v Boyle and Merchant* (1914) 10 Cr App R 180; *R v Clear* [1968] 1 QB 670; *R v Harry* [1974] Crim LR 32; *Benasic v R* (1987) 77 ALR 340.

2. For the offence to be committed it is not necessary that the demand in fact be communicated to the intended recipient. In *Austin v R* (1989) 63 ALJR 413 the accused left a letter of demand in a public telephone box. The letter was intended to be communicated to a state Minister, and threatened an attack on the Pope, who was visiting South Australia at the time. The accused was convicted of demanding money with menaces or threats contrary to s 3(1) of the Kidnapping Act 1960 (SA), and appealed, unsuccessfully, to the High Court. In a joint judgment, Brennan, Deane, Dawson, Toohey and McHugh JJ stated (at 415):

> It is the behaviour of the offender in making a demand with menaces or threats which is the gist of the offence and not actions or events over which the offender may have no control. There are, of course, crimes in which the *actus reus* is incomplete until certain consequences occur as a result of the offender's conduct. Murder by shooting or poisoning, where death is the consequence of the offender's act, are examples. But where the definition of an offence can be construed either to include or to omit the consequences of the offender's act as an element of the offence, the immediacy of the consequences and their subjection to supervening events or actions are material to the construction to be placed upon the definition. Thus it is appropriate to regard the offence of demanding money with menaces or threats as complete when the demand has been made in circumstances apt to achieve its communication to the person to whom it is directed and with the necessary intent. It is inappropriate to regard actual communication as a necessary part of the offence.

See also *Treacy v Director of Public Prosecutions* [1971] AC 537.

Receiving stolen property

7.128 It is a statutory offence to receive stolen property knowing that property to have been stolen: Crimes Act 1900 (NSW) ss 187–189. Stolen property is, by virtue of these provisions, not limited to property obtained by larceny, but extends to property obtained in circumstances which amounted to blackmail, obtaining by false pretences, or embezzlement.

7.129 The offence of receiving implies a principal offender. Thus, if the accused receives property from a child below the age of criminal responsibility, the offence is not made out: *Walters v Lunt* [1951] 2 All ER 645. Of course, it is not a prerequisite for the offence of receiving to be committed that the principal offender be convicted of an offence. The principal offender may be dead or have fled the jurisdiction.

7.130 At the time of the receiving, the property must still have the character of stolen property. If after the stealing, but before the receiving, the goods have been returned to the possession of the owner, or the owner's agent, or some lawful authority, the accused cannot be convicted of receiving: *R v Dolan* (1855) Dears CC 436; 169 ER 794; *R v Schmidt* (1866) LR 1 CCR 15; *R v Villensky* [1892] 2 QB 597.

7.131 For the accused to be guilty of receiving, he or she must have known the property to have been stolen. It is proper for the judge to instruct the jury that they may have regard to what an ordinary reasonable person in the accused's position would have believed in the circumstances and to consider whether the accused wilfully closed her or his eyes to facts that would have led a reasonable person to believe that particular property was stolen. However, juries must be made clearly to understand that they may only consider the hypothetical reasonable person's beliefs for the purpose of helping them decide what the particular accused in fact believed about the property on the particular occasion charged: *R v Dykyj* (1993) 19 NSWLR 671. See also *R v McConnell* (1993) 69 A Crim R 39.

7.132 The prosecution must prove that, at the time the accused received the goods, he or she knew they were stolen. If the accused receives goods innocently and subsequently appropriates them after learning they were stolen, he or she is not guilty of receiving: *R v Johnson* (1911) 6 Cr App R 218; *Murphy v Porter* (1984) 12 A Crim R 38.

7.133 It is not necessary to prove that the accused knew by whom the goods were stolen, or that he or she knew from whom the goods were stolen. It is sufficient that the accused knew them to have been stolen at the time of receipt. Knowledge does not mean certainty. In this context, as in most others, the better view would appear to be that recklessness in the sense of realisation that the goods were probably or likely to have been stolen is sufficient. See *R v White* (1859) 1 F & F 665; 175 ER 898; *Atwal v Massey* [1971] 3 All ER 881; *R v Grainge* [1974] 1 All ER 928; *R v Raad* [1983] 3 NSWLR 344; *R v Schipanski* (1989) 17 NSWLR 618. Compare *R v Havard* (1914) 11 Cr App R 2; *R v Woods* (1968) 53 Cr App R 30.

7.134 A belief on the part of the accused at the time of receiving the goods that he or she has a legal right to them is a complete defence to a charge of receiving: *R v Dickson* (1867) 4 SCR (NSW) 298. Equally, the accused will not be guilty of the offence of receiving if, at the time of receiving the goods, the accused intends to return them to their owner or to the police: *R v Matthews* [1950] 1 All ER 137.

7.135 Sometimes it is unclear whether the accused has stolen property or received it. Where the evidence is unclear as to whether the accused was a thief or a receiver, the usual practice is to charge her or him with both larceny and receiving in alternative counts. In *Gilson v R* (1991) 172 CLR 353, the High Court held that, if at the end of the case, the evidence is consistent with both charges, the jury should be instructed that, if they are satisfied beyond reasonable doubt that the accused is guilty of one or the other of the offences but are unable to say which, they should return a verdict of guilty of the less serious offence. The judge should direct the jury as to which of the offences they should regard as the less serious. Prima facie, the seriousness of the offence will be measured by the maximum penalty that the law attaches to it, and that will be receiving. The circumstances of the case may, however, displace this prima facie approach.

7.136 It is a separate offence to receive goods which were stolen outside the state: Crimes Act 1900 (NSW) s 189A. It is also an offence to take a reward or money corruptly under the pretence of helping to recover property which has been stolen: Crimes Act 1900 (NSW) s 186. It is an offence to advertise a reward for the return of any property which has been stolen, and to intimate in any such advertisement that no questions will be asked about how the person claiming the reward obtained the goods: Crimes Act 1900 (NSW) s 528. Finally, there is a separate summary offence of being in unlawful possession of property reasonably suspected of being stolen: Crimes Act 1900 (NSW) s 527C.

Property Offences: Victoria

CHAPTER 8

INTRODUCTION

8.1 We have seen in **Chapter 7** how, over the centuries, the courts and the legislature developed a complicated patchwork of crimes to deal with offences against property. By the end of the nineteenth century, in one way or another, most varieties of dishonest appropriation of property had been brought within the ambit of the criminal law. However, the structure which had been developed in order to achieve this result was of the most extreme complexity. The various crimes (larceny, larceny as a bailee, larceny by a trick, obtaining by false pretences, embezzlement, fraudulent conversion etc) were often difficult to distinguish. The whole of this area of the law was characterised by undue technicality and often meaningless distinctions.

8.2 Calls for reform of the law relating to property offences were common. In 1959, the newly-created English Criminal Law Revision Committee was asked 'to consider, with a view of providing a simpler and more effective system of law, what alterations in the criminal law are desirable with reference to larceny and kindred offences'.

8.3 This subject occupied the committee for the next seven years. Eventually the committee's Eighth Report, *Theft and Related Offences*, was presented to Parliament in May 1966. The Draft Theft Bill annexed to this report, slightly amended, was the basis of the Theft Bill introduced in the House of Lords in December 1967. After further amendments during its passage, that bill received the Royal Assent in July 1968. The Theft Act 1968 (UK) came into force on 1 January 1969.

8.4 At an early stage in its deliberations, the Criminal Law Revision Committee decided that mere amendment of the existing law would be insufficient. The committee took the view that it would be necessary to create an almost wholly new body of law which would define and conceive of offences of dishonesty in a manner quite different from the common law. The committee stated (p 7):

> [W]e are strongly of the opinion that the time has come for a new law of theft and related offences, based on a fundamental reconsideration of the principles underlying this branch of the law and embodied in a modern statute. We have tried to expose the defects of the present law in the sections of our report relating to each of the offences and to the most important ancillary matters covered by the bill. We have tried not to exaggerate the defects; but if it is agreed that our estimate of them is a fair one, we do not believe that it can be seriously disputed that a new law is necessary … [T]here was no disagreement as to the necessity of rewriting the greater part of the present law or the desirability of including it all in a single Act of Parliament. There have been many demands for a new law of theft and kindred offences. These have been prompted not only by theoretical objections to the anomalies and complications of the present law but also by practical experience of its inadequacy in important respects. Even the advantage of familiarity enjoyed by the present law is a short-term one; and the inconvenience of having to learn and apply a new system will soon be far outweighed, we hope, by its practical advantages and greater simplicity.

8.5 The Theft Act 1968 achieved the committee's aim. The existing myriad of offences, both common law and statutory, was swept away. In place of the offences of simple larceny, larceny as a bailee, embezzlement and fraudulent conversion the Act substituted the single offence of theft. In place of larceny by a trick and obtaining by false pretences, the Act substituted the offence of obtaining property by deception. The Act introduced the new offence of obtaining a pecuniary advantage by deception. In the main these crimes were defined by the use of concepts new to this area of the criminal law. In addition to creating new crimes, the Act redefined old crimes. Thus robbery, burglary, blackmail and handling stolen goods all reappear in the Act, but in considerably modified and simplified form.

8.6 Prior to 1974, the law relating to theft in Victoria was substantially the same as in New South Wales. In a report published in 1972, the Chief Justice's Law Reform Committee recommended that the Victorian law be reformed along the lines of the Theft Act 1968 (UK). Attached to the report was a draft bill embodying the committee's recommendations. That bill differed in only a few respects from the English Act. The most important difference concerned the proposed offence of obtaining a financial advantage by deception (s 82), which is markedly different from its English counterpart.

The committee's draft bill was introduced into the Victorian Parliament and, with one minor change (see **8.24**), enacted as the Crimes (Theft) Act 1973 on 17 April 1973. The Act was proclaimed and came into force on 1 October 1974. In England, the Theft Act 1968 was supplemented by the Theft Act 1978. That latter Act has not been copied in Victoria.

8.7 Similar legislation has been adopted in the Australian Capital Territory and South Australia. The Crimes (Amendment) Ordinance (No 4) 1985 (ACT) was modelled on the Victorian Act. This legislation has now been consolidated in the Crimes Act 1900 (ACT), provisions relating to property offences being contained in Pt IV ss 93–151. In South Australia, the Criminal Law Consolidation (Offences of Dishonesty) Amendment Act 2002 (SA) introduced a new Pt 5, 'Offences of Dishonesty' into the Criminal Law Consolidation Act 1935 (SA). Part 5 of the South Australian Act is modelled on the Victorian legislation, although it incorporates significant changes. Provisions based on the Victorian Act are also to be found in the Criminal Code Act 1983 (NT).

8.8 The Theft Act has been the subject of a great deal of academic discussion in both England and Australia. In Australia, C R Williams, *Property Offences*, 3rd ed, Law Book Co, Sydney, 1999, deals in a comprehensive fashion with the Victorian and Australian Capital Territory legislation. The leading English textbooks are D Ormerod and D Williams (eds), *Smith's Law of Theft*, 9th ed, Oxford University Press, 2007; and E Griew, *The Theft Acts*, 7th ed, Sweet and Maxwell, London, 1995.

THEFT

8.9E **Crimes Act 1958 (Vic)**
(as amended by the Crimes (Theft) Act 1973

PART I — OFFENCES
DIVISION 2 — THEFT AND SIMILAR OR ASSOCIATED OFFENCES

71 Definitions

(1) In this Division —

Gain and *loss* are to be construed as extending only to gain or loss in money or other property, but as extending to any such gain or loss whether temporary or permanent; and —

(a) *gain* includes a gain by keeping what one has, as well as a gain by getting what one has not; and

(b) *loss* includes a loss by not getting what one might get, as well as a loss by parting with what one has;

Goods except in so far as the context otherwise requires, includes money and every other description of property except land and includes things severed from the land by stealing;

Property includes money and all other property real or personal including things in action and other intangible property.

(2) In this Division property shall be regarded as belonging to any person having possession or control of it, or having in it any proprietary right or interest (not being an equitable interest arising only from an agreement to transfer or grant an interest).

72 Basic definition of theft

(1) A person steals if he dishonestly appropriates property belonging to another with the intention of permanently depriving the other of it.

(2) A person who steals is guilty of theft; and *thief* shall be construed accordingly.

73 Further explanation of theft

(1) This section has effect as regards the interpretation and operation of section 72 and, except as otherwise provided in this Division, shall apply only for the purposes of that section and not otherwise.

(2) A person's appropriation of property belonging to another is not to be regarded as dishonest —

(a) if he appropriates the property in the belief that he has in law the right to deprive the other of it, on behalf of himself or of a third person; or

(b) if he appropriates the property in the belief that he would have the other's consent if the other knew of the appropriation and the circumstances of it; or

(c) (except where the property came to him as trustee or personal representative) if he appropriates the property in the belief that the person to whom the property belongs cannot be discovered by taking reasonable steps.

(3) A person's appropriation of property belonging to another may be dishonest notwithstanding that he is willing to pay for the property.

(4) Any assumption by a person of the rights of an owner amounts to an appropriation, and this includes, where he has come by the property (innocently or not) without stealing it, any later assumption of a right to it by keeping or dealing with it as owner.

(5) Where property or a right or interest in property is or purports to be transferred for value to a person acting in good faith, no later assumption by him of rights which he believed himself to be acquiring shall, by reason of any defect in the transferor's title, amount to theft of the property.

(6) A person cannot steal land, or things forming part of land and severed from it by him or by his directions, except in the following cases, that is to say —

(a) when he is a trustee or personal representative, or is authorised by power of attorney, or as liquidator of a company, or otherwise, to sell or dispose of land belonging to another, and he appropriates the land or anything forming part of it by dealing with it in breach of the confidence reposed in him; or

(b) when he is not in possession of the land and appropriates anything forming part of the land by severing it or causing it to be severed, or after it has been severed; or

(c) when, being in possession of the land under a tenancy, he appropriates the whole or part of any fixture or structure let to be used with the land.

For the purposes of this sub-section 'land' does not include incorporeal hereditaments; ***tenancy*** means a tenancy for years or any less period and includes an agreement for such a tenancy, but a person who after the end of a tenancy remains in possession as statutory tenant or otherwise is to be treated as having possession under the tenancy, and 'let' shall be construed accordingly.

(7) Wild creatures, tamed or untamed, shall be regarded as property; but a person cannot steal a wild creature not tamed nor ordinarily kept in captivity, or the carcase of any such creature, unless either it has been reduced into possession by or on behalf of another person and possession of it has not since been lost or abandoned, or another person is in course of reducing it into possession.

(8) Where property is subject to a trust, the persons to whom it belongs shall be regarded as including any person having a right to enforce the trust, and an intention to defeat the trust shall be regarded accordingly as an intention to deprive of the property any person having that right.

(9) Where a person receives property from or on account of another, and is under an obligation to the other to retain and deal with that property or its proceeds in a particular way, the property or proceeds shall be regarded (as against him) as belonging to the other.

(10) Where a person gets property by another's mistake, and is under an obligation to make restoration (in whole or in part) of the property or its proceeds or of the value thereof, then to the extent of that obligation the property or proceeds shall be regarded (as against him) as belonging to the person entitled to restoration, and an intention not to make restoration shall be regarded accordingly as an intention to deprive that person of the property or proceeds.

(11) Property of a corporation sole shall be regarded as belonging to the corporation notwithstanding a vacancy in the corporation.

(12) A person appropriating property belonging to another without meaning the other permanently to lose the thing itself is nevertheless to be regarded as having the intention of permanently depriving the other of it if his intention is to treat the thing as his own to dispose of regardless of the other's rights; and a borrowing or lending of it may amount to so treating it if, but only if, the borrowing or lending is for a period and in circumstances making it equivalent to an outright taking or disposal.

(13) Without prejudice to the generality of sub-section (12) where a person, having possession or control (lawfully or not) of property belonging to another, parts with the property under a condition as to its return which he may not be able to perform, this (if done for purposes of his own and without the other's authority) amounts to treating the property as his own to dispose of regardless of the other's rights.

(14) Notwithstanding anything contained in sub-section (12) in any proceedings —

(a) for stealing a motor vehicle or an aircraft proof that the person charged took or in any manner used the motor vehicle or aircraft without the consent of the owner or person in lawful possession thereof shall be conclusive evidence that the person charged intended to permanently deprive the owner of it; and

(b) for attempting to steal a motor vehicle or an aircraft proof that the person charged attempted to take or in any manner use the motor vehicle or aircraft without the consent of the owner or person in lawful possession thereof shall be conclusive evidence that the person charged intended to permanently deprive the owner of it.

74 Theft

(1) A person guilty of theft is guilty of an indictable offence and liable to level 5 imprisonment (10 years maximum).

(2) Section 80A applies as if the reference in that section to sections 81 87 (both inclusive) were a reference to this section.

80A Extra-territorial offences

(1) If —

(a) a person does, or omits to do, an act or thing referred to in sections 81–87 (both inclusive) outside, or partly outside, Victoria; and

(b) there is a real and substantial link within the meaning of sub-section (2) between doing, or omitting to do, the act or thing and Victoria —

those sections apply to the act or thing or the omission as if it had been done, or omitted to be done, wholly within Victoria.

(2) For the purposes of sub-section (1), there is a real and substantial link with Victoria —

(a) if a significant part of the conduct relating to, or constituting the doing of the act or thing, or the omission, occurred in Victoria; or

(b) where the act or thing was done, or the omission occurred, wholly outside Victoria, if the act or thing was done, or omitted to be done, with the intention that substantial harmful effects arise in Victoria and such effects did arise.

8.10 Although broadly similar in structure, there are many important differences between the Victorian and South Australian provisions. Provisions similar to the Victorian are to be found in the Crimes Act 1900 (ACT). The Victorian provisions will be discussed here.

8.11 To establish the crime of theft, the prosecution must prove the 'actus reus' elements:

(1) that the object of the alleged theft was 'property belonging to another'; and

(2) that the accused appropriated that property;

and the 'mens rea' elements;

(1) that the accused appropriated the property with 'the intention of permanently depriving the other of it'); and

(2) that the accused appropriated the property 'dishonestly'.

The two elements of the actus reus will be dealt with first, and the two mens rea elements second.

Actus reus

Property belonging to another

8.12 The definition of property contained in s 71(1) extends to things having no physical existence; for example a debt, a trademark or a copyright.

Examples include the following:

(1) A is a partner in a firm. A purports to sell on behalf of the firm the right to use a trademark owned by the firm. A is in fact acting on her own behalf. A is guilty of stealing the trademark from the firm.

(2) B owes C $100. A forges an assignment of the debt and presents the assignment to B who pays A the $100. A is guilty of stealing the debt from C.

(3) Putting money into a bank account creates a debt owed by the bank to the customer; that is, there is a relationship of creditor (customer) and debtor (bank), and the debt can be enforced by civil action. The debt is a 'thing in action' and is capable of being stolen. D Company has an account at the XY Bank. E, the company accountant, uses company cheques, without authority, to withdraw money for his own use. E is guilty of stealing the debt. See *R v Kohn* (1979) 69 Cr App R 395.

8.13 D, a civil engineering undergraduate, dishonestly obtained the proof of an examination to be held at his university. He returned the paper from where he had got it after he had read its contents. He was charged by the university authorities with theft of confidential information from the university. Held, the confidential information obtained by D did not fall within the meaning of the expression 'intangible property' (s 71(1) of the Victorian Act), and D was, accordingly, not guilty of theft: *Oxford v Moss* (1978) 68 Cr App R 183.

8.14 In order for property to be capable of being stolen, it must 'belong to another'. Section 71(2) provides that 'property shall be regarded as belonging to any person having possession or control of it, or having in it any proprietary right or interest'. If property does not belong to anyone in any of these senses, it cannot be stolen. Thus a person who takes property which has been abandoned by its owner and is not in the possession or control of anyone, does not commit theft.

8.15 Equally, property cannot be stolen by someone who personally has ownership, possession and control of the property at the time of appropriating it. In *R v Greenberg* [1972] Crim LR 331, the accused was charged with theft from a self-service petrol station. He filled his tank and entered the cashier's office, intending to pay for the petrol. The cashier was busy with another customer and the accused then decided not to pay for the petrol. He left the cashier's office and drove off. It was held that he could not be guilty of theft of the petrol. At the time of putting the petrol in the tank, he intended to pay for it and was, therefore, not acting dishonestly. At the time of dishonestly driving off, the petrol no longer belonged to the proprietors of the petrol station. At this point of time, the accused had the full proprietary interest in the petrol together with possession and control of it. See also *Edwards v Ddin* [1976] 3 All ER 705; *Corcoran v Whent* [1977] Crim LR 52; *R v McHugh* [1977] Crim LR 174; *Davies v Leighton* (1978) 68 Cr App R 4. This gap in the law, however, only applies to interchangeable items (or 'fungibles') such as petrol, coins and sugar. In other cases, there is no such difficulty. The person who accidentally puts an item in their supermarket trolley and decides to keep it when they realise outside the supermarket that they have the item, is guilty of theft because the item is still the property of another (the supermarket) at the time the dishonest intent is formed.

8.16 Can an electronic funds transfer (EFT) be the subject of a theft charge? The United Kingdom House of Lords decided that it could not, in *R v Preddy* [1996] 3 WLR 255. The various accused were charged with obtaining property by deception when they obtained loans by providing false information. Some of the funds were transferred electronically to the accused people's bank accounts and some were paid by cheque. It was held that the electronic transfers were 'property', but they were not property 'belonging to another', because the thing in action (the debt between bank and creditor) was newly created when the funds were credited to the accused's account. More recently, however, the United Kingdom Court of Appeal has held that a funds transfer obtained by fraud could amount to theft, on the basis that the action had reduced the victim's credit balance; that is, had diminished the victim's thing in action: *R v Williams (Roy)* [2001] Cr Ap R 362.

8.17 Section 71(2) does, however, cast a very wide net. Not only proprietary rights are protected, but also possessory rights and even mere physical control. Since all these rights and interests are protected, a single incident may amount to theft from a number of persons. If A lends her or his book to B and, while B is permitting C to examine it, it is snatched from C by D who makes off with it, D steals the book from A (the owner), B (the possessor) and D (the person with control). Clearly, property may be stolen from an owner who has never been in possession. If A sells her or his car to B but the car is taken dishonestly by C before delivery to B, C steals the car both from A (the possessor) and B (the owner) notwithstanding that B has never been in possession of the car.

8.18 Whether a person has a proprietary right or interest in an item of property is, of course, a question of civil law. The expression 'any proprietary right or interest' covers both legal and equitable proprietary interests. Where property is subject to a trust it belongs to both the trustee (legal interest) and the beneficiary (equitable interest) and it may be stolen from either.

8.19 Since property is regarded as belonging to any person having possession, control or any proprietary right or interest, it follows that an accused may be guilty of stealing property in which the accused has a personal proprietary interest. Thus a partner may be guilty of stealing property belonging to the partnership (*R v Bonner* [1970] 2 All ER 907) or a trustee may be guilty of stealing trust property from the beneficiary. Further, it has been held that an owner may even be guilty of stealing property from a person who has no proprietary interest in the property: see *R v Turner (No 2)* [1971] 2 All ER 441 (at **8.25C**).

8.20 Subsections (8), (9) and (10) of s 73 deal with a number of special cases which would not otherwise be covered by the expression 'property belonging to another'. These special cases will now be considered.

8.21 **Purpose trusts** The ordinary case of appropriation of trust property by a trustee is covered by s 71(2) without the necessity for reliance upon s 73(8). The beneficiary under the trust has an equitable proprietary interest and, accordingly, the trust property is regarded as belonging to the beneficiary by virtue of s 71(2). However, in some cases there may be no ascertained beneficiary. This is so in the case of 'purpose trusts', whether charitable or private. Section 73(8) covers such cases by providing that the property is to be regarded as belonging to anyone having a right to enforce the trust. In the case of charitable trusts this will be the state Attorney-General and in the case of non-charitable purposes trusts it will be the person entitled to the residue of the estate.

8.22 Fiduciary ownership A person may receive money or other property in circumstances in which he or she falls under an obligation, either to the person from whom it is received or to some other person, to deal with that property in a particular way. If the person receiving the property holds it as trustee, no problem arises; the property is regarded as belonging to the beneficiary by virtue of s 71(2). However, the receiver may obtain the full legal and equitable interest in the property, yet hold it subject to a fiduciary obligation to deal with it or its proceeds in a particular way. For example, if A collects subscriptions from friends of B in order to buy a birthday present for B, he or she will obtain the full proprietary interest in the money collected. A will, however, be under a fiduciary obligation to deal with the money collected and its proceeds (the present) in a particular way. Such cases are covered by s 73(9).

For consideration of the scope of this provision, see *R v Hall* [1972] 2 All ER 1009 (at **8.27C**) and *R v Meech, Parslow and Jolliffe* [1974] QB 549 (at **8.28C**).

8.23 Mistake Section 73(10) covers the case of the accused who appropriates property which he or she receives from another as a result of that other's mistake. For discussion of this provision, see *R v Gilks* [1972] 3 All ER 280 (at **8.29C**).

8.24 Finally, mention should be made of the case of land and things forming part of land, which can be stolen only in the circumstances set out in s 73(6). Section 73(6)(b) provides that a person not in possession of land may steal anything forming part of the land by severing it or appropriating it after it has been severed. Thus a person who comes on to the land of another and picks mushrooms, wildflowers or plants, commits theft.

8.25C

R v Turner (No 2)

[1971] 2 All ER 441
Court of Appeal (UK)

[The accused took his car to a garage to have it repaired. He subsequently removed the car from outside the garage in order to avoid having to pay for the repairs. In fact, the garage proprietor almost certainly had a repairer's lien over the car, entitling him to continue in possession of it until the repairs were paid for. However, the trial judge directed the jury that they need not be concerned with the question of whether the repairer had a lien. The accused was convicted of theft of the car and appealed to the Court of Appeal. It was argued that, in the absence of proof of a lien, the garage proprietor had no right to possession of the car as against the accused and that, therefore, in taking the car, the accused could not be guilty of theft.]

Lord Parker CJ, **Widgery LJ** and **Bridge J**: As I have said, the judge directed the jury that they were not concerned in any way with lien and the sole question was whether Mr Brown had possession or control. This court is quite satisfied that there is no ground whatever for qualifying the words 'possession or control' in any way. It is sufficient if it is found that the person from whom the property is taken, or to use the words of the Act, appropriated, was at the time in fact in possession or control. At the trial there was a long argument whether that possession or control must be lawful, it being said that by reason of the fact that this car was subject to a hire-purchase agreement, Mr Brown could never even as against the appellant obtain lawful possession or control. As I have said, this court is quite satisfied that the judge was quite correct in telling the jury that they need not bother about lien, and that they need not bother about hire-purchase agreements. The only question was: was Mr Brown in fact in possession or control?

[Appeal dismissed.]

8.26 Notes

1. Does it not appear strange that an owner with the right to take possession of property can be guilty of theft where he or she does take possession, however dishonest her or his intentions? The court may well have been influenced in its decision by the fact that the garage proprietor almost certainly had a lien over the car although, because of the direction given by the trial judge, they were compelled to ignore this fact in giving judgment.
2. The argument rejected in *R v Turner (No 2)* was accepted in a subsequent case at first instance. In *R v Meredith* [1973] Crim LR 253, the accused left his car on a road while he attended a football match. It was removed by police under regulations empowering them to remove cars causing an obstruction. The regulations did not empower the police to detain such cars once they were claimed by their owners. The accused went to the police yard, found his car and forcibly removed a steering lock. He then, without consent or authority from the police, drove the car away. It was held that the accused was not guilty of theft of the car as the police had, as against him, no right to retain it.

8.27C R v Hall

[1972] 2 All ER 1009

Court of Appeal (UK)

[The accused, a partner in a firm of travel agents, received money from clients as deposits and payments for air trips to America. The funds were paid into the firm's general account. The projected flights did not materialise and the money was not refunded. The accused was convicted on seven counts of theft in respect of the money received from clients. On appeal to the Court of Appeal.]

Edmund-Davies, **Stephenson LJJ** and **Boreham J** [Their Lordships quoted the English equivalent of s 73(9) of the Victorian Act (Theft Act 1968 s 5(3)), and continued]:

Counsel for the appellant submitted that in the circumstances arising in these seven cases there arose no such 'obligation' on the appellant. He referred us to a passage in the Eighth Report of the Criminal Law Revision Committee *(Theft and Related Offences,* Cmnd 2977 (1966), p 127) which reads as follows:

> Subsection (3) [of cl 5 'Belonging to Another'] provides for the special case where property is transferred to a person to retain and deal with for a particular purpose and he misapplies it or its proceeds. An example would be the treasurer of a holiday fund. The person in question is in law the owner of the property; but the subsection treats the property, as against him, as belonging to the persons to whom he owes the duty to retain and deal with the property as agreed. He will therefore be guilty of stealing from them if he misapplies the property or its proceeds.

Counsel for the appellant submitted that the example there given is, for all practical purposes, identical with the actual facts in *R v Pulham* (15 June 1971, unreported) where, incidentally, s 5(3) was not discussed, the convictions there being quashed, as we have already indicated, owing to the lack of a proper direction as to the accused's state of mind at the time he appropriated. But he submits that the position of a treasurer of a solitary fund is quite different from that of a person like the appellant, who was in general (and genuine) business as a travel agent, and to whom people pay money in order to achieve a certain object — in the present cases, to obtain charter flights to America. It is true, he concedes, that thereby the travel agent undertakes a contractual obligation in relation to arranging flights and at the proper time paying the airline and any other expenses. Indeed, the appellant throughout acknowledged that this was so, although contending that in some of the seven cases it was the other party who was in breach. But what counsel for the appellant resists is that in such circumstances the travel agent 'is under an obligation' to the client 'to retain and deal with … in a particular way' sums paid to him in such circumstances.

What cannot of itself be decisive of the matter is the fact that the appellant paid the money into the firm's general trading account. As Widgery J said in *R v Yule* [1963] 2 All ER 780 at 784: [1964] 1 QB 5 at 10 decided under s 20(1)(iv) of the Larceny Act 1916:

> The fact that a particular sum is paid into a particular banking account … does not affect the right of persons interested in that sum or any duty of the solicitor either towards his client or towards third parties with regard to disposal of that sum.

Nevertheless, when a client goes to a firm carrying on the business of travel agents and pays them money, he expects that in return he will, in due course, receive the tickets and other documents necessary for him to accomplish the trip for which he is paying, and the firm are 'under an obligation' to perform their part to fulfil his expectation and are liable to pay him damages if they do not. But in our judgment, what was not here established was that these clients expected them 'to retain and deal with that property or its proceeds in a particular way', and that an 'obligation' to do so was undertaken by the appellant.

We must make clear, however, that each case turns on its own facts. Cases could, we suppose, conceivably arise where by some special arrangement (preferably evidenced by documents), the client could impose on the travel agent an 'obligation' falling within s 5(3). But no such special arrangement was made in any of the seven cases here being considered. It is true that in some of them documents were signed by the parties; thus, in respect of counts 1 and 3 incidents there was a clause to the effect that the People to People organisation did not guarantee to refund deposits if withdrawals were made later than a certain date; and in respect of counts 6, 7 and 8 the appellant wrote promising 'a full refund' after the flights paid for failed to materialise. But neither in those nor in the remaining two cases (in relation to which there was no documentary evidence of any kind) was there, in our judgment, such a special arrangement as would give rise to an obligation within s 5(3).

It follows from this that, despite what on any view must be condemned as scandalous conduct by the appellant, in our judgment on this ground alone this appeal must be allowed and the convictions quashed.

[Convictions quashed.]

[See also *R v Clowes (No 2)* [1994] 2 All ER 316; *R v Arnold* [1997] 4 All ER 1.]

8.28C R v Meech, Parslow and Jolliffe

[1974] QB 549

Court of Appeal (Criminal Division) (UK)

[A man named McCord obtained a cheque for £1450 from a finance company by means of a forged instrument. He asked Meech (to whom he owed £40) to cash the cheque for him. Meech, who at this stage was unaware of the fraud, agreed and paid the cheque into his own account. Two days later, after he had become aware that the cheque had been acquired dishonestly, Meech drew and cashed with his bank his own cheque for £1410 (representing £1450 less the amount owed to him). Before doing this, he arranged with two accomplices to stage a fake robbery. Subsequently, the three of them met and divided the £1410. The true facts became known and all three were charged with theft. Apart from s 73(9) (s 5(3) of the Theft Act 1968 (UK)), Meech clearly could not be convicted of theft. He had not stolen the original cheque from the finance company because, at the time of appropriating it by paying into his account, he was unaware that it had been acquired dishonestly. He had not stolen money from the bank having simply withdrawn money from his own account. Nor, apart from s 73(9), could he be guilty of theft of the money from McCord. McCord never obtained possession or control of the money and, upon receiving it from the bank, Meech had obtained the full proprietary interest. The prosecution therefore relied upon s 73(9), arguing that Meech was under an obligation to pay the money to McCord. Meech and his accomplices were convicted and appealed to the Court of Appeal. The liability of the accomplices was dependent upon the liability of Meech.]

Roskill LJ, **Thompson** and **Stocker JJ**: Counsel for all the defendants relied strongly on the series of recent decisions that 'obligation' means 'legal obligation'. The judge so directed the jury. In giving this direction he no doubt had in mind the successive decisions of this court in *R v Hall* [1973] QB 126; *R v Gilks* [1972] 1 WLR 1341 and *R v Pearce* (unreported, November 21 1972) (both the court and counsel were supplied with copies of the judgment). Reliance was also placed on paragraph 76 of Professor Smith's *The Law of Theft* (2nd ed, 1972) — a passage written just before the decisions referred to. Since the judge so directed the jury, we do not find it necessary further to consider those decisions beyond observing that the facts of those cases were vastly different from those of the present case.

Starting from this premise — that 'obligation' means 'legal obligation' — it was argued that even at the time when Meech was ignorant of the dishonest origin of the cheque, as he was at the time when he agreed to cash the cheque and hand the proceeds less the £40 to McCord, McCord could never have enforced that obligation because McCord had acquired the cheque illegally. In our view this submission is unsound in principle. The question has to be looked at from Meech's point of view, not McCord's. Meech plainly assumed an 'obligation' to McCord which, on the facts then known to him, he remained obliged to fulfil and, on the facts as found, he must be taken at that time honestly to have intended to fulfil. The fact that on the true facts if known McCord might not and indeed would not subsequently have been permitted to enforce that obligation in a civil court does not prevent that 'obligation' on Meech having arisen. The argument confuses the creation of the obligation with the subsequent discharge of that obligation either by performance or otherwise. That the obligation might have become impossible of performance by Meech or of enforcement by McCord on grounds of illegality or for reasons of public policy is irrelevant. The opening words of s 5(3) clearly look to the time of the creation of or the acceptance of the obligation by the bailee and not to the time of performance by him of the obligation so created and accepted by him.

It is further to be observed in this connection that this subsection deems property (including the proceeds of property) which does not belong to the bailor to belong to the bailor so as to render a bailee who has accepted an obligation to deal with the property or to account for it in a particular way but then dishonestly fails to fulfil that obligation, liable to be convicted of theft whereas previously he would have been liable to have been convicted of fraudulent conversion though not of larceny. It was not seriously disputed in argument that before 1968 Meech would have had no defence to a charge of fraudulent conversion.

The first branch of the argument therefore clearly fails. The second argument (as already indicated) was that even if Meech initially became under an obligation to McCord, that obligation ceased to bind Meech once Meech discovered McCord had acquired the cheque by fraud. It was argued that once Meech possessed this knowledge, performance of his pre-existing obligation would have involved him in performing an obligation which he knew to be illegal. Thus, it was said, he was discharged from performance and at the time of his dishonest misappropriation had ceased to be bound by his obligation, so that he could not properly be convicted of theft by virtue of s 5(3).

This submission was advanced at considerable length before the judge. It is not necessary to relate those arguments more fully. The judge rejected the arguments and he directed the jury in the following terms so far as relevant. After saying that there were three considerations which Meech said affected his mind and led him not to carry out his agreement with McCord, the judge dealt correctly with the first two of the three matters. He continued as follows:

> Thirdly, he says that he was worried about being involved in the offence of obtaining money by fraud; that he knew this to be, as he described it, a 'dodgy' cheque — knew not at the time that he was handed it, but knew before he drew the cash; that he alleges that from inquiries made on September 11 and 12 he discovered what was seemingly common knowledge among some motor dealers of High Wycombe, that McCord was involved in a dishonest transaction. His knowledge of this was limited and inaccurate, since he thought that there was a name Harris involved. He is not entitled in law to repudiate his agreement merely on the basis of suspicions about McCord. The only basis on which he was entitled to refuse payment was that he refused because if he had honoured the agreement he, Meech, would have committed a criminal offence, or that was his belief. Only if that was the basis — or if you thought on the evidence that may have been the basis — was there no obligation to pay. Otherwise, although you may well think many people had a better right than McCord, so far as Meech was concerned it was his obligation to deal with the proceeds of the cheque in the way that he had agreed with McCord that he would.

The judge thus emphasised that the obligation to McCord remained but that Meech would be excused performance if performance would have involved commission of a criminal offence or if Meech genuinely believed that such performance would involve commission of a criminal offence. Of course if Meech acted as he did honestly and had an honest reason for not performing his obligation and for claiming relief from performance of that obligation, this would clearly be the end of any criminal charge against him. But the jury, as already pointed out, clearly negatived any such honest intention or belief on Meech's part. The argument before this court was that even though he was found to have acted dishonestly, he still could not be convicted of theft.

There was considerable discussion whether if he were not guilty of theft he could have been convicted of any other offence, for example, of conspiracy or of dishonest handling of the proceeds of the cheque which he knew to have been obtained dishonestly. This is not the question. The question is whether he was guilty of theft and not whether if he is not guilty of theft he might have been properly charged with and convicted of some other offence.

The answer to the main contention is that Meech being under the initial obligation already mentioned, the proceeds of the cheque continued as between him and McCord to be deemed to be McCord's property so that if Meech dishonestly misappropriated those proceeds he was, by reason of s 5(3), guilty of theft even though McCord could not have enforced performance of that obligation against Meech in a civil action. Some reliance was placed on a passage in Professor Smith's *The Law of Theft,* p 31, para 76:

> Thus there is no redress in civil or criminal law against a client who is accidentally overpaid by a bookmaker. The same principle no doubt governs other cases where the transaction is void or illegal by statute or at common law. If this is a defect in the law, the fault lies with the civil law and not with the Theft Act. If the civil law says that the defendant is the exclusive owner of the money and under no obligation to repay even an equivalent sum, it would be incongruous for the criminal law to say he had stolen it.

It must be observed that that passage was written with reference to s 5(4) of the Theft Act 1968 and not with reference to s 5(3) of that Act. It immediately follows a discussion of the Gaming Act cases. We do not think the author had a case such as the present in mind. On no view could it be said in the present case that the common law would regard Meech as the 'exclusive owner' of the original cheque or of its proceeds. The true owner of the proceeds was the hire-purchase finance company. They could have sued Meech to judgment for the full value of the original cheque. But Meech having received the original cheque from McCord under the obligation we have mentioned, the criminal law provides that as between him and McCord the cheque and its proceeds are to be deemed to be McCord's property so that a subsequent dishonest misappropriation of the cheque or its proceeds makes Meech liable to be convicted of theft. We are therefore clearly of the view that Meech was properly convicted of theft just as under the old law he would have been liable to have been convicted of fraudulent conversion. We therefore think that the judge was quite right in leaving this case to the jury and that the direction which he gave was correct. If it be open to criticism at all, the criticism might be that the direction was arguably too favourable to the defendants.

Two other separate points were argued on behalf of Parslow and Jolliffe. First, it was said that the £1410 obtained by Meech from his bank by cashing his own cheque were not 'the proceeds' of the original cheque but of Meech's own cheque. The answer to that contention is that it is clear that the money received by Meech when he cashed his own cheque plainly emanated from the original cheque and can properly be regarded on the facts of this case as the proceeds of the original cheque.

Secondly, it was argued for Parslow and Jolliffe that there was a misdirection in relation to appropriation. The judge said:

> As I direct you in law, the time of the appropriation was the time of the fake robbery. Up to that moment, although Meech had drawn the money from the bank, it was still open to him to honour the agreement which he had made with McCord and to pay it over, in due course, to McCord; but once the fake robbery had taken place, that was no longer possible.

It was argued that Meech alone had dishonestly misappropriated the proceeds of the cheque when he drew the money from the bank and that thereafter Parslow and Jolliffe were not guilty of dishonest misappropriation since Meech had already dishonestly misappropriated that money once and for all. It was said that Parslow and Jolliffe were thereafter only liable to be convicted, if at all, of dishonest handling, an offence with which neither was charged.

We think that the judge's direction when he said that the time of the appropriation was the time of the fake robbery was right. A dishonest intention had been formed before the money was withdrawn but the misappropriation only took place when the three men divided up the money at the scene of the fake robbery. It was then that the performance of the obligation by Meech finally became impossible by the dishonest act of these three men acting in concert together.

The convictions must all be affirmed and the appeals dismissed. Meech's application for leave to appeal against sentence is formally refused.

[Appeals dismissed.]

8.29C R v Gilks

[1972] 3 All ER 280
Court of Appeal (Criminal Division) (UK)

[The accused placed a number of bets upon horse races with a bookmaker. When the accused went to collect his winnings, the bookmaker, by mistake, overpaid him by £106. The accused kept the £106 although he knew the bookmaker had made a mistake and that he was not entitled to it. He was convicted of theft of this sum, and appealed to the Court of Appeal.]

Cairns, **Stephenson LJJ** and **Willis J**: The deputy chairman gave rulings in law to the following effect. He ruled that at the moment when the money passed it was money 'belonging to another' and that the ingredient in the definition of theft in s 1(1) of the Act was therefore present. Accordingly, s 5(4) had no application to the case. If he was wrong about that then, he said, 'obligation' in s 5(4) included an obligation which was not a legal obligation. He told the jury that it was open to them to convict the appellant of theft in respect of the mistaken overpayment. And he directed them that the test of dishonesty was whether the appellant believed that 'when dealing with your bookmaker if he makes a mistake you can take the money and keep it and there is nothing dishonest about it'.

In the grounds of appeal it is contended that all these directions were wrong. The main foundation of one branch of the appellant's case at the trial and in this court was the decision of the Court of Appeal in *Morgan v Ashcroft* [1937] 3 All ER 92; [1938] I KB 49. In that case a bookmaker, by mistake, overpaid a client £24. It was held that the bookmaker was not entitled to recover the money by action because that would involve taking account of gaming transactions which were void under the Gaming Act 1845. The argument proceeded as follows. When Ladbrokes paid the appellant they never supposed that they were discharging a legal liability; even if he had won they need not, in law, have paid him. They simply made him a gift of the money. The deputy chairman was wrong in saying that at the moment of payment the money 'belonged to another'. At that very moment its ownership was transferred and therefore the appellant could not be guilty of theft unless the extension given by s 5(4) to the meaning of the words 'belonging to another' could be brought into play. But s 5(4) had no application because under the rule in *Morgan v Ashcroft* the appellant had no obligation to repay.

The deputy chairman did not accept this line of argument. He held that it was unnecessary for the prosecution to rely on s 5(4) because the property in the £106.63 never passed to the appellant. In the view of this court that ruling was right. The subsection introduced a new principle into the law of theft but long before it was enacted it was held in *R v Middleton* (1873) LR 2 CCR 38 that where a person was paid by mistake (in that case by a post office clerk) a sum in excess of that properly payable, the person who accepted the overpayment with knowledge of the excess was guilty of theft. Counsel for the appellant seeks to distinguish the present case from that one on the basis that in *R v Middleton* the depositor was entitled to withdraw 10s from his Post Office Savings Bank account and the clerk made a mistake in thinking he was entitled to withdraw more than £8, whereas in the present case there was no mistake about the appellant's rights — whether his horse won or lost he had no legal right to payment. In our view this argument is fallacious. A bookmaker who pays out money in the belief that a certain horse has won, and who certainly would not have made the payment but for that belief, is paying by mistake just as much as the Post Office clerk in *R v Middleton*.

The gap in the law which s 5(4) was designed to fill was, as the deputy chairman rightly held, that which is illustrated by the case of *Moynes v Coopper* [1956] 1 All ER 450; [1956] 1 QB 439. There a workman received a paypacket containing £7 more than was due to him but did not become aware of the overpayment until he opened the envelope some time later. He then kept the £7. This was held not to be theft because there was no *animus furandi* at the moment of taking, and *R v Middleton* was distinguished on that ground. It was observed ([1956] 1 All ER at 452; [1956] 1 QB at 445) that the law as laid down in *R v Middleton* was reproduced and enacted in s 1(2)(i) of the Larceny Act 1916. It would be strange indeed if s 5(4) of the 1968 Act, which was designed to bring within the net of theft a type of dishonest behaviour which escaped before, were to be held to have created a loophole for another type of dishonest behaviour which was always within the net.

An alternative ground on which the deputy chairman held that the money should be regarded as belonging to Ladbrokes was that 'obligation' in s 5(4) meant an obligation whether a legal one or not. In the opinion of this court that was an incorrect ruling. In a criminal statute, where a person's criminal liability is made dependent on his having an obligation, it would be quite wrong to construe that word so as to cover a moral or social obligation as distinct from a legal one. As, however, we consider that the deputy chairman was right in ruling that the prosecution did not need to rely on s 5(4), his ruling on this alternative point does not affect the result.

[Appeal dismissed.]

8.30 Notes and illustrations

1. Had the accused in *R v Gilks* not become aware of the mistaken overpayment until subsequently, a dishonest intention not to repay the bookmaker would not have rendered him guilty of theft. It should be noted that in Victoria

the position is different as regards the various forms of gambling authorised under the Gambling Regulation Act 2003 (Vic). Such transactions are valid and, accordingly, the punter or patron overpaid is liable to repay the money he or she receives, and a dishonest decision not to do so will amount to theft.

2. D received her salary from her employer by a direct debit system by which the employer's bank account was debited and D's bank account credited, with sums due to D. Because of a mistake by the employer, D's account was credited with a sum for wages and overtime to which she was not entitled. D discovered the overpayment and did nothing about it. Held, D was guilty of theft. As a result of the employer's mistake, D received a thing in action; that is, the right to sue the bank for the amount credited in her name.

   Although she was not under an obligation to restore the property — that is, the thing in action — she was under an obligation to make restoration of the value of the thing in action. Thus the value of the thing in action continued notionally to belong to the employer and, by virtue of the concluding words of s 73(10), D's intention not to make restoration amounted to an intention to deprive the employer of that property: *Attorney-General's Reference (No 1 of 1983)* [1984] 3 All ER 369.

8.31C Attorney-General's Reference (No 1 of 1985)

[1986] QB 491; 2 WLR 733 (UK)
Court of Appeal

[A hotel manager, employed by brewers, contracted with them to sell on their premises only goods supplied by them, and to retain and deal with the proceeds of such sales for the brewers' benefit. He bought some barrels of beer from a wholesaler and intended, by selling it to customers on the brewers' premises, to make a secret profit, as he had done for some time past. The Attorney-General referred to the court the question whether such conduct amounted to theft.]

Lord Lane CJ: … We have to decide whether Parliament intended to bring such behaviour within the ambit of the criminal law and in particular whether, as alleged by the Crown, the illicit profit obtained by A was 'property belonging to another'.

Mr Arlidge bases his submission on two of the subsections to s 5 of the Theft Act 1968. First of all s 5(3), which reads:

> Where a person receives property from or on account of another, and is under an obligation to the other to retain and deal with that property or its proceeds in a particular way, the property or proceeds shall be regarded (as against him) as belonging to the other.

Although, goes the argument, at first sight the money which A receives from selling the beer which he bought seems to belong to him, the effect of this subsection is to make the profit element in the money notionally belong to the employers. Thus when A appropriates the profit, he is guilty of theft, assuming that he is acting dishonestly.

Whether that argument is correct or not depends on whether A can properly be said to have received property (ie, the payment over the counter for the beer he has sold to the customer) 'on account of' the employers. We do not think he can. He received the money on his own account as a result of his private venture. No doubt he is in breach of his contract with the employers; no doubt he is under an obligation to account to the employers at least for the profit he has made out of his venture, but that is a different matter. The fact that A may have to account to B for money he has received from X does not mean necessarily that he received the money on account of B ...

The argument based on s 5(3) of the Theft Act 1968 was a late addition to the reference. We think it is misconceived.

The reference as originally drawn relied solely on arguments based on s 5(1), which reads:

> Property shall be regarded as belonging to any person having possession or control of it, or having in it any proprietary right or interest (not being an equitable interest arising only from an agreement to transfer or grant an interest).

The argument of the Crown is that A was a 'constructive trustee' of the profit element in the money paid by customers over the bar for the 'bought in' beer and that accordingly the money belonged not, as might seem at first sight, to A but to the beneficiary of the trust, namely, the employers. The result of that, it is said, is that when A paid the money into his bank account or otherwise appropriated it, he was guilty of theft (assuming dishonesty).

[His Lordship referred to a number of authorities and continued:]

... There is a clear and important difference between on the one hand a person misappropriating specific property with which he has been entrusted, and on the other hand a person in a fiduciary position who uses that position to make a secret profit for which he will be held accountable. Whether the former is within s 5, we do not have to decide. As to the latter we are firmly of the view that he is not, because he is not a trustee ...

Assuming that, contrary to our views, s 5(1) does import the constructive trust into the Theft Act 1968, on the facts of the case the employers still obtain no proprietary interest. A trustee is not permitted to make a profit from his trust. Therefore if he uses trust property to make a profit from the trust, he is accountable for that profit. If and when such profit is identified as a separate piece of property, he may be a constructive trustee of it. However, until the profit is identifiable as a separate piece of property, it is not trust property and his obligation is to account only.

A used the employers' property and his own money to make a private profit in breach of contract. He received from customers sums of money which represented in part the cost of beer he had bought and in part possible profit for which he was accountable to the employers. This profit element, assuming it existed, never became a separate piece of property of which A could be trustee. It remained part of a mixed fund. Therefore there never was a moment at which A was trustee of a definite fund. It follows that there never was a moment when the employers had any proprietary interest in any of the money. The money did not belong to another. There was therefore no theft.

8.32 Further reading

E Griew, *The Theft Acts*, 7th ed, Sweet & Maxwell, London, 1995, pp 14–41

B McSherry and B Naylor, *Australian Criminal Laws: Critical Perspectives*, Oxford University Press, Melbourne, 2004, pp 263–72, 278–81

D Ormerod and D Williams (ed), *Smith's Law of Theft*, Oxford University Press, 9th ed, 2007, pp 59–75, 76–103

C R Williams, *Property Offences*, 3rd ed, Law Book Co, Sydney, 1999, pp 102–17

The appropriation

8.33C Stein v Henshall

[1976] VR 612
Supreme Court of Victoria

[The accused drove a car which he knew to have been stolen. It was uncertain whether the thief had given the accused the car or merely loaned it to him. The magistrate held that the prosecution had therefore failed to prove an appropriation by the accused and dismissed the information. The prosecution appealed to the Supreme Court by way of order to review.]

Lush J: ... In my opinion, the assumption of the rights of an owner referred to in [*Crimes Act 1958 s 73*] subs (4) involves the taking on one's self of the right to do something which the owner has the right to do by virtue of his ownership. I do not accept the argument that the conduct required to establish an assumption of the rights of an owner extends to establishing an intention to exclude all others, and I think that Mr Uren's argument that subs (14)(a) illustrates this is valid. In my opinion, in order to determine whether there was an 'appropriation' by the defendant in this case, it is not necessary to consider whether the original thief, Graham, gave up all his possessory rights to the defendant or retained them, or lent the car to the defendant so that the defendant was in possession of it by gratuitous bailment.

The question is — and is only — whether the defendant acted in relation to the car in a manner in which the owner would have the right to act. On Wednesday 9 July, and Friday 11 July, the defendant used the car for his own purposes — not for the original thief's purposes or for those of any other person but himself. To make such a use of it was one of the rights of ownership; and the defendant, in my opinion, assumed that right.

Mr Davey's argument, on this view, is not acceptable. An alternative way of explaining its rejection is to say that the rights of the owner included the day-by-day use of the car. The original thief's action in handing the car over to the defendant made it possible for the defendant to exercise that right until the original thief reclaimed the car — if, indeed, he intended to do so. Until that time, the defendant was — even if by the original thief's permission — exercising rights which were rights of the owner.

[Information remitted for rehearing by the Magistrates' Court.]

8.34 Notes and illustrations

1. As will be seen below, the concept of appropriation has given rise to significant issues of interpretation. Section 134(1) of the Criminal Law Consolidation Act 1935 (SA) avoids these problems by providing that theft may be committed by a person who 'deals' with property in a proscribed manner. The expression 'deals' is defined widely by s 130 of the Act.
2. The definition of 'appropriates' contained in s 73(4) of the Crimes Act 1958 (Vic) is apt to cover all the ordinary cases of theft. A person who takes property belonging to another clearly assumes the rights of an owner and this is, of course, the most common instance of appropriation. A person who uses property belonging to another also assumes the rights of an owner. So, too, does a person who destroys or damages property belonging to another. Where property is merely damaged, it may be that theft is not committed because of the absence of an intention permanently to deprive. However, if the damage is substantial, it may constitute a permanent deprivation. To sell or to pledge property belonging to another is also an assumption of the rights of an owner. So, too, is a lending of property belonging to another. A mere retention of property belonging to another may also amount to an assumption of the rights of an owner. Thus a person who refuses to return property to its owner appropriates it.
3. There is no reason why a series of acts in relation to a particular item of property cannot each constitute an appropriation. Thus, an accused who takes property and subsequently destroys it commits two acts of appropriation in respect of that item of property. The accused assumes the rights of an owner over the property when he or she takes it, and the accused again assumes the rights of an owner in respect of the property when he or she subsequently destroys it. The prosecution would be entitled to charge the accused with theft in respect of either appropriation.
4. United Kingdom banks issue customers who wish to use cheques with a 'cheque card' specifying the amount up to which they are authorised to write a cheque. The bank will then honour, or 'guarantee', the payment

of the cheque when presented by the payee. D opened bank accounts in false names and obtained cheque cards. He then drew cheques on these accounts, supported by presentation of the cheque cards, when there was not sufficient money in the accounts to meet those cheques. The trial judge directed the jury that D's conduct amounted to an appropriation of the assets of the banks on which the cheques were drawn. D was convicted and appealed. Held, conviction quashed. There was no assumption by D of the rights of the banks. The use of the cheque card and delivery of the cheque did no more than give the payee a contractual right as against the bank to be paid a specified sum from the bank's fund on presentation of the guaranteed cheque and that was not in itself an assumption of the rights of the bank to that part of the bank's funds to which the sums specified in the cheques corresponded: *R v Navvabi* [1986] 3 All ER 102. D was the accountant for two companies. By means of 10 forged cheques he withdrew money from the companies' bank accounts and caused it to be deposited in his personal account or the account of a business of which he was the sole proprietor. The companies' bank debited their accounts. D was convicted of 10 offences of theft of choses in action; namely, debts owed by the bank to the companies. Held, conviction affirmed. Although the bank had no authority to honour the forged cheques and the companies were entitled to have the amounts debited from their accounts restored, D, by drawing, presenting and negotiating the cheques, had wrongfully assumed some of the companies' rights as owners of the credit in their accounts, and so he had dishonestly appropriated property belonging to the companies: *Chan Man-Sin v R* [1988] 1 WLR 196 (PC on appeal from the Court of Appeal of Hong Kong). Accord *R v Jack* (2002) 148 ACTR 1.

5. D was convicted of theft of a motor car. D had accepted an invitation to go for a ride in a vehicle he knew to have been stolen. Throughout the journey he remained a passenger in the rear seat of the vehicle. Held, conviction affirmed. An appropriation can be committed by the assumption of any of the owner's rights. The act of travelling as a passenger in another's car without the person's consent amounts to a use of the car for one of its ordinary purposes and involves an assumption and usurpation of one of the owner's rights: *W (a child) v Woodrow* [1988] VR 358.

6. On an application to extradite D to Hong Kong under the Fugitive Offenders Act 1967 (UK), questions arose as to where various offences had taken place. Held in *R v Governor of Pentonville Prison; Ex parte Osman* [1989] 3 All ER 701:

   > Where a person, without authority, presents a cheque or sends a telex instruction to a bank to draw on an account in credit or within an agreed overdraft limit, the act of presenting the cheque or sending the telex instruction is the act of theft itself, and not a mere attempt, since it is the

last act which the person has to perform and not a preparatory act, even if the account is in fact never debited. The sending of a telex instruction in such circumstances is therefore an 'appropriation' for the purposes of s 3(1)(a) of the Theft Act 1968, and the place where the telex was dispatched is the place where the chose in action was appropriated. Furthermore, if a crime may have a dual location, it may be that the place where the telex was received may also be regarded as the place of appropriation (see p 717 to p 718, post); dicta of Lord Roskill in *R v Morris* [1983] 3 All ER 288 at 292–3 and of Lord Oliver in *Chan Man-Sin v A-G of Hong Kong* [1988] 1 All ER 1 at 4 applied.

7. On an application to extradite an offender to the United States, the question arose where an appropriation occurred when fraudulent instructions were inserted in a computer, the instructions being inserted via a computer keyboard in Russia and received virtually instantaneously and intended to take effect where the computer was situated in the United States. Held, while it may be that an appropriation may have a dual location, if it was necessary to choose then the appropriation occurred in the United States. In the case of a virtually instantaneous instruction intended to take effect where a computer is situated, it would be artificial to regard the insertion of an instruction onto the disk as having been done only at the remote place where the keyboard was situated: *R v Governor of Brixton Prison; Ex parte Levin* [1996] 1 WLR 657.

8.35C R v Morris

[1984] AC 320
House of Lords

[The accused removed articles from shelves in a self-service store and attached in place or on top of the correct price labels, price labels removed from lower-priced articles in the store. The accused was convicted of theft on the basis that the act of changing the labels amounted to an appropriation. On appeal to the House of Lords.]

Lord Roskill [delivering the judgment of their Lordships]: … The starting point of any consideration of Mr Denison's submissions must, I think, be the decision of this House in *R v Lawrence (Alan)* [1972] AC 626. In the leading speech, Viscount Dilhorne expressly accepted the view of the Court of Appeal (Criminal Division) in that case that the offence of theft involved four elements, (1) a dishonest (2) appropriation (3) of property belonging to another, (4) with the intention of permanently depriving the owner of it. Viscount Dilhorne also rejected the argument that even if these four elements were all present there could not be theft within the section if the owner of the property in question had consented to the acts which were done by the defendant. That there was in that case a dishonest appropriation was beyond question and the House did not have to consider the precise meaning of that word in s 3(1).

Mr Denison submitted that the phrase in s 3(1) 'any assumption by a person of *the rights'* (my emphasis) 'of an owner amounts to an appropriation' must mean any assumption of 'all the rights of an owner'. Since neither respondent had at the time of the removal of the goods from the shelves and of the label switching assumed all the rights of the owner, there was no appropriation and therefore no theft. Mr Jeffreys for the prosecution, on the other hand, contended that *the* rights in this context only meant any of the rights. An owner of goods has many rights — they have been described as 'a bundle or package of rights'. Mr Jeffreys contended that on a fair reading of the subsection it cannot have been the intention that every one of an owner's rights had to be assumed by the alleged thief before an appropriation was proved and that essential ingredient of the offence of theft established.

My Lords, if one reads the words 'the rights' at the opening of s 3(1) literally and in isolation from the rest of the section, Mr Denison's submission undoubtedly has force. But the later words 'any later assumption of a right' in subs (1) and the words in subs (2) 'no later assumption by him of rights' seem to me to militate strongly against the correctness of the submission. Moreover the provisions of s 2(1)(a) also seem to point in the same direction. It follows therefore that it is enough for the prosecution if they have proved in these cases the assumption by the respondents of *any* of the rights of the owner of the goods in question, that is to say, the supermarket concerned, it being common ground in these cases that the other three of the four elements mentioned in Viscount Dilhorne's speech in *R v Lawrence (Alan)* had been fully established.

My Lords, Mr Jeffreys sought to argue that any removal from the shelves of the supermarket, even if unaccompanied by label switching, was without more an appropriation. In one passage in his judgment in *Morris's* case, the learned Lord Chief Justice appears to have accepted the submission, for he said [1983] QB 587 at 596:

> … it seems to us that in taking the article from the shelf the customer is indeed assuming one of the rights of the owner — the right to move the article from its position on the shelf to carry it to the check-out.

With the utmost respect, I cannot accept this statement as correct. If one postulates an honest customer taking goods from a shelf to put in his or her trolley to take to the checkpoint there to pay the proper price, I am unable to see that any of these actions involves any assumption by the shopper of the rights of the supermarket. In the context of s 3(1), the concept of appropriation in my view involves not an act expressly or impliedly authorised by the owner but an act by way of adverse interference with or usurpation of those rights. When the honest shopper acts as I have just described, he or she is acting with the implied authority of the owner of the supermarket to take the goods from the shelf, put them in the trolley, take them to the checkpoint and there pay the correct price, at which moment the property in the goods will pass to the shopper for the first time. It is with the consent of the owners of the supermarket, be that consent express or implied, that the shopper does these acts and thus obtains at least control if not actual possession of the goods preparatory, at a later stage, to obtaining the property in them upon payment of the proper amount at the checkpoint. I do not think that s 3(1) envisages any such act as an 'appropriation', whatever may be the meaning of that word in other fields such as contract or sale of goods law.

If, as I understand all of your Lordships to agree, the concept of appropriation in s 3(1) involves an element of adverse interference with or usurpation of some right of the owner, it is necessary next to consider whether that requirement is satisfied in either of these cases. As I have already said, in my view mere removal from the shelves without more is not an appropriation. Further, if a shopper with some perverted sense of humour, intending only to create confusion and nothing more, both for the supermarket and for other shoppers, switches labels, I do not think that that act of label switching alone is without more an appropriation, though it is not difficult to envisage some cases of dishonest label-switching which could be. In cases such as the present, it is in truth a combination of these actions, the removal from the shelf and the switching of the labels, which evidences adverse interference with or usurpation of the right of the owner. Those acts, therefore, amount to an appropriation and if they are accompanied by proof of the other three elements to which I have referred, the offence of theft is established. Further if they are accompanied by other acts such as putting the goods so removed and relabelled into a receptacle, whether a trolley or the shopper's own bag or basket, proof of appropriation within s 3(1) becomes overwhelming. It is the doing of one or more acts which individually or collectively amount to such adverse interference with or usurpation of the owner's rights which constitute appropriation under s 3(1) and I do not think it matters where there is more than one such act in which order the successive acts take place, or whether there is any interval of time between them. To suggest that it matters whether the mislabelling precedes or succeeds removal from the shelves is to reduce this branch of the law to an absurdity.

...

My Lords, it remains briefly to consider any relationship between s 1 and s 15. If the conclusion I have reached that theft takes place at the moment of appropriation and before any payment is made at the checkpoint be correct it is wrong to assert, as has been asserted, that the same act of appropriation creates two offences one against s 1(1) and the other against s 15(1) because the two offences occur at different points of time; the s 15(1) offence is not committed until payment of the wrong amount is made at the checkpoint while the theft has been committed earlier. It follows that in cases such as *Morris's* two offences were committed. I do not doubt that it was perfectly proper to add the third count under s 15(1) in this case. I think the assistant recorder was right to leave all three counts to the jury. While one may sympathise with his preventing them from returning a verdict on the third count once they convicted on the theft counts if only in the interests of simplification, the counts were not alternative as he appears to have treated them. They were cumulative and once they were left to the jury verdicts should have been taken on all of them.

My Lords, these shoplifting cases by switching labels are essentially simple in their facts and their factual simplicity should not be allowed to be obscured by ingenious legal arguments upon the Theft Act which for some time have bedevilled this branch of the criminal law without noticeably contributing to the efficient administration of justice — rather the reverse. The law to be applied to simple cases, whether in magistrates' courts or the Crown Court, should if possible be equally simple. I see no reason in principle why, when there is clear evidence of both offences being committed, both offences should not be charged. But where a shoplifter has passed the checkpoint and quite clearly has, by deception, obtained goods either without paying or by paying only a lesser price than he should, those concerned with prosecutions may in future think it preferable in the interests of simplicity to charge only an offence against s 15(1). In many cases of that kind it is difficult to see what possible defence there can be and that course may well avoid any opportunity for further ingenious legal arguments upon the first few sections of the Theft Act. Of course when the dishonesty is detected before the defendant has reached the checkpoint and he or she is arrested before that point so that no property has been obtained by deception, then theft is properly charged and if appropriation, within the meaning that I have attributed to that word in this speech, is proved as well as the other three ingredients of the offence of theft, the defendant is plainly guilty of that offence.

My Lords, as already explained I have not gone through all the cases cited though I have mentioned some. Of the rest those inconsistent with this speech must henceforth be treated as overruled.

I would answer the certified questions in this way:

> There is a dishonest appropriation for the purposes of the Theft Act 1968 where by the substitution of a price label showing a lesser price on goods for one showing a greater price, a defendant either by that act alone or by that act in conjunction with another act or other acts (whether done before or after the substitution of the labels) adversely interferes with or usurps the right of the owner to ensure that the goods concerned are sold and paid for at that greater price.

I would dismiss these appeals.

[Appeal dismissed.]

8.36C R v Baruday

[1984] VR 685

Supreme Court of Victoria

[The accused was convicted on a number of counts of theft arising out of the conduct of his business as an insurance broker. Two of the counts involved cheques paid by a client to the accused upon receipt of bogus accounts from the accused for the payment of extra premiums in respect of workers compensation insurance premiums. On appeal to the Supreme Court.]

Southwell J: For the Crown, Mr Weinberg in dealing with counts 2 and 5 submitted that the applicant appropriated the cheques for extra premiums when he received them and paid them into his account. He submitted that *R v Morris* was not authority for the proposition that there can be no appropriation where possession is gained by consent. He further submitted that there was no inconsistency between *Heddich v Dike* and *R v Morris*.

He submitted that in *R v Lawrence* [1972] AC 626 there was an element of deception which vitiated the consent to the taking and that in the present case fraud vitiates the consent to the taking. He submitted that Gobbo J so decided in *Heddich v Dike* and that the decision was correct. It was said that the defence submission involved that there may be deception but nevertheless a true consent and this was unsound in law.

He went on to submit that if there was deception there was appropriation because there was no consent.

In *R v Lawrence* a Mr Occhi, an Italian who spoke little English, arrived at Victoria Station on his first visit to England. He approached the appellant taxi driver, and showed him a piece of paper on which an address was written: the appellant said that it was very far and very expensive, whereupon Mr Occhi took 10s/6d out of his wallet and gave it to the appellant who then, the wallet being still open, took a further £6 out of it. The lawful fare for the journey was about 10s/6d. The appellant was convicted of theft of the £6. The main contention of the appellant was that since Mr Occhi had consented to the taking of the £6 there could be no theft because there could be no appropriation where there was consent to the taking.

In his speech, Viscount Dilhorn, with whom the other members of the House agreed, said that the passage of the Theft Act 1968: 'has relieved the prosecution of the burden of establishing that the taking was without the owner's consent. That is no longer an ingredient of the offence.' After observing that a person is not to be regarded as acting dishonestly if he appropriates another's property believing that with full knowledge of the circumstances that other person has in fact agreed to the appropriation, his Lordship said: 'Belief or the absence of belief that the owner had with such knowledge consented to the appropriation is relevant to the issue of dishonesty, not to the question whether or not there has been an appropriation.' His Lordship went on summarily to dismiss the submission that the £6 was not property 'belonging to another'.

In *Heddich v Dike* (1981) 3 A Crim R 139, the defendant was charged with stealing some offset printing plates which he obtained from an employee of their owner by falsely representing that he was doing so with the authority of the owner. It was submitted that since the plates were handed over by the employee, if any offence was committed it was no more than obtaining property by deception.

Gobbo J, correctly in my view in the circumstances, considered that he ought to follow the decision of the House of Lords in *Lawrence's* case. His Honour went on to adopt the view of the Court of Appeal in *Lawrence's* case that there is such an overlap between the offences in ss 72 and 81 of the *Crimes Act 1958* that every case of obtaining property by deception — save when the subject matter is land — contains the offence of theft.

In *R v Morris* [1983] 3 WLR 697, [1983] 3 All ER 288 two cases were before the House of Lords. In the first case the defendant removed a price label from a joint of pork in a supermarket and attached it to a second more expensive joint. His action was detected at the checkout point before he had paid for the joint. He was convicted of theft. In the second case the defendant took goods from the shelves of a supermarket and replaced the price labels attached to them with labels showing lesser prices. At the checkout point he was asked for and paid the lesser prices. He was charged with theft and with obtaining property by deception. He was convicted of theft but the jury was not asked to return a verdict on the second count. In dismissing the appeals the House of Lords held that to establish an appropriation it was sufficient to prove that the defendant assumed any of the rights of ownership but not necessarily all of them, and the concept of appropriation involved adverse interference with or usurpation of some right of the owner. It was held that the defendants by removing the goods in question from the shelves and switching the labels had adversely interfered with or usurped the rights of the owners of the goods to ensure that they were sold and paid for at the proper prices, and that their acts had constituted an appropriation. It was further held that in the second case the count of obtaining property by deception was not an alternative to the count of theft and that strictly speaking there was no reason why a conviction should not have been recorded on both counts.

Mr Sharp sought to derive some comfort from the speech of Lord Roskill in *R v Morris.* And, as I noted his submission, sought to show that the House in some way distinguished its earlier decision in *R v Lawrence.* The headnotes of the reports of *Morris* refer to *R v Lawrence* as having been applied or approved. I can discern nothing in the speech of Lord Roskill (with whom the other members of the House agreed) to suggest that any doubt was entertained as to the correctness of the decision in *R v Lawrence.* At ([1983] 3 WLR 703) his Lordship said that: 'when an honest customer takes goods from a shelf that customer is acting with the implied authority of the supermarket owner to do so.' Lord Roskill was there dealing with the question whether in the English equivalent to s 73(4) of the Crimes Act the concept of appropriation involved an act expressly or impliedly authorised by the owner or an act by way of adverse interference with the owner's rights. Lord Roskill held that s 73(4) involved the latter. In that case it was a combination of the removal of the goods from the shelf and the switching of the labels which amounted to an appropriation. It is to be implied from the judgment that any consent of the supermarket owner would have to be consent with knowledge of the facts — the deception in switching the labels would vitiate that consent.

In the present case the applicant obtained cheques from the City of Knox in respect to counts 2 and 5 by falsely representing that those sums were due and payable as additional premiums. The authority or consent of the City of Knox to the payment by the applicant of those cheques into his own account was an authority or consent obtained by fraud. Mr Sharp has submitted that a valid distinction is to be drawn between the case of a cheque obtained by deception and goods which were obtained from a supermarket by deception. For my part, I do not see the validity of that distinction. The words of Lord Roskill in *R v Morris,* (at [WLR] 705; [All ER] 295) should be borne steadily in mind: 'These shoplifting cases by switching labels are essentially simple in their facts and their factual simplicity should not be allowed to be obscured by ingenious legal arguments upon the Theft Act which for some time have bedevilled this branch of the criminal law without noticeably contributing to the efficient administration of justice — rather the reverse. The law to be applied in simple cases ... should if possible be equally simple.'

I do not suggest that the present case is 'simple' in the sense there referred to; nevertheless, the cry for simplicity should not be confined only to simple cases. The preparation of a false account calculated to extract a cheque from the victim is doubtless not so simple as the switching of labels on goods in a supermarket, an act calculated to facilitate the removal of goods for a lower than correct price. Nevertheless, I cannot see that the factual difference necessitates the application of a different principle of law.

In my opinion, when the applicant paid the cheques for extra premiums into his account he appropriated them. It is clear that the other elements of the offence of theft were made out to the satisfaction of the jury, and accordingly, the applicant was rightly convicted on counts 2 and 5.

[**Crockett** and **Murray JJ** concurred. Appeal dismissed.]

8.37C R v Roffel

[1985] VR 511
Supreme Court of Victoria

[The accused was convicted on a number of counts of stealing property belonging to a company of which he and his wife were the sole shareholders and directors. The accused alone conducted the day-to-day management of the company. The accused, with intent to defraud creditors of the company, drew cheques on the company's account and used the proceeds of those cheques for his own purposes. On appeal to the Supreme Court.]

Young CJ: That a company is a legal entity separate from its corporators has been trite law at least since *Salomon v Salomon & Co Ltd* [1897] AC 22. Thus there is no doubt that a natural person can steal from a company. Nor is there any reason in logic or in legal theory why a person should not be guilty of stealing from a company of which he was the dominant shareholder and director, although it will not often be possible to prove that he has done so. It is also true that a company which gives property to one of its shareholders or to one of its directors does not by that act alone, without more, commit any offence against the criminal law. Nor is a person who receives a gift from a company by that act alone, without more, guilty of theft from the company even if he owns almost all of the shares and is the governing director with plenary powers.

In the present case it is necessary to ask upon what act of appropriation the Crown relies to prove the theft. Since it is, in the four counts presently under consideration, the theft of money that is alleged, the Crown doubtless relies upon the receipt of the money from the company's bankers as the act of appropriation. But where is the element of usurpation of the company's rights in the act of receiving the money? The cheque was the company's cheque, made payable to cash and in the possession of the applicant who was the de facto controller of the company. There was no evidence to suggest that the company did not intend the applicant to have the money and to use it for his own purposes. If the company decided to give the money to the applicant in order to defeat its creditors, that would be quite irrelevant. The motive of the company in making the gift could not convert the applicant's act in receiving the money into a usurpation of the company's rights. If it be assumed that the act of the company in giving the cheque to the applicant to enable him to obtain the money was beyond the powers of the company, that consideration would not turn the applicant's act of receiving the money into an act of usurpation of the rights of the company. The fact that the applicant was 'the directing mind and will of the company' (see *HL Bolton (Engineering) Co Ltd v TJ Graham & Sons Ltd* [1957] 1 QB 159 at 172, per Lord Denning MR) seems to me to be irrelevant. Though the applicant's purpose may have been the purpose of the company, to treat that purpose as attributable to him as the recipient of the cash which he is alleged to have appropriated seems to me to ignore the fact that the company is a separate legal person. Similarly I would regard the fact that it was *ultra vires* of the company to give the money to the applicant (if it be a fact) as equally irrelevant. If the act of the company were void and the company were able to recover the money from the applicant, it would be able to do so not because the applicant had stolen the money from the company but because he had as the directing mind and will of the company caused the company to apply its money in a manner or towards objects which the company had no power to entertain: cf *Spackman v Evans* (1868) LR 3 HL 171 at 244–5. Thus even if the act of the company were void, the directing mind and will of the company still concurred in the applicant's receiving the money for his own benefit and thereby precluded his receipt of it from being an appropriation within the meaning of the Crimes Act. If this conclusion means that a person whom common sense would regard as a thief is not a thief in law, that result follows from the fact that the law has at least since 1897 treated a company as a legal person entirely separate from and, in law, independent of those who own it or who control or manage its affairs.

I have dealt with the four counts of stealing money but the same reasoning applies to the count charging theft of a cheque. In no case does the evidence justify a conviction and as it was not suggested to us that the Crown could lead any other evidence on a retrial, I would order that a verdict of acquittal be entered.

Crockett J: The applicant appears to me clearly to have been identified with the company at the relevant time. Whether what the company did through the agency of the applicant was dishonest vis-a-vis the trade creditors or was *ultra vires* the company is not to the point. By the instrumentality of the only person through which it could effectively act it consented to entry into the impugned transactions. They were thus not unilateral. Or, to describe it in the terms of *Morris*, by reason of its very acquiescence in the drawing of the cheque on its funds the company was not acting so that it could be said the applicant was adversely interfering with or usurping some right of ownership possessed by it.

[**Brooking J** dissented. Appeal allowed.]

8.38 Notes

D1 and D2 were convicted of a number of offences, including theft from a building society of which D1 was the chairperson of directors. In the course of the trial, the judge ruled that it was possible for the chairperson of directors of a building society to appropriate the property of the building society. On appeal to the Supreme Court of Victoria, held, conviction affirmed. *R v Roffel* (at **8.37C**) decided that where a company has consented to a taking of its property, there is no appropriation of that property within the law relating to theft. The situation of a building society is wholly different. The legislation governing its incorporation is designed to protect the depositors. Not only did D1 not have the consent of the society, but the society could not have given its consent to his taking of its property. Even if a general meeting of the members of the society had resolved that he could take the society's property, such a resolution would have been illegal and a 'consent' which is prohibited by law could hardly amount to a sufficient consent to negative an appropriation for the purposes of the law of theft, particularly where the beneficiary of the taking formed the majority of those who purported to authorise it: *R v Clarkson and Lyon* (1986) 24 A Crim R 54. The case of *Roffel* was considered to be wrongly decided (in obiter) by the High Court of Australia in *Macleod v R* (2003) 214 CLR 230.

8.39C

R v Gomez

[1993] 1 All ER 1
House of Lords

[The accused was employed as the assistant manager of an electrical goods shop. He was approached by B, who asked to be supplied with quantities of electrical goods from the shop in exchange for two stolen building society cheques which were worthless. The accused agreed, and induced the shop manager to authorise the supply of the goods against the cheques which he told the manager were 'as good as cash'. The cheques were then used for the purchase of electrical goods to the value of over £16,000 and were later dishonoured on presentation. The accused was convicted of theft of the goods. The Court of Appeal quashed the conviction on the ground that as the manager had expressly authorised the goods to be removed there had been no appropriation. The Crown appealed to the House of Lords.]

Lord Keith [His Lordship quoted from the judgment of **Lord Roskill** in *R v Morris* (at **8.35C**) and continued]: In my opinion Lord Roskill was undoubtedly right when he said in the course of the passage quoted that the assumption by the defendant of any of the rights of an owner could amount to an appropriation within the meaning of s 3(1), and that the removal of an article from the shelf and the changing of the price label on it constituted the assumption of one of the rights of the owner and hence an appropriation within the meaning of the subsection. But there are observations in the passage which, with the greatest possible respect to Lord Roskill, I must regard as unnecessary for the decision of the case and as being incorrect. In the first place, it seems to me that the switching of price labels on the article is in itself an assumption of one of the rights of the owner, whether or not it is accompanied by some other act such as removing the article from the shelf and placing it in a basket or trolley. No one but the owner has the right to remove a price label from an article or to place a price label upon it. If anyone else does so, he does an act, as Lord Roskill puts it, by way of adverse interference with or usurpation of that right. This is no less so in the case of the practical joker figured by Lord Roskill than in the case of one who makes the switch with dishonest intent. The practical joker, of course, is not guilty of theft because he has not acted dishonestly and does not intend to deprive the owner permanently of the article. So the label switching in itself constitutes an appropriation and so to have held would have been sufficient for the dismissal of both appeals. On the facts of the two cases it was unnecessary to decide whether, as argued by counsel for the prosecution, the mere taking of the article from the shelf and putting it in a trolley or other receptacle amounted to the assumption of one of the rights of the owner, and hence an appropriation. There was much to be said in favour of the view that it did, in respect that doing so gave the shopper control of the article and the capacity to exclude any other shopper from taking it. However, Lord Roskill expressed the opinion that it did not, on the ground that the concept of appropriation in the context of s 3(1) 'involves not an act expressly or impliedly authorised by the owner but an act by way of adverse interference with or usurpation of those rights'. While it is correct to say that appropriation for purposes of s 3(1) includes the latter sort of act, it does not necessarily follow that no other act can amount to an appropriation and in particular that no act expressly or impliedly authorised by the owner can in any circumstances do so. Indeed, *Lawrence's* case is a clear decision to the contrary since it laid down unequivocally that an act may be an appropriation notwithstanding that it is done with the consent of the owner. It does not appear to me that any sensible distinction can be made in this context between consent and authorisation.

In the civil case of *Dobson v General Accident Fire and Life Assurance Corp plc* [1989] 3 All ER 927; [1990] 1 QB 274 a Court of Appeal consisting of Parker and Bingham LJJ considered the apparent conflict between *Lawrence's* case and *R v Morris* and applied the former decision. The facts were that the plaintiff had insured property with the defendant company against, *inter alia*, 'loss or damage caused by theft'. He advertised for sale a watch and ring at the total price of £5,950. A rogue telephoned expressing an interest in buying the articles and the plaintiff provisionally agreed with him that the payment would be by a building society cheque in the plaintiff's favour. The rogue called on the plaintiff the next day and the watch and the ring were handed over to him in exchange for a building society cheque for the agreed amount. The plaintiff paid the cheque into his bank, which informed him that it was stolen and worthless. The defendant company denied liability under its policy of insurance on the ground that the loss of the watch and ring was not caused by theft within the meaning of the 1968 Act. The plaintiff succeeded in the county court in an action to recover the amount of his loss, and the decision was affirmed by the Court of Appeal. One of the arguments for the defendants was that there had been no theft because the plaintiff had agreed to the transaction with the rogue and reliance was placed on Lord Roskill's statement in *R v Morris* [1983] 3 All ER 288 at 293; [1984] AC 320 at 332 that appropriation 'involves not an act expressly or impliedly authorised by the owner but an act by way of adverse interference with or usurpation of those rights'.

In dealing with this argument Parker LJ said ([1989] 3 All ER 927 at 93; [1990] 1 QB 274 at 281):

The difficulties caused by the apparent conflict between the decision in *Lawrence's* case and *R v Morris* have provided, not surprisingly, a basis for much discussion by textbook writers and contributors of articles to law journals. It is, however, clear that their Lordships in *R v Morris* did not regard anything said in that case as conflicting with *Lawrence's* case for it was specifically referred to in Lord Roskill's speech, with which the other members of the Appellate Committee all agreed, without disapproval or qualification. The only comment made was that, in *Lawrence's* case, the House did not have to consider the precise meaning of 'appropriation' in s 3(1) (see [1983] 3 All ER 288 at 292; [1984] AC 320 at 331). With respect, I find this comment hard to follow in the light of the first of the questions asked in *Lawrence's* case and the answer to it, the passages from Viscount Dilhorne's speech already cited, the fact that it was specifically argued that 'appropriates' is meant in a pejorative, rather than a neutral, sense in that the appropriation is against the will of the owner' (see [1972] AC 626 at 631 arg), and finally that dishonesty was common ground. I would have supposed that *the* question in *Lawrence's* case was whether appropriation necessarily involved an absence of consent (Parker LJ's emphasis).

Parker LJ then said that he found other difficulties in Lord Roskill's speech in *R v Morris*, and after setting out the facts of the case and quoting a long passage from that speech (see [1983] 3 All ER 288 at 293; [1984] AC 320 at 332) and also the answer to the certified question he continued ([1989] 3 All ER 927 at 932–3; [1990] 1 QB 274 at 283–4):

> In the first passage Lord Roskill, as it seems to me, impliedly envisages that mere label-switching could be an appropriation and that this is so is confirmed by the answer to the certified question which specifically uses the words 'either by that act alone'. What then is it which would make label-switching alone something which adversely affects or usurps the right of the owner? In that passage it appears to be envisaged that it will depend on the question whether the label-switching was dishonest and coupled with the other elements of the offence of theft or was due to a perverted sense of humour. This, however, appears to run together the elements of dishonesty and appropriation when it is clear from *Lawrence's* case that they are separate. That the two elements were indeed, at any rate to some extent, run together is plain from the fact that the answer to the certified question begins with the words 'there is a dishonest appropriation'. Moreover, on general principles, it would in my judgment be a plain interference with or usurpation of an owner's rights by the customer if he were to remove a label which the owner had placed on goods or put another label on. It would be a trespass to goods and it would be usurping the owner's rights, for only he would have any right to do such an act and no one could contend that there was any implied consent or authority to a customer to do any such thing. There would thus be an appropriation. In the case of the customer with a perverted sense of humour there would however be no theft for there would probably be no dishonesty and certainly no intent permanently to deprive the owner of the goods themselves. The case of

the customer who simply removes foods from the shelves is of course different because the basis on which a supermarket is run is that customers certainly have the consent of the owner to take goods from the shelves and take them to the checkout point, there to pay the proper price for them. Suppose, however, that there were no such consent, in, for example, a shop where goods on display were to be taken from the shelves only by the attendant. In such a case a customer who took from the shelves would clearly be usurping the right of the owner. Indeed he would be doing so if he did no more than move an item from one place on a shelf to another. The only difference appears to be that in the one case there is consent and in the other there is not. Since, however, it was held in *Lawrence's* case that consent is not relevant to appropriation there must, one would have supposed, be no difference between the two cases on that aspect of the offence. There are further matters in *R v Morris* [1983] 3 All ER 288; [1984] AC 320 in which I find difficulty. I mention only two. The first is the observation made in *R v McPherson* [1973] Crim LR 191. That was a case in which the defendant took two bottles of whisky from the shelves and put them in her shopping bag. The sole question in issue was whether there had been an appropriation. It was held in the Court of Appeal that there had been. As to this Lord Roskill said ([1983] 3 All ER 288 at 294; [1984] AC 320 at 333): 'That was not, of course, a label-switching case, but it is a plain case of appropriation effected by the combination of the acts of removing the goods from the shelf and of concealing them in the shopping bag. *R v McPherson* is to my mind clearly correctly decided as are all the cases which have followed it. It is wholly consistent with the principles which I have endeavoured to state in this speech.' Reference to the transcript of the judgment in that case however reveals that the decision did not turn on concealment in the shopping bag but was expressly on the ground that the goods were appropriated when they were taken from the shelves. This indeed was recognised in *Anderton v Wish* (1980) 72 CR App R 23 at 25, where Roskill LJ said: 'The Court of Appeal ... held ... they were guilty of theft because when the bottles were taken there was a dishonest appropriation. If that decision is right and, with respect, it seems to me plainly right ...'. Furthermore in *R v Morris* [1983] 3 All ER 288 at 294; [1984] AC 320 at 334 Lord Roskill said: '... I understand all your Lordships to agree that *Anderton v Wish* was rightly decided for the reasons given.'

Later Parker LJ quoted this passage from the speech of Lord Roskill in *R v Morris* [1983] 3 All ER 288 at 294; [1984] AC 320 at 334:

'... without going into further detail I respectfully suggest that it is on any view wrong to introduce into this branch of the criminal law questions whether particular contracts are void or voidable on the ground of mistake or fraud or whether any mistake is sufficiently fundamental to vitiate a contract. These difficult questions should so far as possible be confined to those fields of law to which they are immediately relevant and I do not regard them as relevant questions under the 1968 Act.' After anxious consideration I have reached the conclusion that whatever *R v Morris* did decide it cannot be regarded as having overruled the very

> plain decision in *Lawrence's* case that appropriation can occur even if the owner consents and that *R v Morris* itself makes it plain that it is no defence to say that the property passed under a voidable contract. (See [1989] 3 All ER 927 at 934; [1990] 1 QB 274 at 285.)

On this ground Park LJ dismissed the appeal.

Bingham LJ plainly took the view that a customer in a supermarket assumes some of the rights of an owner when he takes goods into his possession and exercises control over them by putting them in a basket or trolley, and thus appropriates them (see [1989] 3 All ER 927 at 936; [1990] 1 QB 274 at 287). Later he mentioned that in Lord Roskill's speech in *R v Morris* no reference was made to Viscount Dilhorne's ruling in *Lawrence's* case that appropriation might occur even though the owner has permitted or consented to the property being taken, and continued ([1989] 3 All ER 927 at 937; [1990] 1 QB 274 at 289):

> I do not find it easy to reconcile this ruling of Viscount Dilhorne, which was as I understand central to the answer which the House of Lords gave to the certified question, with the reasoning of the House in *R v Morris*. Since, however, the House in *R v Morris* considered that there had plainly been an appropriation in *Lawrence's* case, this must (I think) have been because the Italian student, although he had permitted or allowed his money to be taken, had not in truth consented to the taxi driver taking anything in excess of the correct fare. This is not a wholly satisfactory reconciliation, since it might be said that a supermarket consents to customers taking goods from its shelves only when they honestly intend to pay and not otherwise. On the facts of the present case, however, it can be said, by analogy with *Lawrence's* case, that although the plaintiff permitted and allowed his property to be taken by the rogue, he had not in truth consented to the rogue becoming owner without giving a valid draft drawn by the building society for the price. On this basis I conclude that the plaintiff is able to show an appropriation sufficient to satisfy s 1(1) of the 1968 Act when the rogue accepted delivery of the articles.

It was argued for the respondent in the present appeal that *Dobson's* case was wrongly decided. I disagree, and on the contrary find myself in full agreement with those parts of the judgment of Parker LJ to which I have referred. As regards the attempted reconciliation by Bingham LJ of the reasoning in *R v Morris* with the ruling in *Lawrence's* case it appears to me that the suggested basis of reconciliation, which is essentially speculative, is unsound. The actual decision in *R v Morris* was correct, but it was erroneous, in addition to being unnecessary for the decision, to indicate that an act expressly or impliedly authorised by the owner could never amount to an appropriation. There is no material distinction between the facts in *Dobson's* case and those in the present case. In each case the owner of the goods was induced by fraud to part with them to the rogue. *Lawrence's* case makes it clear that consent to or authorisation by the owner of the taking by the rogue is irrelevant. The taking amounted to an appropriation within the meaning of s 1(1) of the 1968 Act. *Lawrence's* case also makes it clear that it is no less irrelevant that what happened may also have constituted the offence of obtaining property by deception under s 15(1) of the 1968 Act.

In my opinion it serves no useful purpose at the present time to seek to construe the relevant provisions of the Theft Act by reference to the report which preceded it, namely the eighth report of the Criminal Law Revision Committee, *Theft and Related Offences* (Cmnd 2977 (1966)). The decision in *Lawrence's* case was a clear decision of this House upon the construction of the word 'appropriates' in s 1(1) of the 1968 Act, which had stood for 12 years when doubt was thrown upon it by *obiter dicta* in *R v Morris*. *Lawrence's* case must be regarded as authoritative and correct, and there is no question of it now being right to depart from it.

[**Lord Jauncey, Lord Browne-Wilkinson** and **Lord Slynn** agreed with **Lord Keith. Lord Lowry** dissented. Appeal allowed.]

8.40C R v Hinks

[2001] 2 AC 241; [2000] 4 All ER 833
House of Lords

[The accused was friendly with a man of limited intelligence, describing herself as the main carer for the man. Over a six-month period, the man withdrew sums totalling about £60,000 from his building society account, and those sums were deposited in the account of the accused. The accused was charged with various counts of theft. The prosecution case was that the accused had influenced and coerced the man to withdraw moneys from his account. The accused made a submission of no case to answer, contending that the moneys were a gift to her, that the title in the moneys had passed to her and that, in those circumstances, there could be no theft. The submission was rejected by the judge and the accused was convicted. Her appeal against conviction was dismissed by the Court of Appeal which held that there could be an appropriation even if the owner had consented to the property being taken. On appeal to the House of Lords.]

Lord Steyn: The academic criticism of *R v Gomez* provided in substantial measure the springboard for the present appeal. The certified question before the House is as follows: 'Whether the acquisition of an indefeasible title to property is capable of amounting to an appropriation of property belonging to another for the purposes of s 1(1) of the Theft Act 1968'. In other words, the question is whether a person can 'appropriate' property belonging to another where the other person makes him an indefeasible gift of property, retaining no proprietary interest or any right to resume or recover any proprietary interest in the property.

[His Lordship considered the authorities, and continued:]

It is true of course that the certified question in *R v Gomez* referred to the situation where consent had been obtained by fraud. But the majority judgments do not differentiate between cases of consent induced by fraud and consent given in any other circumstances. The ratio involves a proposition of general application. *R v Gomez* therefore gives effect to s 3(1) of the 1968 Act by treating 'appropriation' as a neutral word comprehending 'any assumption by a person of the rights of an owner'. If the law is as held in *R v Gomez,* it destroys the argument advanced on the present appeal, namely that an indefeasible gift of property cannot amount to an appropriation.

Counsel for the appellant submitted in the first place that the law as expounded in *R v Gomez* and *Lawrence's* case must be qualified to say that there can be no appropriation unless the other party (the owner) retains some proprietary interest, or the right to resume or recover some proprietary interest, in the property. Alternatively, counsel argued that 'appropriates' should be interpreted as if the word 'unlawfully' preceded it. Counsel said that the effect of the decisions in *Lawrence's* case and *R v Gomez* is to reduce the *actus reus* of theft to 'vanishing point' (see Smith and Hogan, *Criminal Law* (9th edn, 1999) p 505). He argued that the result is to bring the criminal law 'into conflict' with the civil law. Moreover, he argued that the decisions in *Lawrence's* case and *R v Gomez* may produce absurd and grotesque results. He argued that the mental requirements of dishonesty and intention of permanently depriving the owner of property are insufficient to filter out some cases of conduct which should not sensibly be regarded as theft. He did not suggest that the appellant's dishonest and repellent conduct came within such a category. Instead he deployed four examples for this purpose, namely the following. (1) S makes a handsome gift to D because he believes that D has obtained a First. D has not and knows that S is acting under that misapprehension. He makes the gift. There is here a motivational mistake which, it is submitted, does not avoid the transaction. (Glanville William's *Textbook of Criminal Law* (1978) p 788). (2) P sees D's painting and, thinking he is getting a bargain, offers D £100,000 for it. D realises that P thinks the painting is a Constable, but knows that it was painted by his sister and is worth no more than £100. He accepts P's offer. D has made an enforceable contract and is entitled to recover and retain the purchase price (Smith and Hogan pp 507–508). (3) A buys a roadside garage business from B, abutting on a public thoroughfare; unknown to A but known to B, it has already been decided to construct a bypass road which will divert substantially the whole of the traffic from passing A's garage. There is an enforceable contract and A is entitled to recover and retain the purchase price. The same would be true if B knew that A was unaware of the intended plan to construct a bypass road. (Compare Lord Atkin in *Bell v Lever Bros Ltd* [1932] AC 161 at 224, [1931] All ER Rep 1 at 30.) (4) An employee agrees to retire before the end of his contract of employment, receiving a sum of money by way of compensation from his employer. Unknown to the employer, the employee has committed serious breaches of contract which would have enabled the employer to dismiss him without compensation. Assuming that the employee's failure to reveal his defaults does not affect the validity of the contract, so that the employee is entitled to sue for the promised compensation, is the employee liable to be arrested for the theft the moment he receives the money? (Glanville Williams, 'Theft and Voidable Title' [1981] *Crim LR* 666 at 672).

My Lords, at first glance these are rather telling examples. They may conceivably have justified a more restricted meaning of s 3(1) than prevailed in *Lawrence's* case and *R v Gomez*. The House ruled otherwise and I am quite unpersuaded that the House overlooked the consequences of its decision. On the facts set out in the examples a jury could possibly find that the acceptance of the transfer took place in the belief that the transferee had the right in law to deprive the other of it within the meaning of s 2(1)(a) of the 1968 Act. Moreover, in such cases a prosecution is hardly likely and, if mounted, is likely to founder on the basis that the jury will not be persuaded that there was dishonesty in the required sense. And one must retain a sense of perspective. At the extremity of the application of legal rules there are sometimes results which may seem strange. A matter of judgment is then involved. The rule may have to be recast. Sir John Smith has eloquently argued that the rule in question ought to be recast. I am unpersuaded. If the law is restated by adopting a narrower definition of appropriation, the outcome is likely to place beyond the reach of the criminal law dishonest persons who should be found guilty of theft. The suggested revisions would unwarrantably restrict the scope of the law of theft and complicate the fair and effective prosecution of theft. In my view the law as settled in *Lawrence's* case and *R v Gomez* does not demand the suggested revision. Those decisions can be applied by judges and juries in a way which, absent human error, does not result in injustice.

Counsel for the appellant further pointed out that the law as stated in *Lawrence's* case and *R v Gomez* creates a tension between the civil and the criminal law. In other words, conduct which is not wrongful in a civil law sense may constitute the crime of theft. Undoubtedly, this is so. The question whether the civil claim to title by a convicted thief, who committed no civil wrong, may be defeated by the principle that nobody may benefit from his own civil or criminal wrong does not arise for decision. Nevertheless there is a more general point, namely that the interaction between criminal law and civil law can cause problems: compare Beatson and Simester, 'Stealing One's Own Property' (1999) 115 *LQR* 372. The purposes of the civil law and the criminal law are somewhat different. In theory the two systems should be in perfect harmony. In a practical world there will sometimes be some disharmony between the two systems. In any event, it would be wrong to assume on *a priori* grounds that the criminal law rather than the civil law is defective. Given the jury's conclusions, one is entitled to observe that the appellant's conduct should constitute theft, the only available charge. The tension between the civil and the criminal law is therefore not in my view a factor which justifies a departure from the law as stated in *Lawrence's* case and *R v Gomez*. Moreover, these decisions of the House have a marked beneficial consequence. While in some contexts of the law of theft a judge cannot avoid explaining civil law concepts to a jury (eg in respect of s 2(1)(a)), the decisions of the House of Lords eliminate the need for such explanations in respect of appropriation. That is a great advantage in an overly complex corner of the law.

My Lords, if it had been demonstrated that in practice *Lawrence's* case and *R v Gomez* were calculated to produce injustice that would have been a compelling reason to revisit the merits of the holdings in those decisions. That is however, not the case. In practice the mental requirements of theft are an adequate protection against injustice. In these circumstances I would not be willing to depart from the clear decisions of the House in *Lawrence's* case and *R v Gomez*. This brings me back to counsels' principal submission, namely that a person does not appropriate property unless the other (the owner) retains, beyond the instant of the alleged theft, some proprietary interest or the right to resume or recover some proprietary interest. This submission is directly contrary to the holdings in *Lawrence's* case and *R v Gomez*. It must be rejected. The alternative submission is that the word 'appropriates' should be interpreted as if the word 'unlawfully' preceded it so that only an act which is unlawful under the general law can be an appropriation. This submission is an invitation to interpolate a word in the carefully crafted language of the 1968 Act. It runs counter to the decisions in *Lawrence's* case and *R v Gomez* and must also be rejected. It follows that the certified question must be answered in the affirmative.

[**Lord Slynn** and **Lord Jauncey** agreed with **Lord Steyn**. **Lord Hutton** and **Lord Hobhouse** dissented. Appeal dismissed.]

8.41 Notes

1. To summarise, the approach taken in the United Kingdom cases of *Gomez* and *Hinks* is that any 'taking' will be an 'appropriation' irrespective of the presence or absence of the victim's consent. This approach is consistent with the wording of the statutory provision. The approach taken in Australia in the cases of *Baruday* and *Roffel* is that the word 'appropriates' in the theft legislation includes the concept of 'without consent', although a taking with consent may amount to an 'appropriation' if the consent was not valid; for example, if obtained by a deception. On the Victorian approach, a fact situation such as that in *Hinks* might arguably lead to acquittal.
2. The Victorian approach, where consent means there has been no appropriation *but* the consent may be negated by any fraud, blurs the distinction between theft and obtaining property by deception. On the other hand, the effect of adopting the approach in *Gomez* and *Hinks* is to place considerable weight on the concept of dishonesty, which becomes the only means of distinguishing between thefts and non-criminal takings. As noted earlier, the High Court of Australia in *Macleod v R* was critical of the decision in *Roffel*, and that decision has subsequently been read down, to have very narrow application only to the type of company involved in that case.

8.42 Further reading

B McSherry and B Naylor, *Australian Criminal Laws: Critical Perspectives*, Oxford University Press, Melbourne, 2004, pp 272–78, 281–83

A Steel, 'Taking Possession: The Defining Element of Theft?' (2008) 32 *Melbourne University Law Review* 1030

G R Sullivan, 'Company Controllers, Company Cheques and Theft' [1983] *Crim LR* 512

P von Nessen, 'Company Controllers, Company Cheques and Theft — An Australian Perspective' [1986] *Crim LR* 154

C R Williams, *Property Offences*, 3rd ed, Law Book Co, Sydney, 1999, pp 117–24

—, 'Reining in the Concept of Appropriation in Theft' (2003) 29 *Mon LR* 261

G Williams, 'Appropriation: A Single or Continuous Act?' [1978] *Crim LR* 69

Mens rea

The intent to deprive permanently

8.43C Sharp v McCormick

[1986] VR 869
Supreme Court of Victoria

[Upon interception by the police, the accused was found in possession of a motor car coil which he admitted he had taken from his employer dishonestly and without permission. The accused stated that he had intended to fit it to his car and added that if it had turned out to be the wrong size he would have returned it to its owner. The accused having been charged with theft, the magistrate upheld a submission that because nothing more than a conditional intention had been proved there was no case to answer. Upon the return of an order nisi.]

Murray J: Before considering the application of the above provisions, which also appear in the English Theft Act 1968, it is desirable to consider the decision of the Court of Appeal in *Easom*. In that case a female sergeant of police, sitting in the aisle in a picture theatre, placed her handbag on the floor beside her. The appellant, sitting behind her, picked up the handbag and examined its contents which were a purse (apparently empty), a notebook, a quantity of tissues, a quantity of cosmetics and a pen. Not finding any of these items to be of value the appellant replaced the handbag with its contents intact on the floor beside the police sergeant. He was later charged with stealing 'one handbag, one purse, one notebook, a quantity of tissues, a quantity of cosmetics and one pen'.

In giving the judgment of the court Edmund Davies LJ held that the evidence only disclosed what his Lordship referred to as a conditional appropriation and that this was not enough to sustain a charge of theft. At ([1971] 2 QB) 319 his Lordship said:

> In the respectful view of this court, the jury were misdirected. In every case of theft the appropriation must be accompanied by the intention of permanently depriving the owner of his property. What may be loosely described as a 'conditional' appropriation will not do. If the appropriator has it in mind merely to deprive the owner of such of his property as, on examination, proves worth taking and then, finding that the booty is valueless to the appropriator, leaves it ready to hand to be repossessed by the owner, the appropriator has not stolen ... In the present case the jury were never invited to consider the possibility that such was the appellant's state of mind or the legal consequences flowing therefrom. Yet the facts are strongly indicative that this was exactly how his mind was working, for he left the handbag and its contents entirely intact and to hand, once he had carried out his exploration. For this reason we hold that conviction of the full offence of theft cannot stand.

In the later part of his judgment his Lordship considered the question of whether the appellant could have been convicted of attempted theft. He pointed out, however, that no attempt had been made to amend the charge and that the case had been conducted solely upon the basis that the appellant was guilty of theft. From some of his Lordship's remarks it is possible to infer that he was of the opinion that if the appellant had been charged with the attempted theft of unspecified articles in the handbag he may well, upon proper directions to the jury, have been convicted.

The decision in *Easom* has by no means escaped discussion by academic writers: for example, Glanville Williams, 'Three Rogues' Charters' [1980] *Crim LR* 263; Laurence Koffman, 'Conditional Intention to Steal' [1980] *Crim LR* 463 and Glanville Williams, 'Temporary Appropriation Should Be Theft' [1981] *Crim LR* 129. In my opinion, however, it is not necessary for this court to pass upon the question of whether it agrees with the decision because the decision is plainly distinguishable in a critical respect. In *Easom's* case the appellant was charged with the theft of the handbag and various specified articles. In relation to the handbag there appears to have been no evidence that the appellant at any time formed an intention to deprive the owner permanently of the handbag because the facts indicate that he took the handbag merely for the purpose of examining its contents. Nor when he opened the handbag and inspected its contents did the evidence establish even a conditional intention of stealing them because by his actions he indicated that he had no such intention. It was these facts which, in my opinion, led Edmund Davies LJ to discuss the question of whether, if the appellant had been charged with an attempt to steal unspecified articles from the handbag such a charge may have been sustainable. In the present case, however, the appellant took the coil and was in the process of taking it home to see whether it fitted his car when he was apprehended. The question, therefore, in the present case is entirely different from the question which fell to be decided in *Easom*.

In argument before the court counsel for the respondent conceded, as he no doubt felt obliged to do, that the evidence established a dishonest appropriation of the coil by the respondent and that the only question which arose was as to his intent.

It is trite law that the intention which falls to be considered is the intention of the accused at the time of the appropriation of property. The question to be decided therefore is whether the evidence established a prima facie case of theft either under s 72(1) alone or under s 72(1) when read with s 73(12) of the Crimes Act. Professor Glanville Williams in *Textbook of Criminal Law*, 1978, p 647 *et seq* scathingly criticises the provisions of s 6(1) of the English Theft Act 1968 which is the equivalent of s 73(12) of the Crimes Act and comes to the conclusion that it is virtually of no practical importance. With great respect to the professor I confess that I do not see all the difficulties which he thinks are so apparent. For example, I do not quite understand why the second limb of subs (12) should have been placed before the first limb or for that matter why the two limbs should have been joined by 'but' rather than by 'and'. I do, however, see considerable difficulty in the application and construction of the second limb. Professor Williams points out that in considering the facts in *R v Easom* [1971] 2 QB 315 the test whether Easom intended to keep the articles unless he later decided to give them back might be expressed in a different way, namely that he intended to give them back unless he later decided to keep them and that differently expressed tests may lead to different legal answers. It appears to me, however, that if the facts in the present case establish that the defendant intended to keep the coil unless he *later* decided to return it then his intention *at the time of the appropriation* is sufficient to establish theft under s 72(1). If the question is posed the other way, namely that the defendant intended to return the coil unless he later decided to keep it, then it appears to me that the appropriation would fall within the first limb of subs (12). His reservation of the probability or possibility of keeping it would amount to an intention to treat the coil as his own to dispose of regardless of the owner's rights. It must be remembered that the operation of subs (12) depends upon the absence of an actual intent permanently to deprive the owner of the property in question at the time of the appropriation.

It follows that what must be examined is the intention of the respondent at the moment he appropriated the coil. The evidence establishes that his intention at that time was to take the coil to see whether it fitted his motor car in which case to retain it and otherwise to return it to his employer. To say that his intention to return it to his employer if it did not fit his motor car was an intention to have regard to the rights of his employer is in my opinion little short of an abuse of language. When the respondent took the coil he was quite clearly treating the coil as his own to dispose of as he saw fit and he was paying no regard to the rights of the true owner. His stated intention of returning it if it did not fit his car was simply a matter of choice on his part which he may or may not have carried out when the time came. The rights of his employer in regard to the property were completely ignored at the time of the appropriation. Despite the criticism of the use of the word 'dispose' (see [1977] *Crim LR* 653) I do not understand why that word would not be appropriate to a disposition of the coil by the respondent either by way of using it in his car or returning it to the factory.

It follows that in my opinion the magistrate was in error in upholding the submission made to him at the close of the case for the prosecution that there was no case for the respondent to answer.

[**Brooking J** and **Nathan J** delivered separate judgments agreeing with **Murray J**. Case remitted to the magistrate for further hearing.]

8.44C

R v Dardovska

(2003) 6 VR 628
Court of Appeal, Supreme Court of Victoria

[The accused was convicted of theft. She had lured the victim to a house, where she and two accomplices had assaulted him and taken a tape recorder and documents. The accused reported her actions to the police, and claimed she had been acting in order to gather incriminating information against the victim which she intended to notify the police about.]

Charles JA: I turn then to s 73(12) which is contained in Division 2 of the *Crimes Act 1958*, and was introduced by the amending provisions of the *Crimes (Theft) Act 1973*, modelled on the Theft Act 1968 of the United Kingdom. The decision to make these amendments to the Victorian Crimes Act followed from a detailed report of the Chief Justice's Law Reform Committee, which recommended what was basically an adoption of the Theft Act 1968 with minor alterations. Sub-sections (12) and (13) of s 73 were taken verbatim from s 6(1) and (2) of the Theft Act 1968.

Before the 1968 legislation was enacted in the United Kingdom, an 'intention permanently to deprive' as an element in the crime of larceny had troubled the courts on many occasions, particularly in circumstances where the accused could only be shown to have had what might be called a conditional or reckless intention to appropriate. There were three situations in which courts had found an intention permanently to deprive in such circumstances: first, where a person took property from the owner intending to return the property only if the owner paid for it, referred to as the 'ransom principle' (*Hall* (1849) 3 Cox CC 245); secondly, where the intention was to return the property only after it had undergone some fundamental change of character, the 'essential quality principle' (*Cabbage* (1815) Russ & Ry 292, 168 ER 809; *Beecham* (1851) 5 Cox CC 181); and thirdly, where a person pawned another's property without his consent, hoping to be able to redeem the pledge, but without being certain of his ability to do so, the 'pawning principle' (*Medland* (1851) 5 Cox CC 292). The intention of the House of Commons when passing the Theft Act 1968 was that s 6 of that Act was to be a 'restatement of the law with regard to those cases which might not literally amount to a deprivation of the ownership, which had been so regarded from time to time'. The passage of the Theft Act and its metamorphosis from the recommendations of the UK Criminal Law Revision Committee into the final form of the Theft Act is traced in an illuminating article by Professor J R Spencer which also explains the pre-existing common law (Spencer, 'The Metamorphosis of Section 6 of the Theft Act' [1977] *Crim LR* 653; see also Smith and Hogan, *Criminal Law*, 10th ed (2002) at 554–555). Professor Spencer said of s 6 that it 'sprouts obscurities at every phrase'. The obscurity then first-mentioned is what is the relationship between the two clauses of s 6(1), namely, whether the first clause of the sub-section lays down a general principle to which the second clause makes a limited exception, in the case of an appropriation by borrowing or lending; or whether the second clause entirely governs the first, restricting the scope of the apparently general principle to cases where property has been borrowed or lent. I think that in Victoria the answer to this question is, for s 73(12), that clearly the first of these two explanations is correct, having regard to the explanatory memorandum which said of the two sections (they were then numbered (13) and (14) that —

> Sub-section (13) states that a person is to be regarded as intending permanently to deprive another of his property if he intends to treat it as his own regardless of the other's rights, even though he does not mean the other permanently to lose the thing itself. Specifically, a borrowing or lending of another's property may amount to a permanent deprivation if and only if the circumstances and the period of time in question make the transaction equivalent to an outright taking or disposal.
>
> Sub-section (14) provides a rider to sub-section (13). It deals with the case of one who, having another's property, parts with it under a condition as to its return which he may not be able to perform, and does so for his own purposes and without the owner's authority. For example, if John, being short of funds, takes William's transistor radio and pawns it, he is to be regarded as having intended to deprive William permanently of his radio. Most of the modern decisions under the present law are to the same effect.

Section 6 of the Theft Act has been subjected to highly critical comment by academic authors. For example, Professor Glanville Williams said of it, *Textbook of Criminal Law,* 2nd ed (1978) 719:

> In view of the grave difficulties of interpretation presented by s 6, a trial judge would be well advised not to introduce it to the jury unless he reaches the conclusion that it will assist them, and even then (it may be suggested) the question he leaves to the jury should not be worded in terms of the generalities of the sub-section but should reflect those generalities as applied to the alleged facts.

These observations were quoted with approval by the Court of Appeal in *R v Lloyd* [1985] 1 QB 829 at 135–836. The suggestion that a judge should exercise caution in referring a jury to s 6 of the Theft Act 1968 and then only with a careful explanation of the application of the section to the alleged facts is made by a number of the commentators (Griew, *The Theft Acts*, 7th ed (1995) at 2–103; A T H Smith, *Property Offences* (1994), 6–27).

[His Honour discussed a number of cases, including *Sharp v McCormick* (at **8.43C**), and continued:]

I have referred at some length to a number of the cases dealing with s 6 of the Theft Act 1968 and s 73(12) for the purpose of demonstrating the nature of the intention which has usually been said to justify the exceptional course of referring a jury hearing a charge of theft to these provisions. The present case is plainly not one of the three types earlier mentioned which at common law established an intention permanently to deprive in the extended sense. There was no suggestion of ransoming or pawning, nor was there any intention that the documents should only be returned after undergoing some fundamental change of character. The applicant, it may at once be accepted, had no legal right to take the documents to the police. But nevertheless I find it surprising that her actions might have been thought to have involved any intention of permanently depriving Akguner ('the victim') of the documents in the relevant sense. Dardovska clearly had no intention of obtaining any form of financial advantage from taking the documents, which were in any case worthless. She had, in the victim's presence, rung the Melton Police Station. There was no reason to doubt her defence that she was outraged that the victim was applying to become a Justice of the Peace and wanted the police to see the documents, to draw their attention to her argument that he should not succeed in that application. There was no obvious reason why the documents would not, once the police had seen and possibly copied them, have been returned to the victim. Insofar as s 73(12) is concerned, although Dardovska had no entitlement to take the documents from the victim, her intention, far from treating the documents as her own to dispose of regardless of the victim's rights, seems to have been rather to insist to the police that they were in fact the victim's documents, and that the police should take notice of them accordingly. Even if the documents had had some value, the action of taking them to the police for them to inspect could not have resulted in any fundamental change to the character of the documents or any reduction in their value.

[**Phillips CJ** and **O'Bryan AJA** agreed with **Charles JA**. Conviction quashed.]

8.45 Notes, illustrations and questions

1. It should be noted that the word 'permanent' must be understood in the light of the owner's particular interest in the property. 'Owner' includes a person with possession or control. Thus if A takes a television set hired by B from C for a period of a month, is aware of the hiring and intends to return the television to C at the expiration of the month, A, although not guilty of stealing the television from C, is guilty of stealing it from B. This is because although he does not intend to deprive C permanently of the television he does intend to deprive B permanently of possession of it.
2. D was involved in mortgage frauds perpetrated on a local authority. The advances were made by cheque, and D was convicted of obtaining the cheques by deception. On appeal to the Court of Appeal it was argued that D had no intention of depriving the authority permanently of the cheques since the cheques would, after payment by the authority's bank on presentation, go back to the authority. Held, appeal dismissed. While a cheque is a piece of paper it changes its character completely once it is paid: *R v Duru* [1973] 3 All ER 715. Accord *Parsons v R* (1999) 190 CLR 619; 160 ALR 531 (at **8.74C**).

In the case of *Oxford v Moss* (1978) 68 Cr App R 183 (see **8.13**) D was charged with theft of confidential information when he obtained an examination paper, read it, and returned it. If D had been charged simply with theft of the examination proofs what would have been the result? Had not the proof, when he returned it, changed its character just as completely as the cheques in *R v Duru*?

3. D took a box of tools belonging to another. He was charged with theft, and his defence was that he intended to return the box in an hour or so. The trial judge, relying on the English equivalent of s 73(12) of the Victorian Act, suggested to the jury that an intention to deprive for a limited but indefinite period of time would be sufficient to justify a conviction for theft. D was convicted and appealed to the Court of Appeal. Held, appeal allowed. An intention to take goods for a limited period only, even though the precise length of the period has not been determined, is not 'equivalent to an outright taking or disposal': *R v Warner* (1970) 55 Cr App R 93. Would the situation have been different if the item was taken at a time when it was of crucial importance to the owner; for example, if a wheelbarrow was taken during a concrete pour, or a wedding dress just prior to the wedding? It is likely that this would still not amount to theft since the items themselves had not been changed in a fundamental way.
4. D1, a cinema projectionist, clandestinely removed feature films due to be shown in the cinema. He lent them to D2, D3 and X, who made master videotape copies of the films. The films were returned before their absence from the cinema was noticed. Many pirated videotape versions of the films were made and sold. The continued success of the Ds' scheme depended on their ability to return the films as rapidly as possible. D1, D2 and D3 were convicted of conspiring to steal feature films. Held, convictions quashed. The intention of D1, D2 and D3 was temporarily to deprive the owners of the films, which was the opposite of an intention permanently to deprive. The borrowing was not for such a period or in such circumstances as made it equivalent to an outright taking or disposal: *R v Lloyd* [1985] 3 WLR 30. These actions would, of course, amount to a breach of copyright, for which criminal sanctions can apply.

8.46 Further reading

E Griew, *The Theft Acts*, 7th ed, Sweet & Maxwell, London, 1995, pp 59–68

B McSherry and B Naylor, *Australian Criminal Laws: Critical Perspectives*, Oxford University Press, Melbourne, 2004, pp 283–8; 307–8

D Ormerod and D Williams (eds), *Smith's Law of Theft*, Oxford University Press, 9th ed, 2007, pp 303–22J

R Spencer, 'The Metamorphosis of Section 6 of the *Theft Act*' [1977] *Crim LR* 653

C R Williams, *Property Offences*, 3rd ed, Law Book Co, Sydney, 1999, pp 124–9

G L Williams, 'Temporary Appropriation Should be Theft' [1981] *Crim LR* 129

Dishonestly

8.47 The meaning of the word 'dishonestly' has caused substantial problems of interpretation. The word is used not just as a defining element of theft, but also of obtaining property by deception (s 81 of the Victorian Act) and obtaining a financial advantage by deception (s 82), as well as a number of less important offences: ss 83, 86, 88. It will be convenient to deal in the present section with cases on dishonesty arising not just in relation to theft, but also in relation to obtaining property by deception and obtaining a financial advantage by deception.

8.48 The adverb 'dishonestly' was deliberately left undefined in the Act. The English Criminal Law Revision Committee took the view that '"dishonesty" is something which laymen can easily recognise when they see it': *Theft and Related Offences*, op cit, p 20. Section 73(2)(a)–(c) of the Victorian Act provides a partial, though negative, definition of dishonesty: that is, an appropriation will not be dishonest if the offender believes they are have the right in law to the property; or if they believe they would have had the owner's consent; or if they believe the owner cannot be found by taking reasonable steps. Section 73(3) provides that an appropriation of property belonging to another may be dishonest notwithstanding a willingness to pay for the property. Paragraph (a) of s 73(2) preserves the common law defence of bona fide claim of legal right: see **7.68**. Paragraphs (b) and (c) of subs (2) and subs (3) are essentially self-explanatory.

8.49 The defence under s 73(2)(a) was accepted in *R v Langham* (1984) 36 SASR 48 (see **7.118C**). Langham had used a shotgun to obtain money he believed he was owed by a sports store. When charged with armed robbery he gave evidence that he believed he was entitled to the cash. The South Australian Supreme Court held that provided an accused honestly believes he or she has a legal right to the money this will be a good defence to a theft or robbery charge, however the right is enforced.

8.50 The partial definition of 'dishonest' which appears in s 73(2) and (3) is deemed, by virtue of s 73(1), to apply to the offence of theft only. What application, if any, do the exemptions contained in s 73(2) have to the crime of obtaining property by deception? In particular, may an accused who uses deception to obtain property to which the accused believes he or she is entitled secure an acquittal to a charge of obtaining property by deception?

8.51 Are there cases, not covered by s 73(2), in which an accused will be able to argue that her or his conduct was not dishonest? Cases in which an accused has appropriated, or obtained by deception, property belonging to another with an intent permanently to deprive, which does not come within s 73(2) and where the accused nonetheless claims that her or his conduct was not dishonest, are obviously fairly rare. However, they certainly occur. An obvious example is the case of the accused who takes money or goods belonging to another, intending to return equivalent money or goods at a later stage. In such a case, the accused will have an intention permanently to deprive because he or she does not intend to return the very money or goods taken. In some cases, this intention to repay may bring the accused within s 73(2)(b), but in others it will not. Nevertheless, the accused may, arguably, be able to argue that her or his conduct was not dishonest.

8.52 Other cases may readily be imagined:

(1) An accused appropriates, or obtains by deception, property in the belief, which may be well-founded, that he or she has a strong moral as opposed to a legal right.

(2) A cook, employed in the officers' mess of the Air Force, takes a left-over cake home to his children rather than see it consigned to the garbage as is the usual practice.

(3) The accused is cleaning up the papers of a friend who has recently died. The accused discovers and destroys letters secreted in the deceased's desk because their contents could cause great distress and humiliation to the deceased's wife and family.

8.53 If there are cases other than those to which s 73(2) refers, in which the accused may be said not to have acted dishonestly, how then is the meaning of that word to be determined? Is its meaning a question to be decided by the judge or by the jury? By what standards are they to determine its meaning?

8.54 As will be seen, the English and the Victorian courts have taken quite different approaches in dealing with these questions, with the English approach being adopted by the legislation in South Australia.

8.55C

R v Feely
[1973] QB 530
Court of Appeal (Criminal Division) (UK)

[The accused was employed as a branch manager by a firm of bookmakers. His employer had sent a circular to all its managers stating that the practice of borrowing from the employer's till was to stop. A month after receiving the circular, the accused took £30 from the firm's safe to give to his father. In a statement to the police, the accused claimed that he intended to pay the money back and that the firm owed him £70 in wages and commission. The trial judge directed the jury that it was no defence for the accused to say that he intended to repay the money and that his employer owed him more than enough to cover what he had taken. At no stage did the trial judge invite the jury to consider whether the accused had acted dishonestly and he stated that: 'if someone does something deliberately knowing that his employers are not prepared to tolerate it, is that not dishonest?' The accused was convicted and appealed.]

Lawton LJ [reading the judgment of the court]: Should the jury have been left to decide whether the defendant had acted dishonestly? The search for an answer must start with the Theft Act 1968, under s 1 of which the defendant had been indicted. The long title of this Act starts with these words: 'An Act to revise the law of England and Wales as to theft and similar or associated offences …' The draftsman seems to have searched the statute book for all the statutes dealing with offences of dishonesty and it is probable that all the old enactments have been repealed so as to enable the Theft Act to deal comprehensively with this branch of the law. The design of the new Act is clear; nearly all the old legal terms to describe offences of dishonesty have been left behind; larceny, embezzlement and fraudulent conversion have become theft; receiving stolen goods has become handling stolen goods; obtaining by false pretences has become obtaining pecuniary advantage by deception. Words in everyday use have replaced legal jargon in many parts of the Act. This is particularly noticeable in the series of sections (1 to 6) defining theft.

'Theft' itself is a word known and used by all and is defined, in what the marginal note to s 1 of the Act of 1968 describes as the basic definition, as follows:

> A person is guilty of theft if he dishonestly appropriates property belonging to another with the intention of permanently depriving the other of it; …

These words swept away all the learning which over the centuries had gathered round the common law concept of larceny and in more modern times around the statutory definition of that offence in s 1(1) of the Larceny Act 1916.

In s 1(1) of the Act of 1968, the word 'dishonestly' can only relate to the state of mind of the person who does the act which amounts to appropriation. Whether an accused person has a particular state of mind is a question of fact which has to be decided by the jury when there is a trial on indictment, and by the magistrates when there are summary proceedings. The Crown did not dispute this proposition, but it was submitted that in some cases (and this, it was said, was such a one) it was necessary for the trial judge to define 'dishonestly' and when the facts fell within the definition he had a duty to tell the jury that if there had been appropriation it must have been dishonestly done.

We do not agree that judges should define what 'dishonestly' means. This word is in common use whereas the word 'fraudulently' which was used in s 1(l) of the Larceny Act 1916 had acquired as a result of case law a special meaning. Jurors, when deciding whether an appropriation was dishonest can be reasonably expected to, and should, apply the current standards of ordinary decent people. In their own lives they have to decide what is and what is not dishonest. We can see no reason why, when in a jury box, they should require the help of a judge to tell them what amounts to dishonesty. We are fortified in this opinion by a passage in the speech of Lord Reid in *Cozens v Brutus* [1972] 3 WLR 521, a case in which the words 'insulting behaviour' in s 5 of the Public Order

Act 1936 had to be construed. The Divisional Court had adjudged that the meaning of the word 'insulting' in this statutory context was a matter of law. Lord Reid's comment was as follows, at 525:

> In my judgment that is not right. The meaning of an ordinary word of the English language is not a question of law. The proper construction of a statute is a question of law. If the context shows that a word is used in an unusual sense the court will determine in other words what that unusual sense is. But here there is in my opinion no question of the word 'insulting' being used in any unusual sense ... It is for the tribunal which decides the case to consider, not as law but as fact, whether in the whole circumstances the words of the statute do or do not as a matter of ordinary usage of the English language cover or apply to the facts which have been proved.

When this trenchant statement of principle is applied to the word 'dishonestly' in s 1(1) of the Theft Act 1968 and to the facts of this case, it is clear in our judgment that the jury should have been left to decide whether the defendant's alleged taking of the money had been dishonest. They were not, with the result that a verdict of guilty was returned without their having given thought to what was probably the most important issue in the case.

[His Lordship discussed the pre-Theft Act cases of *R v Williams* [1953] 1 QB 660 and *R v Cockburn* [1968] WLR 281 and continued:]

We find it impossible to accept that a conviction for stealing, whether it be called larceny or theft, can reveal no moral obloquy. A man so convicted would have difficulty in persuading his friends and neighbours that his reputation had not been gravely damaged. He would be bound to be lowered in the estimation of right thinking people. Further, no reference was made by Winn LJ to the factor of fraud which Lord Goddard CJ in *R v Williams* [1953] 1 QB 660 had said had to be considered. It is this factor, whether it is labelled 'fraudulently' or 'dishonestly', which distinguishes a taking without consent from stealing.

If the principle enunciated in *R v Cockburn* [1968] 1 WLR 281 was right, there would be a strange divergence between the position of a man who obtains cash by passing a cheque on an account which has no funds to meet it and one who takes money from a till. The man who passes the cheque is deemed in law not to act dishonestly if he genuinely believes on reasonable grounds that when it is presented to the paying bank there will be funds to meet it: see *Halstead v Patel* [1972] 1 WLR 661, per Lord Widgery CJ at 665. But, according to the decision in *R v Cockburn,* the man who takes money from a till intending to put it back and genuinely believing on reasonable grounds that he will be able to do so (see Winn LJ at 469) should be convicted of theft. Lawyers may be able to appreciate why one man should be adjudged to be a criminal and the other not; but we doubt whether anyone else would. People who take money from tills and the like without permission are usually thieves; but if they do not admit that they are by pleading guilty, it is for the jury, not the judge, to decide whether they have acted dishonestly.

[Appeal allowed.]

8.56 In *R v Ghosh* [1982] QB 1053, the Court of Appeal placed a further gloss on the test for dishonesty by requiring that the accused must also realise that the conduct was, by 'the ordinary standards of reasonable and honest people' dishonest. The accused, a surgeon, falsely claimed fees for operations which had been performed by others or which had been carried out under the National Health Service. The accused was convicted of obtaining money and attempting to obtain money by deception, and his appeal dismissed by the Court of Appeal. Delivering the judgment of the court, Lord Lane CJ stated (at 1064):

> In determining whether the prosecution has proved that the defendant was acting dishonestly, a jury must first of all decide whether according to the ordinary standards of reasonable and honest people what was done was dishonest. If it was not dishonest by those standards, that is the end of the matter and the prosecution fails. If it was dishonest by those standards, then the jury must consider whether the defendant himself must have realised that what he was doing was by those standards dishonest. In most cases, where the actions are obviously dishonest by ordinary standards, there will be no doubt about it. It will be obvious that the defendant himself knew that he was acting dishonestly. It is dishonest for a defendant to act in a way which he knows ordinary people consider to be dishonest, even if he asserts or genuinely believes that he is morally justified in acting as he did.

8.57C **R v Waterfall**

[1970] 1 QB 148

Court of Appeal (Criminal Division) (UK)

[The accused hired a taxi in Southampton for a journey to London and back for an agreed fare of £14. He did not have the money to pay and when, on arrival in London, the driver asked for an advance of £10, the accused said he would get it from his accountant. No money was forthcoming and the accused was charged with obtaining a financial advantage by deception. The accused's defence was that he had not acted dishonestly since he had believed he would be able to obtain the money from the accountant. The accused was convicted and appealed.]

Lord Parker CJ [delivering the judgment of the court]: Looking at the ingredients of the offence it is clear that there had been an obtaining of a pecuniary advantage, in that the defendant had made himself liable to a debt which he had evaded. Secondly, it is perfectly clear that he did that by deception; not only was the conduct of taking a taxi in those circumstances such as to convey that he had money to pay, but according to the taxi driver there had been a specific assurance that the defendant had money to pay. True, the defendant denied giving that assurance, his case being that he believed and honestly believed that the accountant in Harley Street would provide the money. The sole question as it seems to me in this case revolves around the third ingredient, namely, whether what was done was done dishonestly. In regard to that the deputy recorder directed the jury in this way:

> If on reflection and deliberation you came to the conclusion that this defendant never did have any genuine belief that Mr Tropp [the accountant] would pay the taxi fare, then you would be entitled to convict him. But if you felt on weighing up all of the evidence you have heard that there was some real doubt in your mind, not fantastic but some real doubt in your mind as to whether or not Mr Tropp might have paid, then, of course, he would be entitled to be acquitted.

In other words, in that passage the deputy recorder is telling the jury they had to consider what was in this particular defendant's mind: had he a genuine belief that the accountant would provide the money? That, as it seems to this court, is a perfectly proper direction subject to this, that it would be right to tell the jury that they can use a test, though not a conclusive test, whether there were any reasonable grounds for that belief. Unfortunately, however, just before the jury retired, in two passages the deputy recorder, as it seems to this court, was saying: you cannot hold that this man had a genuine belief unless he had reasonable grounds for that belief. The passage reads thus:

> It is entirely a matter for you to decide; you have to decide not merely whether this man genuinely believed he might get some money from Mr Tropp, but whether he had any reasonable ground for thinking so.

And a little later:

> So what you have to decide in regard to that is not merely was it a genuine belief but was there any reasonable ground for thinking that Mr Tropp would lend him the money.

Having listened to Mr Spokes, who has sought to support this verdict, the court is quite satisfied that those directions cannot be justified. The test here is a subjective test, whether the particular man had an honest belief, and of course whereas the absence of reasonable ground may point strongly to the fact that that belief is not genuine, it is at the end of the day for the jury to say whether or not in the case of this particular man he did have that genuine belief.

In those circumstances, the court has come to the conclusion that the verdict must be quashed.

[Appeal allowed.]

8.58 Notes

1. In England, the procedure to be adopted for determining whether the conduct of an accused has been dishonest in cases to which s 73(2) does not apply is as follows. First, it must be determined what the intentions and beliefs of the accused were. The intentions and beliefs of the reasonable person are not to be imputed to the accused: *R v Waterfall.* Once a decision

has been reached as to the state of mind of the accused at the time of the appropriation, the jury — or in cases tried summarily, the magistrate — determines whether the accused has acted dishonestly by applying the test of the 'current standards of ordinary decent people': *R v Feely*. Further, the accused must be shown personally to have realised that her or his conduct was by those standards dishonest: *R v Ghosh*. The test is an objective one, but what is judged objectively is the propriety of the accused's conduct on the facts as he or she believed them to be.

2. The approach taken by the Court of Appeal in *Feely* and *Ghosh* has been criticised on a number of grounds. First, it is argued that if the question of the honesty of the accused's conduct is left solely to the jury, different juries may well give different answers on facts which are indistinguishable. Second, it is suggested that the task of determining what constitutes dishonesty often involves complex value judgments and questions of policy which are beyond the average jury: see, for example, *R v Greenstein* [1976] 1 All ER 1. Finally, it is argued that it is a function of the court rather than the jury to determine the proper scope to be given to a criminal offence. While the jury may, on occasion, mitigate the strictness of the law by refusing to convict an accused who falls within the definition of an offence, it is an unjustifiable extension of the jury's function to transfer to it the responsibility for determining whether agreed conduct does or does not constitute a criminal offence.

8.59C R v Salvo

[1980] VR 401

Full Court of the Supreme Court of Victoria

[The accused, a car dealer, was charged with obtaining a Ford motor car by deception from one Kapaufs. Kapaufs had purchased the Ford from the accused, trading in a Valiant. Unbeknown to the accused, the Valiant was the subject of a bill of sale to Industrial Acceptance Corporation. The accused sold the Valiant to a third party. Industrial Acceptance Corporation repossessed the Valiant from the third party, who complained to the accused. The accused then bought the Valiant from Industrial Acceptance Corporation, paying off all the money owing, and delivered the car again to the third party.

The accused subsequently learnt that Kapaufs might be interested in selling the Ford. He approached Kapaufs and an agreement for the sale of the car was concluded. The accused paid for the Ford by cheque and took delivery. He then contacted his bank and ordered payment on the cheque to be stopped.

The accused gave evidence at his trial. He did not contest that he had given the cheque to Kapaufs in return for the Ford, nor did he contest that, at the time he gave the cheque to Kapaufs, he had no intention of honouring it. His defence was that he believed that the property in the Ford had not passed to Kapaufs, and that he was entitled to retake possession of it because Kapaufs had obtained it in exchange for a car to which he, Kapaufs, did not have a good title.

The trial judge did not direct the jury that the accused would be entitled to an acquittal if he believed he had a claim of legal right to the Ford. He directed the jury, instead, that the question of whether the accused's conduct amounted to dishonesty or not was entirely a matter for them. His Honour stated:

> [T]he real issue is has the Crown satisfied you beyond reasonable doubt that the accused man was acting dishonestly, in the sense that he knew that what he was doing he had no right to do? That is, take possession of the Ford Falcon …, hand over a valueless cheque for it, which he knew would not be met, and did he know that he had no right to do that? Was he acting dishonestly? Has the Crown satisfied you about that? That is the point.

The accused was convicted and appealed.]

Fullagar J: In my opinion it appears clearly enough from reading s 73 and s 81(3) in their context that 'dishonestly' in the Act of 1973 is not used in its ordinary or primary meaning but in a somewhat special sense. As will appear, I have other and as I think stronger reasons for rejecting any meaning based simply on present-day morality, whatever that phrase may import.

The possible meanings of 'dishonestly' in the statute include at least the following things:

(a) whatever in a particular case it conveys to the mind or minds of the tribunal of fact without any instruction as to the meaning save as to what may be expressly said in a relevant part of the statute to go to construction;
(b) 'discreditably, as being at variance with straightforward or honourable dealing';
(c) something akin to 'fraudulently, as being without any claim of right'.

Whichever one of these meanings was chosen, the test would prima facie have to be applied according to what was in the mind and belief of the actor or accused person. Such an interpretation accords with the modern approach to the notion of guilt of crime. I state the meaning (a) above not because it would appeal to me but because that is what I understand is said to be its meaning by some judges and commentators overseas. In *R v Feely* [1973] QB 530, to which I must later turn in detail, their Lordships were apparently of opinion that judges should not define what 'dishonestly' means and that jurors, in deciding whether an appropriation is dishonest, can be reasonably expected to apply the current standards of ordinary decent people (although considering that the test is 'subjective' because it is the belief or state of mind of the accused that matters), and that 'jurors should not need the help of a judge to tell them what amounts to dishonesty'. Their Lordships were concerned with the English equivalent of the Victorian s 72(l). If I may here interpolate, I am respectfully of opinion that the question was not whether a juror needed the help of a judge to tell him what amounts to dishonesty, but whether a juror should be given some assistance as to what was the necessary element in the new criminal offence which the Crown had to prove and which was imported by the word 'dishonestly' in the context in which it was found in the statute. I think that no juror would be in a position intuitively to know the answer to that question. The proposition, that every juror knows what dishonesty is, is in my opinion too imprecise to be true or false, and it obscures two truths, first that what matters is a point of statutory construction and secondly, that jurors, like judges and magistrates and other people, differ very markedly in their views as to whether particular conduct in particular circumstances is dishonest or is conduct to which moral obloquy attached. Their Lordships in *Feely's* case indicated that moral obloquy did not attach to certain conduct which they predicated. I have the misfortune to disagree with their Lordships also on these questions of morality or of the normal incidence of 'moral obloquy'. The significance of this will later appear.

I am unable to accept the 'meaning' which I have labelled (a). The court must direct the jury as to the meaning of constituent elements in any crime charged, especially if there could be any doubt about the meaning of any word or phrase constituting an element, and certainly in s 81(1), and as I think also in s 72(1), there would be in the jury's mind a very grave doubt about its meaning. The doubt would flow from the intelligence and conscientious approach of the jury, not from any other attribute or any shortcoming of the jury. Five judges in the Court of Appeal in *Feely's* case expressed views, as to whether specified conduct was fraudulent or deserving of moral obloquy, which were opposed to the earlier views thereon (with which I would respectfully agree) of Lord Parker, Lord Justice Winn, Lord Widgery, Forbes J and (before 1973 I think) Melford Stevenson J himself. These conflicts of opinion serve to demonstrate, in my opinion, that to construe the word so as to make 'moral obloquy' the requisite of the new crime is dangerously to base criminal liability on shifting sands.

The second possible meaning (b) must I think be rejected for reasons already indicated — upon this meaning the juror or other tribunal of fact is being asked to distinguish between on the one hand a deprivation-of-property-by-deception which is accompanied by or deserving of moral obloquy and on the other hand a deprivation-of-property-by-deception which is not accompanied by or deserving of moral obloquy. To put the choice more starkly, it is between on the one hand conduct which is at variance with straightforward or honourable dealing *and therefore discreditable* and, on the other hand, conduct which is at variance with straightforward or honourable dealing *and yet not discreditable*.

Some of those who support the moral obloquy test say, in substance, that juries are made up very largely of good and decent and honest people 'and they will know what to do'. The first proposition is doubtless entirely correct, but the second is of uncertain import unless it means that the jury can be trusted to act in accordance with the average moral standards of the day. If it means this last, then the real problem facing them on this test — whether the circumstances were such that the end justified the deceitful means — is a question which could be debated by philosophers as well as jurors from sun-up to sundown without arriving at any satisfactory answer. More than this, since the test must be what the Court of Appeal in *Feely's* case called 'subjective', that is to say that the question must be judged on the state of mind of the accused rather than upon the merely evidentiary existence or absence of reasonable grounds for the state of mind, some people (for example, those who sincerely believe that it is not morally wrong or discreditable to take money from their employer's till despite an express prohibition, provided they intend or believe that they will repay the money later on) may be wrongly and unjustly convicted simply because the jury 'knows what to do' and by its verdict expresses its view of such people or of such beliefs. Indeed, juries might be encouraged to do so — vide the remarks of the Court of Appeal in *Feely's* case [1973] QB at 735, which appear to come close to saying (no doubt unintentionally) that no one need fear the fact that such a person may have a defence in law because experience has shown that he will probably be convicted anyway. It is because of many such considerations (some of which I endeavour to enlarge upon below) that I consider the test of dishonesty in its context in s 81 of the Act cannot be simply a moral test.

I consider that express provisions of the statute like ss 73(1), 73(2), 81(1) itself and 81(3) make it clear that the word 'dishonestly' in the Act is used in a special sense and not in its meaning of 'discreditably as being at variance with straightforward or honourable dealing'. As Lord Reid said in *Cozens v Brutus* [1973] AC 854 at 861, where a word is used in a statute in a special or unusual sense the court will determine what the meaning is, and of course it is in those cases *a fortiori* the duty of the trial judge to explain to the jury, if not the meaning of the word in a judicial definition, at least so far as relevant the constituent element of the crime which is imported by the use of the word, and to relate the facts of the case to that element.

In dealing with indicators that the adverb is here used in a special sense I have already referred to the fact that s 81(1) contemplates an obtaining by deception (with intent permanently to deprive) which may be accomplished honestly. Next there are the express glosses on the word 'dishonestly' contained in s 73, in the form of deeming clauses and with the presence of these glosses must be coupled the fact that most of the glosses, including especially s 73(2)(a), are not to apply to s 81(1) at all, an intention stated by s 73(1) and intractably affirmed by s 81(3). But, as I have foreshadowed, there are more fundamental reasons why I consider that the interpretation of 'dishonestly' adopted in England cannot be accepted, and why the word cannot mean, like Humpty Dumpty's words, whatever meaning the tribunal in a given case chooses secretly to give to it.

The Criminal Law Revision Committee in England, in its recommendations which resulted in the enactment of the Theft Act 1968 of England, expressed the view that 'dishonesty is something which laymen can easily recognise when they see it'. If I may borrow a phrase, this might be called *fons et origo malorum*. Subsequent commentators have spelt out more clearly what the majority of the English Committee must have intended (from their collateral utterances, not the legislation) to convey. Thus Mr C R Williams, in a helpful article in the March 1974 issue of the (Victoria) *Law Institute Journal* said that: 'In cases to which subs (2) (scilicet of s 73) does not apply, it would seem that the meaning of dishonestly is to be determined by the jury expressing the moral standards of the ordinary man. In cases tried summarily those standards will be expressed by the magistrate or justices trying the case. This would appear to have been the intention of the … Committee.'

I must say that this seems to me to be saying that one essential element of a very serious crime, being a felony attracting a maximum penalty of imprisonment for 10 years, is that the actions shall appear to the tribunal of fact at a trial (often not a jury but one judicial officer) to be discreditable as falling short of the moral standards of the day.

Long ago William Blackstone cogently warned against the notion that a judge in a court of law should decide each case in the way that he thinks morally right or just, without founding his decisions on known legal principles: 'The liberty of considering all cases in an equitable light must not be indulged too far, lest thereby we destroy all law, and leave the decision of every question entirely in the breast of the judge. And law without equity, though hard and disagreeable, is much more desirable for the public good than equity without law which would make every judge a legislator and introduce most infinite confusion; and there would then be almost as many different rules of action laid down in our courts as there are differences of capacity and sentiment in the human mind': *Blackstone's Commentaries,* Book 1, p 62.

Much more recently, in 1952, in 85 CLR at XV Dixon CJ said: 'There is I believe a general respect for the Queen's Courts of justice which administer justice according to law, and I believe that there is a trust in them. But it is because they administer justice according to law.'

In my respectful opinion it is contrary to the most fundamental tenets and traditions of the common law, and of the English judicial system itself, that the judges of the courts of law should set themselves up, *or allow themselves to be set up*, as judges of morals or of moral standards. The public respect for the courts, upon which the courts' authority and existence ultimately depend, is held because they decide cases according to known legal principles. It is equally important that the principles applied be legal principles and known principles. Feelings and intuitions as to what constitutes dishonesty, and even as to what dishonesty means, must vary greatly from jury to jury and from judge to judge and from magistrate to magistrate. In *National Insurance Co of New Zealand Ltd v Espagne* (1961) 105 CLR 569 at 572, Dixon CJ said: 'Intuitive feelings for justice seem a poor substitute for a rule antecedently known, *more particularly where all do not have the same intuitions*.' [Emphasis added]

In my opinion, once the courts of law, properly so called, begin to decide cases, especially criminal cases, according to the judge's own view of abstract justice or of current standards of honesty or morality, respect for the courts will be calculated to decline, with dire consequences of a most fundamental character. Justice would no longer be seen to be done, and a judge would be no better qualified than anyone else to decide the cases.

It is for reasons of this kind that the courts of law have consistently refused, wherever possible, to accept from the hands of the legislature any powers of deciding cases upon bases of morality. For example, powers to make such order as the court thinks just are constantly read down and made to depend on known legal principles. Of course the sovereignty of Parliament is fundamental to the continued administration of justice according to law and, if Parliament ever laid it down clearly enough that it did intend the courts to decide on their view of morals and not on their view of the law, the courts of law must, even if it were their last act of deciding according to law, obey the command of Parliament as contained in the statute. But no statute should be so construed unless its language is utterly intractable. Parliament is presumed prima facie not to intend the destruction of the courts of law and their replacement with courts of morals.

It will doubtless be said that the recommendations of the English Committee were substantially that it was the jury and not the judges who should be given the power or duty to say whether the actions of the accused were done dishonestly. But it is simply not true to say that the statute in either country leaves it only to juries. Magistrates have to deal with prosecutions before them under the section and have to decide these questions of morals, and a very large number of cases come before them for decision. The reported cases in England, on appeal, since 1970 show the almost insoluble problems with which this legislation, as interpreted in England, has forced them to wrestle. In my opinion this is calculated to bring the courts into contempt by reason of different decisions being given on similar facts, because this is a particular field where quite demonstrably 'all do not have the same intuitions'. In any event, in my opinion, almost the same objections apply even to allowing juries to decide as to what is or is not dishonest or discreditable or immoral or deserving of moral obloquy, and if they, as well as learned academical commentators, disagree (as the cases show they do) as to the meaning of 'dishonestly' and as to the kind of case which comes within it, it is difficult to see how juries can be expected to have any greater capacity for uniformity. We should soon have as many different decisions upon similar facts 'as there are differences of capacity and sentiment in the human mind'.

Further, in directing a jury as to what are the facts relevant to the element of dishonesty, the judge is always by implication defining, or at all events indicating the connotations of, the element and word and, if the concept is purely one relating to moral obloquy, he necessarily does so by reference to his own view as to morals. And in this very field, of this very statute, it appears that five superior court judges in England have differed from five others. It is my opinion that respect for the law is greatly weakened when offenders receive different treatment as regards conviction, at the hands of different magistrates, justices or juries for almost identical actions in almost identical circumstances. Feelings of great injustice amongst those convicted, in comparing their lot with others acquitted, foster disrespect for and lack of confidence in the law and those charged with the heavy burden of administering it. As I have indicated, a study of the following decided cases shows in my opinion a remarkable, though not unexpected, difference of view between learned and experienced judges as to what is dishonest or fraudulent or deserving of moral obloquy and as to what is not dishonest or fraudulent or deserving of moral obloquy: see *R v Cockburn* [1961] 1 WLR 281; *Halstead v Patel* [1972] 1 WLR 661; *R v Williams* [1953] 1 QB 660; *R v Feely* [1973] QB 530; and *R v Lewis* (1976) 62 CAR 206. On one side are Lord Widgery and Forbes J and Lord Justice Winn and Lord Parker and Lord Goddard (with whose view I would most respectfully agree) and on the other side are the five judges who decided *R v Feely.* But what matters is not who is 'right' and who is 'wrong' so much as the fact that 'intuitions differ' and that therefore charges to the jury must differ, and the consequence will be that some persons will be acquitted on facts not differing in any material respect from those upon which other persons will be convicted. If I am right in thinking that such a consequence is inevitable should the statute be interpreted in this way, then this to my mind is a most cogent reason why it should not be so interpreted.

The alleged proposal of the English Committee as indicated above is in my opinion based upon a clear and fundamental fallacy. Firstly, it is simply untrue to say that every citizen 'knows dishonesty when he sees it' or knows the meaning of the word generally, let alone in the context of a badly drawn statute. Secondly, that is simply not the question that arises under the Acts; it is a different question altogether to ask whether a deprivation by deception has been achieved dishonestly. The word 'dishonestly' is in my opinion used in a somewhat special sense in its special context in the Theft Act 1973 and it is simply not true to say that every citizen knows what the word 'dishonestly' means in the context of this statute.

When discussing the relevant dictionary meanings of relevant words much earlier in these reasons, I reached the position that there were patent difficulties in adopting, as the meaning of dishonestly, 'discreditably, as being at variance with straightforward or honourable dealing', and reached the position that another meaning of the word in the statute was certainly open, viz 'the disposition to take or withhold from another that which it is his right to retain', in substance 'without any claim of right'. In my opinion the discussion just completed shows strong reason for rejecting the former interpretation and for rejecting any interpretation depending upon supposed current morality in the incidence of moral obloquy. The concept of 'without any claim of right' is substantially a known legal principle, and very close in content to a legal principle which has for many years been applied on this very branch of the law.

In my opinion 'dishonestly', in this statute, is used in that sense of 'with disposition to defraud' which means 'with disposition to withhold from a person what is his right' and in the special context thus imports into the offence the element that the actor must obtain 'the property' without any belief that he himself has any legal right to deprive the other of it.

In selecting the criterion by which, in considering a claim of right, wrongfulness and rightfulness can be distinguished, I have given what I consider are strong reasons (however imperfectly expressed) for saying that the court will always prefer to look for legal rightfulness or wrongfulness rather than moral rightfulness or wrongfulness wherever it is possible to do so as upon the proper construction of a statute of this kind.

...

In my opinion the same meaning of 'dishonestly' must apply in s 81(1) as applies in s 72, subject only to the different rules of construction which by s 73 apply to s 72 alone. It would not necessarily be a defence to a charge under s 81(1) that the accused believed that the property was his own in the sense that he was the owner of the goods. If he left his watch with a repairer, and then, after the repairs but before paying for them, he by a deception obtained his own watch with the intention of keeping it without paying for the repairs, the question posed by the critical adverb would be whether the accused believed that he had a legal right to obtain possession of the watch, that is to say, deprive the repairer of the watch, in the subsisting circumstances. If it is asked what is the test of rightfulness, it is in my opinion clear that the answer must be rightfulness in law. The belief which spells innocence is, to use legal language not necessarily to be employed before a jury, the belief that the actor has a legal right to or in respect of 'the property' by reason of which (it is believed) the deprivation of the other does not constitute either a criminal or a civil wrong.

In my opinion the concept involved in 'dishonestly' is very close to the common law requirement of 'intent to defraud', or absence of a claim of right, but it is 'subjective' in the sense in which the Court of Appeal has used the word in this context, and the emphasis is on the intention to 'defraud' the other of (eg) the possession, in the sense of to take without any belief in any legal right to take. Title alone (in the sense of ownership), is not necessarily a defence to a charge under s 81(1). In my opinion ss 73(2)(a) and 73(1) and 81(3) are sufficient on their own to make that clear. But a belief in a legal right in the circumstances to take the goods and deprive the other of possession is a defence to a charge under s 81(1).

As a matter of statutory construction it is in my opinion quite clear that the provisions of s 73(2) have no application whatsoever to the construction of s 81(1), and I would unhesitatingly reject the persistent argument to the contrary submitted for the appellant before us.

In the first place, s 73(1) declares that s 73 shall have effect as regards the interpretation of s 72. Even if no more appeared the conclusion would be almost irresistible that the provisions were intended to have effect as regards s 72 alone. But, secondly, more does appear. Section 73(1) provides expressly that, except as otherwise provided in that division of the Act, the provisions of s 73 shall apply only for the purposes of s 72 and not otherwise. Such a declaration could hardly be clearer. Thirdly, s 73(2) deals expressly with 'appropriation' and not with 'obtaining', a distinction recognised by such provisions as s 81(3). Fourthly (and as it seems to me with absolute conclusiveness) s 81(3) expressly imports, for the purposes of s 81, the provisions of s 73(12) and (13); it omits s 73(2) altogether, and it appears to me that there could hardly be a clearer case than this for the application within s 81 of the maxim *expressio unius est exclusio alterius*, were it not for the fact that, by s 73(1) itself, *alterum* is *expressly* excluded. *[Emphasis added]*

These considerations appear to me to support further the construction which I would put upon the word 'dishonestly' in the Act generally and in s 81(1) in particular. To take first s 72(1), I consider that s 73(2)(a) demonstrates that it is not necessarily a defence to a charge under s 72 that the accused believed he was the owner of the property; for example, the appropriation of property in possession of another, done with the intention of permanently depriving that other of it, may well be an appropriation done dishonestly; what will exonerate is a belief that the accused has a legal right to or in respect of 'the property' which makes or would make it lawful in all the actual circumstances (that is to say, not an infringement of the civil or criminal law) to make the appropriation of possession with intention to deprive.

I may have suggested that the word 'dishonestly' does have the same meaning in all the sections of the Act. This is of course only true in a sense. It is made quite clear by s 73 that the 'meaning' in s 72 is varied by application of special provisions relating to the meaning of that word in s 72. Section 73 can be properly regarded as containing deeming provisions which do not alter the constant import of the word itself. It will be observed however that s 73(2)(a) contains substantially the very thing that is in my opinion constant in the meaning of 'dishonestly' throughout the Act, and in my opinion the reason why it has to be expressly stated in that part of the Act is that the meaning of the word would be otherwise altered by the presence of the other rules of construction in s 73. To have enacted in s 73 subs (2)(b) and (c), and also subs (3), but without subs (2)(a), would have been necessarily to throw open the meaning of dishonestly without any guide at all, from the previous law or the statute, as to what the meaning was. But in my opinion the character of s 73(2), as a matter of drafting, is of the character of a section which provides that: an appropriation is not done dishonestly if it is done (a) honestly, or (b) in a particular belief, or (c) in another particular belief.

If only (b) and (c) were enacted, and not (a), a quite different effect might have to be given to such a section and a different meaning to the word 'dishonestly'.

It is to be observed that in s 78, where the offence is removing property without lawful authority, and where the adverb 'dishonestly' is not used in formulating the offence, subs (3) expressly provides that the offence is not committed by a person who believes that he has authority for the removal, that is to say, by a person who believes he has a legal right to remove the property.

For the reasons that I have given, I have concluded that the element imported by the word 'dishonestly' into the offence created by s 81(1) is the element that the accused person has no belief that he has a legal right to deprive the other of 'the property'. That element the Crown must prove. In my opinion it is the duty of the trial judge, upon a trial for an offence against s 81(1), to convey to the jury, not necessarily in so many words but in some suitable fashion tailored to the occasion, the substance of the requirements of the element I have attempted to define, and to relate it to the facts of the case.

Quite independently of the foregoing, I am of opinion that it simply cannot be correct to leave it to the tribunal of fact to decide for itself what 'dishonestly' means; for there is then no known principle at all.

As neither the Privy Council nor the High Court of Australia nor the Full Court of a State has spoken upon the critical question of construction raised by this case, I turn to the English cases to see how persuasive are any decisions there which might be thought to compel conclusions different from those arrived at above. The English cases show a remarkable divergence of opinion on what constitutes conduct to which moral obloquy should attach, a fact which in my opinion serves to indicate some of the dangers of holding that the adverb imports a conclusion upon morality rather than a conclusion or belief as to the position at law.

[His Honour then discussed and rejected the decision in *R v Feely*, and continued:]

The Court of Appeal in *R v Feely* was in my most respectful opinion correct in considering that *R v Williams* [1953] 1 QB 660 and *R v Cockburn* [1968] 1 WLR 281 were authorities applicable to cases under the Act of 1968. But in my opinion what was said in those two cases in the Reports cited by me was and still is entirely correct and in accordance with unaltered legal principles. In my opinion the law did not drift off course in *Williams*, and it stayed on the right track in *Cockburn*. In *Cockburn* at [1968] 1 WLR 284, Winn LJ (speaking for Lord Parker and Lord Widgery and himself) said: 'The fact of the matter is this, that it is nevertheless quite essential always to remember what are the elements of larceny and what are the complete and total elements of larceny, that is to say, taking the property of another person against the will of that other person *without any claim of right to do so*, and with the intent at the time of taking it permanently to deprive the owner of it.' [Emphasis added]

These elements are in my opinion clear and coherent and capable of ready application by those who have to administer the criminal law. I would not readily construe a new statute as replacing them, or one of them, with a vague requirement which is of no fixed content and which the tribunal can secretly construe for itself as it wishes.

[His Honour referred to a number of other English decisions, and continued:]

In the result, I find nothing in the authorities to compel me, or to persuade me, to adopt conclusions different from those expressed earlier. In *R v Lawrence* [1972] AC 626, where the courts were curiously reluctant to apply the conclusion that a consent obtained by fraud was no consent, the House of Lords expressly said that it was not contended that the acts were done other than dishonestly, and expressed no views upon the meaning of the adverb.

In my opinion the word 'dishonestly' in s 81(1) imports that the accused person must obtain the property (with intent to deprive), without any belief that he has in law the right to deprive the other of the property.

In my opinion Mr Redlich was clearly correct in his contention that 'a claim of right', the test for which is in my opinion imported by the word 'dishonestly' in s 81(1), does not require a belief in the accused in a right to obtain the property *by deception, or by the particular deception employed*. It is the obtaining that the Crown must prove was done dishonestly, not the practising of the deception. This is in part because the law can hardly be thought to give legal rights to deceive. [Emphasis added]

I am finally in a position to deal with the grounds of appeal.

[His Honour considered the direction given by the trial judge, and continued:]

From these directions, and from the charge to the jury as a whole, I consider that the jury almost certainly concluded that all that the Crown had to negative was a belief in the applicant that he had a legal right to get possession of the car *by the deception in fact employed*, whereas in truth the Crown had to go further and to negative any belief in the applicant that he was in all the circumstances legally entitled to deprive Kapaufs of possession of the car. In other words, leaving the onus of proof on one side, a plausible defence of the applicant, namely that he believed he had in all the circumstances a legal right to deprive Kapaufs of possession of the car, was never put clearly to the jury. *[Emphasis added]*

It is in my opinion impossible to say that no injustice was caused by this misdirection of the learned trial judge, understandable as the misdirection was in view of the extraordinary nature of the legislation and the state of judicial authority upon its meaning.

Save as appears above, it is strictly speaking unnecessary for me to deal with the other grounds of appeal, but for the sake of certainty I should say that I have considered all the other grounds of appeal and have concluded that they all should fail.

For these reasons I am of opinion that the application for leave to appeal against conviction should be granted, the appeal treated as heard *instanter* and allowed, the conviction and sentence set aside, and a retrial ordered.

[**Murphy J** delivered a separate judgment agreeing with **Fullagar J**. **McInerney J** dissented. Appeal allowed and a new trial ordered.]

8.60C R v Brow

[1981] VR 783
Full Court of the Supreme Court of Victoria

[The accused, a used car dealer, was convicted on a number of counts of theft and obtaining property by deception. The counts for obtaining property by deception related to transactions in which the accused, by representing to customers that he was the owner of certain motor cars and that those cars were unencumbered, obtained from customers cheques, various sums of money and trade-in vehicles. In fact, the accused either was not the owner of those vehicles, or they were subject to encumbrances. The accused's defence was that he believed that no pecuniary or other disadvantage would accrue to the purchasers. He gave evidence that he intended to pay off the amount owed on the various cars, expected to be able to do so and never intended that any buyer should suffer loss. The counts of theft related to misappropriations by the accused of cheques given to him by purchasers of cars which he held on consignment, which cheques should have been accounted for to the owners of the cars. In answer to these charges, the accused said that he intended to render to the true owner as soon as he could the amounts of the cheques. The trial judge directed the jury that the accused was only entitled to be acquitted on the grounds of lack of dishonesty if he believed he had a legal right to the property in question, which of course he did not.]

Young CJ, **Crockett** and **Tadgell JJ**: In so instructing the jury his Honour was avowedly applying the reasoning of the majority of the members constituting this court in the recent decision of *R v Salvo* [1980] VR 401. The passage from the charge which we have quoted, and the charge as a whole, may fairly be read as meaning not only that it was incumbent on the Crown to prove that the applicant obtained the relevant property without believing he had a legal right to obtain it but that, if the Crown did prove that, then the property was necessarily dishonestly obtained for the purposes of s 81. In other words, his Honour treated the majority judgments in *R v Salvo*, supra, as providing an exclusive definition of 'dishonestly obtains'.

Counsel for the applicant submitted that the trial judge erred in confining the meaning of the word 'dishonestly' in that way and submitted further that the reasoning of the majority in *R v Salvo* did not require it. In so confining the question of dishonesty, it was said, the judge deprived the applicant of a full consideration of his defence. The submission accepted the correctness of the reasoning and the conclusion of the majority judgments in *R v Salvo* but only on the footing that the sole defence in that case was that the accused did believe he had a legal claim of right to obtain the property there in question. In the present case, on the other hand (so it was argued), the defence did not depend upon any belief by the applicant that he had a legal claim of right as such to obtain the relevant property: his defence to the allegation of dishonesty was that he had no dishonest intent because he had no intention when obtaining the property to cause loss to those from whom he obtained it. The argument therefore was that *R v Salvo* does not apply to a case such as this, in which the question of dishonesty was, to use counsel's words, 'at large'. In such cases the jury will not be assisted, it was submitted, by a single reference to an absence of belief of a legal claim of right as a criterion of dishonesty, and the accused will be disadvantaged by it; such a reference tends to put the concept of dishonesty into a strait-jacket. In this case, it was argued, it deprived the accused of the opportunity to have the jury conclude that, although he could not assert a belief of any legal claim of right in the strict sense, he believed that what he did was not dishonest because, having regard to the manner in which he had arranged his business, he honestly believed that no pecuniary or other disadvantage would accrue to those with whom he dealt. Against the background of those submissions counsel for the applicant contended that the question of dishonesty should have been left to the jury by a direction to consider whether the applicant believed that he was entitled to obtain the property in question and whether that belief was reasonable in the light of his business arrangements and all other relevant surrounding circumstances, and having regard to prevailing community standards of honest and decent conduct.

Reduced to essentials the submission for the applicant on this ground was that *R v Salvo* [1980] VR 401 was distinguishable; that in the circumstances of this case the trial judge should have directed the jury as a matter of law that it was not necessarily sufficient, in order to prove that the property was dishonestly obtained, that the Crown negate any belief by the accused of a legal claim of right to obtain the property; and that the jury should have been positively directed that it was open to them not to be satisfied that the applicant obtained the property dishonestly notwithstanding that they were satisfied that he had no such belief.

The submission contained overtones of the reasoning of the Court of Appeal in *R v Feely* [1973] QB 530; [1973] 1 All ER 341 (which was rejected by the majority of the court in *R v Salvo,* supra), that honesty is to be regarded as an amorphous concept a transgression beyond the confines of which will be recognised by a properly instructed jury when they see it. Indeed it was inherent in counsel's argument that the reasoning of the majority in *R v Salvo* was inconsistent with the reasoning in *R v Feely* only in a case where, unlike this case, the only possible defence to an allegation that property was dishonestly obtained is a bona fide belief in a claim of right.

In our opinion these submissions cannot be sustained. It is convenient to consider their validity first in relation to the counts of dishonestly obtaining property in which the property in question was obtained as consideration for a sale by the applicant of a motor vehicle (counts 2, 4, 6, 14 and 15).

If it is proved that a person purports to sell for consideration goods which are the property of another or are encumbered in favour of another knowing (a) that the owner or encumbrancer has no knowledge of the sale and would not consent to it if he had; and (b) that the purchaser has no knowledge of the true ownership or of the encumbrance and would not proceed with the transaction if he had, then in our opinion there is evidence that the consideration is obtained by deception and that the obtaining is dishonest in terms of s 81. We would regard the consideration as none the less dishonestly obtained in those circumstances simply because the vendor at the time of the sale hopes or expects or even intends to deal with the true owner or encumbrancer of the goods with a view ultimately to satisfying his claim as true owner or encumbrancer and thus saving the purchaser from loss.

This is so because the obtaining of property being the consideration for a sale can only be honestly justified by reference to the supposed contractual transaction on which the sale depends. The right of the vendor to obtain the consideration does not depend on an intention that the purchaser should not suffer loss or on any other basis than that afforded by the supposed contract. The right depends upon the vendor's claim that he can satisfy the legal obligations which he believes the contract requires of him. In the circumstances supposed the vendor's obligation must include a right or power on his part to sell unless he believes that the contract absolves him from having that right or power. It follows that unless the vendor believes he can claim the right or power to sell or a contractual absolution from it he cannot point to an honest justification for obtaining the consideration from the purchaser.

The case is therefore quite different from one in which an employee, without his employer's actual consent, 'borrows' money from the till intending that he will replace it after successfully investing it with a bookmaker and that his employer will therefore be caused no loss: cf *R v Williams* [1953] 1 QB 660; [1953] 1 All ER 1068; *R v Cockburn* [1968] 1 All ER 466; [1968] 1 WLR 281. It is also quite different from cases where money which has been obtained by deception might be intended to be subsequently restored: cf *R v McCall (Paul Richard)* (1970) 55 Cr App R 175 CA; *Halstead v Patel* [1972] 2 All ER 147; [1972] 1 WLR 661. It has been suggested by some learned writers that the reasoning in *R v Feely*, supra, should be capable of being applied in such cases to allow a finding of fact inconsistent with dishonesty in circumstances where no intention to cause ultimate loss to the victim can be made out by the Crown. Arguments in favour of that view are to be found in an article by Mr C R Williams in (1980) 54 *LIJ* (Vic) 567, and in Weinberg & Williams, *The Australian Law of Theft* (1977), pp 134–8; Smith, *The Law of Theft* (1972), pp 46–8. *R v Salvo* might or might not leave room for those or similar cases to be regarded on their particular facts as not involving dishonest appropriation or obtaining, as the case may be. It is unnecessary, however, to decide that point here because it does not arise. If there are cases in which a person who by deception obtains property without any bona fide belief of a legal claim of right but who nevertheless does not obtain the property dishonestly in terms of s 81 this is not one of them. This is a case in which the circumstances of the deception proved in relation to counts 2, 4, 6, 14 and 15 are inconsistent with an absence of dishonesty in the obtaining of the property unless the accused believed the circumstances entitled him to claim the property from the various purchasers in the way he did — that they were consenting to his obtaining it.

[The court went on to apply similar reasoning to the counts of theft. Appeal dismissed.]

8.61C R v Bonollo

[1981] VR 633
Full Court of the Supreme Court of Victoria

[The accused was convicted on eight counts of obtaining cheques by deception. She represented to finance companies that she wished to purchase and install furniture and fittings at premises owned by her. Invoices for the goods made out by the proposed vendors were supplied to the finance companies. The finance companies sent cheques to the vendors and then leased the various items to the accused. In fact, the transactions were an elaborate sham on the part of the accused and the vendors. The accused already owned the various items, some of which were the subject of leasing agreements with other finance companies. The invoices supplied to the finance companies thus recorded nonexistent transactions, and the supposed vendors of the goods transferred the money received from the finance companies to the accused.

The accused's defence was that she intended to make payments to the finance companies as they fell due, and that she believed she had the capacity to do so. The trial judge directed the jury that the accused was to be taken as having acted dishonestly if she did not believe that she had any legal right to deprive the finance companies of their cheques.]

Young CJ: I have had the advantage of studying in draft the reasons for judgment prepared by McGarvie J. His Honour has set out the facts fully and there is no need for me to repeat them.

Since the only ground of appeal argued concerned the direction as to the meaning of the word 'dishonestly' I shall turn at once to the question whether the learned judge's direction as to the meaning of that word was in accordance with the law. It is, I think, important that the question should be formulated in that way, for it is not the function of the court to decide what the law ought to be: the function is to say what the law is.

I agree with McGarvie J, that a trial judge should explain to a jury what 'dishonestly' means in s 81. In my view, the proper interpretation of the statute is a matter of law and such a matter must whenever necessary be explained to a jury. It is then for the jury to apply the law to the facts. Although 'dishonestly' is an ordinary English word, I agree with what Murphy J said in *R v Salvo* [1980] VR 401 at 422, viz that the word is clearly used in a special sense in s 81(l): see also per Fullagar J, at 427. Moreover, as Murphy J observed at the same page, a direction to the jury is particularly necessary 'because the very concept of obtaining something by deception and yet not obtaining it dishonestly, is something which few people other than lawyers would normally see to be possible'. Accordingly I am unable with the greatest respect to agree with the observation of Lawton LJ in *R v Feely* [1973] 1 QB 530 at 537; [1973] 1 All ER 341 that judges should not define what dishonestly means.

What then is the special sense in which 'dishonestly' is used in s 81(1)? In my opinion that question has been authoritatively answered by the judgments of the majority in *R v Salvo*, supra, and I think it is the duty of this court to follow that decision, whatever our personal opinions might be as to the correctness of the decision of the majority in that case. As will appear below, it is my opinion that the decision of the majority in

R v Salvo was correct, but that is not the point with which I am presently concerned. It is, I think, of the utmost importance that the principle of *stare decisis* should be upheld. Failure to do so leads to uncertainty in the law and, particularly in the criminal law, uncertainty leads to injustice.

The answer given by the majority in *Salvo's* case, supra, to the question as to the meaning of the word 'dishonestly' is compendiously expressed as 'without a claim of right'. Fullagar J spelled out that meaning at [1980] VR 433 as follows: 'The belief which spells innocence is, to use legal language not necessarily to be employed before a jury, the belief that the actor has a legal right to or in respect of "the property" by reason of which (it is believed) the deprivation of the other does not constitute either a criminal or a civil wrong.'

That sentence, in my opinion, contains the essence of his Honour's decision. Moreover, repeated study of the judgments of the majority in *Salvo's* case has convinced me that Murphy J took the same view. Thus his Honour made it plain (at 420) that a belief in a moral right would not excuse an accused. Murphy J said: 'In this case, the jury should have been told, in my view, that the Crown had to prove beyond reasonable doubt that the accused himself did not believe that he had in all the circumstances a legal right — not a moral right — to deprive Kapaufs of the motor car. I agree with Fullagar J that if the accused sincerely believed that he had a right to take the car — a right not stemming from the law of the land but stemming from some other consideration — it would avail the accused not at all. For example, a sincere belief entertained by the accused that Karma required that he should retake the car would not prevent the retaking from being dishonest. But a sincere belief that the law of the land allowed him to do so would. The subjective aspect of this case was therefore limited to the determination by the jury of the issue whether the accused himself believed he had a legal right in all the circumstances to take the car from Kapaufs. If they were left in reasonable doubt as to this matter then he, the accused, should have been acquitted.'

Again at [1980] VR 423 his Honour said: 'In many cases, as I have said, the resolution of the issue whether the accused has acted "dishonestly" in obtaining property by a deception may be easy, and require no more than a direction from the judge that the Crown must prove that the accused had no belief in a claim of right to the property, for that is the element of the crime, which is added by the adverb.'

The reasoning of their Honours leaves no room in my opinion for acceptance of a view that in some other circumstances a sincere belief by an accused that he had a moral right to obtain the property in question by deception would afford a defence. Nor does it allow for acceptance of a view that anything less than a sincere belief in an entitlement to do what he did without infringement of the law would afford a defence.

The same view of the decision of the majority in *Salvo's* case has been taken by another Full Court in *R v Brow* [1981] VR 783. In the joint judgment of all the members of the court in that case (Young CJ, Crockett and Tadgell JJ) this passage appears:

> Reduced to essentials the submission for the applicant on this ground was that *R v Salvo* was distinguishable, that in the circumstances of this case the trial judge should have directed the jury as a matter of law that it was not necessarily

sufficient, in order to prove that the property was dishonestly obtained, that the Crown negate any belief by the accused of a legal claim of right to obtain the property; and that the jury should have been positively directed that it was open to them not to be satisfied that the applicant obtained the property dishonestly notwithstanding that they were satisfied that he had no such belief.

The submission contained overtones of the reasoning of the Court of Appeal in *R v Feely* [1973] I QB 530 (which was rejected by the majority of the court in *R v Salvo)*, that honesty is to be regarded as an amorphous concept a transgression beyond the confines of which will be recognised by a properly instructed jury when they see it.

Indeed it was inherent in counsel's argument that the reasoning of the majority in *R v Salvo* was inconsistent with the reasoning in *R v Feely* only in a case, where, unlike this case, the only possible defence to an allegation that property was dishonestly obtained is a bona fide belief in a claim of right.

The decision in *R v Brow* reinforces the view, if reinforcement were necessary, that we should follow and apply the reasoning of the majority in *Salvo's* case [1980] VR 401. There is, in my opinion, consistently with the application of *stare decisis*, no room for giving to the word 'dishonestly' any meaning other than that given to it in *Salvo's* case and *Brow's* case.

As I have already indicated I respectfully agree in the reasoning of the majority in *Salvo's* case. I think that the meaning there attributed to 'dishonestly' in s 81(1) was arrived at by the application of the proper principles of statutory interpretation and I see no reason why it should not be applied in the present case. I do not think that the strength of the reasoning of the majority in *Salvo's* case can be impugned by conjuring up imaginary situations in which persons might be charged with offences in circumstances in which right-thinking people would regard the person's conduct as being without moral blameworthiness.

There may be a number of answers that might be made to a suggestion that a person might be prosecuted in some of the supposed circumstances. A trial judge in such a case might well encourage a jury to acquit and in any event juries do not commonly convict in cases in which they think that the prosecution should never have been launched.

I do not mean by these observations to suggest that it is not a legitimate means of testing a proposed interpretation of a statute to consider its operation in particular circumstances. But the process cannot be used to defeat the meaning of the words used by Parliament according to their proper interpretation: see, for example, *Crichton v Victorian Dairies* [1965] VR 49 especially at 53–4, where the unsuccessful argument for the defendant was based on the view that the construction of the statute contended for by the informant could in some circumstances produce absurd results. Reference may also be made to a warning by Fullagar J in *McCarter v Brodie* (1950) 80 CLR 432 at 497, where his Honour said: 'Nothing but futile exaggeration of the difficulties of s 92 can result from an insistence on imagining border-line cases which are excessively unlikely to arise in practice.'

I would, with respect, apply that observation to the word 'dishonestly' in s 81(1).

In the case of many statutory offences it is possible to conjure up situations which, it may readily be assumed, Parliament did not intend to fix with criminal liability. And yet although such supposed situations are within the literal language of the statute creating the offence, it is remarkable that reports of them are not to be found in the books. This situation is not new. Even under the English *Larceny Act 1916* it would not be difficult to think of situations within the Act as interpreted by the courts which right-thinking people would not regard as appropriate for the sanction of the criminal law.

Of course, the decision in every case must be read *secundum subjectam materiam*, but the reasoning of the majority in *Salvo's* case, supra, is not to be defeated by abbreviating that reasoning to the phrase 'without a belief in a claim of right' and treating such an abbreviation as inapplicable to a different set of circumstances. The *ratio decidendi* of the majority is to be found succinctly stated in the passage I have already quoted from Fullagar J's judgment at [1980] VR 433. As his Honour is careful to say, the legal language he uses to express his reasons is not necessarily to be employed before a jury. A trial judge must express the idea in the language which is most appropriate to the case before him. It may not always be sufficient merely to say that 'dishonestly' means 'without a claim of right'. Did the youth who obtained alcoholic liquor from a publican by deceiving the latter as to his age believe that his action involved no offence? Did the employee who obtained an advance from his employer by deception believe that he had a right to do so? Examples may be multiplied but it is unnecessary to do so for I perceive no difficulty in the application of the decision.

In the present case the question for the jury was whether the applicant at the time of obtaining had any genuine belief that in the obtaining she was not committing any breach of the civil or criminal law. Did she obtain the cheque with disposition to take or withhold from First Chicago that which it was First Chicago's right to retain? (See: *Salvo's* case, supra, at 426.) The answer to the latter question must be in the affirmative because she knew that First Chicago owned the money and had the right to retain it against all persons except someone to whom it freely (and not under misapprehension) chose to give it. Her disposition was permanently to deprive First Chicago of the property nonetheless. The fact that she intended or hoped to repay the money is simply irrelevant.

Mr Weinberg, who appeared for the applicant before us, conceded, quite properly, that if we thought that the case was governed by *R v Salvo* no criticism could be directed to the learned judge's charge. It follows that, in my opinion, the application should be dismissed.

McGarvie J [His Honour undertook a detailed analysis of *R v Salvo*, the English cases and the writings of academic commentators, and continued]:

The concept of dishonesty

The length of my reasons and the detailed discussion in them inevitably create the impression that the concept of dishonesty in s 81(1) is an involved and complex one. There has been a wealth of discussion since 1968 upon numerous aspects of the concept of dishonesty and many different views have been expressed by judges and learned writers. On this background, in stating my analysis of the meaning and operation of the concept, I have sought to make clear in a comprehensive way my views on the relevant aspects. It is worth repeating that in my view the concept is very close to the concept of intent to defraud and over many years that concept has not given rise to much complexity. On many of the aspects of the concept of dishonesty which have been treated as doubtful since 1968, the position seems to have been taken for granted upon the concept of intent to defraud. In my view, on most aspects, the controversies are to be determined in a similar way in respect of each of the concepts. The meaning which I have given the word 'dishonesty' is virtually the meaning which the courts have given the words 'intent to defraud'. The concept which I regard as conveyed by the word 'dishonesty' in s 81(1) is a relatively simple one. It is that a person obtaining property by deception obtains it dishonestly if he is conscious that by obtaining it he will produce a consequence affecting the interests of the person deprived of it; and if that consequence is one which would be detrimental of those interests in a significant practical way. To test whether the consequence would be detrimental in that way the question is asked whether an ordinary person, at the time when the property was obtained, would have regarded the particular consequence as one which would be detrimental to the interests of the other person in a significant practical way.

Effect

The word 'dishonestly' operates to free from criminal sanction only the relatively rare case where a person obtaining property by deception is not shown to have believed that he was bringing about a consequence affecting the interests of the other person or, if he believed he was bringing about such a consequence, it is not shown that it was one which would be detrimental to the interests of the other person in a significant practical way. In the great majority of cases of persons obtaining property by deception both those things could be shown. Usually, of course, the main motive of a person who obtains property by deception is self-advantage.

Summary of direction

In summary, the issue of dishonesty in this case required a direction from the trial judge to the jury which in the words and in the order chosen by the judge (1) explained that the question is whether the obtaining was dishonest, not whether the deception was dishonest: *R v Salvo* [1980] VR 401 at 406, 422 and 440; (2) indicated that the accused would have obtained the cheque dishonestly (a) if, at the time she obtained it, she believed that by obtaining it she would produce a consequence affecting the interests of First Chicago, and (b) if, at that time, an ordinary person would have regarded that consequence as one which would be detrimental to the interests of First Chicago in a significant practical way; (3) explained that the Crown case was that the applicant believed that by obtaining the cheque she would produce the consequences (a) that First Chicago would incur a greater financial risk than it understood it was incurring, and (b) that the amount of the cheque was to be used for a purpose different from the purpose for which First Chicago understood it would be used; (4) indicated the evidence and the relevance of the evidence which tended to show (a) whether the applicant believed that by obtaining the cheque she would produce the above consequences and (b) whether an ordinary person would have regarded each of the respective consequences as a consequence which would be detrimental to the interests of First Chicago in a significant practical way.

Provisional conclusion

Faced with the state of the authorities upon the meaning of the word 'dishonestly' in s 81(1) and the pressures of a long and complex trial, the learned judge was placed in a difficult position in deciding upon the proper direction to give upon the element of dishonesty. However, as the jury were not directed to apply the appropriate test and were not directed as to the relevant considerations upon the issue of dishonesty, it would be my view, were it not for the decision of this court in *R v Brow* [1981] VR 783 which I discuss below, that the application should be granted, the appeal against conviction allowed, the conviction quashed and a new trial ordered on the first count.

Mr Fitzgerald took the position that if the court were of the opinion that the jury had not been directed to apply the appropriate test upon the issue of dishonesty, this would not be a case for the application of the proviso to s 568(1) of the *Crimes Act 1958.* I consider that to be the correct approach. See: *Quartermaine v R* (1980) 54 ALJR 453; *R v Waterfall* [1970] 1 QB 148 at 151.

I have discussed this application by reference to the first count of the presentment. My reasons apply in the same way to the other counts on which the applicant was convicted and to the orders with regard to them.

R v Brow

When the draft of my reasons was almost in final form, the joint judgment of Young CJ, Crockett and Tadgell JJ, in *R v Brow* [1981] VR 783 was delivered in this court on 3 December 1980.

[His Honour then discussed *R v Brow* and continued:]

Eventually I have come to the conclusion that the proper implication from the decision in *R v Brow* is that it does bind the court in the present case. In that case the court treated the majority decision in *Salvo's* case as establishing that belief in a claim of right is the test of dishonesty in a case where no such belief was raised as an issue of the trial.

The test which the court held to be the proper test in *Brow's* case, a case where no issue of claim of right was raised, is inconsistent with the test which would have been applied upon my view of the meaning of 'dishonestly' in s 81(1). Upon my view of the meaning of that word the test would have been whether Brow believed that by obtaining the consideration he was producing the consequence that the purchasers, who expected to obtain clear title to cars, were to be left for some limited or indeterminate period, or permanently with no title or an encumbered title, and if so, whether this would be a significant practical detriment to their interests. The court in *Brow's* case must have taken the view that the word 'dishonestly' did not have the constant meaning which I consider it has. As the word presumably has a constant meaning the court must have proceeded on the basis that its meaning is the one which Fullagar J, in *Salvo's* case concluded it has. If, as the court decided in *Brow's* case, the test was whether the accused believed he had a claim of right to the property, I can see no logical distinction between that case and this case which would lead to a different test being applied in this case. Accordingly I conclude that I am bound by part of the *ratio decidendi* in *Brow's* case to decide that this application must be dismissed.

[**McInerney J** concurred in the judgment of **Young CJ**. Appeal dismissed.]

8.62 Notes

1. *R v Salvo* settles that, as a matter of law, the defence of bona fide claim of legal right applies to the offence of obtaining property by deception in the same way as it applies to the offence of theft. This means that s 73(2), which applies to *theft,* is the exhaustive definition of what is 'not dishonest'. It also means that for the *obtaining offences*, where there is no statutory definition of dishonesty, the only defence will be an argument based on bona fide claim of legal right. *R v Salvo*, *R v Brow* and *R v Bonollo* can be said to have settled that *Feely/Ghosh* does not represent the law in Victoria. However, it has been suggested that the authority of the Victorian cases on this point must be regarded as uncertain in consequence of the decision of the High Court in *Peters v R* (1998) 192 CLR 493 (at **7.75C**). In *Peters v R*, Gaudron and Toohey JJ, with whom Kirby J agreed on this point although dissenting in the result, held that the requirement of fraud in conspiracy to defraud incorporates dishonesty, and that, in determining dishonesty, the *Feely/Ghosh* approach should be followed. Their Honours were content to distinguish the Victorian cases, holding they should be confined in their application to the Theft legislation. It can be argued that there is no sound basis in principle for applying *Feely/Ghosh* to offences such as conspiracy to defraud while refusing to apply that approach to offences such as theft and obtaining property by deception.

   In other contexts, also, the courts have chosen to follow *Feely/Ghosh* rather than the Victorian trilogy. In *R v Glenister* [1980] 2 NSWLR 597, the New South Wales Court of Criminal Appeal followed *Feely/Ghosh* in relation to the offence of fraudulently appropriating property belonging to a company. In *R v Lawrence* [1997] 1 VR 459; (1996) 138 ALR 487, Callaway JA, with whom Southwell and Smith AJJA agreed, held in relation to the crime of stealing, misappropriation or conversion of property belonging to the Commonwealth that the *Feely/Ghosh* approach should be adopted rather than the Victorian cases dealing with the Theft legislation. The trilogy of Victorian cases nonetheless appears to continue to represent Victorian law. They have not however been tested and in the future may be further reviewed.

2. It is submitted that the word 'dishonestly' should be regarded as possessing a meaning beyond those cases to which s 73(2) refers. It cannot be correct in principle that an intention to return a specific chattel necessarily leads to an acquittal, while an intention to return an equivalent amount of a fungible such as money does not. It is submitted that the accused should be entitled to an acquittal in both cases. It is submitted that other cases in which the conduct of the accused may involve no significant moral blameworthiness sometimes occur and that in such cases also the accused ought to have a

defence on the grounds of lack of dishonesty. It is submitted that in such cases the question whether the conduct of the accused is properly characterised as dishonest should be determined by the jury by application of the standards of ordinary, decent people.

3. The definition of 'dishonestly' in the Crimes Act 1900 (ACT) incorporates the extension to the negative definition of that adverb adopted by McGarvie J in *R v Bonollo*. Section 96(4)(b) provides that a person's appropriation of property shall not be regarded as dishonest if:

> ... he or she appropriates the property in the belief that the appropriation will not thereby cause any significant practical detriment to the interests of the person to whom the property belongs in relation to that property.

8.63 Further reading

W J Brookbanks, 'Colour of Right and Offences of Dishonesty' (1987) *11 Crim LJ* 153

D W Elliott, 'Dishonesty in Theft: A Dispensable Concept' [1982] *Crim LR* 395

A Halpin, 'The Test for Dishonesty' [1996] *Crim LR* 283

B McSherry and B Naylor, *Australian Criminal Laws: Critical Perspectives*, Oxford University Press, Melbourne, 2004, pp 288–307

D Ormerod and D Williams (eds), *Smith's Law of Theft*, Oxford University Press, 9th ed, 2007, pp 227–36

A Steel, 'The Harms and Wrongs of Stealing: The Harm Principle and Dishonesty in Theft' (2008) 31 *University of New South Wales Law Journal* 712

C R Williams, *Property Offences*, 3rd ed, Law Book Co, Sydney, 1999, pp 129–39

—, 'The Shifting Meaning of Dishonesty' (1999) 23 *Crim LJ* 275

OBTAINING BY DECEPTION

8.64 The two main 'fraud' offences are offences involving obtaining by deception, in ss 81 and 82: the offences of obtaining property, and obtaining a financial advantage, by deception. These will be the focus of this part of the chapter. Other fraud-related offences involve false accounting and falsification of documents.

8.65E Crimes Act 1958 (Vic)

81 Obtaining property by deception

(1) A person who by any deception dishonestly obtains property belonging to another, with the intention of permanently depriving the other of it, is guilty of an indictable offence and liable to level 5 imprisonment (10 years maximum).

(2) For purposes of this section a person is to be treated as obtaining property if he obtains ownership, possession or control of it, and 'obtain' includes obtaining for another or enabling another to obtain or to retain.

(3) Sub-sections (12) and (13) of section 73 shall apply for purposes of this section, with the necessary adaptation of the reference to appropriating, as it applies for purposes of section 72.

(4) For the purposes of this section, ***deception*** —

(a) means any deception (whether deliberate or reckless) by words or conduct as to fact or as to law, including a deception as to the present intentions of the person using the deception or any other person; and

(b) includes an act or thing done or omitted to be done with the intention of causing —

(i) a computer system; or

(ii) a machine that is designed to operate by means of payment or identification

— to make a response that the person doing or omitting to do the act or thing is not authorised to cause the computer system or machine to make.

82 Obtaining financial advantage by deception

(1) A person who by any deception dishonestly obtains for himself or another any financial advantage is guilty of an indictable offence and liable to level 5 imprisonment (10 years maximum).

(2) For purposes of this section 'deception' has the same meaning as in section 81.

83 False accounting

(1) Where a person dishonestly, with a view to gain for himself or another or with intent to cause loss to another —

(a) destroys, defaces, conceals or falsifies any account or any record or document made or required for any accounting purpose; or

(b) in furnishing information for any purpose produces or makes use of any account, or any such record or document as aforesaid, which to his knowledge is or may be misleading, false or deceptive in a material particular —

he is guilty of an indictable offence and liable to level 5 imprisonment (10 years maximum).

(2) For purposes of this section a person who makes or concurs in making in an account or other document an entry which is or may be misleading, false or deceptive in a material particular, or who omits or concurs in omitting a material particular from an account or other document, is to be treated as falsifying the account or document.

83A Falsification of documents

(1) A person must not make a false document with the intention that he or she, or another person, shall use it to induce another person to accept it as genuine, and

by reason of so accepting it to do or not to do some act to that other person's, or to another person's prejudice.

Penalty: Level 5 imprisonment (10 years maximum).

(2) A person must not use a document which is, and which he or she knows to be, false, with the intention of inducing another person to accept it as genuine, and by reason of so accepting it to do or not to do some act to that other person's, or to another person's prejudice.

Penalty: Level 5 imprisonment (10 years maximum).

(3) A person must not make a copy of a document which is, and which he or she knows to be, a false document, with the intention that he or she, or another person, shall use it to induce another person to accept it as a copy of a genuine document and by reason of so accepting it to do or not to do some act to that other person's, or to another person's prejudice.

Penalty: Level 5 imprisonment (10 years maximum).

(4) A person must not use a copy of a document which is, and which he or she knows to be, a false document, with the intention of inducing another person to accept it as a copy of a genuine document and by reason of so accepting it to do or not to do some act to that other person's, or to another person's prejudice.

Penalty: Level 5 imprisonment (10 years maximum).

(5) A person must not have in his or her custody, or under his or her control, a document which is, and which he or she knows to be, false, with the intention that the person or another shall use it to induce another person to accept it as genuine, and by reason of so accepting it to do or not to do some act to that other person's, or to another person's prejudice.

Penalty: Level 5 imprisonment (10 years maximum).

(5A) A person must not, with the intention that he or she may commit an offence against subsection (1), make, or have in his or her custody, or under his or her control, a machine or implement, or paper or other material, which is, and which he or she knows to be, specially designed or adapted for the making of a document which, if made by him or her, would be false.

Penalty: Level 5 imprisonment (10 years maximum).

(5B) A person must not, with the intention that another person may commit an offence against sub-section (1), make, or have in his or her custody, or under his or her control, a machine or implement, or paper or other material, which is, and which he or she knows to be, specially designed or adapted for the making of a document which, if made by that other person, would be false.

Penalty: Level 5 imprisonment (10 years maximum).

(5C) A person must not, without lawful excuse, make or have in his or her custody, or under his or her control, a machine or implement, or paper or other material, which is and which the person knows to be specially designed or adapted for the making of a document which, if made by him or her, would be false.

Penalty: Level 6 imprisonment (5 years maximum).

(6) For the purpose of this section, a document is false if it purports —

(a) to have been made in the form in which it is made by a person who did not in fact make it in that form; or

(b) to have been made in the form in which it is made on the authority of a person who did not in fact authorise its making in that form; or

(c) to have been made in the terms in which it is made by a person who did not in fact make it in those terms; or

(d) to have been made in the terms in which it is made on the authority of a person who did not in fact authorise its making in those terms; or

(e) to have been altered in any respect by a person who did not in fact alter it in that respect; or

(f) to have been altered in any respect on the authority of a person who did not in fact authorise the alteration in that respect; or

(g) to have been made or altered on a date on which, or at a place at which, or otherwise in circumstances in which, it was not in fact made or altered; or

(h) to have been made or altered by an existing person who did not in fact exist.

(7) For the purposes of this section, a person is to be treated as making a false document if the person alters a document so as to make it false in any respect (whether or not it is false in some other respect apart from that alteration).

(8) For the purpose of this section, an act or omission is to a person's prejudice if, and only if, it is one that, if it occurs —

(a) will result —

(i) in the person's temporary or permanent loss of property; or

(ii) in the person's being deprived of an opportunity to earn remuneration or greater remuneration; or

(iii) in the person's being deprived of an opportunity to obtain a financial advantage otherwise than by way of remuneration; or

(b) will result in any person being given an opportunity —

(i) to earn remuneration or greater remuneration from the first-mentioned person; or

(ii) to obtain a financial advantage from the first-mentioned person otherwise than by way of remuneration; or

(c) will be the result of the person's having accepted a false document as genuine, or a copy of a false document as a copy of a genuine one, in connection with the person's performance of a duty.

(9) In this section —

(a) a reference to inducing a person to accept a false document as genuine, or a copy of a false document as a copy of a genuine document, shall be read as including a reference to causing a machine to respond to the document or copy as if it were a genuine document or a copy of a genuine document, as the case may be; and

(b) if —

(i) a machine so responds to a document or copy; and

(ii) the act or omission intended to be caused by the machine's so responding is an act or omission that, if it were an act or omission of a person, would be to a person's prejudice within the meaning of sub-section (1) —

the act or omission intended to be caused by the machine's so responding shall be deemed to be an act or omission to a person's prejudice.

(10) In proceedings for an offence against this section, if it is necessary to allege an intent to induce a person to accept a false document as genuine, or a copy of a false document as a copy of a genuine one, it is not necessary to allege that the accused intended so to induce a particular person.

8.66 Section 83A was inserted into the Crimes Act 1958 (Vic) by the Crimes (Computers) Act 1988 (Vic). See also *Kennison v Daire* (at **7.52C**). That Act also inserted a new s 9A into the Summary Offences Act 1966 (Vic), the offence of computer trespass. For discussion of these provisions, see *Director of Public Prosecutions v Murdoch* [1993] VR 406; *R v Ceylan* (2002) 4 VR 208. Offences relating to misuse of Commonwealth computers and data stored on behalf of the Commonwealth in other computers are contained in the Crimes Act 1914 (Cth) ss 76A–76F; and note *Gilmour v DPP (Cth)* (1995) 134 ALR 631.

8.67 A comprehensive set of provisions relating to computer offences was introduced into the Crimes Act 1958 (Vic) by the Crimes (Property Damage and Computer Offences) Act 2003 (Vic). The following offences were created: unauthorised access, modification or impairment of a computer function with intent to commit a serious offence (s 247B); unauthorised modification of data to cause impairment (s 247C); unauthorised impairment of electronic communication to or from a computer (s 247D); possession of data with intent to commit a serious computer offence (s 247E); producing, supplying or obtaining data with intent to commit a serious computer offence (s 247F); unauthorised access to or modification of restricted data (s 247G); unauthorised impairment of data held in computer disk, credit card or other device (s 247H); and sabotage (s 247K) and threats to sabotage (s 247L).

8.68 The offence of obtaining a financial advantage by deception (s 82) is needed to cover cases in which there is a dishonest obtaining of credit or services by deception, but the offences of theft and obtaining property by deception are not committed because there is no obtaining of 'property': for example, *R v Waterfall* [1970] QB 148 (at **8.57C**).

8.69 Section 82(1) is derived from s 16(1) of the English Theft Act 1968, with the substitution of the word 'financial' for the word 'pecuniary'. This change would appear to be of no significance. Section 16 of the English Act, however, contained a subs (2) which does not appear in the Victorian section, and which provided as follows:

> (2) The cases in which a pecuniary advantage within the meaning of this section is to be regarded as obtained for a person are cases where —
>
> (a) any debt or charge for which he makes himself liable or is or may become liable (including one not legally enforceable) is reduced or in whole or in part evaded or deferred; or

(b) he is allowed to borrow by way of overdraft or to take out any policy of insurance or annuity contract, or obtains an improvement of the terms on which he is allowed to do so; or

(c) he is given the opportunity to earn remuneration or greater remuneration in an office or employment, or to win money by betting.

8.70 That subsection caused considerable difficulties of interpretation in England, and received a great deal of criticism. For this reason, the Victorian Chief Justice's Law Reform Committee decided not to recommend its adoption. The intention of the Chief Justice's Law Reform Committee was clearly to avoid the limitations which subs (2) of the English section placed upon subs (1).

The English Criminal Law Revision Committee in its Thirteenth Report, *Section 16 of the Theft Act 1968* (1977, Cmnd 6733), proposed new legislation to replace the most criticised parts of the section. The recommendations of the committee were implemented by the Theft Act 1978 (UK). That Act repealed s 16(2)(a), and replaced it with three new offences: obtaining services by deception (Theft Act 1978 s 1); evasion of liability by deception (Theft Act 1978 s 2); and making off without payment (Theft Act 1978 s 3). The offence of obtaining a pecuniary advantage by deception remains in respect of the cases referred to in subparas (b) and (c) of s 16(2). The Australian Model Criminal Code Officers Committee in its comprehensive review of Australian criminal laws, recommended the introduction of the offence of 'making off without payment', as it was thought unlikely to be covered by the deception offences. See generally, Model Criminal Code Officers Committee, *Theft, Fraud, Bribery and Related Offences* (1995) pp 89–91, 125–39. This was enacted as s 132.6 Commonwealth Criminal Code 1995. The Commonwealth Criminal Code also enacted an offence of obtaining a financial advantage by deception (s 134.2). 'Obtaining a financial advantage' is defined as occurring when as a result of conduct a person 'obtains a financial advantage for himself or herself from another person; and … the person knows or believes that he or she is not eligible to receive that financial advantage' (s 135.2(aa) and (ab)).

8.71C Director of Public Prosecutions v Ray

[1974] AC 370

House of Lords

Lord MacDermott: My Lords, the respondent with four other young men entered a restaurant on the evening of 30 September 1971, and he and three of his companions then ordered a meal. When this order was given the respondent intended to pay for his meal. The meal was duly served and there were no complaints. But after the respondent and the others had eaten it they had a discussion and decided to run out of the restaurant without paying. Some 10 minutes later they did so while the waiter was absent in the kitchen. By then they had been almost an hour in the restaurant and, until they ran out, had maintained the demeanour of ordinary customers.

On 1 February 1972, the respondent was brought before the magistrates' court sitting at Gainsborough on an information arising out of this incident and alleging an offence under s 16(1) of the Theft Act 1968. The terms of the charge were inapt, but no point was taken about this and before your Lordships counsel for the parties agreed that, in its substance, the offence charged was that the respondent on the occasion in question had dishonestly obtained for himself by deception a pecuniary advantage, namely, the evasion of a debt of 47 pence, the price of the meal he had consumed.

The magistrates' court found that the respondent had practised a deception, and that, having made himself liable for a debt in respect of a meal, had by his deception dishonestly evaded payment. The court accordingly found the case proved, convicted the respondent and fined him £1. It subsequently stated a case for the High Court which set out the facts and findings I have mentioned and asked whether, upon a true construction of s 16 of the Theft Act 1968, the respondent was rightly convicted.

On December 19 1972, a Divisional Court (Lord Widgery CJ, Wills and Talbot JJ) answered this question in the negative. From that decision the Director of Public Prosecutions now appeals by leave to your Lordships' House.

The material parts of subs (1) and (2) of s 16 read:

> (1) A person who by any deception dishonestly obtains for himself or another any pecuniary advantage shall on conviction on indictment be liable to imprisonment for a term not exceeding five years. (2) The cases in which a pecuniary advantage within the meaning of this section is to be regarded as obtained for a person are cases where — (a) any debt or charge for which he makes himself liable or is or may become liable (including one not legally enforceable) is reduced or in whole or in part evaded or deferred; ...

Section 29(2) of the Act of 1968 provides for the summary trial of offences under s 16 with the consent of the accused and subs (3) of s 16 incorporates the meaning of 'deception' contained in subs (4) of s 15 which says that 'deception' means:

> ... any deception (whether deliberate or reckless) by words or conduct as to fact or as to law, including a deception as to the present intentions of the person using the deception or any other person.

To prove the charge against the respondent the prosecution had to show that he (i) by a deception (ii) had dishonestly (iii) obtained for himself (iv) a pecuniary advantage. The last of these ingredients no longer raises, on the facts of this appeal, the problems of interpretation which were recently considered by this House in *R v Turner* [1974] AC 357. By that decision a debt is 'evaded' even if the evasion falls short of being final or permanent and is only for the time being; and a pecuniary advantage has not to be proved in fact as it is enough if the case is brought within s 16(2)(a) or (b) or (c).

On the facts here, this means that the respondent's debt for the meal he had eaten was evaded for the purposes of subs (2)(a); and that in consequence he obtained a pecuniary advantage within the meaning of subs (1). No issue therefore arises on the ingredients I have numbered (iii) and (iv). Nor is there any controversy about ingredient (ii).

If the respondent obtained a pecuniary advantage as described he undoubtedly did so dishonestly. The case is thus narrowed to ingredient (i) and that leaves two questions for consideration. First, do the facts justify a finding that the respondent practised a deception? And secondly, if he did, was his evasion of the debt obtained by that deception?

The first of these questions involves nothing in the way of words spoken or written. If there was deception on the part of the respondent it was by his conduct in the course of an extremely common form of transaction which, because of its nature, leaves much to be implied from conduct. Another circumstance affecting the ambit of this question lies in the fact that, looking only to the period after the meal had been eaten and the respondent and his companions had decided to evade payment, there is nothing that I can find in the discernible conduct of the respondent which would suffice in itself to show that he was then practising a deception. No doubt he and the others stayed in their seats until the waiter went into the kitchen and while doing so gave all the appearance of ordinary customers. But, in my opinion, nothing in this or in anything else which occurred after the change of intention went far enough to afford proof of deception. The picture, as I see it, presented by this last stage of the entire transaction, is simply that of a group which had decided to evade payment and were awaiting the opportunity to do so.

There is, however, no sound reason that I can see for restricting the inquiry to this final phase. One cannot, so to speak, draw a line through the transaction at the point where the intention changed and search for evidence of deception only in what happened before that or only in what happened after that. In my opinion the transaction must for this purpose be regarded in its entirety, beginning with the respondent entering the restaurant and ordering his meal and ending with his running out without paying. The different stages of the transaction are all linked and it would be quite unrealistic to treat them in isolation.

Starting, then, at the beginning one finds in the conduct of the respondent in entering and ordering his meal evidence that he impliedly represented that he had the means and the intention of paying for it before he left. That the respondent did make such a representation was not in dispute and in the absence of evidence to the contrary it would be difficult to reach a different conclusion. If this representation had then been false and matters had proceeded thereafter as they did (but without any change of intention) a conviction for the offence charged would, in my view, have had ample material to support it. But as the representation when originally made in this case was not false there was therefore no deception at that point. Then the meal is served and eaten and the intention to evade the debt replaces the intention to pay. Did this change of mind produce a deception?

My Lords, in my opinion it did. I do not base this conclusion merely on the change of mind that had occurred for that in itself was not manifest at the time and did not amount to 'conduct' on the part of the respondent. But it did falsify the representation which had already been made because that initial representation must, in my view, be regarded not as something then spent and past but as a continuing representation which remained alive and operative and had already resulted in the respondent and his defaulting companions being taken on trust and treated as ordinary, honest customers. It covered the whole transaction up to and including payment and must therefore, in my opinion, be considered as continuing and still active at the time of the change of mind. When that happened, with the respondent taking (as might be expected) no step to bring the change to notice, he practised, to my way of thinking, a deception just as real and just as dishonest as would have been the case if his intention all along had been to go without paying.

Holding for these reasons that the respondent practised a deception, I turn to what I have referred to as the second question. Was the respondent's evasion of the debt obtained by that deception?

I think the material before the justices was enough to show that it was. The obvious effect of the deception was that the respondent and his associates were treated as they had been previously, that is to say as ordinary, honest customers whose conduct did not excite suspicion or call for precautions. In consequences the waiter was off his guard and vanished into the kitchen. That gave the respondent the opportunity of running out without hindrance and he took it. I would therefore answer this second question in the affirmative.

I would, accordingly, allow the appeal and restore the conviction.

Lord Reid [dissenting]: If a person induces a supplier to accept an order for goods or services by a representation of fact, that representation must be held to be a continuing representation lasting until the goods or services are supplied. Normally it would not last any longer. A restaurant supplies both goods and services: it supplies food and drink and the facilities for consuming them. Customers normally remain for a short time after consuming their meal, and I think that it can properly be held that any representation express or implied made with a view of obtaining a meal lasts until the departure of the customers in the normal course.

In my view, where a new customer orders a meal in a restaurant, he must be held to make an implied representation that he can and will pay for it before he leaves. In the present case the accused must be held to have made such a representation. But when he made it it was not dishonest: he thought he would be able to borrow money from one of his companions.

After the meal had been consumed the accused changed his mind. He decided to evade payment. So he and his companions remained seated where they were for a short time until the waiter left the room and then ran out of the restaurant.

Did he thereby commit an offence against s 16 of the Theft Act 1968? It is admitted, and rightly admitted, that if the waiter had not been in the room when he changed his mind and he had immediately run out he would not have committed an offence. Why does his sitting still for a short time in the presence of the waiter make all the difference?

The section requires evasion of his obligation to pay. That is clearly established by his running out without paying. Secondly, it requires dishonesty: that is admitted. There would have been both evasion and dishonesty if he had changed his mind and run out while the waiter was absent.

The crucial question in this case is whether there was evasion 'by any deception'. Clearly there could be no deception until the accused changed his mind. I agree with the following quotation from the judgment of Buckley J in *Re London and Globe Finance Corporation Ltd* [1903] 1 Ch 728 and 732:

> To deceive is, I apprehend, to induce a man to believe that a thing is true which is false, and which the person practising the deceit knows or believes to be false.

So the accused, after he changed his mind, must have done something intended to induce the waiter to believe that he still intended to pay before he left. Deception, to my mind, implies something positive. It is quite true that a man intending to deceive can build up a situation in which his silence is as eloquent as an express statement. But what did the accused do here to create such a situation? He merely sat still.

...

Deception is an essential ingredient of the offence. Dishonest evasion of an obligation to pay is not enough. I cannot see that there was, in fact, any more than that in this case. I agree with the Divisional Court [1973] 1 WLR 317 at 232:

> His plan was totally lacking in the subtlety of deception and to argue that his remaining in the room until the coast was clear amounted to a representation to the waiter is to introduce artificiality which should have no place in the Act.

I would therefore dismiss this appeal.

[**Lord Morris** and **Lord Pearson** delivered separate judgments agreeing with **Lord MacDermott**. **Lord Hodson** delivered a separate judgment agreeing with **Lord Reid**. Appeal allowed and conviction restored.]

8.72C R v Kovacs

[1974] 1 All ER 1236
Court of Appeal (Criminal Division) (UK)

[The accused's account with her bank was overdrawn. The bank wrote to her informing her of this and stating that no further cheques drawn by her would be met. Shortly afterwards, an official of the bank called on her and asked for the return of her chequebook and a cheque card which had been issued to her. She said they were not in her possession. Shortly afterwards, she used cheques drawn on her bank and her cheque card to purchase a railway ticket and a dog. In consequence of the undertaking by the bank in the cheque card, the bank was bound to meet the cheques and the accused's overdraft was increased accordingly. She was convicted of obtaining from the bank a pecuniary advantage by deception and appealed to the Court of Appeal.]

Lawton LJ [reading the judgment of the court]: The appellant's counsel accepted that as a result of his client's conduct she had increased her overdraft by the amounts of the two cheques without the consent and contrary to the intentions of the bank, but he submitted that those results had been brought about by the deception of the railway booking clerk and the pet shop owner, not of the bank. The railway booking clerk and the pet shop owner had been deceived because the appellant in presenting the cheque card with her cheque had represented that she was entitled to be in possession of it and to use it.

When the bank issued the cheque card to the appellant they put her into possession of a document which was an undertaking by them to any person to whom she showed it that they would honour her cheque subject to certain conditions. No question arises in this case whether these conditions had been complied with. This meant that if she was overdrawn on her account when she used her cheque card, she would be allowed by the bank to overdraw further to the extent of the cheque covered by it. She was obtaining a pecuniary advantage as defined by s 16(2)(b) of the Theft Act 1968.

The next question is — how did she obtain this pecuniary advantage? On the facts the answer is clear, namely, by inducing the railway booking clerk and the pet shop owner to believe that she was entitled to use the cheque card when she was not. As a result of this deception they both accepted payment by cheques which the bank was bound to honour pursuant to its undertaking as set out on the face of the cheque card.

In our judgment, the loss suffered by the bank was the result of the appellant's deception of the railway booking clerk and the pet shop owner. Section 16(1) does not provide either expressly or by implication that the person deceived must suffer any loss arising from the deception. What does have to be proved is that the accused by deception obtained for himself or another a pecuniary advantage. What there must be is a causal connection between the deception used and the pecuniary advantage obtained. There was such a connection in this case.

[Appeal dismissed.]

8.73C

R v Lambie

[1982] AC 449; [1981] 2 All ER 776

House of Lords

Lord Roskill: My Lords, on 20 April 1977 the respondent was issued by Barclays Bank Ltd ('the bank') with a Barclaycard ('the card'). That card was what today is commonly known as a credit card. It was issued subject to the Barclaycard current conditions of use, and it was an express condition of its issue that it should be used only within the respondent's credit limit. That credit limit was £200 as the respondent well knew, since that figure had been notified to her in writing when the card was issued. The then current conditions of use included an undertaking by the respondent, as its holder, to return the card to the bank on request. No complaint was, or indeed could be, made of the respondent's use of the card until 18 November 1977. Between that date and 5 December 1977 she used the card for at least 24 separate transactions, thereby incurring a debt of some £533. The bank became aware of this debt and thereupon sought to recover the card. On 6 December 1977 the respondent agreed to return the card on 7 December 1977. She did not, however, do so. By 15 December 1977 she had used the card for at least 43 further transactions, incurring a total debt to the bank of £1005.26.

My Lords, on 15 December 1977 the respondent entered into the transaction out of which this appeal arises. She visited a Mothercare shop in Luton. She produced the card to a departmental manager at Mothercare named Miss Rounding. She selected goods worth £10.35. Miss Rounding completed the voucher, checked that the card was current in date, that it was not on the current stop list and that the respondent's signature on the voucher corresponded with her signature on the card. Thereupon, the respondent took away the goods which she had selected. In due course, Mothercare sent the voucher to the bank and were paid £10.35 less the appropriate commission charged by the bank. On 19 December 1977 the respondent returned the card to the bank.

My Lords, at her trial at the Crown Court at Bedford on 1 and 2 August 1979 before his Honour Judge Counsell and a jury, the respondent faced two charges of obtaining a pecuniary advantage by deception contrary to s 16(1) of the Theft Act 1968. These were specimen charges. The first related to an alleged offence on 5 December 1977 and the second to the events which took place at the Mothercare shop at Luton which I have just related. The particulars of each charge were that she dishonestly obtained for herself a pecuniary advantage 'namely, the evasion of a debt for which she then made herself liable by deception, namely, by false representations that she was authorised to use a Barclaycard ... to obtain goods to the value of £10.35'.

The jury acquitted the respondent on the first charge. She was, however, convicted on the second. The evidence of dishonesty in relation to the Mothercare transaction which was the subject of the second charge was overwhelming, and before your Lordships' House counsel for the respondent did not seek to suggest otherwise. Presumably the acquittal on the first count was because the jury were not certain that at the earlier date, 5 December 1977, the respondent was acting dishonestly.

My Lords, during the hearing in this House your Lordships inquired of counsel for the appellant prosecutor why no count of obtaining property by deception on 15 December 1977 contrary to s 15 of the Theft Act 1968 had been included in the indictment. Your Lordships were told that such a charge had indeed been preferred at the magistrates' court during the committal proceedings but had been rejected by the magistrates on a submission made on behalf of the respondent during those proceedings. My Lords, if this be so, I find it difficult to see on what basis such a submission could properly have succeeded, or what defence there could have been had such a charge been the subject of a further count in the indictment once the jury were convinced, as they were, of the respondent's dishonesty on 15 December 1977. Had that course been taken, the complications which in due course led to the Court of Appeal, Criminal Division, quashing the conviction on the second count, and consequently, to the prosecutor's appeal to this House, with your Lordships' leave, following the grant of a certificate by the Court of Appeal, Criminal Division, would all have been avoided. But the course of adding a count charging an offence against s 15 of the Theft Act 1968 was not followed, and accordingly your Lordships have now to determine whether the Court of Appeal, Criminal Division, was correct in quashing the conviction on the second count. If it was, then, as that court recognised in the concluding paragraph of its judgment, a gateway to successful fraud has been opened for the benefit of the dishonest who in circumstances such as the present cannot be proceeded against and punished at least for offences against s 16 of the Theft Act 1968. ...

My Lords, at the close of the case for the prosecution, counsel for the respondent invited the judge to withdraw both counts from the jury on, it seems from reading the judge's clear ruling on this submission, two grounds: first, that as a matter of law there was no evidence from which a jury might properly draw the inference that the presentation of the card in the circumstances I have described was a representation by the respondent that she was authorised by the bank to use the card to create a contract to which the bank would be a party, and, second, that as a matter of law there was no evidence from which a jury might properly infer that Miss Rounding was induced by any representation which the respondent might have made to allow the transaction to be completed and the respondent to obtain the goods. The foundation for this latter submission was that it was the existence of the agreement between Mothercare and the bank that was the reason for Miss Rounding allowing the transaction to be completed and the goods to be taken by the respondent, since Miss Rounding knew of the arrangement with the bank, so that Mothercare was in any event certain of payment. It was not, it was suggested, any representation by the respondent which induced Miss Rounding to complete the transaction and to allow the respondent to take the goods.

My Lords, the judge rejected these submissions. He was clearly right to do so, as indeed was conceded in argument before your Lordships' House, if the decision of this House in *Metropolitan Police Comr v Charles* [1976] 3 All ER 112; [1977] AC 177 is of direct application. In that appeal this House was concerned with the dishonest use, not as in the present appeal of a credit card, but of a cheque card. The appellant defendant was charged and convicted on two counts of obtaining a pecuniary advantage by deception, contrary to s 16 of the Theft Act 1968. The Court of Appeal, Criminal Division, and your Lordships' House both upheld those convictions. Your Lordships unanimously held that where a drawer of a cheque which is accepted in return for goods, services or cash, uses a cheque card he represents to the payee that he has the actual authority of the bank to enter on its behalf into the contract expressed on the card that it would honour the cheque on presentation for payment.

My Lords, I venture to quote in their entirety three paragraphs from the speech of my noble and learned friend Lord Diplock ([1976] 3 All ER 112 at 114; [1977] AC 177 at 182–3) which, as I venture to think, encapsulate the reasoning of all those members of your Lordships' House who delivered speeches:

> When a cheque card is brought into the transaction, it still remains the fact that all the payee is concerned with is that the cheque should be honoured by the bank. I do not think that the fact that a cheque card is used necessarily displaces the representation to be implied from the act of drawing the cheque which has just been mentioned. It is, however, likely to displace that representation at any rate as the main inducement to the payee to take the cheque, since the use of the cheque card in connection with the transaction gives to the payee a direct contractual right against the bank itself to payment on presentment, provided that the use of the card by the drawer to bind the bank to pay the cheque was within the actual or ostensible authority conferred on him by the bank.
>
> By exhibiting to the payee a cheque card containing the undertaking by the bank to honour cheques drawn in compliance with the conditions endorsed on the back and drawing the cheque accordingly, the drawer represents to the payee that

> he has actual authority from the bank to make a contract with the payee on the bank's behalf that it will honour the cheque on presentment for payment.
>
> It was submitted on behalf of the accused that there is no need to imply a representation that the drawer's authority to bind the bank was actual and not merely ostensible, since ostensible authority alone would suffice to create a contract with the payee that was binding on the bank; and the drawer's possession of the cheque card and the cheque book with the bank's consent would be enough to constitute his ostensible authority. So, the submission goes, the only representation needed to give business efficacy to the transaction would be true. This argument stands the doctrine of ostensible authority on its head. What creates ostensible authority in a person who purports to enter into a contract as agent for a principal is a representation made to the other party that he has the actual authority of the principal for whom he claims to be acting to enter into the contract on that person's behalf. If (1) the other party has believed the representation and on the faith of that belief has acted on it and (2) the person represented to be his principal has so conducted himself towards that other party as to be estopped from denying the truth of the representation then, and only then, is he bound by the contract purportedly made on his behalf. The whole foundation of liability under the doctrine of ostensible authority is a representation, believed by the person to whom it is made, that the person claiming to contract as agent for a principal has the actual authority of the principal to enter into the contract on his behalf.

If one substitutes in the passage the words 'to honour the voucher' for the words 'to pay the cheque' it is not easy to see why *mutatis mutandis* the entire passages are not equally applicable to the dishonest misuse of credit cards as to the dishonest misuse of cheque cards.

But the Court of Appeal in a long and careful judgment delivered by Cumming-Bruce LJ felt reluctantly impelled to reach a different conclusion. The crucial passage in the judgment which the learned Lord Justice delivered reads thus (at [All ER] 339–40; [WLR] 86–7):

> We would pay tribute to the lucidity with which the learned judge presented to the jury the law which the House of Lords had declared in relation to deception in a cheque card transaction. If that analysis can be applied to this credit card deception, the summing up is faultless. But, in our view, there is a relevant distinction between the situation described in *Metropolitan Police Comr v Charles* and the situation devised by Barclays Bank for transactions involving use of their credit cards. By their contract with the bank, Mothercare had bought from the bank the right to sell goods to Barclaycard holders without regard to the question whether the customer was complying with the terms of the contract between the customer and the bank. By her evidence Miss Rounding made it perfectly plain that she made no assumption about the appellant's credit standing at the bank. As she said: 'The company rules exist because of the company's agreement with Barclaycard.' The flaw in the logic is, in our view, demonstrated by the way in

> which the judge put the question of the inducement of Miss Rounding to the jury: 'Is that a reliance by her, Miss Rounding of Mothercare, on the presentation of the card as being due authority within the limits as at that time as with count 1?' In our view, the evidence of Miss Rounding could not found a verdict that necessarily involved a finding of fact that Miss Rounding was induced by a false representation that the appellant's credit standing at the bank gave her authority to use the card.

I should perhaps mention, for the sake of clarity, that the person referred to as the appellant in that passage is the present respondent.

It was for that reason that the Court of Appeal, Criminal Division, allowed the appeal, albeit with hesitation and reluctance. That court accordingly certified the following point of law as of general public importance, namely:

> In view of the proved differences between a cheque card transaction and a credit card transaction, were we right in distinguishing this case from that of *Metropolitan Police Comr v Charles* [1976] 3 All ER 112; [1977] AC 177 on the issue of inducement?

My Lords, as the appellant says in his printed case, the Court of Appeal, Criminal Division, laid too much emphasis on the undoubted, but to my mind irrelevant, fact that Miss Rounding said she made no assumption about the respondent's credit standing with the bank. They reasoned from the absence of assumption that there was no evidence from which the jury could conclude that she was 'induced by a false representation that the [respondent's] credit standing at the bank gave her authority to use the card'. But, my Lords, with profound respect to Cumming-Bruce LJ, that is not the relevant question. Following the decision of this house in *Charles,* it is in my view clear that the representation arising from the presentation of a credit card has nothing to do with the respondent's credit standing at the bank but is a representation of actual authority to make the contract with, in this case, Mothercare on the bank's behalf that the bank will honour the voucher on presentation. On that view, the existence and terms of the agreement between the bank and Mothercare are irrelevant, as is the fact that Mothercare, because of that agreement, would look to the bank for payment.

That being the representation to be implied from the respondent's actions and use of the credit card, the only remaining question is whether Miss Rounding was induced by that representation to complete the transaction and allow the respondent to take away the goods. My Lords, if she had been asked whether, had she known the respondent was acting dishonestly and, in truth, had no authority whatever from the bank to use the credit card in this way, she (Miss Rounding) would have completed the transaction, only one answer is possible: 'No.' Had an affirmative answer been given to this question, Miss Rounding would, of course, have become a participant in furtherance of the respondent's fraud and a conspirator with her to defraud both Mothercare and the bank. Leading counsel for the respondent was ultimately constrained, rightly as I think, to admit that had that question been asked of Miss Rounding and answered, as it must have been, in the negative, this appeal must succeed. But both he and his learned junior strenuously argued that, as

Lord Edmund-Davies pointed out in his speech in *Charles* [1976] 3 All ER 112 at 122; [1977] AC 177 at 192–3, the question whether a person is or is not induced to act in a particular way by a dishonest representation is a question of fact, and, since what they claimed to be the crucial question had not been asked of Miss Rounding, there was no adequate proof of the requisite inducement. In her deposition, Miss Rounding stated, no doubt with complete truth, that she only remembered this particular transaction with the respondent because someone subsequently came and asked her about it after it had taken place. My Lords, credit card frauds are all too frequently perpetrated, and if conviction of offenders for offences against s 15 or s 16 of the Theft Act 1968 can only be obtained if the prosecution are able in each case to call the person on whom the fraud was immediately perpetrated to say that he or she positively remembered the particular transaction and, had the truth been known, would never have entered into that supposedly well-remembered transaction, the guilty would often escape conviction. In some cases, of course, it may be possible to adduce such evidence if the particular transaction is well remembered. But where as in the present case no one could reasonably be expected to remember a particular transaction in detail, and the inference of inducement may well be in all the circumstances quite irresistible, I see no reason in principle why it should not be left to the jury to decide, on the evidence in the case as a whole, whether the inference is in truth irresistible as to my mind it is in the present case. In this connection it is to be noted that the respondent did not go into the witness box to give evidence from which that inference might conceivably have been rebutted.

My Lords, in this respect I find myself in agreement with what was said by Humphreys J giving the judgment of the Court of Criminal Appeal in *R v Sullivan* (1945) 30 Cr App R 132 at 136:

> It is, we think, undoubtedly good law that the question of the inducement acting upon the mind of the person who may be described as the prosecutor is not a matter which can only be proved by the direct evidence of the witness. It can be, and very often is, proved by the witness being asked some question which brings the answer: 'I believed that statement and that is why I parted with my money'; but it is not necessary that there should be that question and answer if the facts are such that it is patent that there was only one reason which anybody could suggest for the person alleged to have been defrauded parting with his money, and that is the false pretence, if it was a false pretence.

It is true that in *R v Laverty* [1970] 3 All ER 432 at 434 Lord Parker CJ said that the Court of Appeal, Criminal Division, was anxious not to extend the principle in *Sullivan* further than was necessary. Of course, the Crown must always prove its case and one element which will always be required to be proved in these cases is the effect of the dishonest representation on the mind of the person to whom it is made. But I see no reason why in cases such as the present, where what Humphreys J called the direct evidence of the witness is not and cannot reasonably be expected to be available, reliance on a dishonest representation cannot be sufficiently established by proof of facts from which an irresistible inference of such reliance can be drawn.

My Lords, I would answer the certified question in the negative and would allow the appeal and restore the conviction of the respondent on the second count in the indictment which she faced at the Crown Court.

[**Lord Diplock, Lord Fraser, Lord Russell** and **Lord Keith** agreed with **Lord Roskill**. Appeal allowed and conviction restored. See also *R v Jenkins* (2002) 6 VR 81.]

8.74C

Parsons v R

(1999) 190 CLR 619; 160 ALR 531
High Court of Australia

[The accused had induced a number of newsagents to give him cheques by false representations that the company for which he worked would provide, for each of them, substantial quantities of cheap copy paper. Some of the cheques were bank cheques made out to the company and others were cheques drawn in favour of the company on the accounts of the newsagents. The accused was convicted of obtaining property by deception in respect of both classes of cheque and the convictions upheld by the Victorian Court of Appeal. On appeal to the High Court.]

[Footnotes to the extract appear at the end of the extract.]

Gleeson CJ, **Gaudron**, **McHugh**, **Gummow** and **Hayne JJ**:

The *Cheques Act 1986*

Before further considering the application of s 81 of the Crimes Act and the supporting definitions to the facts, it is convenient to consider the legal relationships for which the *Cheques Act* (Cth) ('the Cheques Act')[1] provided in respect of the various cheques and bank cheques, the dishonest obtaining of which was the subject of the counts to which the appellant pleaded guilty.

It is convenient first to deal with the particular character of bank cheques. In *Fabre v Ley*,[2] reference was made in the joint judgment of the whole Court to the practice in Australia for a considerable number of years of bankers issuing what have become known as 'bank cheques' at the request of customers who have some reason to provide cash or its equivalent in commercial transactions.[3] Their Honours said:[4]

> These are drafts drawn by a bank usually on itself but occasionally upon another bank: in either case they are issued in the form of cheques. It has been questioned whether a draft of this kind is a cheque within such a provision as s 78 of the *Bills of Exchange Act 1986*.[5] The question arose because the definition of cheque incorporates that of bill of exchange and a cheque drawn by a bank upon itself is not 'addressed by one person to another' within the latter definition (which is now contained in s 8(1) of the Bills of Exchange Act): see *McClintock v Union Bank of Australia Ltd*.[6] In 1932, s 88A was inserted in the Bills of Exchange Act making a banker's draft payable on demand drawn by or on behalf of a bank upon itself a

cheque for the purposes of the crossed cheque provisions of the Bills of Exchange Act. However, although it may be more accurate to refer to a bill of exchange drawn by a bank on itself as a banker's draft, the nomenclature 'bank cheque' is, and has for long been, used in Australia to describe instruments of this kind.

The Bills of Exchange Act has not, since the Cheques Act came into operation, applied to an instrument to which the Cheques Act applies.[7] However, s 5(1) of the Cheques Act provides that, with certain specified exceptions, and unless the contrary intention appears, a reference in that statute to a cheque includes a reference to a bank cheque or a bank draft.[8]

Secondly, the cheques themselves were, within the meaning of the definition in s 10 of the Cheques Act, unconditional orders in writing addressed by the newsagent concerned to its bank, signed by the newsagent and requiring the bank to pay on demand a sum certain in money. The cheques were not wanting in any material particular necessary to render them complete on their face, and so were not inchoate instruments: s 18. Rather, they were bearer cheques and thus were to be taken to require the bank to pay the sum ordered to be paid by the cheques to bearer: s 22.

Thirdly, the drawing of the cheques did not of itself operate as an assignment of funds available in the hands of the drawee bank for the payment of the cheque: s 88. As indicated by Barwick CJ in *Croton v R*,[9] the right of the drawer to recover from the bank the balance standing to the credit of that party in the account with the bank was a chose in action but the effect of s 88 is to emphasise that the drawing of a cheque does not of itself operate as an assignment of that chose in action or of part thereof. Rather, the generally accepted concept of a cheque is that of a 'mandate', addressed by the drawer to the banker directing the banker to effect a *pro tanto* satisfaction of the indebtedness of the banker to the drawer by honouring the cheque drawn on the banker.[10] In this sense, a cheque 'is merely a mandate, not a transfer of rights'.[11]

Fourthly, in its character as such a mandate, the bearer cheques, once drawn, and even in advance of delivery, had intrinsic value as instruments whereby the sums they specified might be drawn from the banks in question.[12]

Fifthly, arising out of the drawing of the cheque, there was, by force of the Cheques Act (ss 25, 71), a contract, incomplete and revocable until delivery, whereby the drawer, the newsagent in question, undertook to compensate the holder or an indorser of the cheque who was compelled to pay it if it were dishonoured when duly presented for payment.[13] Further, s 76 provides that, where a cheque (including by dint of s 5(1) a bank cheque) is dishonoured, the holder, being the bearer in respect of cheques payable to bearer, may recover as damages, from any person liable on the cheque, the face value of the cheque and the amount of interest that in accordance with regulations made under the Cheques Act is payable in respect of that sum.[14]

In *R v Preddy*,[15] Lord Goff of Chieveley said:

> I start with the time when the cheque form is simply a piece of paper in the possession of the drawer. He makes out a cheque in favour of the payee, and delivers it to him. The cheque then constitutes a chose in action of the payee, which he can enforce against the drawer.

The reference in that passage to the chose in action of the payee which can be enforced against the drawer is to be understood, in the Australian context, by reference to ss 25 and 71 of the Cheques Act. However, as indicated in the points made above, a cheque has characteristics which render it more than a chose in action held by the payee against the drawer. The submissions by the appellant rested upon a contrary assumption, and that should not be accepted in construing s 81 of the Crimes Act.

Moreover, the Cheques Act speaks, for example in s 116, of an action or proceeding being brought in a court 'on a cheque', and provision is made in s 116 whereby, on terms, the court may order that the loss or destruction of the cheque not be set up as a defence. Further, it is the cheque as an item in specie which is essential to the operation of negotiability. So, in the present case, every cheque, including any bank cheque, might be transferred by negotiation until it was discharged, the transfer being from the holder to another person in such manner as to constitute that other person the holder within the meaning of the Act (ss 39, 40)[16] ...

Section 81(1) of the Crimes Act and the present case

The contracts arising by operation of ss 25 and 71 of the Cheques Act in respect of the bank cheques had been rendered complete and irrevocable upon their delivery to the newsagent by whom they had been purchased. There is thus no scope for any argument that when, in turn, possession and control of the bank cheques was taken by the appellant there was no pre-existing 'chose in action' which the holder could enforce against the drawer, here the bank of the newsagent concerned.

As to the cheques, at the time of their delivery to the appellant by the newsagents who had drawn them on their banks, the law of negotiable instruments now represented in the Cheques Act imparted to the cheques various legal characteristics giving them then a value beyond what otherwise was their quality as mere pieces of paper. The cheques, being complete in form, contained a mandate by the respective drawer to its bank to reduce the credit of its account by payment in favour of a person answering the statutory description of a holder. Further, arising out of the drawing of the cheques, there was, albeit incomplete and revocable until delivery, the contract by the drawer referred to in ss 25 and 71 of the Cheques Act.

It follows that both the bank cheques and the cheques, at the time they were, by a deception dishonestly obtained by the appellant, were property within the meaning of the definition in s 71(1) of the Crimes Act. These instruments were property belonging to the newsagents within the meaning of s 71(2) because the newsagents had possession or control of them and, in accordance with the above analysis, also had proprietary rights or interests therein.

Possession or control of these instruments was 'obtained' by the appellant and the terms of s 81(2) make it plain that it is no denial of that proposition to say (if it had been the case) that the appellant did so 'for' Canyon Bay into whose account with the ANZ Bank the instruments were deposited. Further, the characteristics which the Cheques Act and the law with respect to conversion attached to the instruments in the hands of a bearer would support the conclusion that there was also an obtaining of what in s 81(2) is called 'ownership'.

However, the appellant submitted that he could not have had the intention of permanently depriving the newsagents of these instruments so that, on that ground alone, the elements of the offence in s 81(1) were not satisfied. The appellant founded this submission upon the observation in *R v Preddy*:[17]

> [T]here can have been no intention on the part of the payee permanently to deprive the drawer of the cheque form, which would on presentation of the cheque for payment be returned to the drawer via his bank.

The appellant here proceeded upon an assumption as to an identity between banking law and practice in England and in Australia. As to the former, in *Charles v Blackwell,* Cockburn CJ said:[18]

> A cheque taken in payment remains the property of the payee only so long as it remains unpaid. When paid the banker is entitled to keep it as a voucher till his account with his customer is settled. After that, the drawer is entitled to it as a voucher between him and the payee.

Earlier, in *R v Watts*, Wilde CJ had said:[19]

> It has always been held that a cheque when paid belongs to the drawer, and that he has a right to have it delivered up to him; and on this ground notice to produce a cheque, which had not been returned from the banker, was held sufficient to warrant the admittance of secondary evidence of its contents.

However, in Australia, banks have asserted the right to retain possession of paid cheques, apparently on the footing that this is an ordinary incident in this country of the relationship between banker and customer.[20] In any event, it is not the practice that cheques be returned, after they have been honoured, to the drawer by the drawer's bank.

Section 68 of the Cheques Act makes provision with respect to the matter which, for present purposes, is inconclusive. Once the drawee bank obtains possession of the relevant cheque, it must retain it unless possession is claimed by the drawer. In that case a copy must be kept for seven years after the date of the cheque: s 68(3A).[21] However, that obligation is stated not to be taken to affect any right that the drawer has against the drawee bank to possession of the cheque: s 68(5)(a).

Accordingly, it may be doubted whether the appellant could deny any intention on his part permanently to deprive the newsagents of the cheques on the footing that, on their presentation for payment by the ANZ Bank as collecting bank for Canyon Bay, the cheques would in the ordinary course be returned to the newsagents by their banks. Nor, in any event, would the English law and practice upon which the appellant relies appear applicable to the bank cheques which he obtained.

Further, as Tadgell JA pointed out in the Court of Appeal:[22]

> The slip of paper that is returned to the drawer's bank has ceased to be a valuable security.

Rather, it has become a record of what the valuable security was.

Applying this reasoning to the terms of s 81(1) of the and their application to the instruments with which this case is concerned, the intention Crimes Act, spoken of in that provision is one of permanently depriving 'the other', namely the newsagents, of those instruments by putting them to a use which will leave them spent and deprived of those characteristics which led or significantly contributed to their classification as property.[23]

[Appeal dismissed.]

Notes:

1. The short title to the Cheques Act was originally the *Cheques and Payment Orders Act* (Cth) but by force of s 3 and item 1 of Pt 1 of Sch to the *Cheques and Payments Orders Amendment Act 1998* (Cth) ('the Cheques Amendment Act') the statute is now to be known as the *Cheques Act 1986* (Cth).
2. (1972) 127 CLR 665.
3. (1972) 127 CLR 665 at 670.
4. (1972) 127 CLR 665 at 670–1. See also Weerasooria, 'The Australian Bank Cheque — Some Legal Aspects' (1976) 2 *Monash University Law Review* 180.
5. Section 78 of the *Bills of Exchange Act 1909* (Cth) ('the Bills of Exchange Act') identifies a cheque as a bill of exchange drawn on a banker payable on demand.
6. (1920) 20 SR (NSW) 494.
7. Sections 2 and 3 of the Bills of Exchange Amendment Act 1986 (Cth).
8. Section 5 was repealed on 1 December 1998 and a fresh s 5 substituted by s 3 and item 13 of Pt 1 of Sch 1 of the *Cheques Amendment Act* but nothing turns upon this change for present purposes.
9. (1967) 117 CLR 326 at 330–1.
10. See Weaver and Craigie, The Law Relating to Banker and Customer in Australia, vol 2, para 9.400.
11. Tyree, *Banking Law in Australia*, 3rd ed (1998), §5.92.
12. cf *Morison v London County and Westminster Bank Ltd* [1914] 3 KB 356 at 379.
13. Section 3(1) defines 'holder' as meaning:
    (a) in relation to a cheque payable to order — the payee or an indorsee who is in possession of the cheque as payee or indorsee, as the case may be; and
    (b) in relation to a cheque payable to bearer — the bearer.
14. The entitlement to interest is subject, by s 76(2), to the power of the court, if it be of opinion that justice so requires, to direct that the interest be withheld in whole or in part. Damages recoverable under s 76 are deemed to be liquidated damages: s 76(3).
15. [1996] AC 815 at 835. See also at 836–7.
16. Sections 39 and 40 are not included among those provisions specified in s 5(1) as not to be read as referring to bank cheques.
17. [1996] AC 815 at 836–7.
18. (1877) 2 CPD 151 at 162–3.
19. (1850) 19 LJMC 192 at 195 (*arguendo*). See also *Lever v Maguire* [1928] VLR 262 at 264.
20. See Tyree, *Banking Law in Australia*, 3rd ed (1998), §5.121.

21. Section 68(3A) was repealed on 1 December 1998 and a fresh s 68(3A) substituted by s 3 and item 24 of Sch 2 to the Cheques Amendment Act but nothing turns upon this change for present purposes.
22. [1998] 2 VR 478 at 491; (1997) 97 A Crim R 267 at 281.
23. cf J C Smith, 'Obtaining Cheques by Deception or Theft' (1997) *Criminal Law Review* 396 at 403–5.

8.75C R v Vasic

(2005) 11 VR 380

Court of Appeal, Supreme Court of Victoria

[The accused was charged with obtaining financial advantage by deception. The accused wrote a cheque for $32,701.23 in pretended payment of an existing debt, knowing the cheque would be dishonoured. Following the presentation of the Crown case, counsel submitted that there was no case to answer. That submission was based on the argument that the mere presentation of a valueless cheque in satisfaction of an antecedent financial obligation does not, without more, constitute the obtaining of a financial advantage. The judge rejected the submission and held that there was a case to answer. The accused thereupon pleaded guilty. The accused sought leave to appeal contending that the judge was wrong in law in holding there was a case to answer.]

[Footnotes to the extract appear at the end of the extract.]

Nettle JA:

The decision below

In his reasons for ruling, Judge Davey said:

> Mr Danos submitted that an element of the offence was not made out. He submitted that although there was evidence of dishonesty in his client's conduct and of deception there was no evidence on which a jury, properly instructed, could find that the accused had obtained a financial advantage. In support of his submission he relied upon two decisions … [*R v Locker*[1] and *Fisher v Bennett*]
>
> The Victorian legislation is very different from the English Act and I must say, after having considered [*R v Locker*], I have not found it of any assistance to me. The second decision *[Fisher v Bennett]* … was an appeal against conviction in the Canberra Magistrates' Court. The legislation there is in very similar terms to the Victorian Act. In that case [Miles CJ] concluded that in the absence of evidence that the appellant's position was improved by the giving of the valueless cheque to the creditor, the prosecution failed.
>
> With the greatest respect to [Miles CJ], I do not think that the law as it appears applied in the ACT is the law in this State. In the case of *Matthews v Fountain*[2] Gray J considered the operation and effect of s 82(1) of the Crimes Act. He held, as the headnote states:

> A person who knowingly proffers a valueless cheque in purport[ed] discharge of an antecedent debt obtains a financial advantage within the meaning of s 82 of the *Crimes Act 1958*.

He went on to say that it did not matter that the person who knowingly proffers a valueless cheque is penniless …

Justice Gray's decision was briefly considered in the Court of [Criminal] Appeal in the case of *John Richard Walsh*.[3] O'Bryan J in delivering the first judgment referred to the judgment of Gray J in *Matthews v Fountain* and stated:

> The concept of financial advantage is a simple one. It is expressed by the use of two common words, each of clear meaning,

and then went on to say and I might say he was there quoting from the judgment of Gray J:

> I agree that the words should be given their plain meaning and that no narrow construction should be given to them,

and then went on to say, and [in so doing] in my view expressed a contrary view to the opinion of Miles CJ:

> It is not to the point that the applicant might have obtained a financial advantage from the errant bank in New York. The critical question indeed an essential element of the charge laid is whether the applicant attempted to obtain a financial advantage from Westpac by his conduct.[4]

On the present facts in my view it is clear that the accused attempted to gain a financial advantage and did in my view obtain a financial advantage in the wide sense in which the term has been interpreted in both the *Matthews* decision and the *Walsh* decision. At the very least the financial advantage was the giving to the accused of further time in which to find another source of finance. In the present circumstances there is, in my view, evidence upon which a properly instructed jury could find the accused guilty of the offence.

The concept of financial advantage

In my opinion Judge Davey was right. Much of what was said by Miles CJ in *Fisher v Bennett* was based on questions posed by Professor David Lanham in his 1977 article on the meaning of financial advantage.[5] They in turn were based upon the rhetorical question posed by Lord Widgery CJ in *R v Turner*[6] as to how it can be said that a penniless man owing a debt which he has no prospect of being able to pay evades the debt by giving the creditor a worthless cheque in pretended payment of it. Miles CJ embraced the question, and the answer which it may be supposed that Lord Widgery might have given to it, as follows:

> … The reference to the financial position of the defendant [in *Matthews v Fountain*] relates to the hypothetical example of the 'penniless man' mentioned initially by Lord Widgery CJ when *Turner's* case was before the Court of Criminal Appeal at [1973] 2 All ER 828 and by Lord Reid in the House of Lords in the passage referred to above. That concept is discussed in an article in (1977) 1 *Crim LJ* 188. In that article the author, Professor Lanham, discusses the example of a

> person [scil a penniless man] who incurs a debt perfectly honestly but practises deception at a later stage in order to obtain relief from the creditor's claim. On p 93 the author observes that in a case of what he calls 'unilateral evasion' the deceitful debtor gains nothing which he could not have obtained by outright refusal to pay or by keeping out of the creditor's way, and that where the debtor passes a valueless cheque, it is hard to see what financial advantage is obtained. The example of unilateral evasion is contrasted by the author with the situation where by deception the debtor secures the agreement of the creditor to reduce or forgive the debt. I think that there is force in the author's remarks.

With respect, however, Gray J explained in *Matthews v Fountain*[7] why Lord Widgery's conception of the penniless man should be avoided for the purposes of s 82 of the Crimes Act. As Gray J said:

> ... the proposition put forward by Lord Widgery presents considerable difficulty. It is difficult to imagine a factual situation in which a creditor is offered cash but is induced by deception to take a valueless cheque. What is a 'penniless person' for this purpose? Is he a man who cannot conveniently pay the debt or one who cannot beg, borrow or steal the amount required? It is difficult to imagine a man in such depleted circumstances that he derives no financial advantage from the evasion of a debt.
>
> It is clear enough that the appellant was not, on the facts stated, a 'penniless person' in any sense. All that the facts show is that he had no funds in a particular bank account at a particular time. ...
>
> The difficulties which would flow from the adoption of Lord Widgery's formulation are touched upon in an interesting article by David Lanham, Obtaining a Financial Advantage by Deception in Victoria, [1977] 1 *Crim LJ* 188. ... The writer points out that if 'pennilessness' is available as a defence, the court would become involved in an investigation of the defendant's financial position. If he takes the defence of an intention not to pay in any event, that issue would have to be investigated.
>
> As already stated, I do not consider that these problems arise. In the commonplace situation of a debtor giving a valueless cheque to gain some time from his pursuers the debtor does, in my opinion, obtain a 'financial advantage' within the meaning of s 82.

It may also be observed in passing that the suggested 'penniless man' exception to obtaining financial advantage by deception is as flawed as a matter of economic theory as it is intractable in practice. Evidently, the idea of the exception depends upon the premise that there is no advantage to a debtor in deferring payment of a debt unless the debtor has the money or the means of obtaining the money with which to pay the debt. According to that conception of things, if a debtor has the money or the means of obtaining it, the delay affords him or her a financial advantage equal to the time value of the debt for the period of the delay; in other words, the return which the money would generate in that period or the cost of borrowing the money for that period. Conversely, if the debtor has no money and no means of obtaining it, the delay affords him nothing; for without money he has no means of obtaining a return on money and if he cannot borrow money he cannot be said to have avoided the costs of borrowing it. But as a matter of economic theory a debtor can always borrow money. In theory it is all just a matter of price, and so everyone can borrow at a price no matter what the level of their credit risk. As the economist would have it, the price elasticity of credit may be hyperbolically sensitive to borrower security, but the gradient of that function never reaches infinity.

And so it is too in reality. For in reality, in the society in which we live, there are no penniless men. Widespread and deep though poverty may be in some sections of our society, all men in it have some money or at least the ability to obtain some money, by work or by the realisation of assets or by borrowing, even at exorbitant rates, or perhaps even in the form of social security entitlements. To that extent, all men obtain a financial advantage by deferring the payment of a debt; no matter how poor they may be. They are relieved of a claim upon such money or ability to generate it as they may have, for the period of the deferral.

In the article by Professor Lanham already mentioned, reference is made[8] to an example (cited by the Criminal Law Revision Committee) of a woman who obtains forbearance by telling a debt collector falsely that her husband is off work sick. The Committee considered that the ordinary man or woman would be surprised to be told that conduct of that kind was criminal and not merely discreditable. Maybe that is so. But as at present advised I am not prepared to exclude the possibility of its criminality. It is one thing to be without the money with which to meet an obligation. Obviously, there is no offence in a debtor responding to a debt collector in those circumstances that he or she is unable to pay the debt. Furthermore, if that is the truth of the matter, and it is that fact alone which causes the creditor to give time, there is nothing necessarily criminal in the debtor embroidering the facts with a story or two as to how the debtor's state of financial embarrassment came about. But it may well be otherwise if the debtor has the money and says that he or she does not have it or, even if the debtor does not have it immediately available, he or she buys time by telling a false story as to how that situation came about. I am inclined to think that most ordinary men and women would agree that the latter as [sic] not only dishonest but possibly also fraudulent.[9]

Section 82 of the Crimes Act

Fortunately, the problem here is not as difficult. We are concerned only with the question of whether it is an offence under the *Crimes Act 1958* for s 82 of a debtor to defer the payment of a debt by giving his creditor a cheque, which the debtor knows to be worthless, in pretended payment of the debt. In my opinion that question should be answered affirmatively, just as it was by Gray J in *Matthews v Fountain*.

Section 82 of the Crimes Act was designedly based on s 16 of the Theft Act 1968 (UK), on the recommendation of the Chief Justice Law Reform Committee, with the intention that it apply to cases of common fraud involving the dishonest obtaining of credit or services.[10] As it was put in the explanatory memorandum:[11]

> [The Chief Justice's Law Reform Committee] decided to recommend the enactment of the English statute with some minor modifications; a few of these modifications

relate to matters of basic principle, but most of them are needed to take account either of the relationship between federal and state spheres of legislative authority or of the general pattern of Victoria legislation. Its decision was based on the fact that the English reform has proved highly successful in practice. The English courts have shown a determination to interpret the new provisions according to their letter and spirit, and to discourage attempts to introduce into new law the technicalities that disfigured the old. Their decisions will be readily available as precedents and guidance for our own courts. ...

Section 82 creates a new offence of obtaining a financial advantage by deception. It is needed because certain types of common fraud, involving a dishonest obtaining of another's services (for example, without any intention of paying for them), are not covered by the offence of theft (section 72) or criminal deception (section 81); since no 'property' is obtained, neither of those sections is available. It was thought undesirable, because of possible unfortunate repercussions, to deal with the problem by defining 'property' so as to include services.

Section 82 was, however, also made different to s 16 of the Theft Act in two respects, so as to overcome problems that had been found in England to result from a proscription in s 16(1) which spoke in terms of obtaining a 'pecuniary advantage' and an exhaustive definition of that expression in s 16(2).[12] The matter was explained in detail in the Committee's Report[13] and in the explanatory memorandum, as follows:

The present section [scil s 82] differs, however, in two respects from its English counterpart [s 16]. The English Act uses the phrase 'pecuniary advantage', and provides a definition for the phrase. This definition is unhappily worded, and has given rise to a set of technicalities described recently by an eminent English judge as a 'judicial nightmare.'[14] It is thought that the proposed section 82 will remove these difficulties.

Sub-section (1) defines the offence as dishonestly obtaining by deception a 'financial advantage'. This phrase is thought more apt to describe what is meant than is the phrase 'pecuniary advantage' used in the English Act; and in order to avoid a repercussion in Victoria of the 'judicial nightmare' no attempt is made to define it. The offence is, in common with all other analogous offences under the Act, declared to be felony. It carries a maximum penalty of 5 years.

Sub-section (2) applies the definition of 'deception' in section 81 to his offence.

Thus as I read the Committee's report and the explanatory memorandum,[15] 'financial advantage' was thought to be a broader notion than 'pecuniary advantage', and so to cover at least all of those things embraced in the extended definition of 'pecuniary advantage' in s 16(2) of the Theft Act, and an exhaustive definition of the kind contained in s 16(2) was eschewed lest it be taken to limit ordinary conceptions of financial advantage. If that be so, it can scarcely be doubted that s 82 was intended to have an operation as broad as s 16 of the Theft Act, if indeed not broader.[16]

At least, in as much as s 82 was enacted in the belief that 'the English reform [had] proved highly successful in practice', and with evident approval of the way in which 'the

English courts [had] shown a determination to interpret the new provisions according to their letter and spirit, and to discourage attempts to introduce into the new law the technicalities that disfigured the old' and in the hope that the English decisions would 'be readily available as precedents and guidance for our own courts', I conclude[17] it was intended that the decisions of the House of Lords in *Turner's* case and *DPP v Ray*[18] should apply as much to s 82 as they do to s 16 of the Theft Act.

[**Vincent JA** and **Cummins AJA** agreed with **Nettle JA**. Appeal dismissed.]

Notes:

1. [1971] 2 QB 321.
2. [1982] VR 1045.
3. *R v Walsh* (1990) 52 A Crim R 80 at 81.
4. See too *Murphy v R* (1987) Tas R 178 (Tas CCA) at [14] per Nettlefold J; cf. *R v Rosar* (1999) Tas R 344 at 346 per Slicer J.
5. Lanham, 'Obtaining a Financial Advantage by Deception in Victoria — The Meaning of Financial Advantage' [1977] 1 *Crim.LJ* 188.
6. [1973] 1 WLR 653 at 656, [1973] 2 All ER 828.
7. [1982] VR 1045.
8. (1977) 1 *Crim LJ* at 193.
9. And see *DPP v Ray* [1974] AC 370 at 382–3; 387; 391.
10. See Crimes (Theft) Bill, Second Reading Speech, Hansard, Legislative Council, Session 1972–3, Vol 311, at 3845, and the Explanatory Memorandum at 8.
11. Which, significantly, was drafted by Professor Peter Brett of the University of Melbourne, who was one of the members of the committee.
12. See Chief Justices Law Reform Committee, *Report on the Law of Theft*, at para 13.
13. ibid.
14. *R v Royle* (1971) 56 Crim.App R 131 at 136, per Edmund-Davies LJ.
15. Pursuant to s 35 of the Interpretation of Legislation Act 1984, see *Catlow v Accident Compensation Commission* (1989) 167 CLR 543 at 549; *Mills v Meeking* (1990) 169 CLR 214 at 235.
16. See Williams, 'The Crimes Theft Act 1973' (1974) 48 *LIJ* 75 at 86; although cf Williams, *Property Offences*, 3rd Ed at 186–187.
17. See Pearce & Geddes, *Statutory Interpretation in Australia*, 5th Ed at [3.39].
18. [1974] AC 370.

8.76 Notes and illustrations

1. D, a steward employed by British Rail, was about to board his train. He had with him his own bread and tomatoes. It was his intention to use these articles, and not British Rail bread and tomatoes, to make sandwiches and to sell the sandwiches to passengers and pocket the proceeds himself. He was charged with having with him articles — that is, the bread and tomatoes

— for use in connection with a 'cheat': for Victorian provision, see Crimes Act 1958 (Vic) s 91. 'Cheat' means to obtain property by deception: in Victoria, Crimes Act 1958 (Vic) s 91(4). The trial judge directed the jury that they should convict D if they were satisfied that the sale of the sandwiches would be a cheat on D's employers. D was convicted and appealed. Held, conviction quashed. To establish an offence had been committed, the Crown had to prove that D intended, by the use of the bread and tomatoes, to practise an effective and operative deception on the passengers, without which they would not have bought the sandwiches, and it was not enough to show that D intended to deceive his employers. Accordingly, the jury should have been directed that a necessary element in D's mens rea was that he believed that passengers would have declined to purchase the sandwiches if they had known that they were made with bread and tomatoes belonging to D and not to British Rail: *R v Rashid* [1977] 2 All ER 237.

2. D was employed as a casual wine waiter at a hotel. He was discovered on the hotel premises with six bottles of wine in his coat pockets. He told the police that if a guest in the restaurant ordered carafe wine, he would substitute his own wine, make out a separate bill and keep the money. He was charged with having with him articles for use in connection with a cheat: in Victoria, see Crimes Act 1958 (Vic) s 91. D was convicted and appealed on the ground that the prosecution evidence did not prove the necessary causal connection between the intended deception and the obtaining of money from the customer. Held, conviction affirmed. It had to be assumed that the hypothetical customer against whom the intended deception was to be practised was reasonably honest. It could not be supposed that such a customer to whom the true situation had been made clear would have willingly made himself a party to what would obviously have been a fraud by the waiter on his employers. It was therefore open to the jury to find that the obtaining of money from the customer would have been caused by the deception practised on him. *R v Rashid* not followed: *R v Doukas* [1978] 1 All ER 1061
3. D, whose account was heavily overdrawn, obtained goods, paying for them by post-dated cheques. No money was paid into his account thereafter and the cheques were dishonoured on presentation. D was convicted of obtaining property by deception. Held, conviction affirmed. By simply giving a cheque, whether post-dated or not, the drawer impliedly represented that the state of facts existing at the date of delivery was such that in the ordinary course of events it would, on presentation for payment on or after the date specified in the cheque, be met: *R v Gilmartin* [1983] 1 All ER 829.
4. There have been difficulties in prosecuting cases where a person has, by fraud, arranged to have an electronic transfer of funds to their bank account (see *R v Preddy* [1996] 3 WLR 255 (at **8.16**)). These can be most simply

and appropriately prosecuted as obtaining by a financial advantage by deception. Alex Steele has commented: 'Practically, there are few instances where any appropriation of a chose in action amounts to an activity that is more characterised by theft than by fraud. … the modern fraud offences adequately cover such behaviours': A Steel 'Problematic and Unnecessary? Issues with the Use of the Theft Offence to Protect Intangible Property' (2008) 30 *Sydney L Rev* 575 at 613.

5. The Crimes Act 1900 (ACT) contains no offence of obtaining property by deception. The effect of s 96(1) is to subsume all cases of obtaining property by deception within the offence of theft. Section 104(1) creates the offence of obtaining a financial advantage by deception (in the same terms as s 82 of the Victorian Act). Subsection (2), however, derogates from this by defining 'financial advantage' in terms similar to those set out in the abortive s 16(2)(b) and (c) of the English Theft Act 1968. Section 105 creates the offence of obtaining the provision of a service by deception. Section 106 creates an offence of evading liability by deception. Section 107 follows the English Theft Act 1978 in creating an offence of dishonestly making off without payment.

8.77 Further reading

D Lanham, 'Obtaining a Financial Advantage by Deception in Victoria — The Meaning of Financial Advantage' (1977) 1 *Crim LJ* 188

S Martin, 'Obtaining Bank Credits and Debits by Deception' (1992) 16 *Crim LJ* 77

B McSherry and B Naylor, *Australian Criminal Laws: Critical Perspectives*, Oxford University Press, Melbourne, 2004, pp 333–57

A Steel, 'Money for Nothing, Cheques for Free? The Meaning of "Financial Advantage" in Fraud Offences' (2007) 31 *Melbourne University Law Review* 8

C R Williams, *Property Offences*, 3rd ed, Law Book Co, Sydney, 1999, pp 171–88

THE RELATIONSHIP BETWEEN THEFT AND OBTAINING PROPERTY BY DECEPTION

8.78C Lawrence v Metropolitan Police Commissioner

[1972] AC 626
House of Lords

Viscount Dilhorne: The appellant was convicted on 2 December 1969, of theft contrary to s 1(1) of the Theft Act 1968. On 1 September 1969, a Mr Occhi, an Italian who spoke little English, arrived at Victoria Station on his first visit to this country. He went up to a taxi driver, the appellant, and showed him a piece of paper on which an address in Ladbroke Grove was written. The appellant said that it was very far and very expensive. Mr Occhi got into the taxi, took £1 out of his wallet and gave it to the appellant who then, the wallet being still open, took a further £6 out of it. He then drove Mr Occhi to Ladbroke Grove. The correct lawful fare for the journey was in the region of 10s 6d. The appellant was charged with and convicted of the theft of the £6.

My Lords, in cross-examination, Mr Occhi, when asked whether he had consented to the money being taken, said that he had 'permitted'. He gave evidence through an interpreter and it does not appear that he was asked to explain what he meant by the use of that word. He had not objected when the £6 was taken. He had not asked for the return of any of it. It may well be that when he used the word 'permitted', he meant no more than that he had allowed the money to be taken. It certainly was not established at the trial that he had agreed to pay to the appellant a sum far in excess of the legal fare for the journey and so had consented to the acquisition by the appellant of the £6.

The main contention of the appellant in this House and in the Court of Appeal was that Mr Occhi had consented to the taking of the £6 and that, consequently, his conviction could not stand. In my opinion, the facts of this case to which I have referred fall far short of establishing that Mr Occhi had so consented.

Prior to the passage of the Theft Act 1968, which made radical changes in and greatly simplified the law relating to theft and some other offences, it was necessary to prove that the property alleged to have been stolen was taken 'without the consent of the owner': Larceny Act 1916 s 1(1).

These words are not included in s 1(1) of the Theft Act, but the appellant contended that the subsection should be construed as if they were, as if they appeared after the word 'appropriates'. Section 1(1) reads as follows:

> A person is guilty of theft if he dishonestly appropriates property belonging to another with the intention of permanently depriving the other of it; and 'thief' and 'steal' shall be construed accordingly.

I see no ground for concluding that the omission of the words 'without the consent of the owner' was inadvertent and not deliberate, and to read the subsection as if they were included is, in my opinion, wholly unwarranted. Parliament by the omission of these words has relieved the prosecution of the burden of establishing that the taking was without the owner's consent. That is no longer an ingredient of the offence.

Megaw LJ, delivering the judgment of the Court of Appeal, said [1971] 1 QB 373 at 376 that the offence created by s 1(1) involved four elements: '(i) a dishonest (ii) appropriation (iii) of property belonging to another (iv) with the intention of permanently depriving the owner of it.'

I agree. That there was appropriation in this case is clear. Section 3(1) states that any assumption by a person of the rights of an owner amounts to an appropriation. Here there was clearly such an assumption. That an appropriation was dishonest may be proved in a number of ways. In this case it was not contended that the appellant had not acted dishonestly. Section 2(1) provides, *inter alia*, that a person's appropriation of property belonging to another is not to be regarded as dishonest if he appropriates the property in the belief that he would have the other's consent if the other knew of the appropriation and the circumstances of it. *A fortiori*, a person is not to be regarded as acting dishonestly if he appropriates another's property believing that with full knowledge of the circumstances that other person has in fact agreed to the appropriation. The appellant, if he believed that Mr Occhi, knowing that £7 was far in excess of the legal fare, had nevertheless agreed to pay him that sum, could not be said to have acted dishonestly in taking it. When Megaw LJ said that if there was true consent, the essential element of dishonesty was not established, I understand him to have meant this. Belief or the absence of belief that the owner had with such knowledge consented to the appropriation is relevant to the issue of dishonesty, not to the question whether or not there has been an appropriation. That may occur even though the owner has permitted or consented to the property being taken. So proof that Mr Occhi had consented to the appropriation of £6 from his wallet without agreeing to pay a sum in excess of the legal fare does not suffice to show that there was not dishonesty in this case. There was ample evidence that there was.

I now turn to the third element 'property belonging to another'. Mr Back QC, for the appellant, contended that if Mr Occhi consented to the appellant taking the £6, he consented to the property in the money passing from him to the appellant and that the appellant had not, therefore, appropriated property belonging to another. He argued that the old distinction between the offence of false pretences and larceny had been preserved. I am unable to agree with this. The new offence of obtaining property by deception created by s 15(1) of the Theft Act also contains the words 'belonging to another'. 'A person who by any deception dishonestly obtains property belonging to another, with the intention of permanently depriving the other of it' commits that offence. 'Belonging to another' in s 1(1) and in s 15(1) in my view signifies no more than that, at the time of the appropriation or the obtaining, the property belonged to another, with the words 'belonging to another' having the extended meaning given by s 5. The short answer to this contention on behalf of the appellant is that the money in the wallet which he appropriated belonged to another, to Mr Occhi.

There was no dispute about the appellant's intention being permanently to deprive Mr Occhi of the money.

The four elements of the offence of theft as defined in the Theft Act were thus clearly established and, in my view, the Court of Appeal was right to dismiss the appeal.

Having done so, they granted a certificate that a point of law of general public importance was involved and granted leave to appeal to this House. Under the Criminal Appeal Act 1968 s 33(2) (which replaced s 1(2) of the Administration of Justice Act 1960), they have power to grant such leave if they think that a point of law of general public importance is involved and also that the point is one which ought to be considered by this House. The certificate granted does not state that they thought that the point was one which ought to be considered by this House but I infer that they were of that opinion from the fact that leave to appeal was granted.

The first question posed in the certificate was:

> Whether s 1(1) of the Theft Act, 1968, is to be construed as though it contained the words 'without having the consent of the owner' or words to that effect.

In my opinion, the answer is clearly no. The second question was:

> Whether the provisions of s 15(1) and s 1(1) of the Theft Act, 1968, are mutually exclusive in the sense that if the facts proved would justify a conviction under s 15(1) there cannot lawfully be a conviction under s 1(1) on those facts.

Again, in my opinion, the answer is no. There is nothing in the Act to suggest that they should be regarded as mutually exclusive and it is by no means uncommon for conduct on the part of an accused to render him liable to conviction for more than one offence. Not infrequently there is some overlapping of offences. In some cases the facts may justify a charge under s 1(1) and also a charge under s 15(1). On the other hand, there are cases which only come within s 1(1) and some which are only within s 15(1). If in this case the appellant had been charged under s 15(1), he would, I expect, have contended that there was no deception, that he had simply appropriated the money and that he ought to have been charged under s 1(1). In my view he was rightly charged under that section.

I must confess to some surprise that a certificate for leave to appeal should have been granted in this case. While it may be true to say that few points of law affecting the general criminal law of the country are not points of general public importance, the second limb of s 1(2) of the Administration of Justice Act 1960 is one to which great regard should be had, namely, that the point is one which ought to be considered by this House.

I can say with some confidence that prior to the Administration of Justice Act 1960 it is most unlikely that the Attorney-General's fiat would have been granted for an appeal to this House in a case such as this.

For the reasons I have stated, in my opinion, this appeal should be dismissed.

[**Lord Donovan**, **Lord Pearson**, **Lord Diplock** and **Lord Cross** agreed with **Viscount Dilhorne**. Appeal dismissed.]

[See also *Heddich v Dike* (1981) 3 A Crim R 139; *Dobson v General Accident Fire and Life Assurance Corporation PLC* [1989] 3 WLR 1066; *R v Gomez* [1992] 3 WLR 1067.]

8.79 Notes

1. In *Lawrence v Metropolitan Police Commissioner,* Viscount Dilhorne stated that some cases which would constitute obtaining property by deception would not constitute theft. However, with the exception of land, which cannot normally be stolen (Crimes Act 1958 (Vic) s 73(6)) but can be obtained by deception, it is difficult to think of any cases in which the offence of obtaining property by deception is committed without the offence of theft also being committed. Remembering that an appropriation is defined as any 'assumption by a person of the rights of an owner' (Crimes Act s 73(4)), it would seem that whenever a person by 'deception dishonestly obtains property' (Crimes Act s 81(1)) he or she also 'dishonestly appropriates property': Crimes Act s 72(1). It is not, of course, true in reverse: many thefts can be carried out without 'deception'.
2. At common law, it was established that, for an accused to be guilty of obtaining by false pretences, the false pretence had to be shown to be a cause of the obtaining: *R v Perera* [1907] VLR 240 (at **7.94**); *R v Clucas* [1949] 2 KB 226 (at **7.96**). This requirement continues under the Theft Act: *R v Laverty* [1970] 3 All ER 432; *R v Rashid* [1977] 2 All ER 237 (at **8.76, note 1**); *R v Doukas* [1978] 1 All ER 1061 (at **8.76, note 2**); *R v King* [1987] 2 WLR 746. Where the prosecution anticipates difficulty in establishing such a connection, it might seek to avoid the problem by charging the accused with theft instead of obtaining property by deception. In the ordinary case, however, where there has been a deception and the deception appears to have been a cause of the obtaining of the property, the proper course for the prosecution to adopt is to charge the accused with the more obvious offence of obtaining property by deception.

8.80 Further reading

B McSherry and B Naylor, *Australian Criminal Laws: Critical Perspectives*, Oxford University Press, Melbourne, 2004, pp 357–60

C R Williams, *Property Offences*, 3rd ed, Law Book Co, Sydney, 1999, pp 188–90

ROBBERY, BURGLARY AND BLACKMAIL

8.81E Crimes Act 1958 (Vic)

75 Robbery

(1) A person is guilty of robbery if he steals, and immediately before or at the time of doing so, and in order to do so, he uses force on any person or puts or seeks to put any person in fear that he or another person will be then and there subjected to force.

(2) A person guilty of robbery, or of an assault with intent to rob, is guilty of an indictable offence and liable to level 4 imprisonment (15 years maximum).

75A Armed robbery

(1) A person is guilty of armed robbery if he commits any robbery and at the time has with him a firearm, imitation firearm, offensive weapon, explosive or imitation explosive within the meaning assigned to those terms for the purposes of section 77(1).

(2) A person guilty of armed robbery is guilty of an indictable offence and liable to level 2 imprisonment (25 years maximum).

76 Burglary

(1) A person is guilty of burglary if he enters any building or part of a building as a trespasser with intent —
   (a) to steal anything in the building or part in question; or
   (b) to commit an offence —
      (i) involving an assault to a person in the building or part in question; or
      (ii) involving any damage to the building or to property in the building or part in question —

which is punishable with imprisonment for a term of five years or more.

(2) References in sub-section (1) to a building shall apply also to an inhabited vehicle or vessel, and shall apply to any such vehicle or vessel at times when the person having a habitation in it is not there as well as at times when he is.

(3) A person guilty of burglary is guilty of an indictable offence and liable to level 5 imprisonment (10 years maximum).

77 Aggravated burglary

(1) A person is guilty of aggravated burglary if he or she commits a burglary and —
   (a) at the time has with him or her any firearm or imitation firearm, any offensive weapon or any explosive or imitation explosive; or
   (b) at the time of entering the building or the part of the building a person was then present in the building or part of the building and he or she knew that a person was then so present or was reckless as to whether or not a person was then so present.

(1A) For the purposes of sub-section (1) —

Explosive means any article manufactured for the purpose of producing a practical effect by explosion, or intended by the person having it with him or her for that purpose;

firearm has the same meaning as in the *Firearms Act 1996;*

'imitation explosive' means any article which might reasonably be taken to be or to contain an explosive;

imitation firearm means anything which has the appearance of being a firearm, whether capable of being discharged or not;

offensive weapon means any article made or adapted for use for causing injury to or incapacitating a person, or which the person having it with him or her intends or threatens to use for such a purpose.

(2) A person guilty of aggravated burglary is guilty of an indictable offence and liable to level 2 imprisonment (25 years maximum).

78 Removal of articles from places open to the public

(1) Subject to sub-sections (2) and (3), where the public have access to a building in order to view the building or part of it, or a collection or part of a collection housed in it, any person who without lawful authority removes from the building or its grounds the whole or part of any article displayed or kept for display to the public in the building or that part of it or in its grounds shall be guilty of an offence.

For this purpose ***collection*** includes a collection got together for a temporary purpose, but references in this section to a collection do not apply to a collection made or exhibited for the purpose of effecting sales or other commercial dealings.

(2) It is immaterial for purposes of sub-section (1) that the public's access to a building is limited to a particular period or particular occasion; but where anything removed from a building or its grounds is there otherwise than as forming part of, or being on loan for exhibition with, a collection intended for permanent exhibition to the public, the person removing it does not thereby commit an offence under this section unless he removes it on a day when the public have access to the building as mentioned in sub-section (1).

(3) A person does not commit an offence under this section if he believes that he has lawful authority for the removal of the thing in question or that he would have it if the person entitled to give it knew of the removal and the circumstances of it.

(4) A person guilty of an offence under this section is guilty of an indictable offence and liable to level 6 imprisonment (5 years maximum).

87 Blackmail

(1) A person is guilty of blackmail if, with a view to gain for himself or another or with intent to cause loss to another, he makes any unwarranted demand with menaces; and for this purpose a demand with menaces is unwarranted unless the person making it does so in the belief —

(a) that he has reasonable grounds for making the demand; and

(b) that the use of the menaces is proper means of reinforcing the demand.

(2) The nature of the act or omission demanded is immaterial, and it is also immaterial whether the menaces relate to action to be taken by the person making the demand.

(3) A person guilty of blackmail is guilty of an indictable offence and liable to level 4 imprisonment (15 years maximum).

8.82C R v Collins

[1973] QB 100
Court of Appeal (Criminal Division) (UK)

Edmund-Davies LJ: This is about as extraordinary a case as my brethren and I have ever heard either on the bench or while at the bar. Stephen William George Collins was convicted on 29 October 1971, at the Essex Assizes of burglary with intent to commit rape and he was sentenced to 21 months' imprisonment. He is a 19-year-old youth, and he appeals against that conviction by the certificate of the judge. The terms in which that certificate is expressed reveal that the judge was clearly troubled about the case and the conviction.

Let me relate the facts. Were they put into a novel or portrayed on the stage, they would be regarded as being so improbable as to be unworthy of serious consideration and as verging at times on farce. At about 2 o'clock in the early morning of Saturday, 24 July 1971, a young lady of 18 went to bed at her mother's home in Colchester. She had spent the evening with her boyfriend. She had taken a certain amount of drink, and it may be that this fact affords some explanation of her inability to answer satisfactorily certain crucial questions put to her at the trial.

She has the habit of sleeping without wearing night apparel in a bed which is very near the lattice-type window of her room. At one stage in her evidence she seemed to be saying that the bed was close up against the window which, in accordance with her practice, was wide open. In the photographs which we have before us, however, there appears to be a gap of some sort between the two, but the bed was clearly quite near the window.

At about 3.30 or 4 o'clock she awoke and she then saw in the moonlight a vague form crouched in the open window. She was unable to remember, and this is important, whether the form was on the outside of the window sill or on that part of the sill which was inside the room, and for reasons which will later become clear, that seemingly narrow point is of crucial importance.

The young lady then realised several things: first of all that the form in the window was that of a male; secondly that he was a naked male; and thirdly that he was a naked male with an erect penis. She also saw in the moonlight that his hair was blond. She thereupon leapt to the conclusion that her boyfriend, with whom for some time she had been on terms of regular and frequent sexual intimacy, was paying her an ardent nocturnal visit. She promptly sat up in bed, and the man descended from the sill and joined her in bed and they had full sexual intercourse. But there was something about him which made her think that things were not as they usually were between her and her boyfriend. The length of his hair, his voice as they had exchanged what was described as 'love talk', and other features led her to the conclusion that somehow there was something different. So she turned on the bedside light, saw that her companion was not her boyfriend and slapped the face of the intruder, who was none other than the defendant. He said to her, 'Give me a good time tonight', and got hold of her arm, but she bit him and told him to go. She then went into the bathroom and he promptly vanished.

The complainant said that she would not have agreed to intercourse if she had known that the person entering her room was not her boyfriend. But there was no suggestion of any force having been used upon her, and the intercourse which took place was undoubtedly effected with no resistance on her part.

The defendant was seen by the police at about 10.30 later that same morning. According to the police, the conversation which took place then elicited these points. He was very lustful the previous night. He had taken a lot of drink, and we may here note that (which to him is a very real problem) had brought this young man into trouble several times before, but never for an offence of this kind. He went on to say that he knew the complainant because he had worked around her house. On this occasion, desiring sexual intercourse — and according to the police evidence he added that he was determined to have a girl, by force if necessary, although that part of the police evidence he challenged — he went on to say that he walked around the house, saw a light in an upstairs bedroom, and he knew that this was the girl's bedroom. He found a step ladder, leaned it against the wall and climbed up and looked into the bedroom. He could see through the wide-open window a girl who was naked and asleep. So he descended the ladder and stripped off all his clothes, with the exception of his socks, because apparently he took the view that if the girl's mother entered the bedroom it would be easier to effect a rapid escape if he had his socks on than if he was in his bare feet. This is a matter about which we are not called upon to express any view, and would in any event find ourselves unable to express one.

Having undressed, he then climbed the ladder and pulled himself up on to the window sill. His version of the matter is that he was pulling himself in when she awoke. She then got up and knelt on the bed, she put her arms around his neck and body, and she seemed to pull him into the bed. He went on:

> I was rather dazed because I didn't think she would want to know me. We kissed and cuddled for about 10 or 15 minutes and then I had it away with her but found it hard because I had had so much to drink.

The police officer said to the defendant:

> It appears that it was your intention to have intercourse with this girl by force if necessary, and it was only pure coincidence that this girl was under the impression that you were her boyfriend and apparently that is why she consented to allowing you to have sexual intercourse with her.

It was alleged that he then said:

> Yes, I feel awful about this. It is the worst day of my life, but I know it could have been worse.

Thereupon the officer said to him — and he challenges this: 'What do you mean, you know it could have been worse?', to which he is alleged to have replied: 'Well, my trouble is drink and I got very frustrated. As I've told you, I only wanted to have it away with a girl and I'm only glad I haven't really hurt her.'

Then he made a statement under caution, in the course of which he said:

> When I stripped off and got up the ladder I made my mind up that I was going to try and have it away with this girl. I feel terrible about this now, but I had too much to drink. I am sorry for what I have done.

In the course of his testimony, the defendant said that he would not have gone into the room if the girl had not knelt on the bed and beckoned him into the room. He said that if she had objected immediately to his being there or to his having intercourse he would not have persisted. While he was keen on having sexual intercourse that night, it was only if he could find someone who was willing. He strongly denied having told the police that he would, if necessary, have pushed over some girl for the purpose of having intercourse.

There was a submission of no case to answer on the ground that the evidence did not support the charge, particularly that ingredient of it which had reference to entry into the house 'as a trespasser'. But the submission was overruled, and, as we have already related, he gave evidence.

Now, one feature of the case which remained at the conclusion of the evidence in great obscurity is where exactly Collins was at the moment when, according to him, the girl manifested that she was welcoming him. Was he kneeling on the sill outside the window or was he already inside the room, having climbed through the window frame, and kneeling upon the inner sill? It was a crucial matter, for there were certainly three ingredients that it was incumbent upon the Crown to establish. Under s 9 of the Theft Act 1968, which renders a person guilty of burglary if he enters any building or part of a building as a trespasser and with the intention of committing rape, the entry of the accused into the building must first be proved. Well, there is no doubt about that, for it is common ground that he did enter the girl's bedroom. Secondly, it must be proved that he entered as a trespasser. We will develop that point a little later. Thirdly, it must be proved that he entered as a trespasser with intent at the time of entry to commit rape therein.

The second ingredient of the offence — the entry must be as a trespasser — is one which has not, to the best of our knowledge, been previously canvassed in the courts. Views as to its ambit have naturally been canvassed by the textbook writers, and it is perhaps not wholly irrelevant to recall that those who were advising the Home Secretary before the Theft Bill was presented to Parliament had it in mind to get rid of some of the frequently absurd technical rules which had been built up in relation to the old requirement in burglary of a 'breaking and entering'. The cases are legion as to what this did or did not amount to, and happily it is not now necessary for us to consider them. But it was in order to get rid of those technical rules that a new test was introduced, namely that the entry must be 'as a trespasser'.

What does that involve? According to the editors of *Archbold's Criminal Pleading Evidence & Practice* (37th ed, 1969), para 1505:

> Any intentional, reckless or negligent entry into a building will, it would appear, constitute a trespass if the building is in the possession of another person who does not consent to the entry. Nor will it make any difference that the entry was the result of a reasonable mistake on the part of the defendant, so far as trespass is concerned.

If that be right, then it would be no defence for this man to say (and even were he believed in saying), 'Well, I honestly thought that this girl was welcoming me into the room and I therefore entered, fully believing that I had her consent to go in'. If *Archbold* is right, he would nevertheless be a trespasser, since the apparent consent of the girl was unreal, she being mistaken as to who was at her window. We disagree. We hold that, for the purposes of s 9 of the Theft Act, a person entering a building is not guilty of trespass if he enters without knowledge that he is trespassing or at least without acting recklessly as to whether or not he is unlawfully entering.

A view contrary to that of the editors of *Archbold* was expressed in Professor Smith's book on *The Law of Theft,* (1st ed, 1968), where, having given an illustration of an entry into premises, the author comments, at para 462:

> It is submitted that ... D should be acquitted on the ground of lack of *mens rea.* Though, under the civil law, he entered as a trespasser, it is submitted that he cannot be convicted of the criminal offence unless he knew of the facts which caused him to be a trespasser or, at least, was reckless.

The matter has also been dealt with by Professor Griew, who in para 4-05 of his work The Theft Act 1968 has this passage:

> What if D wrongly believes that he is not trespassing? His belief may rest on facts which, if true, would mean that he was not trespassing: for instance, he may enter a building by mistake, thinking that it is the one he has been invited to enter. Or his belief may be based on a false view of the legal effect of the known facts: for instance, he may misunderstand the effect of a contract granting him a right of passage through a building. Neither kind of mistake will protect him from tort liability for trespass. In either case, then, D satisfies the literal terms of s 9(1): he 'enters ... as a trespasser'. But for the purposes of criminal liability a man should be judged on the basis of the facts as he believed them to be, and this should include making allowances for a mistake as to rights under the civil law. This is another way of saying that a serious offence like burglary should be held to require *mens rea* in the fullest sense of the phrase: D should be liable for burglary only if he knowingly trespasses or is reckless as to whether he trespasses or not. Unhappily it is common for Parliament to omit to make clear whether *mens rea* is intended to be an element in a statutory offence. It is also, though not equally, common for the courts to supply the mental element by construction of the statute.

We prefer the view expressed by Professor Smith and Professor Griew to that of the editors of *Archbold.* In the judgment of this court there cannot be a conviction for entering premises 'as a trespasser' within the meaning of s 9 of the Theft Act unless the person entering does so knowing that he is a trespasser and nevertheless deliberately enters, or, at the very least, is reckless as to whether or not he is entering the premises of another without the other party's consent.

Having so held, the pivotal point of this appeal is whether the Crown established that this defendant at the moment that he entered the bedroom knew perfectly well that he was not welcome there or, being reckless as to whether he was welcome or not, was nevertheless determined to enter. That in turn involves consideration as to where he was at the time that the complainant indicated that she was welcoming him into her bedroom. If, to take an example that was put in the course of argument, her bed had not been near the window but was on the other side of the bedroom, and he (being determined to have her sexually even against her will) climbed through the window and crossed the bedroom to reach her bed, then the offence charged would have been established. But in this case, as we have related, the layout of the room was different, and it became a point of nicety which had to be conclusively established by the Crown as to where he was when the girl made welcoming signs, as she unquestionably at some stage did.

How did the judge deal with this matter? We have to say regretfully that there was a flaw in his treatment of it. Referring to s 9, he said:

> There are three ingredients. First is the question of entry. Did he enter into that house? Did he enter as a trespasser? That is to say, was the entry, if you are satisfied there was an entry, intentional or reckless? And, finally, and you may think this is the crux of the case as opened to you by Mr Irwin, if you are satisfied that he entered as a trespasser, did he have the intention to rape this girl?

The judge then went on to deal in turn with each of these three ingredients. He first explained what was involved in 'entry' into a building. He then dealt with the second ingredient. But here he unfortunately repeated his earlier observation that the question of entry as a trespasser depended on 'was the entry intentional or reckless?' We have to say that this was putting the matter inaccurately. This mistake may have been derived from a passage in the speech of counsel for the Crown when replying to the submission of 'no case'. Mr Irwin at one stage said: 'Therefore, the first thing that the Crown have got to prove, my Lords, is that there has been a trespass which may be an intentional trespass, or it may be a reckless trespass.' Unfortunately, the judge regarded the matter as though the second ingredient in the burglary charged was whether there had been an intentional or reckless entry, and when he came to develop this topic in his summing up that error was unfortunately perpetuated. The judge told the jury:

> He had no right to be in that house, as you know, certainly from the point of view of the girl's parent. But if you are satisfied about entry, did he enter intentionally or recklessly? What the prosecution say about that is, you do not really have to consider recklessness because when you consider his own evidence he intended to enter that house, and if you accept the evidence I have just pointed out to you, he in fact did so. So, at least, you may think, it was intentional. At the least, you may think it was reckless because as he told you he did not know whether the girl would accept him.

We are compelled to say that we do not think the judge by these observations made sufficiently clear to the jury the nature of the second test about which they had to be satisfied before this young man could be convicted of the offence charged. There was no doubt that his entry into the bedroom was 'intentional'. But what the accused had said was, 'She knelt on the bed, she put her arms around me and then I went in'. If the jury thought he might be truthful in that assertion, they would need to consider whether or not, although entirely surprised by such a reception being accorded to him, this young man might not have been entitled reasonably to regard her action as amounting to an invitation to him to enter. If she in fact appeared to be welcoming him, the Crown do not suggest that he should have realised or even suspected that she was so behaving because, despite the moonlight, she thought he was someone else. Unless the jury were entirely satisfied that the defendant made an effective and substantial entry into the bedroom without the complainant doing or saying anything to cause him to believe that she was consenting to his entering it, he ought not to be convicted of the offence charged. The point is a narrow one, as narrow maybe as the window sill which is crucial to this case. But this is a criminal charge of gravity and, even though one may suspect that his intention was to commit the offence charged, unless the facts show with clarity that he in fact committed it he ought not to remain convicted.

Some question arose as to whether or not the defendant can be regarded as a trespasser *ab initio*. But we are entirely in agreement with the view expressed in *Archbold,* again in para 1505, that the common law doctrine of trespass *ab initio* has no application to burglary under the Theft Act 1968. One further matter that was canvassed ought perhaps to be mentioned. The point was raised that, the complainant not being the tenant or occupier of the dwelling house and her mother being apparently in occupation, this girl herself could not in any event have extended an effective invitation to enter, so that even if she had expressly and with full knowledge of all material facts invited the defendant in, he would nevertheless be a trespasser. Whatever be the position in the law of tort, to regard such a proposition as acceptable in the criminal law would be unthinkable.

We have to say that this appeal must be allowed on the basis that the jury were never invited to consider the vital question whether this young man did enter the premises as a trespasser, that is to say knowing perfectly well that he had no invitation to enter or reckless of whether or not his entry was with permission. The certificate of the judge, as we have already said, demonstrated, that he felt there were points involved calling for further consideration. That consideration we have given to the best of our ability. For the reasons we have stated, the outcome of the appeal is that this young man must be acquitted of the charge preferred against him. The appeal is accordingly allowed and his conviction quashed.

8.83C R v Walkington

[1979] 2 All ER 716
Court of Appeal (Criminal Division) (UK)

[Shortly before closing time in a department store, the store detective and two of his colleagues noticed the accused in a ground floor department. He appeared to them to be interested primarily in the activity at the tills. He went up to a department on the first floor, where there was a till in one of the corners of a rectangle made up of a moveable three-sided counter ('the counter area'). The drawer of the till was partly open. The accused went into the counter area, which was reserved for the store staff, and opened the drawer further. It was empty so he slammed it shut. As he was leaving the building, the accused was detained and was subsequently charged with burglary. At his trial, the trial judge directed the jury that they had to decide (i) whether the counter area was a prohibited area; (ii) whether the accused realised when he entered that area that it was a prohibited area; and (iii) if they decided against the accused on (i) and (ii), whether, at the time he entered the counter area, he intended to steal. The accused was convicted.

On appeal, counsel for the accused contended (i) that the trial judge should have withdrawn the case from the jury because the counter area could not constitute 'part of a building'; and (ii) that, in any event, the accused did not have the necessary mens rea for the purposes of theft because his intention to steal was conditional, depending on whether he found something worth stealing.]

Geoffrey Lane LJ [delivering the judgment of the court]: The first ground of appeal (and indeed before an amendment to the notice of appeal was allowed, the only ground of appeal) was on the basis that the trial judge was wrong in refusing to withdraw the matter from the jury. The way it is put in the notice of appeal is this:

> It would be wrong to divide the store artificially into 'parts' in the way that would be necessary to make a case of burglary out of the situation presented by the prosecution. That being so, the defendant could not be said to have trespassed behind the counter and the count of burglary must fail.

As counsel for the appellant put it before us this morning, what he submits is that the counter area could not have constituted a part of the building for the purposes of burglary. It is perhaps advisable in the first instance to see what it is that s 9 of the Theft Act provides. It reads as follows:

> (1) A person is guilty of burglary if — (a) he enters any building or part of a building as a trespasser and with intent to commit any such offence as is mentioned in subsection (2) below ...
> (2) The offences referred to in subsection (1)(a) above are offences of stealing anything in the building or part of a building in question ...

What the prosecution had to prove here was that the appellant had entered a part of a building as a trespasser with intent to steal anything in that part of the building. Counsel for the appellant submitted that this could not be said to be a part of the building. It wasa submission which we confess we found a little difficult to follow. But it transpired that what counsel for the appellant was principally relying on was a passage in Professor Griew's *The Theft Acts 1968 and 1978* (3rd ed, 1978), p 68, para 4-16) which reads:

> D has the licence that all customers have in a shop to move from counter to counter. He has lawfully entered the shop and bought something at counter 1. He now moves to counter 2, intending to steal at it. If in doing so he is entering a different 'part' of the shop, he may be guilty of burglary, for entry for a purpose other than that for which a licence to enter is granted is a trespassory entry. But

> it does not seem likely that the courts will be hasty to divide buildings artificially into 'parts' in the way that would be necessary to make a case of burglary out of the situation presented here.

With respect to counsel for the appellant it seems to us that that passage is not dealing with the present situation at all. It is dealing with a situation where there is no physical demarcation at all and the only matter which may cause the man to be a trespasser is a change of intention in his own mind. This is not the situation here. Here there is a physical demarcation, and if one turns to the same publication at the passage where Professor Griew is dealing with the situation which exists here, we find this: (ibid, p 64, para 4-07):

> A licence to enter a building may extend to part of the building only. If so, the licensee will trespass if he enters some other part not within the scope of the licence. To do so with intent to commit in that other part one of the specified offences, or to do so and then to commit or attempt to commit one of those offences therein, will be burglary.

That seems to us precisely to fit the circumstances of the present case and really deals the death blow to this part of counsel's submission.

If support is required, it is to be found in Professor J C Smith's book *The Law of Theft* (3rd ed, 1977), p 152, para 329(i) where he says:

> A customer in a shop who goes behind the counter and takes money from the till during a short absence of the shopkeeper would be guilty of burglary even though he entered the shop with the shopkeeper's permission. The permission did not extend to his going behind the counter.

There are similar passages at paras 331 and 334; (ibid, pp 153–4). Paragraph 331 is the only one to which I need refer:

> It would seem that the whole reason for the words 'or part of a building', is that D may enter or be in part of a building without trespass and it is desirable that he should be liable as a burglar if he trespasses in the remainder of the building with the necessary intent. It is submitted that the building need not be physically divided into 'parts'. It ought to be sufficient if a notice in the middle of a hall stated 'No customers beyond this point'. These considerations suggest that, for present purposes, a building falls into two parts only: first, that part in which D was lawfully present and, second, the remainder of the building. This interpretation avoids anomalies which arise if physical divisions within a building are held to create 'parts'.

One really gets two extremes, as it seems to us. First of all you have the part of the building which is shut off by a door so far as the general public is concerned, with a notice saying 'Staff only' or 'No admittance to customers'. At the other end of the scale you have, for example, a single table in the middle of the store, which it would be difficult for any jury to find properly was a part of the building into which the licensor prohibited customers from moving.

The present situation, it seems to us, was that there was a physical partition. Whether it was sufficient to amount to an area from which the public were plainly excluded was a matter for the jury. It seems to us that there was ample evidence on which they could come to the conclusion (i) that the management had impliedly prohibited customers entering that area and (ii) that this particular defendant knew of that prohibition. Whether the jury came to the conclusion that the prosecution made out their case was a matter for them, but there is no dispute that the judge, in those two careful passages which I have read, left the matter fairly and correctly to the jury.

Accordingly it seems to us that this first ground of appeal must necessarily fail. We were referred to the decision in *Anderson v Miller* (1976) 64 Cr App R 178. With respect to counsel for the appellant, we do not think that that decision can assist us in determining this particular point. It was a decision under the Firearms Act 1968 as to the meaning of 'public place' which is defined in the Act at s 57(4). So far as the first ground is concerned, the appeal fails.

The second ground has given us, if we may say so, rather more trouble. The reason why this second ground was not included in the original notice of appeal was that it is based on decisions of this court which had not seen the light of day at the time when the original notice of appeal was drawn. Consequently we deemed it right and fair that counsel for the appellant should have the opportunity of arguing the point and accordingly we gave leave. The additional grounds read as follows:

> 1. When the defendant entered the counter area, there was no evidence that there was anything there capable of being stolen. The defendant could not therefore be convicted of attempted theft.

As to that we make the trite observation that he was not being charged with attempted theft, he was being charged with burglary, which involved him entering this particular area as a trespasser and, at the time when he entered the area in that way, having the intention to steal.

> 2. The evidence also suggested that the defendant intended stealing anything of value which he might find in the counter area. In the event, he found nothing of value and left. As the law presently stands, the defendant's intention to steal was conditional, and a conditional intention falls below the required *mens rea* for the purposes of theft. 3. Similarly, it cannot be said that where the defendant has it in mind to steal only if what he finds is worth stealing he has a present intention to steal.

These submissions are based on the decision of this court in *R v Husseyn* (1977) 67 Cr App R 131n if we may say so respectfully, a most powerful court, because it consisted of Viscount Dilhorne, Lord Scarman and Cusack J. Let me read the introduction:

> On 14 February at Middlesex Crown Court (Judge Solomon) the appellant and one Demetriou, were convicted of attempted theft. On that day Demetriou was

sentenced to three months' detention, and on 7 March 1977, the appellant was also sentenced to three months' detention. The following facts are taken from the judgment: In the early hours of the morning of 27 February 1976, police officers observed in a London street a parked van. They saw the appellant standing in the middle of the road, looking up and down and, as they saw him in the middle of the road, they heard an alarm go off. One of the officers then noticed that another young man appeared to be tampering with the back door of the van. As the officer approached, the young man who was tampering with the back door appeared to attempt to close it and both young men, who proved to be Hussein [sic] and Demetriou, made off at a fast pace. The van belonged to a Mr Johnson ... Inside the door, with which one of these men was tampering, was a holdall, which according to the evidence of Mr Johnson, contained some valuable sub-aqua equipment.

We now turn to the judgment of the court, delivered by Lord Scarman, where he said ((1977) 67 Cr App R 131 n at 132):

> It is well known that to formulate what act or acts constitute an attempt is extremely difficult. It is the subject of a great amount of academic discussion. Suffice it to say that a judge, in summing up, must direct the jury in a way which makes sense in the context of the particular facts of the case. In the present very simple case, there was evidence which, if believed, would establish that these young men, or one of them in league with the other, were trying to open the door of the van. Had they not been interrupted, the next step, and it would have been the next step, would have been picking up the holdall. It seems to this court that it is unnecessary to enter into the realm of jurisprudential definition. Suffice it to say that the direction to the jury in the passage which I have quoted was sufficient in the circumstances. It must be complete common sense that, granted the intention to steal, the opening of a van door immediately prior to taking a holdall which is the other side of the door falls within the external features of an attempt. That point taken by the appellant therefore fails. Very different considerations apply when one comes to consider the way the learned judge summed up the issue of intention. The learned judge said that the jury could infer that what the young men were about was to look into the holdall and, if its contents were valuable, to steal it. In the view of this court that was a misdirection. What has to be established is an intention to steal at the time when the step is taken, which constitutes, or which is alleged to constitute the attempt. Edmund-Davies LJ put the point in *Easom* ([1971] 2 All ER 945 at 947; [1971] 2 QB 315 at 319), in a passage which begins: 'In every case of theft the appropriation must be accompanied by the intention of permanently depriving the owner of his property. What may be *loosely* described as a "conditional" appropriation will not do. If the appropriator has it in mind merely to deprive the owner of such of his property as, on examination, proves worth taking and then, finding that the booty is valueless to the appropriator, leaves it ready to hand to be repossessed by the owner, the appropriator has not stolen.' The direction of the learned judge in this case is

> exactly the contrary. It must be wrong, for it cannot be said that one who has it in mind to steal only if what he finds is worth stealing has a present intention to steal.

What counsel for the appellant suggests to us is that that passage, the last two sentences, meets the situation in this case and that if the facts were that the appellant in this case had it in mind only to steal if what he found was worth stealing, then he had no intention to steal. That is the way he put it.

First of all we would like to say that the particulars of offence in *R v Husseyn* (1977) 67 Cr App R 131n, were that the two men 'attempted to steal a quantity of sub-aqua equipment'. Plainly what considerations have to be applied to a charge of attempting to steal a specific article are different considerations from those which have to be applied when one is considering what a person's intent or intention may be under s 9 of the Theft Act 1968. That, we feel, is sufficient to distinguish our case from *R v Husseyn.*

It is perhaps worth while seeing what it was that Lord Scarman said in *Director of Public Prosecutions v Nock* [1978] 2 All ER 654 at 664; [1978] AC 979 at 1000. The one passage which I need read is as follows:

> Unfortunately, in *R v Husseyn* the issue of intention was summed up in such a way as to suggest that theft, or attempted theft, could be committed by a person who had not yet formed the intention which the statute defines as a necessary part of the offence. An intention to steal can exist even though, unknown to the accused, there is nothing to steal; but, if a man be in two minds as to whether to steal or not, the intention required by the statute is not proved.

That of course provides a gloss on the relevant passage in *R v Husseyn* and seems to us to make it clear that the dictum in *R v Husseyn* has no application to the present circumstances.

In this case there is no doubt that the appellant was not on the evidence in two minds as to whether to steal or not. He was intending to steal when he went to that till and it would be totally unreal to ask oneself, or for the jury to ask themselves, the question, what sort of intent did he have? Was it a conditional intention to steal if there was money in the till or a conditional intention to steal only if what he found there was worth stealing? In this case it was a cash till and what plainly he was intending to steal was the contents of the till, which was cash. The mere fact that the till happened to be empty does not destroy his undoubted intention at the moment when he crossed the boundary between the legitimate part of the store and the illegitimate part of the store. The judge's direction which we have cited already covered that point, and the matter was accurately left to the jury.

[Appeal dismissed.]

[See also *Re Attorney-General's References (Nos 1 and 2 of 1979)* [1979] 3 All ER 143.]

8.84C **Barker v R**

(1983) 153 CLR 338; 47 ALR 1
High Court of Australia

[The accused was convicted of burglary when he removed goods from a neighbour's house. The neighbour had asked the accused to keep an eye on his house while he was away and had told the accused where he kept a concealed key in case the accused needed to enter. The neighbour gave evidence that the accused had authority to enter his house but had no express authority to remove goods, though he conceded in cross-examination that the accused would have had his authority to remove goods had that been necessary for their preservation. The accused's defence, rejected by the jury, was that he had removed the goods for their protection. On appeal to the High Court.]

Mason J: The word 'trespasser' is a basic legal term with an established legal meaning. It should be understood in that sense unless the context reveals that it bears a different meaning: *Attorney-General for NSW v Brewery Employees Union of NSW* (1908) 6 CLR 469 at 531. The context — the creation of a serious criminal offence — unquestionably requires an additional element, *mens rea*. However, the applicant seeks to go much further than that, indeed to persuade us that the word is designed to exclude any person who has any right or authority at all to enter the premises in question.

At the outset it is necessary to examine the common law concept of trespass because the applicant submits, incorrectly in my view, that in any event the common law concept supports his argument as to the effect of s 76(1). The essence of trespass by wrongful entry consists in an entry without right or authority by one person on to the land of another who is in possession, using that word in its strict sense so as to include a person entitled to immediate and exclusive possession: *Thompson v Ward* [1953] 2 QB 153 at 158–9. If the right or authority to enter is limited in scope then an entry which is unrelated to the right or authority will amount to a trespass. Thus a person who has an invitation or permission to enter the land of another for a specific purpose commits a trespass if he enters for any other purpose, especially if that other purpose be an unlawful purpose. For good reason he stands in no better position than the person who enters without any permission at all. So much is established by the cases.

In *R v Pratt* (1855) 4 E & B 860; 119 ER 319 the defendant was convicted under 1 & 2 W 4, c 32, s 30, which made it an illegal trespass to enter or be upon land in search of game. He had entered on a highway, over which there was a public right of way, running through the land of one Bowyer and fired at and missed a pheasant which flew across the road. The defendant was convicted of being on the land in search of game. Lord Campbell CJ spoke in general terms of a right to enter which constitutes a trespass. His Lordship said (4 E & B at 865; 119 ER at 321):

> On these facts I think the magistrates were perfectly justified in concluding that [the defendant] was trespassing on land in the occupation of Mr Bowyer in search of game. ... Then [the defendant], being on that land, was undoubtedly a trespasser if he went there, not in the exercise of the right of way, but for the purpose of seeking game and that only.

And Crompton J said (4 E & B at 868–9; 119 ER at 322): '... I take it to be clear law that, if a man use the land over which there is a right of way for any purpose, lawful or unlawful, other than that of passing and repassing, he is a trespasser.'

Taylor v Jackson (1898) 78 LT 555 was a later case involving a conviction under s 30. The appellants had permission to go on the land of one Cole and hunt for rabbits, but their purpose in going on the land was to course hares. Wills J said (at 556):

> In order to convict there must be a trespass, and a trespass in pursuit of game. Now, there is evidence that the appellants had permission to go on the land and hunt for rabbits ... But there certainly is evidence that they went to hunt for hares, and on that the tribunal may conclude that their real purpose was to course hares. That is evidence of trespass in pursuit of game.

Kennedy J (at 556) also made the point that a limited permission to enter for another purpose does not prevent the conclusion that a person is a trespasser if he has an unlawful purpose in mind.

In *Harrison v Duke of Rutland* [1893] 1 QB 142 the defendant owned a grouse moor crossed by the highway. The plaintiff went on the highway for the purpose of preventing grouse from flying towards the butts occupied by the shooters. The defendant's keepers forcibly prevented the plaintiff from such interference and the plaintiff brought an action for assault. The defendant pleaded justification on the ground that the plaintiff was a trespasser. It was held that, though it was lawful to use the highway to pass and repass (or, in the view of Lord Esher MR, to use it in any of the ordinary and usual modes in which people use a highway), to be on the defendant's land for any other purpose, lawful or unlawful, was a trespass: see at 146–7, 153–4, 158.

The defendant in *Pratt* and the plaintiff in *Harrison* had a right to enter on the land which was the site of the highway. The appellants in *Taylor* had permission to go on the land and hunt for rabbits. The reasoning on which the decisions were based is inconsistent with the suggestion made by the applicant that it is the commission of acts exceeding the limits of the right or authority, not entry for an unlawful or unauthorised purpose, that constitutes the trespass. It is true that both *Pratt* and *Taylor* concerned a statutory definition of trespass, but the reasoning in the judgments is of more general application. The correctness of this reasoning is confirmed by the later decisions relating to licences.

In the Canadian case of *Gross v Wright* [1923] 2 DLR 171 at 185, Anglin J (with whom Davies CJ agreed) said that the defendant:

> ... having obtained a licence to enter upon the plaintiff's land only for a defined purpose, his entry for a different purpose was ... clearly a trespass.

Further, in *Farrington v Thomson & Bridgland* [1959] VR 286 at 297, Smith J said that it is unnecessary to examine the conduct of the entrant on the premises after entry. If he entered for a purpose not within the scope of any invitation or licence that he may have had then that, without more, constitutes him a trespasser.

In *R v Jones & Smith* [1976] 1 WLR 672 the two defendants entered a bungalow belonging to the father of one of the defendants and removed two television sets.

The defendants were charged with burglary under s 9(1)(b) of the Theft Act 1968 (UK), which provides that a person is guilty of burglary if, having entered as a trespasser, he steals or attempts to steal anything or inflicts or attempts to inflict grievous bodily harm on a person. It was submitted that a son to whom a father has given permission generally to enter the father's house cannot be a trespasser if he enters it, even if he enters solely with the intention of committing a theft against the father. The English Court of Appeal rejected the submission, holding (at 675) that:

> … a person is a trespasser for the purpose of s 9(1)(b) of the Theft Act 1968 if he enters premises of another knowing that he is entering in excess of the permission that has been given to him, or being reckless as to whether he is entering in excess of the permission that has been given to him to enter.

The principle expounded in *Jones & Smith* accords with the cases which I have discussed. The court, recognising the necessary element of *mens rea* in the creation of a criminal offence, added the element of knowledge that entry is in excess of permission or of reckless indifference to whether entry is in excess of permission. Whether the application of the principle so as to make the son a trespasser can be supported is another question. The authority of the son to enter his father's house might well have been regarded as so general that his entry for the purpose of theft did not make him a trespasser. But this is not a matter which I need pursue.

Counsel for the applicant submits that the principle established by the earlier cases to which I have referred has been controverted by other decisions. However, on examination they do not affect the principle. In *The Six Carpenters' Case* (1610) 8 Co Rep 146a; 77 ER 695 and *McGrath v Marshall* (1898) 14 WN (NSW) 106 the court refused to apply the distinct and different doctrine known as trespass *ab initio*, a doctrine now said to be obsolete: *Chic Fashions (West Wales) Ltd v Jones* [1968] 2 QB 299 at 313.

In *Byrne v Kinematograph Renters Society Ltd* [1958] 2 All ER 579 cinema inspectors visited a cinema to investigate suspected fraud. The inspectors purchased tickets and saw a performance, but did so only to check numbers on the tickets and count numbers of patrons so as to obtain evidence against the plaintiff. The submission that the inspectors were trespassers was rejected on the ground that their motives were immaterial and they did nothing that they were not invited to do (see at 593). No doubt the invitation by the lessee of the cinema to the public to enter the cinema was in very general terms and could on no view be said to be limited in the way in which it was contended.

The fourth case relied upon by the application is *R v Collins* [1973] 1 QB 100. The defendant looked into an open window of a house and saw the complainant asleep in bed close to the window. The defendant undressed and crouched on the window-sill. The complainant woke up and, assuming that the defendant was her boyfriend, allowed him to enter the room and have sexual intercourse with her. The English Court of Appeal held that the defendant should not have been convicted of burglary under s 9(1)(a) of the Theft Act, which is similar to s 76(1), because the jury had not been invited to consider whether the defendant entered the room knowing that he had no invitation to enter or reckless of whether or not his entry was with permission (see at 107).

It has been suggested that *Collins* is inconsistent with *Jones & Smith*: see Williams, *Textbook of Criminal Law* (1978), pp 810–15. The suggestion seems to turn on the notion, not discussed in the judgments in *Collins* and unsupported by the evidence, that when Collins entered the complainant's bedroom he still had the intention of using force if necessary, notwithstanding the complainant's invitation to him. On this view the effect of the decision in *Collins* is that 'A person who has a licence in fact to enter does not become a trespasser by reason of his criminal intent': see p 812. To my mind the foundation for this conclusion is too frail. It rests on a finding of fact as to intention which was neither made nor discussed in the judgments. The decision and the judgments on which it is based are entirely consistent with the existence of an invitation by the complainant to Collins to enter for the purpose of intercourse and knowledge on his part that he was so invited, with the consequence that his earlier intention to commit rape lapsed. So understood, *Collins* is consistent with the other authorities I have mentioned.

Lord Aitkin in *Hillen and Pettigrew v ICI (Alkali) Ltd* [1936] AC 65 at 69, stated that so far as an invitee 'sets foot on so much of the premises as lie outside the invitation or uses them for purposes which are alien to the invitation he is not an invitee but a trespasser'. This is to say that an invitee whose entry is within the terms of his invitation and who subsequently exceeds the scope of that invitation then becomes a trespasser: cf *Healing (Sales) Pty Ltd v Inglis Electrix Pty Ltd* (1968) 121 CLR 584 at 606, per Kitto J; contra Barwick CJ and Menzies J, at 598–9. The statement says nothing about the person whose entry is quite unrelated to his invitation because it is for an unlawful purpose foreign to the specific purpose contemplated by the invitation.

Accordingly, these cases leave unaffected the common law principle that a person who enters premises for a purpose alien to the terms of a licence given to him to enter the premises enters as a trespasser. It is a matter of determining the scope of the authority to enter, which the licence or invitation confers. If a person enters for a purpose outside the scope of the authority then he stands in no better position than a person who enters with no authority at all. His entry is unrelated to the authority.

The applicant then argues that the words 'enters ... as a trespasser' in s 76 were not intended to carry their common law meaning. He relies upon the Eighth Report on *Theft and Related Offences* by the Criminal Law Revision Committee in the United Kingdom, Cmnd 2977 (1966), which led to the enactment of the Theft Act 1968. There is authority for the proposition that reports of committees investigating the subject matter of legislation, provided the Act does not depart substantially from the committee's recommendations, can be consulted in order to ascertain the mischief with which the Act is concerned: *Black-Clawson Ltd v Papierwerke AG* [1975] AC 591; *Wacal Developments Pty Ltd v Realty Developments Pty Ltd* (1978) 140 CLR 503. Whether this proposition should be extended to embrace the reports of English committees in cases in which Australian legislation is based on United Kingdom legislation is another question. I am willing to assume, without deciding, that the question should be answered in the affirmative. Paragraph 75 of the Report says that the Committee thought of *extending* the scope of what later became s 9 to 'include a person who, having entered lawfully, remained in the building as a trespasser (for example, a person who hid in a shop until after closing time)', but thought it unnecessary 'because the offender is likely to go into a part of the building where he has no right to be, and this will be a trespassory entry into that part'. This passage suggests that the Committee thought that the person who enters a shop with the intention of hiding there until after closing time at which time he will steal something does not *enter* as a trespasser because he has the authority of the owner to enter the shop. If that is what the Committee thought, the Report fails to disclose the reasons for their view. And the suggested inference is at best indirect, arising only from an illustration given by the Committee. It falls far short of establishing that the mischief with which the Committee was concerned in inserting the requirement of entry as a trespasser was to exclude from the scope of the offence of burglary persons entering premises with the limited authority of the owner, but with the intention to steal.

The applicant also submits that, if a person with limited authority to enter who enters with intent to steal must be considered to have entered as a trespasser, the words 'as a trespasser' are superfluous, adding nothing to the requisite entry with intent to steal. I do not agree that the words are superfluous, despite an apparent willingness on the part of the respondent's counsel to concede this point. The words 'as a trespasser' exclude entry by a person who is himself entitled to immediate and exclusive possession of the premises. Thus the owner of a hotel or boarding-house who enters the room of a guest with intent to steal would not enter as a trespasser with intent to steal, unless the guest's contract gives him the right to immediate and exclusive possession. Another possible area of operation of the words is to exclude those who enter premises with intent to steal but also with another intention within the scope of their licence to enter. A person cannot be at the same time a trespasser and a non-trespasser in respect of the same land: *Healing (Sales) Pty Ltd v Inglis Electrix Pty Ltd* at 606, per Kitto J; see also 598–9, per Barwick CJ and Menzies J. If a person enters premises for a purpose which is within the scope of his authority his entry is authorised; it is not made unlawful because he enters with another and alien purpose in mind. The performance of acts with a view to the attainment of that alien purpose does not relate back to his entry so as to endow it with a trespassory character. It is hardly to the point to say that the licensor would not have given that licence, had he known the alien intention of the licensee. It is the effect of the licence actually given that is decisive. I therefore reject the argument that the words 'as a trespasser' are mere surplusage.

The applicant then contends that if the term 'trespasser' is given its common law meaning this will lead to the extraordinary consequence that a mere shoplifter would be an offender under s 76. I am by no means sure that this consequence is extraordinary. True it is that the shoplifter is generally concerned to steal items of small value. This no doubt will be reflected in the imposition of a suitable penalty. Even so I would be inclined to concede that a conviction for burglary would ordinarily convey the impression that an offence more serious than mere shoplifting had been committed. The maximum term of imprisonment for the offence of burglary is fourteen years: s 76(3). On the other hand, the maximum term of imprisonment for the offence of theft is ten years: s 74.

The argument assumes that the shoplifter enters as a trespasser within the meaning of s 76(1)(a). In many instances it will be difficult, if not impossible, to establish that the accused *entered* as a trespasser. His intention to steal may have arisen after entry or it may have been accompanied by another intention or purpose which brought the accused's entry within the ambit of the shopkeeper's implied invitation. There is a strong element of generality in the shopkeeper's invitation to the public to enter his premises. It is not an invitation to enter only for the purpose of doing business or with a view to doing business. The invitation ranges more widely, though it certainly does not amount to an invitation to steal. It will always be necessary to make a close analysis of the implied invitation held out by the shopkeeper and of the belief of the offender as to his right to enter the premises.

These problems do not provide a reason for distorting the words 'as a trespasser' from their ordinary meaning. As we have seen, the character of the provision as one which creates the serious criminal offence of burglary provides a strong reason for introducing the element of *mens rea* so that the section only embraces a person who of his own volition and without any right or authority enters land in the possession of another with intent to steal, knowing that he has no such right or authority or being reckless as to whether he has any such right or authority or not.

I turn to the application of the subsection, as so interpreted, to the facts of the present case. In so far as the *actus reus* of the offence is concerned, the trial judge's direction to the jury was unexceptionable. The jury found, as it was entitled to do, that the applicant entered the building with the intention of stealing, a purpose alien to the authority given to him. His entry was quite unrelated to the invitation or licence which he had with the result that he entered without any right or authority. It remains only for me to say that the sufficiency of the trial judge's charge to the jury on *mens rea* was not an issue at the trial. Nor was it raised in argument before the Court of Criminal Appeal or before this court.

In the result I would grant special leave to appeal and dismiss the appeal.

Brennan and **Deane JJ**: What then are the circumstances in which a person, who has some permission to enter from the person in possession, enters premises as a trespasser for the purposes of s 76(1)? Common sense indicates the answer that entry will be as a trespasser if, as a matter of substance and fact, the entry in question is beyond the scope of the permission. The above discussion compels the conclusion that the law and common sense coincide. The answer to the question is not complicated by artificial notions that a permission must be qualified by reference to authorised purpose or by artificial doctrines of relation back. When the only suggested justification for entry is the permission of the person in possession, the question whether entry was as a trespasser involves no more than identification of the limits of the actual permission, the definition of the actual entry and the determination of whether that entry was within the scope of that permission. If the permission was not subject to any express or implied limitation which excluded the entry from its scope, the entry was not as a trespasser. If the permission was subject to an actual express or implied limitation which excluded the actual entry, the entry was as a trespasser.

It is possible that the question whether a particular entry is within the scope of a limited permission can involve difficulty in the identification of the limits of the permission and the definition of the actual entry. An obvious example is the case where the permission is confined by reference to a particular purpose and an entry is made for that purpose and some other illegitimate purpose: see, generally, *Healing (Sales) Pty Ltd v Inglis Electrix*

Pty Ltd (1968) 121 CLR 584. In such a case, if the permission extends to authorise every entry for the particular purpose, it covers the entry for both purposes since the entry satisfies the requirement that it be for the designated purpose: if the permission extends only to authorise an entry which is exclusively for the particular purpose, entry for both purposes does not satisfy that requirement and is beyond its ambit. Except where an authority under the general law or a question of construction of a written document is involved, the identification of the limits of the authority, like the definition of the actual entry for the purpose of ascertaining whether it comes within those limits, is essentially a question of fact to be determined by reference to the circumstances of the particular case.

The fact that an entry was, in a particular case, as a 'trespasser' within the common law meaning of that word will satisfy that element of the offence created by s 76(1). It will not, however, satisfy the requirement that the *actus reus* must be accompanied by *mens rea* before an offence under s 76(1) will be committed. A person who enters upon another's property as a trespasser, though he has the specific intent mentioned in s 76(1), is not guilty of an offence under that provision unless he knows the facts which make him a trespasser or, at the least, he is reckless as to the existence of those facts. Moreover, as the gist of the offence created by s 76(1) is a trespassory entry, it is an offence with respect to the property entered, and *mens rea* is excluded by an honest claim of right to enter. The common law in this respect is stated 'with complete accuracy' (per Dixon J in *Thomas v R* (1937) 59 CLR 279 at 306) in s 22 of *The Criminal Code 1899* (Qld) which provides:

> ... a person is not criminally responsible, as for an offence relating to property, for an act done or omitted to be done by him with respect to any property in the exercise of an honest claim of right and without intention to defraud.

For present purposes the 'intention to defraud' relates to the act of entering, not to an act which the trespasser intends to do or omit to do thereafter. It is difficult to envisage a case in which that limitation upon the defence of an honest claim of right to enter might operate. A trespasser who enters in exercise of an honest claim of right, even if he knows or is reckless as to the existence of the facts which make him a trespasser, is not liable to conviction though he be wrongheaded in asserting that claim: *R v Pollard* [1962] QWN 13; *R v Gilson & Cohen* (1944) 29 Cr App R 174 at 180. An apparent exception to this doctrine occurred under the game laws in England: it was held in the cases under the Game Acts that an honest claim of right was no defence to entry or presence upon the land unless the accused had reasonable grounds for his belief: *Watkins v Major* (1875) LR 10 CP 662; *Dickinson v Ead* (1914) 111 LT 378. The game laws, however, stood in a special category. Lindley J in *Watkins v Major* said (at 666) that the Game Acts 'are not mere criminal statutes, but are statutes passed for the purpose of protecting the peculiar rights of those entitled to shoot game'. The Game Acts cases are quite anomalous and, as Professor Glanville Williams said in comment on the two last-mentioned cases, 'he would be a bold lawyer who would argue from the Game Acts to any general principle of law': *Criminal Law* (2nd ed, 1961), p 329.

It follows that, even though a jury is satisfied that an accused's entry upon land or into a building or into part of a building in the possession of another was trespassory because the accused did not have any permission to enter or because his permission was so limited that it did not cover the entry charged against him, he cannot be convicted unless the jury is satisfied also that he knew or was reckless as to the existence of the facts which made him a trespasser and that he did not enter in assertion of an honest claim of right to do so.

Dawson J: Burglary, now that the new definition of that crime in the English Theft Act 1968 has been substantially adopted in Victoria, consists of entry by a person upon any building or part of a building as a trespasser with intent to commit any one of certain specified offences. The specified intent which is relevant in this case is 'intent to steal anything in the building or part in question'. See *Crimes Act 1958* (Vic), as amended, s 76(1)(a).

The introduction of entry as a trespasser as an ingredient of burglary was evidently intended to avoid the nice distinctions which had grown up around the older concept of breaking and entering. Trespass is, of course, a creature of the civil law and its meaning must be derived from cases in tort. However, its transposition to the field of crime brings with it at least one modification which is made necessary by the general principle of the criminal law that a crime requires a guilty mind or *mens rea* as well as a guilty act or *actus reus*. This principle must be applied to the trespass which now forms part of the offence of burglary. The requirement of *mens rea* can, of course, be negatived by statute but there can be no suggestion that such is the case with s 76 of the Crimes Act. The Court of Appeal said of the equivalent provision in the Theft Act in *R v Collins* [1973] 1 QB 100 at 105:

> In the judgment of this court there cannot be a conviction for entering premises 'as a trespasser' within the meaning of s 9 of the Theft Act unless the person entering does so knowing that he is a trespasser and nevertheless deliberately enters, or, at the very least, is reckless as to whether or not he is entering the premises of another without the other party's consent.

It is to be observed that the intention which is required by the criminal law is not merely an intention to enter but an intention to enter as a trespasser. By this is meant an appreciation of the lack of consent or other right to enter rather than the legal conclusion which follows. Recklessness as to whether the entry is as a trespasser or not will suffice but, having made that observation, I shall not for the sake of simplicity, continue to refer to recklessness as amounting to a sufficient intent. *Mens rea* consists of an intention to do the forbidden act, the *actus reus*, and with trespass the forbidden act is not entry, but entry without consent or other lawful right.

To require *mens rea* in order to establish entry as a trespasser is to impose a requirement which forms no part of the civil law. Trespass to land, which is the relevant form of trespass for present purposes, consists of a physical interference by one person with the possession of another and the commonest form is a personal entry upon land or buildings occupied by that other. Whether at civil law an entry which is accidental and in that sense unintentional can be a trespass may be a matter of doubt, but it is clear that to constitute a civil trespass the entry does not have to be intentional in the sense of an intentional entry without consent. The civil wrong of trespass can be committed even if the entry is made under a mistake of fact and even though the person entering honestly believes that the land is his own or that he has a right of entry on it. See *Conway v George Wimpey & Co Ltd* [1951] 2 KB 266 at 273, Salmond and Heuston on the *Law of Torts* (18th ed, 1981) pp 36–7.

To establish entry as trespasser for the purposes of s 76 of the Crimes Act requires proof of *mens rea,* that is, intention in the criminal sense, and so entails different or additional considerations from those involved in the proof of entry as a trespasser for the purposes of the civil law.

It is convenient to remark at this point that an intention to enter as a trespasser is not the only intention required by s 76 of the Crimes Act. The offence of burglary is committed only if, at the time of entry as a trespasser, the entrant has an intent to steal. This is not the mental element required generally by the criminal law to constitute *mens rea* namely, an intent to do the act which is forbidden. It is an added requirement of a mental element in the form of a specific intent which must accompany the doing of the forbidden act in order to constitute the whole of the mental element required for the particular offence. Perhaps no great help is to be derived from the use of terms such as basic intent or general intent in order to distinguish the mental element which must generally be proved as part of any criminal offence and the more specific or additional mental element required as part of many crimes. See *R v O'Connor* (1980) 29 ALR 449; 54 ALJR 349. But in any analysis of s 76 of the Crimes Act it is essential to recognise that the offence consists both of an intentional entry as a trespasser and an intent to steal at the time of entry.

The distinction must be maintained because a person accused of burglary may enter premises with an intention to steal but nevertheless in the belief that he is entitled to enter. A person who enters premises with apparent consent but with intent to steal, such as an ordinary shoplifter, is likely to believe at the time he enters the premises that he has the same right of entry as other persons notwithstanding the criminal purpose for which he enters. If intercepted before attempting to steal anything, no doubt he would say that he had done nothing wrong and was entitled to be on the premises. And if he believed that to be so, as he very well might, the mental element required to prove entry as a trespasser would be lacking, notwithstanding evidence of that other aspect of intent required for burglary, an intent to steal at the time of entry. Before there can be burglary there must be an entry as a trespasser with intent to enter as a trespasser as well as with intent to steal.

Because there must be an entry as a trespasser as well as an intention to enter as a trespasser means, of course, that apart from the question of intent, it is necessary to have regard to the requirements of the civil law to find whether or not there was an entry as a trespasser or, to express it in terms of the criminal law, whether there was an *actus reus.* It would, no doubt, be simpler if it could be said that entry as a trespasser is the physical act of entering another's premises without the permission of that other or some other right or entitlement to do so and that it is irrelevant that a person given permission to enter for one purpose may do so for another. That would avoid the introduction to the criminal law of the notion of purpose, which may be something different from intent and in some cases, at least, must look very like motive. Trespass is concerned with the physical violation of possessory rights and it would seem to do no harm to principle to say that there is no violation of possessory rights where the act which would otherwise constitute the violation is permitted even if it is done for a purpose other than the purpose for which the permission was granted. There are, however, cases which say that a person who has a right of entry to the premises of another for a particular purpose commits a trespass if he enters for any other purpose and without any other lawful right or entitlement.

The best known authorities are, perhaps, *R v Pratt* (1855) 4 E & B 860; 119 ER 319 and *Harrison v Duke of Rutland* [1893] 1 QB 142. Each of those cases was concerned with the use by a member of the public of a highway over the land of another for purposes other than passing and repassing which was the extent of the right of way. In the first case the defendant came on to the highway carrying a gun and accompanied by a dog. He waved his hand to the dog, which entered the adjoining cover; a pheasant rose; the defendant, being on the highway, fired at it and missed it. In the second case, the plaintiff interfered with the defendant's shooting of grouse on the defendant's land over which the highway ran, by standing on the highway and doing such things as waving his pocket handkerchief and opening and shutting his umbrella for the purpose of keeping the grouse away. In each case these activities on the highway were said to constitute trespass at common law. I am by no means certain that the cases could not be adequately explained upon the basis that the physical acts involved amounted to more than passage along the highway and so were not acts which were permitted whatever the purpose in committing them. But the judgments speak in terms of purpose. For example, in the latter case, at 146, Lord Esher says:

> Therefore, on the ground that the plaintiff was on the highway, the soil of which belonged to the Duke of Rutland, not for the purpose of using it in order to pass and repass, or for any reasonable or usual mode of using the highway as a highway, I think he was a trespasser.

See also Lopes LJ at 150; Kay LJ at 158. Moreover, there are dicta in other cases which suggest that a person enters another's premises as a trespasser if he enters for a purpose other than the purpose for which he is invited or permitted to enter. See *Taylor v Jackson* (1898) 78 LT 555 at 556; *Hillen and Pettigrew v ICI (Alkali) Ltd* [1936] AC 65 at 69; cf *Byrne v Kinematograph Renters Society Ltd* [1958] 1 WLR 762 at 776. In *Farrington v Thomson and Bridgland* [1959] VR 286 it was held that the second-named defendant trespassed upon the plaintiff's hotel premises when he entered them for a purpose which was not within the scope of any tacit permission or licence that he may have had from the plaintiff. In *Strang v Russell* (1905) 24 NZLR 916 it was held that, although the defendant may have had a licence to enter upon the property of the plaintiff, if he entered not in pursuance of that licence, but with the intention of contesting the plaintiff's right as owner, the licence was no defence in an action for damages for trespass. See also *Gross v Wright* [1923] 2 DLR 171 at 185.

I think that I must, therefore, conclude that entry upon another's premises for a purpose other than a purpose for which permission has been given by that other in the absence of some other lawful right to enter, is entry as a trespasser for the purposes of the civil law and, this concept having been borrowed for the purposes of s 76 of the Crimes Act, it is also entry as a trespasser for the purposes of that section. Of course, where permission is given to enter premises for a limited purpose the limitation must appear expressly or by implication. No unrevealed reservation of purpose by the person giving the permission will restrict its extent if the limitation is not otherwise apparent at the time. Whether or not in any case the permission was limited to entry for a particular purpose will be a question for the jury in all the circumstances.

That, of course, means that a person who enters another's premises with intent to steal will ordinarily enter as a trespasser because permission to enter is not normally given for such a purpose. But it does not necessarily follow that such a person is guilty of burglary, because he must also have intended to enter as a trespasser. Unless that intention is established there is merely an *actus reus* with no *mens rea*.

[**Murphy J** dissented. Appeal dismissed.]

8.85C R v Lambert

[1972] Crim LR 422
Newcastle Crown Court (UK)

[The accused suspected his wife of having an affair with X. He informed X that £250 would buy X's rights to his (the accused's) wife and that, if X did not pay, he (the accused) would inform X's employer and X's wife of his suspicions. The accused was charged with blackmail. The trial judge directed the jury in the following terms:]

The issue here was whether the demand was made with a view to gaining £250 or causing the loss of that sum to X with menaces. 'Menaces' was not defined in the Act but would include a threat or intimidation and must be of such a nature or extent that a person of normal intelligence might succumb to the demand. He further directed the jury that the demand with menaces must be unwarranted and that it is so unless the person making the demand does so in the belief that he has reasonable ground and the use of menaces is a proper means of reinforcing the demand. His belief must be honest. The prosecution have the burden of satisfying the jury that this ingredient of the offence is made out. In other words they must negative any allegation that the defendant believed that he had reasonable ground. The defendant's belief need not be reasonable. The question is whether the defendant honestly held that belief. The test of deciding whether the defendant held this belief is to ask the question — what did the defendant himself believe? His guilt or innocence depends upon his own opinion whether he was acting rightly or wrongly in the circumstances. You have to be satisfied, sure in your own minds before you can convict. Feelings of repugnance must not enter into your deliberations.

The main question in the case was this. Was the demand with menaces unwarranted? Did the defendant honestly believe he had the right or reasonable grounds for making the demand, and did he honestly believe that it was proper to reinforce that demand? The prosecution must show that the defendant made the demand not having that belief.

The prosecution must establish that the defendant did not have the belief. The defendant's guilt or innocence depends upon his own opinion as to whether he was acting rightly or wrongly at the time.

[The accused was acquitted.]

8.86 Notes

1. The nature of the force or threat of force which must be proven as a element of robbery under s 75, and armed robbery under s 75A, is discussed in *R v Galas and Mikhael* (2007) 18 VR 205 (see **4.56C**).
2. A person is only guilty of armed robbery under s 75A if they have with them a 'firearm, imitation firearm, offensive weapon, explosive or imitation explosive' (Crimes Act 1958 (Vic) s 75A(1)). A person can only be said to 'have the weapon with him [or her]' if he or she knows of its presence: *R v Cugullere* [1961] 1 WLR 858. A person was held to 'have with him a firearm' where the firearm was in a locked car outside the place in which the accused intended to commit the robbery, on the basis that it was readily accessible to him: *R v Pawlicki and Swindell* [1992] 1 WLR 827. The weapons referred to are defined in Crimes Act 1958 (Vic) s 77(1A). 'Offensive weapon' means 'an article made or adapted for use for causing injury … or which the person having it with him or her intends or threatens to use for such a purpose'. The last category was held to apply in a case where a plastic soft drink bottle was used to threaten staff in a pharmacy: *R v Nguyen* [1997] 1 VR 551. An item will only be an offensive weapon under this section if it is being carried for this purpose. In *Ohlson v Hylton* [1975] 1 WLR 724 the accused, a carpenter, was on his way home from work with his bag of tools which included a hammer. The trains were very crowded, and the accused got into an argument with another passenger, hitting them on the head with the hammer. His convictions for assault and for having an offensive weapon were quashed on appeal, the Crown Court finding that the offence required proof that the person was carrying the weapon with the pre-existing intent to use it as an offensive weapon. This decision has been followed in Victoria in *Wilson v Kuhl* [1979] VR 315.
3. The acquittal of the accused in *R v Lambert* because he subjectively believed he was entitled to demand money in such circumstances, seems surprising and unsatisfactory. It is submitted that it is correct that the first limb of the twofold test contained in s 87(1) of the Victorian Act (that is, did the accused act in the belief that he or she had reasonable grounds for making the demand) should be subjective in form. It is submitted that the Criminal Law Review Committee was right to make this limb of the twofold test

entirely subjective. However, if an accused makes a demand coupled with a threat to disclose discreditable action on the part of the victim, there seems to be no reason of principle why the accused's guilt or innocence should depend upon his or her own beliefs as to whether the occasion justified the menaces used. It would seem that a subjective test in this context grants an unwarranted advantage to persons of low moral standards. It is submitted that the approach taken in the definition of 'unwarranted' in s 171 of the South Australian legislation, which adopts the test of the standards of ordinary people, is to be preferred.

4. Whatever the accused's own beliefs, the accused will not have a defence where the acts threatened were, themselves, criminal. In South Australia, this is made clear in the definition of unwarranted, and it is submitted that a similar result would be reached in Victoria. In *R v Harvey* (1980) 72 Cr App R 139, the menaces threatened included violence to the victim and to his wife and family. The Court of Appeal held that the accused's beliefs as to the propriety of such threats could not give rise to a defence. Bingham J stated (at 142):

   > In order to exonerate a defendant from liability his belief must be that the use of the menaces is a 'proper' means of reinforcing the demand. 'Proper' is an unusual expression to find in a criminal statute. It is not defined in the Act, and no definition need be attempted here. It is, however, plainly a word of wide meaning, certainly wider than (for example) 'lawful'. But the greater includes the less and no act which was not believed to be lawful could be believed to be proper within the meaning of the subsection. Thus no assistance is given to any defendant, even a fanatic or a deranged idealist, who knows or suspects that his threat, or the act threatened, is criminal, but believes it to be justified by his end or his peculiar circumstances. The test is not what he regards as justified, but what he believes to be proper.

5. The word 'menaces' is derived from the pre-Theft Act provisions. What was said about the word 'menaces' in relation to the New South Wales provisions (see 7.127) is equally applicable in the present context.

6. Note that, in Victoria, the expressions 'gain' and 'loss' are defined by s 71(1) as being limited to 'gain or loss in money or other property'. This limitation on the scope of the offence seems surprising. If A demands with menaces that a woman spends the night with him, he will not be guilty of blackmail because his demand is not made with a view to gain 'in money or other property'. He would be guilty of the offence of procuring by threats under s 57(1) of the Crimes Act 1958 (Vic). However, this offence carries a maximum penalty of only five years' imprisonment. If, however, A were to demand with menaces that the woman spend the night with B, and he were to do so believing that B would pay him for procuring the woman, then he would be guilty

of blackmail, an offence punishable with up to 14 years' imprisonment. He would be guilty of blackmail in this case because he would be acting 'with a view to gain', and s 87(2) provides that '[t]he nature of the act … demanded is immaterial'. Yet the accused's moral culpability seems no greater in this case than in the former.

7. What justification is there for limiting blackmail to cases where the accused acts with a view to gain or intent to cause loss of money or other property? Professor Smith suggests that this limitation is justified as part of a general policy of limiting the provisions of the Act to the protection of economic interests: *The Law of Theft*, op cit, p 176. Such a justification seems inadequate. The offence of burglary extends beyond the protection of economic interests, and there seems no reason in principle why blackmail should not also. It is submitted that the offence should have been drafted so as to cover an accused who, by menaces, obtains sexual gratification or any other non-proprietary gain or advantage, or who causes any non-proprietary loss or disadvantage to the victim. In South Australia, this view has been accepted. Section 171(1) of the Criminal Law Consolidation Act 1935 (SA) defines harm as including physical or mental harm (including humiliation or serious embarrassment).

8.87 Further reading

B McSherry and B Naylor, *Australian Criminal Laws: Critical Perspectives*, Oxford University Press, Melbourne, 2004, pp 308–31

D Ormerod and D Williams (ed), *Smith's Law of Theft*, Oxford University Press, 9th ed, 2007, pp 59–75, 76–103

C R Williams, *Property Offences*, 3rd ed, Law Book Co, Sydney, 1999, pp 207–13, 231–45, 265–70

Drug Offences

CHAPTER 9

INTRODUCTION

9.1 Since at least the mid-1950s the 'drug problem' has been identified as an increasingly significant issue in Australia, as it has been in the rest of the Western world. Of course, mood-altering substances have been used since time immemorial, and some have been seen to have negative consequences for users. Only in the 1950s, however, did the approach to this observation shift from a medical to a criminal response. Since that time, a range of drugs — but not all drugs — have been subject to the criminal law. The usage of illegal drugs, and changes in their usage, is difficult to estimate, with conviction rates for drug offences being related to enforcement and prosecution policies operating at particular points of time. The use of illegal drugs (barbiturates, cannabis, cocaine, heroin, methadone, morphine, ecstasy and methamphetamines, to mention only the more commonly used drugs), nonetheless, clearly constitutes a significant and growing social concern. The Commonwealth Department of Human Services and Health estimated the annual turnover in Australia in 1992 for heroin, cocaine and cannabis alone to be $216.4 million: D Collins and H Lapsley, Department of Human Services and Health (Cth), *The Social Costs of Drug Abuse in Australia in 1988 and 1992*, Report No 30 (February 2006), p 54.

9.2 Any consideration of the issue of illegal drugs must, however, be viewed in the overall context of the steady increase over the past 50 years in the misuse of drugs of all kinds (solvents, alcohol, tobacco, analgesics and other prescription drugs) in our society. In 1988, the Statistical Services Section of the Commonwealth Department of Community Services and Health compiled a detailed set of statistics concerning alcohol usage in Australia. That study showed that in the period from 1956 to 1986 there was a steady increase in alcohol consumption in Australia until 1978, followed by a slight decrease and then a steadying until the end of the period covered. In 2010, statistics compiled for the *National Drug Strategy Household Survey Report* by the Australian Institute of Health and Welfare showed the proportion of Australians who reported drinking alcohol recently in 2010 (80.95%) had declined from a peak in 2004, but was still higher than in 1993 (77.9%). In 2010, one in five people aged 14 years or older consumed alcohol at a level that put them at risk of harm from alcohol-related disease or injury over their lifetime, and this figure remained stable between 2007 (20.3%) and 2010 (20.1%). However, in Australia the number of people drinking alcohol in risky quantities increased from 3.5 million in 2007 to 3.7 million in 2010. Males were far more likely than females to consume alcohol in risky quantities, and those 18–29 years of age were more likely than any other age group to consume alcohol in quantities that placed them at risk of an alcohol-related injury, and of alcohol-related harm over their lifetime. The *National Drug Strategy Household Survey Report* found that the proportion of people who had smoked tobacco in the previous 12 months had steadily declined from 29.1% in 1993 to 18.1% in 2010. In 2010, 15.1% of people in Australia aged 14 years or older were daily smokers, a reduction from 16.6% in 2007 and 24.3% in 1991. Almost 40% of smokers had reduced the amount they smoked in a day in 2010, and 29% had tried unsuccessfully to give up smoking.

9.3 The misuse of lawful drugs in fact causes greater harm than the use of unlawful drugs. The Commonwealth Department of Community Services and Health estimated that in 1987 there were 25,495 deaths caused by drug use. Of these, 18,165 (71%) were due to tobacco use; 6621 (26%) were due to alcohol use (including 805 deaths in traffic accidents involving alcohol); 323 (1%) were due to opiates; and the remaining 2% were due to other drugs, mostly barbiturates: The Drug Offensive, *Statistics on Drug Abuse in Australia 1989*, Australian Government Publishing Service, Canberra, 1990, Table 49. The National Alcohol Indicators Project estimates that 32,696 Australians aged over 15 years died from alcohol-related injury and disease caused by risky/high-risk drinking from 1996–2005: *Trends in Estimated Alcohol-Attributable Deaths and Hospitalisations in Australia* (2009). Statistics for Victoria released in 2012 showed that the rate of alcohol-related deaths per 10,000 people reduced from 1.5 in 2001 to 1.4 in 2007. It should be noted that the rate of alcohol-related deaths for males is much greater than that for females. In 2007, for example, the rate of alcohol-related deaths for males in Victoria was 1.91 per 10,000 and the rate for females was 0.90 per 10,000: Department of Health (Vic), *The Victorian Drug Statistics Handbook: Patterns of Drug Use and Related Harm in Victoria for the Period July 2009 to June 2010*, Report No 13 (2012).

9.4 This picture of lawful drug use is in no way intended to minimise the nature or seriousness of illicit drug use, but rather to emphasise that it is in reality part of a wider community scenario. The 2010 *National Drug Strategy Household Survey Report* found that in 2010, around 7.3 million people in Australia reported having ever used an illicit drug, and almost 3 million had used an illicit drug in the 12 months before the survey. The proportion of people aged 14 years or older who had used an illicit drug in the last 12 months increased from 13.4% in 2007 to 14.7% in 2010. Over 35.4% of Australians over 14 years of age had used cannabis in their lifetime; 7.3% had used cocaine at some point in their life; and 1.4% had used heroin at some stage in their life. Most jurisdictions recorded a slight increase in illicit drug use, but New South Wales was the only state in which this increase was statistically significant. Illicit drug users (whether use was in the previous 12 months or the previous month), were more likely to be diagnosed or treated for a mental illness and report high or very high levels of psychological distress compared with those who had not used an illicit drug in the previous 12 months.

9.5 In Victoria, a decline has been reported in the prevalence of some recent illicit drug use (as distinct from the lifetime-use data reported above) in people over the age of 14 years. *The Victorian Drug Statistics Handbook 2012* reports a decline in reported use of cannabis (from a usage rate of 12.0% in 2001 to 10.0% in 2004 and 9.0% in 2007). The use of heroin has remained steady at 0.3% of Victorians across 2001, 2004 and 2007, and the use of methamphetamines also stabilised at 2.0% in 2001, 3.0% in 2004 and 2.0% in 2007. However, the use of cocaine/crack has increased slightly from 1.0% in 2001 and 2004, to 2.0% in 2007.

9.6 Mortality rates from drug use continue to be dominated by deaths from alcohol and tobacco use. The total number of drug-related deaths in Victoria was 5219 in 2001 and 5012 in 2007. This was largely comprised of tobacco-related deaths (4344 in 2001 and 4199 in 2007) and alcohol-related deaths (723 in 2001 and 728 in 2007): Department of Health (Vic), *The Victorian Drug Statistics Handbook: Patterns of Drug Use and Related Harm in Victoria for the Period July 2009 to June 2010*, Report No 13 (2012). In Victoria between 2001 and 2007, deaths from illicit drugs rose from 93 in 2001 to 156 in 2003, and have since declined steadily to 85 in 2007. Tangible and intangible social costs of drug use across Australia for 2004–05 have been calculated to amount to $15.3 billion for alcohol, $31.5 billion for tobacco, $8.2 billion for illicit drugs, and a further $1.1 billion for alcohol and illicit drugs together: D Collins and H Lapsley, *The Costs of Tobacco, Alcohol and Illicit Drug Abuse to Australian Society in 2004/5*, National Drug Strategy Monograph Series No. 66, 2009.

9.7 It is a mistake to think that the criminal law can ever be more than a part of any concerted move to reduce drug misuse in society. Education, medical treatment and social welfare initiatives are equally, and possibly more, important. This is not, however, to say that the criminal law is not an important part of any attempt to control the increase in drug misuse within our society. Thus, the Williams Royal Commission stated (E S Williams, *Australian Royal Commission of Inquiry into Drugs: Report*, Australian Government Publishing Service, Canberra, 1980, Book D, D13):

> In the Commissions' opinion law enforcement initiatives should be given priority in tackling the drug problem. This observation must not be taken as indicating a belief that the Commission regards treatment and education as less significant. However, law enforcement is capable of immediate improvement … and bears the responsibility for reducing the quantities of commonly abused drugs that are available.

The groundbreaking report of the Victorian Premier's Drug Advisory Council, *Drugs and our Community: Report of the Premier's Drug Advisory Council*, Melbourne, March 1996 (the Pennington Report) proceeded on the basis that prohibition alone could not counter the prevalence of the drug problem. The report contains a detailed set of recommendations, the aim of which is to minimise the harm being done to society. Key recommendations include systematic implementation of school-based education programs about the misuse of licit and illicit drugs; improved information sources for parents to assist them to educate and support their children regarding drug issues; further development of services that are available to support people with drug dependency; improvement in services for young people for whom there is a real possibility of rehabilitation with appropriate support; improvement in the quality of advice to the courts and enhanced capacity to ensure treatment and supervision required by the courts is delivered by a competent organisation; establishment of an Agency for Drug Dependency based on existing services; and complementing Victoria's methadone program by the development of proposals to trial new drugs.

The report recommends decriminalisation of personal use and possession of marijuana. Use and possession of up to 25 grams of marijuana and cultivation of up to five cannabis plants per household for personal use should no longer be an offence. Sale of marijuana should remain an offence, with the sale of small quantities by an adult to an adult incurring a caution for a first offence and an adjourned bond for a second offence. The report recommends the retention of prohibition in the case of other illicit drugs. In the case of drugs such as heroin, cocaine, amphetamines, ecstasy and cannabis products other than marijuana, it recommended that, in the case of a first offence of use or possession, the preferred penalty should be a caution, to be followed by a bond. In the case of drug trafficking, however, it was recommended that existing severe penalties should remain: Victorian Premier's Drug Advisory Council, *Drugs and our Community* (March 1996).

9.8 In June 1996 the Victorian Government announced its intention to accept the key recommendations contained in the Pennington Report other than the decriminalisation of personal use and possession of marijuana. That proposal lapsed and the recommendations have not been adopted to date. Rather than decriminalise cannabis offences, most Australian jurisdictions now have in use a system of cautions to divert minor cannabis offenders from the criminal justice system. For instance, the cannabis cautioning scheme was introduced in Victoria in 1998 and New South Wales in 2000, to provide police with the discretion to formally caution, rather than charge, a person for minor cannabis offences.

9.9 In 2000 in Victoria and New South Wales, a proposal was put forward for the establishment of injecting facilities on a trial basis. Such a facility was established in Kings Cross, Sydney in 2001 on a trial basis. The proposal was not favoured by the Federal Government, and in Victoria it lapsed. The advantages of establishing such facilities are suggested as being reducing the public nuisance of drug addicts injecting in public places and unsafely discarding needles, and a reduction in deaths from overdose by monitoring injection practices. Injecting facilities would also provide access to treatment for addicts wishing to break the habit. The arguments in favour of introducing a number of such facilities in Victoria on a trial basis are dealt with in the report prepared for the Victorian government by the Drug Policy Expert Committee (chaired by Professor David Pennington), *Heroin: Facing the Issues* (2000). It would be necessary for the use of heroin in an approved injecting facility, or possession of heroin for the purpose of use in an approved injecting facility, to no longer be an offence. In 2010 the Drug Misuse and Trafficking Amendment (Medically Supervised Injecting Centre) Act (NSW) was passed, to end the trial period and permanently establish the safe injecting centre in Kings Cross. In the Second Reading Speech to this Act it was estimated that the centre had potentially averted over 300,000 public injections. The aims of the centre were also reaffirmed: to decrease the number of overdose deaths; to provide a gateway to treatment and counselling; to reduce discarded needles and the number of users injecting in public places; and to help reduce the spread of diseases like HIV and hepatitis C. Due to a perception of a high rate of public injecting in the Melbourne inner city suburb of Richmond, the City of Yarra appealed to the state government in 2011 to trial a safe injecting centre. This appeal was strengthened by the Victorian arm of the Australian Medical Association calling in 2012 for the Victorian Government to consider a trial of supervised injecting facilities in Victoria. To date, however, no such facilities have been established in Victoria.

9.10 Many jurisdictions have been developing strategies to address demand, supply, and harm minimisation in the use of drugs. The Australian Government has released the *National Drug Strategy 2010–2015*, New South Wales has the *Drug and Alcohol Plan 2006–2010* and the *Alcohol Services Plan 2009–2013*, and in 2013 the Victorian Government released a 'whole of government strategy to reduce the impact of alcohol and drug abuse on the Victorian community': *Reducing the Alcohol and Drug Toll: Victoria's Plan 2013–2017*.

THE STATUTORY PROVISIONS

9.11 Offences involving the dealing in or use of proscribed drugs are contained in both federal and state legislation. Federal offences are contained in the Criminal Code (Cth) Ch 9. These are detailed provisions covering trafficking, commercial cultivation and selling of controlled plants, manufacturing of controlled drugs and import-export offences. Only a selection of the more important import-export offences are here reproduced. The predecessor of these offences were contained in the Customs Act 1900 (Cth), and were based upon the trade and commerce head of law-making power invested in the Federal Government by s 51 of the Commonwealth of Australia Constitution Act 1900: see *Milicevic v Campbell and Commonwealth of Australia* (1975) 132 CLR 207; 6 ALR 1. Further federal offences are contained in the Crimes (Traffic in Narcotic Drugs and Psychotropic Substances) Act 1990 (Cth). This Act is based upon the external affairs law-making power contained in s 51 of the Constitution. The Act gives force to the United Nations Convention Against Illicit Traffic in Narcotic Drugs and Psychotropic Substances, adopted in Vienna in 1988. Each state has its own legislation dealing with prohibited drugs. In Victoria and New South Wales, the main legislative provisions are contained in the Drugs, Poisons and Controlled Substances Act 1981 (Vic) and the Drug Misuse and Trafficking Act 1985 (NSW). These provisions cover a variety of activities relating to prohibited drugs, including possession and use of drugs, cultivation of drugs, and drug trafficking. In instances, there may be overlap between the federal and state legislation. Such instances of overlap, however, do not amount to inconsistency, and the state legislation has been held to be constitutionally valid: *R v Stevens* (1991) 23 NSWLR 75.

9.12E Criminal Code (Cth)

(Schedule to Criminal Code Act 1995 (Cth))

DIVISION 307 — IMPORT-EXPORT OFFENCES

SUBDIVISION A — IMPORTING AND EXPORTING BORDER CONTROLLED DRUGS OR BORDER CONTROLLED PLANTS

307.1 Importing and exporting commercial quantities of border controlled drugs or border controlled plants

(1) A person commits an offence if:

(a) the person imports or exports a substance; and

(b) the substance is a border controlled drug or border controlled plant; and

(c) the quantity imported or exported is a commercial quantity.

Penalty: Imprisonment for life or 7,500 penalty units, or both.

(2) The fault element for paragraph (1)(b) is recklessness.

(3) Absolute liability applies to paragraph (1)(c).

307.2 Importing and exporting marketable quantities of border controlled drugs or border controlled plants

(1) A person commits an offence if:

(a) the person imports or exports a substance; and

(b) the substance is a border controlled drug or border controlled plant; and

(c) the quantity imported or exported is a marketable quantity.

Penalty: Imprisonment for 25 years or 5,000 penalty units, or both.

(2) The fault element for paragraph (1)(b) is recklessness.

(3) Absolute liability applies to paragraph (1)(c).

(4) Subsection (1) does not apply if the person proves that he or she neither intended, nor believed that another person intended, to sell any of the border controlled drug or any of the border controlled plant or its products.

Note: A defendant bears a legal burden in relation to the matters in subsection (4) (see section 13.4).

307.3 Importing and exporting border controlled drugs or border controlled plants

(1) A person commits an offence if:

(a) the person imports or exports a substance; and

(b) the substance is a border controlled drug or border controlled plant.

Penalty: Imprisonment for 10 years or 2,000 penalty units, or both.

(2) The fault element for paragraph (1)(b) is recklessness.

(3) Subsection (1) does not apply if the person proves that he or she neither intended, nor believed that another person intended, to sell any of the border controlled drug or any of the border controlled plant or its products.

Note: A defendant bears a legal burden in relation to the matters in subsection (3) (see section 13.4).

307.4 Importing and exporting border controlled drugs or border controlled plants — no defence relating to lack of commercial intent

(1) A person commits an offence if:

(a) the person imports or exports a substance; and

(b) the substance is a border controlled drug or border controlled plant, other than a determined border controlled drug or a determined border controlled plant.

Penalty: Imprisonment for 2 years, or 400 penalty units, or both.

(2) The fault element for paragraph (1)(b) is recklessness.

SUBDIVISION B — POSSESSING UNLAWFULLY IMPORTED BORDER CONTROLLED DRUGS OR BORDER CONTROLLED PLANTS

307.5 Possessing commercial quantities of unlawfully imported border controlled drugs or border controlled plants

(1) A person commits an offence if:

(a) the person possesses a substance; and

(b) the substance was unlawfully imported; and

(c) the substance is a border controlled drug or border controlled plant; and

(d) the quantity possessed is a commercial quantity.

Penalty: Imprisonment for life or 7,500 penalty units, or both.

(2) Absolute liability applies to paragraphs (1)(b) and (d).

(3) The fault element for paragraph (1)(c) is recklessness.

(4) Subsection (1) does not apply if the person proves that he or she did not know that the border controlled drug or border controlled plant was unlawfully imported.

Note: A defendant bears a legal burden in relation to the matter in subsection (4) (see section 13.4).

307.6 Possessing marketable quantities of unlawfully imported border controlled drugs or border controlled plants

(1) A person commits an offence if:

(a) the person possesses a substance; and

(b) the substance was unlawfully imported; and

(c) the substance is a border controlled drug or border controlled plant; and

(d) the quantity possessed is a marketable quantity.

Penalty: Imprisonment for 25 years or 5,000 penalty units, or both.

(2) Absolute liability applies to paragraphs (1)(b) and (d).

(3) The fault element for paragraph (1)(c) is recklessness.

(4) Subsection (1) does not apply if the person proves that he or she neither intended, nor believed that another person intended, to sell any of the border controlled drug or any of the border controlled plant or its products.

(5) Subsection (1) does not apply if the person proves that he or she did not know that the border controlled drug or border controlled plant was unlawfully imported.

Note: A defendant bears a legal burden in relation to the matters in subsections (4) and (5) (see section 13.4).

307.7 Possessing unlawfully imported border controlled drugs or border controlled plants

(1) A person commits an offence if:

(a) the person possesses a substance; and

(b) the substance was unlawfully imported; and

(c) the substance is a border controlled drug or border controlled plant, other than a determined border controlled drug or a determined border controlled plant.

Penalty: Imprisonment for 2 years or 400 penalty units, or both.

(2) Absolute liability applies to paragraph (1)(b).

(3) The fault element for paragraph (1)(c) is recklessness.

(4) Subsection (1) does not apply if the person proves that he or she did not know that the border controlled drug or border controlled plant was unlawfully imported.

Note: A defendant bears a legal burden in relation to the matter in subsection (4) (see section 13.4).

SUBDIVISION C — POSSESSING BORDER CONTROLLED DRUGS OR BORDER CONTROLLED PLANTS REASONABLY SUSPECTED OF HAVING BEEN UNLAWFULLY IMPORTED

307.8 Possessing commercial quantities of border controlled drugs or border controlled plants reasonably suspected of having been unlawfully imported

(1) A person commits an offence if:

(a) the person possesses a substance; and

(b) the substance is reasonably suspected of having been unlawfully imported; and

(c) the substance is a border controlled drug or border controlled plant; and

(d) the quantity possessed is a commercial quantity.

Penalty: Imprisonment for life or 7,500 penalty units, or both.

(2) Absolute liability applies to paragraphs (1)(b) and (d).

(3) The fault element for paragraph (1)(c) is recklessness.

(4) Subsection (1) does not apply if the person proves that the border controlled drug or border controlled plant was not unlawfully imported.

Note: A defendant bears a legal burden in relation to the matter in subsection (4) (see section 13.4).

307.9 Possessing marketable quantities of border controlled drugs or border controlled plants reasonably suspected of having been unlawfully imported

(1) A person commits an offence if:

(a) the person possesses a substance; and

(b) the substance is reasonably suspected of having been unlawfully imported; and

(c) the substance is a border controlled drug or border controlled plant; and

(d) the quantity possessed is a marketable quantity.

Penalty: Imprisonment for 25 years or 5,000 penalty units, or both.

(2) Absolute liability applies to paragraphs (1)(b) and (d).

(3) The fault element for paragraph (1)(c) is recklessness.

(4) Subsection (1) does not apply if the person proves that he or she neither intended, nor believed that another person intended, to sell any of the border controlled drug or any of the border controlled plant or its products.

(5) Subsection (1) does not apply if the person proves that the border controlled drug or border controlled plant was not unlawfully imported.

Note: A defendant bears a legal burden in relation to the matters in subsections (4) and (5) (see section 13.4).

307.10 Possessing border controlled drugs or border controlled plants reasonably suspected of having been unlawfully imported

(1) A person commits an offence if:

(a) the person possesses a substance; and

(b) the substance is reasonably suspected of having been unlawfully imported; and

(c) the substance is a border controlled drug or border controlled plant, other than a determined border controlled drug or a determined border controlled plant.

Penalty: Imprisonment for 2 years or 400 penalty units, or both.

(2) Absolute liability applies to paragraph (1)(b).

(3) The fault element for paragraph (1)(c) is recklessness.

(4) Subsection (1) does not apply if the person proves that the border controlled drug or border controlled plant was not unlawfully imported.

Note: A defendant bears a legal burden in relation to the matter in subsection (4) (see section 13.4)

9.13 Border controlled drugs and border controlled plants are defined by s 300.2 as those listed in s 314 or prescribed by regulation. This covers all the more commonly used drugs (barbiturates, cannabis, cocaine, heroin, lysergic acid, mescaline, methadone, morphine and opium), as well as a variety of more esoteric and less well-known substances. Division 314 and regulations specify the commercial, marketable and trafficable quantities of the various drugs.

9.14E Crimes (Traffic in Narcotic Drugs and Psychotropic Substances) Act 1990 (Cth)

PART 1 — PRELIMINARY

…

4 Act extends to external Territories

This Act extends to all external Territories.

4A Application of the Criminal Code

Chapter 2 of the *Criminal Code* applies to all offences against this Act.

Note: Chapter 2 of the *Criminal Code* sets out the general principles of criminal responsibility.

5 Effect of this Act on other laws

(1) This Act is not intended to exclude or limit the operation of any other law of the Commonwealth or any law of a State or Territory.

(2) Where a person has been convicted in a country outside Australia of an offence against the law of that country in respect of any conduct, that person is not liable to be convicted of an offence against this Act in respect of that conduct.

6 Meaning of *dealing in drugs*

(1) For the purposes of this Act, each of the following is a dealing in drugs:

(a) the cultivation of opium poppy, coca bush or cannabis plant with the intention of producing narcotic drugs;

(b) the separation of opium, coca leaves, cannabis or cannabis resin from the plant from which they are obtained;

(c) the manufacture, extraction or preparation of a narcotic drug or psychotropic substance;

(d) the possession of a narcotic drug or psychotropic substance with the intention of the manufacture, extraction or preparation of another such drug or substance;

(e) the sale, supply, or possession with the intention of sale or supply, of a narcotic drug or psychotropic substance;

(f) the importation into Australia, exportation from Australia, or possession with the intention of such importation or exportation, of a narcotic drug or psychotropic substance;

(fa) the manufacture, transport or distribution of any substance listed in Table I or Table II in the Annex to the Convention or of equipment or materials, with the knowledge that the substance, equipment or materials are to be used for a purpose set out in paragraph (a), (b) or (c);

(fb) organising, managing or financing a dealing in drugs referred to in paragraphs (a), (b), (c), (d), (e), (f) or (fa);

(g) the possession of any substance listed in Table I or Table II in the Annex to the Convention or of any equipment or materials, with the knowledge that the substance, equipment or materials are being used or are to be used for a purpose set out in paragraph (a), (b) or (c).

(2) For the purposes of this Act, each of the following is also a dealing in drugs:

(a) a conspiracy or attempt to engage in conduct that is, under subsection (1), a dealing in drugs;

(b) being a party to any dealing in drugs referred to in subsection (1);

(ba) aiding, abetting, counselling or procuring, or being by act or omission in any way directly or indirectly knowingly concerned in, any conduct that is, under subsection (1), a dealing in drugs;

(c) inciting to, urging or encouraging, any conduct that is, under subsection (1), a dealing in drugs.

7 Meaning of *flight* in relation to aircraft

For the purposes of this Act:

(a) a flight of an aircraft commences:

(i) at the time of the closing of the last external door of the aircraft to be closed before the aircraft first moves for the purpose of taking off from any place; or

(ii) if subparagraph (i) is not applicable — at the time at which the aircraft first moves for the purpose of taking off from any place; and

(b) a flight of an aircraft ends:

(i) at the time of the opening of the first external door of the aircraft to be opened after the aircraft comes to rest after its next landing after the commencement of the flight; or

(ii) if subparagraph (i) is not applicable — at the time at which the aircraft comes to rest after its next landing after the commencement of the flight; or, if the aircraft is destroyed, or the flight is abandoned, before either subparagraph (i) or subparagraph (ii) becomes applicable, at the time at which the aircraft is destroyed or the flight is abandoned, as the case may be.

8 Meaning of *ship at sea*

For the purposes of this Act, a ship is taken to be at sea when it is not within:

(a) the limits of a State or Territory; or

(b) the limits of a foreign country.

8A Proof of knowledge, intent or purpose

(1) If a particular knowledge, intent or purpose is an element of an offence against this Act, that knowledge, intent or purpose may be inferred from objective factual circumstances.

(2) Subsection (1) is not intended to exclude or limit any other way of proving knowledge, intent or purpose as an element of an offence for the purposes of a prosecution.

PART 2 — OFFENCES

9 Possession of equipment etc.

(1) A person who has in his or her possession, in Australia, any substance listed in Table I or II in the Annex to the Convention, or any equipment or materials, knowing that

the substance, equipment or materials are being used or are to be used in, or for, a dealing in drugs that:

(a) is referred to in paragraph 6(1)(a), (b) or (c); and

(b) constitutes an offence against:

(i) a law of the Commonwealth; or

(ii) a law of a State or Territory; or

(iii) a law of a foreign country;

is guilty of an offence against this section and is punishable, on conviction, by imprisonment for a period not exceeding:

(c) if the substance, equipment or materials are being used or are to be used in, or for, the manufacture, extraction or preparation of a psychotropic substance referred to in Part 2 of Schedule 3 — 5 years; or

(d) in any other case — 10 years.

(2) For the purposes of an offence against this section, absolute liability applies to the following physical elements of circumstance of the offence:

(a) that the possession is in Australia;

(b) that the substance possessed is listed in Table I or II in the Annex to the Convention;

(c) that the dealing in drugs in which, or for which, the substance, equipment or materials are being used or are to be used is a dealing in drugs described in paragraphs (1)(a) and (b).

10 Dealing in drugs on board an Australian aircraft

(1) A person is guilty of an offence against this section if:

(a) the person, on board an Australian aircraft in flight, whether in or outside Australia, engages in conduct that is a dealing in drugs; and

(b) the conduct would constitute an offence against a law in force in a State or Territory if it were engaged in by the person in that State or Territory.

(2) This section does not apply in relation to conduct engaged in by a person on board an Australian aircraft in flight between 2 places in the same State or in the same Territory.

(3) For the purposes of an offence against this section, absolute liability applies to such of the following physical elements of circumstance as are relevant to the offence:

(a) that the conduct is engaged in on board an Australian aircraft in flight, whether in or outside Australia;

(b) that the conduct would constitute an offence against a law in force in a State or Territory if it were engaged in by the person in that State or Territory;

(c) if paragraph 6(1)(f) applies — that the importation is into Australia, or the exportation is from Australia;

(d) if paragraph 6(1)(fa) or (g) applies — that the substance is listed in Table I or II in the Annex to the Convention.

Note: For *absolute liability*, see section 6.2 of the *Criminal Code*.

11 Dealing in drugs on board an Australian ship

(1) A person is guilty of an offence against this section if:

(a) the person, on board an Australian ship at sea, engages in conduct that is a dealing in drugs; and

(b) the conduct if engaged in by the person in a State or Territory would constitute an offence against a law of the Commonwealth.

(2) For the purposes of an offence against this section, absolute liability applies to such of the following physical elements of circumstance as are relevant to the offence:

(a) that the conduct is engaged in on board an Australian ship at sea;

(b) that the conduct if engaged in by the person in a State or Territory would constitute an offence against a law of the Commonwealth;

(c) if paragraph 6(1)(f) applies — that the importation is into Australia, or the exportation is from Australia;

(d) if paragraph 6(1)(fa) or (g) applies—that the substance is listed in Table I or II in the Annex to the Convention.

12 Dealing in drugs outside Australia

(1) A person is guilty of an offence against this section if:

(a) the person engages, outside Australia, in conduct that is a dealing in drugs; and

(b) the conduct constitutes an offence against the law of a foreign country; and

(c) the conduct would constitute an offence against a law in force in a State or Territory if it were engaged in by the person in that State or Territory.

(2) A person may be charged with an offence against this section only if:

(a) the person is present in Australia; and

(b) if the person is not an Australian citizen:

(i) no steps have been taken by the foreign country referred to in paragraph (1)(b) for the surrender of the person to that country; or

(ii) proceedings taken by that country under the Extradition Act 1988 have not resulted in the person being surrendered to that country.

(3) For the purposes of an offence against this section, absolute liability applies to such of the following physical elements of circumstance as are relevant to the offence:

(a) that the conduct is engaged in outside Australia;

(b) that the conduct constitutes an offence against the law of a foreign country;

(c) that the conduct would constitute an offence against a law in force in a State or Territory if it were engaged in by the person in that State or Territory;

(d) if paragraph 6(1)(f) applies — that the importation is into Australia, or the exportation is from Australia;

(e) if paragraph 6(1)(fa) or (g) applies — that the substance is listed in Table I or II in the Annex to the Convention.

Note: For *absolute liability*, see section 6.2 of the *Criminal Code*.

13 Dealing in drugs outside Australia with a view to commission of offence in Australia etc

(1) A person is guilty of an offence against this section if the person engages, outside Australia, in conduct that is a dealing in drugs with a view to the carrying out:

(a) in Australia; or

(b) on board an Australian aircraft in flight outside Australia; or

(c) on board an Australian ship at sea;

of a dealing in drugs that constitutes an offence against a law of the Commonwealth, of a State or of a Territory.

(2) For the purposes of an offence against this section, absolute liability applies to such of the following physical elements of circumstance as are relevant to the offence:
   (a) that the conduct is engaged in outside Australia;
   (b) that the view to the carrying out of a dealing in drugs with which the conduct is engaged in, is a view to the carrying out of such a dealing:
      (i) in Australia; or
      (ii) on board an Australian aircraft in flight outside Australia; or
      (iii) on board an Australian ship at sea;
   (c) that the carrying out of the dealing in drugs referred to in paragraph (b) constitutes an offence against a law of the Commonwealth, of a State or of a Territory;
   (d) if paragraph 6(1)(f) applies — that the importation is into Australia, or the exportation is from Australia;
   (e) if paragraph 6(1)(fa) or (g) applies — that the substance is listed in Table I or II in the Annex to the Convention.

Note: For *absolute liability*, see section 6.2 of the *Criminal Code*.

14 Conspiracy etc. outside Australia to commit offence inside Australia

(1) A person who, by conduct engaged in outside Australia:
   (a) conspires, or attempts, to carry out in a State or Territory; or
   (b) aids, abets, counsels or procures, or is in any way directly or indirectly knowingly concerned in, or party to, the carrying out in a State or Territory of;

a dealing in drugs referred to in subsection 6(1) that constitutes an offence against a law of that State or Territory is guilty of an offence against this section and is punishable, on conviction, by the same penalty as would be applicable if the person were convicted of the first-mentioned offence.

(2) For the purposes of an offence against this section, absolute liability applies to such of the following physical elements of circumstance as are relevant to the offence:
   (a) that the conduct is engaged in outside Australia;
   (b) that the dealing in drugs is carried out, or is to be carried out, in a State or Territory;
   (c) that the carrying out of the dealing in drugs constitutes an offence against a law of that State or Territory;
   (d) if paragraph 6(1)(f) applies — that the importation is into Australia, or the exportation is from Australia;
   (e) if paragraph 6(1)(fa) or (g) applies — that the substance is listed in Table I or II in the Annex to the Convention.

Note: For *absolute liability*, see section 6.2 of the *Criminal Code*.

15A Knowingly converting etc. property derived from a serious State drug offence

(1) Any person who, knowing that any property was derived from a serious State drug offence, in a State other than a prescribed State or a Territory other than a prescribed Territory:
   (a) converts that property to his or her own use or to the use of another person; or
   (b) transfers that property to another person;

with the intention of:

(c) concealing or disguising that the property was derived from the offence; or

(d) assisting another person involved in the commission of the offence to evade the legal consequences of that involvement;

is guilty of an offence punishable, on conviction, by imprisonment for a period not exceeding 20 years.

(2) For the purposes of an offence against this section, absolute liability applies to the physical element of circumstance of the offence, that the conversion or transfer of property takes place in:

(a) a State other than a prescribed State; or

(b) a Territory other than a prescribed Territory.

Note: For *absolute liability*, see section 6.2 of the *Criminal Code*.

15B Knowingly concealing etc. property derived from a serious State drug offence

(1) Any person who, knowing that any property was derived from a serious State drug offence, in a State other than a prescribed State or a Territory other than a prescribed Territory, conceals or disguises:

(a) the nature, source, or location, of the property; or

(b) any movement of the property; or

(c) the rights of any person with respect to the property; or

(d) the identity of any owner of the property;

is guilty of an offence punishable, on conviction, by imprisonment for a period not exceeding 20 years.

(2) For the purposes of an offence against this section, absolute liability applies to the physical element of circumstance of the offence, that the concealing or disguising takes place in:

(a) a State other than a prescribed State; or

(b) a Territory other than a prescribed Territory.

Note: For *absolute liability*, see section 6.2 of the *Criminal Code*.

15C Knowingly acquiring etc. property derived from a serious State drug offence

(1) If:

(a) a person, in a State other than a prescribed State or a Territory other than a prescribed Territory, acquires, has in his or her possession or uses any property; and

(b) the person knows or knew at the time when he or she receives or received the property that it was derived from a serious State drug offence;

the person is guilty of an offence punishable, on conviction, by imprisonment for a period not exceeding 20 years.

(2) For the purposes of an offence against this section, absolute liability applies to the physical element of circumstance of the offence, that the acquisition, possession or use is in:

(a) a State other than a prescribed State; or

(b) a Territory other than a prescribed Territory.

Note: For *absolute liability*, see section 6.2 of the *Criminal Code*.

9.15 Penalties in respect of the offences contained in ss 10–13 are set out in s 15. The penalties are heavy, ranging from two years for cultivation of small amounts of cannabis plant, to periods of 25 years and life imprisonment for more serious offences.

9.16E Drugs, Poisons and Controlled Substances Act 1981 (Vic)

PART 1 — INTRODUCTORY AND TRANSITIONAL

...

5 Meaning of *possession*

Without restricting the meaning of the word ***possession***, any substance shall be deemed for the purposes of this Act to be in the possession of a person so long as it is upon any land or premises occupied by him or is used, enjoyed or controlled by him in any place whatsoever, unless the person satisfies the court to the contrary.

...

PART V — DRUGS OF DEPENDENCE AND RELATED MATTERS

70 Definitions

(1) In this Part and Part VI, unless inconsistent with the context or subject-matter —

aggregated commercial quantity, in relation to 2 or more drugs of dependence, means a quantity determined as follows —

(a) the quantity of each drug of dependence involved in the alleged offence is determined as a fraction of —

(i) in the case of a drug of dependence which is a narcotic plant, the commercial quantity specified in column 2 of Part 2 of Schedule Eleven in respect of that drug of dependence; and

(ii) in relation to a drug of dependence the name of which is specified in column 1 of Part 3 of Schedule Eleven —

(A) if that drug of dependence is contained in or mixed with another substance and the quantity of that mixture of drug of dependence and other substance is not less than the quantity specified in column 2A of that Part of that Schedule opposite to the name of that drug of dependence, means any amount of that drug of dependence; or

(B) in any other case, means the quantity that is specified in column 2 of that Part of that Schedule opposite to the name of that drug of dependence; and

(b) the fractions determined under paragraph (a) are added together; and

(c) the quantity is an aggregated commercial quantity if the total of those fractions when added together is equal to or greater than the number '1'; [Examples are then given.]

aggregated large commercial quantity, in relation to 2 or more drugs of dependence, means a quantity determined as follows —

(a) the quantity of each drug of dependence involved in the alleged offence is determined as a fraction of —

(i) in the case of a drug of dependence which is a narcotic plant, the large commercial quantity specified in column 1A of Part 2 of Schedule Eleven in respect of that drug of dependence; and

(ii) in relation to a drug of dependence the name of which is specified in column 1 of Part 3 of Schedule Eleven —

(A) if that drug of dependence is contained in or mixed with another substance and the quantity of that mixture of drug of dependence and other substance is not less than the quantity specified in column 1B of that Part of that Schedule opposite to the name of that drug of dependence, means any amount of that drug of dependence; or

(B) in any other case, means the quantity that is specified in column 1A of that Part of that Schedule opposite to the name of that drug of dependence; and

(b) the fractions determined under paragraph (a) are added together; and

(c) the quantity is an aggregated large commercial quantity if the total of those fractions when added together is equal to or greater than the number '1'; [Examples are then given.]

cannabis means any fresh or dried parts of a plant of the genus Cannabis L;

child means a person under 18 years of age;

commercial quantity —

(a) in relation to a drug of dependence the name of which is specified in column 1 of Part 1 of Schedule Eleven, means the quantity that is specified in column 2 of that Part of that Schedule opposite to the name of that drug of dependence;

(b) in relation to a drug of dependence the name of which is specified in column 1 of Part 2 of Schedule Eleven, means the quantity, or the number of plants, that is specified in column 2 of that Part of that Schedule opposite to the name of that drug of dependence;

(c) in relation to a drug of dependence the name of which is specified in column 1 of Part 3 of Schedule Eleven —

(i) if that drug of dependence is contained in or mixed with another substance and the quantity of that mixture of drug of dependence and other substance is not less than the quantity specified in column 2A of that Part of that Schedule opposite to the name of that drug of dependence, means any amount of that drug of dependence; or

(ii) in any other case, means the quantity that is specified in column 2 of that Part of that Schedule opposite to the name of that drug of dependence;

(d) in relation to 2 or more drugs of dependence, means an aggregated commercial quantity of those drugs;

cultivate, in relation to a narcotic plant includes —

(a) sow a seed of a narcotic plant; or

(b) plant, grow, tend, nurture or harvest a narcotic plant; or

(c) graft, divide or transplant a narcotic plant;

large commercial quantity —

(a) in relation to a drug of dependence the name of which is specified in column 1 of Part 2 of Schedule Eleven, means the quantity, or the number of plants, that is specified in column 1A of that Part of that Schedule opposite to the name of that drug of dependence;

(b) in relation to a drug of dependence the name of which is specified in column 1 of Part 3 of Schedule Eleven —

  (i) if that drug of dependence is contained in or mixed with another substance and the quantity of that mixture of drug of dependence and other substance is not less than the quantity specified in column 1B of that Part of that Schedule opposite to the name of that drug of dependence, means any amount of that drug of dependence; or

  (ii) in any other case, means the quantity that is specified in column 1A of that Part of that Schedule opposite to the name of that drug of dependence;

(c) in relation to 2 or more drugs of dependence, means an aggregated large commercial quantity of those drugs;

narcotic plant means any plant the name of which is specified in column 1 of Part 2 of Schedule Eleven and includes a cutting of such a plant, whether or not the cutting has roots;

small quantity —

(a) in relation to any fresh or dried parts of a plant of the genus Cannabis L, means the quantity that is specified in column 4 of Part 2 of Schedule Eleven opposite to the name Cannabis L specified in column 1 of that part of that Schedule; and

(b) in relation to any drug of dependence the name of which is specified in column 1 of Part 3 of Schedule Eleven, means the quantity of that drug, including any other substance in which it is contained or with which it is mixed, that is specified in column 4 of that Part of that Schedule opposite to the name of that drug of dependence;

traffick in relation to a drug of dependence includes —

(a) prepare a drug of dependence for trafficking;

(b) manufacture a drug of dependence; or

(c) sell, exchange, agree to sell, offer for sale or have in possession for sale, a drug of dependence;

traffickable quantity, in relation to a drug of dependence —

(a) the name of which is specified in column 1 of Part 1 of Schedule Eleven, means the quantity that is specified in column 3 of that Part of that Schedule opposite to the name of that drug of dependence;

(b) the name of which is specified in column 1 of Part 2 of Schedule Eleven, means the quantity, or the number of plants, that is specified in column 3 of that Part of that Schedule opposite to the name of that drug of dependence;

(c) the name of which is specified in column 1 of Part 3 of Schedule Eleven —

(i) if that drug of dependence is contained in or mixed with another substance and the quantity of that mixture of drug of dependence and other substance is not less than the quantity specified in column 3 of that Part of that Schedule opposite to the name of that drug of dependence, means any amount of that drug of dependence; or

(ii) in any other case, means the quantity that is specified in column 3A of that Part of that Schedule opposite to the name of that drug of dependence;

use in relation to a drug of dependence means —

(a) smoke a drug of dependence;

(b) inhale the fumes caused by heating or burning a drug of dependence; or

(c) introduce a drug of dependence into the body of a person.

(2) The provisions of section 4(2) and (3) and the interpretations of ***manufacture***, ***sell*** and ***supply*** in section 4(1) do not apply to this Part.

71 Trafficking in a drug or drugs of dependence — large commercial quantity

A person who, without being authorized by or licensed under this Act or the regulations to do so, trafficks or attempts to traffick in a quantity of a drug of dependence or of 2 or more drugs of dependence that is not less than the large commercial quantity applicable to that drug of dependence or those drugs of dependence is guilty of an indictable offence and liable —

(a) to level 1 imprisonment (life); and

(b) in addition to imprisonment, to a penalty of not more than 5000 penalty units.

71AA Trafficking in a drug or drugs of dependence — commercial quantity

A person who, without being authorized by or licensed under this Act or the regulations to do so, trafficks or attempts to traffick in a quantity of a drug of dependence or of 2 or more drugs of dependence that is not less than the commercial quantity applicable to that drug of dependence or those drugs of dependence is guilty of an indictable offence and liable to level 2 imprisonment (25 years maximum).

71AB Trafficking in a drug of dependence to a child

A person who, without being authorized by or licensed under this Act or the regulations to do so, trafficks or attempts to traffick in a drug of dependence to a child is guilty of an indictable offence and liable to level 3 imprisonment (20 years maximum).

71AC Trafficking in a drug of dependence

A person who, without being authorized by or licensed under this Act or the regulations to do so, trafficks or attempts to traffick in a drug of dependence is guilty of an indictable offence and liable to level 4 imprisonment (15 years maximum).

71A Possession of substance, material, documents or equipment for trafficking in a drug of dependence

(1) A person who, without being authorised by or licensed under this Act or the regulations to do so, possesses a substance, material, document containing instructions relating to the preparation, cultivation or manufacture of a drug of dependence or equipment with the intention of using the substance, material, document or equipment for the

purpose of trafficking in a drug of dependence is guilty of an indictable offence and liable to level 5 imprisonment (10 years maximum).

(2) Nothing in this section is limited by section 71C.

(3) Nothing in this section is limited by section 71D.

71B Supply of drug of dependence to a child

(1) A person who, without being authorised by or licensed under this Act or the regulations to do so —

(a) supplies a drug of dependence to a child for the purposes of the supply of that drug of dependence by that child to another person, whether a child or adult; or

(b) supplies a drug of dependence to a child for the use of that drug of dependence by that child —

is guilty of an indictable offence and liable to a penalty of not more than 1000 penalty units or level 4 imprisonment (15 years maximum) or both.

(2) Despite section 70 (2), in this section '***supply***' has the same meaning as in section 4(1) of this Act.

(3) This section does not apply to a person who supplies a drug of dependence to a child if, at the time of supplying that drug, that person was also a child.

(4) It is a defence to a charge under this section for a person charged to prove that he or she believed on reasonable grounds that the person to whom the drug of dependence was supplied was 18 years of age or older.

71C Possession of tablet press

A person who, without being authorized by or licensed under this Act or the regulations (if any) to do so or otherwise without a lawful excuse, possesses a tablet press is guilty of an indictable offence and liable to a penalty of not more than 600 penalty units or level 6 imprisonment (5 years maximum) or both.

71D Possession of precursor chemicals

A person who, without being authorized by or licensed under this Act or the regulations (if any) to do so or otherwise without a lawful excuse, possesses a prescribed precursor chemical in a quantity that is not less than the prescribed quantity applicable to that precursor chemical is guilty of an indictable offence and liable to a penalty of not more than 600 penalty units or level 6 imprisonment (5 years maximum) or both.

72 Cultivation of narcotic plants — large commercial quantity

A person who, without being authorized by or licensed under this Act or the regulations to do so, cultivates or attempts to cultivate a narcotic plant in a quantity of a drug of dependence, being a narcotic plant, that is not less than the large commercial quantity applicable to that narcotic plant is guilty of an indictable offence and liable —

(a) to level 1 imprisonment (life); and

(b) in addition to imprisonment, to a penalty of not more than 5000 penalty units.

72A Cultivation of narcotic plants — commercial quantity

A person who, without being authorized by or licensed under this Act or the regulations to do so, cultivates or attempts to cultivate a narcotic plant in a quantity of a drug of dependence, being a narcotic plant, that is not less than the commercial quantity applicable to that narcotic plant is guilty of an indictable offence and liable to level 2 imprisonment (25 years maximum).

72B Cultivation of narcotic plants

A person who, without being authorized by or licensed under this Act or the regulations to do so, cultivates or attempts to cultivate a narcotic plant is guilty of an indictable offence and liable —

(a) if the trial judge (or magistrate on a summary hearing) is satisfied on the balance of probabilities that the offence was not committed by the person for any purpose related to trafficking in that plant, to level 8 imprisonment (1 year maximum) or a penalty of not more than 20 penalty units or both; or

(b) in any other case, to level 4 imprisonment (15 years maximum).

72C Defence to prosecution for offences involving cultivation

It is a good defence to a prosecution for an offence against section 72, 72A or 72B involving the cultivation of a narcotic plant if the person charged with the offence adduces evidence which satisfies the court on the balance of probabilities that, having regard to all the circumstances (including his or her conduct) in which the matter alleged to constitute the offence arose or preparatory to the alleged commission of the offence, he or she did not know or suspect and could not reasonably have been expected to have known or suspected that the narcotic plant was a narcotic plant.

73 Possession of a drug of dependence

(1) A person who without being authorized by or licensed under this Act or the regulations to do so has or attempts to have in his possession a drug of dependence is guilty of an indictable offence and liable —

(a) where the court is satisfied on the balance of probabilities that —

(i) the offence was committed in relation to a quantity of cannabis or tetrahydrocannabinol that is not more than the small quantity applicable to cannabis or tetrahydrocannabinol;

(ii) the offence was not committed for any purpose related to trafficking in cannabis or tetrahydrocannabinol —

to a penalty of not more than 5 penalty units;

(b) subject to paragraph (a), where the court is satisfied on the balance of probabilities that the offence was not committed by the person for any purpose relating to trafficking in that drug of dependence — to a penalty of not more than 30 penalty units or to level 8 imprisonment (1 year maximum) or to both that penalty and imprisonment; or

(c) in any other case — to a penalty of not more than 400 penalty units or to level 6 imprisonment (5 years maximum) or to both that penalty and imprisonment.

(2) Where a person has in his possession, without being authorized by or licensed under this Act or the regulations to do so, a drug of dependence in a quantity that is not less than the trafficable quantity applicable to that drug of dependence, the possession of that drug of dependence in that quantity is prima facie evidence of trafficking by that person in that drug of dependence.

74 Introduction of a drug of dependence into the body of another person

A person who, without being authorized by or licensed under this Act or the regulations to do so, introduces or attempts to introduce a drug of dependence into the body of another person is guilty of an offence against this Act and liable to a penalty of not more than 30 penalty units or to level 8 imprisonment (1 year maximum) or to both that penalty and imprisonment.

75 Use of drug of dependence

A person who, without being authorized by or licensed under this Act or the regulations to do so uses or attempts to use a drug of dependence is guilty of an offence against this Act and liable —

(a) where the court is satisfied on the balance of probabilities that the offence was committed in relation to cannabis or tetrahydrocannabinol — to a penalty of not more than 5 penalty units; and

(b) in any other case — to a penalty of not more than 30 penalty units or to level 8 imprisonment (1 year maximum) or to both that penalty and imprisonment.

9.17 The above provisions cover the possession and use of drugs as well as cultivation and trafficking in drugs of dependence. Drugs of dependence are those set out in Sch 11 of the Act. The drugs listed there include the more common drugs (amphetamines, barbiturates, cannabis, cocaine, heroin, lysergic acid, mescaline, methadone, morphine), together with a wide variety of less well-known drugs. That Schedule also states the relevant quantities of the various drugs which go to comprise a small quantity, a trafficable quantity, a commercial quantity and a large commercial quantity. The scheme of the legislation is to provide a graduated scale of penalties ranging from possession for personal use (s 73) up to trafficking in commercial quantities (s 71AA) and large commercial quantities (s 71). More severe penalties are provided in the case of supplying to children (s 71B). In specifying a fine of five penalty units only in relation to possession for personal use of a small quantity of cannabis (s 73(1)(a)), the legislation approaches, but does not reach, a position of de facto decriminalisation of possession of that drug for personal use.

9.18E Drug Misuse and Trafficking Act 1985 (NSW)

DIVISION 2 — INDICTABLE OFFENCES

22 Indictable prosecution

(1) Subject to the provisions of this Division and the Criminal Procedure Act 1986, an offence under this Division is to be prosecuted on indictment.

23 Offences with respect to prohibited plants

(1) A person who:

(a) cultivates, or knowingly takes part in the cultivation of, a prohibited plant,

(b) supplies, or knowingly takes part in the supply of, a prohibited plant, or

(c) has a prohibited plant in his or her possession,

is guilty of an offence.

(1A) A person who:

(a) cultivates by enhanced indoor means, or knowingly takes part in the cultivation by enhanced indoor means of, a number of prohibited plants which is:

(i) not less than the small quantity applicable to the prohibited plants, and

(ii) less than the commercial quantity applicable to those prohibited plants, and

(b) cultivates, or knowingly takes part in the cultivation of, those prohibited plants for a commercial purpose,

is guilty of an offence.

(1B) If, on the trial of a person for an offence under subsection (1A), the jury is not satisfied that the number of prohibited plants involved is equal to or more than the small quantity applicable to the prohibited plants, the jury may acquit the person of the offence charged and find the person guilty of an offence under subsection (1)(a), and the person is liable to punishment accordingly.

(1C) If, on the trial of a person for an offence under subsection (1A), the jury is not satisfied that the person cultivated, or knowingly took part in the cultivation of, a prohibited plant for a commercial purpose, the jury may acquit the person of the offence charged and find the person guilty of an offence under subsection (1)(a), and the person is liable to punishment accordingly.

(2) A person who:

(a) cultivates, or knowingly takes part in the cultivation of, a number of prohibited plants which is not less than the commercial quantity applicable to prohibited plants,

(b) supplies, or knowingly takes part in the supply of, a number of prohibited plants which is not less than the commercial quantity applicable to prohibited plants, or

(c) has a number of prohibited plants in his or her possession which is not less than the commercial quantity applicable to prohibited plants,

is guilty of an offence.

(3) If, on the trial of a person for an offence under subsection (2) (other than in relation to the cultivation of prohibited plants by enhanced indoor means), the jury is not satisfied that the number of prohibited plants involved is equal to or more than the commercial quantity applicable to the prohibited plants, the jury may acquit the person of the offence charged and find the person guilty of an offence under subsection (1), and the person is liable to punishment accordingly.

(3A) If, on the trial of a person for an offence under subsection (2) in relation to the cultivation of prohibited plants by enhanced indoor means, the jury is not satisfied that the number of prohibited plants involved is equal to or more than the commercial quantity applicable to the prohibited plants, the jury may acquit the person of the offence charged and find the person guilty of:

(a) an offence under subsection (1A), if the jury is satisfied that the person contravened subsection (1A), or

(b) an offence under subsection (1)(a), if the jury is not satisfied that the person contravened subsection (1A), but is satisfied that the person contravened subsection (1)(a), and the person is liable to punishment accordingly.

(4) Nothing in this section renders unlawful any act relating to the cultivation, supply or possession of a prohibited plant by:

(a) a person:

(i) who informs the court before which the person is prosecuted that the person proposes to adduce evidence as referred to in subparagraph (ii), and

(ii) who adduces evidence which satisfies the court that, having regard to all the circumstances, including the person's conduct, in which the act constituting the offence was done or preparatory to the doing of the act, the person did not know or suspect and could not reasonably be expected to have known or suspected that the prohibited plant was a prohibited plant, or

(b) a person acting in accordance with an authority granted by the Secretary of the Department of Health where the Secretary is satisfied that the cultivation, supply or possession of the prohibited plant is for the purpose of scientific research, instruction, analysis or study, or

(c) a person acting in accordance with a direction given by the Commissioner of Police under section 39RA.

(5) Where a person informs a court as referred to in subsection (4)(a)(i), evidence of any previous conviction of the person for any offence, being evidence which may intend to rebut the evidence referred to in subsection (4)(a)(ii), may, with the leave of the court, be adduced by the prosecutor.

(6) In this section and section 23A, ***cultivating a prohibited plant for a commercial purpose*** includes cultivating the plant:

(a) with the intention of selling it or any of its products, or

(b) with the belief that another person intends to sell it or any of its products.

23A Offences with respect to enhanced indoor cultivation of prohibited plants in presence of children

(1) A person who:

(a) cultivates, or knowingly takes part in the cultivation of, a prohibited plant by enhanced indoor means, and

(b) exposes a child to that cultivation process, or to substances being stored for use in that cultivation process,

is guilty of an offence.

(2) A person who:

(a) cultivates, or knowingly takes part in the cultivation of, a number of prohibited plants by enhanced indoor means which is not less than the commercial quantity applicable to those plants, and

(b) exposes a child to that cultivation process, or to substances being stored for use in that cultivation process,

is guilty of an offence.

(3) A person who:

(a) cultivates by enhanced indoor means, or knowingly takes part in the cultivation by enhanced indoor means of, a number of prohibited plants which is:

(i) not less than the small quantity applicable to the prohibited plants, and

(ii) less than the commercial quantity applicable to those prohibited plants, and

(b) cultivates, or knowingly takes part in the cultivation of, those prohibited plants for a commercial purpose, and

(c) exposes a child to that cultivation process, or to substances being stored for use in that cultivation process,

is guilty of an offence.

(4) If, on the trial of a person for an offence under subsection (2), the jury is not satisfied that the number of prohibited plants involved is equal to or more than the commercial quantity applicable to the prohibited plants, the jury may acquit the person of the offence charged and find the person guilty of:

(a) an offence under subsection (3), if the jury is satisfied that the person contravened subsection (3), or

(b) an offence under subsection (1), if the jury is not satisfied that the person contravened subsection (3), but is satisfied that the person contravened subsection (1),

and the person is liable to punishment accordingly.

(5) If, on the trial of a person for an offence under subsection (3), the jury is not satisfied that the person cultivated, or knowingly took part in the cultivation of, a prohibited plant for a commercial purpose, the jury may acquit the person of the offence charged and find the person guilty of an offence under subsection (1), and the person is liable to punishment accordingly.

(6) It is a defence to a prosecution for an offence under subsection (1), (2) or (3) if the defendant establishes that the exposure of the child to the prohibited plant cultivation process, or to substances being stored for use in that process, did not endanger the health or safety of the child.

(7) If, on the trial of a person for an offence under subsection (1), (2) or (3), the jury:

(a) is not satisfied that a child was exposed to the cultivation of a prohibited plant by enhanced indoor means, or to substances being stored for use in such a cultivation process, or

(b) is satisfied that the defence referred to in subsection (6) has been made out,

the jury may acquit the person of the offence charged and find the person guilty of an offence under section 23(1)(a), (2)(a) or (1A), respectively, and the person is liable to punishment accordingly.

(8) In this section, ***child*** means a person who is under the age of 16 years.

24 Manufacture and production of prohibited drugs

(1) A person who manufactures or produces, or who knowingly takes part in the manufacture or production of, a prohibited drug is guilty of an offence.

(1A) A person who:

(a) manufactures or produces, or who knowingly takes part in the manufacture or production of, a prohibited drug, and

(b) exposes a child to that manufacturing or production process, or to substances being stored for use in that manufacturing or production process,

is guilty of an offence.

(2) A person who manufactures or produces, or who knowingly takes part in the manufacture or production of, an amount of a prohibited drug which is not less than the commercial quantity applicable to the prohibited drug is guilty of an offence.

(2A) A person who:

(a) manufactures or produces, or who knowingly takes part in the manufacture or production of, an amount of a prohibited drug which is not less than the commercial quantity applicable to the prohibited drug, and

(b) exposes a child to that manufacturing or production process, or to substances being stored for use in that manufacturing or production process,

is guilty of an offence.

(3) If, on the trial of a person for an offence under subsection (2) or (2A), the jury are not satisfied that the amount of prohibited drug involved is equal to or more than the commercial quantity applicable to the prohibited drug, the jury may acquit the person of the offence charged and find the person guilty of an offence under subsection (1) or (1A), respectively, and the person is liable to punishment accordingly.

(3A) It is a defence to a prosecution for an offence under subsection (1A) or (2A) if the defendant establishes that the exposure of the child to the prohibited drug manufacturing or production process, or to substances being stored for use in that manufacturing or production process, did not endanger the health or safety of the child.

(3B) If, on the trial of a person for an offence under subsection (1A) or (2A), the jury:

(a) is not satisfied that a child was exposed to a prohibited drug manufacturing or production process, or to substances being stored for use in such a manufacturing or production process, or

(b) is satisfied that the defence referred to in subsection (3A) has been made out, the jury may acquit the person of the offence charged and find the person guilty of an offence under subsection (1) or (2), respectively, and the person is liable to punishment accordingly.

(4) Nothing in this section renders unlawful the manufacture or production of a prohibited drug by:

(a) a person licensed or authorised to do so under the Poisons Act 1966, or

(b) a person acting in accordance with an authority granted by the Secretary of the Department of Health where the Secretary is satisfied that the manufacture or production of the prohibited drug is for the purpose of scientific research, instruction, analysis or study, or renders unlawful the taking part by any other person in the manufacture or production of a prohibited drug by a person to whom paragraph (a) or (b) applies.

(5) In this section, ***child*** means a person who is under the age of 16 years.

24A Possession of precursors and certain apparatus for manufacture or production of prohibited drugs

(1) A person who has possession of:

(a) a precursor, or

(b) a drug manufacture apparatus,

intended by the person for use in the manufacture or production, by that person or another person, of a prohibited drug is guilty of an offence.

(2) Nothing in this section renders unlawful the manufacture or production of a prohibited drug by:

(a) a person licensed or authorised to do so under the *Poisons and Therapeutic Goods Act 1966*, or

(b) a person acting in accordance with an authority granted by the Director-General of the Department of Health where the Director-General is satisfied that the manufacture or production of the prohibited drug is for the purpose of scientific research, instruction, analysis or study,

or renders unlawful the taking part by any other person in the manufacture or production of a prohibited drug by a person to whom paragraph (a) or (b) applies.

(2A) (Repealed)

(3) In this section:

drug manufacture apparatus means an apparatus specified or described in the regulations as a drug manufacture apparatus for the purposes of this section.

precursor means a substance specified or described in the regulations as a precursor for the purposes of this section.

24B Possession of prohibited drug precursors

(1) A person who has in his or her possession a precursor of a quantity not less than the quantity prescribed by the regulations in relation to that precursor is guilty of an offence.

(2) It is a defence to a prosecution for an offence under subsection (1) if the defendant establishes:

(a) that the defendant is in possession of the precursor for the purposes of an activity that is not unlawful, or

(b) that the defendant otherwise has a reasonable excuse for possessing the precursor.

(3) In this section, ***precursor*** means a substance:

(a) that is capable of being used to manufacture or produce a prohibited drug, and

(b) that is specified or described in the regulations as a precursor for the purposes of this section.

25 Supply of prohibited drugs

(1) A person who supplies, or who knowingly takes part in the supply of, a prohibited drug is guilty of an offence.

(1A) A person of or above the age of 18 years who supplies, or who knowingly takes part in the supply of, a prohibited drug (other than cannabis leaf) to a person under the age of 16 years is guilty of an offence.

(2) A person who supplies, or who knowingly takes part in the supply of, an amount of a prohibited drug which is not less than the commercial quantity applicable to the prohibited drug is guilty of an offence.

(2A) A person of or above the age of 18 years who supplies, or who knowingly takes part in the supply of, an amount of a prohibited drug (other than cannabis leaf) which is not less than the commercial quantity applicable to the prohibited drug to a person under the age of 16 years is guilty of an offence.

(2B) Where, on the trial of a person for an offence under subsection (1A) or (2A), the jury are satisfied that the person charged had, at the time the offence is alleged to have been committed, reasonable cause to believe, and did in fact believe, that the person to whom the prohibited drug was supplied was of or above the age of 16 years, they may acquit the person of the offence charged and find the person guilty of an offence under subsection (1) or (2), respectively, and the person is liable to punishment accordingly.

(2C) A person of or above the age of 18 years who procures a person under the age of 16 years to supply, or take part in the supply of, a prohibited drug (other than cannabis leaf) to another person is guilty of an offence.

(2D) A person of or above the age of 18 years who procures a person under the age of 16 years to supply, or take part in the supply of, an amount of a prohibited drug (other than cannabis leaf) which is not less than the commercial quantity applicable to the prohibited drug is guilty of an offence.

(2E) It is a defence to a prosecution for an offence under subsection (2C) or (2D) if the defendant establishes that the defendant had, at the time the offence is alleged to have been committed, reasonable cause to believe, and did in fact believe, that the person who was procured to supply, or take part in the supply of, the prohibited drug was of or above the age of 16 years.

(3) Where, on the trial of a person for an offence under subsection (2) or (2D), the jury are not satisfied that the amount of prohibited drug involved is equal to or more than the commercial quantity applicable to the prohibited drug, they may acquit the person of the offence charged and find the person guilty of an offence under subsection (1) or (2C), respectively, and the person shall be liable to punishment accordingly.

(4) Nothing in this section renders unlawful the supply of a prohibited drug by:

- (a) a person licensed or authorised to do so under the Poisons and Therapeutic Goods Act 1966, or
- (b) a person acting in accordance with an authority granted by the Secretary of the Department of Health where the Secretary is satisfied that the supply of the prohibited drug is for the purpose of scientific research, instruction, analysis or study, or

(c) a person acting in accordance with a direction given by the Commissioner of Police under section 39RA,

or renders unlawful the taking part by any other person in the supply of a prohibited drug by a person to whom paragraph (a), (b) or (c) applies.

(5) Nothing in this section renders unlawful the administration of a prohibited drug to a person being cared for by another person in the circumstances described in section10(2)(d).

25A Offence of supplying prohibited drugs on an ongoing basis

(1) **Offence provision** A person who, on 3 or more separate occasions during any period of 30 consecutive days, supplies a prohibited drug (other than cannabis) for financial or material reward is guilty of an offence. Maximum penalty: 3,500 penalty units or imprisonment for 20 years, or both.

(2) **Same prohibited drug not necessary** A person is liable to be convicted of an offence under this section whether or not the same prohibited drug is supplied on each of the occasions relied on as evidence of commission of the offence.

(3) **Jury must be satisfied as to same 3 occasions of supply** If, on the trial of a person for an offence under this section, more than 3 occasions of supplying a prohibited drug are relied on as evidence of commission of the offence, all the members of the jury must be satisfied as to the same 3 occasions in order to find the person guilty of the offence.

(4) **Alternative verdict — relevant supply offences** If, on the trial of a person for an offence under this section, the jury is not satisfied that the offence is proven but is satisfied that the person has, in respect of any of the occasions relied on as evidence of commission of the offence under this section, committed a relevant supply offence, the jury may acquit the person of the offence charged and find the person guilty of the relevant supply offence, and the person is liable to punishment accordingly.

(5) **Double jeopardy provisions** A person who has been convicted of an offence under this section is not liable to be convicted:

(a) of a relevant supply offence, or

(b) of a separate offence under this section,

on the same, or substantially the same, facts as those relied on as evidence of commission of the offence in respect of which the person has been convicted.

(6) A person who has been acquitted of an offence under this section is not liable to be convicted:

(a) except as provided by subsection (4) — of a relevant supply offence, or

(b) of a separate offence under this section,

on the same, or substantially the same, facts as those relied on as evidence of commission of the offence in respect of which the person has been acquitted.

(7) A person who has been:

(a) convicted of a relevant supply offence, or

(b) acquitted of a relevant supply offence,

is not liable to be convicted for an offence under this section on the same, or substantially the same, facts as those relied on as evidence of commission of the relevant supply offence.

(8) **Liability for relevant supply offences not affected by offence under this section** Subject to subsections (5) and (6), this section does not:
  (a) remove the liability of any person to be convicted of a relevant supply offence, or
  (b) affect the punishment that may be imposed for any such offence.

(9) **Exemption — lawful supply** Nothing in this section renders unlawful the supply of a prohibited drug by:
  (a) a person licensed or authorised to do so under the Poisons and Therapeutic Goods Act 1966 or
  (b) a person acting in accordance with an authority granted by the Director-General of the Department of Health where the Director-General is satisfied that the supply of the prohibited drug is for the purpose of scientific research, instruction, analysis or study.

(10) **Definitions** In this section:
cannabis means cannabis leaf, cannabis oil, cannabis plant and cannabis resin.
relevant supply offence means any offence under this Act (other than under this section) relating to the supply of a prohibited drug.

26 Conspiring

A person who conspires with another person or other persons to commit an offence under this Division is guilty of an offence and liable to the same punishment, pecuniary penalties and forfeiture as the person would be if the person had committed the firstmentioned offence.

27 Aiding, abetting, etc, commission of offence in New South Wales

(1) A person who aids, abets, counsels, procures, solicits or incites the commission of an offence under this Division is guilty of an offence and liable to the same punishment, pecuniary penalties and forfeiture as if the person had committed the firstmentioned offence.

(2) A person does not commit an offence because of this section for any act or omission that is an offence under section 43B.

28 Conspiring to commit and aiding etc commission of offence outside New South Wales

(1) A person who, in New South Wales:
  (a) conspires with another person or persons to commit an offence in any place outside New South Wales, being an offence punishable under the provisions of a law in force in that place which corresponds to a provision of this Division, or
  (b) aids, abets, counsels, procures, solicits or incites the commission of an offence in any place outside New South Wales, being an offence punishable under the provisions of a law in force in that place which corresponds to a provision of this Division,

is guilty of an offence and liable to the same punishment, pecuniary penalties and forfeiture as the person would be if the person had committed the offence which was committed outside New South Wales.

(2) A person does not commit an offence because of this section for any act or omission that is an offence under section 43B.

29 Trafficable quantity — possession deemed to be for supply

A person who has in his or her possession an amount of a prohibited drug which is not less than the traffickable quantity of the prohibited drug shall, for the purposes of this Division, be deemed to have the prohibited drug in his or her possession for supply, unless —

(a) the person proves that he or she had the prohibited drug in his or her possession otherwise than for supply, or

(b) except where the prohibited drug is prepared opium, cannabis leaf, cannabis oil, cannabis resin, heroin or 6-monoacetylmorphine or any other acetylated derivatives of morphine, the person proves that he or she obtained possession of the prohibited drug on and in accordance with the prescription of a medical practitioner, nurse practitioner, dentist or veterinary practitioner.

30 Indictable offences — summary disposal of unless prosecution elects otherwise

(1) This section applies to the following offences:

(a) an offence under section 23(1) or 23A(1),

(b) an offence under section 24(1) or (1A),

(c) an offence under section 25(1), (1A) or (2C),

(c1) an offence under section 26 of conspiring to commit an offence referred to in paragraph (a), (b) or (c),

(d) an offence under section 27 of aiding, abetting, counselling, procuring, soliciting or inciting the commission of an offence referred to in paragraph (a), (b) or (c), and

(e) an offence under section 28 of conspiring to commit, or of aiding, abetting, counselling, procuring, soliciting or inciting the commission of, an offence under a law in force outside New South Wales which corresponds to section 23(1), 23A(1), 24(1) or (1A) or 25(1), (1A) or (2C),

where the court is satisfied on the balance of probabilities that the number or amount of the prohibited plant or prohibited drug concerned in the commission of the offence is not more than the small quantity applicable to the prohibited plant or prohibited drug.

(2) Chapter 5 of the Criminal Procedure Act 1986 (which relates to the summary disposal of certain indictable offences unless an election is made to proceed on indictment)applies to and in respect of an offence to which this section applies.

(3) If such an offence is dealt with summarily, the maximum penalty for the offence is a fine of 50 penalty units or imprisonment for 2 years, or both.

31 Indictable offences — summary disposal of unless prosecution or accused elects otherwise

(1) This section applies to the following offences:

(a) an offence under section 23(1) or 23A(1),

(b) an offence under section 24(1) or (1A),

(c) an offence under section 25(1), (1A) or (2C),

(c1) an offence under section 26 of conspiring to commit an offence referred to in paragraph (a), (b) or (c),

(d) an offence under section 27 of aiding, abetting, counselling, procuring, soliciting or inciting the commission of an offence referred to in paragraph (a), (b) or (c), and

(e) an offence under section 28 of conspiring to commit, or of aiding, abetting, counselling, procuring, soliciting or inciting the commission of, an offence under a law in force outside New South Wales which corresponds to section 23(1), 23A(1), 24(1) or (1A) or 25(1), (1A) or (2C),

where the court is satisfied on the balance of probabilities that the number or amount of the prohibited plant or prohibited drug concerned in the commission of the offence is not more than the indictable quantity applicable to the prohibited plant or prohibited drug.

(1A) This section also applies to an offence under section 24A.

(2) Chapter 5 of the Criminal Procedure Act 1986 (which relates to the summary disposal of certain indictable offences unless an election is made to proceed on indictment)applies to and in respect of an offence to which this section applies.

(3) If such an offence is dealt with summarily, the maximum penalty for the offence is a fine of 100 penalty units or imprisonment for 2 years, or both.

32 Penalty for offences dealt with on indictment not involving commercial quantities

(1) Except as provided by sections 30 and 31, the penalty for:

(a) an offence under section 23(1),

(b) an offence under section 24(1),

(c) an offence under section 25(1) or (1A),

(d) an offence under section 26 of conspiring to commit an offence referred to in paragraph (a), (b) or (c),

(e) an offence under section 27 of aiding, abetting, counselling, procuring, soliciting or inciting the commission of an offence referred to in paragraph (a), (b) or (c), or

(f) an offence under section 28 of conspiring to commit, or of aiding, abetting, counselling, procuring, soliciting or inciting the commission of, an offence under a law in force outside New South Wales which corresponds to section 23(1), 24(1) or 25(1) or (1A), is:

(g) except as provided by paragraph (h), a fine of 2,000 penalty units or imprisonment for a term of 15 years, or both, or

(h) where the offence relates to cannabis plant or cannabis leaf, a fine of 2,000 penalty units or imprisonment for a term of 10 years, or both.

(2) Chapter 5 of the Criminal Procedure Act 1986 (which relates to the summary disposal of certain indictable offences unless an election is made to proceed on indictment) applies to and in respect of an offence referred to in subsection (1) where the offence relates to cannabis plant or cannabis leaf. If such an offence is dealt with summarily, the maximum penalty for the offence is a fine of 100 penalty units or imprisonment for 2 years, or both.

33 Penalty for offences involving commercial quantities

(1) This section applies to the following offences:

(a) an offence under section 23(1A) or (2), 24(2) or 25(2) or (2A),

(b) an offence under section 26 of conspiring to commit an offence referred to in paragraph (a),

(c) an offence under section 27 of aiding, abetting, counselling, procuring, soliciting or inciting the commission of an offence referred to in paragraph (a),

(d) an offence under section 28 of conspiring to commit, or of aiding, abetting, counselling, procuring, soliciting or inciting the commission of, an offence under a law in force outside New South Wales which corresponds to section 23(1A) or (2), 24(2) or 25(2) or (2A).

(2) The penalty for an offence is:

(a) except as provided by paragraph (b), a fine of 3,500 penalty units or imprisonment for 20 years, or both, or

(b) where the offence relates to cannabis plant or cannabis leaf, a fine of 3,500 penalty units or imprisonment for 15 years, or both.

(3) Despite subsection (2), if the court is satisfied that the offence involved not less than the large commercial quantity of the prohibited plant or prohibited drug concerned, the penalty for the offence is:

(a) except as provided by paragraph (b), a fine of 5,000 penalty units or imprisonment for life, or both, or

(b) where the offence relates to cannabis plant or cannabis leaf, a fine of 5,000 penalty units or imprisonment for 20 years, or both.

(4) In this section: ***large commercial quantity***, in relation to a prohibited plant or prohibited drug, means the number or amount, if any, specified opposite the plant or drug in Column 5 of Schedule 1.

9.19 The scheme of the legislation is to create offences covering the cultivation, supply and possession of prohibited plants (s 23), the manufacture and production of prohibited drugs (s 24), and the supply of prohibited drugs (s 25). The plants and drugs prohibited under these provisions are specified in Sch 1 of the Act, which lists all the more commonly used drugs (amphetamines, cannabis, cocaine, heroin, lysergic acid, mescaline, methadone, morphine, and opium), as well as a variety of less well-known drugs. A range of penalties is provided having regard to whether the quantity of the drug involved is classified as being a small quantity, a traffickable quantity, an indictable quantity, a commercial quantity, or a large commercial quantity. The relevant quantities of the various drugs are set out in Sch 1. The penalties range from a fine and maximum term of two years' imprisonment for offences relating to small quantities of drugs, to a maximum term of life imprisonment for offences involving commercial quantities. Section 3 of the Act contains definitions of many of the expressions used in relation to the various offences.

Division 1 of the Act supplements the offences contained in Div 2 with a number of summary offences carrying a maximum penalty of a fine of 20 penalty units and imprisonment for a term of two years (s 21). The offences covered are possession of prohibited drugs (s 10), possession of equipment for administration of prohibited drugs (s 11), sale, supply and display of waterpipes (s 11A), administration of prohibited drugs (ss 12, 13, 14), forging prescriptions (s 15), and obtaining drugs and prescriptions by false representations: ss 16, 17, 18.

SOME PROBLEMS OF INTERPRETATION

Territoriality

9.20C R v Bull

(1974) 131 CLR 203; 3 ALR 171
High Court of Australia

[A ship, on which the four accused were travelling, was intercepted by customs officials at a point within three nautical miles of the Australian coastline. When the officials approached the vessel by helicopter a large quantity of marijuana was thrown overboard. The accused were convicted of (i) importing cannabis contrary to s 233B(1)(b) of the Customs Act 1901 (Cth); (ii) having in possession cannabis contrary to s 233B(1)(a) of the Customs Act 1901 (Cth); and (iii) assembling for the purpose of preventing the seizure of cannabis contrary to s 231(1)(c) of the Customs Act 1901 (Cth). The High Court was asked to consider on a case stated whether these offences could be committed at sea within the three nautical mile limit.]

Gibbs J: No question arises in the present case as to the scope of the legislative power of the Commonwealth. It was not, and could not be, suggested that ss 231(1)(c) and 233B(1)(a) would be beyond power if they applied to acts done at sea between low water mark and the three mile limit or that the Commonwealth Parliament could not validly provide that importation for the purpose of the Act occurs when goods are brought across a line three miles from the coast. The questions are simply questions of construction, and in answering them it is necessary to pay due regard to the objects of the statute and to the context which is afforded by its provisions as a whole.

Section 231(1) provides: 'All persons to the number of two or more assembled for the purpose of — (a) importing prohibited imports; or (b) smuggling; or (c) preventing the seizure, or rescuing after seizure, of any prohibited imports or smuggled goods, shall be guilty of an offence ...'. When the Act was first passed, it was unlikely that goods could have been imported or smuggled into Australia except from the sea. They are still commonly so imported and, it may be supposed, smuggled. Persons who wished to import prohibited imports or to smuggle goods might therefore have been expected to assemble on the sea on those occasions when this might enable them to achieve their unlawful ends. Moreover, the seizure of prohibited imports or smuggled goods may take place on the sea. Prohibited imports and smuggled goods are forfeited to the Crown under s 229(a) and (b) and are therefore liable to seizure under s 203. The power given by that section is to seize, *inter alia*, any forfeited goods 'upon land or water'. The natural meaning of those words would include the sea as well as inland waters and the provisions of other sections of the Act, to which I shall shortly refer, support the conclusion that this meaning was intended. It would therefore be likely that persons desiring to prevent the seizure of prohibited imports or smuggled goods would on occasion assemble on the sea for this purpose, as the accused persons in fact did in the present case. The words of s 231(1) are wide enough to include an assembly on the sea, and having regard to the objects of the section, no reason exists to give those words a restricted meaning.

The context provided by the other sections of the Act fully supports this view. The power to board ships given by the Act clearly extends to ships arriving within three nautical miles of the coast — see ss 59 and 185. Moreover, ships or boats found within three nautical miles of the coast are forfeited if they fail to bring to for boarding upon being lawfully required to do so, or if they hover and do not depart within 12 hours after being required to do so (in which case the cargo also is forfeited), or if they have hiding places or devices adapted for the purpose of running goods — s 228(2), (3), (6); s 229(k). In the light of these express provisions it cannot be doubted that the more general powers given by the Act to board, search and seize ships extend to vessels within the three mile limit or that the provisions of s 231(1) are intended to extend to an assembly within the three mile limit.

Section 233B(1) provides, *inter alia*, that any person who — '(a) without any reasonable excuse (proof whereof shall lie upon him) has in his possession, on board any ship or aircraft, any prohibited imports to which this section applies' shall be guilty of an offence. I can see no justification for construing this provision as referring only to possession on a ship in a river or other enclosed water, and for reasons similar to those given in relation to s 231(1) I consider that no such restriction of the general words of the section was intended. The fact that s 233B(1)(c) is expressly limited to possession of prohibited imports 'which have been imported into Australia in contravention of this Act' supports the view that s 233B(1)(a) is not limited to possession of prohibited imports which have been imported into Australia, but applies to such possession in any place to which the Act extends, including the waters within a distance of three nautical miles from the coast.

For these reasons, in my judgment, offences against ss 231(1)(c) and 233B(1)(a) are committed notwithstanding that the acts done in contravention to those sections occurred at sea within three nautical miles of the coast of Australia.

The question that next falls to be considered is whether goods are imported within s 233B(1)(b), or importation occurs within s 233A, when the goods are brought across a line three nautical miles from the coast of Australia. Section 233B(1) further provides, *inter alia*, that any person who — '(b) imports, or attempts to import, into Australia any prohibited imports to which this section applies' shall be guilty of an offence, and s 233A(1) reads as follows: 'The master of a ship or boat or the pilot of an aircraft shall not use his ship, boat or aircraft, or knowingly suffer her to be used, in smuggling, or in the importation of any goods in contravention of this Act, or in the exportation or conveyance of any goods in contravention of this Act.'

No definition of 'import' or of any derivative of the word is contained in the Act. Its ordinary dictionary meaning is 'To bring in, or cause to be brought in (goods or merchandise) from a foreign country, in international commerce' (*Oxford English Dictionary*). In accordance with this meaning it has been said that the word 'import' in various sections of the Act means 'bring in to the Commonwealth': *Lyons v Smart* (1908) 6 CLR 143 at 150; *Election Importing Co Pty Ltd v Courtice* (1949) 80 CLR 657 at 662. On the basis of these statements, and on the assumption that Australia includes the surrounding sea at least to a distance of three nautical miles, it was submitted by the Crown that to bring goods across the three mile limit is to bring them into Australia and therefore to import them. However, whether or not the sea within three nautical miles of the coast should be regarded as part of Australia for other purposes, it is, in my opinion, clear that goods are not imported simply by bringing them within the three mile limit. It does not conform to ordinary usage to say that goods are imported into a place if they are brought there in the course of transit but with no intention that they should be unloaded there. For example, in ordinary understanding goods would not be thought to have been imported into Australia if they were carried through the waters within three miles of the Australian coast by a ship which did not put into port. Even if goods are brought into port they are not necessarily imported; for example, a cargo being carried from England to New Zealand is not imported into Australia when the ship on which it is carried puts into an Australian port en route: *Wilson v Chambers & Co Pty Ltd* (1926) 38 CLR 131 at 138–9, 147, 150. Similarly, goods are not 'imported into a harbour' by being carried through the limits of the harbour and then landed elsewhere: *Wilson v Robertson* (1855) 24 LJQB 185. However, if goods are brought into port with the intention of being discharged there they are imported: *Wilson v Chambers & Co Pty Ltd*, supra, at 136, 147, 150; and see also *Forbes (Collector of Customs (NSW)) v Traders Finance Corporation Ltd* (1971) 45 ALJR 668 at 673. The words of the Act themselves make it clear that the mere entry into port is not necessarily an importation. Section 30 provides, *inter alia*, that goods shall be subject to the control of customs — '(a) as to all goods imported — from the time of importation ...'. However, s 31 provides, *inter alia*, that all goods on board any ship from parts beyond the seas shall be subject to the control of customs while the ship is within the limits of any port in Australia. If goods were imported once a vessel entered port, the provisions of s 31 to which I have just referred would be quite unnecessary. Of course it is not necessary, to constitute an importation, that the goods should be brought into port — they may be landed in some other way. The remarks made by Isaacs J, at 139, in *Wilson v Chambers & Co Pty Ltd*, supra, with regard to s 68 appear to be a correct general statement of the meaning of importation for the purposes of the Act. After saying that 'the expression "imported goods", in s 68, means goods which in fact are brought from abroad into Australian territory, and in respect of which the carriage is ended or its continuity in some way in fact broken', Isaacs J went on to say:

> The underlying concept appears to me to be as follows: Where, within our territory, some act takes place with regard to goods arriving from abroad, whether in fact they are or are not dutiable or prohibited, which in the absence of some new or further arrangement for carrying them away would make the place of arrival their destination and would therefore result in the goods remaining in Australia, then they are 'imported goods' and it is the duty of the 'owner' to comply with the provisions of s 68.

In the present case the ship was intercepted before it reached its destination and before it had entered port or arrived at the place where it was intended to land the goods. For the reasons I have given, the goods were not imported when they were brought on the ship across a line three nautical miles from the coast and to the place of interception. The fact that the goods were thrown into the sea with the obvious intention of abandoning and destroying them — did not in my opinion mean that they were thereupon imported.

The convictions under ss 233B(1)(b) and 233A therefore cannot stand and should be set aside under the power given by s 73(b) of the Judiciary Act.

It seems probable that the jury returned no verdict on the charges of attempting to import because they were alternative to the charges of importing of which the accused were found guilty. Counsel for the Crown accordingly submitted that we should direct a verdict of guilty to be entered on the former charges if we held that the convictions on the latter must be set aside. To maintain this submission it is necessary to establish that an attempt to import which constitutes an offence against s 233B(1)(b) of the Act can be constituted by acts committed on the waters within three miles of the coast, that in fact the actions of the accused amounted to an attempt to import, that s 73 of the Judiciary Act gives power to order that a verdict of guilty be entered in an appropriate case and that such power ought to be exercised. In my opinion the context and policy of the Act support the view that if acts are done which constitute an attempt to import prohibited imports, an offence against the section will be committed notwithstanding that the attempt takes place on the sea below low water mark at least if within three miles of the coast. However, the case stated does not reveal whether what was done by the accused could reasonably have been regarded by a jury as an attempt to import prohibited imports. Under s 73 of the Judiciary Act the Court may send a case back to be amended or re-stated, but in my opinion we should not take that course here. The accused have been convicted of offences which arise out of the same circumstances as do the alleged attempts. The ends of justice will be sufficiently served if the accused are punished for those offences of which they have been convicted and it is unnecessary to inquire whether, if the accused had not been convicted of those other offences, it would have been possible and appropriate to direct convictions to be entered on the charges of attempting to import or whether we would have exercised the power given by s 73(e) of the Judiciary Act to order a new trial of those charges.

[Separate judgments agreeing with **Gibbs J** were delivered by **Menzies, Stephen** and **Mason JJ**. **Barwick CJ** dissented, holding that none of the offences could be committed at sea within the three nautical mile limit. **McTiernan J** dissented, holding that all three offences could be committed at sea within the three nautical mile limit.]

9.21 The offence of conspiring to import drugs into Australia may be committed notwithstanding that the conspiracy is entered into wholly outside Australia: *R v Fan* (1991) 24 NSWLR 60.

9.22 D was convicted of taking part in the sale of cannabis in South Australia. D purchased cannabis in South Australia and arranged for it to be transferred to New South Wales for sale in that state. Held, the offence is committed when conduct occurs in South Australia that amounts to taking part in the sale of a regulated substance even though the sale is not to occur in South Australia: *Question of Law Reserved (No 4 of 1997)* (1998) 71 SASR 228.

Possession

9.23C R v Boyce

(1976) 15 SASR 40
Supreme Court of South Australia

[The accused was convicted of possessing Indian hemp for sale. The accused had approached an official at an airport and asked to pick up a suitcase being held in the baggage area. He was taken to the baggage area and identified a suitcase which he took from a rack. The area was under police surveillance and as the accused moved towards the door with the suitcase in his hand, he was intercepted by a police officer. The accused admitted the suitcase, which was found to contain a considerable quantity of Indian hemp, was his.]

Bray CJ: Traditionally in juristic analysis possession resolves itself into two elements, the *corpus* and the *animus*, the first consisting in a certain physical relationship between the *propositus* and the thing, the second consisting in a certain mental attitude on his part towards it: cf *Brook v Whitbread* [1966] SASR 310 at 314. In all actual legal systems in practice, or at least in both the English and the Roman, the pure theoretical concept is overlaid and qualified and complicated by technical rules, some applying generally and some to specific situations only.

There is indeed a question as to how far in view of recent authorities, particularly *Director of Public Prosecutions v Brooks* [1974] AC 862, the *animus* is necessary at all in order to constitute possession for the purpose of drug offences. I will make some reference to the matter later on but it is not relevant for the purpose of the present appeal. There was undoubtedly evidence here from which the jury could infer, if they were so minded, that the intention of the appellant was to retain physical custody and control of the case and its contents and to exclude others from interference with it or them except with his consent. According to Detective Birch, he said that the case and contents were his and that he had despatched the case from Sydney.

The argument which Mr Waye forcefully put was directed towards the proof of the *corpus* of possession. He said that the appellant was led into a trap. The case was already suspect. The police were waiting. It was by arrangement with the police that Mr Bastin led the appellant into the baggage area. That area was sealed off by the police. They would never have allowed the appellant to leave it with the case. He had no real exclusive physical control over the case and its contents. He was trapped into picking it up and holding it with the intention that it should almost immediately be taken from him.

If the situation postulated by Mr Waye is granted, nevertheless the appellant had possession of the case and its contents from the time he picked it up until the time the police took it from him. The argument confuses the existence of control with the permanence of control. A precarious possession liable to almost immediate termination is none the less a possession.

A classic hypothetical case of which the jurists are fond is the case of a child with a coin or some other valuable object in his hand which he has just picked up when there is a powerful ruffian looming over him intending to remove it: see Pollock and Wright on *Possession in the Common Law* (1888) pp 12, 15; Paton on *Jurisprudence* (2nd ed, 1951) pp 458–9. Pollock and Wright p 15 quote Holmes J:

> A powerful ruffian may be within equal reach and sight when a child picks up a pocket-book; but if he does nothing, the child has manifested the needful power as well as if it had been backed by a hundred policemen.

I would add, not only if he does nothing but until he does something. The learned authors go on:

> In this case the child's dominion is a very real one for the time being. The ruffian may attempt to seize the pocket-book, but before he can execute his intention the child may tear the book, or throw it into a river, or over a cliff, with the result of it ceasing to exist as the same object, or passing out of human control.

In *R v* Turvey [1946] 2 All ER 60 the Court of Criminal Appeal was dealing with a case where a servant of the Ministry of Works, attempted to be suborned by the defendant, was told by his superiors to hand the property over to the accused so that he could be caught. The learned judges said at 61:

> The other point on which the chairman in his direction to the jury, as we think, went wrong was that he told the jury that these goods always remained under the control of the Ministry, because apparently the police had been warned, and the police were to follow the prisoner once he had stolen them, either to follow him or to go immediately to Newton Abbott and find them in the possession of the receiver. But that will not do. Once the goods were handed over to the appellant the goods were under his control and nobody else's. What was to happen supposing, while he was driving along being followed by the police, the police car broke down? Of course, he would cheerfully drive away with these goods. Of course the goods were under the appellant's control as soon as he went away with the goods.

So here, while the appellant perhaps had not so much liberty of action over such a period of time as did the accused ink *Turvey's* case [1946] 2 All ER 60, nevertheless as long as he had hold of the case he had the exclusive control of it until he was interrupted by the police. He could have thrown it in the air, jumped on it, cut it up with a knife, taken a gun out of his pocket and shot a hole through it, or produced an incendiary apparatus and set alight to it. He was in my view completely in physical de facto custody and control of the thing for a definite, if short, period of time and the fact that a speedy end to that control had been predetermined by the police is immaterial.

In the classic case of *Moors v Burke* (1919) 26 CLR 265 the High Court was dealing with the phrase 'actual possession' in the unlawful possession section of the Victorian *Police Offences Act 1915*. They held that that phrase meant de facto possession as opposed to constructive possession. They said at 274:

> 'Having actual possession' means, in this enactment simply having at the time, in actual fact and without the necessity of taking any further step, the complete present

personal physical control of the property to the exclusion of others not acting in concert with the accused, and whether he has that control by having the property in his present manual custody, or by having it where he alone has the exclusive right or power to place his hands on it, and so have manual custody when he wishes.

At the time, that is during the interval between the picking up of the case and the interception of the police, the present appellant had complete present personal physical control to the exclusion of others by having the case and its contents in his present manual custody, even though others were about to exclude him.

Mr Waye relied on cases where prosecutions for receiving have failed because the stolen goods had passed back under the control of the owner or those acting on his behalf, such as the police, before the accused received them: *R v Dolan* (1855) 6 Cox CC 449; *R v Villensky* [1892] 2 QB 597; *Re Attorney-General's Reference (No 1 of 1974)* [1974] 2 WLR 891. These cases deal with an entirely different matter. If the goods in question have passed back into the power or control of the owner, or his representatives in fact or in law, they are no longer stolen goods and therefore there can be no receiving of stolen goods. In these cases a trap has been laid for the accused and the question is whether what the police did amounted to the taking of control over the goods for the purpose in hand, that is the taking of possession of them. There is a distinction between cases where before the receipt by the accused the police have actually taken control of the goods and cases where they merely stand by, watching and waiting. For a somewhat startling case of the latter kind, see *R v King* [1938] 2 All ER 662.

Here there is no question of the receipt of stolen goods. There is no evidence to show that the police were in possession of the case before the appellant took it up, though TAA probably was. It would not have been material if it had been. The case would still have passed from its possession to that of the appellant when he took it up.

[**Zelling J** concurred with **Bray CJ**. **Bright J** delivered a separate judgment agreeing with **Bray CJ**. Appeal dismissed.]

[See also *R v Frangos* (1979) 21 SASR 331; *R v Conley* (1982) 30 SASR 226.]

9.24 Notes, questions and illustrations

1. D was convicted of having in his possession a hookah pipe containing traces of cannabis resin. Although the amount of cannabis resin contained in the bowl of the pipe was not sufficient to be weighed, chemical tests established the presence of at least 20 micrograms of cannabis. The Court of Appeal upheld D's conviction. In delivering judgment, Lord Widgery CJ in *Bockmg v Roberts* [1974] 1 QB 307 at 309–10 stated:

> This is a difficult and extremely important point. In my judgment it is quite clear that when dealing with a charge of possessing a dangerous drug without

> authority, the ordinary maxim of *de minimis* is not to be applied. In other words, if it is clearly established that the accused had a dangerous drug in his possession without authority, it is no answer for him to say that the quantity of the drug which he possessed was so small that the law should take no account of it. The doctrine of *de minimis* as such in my judgment does not apply, but on the other hand, since the offence is possessing a dangerous drug, it is quite clear that the prosecution have to prove that there was some of the drug in the possession of the defendant to justify the charge, and the distinction which has to be drawn in cases of this kind is whether the quantity of the drug was enough to justify the conclusion that the defendant was possessed of a quantity of the drug or whether, on the other hand, the traces were so slight that they really indicated no more than that at some previous time he had been in possession of the drug. It seems to me that that is the distinction that has to be drawn, although its application to individual cases is by no means easy.

2. D obtained a quantity of heroin in Penang, placed it in some condoms, and gave them to C. The two then travelled back to Australia with the condoms inside C's body. Upon arrival in Australia, C was arrested and the heroin recovered. Held, the facts were not capable of sustaining a finding that D was in possession of the drugs: *Buck v R* [1983] WAR 372. With what offences might D have been successfully charged?
3. D occupied a bedsitter in a house comprised entirely of such accommodation. He instructed his supplier to send a quantity of drugs through the post to him at his address. An envelope containing the drugs was pushed through the letterbox of the house by the postman, and was placed with other letters on the hallway table. D was unaware of the envelope's arrival. Held, D was properly to be regarded as in possession of the envelope and its contents when it arrived through the letterbox of the house in which he was living: *R v Peaston* (1978) 69 Cr App R 203.
4. D placed a bag containing opium under some clothes in a tea-chest belonging to a girl with whom he shared a room and a balcony. The tea-chest was situated on the balcony and D was in a position to recover the bag at will. The girl, although able to resort to the tea-chest at will, was unlikely to discover the bag except by accident. Held, after placing the bag in the tea-chest, D continued to be in possession of the opium within the meaning of s 233B(1)(ca) of the Customs Act 1901 (Cth): *R v Van Swol* [1975] VR 61.
5. D was convicted of possession of heroin contrary to s 233B(1)(ca) of the Customs Act 1901 (Cth). A person carrying a sports bag which contained heroin entered a car and sat in a rear seat. D was seated in the front passenger seat. D was seen to remove a white object from the bag. When police moved in to arrest the occupants of the car, D had a plastic bag containing a quantity

of heroin in his lap. A further quantity of heroin was in the sports bag which was located between the two front bucket seats of the car. D was convicted of possession both of the heroin contained in the bag on his lap and the heroin contained in the sports bag. On appeal, held, appeal dismissed. A person has possession of whatever is, to that person's knowledge, physically in his or her custody or under his or her physical control. The issue for the jury was whether the bag, placed by D between the two front bucket seats in the motor car, was physically in his custody or under his physical control at the time of arrest. A direction in these terms was given to the jury: *R v Maio* [1989] VR 273.

6. D, for two days, had the use of a motorcar belonging to another person, knowing from the time when he took possession of the car that a small bag of Indian hemp was hidden under a seat-cover. There was no evidence that D intended himself to use, or to allow any other person to use, the Indian hemp. Held, D was properly convicted of possession of the Indian hemp: *Bourne v Samuels* (1979) 21 SASR 591.
7. D was arrested by police while seated on a log in a laneway, some five metres from a drain or a hole in which was found a package of heroin. There was evidence that another man had shortly before been supplied with a package of heroin which D had taken from the hole, and that D was where he was so he could keep watch on the remaining package while not having it on him. On appeal, held, the word 'possession' as used in the Drug Misuse and Trafficking Act 1985 (NSW) s 29, is wide enough to include any case where the person alleged to be in possession of a prohibited drug has hidden the thing effectively so that he or she can take it into physical custody whenever he or she wishes and where others are unlikely to discover it except by accident: *R v Delon* (1992) 29 NSWLR 29.
8. Police entered a house and found D1 entering the kitchen and D2 in the kitchen. In the kitchen they found a quantity of heroin, a set of scales, a bag of glucodin and a number of small empty plastic bags. On appeal against conviction for possession of a prohibited import. Held, appeal dismissed. In order to constitute possession, the Crown must prove that each accused had physical control of the drug or the means of exercising dominion and control over the drug, to the exclusion of all others not acting jointly with him or her, and the intention of exercising dominion and control. The mere fact that the accused were found in proximity to the drugs does not necessarily connote possession of them, nor does mere knowledge of the presence of the drugs. Nevertheless, the inference was strong that the accused were engaged in blending, weighing and packaging the drug and, therefore, had dominion and control over it: *Pearce and Carter v DPP (No 2)* (1992) 59 A Crim R 182.

9. D1 was convicted on one count of trafficking heroin and one count of possession of heroin. D1 was apprehended in a van she owned while it was parked outside a factory where she had been living. D2 had left the van and approached the factory with a bag when he was apprehended. The bag contained a large quantity of heroin and over $20,000 in cash. In the van the police found a bag containing $18,000 in cash. Inside the factory the police found a further small quantity of heroin. The trafficking charge related to the heroin in the bag and the possession charge related to the heroin in the factory. D1 denied any knowledge of the drugs and the cash. On appeal it was argued that the judge erred in instructing the jury that D1 could have controlled the heroin in conjunction with D2. Held, appeal dismissed. There was a clear and compelling case of joint possession by D1 and D2 in relation to both amounts of heroin: *R v Doan* (2001) 3 VR 349.
10. D was convicted of supplying a dangerous drug to another contrary to s 6(1) of the Drugs Misuse Act 1986 (Qld). D was an inmate at a correctional facility. D arranged for an acquaintance to visit the correctional facility in order to supply heroin to another inmate for on-supply to D. The heroin was passed to the other inmate, but was not passed on to D. D was convicted on the basis that s 4 of the Act extends the definition of supply to doing any act in furtherance of or for the purpose of supply, and that D had counselled or procured the acquaintance to act for the purpose of supplying D with the heroin. On appeal to the High Court, held, conviction affirmed. The relevant offence was the acquaintance's conduct in supplying the other inmate in preparation for on-supply to D. D was guilty of that offence because he had counselled or procured the acquaintance to commit the offence. The fact that D's conviction did not accord with the ordinary meaning of supply, which requires the supplier to be a different person from the person supplied, was not material in light of the wording of the statutory provision: *Maroney v R* (2003) 216 CLR 31; 202 ALR 405.
11. D was convicted of supplying a prohibited drug to another contrary to s 6(1) of the Misuse of Drugs Act 1981 (WA). D had consigned a box containing the drugs to an air freight operator in Sydney for delivery to a confederate in Perth. At Perth, the drugs were received by police posing as air cargo staff and handed over to the confederate. On appeal to the High Court it was argued that, in these circumstances, the drugs were not supplied to the confederate. Held, appeal dismissed. Section 3(1) of the Act defines to supply as including to send. McHugh and Gummow JJ stated:

> The Drugs Act does not define 'to send'. As a result, and in the absence of any indication to the contrary, the verb must be given its ordinary meaning. The *New Oxford Dictionary of English* relevantly defines to 'send' as to 'arrange for the delivery of, especially by post'. The *New Shorter Oxford English Dictionary* speaks of ordering or causing a thing to be conveyed, transported or

> transmitted by an intermediary to a person or place for a particular purpose. The *Macquarie Dictionary* speaks in similar terms. The definitions focus upon acts initiating, and contributing to, the process of transmission of an object to a particular destination, with a view to the ultimate receipt of the object by a particular person at that destination. None of the definitions suggest that actual receipt of the object by its intended recipient, at the end of the process of transmission, is a necessary element of the expression [*Pinkstone v The Queen* [2004] HCA 23 at [51]].

12. Section 5 of the Drugs, Poisons and Controlled Substances Act 1981 (Vic) provides:

> Without restricting the meaning of the word 'possession', any substance shall be deemed for the purpose of this Act to be in the possession of a person so long as it is upon any land or premises occupied by him or is used, enjoyed or controlled by him in any place whatsoever, unless the person satisfies the court to the contrary.

In *R v Clarke and Johnstone* [1986] VR 643, the Supreme Court of Victoria held that the effect of the section is that a person proved to be in occupation of the relevant land is deemed to be in possession of the substance unless that person proves he or she was not in possession of it. Note also *R v Morabito* (1990) 50 A Crim R 412.

13. In *R v Momcilovic* [2011] HCA 34; (2011) 280 ALR 221, the operation of s 5 was challenged on the grounds that it was inconsistent with the presumption of innocence, which since 2006 has been explicitly articulated in the Victorian Charter of Human Rights and Responsibilities s 25(1): 'A person charged with a criminal offence has the right to be presumed innocent until proved guilty according to law'. The case raised fundamental questions about the power of the courts under s 32 of the Charter to interpret legislation in a way that is consistent with the Charter, and more generally about the balance under the Charter between the courts and parliament. For a discussion of the ramifications of the case, see J Debeljak, 'Who is Sovereign Now? The *Momcilovic* Court Hands Back Power Over Human Rights that Parliament Intended It to Have' (2011) 22 *Public Law Review* 15.

For present purposes, the Court of Appeal made a declaration that s 5 of the Victorian Drugs, Poisons and Controlled Substances Act (1981) was inconsistent with the presumption of innocence (Charter s 25(1)). On appeal to the High Court, the decision of the Court of Appeal was overturned. The High Court pointed out that that s 32 of the Charter only applied where legislation was ambiguous, and held that s 5 was unambiguous in its intent to place the legal burden of proof on an accused person to show that he or she was *not* 'in possession'. The Charter provision was therefore not available to re-interpret the legislation in this instance. However, the

High Court held that s 5 only applied to a charge of possession, and could not be used to support a charge of trafficking ('possession for sale') under s 71AC. The notion of 'possession for sale' under s 71AC was considered to be a 'single and indivisible' phrase, to which the reversal of the onus of proof under s 5 did not apply. As the jury had been incorrectly directed to apply s 5 to a charge under s 71AC, the conviction was quashed and a new trial was ordered. The definition of 'possession' in s 5 therefore continues to operate, but only in relation to the offence of possession, and cannot be used in relation to a charge of trafficking. It remains to be seen whether the Victorian Parliament decides to respond to the decision of the Court of Appeal.

Being knowingly concerned

9.25C

R v Kelly

(1975) 12 SASR 389; 24 FLR 441

Supreme Court of South Australia

[The accused was convicted of being knowingly concerned with the importation of drugs into Australia contrary to s 233B(1)(d) of the Customs Act 1901 (Cth). The accused, while in India, agreed with two men that, upon his return to Australia, he would notify them when certain drugs could be forwarded to him. The accused returned to Australia but, before he notified his accomplices, they forwarded a letter and a package addressed to him. The package was intercepted by Customs Officers and found to contain drugs. The accused replied to the letter, stating that the package had not arrived.]

Hogarth, **Mitchell** and **Zelling JJ**: The ground complains that the trial judge failed to direct the jury in regard to what constitutes in law 'active participation'. The words 'active participation' are not taken from the section, and indeed the learned trial judge in his charge to the jury consistently used the words of the section, namely being 'knowingly concerned'. We think it is a mistake to believe that a man has to be engaged in active participation in some scheme before he can be said to be knowingly concerned. No doubt some act on his part would normally be required in order to prove his knowing concernment. The meaning of the word 'concerned' in a similar context was considered by the Full Court of Western Australia in *Ashbury v Reid* [1961] WAR 49.

Having cited the definition of the word from the *Oxford Dictionary*, the court, in considering whether an act or omission on the part of an individual came within the terms of the section, posed the question 'whether on the facts it can reasonably be said that the act or omission shown to have been done or neglected to be done by the defendant does in truth implicate or involve him in the offence, whether it does show a practical connection between him and the offence'.

It is sufficient if a person remains inactive in Australia, but ready and willing, pursuant to some preconcerted plan, to be the recipient of a parcel when it is delivered to him, in order that he may then embark upon his part in carrying out the plan. It would be sufficient to make out the case for the prosecution if it were established that he was holding himself in readiness to receive the package and to deal with it as had been agreed, even if the package was not sent precisely in accordance with the previous arrangement. In our view the evidence amply justifi es the conclusion that he was holding himself in readiness. This was sufficient to constitute his being 'knowingly concerned' in the importation of the drug. It was not required that he should be actively participating in the scheme at that stage in order for him to fall within the scope of the section. Had the appellant not sent his cable reporting the non-arrival of the package, it might have been dangerous to leave to the jury the question whether his mere inaction was a sufficient base from which to draw the inference that he was standing by waiting to receive the parcel and to deal with it according to the pre-conceived plan. That would have been possible, but perhaps not proved. But his retention of the letter of 25 April and his cable in reply constituted evidence from which the jury was entitled to draw the necessary inference, which clearly it did.

His Honour concluded by putting the question to the jury, 'Was he knowingly and to that extent consciously and deliberately concerned and co-operating in the importation of the prohibited import?'. This, we think, adequately posed the problem which his Honour had previously discussed at length. We think that this was a proper direction on the topic.

[Appeal dismissed.]

[See also *R v Shin Nan Yong* (1975) 7 ALR 271; *R v Toubya* [1993] 1 VR 226.]

Trafficking

9.26C Falconer v Pederson

[1974] VR 185
Supreme Court of Victoria

[The accused was convicted of trafficking in Indian hemp contrary to s 32(a) of the Poisons Act 1962 (Vic) (now repealed). The accused, at the request of a woman and with money supplied by her but without reward to himself, purchased from a man at a hotel a quantity of Indian hemp which he delivered to the woman.]

Anderson J: Section 32(a) of the Poisons Act is cast in very wide terms. The draftsman has collected all the conventional verbs and has attempted to prohibit any association with drugs of addiction not covered by s 27 which prohibits the possession or disposition of such drugs, and s 31 which prohibits their being smoked. In addition, the word 'sell' is described in s 3 as including 'sell whether by wholesale or retail and barter or exchange; also dealing in agreeing to sell or offering or exposing for sale or keeping or having in possession for sale or sending, forwarding, delivering or receiving for sale or on sale or authorising, directing, causing, suffering, permitting or attempting any of such acts or things', and 'sale' and each of the derivatives of 'sell' have corresponding interpretations. This elaboration of the word 'sell' comprehends almost every dealing that can be thought of which is of a commercial nature, yet s 32 in terms prohibits the preparation, manufacture, dealing in and trafficking in Indian hemp, as well as its sale. So lavish is the use of verbs in the definition of 'sell' in s 3 and in s 32 and elsewhere that I do not consider that the expression 'traffic in' appearing in s 32 is to be given a limited meaning which is exclusive of the other expressions in the Act; on the contrary, it is used, I think, in an effort to catch up any transaction in a drug of addiction which may have escaped the wide net cast by the other provisions of the Act. It was said by Lowe J, in *Carter v Mason* [1934] VLR 310 at 314; [1934] ALR 404, that the word 'traffic' as used in the Licensing Act was 'not to be construed as exclusive of the word "sale", but as wider than and as inclusive of "sale"'. I think that the same may be said of 'traffic' in s 32(a) of the Poisons Act; indeed, in my view, 'traffic' is inclusive of other prohibited acts enumerated in the definition of sell and in ss 27 and 32.

I think that the expression 'traffic in' is intended to encompass any association with a drug of addiction not otherwise dealt with and involves at least the handling of such a drug in a conscious manner in the course of a dealing in it. In *Matthews v Towers*, supra, it was held that the making of a gift was not a trafficking. I do not think it relevant in order to constitute trafficking in a drug that the person so accused acted without reward, but if some commercial quality is required for the transaction to constitute trafficking, I think that such an ingredient is supplied in this case by the fact that a sale and purchase of Indian hemp took place and the appellant was involved as the link between the parties to that transaction. The part he played was to obtain the order and the money from the buyer, convey the order and the money to the vendor, pay the vendor and receive the drug, convey the drug and deliver or arrange for the delivery of the drug to the purchaser. The circumstance that only one such series of acts was proved is not material. A single incident in relation to one person may constitute trafficking: *Molyneux v McPherson* (1902) 3 ALR 120; 23 ALT 228. However, the evidence here shows that there was more than an isolated incident for it shows the availability to the appellant of drugs at the hotel, for the previous week he had himself purchased Indian hemp from a man at the same hotel. It was said that the evidence did not show that the person from whom the appellant purchased the Indian hemp, the subject of the charge, was the same person from whom the appellant had purchased Indian hemp at the hotel the previous week. Whether it was the same vendor or not, the appellant evidently knew of the availability of Indian hemp from a person, or persons, at that hotel, and acted as a 'go-between' in the deal.

In the case stated the learned County Court judge found the charge proved because he considered 'that the use of the verb "traffic" in s 32 rendered criminal the acts of a person knowingly engaged in the movement of the drugs specified in the section from the source to the ultimate user in the course of an illicit trade in such drugs, and that this was so whether or not any such acts were performed without reward or on an isolated occasion or at the request of the ultimate user'.

I think that the learned County Court judge has aptly described the operation of the section in respect of the facts of this case. A finding that there was an illicit trade was open on the evidence, and the appellant was knowingly engaged in the movement of the drug from the vendor to the purchaser. The other considerations urged on behalf of the appellant, namely, that he acted without reward and that it was an isolated occasion, are to my mind immaterial, once the trading is established.

[Appeal dismissed.]

9.27 Illustrations

1. D1 and D2 were engaged in growing cannabis on a commercial scale. They were convicted of trafficking in cannabis contrary to s 32 of the Poisons Act 1962 (Vic) (now repealed). Held, allowing the appeal. Trafficking is not constituted merely by growing cannabis, or by being in possession of a growing crop of cannabis, in commercial quantities for the purpose of trafficking: *R v Holman* [1982] VR 471.
2. D, a medical practitioner, wrote hundreds (if not thousands) of prescriptions for drugs of addiction over a period of two years. He was convicted of supplying drugs of addiction contrary to s 21(2A) of the Poisons Act 1966 (NSW) (now repealed, see now Drug Misuse and Trafficking Act 1985 (NSW) s 25). Held, dismissing the appeal. The conduct of a medical practitioner who systematically writes prescriptions for drugs of addiction and hands them over to persons intending to, or with the knowledge that such persons would, procure the drug from a pharmacist, may amount to supplying drugs of addiction, whether or not the person to whom it is handed uses it himself or herself or for sale or both: *R v Coles* [1984] 1 NSWLR 726.
3. D was convicted of trafficking in heroin and possession of heroin contrary to ss 71 and 73, respectively, of the Drugs, Poisons and Controlled Substances Act 1981 (Vic). The charge of trafficking was based on the quantity of drugs which were found in D's premises and on admissions made by D that she had engaged in trafficking, there being no evidence of any sales by D on the day in question. Held, confirming the conviction for trafficking and quashing the conviction for possession. Proof that a particular sale was in contemplation at the material time is not necessary to establish an offence of trafficking where the charge is based on evidence of possession for sale.

D having been convicted of trafficking, it was not proper that she should also be convicted of the separate offence of possession of the same heroin at the same place on the same date: *Reardon v Baker* [1987] VR 887.

4. D was convicted of possession of drugs for the purpose of supply contrary to s 25 of the Drug Misuse and Trafficking Act 1985 (NSW). D admitted having small paper packages containing traffickable amounts of cocaine and hashish in her house but said that the drugs belonged to her sister who had asked her to mind them overnight, stating that she would collect them the next day. On appeal, held, conviction quashed. A person who is in possession of drugs with the intention only of returning the drugs to their owner or the person reasonably believed to be the owner, could not be guilty of supplying them within the meaning of the Act: *R v Carey* (1990) 20 NSWLR 292. Accord *R v Liberti* (1991) 55 A Crim R 120.

5. D was convicted of trafficking in heroin contrary to s 71 of the Drugs, Poisons and Controlled Substances Act 1981 (Vic). D obtained money from another, agreeing to supply that person with heroin in return. D's defence was that he had obtained the money to support his own drug habit, and never intended to supply the heroin. Held, conviction affirmed. If a person offered a drug of dependence for sale, intending at the time the offer was made that the offeree would take the offer seriously, that person made an 'offer for sale' within the meaning of the definition of 'traffick' in s 70 of the Act. It was not necessary for the prosecution to prove that the offeror actually intended to complete the offer or was in a position to do so: *R v Peirce* [1996] 2VR 215.

6. D was charged with knowingly taking part in the manufacture of a prohibited drug contrary to s 24 of the Drug Misuse and Trafficking Act 1985 (NSW). It was established that chemicals being used in the course of trying to produce the prohibited drug, methylamphetamine, were incapable of leading to that result. Held, in circumstances where the chemicals that were being used in the course of trying to produce a prohibited drug were incapable of leading to that result, trying to combine those chemicals was not a step in the process of manufacture of that prohibited drug. The intention of a person engaged in a process that might lead to the production of a prohibited drug is relevant, but it is not sufficient: *R v McCoy* (2001) 51 NSWLR 702.

7. It should be noted that a person can be found to have trafficked in a 'commercial quantity' of a drug on the basis of several transactions involving smaller quantities of the drug; for example, in terms of 'trafficking' between certain dates.

State and federal offences

9.28C R v Nicola

[1987] VR 1040
Supreme Court of Victoria

[The accused was convicted of one count of possession of a prohibited import contrary to s 233B(1)(ca) of the Customs Act 1901 (Cth), and one count of trafficking in a drug of dependence contrary to s 71(1) of the Drugs, Poisons and Controlled Substances Act 1981 (Vic). On appeal it was argued that the trial judge erred in ruling that a Commonwealth and a state count could be tried simultaneously, and that the trial judge ought to have quashed the document bringing the accused before the court and entitled 'Indictment/Presentment'.]

Murray, **McGarvie** and **Nicholson JJ**: The real issue which falls for determination in this case is as to whether it can be said that an indictment under Commonwealth law is identical with a presentment under Victorian law. If it is, then it is difficult to see why state and Commonwealth offences should not be charged on the one document however named. We were informed by counsel that the expression 'presentment' is used only in Victoria and not in other states to describe the method of originating the trial of an indictable offence. It appears, however, that it has a lengthy usage in English law as does the expression 'indictment', the history of which was fully described in the judgments of this court in *R v Parker* [1977] VR 22 at 26–8 per Young CJ; at 31–2 per Gillard J; at 37–8 per Murphy J.

From these judgments it is apparent that the expressions 'presentment' and 'indictment' both find their origins in mediaeval English criminal procedure, but the usage of the two terms does not seem ever to have been governed by a uniform practice. The distinction between the two has not always been reflected in consistency of language. Strictly speaking, an indictment was a document making a formal accusation of crime on the basis of evidence found credible by a grand jury. A presentment was a document of the same character that was based, not upon evidence presented to the grand jury, but upon the grand jury's personal knowledge of the facts. Although this theoretical distinction was still in existence in the early nineteenth century, as indeed was the grand jury procedure in England, the two terms seem by then to have been for practical purposes virtually interchangeable since at least the sixteenth century ...

Assuming that an indictment for Commonwealth purposes is the same as a presentment for Victorian purposes, I am unable to discover any substance in the distinction which counsel for the appellant has sought to draw. The document in question satisfies both the description of an indictment and a presentment, and I can see no reason to construe the two as mutually exclusive. The first count states Mr Morrissey's authority for taking the proceeding, but it is apparent from *Blacklock's* case that this is unnecessary, provided that he did in fact hold the necessary authority pursuant to the Judiciary Act. Similarly, the description of the document as an 'Indictment/Presentment' is irrelevant. It could have been described as either and have been equally efficacious because its substance is what is relevant rather than its form. As Young CJ said in *R v Parker* [1977] VR 22 at 24:

> Thus when s 353 speaks of a prosecutor for the Queen making presentment it means clearly enough that he may make a formal statement as accusation of an indictable offence. He must make it in writing and as the form in the Third Schedule to the Crimes Act shows, he must sign the document containing the allegation or statement in order to authenticate it.

His Honour went on to say that he must also make presentment at the court and it was upon that point that the case turned, but in my view, all that his Honour said of a presentment could equally be said of an indictment in the sense used in the Constitution and the Judiciary Act. The document in question in this case is signed by a person authorised to do so under the law of the Commonwealth and of the state, and in no sense was it argued, nor could it be, that the applicant was placed under any disadvantage as a result of the adoption of this procedure. The argument advanced on his behalf was entirely technical, and must, in my opinion, fail for the reasons given.

[Appeal dismissed.]

THE MENTAL ELEMENT REQUIRED FOR DRUG OFFENCES

9.29 Where a statutory provision is ambiguous as to the mental element required to constitute the crime created, three possible interpretations are open to the courts. First, the offence may be interpreted as imposing 'strict liability', a term used to describe offences which may be committed by an accused who acts without intention, recklessness or negligence. Second, the courts may read into the statute a requirement of mens rea of one form or another (for example, intention or knowledge). In Australia, a third and intermediate approach has sometimes been adopted. Statutes may be interpreted as imposing strict liability in respect of the constituent elements of the particular crime while leaving it open to the accused to rely on any of the general defences. In cases where the accused lacked mens rea (for example, had no intent or knowledge), the defence that will be relied upon is that of honest and reasonable mistake. As with all the general defences, the accused bears the evidential burden of showing the mistake was both honest and reasonable, while the legal burden of proof beyond reasonable doubt remains on the prosecution. The effect of this intermediate approach is that crimes of strict liability become, in substance, crimes of negligence with the evidential burden of showing absence of negligence resting on the accused.

9.30 The problems, both of policy and interpretation, involved in determining which of these three approaches should be adopted in relation to particular statutory provisions are dealt with generally in **Chapter 13**. Statutes dealing with drug offences, however, raise these issues in a particularly acute form and are, therefore, accorded separate treatment in the present section.

9.31C He Kaw Teh v R

(1985) 157 CLR 523; 60 ALR 449
High Court of Australia

[The accused was charged with importing heroin into Australia contrary to s 233B(1)(b) of the Customs Act 1901 (Cth) (now repealed) and possessing heroin contrary to s 233B(1)(c) of that Act (now repealed). The accused travelled from Kuala Lumpur to Melbourne where he was found to be in possession of 2.788 kilograms of heroin in the false bottom of a bag. The trial judge directed the jury that the offences did not require mens rea but that the accused might avail himself of the defence of honest and reasonable mistake. His Honour directed the jury that the legal burden of proving honest and reasonable mistake rested on the accused to the standard of the balance of probabilities. The accused was convicted and appealed unsuccessfully to the Victorian Court of Criminal Appeal. On appeal to the High Court.]

Gibbs CJ: The argument presented on behalf of the applicant raised some fundamental questions of the law relating to criminal responsibility. It was submitted that the learned trial judge erred in directing the jury that the prosecution had no need to prove that a person charged under s 233B(1)(b) acted with guilty knowledge — in particular with knowledge that the baggage he brought into the country contained narcotic goods. Section 233B(1)(b) does not expressly make knowledge an element of the offence. To 'import' simply means to bring into the Commonwealth from abroad: see *Lyons v Smart* (1908) 6 CLR 143 at 150; *R v Bull* (1974) 131 CLR 203 at 254. The word 'import' does not carry its own connotation of knowledge or intention. If one in fact brings goods into Australia from abroad one imports them, whatever one's intention may be and whether or not one knows their nature or quality. Paragraph (b) does not contain any words — such as 'knowingly' — which themselves might reveal that the Parliament intended to make the importation of narcotics an offence only if it was intentionally or knowingly carried out; in that respect it differs from para (d) of s 233B(1), which makes it an offence to be 'knowingly concerned' in the importation of prohibited imports that are narcotic goods.

However, the provision has to be read in the light of the general principles of the common law which govern criminal responsibility. The relevant principle is stated in *Sherras v De Rutzen* [1895] 1 QB 918 at 921, as follows:

> There is a presumption that *mens rea*, an evil intention, or a knowledge of the wrongfulness of the act, is an essential ingredient in every offence; but that presumption is liable to be displaced either by the words of the statute creating the offence or by the subject-matter with which it deals, and both must be considered.

There has in the past been a tendency in Australia to regard this presumption as only a weak one at least in the case of modern regulatory statutes: *Proudman v Dayman* (1941) 67 CLR 536 at 540; *Bergin v Stack* (1953) 88 CLR 248 at 261. However, the principle stated in *Sherras v De Rutzen* has more recently been reaffirmed in the Judicial Committee and the House of Lords (*Lim Chin Aik v R* [1963] AC 160 at 173; *R v Warner*

[1969] AC 256 at 272 and *Gammon Ltd v A-G of Hong Kong* [1984] 3 WLR 437 at 441; [1984] 2 All ER 503 at 507) and in this court: *Cameron v Holt* (1980) 142 CLR 342 at 346, 348. The rule is not always easy to apply. Its application presents two difficulties — first, in deciding whether the Parliament intended that the forbidden conduct should be punishable even in the absence of some blameworthy state of mind and secondly, if it is held that *mens rea* is an element of the offence, in deciding exactly what mental state is imported by that vague expression.

In deciding whether the presumption has been displaced by s 233B(1)(b), and whether the Parliament intended that the offence created by that provision should have no mental ingredient, there are a number of matters to be considered. First, of course, one must have regard to the words of the statute creating the offence. The words of para (b) of s 233B(1) themselves contain no clear indication of Parliament's intention. However they stand in marked contrast to paras (a), (c) and (ca) of the subsection, all of which deal with the possession of prohibited imports in certain circumstances and all of which contain the words 'without reasonable excuse (proof whereof shall lie upon him)'. The absence of those words from para (b) suggests that no reasonable excuse will avail a person who imports narcotics. That would lead to an absurdly Draconian result if it meant that a person who unwittingly brought into Australia narcotics which had been planted in his baggage might be liable to life imprisonment notwithstanding that he was completely innocent of any connection with the narcotics and that he was unaware that he was carrying anything illicit. On the other hand, if guilty knowledge is an ingredient of the offence, it becomes understandable that no excuse should be allowed to a person who has knowingly imported narcotics. This provides an indication, although only a slight one, that by para (b) the Parliament did not intend to displace the presumption of the common law that a blameworthy state of mind is an ingredient of the offence.

The second matter to be considered is the subject matter with which the statute deals. Paragraph (b) of s 233B(1) and the other paragraphs of that subsection deal with a grave social evil which the Parliament naturally intends should be rigorously suppressed. The importation of and trade in narcotics creates a serious threat to the well-being of the Australian community. It has led to a great increase in crime, to corruption and to the ruin of innocent lives. The fact that the consequences of an offence against s 233B(1)(b) may be so serious suggests that the Parliament may have intended to make the offence an absolute one. On the other hand, the subsection does not deal with acts which 'are not criminal in any real sense, but are acts which in the public interest are prohibited under a penalty', to repeat the words used in *Sherras v De Rutzen* at 922, to describe the first of the three classes of exceptions to the general rule which that case laid down. On the contrary, offences of this kind, at least where heroin in commercial quantities is involved, are truly criminal; a convicted offender is exposed to obloquy and disgrace and becomes liable to the highest penalty that may be imposed under the law. It is unlikely that the Parliament intended that the consequences of committing an offence so serious should be visited on a person who had no intention to do anything wrong and no knowledge that he was doing so. A third consideration is that which was mentioned in *Lim Chin Aik v R* at 174:

> It is pertinent also to inquire whether putting the defendant under strict liability will assist in the enforcement of the regulations. That means that there must be something he can do, directly or indirectly ... which will promote the observance of the regulations. Unless this is so, there is no reason in penalising him, and it cannot be inferred that the legislature imposed strict liability merely in order to find a luckless victim.

See also *Sweet v Parsley* [1970] AC 132 at 163 and *Gammon Ltd v A-G of Hong Kong* at 443. A person bringing baggage into a country can no doubt take care to ensure that no drugs are contained in it. The public interest demands that such care should be taken. There is thus an argument, the strength of which I shall later consider, in favour of the view that the Parliament may have intended to penalise importation that was no more than careless. Clearly, however, no good purpose would be served by punishing a person who had taken reasonable care and yet had unknowingly been an innocent agent to import narcotics.

These indications do not all point in the same direction, but at least they suggest the conclusion that the Parliament did not intend that the offence defined in para (b) should be an absolute one.

The expression '*mens rea*' is ambiguous and imprecise. The passage which I have cited from *Sherras v De Rutzen* suggests that it means 'evil intention, or a knowledge of the wrongfulness of the act'. In *Iannella v French* (1968) 119 CLR 84 at 108, 109, Windeyer J approved of the statement in which Jordan CJ in *R v Turnbull* (1943) 44 SR (NSW) 108 at 109, described the *mens rea* of an offender:

> ... assuming his mind to be sufficiently normal for him to be capable of criminal responsibility, it is also necessary at common law for the prosecution to prove that he knew that he was doing the criminal act which is charged against him, that is, that he knew that all the facts constituting the ingredients necessary to make the act criminal were involved in what he was doing.

However, as Lord Diplock pointed out in *Sweet v Parsley* at 162, recklessness may be a sufficient mental element of some offences, and there is no single mental element that is common to all offences. As will be seen, it is a question whether negligence can amount to *mens rea*.

It can hardly be doubted that a person would not commit an offence against s 233B(1)(b) if he did not intend to import either the narcotics themselves or the container in which they were found. The relevance of intention has been recognised in a number of cases. If goods are carried in a ship which sails within Australian territorial waters or into an Australian port, or in an aircraft which flies over Australian airspace or lands at an Australian airfield, with no intention that they should be unloaded in Australia, and they are not in fact unloaded, they will not be imported in the ordinary sense of the term: *R v Bull* at 220, 254. A person may be convicted of an offence against s 233B(1)(b) if he despatches goods to Australia by air from a place outside Australia, with the intention that the goods should be landed in Australia: see *White v Ridley* (1978) 140 CLR 342 esp at 359. Those cases, however, do not answer the question whether the offender must know what he is importing, although *White v Ridley* proceeds on the assumption that an innocent agent — a person who does not know that he is bringing narcotic goods into the country — will not commit the offence. The critical question is whether it is enough that the offender intended to import a bag or parcel, even though he did not know what it contained, or whether knowledge of the nature, and possibly of the quality, of the prohibited thing imported is an element of the offence. Since, as I have indicated, I find it impossible to suppose that the Parliament intended to make the offence one of absolute liability, the only alternative to a requirement of guilty knowledge (by which I include wilful blindness) is that no mental state is an ingredient of the offence, but that an accused is entitled to be acquitted if he honestly and reasonably believed that he was not carrying narcotic goods.

There has developed a principle that an honest and reasonable mistake of fact will be a ground of exculpation in cases in which actual knowledge is not required as an element of an offence. This principle is founded on what was said in *R v Tolson* [1889] 23 QBD 168, particularly per Cave J at 181:

> At common law an honest and reasonable belief in the existence of circumstances, which, if true, would make the act for which a prisoner is indicted an innocent act has always been held to be a good defence. This doctrine is embodied in the somewhat uncouth maxim, '*actus non facit reum, nisi mens sit rea*'. Honest and reasonable mistake stands in fact on the same footing as absence of the reasoning faculty, as in infancy, or perversion of that faculty, as in lunacy ...

In *Bank of New South Wales v Piper* [1897] AC 383 at 389–90, their Lordships said:

> It was strongly urged by the respondent's counsel that in order to the constitution of a crime, whether common law or statutory, there must be *mens rea* on the part of the accused, and that he may avoid conviction by showing that such *mens* did not exist. That is a proposition which their Lordships do not desire to dispute; but the questions whether a particular intent is made an element of the statutory crime, and when that is not the case, whether there was an absence of *mens rea* in the accused, are questions entirely different, and depend upon different considerations. In cases when the statute requires a motive to be proved as an essential element of the crime, the prosecution must fail if it is not proved. On the other hand, the absence of *mens rea* really consists in an honest and reasonable belief entertained by the accused of the existence of facts which, if true, would make the act charged against him innocent.

The implications of these statements were explored in a number of cases in this court particularly *Maher v Musson* (1934) 52 CLR 100, *Thomas v R* (1937) 59 CLR 279 and *Proudman v Dayman*. In the last-mentioned case Dixon J said at 540–1, that even where the statute excludes the necessity for positive knowledge on the part of the accused, honest and reasonable mistake of fact will still be a ground of exculpation. He continued at 541:

> The burden of establishing honest and reasonable mistake is in the first place upon the defendant and he must make it appear that he had reasonable grounds for believing in the existence of a state of facts, which, if true, would take his act outside the operation of the enactment and that on those grounds he did so believe. The burden possibly may not finally rest upon him of satisfying the tribunal in cases of doubt.

These cases establish that if it is held that guilty knowledge is not an ingredient of an offence, it does not follow that the offence is an absolute one. A middle course, between imposing absolute liability and requiring proof of guilty knowledge or intention, is to hold that an accused will not be guilty if he acted under an honest and reasonable mistake as to the existence of facts, which, if true, would have made his act innocent. However there are a number of questions which have not been clearly answered. The first is whether the absence of an honest and reasonable belief in the existence of facts which would have made the act innocent is a form of *mens rea* or whether, on the other hand, an honest and reasonable mistake affords the accused a defence only when he is charged with an offence of which *mens rea* is not an element. A second question is whether the accused bears the onus of proving on the balance of probabilities that he acted under an honest and reasonable mistake of fact or whether it is enough if the evidence raises a reasonable doubt. Thirdly, it is a question whether the so-called defence of honest and reasonable but mistaken belief is available when the offence charged is of a truly criminal character, or whether it applies only to statutory offences of a regulatory kind.

The Supreme Court of Canada, in an important judgment, has given confident answers to these questions. In *R v Sault Ste Marie* [1978] 2 SCR 1299 it was held that where an offence is truly criminal the prosecution must establish a mental element, and negligence is not enough for that purpose. However, it was held, there is a middle position between cases where full *mens rea* is required and cases of absolute liability, namely, cases in which it is a defence for the defendant to prove, on the balance of probabilities, that he was not negligent. Prima facie, 'public welfare offences', or 'regulatory offences', are in this last-mentioned class. Dickson J, who delivered the judgment of the court, accordingly held at 1325–6, that offences could be classified into three categories, as follows:

1. Offences in which *mens rea*, consisting of some positive state of mind such as intent, knowledge, or recklessness, must be proved by the prosecution either as an inference from the nature of the act committed, or by additional evidence.
2. Offences in which there is no necessity for the prosecution to prove the existence of *mens rea;* the doing of the prohibited act prima facie imports the offence, leaving it open to the accused to avoid liability by proving that he took all reasonable care. This involves consideration of what a reasonable man would have done in the circumstances. The defence will be available if the accused reasonably believed in a mistaken set of facts which, if true, would render the act or omission innocent, or if he took all reasonable steps to avoid the particular event. These offences may properly be called offences of strict liability.
3. Offences of absolute liability where it is not open to the accused to exculpate himself by showing that he was free of fault.

The Supreme Court of Canada has further held that in cases in which the prosecution is required to prove mens rea, there can be no conviction if the accused honestly believed that the facts were such as to make his actions innocent, whether or not the mistake was reasonable: *Pappajohn v R* (1980) 14 CR (3d) 243. It is of course clear that if guilty knowledge is an element of an offence, an honest belief, even if unreasonably based, may negative the existence of the guilty knowledge, and thus lead to an acquittal.

It appears that in *R v Tolson* and *Bank of New South Wales v Piper* the absence of *mens rea* was equated with the honest and reasonable but mistaken belief of the accused. Lord Diplock in *Sweet v Parsley* at 163, and Menzies J in *R v Reynhoudt* (1962) 107 CLR 381 at 400, viewed the matter in that way. It may be that little turns on the question whether honest and reasonable mistake should be regarded as a special defence available only in cases not requiring *mens rea,* or as something the absence of which constitutes *mens rea*. The matter is largely one of words. On either view the words of the statute and the nature of the offence must be considered in deciding what mental state is required, and whether an objective test of reasonableness is to be applied together with the subjective test of whether there was a mistaken belief.

I should say immediately that if s 233B(1)(b) does not require the prosecution to prove guilty knowledge, but has the effect that an accused is entitled to be acquitted if he acted with the honest and reasonable belief that his baggage contained no narcotic goods, in my opinion the onus of proving the absence of any such belief lies on the prosecution. *Maher v Musson* suggests the contrary, but that case was decided before *Woolmington v Director of Public Prosecutions* [1935] AC 462. In *Proudman v Dayman* at 541, Dixon J may have intended to say that the accused bore only an evidentiary onus, but his words were somewhat equivocal, and in *Sweet v Parsley* Lord Pearce (at 158) and Lord Diplock (at 164) understood them in different senses. In some later cases judges still spoke as though the onus of proof lay on the accused: see *Dowling v Bowie* (1952) 86 CLR 136 at 141, 149–51; *Bergin v Stack* at 261 and *R v Reynhoudt* at 395–6, 399–400. However, it has now become more generally recognised, consistently with principle, that provided that there is evidence which raises the question the jury cannot convict unless they are satisfied that the accused did not act under the honest and reasonable mistake; see *Iannella v French* at 110–11; *Kidd v Reeves* [1972] VR 563 at 565; *Mayer v Marchant* (1973) 5 SASR 567, but cf *R v Bonnor* [1957] VR 227. This view has also been accepted in New Zealand: *R v Strawbridge* [1970] NZLR 909. As I have said, it is in my opinion the correct view.

I am not sure that we can accept the opinion held in Canada that the defence of honest and reasonable but mistaken belief may be raised only in the case of regulatory offences. *Thomas v R* dealt with a crime that was truly criminal (bigamy) and so possibly did *R v Strawbridge* (the cultivation of marijuana). However, it is more likely that the Parliament will have intended that full *mens rea*, in the sense of guilty intention or guilty knowledge, will be an element if an offence is one of a serious kind.

I have already shown that the offence created by s 233B(1)(b) is treated by the Parliament in some circumstances as being one of the most serious in the criminal calendar. It seems improbable that the Parliament would have intended that it might be committed as a result of mere carelessness, although that would be the case if guilty knowledge was not an element, and an unreasonable although honest mistake would not be sufficient to exculpate the accused. It is true that the penalty of life imprisonment provided by the statute is a maximum one and that a judge who considered that the accused had brought in narcotic goods in the honest but unreasonable belief that his luggage did not contain them would sentence accordingly. Nevertheless, to provide that a sentence of life imprisonment might be imposed for an offence committed merely through negligence would appear to be exceedingly severe. The gravity of the offence suggests that guilty knowledge was intended to be an element of it.

Moreover, it is by no means clear that the creation of liability for negligence would give added efficacy to the prohibition of the importation of narcotics. On any view of the effect of the section, if the suspicions of an incoming traveller are aroused, and he deliberately refrains from making any inquiries for fear that he may learn the truth, his wilful blindness may be treated as equivalent to knowledge. If he is given a bag or parcel to carry into Australia in suspicious circumstances, or if there is something suspicious about the appearance, feel or weight of his own baggage, and he deliberately fails to inquire further, the jury may well be satisfied that he wilfully shut his eyes to the probability that he was carrying narcotics and for that reason should be treated as having the necessary guilty knowledge. If he is innocent of complicity in any attempt to import narcotics, and there is nothing to arouse his suspicions, it is difficult to see what action he could be reasonably expected to take to prevent a stranger from secreting narcotics in his baggage. It would have little point to make negligence a ground of liability.

The present question was considered by the Full Court of the Supreme Court of Queensland in *R v Gardiner* [1981] Qd R 394; (1979) 27 ALR 140 and that court held, by a majority, that on a charge under s 233B(1)(b) the prosecution was not bound to establish *mens rea* or to exclude the operation of 'the defence of ignorance or mistake of fact': see at (CLR) 406; (ALR) 152. The reasons given for the conclusion were summed up by Hoare J (at (CLR) 405; (ALR) 151) very shortly as follows:

> So far as concerns the first charge in the indictment, having regard to the subject matter of the legislation, namely narcotic goods, and the virtual impossibility of proving the state of mind of an importer of narcotic goods in the absence of admissions which would be unlikely to be made by traffickers, while there is much to be said to the contrary, it seems to me that the legislature intended to create the offence by proof of the actual importing or attempting to import.

With all respect I do not consider that the fact that the legislation dealt with narcotic goods supports the view that the Parliament intended to make the offence an absolute one or to make proof of guilty knowledge unnecessary; the gravity of the offence indicates the contrary. Further I am by no means persuaded that it is virtually impossible, or even particularly difficult, to prove the state of mind of an importer of narcotic goods in the absence of admissions. If a person enters Australia carrying a suitcase which has narcotics concealed in it, and offers no convincing explanation of the presence of the narcotics, I should be surprised if a jury would draw any inference other than that he knew that the narcotics were in the case. For these reasons I cannot agree with the conclusion which was reached on this point by the majority of the court in *R v Gardiner* which was followed by the majority of the Supreme Court of Victoria in *R v Parsons*. I accordingly conclude that the presumption that *mens rea* is required before a person can be held guilty of a grave criminal offence is not displaced in relation to s 233B(1)(b) of the *Customs Act* and that the prosecution on a charge under that provision bears the onus of proving that the accused knew that he was importing a narcotic substance.

The next question that falls for consideration is whether on a charge under s 233B(1)(c) the prosecution bears the onus of proving that the accused knew that he had the narcotic goods in his possession. The question bears a different aspect from that which arises in relation to s 233B(1)(b). The words used in s 233B(1)(c) — 'has in his possession' — in their ordinary sense connote a state of mind, in particular some awareness of the existence of the thing that was in fact in the possessor's physical control. In *Director of Public Prosecutions v Brooks* [1974] AC 862 Lord Diplock said at 866:

> Possession is a deceptively simple concept. It denotes a physical control or custody of a thing plus knowledge that you have it in your custody or control. You may possess a thing without knowing or comprehending its nature: but you do not possess it unless you know you have it.

In *Williams v R* (1978) 140 CLR 591 at 610, Aickin J said:

> It is necessary to bear in mind that in possession there is a necessary mental element of intention, involving a sufficient knowledge of the presence of the drug by the accused. No doubt in many cases custody of an object may supply sufficient evidence of possession, including the necessary mental element, but that is because the inference of knowledge may often be properly drawn from surrounding circumstances.

See also *R v Woodrow* (1846) 15 MW 404 at 415, 418; 153 ER 907 at 912, 913; *R v Warner* at 282, 307–8, 310–11. I may digress by saying that we are not concerned in the present case with the situation in which the accused knows that he has the thing in his custody but says that he does not know its nature — eg, if he says that he thought heroin was baking soda — or its qualities — eg, if he knew that he had in his possession a drug, but did not know which drug. In Canada, it has been held that the prosecution must prove that the accused knew that the substance was a drug (*Beaver v R* [1957] SCR 531) but not that it was a drug of the kind mentioned in the charge: *R v Blondin* (1970) 2 CCC (2d) 118; affirmed (1971) 4 CCC (2d) 566. There was no unanimity of opinion on this question in *R v Warner.* I need not discuss these questions further, but may add that I cannot think that in the usual run of cases questions of that kind would present much difficulty to a jury. This is a case in which, if believed, the accused was wholly ignorant that the substance was in his suitcase. Clearly, a person does not have in his possession a narcotic drug which, without his knowledge, is in his baggage or his room.

It would be a misapprehension to think that *Williams v Douglas* (1949) 78 CLR 521 is authority for the view that mere physical custody, without any mental element, amounts to 'possession'. There it was held the words 'possession or control' in the *Gold Buyers Act 1921* (WA), as amended, meant 'de facto possession and actual control' and that gold bars were in the possession of the defendant although he had hidden them in a communal bathroom some distance from his bedroom. When the court spoke of 'de facto possession and actual control' it was intended to exclude cases of constructive possession, 'where the real connection of the accused with the gold was ambiguous and uncertain, and where it would not be fair to throw so great an onus upon him': see at 526. It was clearly not intended to suggest that a person could have possession of something of whose existence he was unaware. On the contrary, the court in that case held that the liability of the defendant depended on whether either he, or his accomplice with his knowledge, had hidden the gold: see at 527, 528. In *Moors v Burke* (1919) 26 CLR 265, which is discussed in *Williams v Douglas*, the defendant was held not to be in actual possession of certain wool suspected of being stolen because he had placed the wool in a locker which was not under his control. It was decided that actual possession meant 'the complete present personal physical control of the property to the exclusion of others not acting in concert with the accused' (see at 274) but this statement did not mean, and the case does not suggest, that knowledge was not a necessary element — in that case of course the defendant had full knowledge of what he had done with the wool.

The effect of the authorities to which I have referred is that where a statute makes it an offence to have possession of particular goods, knowledge by the accused that those goods are in his custody will, in the absence of a sufficient indication of a contrary intention, be a necessary ingredient of the offence, because the words describing the offence ('in his possession') themselves necessarily import a mental element. In such a case it is unnecessary to rely on the common law presumption that *mens rea* is required. The question then is whether the words of the Customs Act contain a sufficient indication that the Parliament intended that knowledge should not be an ingredient of an offence against s 233B(1)(c), notwithstanding the prima facie effect of the words 'in his possession'. The provisions which might be thought to give such an indication are those of the clause 'without reasonable excuse (proof whereof shall lie upon him)' and those of subs (1A).

Before I turn to the authorities in which this question has been considered, it is useful to look at the words of the statute themselves. The words of s 233B(1)(c), read in their ordinary grammatical sense, mean that a person commits an offence if he has narcotic goods in his possession, unless he has reasonable excuse. Plainly the words suggest that no question of reasonable excuse arises until it is proved that the accused had possession of the goods. Since possession imports knowledge, 'reasonable excuse', which falls to be considered only after possession has been proved, does not include mere lack of knowledge. Such a construction does not make the reference to 'reasonable excuse' meaningless or nugatory. A person may have narcotic goods in his possession because he has taken them from an addict and is about to destroy them, or because he has found them and is taking them to the police, or because he is an officer of Customs who has confiscated them, and these circumstances may provide him with reasonable excuse. Subsection (1A) would not appear to bear on the present question. It makes it unnecessary for the prosecution to prove that the accused knew that the goods in his possession had been imported into Australia in contravention of the Act. It does not relieve the prosecution of the burden of proving that the goods were in his possession and that involves proving that he knew of their existence.

A different view has been taken in a number of cases, the first of which was *R v Bush* [1975] 1 NSWLR 298.

[His Honour discussed the decision in *R v Bush*, and continued:]

With all respect I am unable to agree with the reasoning which supports the decision in *R v Bush*, and the cases which have followed it. The critical question, as I have endeavoured to show, is whether the words of s 233B(1)(c) make knowledge an element of the crime a question 'entirely different' from whether there is an absence of *mens rea* when the knowledge is not made an element by the words of the statute themselves: see the passage from *Bank of New South Wales v Piper* cited above. In answering this question it must be remembered that it has two aspects: first, what the word 'possession' ordinarily connotes and secondly, whether there is anything in the statute, or its history, which shows that some other meaning is to be given to the word where it appears in s 233B(1)(c). For the reasons I have already given 'possession' connotes knowledge of the existence of the thing possessed. Further, neither the provisions of para (c) of s 233B(1) nor those of subs (1A) contain any indication either that 'possession' is to be given any other than its ordinary meaning or that the onus of proving an element which that meaning necessarily embraces should be cast upon the accused.

[His Honour then referred to a number of authorities, and continued:]

For the reasons I have given I hold that in a proceeding under para (b) or para (c) of s 233B(1) the prosecution bears the onus of proving that the accused knew of the existence of the goods which he brought into Australia, or which were in a suitcase or other container over which he had exclusive physical control, as the case may be. The proper direction on the first charge was that the prosecution had to prove that the applicant brought the suitcase into Australia, knowing that the heroin was in the case. On the second charge the jury should have been told that they could not find that the applicant had the heroin in his possession, unless they were satisfied that he knew that it was in the suitcase. Whether a direction concerning wilful blindness was also necessary depends on the facts, which were not fully before us. It is rather regrettable that a statutory provision which has assumed so great an importance in law enforcement in Australia should present such difficulties of interpretation. However, I have no fear that the effect which I have given to the section will prove to be a charter for drug traffickers. If that is wrong, the remedy lies with the Parliament.

At first sight it would appear that the misdirection must lead to an order setting aside the conviction and for a new trial. However, the transcript of evidence was not placed before us. The learned trial judge told the jury that they might think that the central issue in the trial was the knowledge of the applicant and there can be no doubt that they found adversely to the applicant on that issue. We are unable to say whether the evidence raised a case so strong that notwithstanding the misdirection no substantial miscarriage of justice occurred. In these circumstances I would grant special leave to appeal, allow the appeal, and refer the matter back to the Full Court of the Supreme Court of Victoria to proceed in accordance with this judgment.

Wilson J [dissenting]: Having, through the medium of a review of many of the relevant cases, exposed the competing considerations that fall to be considered, it is now possible to proceed to draw some conclusions. The central task is to construe s 233B(1)(b) of the

Act. That task is assisted by a consideration of the history of the section, a history which has seen the maximum punishment for an offence under the paragraph move steadily upwards from imprisonment for two years in 1910 to life imprisonment in 1979, and the passage of amendments from time to time which transfer from the prosecution to the defence the burden of proving certain issues relevant to offences under paras (c) and (ca): cf subss (1A) and (1B). Paragraph (b) does not expressly import *mens rea* as an element of the offence; the word 'knowingly' does not appear. Nevertheless, does the presumption referred to by Wright J in *Sherras v De Rutzen* operate? Here the seriousness of the punishment to which an offender is liable is of great materiality. Is it conceivable that the legislature would have created an offence of absolute liability carrying life imprisonment, that is to say, an offence which would be established by proof merely of the importation by the accused of narcotic goods regardless of honest and reasonable mistake or duress or ignorance or the gratuitous act of a stranger or any other reasonable excuse? In considering that question, due regard must be paid to the obvious legislative concern, reflected in the penalty, for the protection of the community from the monstrous evils of the international traffic in heroin and other drugs which are intrinsically nefarious. One cannot lightly dismiss the view of the majority of *Gardiner* that an offence of absolute liability may be justified by the difficulties that any other conclusion would place in the way of law enforcement officers, particularly if guilty knowledge was required to be established in making out a prima facie case. In some of the cases a conclusion in favour of a presumption of *mens rea* as an element of an offence under para (b) has found support in a comparison with the wording of other paragraphs in subs (1). Paragraphs (a), (c) and (ca) expressly import 'without reasonable excuse' in the description of the offence created by each of those paragraphs and in each case the onus of proof of any reasonable excuse is expressly placed upon an accused person. However, I find such phrases inconclusive. It may readily be said that the legislature, having expressly placed an onus on an accused person in these paragraphs, supplies a clear inference that in para (b), where the words do not appear, the legislature intended the onus of proof to remain on the prosecution. But that inference flows only from the presence of the words in parentheses, these being the only words dealing with the question of proof. A competing inference may flow from the express inclusion of the words 'without reasonable excuse'. These are words which clearly import *mens rea* into the offences created by the paragraphs in which they appear. The omission of the words from para (b) could be taken to mean that the legislature intended that in the case of importation no excuse whatever, whether reasonable or otherwise, was to be tolerated. In that case the offence would be one of absolute liability. On the other hand, the presence of subs (1C) in the section recognises the possible application of defences otherwise available to the person charged. The section does not form a code complete in itself.

In my opinion, the omission of the words 'without reasonable excuse' from para (b) has the effect of removing *mens rea* as an element of the offence which is to be positively established by the prosecution in making out a prima facie case. But this is not to constitute the offence as one of absolute liability. It is to give with one qualification the same effect to the omission as Day J, in *Sherras v De Rutzen*, gave to the omission of the word 'knowingly' from the description of one offence in the Act there under consideration whilst the word appeared in another offence in the same section. His Lordship said at 921:

> ... the only effect of this is to shift the burden of proof. In cases under subs 1 it is for the prosecution to prove the knowledge, while in cases under subs 2 the defendant has to prove that he did not know. That is the only inference I draw from the insertion of the word 'knowingly' in the one subsection and its omission in the other.

The qualification is that the word 'prove' in this passage should not in this context be understood to mean any more than to 'adduce evidence of'. In other words, the effect of the omission of the words 'without reasonable excuse' from para (b) is to transfer the evidential burden, the burden of adducing evidence, from the prosecution to the defence. It then remains on the prosecution to rebut that evidence to the satisfaction of the jury beyond a reasonable doubt.

This construction seems to me to most satisfactorily meet the competing considerations to which I have referred. The prosecution is relieved of the necessity of looking into the mind of the alleged offender in an attempt to exclude as part of its case possible states of mind that might point to innocence. Proof of the importation of the drug by the accused person will be prima facie sufficient to establish the charge. But an accused person who lacks any guilty intent will have the opportunity of explaining the incriminating conduct and at the end of the day if the jury is left with a reasonable doubt then an acquittal will follow. It ought not to be assumed that the inference of guilty knowledge arising from the importation of a prohibited drug will be lightly erased. On the other hand, if the consequences of this construction prove inimical to the welfare of the Australian community then it will be for a legislature to make its intention clearer. I should add that in the light of the decision in *Woolmington* and of later authorities I do not think it is possible or desirable to hold that the decision of this court in *Maher v Musson* is determinative of this case. In any event, the seriousness of the offence in *Maher v Musson* bears no comparison with an offence under s 233B(1)(b). It is unnecessary to consider whether the force of that decision remains unimpaired in the case of some minor statutory offences of a strict liability kind which carry a modest penalty. First and foremost it is a question of construction of the particular statute in every case.

In my opinion, then, it should now be taken to be the law in Australia that in order to present a prima facie case of an offence under s 233B(1)(b) of the Act it is not necessary for the Crown to establish guilty knowledge on the part of the accused. In the absence of evidence to the contrary such knowledge will be presumed, but if there is some evidence that an accused person honestly believed on reasonable grounds that his act was innocent then he is entitled to be acquitted unless the jury is satisfied beyond reasonable doubt that this was not so. I have taken the substance of this formulation from the decision of the New Zealand Court of Appeal in *Strawbridge*: at 916. The conclusion is also in line with the opinion of a number of judges within Australia who have had occasion to consider the general problem since *Strawbridge*; Bray CJ and Zelling J in *Mayer v Marchant*; Menhennitt J in *Kidd v Reeves*; Demack J in *Gardiner*; Starke J in *Parsons* (with Young CJ and King J declining to endorse the correctness of the opposing view); and finally by members of this court: Menzies J and Gibbs J in *Samuels v Stokes*; Barwick CJ, Mason and Aickin JJ in *Cameron v Holt*. It may be desirable to add that I am unable as at present advised to draw a distinction between a defence of honest and reasonable mistake and one of honest and reasonable ignorance of the presence or nature of the goods in question. The conclusion also has the merit of bringing the common law in Australia on the question of honest and reasonable mistake into line with the law in the Code states of Queensland, Western Australia and Tasmania: cf *Brimblecombe v Duncan; Ex parte Duncan* [1958] Qd R 8; *Geraldton Fishermen's Co-op Ltd v Munro* [1963] WAR 129. This is an important consideration where the exercise of federal jurisdiction is concerned.

It is next submitted on behalf of the applicant that the trial judge's direction to the jury on the charge of possession under s 233B(1)(c) was erroneous in that his Honour told the jury that the Crown did not have to prove that the applicant was *knowingly* in possession of the heroin. The submission joins issue with the correctness of the unanimous decision of the Court of Criminal Appeal in Victoria in *R v Ditroia and Tucci*. In that case the court held that in a prosecution under s 233B(1)(ca) of the Act if a defendant is found in possession of narcotic goods the Crown is not required to prove knowledge by the defendant of the nature of the narcotic goods: it is for the defendant to establish lack of knowledge of the nature of the goods so that a jury might decide whether such lack of knowledge, if so proved, amounted to a reasonable excuse for possession. In coming to that conclusion, the court followed the decision of the Court of Criminal Appeal in New South Wales in *R v Bush* (1975) 5 ALR 387; [1975] 1 NSWLR 298. The court recognised the desirability of following the decision of an appellate court of co-ordinate jurisdiction in the same exercise of federal jurisdiction, but in addition it expressed its support for the reasoning in the case (at 254):

> However, we think that *Bush's* case ... was correctly decided. In *R v Rawcliffe* [1977] 1 NSWLR 219 a Court of Criminal Appeal consisting of five judges refused to uphold a submission that *Bush's* case was wrongly decided. Since then it has been followed in many cases. See *R v Router* (1977) 14 ALR 365; *R v Malas* (1978) 21 ALR 225 and *R v Kennedy* (1979) 25 ALR 367.

In *Bush*, Nagle J delivered the judgment of the court. In a close analysis of the problem, his Honour first disposed of the submission that *mens rea* was a separate ingredient in the offence created by para (c). It was observed that there was no such express requirement on the Crown to prove that the appellant should have had knowledge of, or reason to suspect, the nature of the contents of the parcel of which he obtained control. Any implication of such a requirement was rejected, having regard to the importance of effective measures to control illicit traffic in narcotic drugs: cf *R v Peel* [1971] 1 NSWLR 247. However, the court held that the section did not exclude the exculpatory principle by which the person charged may prove an honest belief on reasonable grounds in the existence of circumstances which, if true, would make innocent that with which he is charged; their Honours found this exculpation encompassed by the terms of para (c) which allow for any reasonable excuse, proof of which is to lie on the accused. Reference was made to a comment by Barwick CJ in *R v Bull* (1974) 131 CLR 203 at 220 to the effect that knowledge of the nature of the thing possessed is not essential to the commission of the offence under s 233B(1)(a). Thus far the decision merely reinforces in general terms the reasoning which has led me to the conclusion I have expressed in respect of the first submission of the applicant. The distinctive point in his second submission is that the concept of possession as used in para (c) itself imports a mental element requiring knowledge of the nature of the goods allegedly possessed which must be proved by the Crown as part of its case. In *Bush* Nagle J examines a similar submission at great depth. He relies on the decision of this court in *Williams v Douglas* (1949) 78 CLR 521 at 526, 527 in coming to the conclusion that the kind of possession intended when used in relation to dangerous drugs or narcotic goods is limited to de facto possession. His Honour then proceeds to demonstrate persuasively that the mental element involved extends no further than the intention inherent in de facto possession of such goods, namely, the intention to have exclusive physical control of some article which is in fact narcotic goods or of some article or some place wherein such goods are in fact carried or contained or located: at (ALR) 414–15; (NSWLR) 324. It is not inherent in that mental element that an accused should know that an item in his de facto possession is narcotic goods. It is for the accused to advance his ignorance of that fact as a 'reasonable excuse' for his possession. The scope of that defence was illustrated, as the court thought, by the cases of *Poole v Wah Min Charn* and *R v Tawill* [1974] VR 84. As I have already noted, the former case is a decision of this court on s 233(1)(d) of the Act, the provisions of which were similar to s 233B(1)(c). It was held that possession without reasonable excuse of prohibited imports, in itself and independently of any further mental element consisting in knowledge that the goods are prohibited imports, is an offence, but that a defendant may be able to show that he had no reason to believe that the goods were prohibited and thereby provide a reasonable excuse: at 227. Of course, as the court in *Bush* explained, this decision was out of line with the decision in *Hill v Donohoe* with respect to s 233B(1)(c). Harmony was restored by the enactment in 1967 of subs (1A) which in effect overruled *Hill v Donohoe*. *Tawill* was a case involving para (c), but the defence was one of duress. The court held that duress was to be comprehended within 'reasonable excuse'. Referring to the scope of the defence, the court said (at (ALR) 418; (NSWLR) 327:

> The words 'without reasonable excuse' are words of wide import. We see no reason why defences, answers, justifications or excuses recognised by the established principles governing criminal responsibility, such as absence of *mens rea*, mistake, insanity, infancy or duress, do not fall within the ordinary grammatical meaning of those words.

In *Rawcliffe*, provision was made for a court of five judges to review the decision in *Bush*. The court unanimously endorsed the decision. However, in *Kennedy*, a case involving somewhat different facts, Roden J found himself unable to agree with the decision. His Honour's well-reasoned dissent deserves serious consideration. It seems to me that the dissent centres on an acceptance of the proposition that to establish possession there must be shown 'a necessary mental element of intention, involving a sufficient knowledge of the presence of the drug by the accused': per Aickin J in *Williams v R* (1978) 53 ALJR 101 at 108; 22 ALR 195 at 209. It must be borne in mind that Aickin J was dealing with the concept of possession in a different statute and it is readily acknowledged that in construing a word like 'possession' the context is of great importance. With all respect to Roden J, I think the mental element to which he refers is deliberately and expressly taken up by the legislature in the provision for reasonable excuse. Admittedly, the point involves a question of fundamental principle and that the transfer of an onus from the prosecution to an accused person can have serious consequences for that person. As Roden J says at 389:

> If he [the accused] says that he picked it up by mistake, the jury would be directed to convict, even if they entertained a real doubt on that mistake issue; even indeed if 'the scales of probability' were found by them to be evenly balanced and they were unable to decide the issue one way or the other.

However, two things must be borne in mind. First, the social evil to which the section is directed is a very serious one. Secondly, the difficulties of enforcement would be enormous if the Crown were obliged to disprove beyond reasonable doubt any innocent explanation of the proved de facto possession that might possibly be relevant. I think it must follow that the express provision for the accused person to prove the existence of any reasonable excuse for his proved possession of narcotic goods points to the conclusion that the legislature intended to limit the obligation on the prosecution to proof of de facto possession of prohibited imports in the manner found by the court in *Bush* and confirmed in *Rawcliffe*. For these reasons I am unable to endorse the stand taken by Roden J.

The submission for the applicant with respect to the count of possession must be rejected.

[**Mason J** agreed with **Gibbs CJ**. **Brennan J** delivered a separate judgment agreeing with **Gibbs CJ**. **Dawson J** delivered a separate judgment agreeing with **Gibbs CJ** in relation to s 233B(1)(b) but holding that, in relation to s 233B(1)(c), a person may possess narcotic goods if he or she is aware of possessing something but is not aware that what he or she possesses are, in fact, narcotics. The view adopted by **Dawson J** was that, in such a case, the accused's defence will be one of reasonable excuse.]

[See also *R v Baird* [1985] 3 NSWLR 331; *Carlin v Thawat Chidkhunthad* [1985] 4 NSWLR 182; *R v Haddad* (1988) 33 A Crim R 400; *R v Tomasevic* (1990) 51 A Crim R 72; *Davis v R* (1991) 66 ALJR 22; *R v Sleiman (No 1)* (1993) 113 FLR 30; *R v Sleiman (No 2)* (1993) 113 FLR 34; *R v Su* (VCA, 15 December 1995, unreported); *R v Cheng* (1999) 73 SASR 502; *R v Saengsai-Or* (2004) 61 NSWLR 135; *R v Thang Duc Nguyen* (2005) 12 VR 299; *Re Pong Su (No 10)* (2005) 154 A Crim R 19.]

9.32 Notes

1. It is submitted that there is much to be said in favour of the dissenting view of Wilson J that the offences should be interpreted as imposing strict liability subject to the defence of honest and reasonable mistake. The offences formerly contained in s 233B of the Customs Act 1901 (Cth) are extremely

serious and, therefore, clearly not appropriate for the imposition of unqualified strict liability. The drug trade does, however, represent a serious and growing social menace. Those engaged in the trade are frequently sophisticated and experienced criminals, with significant financial and organisational backing. Where persons are found in possession of large quantities of drugs or attempting to import drugs, it is often simple for them to assert those drugs were planted on them. To require the prosecution to prove beyond reasonable doubt in all cases that the accused was not aware he or she possessed the drugs, while placing no burden whatsoever on the accused, may be thought to confer on the accused an advantage not warranted having regard to the community interest in attempting to stamp out the drug trade. Adopting an approach which insists that the accused meet an evidential burden of establishing that he or she believed on reasonable grounds that he or she was not carrying drugs seems a not unreasonable compromise. It allows the blameless accused to escape liability, and involves no infringement of the basic principle that the prosecution must prove its case beyond reasonable doubt. The requirement that the belief be reasonable and that the accused carry the evidential burden of proof, however, lessens the opportunity for the accused successfully to raise bogus defences. In practical terms, the placing of the evidential burden on the accused means that if the defence is to succeed the accused is likely to have to give evidence and, as a consequence, render herself or himself liable to cross-examination. If the prosecution of criminals is to be regarded as a serious affair and not a sporting activity in which the quarry is to be afforded every advantage, such a practical result is not to be regretted.

2. In *Kural v R* (1987) 162 CLR 502; 70 ALR 658, *Saad v R* (1987) 70 ALR 667 and *Pereira v Director of Public Prosecutions* (1988) 82 ALR 217, the High Court gave further guidance to trial judges faced with the task of directing juries as to the mens rea of drug offences. *Kural v R* was concerned with importing drugs contrary to s 233B(1)(b) of the Customs Act 1901 (Cth) (now repealed), and *Saad v R* with possession of prohibited drugs contrary to s 233B(1)(ca) of the Customs Act 1901 (Cth) (now repealed). The court held that, in both cases, it is sufficient to establish intention if the accused realised there was a likelihood that the substance he or she was importing or had in her or his possession was a prohibited drug. In *Kural v R*, Mason CJ, Deane and Dawson JJ stated that a direction along the following lines would be appropriate (at 659):

> Where, as here, it is necessary to show an intention on the part of the accused to import a narcotic drug, that intent is established if the accused knew or was aware that an article which he intentionally brought into Australia comprised or contained narcotic drugs. But that is not to say that actual knowledge or awareness is an essential element in the guilty mind required for the commission of the offence. It is only to say that knowledge or awareness is relevant to the

> existence of the necessary intent. Belief, falling short of actual knowledge, that the article comprised or contained narcotic drugs would obviously sustain an inference of intention. So also would proof that the forbidden act was done in circumstances where it appears beyond reasonable doubt that the accused was aware of the likelihood, in the sense that there was a significant or real chance, that his conduct involved that act and nevertheless persisted in that conduct. As a practical matter, the inference of *mens rea* or a guilty mind will ordinarily be irresistible in cases involving the importation of narcotic drugs if it is proved beyond reasonable doubt that the accused actually imported the drugs and that he was aware, at the time of the alleged commission of the offence, of the likelihood of the existence of the substance in question in what he was importing and of the likelihood that it was a narcotic drug.

In *Saad v R,* their Honours recommended a similar direction be given in cases of possession.

See further *R v Cao* (2006) 65 NSWLR 552 in the New South Wales Court of Criminal Appeal, and the Victorian Court of Appeal case of *DPP Reference (No 1 of 2004) (Vic); R v Nguyen* [2005] VSCA 172; (2005) 154 A Crim R 360.

The approach to proof of mens rea taken in *Kural* and *Saad* was adopted in the case of *DPP Reference (No 1 of 2004) (Vic); R v Nguyen.* The applicant, Duc Thang Nguyen, had been convicted of trafficking in a drug of dependence-commercial quantity under s 71AA of the Drugs, Poisons and Controlled Substances Act 1981 (Vic).The question before the Court of Appeal was whether, in order to prove the commission of an offence under s 71AA, the Crown must prove that the applicant had actual knowledge of the quantity of the drug of dependence in which he or she is alleged to have trafficked. The court confirmed (at [37]) that 'the Crown must prove beyond reasonable doubt that the accused intended to commit the act of trafficking which is alleged and hence that the accused knew or believed that it was, or was likely, that the subject of the act of trafficking was prohibited drugs and that the amount in question was not less than a commercial quantity'. The court further confirmed that a jury will usually decide this by inference from the facts, and that (at [37]) 'subject always to the facts of the particular case, the judge may direct the jury that proof beyond reasonable doubt that the accused believed that there was a significant or real chance that the subject of the act of trafficking was prohibited drugs and that the amount in question was not less than a commercial quantity, is capable of sustaining the inference'. The case therefore confirms that, to be guilty of a charge of trafficking in a specified quantity of a drug, the prosecution must prove the intent both to traffick in the prohibited substance, and to traffick in the particular quantity; that is, to prove that the accused knew both the nature and quantity of the substance. A jury can, however, infer intent if they conclude that the defendant had a belief that there was a 'significant or real chance' that either element existed. See also *Mustica v R* [2011] VSCA 79.

3. In *Pereira v Director of Public Prosecutions* (1988) 82 ALR 217, the High Court clarified the meaning of 'wilful blindness'. The applicant was convicted of being knowingly concerned in the importation of cannabis resin and possessing cannabis resin. The case turned on the accused's alleged lack of knowledge that a parcel she received by post, but did not open, contained cannabis. The trial judge directed the jury as to wilful blindness. In refusing the applicant leave to appeal, the court, comprising Mason CJ, Deane, Dawson, Toohey and Gaudron JJ, elaborated the concept as follows (at 219):

> Even where, as with the present charges, actual knowledge is either a specified element of the offence charged or a necessary element of the guilty mind required for the offence, it may be established as a matter of inference from the circumstances surrounding the commission of the alleged offence. However, three matters should be noted. First, in such cases the question remains one of actual knowledge: *Giorgianni v R* (1985) 156 CLR 473 at 504–7; *He Kaw Teh v R* (1985) 157 CLR 523 at 570. It is never the case that something less than knowledge may be treated as satisfying a requirement of actual knowledge. Second, the question is that of the knowledge of the accused and not that which might be postulated of a hypothetical person in the position of the accused, although, of course, that may not be an irrelevant consideration. Finally, where knowledge is inferred from the circumstances surrounding the commission of the alleged offence, knowledge must be the only rational inference available. All that having been said, the fact remains that a combination of suspicious circumstances and failure to make inquiry may sustain an inference of knowledge of the actual or likely existence of the relevant matter. In a case where a jury is invited to draw such an inference, a failure to make inquiry may sometimes, as a matter of lawyer's shorthand, be referred to as wilful blindness. Where that expression is used, care should be taken to ensure that a jury is not distracted by it from a consideration of the matter in issue as a matter of fact to be proved beyond reasonable doubt.

4. The decision in *He Raw Teh v R* dealt with the mens rea of offences under s 233B of the Act; it did not deal with the status of the general defences in their application to s 233B. In relation to the general defences, two approaches were logically available. They could be treated as governed by ordinary common law principles with the result that the evidential burden of proof would rest upon the accused with the legal burden being placed on the prosecution. Alternatively, they could be classified as matters of 'reasonable excuse' within s 233B, with the result that both the legal and evidential burdens would rest upon the accused. Prior to *He Raw Teh v R*, the latter of these two views had been adopted, most notably by the Supreme Court of Victoria in *R v Tawill* [1974] VR 84. In *R v Brown* (1986) 43 SASR 33, the accused was charged

with possession of prohibited imports contrary to s 233B(1)(ca) of the Act, and raised the defence of duress. The Supreme Court of South Australia held, rejecting the decision in *R v Tawill*, that the legal burden of disproving duress rested on the prosecution. Zelling J stated (at 58):

> [T]he High Court of Australia has held in *He Raw Teh v R* that *mens rea* is not removed as an element of the offence under s 233B(1)(c) of the Act by reason of the words 'without reasonable excuse' and that an issue of honest and reasonable mistake of fact which goes to *mens rea* has to be negatived by the Crown. Subsections (c) and (ca) are in identical verbiage so far as is material and I can't see any way of distinguishing between the two subsections. The decision in *He Raw Teh's* case thereby overrules the view in *Tawill's* case that absence of *mens rea* has to be proved by the defendant because of the words 'without reasonable excuse'. By parity of reasoning, the same applies to duress. And the reason can be put in one of two ways, either duress is something which confesses and avoids the *mens rea* of the offence and is therefore not just a reasonable excuse, but something the Crown must negative beyond reasonable doubt because duress is related to the issue of intention insofar as that intention was only produced by the will of the accused being overborne by threats to the necessary degree. The second and allied way of putting it is that because the Crown has to negative duress beyond reasonable doubt and cannot obtain a conviction until it has done so to the satisfaction of the jury, the defence of reasonable excuse is never reached if the Crown does not first negative duress beyond reasonable doubt.

9.33 Illustrations

1. D was charged with cultivating a commercial quantity of cannabis plants (less than 250 plants) contrary to s 23 of the Drug Misuse and Trafficking Act 1985 (NSW). D admitted cultivating the plants. The trial judge directed an acquittal, taking the view that, in order to be convicted of the offence charged, D had to have an intention to cultivate no fewer than 250 plants. D pleaded guilty to a lesser charge of cultivation. On appeal by the prosecution, held, the trial judge was correct in his conclusion that the onus was on the Crown to prove that D had an intention to cultivate a crop consisting of a number of prohibited plants not less than the commercial quantity. In delivering judgment in *R v CWW* (1993) 32 NSWLR 348, at 355 Sheller JA stated:

   > But evidence that the accused actually knew the crop consisted of a number of plants not less than the commercial quantity is but one way of proving the necessary intention. Intention may be proved by showing beyond reasonable doubt that the accused had a belief, falling short of actual knowledge, or was

aware of the likelihood, in the sense that there was a significant or real chance, that the crop consisted of this number of plants.

2. D was convicted of cultivation of a narcotic plant in not less than a commercial quantity contrary to s 72A of the Drugs, Poisons and Controlled Substances Act 1981 (Vic). The only issue at trial was whether D had the requisite intention to cultivate a commercial quantity of cannabis. D had been cultivating plants weighing 26.35 kilograms, a commercial quantity for the cultivation of cannabis being not less than 25 kilograms. In evidence D stated he believed the plants were below the weight of 25 kilograms. The judge gave a direction on wilful blindness. Held, conviction quashed and D convicted of alternative count of simple cultivation. A direction on the topic of wilful blindness is one that will be appropriate in very few cases. Its introduction in a trial where the critical issue is intention is capable of giving rise to difficulties and, for that reason, it must be very clear that it is an appropriate direction to give in the circumstances of the trial: *R v Garhck (No 2)* (2007) 15 VR 388.

SENTENCING FOR DRUG OFFENCES

9.34C **R v Sorby**
[1986] VR 753
Supreme Court of Victoria

[The applicant was convicted on five counts of conspiring to sell heroin, and sentenced to a total effective sentence of 23 years' imprisonment with a minimum term of 18 years.]

Kaye, **O'Bryan** and **Tadgell JJ**: In our opinion, the effective sentence of 23 years' imprisonment was fully justified for the applicant's five convictions. The sentence properly reflected the role of initiator, controller and supplier which the applicant fulfilled in connection with each conspiracy. Repeatedly this court has stated that crimes connected with the sale of or trafficking in heroin are among the most serious which confront judges whose duty it is to pass sentence upon persons convicted of drug-related offences. The devastating effect upon persons who gain heroin through the activities of those selling or trafficking are notorious. All citizens concerned for the welfare of society are appalled by the activities of those engaged in criminal trading in narcotics. The applicant's purpose for his involvement in these crimes was not to satisfy an addiction; his motive was simply to gain profit from exploiting the needs of those with an addiction for heroin or tempted to experiment with the drug.

From the language employed by him in his unsworn statement, it emerged that the applicant is an articulate man of at least above average intelligence. Yet having served a sentence for a drug-related offence in New Zealand, immediately after coming to Melbourne he became identified with the Australian connection of the pernicious 'Mr Asia Syndicate'. The extent to which his conspiracies have corrupted heroin users — if not led to their premature death — may never be known. Moreover, the extent to which drug traffic breeds collateral criminal conduct cannot be estimated and must be borne in mind in an assessment of the criminality of the offences of the scale now being considered. The element of general deterrence in sentencing traders in heroin has long been recognised by this court as the most important element in the sentence imposed: *R v Zampaglione* (1982) 6 A Crim R 287 at 308. Because of his dominant role in those conspiracies, the large quantities of heroin which were sold as a result of the conspiracies, the large pecuniary gains made by him from those sales, and his previous criminal conviction, the effective sentence passed on the applicant properly reflected the elements of both personal and general deterrence.

[Appeal dismissed.]

9.35C R v Perrier (No 2)

[1991] 1 VR 717

Court of Criminal Appeal, Supreme Court of Victoria

[The applicant, Perrier, was convicted of being knowingly concerned in the importation into Australia of not less than a commercial quantity of heroin, and the respondent, Richardson, was convicted of having imported the heroin, both offences being contrary to s 235(2) of the Customs Act 1901 (Cth). Perrier was an Australian principal concerned in the importation of the heroin and Richardson a courier from overseas who brought the heroin here. Richardson, when detected with the heroin, co-operated with the police so as to bring about the detection and conviction of Perrier. Both Perrier and Richardson were convicted following pleas of not guilty.

Perrier was sentenced to life imprisonment with a minimum term of 22 years. Richardson was sentenced to five years' imprisonment with a minimum term of three years. Perrier sought leave to appeal against the sentence imposed on him, and the Director of Public Prosecutions appealed against the sentence imposed upon Richardson.]

McGarvie J: For the applicant it was stressed that both the sentence of life imprisonment and the minimum term of 22 years are the highest ever imposed in Victoria under the Customs Act. In the nature of things, however, some sentence must be the highest or equal highest.

Recently, this court said in *R v Clune* [1989] VR 567 at 576:

> This court has made it clear over recent years that persons detected in the business of trafficking in heroin can expect little mercy from the courts. Offenders play for high stakes. Such offences cause very considerable misery within the community.

> Persons detected in such offences who may be regarded as key figures in the drug industry deserve condign punishment.

The sentence on this man for this offence is one in respect of which the sentencing aim of deterrence should have full operation. The fact that the applicant was concerned as a Melbourne principal in the commercial importation of heroin within about five years of release from Changi Prison, draws attention both to his high moral culpability in committing the offence and to the need for personal deterrence: see *Veen v R (No 2)* (1988) 164 CLR 465 at 477–8 and *Baumer v R* (1988) 166 CLR 51 at 57–8. Although of much less significance because it occurred more than 20 years before, the conviction in Zurich in 1967 is to be regarded in the same way.

There is reason to doubt whether, with some crimes and some types of persons, sentences in reality have any general deterrent effect. There is no reason to doubt that substantial sentences do deter people who might otherwise be inclined to engage as principals in the commercial importation of heroin. Those who run businesses, legitimate or illegitimate, are constantly guided in deciding whether to take particular commercial courses by their assessments of the economic and other risks and costs involved. In deciding whether to run the risk of pursuing the high returns obtainable from the commercial importation of heroin, the non-addict with the intelligence and ability to organise and operate such a business must count the potential cost. If the contingent cost includes that of forfeiting the whole or a large part of one's remaining life to the prison system, clearly it will operate substantially to discourage selection of the heroin option.

It was argued that life imprisonment was inappropriate because the applicant was not a mastermind of the heroin trade and because such imprisonment should be reserved for large commercial quantities or offences of an aggravated nature.

The maximum penalty is intended for cases falling within the worst category of cases for which the penalty is provided. That does not mean that a lesser penalty must be imposed if it is possible to envisage a worse case: *Veen v R (No 2)* (1988) 164 CLR 465 at 478. As this court said with regard to the maximum sentence of life imprisonment for murder: 'The maximum sentence may be appropriate in a wide variety of cases according to the nature of the offence and the character of the offender': *R v Dumas* [1988] VR 65 at 71.

While the quantity of heroin imported is one of the relevant considerations, it would be artificial to treat either Perrier's moral culpability or the length of appropriate sentence as bearing any direct relationship to the excess of the weight of the heroin over a commercial quantity.

Perrier was a Melbourne principal of the international operation by which the heroin was imported. The relevance of his convictions in Singapore and Zurich has been mentioned. He was a mature, intelligent man, committing the crime solely for profit. Such mitigatory factors as exist carry relatively little weight.

In my opinion, the learned sentencing judge made no error in treating this crime as falling within the worst category of cases for which s 235(c) of the Customs Act provides the penalty, or in imposing the sentence of life imprisonment ...

It is in the community interest in sentencing couriers that the objective of securing their cooperation to implicate principals should substantially prevail when that objective runs counter to the objective of deterring people from acting as couriers by imposing heavy sentences. It should substantially prevail, because it is more likely in the long run to disrupt and break up drug trafficking.

It is true, as stated by Mr G E Fitzgerald QC in the *Report of the Commission of Inquiry into Possible Illegal Activities and Associated Police Misconduct*, 1989, at p 12 when discussing the grant of indemnities from prosecution to some criminals in order to obtain convictions against others, that: 'There is a subliminal message of despair transmitted when crime cannot be solved without the release of some of the criminals in exchange for information.' He added: 'Yet, when the problems are large and intractable, that will often be part of the price that has to be paid.'

Somewhat similar considerations apply to the reduction of the sentences of drug couriers as an incentive for their cooperation in implicating principals.

It is desirable that sentencing policy be directed so as to exert great influence on couriers who are detected in bringing heroin to Australia. The threat of heavy sentences seems to have had limited effect in deterring people from acting as couriers. It seems that many are prepared for the remuneration offered, to run the risk of acting as couriers in the belief that the prospects are high that they will not be caught and will never receive the penalties of the criminal law. This case provides a good example. The court was told that in Thailand, where Richardson commenced to carry the heroin, there are numerous signs in places such as airports reminding everyone that the penalty for its possession is death.

The position changes once a courier is detected with heroin. Recognition of the high prospect of a heavy sentence and the disastrous effect it will have on the courier's life then becomes inescapable. That is the time that the courier's conduct is most susceptible to being influenced by the criminal law. It is in the public interest that at that stage the criminal law exerts its maximum influence so as to lead a courier to follow self-interest by implicating other traffickers. This is best done if the criminal law faces the courier with a clear and compelling alternative: a heavy sentence if there is no cooperation, as against a very substantial reduction in sentence if cooperation is forthcoming and other traffickers are implicated.

The incentive to the heroin courier to cooperate in implicating other traffickers needs to be a very high one. Those who control the cruel heroin trade are persons greatly to be feared. Experience has shown that those who inform against them face high and continuing risks of murder or serious injury. As informers requiring the isolation involved in protective custody, their conditions of serving whatever sentence they receive are particularly harsh. If their homeland is overseas, they are likely to serve the sentence without receiving any visits from friends or relatives. The reluctance of couriers to do other than protect the principal traffickers and seek to deny they have themselves committed an offence is notorious.

For these reasons I consider that it should become known to those associated with the drug trade that in a case such as this, the courier faces a heavy sentence unless cooperation is forthcoming, but if there is cooperation which results in the conviction of a principal trafficker, a courier who admits the offence and pleads guilty might well have the period of sentence reduced by about two-thirds. Of course, the effective operation of such an incentive depends on there being a safe system of witness protection to guard the courier.

In this case, if Richardson had admitted the offence and pleaded guilty, I would have reduced the sentence to the five years he received from the sentencing judge. As he did not do either of those things, he is not entitled to that amount of reduction, but I would reduce his period of sentence to seven years and fix a minimum term of five years.

I would regard a lesser sentence than that as not imposing a proper punishment for a crime of this gravity.

[**Murphy J** concurred. **Brooking J** concurred in dismissing the appeal of the applicant but dissented in respect of the appeal by the Director of Public Prosecutions. Appeal by the applicant Perrier dismissed and sentence upheld. Appeal by the Director of Public Prosecutions allowed and sentence of the respondent Richardson increased.]

[See also *R v Ngui and Tiong* (2001) 1 VR 579.]

9.36 Notes

1. The subject of sentencing is an extremely complex one. In *Drug Users and the Law in Australia*, Law Book Co, Sydney, 1987, p 174, Dr Terry Carney lists the following five variables as being crucial factors in determining the sentence likely to be imposed in drug cases:

(a) the nature of the drug (including type and quantity);

(b) qualities of the offender (including degree of addiction, motive, prior record of drug offences, and age);

(c) the facts of the offence (including the degree, level and character of involvement);

(d) the influence of the legislative context (including the category of offence, and levels of maximum penalties); and

(e) the community impact of the offences (including any moral responsibilities of the offender, deterrence, and the magnitude of social harm).

In *The Quest for Justice*, Scribe, 2010, at p 139 former judge Ken Crispin highlighted the particular dilemmas for the sentencing judge posed by the drug-dependent offender:

> Neither alcoholism nor drug addiction offers any excuse for criminal conduct, and neither is necessarily regarded as a mitigating factor. Yet judges faced with repeat offenders may feel that if the root cause of their behaviour is not addressed, they may remain drug dependent throughout their sentences, and ultimately be released with the same compulsion to obtain money by any means available.

2. As *R v Sorby* and *R v Perrier (No 2)* indicate, the courts are prepared to pass extremely heavy sentences on those engaged in trafficking in hard drugs on a large scale. Similar statements to those made in *R v Sorby* and *R v Perrier (No 2)* have been made in other cases, including *R v Collins* (1979) 21 SASR 38; *R v Press* (1982) 31 SASR 391; *R v Maurie* (1983) 13 A Crim R 440; *R v Moran and Byrnes* (1987) 31 A Crim R 248; *R v Wong and Ng* (1988) 39 A Crim R 1; *R v Sha* (1988) 38 A Crim R 334; *R v Allen* (1989) 41 A Crim R 51; and *R v Ngui and Tiong* (2001) 1 VR 579. As *R v Perrier (No 2)* illustrates, in the case of traffickers who, on apprehension, act as informants against co-conspirators and principals, the courts are willing to allow substantial discounts on the sentences that would otherwise be imposed. Note also *Malvaso v R* (1989) 168 CLR 227; 64 ALJR 44; *R v Nagy* [1992] 1 VR 637.

3. Significant penalties are also imposed by the courts on those engaged in trading in hard drugs on a comparatively small scale. In *R v Rocco* (1985) 37 SASR 512, the accused, a minor dealer in heroin, was found in possession of 6.5 grams of the substance and was convicted of possession of heroin for trading. In increasing the accused's sentence to one of four years and six months, White J stated (at 517):

> I mentioned earlier that substantial penalties are always imposed even though the amounts of heroin discovered in the possession of the offender are usually relatively slight. There are sound reasons for this policy. Street traders and their immediate suppliers are likely, in the nature of things, to possess only relatively small quantities of heroin. Suppliers are not prepared to part with great quantities in case street traders fail to pay for them. In any event, suppliers prefer to carry relatively small quantities on each occasion in case they are detected, in which case they can plead the smallness of their operation. For their part, street traders cannot afford to buy or cannot get credit for larger quantitites of heroin. And it also suits them to have small quantities in case they are detected. Street traders addicted to heroin commonly require 11000–11200 per week to buy the amount of heroin required to sustain their addiction on a continuous basis — one-half of the weekly purchase usually being consumed in purer form, the other half usually being diluted and sold to others in order to raise the purchase price for the next week's supply. Thus it is that offenders are rarely detected with larger quantities of heroin. It is quite fortuitous whether the street trader is detected early in the week when he has 10 to 20 grams or late in the week when he has 2 or 3 grams. The penalty for heroin street traders does not normally fluctuate with the quantity.

See also *R v Le Cerf* (1975) 13 SASR 237; *R v Watson* (1981) 3 A Crim R 254; *R v McLeish* (1982) 30 SASR 486; *R v Suen* (1987) 74 ALR 106.

4. In Victoria, the harm associated with the use of particular drugs is reflected in the quantity of drug required to establish particular offences. Accordingly, an assessment of the general harmfulness of particular drugs is not to be

made by judges in sentencing. In *R v Pidoto and O'Dea* (2006) 14 VR 269, the offenders were convicted of trafficking in not less than a commercial quantity of ecstasy. In sentencing, the judge expressed views as to the effects of the ingestion of ecstasy. The Court of Appeal (at 269) held this was a sentencing error:

> When a person [is] being sentenced for the offence of trafficking in a drug of dependence, as a matter of statutory construction the harmfulness of the particular drug [is] irrelevant to the exercise of the sentencing discretion. Under the Act, trafficking offences [are] classified by quantity. The maximum penalties [are] set accordingly. Had Parliament intended to adopt a harm based classification of trafficking offences, a very different legislative scheme would have been required, along the lines of the scheme then (and now) in force in the United Kingdom and New Zealand. Without a comprehensive harm-based classification of drugs, of the kind established in those other jurisdictions, no individual judge or magistrate [can] evaluate the relative harmfulness of any particular drug, however common its use. Such assessments [require] specialist expertise, [involve] detailed investigation and [must be] based on extensive information on a range of issues. Parliament [cannot] have intended that courts should even attempt the task.

5. Absence of prior convictions is usually a significant factor in sentencing, but in the case of drug offences committed from commercial motives, deterrence is regarded as taking precedence over the offender's prior record: *R v Brodie* (1977) 16 ALR 88; *R v Tait and Bartley* (1979) 24 ALR 473; *R v Strapps* (1979) 22 SASR 59; *R v Lucas* (1982) 31 SASR 375; *R v Elliott* (1983) 32 SASR 22. The fact of addiction may be of significance in determining sentence. In *R v Gronert* (1975) 13 SASR 189 at 193, Bray CJ stated:

> It must always be important to consider the history, particularly the drug history, of the defendant, the quantities and nature of the drug involved, and, very importantly, whether his motives were commercial or gratificatory; whether, in short, he is to be regarded primarily as a dealer or primarily as an addict.

See also *R v Smith and Smith* (1988) 39 A Crim R 48; *R v Lainas* (1989) 50 SASR 461.

In the case of drug dealing on a significant scale, however, the demands of deterrence are regarded as outweighing considerations personal to the accused, and an addict convicted of dealing in heroin will gain little benefit from her or his dependence. The Victorian Sentencing Act 1991 requires that in sentencing for serious drug offences, primarily those involving trafficking and large quantities of illicit drugs, the principal purpose of the sentence should be 'the protection of the community from the offender', and the court may therefore impose a sentence 'longer than that which is proportionate to the gravity of the offence': s 6D.

6. The significance of drug-related offending across the world has led to the development of a range of innovative alternative approaches to sentencing in this area. 'Drug courts' have been established in Victoria, New South Wales, Queensland, South Australia and Western Australia. The rise of Australian drug courts followed the success of drug courts in the United States, first established in Miami in 1981. There are now over 2000 drug courts around the world. The Victorian Drug Court was established in May 2002, as a division of the Magistrates' Court of Victoria. It was designed to introduce a new system of addressing drug use, to largely replace the traditional range of sentencing measures, such as imprisonment. The stated aim of the Victorian Drug Court is 'to improve the safety of the community by focusing on the rehabilitation of offenders with a drug or alcohol dependency and providing assistance in reintegrating them into the community'. Drug courts implement treatment programs tailored to specific offenders, which are then supervised by a judge or magistrate. These programs typically involve sessions designed to help participants overcome fear or shame, a system of rewards for improvements in behaviour, and the prospect of sanctions for behaviour which deviates from the treatment plan. See further G F Roper, 'Introduction to Drug Courts' in J E Lessenger and G F Roper (eds), *Drugs Court: A New Approach to Treatment and Rehabilitation*, Springer, 2007, p 7. Research into drug courts around the world has shown that treatment programs delivered by drug courts lead to lower rates of recidivism, because of their unique focus on the rehabilitation of offenders. A recent study into the Queensland Drug Court by the Australian Institute of Criminology mirrored the international conclusions. It found that the program reduced the 'offending pattern' of drug court participants by 80%: J Payne, *The Queensland Drug Court: A Recidivism Study of the First 100 Graduates*, Australian Institute of Criminology.

9.37 Further reading

T Carney, *Drug Users and the Law in Australia*, Law Book Co, Sydney, 1987, Chs 5 and 6

G Edwards, J Strang and J Jaffe (eds), *Drugs, Alcohol and Tobacco: Making the Science and Policy Connections*, Oxford University Press, Oxford, 1993

R Fox and A Freiberg, *Sentencing: State and Federal Law in Victoria*, 2nd ed, Oxford University Press, Melbourne, 1999

R Fox and I Mathews, *Drugs Policy Fact, Fiction and the Future*, Federation Press, Sydney, 1992

G Nash, D Grace and J Gans, *Bourke's Criminal Law Victoria*, looseleaf, LexisNexis, Australia

New South Wales Bureau of Crime Statistics and Research, *Illicit Drug Use and Property Offending Among Police Detainees* (2012)

T Makkai and J Payne, *Drugs and Crime: A Study of Incarcerated Male Offenders*, Australian Institute of Criminology (2003)

J Payne, S Macgregor and H McDonald, *Prevalence and Issues Relating to Cannabis Use Among Prison Inmates: Key Findings from Australian Research Since 2001*, National Cannabis Prevention and Information Centre, Australia (2013)

F Rinaldi, *Drug Offences in Australia: Sentencing*, Law Book Co, Sydney, 1986

F Rinaldi and P Gillies, *Narcotic Offences*, Law Book Co, Sydney, 1991

Victorian Premier's Drug Advisory Council, *Drugs and Our Community* (March 1996)

For further references on sentencing, see:

J Joudo Larsen, *Responding to Substance Abuse and Offending in Indigenous Communities: Review of Diversion Programs*, Australian Institute of Criminology, 2008

J E Lessenger and G F Roper (eds), *Drugs Court: A New Approach to Treatment and Rehabilitation*, Springer, 2007

D Weatherburn, *The NSW Drug Court: A Re-evaluation of its Effectiveness*, New South Wales Bureau of Crime Statistics and Research, RMIT Publishing, 2008

POLICY OPTIONS FOR THE FUTURE

9.38 Any rational strategy for dealing with the growing problem of illegal drugs in our society must proceed upon the basis that those drugs which are presently illegal constitute only one aspect of a more general problem of drug abuse and misuse. A society which permits the active promotion of alcohol and tobacco cannot, without hypocrisy, claim to be seeking to stamp out drug abuse.

9.39 Assuming that a serious effort is to be made to reduce the level of drug abuse in Australian society by means of public education, improved medical treatment and welfare programs, what role should be played by the criminal law? Some would argue that the criminal law has no role to play: that the decision to take or abstain from drugs is a personal one in relation to which the criminal law should play no part. This is the extreme civil libertarian position adopted by J S Mill. He wrote (*On Liberty*, Everyman ed, pp 72–3):

> The object of this Essay is to assert one very simple principle, as entitled to govern absolutely the dealings of society with the individual in the way of compulsion and control, whether the means used be physical force in the form of legal penalties, or the moral coercion of public opinion. That principle is, that the sole end for which mankind are warranted, individually or collectively, in interfering with the liberty of action of any of their number, is self-protection. That the only purpose for which power can be rightfully exercised over any member of a civilised community, against his will, is to prevent harm to others. His own good, either physical or moral, is not a sufficient warrant. … The only part of the conduct of any one, for which he is amenable to society, is that which concerns others. In the part which merely concerns himself, his independence is, of right, absolute. Over himself, over his own body and mind, the individual is sovereign.

9.40 Such a view may inadequately take into account the fact that the decision to take drugs has ramifications far beyond the individual who makes that decision. This is well illustrated by the case of alcohol and tobacco. The cost to the community in terms of health care and lost productivity in respect of both drugs is enormous. In the case of alcohol, the danger to other members of the community from drunken drivers and from those who become violent when under the influence of alcohol is very great indeed. It is surely legitimate to use the criminal law as a method of seeking to combat an increase in the use of drugs which have not as yet become a part of our culture in the way in which alcohol and tobacco have. Even in so far as the individual user is concerned, a degree of paternalism on the part of the criminal law may be warranted. The authors of a leading American article on the heroin problem put the argument for paternalism in the following terms (J Wilson, M Moore and I D Wheat Jr, 'The Problem of Heroin' (1972) 29 *The Public Interest* 3 at 5):

> Professor Packer recently wrote that a desirable aspect of liberalism is that it allows people to 'choose their own roads to hell if that is where they want to go'. In another view, however, society has an obligation to enhance the 'well being' of each of its citizens even with respect to those aspects of their lives that do not directly impinge on other people's lives. In this conception of the public good, all citizens of a society are bound to be affected, indirectly but perhaps profoundly and permanently, if a significant number are permitted to go to hell in their own way. A society is therefore unworthy if it permits, or is indifferent to, any activity that renders its members inhuman or deprives them of their 'essential' (or 'natural') capacities to judge, choose and act. If heroin use is such an activity, then its use should be proscribed.

9.41 The fact that an activity is socially undesirable is a necessary, but not a sufficient, condition for rendering that activity criminal. The disastrous American experiment with prohibition illustrates what St Thomas Aquinas realised 700 years ago — that certain evils should be tolerated lest more evils should rise from efforts to repress them. With these wise observations in mind, it is submitted that the effective decriminalisation of use and possession of small quantities of cannabis which has been introduced in South Australia, and the proposed decriminalisation which has been recommended for adoption in Victoria by the Pennington Report, represent a sensible and realistic recognition of the widespread social acceptance of that drug.

9.42 Some would go further and argue for legalisation of hard drugs. In a challenging article, I D Leader-Elliott submits that existing criminal laws dealing with hard drugs are both unprincipled and counter-productive: 'Prohibitions Against Heroin Use: Can They Be Justified?' (1986) 19 *Aust and NZ Journal of Criminology* 225. Leader-Elliott presents the argument that opiates, and presumably other hard drugs, should be made available to those dependent upon them. He argues that the present system of criminal prohibition operates, paradoxically, to create a 'congruence of interest between those who enforce the law, and the suppliers who break it, which ensures that the drug is scarce and expensive': at 228. This argument clearly has force.

9.43 Further, as the experience of prohibition in the United States in the 1930s also showed, criminalising a desirable item has the effect of increasing its price, making it attractive to organised crime and more likely to be the subject of corrupt transactions with enforcement officials. The high prices then make it more likely that people addicted to the illegal substance will commit crime to obtain the substance, and may then join a criminalised underclass with all the disadvantages this entails. For further discussion of these complex issues, see T Makkai and J Payne, *Drugs and Crime: A Study of Incarcerated Male Offenders*, Australian Institute of Criminology (2003).

9.44 The cost to society of drug misuse of all kinds is huge, as outlined at the start of this chapter, and this cost includes the cost of using the criminal justice system as a response. In Australia, tangible crime-related costs of alcohol abuse (for example, courts, prisons and police) in 2004–05 were estimated at $1.424 million (together with $1,688.8 million in resources used in abusive consumption). Equivalent crime-related costs of illicit drug use were $3,644.5 million (and $897.7 million). Taken with the intangible costs, such as violence and loss of life, it is estimated that in 2004–05 alcohol-attributable crime cost $1.7 billion, crime attributable to the consumption of illicit drugs cost $5 billion, and crime attributable jointly to both types of drugs cost $0.4 billion: D Collins and H Lapsley, Department of Human Services and Health (Cth), *The Social Costs of Drug Abuse in Australia in 1988 and 1992*, Report No 30 (February 2006). The political, legal and social debates on the role of the criminal law as a response to the abuse of drugs continue.

Attempts

CHAPTER 10

INTRODUCTION

10.1 Attempts to commit crimes were unknown to the early common law as offences in themselves. They first became punishable by the efforts of the Court of Star Chamber, which was established in the late fifteenth century, to stamp out the then prevalent practice of duelling. The victor in a fatal duel was treated by the common law as a murderer, or, in exceptional cases, as at least guilty of manslaughter. The Star Chamber went further and punished anybody who took steps to arrange a duel or took part in one. From these origins there gradually grew the modern preparatory or preliminary crimes of attempt, incitement, and conspiracy: see 10.36 (incitement); 11.43 (conspiracy). These offences are often referred to as 'inchoate crimes' because they are all uncompleted. They became part of the common law when, after the abolition of the Star Chamber in 1641, the Court of King's Bench took over some of its activities.

10.2 At common law, all attempts to commit crimes are punishable as misdemeanours whether the completed crime would be a felony, a misdemeanour or a mere summary offence. The abolition of the distinction between felonies and misdemeanours did not affect the principle that an attempt to commit any crime is itself a crime. In Victoria, s 321S of the Crimes Act 1958 abolishes the offence of attempt at common law. Crimes Act 1900 (NSW) s 344A provides a general offence of attempt.

10.3 Attempts to commit some of the more serious crimes have been made into separate statutory offences: for example, attempted murder and attempt to commit various sexual offences in New South Wales (Crimes Act 1900 s 27 and s 61P, respectively). In Victoria, there are no equivalent provisions.

10.4 In New South Wales, where a maximum penalty is prescribed for any crime by statute, then the same maximum penalty shall apply to attempts: Crimes Act 1900 s 344A. In Victoria, a table of punishments for attempt is set out, the effect of which is that lesser penalties are available for all attempts than would be the case were the crime completed. In cases not covered by the table, the penalty for attempt must not exceed 60% of the maximum penalty for the completed offence: Crimes Act 1958 s 321P.

10.5 A distinction has always been drawn between 'attempts', which are punishable at common law, and 'preparations', which are not. The law has adhered to the view that the individual's freedom should only be circumscribed when her or his activities genuinely endanger the community. A person who engages in merely preliminary activities — the potential burglar who purchases a flashlight and makes plans of the building he or she proposes to enter and the potential passer of bad cheques who purchases a pen — may be doing little more than fantasising. It is only when the accused's activities begin to approach the complete commission of an offence that the law treats the accused as guilty of an attempt. In *R v Smith* [1975] AC 476 (at **10.23**), the House of Lords restated and affirmed the basic distinction between attempts and preparation. However, the utility of this clear conceptual distinction has been much reduced by the rise in popularity of statutory preparatory offences, particularly in anti-terrorism laws. Crimes of preparation are discussed at the end of this chapter.

10.6 In the law of attempts, the key challenge is readily apparent: how much activity is necessary to constitute an attempt as distinct from mere preparation? When is activity sufficiently indicative of danger of criminal purpose to the law-abiding, that it should be punished? It is inherent to the nature of the crime of attempt that it covers only persons who are consciously endeavouring to commit crimes. The accused must intend, in the sense of having it as her or his purpose, to commit the crime he or she is charged with attempting. Therefore, before a person may be guilty of attempting to murder, it must be shown that it was her or his purpose to kill, not merely to cause some harm which, if the victim had died, would have made the accused a murderer in the eyes of the law under, for example, the rule that an intention to cause grievous bodily harm constitutes sufficient malice aforethought in murder: *Alister v R* (1984) 154 CLR 404; *Knight v R* (1992) 175 CLR 495; *McGhee v R* (1995) 183 CLR 82; *Cutter v R* (1997) 143 ALR 498; *R v Pepper* (2007) 16 VR 637. Likewise, a person will not be guilty of attempting a statutory offence of strict liability unless that person knows what he or she is about and intends to carry out the course of conduct proscribed: *Gardner v Akeroyd* [1952] 2 QB 743.

10.7 In Victoria, the law relating to attempts was placed upon a statutory footing by the Crimes (Amendment) Act 1985. Sections 321M and 321N of the Crimes Act 1958, as amended by the Crimes (Amendment) Act 1985, provide:

321M Attempt

A person who attempts to commit an indictable offence is guilty of the indictable offence of attempting to commit that offence.

321N Conduct constituting attempt

(1) A person is not guilty of attempting to commit an offence unless the conduct of the person is —
  (a) more than merely preparatory to the commission of the offence; and
  (b) immediately and not remotely connected with the commission of the offence.

(2) For a person to be guilty of attempting to commit an offence, the person must —
  (a) intend that the offence the subject of the attempt be committed; and
  (b) intend or believe that any fact or circumstance the existence of which is an element of the offence will exist at the time the offence is to take place.

(3) A person may be guilty of attempting to commit an offence despite the existence of facts of which he or she is unaware which make the commission of the offence attempted impossible.

A similar provision is contained in the Crimes Act 1914 (Cth) s 7, as amended by the Crimes Amendment Act 1995 (Cth).

10.8 In New South Wales, the general attempts provision is s 344A of the Crimes Act 1900:

344A Attempts

(1) Subject to this Act, any person who attempts to commit any offence for which a penalty is provided under this Act shall be liable to that penalty.

(2) Where a person is convicted of an attempt to commit an offence and the offence concerned is a serious indictable offence the person shall be deemed to have been convicted of a serious indictable offence.

THE NATURE OF AN ATTEMPT

10.9C **R v Mohan**
[1976] QB 1
Court of Appeal (UK)

[The defendant, in response to a police officer's signal to stop, slowed his car down, but then accelerated and drove the car at the police officer. The police officer jumped aside and the defendant continued on his journey. He was charged with the offence, inter alia, of an attempt by wanton driving to cause bodily harm to the police officer. The trial judge at one stage directed the jury that the prosecution did not have to prove any intention on the part of the defendant to cause bodily harm. In his final direction to the jury, however, the trial judge said that it had to be proved that the defendant deliberately drove wantonly, realizing that such wanton driving would be likely to cause, unless interrupted for some reason, bodily harm to the police officer or that the defendant was reckless as to whether such bodily harm would be caused by his wanton driving. The defendant was convicted. On appeal against conviction.]

James LJ: Mr Bueno's argument for the Crown was that the judge was right in his direction that the Crown did not have to prove, in relation to count 2, any intention in the mind of the defendant. His argument was that where the attempt charged is an attempt to commit a crime which itself involves a specific state of mind, then to prove the attempt the Crown must prove that the accused had that specific state of mind, but where the attempt relates to a crime which does not involve a specific state of mind, the offence of attempt is proved by evidence that the accused committed an act or acts proximate to the commission of the complete offence and which unequivocally point to the completed offence being the result of the act or acts committed. Thus to prove a charge of attempting to cause grievous bodily harm with intent there must be proof that the accused intended to cause grievous bodily harm at the time of the act relied on as the attempt. But, because the offence of causing bodily harm by wanton or furious driving, proscribed by s 35 of the Offences against the Person Act 1861, does not require proof of any intention or other state of mind of the accused, proof of attempt to commit that crime does not involve proof of the accused's state of mind; but only that he drove wantonly and that the wanton driving was proximate to, and pointed unequivocally to, bodily harm being caused thereby.

The attraction of this argument is that it presents a situation in relation to attempts to commit a crime which is simple and logical, for it requires in proof of the attempt no greater burden in respect of *mens rea* than is required in proof of the completed offence. The argument in its extreme form is that an attempt to commit a crime of strict liability is itself a strict liability offence. It is argued that the contrary view involves the proposition that the offence of attempt includes *mens rea* when the offence which is attempted does not and in that respect the attempt takes on a graver aspect than, and requires an additional burden of proof beyond that which relates to, the completed offence.

Mr Glass, for the defendant, does not shrink from his anomalous situation. His argument was expressed in words which he cited from Smith and Hogan, *Criminal Law* (3rd ed; 1973), p 191:

> Whenever the definition of the crime requires that some consequence be brought about by (the defendant's) conduct, it must be proved, on a charge of attempting to commit that crime, that (the defendant) intended that consequence; and this is so even if, on a charge of committing the complete crime, recklessness as to that consequence — or even some lesser degree of *mens rea* — would suffice.

That, Mr Glass argued, is an accurate statement of the law.

In support of his argument he cited the words of Lord Goddard CJ in *R v Whybrow* (1951) 35 Cr App R 141 at 146:

> Therefore, if one person attacks another, inflicting a wound in such a way that an ordinary, reasonable person must know that at least grievous bodily harm will result, and death results, there is the malice aforethought sufficient to support the charge of murder. But, if the charge is one of attempted murder, the intent becomes the principal ingredient of the crime. It may be said that the law, which is not always logical, is somewhat illogical in saying that, if one attacks a person intending to do grievous bodily harm and death results, that is murder, but that if

> one attacks a person and only intends to do grievous bodily harm, and death does not result, it is not attempted murder, but wounding with intent to do grievous bodily harm. It is not really illogical because, in that particular case, the intent is the essence of the crime while, where the death of another is caused, the necessity is to prove malice aforethought, which is supplied in law by proving intent to do grievous bodily harm.

[His Lordship referred to a number of authorities, and continued:]

We find it unnecessary to refer to the remaining authorities (other than *R v Hyam* [1975] AC 55, to which we refer later) cited in the course of argument. In our judgment it is well established law that intent (*mens rea*) is an essential ingredient of the offence of attempt. This principle does not seem to have presented any problems, such as those related to the character of the act relied upon as constituting the attempt, in the earlier cases. In so far as the judge directed the jury that it was not necessary to prove any intent in relation to count 2 he fell into error.

That does not, however, dispose of this appeal. As has been pointed out, the judge varied the terms of the direction in his answer to the jury's question. It has been necessary, therefore, to consider whether taken as a whole the directions did, by the words: '... he must have realised ... that such driving, unless it were to stop, ... was likely to cause bodily harm if he went on, or he was reckless as to whether bodily harm was caused' include the need for proof of the element of *mens rea*. The first question we have to answer is: what is the meaning of 'intention' when that word is used to describe the *mens rea* in attempt? It is to be distinguished from 'motive' in the sense of an emotion leading to action: it has never been suggested that such a meaning is appropriate to 'intention' in this context. It is equally clear that the word means what is often referred to as 'specific intent' and can be defined as 'a decision to bring about a certain consequence' or as the 'aim'.

In *R v Hyam* [1975] AC 55 at 74, Lord Hailsham of St Marylebone cited with approval the judicial interpretation of 'intention' or 'intent' applied by Asquith LJ in *Cunliffe v Goodman* [1950] 2 KB 237 at 253:

> An 'intention' to my mind connotes a state of affairs which the party 'intending' — I will call him X — does more than merely contemplate: it connotes a state of affairs which, on the contrary, he decides, so far as in him lies, to bring about, and which, in point of possibility, he has a reasonable prospect of being able to bring about, by his own act of volition.

If that interpretation of 'intent' is adopted as the meaning of *mens rea* in the offence of attempt, it is not wide enough to justify the direction in the present case. The direction, taken as a whole, can be supported as accurate only if the necessary *mens rea* includes not only specific intent but also the state of mind of one who realises that, if his conduct continues, the likely consequence is the commission of the complete offence and who continues his conduct in that realisation, or the state of mind of one who, knowing that continuation of his conduct is likely to result in the commission of the complete offence, is reckless as to whether or not this is the result.

[His Lordship discussed *R v Hyam* and continued:]

We do not find in the speeches of their Lordships in *R v Hyam* anything which binds us to hold that *mens rea* in the offence of attempt is proved by establishing beyond reasonable doubt that the accused knew or correctly foresaw that the consequences of his act unless interrupted would 'as a high degree of probability', or would be 'likely' to be the commission of the complete offence. Nor do we find authority in that case for the proposition that a reckless state of mind is sufficient to constitute the *mens rea* in the offence of attempt.

Prior to the enactment of s 8 of the Criminal Justice Act 1967, the standard test in English law of a man's state of mind in the commission of an act was the foreseeable or natural consequence of the act. Therefore it could be said that when a person applied his mind to the consequences that did happen and foresaw that they would probably happen he intended them to happen, whether he wanted them to happen or not. So knowledge of the foreseeable consequence could be said to be a form of 'intent'. Section 8 reads:

> A court or jury, in determining whether a person has committed an offence, (a) shall not be bound in law to infer that he intended or foresaw a result of his actions by reason only of its being a natural and probable consequence of those actions; but (b) shall decide whether he did intend or foresee that result by reference to all the evidence, drawing such inferences from the evidence as appear proper in the circumstances.

Thus, upon the question whether or not the accused had the necessary intent in relation to a charge of attempt, evidence tending to establish directly, or by inference, that the accused knew or foresaw that the likely consequence, and, even more so, the highly probable consequence, of his act — unless interrupted — would be the commission of the completed offence, is relevant material for the consideration of the jury. In our judgment, evidence of knowledge of likely consequences, or from which knowledge of likely consequences can be inferred, is evidence by which intent may be established but it is not, in relation to the offence of attempt, to be equated with intent. If the jury find such knowledge established they may and, using common sense, they probably will find intent proved, but it is not the case that they must do so.

An attempt to commit crime is itself an offence. Often it is a grave offence. Often it is as morally culpable as the completed offence which is attempted but not in fact committed. Nevertheless it falls within the class of conduct which is preparatory to the commission of a crime and is one step removed from the offence which is attempted. The court must not strain to bring within the offence of attempt conduct which does not fall within the well-established bounds of the offence. On the contrary, the court must safeguard against extension of those bounds save by the authority of Parliament. The bounds are presently set requiring proof of specific intent, a decision to bring about, in so far as it lies within the accused's power, the commission of the offence which it is alleged the accused attempted to commit, no matter whether the accused desired that consequence of his act or not.

In the present case the final direction was bad in law. Not only did the judge maintain the exclusion of 'intent' as an ingredient of the offence in count 2, but he introduced an alternative basis for a conviction which did not and could not constitute the necessary *mens rea*.

We are indebted to counsel for their arguments.

It is for the above reasons that we allowed the appeal on count 2. Fortunately, in the interests of justice, the jury convicted of dangerous driving and that conviction stands, as does the richly deserved sentence of 12 months' imprisonment.

[See also *Alister v R* (1984) 154 CLR 404 per Gibbs CJ and Brennan J; *R v Millard* [1987] Crim LR 393; *DPP v Stonehouse* [1978] AC 55.]

10.10C R v Evans

(1987) 30 A Crim R 262
Supreme Court of South Australia

[On appeal against a conviction of attempted rape.]

King CJ: The learned trial judge in directing the jury as to the law relating to attempted rape, referred to the mental element in the same terms as the mental element of rape, that is to say, knowledge that the woman was not consenting or reckless indifference as to whether she was consenting or not. Mr Tilmouth argued that the mental element appropriate to the crime of attempted rape differed from that appropriate to the crime of rape. He maintained that in the former reckless indifference was insufficient and that there must be an intention to have intercourse with a person who is known to the assailant to be not consenting. This submission raises the question of the mental element of a crime of attempt. An attempt is necessarily purposive. A person attempts to do something only if he intends to do that thing. The purposive nature of an attempt produces conceptual and practical difficulties in relation to crimes which may be committed in their complete form without an actual intention to perform the forbidden act or to produce the forbidden consequences, or without full advertence to the state of facts or circumstances which render the conduct criminal. Mr Tilmouth argued, in effect, that as the *actus reus* of rape is sexual penetration without consent, conduct can only amount to an attempt to rape if there is an actual intention to penetrate without consent.

There is no authority to provide assistance in the resolution of the question. It arose in *Zorad* [1979] 2 NSWLR 764. There was, of course, no analogue on the statute book of New South Wales of s 48 of the *Criminal Law Consolidation Act 1935* (SA), but I apprehend that the mental element of the crime of rape at common law does not differ from that prescribed by s 48: *Wozniak and Pendry* (1977) 16 SASR 67 at 73–4 esp per Bray CJ. In *Zorad*, Street CJ, with whom the other members of the court agreed, said (at 773):

> The criticism advanced on behalf of the appellant is that the element of intent in a charge of attempted rape requires an omission from what is put to the jury of any reference to a determination to have intercourse, whether the prospective victim was consenting or not. Reference has been made in this regard to a decision in

> *Mohan* [1976] QB 1; (1975) 60 Cr App R 272. I do not regard it as necessary to take time to refer to what was said in *Mohan's* case, or to contrast the nature of the charge there under consideration with a charge of attempted rape. In the present case, the elements necessary to be proved were correctly put by his Honour to the jury. His Honour defined specifically what was involved in the crime of rape, and he accurately told the jury that, in order to convict of an attempt to rape, they must be satisfied that the appellant intended to commit those acts which would go to make up the crime of rape, including, of course, such elements of intent as must be associated with the acts referable to making up the crime of rape. Whatever merit there might have been in the challenge, and in my view there was none, it is dissipated entirely by a subsequent direction which his Honour gave in response to counsel's submission when he said, at p 47 of the summing up, after the jury had been brought back: 'I went on to say that, although the accused realised she may not be consenting, he determined to have penetration of [her] whether she consented or not; and I should perhaps have gone a bit further and said to you, in relation to the attempt to rape, that the Crown must satisfy you that the accused, Zorad, must have had the intent to penetrate the prosecutrix without her consent. The Crown must establish the accused had that purpose and the desire of this consequence.'

This by no means falls short of putting the matter in the most favourable light to the appellant. I would not have been disposed to find error in what his Honour said in the early part of the summing up; but this subsequent, clear and specific direction on the narrower ground for which the appellant now contends, precludes any challenge on the point.

It will be seen from that passage that the terms of the summing up under review made it unnecessary for the court to decide the point which arises on this appeal. Mr Tilmouth sought to reason by analogy from *Whybrow* (1951) 35 Cr App R 141 and *Mohan* [1976] QB 1; (1975) 60 Cr App R 272. *Whybrow* was concerned with an intent to do something other than to cause the particular harm which constituted the complete crime. It was held that an intention to cause grievous bodily harm, although sufficient *mens rea* for murder if death results, is not sufficient for attempted murder. The particular harm which must be caused to constitute murder is death. A person cannot be said to attempt to cause particular harm unless he intends to do so. There being no intent to cause death, there could be no attempt to murder. In *Mohan* the charge under consideration was attempting by wanton driving to cause bodily harm. It was held that the offence could not be committed unless there was an intention to cause bodily harm; recklessness was insufficient. Those cases were concerned with unintended consequences of conduct in the sense that the accused person did not intend the consequence which was required by the definition of the complete crime. A somewhat different view has been taken in Canada (*Lajoie* [1971] 4 CCC (2d) 402; *Ritchie* [1970] 5 CCC 336) but I would treat the English cases as adequate authority for holding that in Australian law an attempt can only be committed if the consequences which are required by the definition of the crime are intended; recklessness as to those consequences is not sufficient.

Both English cases are, however, clearly distinguishable. The problem in the present case is different. It concerns the accused's state of mind not as to the consequences of his conduct but as to a state of facts the existence of which renders his action criminal. The state of facts, the existence of which renders the act of sexual penetration criminal, is the non-consent of the person penetrated. The mental state of the accused in relation to that state of facts, required by the definition of the crime in the section, includes reckless indifference to its existence. There cannot be an attempt to commit a crime involving particular consequences where those consequences are not intended, because the notion of unintended consequences is inconsistent with the notion of attempt to bring about those consequences. That reasoning does not apply, however, to an accused's state of mind as to the existence of circumstances which render an act criminal. There is no reason in principle or logic why steps which are sufficiently proximate to sexual penetration should not constitute an attempt to rape, consent being in fact absent, if the accused has either of the states of mind relative to the consent of the alleged victim which would be sufficient for the complete crime. The distinction in relation to attempt between recklessness as to the consequences of conduct and recklessness as to the existence of facts or circumstances rendering an act criminal is made by the learned authors of Howard, *Criminal Law* (3rd ed), pp 302–6 and of Smith and Hogan, *Criminal Law* (4th ed), p 249. The purposive element of attempt is supplied, in my opinion, by the intention to sexually penetrate irrespective of consent.

Mr Tilmouth argued further that the direction as to the mental element of attempted rape was defective in that the learned judge did not explain to the jury the legal signification of the expression 'recklessly indifferent'. It is essential to a correct summing up that the judge direct the jury in terms of the section: *Sherrin (No 2)* (1979) 21 SASR 250. He is free to explain the meaning of the expression 'recklessly indifferent' along the lines of *Wozniak* and *Pendry* and the cases which preceded that case, if he sees fit to do so, and I think that generally speaking he would be wise to do so. He is not required, however, in my opinion, to add an explanation unless the circumstances of the case require an explanation. The legislature has chosen its expression to denote the state of mind which is required and I do not think that a judge's direction can be criticised because he has confined himself to that expression, unless something in the circumstances of the case or the course of the trial require more. Such a case was *Egan* (1985) 15 A Crim R 20 where the emergence of a concept of 'assumed consent' clearly required a careful explanation of the true meaning of reckless indifference. I think that the direction given in the present case was quite adequate.

[**Jacobs** and **Bollen JJ** delivered separate judgments agreeing with **King CJ**. Appeal dismissed.]

[See also *R v Khan* [1990] 1 WLR 813.]

10.11C

R v Eagleton

(1855) Dears CC 515; 169 ER 826
Court for Crown Cases Reserved

[Eagleton contracted with a local Poor Law authority to supply bread of an agreed weight to poor persons who presented the appropriate tickets. The arrangement made was that Eagleton would then tender these tickets to the authority with a statement of the number of loaves supplied, and the authority would credit Eagleton with 2d for each loaf and pay him a lump sum each month. Eagleton supplied underweight loaves but his fraud was discovered before any payment was made, though his account had already been credited. He was charged with attempting to obtain money by false pretences. The jury found that Eagleton intended to represent that the loaves were of full weight. The case was reserved on the question whether, in law, Eagleton's activity constituted an attempt.]

Parke B [delivering the judgment of the court]: ... The mere intention to commit a misdemeanour is not criminal. Some act is required, and we do not think that all acts towards committing a misdemeanour are indictable. Acts remotely leading towards the commission of the offence are not to be considered as attempts to commit it, but acts immediately connected with it are; and if in this case, after the credit with the relieving officer for the fraudulent over-charge, any further step on the part of the defendant had been necessary to obtain payment, as the making out a further account producing the vouchers to the Board, we should have thought that the obtaining credit in account with the relieving officer would not have been sufficiently proximate to the obtaining the money. But on the statement in this case, no other act on the part of the defendant would have been required. It was the last act, depending on himself, towards the payment of the money, and therefore it ought to be considered as an attempt ...

10.12 Notes, illustrations and questions

1. It would seem that Parke B was posing the test whether the defendant had committed the 'last act, depending on himself' as a sufficient condition of the 'immediate connection' needed to support a conviction for attempt but not as a necessary condition. The *Eagleton* test seems to be appropriate only to the sort of cases where some person other than the accused has to do or omit to do something before the crime attempted may be consummated. What is the 'last act, depending on himself' which the accused does in any situation other than the *Eagleton* situation? Compare *R v Chellingworth* [1954] QWN 35, an arson case in which the 'last act' test was preferred; see also *R v De Silva* [2007] QCA 301.

   D buys a rifle, loads it, walks along a street threatening to kill V, finds V, aims the rifle and is seized. Is D guilty of attempted murder? The last act dependent on D, in this context, is firing the gun, but, equally, surely D's acts demonstrate clearly that her or his purpose is to kill V, and, in such circumstances, he or she is surely attempting to murder.

In *R v Linneker* [1906] 2 KB 99 (CCR), where D was convicted of attempting to discharge a loaded firearm even though his 'victim' had grasped his arm and wrested the revolver from him before D could even raise his arm, Kennedy J put this proposition:

> It is always necessary that the attempt should be evidenced by some overt act forming part of a series of acts which, if not interrupted, would end in the commission of the offence.

This statement of an imaginary continuum has found favour with many judges subsequently.

2. Section 321N (1) of the Crimes Act 1958 (Vic) (see **10.7**) sets out a twofold test. To constitute attempt, it must be shown that the conduct of the accused was more than merely preparatory to the commission of the offence *and* was immediately, and not merely remotely, connected with the commission of the offence. This statutory formulation would not appear to involve any modification of the common law rule. Indeed, the twofold test would appear to constitute little more than alternative ways of expressing the same requirement.
3. D, a jeweller, insured his stock against theft and burglary. He then concealed some jewellery in the shop, tied himself up, and called for help. When police arrived, he told them he had been knocked down and that there had been £1500 worth of stock in the safe, which was found open and empty. The police later found the jewellery hidden in the shop and D confessed that he had intended to get money from his insurers. D was convicted of attempting to obtain money by false pretences but his conviction was quashed by the Court of Criminal Appeal. Lord Reading CJ stated the *Eagleton* proposition and then said that, here, D's acts were only remotely but not immediately connected with the offence of obtaining by false pretences. There was no communication of D's claim and the story supporting it to his insurers: *R v Robinson* [1915] 2 KB 342.

   In *Comer v Bloomfield* (1970) 55 Cr App R 305, D had written to his insurers inquiring whether he could make a claim. Because this was only a preliminary inquiry and he might have desisted before making an actual claim, the Divisional Court held D's acts to be insufficiently proximate. See also *R v Ilyas* (1984) 78 Cr App R 17; *R v Boyle and Boyle* (1987) 84 Cr App R 270; *R v Gullefer* [1987] Crim LR 195. Do these cases accord with *R v Linneker*?
4. D, who lived at premises formerly occupied by A, received cheques payable to A. D took the cheques to a building society and there opened an account in the name of A. D was given a receipt for the cheques and told to come

back in a week's time with identification of herself as A. D did not go back to the building society because she could not obtain the required identification. D was convicted in the magistrates' court of attempting to obtain money by false pretences. On appeal, the conviction was affirmed. As D had admitted that her intention was to commit the substantive offence, the prosecution had proved a sufficiently proximate act to amount to an attempt to commit the offence: *O'Connor v Killian* (1984) 38 SASR 327.

5. D was charged with attempting to sell meat at a price exceeding the maximum permitted under an order made by virtue of the Defence Regulations 1939. P, a Ministry of Food Inspector, had found packages of meat in D's shop refrigerator which bore tickets stating a customer's name, the weight of the meat, and a price which was in accordance with the order. In a drawer, P found another set of tickets relating to the packages bearing a price in excess of that permissible. The justices dismissed the information against D and on a case stated to the Divisional Court, their decision was affirmed (*Hope v Brown* [1954] 1 All ER 330; [1954] 1 WLR 250):

   > [W]hat remained to be done before there could be an attempt was the fixing to the meat of the false tickets. Until that was done, in my opinion the matter remained simply in embryo and in intention.

6. D placed a bet on a greyhound race. Seeing that the dog he had backed was losing, he climbed the fence on to the track in front of the dogs, waving his arms and attempting to distract them. His intention was to have the race declared invalid and to recover from the bookmaker the amount of his bet. D was convicted of attempted theft of the bet. On appeal, held, conviction quashed. There was insufficient evidence for it to be said that D's actions had gone beyond mere preparation: *R v Gullefer* [1990] 1 WLR 1063.

7. D was convicted of attempted murder. On appeal it was submitted that there was insufficient evidence to support the charge because D would have had to perform at least three more acts before the full offence could have been completed, namely removing the safety catch of the sawn-off shotgun that he was pointing at his victim, putting his finger on the trigger and pulling it. The appeal against conviction was dismissed. The court held that there was sufficient evidence to justify a jury finding that D's acts were more than merely preparatory: *R v Jones* [1990] 1 WLR 1057.

8. D grabbed V, pulled her behind a hedge, forced her to the ground and laid full length on top of her. When police arrived, D was on her back, her skirt pulled up to waist level and her undergarments removed. The trial judge directed the jury that to constitute attempted rape there must be some evidence of actual physical attempt at penetration. On appeal to the Court of Appeal, the trial judge's direction was erroneous. Lord Taylor CJ in *Attorney General's Reference (No 1 of 1992)* [1993] 2 All ER 190 stated:

> It is not, in our judgment, necessary, in order to raise a prima facie case of attempted rape, to prove that the defendant with the requisite intent had necessarily gone as far as to attempt physical penetration of the vagina. It is sufficient if there is evidence from which the intent can be inferred and there are proved acts which a jury could properly regard as more than merely preparatory to the commission of the offence.

See also *R v Williams ex parte The Minister for Justice and Attorney-General* [1965] Qd R 86 (attempted rape); *R v Edwards* [1956] QWN 16.

The question of the fault element for attempted rape has caused difficulties in various jurisdictions (see *R v Evans* at **10.10C**). In Victoria, the fault element is dealt with by s 321N(2) of the Crimes Act 1958 (see **10.7**). Does it follow from s 321N(2)(a) that nothing short of an intent to have sexual intercourse without consent will suffice for the accused to be guilty of attempted rape? Or does it follow from s 321N(2)(b) that recklessness as to the possibility of the victim's non-consent (being a 'fact or circumstance the existence of which is an element of the offence') is sufficient? On this issue, note Andrew Ashworth's observation (*Principles of Criminal Law*, 6th ed, Oxford University Press, 2009, p 441):

> [I]f two men set out to have sexual intercourse with two women, not caring whether they consent or not, would it not be absurd if the one who achieved penetration was convicted of rape, while the other, who failed to achieve penetration despite trying, was not liable even for attempted rape.

9. D was convicted of attempting to pervert the course of justice by improperly endeavouring to influence V to plead guilty to a charge of making a false statutory declaration. The Crown case was that D had improperly influenced V by either bribing her or intimidating her or both. It was not established by the Crown that V was not guilty of the offence to which she pleaded guilty. The appeal against conviction was dismissed. A person is guilty of attempting to pervert the course of justice when that person engages in conduct that has the tendency to pervert the course of justice and does so with the intention of perverting the course of justice. It is an attempt to pervert the course of justice to use improper means to secure a plea of guilty. Any conduct designed to intimidate an accused person to plead guilty is improper conduct and necessarily constitutes an attempt to pervert the course of justice even if the intimidator believes that the accused is guilty of the offence with which he or she is charged: *Meissner v R* (1995) 184 CLR 132; 130 ALR 547.

10.13 Further reading

R A Duff, *Trials and Punishments*, Cambridge University Press, 1986

P R Glazebrook, 'Should We Have a Law of Attempted Crime?' (1969) 85 *LQR* 28

K J M Smith, 'Proximity in Attempt: Lord Lane's "Midway Course"' [1991] *Crim LR* 576

R Stuart, 'The *Actus Reus* in Attempts' [1970] *Crim LR* 505

G Williams, 'Wrong Turnings in the Law of Attempt' [1991] *Crim LR* 416

G Yaffe, *Attempts in the Philosophy of Action and the Criminal Law*, Oxford University Press, 2010

10.14C Director of Public Prosecutions v Stonehouse

[1978] AC 55
House of Lords

[The accused was a prominent British politician. He was in serious financial difficulties and decided to fake his death and start his life afresh in Australia under a new identity. In order to provide for his wife who was not aware of his plan, he first insured his life with various companies in England, naming his wife as beneficiary. While in Florida, he carried out his plan and created the appearance of his death in a drowning incident. Five weeks after this incident, he was discovered living in Australia under a false identity. He was extradited to England and tried for a number of offences of dishonesty, including attempting to obtain property by deception from the various life insurance companies. He was convicted on most charges including those of attempting to obtain property by deception. In respect of the attempt convictions, he appealed first to the Court of Appeal and then to the House of Lords. Counsel for the accused argued, inter alia, that the trial judge had been incorrect in instructing the jury that the accused's actions amounted to an attempt.]

Lord Edmund-Davies: While the appellant's counsel did not go so far as to submit to this House that the learned trial judge was wrong in leaving counts 17 to 21 to the jury, he did contend that the actions of the accused in Miami on November 20 1974, did not amount to an attempt. He accepted that they were his final contribution to a fraudulent scheme calculated to induce people in Miami to conclude that he had drowned and to communicate that conclusion to his family and others in England. He nevertheless contended that the appellant had merely made preparation to create a situation in which his wife could in all innocence claim and maybe obtain from the insurance companies moneys which they would have withheld had the true facts been known to them.

Learned counsel relied strongly on *R v Robinson* [1915] 2 KB 342, where a jeweler insured his stock against burglary and then, with the object of obtaining the insurance money, falsely represented to the police that a burglary had been committed and the jewellery stolen. This he did in the hope that they would make a report by which the insurers might be induced to pay, but before the accused had communicated with the insurers the fraud was discovered. His conviction of having attempted to obtain money from the insurers was quashed by the Court of Criminal Appeal, Lord Reading CJ saying at 348–9:

> In the present case the real difficulty lies in the fact that there is no evidence of any act done by the appellant in the nature of a false pretence which ever reached the minds of the underwriters, though they were the persons who were to be induced to part with the money. ... In truth what the appellant did was preparation for the commission of a crime, not a step in the commission of it. ... We think the conviction must be quashed ... upon the broad ground that no communication of any kind of the false pretence was made to them.

The court there founded its judgment on the well-known statement of Parke B in *R v Eagleton*, Dears CC 515 at 538 that:

> Acts remotely leading towards the commission of the offence are not to be considered as attempts to commit it, but acts immediately connected with it are.

But it is open to doubt whether that dictum was properly applied in *R v Robinson*, a decision which has been said to be 'as favourable to the accused as any that can be found in English law; it seems to be too favourable' (Glanville Williams, *Criminal Law, The General Part* (2nd ed, 1961), p 627). In my respectful judgment, the ruling that there cannot be a conviction for an attempt to obtain by false pretences (or, now, of obtaining by deception) unless the pretence or the deception has come to the knowledge of the intended victim should not be followed, and the court was wrong in treating all preceding acts as mere preparation and therefore as not amounting to perpetration of an attempt to commit the full offence.

The much cited *R v Eagleton* has itself been criticised as going further than is called for, in stressing the necessity for the act charged to be 'immediately connected' with the full offence; see, for example, Archbold, *Criminal Pleading, Evidence & Practice* (39th ed, 1976), para 4105, p 1697. In *Stephen's Digest of the Criminal Law* (9th ed, 1950), pp 24–5 it is laid down that:

> An attempt to commit a crime is an act done with intent to commit that crime, and forming part of a series of acts, which would constitute its actual commission if it were not interrupted.

That definition has been repeatedly cited with judicial approval, as by Byrne J in *Hope v Brown* [1954] 1 WLR 250 at 253 and by the Divisional Court in *Davey v Lee* [1968] 1 QB 366. But, as Lord Parker CJ observed in the latter case at 370G, Stephen's definition 'does not help to define the point of time at which the series of acts begins'. Professor Glanville Williams has added [1955] *Crim LR* 68, and rightly in my judgment, that.

> This definition, notwithstanding its judicial commendation, is too narrow, because it is now settled that one may attempt a crime by impossible means, in

> which case the attempt is doomed to failure quite apart from interruption. It is, also, too wide, because many acts that have been held to be mere preparation were part of a series of acts that would have constituted the actual commission of the crime if it were not interrupted.

In the present case, while conceding that the mere act of taking out the insurance policies was, at most, only an act of preparation, counsel for the prosecution submitted that: 'Where a crime is not completed, the principal may be indicted for an attempt to commit the crime, provided that: (a) it is capable of being committed and (b) he has himself or by his agent performed an act or acts which show that he is trying to commit the crime, as distinct from merely getting ready to commit it.' This was a commendable endeavour to embrace the elements (1) of intention, (2) of the necessity for the overt acts charged to be part of a series of acts which would constitute the full offence if uninterrupted, and (3) of proximity, which Lord Hailsham of St Marylebone LC said in *R v Smith (Roger)* [1975] AC 476 at 492 were the true ingredients of a criminal attempt and which I respectfully adopt in the present case.

But what, for my part, I am not prepared to adopt is the view sometimes advanced (eg Glanville Williams, *Criminal Law, The General Part*, p 622, and Smith and Hogan, *Criminal Law* (3rd ed, 1973), p 198) that a man must be guilty of an attempt if he has done the last act which he expects to do and which it is necessary for him to do to achieve the consequence aimed at. This is probably based on the observation of Parke B in *R v Eagleton* Dears CC 515 at 538 regarding a charge of attempting to obtain money from guardians of the poor by false pretences, that:

> … no other act on the part of the defendant would have been required. It was the last act, *depending on himself*, towards the payment of the money, and *therefore* it ought to be considered as an attempt. (Italics supplied.)

But, even so, the wrongdoer may not have progressed a sufficient distance along the intended path, and his actions may still amount (as in *Hope v Brown* [1954] 1 WLR 250) to no more than mere 'preparation'. As Lord Widgery CJ pointed out in the instant case, he may have been given merely 'jobs of a kind which were obviously preparatory and not proximate'. What has always to be borne in mind, as I think, is the nature of the *full* offence alleged to have been attempted. In the instant case, it would not have been that by deception the accused dishonestly obtained a cheque from an insurance company by falsely pretending that he had died, for such a charge would be manifestly ridiculous; and, even if it were not, one can well imagine it being argued on the lines of *R v Robinson* [1915] 2 KB 342, that what the accused did in Miami did not go beyond mere preparation. But the charge actually laid was based on one of the extended meanings of 'obtain' contained in s 15(2) of the Theft Act, viz 'enabling another to obtain'. So, had it been carried through to completion and not been interrupted by his being recognised and arrested in Australia, the full offence charged would have been that the accused dishonestly and by deception enabled his wife to obtain insurance money by the false pretence that he had drowned. Towards the commission of *that* offence, the faking of his death (a) was intended to produce that result; (b) was the final act that he could perform, and (c) went a substantial distance towards the attainment of his goal. In short, in my judgment it was sufficiently proximate thereto to constitute the attempts charged in counts 17 to 21.

[The other members of the House of Lords delivered separate judgments agreeing that the appeal should be dismissed. Three members of the House of Lords (**Lord Salmon, Lord Edmund-Davies** and **Lord Keith**; **Lord Diplock** and **Viscount Dilhorne** dissenting) took the view that the trial judge had been incorrect in telling the jury not that the conduct of the accused could be found by them to constitute an attempt, but that it did amount to an attempt. However, their Lordships upheld the conviction on the basis that no miscarriage of justice could have resulted from the misdirection.]

10.15 Notes

In criticising the direction given by the trial judge in the above case, Lord Edmund-Davies stated (at 88):

> But just as it was for the jury and not the judge to decide whether the necessary *mens rea* had been established, so also it was for them to decide whether the proved acts of the accused were such as to constitute an attempt to commit the full offence of obtaining by deception. My Lords, the erroneous direction in the instant case is but one example of a prevalent (though fortunately not universal) tendency in our courts in these days to withdraw from the jury issues which are solely theirs to determine.

It is submitted that the view adopted by Lord Edmund-Davies and the majority is correct. Whether conduct has gone beyond the stage of mere preparation so as to constitute an attempt involves questions of fact and degree, and as such it is an issue which ought properly to be left for the determination of the jury.

10.16C R v Page

[1933] VLR 351

Full Court of the Supreme Court of Victoria

Mann A-CJ [delivering the judgment of the court — himself, **Lowe** and **Gavan Duffy JJ**]: This was a question of law reserved by a Court of General Sessions, raising a question of some importance with regard to the nature of an attempt to commit a crime. There was also an appeal by the accused, which covers the same point.

The facts are more particularly set out in the case, but shortly the material circumstances were these: The accused induced a young fellow named Partridge to join him in a shopbreaking enterprise at Geelong. The accused kept watch in a lane, while his companion mounted a wall, having armed himself with a lever. Having reached a position where he could open a window, he put the lever under the window-ledge for the purpose of prising it open, but, before using any force, he decided he would not 'continue on with the job'. He dropped the lever to the ground and himself descended, and was arrested with his confederate. The accused admitted the truth of that description of what took place, and the learned trial judge reserved the case, which asks whether what was done by Partridge amounted to an overt act sufficient to constitute an attempt to break into the shop in question. We are of opinion that that question should be answered in the affirmative.

The act in question was one of a series of acts or omissions which would have constituted an offence if they had not been interrupted and are thus to be distinguished on the authorities from a mere preparation to commit an offence. The learned prosecutor for the King, the prisoner being undefended, referred us to the words of a definition of an attempt which seemed to offer a further defence on behalf of the prisoner to the charge as laid. In *Russell on Crimes* (8th ed, 1823), p 148, it said:

> The question in each case is whether the acts relied on constituting the attempt were done with intent to commit the complete offence, and as one or more of a series of acts or omissions directly forming some of the necessary steps towards completing that offence, but falling short of completion by the intervention of causes outside the volition of the accused, or because the offender of his own free will desisted from completion of his criminal purpose for some reason other than mere change of mind.

The concluding words of that definition if they are well founded in law seem to exclude the facts of this case from criminal liability on the part of the accused or his confederate. No authority is cited for that part of the definition, and upon principle it seems difficult to believe that it forms any part of the criminal law. If correct, it would seem to involve the necessity, in almost every case of an unsuccessful attempt to commit a crime, of determining whether the accused desisted from sudden alarm, from a sense of wrongdoing, from failure of resolution, or from any other cause. In the great majority of attempts to commit a crime the persons concerned desist because of causes affecting their volition, and the case we are dealing with is a case in point.

The definition of an attempt is well ascertained in English law, and has been laid down by more than one authority. In *Archbold's Criminal Pleading* (27th ed, 1927), p 1407, there is quoted a definition from a Draft Criminal Code — a document of the very highest legal authority, inasmuch as it was prepared by Lord Blackburn and Barry, Lush and Stephen JJ. That definition is as follows:

> An attempt to commit an offence is an act done or omitted with intent to commit that offence, forming part of a series of acts or omissions which would have constituted the offence if such series of acts or omissions had not been interrupted either by the voluntary determination of the offender not to complete the offence or by some other cause.

That definition is in marked contrast with the passage in *Russell on Crimes*. It was cited, and its authority was approved by Pickford J in *R v Laitwood* (1910) 4 Cr App

R 248; and in *Stephen's Digest of the Criminal Law* (7th ed, 1926), p 52, the rule is laid down in almost identical terms. After defining attempts the learned author concludes with this clause:

> The offence of attempting to commit a crime may be committed in cases in which the offender voluntarily desists from the actual commission of the crime itself.

The author cites for that position the well-known case of *R v Taylor* (1859) 1 F & F 511; 175 ER 831 (Huntingdon Assizes), in which a man struck a match for the purpose of setting fire to a haystack, but desisted and blew out the match on becoming aware that he was watched, and in which Pollock CB laid it down that on those facts there was an attempt to commit a crime. The definition in *Russell* was commented on in *R v Robinson* [1915] 2 KB 342; [1914–15] All ER Rep Ext 1299 (CCA), as being too wide. The position therefore seems to be that there is no authority to support the latter part of the definition in *Russell on Crimes*, while there is high authority for saying that it is an erroneous statement of the law. The more limited definition is approved by our own Full Court in *R v Waugh* [1909] VLR 379 at 383; (1909) 15 ALR 366 at 368.

The result is that the attempt in this case was, in our opinion proved, and the fact that the confederate of the accused desisted of his own volition affords no answer to the charge. Each of the two questions asked by the case will be answered in the affirmative. For the same reasons the appeal against the conviction is dismissed.

IMPOSSIBILITY

10.17 Can a person be guilty of attempting to commit an offence where, for one reason or another, it was not possible for that person to commit the full offence itself? Prior to the decision of the House of Lords in *R v Smith* [1975] AC 476, the balance of authority tended to the conclusion that the answer to this question depended upon whether the impossibility was classified as 'legal impossibility' or 'factual impossibility'. In the former case, the fact that the crime could not be completed would give the accused a defence to a charge of attempt. In the latter, it would not.

10.18 In *R v Smith* (in some reports referred to as *Haughton v Smith*), the House of Lords analysed the problem of impossibility in a significantly different and, in the view of the present authors, incorrect fashion. It is convenient to begin by outlining the principles which, it is submitted, ought to apply in determining whether impossibility gives rise to a defence to a charge of attempt.

10.19 The distinction between 'factual impossibility' and 'legal impossibility' is clearly stated by Jerome Hall in the following passage (in *General Principles of Criminal Law*, 2nd ed, Bobbs-Merrill Co, Indianapolis, 1960, pp 586–7):

> The rules attach liability to attempts which failed because of 'factual impossibility' but they exculpate where the attempt failed because of 'legal impossibility'.

The rationale of the latter is that since the defendant would not have committed any crime even though he had done everything he intended to do, *a fortiori* he cannot be guilty of a criminal attempt if he did less than that. … In sum: (1) unless the intended end is a legally proscribed harm, causing it is not criminal, hence any conduct falling short of that is not a criminal attempt (ie, the principle of legality); and (2) if the intended end is a legally proscribed harm, the failure to effect it because of the lack of a factual condition necessary to its occurrence, is no defence (ie, factual impossibility).

Legal impossibility

10.20 Legal impossibility covers two types of case. First, the accused may believe her or his objective to be criminal when in fact it is not. For example, believing adultery to be a crime, the accused commits adultery. In such a case, the accused is clearly not guilty of a crime. That which the accused has set out to do is not proscribed by the criminal law, and a mere generalised willingness to break the law is not sufficient to constitute the crime of attempt.

The second type of legal impossibility involves accused persons who are outside the class of those defined by the law as capable of committing particular crimes. For example, at common law, a boy under the age of 14 could not be convicted of the crime of rape: see **3.6**. It followed that he could not be guilty of attempted rape: see *R v Williams* [1893] 1 QB 320 per Lord Coleridge CJ; Hawkins J, contra. This common law rule has now been changed by statute. Another example concerns the offence of procuring an abortion, recently repealed in Victoria. Since a woman who is not pregnant cannot (or, in Victoria, could not) be guilty of the offence of administering a poison or other noxious thing with intent to procure her own abortion (Crimes Act 1958 (Vic) s 65 (repealed); Crimes Act 1900 (NSW) s 82), she equally cannot be guilty of attempting to commit this offence. The legislature has determined that women who are not in fact pregnant cannot be guilty of the completed crime of administering such a substance to themselves. It would clearly be contrary to the intention of the legislature for the courts to then hold such a woman guilty of an attempt. A personal incapacity to commit the completed crime must extend to attempts to commit that crime.

Factual impossibility

10.21 All other types of impossibility are classified as cases of 'factual impossibility'. The following constitute examples of some sorts of factual impossibility:

(1) The accused fires a gun into an empty room, intending to kill a person believed to be in the room. The intended victim is, in fact, nowhere in the vicinity. This was held to constitute an attempt in the American case of *State v Mitchell* (1902) 170 Mo 633.

(2) The accused puts her or his hand into another person's pocket, intending to steal a wallet. The pocket is, in fact, empty. *R v Collins* (1864) 9 Cox CC 497 held that the empty pocket situation did not constitute an attempt. This decision was overruled in *R v Brown* (1889) 24 QBD 357 and *R v Ring* (1892) 17 Cox CC 491. See also *R v Miller and Page* (1965) 49 Cr App R 241; *R v Curbishley* (1970) 55 Cr App R 310; *Partington v Williams* [1977] Crim LR 608.

(3) The accused takes an umbrella, believing it to belong to another person. In fact, the umbrella is the accused's own. This example was discussed as a hypothetical in *R v Collins* (1864) 9 Cox CC 497 at 498.

(4) The accused presents a false customs invoice, intending to escape duty. In fact, the goods in question are not dutiable. In *Stephens v Abrahams* (1902) 27 VLR 753, it was held, wrongly it is submitted, that an attempt was not committed on these facts. See also *R v Percy Dalton Ltd* (1949) 33 Cr App R 102.

10.22 It is submitted that in each of the above cases the accused ought properly to be convicted of attempt. The effect of the decision of the House of Lords in *R v Smith*, however, is that in each case the accused would be acquitted.

The principle in R v Smith

10.23 The facts of *R v Smith* were as follows. The police stopped an overloaded van on the highway. It was found to contain stolen corned beef, whereupon the van and its driver were taken to a police station. After a period, it was decided to allow the van to proceed to its destination in order to trap a number of persons who were destined to receive the goods. The van was duly delivered and the accused was one of a group of men who played an active role in arranging for the disposal of the beef at the scene of the delivery. It was not possible to charge the accused with handling stolen goods because the corned beef had ceased to be stolen at the time of handling by virtue of it having been intercepted by the police. The accused was charged with attempting to handle stolen corned beef and convicted. The accused's conviction was quashed by the Court of Appeal and the prosecution's appeal rejected by the House of Lords.

10.24 The main judgment delivered in the House of Lords was that of Lord Hailsham LC. His Lordship approved of a six-fold classification adopted by Turner J in the New Zealand case of *R v Donnelly* [1970] NZLR 980. The six categories and Lord Hailsham's analysis of each of them were as follows:

(1) The accused may change her or his mind before committing any act sufficiently overt to amount to an attempt. Clearly, there would be no criminal attempt in this situation.

(2) The accused may change her or his mind, but too late to deny that she or he had got so far as an attempt. In this situation, there would be a criminal attempt.

(3) The accused may be prevented by some outside agency from doing some act necessary to complete the commission of the crime. For example, a police officer

may interrupt the accused while he or she is endeavouring to force a window open, but before an actual breaking occurs. In this situation, there would be a criminal attempt assuming sufficiently proximate overt acts had occurred.

(4) The accused may suffer no such outside interference, but may fail to complete the crime because of incompetence. For example, the accused may shoot at an intended victim who is out of range, or administer a dose of poison to the intended victim which is insufficiently potent to kill. Cases such as these constitute criminal attempts.

(5) The accused may find that what he or she is proposing to do is after all impossible in a physical sense — it does not fail as a result of any incompetence on the accused's part. The empty pocket case would be an example of this. Lord Hailsham reviewed the authorities, which were in conflict, and concluded that cases falling within this fifth class did not constitute criminal attempts.

(6) The accused may do every act he or she sets out to do but it may transpire that those acts, contrary to the accused's own belief at the time, do not, after all, amount in law to a crime. For example, the accused may believe that duty is payable on a particular commodity and smuggle it past customs officers when, in fact, no duty is payable on that item. In this situation, the accused would not be guilty of attempted smuggling.

10.25 Lord Hailsham concluded that the facts of *R v Smith* probably fell within class 6 but, at the very least, fell within class 5. He therefore held that no criminal attempt was made out. The other members of the House of Lords delivered judgments in essence agreeing with the Lord Chancellor.

10.26 Note that, in commenting on the six-fold classification adopted by *R v Donnelly,* Lord Hailsham took an extremely wide view of the class of legal impossibility (class 6), and further held that, while some cases of factual impossibility do constitute criminal attempts (classes 3 and 4), others do not (class 5). Broadly, the distinction adopted by Lord Hailsham is between relative factual impossibility which does not give rise to a defence (classes 3 and 4), and absolute factual impossibility which does (class 5).

10.27 It may be observed that the distinction drawn by Lord Hailsham is likely to prove difficult to apply. Clearly, to fire a shot at a person just out of range is a case of relative impossibility (class 4), while to fire a shot into an empty room, the intended victim being many miles away at the time, is a case of absolute impossibility (class 5). However, is it a case of absolute or relative impossibility to fire a shot at a man who is a mile away at the time? It is a case of relative impossibility (class 4) to attempt to steal money from a safe by blowing the safe open with an inadequate quantity of explosives. It is a case of absolute impossibility (class 5) to attempt to steal money from an empty safe. Is it a case of absolute or relative impossibility to try and steal money from a heavy safe by attempting to break the safe open with a screwdriver?

10.28 Quite apart from the practical difficulties of drawing the distinction between absolute and relative impossibility, it is difficult to see any reason of principle for wishing to draw such a distinction. The accused's moral culpability is precisely the same in cases of absolute impossibility as in cases of relative impossibility. The deterrent value of punishing the accused is precisely the same in cases of absolute impossibility as in cases of relative impossibility. In both cases, the accused is equally a danger to society. In cases of both absolute and relative impossibility, the accused has failed in her or his attempt to cause harm. However, the danger to society consists of the likelihood that, if unpunished on the instant occasion, the accused will choose more efficacious means of pursuing her or his criminal objects on subsequent occasions. The danger that the accused will learn from her or his mistakes and show more competence in future criminal endeavours appears equally present in cases of absolute impossibility as in cases of relative impossibility. If it is accepted that we should have a law of criminal attempts at all, the authors of this textbook are unable to see any reason of principle for holding cases of factual impossibility, whether absolute or relative, outside the scope of that law.

10.29 Note that in *Director of Public Prosecutions v Nock* [1978] 2 All ER 654, the House of Lords affirmed its decision in *R v Smith* and extended the defence of impossibility to the crime of conspiracy. In *R v Fitzmaurice* [1983] 1 All ER 189, the Court of Appeal held the defence applicable to incitement.

Rejection of the rule in R v Smith

10.30 In England, Victoria and the Commonwealth, the common law providing that factual impossibility is a defence has been abolished by statute: Criminal Attempts Act 1981 (Eng) s 1(2); Crimes Act 1958 (Vic) s 321N(3); Crimes Act 1914 (Cth) s 7(3) (at **10.7**). In this respect, the language of the English and Victorian provisions is virtually identical. Despite the apparent clarity of the language, in *Anderton v Ryan* [1985] 2 WLR 968, the House of Lords held that the decision in *R v Smith* survived the English legislation. In *R v Shivpuri* [1986] 2 WLR 988, however, the House of Lords overruled its earlier decision in *Anderton v Ryan*. In *R v Shivpuri*, the accused was convicted of attempted dealing in heroin. He was in possession of material which he believed to be heroin, but which was in reality vegetable material akin to snuff. The House of Lords held that, on its true construction, the statutory offence of attempt required an act which was more than merely preparatory to the commission of an offence and which the accused did with the intention of committing an offence, notwithstanding that the commission of the actual offence was, on the true facts, impossible. See also *R v Tulloch* (1986) 83 Cr App R 166; *R v Smith and Smith* [1986] Crim LR 166.

10.31 The best view is that *R v Smith* does not represent Australian common law. The Supreme Court of Victoria, in dealing with federal offences (to which the Crimes Act 1958 (Vic) does not apply), has adopted the view that *R v Smith* should not be followed: *Britten v Alpogut* [1987] VR 929 (at **10.35C**). In *R v Mai* (1991) 26 NSWLR 371, the New South Wales Court of Criminal Appeal rejected earlier New South Wales decisions in favour of following *Britten v Alpogut*. The definitive demise of the common law approach to impossible attempts reflects the rise of the principle of subjectivism, according to which the key ingredient of liability is what the defendant himself or herself intended, knew, or believed. On this basis, what matters in a case of impossible attempt is what the facts would have been had they been as the defendant believed them to be.

10.32 For an illustration of the difficulties occasioned by the application of the rule in *R v Smith*, consider *R v Collingridge* (1976) 16 SASR 117. In this case, the accused was charged with the attempted murder of his wife. While his wife was bathing, the accused entered the bathroom and threw the bared end of a live electric wire into the water behind her. The wire did not touch her body and he did not attempt to bring it into contact with her body. At trial, scientific evidence was adduced to the effect that the wire in question could not have killed the wife, so long as it was not in contact with her body. If, however, the wire had contacted her body she might have been killed. The accused was convicted of murder, and appealed to the Supreme Court of South Australia. On appeal, Bray CJ in the Supreme Court of South Australia considered at length whether the case was one of relative impossibility (because the current was insufficient on the facts) or absolute impossibility (because it was absolutely impossible that an electric wire placed as it was could have led to the victim's death). He held that it was one of relative impossibility. Hence, the appeal against conviction was dismissed.

10.33 Clearly Bray CJ was correct in classifying the case before him as one of relative impossibility (class 4) rather than absolute impossibility (class 5). The approach taken by his Honour was to restrict fairly narrowly the sphere of operation of absolute impossibility (class 5) and, consequently, to widen the scope of relative impossibility (classes 3 and 4). It is not clear, however, why Bray CJ was prepared to follow and approve the decision in *R v Smith*. Being a decision of the House of Lords, it is, of course, not strictly binding on a state Supreme Court. His Honour was certainly aware of the unsatisfactory results which an application of the classification adopted by Lord Hailsham LC might lead to.

10.34 His Honour may well have been influenced by the possibility, adverted to in his judgment, that to hold that factual impossibility can never constitute a defence might lead to the conviction of harmless cranks such as the person who thinks he or she can kill by witchcraft or by prayer. Such people are, of course, not necessarily harmless. Their methods may be highly effective if the victim is aware of their activities and shares their belief. Further, there is the possibility that when the accused realises her or his efforts at murder by prayer or witchcraft are proving fruitless, the accused may turn to more conventional methods of bringing about the death of the victim. In any event, it is submitted that such exceptional cases as these should be left to be dealt with by prosecutorial discretion and the discretion of the trial judge in relation to sentencing. The possibility of such exceptional cases occurring ought not to lead to the creation of substantive rules of law allowing the acquittal of socially dangerous individuals such as the accused who plunges her or his hand into an empty pocket believing it to contain a wallet, the accused who fires a gun into an empty room believing her or his intended victim to be in the room, and the accused who handles goods which he or she mistakenly believes to be stolen.

10.35C Britten v Alpogut

[1987] VR 929

Supreme Court of Victoria

[The defendant was charged with attempting to import prohibited imports into Australia contrary to s 233B of the Customs Act 1901 (Cth). The defendant believed that he was importing, and intended to import, into Australia a prohibited import, namely cannabis, but the substance which he believed to be cannabis and which he imported was another substance which was not a prohibited import within s 233B of the Customs Act 1901 (Cth). The magistrate dismissed the information. The prosecution sought an Order to Review.]

Murphy J: It will be seen that in the law of attempt the emphasis lies on the criminal intent of the actor, rather than on the patent criminality of the act which he performed. The act itself may be innocuous.

The intention which the Crown must prove is an intention to bring about each element of the crime alleged to be attempted, and it must be proven that this intention is accompanied side by side by an act sufficiently proximate to the offence attempted to take it out of the class of mere preparatory acts.

The latter consideration has been developed in many subsequent cases and is not a matter of any moment in the present case.

If a charge of attempting to commit a crime is to lie, it is of course usual (though perhaps not necessary cf *Webley v Buxton* [1977] 2 QB 481) that the crime attempted fails, for one reason or another. That the crime attempted fails also assists to emphasise that the law, in punishing criminal attempts, is really punishing the person concerned for his criminal intention, so as to deter or neutralise dangerous individuals, and does not punish to deter dangerous acts as such: cf US *Model Penal Code*.

This is so even though: 'The mere intent to commit a misdemeanour is not criminal — some act is required': see *R v Eagleton* (1855) Dears CC 515 at 538, per Baron Parke. Thus John Austin wrote, in *Lectures in Jurisprudence*, 1861 p 120, 'where a criminal intent is evidenced by an attempt, the party is punished in respect of the criminal intention'. See also J W C Turner, 'Attempts to Commit Crime' (1933) 5 *Camb LJ* 230 at p 235; *Russell on Crime*, 10th ed, p 1784; P J Fitzgerald, *Criminal Law Punishment*, 1962, pp 97–8.

The English Law Commission in its report on Criminal Law: Attempt *and Impossibility in Relation to Attempt Conspiracy and Incitement (Report No 102 (1980))*, p 6 reported that 'the main justification for the retention of inchoate offences is the need to permit the law to impose criminal sanctions in certain cases where a crime has been contemplated but not in fact committed'.

But this view was expressed after the decision in *Haughton v Smith* [1975] AC 476.

In my opinion, it can be said that before *Haughton v Smith* the law of attempt punished a manifest criminal intention to commit a crime which was not accomplished.

For some inexplicable reason the law of attempt became involved with the question whether or not the crime attempted could have been in fact accomplished by the accused.

It was thought by some that the accused could not be convicted of an attempt to commit a particular crime, when on the facts of the case it would not have been possible for the accused to commit the crime in question.

Immediately, there was a confusion demonstrated between a relevant step in the commission of a possible crime and a relevant step in the commission of an intended crime, but one not capable of being accomplished.

Courts began to ignore the importance of the intention of the accused and tended to concentrate on the question whether what was done was a step towards a crime, which if uninterrupted, would have been committed: cf *R v Percy Dalton (London) Ltd* (1949) 33 Cr App R 102 at 110.

It was at this stage that the embryo of the heresy in *Haughton v Smith* was conceived.

Courts spoke of attempts as interruptions in the commission of acts which, if not interrupted, would have amounted to the crime intended. Clearly, if accompanied by the necessary and vital intent, such acts, if performed sufficiently proximately, would amount to an attempt. But the emphasis in thinking wrongly changed from the element of subjective intent, to the element of objective doing of a forward or proximate act in the actual commission of the crime itself.

It tended to be forgotten that the crime of attempt derives its criminality from the conduct intended or sought to be done: cf *Gillies Criminal Law*, 1985, p 519.

However, the submission on behalf of the Crown in this case is that in 1910 when s 233 was first introduced into the *Customs Act 1901* (cf *Beckwith v R* (1976) 135 CLR 569 at 578–80, per Mason J) the common law of attempt was that anyone who, believing that a certain state of facts exists, does an act the doing of which would, if that state of facts existed, be an attempt to commit an offence, attempts to commit that offence, although its commission in the manner proposed was by reason of the actual state of affairs impossible.

Mr Weinberg of counsel for the applicant took this statement from the 1879 *Draft Criminal Code*, s 74. He also relied in support of it upon *R v Brown* (1889) 24 QB 357; *R v Ring* (1892) 17 Cox CC 491; *McMillan v Reeves* (1945) 62 WN (NSW) 126; *O'Sullivan v Peters* [1951] SASR 54; *Haas v R* [1964] Tas SR 1; *R v Perera* [1907] VLR 240; *Stephens v Abrahams* (1902) 27 VLR 753.

It should however be noted that in the *Draft Code* appended by the Criminal Code Bill Commissioners to their report, this passage coming after the definition of an attempt bears an asterisk, which in the margin attracts the comment by the Commissioners:

> This declares the law differently from *R v Collins* L & C 471 where it was held that a person who put his hand into the pocket in order to steal, was not guilty of an attempt to steal, because it happened that that pocket was empty.

In the body of their report the Commissioners state as to this proposed section, 'This alters the law from what it has been held to be'. The Commissioners were Lord Blackburn, Barry J, Lush J and Sir James Fitzjames Stephen QC.

It was shortly after that report that *R v Brown* and *R v Ring* were decided.

In *R v Brown* (1889) 24 QBD 357 at 359. Lord Coleridge CJ, Pollock B, Field, Manisty, Cave, Day and Granham JJ stated bluntly that *R v Collins* 'is no longer law'. Nor was *R v Dodd* (unreported) which 'proceeded upon the same view that a person could not be convicted of an attempt to commit an offence which he could not actually commit. Some of the judges, I know, yielded with great reluctance to the authority of *R v Collins*, and thought that decision was wrong.'

Then again in another Crown case reserved, *R v Ring* (1892) 17 Cox CC 491 before Lord Coleridge CJ, Hawkins, Wills, Lawrence and Wright JJ, the prisoners were charged with an attempt to steal from the person of a person unknown. Apparently, it is assumed that they were unable to find the pocket of the dress of their victim. They were convicted at Quarter Sessions and the case was stated, following the Deputy Chairman's ruling that *R v Collins* had been overruled by *R v Brown*. Lord Coleridge said, at 149:

> The case was stated to ascertain whether or not *R v Collins* is good law. That case was overruled by the decision in *R v Brown*, a case decided by five judges [*The reporter notes that this should be seven, although the reporter includes Charles J instead of Day J*] and since this case will also be decided by five judges, one of whom was one of the judges who decided *R v Brown* the learned judge who stated the case will have the satisfaction of knowing that now nine judges hold that *R v Collins* is bad law.

The number of judges should of course have been eleven, all, I think, recognised to be judges of great experience in the criminal law. It has been submitted that as the crime of attempting to import into Australia any prohibited imports to which the section (s 233B(1)(b) of the *Customs Act 1901*) applies, is a statutory offence, the only possible attempt of which the accused could have been guilty would be an attempt to do that which is forbidden by the legislature.

But if the word 'attempt' is used in s 233B(1)(b) in its common law sense, as I believe that it is, then it is to beg the question to say that it is only if the goods imported or sought to be imported, are in fact prohibited imports that an 'attempt' within the meaning of the subsection can be committed.

For if the evil intent of the actor can make a sufficiently proximate though objectively innocent act criminal, so as to amount to an attempt, it would seem irrelevant to have to go on to see whether the attempt could or would have succeeded. At common law, if the intent was to commit a recognized and not an imagined crime, and the act done was not merely preparatory but sufficiently proximate, then at that stage an attempt to commit the recognized crime has been committed, and it seems to me it is not necessary to go further.

It follows, in my view, that to prove the statutory crime created by s 233B(1)(b) of the *Customs Act*, of attempting to import prohibited imports into Australia, the Crown must prove that the accused at all material times intended to import something which was as a matter of law a prohibited import and known by him to be so, and that pursuant to this intention he did an act or acts (including omissions) not merely preparatory but sufficiently proximate to the intended commission of the crime.

[His Honour considered a number of cases and continued:]

It is my opinion, sitting in this court, that we ought to say that we are unable to accept the law as to criminal attempts set forth in *Haughton v Smith*, and that we should affirm the general body of the law on this subject as it stood preceding *R v Percy Dalton (London) Ltd* (1949) 33 Cr App R 102.

This would be, in my opinion, to affirm the reasoning apparent in our own Full Court in decisions preceding *Haughton v Smith* (for example, *R v Perera* [1907] VLR 240) and to accord with the revised general reasoning of the House of Lords in *R v Shivpuri* [1986] 2 All ER 334; [1986] 2 WLR 988.

It would also be to recognise that at common law a criminal attempt is committed if it is proven that the accused had at all material times the guilty intent to commit a recognized crime and it is proven that at the same time he did an act or acts (which in appropriate circumstances would include omissions) which are seen to be sufficiently proximate to the commission of the said crime and are not seen to be merely preparatory to it. The 'objective innocence' or otherwise of those acts is irrelevant.

Impossibility is also irrelevant, unless it be that the so-called crime intended is not a crime known to the law, in which case a criminal attempt to commit it cannot be made.

In my opinion, the order *nisi* should be made absolute and the case remitted to the magistrate, to be tried according to law, there being a case to answer on the evidence.

[**Fullagar J** delivered a separate judgment agreeing with **Murphy J. Gobbo J** concurred. Order made absolute.]

[See also *R v Mai* (1992) 26 NSWLR 371.]

OTHER INCHOATE CRIMES

Incitement

10.36 It is a common law misdemeanour to solicit or incite any person to commit any indictable offence. A person who incites is one who 'counsels, commands or advises' the commission of a crime; and that person is guilty of the offence, though the person incited does nothing whatsoever in pursuit of the criminal purpose, provided the latter person has heard and comprehended the words of incitement. In *R v Quail* (1866) 4 F & F 1076; 176 ER 914, the accused was convicted of inciting to larceny a servant who had no intention of obeying his exhortations and was only interested in helping his employer to entrap Quail. See also *R v Dimozantos* (1991) 56 A Crim

R 345. If the person incited commits a lesser crime than he or she was encouraged to commit, the inciter remains guilty of incitement of the more serious offence. Therefore, in *R v Howe* [1987] 2 WLR 568, the House of Lords held that an accused who incites another to kill is guilty of incitement to commit murder notwithstanding that the actual killer is convicted of manslaughter only. If, however, the incitement does not come to the notice of the person to whom it is addressed, there can be no conviction for incitement but there may be a conviction for attempting to incite: *R v Ransford* (1874) 13 Cox CC 9. In *R v Andrews* [1973] QB 422, the Court of Appeal held that there may be an incitement to pervert the course of judicial proceedings.

10.37 It has been said that the crime of incitement covers exhortation addressed to the world in general. The principal decision is *R v Most* (1881) 7 QBD 244 in which the accused's conviction for incitement to murder was upheld. Most was an exile living in England who edited and published a German-language newspaper called *Freiheit*. After the assassination of the Czar Alexander II, he published an article warmly praising the deed and containing phrases which contemplated with approval the likelihood that other assassinations of political rulers would follow. The court discussed the charge of incitement without any consideration of the limits of political speech; and it may, accordingly, be questioned whether the decision would be followed at the present day. It is, of course, debatable whether freedom of speech should extend to the publication of material of this kind. Nevertheless, it would seem that there are better ways of suppressing such publications, if that is desired, than using the device of incitement charges, at any rate in cases where the encouragement is addressed to the world at large and advocates the commission of crime in general terms without reference to any specific time, place, or circumstance.

10.38 If the solicitation or incitement should prove successful so that the crime is actually carried out by the addressee, then the solicitor or inciter will, in most instances, personally be guilty of the completed crime as an accomplice. Liability in this capacity is discussed fully in **Chapter 11**.

10.39 In Victoria, the crime of incitement was placed upon a statutory footing by the Crimes (Conspiracy and Incitement Act) 1984. That Act abolished the common law offence of incitement. Section 321G of the Crimes Act 1958 (Vic) now provides:

> (1) Subject to this Act, where a person in Victoria or elsewhere incites any other person to pursue a course of conduct which will involve the commission of an offence by —
> (a) the person incited;
> (b) the inciter; or
> (c) both the inciter and the person incited —
> if the inciting is acted on in accordance with the inciter's intention, the inciter is guilty of the indictable offence of incitement.
>
> (2) For a person to be guilty under sub-section (1) of incitement the person —
> (a) must intend that the offence the subject of the incitement be committed; and

(b) must intend or believe that any fact or circumstance the existence of which is an element of the offence in question will exist at the time when the conduct constituting the offence is to take place.

(3) A person may be guilty under sub-section (1) of incitement notwithstanding the existence of facts of which the person is unaware which make commission of the offence in question by the course of conduct incited impossible.

10.40 In New South Wales, incitement has not been placed on a statutory footing, although there are exceptions, including incitement to commit certain sexual offences (under Crimes Act 1900 (NSW) s 80G) and under the Crimes Prevention Act 1916 (NSW) (which contains a general provision that makes it an offence to incite, urge, aid or encourage the commission of crimes, or to incite the carrying on of any operations for or by the commission of crimes, but it is seldom used).

Crimes of preparation

10.41 It should be clear from what has already been said that it may be possible for a person to take steps towards the commission of a crime or series of crimes without being punishable for an attempt, or indeed for any crime known to the common law, if that person is apprehended before approaching completion of the crime. For this reason, the legislature has often intervened and made preliminary steps which fall short of an attempt themselves punishable as distinct offences. These types of offences are generally known as preparatory offences. Thus, the possession of instruments commonly used for forging or counterfeiting is itself made a substantive offence by the same statutes which provide for the punishment of the actual forging or counterfeiting when carried out. Other examples include being armed with intent to commit an indictable offence or being in possession of implements of housebreaking, safebreaking or car theft (Crimes Act 1900 (NSW) s 114), and being equipped for stealing (Crimes Act 1958 (Vic) s 91).

The creation of preparatory offences has accelerated in recent years, particularly in the context of terrorism. The Criminal Code (Cth) contains numerous offences related to terrorism, some of which criminalise acts preparatory to the commission of a terrorist act. Clearly, the existence of such offences raises significant policy issues. In *Faheem Khalid Lodhi* [2006] NSWCCA 121, the court observed (at [66]) that:

> Preparatory acts are not often made into criminal offences. The particular nature of terrorism has resulted in a special, and in many ways unique, legislative regime. It was, in my opinion, the clear intention of Parliament to create offences where an offender has not decided precisely what he or she intends to do. A policy judgment has been made that the prevention of terrorism requires criminal responsibility to arise at an earlier stage than is usually the case for other kinds of criminal conduct, for example, well before an agreement has been reached for a conspiracy charge. The courts must respect that legislative policy.

Extending Criminal Liability: Participation in Crime

CHAPTER 11

INTRODUCTION: THE PROBLEM OF COMPLICITY IN CRIME

11.1 Gang violence has always drawn media and legislative attention. It has a dangerous tendency to escalate beyond the original intentions of the perpetrators. However, it is hard not to feel some sympathy for the naïve, overly trusting or intimidated individuals who find themselves swept up in criminal enterprises over which they have little control. Equally, while the law should be equipped to deal with the 'Mr Bigs' who organise or procure crime, it should not be unduly harsh on the 'minnows'. Added to this is the basic principle that the criminal law should only punish offenders who possess both the mens rea and actus reus for the offence alleged against them — a principle that is difficult to apply where the person being tried is associated with the criminal offence committed, but has not necessarily committed the physical act constituting the offence.

An alternative approach is to punish a person by virtue of his or her association with known or suspected criminals. For the prosecution, this approach has the virtue of obviating the need to prove actual involvement in a criminal act. However, it flies in the face of hard-won civil liberties and rights of the defendant, in particular the notion that a person should only be punished when it can be proved they have committed a crime. Historically, the common law developed a suite of what are generally known as 'public order' offences designed to police drunks, vagrants, and other disorderly elements for the benefit of the 'respectable' classes. These laws, which include loitering and 'move-on' powers, as well as more serious offences such as habitually consorting with known criminals, are still contained in the summary offences laws of some Australian jurisdictions, but have now broadly fallen into disuse.

Nevertheless, the notion of punishing people by virtue of their association with an unpopular or suspected criminal element keeps reappearing in public debate, and consequently on the statute-books. One recent example of this is the New South Wales laws commonly known as the bikie laws, because they were prompted by a concern over crime and violence linked to bikie gangs. However, they apply to criminal organisations more broadly (see Crimes Act 1900 (NSW) s 93S).

In New South Wales, the Crimes Act 1900 ss 93S(2)(b) and 93T provide that a person can be convicted as a member of a criminal group, even though 'only some of the people involved in the group are involved in planning, organising or carrying out any particular activity' so long as the person knows or ought reasonably to know that it is a criminal group and 'his or her participation in that group contributes to the occurrence of any criminal activity'. There are also new consorting offences for people who consort with convicted offenders (on at least two occasions) and consort after receiving an official warning (Crimes Act 1900 (NSW) s 93X). In Victoria, the Criminal Organisations Control Bill introduced into Parliament in November 2012 allows certain groups to be declared 'criminal organisations' which can be subject to control orders banning members of that group from associating or participating in gang activities. At the time of writing, this bill was still before parliament.

Despite such recent developments, the main rules governing the criminal liability of those who assist or encourage others to commit criminal offences continue to be the laws of criminal complicity.

HISTORY AND OUTLINE OF THE RULES OF COMPLICITY

11.2 Responsibility for a criminal offence extends beyond the person who commits the crime to cover others who, in one way or another, assist that person. At common law, the actual offender was known as a 'principal in the first degree'. A person who was present at the commission of the crime, aiding and abetting the principal in the first degree, was known as a principal in the second degree. A person who encouraged the commission of the crime, but was not present at its commission, was known as an accessory before the fact. A person who assisted a principal offender subsequent to the commission of the offence was known as an accessory after the fact.

11.3 In Victoria, principals in the second degree and accessories before the fact have been subsumed under the single category of abettors. Section 323 of the Crimes Act 1958 (Vic) provides:

> A person who aids, abets, counsels or procures the commission of an indictable offence may be tried, indicted or presented and punished as a principal offender.

This provision would appear to affect terminology only. In Victoria, the correct division is thus principals in the first degree (or 'principal offenders'), abettors (sometimes referred to as principals in the second degree, or as accessories before the fact) and accessories after the fact.

11.4 There may, of course, be two or more principal offenders to the same crime. Joint principal offenders occur in two types of cases:

(1) first, if two or more persons each play a part in performing the acts which go to constitute the crime. Thus if a number of individuals attack another, intending to kill their victim, and the combined effect of their blows is to cause death, each are

principals in the first degree: *Macklin and Murphy's* case (1838) 2 Lew CC 225; 168 ER 1136; *R v McDonald* [1904] St R Qd 151;

(2) second, even if only one participant performed the acts constituting the crime, each will be guilty as principals in the first degree if the acts were performed in the presence of all and pursuant to a preconceived plan. In this case, the parties are said to be acting in concert. 'Acting in concert' is sometimes also known as joint criminal enterprise or common purpose. In *R v Lowery and King (No 2)* [1972] VR 560 Smith J stated the law as follows:

> The law says that if two or more persons reach an understanding or arrangement that together they will commit a crime and then, while that understanding or arrangement is still on foot and has not been called off, they are both present at the scene of the crime and one or the other of them does, or they do between them, in accordance with their understanding or arrangement, all things that are necessary to constitute the crime, they are equally guilty of that crime regardless of what part each played in its commission. In such cases they are said to have been acting in concert in committing the crime.

See also *R v Jensen and Ward* [1980] VR 194; *Osland v R* (1998) 197 CLR 316; 159 ALR 170 (at 11.13C); *Likiardopoulos v The Queen* [2012] HCA 37 (14 September 2012); *Huynh, Duong and Sem v The Queen* [2013] HCA 6 (13 March 2013) at 8.

11.5 Principals in the second degree need not be physically present at the offence. Foster defines 'principal in the second degree' as follows (*Crown Law*, 3rd ed, 1809, pp 349–50):

> When the law requireth the presence of the accomplice at the perpetration of the fact, in order to render him a principal, it *doth not require a strict, actual, immediate presence*, such a presence as would make him an eye or ear witness of what passeth. Several persons set out together, or in small parties, upon one common design, be it murder or other felony, or for any other purpose unlawful in itself, and each taketh the part assigned him; some to commit the fact, others to watch at proper distances and stations to prevent a surprise, or to favour, if need be, the escape of those who are more immediately engaged. They are all, provided the fact be committed, in the eye of the law present at it: for it was made a common cause with them, each man operated in his station at one and the same instance towards the same common end; and the part each man took tended to give countenance, encouragement, and protection to the whole gang, and to insure the success of their common enterprise. I will not here multiply cases upon the head of constructive presence. This may be sufficient by way of illustration. Others founded in the same principle of mutual concert, aid, and protection will fall in their proper places.

11.6 Consider the following situation in relation to principal in the second degree: D1 and D2 agree to burgle the house of V. Knowing that V is normally at home in the evenings, D2 telephones V and arranges an appointment with him at a rendezvous some 30 kilometres away to discuss some alleged business matter of great urgency. V goes to the rendezvous where D2 meets him and engages him in conversation for two or three hours, during which time D1 burgles the house. Based on Foster's broad formulation, D2 would be regarded as a principal in the second degree, although he is 30 kilometres away at the time of the burglary.

11.7 A person who acts through an innocent agent is a principal in the first degree rather than an abettor. The innocent agent may be either one who is unaware of what he or she is doing (as in the case of a person who administers poison, believing it to be harmless) or one who is (in a sense) aware of what he or she is doing but, for some reason, is not amenable to the criminal law. This could arise in various ways; the agent might be insane, or might be excused on some ground such as duress or infancy.

11.8 Accessories before the fact encourage or assist the principal offender before the commission of a crime, whereas accessories after the fact knowingly assist an offender after a crime has been committed. Blackstone states the common law in relation to accessories before and after the fact. He states that an accessory *before* the fact is 'absent at the time of the crime committed' but 'procure[s], counsel[s], or command[s] another to commit a crime'. Clearly, if this accessory was present, it would make her or him guilty as a principal in the first degree. The following example of an accessory before the fact is provided by Blackstone: If A advises B to kill another, and B does it in the absence of A, B is principal and A is accessory in the murder. A is an accessory to the crime committed by B and all acts of a consequential or collateral nature, although not ones that are wholly distinct (such as B robbing a house when A advised merely to burn the house).

11.9 Blackstone's description of an accessory *after* the fact is 'where a person, knowing a felony to have been committed, receives, relieves, comforts, or assists the felon'. Therefore, to be an accessory after the fact, the person must know of the crime committed; receive, relieve, comfort or assist the criminal; and help in preventing the criminal from being apprehended, tried or punished. This can include helping the offender to escape police or prison guards or providing a shelter to conceal the offender. To be charged as an accessory after the fact, the crime must be complete, otherwise there is no relevant offender to assist (Blackstone, 4 *B1 Comm* 34).

11.10 At common law, a principal in the second degree was regarded, so to speak, as an offender in her or his own right, and could be tried and convicted although the principal in the first degree could not, for some reason, be proceeded against. However, an accessory was regarded as an ancillary criminal and could not be convicted unless the principal crime was established. An accessory could be tried and convicted with the principal, or after the latter had been convicted or outlawed or attainted, but if the principal had been neither outlawed nor attainted, the accessory could not be tried before her or him.

These procedural rules have now been abolished by statute: see Crimes Act 1958 (Vic) ss 323–325; Crimes Act 1900 (NSW) ss 346–347.

11.11 Can an abettor be guilty of a higher crime than the principal in the first degree? The answer is yes, as held by the House of Lords in *R v Howe* [1987] 2 WLR 568. This would make sense in the following scenario: D1, in response to serious provocation, attacks V with intent to cause V death or grievous bodily harm. D2, who is unaware of the provocative incident, comes on the scene and encourages D1 to continue the attack. D1 does so and V dies as a consequence. In this situation, clearly, D2 should be guilty of murder, notwithstanding that, in jurisdictions which retain the partial defence, D1 is guilty of manslaughter only by reason of the provocation received from V. Referring to such an example, Lord Mackay in *R v Howe* stated (at 603):

> The mere fact that the actual killer may be convicted only of the reduced charge of manslaughter for some reason special to himself does not, in my opinion in any way, result in a compulsory reduction for the other participant.

See also *Hui-Chi Ming v The Queen* [1992] 1 AC 34, an appeal to the Privy Council from the Court of Appeal of Hong Kong. The defendant had participated in a joint enterprise in which the principal offender (a man named Ah Po) had killed the victim. Ah Po and Hui-Chi Ming were tried separately. At his trial, Ah Po was found guilty of manslaughter only; however, the defendant's conviction for murder was upheld on appeal. The fact that a different jury had found the principal offender guilty of manslaughter only did not mean that Hui-Chi Ming could not be convicted of murder.

11.12 Abettors (including accessories before the fact) are liable to be punished in the same way as principals in the first degree: Crimes Act 1958 (Vic) ss 323–324; Crimes Act 1900 (NSW) ss 345–346, 351. Accessories after the fact are commonly liable to lesser penalties than the principal offender: Crimes Act 1958 (Vic) ss 325–326; Crimes Act 1900 (NSW) ss 348–350.

PRINCIPAL OFFENDERS

11.13C

Osland v R

(1998) 197 CLR 316; 159 ALR 170
High Court of Australia

[The appellant and her son, Albion, were charged with the murder of the deceased, the appellant's husband and Albion's step-father. The prosecution case was that the two had together planned to murder the deceased, that on a particular day they dug a grave for him, that in the evening the appellant mixed sedatives in with the deceased's dinner in sufficient quantity to induce sleep and that, after the deceased went to bed, Albion fatally hit him over the head with a pipe in the presence of the appellant. The appellant and Albion admitted that they killed the deceased and relied on self-defence and provocation. These defences were raised against an evidentiary background of tyrannical and violent behaviour by the deceased towards the appellant over many years. Expert evidence of battered women syndrome and that the appellant was affected by it was admitted by the trial judge. This aspect of the case is dealt with at **12.20, note 2**. The jury convicted the appellant of murder. They were unable to reach a verdict with respect to Albion, who was subsequently retried and acquitted. On appeal to the High Court, the appellant contended, inter alia, that her conviction was inconsistent with the jury's failure to convict Albion.]

[Footnotes to the extract appear at the end of the extract.]

McHugh J:

Criminal complicity

Much of the argument for Mrs Osland in this court was characterised by a failure to distinguish between, on the one hand, the criminal liability of a person who is present at the scene of a crime and is acting in concert with another and, on the other, the criminal liability of one who is present but not acting in concert with that person. Much of the criticism — express and implied — of the trial judge's directions, and most of the argument that was relied on to urge that the conviction and the failure to agree were inconsistent, resulted from the failure to accept the existence of that distinction. Because that is so, it is first necessary to refer briefly to the principles of criminal liability applicable when a crime is committed by persons acting in concert.

At common law, a person who commits the acts which form the whole or part[1] of the *actus reus* of the crime is known as a 'principal in the first degree'. There can be more than one principal in the first degree.[2] However, a person may incur criminal liability not only for his or her own acts that constitute the whole or part of the *actus reus* of a crime but also for the acts of others that do so. The liability may be primary or derivative. In earlier times, when it was alleged that a person should be held criminally liable for the acts of another, it mattered whether the crime was a felony or a misdemeanour. In Victoria, the distinction between felonies and misdemeanours has been abolished.[3] There is no longer any need to draw a distinction between the two categories of crime.[4]

Those who aided the commission of a crime but were not present at the scene of the crime were regarded as accessories before the fact or principals in the third degree. Their liability was purely derivative and was dependent upon the guilt of the person who had been aided and abetted in committing the crime.[5] Those who were merely present, encouraging[6] but not participating physically,[7] or whose acts were not a substantial cause of death,[8] were regarded as principals in the second degree.[9] They could only be convicted of the crime of which the principal offender was found guilty. If that person was not guilty, the principal in the second degree could not be guilty.[10] Their liability was, accordingly, also derivative.

However, there is[11] a third category where a person was not only present at the scene with the person who committed the acts alleged to constitute the crime but was there by reason of a pre-concert or agreement with that person to commit the crime.[12] In that category, the liability of each person present as the result of the concert is not derivative but primary. He or she is a principal in the first degree. In that category each of the persons acting in concert[13] is equally responsible for the acts of the other or others. The general principle was clearly stated in *R v Lowery and King (No 2)*[14] by Smith J who directed the jury in the following terms:

> The law says that if two or more persons reach an understanding or arrangement that together they will commit a crime and then, while that understanding or arrangement is still on foot and has not been called off, they are both present at the scene of the crime and one or other of them does, or they do between them, in accordance with their understanding or arrangement, all the things that are necessary to constitute the crime, they are all equally guilty of that crime regardless of what part each played in its commission. In such cases they are said to have been acting in concert in committing the crime.

In that case, his Honour directed the jury that 'they are all equally guilty of that crime'. But as subsequent cases show, and as principle requires, the correct statement is that they are all equally liable for the acts that constitute the *actus reus* of the crime. The principle is accurately stated by Brett, Waller and Williams in the 8th edition of their work on *Criminal Law:*[15]

> [E]ven if only one participant performed the acts constituting the crime, each will be guilty *as principals in the first degree* if the acts were performed in the presence of all and pursuant to a preconceived plan. In this case, the parties are said to be acting in concert (emphasis added).

So far as is presently relevant, these principles were accurately and more fully stated by the New South Wales Court of Criminal Appeal in *Tangye.*[16] The court said:[17]

> (1) The law is that, where two or more persons carry out a joint criminal enterprise, *each is responsible for the acts of the other or others in carrying out that enterprise.* The Crown must establish both the existence of that joint criminal enterprise and the participation in it by the accused.
>
> (2) A joint criminal enterprise exists where two or more persons reach an understanding or arrangement amounting to an agreement between them that they will commit a crime. The understanding or arrangement need not be express, and its existence may be inferred from all the circumstances. It need not have been reached at any time before the crime is committed. The circumstances in which two or more persons are participating together in the commission of a particular crime may themselves establish an unspoken understanding or arrangement amounting to an agreement formed between them then and there to commit that crime.
>
> (3) A person participates in that joint criminal enterprise either by committing the agreed crime itself or simply by being present at the time when the crime is committed (emphasis added).

In accordance with the New South Wales practice, the court referred to 'carrying out a criminal enterprise' rather than acting in concert. The principles, however, are the same.

As a result, a person may be found guilty of murder although he or she did not commit the acts which physically caused the death of the victim and the person who did is found guilty only of manslaughter.[18] In *R v Howe*,[19] all their Lordships were of the opinion that

R v Richards,[20] which had held that the person who did not perform the acts could not be guilty of a more serious charge than the actual perpetrator, was wrongly decided. Lord Mackay said:[21]

> [W]here a person has been killed and that result is the result intended by another participant, the mere fact that the actual killer may be convicted only of the reduced charge of manslaughter for some reason special to himself does not, in my opinion in any way, result in a compulsory reduction for the other participant.

This statement is conclusive in England, at all events, in showing that it is the acts, and not the crime, of the actual perpetrator which are attributed to the person acting in concert. If the latter person has the relevant *mens rea,* he or she is guilty of the principal offence because the *actus reus* is attributed to him or her by reason of the agreement and presence at the scene. It is irrelevant that the actual perpetrator cannot be convicted of that crime because he or she has a defence such as lack of *mens rea*, self-defence, provocation, duress or insanity. ...

The principle that those who act in concert and are present at the scene are responsible for the acts of the actual perpetrator operates to make a person guilty of the principal crime, even though the actual perpetrator is acquitted completely. Thus, the person who did the act may be legally insane. Yet as long as that person had sufficient mental capacity to enter into the arrangement or common understanding, the other participant present at the scene will be guilty of committing the principal crime if he or she has the relevant *mens rea.*[22] In *Matusevich v R*,[23] this court decided that, when two persons are said to be acting in concert, the fact that the actual perpetrator is legally insane does not necessarily mean that the conviction of the other, who was present at the scene, should be quashed. If the actual perpetrator has sufficient capacity to enter into the agreement or understanding, the person present at the scene who was acting in concert may be convicted of the offence.

Professor Lanham in his article 'Complicity, Concert and Conspiracy'[24] is critical of *Matusevich*, but he accepts that it is an authority for the proposition that, in cases of concert, a non-participant present at the scene of the *actus reus* may be convicted as a primary and not as a derivative offender. He says:[25]

> The overall result of *Matusevich v R* is that the High Court has left open whether an aider and abettor's liability is dependent on that of the perpetrator, [which] has thrown some doubt on the use of innocent agency as a solution but '*has given clear approval to the use of the principle of acting in concert to convict secondary parties when the principal is not personally liable*' (emphasis added).

He also notes that:[26]

> Australian cases which in effect treat those acting in concert as principals in the first degree stress the requirement of presence and show no disposition to extend the concept to those absent from the offence.

Markby v R[27] also supports the conclusion that it is the wrongful acts of the perpetrator which are attributed to the person acting in concert and present at the scene. *Markby* establishes that if violence is one of the contemplated incidents of a joint criminal enterprise and one of the accused kills a person, the other accused can be convicted of manslaughter even though the killer is guilty of murder. This decision is consistent only with the conclusion that it is the acts constituting the *actus reus,* and not the crime, of the actual offender which are attributed to the other party. The liability is direct or primary, not derivative. …

Counsel for the appellant relied on *R v Demirian*[28] where a majority of the Full Court of the Supreme Court of Victoria said that, even if it could have been established that the accused in that case was present at the scene of a bomb explosion and was acting in concert with the person who exploded the bomb, the accused could not have been convicted as a principal in the first degree. Upon the facts of that case, the statement may be correct. However, it is plain that their Honours were seeking to lay down a general proposition. In my opinion it is not an accurate statement of the modern law. Moreover, the proposition was not necessary for the decision. Curiously, the majority of the Full Court preferred to follow the decision of the English Court of Appeal in *Richards*[29] notwithstanding that in *Howe*[30] the House of Lords said that Richards was wrongly decided. The majority in *Demirian*[31] also appears to have treated *Matusevich,*[32] wrongly in my opinion, as a case of innocent agency.

In my opinion, the statement in *Demirian* is inconsistent with the principles which underly the decisions in *R v Hurse,*[33] *Bourne,*[34] *Lowery and King,*[35] *Matusevich,*[36] *Markby,*[37] *Hui Chi-ming,*[38] *Johns*[39] and *Chan Wing-Siu*[40] and the statements of principle in *Howe*[41] and *Tangye.*[42] And there is no policy reason why *Demirian* should be followed in preference to the statements in *Howe.*

Where the parties are acting as the result of an arrangement or understanding, there is nothing contrary to the objects of the criminal law in making the parties liable for each other's acts and the case for doing so is even stronger when they are at the scene together. If any of those acting in concert but not being the actual perpetrator has the relevant *mens rea,* it does not seem wrong in principle or as a matter of policy to hold that person liable as a principal in the first degree. Once the parties have agreed to do the acts which constitute the *actus reus* of the offence and are present acting in concert when the acts are committed, the criminal liability of each should depend upon the existence or non-existence of *mens rea* or upon their having a lawful justification for the acts, not upon the criminal liability of the actual perpetrator. So even if the actual perpetrator of the acts is acquitted, there is no reason in principle why others acting in concert cannot be convicted of the principal offence. They are responsible for the acts (because they have agreed to them being done) and they have the *mens rea* which is necessary to complete the commission of the crime.

In my opinion, the statement in *Demirian* should not be followed in the common law jurisdictions in this country. It may be that the statement accurately reflects the early common law. It is not, however, possible to reconcile it with the modern cases.

Counsel for Mrs Osland also relied on *Surujpaul*[43] as authority for the proposition that when persons are jointly charged with murder they cannot be convicted as accessories unless one or more of them has been convicted as a principal. But the conviction in that case was as an accessory before the fact. As I pointed out earlier, the liability of an accessory before the fact is derivative. There can be no conviction as an accessory before the fact unless there is a principal offender. In *Surujpaul*, all the co-accused were acquitted both as principals and as accessories before the fact. That case has no bearing on the criminal responsibility of a person for the acts of the actual perpetrator when the former is alleged to be acting in concert and present at the scene with the latter.

The explanation of the conviction and the failure [of the jury] to agree [on the verdict of *Albion*]

I have already indicated that it is likely that the jury found beyond reasonable doubt that Mrs Osland and her son killed the deceased in accordance with a common understanding or arrangement and that they also found that Mrs Osland was not acting in self-defence or as the result of provocation when she participated in the killing. I have also suggested that one or more jurors may have had a reasonable doubt as to whether her son was acting in self-defence. If the jury so reasoned, they reached their verdict of conviction in respect of Mrs Osland in accordance with the way that the Crown and the accused persons conducted the case and in accordance with the directions of the trial judge.

[**Kirby** and **Callinan JJ** delivered separate judgments agreeing that the conviction of the appellant was not inconsistent with the jury's failure to reach a verdict in respect of Albion in the first trial and with his acquittal in his second trial. **Kirby J** agreed with **McHugh J** on the liability of persons acting in concert and present at the scene of the crime (at 383). **Callinan J** held that where two or more people act in concert, the question whether each is liable for the completed offence is one of causation; that is, whether the acts of each has sufficiently significantly contributed to the offence (at 402–3). **Gaudron** and **Gummow JJ** dissented.]

[See also *R v Phan* (2001) 53 NSWLR 480.]

Notes:

1. *R v Bingley* (1821) Russ & Ry 446; 168 ER 890 (Bingley's part was to impress the date lines and numbers on forged bank notes; other associates were responsible for the printing and signatures); *R v Ferguson* (1916) 17 SR (NSW) 69 at 76 (assisting in making a plate to be used for printing counterfeit notes).
2. *Errington and Others' Case* (1838) 2 Lewin 217; 168 ER 1133; *R v Clarke* [1959] VR 645.
3. *Crimes Act 1958* (Vic) s 322B.
4. *Crimes Act 1958* (Vic) s 323.
5. *R v Higgins* (1801) 2 East 5 at 19; 102 ER 269 at 274–5; *R v See Lun* (1932) 32 SR (NSW) 363 at 364; *Howell v Doyle* [1952] VLR 128 at 133/ *Jackson v Horne* (1965) 114 CLR 82 at 94.
6. *Kupferberg* (1918) 13 Cr App R 166; *R v Clarkson* [1971] 1 WLR 1402; [1971] 3 All ER 344.
7. *R v Coney* (1882) 8 QBD 534; *Wilcox v Jeffery* [1951] 1 All ER 464.
8. *Mohan v R* [1967] 2 AC 187.

9. Lanham, 'Limitations on Accomplice Liability' (1982) 6 *Criminal Law Journal* 306 at 313.
10. *R v Dunn* (1930) 30 SR (NSW) 210 at 213.
11. I say 'is' because it may be that this third category is a late development of the common law which owes its impetus to the enactment of the Accessories and Abettors Act 1861 (UK) and its counterparts in other jurisdictions, such as s 323 of the *Crimes Act 1958* (Vic), and the abolition of the distinction between felonies and misdemeanours.
12. *R v Lowery and King (No 2) [1972] VR 560.*
13. In *R v Hurse* (1841) 2 M & Rob 360 at 361; 174 ER 316 at 317, which was a case of misdemeanour, Erskine J directed the jury 'that if two persons, having jointly prepared counterfeit coin, plan the uttering, and go on a joint expedition and utter in concert and by previous arrangement the different pieces of coin, then the act of one would be the act of both, though they might not be proved to be actually together at each uttering'.
14. [1972] VR 560 at 560.
15. (1997) at 465.
16. *Tangye* (1997) 92 A Crim R 545.
17. *Tangye* (1997) 92 A Crim R 545 at 556–7.
18. *R v Howe* [1987] AC 417 at 426, 436, 438, 446, 458.
19. [1987] AC 417.
20. [1974] QB 776.
21. [1987] AC 417 at 458.
22. *Matusevich v R* (1977) 137 CLR 633.
23. (1977) 137 CLR 633.
24. (1980) 4 *Criminal Law Journal* 276 at 282.
25. Lanham, 'Complicity, Concert and Conspiracy' (1980) 4 *Criminal Law Journal* 276 at 282
26. Lanham at 287.
27. (1978) 140 CLR 108.
28. [1989] VR 97 at 123–4.
29. [1974] QB 776.
30. [1987] AC 417.
31. [1989] VR 97 at 124.
32. (1997) 137 CLR 633.
33. [1841] 2 M & Rob 360; 174 ER 316.
34. [1952] 36 CR App R 125.
35. [1972] VR 560.
36. (1977) 137 CLR 633.
37. (1978) 140 CLR 108.
38. [1992] 1 AC 34.
39. (1980) 143 CLR 108.
40. [1985] AC 168.
41. [1987] AC 417
42. (1997) 92 A Crim R 545.(1997) 92 A Crim R 545.
43. [1958] 42 Cr App R 266.

11.14 Illustrations and questions

1. D was charged with the murder of his wife and two infant children. All three had died by drowning late one evening in a public swimming pool. The Crown case was that the accused had deliberately drowned each of them. D gave evidence that, following a quarrel, his wife had drowned herself and the children and that he had unsuccessfully tried to rescue them. After the jury retired, they returned and the foreman asked the judge what the position would be if 'the woman took the children into the water without the assistance of putting them in the water by the man, but that he stood by, conniving to the act?' The judge directed the jury that a failure to discharge his parental duty to seek to prevent his wife from killing the children would render D guilty of manslaughter. The judge further directed the jury that if D was encouraging and persuading his wife to commit suicide and to do away with the children at the same time, then he would be guilty of murder. The jury returned a verdict of guilty on three counts of manslaughter. On appeal the Supreme Court of Victoria unanimously dismissed the appeal in relation to the children, and by a majority in relation to the wife (Cussen ACJ and Mann J, McArthur J dissenting): *R v Russell* [1933] VLR 59. Cussen ACJ stated (at 66):

   > I am of opinion (1) that if a person present at the commission of a crime in the opinion of the jury on sufficient evidence shows his assent to such commission, he is guilty as a principal, and (2) that assent may in some cases be properly found by the jury to be shown by the absence of dissent, or in the absence of what may be called an effective dissent.

   Note that Cussen ACJ's reasoning could no longer be applied in respect of the wife if such a case were to occur again, since suicide is, of course, no longer a crime. Why do you think the jury found the accused guilty of manslaughter of all three? Possibly they misunderstood the trial judge's direction in relation to parental duty as applying to the wife as well as the children and convicted on this basis. If this is a real possibility, then was not the accused entitled to an acquittal in respect of the wife? Alternatively, the jury viewed the accused as encouraging his wife at the time of her suicide.

2. *R v Russell* was followed and applied in *R v Clarke and Wilton* [1959] VR 645 where the defendants were convicted of the manslaughter of a child to whom they stood in loco parentis. The evidence showed that the child had died from injuries received as the result of one or more of a series of blows struck on different occasions by each of the defendants. On each occasion the other defendant was present. Although the evidence failed to establish which blow was fatal and who had inflicted it, it was held that both were properly convicted, on the basis either that they were acting in concert in

beating the child or that each had failed in his or her parental duty to protect the child from harm inflicted unlawfully by the other.

3. D was convicted of murder. Many injuries were inflicted upon V over a long period during which V was held prisoner, some by D personally and others by other persons, often while D was absent. The basis of the Crown case was that death had been caused by the combined effect of all the injuries and that all the injuries had been inflicted by D personally or by persons under his control. The trial judge directed the jury that D was criminally responsible for his own acts and for the acts of other persons who were under his control. The jury was not directed on the basis that D and the others acted in concert or that D counselled or procured, or aided and abetted, the others. Held, the judge's direction constituted misdirection. It was wrong to say that D, by reason of the 'control' which he exercised, should have the acts of the other men attributed to him so that he might be regarded as having caused the injuries which they inflicted. Except in the case of innocent agency and vicarious liability, the acts of a person may not be attributed to another as a matter of causation so as to render the other criminally liable. For the purposes of the criminal law, one person does not cause another to act where the act of that other is wholly voluntary. However, the misdirection on complicity did not cause a miscarriage of justice. On the evidence (including admissions by D's counsel at trial) no reasonable jury could have failed to find that the injuries inflicted upon V personally by D were a substantial cause of death and that D inflicted those injuries with intent to cause really serious bodily injury: *R v Franklin* (2001) 3 VR 9.
4. For another case on somewhat similar facts to *Franklin*, see *Likiardopoulos v The Queen* [2012] HCA 37. In *Likiardopoulos*, the appellant was one of a number of people involved in the sustained, brutal beating of an intellectually handicapped man, who subsequently died of injuries sustained. The appellant was the only person to be charged with murder, the others accepting guilty pleas to lesser offences. He appealed to the Court of Appeal in Victoria against his conviction for murder on the basis (inter alia) that the Crown had not established that he had been present when the act or acts causing death were carried out. The appellant was 47-years-old, and in a position of dominance over the other parties to the assaults. He had urged his co-accused to redouble their assaults on the victim. The Court of Appeal agreed with the trial judge that the appellant was liable as a principal offender if he was a party to an understanding or arrangement to inflict really serious injury to the deceased, and that while that arrangement was on foot, one or more of the parties to the arrangement did the acts which caused death intending to do really serious injury to the deceased. It was not necessary to prove that the appellant had been present throughout the whole of the

time during which the assaults took place. The High Court agreed with the Court of Appeal (at 6–7 per Gummow, Hayne, Crennan, Kiefel and Bell JJ).

5. Two men took part in a prize fight — that is, a fight with bare fists — in the presence of a large crowd. The accused were among the crowd but it was not shown that they took any part in its management or said or did anything. They were tried for common assault and convicted after the chairman of quarter sessions had directed the jury that all persons who went to see a prize fight and were present when it took place were guilty as aiders and abettors. On case reserved, held, the convictions could not stand. The fight being with bare fists, and not with gloves, each blow struck constituted an assault. However, mere accidental presence at the scene of an assault was not even evidence of aiding and abetting; and presence which was not prima facie accidental could be no more than evidence of aiding and abetting from which a jury might, but were not bound to, draw a conclusion that there was encouragement: *R v Coney* (1882) 8 QBD 534 (CCR). Accord *R v Jones and Mirrless* (1977) 65 Cr App R 250.

6. D, hearing a noise, entered a room where a woman was being raped by several fellow soldiers. D stood and watched, but did no more. Held, before D could be convicted as a principal in the second degree to rape, it must be shown that he had intended to encourage and had encouraged the offence. It is not enough that his presence did encourage the others, for D might not have realised this: *R v Clarkson* [1971] 3 All ER 344. Cf *R v Brougham* (1986) 43 SASR 187.

7. Police officers who unlawfully seized property defended a civil claim for its return on the ground that, if returned, the property would be used for the commission of an offence under the Indecent Articles and Classified Publications Act 1975 (NSW). Held, rejecting the defence, an act of a person who holds property of another in returning that property to the owner in simple compliance with a demand will not make that person an accessory, even if he or she knows that the owner proposes to commit some crime with the property, provided he or she does not act with the intention of encouraging or facilitating the commission of the offence: *Gollan v Nugent* (1987) 8 NSWLR 166. On appeal the High Court affirmed the decision of the Court of Appeal of New South Wales on this point: *Gollan v Nugent* (1988) 166 CLR 18; 82 ALR 193.

8. It is a general rule that the enactment of a statutory offence automatically carries with it the liability of principals in the second degree and of accessories, even though the legislature does not expressly mention such liability. It is, however, questionable whether this general rule should be applied where the offence is one which necessarily involves two parties and the legislature

expressly penalises only one of them. Thus, a performance requires an audience. Can it be argued that to expressly penalise the performer, without mention of the audience, carries an implication that the latter are not to be criminally liable? If Parliament makes it an offence to sell something, is the buyer liable as a principal in the second degree, or should the maxim *expressio unius est exclusio alterius* be applied, so as to exclude liability on her or his part under the general rule?

In *R v Tyrell* [1894] 1 QB 710, D, a girl between the ages of 13 and 16, abetted F to have sexual intercourse with her contrary to s 5 of the Criminal Law Amendment Act 1885 (Eng). It was held that D could not be guilty as a principal in the second degree to the offence committed by F. Lord Coleridge CJ stated (at 712):

> … it is impossible to say that the Act, which is absolutely silent about aiding or abetting, or soliciting or inciting, can have intended that the girls for whose protection it was passed should be punishable under it for the offences committed upon themselves.

Accord *R v Whitehouse* [1977] 2 WLR 925. In *Scott v Killian* (1984) 36 SASR 438, on a charge of receiving money paid in a brothel in respect of prostitution, it was held that the client was not an accomplice so as to require that a warning be given as to the possible veracity of his evidence.

On the other hand, in a South Australian case, a victim of domestic violence was convicted of aiding and abetting the offence of breaching a restraining order, where she admitted a violent partner into her home: *Michelle Fay Keane* (1997) 95 A Crim R 593. This was done for 'reasons of justice and convenience', including that 'where an order is made for a person's benefit, it would seem to be unjust that the person should be able to encourage or facilitate a breach of the order thereby causing another to commit an offence … In the present case the appellant's actions, in addition to causing distress to the children, resulted in the police having to come to the house to remove the offender' (at 596).

11.15C R v Hewitt

[1997] 1 VR 301

Court of Appeal, Supreme Court of Victoria

[The accused and co-accused were charged on three counts of rape with aggravating circumstances. The accused had arranged a rendezvous with the complainant. He lured her into his vehicle and drove her to an isolated spot in a forest, picking up the co-accused on the way. The accused, when not in the presence of the co-accused, insisted to the complainant that she permit the co-accused to have sex with her and three acts of penetration were performed by the co-accused upon the complainant. The accused did not himself engage in sexual acts with the complainant resulting in penetration. The prosecution case was that the accused and co-accused had acted in concert. The trial judge, however, raised the possibility of a case against the accused as principal through the 'innocent agency' of the co-accused.

The trial judge directed the jury that they could convict the accused while acquitting the co-accused, on the basis that the accused had set up the situation, got the victim out in the forest and forced her to indulge in acts of sexual activity with the co-accused, knowing she did not consent. The jury acquitted the co-accused on all counts but found the accused guilty of rape on each count.]

Winneke P: For my own part I can see no reason in principle why a person should not be convicted of the crime of rape if that person causes and intends another to have intercourse with the innocent victim whom the 'controller' knows is not consenting. The principle which I believe to be at the core of *Cogan's* case [1976] 1 QB 217 (ie the 'innocent agent' principle) has been cited with apparent approval (albeit in different circumstances) by several courts in Australia, including our own Court of Criminal Appeal: see *R v Matusevich and Thompson* [1976] VR 470 at 478, 480; *R v Demirian* [1989] VR 97 at 118; *Giorgianni v R* (1981) 7 A Crim R 204; *Schultz v Pettitt* (1980) 25 SASR 427. The principle has also been applied, in a rape case, in the Republic of South Africa: see *S v Ncanywa* 1993 (2) SA 567 at 576.

It is true that, in the cases of *Matusevich, Giorgianni* and *Schultz v Pettitt,* the courts appeared to regard *Cogan's* case as authority for the proposition that an accused person could be convicted as an aider and abettor even though the principal offender had been acquitted: *Matusevich* at 430, *Giorgianni* at 205 and *Schultz v Pettitt* at 437–8. However when the case of *Matusevich* went on appeal to the High Court ((1977) 137 CLR 633), the Chief Justice (Sir Harry Gibbs) was the only member of the court who specifically commented on this aspect of the Court of Criminal Appeal's decision. He said at 638:

> However, the reasoning in *R v Bourne* ... suggests that there are cases in which a person may be liable for aiding and abetting another to commit a crime, although the actual perpetrator is not criminally responsible. The law on this question remains unsettled (see *R v Cogan*) but it is unnecessary to pursue this matter.

As I have already said, I have some conceptual difficulty in supporting the proposition that a person can be convicted as an aider and abettor when the principal offender has been acquitted. The proposition appears to have been justified on the basis that if the principal offender's act has been wrongful but excusable (eg on the grounds of insanity or duress or status or mistaken belief) a conviction of a co-accused as an aider and abettor is nonetheless supportable provided that the aider and abettor has the requisite *mens rea:* see Professor Fletcher, *Rethinking Criminal Law,* (1978), pp 664–5; R D Taylor,

'Complicity and Excuses' [1983] *Crim LR* 656. Indeed it would seem that this was the justification for supporting the convictions in such cases as *Bourne* and *R v Austin* [1981] 1 All ER 374.

However, it seems to me that the principle so espoused runs counter to the basic proposition of the common law that the liability of the accessory is derivative from the liability of the principal offender. The general rule is, and so far as I am aware, always has been that unless there is a perpetrator of a crime, there cannot be an accessory: *R v Tyler and Price* (1838) 8 Car & P 616; 173 ER 643; *Cain v Doyle* (1946) 72 CLR 409. As Professor Glanville Williams commented in his aforesaid *Textbook of Criminal Law* at p 368:

> The general rule is not merely a piece of pedantry. The law of complicity cannot turn non- crimes into crimes.

Notwithstanding, there does appear to be a growing body of authority to support the view that, in some circumstances, an accused person can be convicted of aiding and abetting when the principal offender has been acquitted: cf per Street CJ in *Giorgianni* at 205. It is unnecessary in the resolution of this case to determine whether that is correct or what those circumstances might be.

It is my view, as I have already indicated, that the true basis for sustaining the conviction of Leak in the case of *Cogan and Leak* did not depend on accessorial liability but rather liability as a principal offender through the doctrine of 'innocent agency'. Understood in these terms the decision in *Cogan* is consistent with authority: see Gillies, *The Law of Criminal Complicity* (1980) p 141; where the author attacks the criticism of *Cogan* as 'unduly narrow'. The concept of the 'innocent agent' is a concept well known to the common law and has long been used to support the conviction of a person as a principal in the first degree, of a crime where the 'agent' was merely the instrument used by the accused to commit the crime: see *R v Paterson* [1976] 2 NZLR 394 at 396. For the purposes of the doctrine the 'innocence' of the 'agent' is not to be regarded as requiring the absence of moral responsibility or fault. In my view there is no reason why this principle cannot apply to the crime of rape where the circumstances justify it, as they did in *Cogan and Leak.* This is certainly so now in this state, where the legislature has re-defined the crime of rape as one which is 'gender neutral'. What has to be demonstrated in order to support a conviction on this basis (as the court said in *Cogan and Leak)* is that the accused wanted and intended the act of intercourse by 'the agent' to take place and, by his conduct, caused the act to occur when he knew that the victim was not consenting.

[**Callaway JA** delivered a separate judgment agreeing with **Winneke P. Hampel AJA** agreed.]

[See also *R v Bourne* (1952) 36 Cr App R 125; *R v D* 1969 (2) SA 591; *R v Cogan and Leak* [1976] 1 QB 217.]

11.16C Matusevich v R

(1977) 137 CLR 633; 15 ALR 117
High Court of Australia

[The accused and one Thompson were jointly charged with murder. The accused, Thompson, and the deceased were in the same ward of a division of Pentridge Gaol, and were the only prisoners in that ward. The deceased was killed by blows inflicted with an axe. When interviewed by the police, Thompson stated that his memory was vague but that he remembered losing his head and hitting the deceased on the head with the axe. At the trial of the two accused, the principal issues in dispute concerned which of the two struck the blows which killed the deceased and whether there had been concert between them in the commission of the crime.

Thompson's counsel cross-examined the accused with a view to suggesting that the accused was solely responsible for the killing, but the accused made no significant concessions in the course of that cross-examination. On behalf of Thompson, evidence was called to show that he was legally insane at the time of the killing. The accused gave evidence in which he said, in effect, that he was locked up in the ward with a madman, Thompson, who not only killed the deceased but threatened to kill him if he gave the alarm.

The trial judge directed the jury that insanity was not relevant to whether the accused and Thompson had acted in concert. He stated that should the jury find Thompson not guilty on the ground of insanity, they could not then find the accused guilty of aiding and abetting (that is, as a principal in the second degree) — this did not apply in relation to acting in concert.

Both Thompson and the accused were convicted of murder. They appealed to the Court of Criminal Appeal (Vic). That court took the view that the jury had not been properly instructed on the issue of insanity and that the verdict against Thompson should be set aside and a new trial ordered. On the new trial of Thompson, a properly instructed jury found him not guilty on the ground of insanity. The accused did not succeed in his appeal.

The accused then appealed to the High Court on the ground, inter alia, that it was not possible to act in concert with an insane person in the commission of a crime. The accused's appeal was allowed on the ground that, when cross-examined by counsel for Thompson, he had been improperly asked questions relating to his prior criminal convictions and bad character. A new trial was ordered.

In the course of giving judgment, several members of the High Court discussed the liability of an accused who engages in the commission of a crime with an insane person.]

Gibbs ACJ: Since there may be a new trial I shall briefly express my views on certain other questions that have been raised. It was submitted on behalf of the applicant that the fact that the other accused man (Thompson) was insane meant that the jury could not properly find that the two accused acted in concert. The law as to the liability of persons who act in concert in committing a crime was stated by Smith J in *R v Lowery and King (No 2)* [1972] VR 560 as follows:

> The law says that if two or more persons reach an understanding or arrangement that together they will commit a crime and then, while that understanding or

> arrangement is still on foot and has not been called off, they are both present at the scene of the crime and one or other of them does, or they do between them, in accordance with their understanding or arrangement, all the things that are necessary to constitute the crime, they are all equally guilty of that crime regardless of what part each played in its commission.

What is necessary, for this principle to apply, is that the two or more persons concerned had a common design, or in other words had formed a common intention and were acting together in a common enterprise to achieve an object which was in law criminal. The question whether two persons have entered into an agreement, or have made an arrangement, or formed an understanding, to pursue a particular object is simply one of fact. The circumstance that one of the persons concerned is insane is relevant to that issue, but insanity sufficient to amount to a defence to a criminal charge does not necessarily render the person whose mind is diseased incapable of making an agreement or arrangement or reaching an understanding with another. Whether insanity will have that effect will no doubt depend, amongst other things, on the form which the disease takes. For example, a man who suffers from such a defect of reason from disease of the mind as not to know that it is wrong to kill may nevertheless be quite capable of agreeing with another person to kill a third person.

But if the insanity of Thompson was such that he was incapable of reaching any agreement, arrangement or understanding with the applicant, it does not follow that the latter must be acquitted if the death of Whateley was caused by the acts of Thompson. If the applicant incited Thompson to kill Whateley, the applicant would be guilty of murder, since Thompson, if insane, would then be treated as the applicant's innocent agent. If there was no preconcert between the two accused, and the applicant did not influence Thompson to act as he did, the applicant may nevertheless be convicted if he was present and assisted Thompson when the latter struck the fatal blows. The learned trial judge directed the jury that if they found Thompson not guilty on the ground of insanity they could not find the applicant guilty of aiding and abetting. The view that a person cannot be convicted on a charge of aiding and abetting another to commit a crime when the person who actually perpetrated the criminal act was of unsound mind, and was therefore himself not criminally responsible, is supported by *R v Tyler and Price* (1838) 8 C&P 616; 173 ER 643, where Lord Denman CJ (at 618, 644 of ER) told the jury that in such a case 'there will be no foundation on which the accessory crime can rest'. However, the reasoning in *R v Bourne* (1952) 36 Cr App R 125 suggests that there are cases in which a person may be liable for aiding and abetting another to commit a crime, although the actual perpetrator is not criminally responsible. The law on this question remains unsettled (see *R v Cogan* [1975] 3 WLR 316 at 319; [1975] 2 All ER 1059 at 1061), but it is unnecessary to pursue the matter. If the applicant knew that Thompson intended to strike Whateley blows of considerable severity with an axe, and, himself intending that Whateley should be killed or seriously injured, assisted Thompson, the applicant would be guilty of murder. It would be an affront to justice and to common sense that Thompson's insanity should exculpate the applicant in those circumstances. If authority is needed to show that the applicant would be guilty in such a case, *R v Tyler and Price* provides it. Opinions may differ as to the basis of that decision. It may be that the lunatic there was regarded as the innocent agent of the accused. Or it may be that the case establishes that an accused person may act in concert with a lunatic even if the latter is, for his part, not capable of making an agreement.

The jury on a new trial need not be troubled by a charge which endeavours to explain these niceties. Nor should they be asked for special findings. What would be necessary would be to instruct them clearly as to the facts of whose existence they would have to be satisfied before they could convict. If upon a new trial the jury find that Thompson and not the applicant struck the blows that killed Whateley, they may convict the applicant of murder, notwithstanding that Thompson was insane, if they are satisfied either that the two men acted in concert or that, whether there was preconcert or not, the applicant, intending that Whateley should be killed or seriously injured, procured Thompson to strike him with an axe, or assisted him when he did so.

Aickin J: Although the point already dealt with is sufficient to dispose of this case, the other two points are likely to arise in a further trial of the applicant and should therefore be dealt with. The first of the three points argued before us was whether it was possible to act in concert with a lunatic and involves inquiring as to what is meant by 'consensus' or 'concert' and the significance of *mens rea* in a 'consensus'. It was argued that concert in this sense exists only when two or more persons agree to carry out some crime. If they have not in fact so agreed then, in such a case as this, one may be a principal and the other merely an aider or abettor. The question is what is the scope of the agreement required to make the act done something which is done in concert. It was argued that where intention is a necessary element in the crime there must be sharing of that intention, and that it was not enough to show agreement to do the physical act only without the agreement extending to a common criminal intention. It was then said that insanity affects the capacity to have the necessary intention and that if you cannot find the sharing of that intention you cannot find that the acts are done in concert. As an alternative it was put that the jury should be told to consider the nature of the insanity in question in order that they should consider whether that insanity was such as to make it impossible for the formation of a common criminal intent. The trial judge directed the jury that insanity was not relevant to the intention with which an act was done and was not relevant to whether or not there was a concert.

The Court of Criminal Appeal said that the necessary concert is:

> ... constituted by the assent together of the participants to do the act [ie the *actus reus* alone] and that it may be evidenced by their conduct. The fact that a man is insane for the purposes of the criminal law does not necessarily mean that he is incapable of assenting together with another man to an act. He may not know that the act is wrong but he may still assent to do it.

The court referred to the distinction between the *actus reus* and the *mens rea* which together constitute the crime of murder and said:

> In this case the *actus reus* was made up of the unlawful striking of the blow or blows which caused the death of the deceased, and the resultant death itself. Leaving

> aside for the moment the effect of the insanity of one man, if the two men assented together to the striking of the blow or blows, then once it was established that the striking was unlawful and that death resulted from it, the two men were acting in concert in the *actus reus* of the crime. Any question as to their knowledge that the striking was unlawful or that death would or might result or as to their respective intentions would arise only in determining whether either had a *mens rea*.

And they therefore held that the assent of a sane man and an insane man to do the physical acts which constitute the *actus reus* makes the sane man guilty if he had the necessary *mens rea,* although the insane man is not guilty. …

The question whether there can be a common intent with respect to the commission of a crime between a sane man and a lunatic is almost devoid of direct authority and no material discussion is to be found in the textbooks. I do not think, however, that the problem of whether there can be the requisite concert can always be solved by reference to the so-called doctrine of the 'innocent agent'.

I am in agreement with the views of the Court of Criminal Appeal when they say that:

> … the question whether in a particular case the sane and the insane man were acting in concert requires of course an examination of the evidence. The nature of the insanity may preclude the insane man from being capable of the assent which is necessary for the two men to be acting in concert.

They go on to say:

> That would not mean that the sane man would not be guilty in respect of his own participation in the events which caused the death and the concept of innocent agency might well apply to make him liable for the acts of the insane man. But in such a case, the matter could not be put on the basis of acting in concert.

The evidence given at the trial, however, would not have justified the view that there was anything in the nature of innocent agency in the present case. The difficulty is that all that the trial judge said in the course of his charge was that, although if the jury found Thompson not guilty on the ground of insanity they could not find Matusevich guilty of aiding and abetting (whether that is right or wrong is not material), 'that does not apply in relation to concert'. This appears to me to be inadequate, although in the event the jury did not act on that, or rather had no occasion to act upon it, because they did not find Thompson to be insane. A proper direction, however, would have to advert to the question whether the nature of the insanity may preclude the insane man from being capable of the necessary assent to produce action in concert. It would not be enough to say that all the jury had to consider was whether the condition of the insane man was such that his mind went with the doing of the *actus reus.* The jury should also be told that they must consider whether the nature of the insanity, if they find insanity, is such as to make it impossible for there to be any concert between the two accused. They should be told that if they find that one accused did not understand the nature or quality of the act which he in fact did, then there could be no concert between the two accused. They should also be told that, if the basis for their finding of insanity was that the accused did not know that what he did was wrong, they may find that the two accused acted in concert, if they are satisfied that there was an actual agreement or common understanding. The way in which such a matter should be expressed in a charge cannot usefully be considered further in the abstract, as it must depend upon the particular evidence in the particular case.

[**Mason** and **Murphy JJ** delivered judgments in which they agreed with the views of **Aickin J**. **Stephen J** expressed his agreement with the views of **Aickin J** and **Gibbs ACJ**. Appeal allowed and a new trial ordered.]

11.17 Further reading

G Hubble, 'Rape by Innocent Agent' (1997) 21 *Crim LJ* 204

D Lanham, 'Three Cases of Accessorial Absurdity?' (1990) 53 *MULR* 75

SCOPE OF THE OFFENCE AND RESPONSIBILITY OF PARTIES

11.18 As a matter of principle, a person should only be guilty of a criminal offence if he or she has a guilty mind. In the context of accessorial liability, this has been held to mean that an accessory is only liable if they have intentionally assisted or encouraged the principal offender. As the High Court said in *Giorgianni* (1985) 156 CLR 473 at 505 (see **11.31C**): '[A]iding, abetting, counseling or procuring the commission of an offence requires the intentional assistance or encouragement of the doing of those things which go to make up the offence'.

This formulation has been criticised as too restrictive, imposing a more stringent standard for the criminal liability of an accessory than that imposed for a principal offender, making it unduly difficult for the prosecution to prove an accessory's guilt. That this is not always the case is illustrated by the application of the *Giorgianni* principle to felony murder or constructive murder cases: see, for example, *R v R* (1995) 63 SASR 417 (see **11.20**).

Different principles apply where the crime committed by the principal offender is different from or beyond that actually agreed between the parties. At common law, the situation is governed by the so-called doctrine of common purpose. According to this doctrine, each party is liable not only for what was agreed, but also for possible consequences which were within the contemplation of the parties (see *McAuliffe* (1995) 183 CLR 108 at 115 (at **11.23C**)). In addition, a series of High Court cases since *McAuliffe* has established that the accessory is liable for offences that are outside the scope of the common purpose, but that he or she has foreseen (see *Gillard* (2003) 219 CLR 1 (at **11.24C**); *Clayton; Hardwick* (2006) 231 ALR 500 (at **11.25C**)).

This doctrine, known as the doctrine of 'extended common purpose', has been criticised as a form of 'constructive guilt' or 'guilt by criminal association'. Arguably, it is illogical and unfair to convict an accessory on the basis of foresight alone, where intent or recklessness is required of the principal offender. Kirby J in dissent in *Clayton; Hartwick* suggested a compromise solution in which the prosecution would have to prove that the defendant knew it was virtually certain (as opposed to merely possible) that the principal offender would act as he or she did ((2006) 231 ALR 500 at 532). However, this approach has not found favour in Australia or England (see *Powell* [1997] 3 WLR 959; A Simester, 'The Mental Element in Complicity' (2006) 122 *LQR* 578).

In general, therefore, where two or more persons are parties to a joint criminal enterprise, each is equally liable for the consequences of such acts of the other as are performed as part of that enterprise. Thus if A and B agree to assault C, and the assault is committed by A and C dies, A and B are responsible for the death of C. This does not mean that they will each be guilty of the same crime in respect of that death. If A intended an assault involving grievous bodily harm and B intended an assault involving lesser injury only, then A will be guilty of the murder of C and B will be guilty of the manslaughter of C. If, however, the principal actor goes beyond what was counselled or agreed upon, so that he or she is in effect engaged upon a different criminal enterprise, then an abettor is not liable for the consequences of that unauthorised act. Thus if A and B agree to steal from C, the agreement involving neither violence nor the use of any weapon but, unknown to B, A carries a gun and deliberately shoots and kills C, the difference between what was agreed and what occurred is such that B will bear no responsibility for the death of C.

The following cases deal with issues as to the responsibility of different parties to a criminal enterprise, and with the issues involved in distinguishing between what is a consequence of an agreed criminal enterprise and what in fact amounts to a different enterprise.

11.19C

Varley v R

(1976) 12 ALR 347
High Court of Australia

[The accused was charged with murder and convicted of manslaughter. He and two police officers went to the deceased's residence to beat him up in order to compel him to pay over part of the proceeds of illegal transactions in which all three, as well as others, were engaged. There was evidence that a police baton was in the vehicle which took them to the residence of the deceased, and that this baton was used in the fatal assault on the deceased. The accused's defence, rejected by the jury, was that he had been no more than an unwilling spectator of the assault, coerced by the police into being there at all.

The trial judge directed the jury in relation to manslaughter to the effect that if they concluded that there was a joint enterprise to give the deceased a hiding not amounting to grievous bodily harm and if, during the enterprise, the police used a baton to inflict a degree of force which was beyond what Varley had expected, the police would be guilty of murder and Varley guilty of manslaughter. On appeal to the High Court the accused submitted that the use of the baton was beyond the scope of the criminal enterprise so that the accused was not criminally liable for the consequences of such use.]

Barwick CJ: The appellant's submission is that the use of the baton, or cosh, was beyond the scope of the common enterprise, so that the appellant was not criminally liable for the consequences of such use: and that, in any case, the jury ought specifically to have been told that they must be satisfied that the use of a baton or cosh was within the scope of the common enterprise.

I am clearly of opinion, however, that, even on the assumption that the appellant did not know of the availability of the baton or cosh, or of its intended use (an assumption the jury were not bound to accept), it could not reasonably be held that the use of such an instrument or weapon as a baton or cosh was not in all the circumstances within the scope of the common design to beat or 'rough up' the deceased. The judge, in my opinion, placed the use of the weapon in its correct perspective when he treated it, if its use was not foreseen by the appellant, as no more than an unexpected incident in carrying out the common design. The circumstances of the case are not the same as those in *R v Anderson and Morris* [1966] 2 QB 110, [1966] 2 All ER 644, which was pressed upon us by the appellant's counsel. There a knife was carried and used with intent to kill by stabbing. It was there possible to regard its use as beyond the scope of the common design to which it was established the accused in that case was a party. Here the use of the baton or cosh, even if not actually contemplated, was clearly a likely means of carrying out the plan of beating up Burton: and obviously within the scope of that plan. There is therefore no need to discuss the question whether or not the judge gave specific attention in his summing up to the scope of the common design.

[**Stephen**, **Mason**, **Jacobs** and **Aickin JJ** agreed with **Barwick CJ**. Appeal dismissed.]

11.20 Illustrations

1. Because of dire financial distress and for the purpose of insurance gain for his widow, W, and to avoid imprisonment for fraud, V conspired with D1, W and D2 that he be shot. D1 was to do the shooting and V agreed to go on with the plan 'no matter what happens'. The four drove to the agreed place. At the last moment, V withdrew his consent to die. D1 then shot him. D1, W and D2 were convicted of murder. On appeal to the Supreme Court of South Africa. Held, by Steyn CJ and Potgieter JA, that the common purpose was murder with the consent of V, and that D1 had acted outside that common purpose. W and D2, accordingly, were not guilty of murder. They were, however, guilty of attempted murder, since D1 had reached the stage of an attempt before V withdrew his consent. Holmes JA, dissenting, stated: 'Looking squarely at the whole train of events, the conspiracy was fulfilled in death, and there is no room for exquisite niceties of logic about

the exact limits of the mandate in the conspiratorial common purpose': *R v Robinson* 1968 (1) SA 666.

2. B and E agreed that, while armed with loaded weapons, they would go to a house and threaten the occupants with those weapons. In the course of doing this, B shot a dog. B also went into an occupied room and fired two shots at a wall. E went into another room and murdered the occupant of it. The trial judge directed the jury, in relation to B, that if he foresaw a substantial risk that E would, in the course of the enterprise, shoot someone with the intention of at least causing really serious harm, then B should be found guilty of murder. Both B and E were convicted of murder. On appeal, held, the trial judge was correct in his direction: *R v Britten and Eger* (1988) 49 SASR 47.
3. D1 and D2 were convicted of murder. They had entered a restaurant, run by V and his wife, armed with knives and wearing balaclavas. They intended to rob the restaurant. In the course of a scuffle, V was fatally stabbed. D2 gave evidence that D1 stabbed the victim and that he neither believed that the knives would be used nor considered the possibility of violence taking place. The trial judge directed the jury that the perpetrator was guilty of felony murder if he caused the victim's death by a deliberate stab wound that occurred in the course of, or in furtherance of, a felony involving violence or danger. The trial judge told the jury that the perpetrator's companion also would be guilty of felony murder if he was party to a joint criminal enterprise to commit a felony that involved violence and danger to life, and that death occurred in the course of, or in furtherance of, that felony. On appeal by D2, held, conviction affirmed. If the policy is accepted that the actual perpetrator should be liable for the unintended consequences of her or his actions in the course of the felony, there appears to be no reason of policy why other participants in the felony should not also have to accept the same responsibility: *R v R* (1995) 63 SASR 417.
4. D was charged with the murder of two people and convicted of the manslaughter of both. The case for the Crown was that the victims were killed by a co-offender and that D was guilty of murder via common purpose or joint enterprise and that D was present when the victims were killed. Held, conviction set aside and a new trial ordered. In cases of homicide by joint enterprise or common design, the general principle is that if the common design incorporates the intention to use force or grievous bodily harm on the victim and if the victim is killed, then the parties are all guilty of murder. If, however, the agreement was such that the participants would be guilty of manslaughter, or the use of the weapon was no more than an unexpected incident in carrying out the common design, the inactive participant may be convicted of manslaughter. Where the principal assailant has gone completely beyond the scope of the common design and acted in

a way that no party to the common design could suspect, the inactive party may be not guilty of homicide at all. The direction of the trial judge had not adequately dealt with the need to consider the scope of the joint enterprise: *R v Zappia* (2002) 84 SASR 206.

11.21C Johns v R

(1980) 143 CLR 108; 28 ALR 155
High Court of Australia

[The accused joined with two others in planning an armed robbery of a well-known receiver of stolen property. The accused drove one of the principal offenders to a point near the block of flats in which the victim lived. There they met the other principal offender. The accused waited in his vehicle while the two proceeded to carry out the robbery. The accused knew one of the principal offenders was carrying a pistol, and he expected the pistol to be loaded. He knew the principal offender to be quick-tempered and violent, and he had heard the principal offender say he did not intend to let the victim 'get on top of him'. The plan was that when the robbery had been completed, the principal offenders would rejoin the accused and would hand over the proceeds to him. The accused would then take them to a pre-arranged hiding place. The plan miscarried. When the principal offenders encountered the victim outside his residence, there was a struggle and the victim was shot and killed. The accused was charged as an accessory before the fact to murder. The trial judge directed the jury that an accessory may be held liable for acts performed by the principal offender if those acts, whilst differing from what was directly and specifically intended by the accessory, were within the contemplation of the parties as acts which might be done in the course of carrying out their primary criminal intention. The accused was convicted and appealed unsuccessfully to the Supreme Court of New South Wales. On appeal to the High Court.]

Stephen J: The trial judge, in charging the jury, referred to the doctrine of common purpose as applicable to both defendants alike. He told the jury to consider for themselves the nature and extent of the joint enterprise alleged by the prosecution and, in the case of a crime of violence involving the carrying of a firearm, said that it was for them:

> ... to consider whether the parties must have had in mind the contingency that for the purpose of carrying it out or attempting to carry it out the firearm might be discharged and kill somebody. If the jury considers that a party to such a design to carry out such a crime must have been aware of such a *possibility* or *contingency* then he is responsible for the death whether he was present assisting or encouraging as a principal in the second degree, or had given assent and encouragement as an accessory before the fact (emphasis added).

Johns says that while such a direction may have been well enough in the case of Dodge, who was present at the killing aiding Watson, it was wrong in his case, that of a mere accessory before the fact not present at the killing. He should, he said, only be liable to be convicted of the murder of Morris if found by the jury to have known that, in carrying out the common purpose of robbery, it was *likely* or *probable*, and not merely 'a possibility or contingency', that Morris would be killed.

There are two main features of the applicant's argument. The first is a submission that the criminal responsibility of an accessory *before* the fact should be judged by a standard different from that of an accessory at the fact, a principal in the second degree. The second is that, according to this different standard, an accessory before the fact will only be liable for the crimes of a principal offender if they were within his contemplation as a *probable* consequence of the common purpose of the parties. ...

No trace of the distinction suggested by the applicant has ever existed in our criminal law, so carefully summarised in the judgment of Street CJ [in the Court of Criminal Appeal [1987] 1 NSWLR 282 at 284–90] and which is described in detail in Holdsworth, *A History of English Law*, vol 3, p 207 et seq; Pollock and Maitland, *The History of English Law*, vol 2, p 509 et seq and Stephen, *A History of the Criminal Law of England*, vol 2, p 229 et seq. The relative positions of accessories before the fact and of principals of both degrees may, as a broad generalisation, be summarised in the words of Glanville Williams, again p 404, where he says: 'The distinction between principals in the first and in the second degree, and between principals and accessories, generally has no legal importance.'

In the absence of any authority or of any considerations of principle supporting the applicant's suggested distinction, it must be rejected.

Counsel for the applicant did not suggest that the trial judge in any way misstated the criterion of complicity applicable to Dodge, a principal in the second degree: if, as I have concluded, no relevant distinction exists between accessories before the fact and principals in the second degree, it follows that that is enough to dispose of the present application. However, since what I have called the second feature of the applicant's submissions suggests a criterion of liability based upon probable, rather than possible, consequences, it merits consideration as a basis of liability for accomplices generally, if only for the purpose of exposing features which I regard as making it unacceptable. I turn therefore to this second feature.

The criminal responsibility here under discussion is not that relating to the crime which is the prime object of a criminal venture. As to that crime, one who, while not actually physically present and participating in its commission, nevertheless knows what is contemplated, and both approves of it and in some way encourages it thereby becomes an accessory before the act *Russell on Crime* (12th ed), vol 1, p 151. His knowledge, coupled with his actions, involves him in complicity in that crime. But if, in carrying out that contemplated crime, another crime is committed there arises the question of the complicity of those not directly engaged in its commission. The concept of common purpose provides the measure of complicity, the scope of that common purpose determining whether the accessory before the fact to the original crime is also to share in complicity in the other crime. If the scope of the purpose common both to the principal offender and to the accessory is found to include the other crime, the accessory will be fixed with criminal responsibility for it. In determining scope, it may either be restricted to what the accessory regarded as probable consequences of the criminal venture or may be extended to include what he regarded as possibly involved in the venture. To apply to such a situation a criterion of what is probable, as contrasted with what is merely possible, seems singularly inappropriate. The commission of that other crime will not have been the prime object of the criminal venture; it will in all probability have been committed as a reaction to whatever response is made by the victim, or by others who attempt to frustrate the venture, upon suddenly being confronted by the criminals. There will usually be a variety of possible responses to the criminal act. With each of these contingencies the criminals will have to reckon, if they are at all to plan their future action. What they conceive of as contingent reactions to each possible response will have, interposed between these reactions and the planned crime, at least one and perhaps a whole sequence of spontaneous and relatively unpredictable events.

In those circumstances it is understandable that criminal liability should be made to depend upon the jury's assessment of whether or not the accessory before the fact must have been aware of the *possibility* that responses by the victim or by third parties would produce the reaction by the principal offender which led to the other crime. In such a speculative area, it would be remarkable were the accessory's liability for the other crime to depend upon the jury assessing, in terms of 'more probable than not' the degree of probability or improbability which the accessory attached to the happening of the particular reaction by the principal offender which in fact occurred, itself dependent upon the intervening uncertain responses of victim or third parties. Yet that is what would be required were an accessory's responsibility to depend upon such a criterion of probability, necessarily involving a balancing process and often a nice assessment of odds. I have spoken of intervening contingencies dependent upon human responses; however to these must be added those contingencies which may arise without any human intervention.

Another and perhaps more substantial objection to the suggested criterion of probability lies in the standard of blameworthiness and responsibility which it presupposes. If applied, it would mean that an accessory before the fact to say, armed robbery, who well knows that the robber is armed with a deadly weapon and is ready to use it on his victim if the need arises, will bear no criminal responsibility for the killing which in fact ensues so long as his state of mind was that, on balance, he thought it rather less likely than not that the occasion for the killing would arise. Yet his complicity seems clear enough; the killing was within the contemplation of the parties, who contemplated 'a substantial risk' that the killing would occur: Howard, *Criminal Law*, (3rd ed), p 276. …

It is for these reasons that I agree with the approval given in my brothers' joint judgment to the passage which they cite from the judgment of Street CJ as to the criminal liability of an accessory before the fact.

I would grant special leave and dismiss the appeal.

Mason, **Murphy** and **Wilson JJ**: The Crown relied upon the doctrine of common purpose or common design in order to involve Dodge with complicity as a principal in the second degree and the applicant as an accessory before the fact. It thus became necessary for the trial judge to direct the jury on the meaning and effect of that doctrine in its application to the facts as the jury might find them. The judge directed the jury that a principal in the second degree may be held liable pursuant to the doctrine of common purpose if the act constituting the offence committed was one which the jury might regard as being within the contemplation of the parties as an act done in the course of carrying out the particular venture upon which they had embarked. The judge gave this direction and applied it not only to Dodge as a principal in the second degree but also to the applicant as an accessory before the fact. It is evident from an examination of the summing-up that the trial judge did not distinguish between Dodge and the applicant in expressing the meaning and effect of the doctrine of common purpose.

It is to this aspect of the summing-up that the applicant takes exception. The applicant's case is that the jury should have been instructed that as the applicant was an accessory before the fact, it was necessary, in order to find him guilty, for the jury to conclude that it was a likely or probable consequence of the way in which the crime was to be committed, that is, of the common purpose, that the gun would be discharged so as to kill the deceased. The applicant concedes that the doctrine of common purpose as applied to a principal in the second degree will involve him in complicity if the act constituting the offence charged was contemplated as a possibility by the parties in arriving at their common purpose or design, or if it was incidental to the execution of that purpose or design, but says that the doctrine differs when it is applied to an accessory before the fact.

The argument does not reveal any reason why as a matter of legal principle or legal conception there should be such a difference. True it is that the common law distinguishes for the purposes of classification between the accessory before the fact and the principal in the second degree, but this classification is quite unrelated to the doctrine of common purpose. The object of the doctrine is to fix with complicity for the crime committed by the perpetrator those persons who encouraged, aided or assisted him, whether they be accessories or principals. Broadly speaking, the doctrine looks to the scope of the common purpose or design as the gravamen of complicity and criminal liability. There is nothing in this to suggest that the criterion of complicity and liability should differ as between accessory and principal in the second degree. If they are both parties to the same purpose or design and that purpose or design is the only basis of complicity relied upon against each of them, there is no evident reason why one should be held liable and the other not. In each case liability must depend on the scope of the common purpose. Did it extend to the commission of the act constituting the offence charged? This is the critical question. It would make nonsense to say that the common purpose included the commission of the act in the case of the principal in the second degree but that the same common purpose did not include the commission of the same act in the case of the accessory before the fact. Yet this is precisely what the applicant's submission does say. A telling answer to it is the example given by Street CJ in his judgment in this case ([1978] 1 NSWLR 282 at 290), where he speaks of the three men who set out to carry out an armed robbery on a bank, two intending to enter the bank with loaded firearms whilst the third remains outside to drive the getaway car. In the course of the robbery a bank officer is shot and killed. The driver of the getaway car would be held liable as a principal in the second degree for the killing. If, however, the plan had involved the driver merely dropping the two armed men outside the bank and then driving off, the car driver would be an accessory before the fact. There would, as his Honour says, be no logical or legal justification for distinguishing between the complicity and liability of the driver whether he be a principal in the second degree or an accessory before the fact.

The problem here is one of expressing the degree of connection between the common purpose and the act constituting the offence charged which is required to involve the accessory and the principal in the second degree in complicity. The applicant referred to some cases in which reference has been made to the offence charged as a 'probable' consequence of the common purpose and sought to gain support from them. Two comments should be made about these cases. One is that none of them lends any countenance to the notion that the doctrine differs in its application to an accessory before the fact as compared with a principal in the second degree. The second comment is that the observations in the two cases on which the applicant principally relies relate, not to the common law, but to the interpretation of one only of two relevant provisions in statutory criminal codes. It should be noted, as will be mentioned later, that there is support for the view that the relevant code provisions reflect the common law.

[Their Honours then discussed *Brennan v R* (1936) 55 CLR 253 and *R v Guay* [1957] OR 120, cases decided respectively under the Western Australian and Canadian Criminal Codes and continued:]

The applicant derives no support from the common law cases. Indeed, the recent decisions in England and New South Wales are against him. In *R v Surridge* (1942) 42 SR (NSW) 278, Jordan CJ said (at 282):

> If two combine to effect a common criminal purpose, each is liable for any act done by the other in order to effect the purpose which was common to both of them, but not for anything done by the other which was not incidental to the carrying out of their common purpose. A person is an accomplice in the crime charged if he took part in its commission, and was 'privy to the criminal intent of the thing done': *R v Cramp* (1880) 14 Cox's Cr Cases 390–3, ie if he aided not only in the commission of what he knew to be a criminal act, but in the commission of what he knew to be, or to be likely to involve, the particular criminal act charged, so that what was done was in the course of carrying out a common purpose.

The first sentence in this passage indicates that the Chief Justice was not saying that the accused is guilty if, and only if, it was more probable than not that the criminal act charged would take place.

In *R v Smith* [1963] 1 WLR 1200, [1963] 3 All ER 597, the appellant was a participant in a concerted attack on a public-house. A barman was killed with a knife by one of the attackers inside the public-house whilst the appellant remained outside. The appellant knew that the man who stabbed the barman was carrying a knife. It was held by a bench of five judges that a conviction of manslaughter could be sustained on the ground that it must have been within the appellant's contemplation that the knife might be used and that the use was therefore within the scope of the concerted action.

In *R v Vandine* [1970] 1 NSWR 252, the appellant, a principal in the second degree, was convicted of murder. He had agreed with S and M to rob a messenger who was killed when struck by M with an iron bar which, to the appellant's knowledge, M brought to the scene of the crime. Herron CJ said (at 256):

> It seems to me to have been a matter for a common-sense jury to decide whether or not a wounding of the victim with the bar was a consequence of the conspiracy to rob. It seems to me that there was evidence fit for the jury to consider that the appellant knew that McCoy had the bar and must have known that it was intended to be used as a natural consequence if the occasion presented itself to McCoy as necessary to effect their purpose.

See also *R v Radalyski* (1899) 24 VLR 687 at 692 and *R v Murray* [1924] VLR 374.

In our opinion these decisions support the conclusion reached by Street CJ, namely:

> ... that an accessory before the fact bears, as does a principal in the second degree, a criminal liability for an act which was within the contemplation of both himself and the principal in the first degree as an act which might be done in the course of carrying out the primary criminal intention — an act contemplated as a possible incident of the originally planned particular venture: [1978] 1 NSWLR 282 at 290.

Such an act is one which falls within the parties' own purpose and design precisely because it is within their contemplation and is foreseen as a possible incident of the execution of their planned enterprise. ...

The narrow test of criminal liability proposed by the applicant is plainly unacceptable for the reason that it stakes everything on the probability or improbability of an act, admittedly contemplated, occurring. Suppose a plan made by A, the principal offender, and B, the accessory before the fact, to rob premises, according to which A is to carry out the robbery. It is agreed that A will carry a loaded revolver and use it to overcome resistance in the unlikely event that the premises are attended, previous surveillance having established that the premises are invariably unattended at the time when the robbery is to be carried out. As it happens a security officer is in attendance when A enters the premises and is shot by A. It would make nonsense to say that B is not guilty merely because it was an unlikely or improbable contingency that the premises would be attended at the time of the robbery, when we know that B assented to the shooting in the event that occurred.

In the present case there was ample evidence from which the jury could infer that the applicant gave his assent to a criminal enterprise which involved the use, that is the discharge, of a loaded gun, in the event that Morris resisted or sought to summon assistance. We need not recapitulate the evidence to which we have already referred. The jury could therefore conclude that the common purpose involved resorting to violence of this kind, should the occasion arise, and that the violence contemplated amounted to grievous bodily harm or homicide.

[**Barwick CJ** delivered a separate judgment in which he agreed with the views expressed by the other members of the court. Appeal dismissed.]

[In *Mills v R* (1986) 68 ALR 455, the High Court affirmed its decision in *Johns v R*. In *Chan Wing-siu v R* [1984] 3 All ER 877, the Privy Council followed and approved *Johns v R*.]

11.22C Miller v R

(1980) 32 ALR 321
High Court of Australia

[The accused was a close friend of one Worrell. On many occasions he drove Worrell around looking for girls whom Worrell could pick up. Once this had been achieved, he would drive Worrell and the girl to a deserted place and then leave the car whilst Worrell had sexual intercourse with the girl. On an occasion in December 1976, whilst the accused was thus away from the car, Worrell murdered the girl with him. During the following months, the accused continued to drive Worrell about for the purpose of picking up girls. On six further occasions, Worrell murdered the girls in question. On most occasions, however, no harm came to the girl with him. The accused was charged with seven counts of murder.

The case against the accused was put in two ways. First, that he had been acting in concert with Worrell in pursuance of an agreement or understanding to kill (that is, that he was a principal in the first degree) or, second, that he had aided and abetted Worrell in the murders (that is, that he was a principal in the second degree).

The trial judge directed the jury that 'if it was within the contemplation of Miller that that particular girl might be murdered, he is guilty of murder'. The accused was acquitted on the first charge, and convicted on the remaining six. He appealed unsuccessfully to the Full Court of the Supreme Court of South Australia, and then to the High Court.]

Gibbs, **Stephen**, **Mason**, **Murphy** and **Aickin JJ**: It is because we were of opinion that the last sentence of the passage containing the redirection did not contain a misdirection that we considered it necessary to express briefly our reason for refusing special leave to appeal. It was argued on behalf of the applicant that this sentence misdirected the jury as to the first basis of the Crown case — that the applicant Worrell acted in concert; it was accepted that there was no misdirection as to the aiding and abetting. The argument was that in the circumstances the applicant would be guilty of murder only if there was an agreement or understanding between himself and Worrell that the latter might murder any girl who was picked up if he wished to do so, or if the applicant foresaw that it was probable that the girl would be killed on the occasion in question. It was not enough, so it was submitted, that it was within the contemplation of the applicant that the girl might be murdered. It was said that the common design, or concert, referred to by the learned trial judge in his redirection was simply to pick up a girl, that is, a design to do something not in itself unlawful. It was wrong, so it was submitted, to tell the jury that the applicant, although not a party to any unlawful arrangement or understanding, might be convicted of murder if it was within his contemplation that the girl picked up might be murdered. It was pointed out that on most occasions the applicant drove Worrell the girl who was persuaded to enter the vehicle left it unharmed, so that on any particular occasion there was no more than a possibility that murder would be committed. Finally it was submitted that the judgments in *Johns v R* (1980) 28 ALR 155, 54 ALJR 166, provide no guidance in the present case, because in that case the parties were acting in concert to commit one crime, and in the course of the execution of their unlawful common purpose another crime was committed. [Their Honours quoted from *Johns v R* (at **10.29C**) and continued:]

It is true that these remarks were directed to a case where one of the parties to a design to commit a particular crime committed another crime in the course of the execution of that design. However, in the present case, one ground on which the case against the applicant was rested was that he was acting in concert with Worrell, and on that basis the liability of the applicant depended on the scope of the common purpose he had formed with Worrell. For the reasons about to be stated, if it was within the contemplation of himself and Worrell that the girl the subject of the charge might be murdered, he would be guilty of murder if she were murdered, notwithstanding that, on any particular occasion, it might be more probable than not that no murder would occur.

The scope of the common purpose of the applicant and Worrell, as it applied to each occasion upon which Worrell murdered a girl, would, on any view, have included the following: The applicant driving the car throughout the enterprise; Worrell finding a suitable girl and inducing her to get into the car; the applicant driving it to a secluded site and then leaving Worrell and the girl together so that they might have sexual intercourse. It was open to the jury to conclude that after the first murder had occurred the scope of the common purpose had altered. Miller now knew that Worrell not only intended sexual intercourse with the girls but might also murder them, while Worrell knew that when Miller participated in further expeditions he was fully aware of the fatal outcome of earlier expeditions. Because of these additional elements the jury might conclude that the purpose common to them both on these subsequent expeditions had altered. Because of their knowledge of one another's state of mind a new factor would be present in the recurring common purpose of the pair: when Miller would leave Worrell and a girl together, he would no longer be leaving them merely so that they might have sexual intercourse but also so that, if the mood took him, Worrell might, in Miller's absence, murder the girl. The intended role of the girl was no longer merely that of Worrell's partner in intercourse, she had become also a possible murder victim. It is significant that Miller's evidence was that he found Worrell's murderous moods to be wholly unpredictable, sudden in their onset and due to no apparent cause, thus to his knowledge putting each girl in turn at risk of death.

It, of course, requires no evidence of express agreement to establish the existence and scope of a criminal common purpose; it may be deduced from all the proven circumstances. In what was necessarily a lengthy summing up, the trial judge had dealt fully with the evidence and with the principles of law which the jury would have to apply. When the jury sought further clarification of 'the law relating to murder in relation to acting in concert' his Honour repeated to them what he had earlier told them, based upon the directions of Smith J in *R v Lowery and King (No 2)* [1972] VR 560. In his final remarks he sought to crystallise the problem before them in the light of all that had already been said to them. He referred to the original common purpose, that which prevailed before the first murder, when he spoke of the pair 'acting in concert to pick up a girl'. To that he added a further element, the contemplation of Miller that the particular girl might be murdered. If the jury were satisfied beyond reasonable doubt as to each of these then, he told them, the applicant was guilty of murder.

By his introduction of Miller's new state of mind, arising after he had discovered Worrell's killing of his first victim, his Honour brought to the minds of the jury the most material of the elements going to make up the new, extended common purpose. Had his Honour also referred to what was perhaps too obvious to require mention, Worrell's knowledge of Miller's awareness of the circumstances of the earlier murders, all the circumstances necessary for the extended common purpose would have been restated to the jury: and if they had been satisfied of the existence of that extended common purpose it would have so involved the applicant in complicity as to make him guilty of murder.

The failure to refer to Worrell's knowledge is to be viewed not only in the light of the exhaustive exposition of the fact which had taken place before the jury but also having regard to the fact that it was not Worrell but the applicant who was on trial. It might have added formal symmetry to have included a reference to Worrell's knowledge and to the way in which it operated to extend the scope of the common purpose. But to omit to do so did not result in any misdirection of the jury. The direction should reasonably have been understood as referring to a plan which included the possible murder of the girls, so that the parties to the plan contemplated, as a substantial risk, the murder of any girl who was picked up, even though it was not contemplated that murder would occur in the course of every drive. So understood, the direction was correct. The jury appear to have understood the direction in this sense. They acquitted the accused on the first charge, presumably on the footing that there was no acceptable evidence that the accused contemplated murder as a possibility. They convicted him on the other charges, no doubt on the basis that thereafter murder was contemplated as a possible outcome of the expedition. ...

Having formed the opinion that the summing up was not open to objection, we did not need to consider the possible application of the proviso. We accordingly refused special leave to appeal.

11.23C McAuliffe v R

(1995) 183 CLR 108; 130 ALR 26
High Court of Australia

[The two appellants, who were brothers, went with one Davis to a park for the purpose of robbing or bashing someone. They attacked the deceased and another, each of the three playing a role in the attack. In directing the jury, the trial judge stated that even if the common purpose of the three did not embrace the intentional infliction of grievous bodily harm, there was a sufficient intent on the part of either appellant for the purposes of murder if he contemplated the intentional infliction of grievous bodily harm by one of the other participants as a possible incident in the carrying out of their joint enterprise and continued to participate in that enterprise. The three were convicted of murder, and the appellants appealed to the High Court.]

[Footnotes to the extract appear at the end of the extract.]

Brennan CJ, **Deane**, **Dawson**, **Toohey** and **Gummow JJ**: ... The appellants contend that the trial judge was wrong in giving those directions. They submit that in a case such as the present the doctrine of common purpose requires that the intentional infliction of grievous bodily harm be part of the common purpose — that is, that it be agreed expressly or tacitly between the parties as at least a possible incident — before one party can be liable for murder arising out of the act of another committed in the course of executing the common design. In other words, the appellants contend that the realisation by one of the parties to a common design that the intentional infliction of grievous bodily harm by another party is a possible incident of the joint enterprise is not sufficient to render that party liable for a murder committed by that other party in the course of executing the common design unless that possibility was within the contemplation of all parties so as to form part of the common purpose. In our view that contention must be rejected.

The doctrine of common purpose applies where a venture is undertaken by more than one person acting in concert in pursuit of a common criminal design. Such a venture may be described as a joint criminal enterprise. Those terms — common purpose, common design, concert, joint criminal enterprise — are used more or less interchangeably to invoke the doctrine which provides a means, often an additional means, of establishing the complicity of a secondary party in the commission of a crime. The liability which attaches to the traditional classifications of accessory before the fact and principal in the second degree may be enough to establish the guilt of a secondary party: in the case of an accessory before the fact where that party counsels or procures the commission of the crime and in the case of a principal in the second degree where that party, being present at the scene, aids or abets its commission.[1] But the complicity of a secondary party may also be established by reason of a common purpose shared with the principal offender or with that offender and others. Such a common purpose arises where a person reaches an understanding or arrangement amounting to an agreement between that person and another or others that they will commit a crime. The understanding or arrangement need not be express and may be inferred from all the circumstances. If one or other of the parties to the understanding or arrangement does, or they do between them, in accordance with the continuing understanding or arrangement, all those things which are necessary to constitute the crime, they are all equally guilty of the crime regardless of the part played by each in its commission.[2]

Not only that, but each of the parties to the arrangement or understanding is guilty of any other crime falling within the scope of the common purpose which is committed in carrying out that purpose. Initially the test of what fell within the scope of the common purpose was determined objectively so that liability was imposed for other crimes committed as a consequence of the commission of the crime which was the primary object of the criminal venture, whether or not those other crimes were contemplated by the parties to that venture.[3] However, in accordance with the emphasis which the law now places upon the actual state of mind of an accused person, the test has become a subjective one and the scope of the common purpose is to be determined by what was contemplated by the parties sharing that purpose.[4]

[The court considered *Johns v R* (1980) 28 ALR 155 (at **11.21C**) and a number of other cases, and continued:]

In *Johns* this court was concerned with the common purpose of a joint criminal enterprise. In particular, it was concerned with whether the scope of the common purpose extended to possible as well as probable incidents of the venture. The scope of the common purpose is no different from the scope of the understanding or arrangement which constitutes the joint enterprise; they are merely different ways of referring to the same thing. Whatever is comprehended by the understanding or arrangement, expressly or tacitly, is necessarily within the contemplation of the parties to the understanding or arrangement. That is why the majority in *Johns* in the passage which we have cited above spoke in terms of an act which was in the contemplation of both the secondary offender and the principal offender. There was no occasion for the court to turn its attention to the situation where one party foresees, but does not agree to, a crime other than that which is planned, and continues to participate in the venture. However, the secondary offender in that situation is as much a party to the crime which is an incident of the agreed venture as he is when the incidental crime falls within the common purpose. Of course, in that situation the prosecution must prove that the individual concerned foresaw that the incidental crime might be committed and cannot rely upon the existence of the common purpose as establishing that state of mind. But there is no other relevant distinction. As Sir Robin Cooke observed, the criminal culpability lies in the participation in the joint criminal enterprise with the necessary foresight and that is so whether the foresight is that of an individual party or is shared by all parties. That is in accordance with the general principle of the criminal law that a person who intentionally assists in the commission of a crime or encourages its commission may be convicted as a party to it.

For these reasons, the trial judge was not in error in directing the jury that if the appellants were engaged in a joint criminal enterprise with Davis, a shared common intention — that is, a common purpose — to inflict grievous bodily harm or an individual contemplation of the intentional infliction of grievous bodily harm as a possible incident of the venture would be a sufficient intention on the part of either of them for the purpose of murder.

[Appeal dismissed.]

Notes:

1. See *Giorgianni v R* (1985) 156 CLR 473.
2. Cf *R v Lowery and King [No 2]* [1972] VR 560 at 560 per Smith J.
3. *Mansell* (1556) 2 Dyer 128b; 73 ER 279; *Ashton's Case* (1698) 12 Mod 256; 88 ER 1304; *R v Radalyski* (1899) 24 VLR 687; *R v Kalinowski* (1930) 31 SR (NSW) 377. See generally Smith, *A Modern Treatise on the Law of Criminal Complicity* (1991) at pp 209–14.
4. See *R v Johns* [1978] 1 NSWLR 282 at 287–90 per Street CJ.

11.24C

Gillard v R

(2003) 219 CLR 1; 202 ALR 202
High Court of Australia

[The appellant and a co-offender (Preston) were jointly tried and convicted of the murder of two men and the attempted murder of another. The co-offender shot the victims as part of a contract killing. At the request of the co-offender, the appelllant stole a van and used it to drive the co-offender to the place where the killings took place. The prosecution submitted that the appellant was a party to the plan to kill the deceased. However, the appellant maintained that he had no knowledge of the co-offender's plan and held the belief that the co-offender was going to commit an armed robbery. The trial judge did not consider a verdict of manslaughter to be reasonably open to the jury and, therefore, did not direct the jury about the availability of that verdict in relation to the facts of the case. As a result, the only options open to the jury were conviction for murder and acquittal. An appeal to the South Australian Court of Criminal Appeal was dismissed. On appeal to the High Court it was argued that an error of law had occurred due to the trial judge's failure to direct the jury that manslaughter was an available verdict.]

[Footnotes to the extract appear at the end of the extract.]

Gleeson CJ and **Callinan J**: … In the present context, we are concerned with the culpability of the appellant by reason of his complicity in the conduct of Preston. The Full Court said that, upon the robbery hypothesis, 'Gillard had been duped by Preston'. But the case is not about the vitiating effect of misrepresentation upon a contractual agreement. The question is whether, if the appellant thought he was participating in an armed hold-up, and Preston intended from the outset to kill Knowles, the appellant can be liable for culpable homicide by reason of such common purpose as they entertained. To say that Preston's purpose was different from that of the appellant does not answer the question. There was a substantial commonality of purpose, and the question is as to the legal significance of the difference.

It is established that, consistently with the principles stated in *McAuliffe* (or statutory provisions to similar effect), where death results from a joint enterprise involving violence, and the level of violence contemplated by one participant exceeds that contemplated by another, one may be guilty of murder and the other guilty of manslaughter. *Gilbert* was such a case. Examples from various jurisdictions were examined in *R v Barlow*.[1]

In *Markby v R*,[2] Gibbs ACJ said (omitting references):

> If … two men attack another without any intention to cause death or grievous bodily harm, and during the course of the attack one man forms an intention to kill the victim, and strikes the fatal blow with that intention, he may be convicted of murder while the other participant in the plan may be convicted of manslaughter. The reason why the principal assailant is guilty of murder and the other participant only of manslaughter in such a case is that the former had an actual intention to kill whereas the latter never intended that death or grievous bodily harm be caused to the victim, and if there had not been a departure from the common

> purpose the death of the victim would have rendered the two participants guilty of manslaughter only. In some cases the inactive participant in the common design may escape liability either for murder or manslaughter. If the principal assailant has gone completely beyond the scope of the common design, and for example 'has used a weapon and acted in a way which no party to that common design could suspect', the inactive participant is not guilty of either murder or manslaughter. If however the use of the weapon, even if its existence was unknown to the other party, is rightly regarded as no more than an unexpected incident in carrying out the common design the inactive participant may be convicted of manslaughter.[3]

The concluding sentence of that passage, raises what, as it appears to us, is the potential significance of the supposition that Preston 'duped' the appellant, although the reference to the possibility that the existence of the weapon was unknown to the other party is not presently material.

[Their Honours referred to *R v Collie* (1991) 56 SASR 302, and continued:]

A question that arose was whether the death of Knowles was causally related to an act for which the appellant was criminally responsible. The act causing his death was the presentation and discharge of the weapon by Preston. The issue is whether, and to what extent, the appellant was criminally responsible for that act. The resolution of that issue depends upon the scope of the common criminal design, and the foresight of the appellant.

Collie was not followed in a recent decision of the Full Court of the Supreme Court of South Australia. In *R v Zappia*,[4] a case decided after the Full Court's decision in the present case, the appellant was convicted of manslaughter. The appellant and a co-offender went to the deceased's apartment. The appellant's case was that he knew the co-offender intended to threaten the deceased with a gun. There was evidence that the appellant knew the gun was or might be loaded. The co-accused shot and killed the deceased. The appellant said he did not expect this to happen. The conviction was upheld. Doyle CJ, with whom Lander J and Martin J agreed, referred to counsel's submission that if, unknown to the appellant, the co- offender intended to kill the victim from the outset, and then killed the victim deliberately, the jury could not convict of manslaughter unless satisfied that the deliberate killing of the victim 'was not an unexpected event completely outside the scope of the joint enterprise'.[5] The submission was put alternatively in terms of causation. Reliance was placed upon *Collie*. Doyle CJ distinguished that case as turning on its own facts and preferred to follow the statement of principle made by Gibbs ACJ in *Markby*.[6]

He said:[7]

> As I observed earlier, the relevant direction was given on the basis that the jury was satisfied that Mr Zappia knew Mr Kamleh was carrying a loaded gun and intended to use it to threaten Mr Rasti. That is an important point. Mr Zappia knew that a dangerous weapon was being taken to the scene. Having regard to the nature of the joint enterprise … an inevitable conclusion was that if, in the course of the confrontation, Mr Kamleh formed an intention to kill, that was no more than an unexpected incident in the carrying out of the common design … Would

> it make any difference if it were a reasonable possibility that Mr Kamleh formed the intention to kill relatively early in the piece, perhaps shortly before, or as the men entered the apartment? My view is that in the circumstances of this case it would not. The joint enterprise that is posited was, all along, to confront Mr Rasti, and to use the loaded pistol to threaten him. I do not consider that it makes any difference when Mr Kamleh formed the intention to kill.

We agree with that approach. The present case illustrates the artificiality of a distinction, in the circumstances under consideration, based upon when an intention to kill was formed by a primary offender. The appellant stole a van and used it to deliver Preston to Knowles' premises, having first checked to make sure that Knowles was present. On the assumed facts, he knew that Preston was armed with a loaded gun. He waited outside the premises to assist Preston to escape. Preston shot Knowles with intent to kill. There is no reason why the existence and degree of the responsibility of the appellant for the killing of Knowles should depend upon whether Preston decided to kill him on the spur of the moment, or shortly before they arrived at the premises, or whether that was his intention from the time when he arranged for the appellant to assist him.

In *McAuliffe*,[8] the court said:

> There was no occasion [in *Johns v R*[9]] for the Court to turn its attention to the situation where one party foresees, but does not agree to, a crime other than that which is planned, and continues to participate in the venture. However, the secondary offender in that situation is as much a party to the crime which is an incident of the agreed venture as he is when the incidental crime falls within the common purpose. Of course, in that situation the prosecution must prove that the individual concerned foresaw that the incidental crime might be committed and cannot rely upon the existence of the common purpose as establishing that state of mind ... As Sir Robin Cooke observed, the criminal culpability lies in the participation in the joint criminal enterprise with the necessary foresight ... That is in accordance with the general principle of the criminal law that a person who intentionally assists in the commission of a crime or encourages its commission may be convicted as a party to it.

The general principle there referred to extends to the possibility that a person who intentionally assists in homicide may be guilty of manslaughter even though the principal offender is guilty of murder. The existence of that possibility assumes a difference in the intentions of the two parties. The secondary party may not know of, or foresee, the principal offender's murderous intention, but may foresee the possibility of the act causing death as an incident of the common design. The essence of the reasoning in the above passage is that, when the secondary party continues to participate in the venture without having agreed to, but foreseeing as a possibility, the act causing death, that party is regarded as intentionally assisting in the commission of a crime. In the present case, if a jury decided that the appellant foresaw as a possibility that Preston would fire the loaded gun at Knowles, and continued to participate with that foresight, then he would be intentionally assisting in the commission of culpable homicide. The level of his own culpability would depend upon whether he foresaw that Preston might act with intent to kill or cause grievous bodily harm.

In our view, there was a viable case of manslaughter to be left to the jury, and the refusal to leave that case was a wrong decision on a question of law.

This raises the question of the proviso. *Gilbert* decides that it is not an answer to the appellant's argument to point out that, since the jury were properly (albeit conservatively) instructed on the elements of murder, and since they convicted the appellant of murder, there is, on that account alone, no miscarriage of justice. It is unnecessary to repeat the reasons for that. The jury were wrongly deprived of an opportunity to consider an intermediate position.

[**Kirby** and **Hayne JJ** delivered separate judgments agreeing that the appeal should be allowed. **Gummow J** agreed with **Hayne J**. Appeal allowed and a new trial ordered.]

Notes:

1. (1997) 188 CLR 1.
2. (1978) 140 CLR 108 at 112–113.
3. See also *Reid* (1975) 62 Cr App R 109 at 112.
4. (2002) 84 SASR 206.
5. *R v Zappia* (2002) 84 SASR 206 at 221.
6. *R v Zappia* (2002) 84 SASR 206 at 227.
7. *R v Zappia* (2002) 84 SASR 206 at 227.
8. (1995) 183 CLR 108 at 117–118.
9. (1980) 143 CLR 108 at 130–131.

11.25C Clayton v R; Hardwick v R; Hardwick v R

(2006) 231 ALR 500
High Court of Australia

[The three applicants were convicted of murder and of intentionally causing serious injury to the partner of the murdered man. Mr and Mrs Hardwick had been married but, at the relevant time, were divorced. Ms Clayton was a friend of Mrs Hardwick. Following a quarrel between Mrs Hardwick and Ms Clayton and the partner of the deceased, the deceased had driven a stolen car to the house of Mrs Hardwick and had smashed the car into the rear of Ms Clayton's rental car. When the three applicants discovered what had occurred, they armed themselves with knives, metal poles and pieces of wood and drove to the house of the partner. The deceased left the house by the back door when the applicants arrived. The partner was assaulted, and the deceased severely beaten and stabbed a number of times in the course of an attack which lasted between 30 and 40 minutes. He died a short time later as a result of one of the stab wounds. On appeal to the High Court.]

[Footnotes to the extract appear at the end of the extract.]

Gleeson CJ, **Gummow**, **Hayne**, **Callinan**, **Heydon** and **Crennan JJ**: … The prosecution's case at trial was that, although it could not identify which of the applicants inflicted the fatal stab wound, each was guilty of murder. This contention was put in three ways. First, it was said that the killing occurred in the course of the applicants' implementation of a plan to cause really serious injury to the deceased. That is, the prosecution alleged that each applicant had participated in a joint enterprise. Alternatively, the prosecution argued that each applicant was guilty of murder because each had agreed to assault the deceased using weapons, and reasonably foresaw the possibility that death or really serious injury might be intentionally inflicted on the victim by one of them in the course of their carrying out the agreed assault. It is this second way of putting the case ('extended common purpose') that engaged the principles described in *McAuliffe* and *Gillard.* Finally, the prosecution argued that the two applicants who did not inflict the fatal wound had aided and abetted the person who did, by intentionally helping, encouraging or conveying their assent to that person in his or her commission of the murder. This third contention depended upon principles of accessorial liability. ...

Questions of extended common purpose had to be considered at trial. The principles authoritatively established in *McAuliffe* and *Gillard* were to be applied both at trial and by the Court of Appeal and there was, and could be, no argument to the contrary. The applicants sought special leave to appeal to contend that those principles, which had to be applied in the courts below, should now be abandoned or at least substantially modified, presumably on the basis that 'on any ground there was a miscarriage of justice'.[1]

There are several reasons for the Court not to reconsider what was said in *McAuliffe* or *Gillard* about extended common purpose. First, contrary to the applicants' central submission, it is not demonstrated that the application of the principles stated in those cases has led to any miscarriage of justice in this case or, more generally, has occasioned injustice in the application of the law of homicide. The applicants pointed to no decided case said to reveal the alleged injustice. Rather, for the most part, the argument was advanced in a wholly abstract form.

The applicants' contentions about 'unjust' results, or results said to demonstrate disconformity between legal and moral responsibility, proceeded, in the main, from an unstated premise that the crime of murder should be confined to cases in which the accused intended the death of the victim. The allegation of injustice or disconformity, though variously expressed, fastened upon the fact that applying principles of extended common purpose could result in a person being found guilty of murder where that person did not agree or intend that death should result, but foresaw only the possibility that an assault with intent to kill or cause really serious injury might be made in the course of the joint enterprise. The applicants sought to compare this outcome with the case of a person assaulting another, knowing of the possibility, but not intending, that death or really serious injury might result. Such a person, the applicants submitted, would be guilty only of manslaughter.

A person who does not intend the death of the victim, but does intend to do really serious injury to the victim, will be guilty of murder if the victim dies. If a party to a joint criminal enterprise foresees the possibility that another might be assaulted with intention to kill or cause really serious injury to that person, and, despite that foresight, continues to participate in the venture, the criminal culpability lies in the continued participation in the joint enterprise with the necessary foresight.[2] That the participant does not wish or intend that the victim be killed is of no greater significance than the observation that the person committing the assault need not wish or intend that result, yet be guilty of the crime of murder.

Secondly, the applicants could point to no other court of final appeal accepting the proposition that the applicants put at the forefront of their submission, namely, that the doctrine of extended common purpose should be abolished or modified by replacing foresight of the possibility of a murderous assault with foresight of the probability of such an assault. Other common law countries continue to apply[3] generally similar principles to those stated in *McAuliffe* and *Gillard*.

Thirdly, if there are to be changes in this area of the law (and we are not to be taken as suggesting that there should be) there could be no change undertaken to the law of extended common purpose without examining whether what was being either sought or achieved was in truth some alteration to the law of homicide depending upon distinguishing between cases in which the accused acts with an intention to kill and cases in which the accused intends to do really serious injury or is reckless as to the possibility of death or really serious injury.[4] That is a task for legislatures and law reform commissions. It is not a step that can or should be taken in the development of the common law. The nature and extent of the difficulties that are encountered in adopting some other principle are revealed in the report of the United Kingdom Law Commission *Inchoate Liability for Assisting and Encouraging Crime*.[5] The Law Commission rejected a proposal to abolish what it described[6] as secondary liability for a collateral offence committed in the course of a joint venture.

Further, no change could be undertaken to the law of extended common purpose without examining the whole of the law with respect to secondary liability for crime. The history of the distinction between joint enterprise liability and secondary liability as an aider, abettor, counsellor or procurer of an offence has recently been traced by Professor Simester.[7] As that author demonstrates,[8] liability as an aider and abettor is grounded in the secondary party's contribution to another's crime. By contrast, in joint enterprise cases, the wrong lies in the mutual embarkation on a crime, and the participants are liable for what they foresee as the possible results of that venture. In some cases, the accused may be guilty both as an aider and abettor, and as participant in a joint criminal enterprise. That factual intersection of the two different sets of principles does not deny their separate utility.

Finally, it was submitted that the doctrine of extended common purpose should be discarded because it renders the trial of homicide too complex. The trial of these applicants was said to provide a good example of the complexities that arise. But upon examination, this trial does not support this particular criticism.

[**Kirby J** delivered a dissenting judgment. Appeal dismissed.]

Notes:

1. *Crimes Act 1958* (Vic), s 568(1).
2. *McAuliffe v The Queen* (1995) 183 CLR 108 at 118; *Gillard v The Queen* (2003) 219 LR 1 at 36 [112].
3. See, for example, *Chan Wing-Siu v The Queen* [1985] AC 168; *Hui Chi-ming v The Queen* [1992] 1 AC 34; *R v Powell* [1999] 1 AC 1.

4. *R v Crabbe* (1985) 156 CLR 464.
5. United Kingdom, The Law Commission, *Inchoate Liability for Assisting and Encouraging Crime*, Law Com No 300, (July 2006) Cm 6878.
6. United Kingdom, The Law Commission, *Inchoate Liability for Assisting and Encouraging Crime*, Law Com No 300, (July 2006) Cm 6878 at 19 [2.24]–[2.25].
7. Simester, 'The Mental Element in Complicity', (2006) 122 *Law Quarterly Review* 578 at 596–598.
8. Simester, 'The Mental Element in Complicity', (2006) 122 *Law Quarterly Review* 578 at 598–599.

[See also *Darkan v R* (2006) 227 CLR 373; 228 ALR 334; *R v Taufahema* (2007) 228 CLR 232; 234 ALR 1.]

ABANDONMENT OF CRIMINAL PARTICIPATION

11.26C **R v Rook**

[1993] 2 All ER 955

Court of Appeal (Criminal Division) (UK)

[The accused agreed with A, L and MA to kill MA's wife in return for MA paying them £20,000. The four men met the evening before the killing and agreed that the next day MA would pick up the three men and drive them to a lake, and that when they were ready, he would bring his wife to the lake in his car. The accused did not turn up the next day as arranged and the killing was carried out by the other two men. All four men were jointly charged with the murder of MA's wife. The accused's defence was that he had never intended the woman to be killed, that he hoped to get some money 'up front' from MA and then disappear, that he had never intended to go through with the killing himself and that he had deliberately absented himself on the day of the killing because he thought that if he were not there the other two would not go ahead with the crime. In directing the jury, the trial judge stated that while a person who has embarked on a criminal enterprise may withdraw from it and save himself from criminal liability, 'more than mere inactivity is required to destroy the criminal liability which flows from the earlier acts, in this case of encouragement or advice, to lead to a verdict in your case of not guilty'. The accused was convicted and appealed to the Court of Appeal.]

Lloyd LJ [delivering the judgment of the court]: ... Mr Maxwell QC submits that where a person has given assistance, for example by providing a gun, in circumstances which would render him liable as a secondary party if he does not withdraw, then in order to escape liability he must 'neutralise' his assistance. He must, so it was said, break the chain of causation between his act of assistance, and the subsequent crime, by recovering the gun, or by warning the victim to stay away, or by going to the police. Mr Hockman submits, on the other hand, that the Crown must prove that the defendant continued ready to help until the moment the crime is committed; and if there is doubt as to the defendant's state of mind on the day in question, or his willingness to provide further help if required, then the jury must acquit.

As between these two extreme views, we have no hesitation in rejecting the latter. In *R v Croft* [1944] 2 All ER 483, [1944] KB 295 the surviving party of a suicide pact was held to be guilty of murder. Lawrence J, giving the judgment of the court, said ([1944] KB 295 at 298, cf [1944] 2 All ER 483 at 485):

> The authorities, however, such as they are, show, in our opinion, that the appellant, to escape being held guilty as an accessory before the fact must establish that he expressly countermanded or revoked the advising, counselling, procuring or abetting which he had previously given.

In *R v Whitehouse* [1941] 1 WWR 112 at 115 Sloan JA said:

> Can it be said on the facts of this case that a mere change of mental intention and a quitting of the scene of the crime just immediately prior to the striking of the fatal blow will absolve those who participate in the commission of the crime by overt acts up to that moment from all the consequences of its accomplishment by the one who strikes in ignorance of his companions' change of heart? I think not. After a crime has been committed and before a prior abandonment of the common enterprise may be found by a jury there must be, in my view, in the absence of exceptional circumstances, something more than a mere mental change of intention and physical change of place by those associates who wish to dissociate themselves from the consequences attendant upon their willing assistance up to the moment of the actual commission of that crime. I would not attempt to define too closely what must be done in criminal matters involving participation in a common unlawful purpose to break the chain of causation and responsibility. That must depend upon the circumstances of each case but it seems to me that one essential element ought to be established in a case of this kind: Where practicable and reasonable there must be timely communication of the intention to abandon the common purpose from those who wish to dissociate themselves from the contemplated crime to those who desire to continue in it. What is 'timely communication' must be determined by the facts of each case but where practicable and reasonable it ought to be such communication, verbal or otherwise, that will serve unequivocal notice upon the other party to the common unlawful cause that if he proceeds upon it he does so without the further aid and assistance of those who withdraw. The unlawful purpose of him who continues alone is then his own and not one in common with those who are no longer parties to it nor liable to its full and final consequences.

In *R v Becerra* (1975) 62 Cr App R 212, this court approved that passage as a correct statement of the law. The facts of *R v Becerra* were that the victim was killed in the course of a burglary. The appellant had provided the knife shortly before the murder. The court held that the appellant's sudden departure from the scene of the crime with the words 'Come on let's go' was an insufficient communication of withdrawal. So the appellant's conviction as a secondary party to the murder was upheld. In *R v Whitefield* (1983) 79 Cr App R 36 at 39–40 Dunn LJ stated the law as follows:

If a person has counselled another to commit a crime, he may escape liability by withdrawal before the crime is committed, but it is not sufficient that he should merely repent or change his mind. If his participation is confined to advice or encouragement, he must at least communicate his change of mind to the other, and the communication must be such as 'will serve unequivocal notice upon the other party to the common unlawful cause that if he proceeds upon it he does so without the aid and assistance of those who withdraw'.

In the present case the appellant never told the others that he was not going ahead with the crime. His absence on the day could not possibly amount to 'unequivocal communication' of his withdrawal. In his evidence-in-chief, in a passage already quoted, he said that he made it quite clear to *himself* that he did not want to be there on the day. But he did not make it clear to the others. So the minimum necessary for withdrawal from the crime was not established on the facts. In these circumstances, as in *R v Becerra*, it is unnecessary for us to consider whether communication of his withdrawal would have been enough, or whether he would have had to take steps to 'neutralise' the assistance he had already given.

Mr Maxwell rightly drew our attention to a sentence in the judgment of Sloan JA, already quoted, where he refers to the service of notice on the other party that if he proceeds he does so without *further* aid from those who withdraw. This may suggest that aid *already* afforded need not be neutralised. We agree with Mr Maxwell that this attaches too much importance to a single word. But that is as far as we are prepared to go in this case. We are not prepared, as at present advised, to give our approval to his proposition in its extreme form. In *Criminal Law: The General Part* (2nd ed, 1961), para 127, Glanville Williams quotes a graphic phrase from an American authority (*Eldredge v US* (1932) 62 F 2d 449 per McDermott J): 'A declared intent to withdraw from a conspiracy to dynamite a building is not enough, if the fuse has been set; he must step on the fuse.' It may be that this goes too far. It may be that it is enough that he should have done his best to step on the fuse. Since this is as much a question of policy as a question of law, and since it does not arise on the facts of the present case, we say no more about it.

[Appeal dismissed.]

[See also *R v Tietie, Tulele and Bolamatu* (1988) 34 A Crim R 438.]

11.27 Notes

1. The question of the liability of an accused who seeks to withdraw from a planned criminal enterprise arose in a quite different context in *White v Ridley* (1978) 140 CLR 342; 21 ALR 661. While in Singapore, the accused used a false name to airfreight a box containing a stereo receiver in which was concealed a quantity of cannabis to a fictitious person in Australia. The accused travelled to Australia in advance of the box. On his arrival in Sydney, he was searched by Customs officials who found that he was in possession

of a document which evidenced the consignment of the box and who questioned him about the document. Being apprehensive as a result of the search and the questioning, the accused, in the name of the 'consignee', sent a telex marked 'urgent' to the airline in Singapore to stop the consignment. The message arrived too late for action by the airline, with the consequence that the box was, in fact, transported to Australia. The accused was convicted in a Magistrates' Court of importing into Australia a prohibited import. He appealed unsuccessfully to the County Court of Victoria and then by way of case stated to the Full Court of the Supreme Court of Victoria. The accused then sought special leave to appeal to the High Court. By a majority of three to two (Gibbs, Stephen and Aickin JJ; Jacobs and Murphy JJ dissenting), the High Court granted special leave to appeal but dismissed the appeal.

2. Gibbs J took the view that the accused's position was analogous to that of a person who, having counselled or procured another to commit a crime, countermands his counselling or procuring before the crime is committed, or to that of a person who, having engaged with others in a common criminal enterprise, withdraws before the enterprise is carried to completion. His Honour stated (at 669):

> Where the accused has requested a person who is of sound and mature mind to do an act which the accused knows, but the agent does not know, is illegal, the accused will not be liable if he has given timely countermand of his request. The countermand must have been manifested by words or conduct sufficiently clear to bring it home to the mind of the agent that the accused no longer desires the agent to do what he was previously asked to do; a vague, ambiguous or perfunctory countermand would not be enough. And the accused must have done or said whatever was reasonably possible to counteract the effect of his earlier request. The countermand will not have been timely if it was given when it was too late to stop the train of events which was started by his request.

On the facts of the case, his Honour held that it was not clear that the countermanding of the request to airfreight the box was not timely. However, his Honour held that it was clear that the accused did not do all that he reasonably could do to attempt to prevent the airline from effecting the carriage which he had requested it to perform. He did not disclose to the airline, in his telex, that the box, in fact, contained cannabis. If he had done so, the airline would have become aware of the importance of stopping the carriage. The sending of the telex was, therefore, not sufficient to absolve the accused from responsibility when the airline, acting upon his previous instructions, brought the box into Australia.

3. Stephen J, with whom Aickin J agreed, preferred to analyse the liability of the accused in terms of causation. His Honour held that only the intervention of some new cause so as to deprive the accused's arrangement

with the airline of its incriminating character would be sufficient to displace the original arrangement as the event to which the importation could be causally assigned. The accused's ineffective attempt to stop the importation gave rise to no new cause which displaced, as the cause of importation, his original arrangement with the airline. It followed that this attempt had no effect in law upon his criminal liability.

4. It is doubtful if the difference in approach taken by Gibbs J and by Stephen J would, in fact, be likely to lead to different results in any given case. It is submitted, however, that the approach taken by Gibbs J has the merit that it is more likely to be readily understood by a jury. His Honour stated (at 669):

> A trial judge or a jury need not, in my opinion, decide a case such as this by considering questions of causation. It may be true that the rules relating to countermand may be explained by reference to the principles of causation, and that if after a sufficient countermand the agent nevertheless proceeds to act in accordance with the request originally made, his acts may be regarded as resulting from a new and intervening cause. But it is enough to apply directly the rules I have endeavoured to state; for a trial judge or jury to go behind them, and consider questions of causation, is more likely to lead to confusion than to provide assistance.

11.28 Further reading

D Lanham, 'Accomplices and Withdrawal' (1981) 97 *LQR* 575

ABETTORS

11.29C R v Bainbridge

[1960] 1 QB 129; [1959] 3 All ER 200
Court of Criminal Appeal (UK)

Lord Parker CJ [delivering the judgment of the court]: The appellant in this case was convicted at the Central Criminal Court of being accessory before the fact to office-breaking and was sentenced to four years' imprisonment. He now appeals against his conviction only on a point of law.

The facts were these. On the night of 30 October 1958 the Stoke Newington branch of the Midland Bank was broken into by cutting the bars of a window, the doors of the strong room and of a safe inside the strong room. They were opened by means of oxygen cutting equipment and nearly £18,000 was stolen. The cutting equipment was all left behind, and it was later found that that cutting equipment so left behind by the thieves had been purchased by the appellant some six weeks earlier. The case against him was that he had bought this cutting equipment on behalf of one of more of the thieves with full knowledge that it was going to be used, if not against the Stoke Newington branch of the Midland Bank, at any rate for the purposes of breaking and entering premises. The appellant's case, as given in his evidence, was this:

> True, I had bought this equipment from two different firms. I had gone there with a man called Shakeshaft to buy it for him. As a result of conversation which I had with him, I was suspicious that he wanted it for something illegal. I thought it was for breaking up stolen goods which Shakeshaft had received, and, as the result, in making those purchases I gave false names and addresses; but I had no knowledge that the equipment was going to be used for any such purpose as that for which it was used.

The complaint here is that Aarvold J, who tried the case, gave the jury a wrong direction in regard to what it was necessary for them to be satisfied of in order to hold the appellant guilty of being an accessory before the fact. The passages in question are these:

> To prove that, the prosecution have to prove these matters: first of all, they have to prove that the felony itself was committed. Of that there is no doubt. That is not contested. Secondly, they have to prove that the *[appellant]* knew that a felony of that kind was intended and was going to be committed, and with that knowledge he did something to help the felons commit the crime. The knowledge that is required to be proved in the mind of [the appellant] is not the knowledge of the precise crime. In other words, it need not be proved that he knew that the Midland Bank, Stoke Newington branch, was going to be broken and entered, and money stolen from that particular bank, but he must know the type of crime that was in fact committed. In this case it is a breaking and entering of premises and the stealing of property from those premises. It must be proved that he knew that that sort of crime was intended and was going to be committed. It is not enough to show that he either suspected or knew that some crime was going to be committed, some crime which might have been a breaking and entering or might have been disposing of stolen property or anything of that kind. That is not enough. It must be proved that he knew that the type of crime which was in fact committed was intended.

There are other passages to the same effect; in particular, when the jury returned for further directions before they came to their verdict, the learned judge said this:

> If in fact, before it has happened, *[the appellant]*, knowing what is going to happen with full knowledge that a felony of that kind is going to take place, deliberately and wilfully helps it on its way, he is an accessory ... If he was not present he would not be guilty as a principal, but then you would have to decide

whether he helped in purchasing this equipment for Shakeshaft knowing full well the type of offence for which it was going to be used, and, with that knowledge, buying it and helping in that way.

Counsel for the appellant, who argued this case very well, contended that that direction was wrong. As he put it, in order that a person should be convicted of being accessory before the fact, it must be shown that, at the time when he bought the equipment in a case such as this, he knew that a particular crime was going to be committed; and by 'a particular crime' counsel meant that the premises in this case which were going to be broken into were known to the appellant and contemplated by him, and not only the premises in question but the date when the crime was going to occur; in other words, that he must have known that on a particular date the Stoke Newington branch of the Midland Bank was intended to be broken into.

The court fully appreciates that it is not enough that it should be shown that a person knew that some illegal venture was intended. To take this case, it would not be enough if the appellant knew — he says that he only suspected — that the equipment was going to be used to dispose of stolen property. That would not be enough. Equally, this court is quite satisfied that it is unnecessary that knowledge of the intention to commit the particular crime which was in fact committed should be shown, and by 'particular crime' I am using the words in the same way as that in which counsel for the appellant used them, namely, on a particular date and particular premises.

It is not altogether easy to lay down a precise form of words which will cover every case that can be contemplated, but, having considered the cases and the law, this court is quite clear that the direction of Aarvold J in this case cannot be criticised. Indeed, it might well have been made with the passage in Foster's *Crown Cases* (3rd ed, 1792), p 369, in mind, because there the learned author says: 'If the principal totally and substantially varieth, if being solicited to commit a felony of one kind he *wilfully and knowingly* committeth a felony of another, he will stand single in that offence, and the person soliciting will not be involved in his guilt. For on his part it was no more than a fruitless ineffectual temptation', the converse of course is that, if the principal does not totally and substantially vary the advice or the help and does not wilfully and knowingly commit a different form of felony altogether, the man who has advised or helped, aided or abetted, will be guilty as an accessory before the fact. *[Emphasis added]*

Aarvold J in this case, in the passages to which I have referred, makes it clear that there must be not merely suspicion but knowledge that a crime of the type in question was intended, and that the equipment was bought with that in view. In his reference to the felony of the type intended it was, as he states, the felony of breaking and entering premises and the stealing of property from those premises. The court can see nothing wrong in that direction.

[Appeal dismissed.]

[See also *R v Bullock* [1955] 1 All ER 15.]

11.30 Notes and illustrations

1. D2 assisted D1 to open a bank account by fraudulent means. Subsequently, D1 forged a cheque and paid it into the credit of the account. D2 was convicted of aiding and abetting D1 in the fraudulent use of the forged cheque. The only rational hypothesis which would account for the evidence concerning D2's conduct was that D2 knew when the account was opened that it would be used by D1 in fraudulent transactions of this kind, namely, ones involving the use of forged cheques. On appeal, D2's conviction was upheld despite the fact that the forged cheque had not come into existence when the account was opened: *Thambiah v R* [1966] AC 37 (PC). In the course of judgment, Lord Pearce stated (at 46):

   > One man may abet another by helping to set the stage even before the victim has been found. If a man helps another in preparation for crimes of a certain nature with the intention that the other shall commit crimes of that nature he may abet those crimes when they come to be committed. Moreover in the present case at the time when the cheque was fraudulently used the account still owed not only its origin but also its maintained existence to the appellant.

2. D1 and D2, believing that D1's mother was a witch, hired a witch doctor, D3, to kill her by means of a magic gun. D3 loaded a gun with bullets and fired at the victim, killing her. D1 believed that the gun was to be pointed at the sun and would thus bring about the death by witchcraft; but D2 knew that the gun was loaded with bullets. Held, D1 was accessory to the murder, since he intended to kill by one means and it was immaterial that the killing was by another means: *Twelve v R* [1957] Rhod & Nyas LR 265.

3. D counselled Z to murder V. Z pleaded guilty and gave evidence for the prosecution. Z testified that he had decided not to kill V but had then gone berserk and had done so. D was convicted. Held, conviction affirmed. 'So long as there is counselling … so long as the principal offence is committed by the one counselled, and so long as the one counselled is acting within the scope of her or his authority', the offence is committed. It is not necessary that there be a substantial causal connection between the acts of the counsellor and the commission of the offence: *R v Calhaem* [1985] 2 WLR 826.

11.31C Giorgianni v R

(1985) 156 CLR 473; 58 ALR 641

High Court of Australia

[The accused was convicted under s 52A of the Crimes Act 1900 (NSW) on five charges of dangerous driving causing death and one charge of dangerous driving occasioning grievous bodily harm. A coal truck driven by an employee of the accused had collided with other vehicles causing the death of five persons and serious injury to another when the brakes of the truck had failed. The Crown's case was that the brakes were obviously defective and that the employee, by driving it in that condition, was driving in a manner dangerous to the public within the terms of s 52A. The accused had, the Crown alleged, procured the employee to drive the truck in its defective condition and was, therefore, by virtue of s 351 of the Crimes Act 1900 (NSW), liable to be convicted and punished as a principal offender. The trial judge directed the jury that the accused would be guilty if he knew of the defective condition of the brakes or if he had acted recklessly not caring whether the brakes were defective or not.]

Wilson, **Deane** and **Dawson JJ**: Section 52A of the Crimes Act, under the heading 'Culpable driving', provides:

> (1) Where the death of, or grievous bodily harm to, any person is occasioned through
>
> (c) impact with a motor vehicle; or
>
> and the motor vehicle was at the time of the impact, or at the time of overturning or leaving the highway, being driven by another person —
>
> (e) under the influence of intoxicating liquor or of a drug;
>
> (f) at a speed or in a manner dangerous to the public, the person who was so driving the motor vehicle shall be guilty of the misdemeanour of culpable driving.
>
> (3) It shall be a defence to any charge under this section that the death or the grievous bodily harm occasioned, as the case may be, was not in any way attributable to the fact that the person charged was under the influence of intoxicating liquor or of a drug or, as the case may be, to the speed at which or the manner in which the vehicle was driven.

The manner in which a vehicle may be driven includes its mechanical condition and if that condition is defective, it may, by reason of that fact, be driven in a manner dangerous to the public. See *R v Coventry* (1938) 59 CLR 633 esp at 639; *R v Spurge* [1961] 2 QB 205; *R v Robert Millar Ltd* [1970] 2 QB 54. The offence created by s 52A does not require the prosecution to prove any state of mind on the part of the driver, although his act of driving must be conscious and voluntary and he may have a defence of mistake of fact on reasonable grounds: *R v Coventry* at 638. It is unnecessary to pursue in this case whether the driver must establish such a defence or whether the effect of his raising it is to cast upon the Crown the ultimate burden of disproving it beyond reasonable doubt. It is sufficient to observe that the defence is available. Otherwise the mental state of the driver is irrelevant, for the section `imports an objective standard by which his driving is to be judged.

No question was, however, raised in this case that the actions of Renshaw were other than conscious and voluntary and no reliance appears to have been placed upon any exculpatory belief which may have been entertained by him. The accident occurred when the brakes failed on the appellant's vehicle and it careered down a steep descent unable to slow down or stop. Seconds before the accident, the vehicle collided with another truck which had been intentionally placed in its path in an effort to avoid the collisions which nevertheless ensued. Renshaw gave evidence that, after colliding with the other truck, the steering mechanism of the appellant's vehicle failed and he lost control of it. Thereafter the vehicle veered on to the wrong side of the road and collided with other vehicles, including those in which the five people died and the sixth was injured. The question was raised whether Renshaw was driving the appellant's vehicle at the time of the impact with the latter vehicles, having regard to the collision with the other truck and his loss of control, but, as Barwick CJ pointed out in *McBride v R* (1966) 115 CLR 44 at 47, '... the interval of time between the driving which is in breach of the section and the impact may be so short that the offending driving can be regarded as persisting to the moment of impact'. It was a question for the jury and the learned trial judge drew their attention to it in clear terms. There was evidence upon which the jury could find that Renshaw was still driving the appellant's vehicle at the time of the two impacts in question and it is clear that they did so find.

It is necessary, therefore, to proceed upon the basis that the offences of culpable driving were committed by Renshaw. It is those offences which the appellant was alleged to have aided, abetted, counselled or procured. To have done so he must have intentionally participated in the principal offences and so must have had knowledge of the essential matters which went to make up the offences of culpable driving on the occasion in question, whether or not he knew that those matters amounted to a crime. See *Johnson v Youden* [1950] 1 KB 544 at 546; *R v Churchill* [1967] 2 AC 224. As Viscount Dilhorne put it in *R v Maxwell* at 1355 of WLR, 1144 of All ER, '... it is clear that a person cannot properly be convicted of aiding and abetting in the commission of acts which he does not know may be or are intended'. See also *Abley v Crosaro* [1946] VLR 53; *Blackmore v Linton* [1961] VR 374; *Dennis v Pight* (1968) 11 FLR 458. The requirement of intention on the part of an aider, abettor, counsellor or procurer or, if we may use the term, a secondary participant in a crime, is a requirement at common law and it is a requirement which is not affected by s 351 of the Crimes Act. That section merely restates the common law by providing, in effect, that in proceedings against a secondary participant in a misdemeanor, no distinction is to be drawn between the principal offender and the secondary participant. See *Du Cros v Lambourne* [1907] 1 KB 40; *Gould & Co v Houghton* [1921] 1 KB 509; *Carter Patersons & Pickfords Carriers, Ltd v Wessel* [1947] KB 849 at 852; *Richards v McPherson* [1943] VLR 44; *Ex parte Coorey* (1944) 45 SR (NSW) 287 at 295. Whilst in the case of felonies, separate offences are committed by principals in the second degree (aiders and abettors) and accessories before the fact (counsellors and procurers), a person who aids, abets, counsels or procures the commission of a misdemeanour may at common law be proceeded against as a principal because '... it is not worthwhile to regard inferior criminals through a microscope, or to classify them scientifically, as felons were treated when most felonies were capital offences so far as the principals were concerned'. See *Gould & Co v Houghton* at 520 per Darling J. It is the common law position which s 351 of the Crimes Act expresses and in so doing it does not exclude a guilty mind as a necessary ingredient of secondary participation in the commission of a misdemeanour.

We have mentioned at the outset the requirement of intent on the part of a secondary participant, because in each count, the principal offence, culpable driving, is, in the sense in which we have explained it, an offence involving strict liability: the prosecution is not required to prove any mental state on the part of the driver. That does not, however, relieve the prosecution of the burden of proving intention on the part of a secondary participant and it is this consideration which we think lies behind a submission that the offence of culpable driving created by s 52A of the Crimes Act is of such a nature as to preclude secondary participation in it with the result that the application of s 351 is excluded. The application of that section may be excluded by necessary implication (see *Mallan v Lee* (1949) 80 CLR 198 at 216 per Dixon J; *Morris v Tolman* [1923] 1 KB 166; *Ellis v Guerin* [1925] SASR 282) and it would be excluded if it appeared that the offence of culpable driving created by the legislature was intended to apply only to the driver of the vehicle involved and not to a secondary participant. The mere absence in the section of any reference to secondary participation does not, however, show any intention to exclude it. See *Hale's Pleas of the Crown,* vol 1 (1800), p 704; *R v Potts* (1818) Russ & Ry 353; 168 ER 841.

There is no difficulty in the proposition that a person may intentionally aid, abet, counsel or procure the driving of a vehicle in a particular manner or whilst the driver is in a particular state. Thus there may be secondary participation in the offence of driving in a manner dangerous to the public or of driving whilst under the influence of intoxicating liquor or of a drug. Those offences are created by s 4(1) and s 5(2) of the *Motor Traffic Act 1909* (NSW). But the offence of culpable driving is something more than those offences. It includes the acts necessary to constitute those offences but requires in addition that the driving should be attended by death or grievous bodily harm occasioned through impact with the vehicle being driven. Although it is clear that a person may intend to aid, abet, counsel or procure the driving of a vehicle in a dangerous manner or whilst the driver is under the influence of intoxicating liquor, it is not to be expected, except, perhaps, in rare instances, that in so doing he would intend that there should be an impact occasioning death or grievous bodily harm. So it is said, as we understand the submission, that whilst the driver of the vehicle may be guilty of culpable driving because the offence does not involve any mental state on his part, he cannot be aided, abetted, counselled or procured to commit the offence because that would require on the part of the secondary participant an intention which encompassed the occurrence of death or grievous bodily harm. It may be enough to answer the submission to point to the rare instances — intentionally encouraging a driver to drive in the face of oncoming traffic, for example — where the intent of the secondary participant may be said to extend to an impact occasioning death or grievous bodily harm, but the real answer lies elsewhere.

Before the introduction of the offence of culpable driving, motorists who caused death in the course of committing unlawful acts on the roads were charged with manslaughter. Although the manslaughter charged was involuntary manslaughter, juries were nevertheless reluctant to convict and the less grave offence of culpable driving was conceived. See *A-G v Bindoff* (1953) 53 SR (NSW) 489 at 490. As with involuntary manslaughter, culpable driving does not require that the death, if it is a case involving death, should be intended. It is merely a consequence which serves to convert what would otherwise amount to one offence — driving in a manner dangerous to the public, for instance — into another and more serious offence. The same may be said of grievous bodily harm if it is a case of grievous bodily harm. Just as an unintended death may convert a crime such as an assault into involuntary manslaughter, so death or grievous bodily harm may convert a lesser driving offence into culpable driving, even if the death or grievous bodily harm is unintended.

At one time there may have been some basis for the proposition that no offence is known to the law of being an accessory before the fact to involuntary manslaughter. See *Hale's Pleas of the Crown*, vol 1 (1800), p 436. The proposition is based upon the notion that a man cannot counsel or procure what he does not intend and he cannot intend an accidental killing. But in *Blackstone's Commentaries* (21st ed, 1844) vol 4, pp 36–7, it was said:

> And it is also settled, that whoever procureth a felony to be committed, though it be by the intervention of a third person, is an accessory before the fact. It is likewise a rule, that he who in any wise commands or counsels another to commit an unlawful act, is accessory to all that ensues upon that unlawful act; but is not accessory to any act distinct from the other.

And Bramwell B in *R v Gaylor* (1857) Dears & Bell 288 at 291; 169 ER 1011 at 1012 apparently thought that there was only one answer to the question:

> Suppose a man, for mischief, gives another a strong dose of medicine, not intending any further injury than causing him to be sick and uncomfortable, and death ensues, would not that be manslaughter? Suppose, then, another had counselled him to do it, would not he who counselled be an accessory before the fact?

See also *R v Taylor* (1875) 13 Cox CC 68; *R v Buck and Buck* (1960) 44 Cr App R 213. In *R v Creamer* [1966] 1 QB 72 at 82, the Court of Criminal Appeal reviewed the authorities and expressed the law to be as follows:

> A man is guilty of involuntary manslaughter when he intends an unlawful act and one likely to do harm to the person and death results which was neither foreseen nor intended. It is the accident of death resulting which makes him guilty of manslaughter as opposed to some lesser offence such as assault, or, in the present case, abortion. This can no doubt be said to be illogical, since the culpability is the same, but nevertheless, it is an illogicality which runs throughout the whole of our law, both the common law and the statute law. A comparatively recent example is clearly that of dangerous driving and causing death by dangerous driving. Bearing that in mind, it is quite consistent that a man who has counselled and procured such an illegal and dangerous act from which death, unintended, results should be guilty of being accessory before the fact to manslaughter.

That seems to us to be an accurate statement of the law and it follows that, although a person cannot aid, abet, counsel or procure the commission of an offence, even a statutory offence involving strict liability, without intent based upon knowledge of the essential facts which constitute the offence, the requisite intent and knowledge do not, in the case of culpable driving, extend to the occurrence of the death or grievous bodily harm which 'ensues upon' the unlawful act the commission of which was aided, abetted, counselled or procured. The application of s 351 of the Crimes Act to the offence of culpable driving is not, therefore, excluded by necessary implication. Cf *R v Robert Millar (Contractors) Ltd.*

The second main submission made on behalf of the appellant was that the learned trial judge misdirected the jury in charging them that it was sufficient to establish intent on the part of the accused if his vehicle was being driven by Renshaw with defective brakes and the applicant:

> ... ought to have known of the defect by the exercise of his reasonable care and diligence, that the accused knew or ought to have known by the exercise of reasonable care and diligence of the danger thereby to the public, and that the accused either ignored it or knowingly took such negligent measures to cope with it to make his conduct in employing the driver so to drive in a manner dangerous to the public.

Elsewhere in the charge the learned trial judge referred to the possibility of 'imputed knowledge' or 'presumed knowledge' of the applicant of the defective state of his vehicle's brake and finally in a re-direction he qualified his former remarks by saying:

> I qualify that by limiting the words, 'Ought to have known by the exercise of reasonable care and diligence' by saying that a mere failure to make an inquiry which would yield knowledge of an essential fact is not in itself sufficient, for to act negligently does not make a person an aider or abettor. The prosecution for its part must show that he knew on 18 May that the brakes were defective and could constitute the driving of the vehicle to be driving in a manner dangerous to the public ... or on 18 May he acted so recklessly not caring whether these facts existed or not.

In giving these directions, the trial judge no doubt had in mind the judgment of the New South Wales Court of Criminal Appeal in *R v Glennan* (1970) 91 WN (NSW) 609 in which the following passage appears (at p 614):

> It may, therefore, be concluded that, in the case of statutory offences in which intention is not a necessary element, the law does not require actual knowledge on the part of the aider and abettor of all the essential facts of the offence. The element of knowledge or intention required of an aider and abettor might perhaps be more accurately expressed by saying that it must be shown that he either knew or suspected the existence of facts which would constitute the commission of the offence or, perhaps, that he acted recklessly, not caring whether the facts existed or not. Mere failure to make an inquiry which, if made, would yield knowledge of an essential fact, is not in itself enough to constitute knowledge of the fact, for it is accepted that to act negligently does not make a person an aider

> and abettor. ... But the circumstances of a given case may be such as to reveal not merely a failure to make an inquiry, but a failure to make an inquiry which is of such a kind as to suggest that the defendant has deliberately abstained from acquiring knowledge because he suspected the existence of a fact which would have been ascertained on inquiry, or that the defendant has acted recklessly in the sense that he did not care whether the facts existed or not: *Carter v Mace* [1949] 2 All ER 714; cf *Davies, Turner & Co Ltd v Brodie* [1954] 1 WLR 1364; [1954] 3 All ER 283.

A number of things might be said about that passage. In the first place, there is no basis upon which it can be said that where a statutory offence requires no proof of intent, it is unnecessary in order to establish secondary participation in the commission of that offence to prove actual knowledge of all the essential facts of the offence. Intent is an ingredient of the offence of aiding and abetting or counselling and procuring and knowledge of the essential facts of the principal offence is necessary before there can be intent. It is actual knowledge which is required and the law does not presume knowledge or impute it to an accused person where possession of knowledge is necessary for the formation of a criminal intent. Secondly, although it may be a proper inference from the fact that a person has deliberately abstained from making an inquiry about some matter that he knew of it and, perhaps, that he refrained from inquiry so that he could deny knowledge, it is nevertheless actual knowledge which must be proved and not knowledge which is imputed or presumed.

The third question raised by the passage which we have cited from *R v Glennan* is whether it is possible to aid, abet, counsel or procure the commission of an offence by acting recklessly. Aiding, abetting, counselling or procuring the commission of an offence requires the intentional assistance or encouragement of the doing of those things which go to make up the offence. The necessary intent is absent if the person alleged to be a secondary participant lacks knowledge that the principal offender is doing something or is about to do something which amounts to an offence. We have already referred to *Johnson v Youden* and the other cases in which this point is made clearly. The same point was expressed differently but with equal clarity by Lord Goddard CJ in *Thomas v Lindop* [1950] 1 All ER 966 at 968, where he said:

> More than once this court has pointed out that it is impossible to convict persons of aiding and abetting the commission of an offence unless they know the facts which must be proved to show that an offence has been committed ... It is, of course, not necessary to show that the person knew that it was an offence, because he cannot plead ignorance of the law, but where anyone is charged with aiding and abetting a person to commit an offence, it must, at least, be shown that he knew what that person was doing. A person who does not know of the acts which another person is doing cannot be charged with aiding and abetting him because he does not know that he is doing acts which amount to an offence.

There are, of course, those cases which hold that the requisite knowledge need not extend to the precise crime which is in fact committed, although some crime must be in contemplation at the time secondary participation is alleged to occur, a general criminal purpose being insufficient. See *R v Lomas* (1913) 9 Cr App R 220; *R v Bullock* [1955] 1 WLR 1; [1955] 1 All ER 15; *R v Bainbridge* [1960] 1 KB 129; *R v Maxwell* [1978] 1 WLR 1350; [1978] 3 All ER 1140. The questions which these cases raise do not arise in this case and it is unnecessary to do more than refer to them.

In this case, the Crown contends that the appellant procured the commission of the offences of culpable driving by Renshaw by sending him on to the road in a vehicle with defective brakes. It contends that, even if the appellant had no knowledge of the state of the vehicle's brakes, it was sufficient that he acted recklessly in doing what he did. The precise nature of the recklessness relied upon is not entirely clear and it is understandable that it occasioned the learned trial judge some difficulty in attempting to explain it to the jury. It cannot have been inadvertent carelessness, however gross, for it can hardly be suggested that a person can accidentally become a secondary participant in the commission of a crime. The recklessness contemplated must have involved some foresight on the part of the appellant that the driving of the vehicle on the road would probably (or possibly — it was not clear which) be dangerous, because of the defective condition of the brakes. In effect, that would mean, if the Crown were correct, that it would have proved a sufficient intent on the part of the appellant in all the circumstances if it established that he knew that the brakes on the vehicle were probably (or possibly) defective.

For the purposes of many offences it may be true to say that if an act is done with foresight of its probable consequences there is sufficient intent in law even if such intent may more properly be described as a form of recklessness. There are, however, offences in which it is not possible to speak of recklessness as constituting a sufficient intent. Attempt is one and conspiracy is another. And we think the offences of aiding and abetting and counselling and procuring are others. Those offences require intentional participation in a crime by lending assistance or encouragement. They do not, of course, require knowledge of the law and it is necessary to distinguish between knowledge of or belief in the existence of facts which constitute a criminal offence and knowledge or belief that those facts are made a criminal offence under the law. The necessary intent is absent if the person alleged to be a secondary participant does not know or believe that what he is assisting or encouraging is something which goes to make up the facts which constitute the commission of the relevant criminal offence. He need not recognise the criminal offence as such, but his participation must be intentionally aimed at the commission of the acts which constitute it. It is not sufficient if his knowledge or belief extends only to the possibility or even probability that the acts which he is assisting or encouraging are such, whether he realises it or not, as to constitute the factual ingredients of a crime. If that were sufficient, a person might be guilty of aiding, abetting, counselling or procuring the commission of an offence which formed no part of his design. Intent is required and it is an intent which must be based upon knowledge or belief of the necessary facts. To the extent that *R v Glennan* suggests the contrary, it is not, in our view, in accordance with principle and does not correctly state the law.

The authorities relied upon in the passage which we have cited in *R v Glennan* do not appear to us to provide adequate support for the propositions which it contains. *Carter v Mace* was a case in which the appellant was alleged to have aided and abetted the commission of the statutory offence of failing to comply with the conditions of a licence to carry goods. The principal offence was committed by the owner of a lorry which the appellant, who carried on the business of a transport clearing house, hired to carry goods for him. A Divisional Court held that if the appellant undertook this class of business he was bound to see that contracts were carried out in a legal manner and, having failed to do so, was guilty of aiding and abetting the commission of a statutory offence. The precise basis of the decision is difficult to discern. In *Davies, Turner & Co Ltd v Brodie*, a Divisional Court was referred to *Carter v Mace* and it expressed the view that it was a decision on its own particular facts and laid down no proposition of law. In *Davies, Turner & Co Ltd v Brodie*, the defendant was charged with aiding and abetting the commission of the offence of using a goods vehicle without the required permit. The defendant had obtained an assurance from the driver of the vehicle that he had the necessary permit. The court held that because the appellant '... had no reason to suppose that the facts were present which would constitute an offence ...', the offence of aiding and abetting was not made out. Lord Goddard C J, who also presided in *Carter v Mace,* said at 1367 of WLR; cf 286 of All ER:

> If a person shuts his eyes to the obvious or refrains from making any inquiry where a reasonably sensible man would make inquiry. I think the court can find that he was aiding and abetting, certainly if he shuts his eyes to the obvious.

The fact of exposure to the obvious may warrant the inference of knowledge. The shutting of one's eyes to the obvious is not, however, an alternative to the actual knowledge which is required as the basis of intent to aid, abet, counsel or procure. Lord Goddard appears to have recognised this by concluding his judgment with the words: '... that is the point: you must know the essential matters which constitute the offence.'

The Court of Criminal Appeal in *R v Glennan* also referred in its judgment to *Poultry World Ltd v Conder* [1975] Crim LR 803 and *Bateman v Evans* (1964) 108 SJ 522. In the report of *Poultry World Ltd v Conder*, a Divisional Court is said to have decided that a person could not be convicted of aiding and abetting unless he had knowledge of the facts which constitute the offence or unless he deliberately abstained from obtaining such knowledge. In the commentary upon the decision, however, it is made clear that the court took the view that the offence of aiding and abetting could not be established unless there was proof of knowledge or '... such negligence as to amount to deliberate shutting of the eyes, ie connivance'. Connivance can, of course, only be established on the basis of knowledge, whether proved directly or by inference.

In *Bateman v Evans*, the defendant was convicted of aiding and abetting the commission of the offence of driving while disqualified. The defendant believed the driver's assurance that he had lodged an appeal against his disqualification and was permitted to drive. On a case stated by justices of a Divisional Court, it was held that the conviction should be quashed upon the basis '... that A had a bona fide belief that B was entitled to drive, and the case fell within *Davies, Turner & Co Ltd v Brodie*'.

The passage which we have cited from *R v Glennan* was unnecessary for the decision in that case, which held that a person charged with aiding and abetting the offence of driving with a prescribed percentage of alcohol in the blood did not have to know the percentage in order to know all the facts which gave rise to the commission of the principal offence.

It follows that, in our view, the trial judge was wrong in directing the jury that reckless behaviour on the part of the appellant would suffice to establish the intent necessary to constitute him the procurer of the offences of culpable driving. That is sufficient to determine this case and no point is to be served in examining the terms of the direction given. Since there was evidence, not without its weaknesses, from which the jury might have inferred that the appellant knew the facts which went to make up the offence of culpable driving, there was a case to answer. The proper course is, therefore, for this court to grant special leave, allow the appeal, quash the conviction and order a new trial.

Gibbs CJ: Suspicion of the existence of facts, although relevant when the accused has deliberately shut his eyes, does not by itself amount to or take the place of knowledge for present purposes. Further it is not correct to say that a person may be convicted of aiding, abetting, counselling or procuring the commission of an offence simply because he has acted recklessly. Dr Edwards, in *Mens Rea in Statutory Offences* (1955) pp 196–205, asserts that a person who deliberately closes his eyes to what is going on connives at it and that there is a close analogy between connivance and recklessness. However, connivance, or wilful blindness, is only relevant to the liability of a secondary party to an offence because it virtually amounts to knowledge. Recklessness, in the sense of not caring whether the facts exist or not, would be relevant only if it too was virtually equivalent to knowledge, in other words only if it amounted to wilful blindness.

It is true that there are some remarks in the judgment of the members of the Divisional Court in *Carter v Richardson* at 317–18, which suggest that it is enough that an aider and abettor was reckless as to whether the principal offender had consumed an excessive amount of alcohol before driving a motor vehicle. However, the ratio of that case was expressed in the following words at 318:

> The justices were right if they took the view that it was sufficient if the defendant was aware that the principal offender had consumed excessive alcohol even though the precise amount had not been determined.

It can never be right to direct a jury that recklessness is enough to constitute a person an aider, abettor, counsellor or procurer. Indeed in many, if not most cases it will be unnecessary to introduce the subject of wilful blindness into a summing up and it would only be confusing to direct a jury on that subject if the facts of the case did not require it.

My view of the law may be summed up very shortly. No one may be convicted of aiding, abetting, counselling or procuring the commission of an offence unless, knowing all the essential facts which made what was done a crime, he intentionally aided, abetted, counselled or procured the acts of the principal offender. Wilful blindness, in the sense that I have described, is treated as equivalent to knowledge but neither negligence nor recklessness is sufficient.

[**Mason J** delivered a separate concurring judgment. Appeal allowed and a new trial ordered.]

ACCESSORIES AFTER THE FACT

11.32 At common law, an accused can only be convicted as an accessory after the fact if it is established that he or she had knowledge of all the relevant facts or acts that established the precise offence with respect to which the Crown alleged the accused was an accessory: *R v Stone* [1981] VR 737. If it appears that the principal offender was guilty only of a different, although related or similar, offence, the accused could not be convicted as an accessory after the fact. This rule applies in New South Wales for accessories after the fact generally and in Victoria for offences other than serious indictable offences.

11.33 In Victoria, where the principal offender has committed a serious indictable offence it is no longer necessary for the prosecution to show that an accessory after the fact was aware of the precise crime committed by the principal offender. Section 325 of the Crimes Act 1958 (Vic) provides:

> (1) Where a person (in this section called 'the principal offender') has committed a serious indictable offence (in this section called 'the principal offence'), any other person who, knowing or believing the principal offender to be guilty of the principal offence or some other serious indictable offence, without lawful authority or reasonable excuse does any act with the purpose of impeding the apprehension, prosecution, conviction or punishment of the principal offender shall be guilty of an indictable offence.
> (2) If, on the trial of any person for a serious indictable offence, the jury are satisfied that the offence charged (or some other serious indictable offence of which the accused might on that charge be found guilty) was committed, but find the accused not guilty of it, they may find him guilty of any offence under sub-section (1) of which they are satisfied that he is guilty in relation to the offence charged (or that other offence).
> (3) A person charged with an offence against sub-section (1) may be indicted or presented and convicted together with or before or after the principal offender and whether or not the principal offender is amenable to justice.
> (4) A person convicted of an offence against sub-section (1) shall be liable —
> (a) if the principal offence is one for which the penalty is level 1 imprisonment (life) to level 3 imprisonment (20 years maximum); or
> (b) in any other case, to imprisonment for a term which is neither —
> (i) more than 5 years in length; nor
> (ii) more than one-half the length of the longest term which may be imposed on first conviction for the principal offence.
>
> …
>
> (5) In this section, 'serious indictable offence' means an indictable offence which, by virtue of any enactment, is punishable on first conviction with imprisonment for life or for a term of five years or more.

Note that s 338 of the Crimes Act 1958 (Vic) provides that a married person who assists or encourages a spouse who has committed an indictable offence is not an accessory after the fact to that offence.

11.34 The Crimes Act 1900 (NSW) s 347 is a more general provision for accessories after the fact for serious indictable offences:

> Every accessory after the fact to a serious indictable offence may be indicted, convicted, and sentenced as such accessory, either before, or together with, or after the trial of the principal offender, whether the principal offender has been previously tried or not, or is amenable to justice or not.

The penalty for an accessory after the fact for treason is two years; for murder, 25 years; for armed robbery and kidnapping, 14 years; and for all other indicatable offences, five years (ss 348–350). The spousal immunity, however, has been abolished in New South Wales. Section 347A states that 'a wife may be accessory after fact to husband's felony'.

11.35 Illustrations

1. D was convicted of being an accessory after the fact to various offences of receiving stolen goods committed by his wife, she being convicted of these offences at their joint trial. The only evidence against D was the fact that when police officers had visited his house and found stolen articles there, he had made untrue and evasive statements to them. On appeal, held, reversed — the recorder at the trial had failed to make clear to the jury the nature of the active steps which must be proved to have been taken by the accused to assist the offender and, in particular, he had failed to make it clear that there could be no conviction if the jury thought that D's motive in making the untrue statements was to avoid the possibility of himself being arrested: *R v Jones* [1949] 1 KB 194. See also *R v Andrews* [1962] 3 All ER 961.
2. D was charged with being an accessory after the fact to the larceny of a motor car by B. D had accepted a lift in the car, realising that B had stolen it. Held, mere enjoyment of the use of the proceeds of a crime, with knowledge of the crime at the time of the subsequent use, does not of itself render one an accessory after the fact in the original crime; the added ingredient of acting for the purpose of assisting the principal offender to escape conviction is necessary: *R v Barlow* (1962) 79 WN (NSW) 756.
3. X shot and wounded V, and at once Ds drove X out of town and tried to dissuade officers from arresting him. V died from the wound the next day. Ds were convicted of being accessories after the fact to the murder. On appeal, held, reversed — the murder was not complete until V died, and all the acts charged against Ds were committed before that time: *State v Williams* 49 SE 2d 617 (NC 1948).

CRIMES INVOLVING PARTICIPATION OTHERWISE THAN AS PRINCIPAL OR ACCESSORY

Subornation and perjury

11.36 Mainly for historical reasons, one who has successfully advised the commission of perjury is known as a suborner, and is said to have committed the substantive offence of subornation of perjury. If the suborner's incitement or advice was fruitless, he or she is guilty only of the crime of incitement: see **10.36**.

Perjury itself was a 'Star Chamber crime' which later found its way into the common law. It consists of wilfully making a false statement on oath in a judicial proceeding. The requirement of wilfulness is satisfied by showing that the accused, when making the statement, either knew it to be false or did not believe it to be true. The statement must have been material; but this requirement is treated very broadly, and only a completely irrelevant statement would fail to satisfy it.

As the crime was limited to statements by those lawfully sworn in a judicial proceeding, it has had to be extended by statute. There are now analogous statutory offences concerning the false making of affidavits and statutory declarations, and of false statements made in proceedings which are not strictly judicial, or made by witnesses who are lawfully testifying without being sworn. See, for example, Evidence Act 1958 (Vic) s 141; Crimes Act 1900 (NSW) ss 335–337.

Perjury and subornation are both now dealt with in Victoria by ss 314–315 of the Crimes Act 1958 and in New South Wales by ss 327–335, 338–339 of the Crimes Act 1900.

Misprision: concealing an offence

11.37 A person may be constituted as an accessory after the fact if it is established that he or she took some active step by way of assistance. What if this was not done, but he or she merely concealed knowledge of the transaction from the authorities? At common law, if the transaction amounted to a felony, mere non-disclosure could amount to the offence of misprision of felony: *R v Crimmins* [1959] VR 270; *R v Stone* [1981] VR 737; *R v Lovegrove and Kennedy* (1983) 33 SASR 332; *R v James* (1983) 36 SASR 215; *R v Dam* (1986) 43 SASR 422; *R v Wozniak* (1989) 16 NSWLR 185. At common law there was also an offence of misprision of treason but not misprision of misdemeanour.

11.38 In each of the common law jurisdictions, the offence of misprision of felony was abolished with the abolition of the classification of crimes into felonies and misdemeanours. In Victoria, misprision of felony was replaced by the more limited offence of concealing an offence for a benefit. Section 326 of the Crimes Act 1958 (Vic) provides:

> (1) Where a person has committed a serious indictable offence, any other person who, knowing or believing that the offence, or some other serious indictable

offence, has been committed and that he has information which might be of material assistance in securing the prosecution or conviction of an offender for it, accepts any benefit for not disclosing that information shall be guilty of a summary offence and liable to level 8 imprisonment (1 year maximum).

(2) Notwithstanding anything to the contrary in sub-section (1), it is no offence against this section to fail to disclose the commission of any offence against —
  (a) Division 2 of Part I; or
  (b) sub-division (1), (2) or (3) of Division 3 of Part I —

  if the only benefit accepted in return for failing to disclose the commission of the offence is the making good of any loss or injury caused by its commission or the making of reasonable compensation for any such loss or injury.

(3) For the purposes of this section a person shall be deemed to accept a benefit if he accepts or agrees to accept any benefit or advantage, or the promise of any benefit or advantage, either to himself or to another, whether or not the benefit or advantage is in money or money's worth.

(5) The compounding of an offence other than treason shall not be an offence otherwise than under this section.

(6) In this section 'serious indictable offence' has the same meaning as it has in section 325.

No equivalent offence was introduced in New South Wales.

Unlawful assemblies

11.39 It is a common law misdemeanour, called 'unlawful assembly', for three or more persons to gather together either for the purpose of committing or preparing to commit a crime involving the use of violence or in order to carry out any purpose in an unlawful manner. The essence of this offence is that it has a tendency to create a breach of the peace.

Rout

11.40 If the persons gathered in an unlawful assembly begin to move towards the achievement of their object, in however small a way, they thereupon become guilty of the common law offence known as 'rout'.

Riot

11.41 When the assembly has begun to execute the common purpose and, in so doing, displayed such violence as to alarm at least one person of reasonable firmness and courage, its members will, if they can be shown to intend to help one another by force if necessary, become guilty of the common law crime of riot. In New South Wales, the offence of rout has been abolished and the crime of riot placed upon a statutory footing: Crimes Act 1900 (NSW) ss 93A–93D.

The Riot Act

11.42 These common law provisions as to riotous assemblies were found to be insufficient to cope with the disturbances in England which followed upon the accession of the first of the Hanoverian Kings, and they were, therefore, greatly extended by the Riot Act 1714. This statute provided that if 12 or more persons remained assembled in a riot for one hour after a proclamation prescribed by the statute had been read to them by a magistrate, they should be guilty of felony without benefit of clergy, and be liable to suffer death: hence the popular phrase 'read the riot act'. The Act also provided for the immunity of those who might kill or injure persons taking part in such a riotous assembly while endeavouring to disperse it.

These provisions formed part of the statute law which was received into the Australian colonies on the occasion of their settlement. They have now been replaced by more recent legislation in Victoria and New South Wales: see the Unlawful Assemblies and Processions Act 1958 (Vic); Crimes Act 1900 (NSW) s 545C; and note *Black v Corkery* (1988) 33 A Crim R 134.

CONSPIRACY

Introduction

11.43 Although the old common law knew an offence of conspiring to accuse a person falsely, the modern crime of conspiracy was developed by the Court of Star Chamber. After the Restoration and the demise of the Court of Star Chamber, the Court of King's Bench took over its powers including the power to develop the crime of conspiracy. Conspiracy has commonly been defined as 'an agreement to do an unlawful act or a lawful act by unlawful means': per Lord Denman in *R v Jones* (1832) 4 B & Ad 345 at 349; 110 ER 485 at 487. The two limbs of this proposition in fact appear to be different ways of stating the same thing. The definition is very wide. Plainly, a conspiracy to commit any crime is itself criminal. The cases and discussions on the matter really centre on the difficult question, to what extent will the courts recognise the crime of conspiracy as extending to cover agreements to engage in conduct which would not be criminal if carried out by an individual without prior agreement? One common type of conspiracy is that which is generally called conspiracy to pervert the course of justice. Examples of the offence are agreements to tamper with evidence or to suborn witnesses to give false evidence. However, since there exists a substantive offence of perverting or attempting to pervert the course of justice (see *R v Rogerson* (1992) 174 CLR 268; 107 ALR 225), this form of conspiracy may be regarded as simply an example of conspiracy to commit a crime. The offence of conspiracy to defraud, or to 'cheat and defraud' as it is sometimes termed, is well established at common law: see below. In England, the House of Lords has affirmed the existence of offences of conspiracy to corrupt public morals and conspiracy to outrage public decency; *Shaw v Director of Public Prosecutions* [1962] AC 220; *Knuller (Publishing, Printing and Promotions) Ltd v Director of Public Prosecutions* [1973] AC 435 (at **11.45**). These decisions would be unlikely to be now followed in Australia. The House of Lords held in *Director of Public Prosecutions v Withers* [1975] AC 842 (at 11.45) that there is no offence known to the law of conspiracy to effect a public mischief, and it is clear that a similar view would be taken in Australia. Likewise, it seems certain now that old decisions affirming the existence of crimes of conspiracy to commit an immoral act, conspiracy to break a contract and conspiracy to commit a tort (see *Kamara v Director of Public Prosecutions* [1974] AC 104 for a modern affirmation of the existence of this offence) would not be followed in Australia.

Conspiracy to defraud

11.44 In *Scott v Metropolitan Police Commissioner* [1975] AC 819, the House of Lords distinguished two categories of conspiracy to defraud. The first is conspiracy involving the infliction of economic harm. Viscount Dilhorne stated (at 840):

> [I]n my opinion it is clearly the law that an agreement by two or more by dishonesty to deprive a person of something which is his or to which he is or would be or might be entitled and an agreement by two or more by dishonesty to injure some proprietary right of his, suffices to constitute the offence of conspiracy to defraud.

The second category is conspiracy involving interference with the due performance of a public duty. Lord Diplock stated (at 841):

> Where the intended victim of a 'conspiracy to defraud' is a person performing public duties as distinct from a private individual it is sufficient if the purpose is to cause him to act contrary to his public duty, and the intended means of achieving this purpose are dishonest. The purpose need not involve causing economic loss to anyone.

In the case of the first category, the scope of the law relating to offences against property is such that there will be few cases in which this form of conspiracy to defraud does not involve a conspiracy to commit what is an independent crime. The offence is, however, wide and certainly encompasses some situations where that which it is agreed to do would not constitute a crime if carried out by an individual. In *Peters v R* (1998) 192 CLR 493; 151 ALR 51 (at 7.75C), Toohey and Gaudron JJ stated (at ALR 57) that there were 'difficulties in the path of an exhaustive statement as to what is involved in the offence of conspiracy to defraud'. They continued (at ALR 58–9):

> The offence of conspiracy to defraud is not limited to an agreement involving an intention to cause economic loss, even where the intended victim is a private person. It has always been sufficient that the accused be aware that there is a risk of economic loss. And even where the victim is a private person, there may be cases of fraud which do not involve an intention to put another person's economic interests at risk in any ordinary sense of that term. To take an example given by King CJ in *R v Kastratovic* (1985) 42 SASR 59, someone who believes that a person is indebted

to him and that a defence which that person is genuinely asserting is without merit, nevertheless has an intention to defraud if he intends by dishonest means to deprive that other person of the opportunity of having the matter adjudicated.

Conspiracy to corrupt morals and effect a public mischief

11.45 In *Shaw v Director of Public Prosecutions* [1962] AC 220, the accused published a booklet called *The Ladies' Directory,* a directory of prostitutes together with photographs and indications of particular practices individual prostitutes were prepared to engage in. The House of Lords upheld the conviction of the accused for conspiracy to corrupt public morals. *Shaw* was followed by the House of Lords in *Knuller (Publishing, Printing and Promotions) Ltd v Director of Public Prosecutions* [1973] AC 435. In *Knuller*, the accused had taken part in the publication of a homosexual contact magazine. Sexual mores have changed dramatically since the decisions in *Shaw* and *Knuller* and they are decisions that would almost certainly not be followed by Australian courts in the twenty-first century. Apart from the issue of an unwarranted extension of the criminal law into areas best regarded the province of private morality, *Shaw* and *Knuller* involved, it is submitted, a degree of law creation best left to the legislature. In *Director of Public Prosecutions v Withers* [1975] AC 842, the House of Lords declined to extend the reasoning of those decisions and held that there exists no crime of conspiracy to effect a public mischief. The accused, in the course of their business as an investigating agency, made reports for clients about the status and financial standing of third parties. To obtain the necessary information, they made inquiries, usually by telephone, to banks, building societies, government departments and local authorities and, to induce the officials or public servants to disclose confidential information, they pretended to be acting in an official capacity. They were charged with conspiracy to effect a public mischief. The judge directed the jury that if the accused agreed to do deceitful acts which would cause extreme injury to the community as a whole, they would be guilty of conspiracy to effect a public mischief. The accused were convicted and appealed unsuccessfully to the Court of Appeal. On appeal to the House of Lords the convictions were quashed, their Lordships holding that there exists no offence of conspiracy to effect a public mischief. Lord Diplock stated (at 862):

> It would be disingenuous to try to conceal my personal conviction that this branch of the criminal law of England is irrational in treating as a criminal offence an agreement to do that which, if done, is not a crime; and that its irrationality becomes injustice if it takes days of legal argument and historical research on appeal to your Lordship's House to discover whether any crime has been committed even though the facts are undisputed. … I am glad to agree with your Lordships that this House is not compelled by previous authority to recognise the existence of a generalised offence of 'conspiracy to effect a public mischief', or to hold that the particulars of offence under count 1 disclose an offence known to the common law. If what the defendants did ought to be made a crime it is for Parliament to legislate accordingly.

11.46 The Australian courts have shown no inclination to widen the scope of the crime of conspiracy to encompass activities which might be thought generally undesirable. In *R v Cahill* [1978] 2 NSWLR 453; (1978) 22 ALR 361, three Australian women agreed to marry three Chinese men for the purpose of enhancing the chances of the men to avoid being deported from Australia as prohibited immigrants. One marriage took place but police aborted the other two ceremonies. The actual and contemplated marriages were valid and effective at law and involved no deception or misrepresentation. Under the Migration Act 1985 (Cth), the Minister for Immigration and Ethnic Affairs had a complete discretion to deport or allow the men to stay in Australia. The men and women were each charged with and convicted of an offence under s 86(1)(b) of the Crimes Act 1914 (Cth) of conspiracy to prevent the enforcement of a law of the Commonwealth. At trial and on appeal by way of case stated to the Court of Appeal of New South Wales, the Crown argued that the general law of conspiracy was applicable, and that if the jury found that the agreement between the accused contemplated conduct so offensive to public morality that it could be said to be unlawful, then the jury would be entitled to convict the accused because they had conspired together to achieve a lawful object by unlawful means. The court overturned the convictions. Street CJ stated (at ALR 363):

> It has always been permissible in many fields so to order one's affairs as to avoid attracting the operation of a law, whether it be a law of the Commonwealth or a law of the state. Equally, it has always been permissible to bring about circumstances which will create a climate favourable to the person concerned in respect of a statutory discretion which might be exercised for or against his interests. It is not necessary to canvass the many areas where such planning and action is both commonplace and legitimate, but the revenue field comes at once to mind. For these reasons I would regard the present convictions as unfounded.

Elements of criminal conspiracy

11.47 As well as the serious problems associated with the scope of criminal conspiracy, there are other important ones even in relation to conspiracies to commit crimes. What kind of conduct is needed to constitute a conspiracy? It is usually said that an agreement is needed to constitute it. But this statement is misleading, for it is plain from the decisions that no evidence of any formal agreement is necessary. It is more accurate to say that if there is evidence that two or more people are pursuing the same unlawful purpose, and doing so in combination (as opposed to acting in complete independence of each other), then it may be inferred that they are acting as a result of a prior agreement amongst themselves, that is, that they are parties to a conspiracy. Moreover, persons who can be shown to have agreed on an unlawful purpose, or to have unlawfully combined, may be convicted of conspiracy even though they have not taken any positive steps to carrying out the purpose; for it is the agreement or combination that is unlawful, not the action taken pursuant to it (which may also be unlawful, of course). Naturally, if two persons mentally agree on a common unlawful purpose, but conceal their agreement in their heads, they cannot be convicted — but this is because there will be no evidence from which the agreement can be inferred. An *overt act*, that is, some piece of human behaviour (about which evidence can be given) from which the conspiracy can be inferred, must be proved. It used to be the practice to include in the indictment a statement of the overt act intended to be proved, although this was not a formal requirement. Nowadays the overt act is not always set out.

In practice, although a conspiracy consists of an agreement or combination, it often turns out to be a very shadowy affair. The only thing which clearly emerges is that where the unlawful purpose is the commission of a crime which is actually committed, all persons who are parties to the crime (that is, accessories before the fact and principals) are (almost always) also conspirators; but conspirators to commit a crime are often not parties to its commission.

Evidential and procedural problems in criminal conspiracy

11.48 Defence lawyers often claim that conspiracy prosecutions are unfair. This is because of two rules of evidence which have a peculiar 'bite' in conspiracy trials.

It is a general rule of evidence that the evidence presented at a trial must be relevant to the issues being tried. If irrelevant evidence is presented, and if that evidence may have had a prejudicial effect, then an appellate court will quash the conviction. However, in practice it is difficult to ensure at a trial that every piece of evidence is strictly relevant. For example, counsel will present a witness to prove a particular point which is relevant only if another point is also proved. He or she is allowed to do this if counsel assures the trial judge that he or she will later call other witnesses to prove the second point, or (to use the standard phrase) to establish the connection between that point for which evidence is tendered now and the ultimate issues being tried. For example, a witness at a trial for burglary may be called to show that certain fingerprints are identical with those of the accused. Such evidence is irrelevant, unless (for example) it is shown that these fingerprints were found on the burgled premises. A second witness may be needed to prove the latter point, and when he or she is called, the evidence of the first witness becomes relevant evidence.

At a conspiracy trial, evidence about the alleged conspiracy and what was done pursuant to it is irrelevant unless it can be shown that the accused was a party to the conspiracy. Counsel is, however, often allowed to call such evidence on an undertaking to prove the accused's membership later. This may cause complications, because the proof of the membership may be available only by inference from proof of the conspiracy itself. It is particularly easy in a conspiracy case to become involved in the logical fallacy of *petitio principii*, or lifting oneself up by one's own bootstraps.

11.49 It is also a general rule of evidence that one may not use the out-of-court statements of witnesses or others in order to establish the truth of the matter stated. For example, if it is necessary to prove that A was present at a certain place, it is useless to call a witness to say that 'B told me that he saw A there'. B must be called to prove the fact himself. This is the famous hearsay rule. It is subject to numerous exceptions, among which is a rule which allows the hearsay (out-of-court) statements of A to be used as evidence against B if A is B's authorised agent to make such statements. In the same way as B's own out-of-court admissions may be used against him, so may those of his agent A. In a conspiracy trial, every conspirator (whether charged or not) is regarded as the authorised agent of every other conspirator, so that everything said or done by any conspirator in pursuance of the conspiracy is admissible evidence. In practice, the result may well be the admission of much evidence which would normally be regarded as inadmissible hearsay; see *Ahern v R* (1988) 165 CLR 87; *R v Pektas* [1989] VR 239. The use of separate trials has been recommended by the High Court in cases where evidence clearly admissible against one alleged conspirator is equally not admissible against another: see *R v Darby* (1982) 148 CLR 668; 40 ALR 594 at 598 (at 11.51). And see J C Smith 'Proving Conspiracy' [1996] *Crim LR* 386.

The advantages which may accordingly flow from the inclusion of a conspiracy charge in an indictment often tempt prosecutors to add such a charge to a series of charges of substantive offences allegedly committed by two or more persons in concert. This practice has earned from the judges many expressions of strong disapproval: see *Board of Trade v Owen* [1957] AC 602; *Verrier v Director of Public Prosecutions* [1967] 2 AC 195.

Nevertheless one cannot help feeling aware, in reading these protests and admonitions, that judges have created, on this matter, something in the nature of a 'credibility gap'. For they have insisted with equal force that the choice whether to add a conspiracy charge or not is entirely one for the prosecuting authorities: see *R v Weaver* (1931) 45 CLR 321 and *R v McDonnell* [1966] 1 QB 233.

11.50 Prosecutors stand to gain much more than they stand to lose by adding a conspiracy charge. The procedural advantages have already been mentioned, but the considerations which might be offset against them need to be stated. If both the conspiracy and the substantive charges fail, either at the trial or on appeal, nothing is lost. If the substantive charges fail, but the conspiracy charge succeeds at the trial and survives appellate scrutiny, something is gained; and if the conspiracy charge is quashed on appeal, nothing is lost, once again. It is only in the comparatively rare case where the convictions on the substantive charges are quashed on appeal because of the misuse of evidence introduced to support a conspiracy charge which fails that the prosecution clearly loses what it might have gained by omitting the conspiracy charge.

In most instances, therefore, the courts allow the prosecution to play under rules of the 'heads I win, tails you lose' type. It is scarcely surprising that prosecutors seize the opportunity they are given; but there seems to be nothing meritorious about judicial criticism of prosecutors for succumbing to the temptations offered by judicial inaction.

The Criminal Code Act 1995 (Cth) provides specific safeguards against abuse in this connection. First, a person cannot be found guilty of conspiracy to commit an offence if all other parties to the agreement have been acquitted of the conspiracy and a finding of guilt would be inconsistent with their acquittal: s 11.4(a). Second, a 'court may dismiss a charge of conspiracy if it thinks that the interests of justice require it to do so': s 11.5(6). Third, a conspiracy prosecution may not be started without the consent of the Director of Public Prosecutions: s 11.5(8).

11.51 Since agreement is of the essence in conspiracy, the prosecution must prove the accused conspired with some other person. The other person need not be tried or even identified, but may be described in the indictment as a person unknown. Nonetheless, if the involvement of another party is not proved there is no agreement and, therefore, no conspiracy. The requirement of an agreement led the courts at one stage to adopt the view that if the only person the accused was alleged to have conspired with was acquitted, the accused must also be acquitted: *Dharmasena v R* [1951] AC 1; *Director of Public Prosecutions v Shannon* [1975] AC 717. Such a view is, it is submitted, incorrect. An acquittal is not a finding of innocence, but rather a finding that a person has not, on the basis of evidence admissible against that person, been proven guilty beyond a reasonable doubt. Thus, evidence admissible against A may establish A conspired with B, but evidence admissible against B might not establish B conspired with A. This possible scenario was recognised by the High Court in *R v Darby* (1982) 148 CLR 668; 40 ALR 594. The accused and T were tried together and convicted of conspiring to commit armed robbery. At trial evidence was given of admissions made by the accused that the object of the conspiracy was, in fact, armed robbery. On appeal by T, his conviction was quashed on the ground that the evidence against T (the admissions by the accused were admissible evidence against the accused only) fell short of establishing what crime the two had agreed to commit. The accused then appealed against his conviction, relying on the fact of T's acquittal. By a majority of four to one (Gibbs CJ, Aickin, Wilson and Brennan JJ; Murphy J dissenting), the court dismissed the appeal. The majority held that, whether tried separately or together, the acquittal of one co-accused does not necessarily mean that the other co-accused cannot be convicted. In a joint judgment, the majority stated (at 601):

> [T]he conviction of a conspirator whether tried together with or separately from an alleged co-conspirator may stand notwithstanding that the latter is or may be acquitted unless in all the circumstances of the case his conviction is inconsistent with the acquittal of the other person.

The justification of conspiracy

11.52 It appears then that conspiracy trials often involve considerable dangers of unfairness to accused persons. What then are the justifications for retaining conspiracy as a separate offence? They would appear to be twofold.

11.53 First, the offence of conspiracy serves the purpose of enabling criminal enterprises to be nipped in the bud. The offence can be used to prevent crimes from occurring. To abolish it would be to create a gap in the law that the offences of attempt and incitement would be inadequate to fill.

11.54 Second, the offence of conspiracy makes it easier to punish persons who plan and organise crimes but take no part in their actual commission. To a considerable extent, the criminal 'ring', indulging in large-scale murder and theft, masterminded by a directorate of 'arch-criminals', belongs more to the world of fiction than that of reality. However, in our society, the existence of organised crime is well established.

The existence of such criminal organisations is usually derived directly from the existence of legislation which prevents certain demands of certain people from being legally met. The demand for illicit drugs is the most obvious example. It is a matter of common experience that the demands will be met, whether or not the law approves; and so, if the law prohibits the meeting of the demand above ground, the purveyors of the supplies will continue their activities underground. The American experience with prohibition amply demonstrated this truth and some current Australian experiences seem also to substantiate it. It is foolish either to deny the existence of this demand, or to believe that it can be eradicated by repressive legislation. As St Augustine observed (in the context of the then laws against prostitution): '[I]f you do away with harlots, the world will be convulsed with lust'. St Thomas Aquinas, echoing his remark, observed that some evils have to be tolerated lest greater evils be incurred in trying to repress them.

11.55 Those who direct the general supply of vice and narcotics are usually too remote from the individual acts of supply to be struck at by the laws which govern the complicity of parties. If the organisation is large enough, they do not concern themselves with individual details and acts. They are concerned with the task of general organisation. The law of conspiracy is an extremely useful weapon with which to fight them; see *R v Sorby* [1986] VR 753.

The Australia-wide introduction of broad legislation establishing procedures for the freezing or forfeiture of the proceeds of crime has been accomplished by the enactment of the Proceeds of Crime Act 2002 (Cth), the Confiscation Act 1997 (Vic), and the Criminal Assets Recovery Act 1990 (NSW).

Statutory reform in Victoria

11.56E **Crimes Act 1958 (Vic)**

as amended by the Crimes (Conspiracy and Incitement) Act 1984
and the Crimes (Amendment) Act 1985
DIVISION 10 — CONSPIRACY

321 Conspiracy to commit an offence

(1) Subject to this Act, if a person agrees with any other person or persons that a course of conduct shall be pursued which will involve the commission of an offence by one or more of the parties to the agreement, he is guilty of the indictable offence of conspiracy to commit that offence.

(2) For a person to be guilty under sub-section (1) of conspiracy to commit a particular offence both he and at least one other party to the agreement —

(a) must intend that the offence the subject of the agreement be committed; and

(b) must intend or believe that any fact or circumstances the existence of which is an element of the offence will exist at the time when the conduct constituting the offence is to take place.

(3) A person may be guilty under sub-section (1) of conspiracy to commit an offence notwithstanding the existence of facts of which he is unaware which make commission of the offence by the agreed course of conduct impossible.

(4) A presentment at the Supreme Court or the County Court of a person for an offence against this section shall not be made without the approval of the Director of Public Prosecutions or of a person authorised by the Director of Public Prosecutions to give approval for the purposes of this sub-section.

321A Agreements to commit offences outside Victoria

(1) The expression 'the commission of an offence' in section 321(1) extends to the commission of an offence against a law in force only in a place outside Victoria if, but only if —

(a) the necessary elements of that offence include elements which, if present or occurring in Victoria, would constitute an offence against a law in Victoria; and

(b) one or more of the persons referred to in section 321(1) is or are in Victoria when the agreement referred to in that sub-section is made.

(2) Where all parties to an agreement are outside Victoria when it is made, section 321 shall apply in relation to it if, but only if, that agreement is to pursue a course of conduct which, if the agreement is carried out in accordance with their intentions, will necessarily amount to or involve the commission of an offence against a law in force in Victoria.

321B As to consequences of acquittal of co-conspirators

It is hereby declared that the conviction of a conspirator whether tried together with or separately from another alleged conspirator or other alleged conspirators may stand notwithstanding that the other alleged conspirator or conspirators is are or may be acquitted unless in all the circumstances of the case the conviction is inconsistent with the acquittal of the other alleged conspirator or conspirators.

321C Penalties for conspiracy

(1) Where a person is convicted under section 321 of conspiracy to commit an offence or offences against a law or laws in force in Victoria —

(a) if the penalty for the relevant offence is fixed by law, the person shall be liable to a penalty not exceeding the penalty for the relevant offence;

(b) if the relevant offence, or any of the relevant offences, is an offence for which the penalty is imprisonment for a term the maximum length of which is not prescribed by law, the person shall be liable to level 4 imprisonment;

(ba) despite paragraph (b), if the relevant offence, or any of the relevant offences, is murder or treason, the person is liable to —

(i) level 1 imprisonment; or

(ii) imprisonment for such other term as is fixed by the court — as the court determines;

(c) subject to paragraphs (a), (b), (ba) and (d), if the relevant offence, or any of the relevant offences, is an offence for which a maximum penalty is prescribed by law, the person shall be liable to a penalty not exceeding that maximum penalty or the accumulated maximum penalties, as the case may be; or

(d) if the relevant offence, or each of the relevant offences, is triable only in the Magistrates' Court, the person shall be liable to:

(i) level 6 imprisonment; or

(ii) imprisonment for a term not exceeding the maximum term of imprisonment (if any) prescribed in respect of the relevant offence or the greatest of the maximum terms prescribed in respect of any of the relevant offences, as the case requires —

whichever is the greater.

(2) Where a person is convicted under section 321 of conspiracy to commit an offence or offences against a law or laws in force only in a place outside Victoria —

(a) the person shall, if the relevant offence, or any of the relevant offences, is punishable by a term of imprisonment, be liable to a term of imprisonment not exceeding the maximum term of imprisonment prescribed in respect of the relevant offence; and

(b) the person shall, in any other case, be liable to a level 6 fine.

321D Application of certain provisions

Sections 321(2) and (3) and 321B shall apply, so far as they are capable of doing so and with such changes as are necessary, for the purpose of determining whether a person is guilty of conspiracy under any enactment other than section 321 or of conspiracy to cheat and defraud or of conspiracy to defraud.

321E Limitations on prosecution

(1) Where any enactment prohibits the institution or continuance of proceedings for an offence otherwise than by or with the consent of any person, the prohibition shall apply in relation to proceedings under section 321 for conspiracy to commit that offence.

(2) Where —

(a) an indictable offence has been committed in pursuance of an agreement; and

(b) proceedings may not be instituted for that offence because a time limit applicable to the institution of such proceedings has expired —

proceedings under section 321 for conspiracy to commit that offence shall not be instituted against any person on the basis of that agreement.

(3) A person shall not be liable to be convicted in respect of the same agreement of both
- (a) conspiracy under section 321; and
- (b) conspiracy under any enactment other than section 321 or of conspiracy to cheat and defraud or of conspiracy to defraud.

321F Abolition of certain offences of conspiracy at common law

(1) The offence of conspiracy at common law is hereby abolished.

(2) Nothing in sub-section (1) shall affect the offence of conspiracy at common law so far as it relates to conspiracy to cheat and defraud and conspiracy to defraud.

(3) Any offence at common law of incitement to commit the offence of conspiracy or attempt to commit the offence of conspiracy (whether the offence of conspiracy incited or attempted would be an offence at common law or under section 321 or any other enactment) is hereby abolished.

(4) A presentment at the Supreme Court or the County Court of a person for an offence of conspiracy to cheat and defraud or conspiracy to defraud shall not be made without the approval of the Director of Public Prosecutions or of a person authorised by the Director of Public Prosecutions to give approval for the purposes of this sub-section.

11.57 These provisions are substantially based upon the English Criminal Law Act 1977. In stating the elements of conspiracy, s 321(1) and (2) follow the common law. Section 321(3) makes clear that factual impossibility is no defence to a charge of conspiracy. Section 321B incorporates the holding in *R v Darby* (see **11.51**). Section 321F(1) abolishes the crime of conspiracy at common law. Therefore, in Victoria, it is not possible to argue for the existence of crimes such as conspiracy to corrupt public morals, conspiracy to commit a public mischief or conspiracy to commit a tort. Section 321F(2), however, preserves the common law crime of conspiracy to defraud.

PART 3

Defences

Self-Defence, Necessity, Duress, Superior Orders and Coercion

CHAPTER 12

INTRODUCTION

12.1 This chapter deals with a group of general defences to criminal charges which all share one characteristic. In the prototype cases in which the defences are proposed, the accused asserts that he or she has been compelled by extreme circumstances or the threats of another to break the law.

SELF-DEFENCE

12.2 The defence of self-defence is available to crimes involving the use of, or threat of, force to the person, most commonly homicide and assault offences. A successful defence of self-defence will result in a complete acquittal. The definition of self-defence varies in New South Wales and Victoria, but in general, a person may raise the defence if she or he acted for one of the following purposes:

(1) in order to defend herself or himself from unlawful violence;

(2) in order to defend another from unlawful violence;

(3) in order to prevent the commission of a crime; and

(4) in order to exercise a power of lawful arrest.

Similar principles apply in respect of each of these types of case: *R v Chisam* (1963) 47 Cr App R 130; *R v Duffy* [1967] 1 QB 63; *R v Redman* [1978] VR 178.

12.3 In such cases, the accused will be entitled to a complete acquittal if three conditions are satisfied:

(1) the accused was genuinely acting for one of these purposes. Obviously, the accused may not take advantage of such a situation arising in order to do away with an enemy;

(2) the accused used no greater degree of force than he or she honestly believed to be necessary in the circumstances of the case. This condition poses a test which is

subjective in nature; the question is whether the accused believed that the force used was proportionate to the necessity of the situation in which that person was placed; and

(3) the accused used no greater degree of force than a reasonable person would have regarded as necessary in the circumstances of the case. This condition poses a test which is objective in nature; the question is not what the accused believed to be reasonably necessary, but what an ordinary person would have regarded as necessary.

Self-defence is open-ended in its formulation in the sense that there are few substantive rules limiting its scope and it is very much a matter for the jury to decide: *DPP Reference (No 1 of 1991)* (1992) 60 A Crim R 43 at 46.

Considerable controversy has existed over the question of the liability of an accused who satisfies conditions one and two (the subjective requirements), but who fails to satisfy condition three (the objective requirement). In *R v Howe* (1958) 100 CLR 448, the High Court held that in such a case the accused would be guilty of manslaughter. In *Palmer v R* [1971] AC 814, the Privy Council took the view that in such a case the accused's defence would fail altogether, and he or she would be guilty of murder. In *Viro v R* (1978) 18 ALR 257, a majority of the High Court affirmed its earlier decision in *R v Howe*. Finally, in *Zecevic v Director of Public Prosecutions (Vic)* (1987) 162 CLR 645; 71 ALR 641 (at **12.4.C**), the High Court disapproved of its earlier decisions and chose to follow the approach taken 16 years earlier by the Privy Council and by the English Court of Appeal, Criminal Division. It is not, overall, a laudable example of the genius of the common law, in relation to a subject of great general importance in the administration of criminal justice. In New South Wales and Victoria, however, the defence of excessive self-defence (or in Victoria, defensive homicide) reducing murder to manslaughter has been re-introduced by statute (see **12.5**).

For crimes other than murder and manslaughter, the common law of self-defence, as enunciated by *Zecevic*, below, is applied in Victoria. New South Wales has replaced the common law with a statutory defence (at **12.5**).

12.4C Zecevic v Director of Public Prosecutions (Vic)[1]

(1987) 162 CLR 645; 71 ALR 641
High Court of Australia

Wilson, Dawson and **Toohey JJ**: The appellant, Fadil Zecevic, was convicted in the Supreme Court of Victoria of having murdered Harold Peter Triebel on 16 July 1983 at Ascot Vale in Melbourne. This appeal is against the judgment of the Full Court of the Supreme Court dismissing an appeal against that conviction.

1. The judgment of the Chief Justice appears before that of Wilson, Dawson and Toohey JJ in the report of this decision. It has been printed after their judgment in this extract, because Mason CJ accepted that judgment as correctly stating the law of self-defence in Australia.

The appellant and his family, consisting of his parents, four brothers and one of his sisters, were migrants from Albania to this country. In 1982 the parents and the brothers all moved into a block of units which they had built at Ascot Vale. The brothers were by this time married and occupied separate units. The appellant and his wife moved into Unit 5. In addition to the units occupied by the family, two units were available for rental and one of them, Unit 6 which adjoined Unit 5, was rented by the deceased and occupied by him and his girlfriend.

The relationship between the deceased and the Zecevic family, which was initially pleasant, began to deteriorate, largely, it seems, because of the deceased's repeated failure to close the security gates to the courtyard around which the units were erected and his failure to place his car in the garage provided.

On 16 July 1983, there was an altercation between the appellant and the deceased after the deceased had again left the gates open and left his car outside the garage. The appellant in his unsworn statement described that altercation and the events leading to the shooting of the deceased. He said that he had bought some bread and milk at a shop and returned home. He continued as follows:

> I asked him why he didn't close the doors and why he didn't put his car in the garage. He got very angry with me and say, 'What's it to you, I do what I like, I pay rent'. I say, 'Why do you think I spend so much money on the doors?' and he said, 'It's none of your business, I do what I like, I pay $115 rent'. He won't close the doors and he went to his unit. I went to my unit and opened the door and I put the bread and milk on the steps. Then I went and knocked on his door. I was upset with him because he won't shut the gates. When I knocked on his door, the glass broke. He come to the door and looked very angry. His colour had changed and he was white. I asked him why he did not close the doors and why he did not put his car in the garage, and he say, 'Wait a second', and went back inside. I stood back from his door and he come with his hands behind in his back and stabbed me. He stabbed me in the chest on the left side, on the left side, but I did not see the knife. I thought — I didn't know how bad I was stabbed. I was angry and very much scared. I ran inside to my unit.
>
> He say, 'I blow your head off'. I believed he had a knife, and I thought he might have a shotgun in the car. I ran up to my bedroom. I was very angry and very frightened. I was not sure what I was doing at that stage. I got the gun and shells and went downstairs and loaded the gun. I could see Harry and I was very scared and upset. He was near his car, and I thought Harry was going to do something to me, and he was going to, he was going to kill me. I had been stabbed already, and I thought he might have had a gun or something in the car.
>
> After that I don't remember exactly what happened. I was lost. I remember I see him there and I shot. He was facing me and I start to shoot. I don't remember how many times, I don't remember how many time I shoot. At that time I was very frightened and angry and I wasn't myself at all. I knew I didn't want to kill him. I wanted to protect myself because I thought he was going to kill me.

Elsewhere in his unsworn statement the appellant said that the deceased, who was some years younger than him, had told him that he had a black belt in karate, that he was a boxer and lifted weights and that he kept something for protection in his car. There was some evidence given by the deceased's girlfriend that those facts were true, the article in the car being a large stainless steel barbecue fork.

Evidence was given by the appellant's brother that immediately after the shooting they observed the deceased's body on the ground with a knife in his hand. The prosecution, however, led evidence from which it might be inferred that the knife came from the appellant's own unit and had been placed in the deceased's hand after the killing.

The issue of self-defence was raised but, notwithstanding the matters which the appellant asserted in his unsworn statement, that issue was withdrawn from the jury by the trial judge. His Honour took this course because he concluded that the only inference open upon the evidence was that the appellant did not reasonably believe that an unlawful attack which threatened him with death or serious bodily harm was being or was about to be made upon him. In so ruling the trial judge apparently had regard to the first of the propositions laid down in *Viro v R* (1978) 141 CLR 88, 18 ALR 257 in the judgment of Mason J (CLR at 146–7, ALR at 303). It is convenient at this point to set out those propositions because, as will emerge, their relevance in this case extends beyond the first of them. They are as follows:

1. (a) It is for the jury first to consider whether when the accused killed the deceased the accused reasonably believed that an unlawful attack which threatened him with death or serious bodily harm was being or was about to be made upon him. (b) By the expression 'reasonably believed' is meant, not what a reasonable man would have believed, but what the accused himself might reasonably believe in all the circumstances in which he found himself.
2. If the jury is satisfied beyond reasonable doubt that there was no reasonable belief by the accused of such an attack no question of self-defence arises.
3. If the jury is not satisfied beyond reasonable doubt that there was no such reasonable belief by the accused, it must then consider whether the force in fact used by the accused was reasonably proportionate to the danger which he believed he faced.
4. If the jury is not satisfied beyond reasonable doubt that more force was used than was reasonably proportionate it should acquit.
5. If the jury is satisfied beyond reasonable doubt that more force was used, its verdict should be either manslaughter or murder, that depending upon the answer to the final question for the jury — did the accused believe that the force which he used was reasonably proportionate to the danger which he believed he faced?
6. If the jury is satisfied beyond reasonable doubt that the accused did not have such a belief the verdict will be murder. If it is not satisfied beyond reasonable doubt that the accused did not have that belief the verdict will be manslaughter.

Counsel for the appellant contended that, even accepting the requirements of the first proposition, the evidence was sufficient in this case to require the issue of self-defence to be left to the jury, but he also submitted that the law relating to self-defence should not require that an accused person's belief that he is being threatened with death or serious bodily harm be a reasonable belief. It is sufficient, so it was contended, that an accused person hold an actual belief of that kind whether reasonable or not. That submission was dependent upon a contention that no distinction should be drawn between the definitional and defence elements of the crime. It was put that, notwithstanding that a plea of self-defence is by way of justification or excuse and therefore a defence to the charge, a rule creating such a defence merely supplies additional details of the scope of the relevant offence. The defence is a negative condition of the offence and is therefore an integral part of it: see Glanville Williams, *Textbook of Criminal Law*, 2nd ed (1983), pp 137–8. For that reason, so the argument continued, the mental element necessary to raise the plea bears, in a negative sense, upon the *mens rea* of the offence itself making it inappropriate in cases of homicide to require, in addition to the subjective requirement that the accused should believe that he is threatened with death or serious bodily harm, an objective requirement that the belief should be reasonable.

Although self-defence is still commonly referred to as a defence, the ultimate onus of proof with respect to self-defence does not rest on the accused. Since *Woolmington v Director of Public Prosecutions* [1935] AC 462, it has been clearly established that once the evidence discloses the possibility that the fatal act was done in self-defence, a burden falls upon the prosecution to disprove that fact, that is to say, to prove beyond reasonable doubt that the fatal act was not done in self-defence. The jury must be instructed accordingly whether or not the plea is actually raised by the accused: *Director of Public Prosecutions v Walker* [1974] 1 WLR 1090 at 1094.

Nevertheless, the modern law of self-defence has its origin in rules which distinguished between justifiable and excusable homicide. The importance of the distinction lay largely in the different consequences of successful pleas of justification and excuse and now is a matter of history. Justifiable homicide carried with it commendation rather than blame and accordingly entitled the accused to total acquittal, entailing no forfeiture and requiring no pardon. It extended to killing done in the execution of justice, which came to include both the apprehension of felons and the prevention of felonies and thus those cases of self-defence which were in response to a felonious attack by the deceased. Excusable homicide, on the other hand, was not entirely without blame and merely excused rather than acquitted, requiring, at first, a pardon and involving, for a somewhat longer period, forfeiture. It was concerned, not with the execution of justice, but with a necessary and reasonable response to a threat to life and limb, see *R v Lawson and Forsythe* [1986] VR 515 at 554–68, per Ormiston J; Dixon, 'The Development of the Law of Homicide' (1935) 9 *ALJ (Supp)* 64; Snelling, 'Killing in Self-Defence' (1960) 34 *ALJ* 130. Any practical distinction between justifiable homicide and excusable homicide disappeared with the abolition of forfeiture by statute in 1828 and today it is no part of the law in Australia to differentiate between the two: see 9 Geo IV, ch 31, s 10, (UK) enacted in Victoria from time to time; cf *Crimes Act 1958* (Vic) s 7, repealed by the *Crimes (Classification of Offences) Act 1981* (Vic) s 11(1). But the history of the matter serves to explain why the requirement of reasonableness, which was a requirement of excusable homicide, has remained part of the law of self defence. Moreover, it establishes why that requirement ought not be regarded as a definitional element of the offence in question but as going rather to exculpation. True it is that in result a successful plea of self-defence resembles justification rather than excuse because it entitles the accused to a full acquittal, but in scope and in practice nowadays the plea has a greater connection with excusable homicide, being in most cases, related to the preservation of life and limb rather than the execution of justice.

To require as part of the law of self-defence that the accused should reasonably have believed that he was threatened with death or serious bodily harm was said by counsel for the appellant to be a misapplication, presumably by analogy, of the common law defence of mistake of fact which requires the mistake to be both honest and reasonable. Whilst it was conceded that a requirement of reasonableness was appropriate in the case of a defence to an offence of strict liability, it was submitted that it was entirely inappropriate in the case of a plea of self-defence which operates as a defence to offences requiring *mens rea*. However, the history and purpose of the law of self-defence do not support the suggestion made. Self-defence, as we know it, was essentially exculpatory in its origin and the fact that it now falls to be excluded by the prosecution rather than proved by the defence does not alter its true nature. Moreover, after a period of some uncertainty it has been established in *He Kaw Teh v R* (1985) 157 CLR 523, 60 ALR 449 that if the question of honest and reasonable mistake arises, the ultimate burden rests upon the prosecution to prove the absence of the exculpatory belief. As Brennan J put it in the case cited (CLR at 580, ALR at 490): '... the absence of an exculpatory belief is now seen as a form of *mens rea* implied in certain circumstances as an element in a statutory offence the onus of proving which rests on the prosecution.' See also per Gibbs CJ (CLR) at 534, Wilson J at 553, 558 and Dawson J at 593–4. There is, therefore, no relevant distinction between honest and reasonable mistake and self-defence which lends support to the appellant's argument.

Putting to one side the question of the sufficiency of the evidence, what we have said would be enough to dispose of the submissions made on behalf of the appellant which were directed against the first of the six propositions formulated by Mason J and accepted by a majority in *Viro*. However, argument extended to the re-examination of all of those propositions, this being in accordance with the basis upon which special leave to appeal was granted.

The six propositions were intended to state in summary form the issues which arise for the determination of a jury when a plea of self-defence is raised in a case of homicide. To the extent that they deal with the use of excessive force, they are based upon the view expressed by Dixon CJ in *R v Howe* (1958) 100 CLR 448 at 460–1. In expressing that view, Dixon CJ assumed that an occasion for self-defence had arisen and that the force or violence used went beyond what was needed for the protection of the accused or what the accused could reasonably have believed was necessary for his protection. Upon those assumptions Dixon CJ asked what crime was committed as a result and his reply, at 461, was as follows:

> There is no clear and definite judicial decision providing an answer to this question but it seems reasonable in principle to regard such a homicide as reduced to manslaughter, and that view has the support of not a few judicial statements to be found in the reports.

That view, which in *Howe* was adopted by McTiernan and Fullagar JJ, was not accepted by the Privy Council in *Palmer v R* [1971] AC 814 but in *Viro* it was unanimously held that this court is no longer bound by decisions of the Privy Council. Whilst the correctness of the decision in *Howe* was the basis upon which Mason J enunciated certain of the propositions in *Viro*, those propositions were accepted by Gibbs J (CLR at 128), Jacobs J (CLR at 158) and Murphy J (CLR at 171) only for the purpose of achieving a measure of certainty in a situation of diversity of opinion and Barwick CJ was in dissent. The status of *Viro* as an authority upon the use of excessive force in self-defence is, for this reason, open to question. Moreover, it is apparent that difficulties have been experienced in instructing juries in accordance with the fifth and sixth propositions in *Viro* which, being based upon *Howe*, necessarily contain refinements which cannot be expressed in a way which makes them readily understandable. It is for these reasons that it is appropriate to turn once again to *Viro*.

The relevant issue in *Viro* was whether manslaughter is the appropriate verdict where only the use of excessive force stands in the way of an acquittal upon a charge of murder. Only three justices (Stephen, Mason and Aickin JJ) were of the view that manslaughter was the appropriate verdict and in so holding relied upon *Howe* and the rationale that 'the moral culpability of a person who kills another in defending himself but who fails in a plea of self-defence only because the force which he believed to be necessary exceeded that which was reasonably necessary falls short of the moral culpability ordinarily associated with murder': *Viro* (CLR at 139) per Mason J. On the other hand, the remaining four justices (Barwick CJ, Gibbs, Jacobs and Murphy JJ) were, for differing reasons, of the view that *Howe* should not be followed and that the 'defence of self-defence either succeeds so as to result in an acquittal or it is disproved in which case as a defence it is rejected': see *Palmer* at 832. Barwick CJ and Gibbs J preferred the approach of the Privy Council in *Palmer* at 831: 'It is both good law and good sense that a man who is attacked may defend himself. It is both good law and good sense that he may do, but may only do, what is reasonably necessary. But everything will depend upon the particular facts and circumstances.'

Jacobs J gave the defence a wider scope by saying that as long as the accused believed that he had used only the necessary amount of force in self-defence, then there should be an acquittal, provided that the belief was not irrational: see CLR at 156–8. Murphy J went even further and abandoned any objective test, holding that a belief on the part of the accused that he was defending himself was sufficient to lead to acquittal: see CLR at 168.

In those circumstances, it seems desirable to restate the law relating to self-defence with such assistance as might be gained from *Howe*, *Palmer* and *Viro*. It is, we think, unnecessary to go to the earlier cases touching upon the consequences of the use of excessive force in self-defence. As Dixon CJ recognised in *Howe*, they provide no clear and definite result and they in fact led to different conclusions in *Howe* and *Palmer*. Perhaps, however, some mention should be made of *R v McKay* [1957] VR 560 in which Lowe J, at 563, laid down the proposition: 'If the occasion warrants action in self-defence or for the prevention of felony or the apprehension of the felon, but the person taking action acts beyond the necessity of the occasion and kills the offender, the crime is manslaughter — not murder.'

The Full Court of the Supreme Court of South Australia in *R v Howe* [1958] SASR 95 placed considerable reliance upon this passage and it was the view of that court which was upheld in *Howe*. However, the proposition laid down in *McKay* suffers from a serious defect in that it does not require the accused to have believed that the excessive force was necessary. There may be some explanation for this inadequacy, though hardly satisfactory, in the fact that *McKay* was a case of the apprehension of a felon rather than a case of self-defence. But it is a shortcoming which, as Taylor J observed in *Howe* at 467, weakens considerably any support which may be derived from *McKay* for the test ultimately propounded by the majority in *Howe*.

It is apparent, we think, from the difficulties which appear to have been experienced in the application of *Viro*, that there is wisdom in the observation of the Privy Council in *Palmer* that an explanation of the law of self-defence requires no set words or formula. The question to be asked in the end is quite simple. It is whether the accused believed upon reasonable grounds that it was necessary in self-defence to do what he did. If he had that belief and there were reasonable grounds for it, or if the jury is left in reasonable doubt about the matter, then he is entitled to an acquittal. Stated in that form, the question is one of general application and is not limited to cases of homicide. Where homicide is involved some elaboration may be necessary.

Murder consists of an unlawful killing done with intent to kill or to do grievous bodily harm. Recklessness may be put to one side as having no apparent relevance in the context of self-defence. Manslaughter also consists of an unlawful killing, but without such an intent. A killing which is done in self-defence is done with justification or excuse and is not unlawful, though it be done with intent to kill or do grievous bodily harm. However, a person who kills with the intention of killing or of doing serious bodily harm can hardly believe on reasonable grounds that it is necessary to do so in order to defend himself unless he perceives a threat which calls for that response. A threat does not ordinarily call for that response unless it causes a reasonable apprehension on the part of that person of death or serious bodily harm. If the response of an accused goes beyond what he believed to be necessary to defend himself or if there were no reasonable grounds for a belief on his part that the response was necessary in defence of himself, then the occasion will not have been one which would support a plea of self-defence. That is to say, the killing will have been without justification or excuse and it will be for the jury to determine how it must be regarded. If it was done with intent to kill or to do grievous bodily harm, then unless there was provocation reducing it to manslaughter, it will be murder. In the absence of such an intent it will be manslaughter: see *Viro* (CLR at 101).

When upon the evidence the question of self-defence arises, the trial judge should in his charge to the jury place the question in its factual setting, identifying those considerations which may assist the jury to reach its conclusion. In attempting to identify those considerations in any abstract manner here, there is a danger of appearing to elevate matters of evidence to rules of law. For example, it will in many cases be appropriate for a jury to be told that, in determining whether the accused believed that his actions were necessary in order to defend himself and whether he held that belief on reasonable grounds, it should consider whether the force used by the accused was proportionate to the threat offered. However, the whole of the circumstances should be considered, of which the degree of force used may be only part. There is no rule which dictates the use which the jury must make of the evidence and the ultimate question is for it alone. The trial judge should also offer such assistance by way of comment as is called for in the particular case. No doubt it will often also be desirable to remind the jury that in the context of self-defence it should approach its task in a practical manner and without undue nicety, giving proper weight to the predicament of the accused which may have afforded little, if any, opportunity for calm deliberation or detached reflection.

There is, however, one situation which requires particular mention. It should, we think, be regarded as raising only evidentiary matters to be considered in arriving at an answer to the ultimate question, although in the code States it is treated as raising matters of law: see s 272 of the *Criminal Code 1899* (Qld); s 249 of the *Criminal Code 1913* (WA); s 47 of the *Criminal Code 1924* (Tas). Where an accused person raising a plea of self-defence was the original aggressor and induced or provoked the assault against which he claims the right to defend himself, it will be for the jury to consider whether the original aggression had ceased so as to have enabled the accused to form a belief, upon reasonable grounds, that his actions were necessary in self-defence. For this purpose, it will be relevant to consider the extent to which the accused declined further conflict and quit the use of force or retreated from it, these being matters which may bear upon the nature of the occasion and the use which the accused made of it. Indeed, even in circumstances in which the accused was not the original aggressor, retreat in the face of a threat of violence before resort to force may be relevant to the belief of the accused or the reasonableness of the grounds upon which the accused based his belief. There is, however, no longer any rule that the accused must have retreated as far as possible before attempting to defend himself. It is a circumstance to be considered with all the others in determining whether the accused believed upon reasonable grounds that what he did was necessary in self-defence: *Howe* at 462–4 per Dixon CJ; *Viro* (CLR at 115–16) per Gibbs J.

What we have said involves a departure from the propositions which were accepted in *Viro,* but it is necessary to refer specifically to only two of the differences. In *Viro* self-defence is confined to a response to an unlawful attack, whereas the law as we have explained it is not so confined. Whilst in most cases in which self-defence is raised the attack said to give rise to the need for the accused to defend himself will have been unlawful, as a matter of law there is no requirement that it should have been so. This is demonstrated by the exhaustive examination of authority carried out by Ormiston J in *R v Lawson* and *Forsythe*. Thus, for example, self-defence is available against an attack by a person who, by reason of insanity, is incapable of forming the necessary intent to commit a crime. It is, however, only in an unusual situation that an attack which is not unlawful will provide reasonable grounds for resort to violence in self defence. The whole of the surrounding circumstances are to be taken into account and where an accused person has created the situation in which force might lawfully be applied to apprehend him or cause him to desist — where, for example, he is engaged in criminal behaviour of a violent kind — then the only reasonable view of his resistance to that force will be that he is acting, not in self-defence, but as an aggressor in pursuit of his original design. A person may not create a continuing situation of emergency and provoke a lawful attack upon himself and yet claim upon reasonable grounds the right to defend himself against that attack.

The second difference lies in the treatment of the use of excessive or disproportionate force. As we have expressed the law, the use of excessive force in the belief that it was necessary in self-defence will not automatically result in a verdict of manslaughter. If the jury concludes that there were no reasonable grounds for a belief that the degree of force used was necessary, the defence of self-defence will fail and the circumstances will fall to be considered by the jury without reference to that plea. There is some force in the view, adopted by Stephen, Mason and Aickin JJ in *Viro*, that this may result in the conviction for murder of a person lacking the moral culpability associated with that crime. Experience would suggest, however, that such a result is unlikely in practice. As the Court of Appeal in England pointed out in *R v McInnes* (1971) 55 Cr App Rep 551 at 562: '... it is important to stress that the facts upon which the plea of self-defence is unsuccessfully sought to be based may nevertheless serve the accused in good stead. They may, for example, go to show that he may have acted under provocation or that, although acting unlawfully, he may have lacked the intent to kill or cause serious bodily harm, and in that way render the proper verdict one of manslaughter.'

And, as we have already said, an accused person is not liable to be convicted of murder unless the jury is satisfied beyond reasonable doubt that there was an intention to kill or do grievous bodily harm.

We have anxiously considered whether the departures which we propose from *Howe* and *Viro* could occasion injustice to persons presently awaiting trial for offences where self-defence may be raised, including the present appellant in the event of a new trial. For the reasons which we have given we think this unlikely. Of course, the risk of injustice, however slight, must be weighed carefully. On the other hand, there are compelling reasons for the course which we propose. Special leave was granted in this case to enable a review of the common law relating to self-defence as it was expounded in *Viro*. A Full Court of seven members was convened for the purpose. Believing, as we do, that the law as we have set it out is dictated by basic principle upon a matter of fundamental importance, it is unthinkable that the court should abdicate its responsibility by declining to declare it accordingly. It has the virtue of being readily understandable by a jury. It restores consistency to the law relating to self-defence whether raised in a case of homicide or otherwise. Finally, it has the effect of expressing the common law in terms which are in accord with the views expressed in *Palmer* (adopted in England in *McInnes*) and which are generally consonant with the law in the code States.

Turning to the evidence in this case, it is necessary to bear in mind that it was entirely for the jury to determine whether the appellant's version of events was true: *Lee Chun-Chuen v R* [1963] AC 220 at 230. Moreover, the appellant had only to raise a reasonable doubt in the minds of the jury to entitle him to succeed in his defence. As Gibbs J observed in *R v Muratovic* [1967] Qd R 15 at 20, '... the plea of self-defence may seem to a judge to be weak and tenuous, but it is for a jury not a judge to decide upon a plea of this kind, as upon any other question of fact, provided … that there is evidence on which a reasonable jury could decide the issue favourably to the accused'.

The issue of self-defence was squarely raised. Clearly there was evidence upon which the jury could conclude that the appellant believed it was necessary to do what he did in order to defend himself. There was also evidence of the grounds for that belief. Whether those grounds were reasonable was a matter for the jury. Upon the account given by the appellant in his unsworn statement, he had been stabbed by the deceased a short time before he fired the fatal shots. There was evidence of an injury consistent with his statement. The appellant said that the deceased had threatened to 'blow his head off'. He said that he believed that the deceased may have had a shotgun in his car and that it was necessary to act in order to defend himself. The weakness in the appellant's case was the fact that he went to his own flat after the deceased threatened him and, after an interval of time had elapsed, re-emerged at the scene of the shooting. However, if the jury believed the appellant, it is not inconceivable that it might have adopted a view of the facts which would have favoured him in his defence of self-defence. The issue should have been left to the jury.

We would allow the appeal.

Mason CJ: … I am unable to accept the submission that self-defence lacks an objective element. *Howe, Palmer* and five of the judgments in *Viro* assert the existence of an objective element. And, as Wilson, Dawson and Toohey JJ point out in their reasons for judgment in the present case, neither the history of the law of self-defence nor its exculpatory character support the appellant's submission. Nor does that history or the character of the defence assist the appellant's claim that the requirement that the accused should reasonably have believed that he was threatened with death or serious bodily harm has in some way or other developed analogically, though incorrectly, from the common law defence of honest and reasonable mistake of fact.

Although I would reject the appellant's principal submission, there remains the question whether the court should continue to adhere to *Howe* and *Viro*. In *Viro* I considered that we should accept and follow *Howe* because: '… the moral culpability of a person who kills another in defending himself but who fails in a plea of self-defence only because the force which he believed to be necessary exceeded that which was reasonably necessary falls short of the moral culpability ordinarily associated with murder' ((CLR) at 139, (ALR) at 297).

And I thought that much of the uncertainty that was said to be inherent in the application of the principle enunciated in *Howe* would disappear as the principle came to be refined and elaborated in later cases.

Regrettably this has not taken place. Instead trial judges have continued to encounter difficulties in explaining the elements of the *Viro* formulation to juries: see *R v McManus* (1985) 2 NSWLR 448 at 461–2; *R v Lawson and Forsythe* [1986] VR 515 at 547–9. With the benefit of hindsight it can be seen that it was a mistake to attempt to state the law of self-defence in a form which sought to take account of the onus of proof. This attempt led to complexity which might otherwise have been avoided. And the same comment might be made about the inclusion in the formulation of three separate elements of reasonableness. But that was the doctrine according to *Howe*. Quite apart from these aspects of the matter, the need to make findings about the accused's reasonable belief and his subjective belief rendered the jury's already difficult task even more complex. I am not confident that a reformation of the *Viro* formulation will enable trial judges to explain simply to juries the issue which they are called upon to determine according to the *Howe* doctrine. It is interesting to observe that the Judicial Committee in *Palmer*, well in advance of the *Viro* formulation, described the *Howe* doctrine as 'requiring a jury to go through a complicated and difficult process' (at 831). Obviously this evaluation of *Howe* played a decisive part in its rejection because Lord Morris went on to speak (at 831) of the version of the defence vindicated in *Palmer* as 'one which can be and will be readily understood by any jury', as 'a straightforward conception', involving 'no abstruse legal thought'.

I still believe that the doctrine enunciated in *Howe* and *Viro* expresses a concept of self-defence which best accords with acceptable standards of culpability, so that an accused whose only error is that he lacks reasonable grounds for his belief that the degree of force used was necessary for his self-defence is guilty of manslaughter, not murder. But in the light of experience since *Viro*, which is in my view not wholly to be accounted for by the complexity of the summary formulation at the end of my judgment, I recognise that the doctrine imposes an onerous burden on trial judges and juries. In this respect I take note of the fact that in this case Wilson, Brennan, Dawson and Toohey JJ have concluded that the doctrine of self-defence enunciated in *Howe* creates difficult problems for trial judges and juries. For this reason there is a serious risk that the doctrine will not achieve its desired goal.

In the result I now consider that we should accept that the joint judgment of Wilson, Dawson and Toohey JJ correctly states the law of self-defence. The law on this topic in Australia will then conform to the law in the United Kingdom as expounded in *Palmer* and *R v McInnes* [1971] 1 WLR 1600; [1971] 3 All ER 295, and in other jurisdictions. The risk that an accused person may be convicted of murder when he lacks reasonable grounds for his belief that the degree of force used was necessary for his self-defence will be alleviated by several factors. It is for the Crown to establish that there was an absence of reasonable grounds for the accused's belief. A jury will be slow to make such a finding if the Crown has failed to satisfy them that the accused did not honestly believe that the force used was necessary. And the jury will not return a verdict of murder unless it is satisfied that there was an intention to kill or to do grievous bodily harm.

For the reasons given by Wilson, Dawson and Toohey JJ I would allow the appeal.

[**Deane** and **Gaudron JJ** delivered separate judgments in which they agreed the appeal be allowed and a new trial ordered. **Brennan J** delivered a separate judgment agreeing with **Wilson, Dawson** and **Toohey JJ**. Appeal allowed.]

[See *R v Hawes* (1994) 35 NSWLR 294.]

12.5 Notes and questions

1. Does the argument that a *Viro* direction creates an unduly difficult task for trial judges and for juries justify a departure from a basic principle of criminal responsibility as it applies to murder? Could not the difficulties in the language employed by Mason J in *Viro* have been dealt with by an effective reformulation in plain English of the direction?
2. In New South Wales, the defence of self-defence has been placed upon a statutory footing. The legislation re-establishes the doctrine of excessive self-defence reducing murder to manslaughter. The Crimes Act 1900 (NSW), as amended by the Crimes Amendment (Self-Defence) Act 2001 (NSW), provides:

418 Self-defence — when available

(1) A person is not criminally responsible for an offence if the person carries out the conduct constituting the offence in self-defence.

(2) A person carries out conduct in self-defence if and only if the person believes the conduct is necessary:

a) to defend himself or herself or another person, or

b) to prevent or terminate the unlawful deprivation of his or her liberty or the liberty of another person, or

c) to protect property from unlawful taking, destruction, damage or interference, or

d) to prevent criminal trespass to any land or premises or to remove a person committing any such criminal trespass,

and the conduct is a reasonable response in the circumstances as he or she perceives them.

419 Self-defence — onus of proof

In any criminal proceedings in which the application of this Division is raised, the prosecution has the onus of proving, beyond reasonable doubt, that the person did not carry out the conduct in self-defence.

420 Self-defence — not available if death inflicted to protect property or trespass to property

This Division does not apply if the person uses force that involves the intentional or reckless infliction of death only:

a) to protect property, or

b) to prevent criminal trespass or to remove a person committing criminal trespass.

421 Self-defence — excessive force that inflicts death

(1) This section applies if:

a) the person uses force that involves the infliction of death, and

b) the conduct is not a reasonable response in the circumstances as he or she perceives them,
c) but the person believes the conduct is necessary:
d) to defend himself or herself or another person, or
e) to prevent or terminate the unlawful deprivation of his or her liberty or the liberty of another person.

(2) The person is not criminally responsible for murder but, on a trial for murder, the person is to be found guilty of manslaughter if the person is otherwise criminally responsible for manslaughter.

According to *R v Katarzynski* [2002] NSWSC 613, in New South Wales the questions now to be considered by the jury when self-defence is raised are:

(a) is there a reasonable possibility that the accused believed that his or her conduct was necessary in order to defend him or herself; and
(b) if there was, is there also a reasonable possibility that what the accused did was a reasonable response in the circumstances as she or he perceived them to be?

The first question is determined from a completely subjective point of view considering all the personal characteristics of the accused at the time he or she carried out the conduct. The second question is determined by an entirely objective assessment of the proportionality of the accused's response to the situation the accused believed he or she faced. The Crown would negate self-defence if it proves either (a) that the accused did not genuinely believe that it was necessary to act as he or she did in his or her own defence; or (b) that what the accused did was not a reasonable response to the danger as he or she perceived it to be.

Katarzynski also considered the relevance of self-induced intoxication to a defence of self-defence. It was held that intoxication is relevant to the first, subjective question to be determined by the jury, that is, whether it is reasonably possible that the accused believed it was necessary to do what was done in self-defence, but not to the second question, being whether the response was reasonable.

3. In Victoria also, the defence of self-defence has been placed upon a statutory footing. The legislation re-establishes the doctrine of excessive self-defence by introduction of a new, lesser offence of defensive homicide. The Crimes Act 1958 (Vic), as amended by the Crimes (Homicide) Act 2005 (Vic), provides:

4 Alternative verdict of defensive homicide on charge for murder

(1) If on the trial of a person for murder the jury are not satisfied that he or she is guilty of murder but are satisfied that he or she is guilty of an

offence against section 9AD (defensive homicide), the jury may acquit the accused of murder and find him or her guilty of defensive homicide and he or she is liable to punishment accordingly.

9AC Murder — 'self-defence'

A person is not guilty of murder if he or she carries out the conduct that would otherwise constitute murder while believing the conduct to be necessary to defend himself or herself or another person from the infliction of death or really serious injury.

9AD Defensive homicide

A person who, by his or her conduct, kills another person in circumstances that, but for section 9AC, would constitute murder, is guilty of an indictable offence (defensive homicide) and liable to level 3 imprisonment (20 years maximum) if he or she did not have reasonable grounds for the belief referred to in that section.

9AE Manslaughter — 'self-defence'

A person is not guilty of manslaughter if he or she carries out the conduct that would otherwise constitute manslaughter while believing the conduct to be necessary

(a) to defend himself or herself or another person; or

(b) to prevent or terminate the unlawful deprivation of his or her liberty or the liberty of another person —

and he or she had reasonable grounds for that belief.

9AF Self-defence exceptions do not apply in the case of lawful conduct

Sections 9AC and 9AE do not apply if —

(a) the person is responding to lawful conduct; and

(b) at the time of his or her response, the person knows that the conduct is lawful.

9AH Family violence

(1) Without limiting section 9AC, 9AD or 9AE, for the purposes of murder, defensive homicide or manslaughter, in circumstances where family violence is alleged a person may believe, and may have reasonable grounds for believing, that his or her conduct is necessary —

(a) to defend himself or herself or another person; or

(b) to prevent or terminate the unlawful deprivation of his or her liberty or the liberty of another person —

even if —

(c) he or she is responding to a harm that is not immediate; or

(d) his or her response involves the use of force in excess of the force involved in the harm or threatened harm.

(2) Without limiting the evidence that may be adduced, in circumstances where family violence is alleged evidence of a kind referred to in subsection (3) may be relevant in determining whether —

(a) a person has carried out conduct while believing it to be necessary for a purpose referred to in sub-section (1)(a) or (b); or

(b) a person had reasonable grounds for a belief held by him or her that conduct is necessary for a purpose referred to in sub-section (1)(a) or (b); or

(c) a person has carried out conduct under duress.

(3) Evidence of —

(a) the history of the relationship between the person and a family member, including violence by the family member towards the person or by the person towards the family member or by the family member or the person in relation to any other family member;

(b) the cumulative effect, including psychological effect, on the person or a family member of that violence;

(c) social, cultural or economic factors that impact on the person or a family member who has been affected by family violence;

(d) the general nature and dynamics of relationships affected by family violence, including the possible consequences of separation from the abuser;

(e) the psychological effect of violence on people who are or have been in a relationship affected by family violence;

(f) social or economic factors that impact on people who are or have been in a relationship affected by family violence.

(4) In this section —

child means a person who is under the age of 18 years;

family member, in relation to a person, includes —

(a) a person who is or has been married to the person; or

(b) a person who has or has had an intimate personal relationship with the person; or

(c) a person who is or has been the father, mother, step-father or step-mother of the person; or

(d) a child who normally or regularly resides with the person; or

(e) a guardian of the person; or

(f) another person who is or has been ordinarily a member of the household of the person; ***family violence***, in relation to a person, means violence against that person by a family member; ***violence*** means —

(a) physical abuse;

(b) sexual abuse;

(c) psychological abuse (which need not involve actual or threatened physical or sexual abuse), including but not limited to —

(i) intimidation;

(ii) harassment;

(iii) damage to property;

(iv) threats of physical abuse, sexual abuse or psychological abuse;

(v) in relation to a child —
   (A) causing or allowing the child to see or hear the physical, sexual or psychological abuse of a person by a family member; or
   (B) putting the child, or allowing the child to be put, at real risk of seeing or hearing that abuse occurring.

(5) Without limiting the definition of ***violence*** in sub-section (4) —
   (a) a single act may amount to abuse for the purposes of that definition;
   (b) a number of acts that form part of a pattern of behaviour may amount to abuse for that purpose, even though some or all of those acts, when viewed in isolation, may appear to be minor or trivial.

4. In *Babic v The Queen* [2010] VSCA 198, the defendant appealed against his conviction for murder on the basis that the trial judge had erred by not leaving the defence of self-defence at common law to the jury. He argued that the defence created by s 9AC is more restrictive than common law self-defence. In particular, the common law requirement that the conduct be 'reasonably necessary' in self-defence arguably leaves open the possibility of the defence succeeding where the threat is not one of death or really serious injury. This possibility is not left open in the formulation under s 9AC. The court rejected this argument, holding that the statutory formulation has the effect of abolishing self-defence at common law for the offences it covers; that is, murder and manslaughter.

5. Note that an additional argument under s 462A of the Crimes Act 1958 (Vic) may be available to some people who kill in situations analogous to self-defence. Section 462A provides as follows:

> **462A Use of force to prevent the commission of an indictable offence**
>
> A person may use such force not disproportionate to the objective as he believes on reasonable grounds to be necessary to prevent the commission, continuance or completion of an indictable offence or to effect or assist in effecting the lawful arrest of a person committing or suspected of committing any offence

This section would cover police officers and others who kill in life-threatening situations, or circumstances believed to be life-threatening, such as in attempting to carry out an arrest. Like self-defence at common law, it does not require that the threat be one of death or really serious injury.

6. The matter of self-defence has also been dealt with by the Federal Parliament. The Criminal Code Act 1995 (Cth), enacted after substantial and extended preparatory work by the Model Criminal Code Officers Committee of the Standing Committee of Attorneys-General (federal, state and territories), deals with general principles of criminal responsibility. Section 10.4 provides for self-defence as a circumstance in which there is no criminal responsibility. The section is of general application. It provides that 'conduct in self-defence' is an act done if the defendant believes the conduct is necessary and believes it is a reasonable response in the circumstances as perceived by the defendant. The section does not apply to the use of force intentionally to cause death or really serious injury for the protection of property or the prevention of trespass.

NECESSITY

12.6 The defence of necessity involves a claim by an accused that he or she was compelled to do what he or she did because of some extraordinary emergency. Necessity is a complete defence.

The difference between the defences of duress and necessity is that in cases of duress, X must explicitly or implicitly nominate that D commits a *particular* crime. In contrast, in the defence of necessity D reacts to threats or extraordinary circumstances and chooses which crime to commit. Thus, in *R v Cole* [1994] Crim LR 582, D was ordered by X to make a repayment of a debt or suffer serious harm. Consequently, D robbed a bank in order to get money for repayment. D was refused a defence of duress because X had not nominated, expressly or impliedly, the crime D should commit. Robbing a bank was, rather, D's response to the predicament posed by X. In New South Wales (and probably in Victoria), D would be able to argue the defence of necessity in these circumstances.

12.7 Thomas Hobbes, who was Lord Bacon's secretary, has the following to say in *Leviathan* (1651):

> If a man by the terrour of present death, be compelled to doe a fact against the Law, he is totally Excused; because no Law can oblige a man to abandon his own preservation. And supposing such a Law were obligatory; yet a man would reason thus, If I doe it not, I die presently; if I doe it, I die afterwards; therefore by doing it, there is time of life gained; Nature therefore compells him to the fact.
>
> When a man is destitute of food or other thing necessary for his life, and cannot preserve himselfe any other way, but by some fact against the law; as if in a great famine he take the food by force, or stealth, which he cannot obtain for mony nor charity; or in defence of his life, snatch away another mans Sword, he is totally Excused, for the reason next before alleged.

12.8C **R v Dudley and Stephens**

(1884) 14 QBD 273

Queen's Bench Division

[Thomas Dudley and Edwin Stephens were charged with the murder of Richard Parker. The killing took place on the high seas. Dudley, Stephens, the deceased Parker (a boy between 17 and 18 years of age), and one Brooks were all members of the crew of an English yacht,

Mignonette, sailing to Sydney. This foundered in a storm on 5 July 1884, some 1600 miles from the Cape of Good Hope, and the three men and the boy were compelled to put off in an open boat belonging to the yacht. The boat had no supply of either water or food except for two one-pound tins of turnips. For the first three days, the four shipwrecked mariners subsisted on the turnips. On the fourth day, they caught a small turtle and subsisted on this for the next eight days, by which time nothing remained. For the eight following days, they had nothing to eat and they had no fresh water, except such rain as they could from time to time catch in their oilskin capes. During all this time, the boat was drifting on the ocean, probably more than a thousand miles from land. On the eighteenth day, when they had been seven days without food and five without water, Dudley and Stephens spoke to Brooks. They suggested that if no help came, one of the four should be sacrificed to save the rest. Brooks disagreed, and Parker (the 'one of the four' understood to be referred to in this conversation) was not consulted. On the nineteenth day, Dudley proposed to Stephens and Brooks that lots should be cast to decide who should be put to death to save the rest; Brooks refused to agree and the matter was not put to Parker. In fact, there was no drawing of lots. On the same day, Dudley and Stephens spoke of their families and Dudley proposed that action should be taken the next day if no vessel was in sight.

On the twentieth day, no vessel having appeared, Dudley told Brooks to go and have a sleep and, by signs, showed Stephens and Brooks that he thought Parker had better be killed. Stephens agreed, but Brooks dissented. At this time, Parker was lying at the bottom of the boat quite helpless, extremely weakened by famine and by drinking sea water, and unable to make any resistance. Dudley offered up a prayer for forgiveness and then, with Stephens' assent, went to Parker, told him that his time was come and killed him by putting a knife in his throat.

For the next four days, Dudley, Stephens and Brooks fed upon Parker's body and blood. On the fourth day, their boat was picked up by a passing vessel and they were rescued in the lowest state of prostration. They were taken to Falmouth, and Dudley and Stephens were committed for trial at Exeter. At the trial, the jury found that if the men had not fed upon the boy's body they probably would not have survived to be rescued; that Parker was likely to have died before them; that at the time of the killing there was no sail in sight nor any reasonable prospect of relief; that under these circumstances there appeared to the prisoners every probability that unless they then fed, or very soon fed, upon the boy or one of themselves, they would die of starvation; that there was no appreciable chance of saving life except by killing someone for the others to eat; and that, assuming any necessity to kill anybody, there was no greater necessity for killing Parker than any of the other three.

The jurors found all these facts by way of a special verdict at the trial of Dudley and Stephens on 7 November 1884, but they declined to give their view whether these facts amounted to murder. Instead, they prayed the advice of the court (**Huddleston B**). The court reserved the question for argument before a court of five judges of the Queen's Bench Division (**Lord Coleridge CJ**, **Grove** and **Denman JJ**, and **Pollock** and **Huddleston BB**). After hearing full argument by counsel, the court, on 9 December, held that the prisoners were guilty of murder and sentenced them to death.]

Lord Coleridge CJ [delivering the judgment of the court]: ... From these facts, stated with the cold precision of a special verdict, it appears sufficiently that the prisoners were subject to terrible temptation, to sufferings which might break down the bodily power of the strongest man, and try the conscience of the best. Other details yet more harrowing, facts still more loathsome and appalling, were presented to the jury, and are to be found recorded in my learned brother's notes. But nevertheless this is clear, that the prisoners put to death a weak and unoffending boy upon the chance of preserving their own lives by feeding upon his flesh and blood after he was killed, and with the certainty of depriving *him* of any possible chance of survival. The verdict finds in terms that 'if the men had not fed upon the body of the boy they would *probably* not have survived', and that 'the boy being in a much weaker condition was *likely* to have died before them'. They might possibly have been picked up next day by a passing ship; they might possibly not have been picked up at all; in either case it is obvious that the killing of the boy would have been an unnecessary and profitless act. It is found by the verdict that the boy was incapable of resistance, and, in fact, made none; and it is not even suggested that his death was due to any violence on his part attempted against, or even so much as feared by, those who killed him. Under these circumstances the jury say that they are ignorant whether those who killed him were guilty of murder, and have referred it to this court to determine what is the legal consequence which follows from the facts which they have found.

There remains to be considered the real question in the case — whether killing under the circumstances set forth in the verdict be or be not murder. The contention that it could be anything else was, to the minds of us all, both new and strange, and we stopped the Attorney-General in his negative argument in order that we might hear what could be said in support of a proposition which appeared to us to be at once dangerous, immoral, and opposed to all legal principle and analogy. All, no doubt, that can be said has been urged before us, and we are now to consider and determine what it amounts to. First it is said that it follows from various definitions of murder in books of authority, which definitions imply, if they do not state, the doctrine, that in order to save your own life you may lawfully take away the life of another, when that other is neither attempting nor threatening yours, nor is guilty of any illegal act whatever towards you or any one else. But if these definitions be looked at they will not be found to sustain this contention. The earliest in point of date is the passage cited to us from Bracton, who lived in the reign of Henry III. It was at one time the fashion to discredit Bracton, as Mr Reeve tells us, because he was supposed to mingle too much of the canonist and civilian with the common lawyer. There is now no such feeling, but the passage upon homicide, on which reliance is placed, is a remarkable example of the kind of writing which may explain it. Sin and crime are spoken of as apparently equally illegal, and the crime of murder, it is expressly declared, may be committed *lingua vel facto*; so that a man, like Hero 'done to death by slanderous tongues', would, it seems, in the opinion of Bracton, be a person in respect of whom might be grounded a legal indictment for murder. But in the very passage as to necessity, on which reliance has been placed, it is clear that Bracton is speaking of necessity in the ordinary sense — the repelling by violence, violence justified so far as it was necessary for the object, any illegal violence used towards oneself. If, say[s] Bracton, the necessity be *evitabilis, et evadere posset absque occisione, tunc erit reus homicidii* — words which shew clearly that he is thinking of physical danger from which escape may be possible, and that the *inevitabilis necessitas* of which he speaks as justifying homicide is a necessity of the same nature.

It is, if possible, yet clearer that the doctrine contended for receives no support from the great authority of Lord Hale. It is plain that in his view the necessity which justified homicide is that only which has always been and is now considered a justification.

> In all these cases of homicide by necessity, [says he] as in pursuit of a felon, in killing him that assaults to rob, or comes to burn or break a house, or the like, which are in themselves no felony: 1 Hale *PC* 491.

Again, he says that:

> ... the necessity which justifies homicide is of two kinds: (1) the necessity which is of a private nature; (2) the necessity which relates to the public justice and safety. The former is that necessity which obligeth a man to his own defence and safeguard, and this takes in these inquiries: (1) What may be done for the safeguard of a man's own life; ...

and then follow three other heads not necessary to pursue. Then Lord Hale proceeds:

> As touching the first of these — viz, homicide in defence of a man's own life, which is usually styled *se defendendo*.

It is not possible to use words more clear to shew that Lord Hale regarded the private necessity which justified, and alone justified, the taking the life of another for the safeguard of one's own to be what is commonly called 'self-defence': 1 Hale *PC* 478.

But if this could be even doubtful upon Lord Hale's words, Lord Hale himself has made it clear. For in the chapter in which he deals with the exemption created by compulsion or necessity he thus expresses himself:

> If a man be desperately assaulted and in peril of death, and cannot otherwise escape unless, to satisfy his assailant's fury, he will kill an innocent person then present, the fear and actual force will not acquit him of the crime and punishment of murder, if he commit the fact, for he ought rather to die himself than kill an innocent; but if he cannot otherwise save his own life the law permits him in his own defence to kill the assailant, for by the violence of the assault, and the offence committed upon him by the assailant himself, the law of nature, and necessity, hath made him his own protector *cum debito moderamine inculpatae tutelae*: 1 Hale *PC* 51.

But, further still, Lord Hale in the following chapter deals with the position asserted by the casuists, and sanctioned, as he says, by Grotius and Puffendorf, that in a case of extreme necessity, either of hunger or clothing:

> ... theft is no theft, or at least not punishable as theft, as some even of our own lawyers have asserted the same. But [says Lord Hale] I take it that here in England, that rule, at least by the laws of England, is false; and therefore, if a

> person, being under necessity for want of victuals or clothes, shall upon that account clandestinely and *animo furandi* steal another man's goods, it is felony, and a crime by the laws of England punishable with death: 1 Hale *PC* 54.

If, therefore, Lord Hale is clear — as he is — that extreme necessity of hunger does not justify larceny, what would he have said to the doctrine that it justified murder?

It is satisfactory to find that another great authority, second, probably, only to Lord Hale, speaks with the same unhesitating clearness on this matter. Sir Michael Foster, in the 3rd chapter of his 'Discourse on Homicide' (*Crown Law*, 3rd ed, 1809, pp 253–337), deals with the subject of 'homicide founded in necessity'; and the whole chapter implies, and is insensible unless it does imply, that in the view of Sir Michael Foster 'necessity and self-defence' (which he defines as 'opposing force to force even to the death') are convertible terms. There is no hint, no trace, of the doctrine now contended for; the whole reasoning of the chapter is entirely inconsistent with it.

In 1 East *PC* 271, the whole chapter on homicide by necessity is taken up with an elaborate discussion of the limits within which necessity in Sir Michael Foster's sense (given above) of self-defence is a justification of or excuse for homicide. There is a short section at the end very generally and very doubtfully expressed, in which the only instance discussed is the well-known one of two shipwrecked men on a plank able to sustain only one of them, and the conclusion is left by Sir Edward East entirely undetermined.

What is true of Sir Edward East is true also of Mr Serjeant Hawkins. The whole of his chapter on justifiable homicide assumes that the only justifiable homicide of a private nature is the defence against force of a man's person, house, or goods. In the 26th section we find again the case of the two shipwrecked men and the single plank, with the significant expression from a careful writer, '*It is said* to be justifiable'. So, too, Dalton, c 150, clearly considers necessity and self-defence in Sir Michael Foster's sense of that expression, to be convertible terms, though he prints without comment Lord Bacon's instance of the two men on one plank as a quotation from Lord Bacon, adding nothing whatever to it on his own. And there is a remarkable passage, at p 339, in which he says that even in the case of a murderous assault upon a man, yet before he may take the life of the man who assaults him even in self-defence, *cuncta prius tentanda*.

The passage in Staundforde, on which almost the whole of the dicta we have been considering are built, when it comes to be examined, does not warrant the conclusion which has been derived from it. The necessity to justify homicide must be, he says, inevitable, and the example which he gives to illustrate his meaning is the very same which has just been cited from Dalton, shewing that the necessity he was speaking of was a physical necessity, and the self-defence a defence against physical violence. Russell merely repeats the language of the old textbooks, and adds no new authority, nor any fresh considerations.

Is there, then, any authority for the proposition which has been presented to us? Decided cases there are none. The case of the seven English sailors referred to by the commentator on Grotius and by Puffendorf has been discovered by a gentleman at the Bar, who communicated with my brother Huddleston, to convey the authority (if it conveys so much) of a single judge of the island of St Kitts, when that island was possessed partly by France and partly by this country, somewhere about the year 1641. It is mentioned in a medical treatise published at Amsterdam, and is altogether, as authority in an English court, as unsatisfactory as possible. The American case cited by my brother Stephen in his *Digest*, from *Wharton on Homicide*, in which it was decided, correctly indeed, that sailors had no right to throw passengers overboard to save themselves, but on the somewhat strange ground that the proper mode of determining who was to be sacrificed was to vote upon the subject by ballot, can hardly, as my brother Stephen says, be an authority satisfactory to a court in this country. The observations of Lord Mansfield in the case of *R v Stratton* (21 How St Tr 1046 at 1223 (KB 1779)), striking and excellent as they are, were delivered in a political trial, where the question was whether a political necessity had arisen for deposing a Governor of Madras. But they have little application to the case before us, which must be decided on very different considerations.

The one real authority of former time is Lord Bacon, who, in his commentary on the maxim, *necessitas inducit privilegium quoad jura privata*, lays down the law as follows:

> Necessity carrieth a privilege in itself. Necessity is of three sorts — necessity of conservation of life, necessity of obedience, and necessity of the act of God or of a stranger. First of conservation of life; if a man steal viands to satisfy his present hunger, this is no felony nor larceny. So if divers be in danger of drowning by the casting away of some boat or barge, and one of them get to some plank, or on the boat's side to keep himself above water and another to save his life thrust him from it, whereby he is drowned, this is neither *se defendendo* nor by misadventure, but justifiable.

On this it is to be observed that Lord Bacon's proposition that stealing to satisfy hunger is no larceny is hardly supported by Staundforde, whom he cites for it, and is expressly contradicted by Lord Hale in the passage already cited. And for the proposition as to the plank or boat, it is said to be derived from the canonists. At any rate he cites no authority for it, and it must stand upon his own. Lord Bacon was great even as a lawyer, but it is permissible to much smaller men, relying upon principle and on the authority of others, the equals and even the superiors of Lord Bacon as lawyers, to question the soundness of his dictum. There are many conceivable states of things in which it might possibly be true, but if Lord Bacon meant to lay down the broad proposition that a man may save his life by killing, if necessary, an innocent and unoffending neighbour, it certainly is not law at the present day.

There remains the authority of my brother Stephen, who, both in his *Digest* and in his *History of the Criminal Law*, uses language perhaps wide enough to cover this case. The language is somewhat vague in both places, but it does not in either place cover this case of necessity, and we have the best authority for saying that it was not meant to cover it. If it had been necessary, we must with true deference have differed from him, but it is satisfactory to know that we have, probably at least, arrived at no conclusion in which if he had been a member of the court he would have been unable to agree. Neither are we in conflict with any opinion expressed upon the subject by the learned persons who formed the commission for preparing the Criminal Code. They say on this subject:

> We are certainly not prepared to suggest that necessity should in every case be a justification. We are equally unprepared to suggest that necessity should in no case be a defence; we judge it better to leave such questions to be dealt with when, if ever, they arise in practice by applying the principles of law to the circumstances of the particular case.

It would have been satisfactory to us if these eminent persons could have told us whether the received definitions of legal necessity were in their judgment correct and exhaustive, and if not, in what way they should be amended, but as it is we have, as they say, 'to apply the principles of law to the circumstances of this particular case'.

Now, except for the purpose of testing how far the conservation of a man's own life is in all cases and under all circumstances, an absolute, unqualified, and paramount duty, we exclude from our consideration all the incidents of war. We are dealing with a case of private homicide, not one imposed upon men in the service of their Sovereign and in the defence of their country. Now it is admitted that the deliberate killing of this unoffending and unresisting boy was clearly murder, unless the killing can be justified by some well-recognised excuse admitted by the law. It is further admitted that there was in this case no such excuse, unless the killing was justified by what has been called 'necessity'. But the temptation to the act which existed here was not what the law has ever called necessity. Nor is this to be regretted. Though law and morality are not the same, and many things may be immoral which are not necessarily illegal, yet the absolute divorce of law from morality would be of fatal consequence; and such divorce would follow if the temptation to murder in this case were to be held by law an absolute defence of it. It is not so. To preserve one's life is generally speaking a duty, but it may be the plainest and the highest duty to sacrifice it. War is full of instances in which it is a man's duty not to live, but to die. The duty, in case of shipwreck, of a captain to his crew, of the crew to the passengers, of soldiers to women and children, as in the noble case of the *Birkenhead*; these duties impose on men the moral necessity, not of the preservation but of the sacrifice of their lives for others, from which in no country, least of all, it is to be hoped, in England, will men ever shrink, as indeed, they have not shrunk. It is not correct, therefore, to say that there is any absolute or unqualified necessity to preserve one's life. *Necesse est ut eam, non ut vivam*, is a saying of a Roman officer quoted by Lord Bacon himself with high eulogy in the very chapter on necessity to which so much reference has been made. It would be a very easy and cheap display of commonplace learning to quote from Greek and Latin authors, from Horace, from Juvenal, from Cicero, from Euripides, passage after passage, in which the duty of dying for others has been laid down in glowing and emphatic language as resulting from the principles of heathen ethics; it is enough in a Christian country to remind ourselves of the Great Example whom we profess to follow. It is not needful to point out the awful danger of admitting the principle which has been contended for. Who is to be the judge of this sort of necessity? By what measure is the comparative value of lives to be measured? Is it to be strength, or intellect, or what? It is plain that the principle leaves to him who is to profit by it to determine the necessity which will justify him in deliberately taking another's life to save his own. In this case the weakest, the youngest, the most unresisting, was chosen. Was it more necessary to kill him than one of the grown men? The answer must be 'No':

> So spake the Fiend, and with necessity,
> The tyrant's plea, excused his devilish deeds.

It is not suggested that in this particular case the deeds were 'devilish', but it is quite plain that such a principle once admitted might be made the legal cloak for unbridled passion and atrocious crime. There is no safe path for judges to tread but to ascertain the law to the best of their ability and to declare it according to their judgment; and if in any case the law appears to be too severe on individuals, to leave it to the Sovereign to exercise that prerogative of mercy which the Constitution has intrusted to the hands fittest to dispense it.

It must not be supposed that in refusing to admit temptation to be an excuse for crime it is forgotten how terrible that temptation was; how awful the suffering; how hard in such trials to keep the judgment straight and the conduct pure. We are often compelled to set up standards we cannot reach ourselves, and to lay down the rules which we could not ourselves satisfy. But a man has no right to declare temptation to be an excuse, though he might himself have yielded to it, nor allow compassion for the criminal to change or weaken in any manner the legal definition of the crime. It is therefore our duty to declare that the prisoners' act in this case was wilful murder, that the facts as stated in the verdict are no legal justification of the homicide; and to say that in our unanimous opinion the prisoners are upon this special verdict guilty of murder.[1]

Notes:

1. My brother Grove has furnished me with the following suggestion, too late to be embodied in the judgment but well worth preserving: 'If the two accused men were justified in killing Parker, then if not rescued in time, two of the three survivors would be justified in killing the third, and of the two who remained the stronger would be justified in killing the weaker, so that three men might be justifiably killed to give the fourth a chance of surviving.' — C.

12.9C United States v Holmes

Fed Cas No 15383 (CCED Pa, 1842)
Circuit Court Eastern District, Pennsylvania (USA)

[In the judgment in *Dudley and Stephens*, the court referred to this American case. The prosecution arose out of the shipwreck of the merchant ship *William Brown* on a voyage from Liverpool to the United States. The ship carried a heavy cargo, a crew of 17 and 65 passengers. Some 250 miles from the coast of Newfoundland, she struck an iceberg and it became evident that she was soon going down. Accordingly, the long boat and the jolly-boat were lowered. The captain, the second mate, seven of the crew and one passenger got into the jolly-boat. The first mate, eight other members of the crew (including a negro supernumerary cook) and 32 passengers got into the long-boat. The remaining 31 passengers had to remain aboard the ship and went down with her an hour and a half after the iceberg was struck. The wreck occurred on a Monday and on the Tuesday morning, the two boats parted company. Before doing so, the captain gave the crew of the long-boat directions, including an advice to obey all the orders of the mate, which the crew promised they would do. The long-boat had been believed to be in good condition but, as soon as she was launched, she began to leak and continued to leak the whole time. The passengers had buckets and tins, and, by bailing, were able to make her hold her own. The plug came out more than once and finally got lost, but was replaced by various expedients. Holmes, a crewman, was one of those who manned the long-boat.

At Holmes' trial, the captain and the second mate gave evidence to show that, loaded as the long-boat was on the Tuesday morning, the chances of survival were much against her. Nevertheless, she did survive fully loaded until 10 o'clock on the Tuesday night. The crew rowed and the passengers bailed. On Tuesday morning, after the two boats had parted, it began to rain and continued to do so throughout the whole day and night. At night a storm sprang up and waves began to splash over the boat's bow. Although little evidence was given at the trial as to the degree of danger on the Tuesday night, it seems that by this time everyone on board was partially naked, and, the water being cold and the rain falling heavily, was considerably overpowered by exhaustion and cold. At 10 o'clock on Tuesday night, with the sea freshening and the rain falling heavily, and the boat having considerable water in it, the mate gave up bailing and said: 'This work won't do. Help me, God. Men, go to work.' At the same time, some of the passengers cried out that the boat was sinking and called upon God for mercy. Neither Holmes nor any of the crew took any immediate action but, after a little while, the mate said again: 'Men, you must go to work, or we shall all perish.' At this stage, the crew went to work and during the next few hours they threw overboard 16 passengers (14 men and two women). The mate directed the crew 'not to part man and wife, and not to throw over any women'. There was no evidence of combination among the crew, no lots were cast, and the passengers had not previously been informed or consulted. All the men passengers, except two married men and a small boy, were thrown overboard. Not one of the crew was cast over. The two women thrown over were perhaps (the witnesses were not clear about this) so treated at their own request, as an act of devotion to their brother, who struggled violently before being cast over. Two of the men were discovered and thrown over only on the Wednesday morning, when the peril had ceased. Witnesses differed as to whether these men were, at the time, so frozen as to have been past hope of recovery. Holmes was one of the seamen who assisted in the work. He was of excellent character, and had gone back to the ship, after the wreck, to rescue a child. After the long-boat had been rescued, he was brought to trial for manslaughter. The following is an extract from the charge of **Baldwin CJ** to the jury.]

Baldwin CJ: ... it is one thing to give a favourable interpretation of evidence in order to mitigate an offence. It is a different thing, when we are asked, not to extenuate, but to justify, the act. In the former case, as I have said, our decision may in some degree be swayed by feelings of humanity; while in the latter, it is the law of necessity alone which can disarm the vindicatory justice of the country. Where, indeed, a case does arise, embraced by this 'law of necessity', the penal laws pass over such case in silence; for law is made to meet but the ordinary exigencies of life. But the case does not become a 'case of necessity' unless all ordinary means of self-preservation have been exhausted. The peril must be instant, overwhelming, leaving no alternative but to lose our own life, or to take the life of another person. An illustration of this principle occurs in the ordinary case of self-defence against lawless violence, aiming at the destruction of life, or designing to inflict grievous injury to the person; and within this range may fall the taking of life under other circumstances where the act is indispensably requisite to self-existence. For example, suppose that two persons who owe no duty to one another that is not mutual, should, by accident not attributable to either, be placed in a situation where both cannot survive. Neither is bound to save the other's life by sacrificing his own, nor would either commit a crime in saving his own life in a struggle for the only means of safety. Of this description of cases are those which have been cited to you by counsel, from writers on natural law — cases which we rather leave to your imagination than attempt minutely to describe. And I again state that when this great 'law of necessity' does apply, and is not improperly exercised, the taking of life is divested of unlawfulness.

But in applying this law, we must look, not only to the jeopardy in which the parties are, but also to the relations in which they stand. The slayer must be under no obligation to make his own safety secondary to the safety of others. A familiar application of this principle presents itself in the obligations which rest upon the owners of stages, steamboats, and other vehicles of transportation. In consideration of the payment of fare, the owners of the vehicle are bound to transport the passengers to the place of contemplated destination. Having, in all emergencies, the conduct of the journey, and the control of the passengers, the owners rest under every obligation for care, skill, and general capacity; and if, from defect of any of these requisites, grievous injury is done to the passenger, the persons employed are liable. The passenger owes no duty but submission. He is under no obligation to protect and keep the conductor in safety, nor is the passenger bound to labour, except in cases of emergency, where his services are required by unanticipated and uncommon danger. Such ... is the relation which exists on shipboard. The passenger stands in a position different from that of the officers and seamen. It is the sailor who must encounter the hardships and perils of the voyage. Nor can this relation be changed when the ship is lost by tempest or other danger of the sea, and all on board have betaken themselves, for safety to the small boats; for imminence of danger can not absolve from duty. The sailor is bound, as before, to undergo whatever hazard is necessary to preserve the boat and the passengers. Should the emergency become so extreme as to call for the sacrifice of life, there can be no reason why the law does not still remain the same. The passenger, not being bound either to labour or to incur the risk of life, cannot be bound to sacrifice his existence to preserve the sailor's. The captain, indeed, and a sufficient number of seamen to navigate the boat, must be preserved; for, except these abide in the ship, all will perish. But if there be more seamen than are necessary to manage the boat, the supernumerary sailors have no right, for their safety, to sacrifice the passengers. The sailors and passengers, in fact, cannot be regarded as in equal positions. The sailor (to use the language of a distinguished writer) owes more benevolence to another than to himself. He is bound to set a greater value on the life of others than on his own. And while we admit that sailor and sailor may lawfully struggle with each other for the plank which can save but one, we think that, if the passenger is on the plank, even 'the law of necessity' justifies not the sailor who takes it from him. This rule may be deemed a harsh one towards the sailor, who may have thus far done his duty, but when the danger is so extreme, that the only hope is in sacrificing either a sailor or a passenger, any alternative is hard; and would it not be the hardest of any to sacrifice a passenger in order to save a supernumerary sailor?

But in addition, if the source of the danger has been obvious, and destruction ascertained to be certainly about to arrive, though at a future time, there should be consultation, and some mode of selection fixed, by which those in equal relations may have equal chance for their life. By what mode, then, should selection be made? The question is not without difficulty; nor do we know of any rule prescribed, either by statute or by common law, or even by speculative writers on the law of nature. In fact, no rule of general application can be prescribed for contingencies which are wholly unforeseen. There is however, one condition of extremity for which all writers have prescribed the same rule. When the ship is in no danger of sinking, but all sustenance is exhausted, and a sacrifice of one person is necessary to appease the hunger of others, the selection is by lot. This mode is resorted to as the fairest mode, and, in some sort, as an appeal to God, for selection of the victim. This manner, obviously, was regarded by the mate, in parting with the captain, as the one which it was proper to adopt, in case the long-boat could not live with all who were on board on Tuesday morning. The same manner, as would appear from the response given to the mate, had already suggested itself to the captain. For ourselves, we can conceive of no mode so consonant both to humanity and to justice; and the occasion, we think, must be peculiar which will dispense with its exercise. If, indeed, the peril be instant and overwhelming, leaving no chance of means, and no moment for deliberation, then, of course, there is no power to consult, to cast lots, or in any such way to decide; but even where the final disaster is thus sudden, if it have been foreseen as certainly about to arrive, if no new cause of danger have arisen to bring on the closing catastrophe, if time have existed to cast lots, and to select the victims, then as we have said, sortition should be adopted. In no other than this or some like way are those having equal rights put upon equal footing, and in no other way is it possible to guard against partiality and oppression, violence and conflict ...

When the selection has been made by lots, the victim yields of course to his fate, or, if he resists, force may be employed to coerce submission ...

[The jury were, at first, unable to agree but, after 16 hours, they found a verdict of guilty and recommended Holmes to the mercy of the court. After hearing further argument, Holmes was brought up for sentence and the judge sentenced him to undergo six months' hard labour in the penitentiary and to pay a fine of $20. The maximum authorised penalty was three years' hard labour and a fine of $1000; however, at the time of the sentence, Holmes had already been in gaol for several months. An effort was made to obtain a pardon for him, but as the court would not join in the application, **President Tyler** refused to grant it. The penalty was subsequently remitted.]

12.10 Notes

1. Holmes was not charged with murder, but with manslaughter. Should the same course have been taken in relation to *Dudley and Stephens*? The English court assumed that the case was one of either murder or excusable homicide. Is this correct? While it is true that most of the decisions speak of 'provocation' as being the only factor which will mitigate an intentional killing from murder to manslaughter, it does not appear to have been finally and authoritatively decided that provocation is the only mitigating factor recognised by the law — at least apart from the conclusions which may be drawn from the decision in *Dudley and Stephens*. Professor R Perkins, in *Cases and Materials on Criminal Law and Procedure*, The Foundation Press Inc, Brooklyn, 1952, p 490, says:

   > Strangely enough the possibility of manslaughter rather than murder in such cases seems never to have had adequate consideration. The killing is intentional, to be sure, and there is no legally recognised *provocation*. But the circumstances are extremely *mitigating*. The mitigation in such a case is entitled to greater recognition than that in most instances of voluntary manslaughter committed in the sudden heat of passion. The state of mind of one who reluctantly takes a life of an innocent person as the only means of saving his own, while not guiltless, is certainly not malice aforethought.

   This line of thought is strongly supported by the cases on excessive force used in self-defence or in the advancement of justice. Despite the decision of the High Court of Australia in *Zecevic v DPP* (at **12.4C**), in each of the common law states the doctrine, or a variation of it in the case of Victoria, has been re-introduced by statute: see **12.5**.

   Note that the mandatory death sentence imposed in *Dudley and Stephens* was later commuted by the Executive to six months' imprisonment.

2. Three Australian states — Queensland, Tasmania and Western Australia — have enacted comprehensive Criminal Codes. The Queensland Code was drafted by Sir Samuel Griffith CJ, and the Western Australian Code is an almost exact copy of it. Section 25 of each of these Codes provides that:

   > Subject to the express provisions of this Code relating to acts done upon compulsion or provocation or in self-defence, a person is not criminally responsible for an act or omission done or made under such circumstances of sudden or extraordinary emergency that an ordinary person possessing ordinary power of self-control could not reasonably be expected to act otherwise.

   In his report to the Attorney-General of Queensland which accompanied his draft Code, Sir Samuel justified this provision on the ground that no man should be expected to be wiser than the ordinary run of mankind; he acknowledged, however, that the provision had no common law basis. The Tasmanian Code, which was drafted considerably later, contains no provision of this kind.

The Commonwealth Criminal Code Act 1995 contains the following general provision in s 10.3:

> (1) A person is not criminally responsible for an offence if he or she carries out the conduct constituting the offence in response to circumstances of sudden or extraordinary emergency.

But s 10.3(2) qualifies this general defence by providing that it is only available where the defendant 'reasonably believes' that those circumstances exist, and that the only reasonable way to deal with the emergency is by committing the offence, and 'the conduct is a reasonable response to the emergency'.

3. In Victoria, a defence of sudden or extraordinary emergency has been introduced as an available defence in homicide cases. Section 9AI of the Crimes Act 1958, as amended by the Crimes (Homicide) Act 2005 (Vic), provides:

> (1) A person is not guilty of a relevant offence in respect of conduct carried out by him or her in response to circumstances of sudden or extraordinary emergency.
> (2) This section applies if and only if the person carrying out the conduct reasonably believes that —
> (a) circumstances of sudden or extraordinary emergency exist; and
> (b) committing the offence is the only reasonable way to deal with the emergency; and
> (c) the conduct is a reasonable response to the emergency.
> (3) This section only applies in the case of murder if the emergency involves a risk of death or really serious injury.

'Relevant offence' is defined by s 9AB as meaning murder, manslaughter or defensive homicide. Although introduced in 2005, s 9AI incorporates recommendations made by Victoria's Law Reform Commission considerably earlier: Report No 9, *Duress, Necessity and Coercion* (1980); Report No 40, *Homicide* (1991).

12.11 Further reading

A W Brian Simpson, *Cannibalism and the Common Law*, Penguin Books, Harmondsworth, 1986

P Crofts, *Wickedness and Crime: Laws of Homicide and Malice*, Routledge, 2013

R Cross, 'Necessity Knows No Law' (1968) 3 *Univ Tas LR* 1

WD W Elliott, 'Necessity, Duress and Self-Defence' [1989] *Crim LR* 611

L Fuller, 'The Case of the Speluncean Explorers' (1949) 62 *Harv LR* 616

The development of the defence of necessity

12.12C **R v Davidson**

[1969] VR 667

Supreme Court of Victoria

Menhennitt J: The accused is charged on four counts of unlawfully using an instrument or other means with intent to procure the miscarriage of a woman and one count of conspiring unlawfully to procure the miscarriage of a woman. The trial is in its eighth day. The Crown is about to call medical witnesses to give expert evidence. In order to determine questions of admissibility of evidence which may well arise, it is necessary that an aspect of the relevant law relating to the charges be stated. Accordingly, I invited counsel to make submissions so that I could then make appropriate rulings. The particular matter as to which I have heard submissions and on which I make this ruling is as to the element of unlawfulness in the charges.

The relevant portion of s 65 of the *Crimes Act 1958*, under which the first four counts are laid and which is the basis of the conspiracy charge in the fifth count, is as follows:

> Whosoever … with intent to procure the miscarriage of any woman whether she is or is not with child unlawfully administers to her or causes to be taken by her any poison or other noxious thing, or unlawfully uses any instrument or other means with the like intent, shall be guilty of felony, and shall be liable to imprisonment for a term of not more than fifteen years.

The use of the word 'unlawfully' in the section implies that in certain circumstances the use of an instrument or other means to procure a miscarriage may be lawful. The word 'unlawfully' is nowhere statutorily defined …

The only decision of which I am aware in which the meaning of the word 'unlawfully' in s 65 of the *Crimes Act 1958*, or its equivalent elsewhere, has been deliberately construed is *R v Bourne* [1939] 1 KB 687, [1938] 3 All ER 615 (CCC) …

R v Bourne, supra, was a trial of an eminent surgeon who openly in a public hospital operated to terminate the pregnancy of a 14-year-old girl who had become pregnant in consequence of a violent rape. Macnaghten J, the trial judge, in the course of his charge to the jury said (at [KB] 690–1; [All ER] 616–17):

> Nine years ago Parliament passed an Act called the Infant Life (Preservation) Act 1929 (19 & 20 Geo 5 c 34). Section 1(1) of that Act provides that 'any person who, with intent to destroy the life of a child capable of being born alive, by any wilful act causes a child to die before it has an existence independent of its mother, shall be guilty of felony, to wit of child destruction, and shall be liable on conviction thereof on indictment to penal servitude for life: Provided that no person shall be found guilty of an offence under this section unless it is proved that the act which caused the death of the child was not done in good faith for the purpose only of preserving the life of the mother.' It is true, as Mr Oliver [counsel for the defendant] has said, that this enactment provides for the case where a child is killed by a

> wilful act at the time when it is being delivered in the ordinary course of nature; but in my view the proviso that it is necessary for the Crown to prove that the act was not done in good faith for the purpose only of preserving the life of the mother is in accordance with what has always been the common law of England with regard to the killing of an unborn child. No such proviso is in fact set out in s 58 of the Offences against the Person Act 1861; but the words of that section are that any person who 'unlawfully' uses an instrument with intent to procure a miscarriage shall be guilty of felony. In my opinion the word 'unlawfully' is not, in that section, a meaningless word. I think it imports the meaning expressed by the proviso in s 1(1) of the Infant Life (Preservation) Act 1929, and that s 58 of the Offences against the Person Act 1861 must be read as if the words making it an offence to use an instrument with intent to procure a miscarriage were qualified by a similar proviso.

Later he said (at [KB] 693–4; [All ER] 619):

> It permits the termination of pregnancy for the purpose of preserving the life of the mother. As I have said, I think those words ought to be construed in a reasonable sense, and, if the doctor is of opinion, on reasonable grounds and with adequate knowledge, that the probable consequence of the continuance of the pregnancy will be to make the woman a physical or mental wreck, the jury are quite entitled to take the view that the doctor who, under those circumstances and in that honest belief, operates, is operating for the purpose of preserving the life of the mother.

It is to be noted that s 2 of the English Infant Life (Preservation) Act 1929 provided that on a trial for, *inter alia*, an offence under s 58 of the 1861 Act (unlawfully using an instrument to procure a miscarriage) a jury could convict under s 1 of the 1929 Act and that on a trial under s 1 of that Act a jury could convict, *inter alia*, of an offence under s 58 of the 1861 Act and it might be argued that what was to be negated by the Crown by reason of the proviso to s 1 in relation to child destruction should also have to be negated, by reason of the word 'unlawfully', in the less grave crime (although with the same penalty of life imprisonment) of unlawful abortion.

Mr J V Barry (as he then was, now Barry J), in an address delivered on 26 November 1938, entitled 'The Law of Therapeutic Abortion' (recorded in *The Proceedings of the Medico-Legal Society of Victoria*, vol 3, pp 211–33), which, if I may say so with respect, includes, *inter alia,* a most comprehensive survey of the law relating to abortion going back to Roman law, pp 228–9, criticises the fact that Macnaghten J, should have founded himself so narrowly on a much later Act in considering the Act of 1861. At pp 220–3 and 228–9 of that paper, the learned author said that his view was that the proper approach to the problem is to be found in the application of the principle of necessity and he cited Stephen's statement of that principle in Art 32 of his *Digest of the Criminal Law* (1st ed, 1877).

The position in this state is that in the Victorian equivalent of the English Infant Life (Preservation) Act 1929, namely s 5 of the *Crimes Act 1949*, now s 10 of the *Crimes Act 1958*, there is the significant difference that the proviso to s 1 of the English Act does not appear but the word 'unlawfully', which does not appear in the English Act, does appear. Accordingly, in so far as the decision in *R v Bourne* is founded upon the proviso to s 1 of the

1929 English statute, that basis for the decision is absent from Victorian law. Accordingly, what is lawful and what is unlawful must be determined by other legal principles …

Whilst necessity is not a justification for every act which would otherwise be criminal (*Halsbury's Laws of England* (Simonds ed) vol 10, p 291; *Archbold's Criminal Pleading, Evidence and Practice* (36th ed, 1966), p 924), none the less the concept of necessity finds its place in various branches of the criminal law. Examples are the prevention of a felony and the apprehension of a felon …

Having regard to the deliberate and repeated use of the word 'unlawfully' in s 65 of the *Crimes Act 1958* and the nature of the offence created and the history thereof and in the light of the authorities and views of learned authors to which I have referred, it appears to me that necessity is the appropriate principle to apply to determine whether a therapeutic abortion is lawful or unlawful within the meaning of s 65.

The principle of necessity as stated by Stephen contains within it the two elements of necessity and proportion.

[His Honour discussed certain cases and continued:]

The principle of necessity imported by the use of the word 'unlawfully' in s 65 of the *Crimes Act 1958*, in my view, imports the two elements of necessity and proportion.

One aspect of the element of necessity in relation to prevention of a felony or arrest of a felon or self-defence is that the accused should honestly believe on reasonable grounds that what he did was necessary. In principle, it appears to me that the same concepts should apply to the element of necessity in relation to unlawfulness in s 65 of the *Crimes Act 1958*. In *R v Bourne* Macnaghten J in the second passage I have cited above, in stating the relevant test, used the expressions 'if the doctor is of opinion on reasonable grounds and with adequate knowledge' and 'in that honest belief'.

In the next place, for therapeutic abortion to be lawful I think that the accused must have honestly believed on reasonable grounds that the act done by him was necessary to preserve the woman from some serious danger. As to this element of danger, it appears to me in principle that it should not be confined to danger to life but should apply equally to danger to physical or mental health provided it is a serious danger not being merely the normal dangers of pregnancy and childbirth. In *R v Bourne* Macnaghten J extends the principle to cover the case where the woman would be a physical or mental wreck. In *R v Trim* [1943] VLR 109 at 116–17; [1943] ALR 236 at 240 Martin and O'Bryan JJ held that the facts did not raise any question of the act being lawful because done in good faith for the purpose only of preserving the life or health of the deceased. In *R v Newton and Stungo* [1958] Crim LR 469 (CCC), Ashworth J said that the use of an instrument to procure a miscarriage 'is unlawful unless the use is made in good faith for the purpose of preserving the life or health of the woman'. See also Glanville Williams, *The Sanctity of Life and the Criminal Law* (1958), pp 153–63.

As to the element of proportion, it seems to me in principle that this should apply to the element of unlawfulness in s 65 of the Crimes Act as it does to the element of necessity in prevention of felony, arrest of a felon and self-defence. Proportion is an aspect of the principle of necessity as stated by Stephen. The concept of proportion underlay what Macnaghten J said in *R v Bourne* [1939] 1 KB at 694–5; [1938] 3 All ER at 619–20.

The two elements of necessity and proportion involve, I think, subjective tests, subject to the beliefs being held on reasonable grounds.

In the present case, no issue as to lawfulness on grounds other than therapeutic grounds has emerged. On the basis of all the foregoing, I accordingly decide that the relevant law in relation to unlawfulness is as follows:

> For the use of an instrument with intent to procure a miscarriage to be lawful the accused must have honestly believed on reasonable grounds that the act done by him was (a) necessary to preserve the woman from a serious danger to her life or her physical or mental health (not being merely the normal dangers of pregnancy and childbirth) which the continuance of the pregnancy would entail; and (b) in the circumstances not out of proportion to the danger to be averted.

Accordingly, to establish that the use of an instrument with intent to procure a miscarriage was unlawful, the Crown must establish either (a) that the accused did not honestly believe on reasonable grounds that the act done by him was necessary to preserve the woman from a serious danger to her life or her physical or mental health (not being merely the normal dangers of pregnancy and childbirth) which the continuance of the pregnancy would entail; or (b) that the accused did not honestly believe on reasonable grounds that the act done by him was in the circumstances proportionate to the need to preserve the woman from a serious danger to her life or her physical or mental health (not being merely the normal dangers of pregnancy and childbirth) which the continuance of the pregnancy would entail.

[On 3 June 1969, the jury found the accused not guilty on each of the abovementioned five counts on which he was charged.]

12.13 Notes

Of the two elements referred to in Menhennitt J's ruling, that of necessity requires no comment. It seems likely that the second, the element of proportion, will require principally, though perhaps not exclusively, a weighing of the risks involved in carrying out the abortion against those involved in a continuation of the pregnancy. It must be remembered that some abortions are still performed by unqualified persons using dangerous methods in hazardous conditions: see *R v Salika* [1973] VR 272, and the discussion on abortion at **4.15**. For a similar ruling in New South Wales, see *R v Wald* (1971) 3 DCR (NSW) 25. See L Waller, 'Any Reasonable Creature in Being' (1987) 13 *Mon L Rev* 37. See also *Gillick v West Norfolk and Wisbech AHA* [1986] AC 112.

In Victoria, the decision in *Davidson* is no longer relevant to abortion, having been superseded by statutory provisions considered above: see **4.16**. It continues to be the basis for the law governing abortion in New South Wales.

12.14C R v Loughnan

[1981] VR 443
Supreme Court of Victoria

[The accused was tried and convicted before the County Court on a charge of escaping from Pentridge Prison contrary to s 132(1) of the Community Welfare Services Act 1970 ('the Act'). The Crown case established that the accused was lawfully detained at Pentridge, that Pentridge is a prison under the Act, and that he had escaped from it. The accused escaped along with three other prisoners. Prior to the escape and at all material times, the accused had been in 'B' division of the prison. The escape involved reaching a catwalk for guards on the prison wall, and jumping down and out from this wall over a cyclone-wire fence. In performing this act, the applicant broke both his ankles. He was apprehended on the following day at Ferntree Gully Hospital. When interviewed by the police that day, he made complete admissions, saying that he would not have been recaptured if he had not broken his ankles. He said that he would plead guilty. He said that he had known long ago of the plan of the other three prisoners to escape and that he had decided to go with them a couple of days before the interview.

At his trial, the accused relied on the defence of necessity. He called four prisoners and a prison officer as witnesses and made an unsworn statement from the dock. His case was that he had hidden a gun and some bullets in a stool; that through another prisoner, the stool had found its way into the cell of one Regan; that the gun and the bullets were found in the stool while it was in Regan's cell; that Regan was sent to the prison's 'H' division and that, in these circumstances, other prisoners believed that the accused was either working for the prison officers or an informer. He said that he had twice asked to go into the prison's 'H' division in the place of Regan in order to demonstrate the untruth of the allegations of his fellow prisoners, and the refusal of this request fortified these prisoners in their unfavourable opinion of him. At the trial, prison officers agreed that he had sought to move to 'H' division, in Regan's place. Regan was at that time eligible for parole. There was no evidence that the accused had ever told prison officers that he feared for his life. The accused said that he had been insulted and threatened, and that on the day of his escape he had been told that he would be killed that night. He had heard rumours of the escape and joined in, without prior arrangements, to avoid the threatened attack. He would not have done so had he not thought that he would be killed. He claimed not to have been otherwise connected to these prisoners or these plans. He did not challenge the accuracy of the evidence as to what he said to police on the day of his recapture.

The trial judge said that there was no evidence fit to be left to the jury on the question of necessity.]

Young CJ and **King J**: The only ground relied upon in support of the present application is that the learned judge was wrong in law in refusing to allow the defence or defences of duress or necessity to be considered by the jury. So far as duress was concerned Mr Sharp conceded that unless the court was prepared to reconsider the recent decision of *R v Dawson* [1978] VR 536, he could not succeed. In that case this court (Starke, Anderson and Harris JJ) held that the defence of duress is confined to cases where the accused is compelled to perform some criminal action under threat of physical harm. The defence is not available to exculpate an accused who commits a crime in order to evade the possible consequences of a threat made against him. The court indicated that it was not prepared to reconsider that decision and the argument therefore proceeded without further reference to duress.

In *Dawson's* case, supra, necessity was also raised as a defence, but the court was able to dispose of the application for leave to appeal without deciding whether a defence of necessity might serve to exculpate a prisoner otherwise guilty of escape. Their Honours held that in that case 'very few, if any, of the elements which would be required to found the defence of necessity' were present and that it would be mischievous to allow such a defence to go to the jury: see ([1978] VR) at 539–40.

Mr Sharp contended that the defence of necessity was recognised by our law and that the elements of it of which there had been no evidence in *Dawson's* case, supra, had been established in this case or at any rate that there was evidence fit to be considered by the jury which if accepted by them would establish those elements.

There does not appear to be any reported case which is binding upon us in which a defence of necessity has *eo nomine* been accepted. There are, however, statements going back very many years by writers of distinction to some of which we shall refer, which recognise the defence. There is also a sharp controversy between academic writers: see Glanville Williams *Criminal Law: The General Part* (2nd ed, 1961), p 724, para 231 where it is confidently submitted that the defence is recognised in English law and, on the other hand, P R Glazebrook, 'The Necessity Plea in English Criminal Law' [1972] *Camb LJ* 87 where an opposing view is taken.

In this case we have come to the conclusion that the application should fail because even if there be a defence of necessity available to a prisoner who escapes from lawful custody we do not think that the facts adduced justified the leaving of the defence to the jury. If there be no such defence recognised by the law, of course, *cadit quaestio*. However since we are of the opinion that a prisoner who escapes may in certain circumstances raise a defence of necessity, we think it is necessary or at any rate desirable that we should state briefly the foundation for the conclusion which we have reached.

We do not find it difficult to accept a general proposition to the effect that the law in some cases does recognise a defence of necessity. The difficulty is to describe the elements of the defence and there is a great danger in attempting to describe those elements in general terms, that is to say, in terms applicable to crimes in general or to a particular class of crimes. In *Halsbury's Laws of England*, 4th ed, vol 11, p 26, para 26, it is said that there is no general rule giving rise to a defence of necessity but this may be intended as no more than a cautious statement of the position. On the other hand, 'there is authority for saying that in case of great and imminent danger, in order to preserve life, the law will permit an encroachment on private property', per Lord Denning MR in *Southwark LBC v Williams* [1971] Ch 734 at 743, where his Lordship cited *Mouse's* case (1608) 12 Co Rep 63. Lord Denning also said that 'the doctrine so enunciated must, however, be carefully circumscribed. Else necessity would open the door to many an excuse'.

In *R v Davidson* [1969] VR 667 at 670, Menhennitt J quoted Sir James Fitzjames Stephen's view as follows:

> The principle of necessity is stated by Stephen in his *Digest of the Criminal Law* (1st ed, ch 3, art 43; 9th ed, ch 2, art 11) in the following terms: 'An act which would otherwise be a crime may in some cases be excused if the person accused can show that it was done only in order to avoid consequences which could not otherwise be avoided, and which, if they had followed, would have inflicted upon him or upon others whom he was bound to protect inevitable and irreparable evil, that no more was done than was reasonably necessary for that purpose, and that the evil inflicted by it was not disproportionate to the evil avoided. The extent of this principle is unascertained'.

Menhennitt J went on to point out at the same page that the concept of necessity finds its place in various branches of the criminal law: see the authorities which are there cited. There is also much reference to the question in academic writings not all of which are readily available here, but we mention some of those that we have consulted in addition to those already mentioned: Gardner, 'The Defence of Necessity and the Right to Escape from Prison' 49 *SCLR* 110; Davies, 'Law of Abortion and Necessity' (1939) 2 *Mod LR* 126; Edwards, 'Compulsion, Coercion and Criminal Responsibility' (1951) 14 *Mod LR* 297.

It will be seen from the statement by Sir James Fitzjames Stephen that there are three elements involved in the defence of necessity. First, the criminal act or acts must have been done only in order to avoid certain consequences which would have inflicted irreparable evil upon the accused or upon others whom he was bound to protect. The limits of this element are at present ill defined and where those limits should lie is a matter of debate. But we need not discuss this element further because the irreparable evil relied upon in the present case was a threat of death and if the law recognises the defence of necessity in any case it must surely do so where the consequence to be avoided was the death of the accused. We prefer to reserve for consideration if it should arise what other consequence might be sufficient to justify the defence: cf *People v Lovercamp* (1975) 43 California Appeals 3d 823, in which the consequence to be avoided was forcible homosexual activity.

The other two elements involved, which were identified by Menhennitt J in *R v Davidson*, supra, at 671 can for convenience be given the labels, immediate peril and proportion, although the expression of what is embodied in those two elements will necessarily vary from one type of situation to another.

The element of imminent peril means that the accused must honestly believe on reasonable grounds that he was placed in a situation of imminent peril. As Edmund Davies LJ (as he then was) pointed out in *Southwark LBC v Williams*, supra, at 746, all the cases in which a plea of necessity had succeeded are cases which deal with an urgent situation of imminent peril. Thus if there is an interval of time between the threat and its expected execution it will be very rarely if ever that a defence of necessity can succeed.

The element of proportion simply means that the acts done to avoid the imminent peril must not be out of proportion to the peril to be avoided. Put in another way, the test is: would a reasonable man in the position of the accused have considered that he had any alternative to doing what he did to avoid the peril? The two tests of imminent peril and proportion we have adapted from the tests propounded by Smith J in *R v McKay* [1957] VR 560 at 572–3, where they are referred to as necessity and proportion. It will be seen that in the application of the defence of necessity to a given situation these two elements may become interwoven. A person who receives a threat that he will be killed on a future day cannot seek out the person making the threat and kill him and escape liability on the ground that the killing was necessary in order to avoid his own death unless no other way of avoiding the danger was open to him. In such a case the accused will not be held to have had reasonable grounds for believing that it was necessary for him to do as he did in order to avoid the peril feared and it would also be held that his killing was in the circumstances out of proportion to the threat made to him.

A further example may be taken from *R v Kitson* (1955) 39 Cr App R 66 where a passenger awoke in a car to find that the driver had left and the car was moving. He managed to steer the car for some 300 yards on to a grass verge although he himself was intoxicated. Upon being charged with driving whilst under the influence of drink the defence of necessity was apparently not raised. If it had been, it might have succeeded. It might have been held that the accused was in a situation of imminent peril and that he had no reasonable alternative to doing what he did to avoid the peril. But if having placed himself in the driver's seat the accused had decided to drive himself home his actions would clearly have gone beyond what was reasonably necessary to avoid the imminent peril.

The well-known defence of self-defence, if not capable of being brought within the general description of a defence of necessity, is at least analogous to it, but in comparing the kind of necessity which requires self-defence with the necessity which requires escape from prison there is, of course, an essential difference in that in the former the accused will always or almost always attack the person threatening him whereas in a case where a prisoner pleads necessity as a justification for escaping, the criminal act which he commits is not directed to the person making the threat. But we do not see any reason why the same two elements should not be involved. First, an urgent situation of imminent peril must exist in which the accused must honestly believe on reasonable grounds that it is necessary for him to do the acts which are alleged to constitute the offence in order to avoid the threatened danger. Secondly, those acts must not be disproportionate to the threatened danger. In other words, if a prisoner were confined in a small country gaol and were placed in a position where he honestly believed on reasonable grounds that to preserve his own life he had to escape from the place where he was confined, he might be allowed with impunity to escape to the outside world. But if he were confined in a large metropolitan prison containing many divisions a similar threat might only be held to justify escape from the particular division in which he was confined. In such a case the accused might not of course be charged with escaping from lawful custody but no doubt he might be open to a charge of some lesser offence.

We shall not attempt to fit the decision in the well-known case of *R v Dudley and Stephens* (1884) 14 QBD 273 into the views here expressed. That case has been elaborately considered and discussed by Glanville Williams, op cit, pp 741–5, para 237.

It is sufficient to say that the decision does not require us to hold that a defence of necessity can never excuse a charge of escaping from lawful custody.

A question was raised during the argument whether a defence of necessity can be raised to a statutory offence such as that with which the applicant was charged. The offence of escaping from prison is created by s 132(1) of the *Community Welfare Services Act 1970* which reads:

> 132. (1) Every prisoner who escapes or attempts to escape:
> (a) from a prison or police gaol; or
> (b) from the custody of a member of the police force or a prison officer in whose legal custody he is or is deemed to be:
>
> shall be guilty of an indictable offence.
> Penalty: Imprisonment for five years.

The section does not attach the word 'unlawfully' to the word 'escapes' but in our opinion the failure to do so does not exclude the possibility that a lawful justification or excuse may provide an answer to a charge under it. Many indictable offences are created without the use of the word 'unlawfully' or some word of similar effect and yet the law has allowed the absence of *mens rea* or some unlawful justification or excuse to be raised by way of defence. In Victoria indictable offences are generally created without an attempt to set out in the statute all the elements of the offence and where what would otherwise be a defence is to be excluded, it is expressly so enacted: see, eg, Crimes Act s 49 (consent no defence to a charge of carnal knowledge of a female under the age of 16 years). See generally Glazebrook, 'The Necessity Pleas in English Criminal Law' [1972] *Camb LJ* 87 at 93 et seq. We therefore think that a defence of necessity is open to a person accused of escaping from prison contrary to s 132(1) of the Community Welfare Services Act.

Before turning to consider whether the present applicant raised a prima facie case of necessity, we should notice *People v Lovercamp*, supra, to which Mr Sharp referred us. That was a decision of the Court of Appeal of California in a case in which a defendant to a charge of escape sought to show that two female prisoners, who had been subjected to demands for lesbian activities of which they had complained many times to the authorities, escaped from prison in fear of their lives. The trial court rejected their evidence but the Court of Appeal held that they should have been allowed to raise a defence of necessity. The judgment of the court included the following summary:

... we hold that the proper rule is that a limited defence of necessity is available if the following conditions exist:

(1) The prisoner is faced with a specific threat of death, forcible sexual attack or substantial bodily injury in the immediate future;
(2) There is no time for a complaint to the authorities or there exists a history of futile complaints which make any result from such complaints illusory;
(3) There is no time or opportunity to resort to the courts;

(4) There is no evidence of force or violence used towards prison personnel or other 'innocent' persons in the escape; and

(5) The prisoner immediately reports to the proper authorities when he has attained a position of safety from the immediate threat.

All that we need say about that decision, which is not of course binding upon us, is that the first proposition states in substance what we understand to be one of the elements of the defence in our law, although we have earlier reserved for future consideration the exact limits of the consequences for the avoidance of which the defence may be raised. The remaining propositions deal essentially with matters which may have evidentiary significance. We could not accept them as propositions of law applicable in this state. In particular the fifth proposition does not appear to us to be based upon principle or authority although evidence of whether or not a prisoner who escapes does voluntarily report to the authorities as soon as possible after attaining his freedom may have a considerable evidentiary significance, in particular upon the question whether the acts of the accused are proportionate to the danger to be avoided.

Next it is necessary to consider whether there was in this case sufficient evidence to justify leaving the defence of necessity to the jury. There was we think evidence from which if accepted the conclusion might have been reached that when the applicant was in the chapel there was an urgent situation of imminent peril in which the applicant honestly believed on reasonable grounds that it was necessary for him to take the opportunity which presented itself of escaping from 'B' division. But when the other element of the defence is considered, namely, whether his acts were proportionate to the danger which he feared, we think that the inevitable conclusion must be that they were not. Once the applicant was clear of 'B' division and on the catwalk, he had put himself out of reach of the danger which he feared and there was no necessity for him to go further. It may readily be inferred that the applicant knew that as a result of what he had done he would have been confined in 'H' division, the very result that he said he was seeking. The applicant said in his unsworn statement that he joined in the escape believing that it would not work, that it would not be successful. He gave his reasons for so thinking, and continued: 'I saw it was an out and a good out. And I believed honestly we would be caught out on the grounds and I would be taken to "H" division. As you have heard, I tried everything to get to "H" division, to get out of "B" division.' It was thus never part of the applicant's case that he had to put himself beyond the prison walls to be safe from the threat which he feared.

Ordinarily it is a question for the jury to say whether acts of an accused are no more than are necessary to avoid the threatened danger. But in this case there was no evidence upon which the jury could have found that the applicant's escape from the prison was reasonably proportionate to the threat which he said he feared. If the matter had been left to the jury they could not properly have concluded on the evidence that he had no alternative to escaping from the prison in order to avoid the peril which he said he feared.

If our analysis of the case is correct there was thus no basis upon which the learned judge was required to leave the defence of necessity to the jury. But if we were wrong on this question we would nevertheless be of the opinion that the application should fail, for his Honour's refusal to leave the defence of necessity to the jury cannot have involved a substantial miscarriage of justice. In other words, we think that the proviso to s 568(1) of the Crimes Act should be applied. The test for the application of that provision has been stringently expressed, but we are satisfied that any reasonable jury properly instructed would have inevitably come to the same conclusion even if the matter had been left to them. We have reached a firm conviction on this point from a study of the whole of the evidence but we have been fortified in the conclusion we have reached by the fact that the learned trial judge clearly thought that even if there were a defence of necessity which he should leave to the jury the evidence would not have justified the jury in concluding that the defence had been made out or that the Crown had failed to exclude it. His Honour did not, of course, take the matter away from the jury on that ground but that that was his view of the evidence emerges clearly from the discussion which preceded his ruling that the defence of necessity was not open to the applicant. Moreover, in his ruling his Honour said: 'In my view, on the facts of this case, no reasonable jury of 12 men could find this defence sustained.'

We think the application should be refused.

[**Crockett J** delivered a separate judgment agreeing that the appeal should be dismissed. Appeal dismissed.]

[See also *Re Appeal of White* (1987) 9 NSWLR 427.]

12.15 Notes

1. The case of *R v Loughnan* outlines the elements of the defence of necessity, with a mix of subjective and objective elements.
2. While the decisions in *R v Davidson* and *R v Loughnan* establish the existence of a defence of necessity (at least in cases other than murder) in Australia, the English courts have been more restrictive in their approach to the doctrine. For examples of this attitude, see *London Borough of Southwark v Williams* [1971] 2 All ER 175 and *Buckoke v Greater London Council* [1971] 2 All ER 254. In the former case, Edmund Davies LJ stated (at 181):

   > ... the law regards with the deepest suspicion any remedies of self-help, and permits these remedies to be resorted to only in very special circumstances. The reason for such circumspection is clear — necessity can very easily become simply a mask for anarchy.

   The Court of Appeal has expanded the defence of duress to cover cases of 'duress of circumstances': see particularly *R v Martin* [1989] 1 All ER 652; *Woodward v Morgan* (1990) 10 MVR 474.

DURESS

The general defence

12.16 A useful formulation of the general defence of duress is contained in the judgment of Mr Justice Murnaghan in the Irish case of *Attorney-General v Whelan* [1934] IR 518 at 526:

> [T]hreats of immediate death or serious personal violence so great as to overbear the ordinary power of human resistance should be accepted as a justification for acts which would otherwise be criminal. … Where the excuse of duress is applicable it must … be clearly shown that the overpowering of the will was operative at the time the crime was actually committed, and, if there were reasonable opportunity for the will to reassert itself, no justification can be found in antecedent threats.

In order to argue the defence of duress, X must have nominated the type of crime D committed: *R v Cole* [1994] Crim LR 582. The defence is recognised at common law in New South Wales and Victoria. If duress is successful, the accused will be acquitted. In New South Wales, duress is not available as a defence to murder. In Victoria, duress is available in homicide cases by virtue of s 9AG of the Crimes Act 1958 (Vic) (discussed further at **12.29**). It is unclear at common law whether the defence is open to an accessory in relation to a charge of attempted murder. The weight of opinion seems to be that it is not available: *R v Gotts* [1992] AC 412.

12.17C R v Lawrence

[1980] 1 NSWLR 122; (1980) 32 ALR 72
Court of Criminal Appeal, Supreme Court of New South Wales

[A number of the accused were convicted of conspiring to import a large quantity of cannabis into Australia. One of the accused, the navigator for the two ships involved in the operation, asserted that he initially entered into the venture innocently and that, after he became aware of the true purpose of the voyage, he was compelled by threats to continue. In directing the jury, the trial judge left to them not only the question whether the threats were made and the mind of the accused overborne, but also the question whether the threats, in the circumstances, were such that the mind of a reasonable person would have been overborne. He stated: 'It must appear in the evidence that the duress was of such a kind that a person of ordinary firmness of character would be likely to yield in the way the accused did.' His Honour further directed the jury that the defence was not made out if there was a reasonable opportunity for the accused to take action (such as informing the authorities) so that his will was reasserted.

On appeal it was argued that the test for duress should be entirely subjective in nature, that is it should be simply: 'Was the accused's will in fact overborne at the time of the commission of the offence?'.]

Moffitt P [His Honour examined the authorities in detail, and rejected the argument of counsel for the accused. His Honour expressed his conclusions as follows]:

The law of duress relevant to the present case is as follows:

(1) Where a person does acts otherwise criminal by reason only of his mind being then overborne by threats of death or serious bodily violence, whether to himself or to another, the defence of duress will be available provided an average person of ordinary firmness of mind of a like age and sex in like circumstances would have done the acts.

(2) Where it appears that the accused person fails to avail himself of an opportunity reasonably open to him for his will to be reasserted the defence will not be available to him. Answer to this question will depend upon whether an average person of ordinary firmness to mind of like age and sex in like circumstances involving like risks in respect of the alternatives open would have availed himself of the opportunity in question.

(3) The extent to which it will be appropriate to give directions to the jury in relation to the relevance of particular circumstances, including any relevant risks, if the threat is ignored, or the opportunity availed of and in relation to the age and sex of the accused will depend on the facts of the particular case and the conduct of the trial. Although not necessary for decision in the present appeal, it should be added:

(4) Consistency in the law would be served by applying the criteria in (1) and (2) where the law admits a threat of any other description as a possible basis for the defence of duress. In the present state of the law, it is unclear what other threats will be so admitted and on what policy or criteria the law will admit some but exclude other threats and in relation to what crimes and in what circumstances. It is not clear which cases will be left outside duress as a defence to guilt so it is left to be dealt with as a matter for mitigation of punishment, eg a threat to damage property. It would be consistent with common law principles that so far as duress as a defence is to be admitted this branch of the law should depend upon a rule of general application and that any such rule should conform to standards regarded as acceptable by the general body of the community. The principles of the common law would be served if the question whether the nature of the threat, taken with the circumstances and with the nature of the crime committed under the influence of the threat, is sufficient for the defence to be available were determined in accordance with (1) above. It would have a parallel in the general principles applied in relation to the law regarding provocation. Such an approach would accommodate too the anomalies which concerned Lord Simon of Glaisdale in *Lynch* quoted above. It would not be inconsistent with this approach that there be excluded as a matter of law from the defence some classes of threat. This might consistently be done either for particular policy reasons (as in *Abbott*) or by it being ruled as a matter of law that it was not to be open to a jury to find in such a case that an average person of ordinary firmness would have responded to such a threat to commit the particular crime.

It follows from these conclusions (1), (2) and (3) that Begg J did not err as alleged in the directions of law given by him concerning the defence of duress as to whether it was originally available and also as to whether it had been lost by failure of the accused to avail himself of a relevant opportunity to render the threats ineffective.

[**Nagle CJ** and **Yeldham J** delivered a separate joint judgment adopting the same views as **Moffitt P**. Appeal dismissed.]

12.18 Illustrations

1. D was charged with escaping from prison, and raised the defences of duress and necessity. He led evidence that he escaped because he feared for his life as a result of threats made against him in the prison. The trial judge ruled that these defences were not available. The accused was convicted and appealed to the Full Supreme Court of Victoria. Held, appeal dismissed. For the defence of duress to be available the threat must be 'present and continuing, imminent and impending', and the accused must have 'no means, with safety to himself, of preventing the execution of the threat'. In the instant case, the threat was not immediate. The threats had not been made directly to the accused, but had been relayed to him. There was no evidence that, at any time, any of those who had made the threats were near or in the presence of the accused. Further, the accused had available to him means of preventing the carrying out of the threats which he did not avail himself of; namely, he could have reported the matter to the authorities. Held further that D's defence was properly categorised as one of necessity rather than duress. However, the requirements of immediacy and unavoidability are equally requirements of the defence of necessity as they are of duress: *R v Dawson* [1978] VR 536. Note, this case is discussed in *R v Loughnan* (at **12.14C**).
2. D, a married woman, was convicted of presenting false forms to the Department of Social Security. The magistrate accepted evidence that D had received beatings and threats from her husband which caused her to hand in the forms, but found that she could have avoided committing the offences by complaining to the police or leaving her husband. The magistrate convicted D. On appeal to a single judge, the decision of the magistrate was reversed. The Crown appealed to the Full Court of the Supreme Court of South Australia. Held, decision of the single judge affirmed. The court stated in *Osborne v Goddard* (1978) 21 ALR 189:

   > Like the learned judge we do not think that a court requires a wife to terminate her marriage to escape bodily injury and the compulsion of committing these offences. We say 'these offences' because it is obvious that an offence of the

gravity of treason or murder might require different answers. In any case … it is notorious to all those who have had to hear accounts of family disputes in the courts, that the police do their utmost not to get involved in such disputes, so that purely as a matter of fact the respondent had no guarantee at all that an application to the police for her safety would necessarily result in police action. In any case, as is pointed out in *R v Hudson* [1971] 2 QB 202 at 207, the police cannot provide effective protection 24 hours a day and a complaint to them even if immediately efficacious, might not have saved her from the 'belting' that she feared. In our opinion the learned judge was right in the conclusion to which he came and the respondent did make out a defence of duress according to law.

See also **12.38** on the question of marital coercion.

3. D was a member of a gang which robbed post offices. H, another member, shot and killed the postmaster in the last of the robberies. H was convicted of murder and D of manslaughter. At an earlier robbery, H fired one shot which hit another gang member. D stated that he had not wanted to participate in the final robbery when he saw that guns were being carried, but H had threatened him. He sought to rely on the defence of duress. Held, appeal dismissed. Where a person had voluntarily and knowingly joined an organisation or a gang which he or she realised might exert pressure upon or level threats at that person to continue to participate, and was an active member of the gang at the time of the threats, the defence of duress will not be available: *R v Sharp* [1987] QB 853. See also *R v Shepherd* [1987] Crim LR 686, where it was held that the jury must be allowed to consider the nature and timing of threats and the nature and persistence of the offences in question in order to decide whether the defence of duress was made out. While a defendant who voluntarily joined a gang of armed robbers, or a para-military organisation, must know what could happen if, in a particular episode, that defendant loses his or her nerve or desires to withdraw for reasons of conscience, there are certain kinds of criminal activities into which a person may enter without any foreknowledge that thinking better of it will lead to serious threats to the defendant or his or her family. See K J M Smith, 'Must Heroes Behave Heroically?' [1989] *Crim LR* 622.

12.19C

R v Runjanjic and Kontinnen

(1991) 56 SASR 114

Supreme Court of South Australia

King CJ: The appellants were tried in the Supreme Court on an information containing a count of false imprisonment and a count of causing grievous bodily harm with intent to do grievous bodily harm. They were found guilty on each count. There was a third count of assault occasioning actual bodily harm but that was an alternative to the second count and no verdict was taken upon it. The appellants have appealed against those convictions.

The offences were alleged to have been committed against one Patricia Hunter at a property at Swan Reach where Runjanjic and a man by the name of Hill lived together on a de facto basis. Hill was originally jointly charged with the appellants but died suddenly in January of this year.

Runjanjic is 30 years of age. She worked in various jobs after leaving school. She met Hill in 1981 and commenced her de facto relationship with him. The relationship was undoubtedly marked by Hill's dominance and Runjanjic's subservience. He put her to work as a prostitute. There was a consistent pattern of domineering and violent conduct by Hill towards Runjanjic. She was expected to attend to his every need, including quite trivial needs, and the price of disobedience was severe beating. Nevertheless it is clear that she loved Hill and was intensely loyal to him. She bore his child in 1989.

Kontinnen is 26 years of age. She first met Hill when she was keeping company with Hill's cousin. That friendship broke up when Kontinnen was about 22 years of age. It appears that from that time Hill began to exert an influence over Kontinnen and he engaged her to conduct a business known as 'Fantasy Phonecall Service'. She also had a job at Bridgestones. Kontinnen joined with Hill and Runjanjic in purchasing the property at Swan Reach. A sexual relationship developed between Hill and Kontinnen and he prevailed upon her to work as a prostitute. From that time on Hill looked upon both the appellants as his women and designated them No 1 and No 2. His conduct towards Kontinnen was also domineering and marked by habitual violence. The two appellants and Hill had lived as one household on occasions, but at the time of these alleged offences Hill and Runjanjic were living at Swan Reach and Kontinnen was living in Adelaide.

The alleged victim, Patricia Hunter, had been a friend of Kontinnen for many years. Their friendship seems to have cooled somewhat as the result of Kontinnen's relationship with Hill and Hill's influence on her, but they remained friends and Kontinnen knew that Patricia Hunter would help her if needed. It appears that shortly before the commission of these alleged offences, some articles were stolen from the house occupied by Kontinnen. As I understand the evidence, this was a house in which Hill and Runjanjic also resided when they were in Adelaide. A friend told Kontinnen that Hunter had possession of some of the stolen articles. Kontinnen told Hill of this information.

Hill directed Runjanjic to telephone Kontinnen with instructions to get Hunter up to Swan Reach. This was to be accomplished by telling a false story to her. The story which Hill invented and which was relayed by Runjanjic to Kontinnen was that Kontinnen had spent some money which Hill had entrusted to her and that it was necessary for her to get some money quickly to replace that which she had spent in order to avoid a beating. She was to ask Hunter to accompany her to Swan Reach in order to assist her to sell some furniture and some Indian hemp to enable her to raise the necessary money. She was to tell Hunter that Hill and Runjanjic were absent from the property.

Kontinnen duly told this story to Hunter and persuaded her to accompany her to Swan Reach. On arrival there Hill and Runjanjic were waiting for her. Hill beat Hunter severely with a shotgun and inflicted other forms of violence on her. She suffered quite severe injuries including a broken arm.

The events which followed the initial beating are in dispute. Hunter said that she was detained at the property against her will. At one stage she was handcuffed to a bed. She was subjected to verbal and physical ill-treatment and was made to gather firewood in her injured condition. She was interrogated about the alleged theft, about who was implicated and where the stolen property was. At one stage rings were cut from her swollen fingers against her will. Hunter said that she was kept against her will at one property at Swan Reach from the time of her arrival on a Tuesday until the Wednesday night. She was then taken to another property and kept there against her will until the Friday. Hill, Runjanjic and Kontinnen were present during most of this period. On the Friday Hill and Kontinnen had left and Hunter was left alone with Runjanjic. Runjanjic told her that they had to go to the other property and took her in a truck. There was a shotgun in the truck. The truck broke down and Hunter made her escape on foot. She hailed a car on the main road but Runjanjic arrived on the scene and tried to drag her back to the truck. Runjanjic told the occupants of the car Hunter had been involved in an accident and to take no notice of her. The occupants of the car, however, took her to a police station.

The appellants in their evidence admitted being parties to deceiving Hunter into going to Swan Reach. They denied, however, that they anticipated that Hill would use violence towards her and denied that they were part of any plan involving the use of violence. Their evidence was that the purpose of the plan from their point of view was simply to persuade Hunter to disclose information about the supposed theft. They claimed that Hunter remained at Swan Reach willingly and denied that she was under restraint or that handcuffs were used. They explained their apparent co-operation with Hill by stating that they would face violence from him if they disobeyed him.

The primary defence, as it was put to the jury, was that the appellants were not parties to any plan involving the imprisonment or violence and that Hill's assault on Hunter was not anticipated by them. Alternatively, it was contended on their behalf that their wills were overborne by fear of Hill's violence and that they acted under duress.

Mr Borick, who was counsel for Kontinnen at the trial and for both appellants on the appeal, argued that the verdicts were unsafe and unsatisfactory. It seems to me, however, that it was quite open to a reasonable jury to reach verdicts of guilty beyond reasonable doubt. There can be little doubt that Hill was a domineering man and that the appellants were under his influence to a considerable extent. Nevertheless there was a considerable body of evidence from which the jury could reasonably infer that they both willingly cooperated in the plan to inveigle Hunter to Swan Reach knowing that Hill intended to attempt to beat information out of her regarding the supposed theft. It is difficult to see why it was necessary to inveigle Hunter to the property at Swan Reach unless unlawful force was intended to be used. Runjanjic told Kontinnen that the purpose was to teach Hunter a lesson. Hunter's evidence was that Runjanjic joined in the infliction of violence to the extent of punching her. The two appellants joined in the questioning of Hunter following the violence and they participated in the cutting of the rings from her swollen fingers. Kontinnen went to Adelaide and brought Hunter's children to the Swan Reach property on the Wednesday. Clearly Runjanjic was left to guard Hunter on the Friday and was engaged in doing that when the truck broke down. She attempted to prevent Hunter's escape. It is not surprising that the jury rejected the appellants' evidence that they were unaware that Hill intended to use violence towards Hunter and even less surprising that they rejected their evidence that Hunter was not detained against her will but was quite willing to remain at the property notwithstanding the ill-treatment she had received and the severe injuries from which she was suffering.

The defence of duress was a matter for the consideration of the jury. Its force was greatly weakened, however, by the fact that the appellants did not claim to have participated in a plan involving imprisonment and violence out of fear, but had denied such participation together. Their credibility must have been severely weakened in the eyes of the jury by what were seen to be false denials and that must have greatly influenced the jury's assessment of the story that, to the extent that they cooperated with Hill, they did so only out of fear.

I do not think that, on the evidence given in the case, the verdict could be regarded as unsafe or unsatisfactory and that ground of appeal must fail.

There was another ground of appeal which raises an important question of admissibility of evidence. At the trial Mr Borick sought to call a Mr Fugler, a professional psychologist, to give evidence of what Mr Borick described on the appeal as 'the battered woman syndrome'. The learned trial judge ruled that the evidence was inadmissible and Mr Borick has argued on the appeal that that ruling was wrong.

Mr Fugler was not sworn and the judge was not provided with a proof of the evidence which he proposed to give. Mr Borick summarised the proposed evidence for the judge. He described Mr Fugler as a clinical forensic psychologist of 20 years experience. He described the proposed evidence on the following terms:

> Our basic submission is that there are certain behaviour patterns displayed by women who are battered in the way these women have been battered and it leads to certain inabilities to handle situations in the way ordinary people would, and in brief what they have undergone is beyond ordinary experience and the jury would require assistance from someone like Mr Fugler to explain.
>
> The sort of behaviour patterns that in general terms Mr Fugler would talk about would be that it starts with what he described as a role induction whereby they become accustomed to violence and begin to rationalise violence. It is associated with a loss of self-esteem and confidence which robs them of the ability to cope with infliction of violence in the way that an ordinary person would. Violence becomes normal. Then there is the effect of long-term fear arising out of threats of death or severe injuries over a period of time. Mr Fugler says that leads to a type of dependence where they become dependent upon their assailant. He says their emotional responses are blocked and the expectation of violence which is abnormal to an ordinary person becomes normal to them. Their anxiety level robs them of the ability to make decisions and that is an important aspect of the evidence from the psychologist.

I think that it is reasonable to suppose that Mr Borick's summary of the evidence which Mr Fugler would give was by no means complete. He would have given evidence no doubt of what is now known by psychologists as the 'battered woman syndrome'. There is now a considerable body of literature on this topic and a perusal of that literature enables one to flesh out from Mr Borick's bare summary the sort of evidence which Mr Fugler might have been expected to give if he had been permitted to do so. I propose to refer to the features of the 'battered woman syndrome' as it is described in the literature. As I have said, the body of literature on the topic, particularly in the United States of America, is considerable. I have selected for citation from the mass of available material articles which I have found to be most useful because they relate features of the syndrome to legal issues which arise in criminal trials. Those articles are cited at 122, in the footnote to these reasons. I draw attention particularly to two articles which, I think, sufficiently describe the syndrome for present purposes. I refer to an article by Daniel J Brodsky, 'Educating Juries: The Battered Woman Defence in Canada' (1987) 25 No 3 *Alberta Law Review* 461, and an article by Annie E Thar, 'The Admissibility of Expert Testimony on Battered Wife Syndrome: An Evidentiary Analysis' (1982) 77 No 3 *Northwestern University Law Review* 348.

I gather from the literature that the idea of the battered woman syndrome was pioneered by Dr Lenore Walker in a publication entitled *The Battered Woman* (1979). She is the author of *The Battered Woman Syndrome* (1984). It now appears to be a recognised facet of clinical psychology in the United States and Canada. It emerges from the literature that methodical studies by trained psychologists of situations of domestic violence have revealed typical patterns of behaviour on the part of the male batterer and the female victim, and typical responses on the part of the female victim. It has been revealed, so it appears, that women who have suffered habitual domestic violence are typically affected psychologically to the extent that their reactions and responses differ from those which might be expected by persons who lack the advantage of an acquaintance with the result of those studies.

Repeated acts of violence, alternating very often with phases of kindness and loving behaviour, commonly leave the battered woman in a psychological condition described as 'learned helplessness'. She cannot predict or control the occurrence of acute outbreaks of violence and often clings to the hope that the kind and loving phases will become the norm. This is often reinforced by financial dependence, children and feelings of guilt. The battered woman rarely seeks outside help because of fear of further violence. It is not uncommon for such women to experience feelings for their mate which they describe as love. There is often an all-pervasive feeling that it is impossible to escape the dominance and violence of the mate. There is a sense of constant fear with a perceived inability to escape the situation.

An essential prerequisite to the admission of expert evidence as to the battered woman syndrome is that it be accepted by experts competent in the field of psychology or psychiatry as a scientifically established facet of psychology. This must be established by appropriate evidence. Because the learned trial judge ruled the evidence to be inadmissible on other grounds, Mr Fugler was not examined on this point and no finding was made. A perusal of the literature to which I have referred, however, indicates a wide acceptance of the syndrome as having a valid existence. The attitudes of various courts in the United States are discussed in a number of the articles cited at 122. Two citations will suffice.

In *People (New York) v Torres* 488 NYS 2d 358 (1985), the trial judge, Bernstein J, admitted expert evidence of the battered woman syndrome. He said (at 363):

> Upon careful reflection and analysis, however, it is the opinion of this court that the theory underlying the battered woman's syndrome has indeed passed beyond the experimental stage and gained a substantial enough scientific acceptance to warrant admissibility. According to Dr Blackman, numerous articles and books have been published about the battered woman's syndrome; and recent findings of researchers in the field have confirmed its presence and thereby indicated that the scientific community accepts its underlying premises.

This passage was cited with approval by the Court of Appeals of New Mexico in *State (New Mexico) v Gallegos* 719 P 2d 1268 (1986) at 1274, and the court added:

> In our case, the trial court apparently found the psychologist qualified to testify in her area of expertise. The court evidently also determined that the 'battered wife syndrome' had gained general recognition and acceptance in the field of psychology. We, therefore, see no reason for excluding use of a recognised term to describe the phenomenon. Certainly the term used to describe this condition could be no more inflammatory than its symptoms, and far less than its causes.
>
> Accordingly, we hold that the trial court should not have excluded, during the expert's testimony, use of the term 'battered wife syndrome'.

The same view has been taken in Canada: see *Lavallee v R* (1990) 55 CCC (3d) 97, a case to which I shall return later. I am not aware of any case on the subject in Australia or in any other common law country.

Evidence of the kind under discussion is relevant, in my opinion, to issues arising in this case. It was necessary on the evidence for the jury to consider whether the appellants were constrained by duress to participate in the crimes charged. The learned trial judge left that issue to the jury. The defence of duress exists:

> … when the otherwise criminal acts are committed not out of choice but because the will of the accused is overborne by threats of death or serious physical injury in such circumstances that the will of a person of reasonable firmness might be similarly overborne: see *R v Brown* (1986) 43 SASR 33 at 37.

The availability of the defence is subject to a condition that the accused has not failed to avail himself of an opportunity which was reasonably open to him to render the threat ineffective: see *Brown* supra at 39. There is therefore a subjective and an objective aspect of the test. There is the question whether the will of the accused was actually overborne. There is then the further question whether the will of a person of reasonable firmness in his situation would have been overborne.

The learned judge ruled the proffered evidence to be inadmissible on the ground that the test is objective and that expert evidence of the state of mind of the appellants was therefore irrelevant. I do not think that that is a sound basis for excluding the evidence. In the first place it ignores the subjective aspect of the test. Even if the evidence had no bearing on the objective aspect, it would be relevant to the question whether the wills of these appellants were in fact overborne. But it also misapprehends, in my opinion, an important thrust of the proffered evidence. It may be that the expert is in a position to express an opinion as to the condition of mind of these appellants, but the primary thrust of the evidence is to establish a pattern of responses commonly exhibited by battered women. The proffered evidence is concerned not so much with the particular responses of these appellants as with what would be expected of women generally, that is to say, women of reasonable firmness, who should find themselves in a domestic situation such as that in which the appellants were. It is designed to assist the court in assessing whether women of reasonable firmness would succumb to the pressure to participate in the offences. It also serves to explain why even a woman of reasonable firmness would not escape the situation rather than participate in criminal activity. As such it is relevant.

Not all knowledge, however, which is relevant to an issue and which forms part of an organised field of knowledge may be imparted to a court by means of expert testimony. The law jealously guards the role of the jury, or the court where it is the trier of the facts, as the judge of human nature, of the behaviour of normal people and situations which are within the experience of ordinary persons or are capable of being understood by them: see *R v Turner* [1975] QB 834. It is not sufficient, in order to justify the admission of expert evidence of the battered woman syndrome, as was argued by counsel for the appellant, that the ordinary juror would have no experience of the situation of a battered woman. Jurors are constantly expected to judge of situations, and of the behaviour of people in situations, which are outside their experience. Much conduct which occupies the attention of the criminal courts occurs in the criminal underworld, or in sordid conditions and situations, of which jurors would generally have no experience. It is not considered to be beyond the capacity of juries, or of the court if it is the trier of the facts, to judge of the reactions and behaviour of people in those situations. Expert evidence of how life in criminal or sordid conditions might affect a person's responses to situations would not be admitted.

Nevertheless, some human situations or relations, or the attitudes or behaviour of some categories of persons, may be so special and so outside the experience of jurors, or of the court if it is the trier of facts, that evidence of methodical studies of behaviour or attitudes in such situations or relations, or of the attitudes or behaviour of those categories of persons, may be admissible. The fact that the accused person cannot be characterised as an abnormal person or that the evidence relates to the behaviour of normal persons in special situations is not necessarily a bar to the admission of such evidence: see *Murphy v R* (1989) 167 CLR 94, per Mason CJ and Toohey J (at 112), per Dawson J (at 130–1).

This is an area in which the courts must move with great caution. The admission of expert evidence of patterns of behaviour of normal human beings, even in abnormal situations or relations, is fraught with danger for the integrity of the trial process. The risk that, by degrees, trials, especially criminal trials, will become battle grounds for experts and that the capacity of juries and courts to discharge their fact-finding functions will be thereby impaired is to be taken seriously. I have considered anxiously whether the situation of the habitually battered woman is so special and so outside ordinary experience that the knowledge of experts should be made available to courts and juries called upon to judge behaviour in such situations. In the end, I have been impressed by what I have read of the insights which have been gained by special study of the subject, insights which I am sure would not be shared or shared fully by ordinary jurors. It seems to me that a just judgment of the actions of women in those situations requires that the court or jury have the benefit of the insights which have been gained.

I am fortified in the conclusion to which I have come not only by the trend of authority in the United States of America but by the decision of the Supreme Court of Canada in *Lavallee*, supra. The court upheld the admission of expert evidence of the battered woman syndrome on the issue of self-defence in a case in which a woman was charged with the murder of her husband. In a strongly, at times passionately, expressed judgment, Wilson J, with whose judgment the other members of the court agreed, stated the reasons for the decision. Wilson J said (at 112):

> Expert evidence on the psychological effect of battering on wives and common law partners must, it seems to me, be both relevant and necessary in the context of the present case. How can the mental state of the appellant be appreciated without it? The average member of the public (or of the jury) can be forgiven for asking: Why would a woman put up with this kind of treatment? Why should she continue to live with such a man? How could she love a partner who beat her to the point of requiring hospitalisation? We would expect the woman to pack her bags and go. Where is her self-respect? Why does she not cut loose and make a new life for herself? Such is the reaction of the average person confronted with the so-called 'battered wife syndrome'. We need help to understand it and help is available from trained professionals.

Lavellee was a case of self-defence to a charge of murder. All the American cases which I have seen in which evidence of the battered woman syndrome has been admitted have been cases in which the issue was self-defence or provocation on a charge of murder. It would appear, however, that, on the trial of Patti Hearst for armed robbery, expert evidence was admitted, as relevant to a defence of duress, of the psychological effect of a period of prolonged captivity and coercion on a normal person, and this was approved by the United States Court of Appeals, Ninth Circuit: see *United States v Hearst* 563 Fed 2d 1331 (1977) at 1351. I can see no distinction in principle between the admission of expert evidence of the battered woman syndrome on the issues of self-defence and provocation and on the issue of duress.

I consider therefore that the ruling excluding the evidence on the ground upon which it was made was in error. The evidence was admissible, in my opinion, subject to satisfactory proof that its subject matter is regarded by experts competent in the field as an accepted field of scientific knowledge and subject, of course, to the proposed expert witness or witnesses being qualified as expert in this particular field.

I think that the exclusion of this potentially important body of evidence has vitiated the trial. Although the verdict was properly open to the jury on the evidence given at the trial, it might have been affected by the excluded evidence.

I would therefore allow the appeal, set aside the convictions and order a new trial of the appellants on the information.

[**Legoe** and **Bollen JJ** delivered concurring judgments. Appeal allowed. Order for a new trial.]

12.20 Notes

1. The importance of this case lies primarily in the judicial recognition of the battered woman syndrome as an established facet of human psychology, in respect of which expert evidence will be admissible.

   There is, however, no doubt of the significance of the case in reaffirming the firm place of the defence of duress in the criminal law of Australia's common law jurisdictions.

   On the syndrome, see K O'Donovan, 'Law's Knowledge: The Judge, the Expert, the Battered Woman and Her Syndrome' (1993) 29 *JL & Soc* 427; I Leader-Elliott, 'Battered but Not Beaten: Women Who Kill in Self Defence' (1993) 15 *SydLR* 403; I Freckelton, 'Contemporary Comment: When Plight Makes Right — The Forensic Abuse Syndrome' (1994) 18 *Crim LJ* 29. See also *R v J* (1994) 75 A Crim R 522; P Easteal, 'Battered Women Syndrome: What is Reasonable?' (1992) 17 *Alternative Law Journal* 203; E Sheehy, J Stubbs and J Tolmie, 'Defending Battered Women on Trial: The Battered Women Syndrome and its Limitations' (1992) *Criminal Law Journal* 369.

2. The case should be considered in the larger context of domestic violence. This subject is considered at 2.19. In *Osland v R* (1998) 197 CLR 316; 159 ALR 170 (see 11.13C), several members of the High Court considered the nature and quality of the battered woman syndrome. Expert evidence of the syndrome affecting the appellant, who was convicted of the murder of her husband, had been admitted by the trial judge. Gaudron and Gummow JJ, who dissented from the decision to dismiss the appeal, and Kirby J all agreed that the trial judge had not erred in his direction to the jury on the use to which the evidence of the syndrome might be put. It permitted the jury, if they chose to accept the evidence, to draw conclusions about the appellant's behaviour, in the context of the specific defences of self-defence and provocation which were advanced by her.

Duress and murder

12.21 The view of the institutional writers was that duress could never be a defence to a charge of murder. Thus in Blackstone's *Commentaries* it is stated (vol 4, p 30):

> … though a man be violently assaulted, and hath no other possible means of escaping death, but by killing an innocent person; this fear and force shall not acquit him of murder; for he ought rather to die himself, than escape by murder of an innocent.

12.22 In *R v Brown and Morley* [1968] SASR 467, the majority of the Supreme Court of South Australia held that duress could not be a defence to a charge of murder.

A powerful dissent, however, was delivered by Bray CJ. A similar view was adopted by the Full Court of the Supreme Court of Victoria in *R v Harding* [1976] VR 129.

12.23 In *Director of Public Prosecutions for Northern Ireland v Lynch* [1975] AC 653, a majority of the House of Lords decided that the defence of duress was available in certain circumstances to a person charged as a principal in the second degree to murder, leaving open the issue of its availability to a person charged as a principal in the first degree. Lord Simon delivered a powerful dissenting speech, and Lord Kilbrandon also dissented. Shortly afterwards, in *Abbott v R* [1977] AC 755, the Judicial Committee of the Privy Council, in a majority opinion delivered by Lord Salmon, Lord Hailsham and Lord Kilbrandon, decided that the appellant, whom they characterised as a principal in the first degree to murder, could not avail himself of the defence of duress. They subjected the *Lynch* decision to strong criticism. Lord Wilberforce and Lord Edmund-Davies who, with Lord Morris, constituted the majority in *Lynch's* case, delivered an equally powerful dissenting opinion.

12.24 The development of the law in the Australian common law states after these conflicting and 'much discussed decisions' of two final courts of appeal (remembering that *Abbott v R* was decided before the enactment of the Australia Act 1986) is illustrated by the following case.

12.25C R v Darrington and McGauley

[1980] VR 353
Supreme Court of Victoria

[The deceased was shot while a passenger in a car driven by the female accused, Darrington. The shot was fired by McGauley. The body of the victim was removed from the car, and Darrington then drove the car over it several times. There was evidence to support a conclusion that the victim had died before the car first passed over his body, and also evidence to support a conclusion that he was alive when the car was first driven over him.

The trial judge did not direct the jury as to a possible defence of duress. At the trial, Darrington had made an unsworn statement, according to which her conduct in driving over the body of the victim was in response to McGauley pointing the gun at her and threatening to kill her. On Darrington's own account of the incidents leading to the victim's death, no threats were made to her prior to this time. The firing of the shot had, she said, come as a complete surprise to her, she believing that the victim was being taken to McGauley's father who was to settle an issue between them.]

Jenkinson J: The first ground of the application by Kaye Darrington for leave to appeal against her conviction was that the learned trial judge had erred 'in not leaving to the jury the defence of duress'.

It was the submission of Mr Kelly QC, who appeared with Mr Morrish for Kaye Darrington, that this court must — or at least ought — now hold, in consequence of what was decided and of what was said in *Director of Public Prosecutions for Northern Ireland v Lynch* [1975] AC 653; [1975] 1 All ER 913 and in *Abbott v R* [1977] AC 755; [1976] 3 All ER 740, that the defence of duress is not denied to any party to murder except a principal in the first degree. Those two decisions required, or at least authorised, such a departure from what was decided by this court in *R v Harding* [1976] VR 129, Mr Kelly submitted.

In *Harding's* case this court held duress not to be an answer in law by a principal in the second degree of murder. All three members of the court gave prolonged consideration to the question in reserved judgments. The contrary conclusion of the House of Lords in *Lynch's* case does not bind this court and that contrary conclusion is not in my opinion a necessary element in the reasoning by which the decision of the Privy Council was reached in *Abbott's* case, that the defence of duress is not available to one who participates physically in the acts causing death as a principal in the first degree to murder. It is true that the reasons for judgment of the majority in the Judicial Committee included the observation that they 'feel bound to accept the decision of the House of Lords in *Lynch's* case': at [1977] AC 763. It is true that the majority in *Abbott's* case examined the speeches in *Lynch's* case in order to determine whether the authority could be found for or against allowing duress as a defence to a principal in the first degree to murder; and that they found nothing pro and something contra. They found that, if some observations by two of the majority were added to observations by each of the two members of the House who were in the minority, it seemed that 'the majority of the House' was against allowing duress as a defence to 'anyone proved to have done the actual killing': at [1977] AC 764. But that circumstance was not said to have persuaded the majority in the Judicial Committee to their conclusion. And nothing of the reasoning by which the conclusion in *Lynch's* case was reached finds expression in the reasoning of the majority in *Abbott's* case, unless it be the observation that participation under duress in the actual killing usually attracts a graver moral censure than other acts under duress by which participation in homicide is effected. The observation had an influence upon the conclusion in each of the two cases, but could not be said to have been determinative of either conclusion.

This court is not bound to follow the decision of the House of Lords in *Lynch's* case. The questions whether, and in what circumstances, a State Supreme Court exercising appellate jurisdiction in its Full Court or in its Court of Appeal might decline to follow a decision of the House of Lords have been recently considered: *Kelly v Sweeney* [1975] 2 NSWLR 720; *Thompson v Nix* [1976] WAR 141; *Brisbane v Cross* [1978] VR 49. Those cases were decided before the reasons for judgment of the members of the High Court in *Viro v R* (1978) 52 ALJR 418 were published. Those reasons expose the difficulties which the enactment by the Commonwealth Parliament of the *Privy Council (Appeals from the High Court) Act 1975* creates for the State Supreme Courts in their application of the rules of precedent to decisions of the Privy Council. Those difficulties have also a significance in any consideration of the course to be taken when a recent, considered decision of this court, not at variance with any reasoning of a judge of the High Court, nor shown to be 'clearly wrong' (see *Daniell v Robotham* (1883) 9 VLR (L) 215), is contradicted by a decision of the House of Lords. Those difficulties are of particular significance when the decision of the House of Lords is the result of what Windeyer J called 'the creative element' in the work of the House: see *Brisbane v Cross* [1978] VR 49 at 52–5. The decision in *Lynch's* case is no declaration of what might be deduced from established principles of the common law. It is a conclusion based upon considerations drawn from moral and political philosophy which were thought to be appropriate in the United Kingdom now. The Judicial Committee has itself recognised that the resolution of such considerations for England may be inappropriate for other parts of the Queen's dominions: *Australian Consolidated Press Ltd v Uren* [1969] 1 AC 590 at 641; [1967] 3 All ER 523; *Abbott's* case [1977] AC 755 at 768; [1976] 3 All ER 740. It is of course not ordinarily the function of this court to determine for itself whether such considerations are to be resolved in the same sense here: that is for the High Court of Australia and the Privy Council. At the time when there is uncertainty of precedent by reason of the circumstances discussed in *Viro's* case, this court might be thought to fulfil its function best by applying the decision in *Harding's* case in disregard of *Lynch's* case. But the practice of this court has been to follow a decision of the House of Lords in preference to its own decision, unless compelled to another course by a decision or reasoning of the Privy Council or of the High Court. The practice is in conformity with the advice expressed by Owen J (in which Taylor J concurred) in *Skelton v Collins* (1966) 115 CLR 94 at 122, 139 and by Barwick CJ and Gibbs J in *Public Transport Commission (NSW) v Murray-More (NSW) Pty Ltd* (1975) 132 CLR 336 at 341, 349. That advice has not been countermanded by any more recent, unequivocal guidance by the High Court: see *Viro v R* (1978) 52 ALJR 418 at 430, 447. In those circumstances I think that we should not depart from the existing practice, but should follow *Lynch's* case …

The decision of the Judicial Committee in *Abbott's* case, no less than the decision of this court in *Harding's* case, denies Kaye Darrington any defence of duress in respect of the acts whereby she caused the car to pass over Peter Darrington's body, considered as acts inculpating her as principal in the first degree. And her own unambiguous, not to say emphatic, account to the jury of her belief that David McGauley's intention was to accompany Peter Darrington to his father — 'I really thought he was taking Peter to see his father' — made it appropriate, in my opinion, for the learned trial judge to direct the jury concerning the defence of duress in relation to the acts she did between the time when David McGauley proposed the journey to his father and the time when she heard the noise of the discharging rifle.

[**Young CJ** agreed with **Jenkinson J. Anderson J** delivered a separate judgment agreeing that the appeal should be dismissed. Appeal dismissed.]

12.26 Notes

The view taken in *Abbott v R* was anticipated in the earlier decision of the New South Wales Court of Criminal Appeal in *R v McConnell* [1977] 1 NSWLR 714. The three accused were charged as principals in the first degree to murder. Each had participated in the stabbing and drowning of the deceased. Two of the accused claimed that they had participated in the killing because of threats made to them by the third accused. The court held that while duress is available to a person charged with murder as a principal in the second degree, it is not available to a principal in the first degree.

Subsequently, the House of Lords unanimously decided to use its rarely employed power to overrule *Director of Public Prosecutions for Northern Ireland v Lynch* [1975] AC 653. The text of that decision is set out in *R v Howe; R v Bannister; R v Burke; R v Clarkson*, below.

12.27C R v Howe; R v Bannister; R v Burke; R v Clarkson

[1987] 1 All ER 771
House of Lords

Lord Hailsham of St Marylebone LC: My Lords, these appeals arise from two cases, one originating from a trial in the Manchester Crown Court before Jupp J and a jury (Howe and Bannister), and one in the Central Criminal Court before the then Common Serjeant, Judge Tudor Price and a jury (Burke and Clarkson).

Howe and Bannister were tried with two other defendants (Murray and Bailey) both of whom during the trial changed their plea to one of duress.

The indictment in the case of Howe, Bannister, Murray and Bailey accused the four men of two murders (Elgar and Pollitt) and a conspiracy to murder (Redfern, an intended victim who escaped in time). The three counts related to three successive days, respectively 10, 11 and 12 October 1983.

Burke and Clarkson were charged with the murder of a single victim (Botton) on 9 July 1983.

The four current appellants appealed against their convictions to the Court of Appeal (Criminal Division) [1968] QB 626 who dismissed all four appeals in a judgment delivered on 27 January 1986. In giving leave to appeal to your Lordships' House the Court of Appeal (Lord Lane CJ, Russell and Taylor JJ) certified three questions of law of general public importance as involved in the decision. The three certified questions are: (1) Is duress available as a defence to a person charged with murder as a principal in the first degree (the actual killer)? (2) Can one who incites or procures by duress another to kill or to be a party to a killing be convicted of murder if that other is acquitted by reason of duress? (3) Does the defence of duress fail if the prosecution prove that a person of reasonable firmness sharing the characteristics of the defendant would not have given way to the threats as did the defendant?

The first of these questions involves a reconsideration of the much discussed decisions in *Director of Public Prosecutions for Northern Ireland v Lynch* [1975] AC 653 and *Abbott v R* [1977] AC 755.

In answering the second question, the Court of Appeal invited us to reconsider the decision of the Court of Appeal in *R v Richards* [1974] QB 776, by which it considered itself bound.

In the arguments presented before your Lordships many other reported authorities and citations from established writers, including Law Commission Report, Criminal Law, Report on Defences of General Application (Law Com No 83) printed by order of the House of Commons, dated 27 July 1977, were cited. Reference to other cases will be made as and where appropriate.

I take the facts of these truly horrible cases almost verbatim from the judgment of Lord Lane CJ [1986] QB 626 in the instant appeal. First, as to the case of Howe and Bannister, Murray and Bailey, the facts were as follows. At the time of the offences Howe and Bailey were 19, Bannister was 20 and Murray was 35. Howe had one minor conviction for motoring offences. Bannister had convictions for theft and burglary but none for violence. He was on probation. Bailey had convictions for burglary and theft. Murray had 25 previous court appearances, including two convictions for assault occasioning actual bodily harm, and in 1974 he had been convicted of assault with intent to rob and robbery in respect of which he had been sentenced to eight years' imprisonment.

Bannister met Murray in Risley Remand Centre. Howe and Bailey met in Stockport when Bailey was living in a hostel and Howe happened to be living next door with his grandmother. Murray came to visit Bailey when he was on six days' home leave from a sentence of two and a half years' imprisonment. Bailey introduced Howe to Murray. Lord Lane CJ continued, at 635–6:

> *Count 1: murder of Elgar.* The first victim was a 17-year-old youth called Elgar. He was offered a job as a driver by Murray. On the evening of 10 October 1983 all five men were driven by Murray up into the hills between Stockport and Buxton, eventually stopping at some public lavatories at a remote spot called Goytsclough. Murray at some stage told both appellants in effect that Elgar was a 'grass', and that they were going to kill him. Bannister was threatened with violence if he did not give Elgar 'a bit of a battering'. From thenceforwards Elgar, who was naked, sobbing and begging for mercy, was tortured, compelled to undergo appalling sexual perversions and indignities, he was kicked and punched. Bannister and Howe were doing the kicking and punching. The coup de grace was executed by Bailey who strangled Elgar with a headlock. It is unnecessary to go into further details of the attack on Elgar which are positively nauseating. In brief the two appellants asserted that they had only acted as they did through fear of Murray, believing that they would be treated in the same way as Elgar had been treated if they did not comply with Murray's directions. The prosecution were content to assent to the proposition that death had been caused by Bailey strangling the victim, although the kicks and punches would have resulted in death moments later even in the absence of the strangulation. The body was hidden by the appellants and the other two men. On this basis the appellants were in the position of what would have earlier been principals in the second degree and duress was left to the jury as an issue on this count.
>
> *Count 2: murder of Pollitt.* Very much the same course of conduct took place as with Elgar. On 11 October 1983 the men picked up Pollitt, a 19-year-old labourer, and took him to the same place where all four men kicked and punched the youth. Murray told Howe and Bannister to kill Pollitt, which they did by strangling him

> with Bannister's shoe lace. As the appellants were in the position of principals in the first degree, the judge did not leave duress to the jury on this count.
>
> *Count 3: conspiracy to murder Redfern.* The third intended victim was a 21-year-old man. The same procedure was followed, but Redfern suspected that something was afoot and managed with some skill to escape on his motorcycle from what would otherwise have inevitably been another horrible murder. The judge left the defence of duress to the jury on this charge of conspiracy to murder.
>
> The grounds of appeal, which are the same in respect of each of the appellants, are as follows. That the judge erred in directing the jury (1) in respect of count 2, that the defence of duress was not available to a principal in the first degree to the actual killing; (2) in respect of counts 1 and 3, that the test as to whether the appellants were acting under duress contains an 'objective' element; that is to say, if the prosecution prove that a reasonable man in the position of the defendant would not have felt himself forced to comply with the threats, the defence fails.

So much for the facts relating to the appellants Howe and Bannister. Lord Lane CJ then turned to the case of Burke and Clarkson. In the case of Howe and Bannister the defence of duress was left to the jury by Jupp J on the third count of conspiracy to murder and rejected by the jury. However, Jupp J had directed the jury in relation to duress. In this case Burke dressed as a policeman had killed Botton with a sawn off shotgun at the entrance of Botton's house. The Lord Chief Justice continued, at 637:

> The prosecution's case was that Burke had done this at the request of Clarkson, who was anxious to prevent Botton from giving evidence against him. Clarkson's defence was that he had nothing to do with the shooting at all. Burke's defence was that he had agreed to shoot Botton because of his fear that Clarkson would kill him if he did not, but when it came to the event, the gun went off accidentally and the killing therefore was unintentional and amounted to no more than manslaughter.

This defence was evidently rejected by the judge as inadmissible, but his defence in respect of manslaughter was left to the jury.

A further submission on behalf of Burke was not argued before us. On the third certified question Jupp J's direction to the jury on the nature of duress, although not identical with that of Judge Tudor Price equally raised the question of the objective element in the threats required raised by the third question certified by the Court of Appeal. The only ground of appeal separately argued before your Lordships on the part of Clarkson depends on the answer to be given to the second certified question to which I will return later.

On the third certified question Mr Self on behalf of the appellants other than Clarkson addressed to us an impressive argument that the test applied is not objective, ie not:

> … whether the threat was of such gravity that it might well have caused a reasonable man placed in the same situation as the defendants to act as the defendant did' nor 'would a sober person of reasonable firmness sharing the defendant's characteristics have responded to the threats by taking part in the killing?

Mr Self's submission was to the effect that where the defence of duress is available to an accused, the test of duress does not contain either of these objective elements but is purely subjective to the accused and depends solely on the effect which the actual threat had on the mind of the particular accused.

From the above, it will be seen that each of the appellants other than Clarkson were actual participants, whether as principal in the first or second degree, in the perpetration of the actual killing of the respective victims in respect of the counts of murder. Clarkson's defence, which was that he had nothing whatever to do with the murder of Botton was rejected by the jury and nothing turned on this at all except that the jury's verdict means that he was the real villain of the piece, since, on any view of the facts, Burke acted at his suggestion and was very much under his influence. The success of Clarkson's appeal depends solely on the answer to the second certified question, and only arises in the event that Burke's appeal on the first or third question succeeds or succeeds to the extent that a conviction of Burke for manslaughter should be substituted in the case for the verdict of murder. Counsel for Clarkson very properly conceded that the decision of the second question was free from authority binding on this House and open to your Lordships, both on principle and authority, since *R v Richards* [1974] QB 776, by which the Court of Appeal regarded itself as bound, is not binding on your Lordships' House. It was conceded that, on the facts as they must be assumed to be for the purposes of the second question, apart from authority the point was totally devoid of merit, and, despite the advocacy of counsel, their Lordships did not think fit to trouble counsel for the respondent on this question. The Court of Appeal does not appear to have referred directly (although it was mentioned in argument), to the horrible case of *R v Cogan* [1976] QB 217, which, if the answer had not been otherwise obvious, seems to me to dispose of the matter. In the event, we also did not call upon the respondent to argue the third certified question since, in my opinion, and, I believe, that of my noble and learned friends, the definition of duress, whether applicable to murder or not, was correctly stated by both trial judges to contain an objective element on the lines of their respective directions and this must involve a threat of such a degree of violence that 'a person of reasonable firmness' with the characteristics and in the situation of the defendant could not have been expected to resist. No doubt there are subjective elements as well, but, unless the test is purely subjective to the defendant which, in my view, it is not, the answer to the third certified question, like that to the second, must be 'yes'.

This leaves us free to discuss the first, and principal, issue in the appeal which is the answer to be given to the first of the three certified questions. In my opinion, this must be decided on principle and authority, and the answer must in the end demand a reconsideration of the two authorities of *Director of Public Prosecutions for Northern Ireland v Lynch* [1975] AC 653 and *Abbott v R* [1977] AC 755. Having been myself a party to *Abbott,* I feel I owe it to the two noble and learned friends then with me in the majority to say that we were very conscious of the fact that our decision would only be of persuasive authority in the English jurisdiction whilst the decision in *Lynch*, though a Northern Irish case, which distinguished for the purposes of duress between principals in the first degree on the one hand, and principals in the second degree and aiders and abettors on the other, being a decision of the House of Lords would be likely to be treated as binding throughout England and Wales as well as Northern Ireland. We did, however, say, at 763:

> Whilst their Lordships feel bound to accept the decision of the House of Lords in *Lynch's* case they find themselves constrained to say that had they considered (which they do not) that that decision is an authority which requires the extension of the doctrine to cover cases like the present they would not have accepted it.

Speaking only for myself, it was precisely because the three noble and learned Lords in the majority in *Lynch* had expressly left open the availability of duress as a defence to the actual participant in a murder that I found it possible to accept the decision in *Lynch* without criticism, and then only because the *Abbott* appeal was solely concerned with the question so expressly left open. One only needs to read the facts in *Abbott* to be aware of exactly what the Board was being asked to do if it extended *Lynch* and allowed the appeal.

The present case, in my opinion, affords an ideal and never to be repeated opportunity to consider as we were invited expressly to do by the respondent, the whole question afresh, if necessary, by applying the Practice Statement (Judicial Precedent) [1966] 1 WLR 1234 to the decision in *Lynch*.

I therefore consider the matter first from the point of view of authority. On this I can only say that at the time when *Lynch* was decided the balance of weight in an unbroken tradition of authority dating back to Hale and Blackstone seems to have been accepted to have been that duress was not available to a defendant accused of murder. I quote only from Hale and Blackstone. Thus *Hales Pleas of the Crown* (1736), vol 1, p 51:

> ... if a man be desperately assaulted, and in peril of death, and cannot otherwise escape, unless to satisfy his assailant's fury he will kill an innocent person then present, the fear and actual force will not acquit him of the crime and punishment of murder, if he commit the fact; for he ought rather to die himself, than kill an innocent: ...

Blackstone, *Commentaries on the Laws of England* (1857 ed), vol 4, p 28 was to the same effect. He wrote that a man under duress: 'ought rather to die himself than escape by the murder of an innocent.'

I forbear to quote the eloquent and agonised passage in the dissenting speech of Lord Salmon of Glaisdale in *Lynch* [1975] AC 653 at 695, or the more restrained exposition of Lord Kilbrandon, at 702, on the law as expressed in *R v Dudley and Stephens* (1884) 14 QBD 273. These quotations are unnecessary since it seems to have been accepted both by the majority in *Lynch* and the minority in *Abbott*, that, to say the least, prior to *Lynch* there was a heavy preponderance of authority against the availability of the defence of duress in cases of murder.

I would only add that article 8 of the Charter of the International Military Tribunal, Treaty Series No 27 of 1946 at Nuremberg (Cmnd 6903), which was, at the time, universally accepted, save for its reference to mitigation, as an accurate statement of the common law both in England and the United States of America that:

> The fact that the defendant acted pursuant to the order of his government or of a superior shall not free him from responsibility, but may be considered in mitigation of punishment if the tribunal determines that justice so requires.

'Superior orders' is not identical with 'duress', but, in the circumstances of the Nazi regime, the difference must often have been negligible. I should point out that under article 6, the expression 'war crimes' expressly included that of murder; which, of course, does not include the killing of combatants engaged in combat.

What then is said on the other side? I accept, of course, that duress for almost all other crimes had been held to be a complete defence. I need not cite cases. They are carefully reviewed in *Lynch* and establish I believe that the defence is of venerable antiquity and wide extent. I pause only to say that although duress has, in my view, never been defined with adequate precision, two views of its nature can no longer be viewed as correct in the light of reported authority. The first is that of Stephen in his *History of the Criminal Law of England* (1883), vol 2, p 108 who first promulgated the opinion that duress was not a defence at all but, as in the Nuremberg statute, only a matter of mitigation. The fact is that, where it is applicable at all, in a long line of cases duress has been treated as a matter of defence entitling an accused to a complete acquittal. But in almost every instance where duress is so treated a cautionary note has been sounded excluding murder in terms sometimes more, and sometimes less emphatic, from the number of crimes where it can be put forward.

The second unacceptable view is that, possibly owing to a misunderstanding which has been read into some judgments, duress as a defence affects only the existence or absence of *mens rea*. The true view is stated by Lord Kilbrandon (of the minority) in *Lynch* [1975] AC 653 and by Lord Edmund-Davies (of the majority) in his analysis, at 709. Lord Kilbrandon said, at 703:

> ... the decision of the threatened man whose constancy is overborne so that he yields to the threat, is a *calculated decision to do what he knows to be wrong*, and is therefore that of a man with, perhaps to some exceptionally limited extent, a 'guilty mind'. But he is at the same time a man whose mind is less guilty than is his who acts as he does but under no such constraint. (Emphasis mine.)

In coming to the same conclusion Lord Edmund-Davies, at 709–10, quoted from Professor Glanville Williams' well known treatise *Criminal Law*, 2nd ed, 1961, p 751, para 242:

> True duress is not inconsistent with act and will as a matter of legal definition, the maxim being *coactus volui*. Fear of violence does not differ in kind from fear of economic ills, fear of displeasing others, or any other determinant of choice, it would be inconvenient to regard a particular type of motive as negativing of will.

After approving a paragraph from Lowry CJ, Lord Edmund-Davies went on to say that two quotations from Lord Goddard CJ in the disgusting case of *R v Bourne* (1952) 36 Cr App R 125 were subject to criticism on this score: see *Lynch* [1975] AC 653 at 710.

Before I leave the question of reported authority I must refer to two other cases. The first is *R v Kray (Ronald)* (1969) 53 Cr App R 569 which was, to some extent, relied on by the majority in *Lynch*, on the score of an *obiter dictum* of Widgery LJ, at 578. I do not myself regard this passage as authoritative. It depends on a concession by the Crown regarding a party who was not before the Court of Appeal as his case had been disposed of at first instance in order to found a submission by the appellants. The *dictum* is also open to the criticism that Widgery LJ appeared to treat duress as making a person otherwise than an 'independent actor' which is contrary to the analysis which I have accepted above.

The other reported authority is the famous and important case of *R v Dudley and Stephens* (1884) 14 QBD 273. This is generally and, in my view correctly, regarded as an authority on the availability of the supposed defence of necessity rather than duress. But I must say frankly that, if we were to allow this appeal, we should, I think, also have to say that *Dudley and Stephens* was bad law. There is, of course, an obvious distinction between duress and necessity as potential defences; duress arises from the wrongful threats or violence of another human being and necessity arises from any other objective dangers threatening the accused. This, however, is, in my view a distinction without a relevant difference, since on this view duress is only that species of the genus of necessity which is caused by wrongful threats. I cannot see that there is any way in which a person of ordinary fortitude can be excused from the one type of pressure on his will rather than the other.

I shall revert to *Dudley and Stephens* when I come to consider some of the issues of principle involved in our response to the first certified question. But at this stage I feel that I should say that in *Abbott* I would have been prepared to accept a distinction between *Abbott* [1977] AC 755 and *Lynch* [1975] AC 653 on the basis of the argument which appeared to attract Lord Morris of Borth-y-Gest at 671–2 of *Lynch*. I would not myself have immersed myself in the somewhat arcane terminology of accessory, principal in the second degree, and aiding and abetting. But it did seem to me then, and it seems to me now, that there is a valid distinction to be drawn in ordinary language between a man who actually participates in the irrevocable act of murder to save his own skin or that of his nearest and dearest and a man who simply participates before or after the event in the necessary preparation for it or the escape of the actual offender. It is as well to remember that, in *Abbott* the facts were that Abbott had dug a pit, thrown the victim into it, subjected her in cooperation with others to murderous blows and stab wounds and then buried her alive. It seems to me that those academics who see no difference between that case and the comparatively modest part alleged (falsely as is now known) in *Lynch* to have been played by the defendant under duress have parted company with a full sense of reality. Nevertheless and in spite of this, and in the face of the somewhat intemperate criticism to which this type of distinction has sometimes been subjected since *Abbott* I am somewhat relieved to know that the views of my noble and learned friends on the main issue permit me to escape from such niceties and simply to say that I do not think that the decision in *Lynch* can be justified on authority and that, exercising to the extent necessary, the freedom given to us by the Practice Statement (Judicial Precedent) [1966] 1 WLR 1234 which counsel for the respondent urged us to apply, I consider that the right course in the instant appeal is to restore the law to the condition in which it was almost universally thought to be prior to *Lynch*. It may well be that that law was to a certain extent unclear and to some extent gave rise to anomaly. But these anomalies I believe to be due to a number of factors extraneous to the present appeal and to the intrinsic nature of duress. The first is the mandatory nature of the sentence in murder. The second resides in the fact that murder being a 'result' crime, only being complete if the victim dies within the traditional period of a year and a day and that, in consequence, a different crime may be charged according to whether or not the victim actually succumbs during the prescribed period. The third lies in the fact (fully discussed amongst many authorities in *R v Hyam* [1975] AC 55) that, as matters stand, the *mens rea* in murder consists not simply in an intention to kill, but may include an intent to commit grievous bodily harm. It has always been possible for Parliament to clear up this branch of the law (or indeed to define more closely the nature and extent of the availability of duress as a defence). But Parliament has conspicuously, and perhaps deliberately, declined to do so. In the meantime, I must say that the attempt made in *Lynch* to clear up this situation by judicial legislation has proved to be an excessive and perhaps improvident use of the undoubted power of the courts to create new law by creating precedents in individual cases.

This brings me back to the question of principle. I begin by affirming that, while there can never be a direct correspondence between law and morality, an attempt to divorce the two entirely is and has always proved to be, doomed to failure, and, in the present case, the overriding objects of the criminal law must be to protect innocent lives and to set a standard of conduct which ordinary men and women are expected to observe if they are to avoid criminal responsibility.

No one, who has read *Dudley and Stephens* whether in the Law Reports, or in the more popular and discursive volume published by Professor Simpson *Cannibalism in the Common Law* (1984), can fail to be moved by the poignant and anguished situation to which the two shipwrecked mariners with Brooks (who was not guilty) and the innocent boy of 17, who was the victim, were exposed and which led the Home Secretary of the day to commute a death sentence for murder to one of six months' imprisonment. Nevertheless, when one comes to examine the case as one of legal principle it is, I believe, the case that the conclusion reached by the judges of the Queen's Bench Division and voiced by Lord Coleridge CJ, not without manifest compassion, has met with very wide acceptance. I quote from 14 QBD 273 at 286–8:

> Now it is admitted that the deliberate killing of this unoffending and unresisting boy was clearly murder, unless the killing can be justified by some well-recognised excuse admitted by the law. It is further admitted that there was in this case no such excuse, unless the killing was justified by what has been called 'necessity'. But the temptation to the act which existed here was not what the law has ever called necessity. Nor is this to be regretted. Though law and morality are not the same, and many things may be immoral which are not necessarily illegal, yet the absolute divorce of law from morality would be of fatal consequence; and such divorce would follow if the temptation to murder in this case were to be held by law an absolute defence of it. It is not so. To preserve one's life is generally speaking a duty, but it may be the plainest and the highest duty to sacrifice it.

> War is full of instances in which it is a man's duty not to live, but to die. The duty, in case of shipwreck, of a captain to his crew, of the crew to the passengers, of soldiers to women and children, as in the noble case of the *Birkenhead,* these duties impose on men the moral necessity, not of the preservation, but of the sacrifice of their lives for others, from which in no country, least of all, it is to be hoped, in England, will men ever shrink, as indeed, they have not shrunk ... It is not needful to point out the awful danger of admitting the principle which has been contended for. Who is to be the judge of this sort of necessity? By what measure is the comparative value of lives to be measured? Is it to be strength, or intellect, or what? It is plain that the principle leaves to him who is to profit by it to determine the necessity which will justify him in deliberately taking another's life to save his own. In this case the weakest, the youngest, the most unresisting, was chosen. Was it more necessary to kill him than one of the grown men? The answer must be No. ...

It was pointed out in a footnote in this case at 288 (attributed to Grove J) that if the principle were once admitted and the castaways not rescued, in the meantime it would have been lawful for the strongest of the four men to eat his way through the whole crew of the drifting boat, in order to be rescued himself.

I must dissent profoundly from the statement of my predecessor Bacon, a greater moralist perhaps in theory than in practice, where, quoted by Lord Coleridge CJ in *Dudley and Stephens*, in his commentary on the maxim '*necessitas inducit privilegium quoad jura privata*' he writes, at 285:

> ... If divers be in danger of drowning by the casting away of some boat or barge, and one of them get to some plank, or on the boat's side to keep himself above water, and another to save his life thrust him from it, whereby he is drowned, this is neither *se defendendo* nor by misadventure, but justifiable.

I also dissociate myself from the view of Rumpff JA in the South African case S *v Goliath* 1972 (3) SA 1, 465 at 480 (based, however, on Roman Dutch law) and quoted in *Abbott* [1977] AC 755 at 771 as a justification for the opinion of the dissenting minority:

> It is generally accepted ... that for the ordinary person in general his life is more valuable than that of another. Only they who possess the quality of heroism will intentionally offer their lives for another. Should the criminal law then state that compulsion could never be a defence to a charge of murder, it would demand that a person who killed another under duress, whatever the circumstances, would have to comply with a higher standard than that demanded of the average person. I do not think that such an exception to the general rule which applies in criminal law, is justified.

In general, I must say that I do not at all accept in relation to the defence of murder it is either good morals, good policy or good law to suggest, as did the majority in *Lynch* and the minority in *Abbott* that the ordinary man of reasonable fortitude is not to be supposed to be capable of heroism if he is asked to take an innocent life rather than sacrifice his own. Doubtless in actual practice many will succumb to temptation, as they did in *Dudley and Stephens*. But many will not, and I do not believe that as a 'concession to human frailty' the former should be exempt from liability to criminal sanctions if they do. I have known in my own lifetime of too many acts of heroism by ordinary human beings of no more than ordinary fortitude to regard a law as either 'just or humane' which withdraws the protection of the criminal law from the innocent victim and casts the cloak of its protection upon the coward and the poltroon in the name of a 'concession to human frailty'.

I must not, however, underestimate the force of the arguments on the other side, advanced as they have been with such force and such persuasiveness by some of the most eminent legal minds, judicial and academic, in the country.

First, amongst these is, perhaps, the argument from logic and consistency. A long line of cases, it is said, carefully researched and closely analysed, establish duress as an available defence in a wide range of crimes, some at least, like wounding with intent to commit grievous bodily harm, carrying the heaviest penalties commensurate with their gravity. To cap this, it is pointed out that at least in theory, a defendant accused of this crime under s 18 of the Offences against the Person Act 1861, but acquitted on the grounds of duress, will still be liable to a charge of murder if the victim dies within the traditional period of one year and a day. I am not, perhaps, persuaded of this last point as much as I should. It is not simply an anomaly based on the defence of duress. It is a product of the peculiar *mens rea* allowed on a charge of murder which is not confined to an intent to kill. More persuasive, perhaps, is the point based on the availability of the defence of duress on a charge of attempted murder, where the actual intent to kill is an essential prerequisite. It may be that we must meet this *casus omissus* in your Lordships' House when we come to it. It may require reconsideration of the availability of the defence in that case too.

I would, however, prefer to meet the case of alleged inconsistency head on. Consistency and logic, though inherently desirable, are not always prime characteristics of a penal code based like the common law on custom and precedent. Law so based is not an exact science. All the same, I feel I am required to give some answer to the question posed. If duress is available as a defence to some crimes of the most grave why, it may legitimately be asked, stop at murder, whether an accessory or principal and whether in the second or the first degree? But surely I am entitled, as in the view of the Common Serjeant in the instant case of Clarkson and Burke, to believe that some degree of proportionality between the threat and the offence must, at least to some extent, be a prerequisite of the defence under existing law. Few would resist threats to the life of a loved one if the alternative were driving across the red lights or in excess of 70 mph on the motorway. But, to use the Common Serjeant's analogy, it would take rather more than the threat of a slap on the wrist or even moderate pain or injury to discharge the evidential burden even in the case of a fairly serious assault. In such a case the 'concession to human frailty' is no more than to say that in such circumstances a reasonable man of average courage is entitled to embrace as a matter of choice the alternative which a reasonable man could regard as the lesser of two evils. Other considerations necessarily arise where the choice is between the threat of death or *a fortiori* of serious injury and deliberately taking an innocent life. In such a case a reasonable man might reflect that one innocent human life is at least as valuable as his own or that of his loved one. In such a case a man cannot claim that he is choosing the lesser of two evils. Instead he is embracing the cognate but morally disreputable principle that the end justifies the means.

I am not so shocked as some of the judicial opinions have been at the need, if this be the conclusion, to invoke the availability of administrative as distinct from purely judicial remedies for the hardships which might otherwise occur in the most agonising cases. Even in *Dudley and Stephens* in 1884 when the death penalty was mandatory and frequently inflicted, the prerogative was used to reduce a sentence of death by hanging to one of six months in prison. In murder cases the available mechanisms are today both more flexible and more sophisticated. The trial judge may make no minimum recommendation. He will always report to the Home Secretary, as he did in the present case of Clarkson and Burke.

The Parole Board will always consider a case of this kind with a High Court judge brought into consultation. In the background is always the prerogative and, it may not unreasonably be suggested, that is exactly what the prerogative is for. If the law seems to bear harshly in its operation in the case of a mandatory sentence on any particular offender there has never been a period of time when there were more effective means of mitigating its effect than at the present day. It may well be thought that the loss of a clear right to a defence justifying or excusing the deliberate taking of an innocent life in order to emphasise to all the sanctity of a human life is not an excessive price to pay in the light of these mechanisms. Murder, as every practitioner of the law knows, though often described as one of the utmost heinousness, is not in fact necessarily so, but consists in a whole bundle of offences of vastly differing degrees of culpability, ranging from brutal, cynical and repeated offences like the so-called Moors murders to the almost venial, if objectively immoral, 'mercy killing' of a beloved partner.

Far less convincing than the argument based on consistency is the belief which appears in some of the judgments that the law must 'move with the times' in order to keep pace with the immense political and social changes since what are alleged to have been the bad old days of Blackstone and Hale. I have already dealt with this argument in my respectful criticism of the dissent in *R v Hyam* [1975] AC 55. The argument is based on the false assumption that violence to innocent victims is now less prevalent than in the days of Hale or Blackstone. But I doubt whether this is so. We live in the age of the holocaust of the Jews, of international terrorism on the scale of massacre, of the explosion of aircraft in mid-air, and murder sometimes at least as obscene as anything experienced in Blackstone's day. Indeed one of the present appeals may provide an example. I have already mentioned the so-called Moors murders. But within weeks of hearing this appeal a man was convicted at the Central Criminal Court (*R v Hindawi, The Times*, 25 October 1986) of sending his pregnant mistress on board an international aircraft at Heathrow, with her suitcase packed with a bomb and with the deliberate intention of sending the 250 occupants, crew, passengers, mistress and all to a horrible death in midair. I cannot forbear to say that if *Abbott* [1977] AC 755 was wrongly decided, and had the attempt succeeded, the miscreant who did this would have been free to escape scot free had he been in a position to discharge the evidential burden on duress and had the prosecution, on the normal *Woolmington* principles (*Woolmington v Director of Public Prosecutions*

[1935] AC 462 at 482), been unable to exclude beyond reasonable doubt the possibility of his uncorroborated word being true. I must also point out in this context that known terrorists are more and not less vulnerable to threats than the ordinary man and that a plea of duress in such a case may be all the more plausible on that account. To say this is not to cast doubt on the reliability and steadfastness of juries. Counsel for the appellants was able to say with perfect truth that, where duress in fact has been put forward in cases where it was available, juries have been commendably robust as they were in the instant cases in rejecting it where appropriate. The question is not one of the reliability of juries. It is one of principle. Should the offence of duress be available in principle in such a case as that of *R v Hindawi* where, of course, it was not put forward? The point which I am at the moment concerned to make is that it is not clear to me that the observations of Blackstone and Hale, and almost every respectable authority, academic or judicial, prior to *Lynch* are necessarily to be regarded in this present age as obsolescent or inhumane or unjust owing to some supposed improvement in the respect for innocent human life since their time which unfortunately I am too blind to be able for myself to perceive. Still less am I able to see that a law which denies such a defence in such a case must be condemned as lacking in justice or humanity rather than as respectable in its concern for the sanctity of innocent lives. I must add that, at least in my view, if *Abbott* were wrongly decided some hundreds who suffered the death penalty at Nuremberg for murders were surely the victims of judicial murder at the hands of their conquerors owing to the operation of article 8. Social change is not always for the better and it ill becomes those of us who have participated in the cruel events of the twentieth century to condemn as out of date those who wrote in defence of innocent lives in the eighteenth century.

During the course of argument it was suggested that there was available to the House some sort of half way house between allowing these appeals and dismissing them. The argument ran that we might treat duress in murder as analogous to provocation, or perhaps diminished responsibility, and say that, in indictments for murder, duress might reduce the crime to one of manslaughter. I find myself quite unable to accept this. The cases show that duress, if available and made out, entitles the accused to a clean acquittal, without, it has been said, the 'stigma' of a conviction. Whatever other merits it may have, at least the suggestion makes nonsense of any pretence of logic or consistency in the criminal law. It is also contrary to principle. Unlike the doctrine of provocation, which is based on emotional loss of control, the defence of duress, as I have already shown, is put forward as a 'concession to human frailty' whereby a conscious decision, it may be coolly undertaken, to sacrifice an innocent human life is made as an evil lesser than a wrong which might otherwise be suffered by the accused or his loved ones at the hands of a wrong doer. The defence of diminished responsibility (which might well, had it then been available to Dudley and Stephens, have prevailed there) is statutory in England though customary in Scotland, the land of its origin. But in England at least it has a conceptual basis defined in the Homicide Act 1957 which is totally distinct from that of duress if duress be properly analysed and understood. Provocation (unique to murder and not extending even to 'section 18' offences) is a concession to human frailty due to the extent that even a reasonable man may, under sufficient provocation temporarily lose his self control towards the person who has provoked him enough. Duress, as I have already pointed out, is a concession to human frailty in that it allows a reasonable man to make a conscious choice between the reality of the immediate threat and what he may reasonably regard as the lesser of two evils. Diminished responsibility as defined in the Homicide Act 1957 depends on abnormality of mind impairing mental responsibility. It may overlap duress or even necessity. But it is not what we are discussing in the instant appeal.

I must add that, had I taken a different view, in the cases of Bannister and Howe and, for rather different reasons, in the case of Burke, I would have gone on to consider the questions whether in any of these appeals the appellants had discharged the evidential burden in duress, or whether, if they had, on the facts described in the judgment of Lord Lane CJ, the proviso should not have been applied in every case. The case of Clarkson is surely beyond dispute on the assumption that the second certified question is not answered in his favour. But whatever may be the characteristics of duress, even on the existing law the ingredients of immediacy and absence of voluntary association (see *R v Fitzpatrick* [1977] NI 20), must be essential components of the evidential burden more or less on the lines of the draft bill annexed to the Law Commission Report No 83, to which I have referred above. Even apart from this and on the assumption that the matter should properly have been left to the jury, I am rather more than doubtful whether any properly instructed jury could have acquitted on the murder charges in either of the instant cases or on the facts of *Abbott*. It is not necessary to express a concluded opinion on this since, for reasons I have adumbrated above, I consider that these appeals should be dismissed and the certified questions answered respectively (1) no, (2) yes, (3) yes. If so, the questions relating to the proviso and evidential burden do not arise. So far as I have indicated, the decision of this House in *Lynch* [1975] AC 653 should be regarded as unsatisfactory and the law left as it was before *Lynch* came up for decision. The decision in *Abbott* [1977] AC 755 should be followed, and unless it can be distinguished on the facts, that in *R v Richards* [1974] QB 776 should be overruled.

[**Lord Mackay, Lord Bridge, Lord Brandon** and **Lord Griffiths** delivered separate judgments agreeing with **Lord Hailsham LC**. Appeals dismissed.]

12.28 Despite the clarity and certainty achieved finally in England by the decision in *R v Howe*, serious misgivings remain about the justice of the rule of law pronounced in that case. This is clearly adverted to in *R v Howe*, where Lord Hailsham LC says that he is 'not so shocked as some of the judicial opinions have been at the need, if this be the conclusion, to invoke the availability of administrative as distinct from purely judicial remedies for the hardships which might otherwise occur in the most agonising cases'. In *R v Gotts* [1992] 2 AC 412, the House of Lords decided that there was no justification in logic, morality or law for allowing the defence of duress to a person charged with attempted murder, since it was not available to a person charged with murder. Lord Keith and Lord Lowry dissented.

12.29 In Victoria, the defence of duress has been made available in homicide cases by statute. Section 9AG of the Crimes Act 1958, as amended by the Crimes (Homicide) Act 2005 (Vic), provides:

(1) A person is not guilty of a relevant offence in respect of conduct carried out by him or her under duress.
(2) A person carries out conduct under duress if and only if the person reasonably believes that —
  (a) subject to subsection (3), a threat has been made that will be carried out unless an offence is committed; and
  (b) carrying out the conduct is the only reasonable way that the threatened harm can be avoided; and
  (c) she conduct is a reasonable response to the threat.
(3) However, a person does not carry out conduct under duress if the threat is made by or on behalf of a person with whom the person is voluntarily associating for the purpose of carrying out violent conduct.
(4) This section only applies in the case of murder if the threat is to inflict death or really serious injury.

Note: See section 9AH for evidentiary provisions where family violence is alleged.

This provision incorporates recommendations made by Victoria's Law Reform Commissioner in Report No 40, *Homicide* (1991).

12.30 The Criminal Code Act 1995 (Cth) contains the following general defence of duress, in s 10.2: 'A person is not criminally responsible for an offence if he or she carries out the conduct constituting the offence under duress'.

The defence has no limitations related to any particular crime, such as murder or treason. It has, however, both subjective and objective elements in it. Section 10.2(2) provides that 'under duress' means that the defendant reasonably believed that a threat had been made that would have been carried out unless the offence was committed; that there was no *reasonable* way that the threat could be rendered ineffective; and that the defendant's conduct was a *reasonable* response to that threat. Furthermore, s 10.2(3) precludes a defendant who has voluntarily entered into an association with the person who makes the threat, for the very purpose of carrying out conduct of the kind perpetrated. Note *R v Oblach* (2005) 65 NSWLR 75.

In their Final Report, *Model Criminal Code — Chapters 1 and 2 — General Principles of Criminal Responsibility* (December 1992), the Criminal Law Officers Committee wrote that they rejected the reasoning of the House of Lords in *Howe's* case and its reiteration and further specific application in *Gott's* case. They favoured a comprehensive provision, and they ended their commentary thus (at 65): 'The objective test should provide a sufficient safeguard against abuse of the defence.'

NECESSITY AND DURESS: CRITICAL COMMENT

12.31 Despite the longevity of the compulsion defences, they are the continued subject of many judicial and academic debates. Particular controversy has surrounded the defences of duress and necessity, including their justification, rationale, parameters and desirability. In *Wickedness and Crime: Laws of Homicide and Malice* (Routledge,

2013), Penny Crofts has argued that the defences of necessity and duress are particularly problematic for the law because of the absence of malice of the victim. Drawing on historic structures of malice, Crofts highlights that in self-defence (and provocation), the victim of the accused is explicitly or implicitly structured as malicious. The doctrine of self-defence emphasises the malice of the victim, a malice that was evident in manifest conduct such as the victim charging at the accused with a knife. In self-defence cases, one is acting directly against the person to protect values that the law would protect if it could have done so. In self-defence cases, the accused is addressing the source of the peril. In most cases of self-defence, the malice of the victim is part of the calculus of the accused's responsibility. An accused is thus asserting an absence of malice, identification with the law, and a malicious victim.

In cases of duress and necessity, there is no such parity between an innocent accused acting against a malevolent victim. Unlike self-defence, the person against whom the accused has acted in cases of duress and necessity has nothing to do with the threats that originally compelled the accused to take the steps that she or he took. The actions of an accused are the same in cases of self-defence, duress and necessity, but different culpability is attached based on the malice (or lack thereof) of the victim. This provides an explanation for the complexity and technicality of rules and limits placed on the defences of duress and necessity, especially when compared with the rules of self-defence. It provides an explanation for the historical principle that the defences of necessity and duress are not available for the offence of murder. Hale asserted that killing an innocent cannot be justified or excused because 'he ought rather to die himself, than kill an innocent' (Hale, *Pleas of the Crown*, 1713, p 434). Crofts argues that the absence of a malicious victim in necessity and duress cases means that the law is effectively confronted with two innocent legal subjects — an innocent victim of extreme circumstances or an outlaw *and* an innocent victim of the accused's actions. Duress and necessity cases thus demand that the law choose between legal subjects who are innocent and identify with the law. The law expresses empathy for the agonising choice between two evils that a legal subject acting under compulsion is forced to make. The choice between evils underlines that in some cases, no good choice or outcome can be made. The passionate language of the judiciary describing the impossible choice made by defendants under compulsion reflects the decision that the judges regard themselves as having to make. It is a 'poignant and anguished situation' (*R v Howe* (1987) 1 All ER 771 at 780), a 'terrible, agonizing choice of evils' (ibid at 779). Crofts argues that cases of compulsion highlight the limits of the law. In these cases, the law has failed to protect not only the accused, who was confronted by a threat by an outlaw or extreme circumstances, but also the victim, who suffered at the hands of the accused.

SUPERIOR ORDERS

12.32 A favourite problem of many writers in criminal law is the extent to which a member of the armed forces, charged with crime, can rely on the fact that the service person acted under the orders of someone whom he or she was bound to obey.

12.33 A member of the armed forces is, of course, bound to obey the criminal law like anyone else. He or she is equally bound by the provisions of the various statutes regulating that force to obey a superior officer's lawful commands. It may be put that there is no difficulty here. If the member obeys only lawful commands he or she will not infringe either the criminal or the military law. However, Stephen saw that this answer was not complete despite its apparent simplicity (1 *Hist Crim Law* (1883), p 205):

> The hardship upon soldiers is, that if a soldier kills a man in obedience to his officer's orders, the question whether what was done was more than was reasonably necessary to quell civil disturbance has to be decided by a jury, probably upon a trial for murder. Whereas, if he disobeys his officer's orders to fire because he regards them as unlawful, the question whether they were unlawful as having commanded something not reasonably necessary would have to be decided by a court martial upon the trial of the soldier for disobeying orders, and for obvious reasons the jury and the court martial are likely to take different views as to the reasonable necessity and therefore as to the lawfulness of such an order.

12.34 It is true that if the military command is clearly unlawful, the soldier obeys it at peril. Obedience will afford him or her no answer at the criminal trial before a civil (that is, non-military) court. The North Carolinian case of *State v Roy* (1951) 233 NC 558, affords an example. In that case, D1 and D2 were respectively charged with, and convicted of, assault on a female with intent to commit rape, and assault on a female. At the material times, D1 was a sergeant and D2 a private in the United States Army. On appeal D2 contended that he was acting throughout on the command of his superior, D1. The Supreme Court of North Carolina tersely held that his contention had no merit:

> The duty of a subordinate to obey a superior officer, while one is subject to military law, has reference only to lawful commands of such superior officer, in matters relating to military duty. And there is certainly nothing on this record to indicate that either of these defendants were engaged in any activity relating to military duties on the night in question.

12.35 The simple 'lawful command' rule leaves the soldier in an unhappy situation where the order given is actually unlawful, but not obviously so, nor is it known to be so to the soldier. Perhaps nowhere is this so unhappy as where the lawfulness of the order turns on a judgment of what is reasonable or necessary to preserve law and order in particular circumstances in the repression of riots or serious civil disorders. It is surely unjust that the soldier is to be criminally liable in every case of obedience to an order in fact unlawful. At the same time, even a disciplined person should not escape responsibility in every case by reliance on an unlawful command which he or she obeyed blindly. Where is the line of responsibility to be drawn? The case which follows may provide some answers.

12.36C Commonwealth ex rel Wadsworth v Shortall

(1903) 206 Pa 165
Supreme Court of Pennsylvania (USA)

[Wadsworth was a member of the National Guard, the state volunteer militia. The Governor of Pennsylvania called out the guard to aid in the suppression of violence engendered by a widespread miners' strike. During the strike several houses occupied by non-unionists were blown up, and attempts made to dynamite others. The commander of Wadsworth's regiment ordered that a guard be posted at one house so attacked, which was occupied by a woman and four children. The guard was expressly ordered that:

> … if any attempt is made to dynamite [it], or they [the guard] are shot at, or stoned, or any suspicious characters prowl around, particularly in the rear of the house, who fail to halt when directed by the guard, the guard shall shoot, and shoot to kill.

Wadsworth was a member of the guard. At about 11.30 pm he saw a man coming along the side of the house. He ordered the man to halt four times, but the man opened the gate and entered the yard of the house, whereupon Wadsworth shot him dead. At the inquest, the coroner's jury found the shooting was 'hasty and unjustifiable', and recommended that the matter be investigated by the district attorney. Wadsworth was arrested when he returned from service, and brought a writ of habeas corpus to determine whether he was properly held in custody. The following extract from the opinion deals with the question of superior orders as a defence to a criminal charge.]

Mitchell J: … Coming now to the position of the relator in regard to responsibility, we find the law well settled.

> A subordinate stands, as regards the application of these principles, in a different position from the superior whom he obeys, and may be absolved from liability for executing an order which it was criminal to give. The question is, as we have seen, had the accused reasonable cause for believing in the necessity of the act which is impugned, and in determining this point a soldier or member of the *posse comitatus* may obviously take the orders of the person in command into view as proceeding from one who is better able to judge and well informed; and, if the circumstances are such that the command may be justifiable, he should not be held guilty for declining to decide that it is wrong with the responsibility incident to disobedience, unless the case is so plain as not to admit of a reasonable doubt. A soldier consequently runs little risk in obeying any order which a man of common sense so placed would regard as warranted by the circumstances: Hare, *Const Law*, p 920.

The cases in this country have usually arisen in the army and been determined in the United States courts. But by the articles of war (art 59), under the acts of Congress, officers or soldiers charged with offences punishable by the laws of the land are required (except in time of war) to be delivered over to the civil (ie in distinction from military) authorities, and the courts proceed upon the principles of the common (and statute) law: *US v Clark* 31 Fed 710 at 711 (CCED Mich 1887). The decisions, therefore, are precedents applicable here.

A leading case is *US v Clark*, supra. A soldier on the military reservation at Ft Wayne had been convicted by court martial, and when brought out of the guardhouse with other prisoners at 'retreat' broke from the ranks, and was in the act of escaping, when Clark, who was the sergeant of the guard, fired and killed him. Clark was charged with homicide, and brought before the United States District Judge, sitting as a committing magistrate. Judge Brown, now of the Supreme Court of the United States, delivered an elaborate and well-considered opinion, which has ever since been quoted as authoritative. In it he said:

> The case then reduces itself to the naked legal proposition whether the prisoner is excused in law in killing the deceased: 31 Fed at 712.

Then, after referring to the common-law principle that an officer having custody of a prisoner charged with felony may take his life if it becomes absolutely necessary to do so to prevent his escape, and pointing out the peculiarities of the military code, which practically abolish the distinction between felonies and misdemeanours, he continued:

> I have no doubt the same principle would apply to the acts of a subordinate officer, performed in compliance with his supposed duty as a soldier; and unless the act were manifestly beyond the scope of his authority, or ... were such that a man of ordinary sense and understanding would know that it was illegal, that it would be a protection to him, if he acted in good faith and without malice: 31 Fed at 717.

In *McCall v McDowell* Fed Cas No 8673 (1867), where an action was brought by a plaintiff against Gen McDowell and Capt Douglas for false imprisonment under a general order of the former for the arrest of persons publicly exulting over the assassination of President Lincoln, the court said:

> Except in a plain case of excess of authority, where at first blush it is apparent and palpable to the commonest understanding that the order is illegal, I cannot but think that the law will excuse a military subordinate, when acting in obedience to the order of his commander; otherwise he is placed in a dangerous dilemma of being liable to damages to third persons for obedience to the order, or for the loss of his commission and disgrace for disobedience thereto ... Between an order plainly legal and one palpably otherwise there is a wide middle ground, where the ultimate legality and propriety of orders depend or may depend upon circumstances and conditions, of which it cannot be expected that the inferior is informed or advised. In such cases justice to the subordinate demands, and the necessities and efficiency of the public service require, that the order of the superior would protect the inferior, leaving the responsibility to rest where it properly belongs, upon the officer who gave the command.

The court, sitting without a jury, accordingly gave judgment for Capt Douglas, though finding damages against Gen McDowell.

In *US v Carr* Fed Cas No 14732 (1872), which was a case of the shooting of a soldier in Fort Pulaski by the prisoner, who was sergeant of the guard, Woods J, afterwards of the Supreme Court of the United States, charged the jury:

> Place yourself in the position of the prisoner at the time of the homicide. Inquire whether at the moment he fired his piece at the deceased, with his surroundings at the time, he had reasonable ground to believe, and did believe, that the killing or serious wounding of the deceased was necessary to the suppression of a mutiny then and there existing, or of a disorder which threatened to ripen into mutiny. If he had reasonable ground so to believe, then the killing was not unlawful. But if, on the other hand, the mutinous conduct of the soldiers, if there was any such, had ceased, and it so appeared to the prisoner, or if he could reasonably have suppressed the disorder without the resort to such violent means as the taking of the life of the deceased, and it would so have appeared to a reasonable man under like circumstances, then the killing was unlawful. But it must be understood that the law will not require an officer charged with the order and discipline of a camp or fort to weigh with scrupulous nicety the amount of force necessary to suppress disorder. The exercise of a reasonable discretion is all that is required.

In *Riggs v State* 91 Am Dec 272 (Tenn 1866), the Supreme Court of Tennessee held to be correct an instruction to the jury that:

> ... any order given by an officer to his private, which does not expressly and clearly show on its face or in the body thereof its own illegality, the soldier would be bound to obey, and such order would be a protection to him: 91 Am Dec at 273.

These are the principal American cases, and they are in entire accord with the long line of established authorities in England.

Applying these principles to the act of the relator, it is clear that he was not guilty of any crime. The situation, as already shown, was one of martial law, in which the commanding general was authorised to use as forcible military means for which the repression of violence as his judgment dictated to be necessary. The house had been dynamited at night and threatened again. With an agent so destructive, in hands so lawless, the duty of precaution was correspondingly great. There was no ground, therefore, for doubt as to the legality of the order to shoot. The relator was a private soldier, and his first duty was obedience. His orders were clear and specific, and the evidence does not show that he went beyond them in his action. There was no malice, for it appears affirmatively that he did not know the deceased, and acted only on his orders when the situation appeared to call for action under them. The unfortunate man who was killed was not shown to have been one of the mob gathered in the vicinity, though why he should have turned into the gate is not known. The occurrence, deplorable as it was, was an illustration of the dangers of the lawless condition of the community, or of the minority who were allowed to control it, and must be classed with the numerous instances in riots and mobs where mere spectators and even distant noncombatants get hurt without apparent fault of their own.

Whenever a homicide occurs, it is not only proper, but obligatory, that an official inquiry should be made by the legal authorities. Such an inquiry was had here at the coroner's inquest, and if there were any doubt about the facts we should remand the relator to the custody of the constable under his warrant, for a further hearing before the justice of the peace. But there was no conflict in the evidence before the coroner, and the commonwealth's officer makes no claim here that anything further can be shown. The facts, therefore, are not in dispute, and the question of the relator's liability depends on whether he had reasonable cause to believe in the necessity of action under his orders. As said by Judge Hare, citing Lord Mansfield, in *Mostyn v Fabrigas* (1775) 1 Cowp 161, 98 ER 1021 (KB):

> The question of probable cause in this as in most other instances is one of law for the Court. The facts are for the jury; but it is for the Judges to say whether, if found, they amount to probable cause: Hare, *Const Law* 919.

In *US v Clark*, supra, Mr Justice Brown said:

> It may be said that it is a question for a jury, in each case whether the prisoner was justified by the circumstances in making use of his musket, and if this were a jury trial I should submit that question of them; but … as I would, acting in another capacity, set aside a conviction, if a verdict of guilty were rendered, I shall assume the responsibility of directing his discharge: 21 Fed at 717.

This court, either sitting as a committing magistrate or by virtue of its supervisory jurisdiction over the proceedings of all subordinate tribunals (*Gosline v Place* 32 Pa St 520 (1859)), has the authority and the duty, on *habeas corpus* in favour of a prisoner held on a criminal charge, to see that at least a prima facie case of guilt is supported by the evidence against him. In the relator's case the facts presented by the evidence are undisputed, and on them the law is clear and settled. If the case was before a jury, we should be bound to direct a verdict of not guilty, and to set aside a contrary verdict if rendered. It is therefore our duty now to say that there is no legal ground for subjecting him to trial, and he is accordingly discharged …

[**Dean, Fell, Brown, Mestrezat** and **Potter JJ** concurred.]

12.37 Notes and illustrations

1. D, a soldier in the British Army in South Africa, was ordered by his officer to shoot a farm labourer, V, who refused to fetch a bridle for a horse. D did so. At his trial for murder, Solomon J said:

   > I think it is a safe rule to lay down that if a soldier believes he is doing his duty in obeying the commands of his superior, and if the orders are not so manifestly illegal that he must or ought to have known they are unlawful, the private soldier would be protected by the orders of his superior officer.

D was acquitted: *R v Smith* (1900) 17 SCR 561 (Special Ct of Cape Colony).

2. In October 1956, just before Israel's Sinai offensive, D1, the commander of a unit of the Border Police, was ordered by his superior officer to place the Arab village of Kafr Kassim under curfew, and to shoot to kill, and specifically not to arrest, any person moving outside the houses in the village after curfew. D1 communicated this order to D2, an officer, who, with a corporal and eight privates, killed some 40 people returning from work in the fields, with no knowledge of the imposition of a curfew. At their trial for the murder of the villagers, D1 and his co-defendants pleaded that they had acted in obedience to superior orders, invoking s 19(b) of the Israeli Criminal Code, which provides that:

   > A person is not criminally responsible for an act … if he does the act … in obedience to the order of a competent authority which he is bound by law to obey, unless the order is manifestly unlawful.

   The Code further provides that the question of whether or not the order is manifestly unlawful is a question of law. The court, in convicting eight of the defendants, including D1 and D2, said the 'shoot to kill' order was manifestly unlawful and offered no defence. A manifestly unlawful order was one which:

   > … in itself, or by virtue of what it requires to be done [is] so clearly and unequivocally illegal that its illegality strikes the eye and stirs the heart of any but the blindest and most corrupt … The order … was an open invitation to murder civilians — and was, therefore, manifestly unlawful in all circumstances, even in time of war. For even during a war the lives of civilians in a military area are not at the disposal of the commander of the area … The lives … of civilian non-combatants are sacrosanct.

   On appeal, the Appeal Court Martial affirmed the lower court's finding that the order was manifestly unlawful: *Military Prosecutor v Malinki*, *Jerusalem Post*, 16–18 October 1958; 22, 24 November 1959 (Jerusalem Military District Tribunal, 1958; Appeal Court Martial, 1959).

3. The Charter of the International Military Tribunal established to try Nazis charged with war crimes in the Second World War expressly provided that superior orders were no defence to the various charges, but might be adduced in mitigation of penalties.

4. The plea of superior orders was advanced by Adolf Eichmann at his trial in Israel in 1961. He was accused of major participation in the extermination of millions of European Jews in the Second World War, between 1940 and 1945. Under s 11a of the Nazi and Nazi Collaborators (Punishment) Law 1950 (Israel), its only effect could have been in mitigation of punishment;

but, in any event, the Jerusalem District Court stated that, on the evidence adduced, the plea must have failed, even applying the principles of German military law. See Lord Russell of Liverpool, *The Trial of Adolf Eichmann*, Heinemann, London, 1962, pp 299–302; and compare the German case of *The Llandovery Castle* [1923–24] Ann Dig Pub Int Law Cas 436.

5. In Australia, the Defence Force Discipline Act 1982 (Cth) provides for a limited defence of superior orders in relation to military offences: see s 14(b).
6. In *A v Hayden (No 2)* (1984) 156 CLR 532; 56 ALR 82, the High Court stated that the defence of superior orders is not available as an absolute answer to a charge under the criminal law of Victoria. 'The criminal law of this country has no place for a general defence of superior orders or of Crown or Executive fiat': per Deane J at 126. This case arose from an Australian Security Intelligence Service exercise which took the form of a raid on the unsuspecting staff and guests of a Melbourne hotel, compared by Mason J to a Maxwell Smart TV show episode. Despite the clear rejection of a defence of superior orders *in limine*, Murphy J considered that a defence based on the contention that the agents acted 'in obedience to orders which were not apparently unlawful may arise in other proceedings': at 101. In *Yip Chiu-Cheung v The Queen* [1995] 1 AC 111, the Privy Council followed the decision of the High Court.

   The Queensland and the Western Australian Codes provide a defence to a person who acts in obedience to the order of a competent authority 'unless the order is manifestly unlawful': s 31(1)(b).

THE POSITION OF MARRIED WOMEN

12.38 The common law recognised a general defence of marital coercion. If a married woman established that a criminal act committed by her was committed in the presence of her husband, the fact of his presence raised a presumption that she was acting under his coercion rather than of her own free will. She was then entitled to be excused unless the presumption was rebutted by evidence showing that she was, in fact, acting of her own volition. The presumption applied also in relation to a wife acting as an accessory after the fact to a felony committed by the husband. The defence was not available in cases of treason or murder. For general discussion of the common law position, see *Ewart v Fox* [1954] VLR 699.

12.39 The common law rule has been abolished in each of the Australian states. Section 407A of the Crimes Act 1900 (NSW) simply abolishes the presumption of marital coercion.

12.40 In Victoria, the common law rule was abolished and replaced by detailed statutory provisions in 1977. These statutory provisions adopted recommendations made by Victoria's Law Reform Commissioner in Report No 5, *Criminal Liability of Married Persons* (1975).

12.41E **Crimes Act 1958 (Vic)**

as amended by the Crimes (Married Persons' Liability) Act 1977 (Vic)

DIVISION 3 — CRIMINAL LIABILITY OF MARRIED PERSONS

336 Marital coercion

(1) Any presumption that an offence committed by a wife in the presence of her husband is committed under his coercion is hereby abolished.

(2) Where a woman is charged with an offence other than treason or murder, that woman shall have a complete defence to such charge if her action or inaction (as the case may be) was due to coercion by a man to whom she was then married.

(3) For the purposes of this section 'coercion' means pressure, whether in the form of threats or in any other form, sufficient to cause a woman of ordinary good character and normal firmness of mind, placed in the circumstances in which the woman was placed, to conduct herself in the manner charged.

(4) Without limiting the generality of the expression 'the circumstances in which the woman was placed' in sub-section (3), such circumstances shall include the degree of dependence, whether economic or otherwise, of the woman on her husband.

(5) The accused shall bear the burden of adducing evidence that she conducted herself in the manner charged because she was coerced by her husband, but if such evidence has been adduced, the prosecution shall bear the burden of proving that the action or inaction charged was not due to coercion by the husband.

(6) This section shall operate in substitution for the common law as to any presumption or defence of marital coercion.

(7) This section shall not affect the law relating to the defence of duress.

337 Misprision

A married person shall not become guilty of misprision by concealing or failing to disclose the commission of an indictable offence by his or her spouse, or by the spouse and another party or parties, nor by concealing or failing to disclose facts which might lead to the apprehension of the spouse, or the spouse and such other or others, in respect of the offence.

338 Accessory after the fact

A married person shall not become an accessory to any indictable offence by receiving, relieving, comforting or assisting his or her spouse, or the spouse and another person or persons, though with knowledge that the spouse, whether alone or with the other person or persons, has committed an offence and though the purpose of what is done is to enable the spouse, or the spouse and the other person or persons, to escape being apprehended, tried or punished.

339 Conspiracy and incitement

(1) A married person shall be criminally responsible for incitement or conspiracy to commit treason or murder and for any offence specified in s 4 as if he or she were unmarried.

(2) Subject to sub-section (1), a married person shall not be criminally responsible for conspiracy with his or her spouse alone, nor for incitement of his or her spouse to commit a criminal offence.

Nothing in sub-section (2) shall affect the liability of a married person as a principal offender in any offence except conspiracy or incitement.

12.42 The common law rule which prevented a spouse being charged with conspiracy with the other spouse has been abolished in New South Wales: Crimes Act 1900 (NSW) s 580D.

Mistake and Strict Liability

CHAPTER 13

INTRODUCTION

13.1 This chapter considers two related issues. These are, first, the availability of a defence of mistake to an accused person charged with a criminal offence; and second — and relatedly — the question when the courts will interpret a statutory offence as being proven without evidence of mens rea. This latter issue is known as strict liability. The two issues are linked: if a court concludes that a statutory provision creating an offence excludes the requirement to prove mens rea, it may still conclude that the accused can raise a defence based on mistake. The issues are of growing importance as parliaments are increasingly inclined to create statutory offences which make no reference to mens rea, such as those dealing with regulation of public welfare, such as food safety and traffic matters, and compliance to an increasing range of regulatory requirements.

THE DOCTRINE OF MISTAKE

13.2 Blackstone saw both ignorance and mistake as one issue. He wrote (4 *Bl Comm* 27):

> *[I]gnorance or mistake* is another defect of will; when a man, intending to do a lawful act, does that which is unlawful. For here the deed and the will acting separately, there is not that conjunction between them, which is necessary to form a criminal act. But this must be an ignorance or mistake of fact, and not an error in point of law. As if a man, intending to kill a thief or housebreaker in his own house, by mistake kills one of his own family, this is no criminal action: but if a man thinks he has a right to kill a person excommunicated or outlawed, wherever he meets him, and does so; this is wilful murder. For a mistake in point of law, which every person of discretion not only may, but is bound and presumed to know, is in criminal cases no sort of defence. *Ignorantia juris, quod quisque tenetur scire, neminem excusat*, is as well the maxim of our own law, as it was of the Roman.

As this comment makes clear, there is a distinction between mistakes about matters of law and mistakes about matters of fact. These are treated differently in the criminal law.

13.3C CTM v R

(2008) 247 ALR 1; [2008] HCA 25
High Court of Australia

[The complainant, a 15-year-old girl, had been out drinking with two friends and went to the flat of the accused where he was also drinking with companions. The girl fell asleep and was taken to a bedroom and her friends left. The accused and two of his companions allegedly sexually assaulted her. The accused and the complainant had become known to one another that year through attending the same high school. The accused was aged 17 and in year 11. He told police he thought the girl was in year 10 (she was, in fact, in year 9), and that she had told him some time before that she was 16. The accused denied having sex with the complainant. The accused was charged with sexual intercourse with the complainant, knowing she was not consenting. In the New South Wales District Court, he was acquitted of this charge, but was found guilty of the alternative charge of sexual intercourse with a person aged between 14 and 16, contrary to s 66C(3) of the Crimes Act 1900 (NSW). He was given a suspended 18-month sentence. Before the Act was amended in 2003, it provided a defence to heterosexual acts with under-age people if the offender reasonably believed that the child to whom the charge related was aged at least 16, and provided that the child was at least 14 and had consented to the sexual activity. After the 2003 amendments, the Act said nothing expressly about mistake as to age. The accused appealed unsuccessfully to the Court of Criminal Appeal against both conviction and sentence. On appeal to the High Court against conviction.]

[Footnotes to the extract appear at the end of the extract.]

Gleeson CJ, **Gummow**, **Crennan** and **Kiefel JJ**: In 1897, Sir Samuel Griffith, then Chief Justice of Queensland, prepared for the Government of Queensland a Draft Code of Criminal Law. In a letter to the Attorney-General, enclosing this monumental work, Sir Samuel wrote:[1]

> *Criminal Responsibility.* — This most important and difficult branch of the law is dealt with in Chapter V. I have appended to several of the sections Notes to which I invite special attention. No part of the Draft Code has occasioned me more anxiety, but I may add that I regard no part of the work with more satisfaction.

Chapter V of the Draft Code dealt, among other things, with the mental element necessary to attract criminal responsibility. It included the following provision:

> 26. A person who does or omits to do an act under an honest and reasonable, but mistaken, belief in the existence of any state of things is not criminally responsible for the act or omission to any greater extent than if the real state of things had been such as he believed to exist.

The operation of this rule may be excluded by the express or implied provision of the law relating to the subject.

In a marginal note against that provision, Sir Samuel wrote: 'Common Law'.[2] The provision was enacted as s 24 of the Criminal Code (Q). In *Thomas v The King*,[3] Dixon J said that the language of the Code, which was also taken up in the other Code States of Tasmania and Western Australia, in this respect reflected the common law with complete accuracy.[4] Clause 26 appears to have been taken substantially from *Stephen's Digest of the Criminal Law*,[5] and was in accordance with what Cave J said in *R v Tolson*[6] (a bigamy case in which the accused, at the time of the second marriage, believed on reasonable grounds that her husband was dead):

> At common law an honest and reasonable belief in the existence of circumstances, which, if true, would make the act for which a prisoner is indicted an innocent act has always been held to be a good defence.

In the same case, Cave J explained the reason for the principle:[7]

> Now it is undoubtedly within the competence of the legislature to enact that a man shall be branded as a felon and punished for doing an act which he honestly and reasonably believes to be lawful and right; just as the legislature may enact that a child or a lunatic shall be punished criminally for an act which he has been led to commit by the immaturity or perversion of his reasoning faculty. But such a result seems so revolting to the moral sense that we ought to require the clearest and most indisputable evidence that such is the meaning of the Act.

What is involved is a basic legal principle of criminal responsibility which informs our understanding, and interpretation, of the criminal law. That law is, to a large extent, although in most Australian jurisdictions not completely, governed by statute. The *Crimes Act 1900* (NSW) ('the Crimes Act') is not a code, but it contains provisions dealing with most serious offences against the person. The legal effect of some of those provisions, of which those relating to homicide are a well-known example, can be understood only against a background of common law principle.[8] Where the problem is one of interpretation of what Parliament has enacted, general principles of criminal responsibility inform such interpretation, but ultimately it is the language of the statute that is controlling. A principle as to criminal responsibility, such as that described above, as is acknowledged, may be excluded by a sufficiently plain manifestation of legislative intention.

Cave J's description of a mistaken belief of the kind he was discussing as a 'defence', and Sir Samuel Griffith's Draft Code, preceded *Woolmington v Director of Public Prosecutions*[9] by almost 40 years. Questions of onus and standard of proof now need to be considered in the light of later developments in the law. References to arguments raised on behalf of the accused at a criminal trial as a defence, or a ground of exculpation, may be harmless enough if they do not pre-empt questions of onus of proof. People understandably feel the need to call them something, and the adversarial setting of a trial leads judges and practitioners sometimes to refer to any point relied upon by an accused as a defence. So, for example, in the plurality judgment in this Court in *Jiminez v The Queen*,[10] honest and reasonable mistake was referred to as an 'excuse' and a 'defence'. By reference to a leading decision of this Court on the subject, it is sometimes called 'the *Proudman v Dayman* defence'. Such descriptions have their dangers, but the shorthand may be convenient provided it is understood for what it is.

Honest and reasonable mistakes of fact do not cover the whole field of risk of criminal liability to which a person may be exposed by making an error. Mistakes of law are not a ground of exculpation: ignorance of the law is no excuse.[11] Moreover, the moral sense invoked by Cave J, at least in Australian law, does not extend to cover unreasonable mistakes.[12] The concept of mistake itself is protean.[13] The state of mind that, in a given set of circumstances, will qualify as a mistaken belief in a fact or state of affairs may be a matter of difficulty. An honest and reasonable belief in a certain fact or state of affairs may be very different from an absence of concern. Even so, the point made by Cave J at the end of the second passage quoted above continues to be of fundamental importance to the function of courts in seeking to find and give effect to the meaning of criminal legislation. While the strength of the consideration may vary according to the subject matter of the legislation,[14] when an offence created by Parliament carries serious penal consequences, the courts look to Parliament to spell out in clear terms any intention to make a person criminally responsible for conduct which is based on an honest and reasonable mistake. This appears to us to be closely related to the principle of statutory interpretation which was discussed in *Plaintiff S157/2002 v The Commonwealth*,[15] *Al-Kateb v Godwin*,[16] and *Electrolux Home Products Pty Ltd v Australian Workers' Union*,[17] and which was applied by the whole Court in the several judgments in *Daniels Corporation International Pty Ltd v Australian Competition and Consumer Commission*.[18] There is no present need to expand upon that discussion.

Where it is a ground of exculpation, the law in Australia requires that the honest and reasonable, but mistaken, belief be in a state of affairs such that, if the belief were correct, the conduct of the accused would be innocent. In that context, the word 'innocent' means not guilty of a criminal offence. In the case of an offence, or a series of offences, defined by statute, it means that, if the belief were true, the conduct of the accused would be 'outside the operation of the enactment'.[19] As explained in *He Kaw Teh v The Queen*,[20] the evidentiary onus of raising the ground of exculpation is on the accused, but, once that occurs, the ultimate legal onus of displacing the ground lies on the prosecution. The concept of evidentiary onus itself needs to be understood in the light of the subject matter to which it applies; here, honest and reasonable belief, a concept that has a subjective element of a kind that ordinarily is peculiarly within the knowledge of the accused, and an objective element that must be capable of being measured against the evidence by a tribunal of fact.

Sir Samuel Griffith's qualification, that the operation of the rule stated in the first paragraph of cl 26 (later s 24) may be excluded by the express or implied provisions of the law relating to the subject, was exemplified by the provisions of his Draft Code concerning the topic with which the present appeal is concerned, a topic which used to be described as carnal knowledge by a male of a female under the age of consent.

There is a long history, in Australia, of criminal statutes which punished not only rape, that is, unlawful carnal knowledge of a female of any age without her consent, but also any unlawful carnal knowledge of a female below a certain age. (We are not presently concerned with sexual abuse of infants of tender years, or others for whom the concept of consent may have no practical meaning.) There is an obvious question which arises in the case of any such law: when Parliament specifies an age below which consent is no answer to a charge, what is the position of an accused who honestly and reasonably believed that the female concerned was above that age? …

We have referred to Sir Samuel Griffith's Draft Code as a convenient reference point to illustrate certain considerations that might reasonably be expected to be present in the mind of anyone framing legislation on this topic. Legislation making it an offence for a male to have sexual relations with a female under a certain age commonly has differentiated between females of various ages, ranging through degrees, from infants of tender years, to people who might be mature adolescents. (Concepts of maturity themselves vary over time. There was a time when the age at which a female could marry was 12;[21] hence the need to distinguish 'unlawful' carnal knowledge.) We leave to one side, for the moment, the way in which such laws differentiated between heterosexual and homosexual activity. In dealing with conduct involving sexual relations with a female at the higher end of whatever range is chosen, such legislation typically addressed the possibility of an honest and reasonable mistake as to age. This is a problem inherent in the nature of the issue with which such legislation is concerned. When Parliament stipulates that, regardless of any question of consent, it is a serious crime for a male to have sexual relations with a female under a certain age, it is impossible to ignore the case of an alleged offender who honestly and reasonably believes that the female is above the specified age. It would be absurd to suggest that honest and reasonable mistakes of that kind are never made. When they occur, how is the law to deal with them? A similar (but not identical) answer was given in almost all examples of legislation on this topic in Australian jurisdictions, and in countries of a similar legal background.

A related matter is how the law is to deal with the not uncommon case of the offender who is approximately the same age as the victim. The present appeal provides an example. At the relevant time, the appellant was 17, and the complainant was 15. The term 'sexual predator' may be appropriate to describe some people who engage in sexual activity with consenting 15-year-old females, but it is hardly of universal application. The present appellant was himself, in the eyes of the law, a child, and this was potentially relevant both to the procedures that governed his prosecution and to questions of penalty. The facts of the present case illustrate a kind of adolescent behaviour that lies within the spectrum of conduct which the New South Wales Parliament must have had in contemplation when it enacted the legislative changes that give rise to the primary issue in this appeal.

[Their Honours dealt with the background to the current legislation, and continued:]

The 2003 amendments

The *Crimes Amendment (Sexual Offences) Act 2003* (NSW) made substantial amendments to the sexual offences provisions of the Crimes Act. Of direct relevance to the present case are the amendments made to ss 66C and 77. Of indirect, but substantial, relevance are other amendments designed to give effect to one of the purposes stated in the long title to the Act, 'to provide for the equal treatment of sexual offences against males and females'. In that respect, it established what the Attorney-General described as 'an equal age of consent'. The Attorney-General said:[22]

> Equalising the age of consent to 16 is just one of the many objectives of the bill ...
>
> The safeguards now include the removal of the express defence [to a charge] of carnal knowledge based on reasonable mistake of age.

In an earlier speech in Parliament on the same Bill, the Attorney-General said:[23]

> The bill eliminates the defence currently available to consensual sexual activity with young people aged between 14 and 16 years, formerly known as carnal knowledge.
>
> The bill removes the express statutory defence presently provided in section 77(2)(c) of the Crimes Act that the person charged had reasonable cause to believe, and did in fact believe, that the child was of or above the age of 16 years. As a consequence, it will no longer be possible to argue that a uniform age of consent of 16 years creates an effective age of consent of 14 years.

What the Attorney-General did not say was that the 'express defence' in s 77(2) was a statutory narrowing of a wider potential ground of exculpation that, according to established principle, would at least arguably have been available otherwise and that, in 1988, had been held to be available in the case of certain homosexual offences.

The 2003 legislation amended s 66C to make it, as it were, gender neutral, but otherwise retained, in terms of offences, and penalties, the distinction between offences against children under 10, children between 10 and 14, and children between 14 and 16. It also amended s 77 by deleting s 77(2), and the opening words of s 77(1).

Section 66C, following amendment, and so far as is presently relevant, dealt, in subs (1), with sexual intercourse with a person aged between 10 and 14, in subs (2) with sexual intercourse with a person aged between 10 and 14 in (defined) circumstances of aggravation and, in subs (3), with sexual intercourse with a person aged between 14 and 16. We are presently concerned directly with s 66C(3), which provided that any person who has sexual intercourse with another person who is of or above the age of 14 years and under the age of 16 years is liable to imprisonment for 10 years.

The question arises: what does the law now provide if a person charged with an offence against s 66C(3) honestly believed, on reasonable grounds, that the complainant was aged 16 years or over? It has already been noted with reference to what was said by Dixon J in *Proudman v Dayman*[24] that the potential ground of exculpation requires an honest and reasonable belief in a state of affairs which, had it existed, would be such that the accused's conduct was innocent, in the sense earlier explained. It would therefore not assist an accused to believe that a child was aged between 10 and 14, or between 14 and 16; for if the child were of that age, it would merely take the case out of one prohibition into another. The act of consensual sexual intercourse is not of itself an offence. The offence consists in a particular accompanying state of affairs or circumstance (relevantly, age). An honest mistake about the extent to which a child is under-age would merely be a mistake about the kind of offence that is being committed.

That would be legally irrelevant to guilt, although it could possibly have some consequence for sentencing purposes. Furthermore, the belief, to be exculpatory, must be reasonable. The greater the gap between the child's true age and the age of 16 years, the less likely it may be, in practice, that such a belief was reasonable.

The Attorney-General's speech in Parliament reveals a concern about an argument that, in the case of homosexual intercourse, to reduce the 'age of consent' from 18 years to 16 years was, in practice, to reduce it to 14 years. The problem, however, was more complex than that.

In the Court of Criminal Appeal, Howie J said:

> It has to be said at the outset that I find it remarkable that a section [s 77(2)] that had existed from time immemorial should be repealed without a clear and uncompromising statement being made, either by the draftsperson or by the Minister responsible for the repeal, as to its intended effect. On the face of it a defence to a number of serious criminal offences, carrying substantial sentences of imprisonment as the maximum penalties, was being repealed and yet nothing is expressly stated to indicate any clear understanding by Parliament of the consequence of that repeal. And this in an area of the criminal law which is of continuing concern to the community and, hence, the Parliament. There is probably no part of the Crimes Act that has been subject to more change in recent years than the provisions dealing with sexual assaults against children, much of those changes intended to increase penalties for the offences and to make it easier for children to give evidence and, thereby, easier to secure convictions.

Those sentiments are understandable, although it needs to be remembered that a court, knowing nothing of the political considerations at work, may not be well placed to draw inferences from silence, even on a topic that seems to demand attention.[25] In politics, compromise is sometimes achieved by reticence. This may create a problem for courts that have to deal with the outcome of the compromise, but that is the way of the democratic process. In the equalisation undertaken in 2003, the New South Wales Parliament regarded the 'express defence' in s 77(2) as no longer appropriate. It was a defence that, in its terms, differentiated between homosexual and heterosexual activity, so it at least had to be changed if there were to be the desired equalisation. It could not have been left as it was. Yet the problem to which that provision was addressed did not disappear; and the long-standing and well-understood principle which provided an alternative response to the same problem remained potentially applicable in the absence of 'the clearest and most indisputable evidence [concerning] the meaning of the Act.'[26]

One of the reasons why, for more than a century, in most common law jurisdictions, including the Australian colonies and, later, States, the problem of mistake in connection with age-related sexual offences was dealt with by a separate and more specific legislative provision was that Parliament was thereby enabled to deal with issues such as onus of proof, consent, and mistake about age in a manner tailored to the particular kind of offence in question. One practical matter, discussed by Howie J in the Court of Criminal Appeal, is exemplified by this case. As often happens, the appellant was charged with sexual intercourse with the complainant, knowing she was not consenting. He was acquitted of that charge. The offence of which he was convicted (sexual intercourse with a person over 14 and under 16, contrary to s 66C(3)) was left to the jury as an alternative verdict. In such a case, where the complainant alleges she was not consenting, the prosecution sets out in support of its primary charge (in the language of former times, rape) to establish absence of consent. For the alternative charge (in the language of former times, carnal knowledge), it did not need to prove lack of consent. By the time the jury came to consider the s 66C issue, the matter of consent had been dealt with. Absence of consent was not an element of the s 66C(3) offence, and s 77(1) declared that presence of consent was no answer. The supposed mistake was about age, not consent. The defence previously provided by s 77(2) made the existence of consent, like the fact of an age in excess of 14 years, a condition of the availability of a defence based on a mistake as to age. The potential *Proudman v Dayman* ground of exculpation was not so conditioned.

When, in the context of equalisation of laws relating to heterosexual and homosexual activity, in 2003, the New South Wales Parliament repealed s 77(2), and thereby abandoned the special defence that previously applied to heterosexual acts with under-age persons, it necessarily raised the problem of the possible application, to the now equalised, age-related, offences, of the *Proudman v Dayman* ground of exculpation, that is to say, honest and reasonable mistake of fact. Such mistakes were still going to happen. The question that Parliament left for the courts to decide was whether they were to be treated as irrelevant, or whether they would constitute, in accordance with the long-established principle referred to at the commencement of these reasons, a potential answer to a charge.

Howie J said:

> The immediate reaction to the Crown submission is surprise, if not shock, at the suggestion that the Crimes Act can have what are in effect absolute liability offences carrying substantial gaol penalties. Of course that was always so with a child under 14 but there can be no denying that as the child becomes older the likelihood of an innocent mistake becomes more likely. I also accept that it is notoriously difficult to tell the age of [a] person with such accuracy as an absolute offence would require, and it is not uncommon for children approaching the age of 16 to disguise or lie about their age in order to be treated more favourably as an adult.

He could have added that sexual activity with persons under 16 may be engaged in, not by adult sexual predators, but by other persons who themselves are adolescents. (This is not to overlook the possibility that some adolescents are capable of predatory behaviour.) Nevertheless, Howie J, and Hodgson JA and Price J who agreed with him, felt compelled to conclude that there was a legislative intent that, following the repeal of s 77(2), honest and reasonable mistake would be irrelevant to a charge of an offence against s 66C(3). We accept that, in the face of the legislative silence earlier referred to by Howie J, there are powerful arguments in support of that conclusion. There is, however, what appears to us to be a compelling argument to the contrary. It is that foreshadowed by Cave J in *R v Tolson*, and it concerns the relationship between the courts and Parliament.

The common law principle in question reflects fundamental values as to criminal responsibility. The courts should expect that, if Parliament intends to abrogate that principle, it will make its intention plain by express language or necessary implication. We would, therefore, construe the legislation in the light of the principle of criminal responsibility stated at the outset of these reasons. An honest and reasonable belief that the other party to sexual activity is above the age of 16 years is an answer to a charge of a contravention of s 66C(3). The evidential burden of establishing such a belief is in the first place upon an accused. If that evidential burden is satisfied, then ultimately it is for the prosecution to prove beyond reasonable doubt that the accused did not honestly believe, on reasonable grounds, that the other party was consenting and was above the age of 16 years. The outcome of the present appeal turns upon what is involved in the concept of evidential burden in the context of the particular offence, and the particular ground of exculpation.

The present case

The facts, and the course of proceedings, appear from the reasons of Hayne J. We agree with Hayne J that the circumstance that, in answer to a police question in the course of an interview, the appellant said that the complainant was 16 and that she had told him that was her age did not, in the light of the course of evidence, and absence of evidence, at trial, discharge the evidentiary burden involved in reliance on honest and reasonable mistake of fact as a ground of exculpation. This was a point that was left unresolved by the Court of Criminal Appeal. However, it arises once it is decided that what Howie J called 'the common law defence' is left open by the statute.

In *Jiminez v The Queen*,[27] the plurality reasons for judgment examined in some detail the circumstantial evidence in the case which suggested that the driver of a motor car honestly believed on reasonable grounds that it was safe for him to drive. The material referred to was such as to enable a tribunal of fact not only to decide whether such a belief might have been honestly held, but also to evaluate its reasonableness. The reasons did not merely rely on the driver's claim that he had no warning of the onset of sleep. They tested that claim against the facts and circumstances proved in evidence, and the inferences available from the evidence, and concluded that, in the light of the whole of the evidence, there was a serious issue to be decided.

Here, the fact that the defence case at trial (unsupported by sworn evidence of the appellant) was that no intercourse occurred did not of itself make the point unavailable, especially where, according to the defence case, the only reason no intercourse occurred was that the appellant's plans in that regard were interrupted. There was, however, nothing to support the honesty and reasonableness of a suggested belief in the truth of his out-of-court assertion that the complainant had told him what would have been a lie about her age. The complainant (who was in fact 15) gave evidence that she was in year 9 at school. The appellant, aged 17, was in year 11. In his record of interview the appellant, when asked by the police how old the complainant was, said '16'. When asked how he knew that, he said that the complainant had told him. He also said the complainant was, he thought, in year 10. It was not suggested to the complainant in cross-examination that she had lied to the appellant about her age or, for that matter, that she had discussed it with him.

Honesty and reasonableness are essential features of the mistaken belief relied upon as a ground of exculpation. The belief of the appellant was a matter peculiarly within his own knowledge, but he gave no sworn testimony about it. The reasonableness of his belief was based on an out-of-court assertion as to what the complainant allegedly said, but this was not put to her in cross-examination. A tentative out-of-court suggestion by the appellant as to the complainant's class at school, which would have been consistent with his case, was shown by the evidence to be wrong. The evidential burden was not satisfied.

Conclusion

The appeal should be dismissed.

[**Hayne J** delivered a separate judgment agreeing with the majority. **Heydon J** held the defence of mistake was not available. **Kirby J** dissented. Appeal dismissed.]

Notes:

1. Griffith, *Draft of a Code of Criminal Law*, (1897) at x.
2. Griffith, *Draft of a Code of Criminal Law*, (1897) at 13.
3. (1937) 59 CLR 279 at 305–306; [1937] HCA 83.
4. For later acceptance of the common law principle in this Court, see, for example, *Proudman v Dayman* (1941) 67 CLR 536; [1941] HCA 28; *He Kaw Teh v The Queen* (1985) 157 CLR 523; [1985] HCA 43; *Jiminez v The Queen* (1992) 173 CLR 572; [1992] HCA 14; *Macleod v The Queen* (2003) 214 CLR 230; [2003] HCA 24.
5. *Stephen's Digest of the Criminal Law*, 3rd ed (1883) at 26.
6. (1889) 23 QBD 168 at 181.
7. (1889) 23 QBD 168 at 182.
8. See, for example, *R v Lavender* (2005) 222 CLR 67; [2005] HCA 37.
9. [1935] AC 462.
10. (1992) 173 CLR 572 at 581–582.
11. See, for example, *Ostrowski v Palmer* (2004) 218 CLR 493; [2004] HCA 30.
12. *Thomas v The King* (1937) 59 CLR 279; *Proudman v Dayman* (1941) 67 CLR 536; *He Kaw Teh v The Queen* (1985) 157 CLR 523.
13. *State Rail Authority of NSW v Hunter Water Board* (1992) 28 NSWLR 721 at 724.
14. As explained by Dixon J in *Proudman v Dayman* (1941) 67 CLR 536 at 540.
15. (2003) 211 CLR 476 at 492 [30]; [2003] HCA 2.
16. (2004) 219 CLR 562 at 577 [19]; [2004] HCA 37.
17. (2004) 221 CLR 309 at 328–329 [19]–[21]; [2004] HCA 40.
18. (2002) 213 CLR 543 at 553 [11], 562–563 [43], 576 [88], 592–593 [134]; [2002] HCA 49.
19. *Proudman v Dayman* (1941) 67 CLR 536 at 541.
20. (1985) 157 CLR 523 at 534–535.
21. Joske, *Matrimonial Causes and Marriage: Law and Practice*, 5th ed (1969) at 149.
22. New South Wales, Legislative Assembly, *Parliamentary Debates* (Hansard), 21 May 2003 at 898–899.

23. New South Wales, Legislative Assembly, *Parliamentary Debates* (Hansard), 7 May 2003 at 376.
24. (1941) 67 CLR 536 at 541.
25. See *Byrne v Australian Airlines Ltd* (1995) 185 CLR 410 at 459; [1995] HCA 24; *Wik Peoples v Queensland* (1996) 187 CLR 1 at 168–169; [1996] HCA 40.
26. *R v Tolson* (1889) 23 QBD 168 at 182.
27. (1992) 173 CLR 572 at 583–584.

13.4 Notes

1. In their judgment in *CTM v R*, Gleeson CJ, Gummow, Crennan and Kiefel JJ refer to the requirement that the accused's mistaken belief be as to the existence of circumstances which would make the act 'innocent'. This word is ambiguous, for it could mean:

(a) legally innocent — that is, not in contravention of the criminal law;

(b) morally innocent; or

(c) both legally and morally innocent.

Although statements in some of the old cases appear to adopt the third view (see, for example, the judgment of Bramwell B in *R v Prince* (1875) LR 2 CCR 154), it seems clear that innocent in this context means 'legally innocent': *Director of Public Prosecutions (NSW) v Bone* (2005) 64 NSWLR 735. Were this view not adopted, the courts would be compelled to attempt to make decisions, inevitably controversial and divisive, as to what acts legally permitted can properly be described as immoral.

2. In many situations where the accused acted under a 'mistake', he or she will rely not upon the defence of honest and reasonable mistake, but rather upon a denial that he or she possessed the mens rea required to constitute the crime charged. Therefore, an accused who is charged with theft or with larceny, and who asserts that a belief that the property taken belonged to her or to him in fact, is not relying on the general defence of mistake, but is simply denying an intention to steal. An accused who is charged with rape who claims he believed the victim was consenting is not relying on the defence of mistake, but is denying that he intended to have intercourse with the victim without consent. The difference between the majority and the minority in *Director of Public Prosecutions v Morgan* [1976] AC 182 (at **3.19C**) was over the question of whether knowledge of the victim's non-consent, or recklessness as to her possible non-consent, was part of the mens rea of the crime of rape, or whether such lack of knowledge must be raised by way of the defence of mistake.

3. The question of whether an error on the part of the accused amounts to a denial of the mens rea of the crime charged or to the raising of the affirmative defence of mistake is no mere argument of semantics or quibble over classification. Two significant consequences follow from it.

   First, if the mistake is raised by way of denial of the mens rea of the crime charged, then the mistake need only be genuine. The reasonableness of the mistake will have substantial practical significance; an accused who asserts such a belief which is regarded by the jury as unreasonable may well not be believed. Nonetheless, if the jury has a reasonable doubt as to the possibility that the accused held such a belief, he or she will be entitled to an acquittal. If, however, the mistake is raised by way of the affirmative defence of honest and reasonable mistake the mistake must be 'reasonable'. If the jury form the view that the accused acted under the mistake, but are satisfied beyond reasonable doubt that he or she did not have reasonable grounds for that mistaken belief, then the accused may be convicted. Since the opinion of the Privy Council in *Beckford v R* [1988] AC 130, where it was held that a mistaken belief in self-defence can be a defence to certain criminal charges, even though that belief was unreasonable, there has been initiated a wider move away from the specific requirement that a mistake must be 'reasonable' as a matter of law, rather than as an evidentiary element.

   Second, whether a mistake is relied on by way of denial of the mens rea of the crime charged or by way of affirmative defence has a significance in relation to burden of proof and, as a consequence, in relation to the trial judge's power to withdraw the issue of mistake from the jury. The distinction between the evidential burden of proof and the legal burden of proof was dealt with at **1.71–1.79**. Where the mistake is raised by way of denial of part of the mens rea of the crime charged, then the prosecution bears both the legal and the evidential burden of showing that the mistake was not made. Where the affirmative defence of honest and reasonable mistake of fact is relied on, however, the accused bears the evidential burden of showing that there is evidence fit for the jury's consideration that he or she acted both under the mistaken belief and had reasonable grounds for that belief. If the accused is not able to satisfy this evidential burden, then the trial judge will withdraw the issue of mistake from the jury. It was at one stage argued that not only the evidential burden but also the legal burden of proving mistake to the standard of the balance of probabilities rests on the accused. The decisions of the High Court of Australia in *He Kaw Teh v R* (1985) 157 CLR 523; 60 ALR 449 (at **9.31C**) and *CTM v R* (at **13.3C**) have settled this question. The legal burden is upon the prosecution.

4. It follows from the above that the defence of honest and reasonable mistake only has an effective application in relation to offences which

involve some element of strict liability; that is, to crimes which do not require mens rea in the form of intention, recklessness or negligence in relation to all their defining elements and surrounding circumstances. Thus the nature, scope and availability of the defence of mistake will be considered in this chapter in relation to crimes of strict liability: see 13.27–13.40. However, before that examination is undertaken, the distinction between mistake of fact and mistake of law, clearly enunciated in *CTM v R* (at 13.3C), will be explored.

THE BOUNDARIES OF THE DEFENCE OF MISTAKE

13.5 Of the many questions arising in connection with the defence of ignorance or mistake, at least three stand out as being of particular importance:

(1) Is it really possible to have a workable rule founded upon a distinction between law and fact?

(2) Assuming that it is possible, to what extent should a defendant be permitted to excuse himself or herself by showing a reliance on mistaken but supposedly expert advice as to the law?

(3) What is the justification for the *ignorantia juris* rule; that is, the rule that ignorance or mistake of law does not excuse?

Fact and law

13.6 The proposition that, for the defence of honest and reasonable mistake to be available, the mistake must be one of fact is well settled. In *R v Esop* (1836) 173 ER 203, the accused was indicted for sodomy, allegedly committed on board an East India ship lying in St Katherine's Docks. It was argued that in the country from which the prisoner came sodomy was not a crime, and that the prisoner may not have been aware it was in England. The judges of the Central Criminal Court held that mistake as to the state of the law was no defence.

13.7 The distinction between law and fact is, however, by no means always so clear. In *Thomas v R* (1937) 59 CLR 279, the accused was charged with bigamy. The accused had married his wife (Ms Westacott) in the belief that her earlier marriage had been dissolved. This was true. His wife subsequently told the accused repeatedly that this dissolution had not been effective, and that she was not his wife. Eventually, still protesting that her marriage with the accused was no marriage, Ms Westacott went off with another man.

The accused then met and, believing he was free to do so, married, another woman (Ms Deed). The accused was convicted of bigamy in respect of this marriage, and appealed successfully to the High Court. The bigamy statute made no reference to mens rea or to any defence of mistake. The majority of the High Court (Latham CJ, Dixon and Rich JJ, Starke and Evatt JJ dissenting) held the defence of honest and reasonable mistake of fact was available. As a matter of logic, the mistake of the accused may be classified as being either one of fact or as to the law. At the time of his bigamous marriage to Ms Deed, the accused believed he was free to marry. That factual belief, however, came about as a consequence of his belief that the earlier marriage of Ms Westacott had not been legally dissolved at the time he married her. The majority held the belief of the accused — that he was free to marry Ms Deed — was a mistake of fact rather than one of law. Dixon J stated, at 306:

> He knew that, unless [Ms Westacott] was effectively divorced, his own marriage with her was a nullity. He rightly supposed that in point of law her divorce was not effective unless it were made absolute, completed, or, as he called it, 'entered in the court'. According to the jury, he honestly and reasonably supposed this had not been done. Whether it had been done or not was a matter of fact, not law. But, in any case, in the distinction between mistakes of fact and of law, a mistake as to the existence of a compound event consisting of law and fact is in general one of fact and not a mistake of law. This is brought out by an apposite passage in the judgment of Jessel MR, in *Eaglesfield v Marquis of Londonderry* (1875) 4 Ch D 693 at 702, 703:
>
> > A misrepresentation of law is this: when you state the facts and state a conclusion of law, so as to distinguish between facts and law. The man who knows the facts is taken to know the law; but when you state that as a fact which no doubt involves, as most facts do, a conclusion of law, there is still a statement of fact and not a statement of law.

13.8 The view of Dixon J in *Thomas v R* is, on principle, correct. The alternatives would seem to be (a) to treat such mixed questions as questions of law, which would be far too harsh; or (b) to distinguish between cases where the person who makes the mistake merely asserts a conclusion and cases where he or she sets out the reasoning. One would be forced by such a distinction to say that if a person says 'I am not married' this is an assertion of fact, while if she or he says, 'I am not married, because …' this may be making an assertion of law.

13.9 The difficulties in making the distinction between questions of law and of fact are illustrated by the High Court case of *Iannella v French* (1968) 119 CLR 84. The accused owned a house which, as he knew, was subject to rent controls under the Housing Improvement Act 1940 (SA). He read in the newspaper that another Act, the Landlord and Tenant (Control of Rents) Act 1942–1961 (SA) had expired. Wrongly believing that he was now free of the rent controls, he subsequently let the house at a higher rental. He was charged with breach of the Housing Improvements Act.

That Act made wilful demand of a rent greater than the statutory maximum a summary offence. At the trial, a government officer testified that he had interviewed the accused and was convinced the accused had honestly believed he was free to charge the higher rent. The accused was convicted and appealed, ultimately, to the High Court. The High Court quashed the conviction (4:1) on other grounds, but the four judges in the majority disagreed over whether the mistake alleged was one of fact or law. Taylor and Owen JJ said as a mistake as to the general state of the law — whether or not a statute existed — it involved a question of law. Barwick CJ and Windeyer J, on the other hand, said that the mistake was as to whether the house was rent-controlled, and this was a question of fact.

13.10 In *Ostrowski v Palmer* (2004) 218 CLR 493; 206 ALR 422, the High Court once again examined the question of characterising a mistake as one of fact or one of law. D was a professional fisherman with an appropriate valid commercial licence. He was accordingly entitled to fish commercially in the terms of the Fish Resources Management Act 1994 (WA) and the Regulations made under the statute. D wished to fish for lobster in a particular area of the Indian Ocean. Lobster fishing was carefully regulated and D knew that, even in a prescribed fishing zone, there were areas which might be closed to commercial fishing. He asked the local office of Fisheries WA, the relevant government agency, for comprehensive documentation. He was given documents which were deficient in that a regulation proscribing a specific area closed to lobster fishing was not included. D was told that the documents he received were sufficient for his purposes. He fished in the prohibited area and was charged with a statutory offence. D relied on the defence of mistake of fact created by s 24 of the Criminal Code (WA), but the magistrate rejected his defence, even though he accepted that D had honestly and reasonably believed he was entitled to fish in the closed zone. The Full Court of the Supreme Court of Western Australia set aside the decision and the prosecution appealed to the High Court.

The High Court held that D had made a mistake of law; he did not know that a regulation had been made which rendered his action unlawful. The erroneous information supplied to D did not affect this conclusion. The appeal was allowed.

In their joint judgment, Callinan and Heydon JJ said (at 444): 'It is impossible not to sympathise with the respondent. On any fair and objective view he was not culpable in any way. To the contrary he was most diligent'. The prosecution had given an undertaking that if the appeal succeeded the government would advise the Governor in Council to remit all penalties and orders for costs, and this would 'cure any perceived injustice to [D]'. Callinan and Heydon JJ observed that D would still stand convicted of the offence. Under the provisions of the fisheries legislation, he was in jeopardy of mandatory licence cancellation if convicted of three or more offences in a 10-year period.

It is difficult to understand why the High Court was not prepared to characterise D's mistake as a mixed one of fact and law, and thus to be labelled a mistake within the terms of s 24 of the Code.

Misstated law and mistake of law

13.11 Assuming that the existing rule is to be retained, and that the mistake of the accused can clearly be recognised as one of law, it must next be asked how far, if at all, the accused can plead that he or she was acting under supposedly expert advice. There are three main situations where this may occur.

13.12 First, suppose the accused has acted under the advice of a lawyer to the effect that the proposed activity was not contrary to law. For this purpose, it must be assumed that the legal practitioner was consulted and gave advice in good faith, after full disclosure to him or her of all relevant facts. In such a situation, should the accused be convicted if the advice was wrong? There seems to be no English authority dealing with this situation. In Australia, the decision in *Crichton v Victorian Dairies Ltd* [1965] VR 49 is perhaps authority for convicting in these circumstances. But American courts have given different answers to the question. In *People v McCalla* (1923) 220 Pac 436, the California District Court of Appeal rejected such a defence, saying that:

> … if the advice of counsel could afford immunity to one accused of the violation of a penal statute it would result in the advice of an attorney being paramount to the law.

This is probably the majority view. But in *Long v State* (1949) 65 A 489, the Supreme Court of Delaware said that the defence might be recognised where:

> … before engaging in the conduct, the defendant made a bona fide, diligent effort, adopting a course and resorting to sources and means at least as appropriate as any afforded under our legal system, to ascertain and abide by the law, and where he acted in good faith reliance upon the results of such effort.

Which is the better view? In considering this question, it is appropriate to ask what steps the accused could take in self-protection, apart from relying upon legal advice. If a defendant is to act at his or her peril unless a favourable court decision has already been given, by what procedure could he or she obtain a court decision dealing with that personal position? A court would not normally hear proceedings brought to ascertain the legality of proposed future action on the ground that courts do not answer hypothetical questions or give advisory opinions. So is it fair to tell the defendant that 'You must run the risk of conviction if the advice you receive, from the only source from which you can obtain it, proves to be incorrect'?

13.13 Second, suppose the accused has acted on advice of a government official charged with the implementation of the relevant statute. For example, a statute requires that a person wishing to engage in a defined transaction must first obtain a licence. The accused applies to the appropriate department or official for a licence and is told that what is proposed is outside the statute, so that the person does not need a licence. If the accused goes ahead, and the official is wrong, can he or she be prosecuted for breach of the statute?

As a preliminary question, one might ask what sense it would make to prosecute the person. What more could he or she reasonably be expected to have done? True, in the case supposed, he or she might have gone to the court and asked for a writ of mandamus, commanding the official to consider the licence application; in this way he or she would be able to get, not a licence, but a decision whether one was needed. But why should the defendant be required by the law to assume that responsible government officials do not know their own business?

13.14 In *Falmouth Boat Construction Co v Howell* [1950] 2 KB 16 at 26, Denning LJ answered this question by laying down the principle that:

> ... whenever government officers, in their dealing with a subject, take on themselves to assume authority in a matter with which he is concerned, the subject is entitled to rely on their having the authority which they assume.

It may be thought that this is too wide. The subject ought, perhaps, not be entitled to rely on an official's statement concerning some matter which appears clearly to be outside the range of the official's duties; although Denning LJ answered this by observing that the process of government is of such complication that the official may be assumed to know the scope of his or her duties and authority better than the subject with whom that official deals. It might also further be said that everyone should be taken to know that government officers do not have authority to interpret the law, this being a matter committed to the judges.

The case went on appeal to the House of Lords: *sub nom Howell v Falmouth Boat Construction Co* [1951] AC 837. Although the actual decision was upheld, it was on a different ground, and Lord Simonds adverted to Denning LJ's remarks, saying that he knew no authority for them. He added (at 845) that:

> The illegality of an act is the same whether or not the actor has been misled by an assumption of authority on the part of a government officer however high or low in the hierarchy. I do not doubt that in criminal proceedings it would be a material factor that the actor had thus been misled, *if knowledge is a necessary element of the offence*, and in any case it would have a bearing on the sentence to be imposed [emphasis added].

Lord Normand also expressed his view that such facts would not afford a defence to a criminal prosecution. The remaining Lords agreed with the views of these two.

The question under discussion arose again in *Surrey County Council v Battersby* [1965] 2 QB 194. The Divisional Court, in remitting the case to the justices with an order that they should convict, devoted all its attention to the substantive question of law involved. It assumed without discussion that the fact that the respondent acted on the advice of a council official could not afford her a defence. A similar view was expressed in *Cambridgeshire County Council v Rush* [1972] 2 QB 426.

13.15 In *Ostrowski v Palmer* (see 13.10), the High Court had the opportunity to consider whether what the court characterised as a mistake of law should nonetheless be a ground of exculpation where it was patent that the mistake resulted from misleading advice by, and careless behaviour of, a government official. D's conduct was directly occasioned by that official misbehaviour. McHugh J examined this issue and decided (at 436) that it was 'irrelevant that [D's] mistake was induced by the conduct of an employee of Fisheries WA'. Gleeson CJ and Kirby J, in their joint judgment, stated (at 425) that since the issue of an officially induced error had not been raised in the Magistrates' Court, the Full Court was right in its decision not to allow it to be raised on appeal.

13.16 Maule J is supposed to have said that 'everybody is presumed to know the law except His Majesty's judges, who have a Court of Appeal set over them to put them right': see G L Williams, *Criminal Law — The General Part*, 2nd ed, Stevens & Sons Ltd, London, 1961, p 290. If the remarks in the *Howell* case are correct, the rule should now be that everybody is presumed to know the law, except the judges and the executive officials who are particularly charged with implementing it. This seems so absurd that one is forced to question whether Lords Simonds and Normand were correct. They were dealing with a civil case, and thus their remarks may be considered to be obiter. The effect of their view is that the government is permitted to shift the responsibility for its own errors onto the shoulders of its citizens. Such a holding has little if anything to commend it, and the injustice thereby created is not avoided by saying that the facts may go towards mitigation of punishment. The latter observation reveals a complete insensitiveness to the fact that a person who has been convicted has been publicly labelled a criminal, and that the stigma will remain even if he or she is not punished. The decision, and some of the specific statements in the judgments in *Ostrowski v Palmer* (see 13.10), sadly espouse this approach in contemporary Australian jurisprudence.

13.17 A third scenario arises where an accused acted in reliance on decisions of a court which later turn out to be incorrect. Consider the following hypothetical situation. D1 is prosecuted for a violation of the Liquor Control Reform Act 1998 (Vic). He is convicted by a magistrate but, on appeal, a single justice of the Supreme Court of Victoria holds that that particular activity is not a violation of the Act. The Crown does not proceed further. However, some months later, it feels that the judge's decision has opened up a loophole in the Act and would like to get it reversed. Accordingly, D2 is prosecuted for performing acts in no material way different from those of D1. This time, when the magistrate acquits, the case is carried to the High Court of Australia. That court holds that the Victorian judge was wrong on the previous occasion. In this way, the interests of the Crown are safeguarded and satisfied. But why should it follow that to achieve this result D2 must be branded a criminal? What conceivable harm could be done to the interests of the state or to the integrity of the judicial system if it were plainly recognised that, in such a situation, D2 is an innocent person?

13.18 It seems that the sensible course for the court to take would be to declare that prima facie D2's activities constituted a violation of the statute; but that D2 was entitled to be acquitted on the grounds (assuming it to be proved) that she acted in reliance on the previous court decision. There appears to be no clear authority for such a result in the Commonwealth. The normal practice would be for the matter to be dealt with by finding D2 guilty but imposing a minimum, or no, punishment. However, is this not a mean compromise indulged in by courts which are unable to see beyond the literal interpretation of an old maxim into a wider horizon of justice?

In a number of United States jurisdictions, where a problem of this kind has come up, the court has acquitted the defendant because of his or her reliance on court decisions, while announcing that similar conduct in the future would be a violation: see *State v Jones* (1940) 44 N Mex 623. See now, for a review and evaluation of the authorities, E M Campbell, 'Reliance on Official Representations and Criminal Liability' (1994) 1 *Cambridge LR* 15.

The future of ignorantia juris

13.19 To this point in the discussion it has been assumed that sound policy underlies the rule that ignorance of the law does not excuse. But is this the case? And what is the policy involved? In *The Common Law* (Little, Brown and Company, Boston, 1881), Oliver Wendell Holmes Jr wrote (at pp 47–8):

> Ignorance of the law is no excuse for breaking it. This substantive principle is sometimes put in the form of a rule of evidence, that every one is presumed to know the law. It has accordingly been defended by Austin and others, on the ground of difficulty of proof. If justice requires the fact to be ascertained, the difficulty of doing so is no ground for refusing to try. But every one must feel that ignorance of the law could never be admitted as an excuse, even if the fact could be proved by sight and hearing in every case. Furthermore, now that parties can testify, it may be doubted whether a man's knowledge of the law is any harder to investigate than many questions which are gone into. The difficulty, such as it is, would be met by throwing the burden of proving ignorance on the lawbreaker.
>
> The principle cannot be explained by saying that we are not only commanded to abstain from certain acts, but also to find out that we are commanded. For if there were such a second command, it is very clear that the guilt of failing to obey it would bear no proportion to that of disobeying the principal command if known, yet the failure to know would receive the same punishment as the failure to obey the principal law.
>
> The true explanation of the rule is the same as that which accounts for the law's indifference to a man's particular temperament, faculties, and so forth. Public policy sacrifices the individual to the general good. It is desirable that the burden of all should be equal, but it is still more desirable to put an end to robbery and murder. It is no doubt true that there are many cases in which the criminal could not have known that he was breaking the law, but to admit the excuse at all would be to

encourage ignorance where the lawmaker has determined to make men know and obey, and justice to the individual is rightly outweighed by the larger interests on the other side of the scales.

13.20 In this passage, Holmes justifies the rule as being an integral part of the fabric, which he wove so tenaciously, of objective liability. While elements of objectivity continue to play a significant role in some areas of the criminal law, there has, in Australia, been a continuing trend towards subjectivity since the landmark decision of the High Court in *Parker v R* (1963) 11 CLR 610. However, whether as part of his theory or not, Holmes makes it plain that the rule that ignorance of the law does not excuse can be supported only on the ground that some innocent people should be condemned so that too many guilty people shall not escape. Such a view certainly offends basic concepts of justice. Further, it is to be doubted whether these considerations really demand the doctrine of *ignorantia juris*.

13.21 Offences may be categorised in different ways. Broadly speaking, when it comes to the seriousness of the offence, it is possible to characterise offences as one or other of two main types. One type consists of a contravention of a rule of conduct which, one may say without exaggeration, is recognised throughout Western society — indeed, perhaps throughout the world. Murder, rape, assault, and the various theft offences are of this type. One does not need to go to a law book or a statute to learn that intentional killing is wrong. Indeed, one does not normally look to such a source to find out what one may not do in matters of this kind. The learning on such matters is derived from the 'folkways' of the community.

The other type of offence is of a somewhat different order. It is a breach of a prohibition relating to conduct, not intrinsically wrong in itself, but deemed necessary by the legislature for the welfare of the community. Liquor offences or some driving offences afford a good example of crimes of this type. With such offences, one may indeed learn in a vague way from living in a community — from social norms and practices — that some form of prohibition exists. However, one has to go to the statute book to find out its limits. These types of offences are further considered later in this chapter.

13.22 The distinction here being made is akin to that made by the older writers and judges, and American scholars, between *mala in se* (broadly meaning, wrong 'in themselves' or 'morally wrong') and *mala quia prohibita* (that is, wrong only because prohibited by law). It is a distinction which has been much criticised by the analytical writers on law, principally because it is not capable of precise definition. Admittedly, there is no clear line of demarcation. Borderline cases will occur in which it is difficult to decide whether a crime is of the one kind or the other, but these difficulties do not require complete disregard of the broad general distinction.

One point should be noted, however. It must not be assumed that because, when it is first enacted, a crime clearly comes within the category of *mala quia prohibita*, it will always remain in that category. Many legislative prohibitions ultimately seep into social norms and practices, and when this occurs they may be regarded as having been transmuted into *mala in se*. Consider the case of obtaining property by false pretences or by deception. At the beginning of the eighteenth century such activity was apparently regarded by community practice as permissible, but at the present time it may be generally assumed to be regarded as dishonest and wrong.

13.23 Once these distinctions are understood, it becomes easy to see why a person accused of murder will not be allowed to say 'I did not know that murder was prohibited by the criminal law', for such an answer would be utterly irrelevant. The law against murder does no more than provide an official means of enforcing the rule of the folkways. What the person is really saying is that he or she did not know that the state could punish the wrongful deed. This does not make the deed an innocent one. It merely shows that, although the person appreciated that his or her act was wrong, the person was mistaken as to the precise *degree* of wrongfulness. This has never been regarded as an excuse.

13.24 When, however, an offence of the second type is under consideration, then the most that social norms and practices require is that the accused should have endeavoured to comply with the law. If a person has done that — if he or she has looked to the statute, or genuinely sought legal advice — that person should be excused when it ultimately turns out that he or she has made a mistake. The public communication by the court of that mistake is sufficient to ensure, as far as possible, that the mistake will not be repeated in future by that person or by others (at least, by those others who genuinely seek to find out what they are forbidden to do).

STRICT LIABILITY — AN INTRODUCTION

13.25 Mens rea is, of course, a central component of criminal liability, as discussed in **Chapter 1**. There is, however, a category of offence which may be committed by an accused who acts without intention, recklessness or negligence. That is, it may be possible to convict someone of one of these offences without having to prove a mens rea component of the offence. These are referred to as crimes of strict liability. Such offences are almost entirely the creation of statute. Statutes said to create crimes of strict liability may be ambiguous and the justifications for imposing strict liability are thus to be found in principles of interpretation based on considerations of public policy accepted by the courts. Strict liability is most often imposed in respect of commonly recurring and what are usually regarded as less serious offences (illegal sales of liquor, sales of impure or adulterated food or drugs, violation of traffic regulations, violation of regulations designed to protect public health or safety, etc). This is, however, not always so. On occasion, quite serious offences are interpreted as involving strict liability: see, for example, *R v Kennedy* [1981] VR 565 (although this case must be regarded as incorrectly decided in the light of *CTM v R* (at **13.3C**): see now *Burns v R* [2012] HCA 35; (2012) 246 CLR 334.

13.26 Increasing numbers of crimes are being created by statute without reference to any mens rea. This raises important issues. The existence of crimes of strict liability constitutes an important and wide-ranging exception to the general principle that an accused ought not to be convicted of an offence where his or her conduct did not involve an element of moral culpability. The growth of the phenomenon, and the approach taken by the courts to the interpretation of such statutes, will be considered in the following section. The modern cases propound, in fact, a further classification of crimes as ones of absolute liability. The terminology has not been used consistently in the case law, but an important distinction can now be drawn between 'strict' and 'absolute' liability, discussed at 13.48–13.54.

CASES ON STRICT LIABILITY

13.27C **R v Woodrow**

(1846) 15 M & W 404; 153 ER 907

Court of Exchequer

[By an Act of 1842 it was provided that:

> … every … dealer in, or retailer of tobacco, who shall … have in his possession … any tobacco or snuff which shall have been manufactured with, or shall have had added thereto or mixed therewith, or into or amongst which there shall have been put, either before or after being manufactured, or in which there shall be found on examination thereof, any other material, liquid, substance, matter or thing, then, as respects tobacco, water only …

should forfeit £200. This Act was, by its preamble, stated to have been enacted for the protection of the revenue. The administration of the Act was confined to the Commissioners of Excise, whose general powers and duties were set out in an earlier statute. Under s 98 of that statute, as was pointed out by Rolfe B during the argument of this case, the Commissioners were empowered to forbear from prosecuting an offence if it should appear to their satisfaction that any penalty or forfeiture had been incurred 'without any intention of fraud, or of offending against this Act'.

Hedges, an officer of excise, found, in the possession of Woodrow, 54 pounds of tobacco which was proved to have been adulterated with sugar and molasses. He accordingly laid an information against Woodrow, claiming the penalty of £200 and the forfeiture of the tobacco. The information was heard by justices at petty sessions and was dismissed. At the hearing, Marks, another officer of excise, appeared and conducted the case, Hedges not being present. Marks signed and served notices of appeal to Quarter Sessions; and, in due course, notice of the trial of the appeal was signed and served by Hedges. At the trial of the appeal, Woodrow objected that, since the two notices were signed by different persons, the proceeding was defective. Quarter Sessions overruled this objection; they then heard the case. On the merits, they found that the adulteration of the tobacco had occurred in the course of its manufacture, but that Woodrow had purchased the tobacco as genuine tobacco; and that he believed the tobacco was genuine and had no knowledge or cause to suspect that it had been adulterated. They accordingly dismissed the appeal, but stated a case for the Court of Exchequer, raising both the procedural and the substantive point.

In the event, the Court of Exchequer gave judgment for the Crown. The following extracts from the judgments relate to the merits of the case only.]

Pollock CB: ... Then the next question is, whether the respondent has been guilty of the offence charged in the information. It appears to me, that, in this case, it being within the personal knowledge of the party that he was in possession of the tobacco (indeed, a man can hardly be said to be in possession of anything without knowing it), it is not necessary that he should know that the tobacco was adulterated; for reasons probably very sound, and not applicable to this case only, but to many other branches of the law, persons who deal in an article are made responsible for its being of a certain quality. If this were the case of provisions, or of any matter that affected the public health, it would not be at all unreasonable to require persons dealing in them to be aware of their character and quality, and to be responsible for their goodness, whether they know it or not; they are bound to take care. It appears to me that the section referred to, which creates this offence, namely the 3rd section of the 5 & 6 Vict, c 93, applies to this case, whether the party knows it or not. The section pointed out by my Brother Rolfe, in the course of the argument [that is, s 98 of the general Act], strongly confirms that, if it were necessary to have any confirmation in addition to the express language of the section itself. It may be said, that in this particular instance it works a great hardship, because it is expressly found, I may take it, that the magistrates, who in the first instance dismissed the information, and the Court of Quarter Sessions, who decided in favour of the defendant, were of the opinion that he personally had no knowledge of this violation of the law. If the law in a particular case works any hardship, it is either for the legislature to alter the law, or for the executive department of this branch of the revenue law to abstain from calling for the enforcement of the statute. But if we are called upon to put our construction upon it, I believe we are all of opinion that the due construction of the 3rd and 4th sections is, that this tobacco was forfeited, and that the party is liable to the penalty, whether he is or is not aware that the commodity has been adulterated in the manner in which this turns out to be. In reality, a prudent man who conducts this business, will take care to guard the injury he complains of, and which Mr Crompton [counsel for Woodrow] says he has a right to complain of, and he would not be exposed to it. If he examines the article, he may reject it, and not keep it in his possession; or if he is incompetent to do that, he may take a guarantee that shall render the person with whom he is dealing responsible for all the consequences of a prosecution ...

Parke B: ... With respect to the offence itself, I have not the least doubt that the ordinary grammatical construction of this clause is the true one. It is very true that in particular instances it may produce mischief, because an innocent man may suffer from his want of care in not examining the tobacco he has received, and not taking a warranty; but the public inconvenience would be much greater, if in every case the officers were obliged to prove knowledge. They would be very seldom able to do so. The legislature have made a stringent provision for the purpose of protecting the revenue, and have used very plain words. If a man is in possession of an article as the defendant was in this case, and that article falls within the terms mentioned in the statute, there is no question but that the offence is proved. If there is any hardship in the case, it does not rest with those who have only to carry the law into effect to remedy it. There is a provision, referred to by my brother Rolfe, which enables the commissioners to meet such a case. I have not the least doubt that the defendant has been guilty of the offence described in the 3rd section ...

Alderson B: ... As to the merits of the case, I think the court was wrong; because the words of the Act, though they are no doubt very stringent, are nevertheless very clear, and any retailer of tobacco who has an adulterated article in his possession is liable to the penalty. I cannot say that this man had not the tobacco in his possession, because he clearly knew it. He did not know it was in an adulterated state, but he knew he had it in his possession; and the question of 'knowingly', it appears to me, is involved in the word possession. That is, a man has not in his possession that which he does not know to be about him. I am not in possession of anything which a person has put into my stable without my knowledge. It is clear, therefore, that possession includes a knowledge of the facts as far as the possession of the article is concerned.

[**Rolfe B** concurred.]

13.28 Illustrations

1. D was charged under the Licensing Act 1872 (Eng) with, being a keeper of licensed premises, having sold intoxicating liquor to a drunken person. At the hearing of the charge, D proved that neither he nor his servants had noticed that the person served was drunk and that the person served had, whilst in the premises, been quiet and done nothing to indicate his insobriety. The magistrate held that the offence was complete on proof of the sale and of the fact that the person served was drunk. He accordingly convicted D. On appeal, held, conviction affirmed. The prohibition was absolute. Knowledge of the condition of the person served with liquor was not necessary to constitute the offence: *Cundy v Le Cocq* (1884) 13 QBD 207.
2. D was convicted under the Licensing Act 1872 (Eng) with having supplied liquor to a constable on duty. D's public house was nearly opposite a police station and was frequently used by police from that station when off duty. On the day in question, the constable, who was well known to D and his daughter, entered the public house while on duty and was served with liquor by the daughter in D's presence. Before entering the public house, the constable had taken off his armlet, and, it being known to D and his daughter that a constable removed his armlet when going off duty (this

fact was common knowledge among Londoners), both of them took it for granted that this particular constable was off duty and neither of them asked for confirmation of that fact. On appeal, held, conviction quashed. The offence is not committed where the licensee bona fide believes that the police constable is off duty: *Sherras v De Rutzen* [1895] 1 QB 918.

3. D, a dairyman, entered into a contract for the sale of milk. He delivered churns of pure milk to a railway station near his farm, for transport to London. Under the contract, the property in the milk passed when it was delivered in London. The milk, when tested in London, contained 9% of added water. D was found guilty of selling adulterated milk, contrary to s 6 of the Food and Drugs Act 1875, and the conviction was upheld by the Divisional Court: *Parker v Alder* [1899] 1 QB 20. What more could D have done?
4. D, a French subject, was permitted to land in the United Kingdom. Her passport was endorsed with a permit to land upon certain conditions. These conditions were subsequently varied by a condition requiring her to depart from the United Kingdom not later than a certain date. On that date, she went to the Irish Free State. An order for her deportation from the Irish Free State was made by the executive authorities of that country, and she was subsequently brought back to Holyhead in the custody of the Irish Free State police, who there handed her over to the police of the United Kingdom, by whom she was detained. She was convicted under the Aliens Order 1920 of being an alien, to whom leave to land in the United Kingdom had been refused, being found in the United Kingdom. On appeal, held, conviction affirmed. She had committed the offence with which she was charged, the circumstances in which she returned to the United Kingdom being immaterial: *R v Larsonneur* (1933) 24 Cr App R 74. Note D Lanham, '*Larsonneur* Revisited' [1976] *Crim LR* 276. The decision has been much criticised as 'the acme of injustice', but see now R C Doeger, 'Strict Liability in Criminal Law, and *Larsonneur* Reassessed' [1998] *Crim LR* 791, and the rejoinder by J C Smith in '*R v Larsonneur*' [1999] *Crim LR* 100.

13.29C Proudman v Dayman

(1941) 67 CLR 536; [1944] ALR 64
High Court of Australia

[Dayman laid an information against Mrs Proudman, charging her with the statutory offence of permitting an unlicensed driver to drive a motor car. She was convicted and appealed to the Supreme Court of South Australia. Cleland J set aside the conviction on the ground that the evidence showed her to have believed, on reasonable grounds, that the driver was licensed. On further appeal to the Full Court, the conviction was restored. Mrs Proudman then sought special leave to appeal to the High Court of Australia.]

Dixon J: The applicant was convicted summarily of an offence against s 30 of the *Road Traffic Act 1934–39* (SA). The charge was that she permitted a person, not being the holder of a licence for the time being in force, to drive a motor vehicle on a road. She appealed against that conviction to the Supreme Court. Cleland J, who heard her appeal, set aside the conviction on the ground that she believed that the driver in question held a licence which was in force and that she had reasonable grounds for her belief. His Honour appears further to have considered that she could not be said to have permitted him, as a person not holding such a licence, to drive the motor vehicle unless she knew that he was unlicensed, quite independently of the question of the reasonableness of her belief to the contrary.

The Full Court of the Supreme Court, consisting of Murray CJ, Angas Parsons and Napier JJ, allowed the appeal and restored the conviction. Their Honours were of all of the opinion that the applicant had not made out in fact any defence of mistake on reasonable grounds and that under the provisions of s 30 it was not incumbent upon the prosecution to establish that the applicant knew that a licence for the time being in force was not held by the person whom she permitted to drive the motor vehicle.

Murray CJ, went further and decided that under s 30 mistake would not afford a defence, that is to say, it would not amount to an answer to the charge of permitting if a defendant proved that on reasonable grounds he honestly believed that the person he permitted to drive his car held a licence then in force.

From the decision of the Full Court the applicant now seeks special leave to appeal to this court.

A consideration of the provisions of the statute and of the authorities cited in a somewhat full argument has not disclosed any reason for doubting the correctness of the conclusion of the Full Court. It is not necessary to go as far as Murray CJ, and hold that a defence of honest mistake on reasonable grounds cannot be available under s 30.

It is one thing to deny that a necessary ingredient of the offence is positive knowledge of the fact that the driver holds no subsisting licence. It is another to say that an honest belief founded on reasonable grounds that he is licensed cannot exculpate a person who permits him to drive. As a general rule an honest and reasonable belief in a state of facts which, if they existed, would make the defendant's act innocent affords an excuse for doing what would otherwise be an offence.

The strength of the presumption that the rule applies to the statutory offence newly created varies with the nature of the offence and the scope of the statute. If the purpose of the statute is to add a new crime to the general criminal law, it is natural to suppose that it is to be read subject to the general principles according to which that law is administered. But other considerations arise where in matters of police, of health, of safety or the like the legislature adopts penal measures in order to cast on the individual the responsibility of so conducting his affairs that the general welfare will not be prejudiced. In such cases there is less ground, either in reason or in actual probability, for presuming an intention that the general rule should apply making honest and reasonable mistake a ground of exoneration, and the presumption is but a weak one.

Indeed, there has been a marked and growing tendency to treat the prima facie rule as excluded or rebutted in the case of summary offences created by modern statutes, particularly those dealing with social and industrial regulation. But, although it has been said that in construing a modern statute a presumption as to *mens rea* does not exist (per Kennedy LJ, *Hobbs v Winchester Corporation* [1910] 2 KB 471 at 483 (CA)), it is probably still true that, unless from the words, context, subject matter, or general nature of the enactment some reason to the contrary appears, you are to treat honest and reasonable mistake as a ground of exculpation, even from a summary offence.

There may be no longer any presumption that *mens rea*, in the sense of a specific state of mind, whether of motive, intention, knowledge or advertence, is an ingredient in an offence created by a modern statute; but to concede that the weakening of the older understanding of the rule of interpretation has left us with no prima facie presumption that some mental element is implied in the definition of any new statutory offence does not mean that the rule that honest and reasonable mistake is prima facie admissible as an exculpation has lost its application also.

Doubtless over a wide description of legislation the presumption in favour of its application is but a weak one. See *Maher v Musson* (1934) 52 CLR 100; [1935] ALR 80; *Thomas v R* (1937) 59 CLR 279; [1938] ALR 37, and three papers referred to in that report. But it still remains a presumption, and in relation to s 30 there appears to be no sufficient reason for treating it as rebutted.

The burden of establishing honest and reasonable mistake is in the first place upon the defendant and he must make it appear that he had reasonable grounds for believing in the existence of a state of facts, which, if true, would take his act outside the operation of the enactment and that on those grounds he did so believe. The burden possibly may not finally rest upon him of satisfying the tribunal in case of doubt. But, in the present case, the applicant assigned reasons for her alleged belief which neither the magistrate nor the Full Court found convincing or sufficient. Indeed, it may be doubted if she thought at all upon the question whether the person she permitted to drive her car did or did not hold a subsisting licence.

Agreeing as we all do in the view of the Full Court on this question of fact, it is enough to say that there is no support in the circumstances of the case for the defence of honest and reasonable mistake.

The applicant contended, however, that, upon a charge under s 30 of permitting a person not being the holder of a licence for the time being in force to drive a motor vehicle on any road, it must be shown, not merely that the driver was unlicensed, but also that the defendant knew it or at all events was indifferent to the question whether he was licensed or not.

This contention was based upon the ground that the very idea of permission connotes knowledge of or advertence to the act or thing permitted. In other words, you cannot permit without consenting and consent involves a consciousness or understanding of the act or conduct to which it is directed. Be it so. Nevertheless the contention fails in its application to the actual terms of the provision. The material words of s 30 are: '… employs or permits any person not being the holder of such a licence to drive a motor vehicle on any road.' It may be conceded that unless a defendant meant to consent to the three conditions involved in the words (1) drive, (2) a motor vehicle, (3) on a road, he could not be said to have permitted the doing of that thing. But it is to that act that the permission must be directed, not to the absence of a licence. The words 'not being the holder of such a licence' do not form part of the act permitted. They are a negative qualification upon the word 'person', and operate to exclude persons so licensed from the class who may not be permitted to drive. There is nothing in the language of the section to suggest that the consent must be directed to the failure of the driver to hold a licence, and the form in which the section is cast indicates the contrary. It is the driving which must not be permitted, that is, unless the driver holds a licence.

The application should be refused.

[**Rich ACJ** and **McTiernan J** delivered separate concurring judgments. Special leave to appeal refused.]

13.30C Sweet v Parsley

[1970] AC 132; [1969] 1 All ER 347
House of Lords

[The appellant was convicted of an offence against s 5(b) of the Dangerous Drugs Act 1965 (UK), which made it an offence for a person to be concerned in the management of any premises used for the smoking of cannabis (marijuana). She was fined £25 and ordered to pay costs. She was the sub-tenant of a farmhouse where she let rooms to tenants who shared the kitchen with her. She later left the farm, coming intermittently to collect the rent and mail. Cannabis was found on the premises. The appellant conceded that the premises had been used for smoking cannabis; the prosecution conceded she did not know they had been so used. The Divisional Court dismissed her appeal, and (having obtained leave) she appealed to the House of Lords.]

Lord Reid: My Lords, a Divisional Court dismissed [the appellant's] appeal, holding that she had been concerned in the management of those premises. The reasons given for holding that she was managing the property were that she was in a position to choose her tenants: that she could put them under as long or as short a tenancy as she desired: and that she could make it a term of any letting that smoking of cannabis was not to take place. All these reasons would apply to every occupier who lets out parts of his house or takes lodgers or paying guests. But this was held to be an absolute offence, following the earlier decision in *Yeandel v Fisher* [1966] 1 QB 440; [1965] 3 All ER 158 (Div Ct).

How has it come about that the Divisional Court has felt bound to reach such an obviously unjust result? It has in effect held that it was carrying out the will of Parliament because Parliament has chosen to make this an absolute offence. And, of course, if Parliament has so chosen the courts must carry out its will, and they cannot be blamed for any unjust consequences. But has Parliament so chosen?

I dealt with this matter at some length in *Warner's* case [1969] 2 AC 256; [1968] 2 All ER 356 (HL). On reconsideration I see no reason to alter anything which I there said. But I think that some amplification is necessary. Our first duty is to consider the words of the Act: if they show a clear intention to create an absolute offence that is an end of the matter. But such cases are very rare. Sometimes the words of the section which creates a particular offence make it clear that *mens rea* is required in one form or another. Such cases are quite frequent. But in a very large number of cases there is no clear indication either way. In such cases there has for centuries been a presumption that Parliament did not intend to make criminals of persons who were in no way blameworthy in what they did. That means that whenever a section is silent to the *mens rea* there is a presumption that, in order to give effect to the will of Parliament, we must read in words appropriate to require *mens rea*.

Where it is contended that an absolute offence has been created, the words of Alderson B, in *Attorney-General v Lockwood* (1842) 9 M & W 378 at 398; 152 ER 160 at 168–9 (Exch), have often been quoted:

> The rule of law, I take it, upon the construction of all statutes, and therefore applicable to the construction of this, is, whether they be penal or remedial, to construe them according to the plain, literal, and grammatical meaning of the words in which they are expressed, unless that construction leads to a plain and clear contradiction of the apparent purpose of the Act, or to some palpable and evident absurdity.

This is perfectly right as a general rule and where there is no legal presumption. But what about the multitude of criminal enactments where the words of the Act simply make it an offence to do certain things but where everyone agrees that there cannot be conviction without proof or *mens rea* in some form? This passage, if applied to the present problem, would mean that there is no need to prove *mens rea* unless it would be 'a plain and clear contradiction of the apparent purpose of the Act' to convict without proof of *mens rea*. But that would be putting the presumption the wrong way round: for it is firmly established by a host of authorities that *mens rea* is an essential ingredient of every offence unless some reason can be found for holding that that is not necessary.

It is also firmly established that the fact that other sections of the Act expressly require *mens rea*, for example because they contain the word 'knowingly', is not in itself sufficient to justify a decision that a section which is silent as to *mens rea* created an absolute offence. In the absence of a clear indication in the Act that an offence is intended to be an absolute offence, it is necessary to go outside the Act and examine all relevant circumstances in order to establish that this must have been the intention of Parliament. I say 'must have been' because it is a universal principle that if a penal provision is reasonably capable of two interpretations, that interpretation which is most favourable to the accused must be adopted.

What, then, are the circumstances which it is proper to take into account? In the well known case of *Sherras v De Rutzen* [1895] 1 QB 918; [1895–99] All ER Rep 1167 (Div Ct), Wright J only mentioned the subject matter with which the Act deals. But he was there dealing with something which was one of a class of acts which 'are not criminal in any real sense, but are acts which in the public interest are prohibited under a penalty' ([1895] 1 QB at 922; [1895–99] All ER Rep at 1169). It does not in the least follow that when one is dealing with a truly criminal act it is sufficient merely to have regard to the subject matter of the enactment. One must put oneself in a position of a legislator. It has long been the practice to recognise absolute offences in this class of quasi-criminal acts, and one can safely assume that, when Parliament is passing new legislation dealing with this class of offences, its silence as to *mens rea* means that the old practice is to apply. But when one comes to acts of a truly criminal character, it appears to me that there are at least two other factors which any reasonable legislator would have in mind. In the first place a stigma still attaches to any person convicted of a truly criminal offence, and the more serious or more disgraceful the offence the greater the stigma. So he would have to consider whether, in a case of this gravity, the public interest really requires that an innocent person should be prevented from proving his innocence in order that fewer guilty men may escape. And equally important is the fact that fortunately the Press in this country are vigilant to expose injustice and every manifestly unjust conviction made known to the public tends to injure the body politic by undermining public confidence in the justice of the law of its administration. But I regret to observe that, in some recent cases where serious offences have been held to be absolute offences, the court has taken into account no more than the wording of the Act and the character and seriousness of the mischief which constitutes the offence.

The choice would be much more difficult if there were no other way open than either *mens rea* in the full sense or an absolute offence; for there are many kinds of case where putting on the prosecutor the full burden of proving *mens rea* creates great difficulties and may lead to many unjust acquittals. But there are at least two other possibilities. Parliament has not infrequently transferred the onus as regards *mens rea* to the accused, so that, once the necessary facts are proved, he must convince the jury that on balance of probabilities he is innocent of any criminal intention. I find it a little surprising that more use has not been made of this method: but one of the bad effects of the decision of this House in *Woolmington v Director of Public Prosecutions* [1935] AC 462; [1935] All ER Rep 1, may have been to discourage its use. The other method would be in effect to substitute in appropriate classes of cases gross negligence for *mens rea* in the full sense as the mental element necessary to constitute the crime. It would often be much easier to infer that Parliament must have meant that gross negligence should be the necessary mental element than to infer that Parliament intended to create an absolute offence. A variant of this would be to accept the view of Cave J, in *R v Tolson* (1889) 23 QBD 168 at 181; [1886–90] All ER Rep 26 at 34 (CCR). This appears to have been done in Australia where authority appears to support what Dixon J said in *Proudman v Dayman* (1941) 67 CLR 536 at 540; [1944] ALR at 65:

> As a general rule an honest and reasonable belief in a state of facts which, if they existed, would make the defendant's act innocent affords an excuse for doing what would otherwise be an offence.

It may be that none of these methods is wholly satisfactory but at least the public scandal of convicting on a serious charge persons who are in no way blameworthy would be avoided.

If this section means what the Divisional Court have held that it means, then hundreds of thousands of people who sublet part of their premises or take in lodgers or are concerned in the management of residential premises or institutions are daily incurring a risk of being convicted of a serious offence in circumstances where they are in no way to blame. For the greatest vigilance cannot prevent tenants, lodgers or inmates or guests whom they bring in from smoking cannabis cigarettes in their own rooms. It was suggested in argument that this appellant brought this conviction on herself because it is found as a fact that when the police searched the premises there were people there of the 'beatnik fraternity'. But surely it would be going a very long way to say that persons managing premises of any kind ought to safeguard themselves by refusing accommodation to all who are of slovenly or exotic appearance, or who bring in guests of that kind. And unfortunately, drug taking is by no means confined to those of unusual appearance.

Speaking from a rather long experience of membership of both Houses, I assert with confidence that no Parliament within my recollection would have agreed to make an offence of this kind an absolute offence if the matter had been fully explained to it. So, if the court ought only to hold an offence to be absolute offence where it appears that that must have been the intention of Parliament, offences of this kind are very far removed from those which it is proper to hold to be absolute offences.

I must now turn to the question what is the true meaning of s 5 of the 1965 Act. It provides:

> If a person — (a) being the occupier of any premises, permits those premises to be used for the purpose of smoking cannabis or cannabis resin or of dealing in cannabis or cannabis resin (whether by sale or otherwise); or (b) is concerned in the management of any premises used for any such purpose as aforesaid; he shall be guilty of an offence against this Act.

We are particularly concerned with para (b), and the first question is what is meant by 'used for any such purpose'. Is the 'purpose' the purpose of the smoker or the purpose of the management? When in *Warner's* case, supra, I dealt briefly with *Yeandel's* case, supra, I thought it was the purpose of the smoker, but fuller argument in the present case brought out that an identical provision occurs in s 8(d) which deals with opium. This latter provision has been carried on from the Dangerous Drugs Act 1920, and has obviously been copied into the later legislation relating to cannabis. It would require strong reasons — and there are none — to justify giving this provision a new meaning in s 5 different from that which it had in the 1920 Act and now has in s 8 of the 1965 Act. I think that in s 8 it is clear that the purpose is the purpose of the management. The first purpose mentioned is the purpose of the preparation of opium for smoking which can only be a purpose of the management. I believe that opium cannot be smoked casually anywhere at any time as can a cannabis cigarette. The section is dealing with 'opium dens' and the like when the use of opium is the main purpose for which the premises are used. But it is a somewhat strained use of language to say that an ordinary room in a house is 'used for the purpose' of smoking cannabis when all that happens is that some visitor lights a cannabis cigarette there. Looking to the origin and context of this provision, I have come to the conclusion that it cannot be given this wide meaning. No doubt this greatly reduces the scope of this provision when applied to the use of cannabis. But that is apt to happen when a draftsman simply copies an existing provision without regard to the different circumstances in which it is to operate. So, if the purpose is the purpose of the management, the question whether the offence with regard to opium in 1920, and now with regard to cannabis, is absolute can hardly arise. It could only arise if, although the manager not only knew about cannabis smoking and conducted the premises for that purpose, some person concerned in the management had no knowledge of that. One would first have to decide whether a person who is not actually assisting in the management can be regarded as being 'concerned in the management', although ignorant of the purpose for which the manager was using the premises. Even if such a person could be regarded as 'concerned in the management', I am of opinion that, for the reasons which I have given, he could not be convicted without proof of *mens rea*.

I would allow the appeal and quash the appellant's conviction.

Lord Pearce: My Lords, the prosecution contend that any person who is concerned in the management of premises where cannabis is in fact smoked even once, is liable, though he had no knowledge and no guilty mind. This is, they argue, a practical Act intended to prevent a practical evil. Only by convicting some innocents along with the guilty can sufficient pressure be put upon those who make their living by being concerned in the management of premises. Only thus can they be made alert to prevent cannabis being smoked there. And if the prosecution have to prove knowledge of *mens rea*, many prosecutions will fail and many of the guilty will escape. I find that argument wholly unacceptable.

The notion that some guilty mind is a constituent part of crime and punishment goes back far beyond our common law. And at common law *mens rea* is a necessary element in a crime. Since the Industrial Revolution the increasing complexity of life called into being new duties and crimes which took no account of intent. Those who undertake various industrial and other activities, especially where these affect the life and health of the citizen, may find themselves liable to statutory punishment regardless of knowledge or intent, both in respect of their own acts or neglect and those of their servants. But one must remember that normally *mens rea* is still an ingredient of any offence. Before the court will dispense with the necessity for *mens rea* it has to be satisfied that Parliament so intended. The mere absence of the word 'knowingly' is not enough. But the nature of the crime, the punishment, the absence of social obloquy, the particular mischief and the field of activity in which it occurs, and the wording of the particular section and its context, may show that Parliament intended that the act should be prevented by punishment regardless of intent or knowledge.

Viewing the matter on these principles, it is not possible to accept the prosecution's contention. Even granted that this were in the public health class of case, such as, for instance, are offences created to ensure that food shall be clean, it would be quite unreasonable. It is one thing to make a man absolutely responsible for all his own acts and even vicariously liable for his servants if he engages in a certain type of activity. But it is quite another matter to make him liable for persons over whom he has no control.

The innocent hotel keeper, the lady who keeps lodgings or takes paying guests, the manager of a cinema, the warden of a hostel, the matron of a hospital, the house-master and matron of a boarding school, all these, it is conceded, are, on the prosecution's argument, liable to conviction the moment that irresponsible occupants smoke cannabis cigarettes. And for what purpose is this harsh imposition laid on their backs? No vigilance by night or day can make them safe. The most that vigilance can attain is advance knowledge of their own guilt. If a smell of cannabis comes from a sitting-room, they know that they have committed the offence. Should they then go at once to the police and confess their guilt in the hope that they will not be prosecuted? They may think it easier to conceal the matter in the hope that it may never be found out. For if, though morally innocent, they are prosecuted they may lose their livelihood, since thereafter, even though not punished, they are objects of suspicion. I see no real, useful object achieved by such hardship to the innocent. And so wide a possibility of injustice to the innocent could not be justified by any benefit achieved in the determent and punishment of the guilty. If, therefore, the words creating the offence are as wide in their application as the prosecution contend, Parliament cannot have intended an offence to which absence of knowledge or *mens rea* is no defence.

Parliament might, of course, have taken what was conceded in argument to be a fair and sensible course. It could have said, in appropriate words, that a person is to be liable unless he proves that he had no knowledge or guilty mind. Admittedly, if the prosecution have to prove a defendant's knowledge beyond reasonable doubt, it may be easy for the guilty to escape. But it would be very much harder for the guilty to escape if the burden of disproving *mens rea* or knowledge is thrown on the defendant. And if that were done, innocent people could satisfy a jury of their innocence on a balance of probabilities. It has been said that a jury might be confused by the different nature of the onus of satisfying 'beyond reasonable doubt' which the prosecution have to discharge and the onus 'on a balance of probabilities' which lies on a defendant in proving that he had no knowledge or guilt. I do not believe that this would be so in this kind of case. Most people can easily understand rules that express in greater detail that which their own hearts and minds already feel to be fair and sensible. What they find hard to understand is rules that go 'against the grain' of their own common sense. If a judge on a drug case, feeling disheartened, perhaps, after a close study of *Warner's* case [1969] 2 AC 256; [1968] 2 All ER 356 (HL), had given the jury no direction as to the law, and had simply said that they must consider the facts and do their best with the charge, I believe that they would evolve their duty in some such form as this: 'First, I suppose, we must make sure that there really was drug smoking on the premises' (or 'that he *really* had drugs on him' or whatever the charge may be) 'and then it is up to the defendant to persuade us that he did not know, or was not guilty for some other good reason'. If I am right in this surmise any judicial elaboration of their own instinctive reactions would be quite easy for them to understand.

If it were possible in some so-called absolute offence to take this sensible half-way house, I think that the courts should do so. This has been referred to in *Warner's* case, supra. I see no difficulty in it apart from the opinion of Viscount Sankey LC, in *Woolmington v Director of Public Prosecutions* [1935] AC 462; [1935] All ER Rep 1 (HL). But so long as the full width of that opinion is maintained, I see difficulty. There are many cases where the width of that opinion has caused awkward problems. But before reducing that width your Lordships would obviously have to consider all the aspects of so far-reaching a problem. In the present case Miss Heilbron was wisely loth to involve herself in this when she had easier and surer paths to pursue.

The Australian High Court, rounding on Cave J, and Wills J, in *R v Tolson* (1889) 23 QBD 168 at 175, 181; [1886–90] All ER Rep 26 at 30, 34 (CCR), have evolved a defence of reasonable mistake of fact, and the burden of proving this on a balance of probabilities rests upon the defendant. The whole matter is discussed in an interesting article, 'Strict Responsibility in the High Court of Australia', by Professor Colin Howard in (1960) 76 *LQR* 547. He concludes at 566:

> Where a statutory prohibition is cast in terms which at first sight appear to impose strict responsibility, they should be understood merely as imposing responsibility for negligence but emphasising that the burden of rebutting negligence by affirmative proof of reasonable mistake rests upon the defendant.

He cites *Maher v Musson* (1934) 25 CLR 100 at 105; [1935] ALR 80 at 81, per Dixon J, and per Evatt and McTiernan JJ, (at (CLR) 108; (ALR) 82): *Sherras v De Rutzen* [1895] 1 QB 918 at 921; [1895–99] All ER Rep 1167 at 1169 (Div Ct), per Day J. That decision was before *Woolmington's* case, supra. In *Thomas v R* (1937) 59 CLR 279; [1938] ALR 37 (1937), the matter was further discussed, but I see no reference to *Woolmington's* case, supra. I should be happy to be persuaded either that it does not prevent us from adopting such a satisfactory concept as the Australian courts have evolved or that its wide effect should be limited. But it has not been necessary for the purposes of the present case to go fully into that aspect of the matter.

Although the subsection cannot constitute an absolute offence in the wide application for which the prosecution contend, it does not follow that on a narrower construction it may not constitute an absolute offence. By the term 'absolute' I mean an offence to which the normal assumption of *mens rea* does not apply, but in which the actual words of the offence (without any additional implication of *mens rea*) may well import some degree of knowledge, as, for example, the word 'possession' as in *Warner's* case, supra. In saying that the section relating to possession (which was there under discussion) was absolute, I was using it (as the context was intended to show) in that loose and convenient sense which had been used in the argument.

The history of the subsection and the words themselves lend strong support to the view that a narrow meaning was intended. In the Dangerous Drugs Act 1920, s 4(c) and (d), identical words are used save that the 'purpose' there was 'the preparation of opium for smoking or the sale or smoking of prepared opium' instead of 'the purpose of smoking cannabis or cannabis resin or of dealing in cannabis or cannabis resin whether by sale or otherwise'. Section 4 of the 1920 Act was in fact re-enacted in s 8 of the 1965 Act now under consideration. The words thus taken from the 1920 Act cannot have a different sense when used in the 1965 Act, especially when they are re-enacted in another part of the 1965 Act itself. Any guide provided by their context in 1920 can, therefore, be useful in deciding their meaning in 1965, when applied to cannabis smoking. The prosecution point out that opium smoking needs more paraphernalia and preparation (in what are sometimes called 'opium dens') and that considerations applicable to them are out of place in dealing with cannabis, which may be smoked casually and without preparation. Anyone may carry a cannabis cigarette and light it in the normal places and in normal circumstances of life. But that very fact makes it the more unlikely that responsibility for such casual acts of invitees or licensees should fall on those who manage premises unless they are managing them for just such a purpose.

The whole context and content of the original s 5 of the 1920 Act show that it was considering premises one of whose 'purposes' was opium smoking. The 'purpose' there referred to is thus the purpose of the management or a purpose known to or acquiesced in by them. I think that the words which were lifted from that section and enacted in relation to cannabis in s 5 of the Dangerous Drugs Act 1965 must be given a similar narrow construction. There was no need to insert the word 'purpose', if all that was intended was premises where cannabis is in fact smoked. Being concerned in the management of premises used for the purpose of smoking cannabis necessarily imports some knowledge of the use of the premises for the purpose. Admittedly Miss Sweet had no knowledge.

I appreciate that this limitation will, as the prosecution contend, rob the section of much of its force. If a wider application or efficiency were desired it could be achieved by a change of onus and a consideration of what exactly is being required of landladies and the like. They cannot reasonably be branded with guilt whenever there happens to be on their premises someone who without their knowledge or assent smokes cannabis.

I would allow the appeal.

[**Lord Morris**, **Lord Diplock** and **Lord Wilberforce** delivered separate judgments in which they agreed in allowing the appeal.]

13.31C

Mayer v Marchant

(1973) 5 SASR 567

Supreme Court of South Australia

[The respondent was charged with being the owner of a vehicle driven on a road without complying with the requirements of ss 145–149 of the Road Traffic Act 1961 (SA), in that the weight on the axles of the vehicle in question exceeded the permitted weight of 32 tons. The vehicle was driven on a road by one of the respondent's employees with a load of 6410 gallons of distillate weighing 33 tons. The vehicle had previously carried 6400 gallons of distillate, and on such occasions it had been found that the weight had sometimes been slightly over, and sometimes slightly under, the permitted weight. No action had been taken by the relevant authorities about any excessive weight. On the occasion which gave rise to the charge, the extra weight was caused by a variation in the density of the distillate. The driver of the vehicle was unaware of this variation in density, and assumed that the distillate would be of the usual density and that any excess weight would, as on previous occasions, only amount to two or three hundredweight.

The appeal from the dismissal by the magistrate was referred to the Full Court of the Supreme Court by a single Justice of the Supreme Court.]

Bray CJ: In *Kain & Shelton Pty Ltd v McDonald* (1971) 1 SASR 39, we held that it was not necessary for the prosecution to prove *mens rea* in a charge of an offence against s 144 of the *Road Traffic Act 1961–1972* (as amended by s 26 of the amending Act of 1969). We left open the question of the availability of certain defences to such a charge. It is now necessary to consider some of those matters.

In general I adhere to the views I expressed in *Kain & Shelton's* case. Two possible defences arise in this case: the defence of honest and reasonable mistake of fact, commonly called the *Proudman v Dayman* defence (*Proudman v Dayman* (1941) 67 CLR 536), and the defence of what is sometimes, though, I think, imprecisely, called act of a stranger, commonly called in this state the *Snell v Ryan* defence (*Snell v Ryan* [1951] SASR 59).

I agree that the first defence is not open here on the facts, even if all arguable points of law are resolved in the respondent's favour. The defence has been variously expressed. For the present purpose I am content to adopt the formula of Cave J in *R v Tolson* (1889) 23 QBD 168 at 181, 'an honest and reasonable belief in the existence of circumstances which, if true, would make the act for which the prisoner is indicted an innocent act'. Here the respondent did not have a belief in circumstances which, if true, would make the act an innocent act. He believed, and probably on reasonable grounds, that if the load exceeded the statutory 32 tons by one, two or three hundredweight the authorities would take no action. Assume he had that belief on this occasion. Still that is not a belief in the existence of circumstances which, if true, would make the act innocent: it is only a belief in the existence of circumstances which, if true, would make the act one that could be committed with impunity. It relates to factual immunity, not legal immunity. Like Zelling J, I cannot agree with the learned Special Magistrate that it was a fair inference that the complaisance with which the authorities were prepared to regard an overload of two or three hundredweight was due to the possibility of error in the weighbridge. The *Weights and Measures Act 1971*, and the regulations thereunder, which were referred to before us, make it clear that the allowable tolerance for the possibility of error on a load of this size was only about 32 pounds at the most, far short of two or three hundredweight.

It is not, therefore, strictly necessary to say anything about the availability of the defence in law. But since the matter has been canvassed I desire to make some comments.

I think that the defence is open on a charge of a breach of s 144 notwithstanding that the offence is a so-called status offence, ie that as far as verbal form goes, what is penalised is the connection of the defendant with a vehicle in a certain condition in certain circumstances, not any act or omission of his. I adhere to what I said about status offences in *Kain & Shelton's* case (1971) 1 SASR 39. Such a statutory wording has been held to foreclose all inquiry into the state of the defendant's mind: *Maher v Musson* (1934) 52 CLR 100; *Bond v Foran* (1934) 52 CLR 364 per Rich J at 369. In truth it is a mistake to segregate 'mistake' from other general defences to criminal charges. I will cite again from Cave J in *Tolson's* case (1889) 23 QBD 168 at 181:

> Honest and reasonable mistake stands in fact on the same footing as absence of the reasoning faculty, as in infancy, or perversion of that faculty, as in lunacy

> ... So far as I am aware it has never been suggested that these exceptions do not equally apply in the case of statutory offences unless they are excluded expressly or by necessary implication.

See also *Handmer v Taylor* [1971] VR 308. Of course, Parliament can exclude the defence expressly and no doubt it can also exclude it impliedly, but, as I said in *Kain & Shelton's* case (1971) 1 SASR 39, when Parliament has not seen fit to make any express exclusion I would be very loath to draw any such implication, except in unusual circumstances. I see no reason to draw any such general inference with regard to the Road Traffic Act as a whole, or with regard to s 144 in particular, by reason of the specific reference to particular defences to charges under particular sections in the various parts of the Act to which we have been referred.

I agree that where the defence is applicable it is sufficient if there is a general belief in a general proposition covering the relevant circumstances, such as that a certain number of gallons of distillate loaded on to a vehicle of a certain type will produce a load of a certain weight, and that it is not necessary that there should be conscious advertence to each practical application of that proposition, such as that a particular vehicle on a particular day at a particular stage of its journey carried a particular load. To require this would, I think be to deprive the defence of practical effect in a case like the present.

I think that before this defence falls to be considered by a court in any particular case, the defendant has to discharge an evidential onus by pointing to some evidence, either in his case or that of the prosecution, sufficient to raise it. Once that is done I think that the ultimate onus of negativing it passes to the Crown. To put it another way, it is sufficient for the defence to raise a reasonable doubt about the proposition. Again, this is only to put the defence into the same class as other general defences, such as provocation, self-defence and the like. I know that eminent authorities have taken the contrary view, but it seems to me that the weight of judicial opinion is now in favour of the proposition as I have stated it. It was indeed mooted as a possibility by Dixon J, as he then was, in *Proudman v Dayman* (1941) 67 CLR 536 itself. The learned judge said, at 541:

> The burden of establishing honest and reasonable mistake is in the first place on the defendant and he must make it appear that he had reasonable grounds for believing in the existence of a state of facts, which, if true, would take his act outside the operation of the enactment and that on those grounds he did so believe. The burden possibly may not finally rest upon him of satisfying the tribunal in case of doubt.

The implications of *Woolmington's* case [1935] AC 462 have only gradually been recognised, not, on occasions, without disquiet at their width; see, for example, *Sweet v Parsley* [1970] AC 132, per Lord Pearce at 158. Once they are, it must, in my view, be accepted that the ultimate onus is always on the Crown, except in the case of insanity or where the onus is shifted by statute, and it does not matter whether the offence is the creature of common law or of statute. There is a wide range of authority to this effect both generally: *R v Spurge* [1961] 2 QB 205 at 210; *Burns v Bidder* [1966] 3 All ER 29; *Stokes v Samuels* (1973) 5 SASR 18; and with specific reference to the defence of mistake: *Geraldton Fisherman's Co-operative Ltd v Munro* [1963] WAR 129 at 134–5 (it is true that this was a case under the Western Australian Criminal Code, but I do not think that is a material distinction); *R v Strawbridge* [1970] NZLR 909; *Kidd v Reeves* [1972] VR 563; *Sweet v Parsley* [1970] AC 312, per Lord Diplock at 164. This was also the view of Chamberlain J in *Norcock v Bowey* [1966] SASR 250 at 257, and, with respect, I agree. The argument to the contrary, it seems to me, is largely based on considerations of policy, because, it is said, the facts in most cases are peculiarly within the knowledge of the defendant (see Howard, *Strict Responsibility* (1963) pp 40–3), but with respect to those who take this view, I think there are two answers to that. One is that those policy considerations are largely answered by leaving the evidential onus on the defendant, but the stronger answer is, in my view, that the logic of *Woolmington's* case [1935] AC 462 is compelling and I for one would be loath to tarnish the golden thread.

Since drafting these reasons I have had the advantage of reading the reasons for judgment of Hogarth J. It is true that the learned judges of the High Court in *Maher v Musson* (1934) 52 CLR 100 spoke as if, in the case of a statute framed in apparently absolute terms, the onus was on the defendant to prove the defence on the balance of probabilities. But that case was decided before *Woolmington's* case [1935] AC 462, which, I think, has been generally accepted in Australia, with the consequence that pre-existing ideas about the passing of the onus to the defence in criminal cases have been greatly modified and in some respects abandoned. I think that in the passage from *Proudman v Dayman* (1941) 67 CLR 536 at 541 which I have previously cited Dixon J, who was a party to the decision in *Maher v Musson* (1934) 52 CLR 100, was acknowledging this.

I think that we are bound to hold that to make out the defence the belief must be reasonable as well as honest: see *Handmer v Taylor* [1971] VR 308, per McInerney J at 312–15. There is, in my view, a contrast here with *mens rea*. If that is an essential element of the offence, a genuine belief of fact, even if it is also an unreasonable belief, may well exclude it.

I do not think the case raises the question of honest and reasonable ignorance as opposed to honest and reasonable mistake. On this topic I refer to what I said in *Kain & Shelton's* case (1971) 1 SASR 39 at 45; but cf *Gherashe v Boase* [1959] ALR 218. The respondent clearly enough had a belief about the weights of loads of distillate on his vehicle, even though it was a general belief and he may not have adverted to this particular load.

It is not correct, with respect to those who hold the contrary view, to say that to allow the defence of mistake with the ultimate onus of proof on the prosecution, while holding that the statute has excluded *mens rea* as an element in the case to be established by the prosecution, is to let in through the back door what you shut out by the front door. There are real differences. One is that, in my view, an honest belief may exclude *mens rea*, but to establish the defence as the authorities now stand the mistake must be reasonable as well as honest. Another, and perhaps more important, answer is that the exclusion of *mens rea* dispenses the prosecution from having to prove the mental state of the defendant as part of its own case, and that means that, except in the unusual event of material sufficient to raise the defence of mistake appearing from the evidence of the prosecution, a submission that there is no case to answer at the end of the prosecution case on any ground connected with the defendant's mental state will seldom succeed.

However, for the reasons I have given, I do not think that the defence of mistake arises here. I turn now to the defence that the overloading was due to the act of a stranger, namely, the supplier of the distillate. This type of defence was recognised by Napier CJ in *Snell v Ryan* [1951] SASR 59 and by the Full Court in *Norcock v Bowey* [1966] SASR 250, and I think it applies to this charge. It remains, however, to decide its definition and scope. In *Snell v Ryan* Napier CJ referred to what was said by Griffith CJ in *Hardgrave v R* (1906) 4 CLR 232 at 237. There the learned Chief Justice said:

> The general rule is that a person is not criminally responsible for an act which is done independently of the exercise of his will or by accident. It is also a general rule that a person who does an act under a reasonable misapprehension of fact is not criminally responsible for it even if the facts which he believed did not exist. I do not think the first rule has ever been excluded by any statute.

It is quite true, as pointed out by Chamberlain J in *Norcock v Bowey* [1966] SASR 250 at 255, that *Hardgrave v R* was a case of an indictable offence. But the important consideration for the present purpose, as I see it, is that in that citation the defence in question is advanced as a general defence to criminal charges and one sharply separated from the defence of mistake, and I think that whenever that defence applies to a statutory offence then *a fortiori* the former defence does too and it may well apply even if mistake is excluded. Of course in most cases the question will not arise because the offence is usually defined in terms which preclude any argument that the defendant is liable for acts which occur independently of his will.

Sir Samuel Griffith's remarks about accident are not, of course, to be construed as excluding in an appropriate case criminal liability for negligence. But there is nothing to indicate that an act done independently of the will of the defendant by a stranger must be wrongful on the stranger's part in order to be of avail. On the other hand, there may, no doubt, be statutory offences where the defendant is expected by the legislature to foresee the possible intervention of other people and guard against its consequences. I cannot agree that the wrongful nature of the intervention is a necessary criterion for the establishment of the defence. *Snell v Ryan* [1951] SASR 59 was a case of a charge against s 46 of the *Impounding Act 1920–47*, which provided that if any cattle were found straying in a street or public place the owner should be liable to a penalty. The cow had got out on to the road as a result of the gate being left open by a trespassing stranger. If in that case the cow had escaped on to the road through a gate left open, not by a trespassing stranger but by an official inspector of the property with a legal right to enter, I do not think the result would have been different, at least if the defendant had no reason to foresee or guard against the visit or the leaving open of the gate. On the other hand, if the gate had been left open by a departing visitor and the defendant had neglected to tell him to shut it behind him, the result might have been different. And, like Walters J in *Norcock v Bowey* [1966] SASR 250 at 269, I think that events independent of any human activity, such, for instance, as were in a more reverend age classified as acts of God, stand on the same footing as acts of a stranger.

I would prefer to formulate the proposition in this way: that normally speaking it is a defence to a criminal charge, whether under the provisions of the common law or of any statute, to show that the forbidden act occurred as the result of an act of a stranger, or as the result of non-human activity, over which the defendant had no control and against which he could not reasonably have been expected to guard. This proposition, of course, has nothing to say to the question of vicarious liability which, in appropriate cases, it may well have been the intention of the legislature to impose.

The onus of proof of this defence is, in my view, exactly the same as in the case of mistake or any other general defence. The onus is on the defendant to point to some evidence capable of raising it. Once that has happened the ultimate onus is on the prosecution to exclude it so that a reasonable doubt as to its existence will result in an acquittal. I refer to what I have already said on this matter.

The remaining question is whether the evidence here is capable of raising the defence. I have hesitated about this. But the learned Special Magistrate has found that the density of the distillate on this occasion was unusually high and not reasonably to be anticipated. As I read the evidence of the driver Duncan, he went to the BP depot on the day in question and got the slip, Exhibit D 2, which simply refers to 6400 gallons for OTC, ie Overseas Telecommunications Centre. Armed with that he filled up the tanker himself. There was nothing, as I see it, to indicate to him that unusually heavy distillate would be supplied. I think the supply without notice of unusually heavy distillate when distillate of normal density was expected would be the unauthorised act of a stranger over which the respondent had no control and against which, prima facie at any rate, he could not reasonably be expected to guard. To supply without warning to a purchaser a product different from that impliedly ordered, the difference not being detectable by him, seems to me to be the positive act of a stranger for the present purpose, if it was the cause of the commission of the forbidden act, and not merely a circumstance inducing a mistaken belief. But I have had some doubt as to whether it was solely the supply of unusually heavy distillate which made the load overweight, or whether it would not still have been overweight with fuel of ordinary density, albeit to a much lesser extent. But Zelling J has analysed the evidence about this and I am content to abide by his conclusions.

The only other matter to which I desire to refer is the passage from the judgment of Evatt and McTiernan JJ in *Maher v Musson* (1934) 52 CLR 100 at 109, set out by me in *Kain & Shelton's* case (1971) 1 SASR 39 at 45–6, and referred to by the learned Special Magistrate. That passage could be used to support the existence of a defence of honest and reasonable ignorance of fact as opposed to honest and reasonable mistake. It may be that such a defence exists. It may be, on the other hand, that the only two relevant defences are honest and reasonable mistake and act of a stranger. It is fortunately not necessary to canvass that now.

[**Zelling J** delivered a separate judgment agreeing with the views of **Bray CJ**. **Hogarth J** dissented. Appeal by the complainant dismissed.]

13.32C B (a minor) v Director of Public Prosecutions

[2000] 1 All ER 833; 2 WLR 452
House of Lords

[B, aged 15, asked V, a girl aged 13, to perform oral sex on him. She repeatedly refused. B was charged with inciting a girl under the age of 14 to commit an act of gross indecency with him, contrary to s 1(1) of the Indecency with Children Act 1960 (UK). B pleaded not guilty; it was accepted that he honestly believed V was over 14 years old. B changed his plea to guilty when told his belief did not constitute a defence to the charges. B's appeal to the Divisional Court of the Queen's Bench Division was dismissed.]

Lord Steyn: My Lords, the first certified question is whether a defendant is entitled to be acquitted of the offence of inciting a child under 14 to commit an act of gross indecency, contrary to s 1(1) of the Indecency with Children Act 1960, if he holds or may hold an honest belief that the child was 14 years or over. In other words, the question of statutory interpretation before the House is whether *mens rea* is an ingredient of the offence or whether the subsection creates an offence of strict liability.

...

The genesis of s 1(1) of the 1960 Act

Before the enactment of the 1960 Act there was already in existence a relatively comprehensive statute, the Sexual Offences Act 1956, which served to protect young children against sexual exploitation. In particular the Act of 1956 contained provisions making it an offence to commit an indecent assault on a man or a woman: ss 14 and 15. The statute provided that girls and boys under 16 cannot in law give consent which would prevent the act being an assault. These provisions were effective so far as they went but decided cases revealed a gap in the protective net of the 1956 Act: *Fairclough v Whipp* [1951] 2 All ER 834 and *Director of Public Prosecutions v Rogers* [1953] 2 All ER 644, [1953] 1 WLR 1017. The statute made no provision for cases where an adult invited a child to touch or handle him indecently: in such cases there was sometimes no ingredient of assault which could trigger the indecent assault provisions of the 1956 Act, namely ss 14 and 15. In 1959 the Home Secretary invited the Criminal Law Revision Committee to consider the point and to make recommendations for an amendment of the law. The committee produced a clear and succinct report dated 18 June 1959: *First Report (Indecency with Children)* (Cmnd 835). The committee cautioned itself against recommending too broad a provision, instead it concentrated on the gap in the 1956 Act. It considered the appropriate age limit. The committee recommended the creation of an entirely new offence in respect of acts of gross indecency towards children under the age of 14. The committee annexed a draft bill to its report. Clause 1(1) of the draft bill was in due course enacted as s 1(1) of the 1960 Act. There is no discussion in the report of the question whether the proposed new offence would be one of strict liability or not.

Section 1(1)

The long title of the 1960 Act describes it as an Act 'to make further provision for the punishment of indecent conduct towards young children'. Section 1(1) provides:

> Any person who commits an act of gross indecency with or towards a child under the age of fourteen, or who incites a child under that age to such an act with him or another, shall be liable on conviction on indictment to imprisonment for a term not exceeding two years, or on summary conviction to imprisonment for a term not exceeding six months, to a fine not exceeding [the prescribed sum], or to both.

Section 1(1) creates an age-based offence. It is of the essence of the offence that the child is under the age of 14 years. The offence is an exception to the general law which does not make it an offence to commit or to incite another to commit an act of indecency or gross indecency. The only criminalisation of acts of gross indecency in the 1956 Act is to be found in s 13 which makes acts of indecency between men an offence. This is, however, not an age-based offence. It is common ground that this link between the two Acts is neutral and throws no light on the problem before the House.

The 1956 Act

In the Divisional Court ([1998] 4 All ER 265 at 270, [1999] 3 WLR 116 at 122D) Rougier J described the 1960 Act as an appendix to the 1956 Act and I would adopt this description. At the hearing of the appeal to the House counsel for the appellant demonstrated how the 1956 Act consists of a collection of disparate offences deriving from diverse earlier enactments. Leaving to one side procedural provisions in the 1956 Act regarding the powers and procedure for dealing with offences and powers of arrest and search, and concentrating on the substantive provisions, the immediate precursors of the present-day offences are to be found in legislation dating from 1861, 1885, 1889, 1912, 1913, 1922, 1929 and 1933. And the precursors of some of the sexual offences in the Offences against the Person Act 1861 go back to medieval times. The Crown accepts that it would be wrong to describe the 1956 Act as the product of a legislative initiative designed to devise a more rational system. It would be more accurate to describe it as the bringing together in one statute of a range of offences pragmatically created at different times in response, no doubt, to the perceived demands of public interest at the time. But, as counsel for the Crown pointed out, there is nevertheless a strong theme running through the various provisions of the Act of 1956, namely the protection of young children from sexual depredations.

For present purposes it is unnecessary to review all the detailed substantive provisions of the 1956 Act. But three matters need to be mentioned. First, ss 5 and 6 create a 'pair' of offences, namely offences of having sexual intercourse with girls under 13 (s 5) and with girls under 16 (s 6). Under s 6(3) there is a so-called 'young man's defence'. That is a defence available to men under the age of 24, who have not previously been charged with a like offence, who act in the belief that the girl is of the age of 16 or over and have reasonable cause for such a view. This defence is not available upon a charge under s 5 which plainly, creates an offence of strict liability. Secondly, in the statement of facts and issues and in oral argument counsel described ss 14 and 15 of the 1956 Act as for present purposes the most relevant comparators in the 1956 Act. They provide:

> 14(1) It is an offence, subject to the exception mentioned in subsection (3) of this section, for a person to make an indecent assault on a woman.

(2) A girl under the age of sixteen cannot in law give any consent which would prevent an act being an assault for the purposes of this section.

(3) Where a marriage is invalid under section two of the Marriage Act 1949, or section one of the Age of Marriage Act 1929, (the wife being a girl under the age of sixteen), the invalidity does not make the husband guilty of any offence under this section by reason of her incapacity to consent while under that age, if he believes her to be his wife and has reasonable cause for the belief.

(4) A woman who is a defective cannot in law give any consent which would prevent an act being an assault for the purposes of this section, but a person is only to be treated as guilty of an indecent assault on a defective by reason of that incapacity to consent, if that person knew or had reason to suspect her to be a defective.

15(1) It is an offence for a person to make an indecent assault on a man.

(2) A boy under the age of sixteen cannot in law give any consent which would prevent an act being an assault for the purposes of this section.

(3) A man who is a defective cannot in law give any consent which would prevent an act being an assault for the purposes of this section, but a person is only to be treated as guilty of an indecent assault on a defective by reason of that incapacity to consent, if that person knew or had reason to suspect him to be a defective.

(4) Section thirty-nine of this Act (which relates to the competence as a witness of the wife or husband of the accused) does not apply in the case of this section, except on a charge of indecent assault on a boy under the age of seventeen.

(5) For the purposes of the last foregoing subsection a person shall be presumed, unless the contrary is proved, to have been under the age of seventeen at the time of the offence charged if he is stated in the charge or indictment, and appears to the court, to have been so.

It has been held that it is no defence on charges under ss 14 and 15 that the defendant believed the girl or boy to be over 16 and to be consenting: *R v Forde* [1923] 2 KB 400 and *R v Maughan* (1934) 24 Cr App R 130. Counsel for the appellant challenged the correctness of these decisions. The third point is a more general one. Counsel for the Crown submitted that a study of the 1956 Act reveals a general legislative policy to protect young children under the age of 16 years from sexual abuse. This proposition is uncontroversial: the legislative policy described by counsel is evidenced by numerous provisions of the 1956 Act. In these circumstances it is unnecessary to refer to other provisions of the 1956 Act.

The correct approach

My Lords, it will be convenient to turn to the approach to be adopted to the construction of s 1(1) of the 1960 Act. While broader considerations will ultimately have to be taken into account, the essential point of departure must be the words of s 1(1). The language, is general and nothing on the face of s 1(1) indicates one way or the other whether s 1(1) creates an offence of strict liability. In enacting such a provision Parliament does not write on a blank sheet. The sovereignty of Parliament is the paramount principle of our constitution. But Parliament legislates against the background of the principle of legality. In *R v Secretary of State for the Home Department; Ex parte Pierson* [1998] AC 539 many illustrations of the application of the principle were given in the speech of Lord Browne-Wilkinson and in my speech: at 573–5, 587–90. Recently, in *R v Secretary of State for the Home Department; Ex parte Simms* [1999] 3 WLR 328 the House applied the principle to subordinate legislation: see in particular the speeches of Lord Hoffmann at 341F–G, myself at 340G–H and Lord Browne-Wilkinson at 330E. In *Ex parte Simms* Lord Hoffmann explained the principle as follows (at 341):

> But the principle of legality means that Parliament must squarely confront what it is doing and accept the political cost. Fundamental rights cannot be overridden by general or ambiguous words. This is because there is too great a risk that the full implications of their unqualified meaning may have passed unnoticed in the democratic process. In the absence of express language or necessary implication to the contrary, the courts therefore presume that even the most general words were intended to be subject to the basic rights of the individual.

This passage admirably captures, if I may say so, the rationale of the principle of legality. In successive editions of his classic work Professor Sir Rupert Cross cited as the paradigm of the principle the 'presumption' that *mens rea* is required in the case of statutory crimes': *Statutory Interpretation*, 3rd ed (1995), p 166. Sir Rupert explained that such presumptions are of general application and are not dependent on finding an ambiguity in the text. He said they:

> ... not only supplement the text, they also operate at a higher level as expressions of fundamental principles governing both civil liberties and the relations between Parliament, the executive and the courts. They operate as constitutional principles which are not easily displaced by a statutory text.

In other words, in the absence of express words or a truly necessary implication, Parliament must be presumed to legislate on the assumption that the principle of legality will supplement the text. This is the theoretical framework against which s 1(1) must be interpreted.

It is now necessary to examine the practical application of the principle as explained by the House in *Sweet v Parsley* [1970] AC 132. The decision is of great importance not for the actual decision but for the clear statement of general principle in the speeches. ... Lord Reid (at 149F) drew a distinction between 'a truly, criminal act' and acts which are not truly criminal in any real sense, but are 'acts which in the public interest are prohibited under a penalty'. He reaffirmed his observations in *Warner v Metropolitan Police Comr* [1969] 2 AC 256 where he gave examples of the latter category of offences. In *Sweet v Parsley* he said (at 150) that in cases of truly criminal acts it is wrong to take into account 'no more than the wording of the Act and the character and seriousness of the mischief which constitutes the offence'. Lord Morris of Borth-y-Gest and Lord Pearce delivered concurring speeches which do not differ in any material way from the approach outlined by Lord Reid. Lord Wilberforce dealt with the case on a narrower basis. Subject to one qualification the speech of Lord Diplock is to the same effect as the speech of Lord Reid. Lord Diplock invoked (at 163):

> ... a general principle of construction of any enactment, which creates a criminal offence that, even where the words used to describe the prohibited conduct would not in any other context connote the necessity for any particular mental element, they are nevertheless to be read as subject to the implication that a necessary element in the offence is the absence of a belief, held honestly *and on reasonable grounds* in the existence of facts which, if true, would make the act innocent (my emphasis).

The qualification is contained in the emphasised words. It is not to be found in the other speeches in *Sweet v Parsley*. It is a point to which I will return later in this judgment. Counsel for the Crown accepted that the approach as outlined in *Sweet v Parsley*, and in particular in the speech of Lord Reid, is an authoritative and accurate statement of the law. It is only necessary to refer to one further decision. In *Lim Chin Aik v R* [1963] AC 160 at 174, the Privy Council observed that in considering how the presumption can be displaced 'it is not enough in their Lordships' opinions merely to label the statute as one dealing with a grave social evil and from that to infer that strict liability was intended'. Their Lordships no doubt had in mind that the prevalence of even a grave social evil does not necessarily throw light on the question of what technique was adopted to combat the evil, viz the creation of an offence of strict liability or an offence of which *mens rea* is an ingredient.

Concentrating still on the wording of s 1(1) of the 1960 Act, I now address directly the question whether the presumption is prima facie applicable. Two distinctive features of s 1(1) must be taken into account. First, the *actus reus* is widely defined. Unlike the position under ss 14 and 15 of the 1956 Act, an assault is not an ingredient of the offence under s 1(1). Any act of gross indecency with or towards a child under the age of 14, or incitement to such an act, whether committed in public or private, is within its scope. The subsection is apt to cover acts of paedophilia and all responsible citizens will welcome effective legislation in respect of such a great social evil. But it also covers any heterosexual or homosexual contact between teenagers if one of them is under 14. And the *actus reus* extends to incitement of a child under 14 — words are enough. The subsection therefore extends to any verbal sexual overtures between teenagers if one of them is under 14. see the telling examples given by Brooke LJ in the instant case [1998] 4 All ER 265 at 277, [1999] 3 WLR 116 at 128H–129C. For the law to criminalise such conduct of teenagers *by offences of strict liability* would be far reaching and controversial. The second factor is that s 1(1) creates an offence of a truly criminal character. It was initially punishable on indictment by a custodial term of up to two years and by subsequent amendment the maximum term has been increased to 10 years' imprisonment. Moreover, as Lord Reid observed in *Sweet v Parsley* [1970] AC 132 at 149, 'a stigma still attaches to any person convicted of a truly criminal offence, and the more serious or disgraceful the offence the greater the stigma'. Taking into account the cumulative effect of these two factors, I am persuaded that, if one concentrates on the language of s 1(1), the presumption is prima facie applicable. It is, however, now necessary to examine weighty contrary arguments based on the broader context in which s 1(1) must be seen. Since counsel for the Crown adopted as part of his argument the reasoning of the Divisional Court, and in particular the reasoning of Rougier J, it is unnecessary to summarise the judgments. Instead I propose to examine directly the major planks of the reasoning contained in the judgments of the Divisional Court and in the submissions of counsel for the Crown. But I would respectfully record my tribute to the careful and elegant judgments in the Divisional Court.

The 1960 and 1956 Acts are a code

Counsel for the Crown submitted that the 1960 and 1956 Acts are a code of sexual offences. He said that the two Acts should be read as one always speaking statute to be interpreted in the world of today: *R v Ireland* [1998] AC 147 at 158D–G. I regard this approach as sound but by itself it constitutes no positive reason in favour of the displacement of the presumption. If the 1956 Act is to impress a particular meaning on the 1960 Act it must be on the basis that its concrete terms provide a consistency of theme.

Counsel for the Crown was faced with the immediate difficulty that the weight to be attached to a comparison of the language of the two statutes is materially diminished by the history of the evolution of the legislation, which I have already described. The point can be illustrated from a citation in *R v Ireland* at 159. The context was an argument based on differences in the wording of ss 18, 20 and 47 of the 1861 Act. Observing that the difference in language was not a significant factor, I quoted in my judgment, which was given with the approval of all members of the Appellate Committee, from the commentary of Greaves, the draftsman, *The Criminal Law Consolidation and Amendment Acts* (2nd ed, 1862, pp 3–4). For convenience I set the passage out:

> If any question should arise in which any comparison may be instituted between sections of any one or several of these Acts, it must be carefully borne in mind in what manner these Acts were framed. None of them was rewritten; on the contrary, each contains enactments taken from different Acts passed at different times and with different views, and frequently varying from each other in phraseology, and ... these enactments, for the most part, stand in these Acts with little or no variation in their phraseology, and, consequently, their differences in that respect will be found generally to remain in these Acts. It follows, therefore, from hence, that any argument as to a difference in the intention of the legislature, which may be drawn from a difference in the terms of one clause from those in another, will be entitled to no weight in the construction of such clauses; for that argument can only apply with force where an Act is framed from beginning to end with one and the same view, and with the intention of making it thoroughly consistent throughout.

This explanation led to the description of the 1861 Act (a precursor of the 1956 Act) as containing 'a rag-bag of offences brought together from a variety of sources with no attempt, as the draftsman frankly acknowledged, to introduce consistency as to substance or as to form': *R v Parmenter* [1992] 1 AC 699 at 752 per Lord Ackner, quoting Professor J C Smith QC [1991] *Crim LR*. 43. Counsel for the Crown accepted that this is an accurate characterisation of the genesis of the 1960 and 1956 Acts read together.

The express provision in the 1956 Act
Adopting the reasoning of Rougier J, counsel for the Crown laid stress on express provisions in the 1956 Act allowing a defence of mistake. The argument is that where the legislature has been silent on mistake the offence must be one of strict liability. Counsel drew attention to the following provisions. Section 6(3) permits a statutory defence for young men who believe on reasonable grounds a girl to be aged 16 or over. Section 7(2) (as substituted by s 127(1)(a) of the Mental Health Act 1959) provides for proof of knowledge in the case of intercourse with an idiot or imbecile. The same applies to procurement of a defective: s 9(2). It also applies to indecent assault on a female defective: s 14(4). Finally, there is such a defence in respect of the offence of permitting a defective to use premises for intercourse: s 27(2). This argument fails to make adequate allowance for the haphazard way in which the 1956 Act evolved. It is not the product of a rational scheme. The appeal to its diverse provisions enacted in response to the felt necessities of different times does not deserve the weight which the Divisional Court and counsel for the Crown put on it. Moreover, it fails to take account of the force of the presumption, and in particular Lord Reid's observation in *Sweet v Parsley* [1970] AC 132 at 149 that it is:

> ... firmly established that the fact that other sections of the Act expressly require *mens rea*, for example because they contain the word 'knowingly', is not in itself sufficient to justify a decision that a section which is silent as to *mens rea* creates an absolute offence.

In my view the express references to knowledge in the 1956 Act do not sufficiently clearly displace the presumption.

Sections 14 and 15 of the 1956 Act
Counsel for the Crown also put forward a narrower but more formidable argument. Section 13 of the 1956 Act, which deals with acts of gross indecency between men, is the closest comparator to s 1(1) of the 1960 Act. But, it does involve an age-based offence. In these circumstances he described ss 14 and 15 as the most significant comparators in the present context. He relied on the fact that it had been held in *R v Forde* [1923] 2 KB 400 and *R v Maughan* (1934) 24 Cr App R 130 that an honest belief that the girl or boy is over 16 is no defence. On that basis he rhetorically asked: why should the same not apply to s 1(1) of the 1960 Act? As I have already pointed out counsel for the appellant challenged the correctness of these decisions. For my part it is not necessary to examine the legal position under ss 14 and 15. While I accept that the matter is finely balanced, I am persuaded that the balance of arguments point to a rejection of this submission. The scope of ss 14 and 15 is markedly narrower than s 1(1) with which this case is concerned. Under ss 14 and 15, an assault is an ingredient of the offence. And an assault necessarily

requires an intentional act: an accidental contact would not be an assault. To that extent at least *mens rea* is an ingredient. By contrast ss (1) does not require an assault. It criminalises a far wider spectrum of acts. And the age of the victim is of the essence of the offence. Absent the age factor, such conduct is not criminal. By contrast any indecent assault has been a crime for centuries. In my view a comparison of the language of ss 14 and 15 and s 1(1) does not point towards the displacement of the presumption. It is not a solid basis for a necessary implication rendering the principle enunciated in *Sweet v Parsley* inapplicable.

The legislative policy of the 1956 Act

Counsel for the Crown next submitted that a necessary implication negativing *mens rea* as an ingredient of the offence is to be found in the general legislative policy of the 1956 Act to protect girls under the age of 16: see ss 5, 6, 14, 15, 26 and 28. It is undoubtedly right that there is a clear legislative policy prohibiting the sexual exploitation of girls. It is unquestionably a great social evil as Lord Hutton has so clearly explained. Whatever can be done sensibly and justly to stamp it out ought to be done. The real question is: what does this policy tell us about the critical question whether s 1(1) is an offence of strict liability or not? It is not enough to label the statute as one dealing with a grave social evil and from that to infer that strict liability was intended: see *Lim Chin Aik v R* [1963] AC 160 at 174. Moreover, upon analysis the argument is far from compelling. It infers from the premise of the legislative policy directed against the mischief a conclusion that the legislature gave clear expression to a choice of the solution of creating an offence of strict liability rather than an offence containing *mens rea* as an ingredient. The cardinal principle of construction described by Lord Reid in *Sweet v Parsley* is not to be displaced by such speculative considerations as to the chosen legislative technique. I would reject this argument.

Prince's case

Counsel for the Crown also relied on what he described as a principle of construction established in *R v Prince* (1875) LR 2 CCR 154. In *Prince's* case the defendant was convicted under a Victorian statute of unlawfully taking an unmarried girl under the age of 16 out of the possession of her father. The defendant bona fide and on reasonable grounds believed that the girl was over 16. The judge referred the question of the availability of the defence to the Court for Crown Cases Reserved. The court consisted of 16 judges. The prisoner was not represented. By a majority of 15 to 1 the court held that there was no such defence. The leading judgment was given by Blackburn J with the concurrence of nine other judges. Blackburn J relied strongly on a drafting flaw in ss 50 and 51 of the 1861 Act. The two sections respectively provided for offences of sexual intercourse with a girl under 10 (s 50) and above the age of 10 years and under the age of 12 years (s 51). The first was a felony and the latter a misdemeanour. Blackburn J produced what Professor Sir Rupert Cross in a magisterial article described as a 'knock-out' argument: 'Centenary Reflections on *Prince's* case' (1975) 91 *LQR* 540 at 542. The passage in Blackburn J's judgment reads:

> It seems impossible to suppose that the intention of the legislature in those two sections could have been to make the crime depend upon the knowledge of

> the prisoner of the girl's actual age. It would produce the monstrous result that a man who had carnal connection with a girl, in reality not quite 10 years old, but whom he on reasonable grounds believed to be a little more than 10, was to escape altogether. He could not, in that view of the statute, be convicted of the felony, for he did not know her to be under 10. He could not be convicted of the misdemeanour, because she was in fact not above the age of 10. It seems to us that the intention of the legislature was to punish those who had connection with young girls, though with their consent, unless the girl was in fact old enough to give a valid consent. The man who has connection with a child, relying on her consent, does it at his peril, if she is below the statutable age. The 55th section, on which the present case arises, uses precisely the same words as those in ss 50 and 51, and must be construed in the same way ...

Eventually the distinction between felonies and misdemeanours was abolished and the drafting flaw in the earlier legislation no longer exists. The principal ground of the decision of Blackburn J has disappeared. It is true that Bramwell B gave a separate judgment in which seven judges concurred. This judgment is largely based on the view that the defendant was guilty in law because if the facts had been as he supposed he would have acted immorally. For the further reasons given by Sir Rupert Cross in his article one can be confident that the reasoning of Bramwell B, if tested in a modern court, would not be upheld: see also *R v Morgan* [1976] AC 182 at 238 per Lord Fraser of Tullybelton; and the valuable discussion by Brooke LJ [1999] 3 WLR 116 at 130B–132B of the context of *Prince's* case. Significantly, *Prince's* case was cited in *Sweet v Parsley* [1970] AC 132 but was not mentioned in any of the judgments. The view may have prevailed that it was not necessary to overrule it because its basis had gone and that the principle laid down in *Sweet v Parsley* would in future be the controlling one. In any event, I would reject the contention that there is a special rule of construction in respect of age-based sexual offences which is untouched by the presumption as explained in *Sweet v Parsley*. Moreover, *Prince's* case is out of line with the modern trend in criminal law which is that a defendant should be judged on the facts as he believes them to be: *R v Morgan*; *R v Williams (Gladstone)* [1987] 3 All ER 411 and *Beckford v R* [1988] AC 130. This development has led the Criminal Law Revision Committee to recommend that the rules be harmonised and that the prosecution should prove that the man realised that the girl was under 16: *Fifteenth Report: Sexual Offences* (1984) (Cmnd 9213), paras. 5.5–5.15. Its recommendation was repeated by Brooke LJ at 136B–E. For all these reasons I would reject counsel's attempt to reinvigorate *Prince's* case — it is a relic from an age dead and gone. It is no longer possible to extract from *Prince's* case a special principle of construction applicable only to age-based sexual offences.

Practical difficulties

Counsel for the Crown finally submitted that it would in practice be difficult for the Crown to disprove defences of lack of knowledge of the age of the victim. In my view counsel has overstated the difficulties. After all, the legislature expressly made available such an excuse in the case of the so-called 'young man's defence' under s 6(3). Moreover, as Brooke LJ pointed out (at 129B) recklessness or indifference as to the existence of the prohibited circumstance would be sufficient for guilt. And in practice the Crown would only have to shoulder the burden of proving that the defendant was aware of the age of the victim if there was some evidential material before the jury or magistrates suggesting the possibility of an honest belief that the child was over 14. In these circumstances the suggested evidential difficulties ought not to divert the House from a principled approach to the problem.

Conclusion

My Lords, for these reasons, as well as reasons given by Lord Hutton, I would answer the principal certified question in the affirmative.

The supplementary certified questions

Given my conclusion on the first certified question the following supplementary certified questions arise. (a) Must the belief be held on reasonable grounds? (b) On whom does the burden of proof lie? Counsel for the Crown did not argue, in the alternative, that the belief must be held on reasonable grounds. Nevertheless, I initially regarded such a requirement as an acceptable solution. A basis for this view would be Lord Diplock's observation in *Sweet v Parsley* [1970] AC 132 at 163. This view is however contrary to the way in which our criminal law has subsequently developed. In *R v Morgan* [1976] AC 182 the House of Lords held by a majority of three to two that when a defendant had sexual intercourse with a woman without her consent, genuinely believing that she did consent, he was not guilty of rape, even if he had no reasonable grounds for his belief. The importance of this decision for the coherent development of English law was not immediately appreciated. The next stage in the development was the decision of the Court of Appeal in *R v Williams (Gladstone)* [1987] 3 All ER 411. The charge was assault. The defendant argued that he used force in the honest belief that he was protecting somebody else from an unlawful assault. Holding that the jury had been materially misdirected, the Court of Appeal, applying the logic of *Morgan's* case, held that if the defendant believed, reasonably or not, in the existence of facts which would justify the force used in self-defence, he did not intend to use *unlawful* force. The decision in *Williams's* case was followed and approved and applied by the Privy Council in *Beckford v R* [1988] AC 130. It was held that if the defendant honestly believed the circumstances to be such as would, if true, justify his use of force to defend himself from attack and the force was no more than reasonable to resist the attack, he was entitled to be acquitted of murder, since the intent to act unlawfully would be negatived by his belief, however mistaken or unreasonable. *Morgan's* case was described, as 'a landmark decision in the development of the common law': *Beckford v R* [1988] AC 130 at 145. There has been a general shift from objectivism to subjectivism in this branch of the law. It is now settled as a matter of general principle that mistake, whether reasonable or not, is a defence where it prevents the defendant from having the *mens rea* which the law requires for the crime with which he is charged. It would be in disharmony with this development now to rule that in respect of a defence under s 1(1) of the 1960 Act the belief must be based on reasonable grounds. Moreover, if such a special solution were to be adopted, it would almost certainly create uncertainty in other parts of the criminal law. It would be difficult to confine it on a principled basis to s 1(1). I would answer question (a) in the negative.

That leaves question (b). In *Woolmington v Director of Public Prosecutions* [1935] AC 462 at 481 Viscount Sankey LC observed that 'Throughout the web of the English criminal law one golden thread is to be seen, that it is the duty of the prosecution to prove the prisoner's guilt …'. It provides the answer to question (b). There is no legally sound basis on which it would be possible to rule that the burden is on the defendant to prove an honest belief that the victim was over 14 years. …

[**Lord Nicholls** and **Lord Hutton** delivered separate judgments in which they agreed in allowing the appeal and quashing the conviction. **Lord Irvine LC** expressly concurred in the judgment of **Lord Nicholls**. **Lord Mackay** concurred in the judgments of **Lord Nicholls, Lord Steyn** and **Lord Hutton**.]

13.33 Notes

Prince's case has now been effectively overruled by the House of Lords. For further confirmation of this conclusion, see *R v K* [2002] 1 AC 462. Its authority in Australia was undermined by the case of *He Kaw Teh v R*, the most significant Australian case on strict liability and the subject of the next section of this chapter.

HE KAW TEH V R AND ITS AFTERMATH

13.34 The important decision of the High Court in *He Kaw Teh v R* (1985) 157 CLR 523; 60 ALR 449 is extracted at **9.31C**. That decision is, however, of great significance in relation to the doctrines of mistake and strict liability, and, therefore, warrants comment in the present chapter. The accused travelled from Kuala Lumpur to Melbourne, where he was found to be in possession of 2.788 kilograms of heroin in the false bottom of a bag. He was charged with importing heroin into Australia contrary to s 233B(1)(b) of the Customs Act 1901 (Cth), and with possessing heroin contrary to s 233B(1)(c). Those subsections, which have since been repealed and replaced by provisions in the Criminal Code (Cth), provided:

> Any person who —
> (b) imports, or attempts to import, into Australia any prohibited imports to which this section applies or exports, or attempts to export, from Australia any prohibited exports to which this section applies; or
> (c) without reasonable excuse (proof whereof shall lie upon him) has in his possession, or attempts to obtain possession of, any prohibited imports to which this section applies which have been imported into Australia in contravention of this Act;
>
> shall be guilty of an offence.

Section 235 provides a range of penalties up to, in the case of commercial quantities of heroin, imprisonment for life.

13.35 The trial judge directed the jury that the offence did not require mens rea but that the accused might avail himself of the defence of honest and reasonable mistake. He directed the jury that the legal burden of proving honest and reasonable mistake rested on the accused to the standard of the balance of probabilities. The accused was convicted and appealed unsuccessfully to the Victorian Court of Criminal Appeal. He then appealed to the High Court where, by a majority of four to one, the appeal was allowed and the case remitted to the Victorian Court of Criminal Appeal to consider whether the proviso that there had been no substantial miscarriage of justice might be applicable: see s 568(1) of the Crimes Act 1958 (Vic).

13.36 All members of the court took the view that, were the offences ones of strict liability to which the *Proudman v Dayman* defence was applicable, the evidential burden only of proving honest and reasonable mistake would rest on the accused. If the accused satisfied that burden, the legal burden would rest on the prosecution. In adopting this view, the court was correct. This point is considered further at **13.55–13.57**.

13.37 Separate majority judgments were delivered by Gibbs CJ, and Brennan and Dawson JJ. Mason J agreed with Gibbs CJ. Wilson J dissented. It will be convenient to concentrate upon the judgment of Gibbs CJ. The Chief Justice dealt first with s 233B(1)(b), and adopted, as his starting point, the principle that statutes should be read in the light of the general principles which govern criminal responsibility. Thus a statute should prima facie be presumed not to dispense with a requirement of mens rea. Having regard to the seriousness of the offence, he held that it was unlikely that parliament intended to impose strict liability and that the seriousness of the offence made it unlikely that parliament intended even to impose strict liability subject to the *Proudman v Dayman* defence. Gibbs CJ stated:

> [T]he offence created by s 233B(1)(b) is treated by the Parliament in some circumstances as being one of the most serious in the criminal calendar. It seems improbable that the Parliament would have intended that it might be committed as a result of mere carelessness, although that would be the case if guilty knowledge was not an element, and an unreasonable although honest mistake would not be sufficient to exculpate the accused … The gravity of the offence suggests that guilty knowledge was intended to be an element of it … I accordingly conclude that the presumption that *mens rea* is required before a person can be held guilty of a grave criminal offence is not displaced in relation to s 233B(1)(b) of the Customs Act and that the prosecution on a charge under that provision bears the onus of proving that the accused knew that he was importing a narcotic substance.

He then considered s 233B(1)(c). As a starting point, he adopted the following proposition:

> [W]here a statute makes it an offence to have possession of particular goods, knowledge by the accused that those goods are in his custody will, in the absence

> of a sufficient indication of a contrary intention, be a necessary ingredient of the offence, because the words describing the offence ('in his possession') themselves necessarily import a mental element. In such a case it is unnecessary to rely on the common law presumption that *mens rea* is required.

Gibbs CJ held that the words 'without reasonable excuse (proof whereof shall lie upon him)' were not a sufficient indication that parliament intended that knowledge should not be an ingredient of the offence, and that accordingly the basic presumption was not displaced.

13.38 Brennan J delivered a separate judgment agreeing, in substance, with Gibbs CJ. Dawson J delivered a separate judgment agreeing with Gibbs CJ in relation to s 233B(1)(b), but holding that, in relation to s 233B(1)(c), a person may possess narcotic goods if he or she is aware of possessing something but is not aware that what he or she possesses are, in fact, narcotics. In such a case, the accused's defence will be one of reasonable excuse.

13.39 Wilson J dissented, taking the view that both offences should be interpreted as imposing strict liability subject to the possibility of a *Proudman v Dayman* defence. In relation to s 233B(1)(b), his Honour stated:

> In my opinion, then, it should now be taken to be the law in Australia that in order to present a prima facie case of an offence under s 233B(1)(b) of the Act it is not necessary for the Crown to establish guilty knowledge on the part of the accused. In the absence of evidence to the contrary such knowledge will be presumed, but if there is some evidence that an accused person honestly believed on reasonable grounds that his act was innocent then he is entitled to be acquitted unless the jury is satisfied beyond reasonable doubt that this was not so.

13.40 The decision of the High Court in *He Kaw Teh v R* marked a significant recalibration of the place of strict liability in criminal law on the part of the High Court. This move is illustrated by the case of *CTM v R* (at **13.3C**), the most recent decision of the High Court dealing with issues of mistake and strict liability.

13.41C Allen v United Carpet Mills Pty Ltd

[1989] VR 323
Supreme Court of Victoria

Nathan J: In July 1985 the Darebin Creek at Northcote flowed with the colour and consistency of milk. This event not only startled the good burghers of Northcote, but diminished their enjoyment and use of the creek as a recreational area. Also, and not surprisingly, it harmed aquatic life in the creek. The cause of those events, and so much is admitted by all defendants, was a discharge of rubber latex, used as a backing for carpets, into the creek.

On the day before the discolouration was noticed, Davis, the owner and operator of a prime mover, attempted to deliver a quantity of rubber latex from a liquid haulage tanker owned by the second respondent (RL) to the premises of the first respondent (UCM), a factory occupying a site near the creek and from which it conducted its business of manufacturing carpets. It is conceded that Davis incorrectly hooked up the hoses leading from RL's tanker to UCM's storage tanks, in such a way that rubber latex flowed out of the top of the haulage tanker down its sides and on to the ground where Davis hosed it into a stormwater drain. From that drain the latex found its way into the creek. On the day the discharge was noticed the informant, an inspector from the Environment Protection Authority, went to UCM's factory and saw Davis hosing the residue of the latex into the stormwater drain. After a less than friendly exchange, Davis desisted and some days later the creek returned to its normal flow and colour.

RL provided the latex to UCM in the course of its business and had retained Davis to drive its tanker with his prime mover through an intermediary trucking company known as Beacon Transport. RL knew of the peculiarities of UCM's hose and valve system for the delivery of latex into UCM's storage tanks, but had allowed Davis to attempt to deliver the latex without supervision or thorough instruction. RL certainly did not instruct Davis to hose the spilt latex into the stormwater drain. Similarly, UCM which did not have any direct contractual relationship with Davis, permitted him to use its water and hoses for the purposes of dispersing the spilt latex, but did not intend it be hosed into the stormwater system and hence into the creek. In fact UCM had a system to prevent this occurring, but it was not able to cope with the independent actions of Davis. Allen subsequently charged UCM, RL and Davis with an offence of causing pollution to waters under the terms of the *Environment Protection Act 1970* (the Act).

Section 39(1) of the Act, as appropriately edited, reads as follows:

(1) A person shall not cause or permit any waters to be polluted so that the physical, chemical or biological condition of the water is so changed as to make or be reasonably expected to make those waters —

...

(d) ... harmful or potentially harmful to ... fish or other aquatic life;

...

(e) detrimental to any beneficial use made of those waters.

As I have already noted, the defendants conceded that the latex was harmful to the aquatic life, including crustaceans of the creek. 'Beneficial use' is defined in the Act in sufficiently wide terms to encompass the disturbance and startlement of the good burghers using the creek for recreational purposes.

Davis pleaded guilty, the other respondents did not, and the magistrate dismissed the informations against them. It is from those orders that the informant has obtained an order to review, and I turn now to the magistrate's findings and decision, and then, to the grounds upon which the order to review was obtained.

The charge against RL was dismissed by the magistrate after a no case submission. The magistrate found that RL could not be held vicariously liable for this offence unless the prosecution could establish that RL had in some way by its act or omission caused or permitted the pollution. The magistrate found the prosecution had not discharged its onus in establishing such a failure or omission.

UCM also made a no case submission which was unsuccessful, however, it then elected not to call evidence, and the charge against it was dismissed. The magistrate held the discharge of pollution had not been the result of a failure or omission on the part of UCM. The magistrate then considered the import of s 63(2) of the Act relied upon by the informant. Section 63(2) reads:

> Where any segment or element of the environment is polluted as a result of a discharge, emission or deposit of waste from or on any premises on which there is conducted any commercial or industrial undertaking the occupier of the premises shall be deemed to have caused the discharge or emission unless the occupier proves that the discharge or emission was unrelated to any commercial or industrial undertaking. [The deeming provision.]

The magistrate found, despite the fact that latex was brought on to UCM's premises as a direct consequence of its commercial undertaking, that this act was unrelated to the eventual spillage. He further found the deeming provision, which enables a prima facie case to be established in circumstances where facts might be peculiarly within the knowledge of a defendant, was a rebuttable presumption. On his findings of fact, the presumption was rebutted and the charge was dismissed.

Pursuant to Pt XI of the *Magistrates' Court Act 1958*, orders *nisi* to review were obtained against RL and UCM before a master of this court. These matters now come before me for my consideration as to whether the orders nisi should be made absolute.

The grounds of review with respect to RL, as stated in the order *nisi*, are as follows:

1. The learned magistrate erred in finding that reasonable precautions is a defence to an offence under the *Environment Protection Act 1970*.
2. The learned magistrate erred in holding that the respondent was not vicariously liable for the actions of its independent contractor, Davis.
3. The learned magistrate erred in rejecting the submission that when Mr. Davis caused the discharge of latex, he was not acting within the scope of his employment.

The order *nisi* with respect to UCM reads:

1. The learned magistrate erred in holding that the respondent did not 'cause the waters of the Darebin Creek to be polluted' in the sense in which that term has been interpreted by the case law.
2. The learned magistrate erred in holding that the discharge of latex was unrelated to the commercial or industrial undertaking of the respondent in terms of s 63(2) of the *Environment Protection Act 1970*.

I now turn to the first ground of the order *nisi* with respect to RL. Is the taking of reasonable precautions or reasonable care and due diligence a defence under the Act? In order to consider this question, it is necessary to analyse the character of s 39. Does it create an offence of which *mens rea* is an element, or is it one of absolute liability, or, is it in that 'halfway house' of strict liability, as described by Asche J in *Chiou Yaou Fa v Morris* (1987) 46 NTR 1, where the defence may be applicable.

The High Court was called upon to consider these various categories of offences in *He Kaw Teh v R* (1985) 157 CLR 523; 60 ALR 449. ...

It was held by the court, Wilson J dissenting, the presumption that *mens rea* is required before a person can be held guilty of a criminal offence was not displaced by this section. Further, the prosecution has the onus of proving that the accused knew he was importing a prohibited import.

The High Court recognised a tripartite categorisation of statutory offences, so far as the mental ingredient necessary for conviction was concerned. They are conveniently summarised by Asche J in *Chiou Yaou Fa's* case as follows (at 19):

(1) that *mens rea* applies in full;
(2) that the offence is one of strict liability so that the prosecution does not have to rebut *mens rea* in proving the *actus reus*; but if the evidence raises a likelihood of honest and reasonable mistake the prosecution must rebut that beyond reasonable doubt;
(3) that the offence creates absolute liability.

It was conceded by all parties before me that s 39 offences do not fall within the first category, namely, offences in which *mens rea*, per se, is an element. The respondents have submitted the offence is one of strict not absolute liability, therefore the defence of honest and reasonable mistake is available. The defence, it was contended, should also be extended to a defendant who has acted with all reasonable and proper care and diligence. Such an extension of the defence of honest and reasonable mistake was suggested by the full court of the Canadian Supreme Court in *R v Sault Ste Marie* [1978] 2 SCR 1299, where Dickson J, reading the judgment of the court, said (at 181–2): '1. The defence (to an offence of strict liability) will be available if the accused reasonably believes in a mistaken set of facts which, if true, would render the act or omission innocent, or if he *took all reasonable steps to avoid the particular event*.' [Emphasis added]

This decision was considered in *Teh's* case and *Chiou Yaou Fa's* case and followed in New Zealand in *Hastings City Council v Simons* [1984] 2 NZLR 502.

I consider that a defence of taking all reasonable care and diligence is within the scope of the concept of honest and reasonable mistake and should be available to offences carrying strict liability. This being so, if s 39 is an offence of strict liability, the magistrate would have been entitled (subject to satisfactory evidence being available) to dismiss the charge against RL. I should add here, that although the term 'defence' has been used by me and in other authorities when discussing honest and reasonable mistake, the accused has an evidentiary onus only to discharge, so as to raise a defence of honest and reasonable mistake or reasonable and proper care and diligence. Once the evidentiary onus is discharged by the accused, it is then required to be displaced by the prosecution beyond reasonable doubt.

The applicant submitted the offence was of the third category, namely, one of absolute liability, where no defence of honest and reasonable mistake or any extension of that concept was available. He referred to *Alphacell Ltd v Woodward* [1972] AC 824.

In *Alphacell's* case, the House of Lords was required to examine the Prevention of Pollution Act 1951 s 2(1), which appropriately edited, read:

> Subject to this Act, a person commits an offence punishable under this section —
> (a) if he causes or knowingly permits to enter a stream any poisonous, noxious or polluting matter.

Alphacell, a paper manufacturer, was charged with causing effluent to enter a river contrary to this section. The defendant argued it should be acquitted as the overflow of effluent into the river was caused without its knowledge and without its negligence. Their Lordships, however, on a reading of this section, held that the 'causes' did not include the concept of mens rea. Therefore, even assuming the escape of effluent occurred without the defendant's negligence, that was not sufficient to exclude it from the force of the section.

I consider this case to be of limited assistance. Their Lordships, in the interpretation of the word 'causes', gave great weight to the fact that the legislature had chosen the phrase 'knowingly permits' in the same section. As the legislature had not elected to put 'knowingly' prior to the word 'causes', it was considered inappropriate to read into the meaning of 'causes' the concept of *mens rea*. A further difficulty with the English authorities in this area is that they have not developed, to the same extent and clarity, the tripartite categorisation of criminal offences as was adopted in *Teh's* case and accordingly, the terms 'strict liability' and 'absolute liability' have tended to be used by the English authorities interchangeably.

It was submitted by the respondents I should adopt the interpretation of 'cause' as held in *O'Sullivan v Truth and Sportsman Ltd* (1957) 96 CLR 220. In this case the High Court was required to interpret the meaning of 'cause' as found in the *Police Offences Act 1953* (SA) s 35(1), which made it an offence to 'offer for sale, sell or cause to be offered for sale or sold to any person' any newspapers containing a report relating to sexual morality which occupied more than a given space or carried type exceeding a given size. The court held that 'cause' included the notion that the accused must 'contemplate or desire that the prohibited act will ensue' (joint judgment of Dixon CJ, Williams, Webb and Fullagar JJ, at 228). This approach tends to suggest that some degree of *mens rea* is required in an interpretation of the word 'cause'. However, the difference in legislative subject matter in *Truth and Sportsman Ltd* and this case is stark, and to my mind critical. The section in *Truth and Sportsman Ltd* involved 'causing' the sale, or offering for sale, involved creating contractual relations between parties. It would be difficult to contemplate how such transactions could take place without a party's intent to achieve such a result. In contrast, pollution is frequently 'caused', not only intentionally, but also unintentionally and accidentally. The prohibition here is the social and environmental detriment of pollution. In the *Truth* case, it was regulating the salacious content and concomitant sale of prurient newspapers.

Returning to *Teh's* case and *Chiou Yaou Fa's* case, both pointed out the prima facie presumption that *mens rea* is an element of any criminal offence, and that the onus rests on the prosecution at all times to establish that element beyond reasonable doubt. A court requires good grounds for moving away from such a presumption. Further to this proposition, as stated by Asche J in *Chiou Yaou Fa's* case (at (NTR) 22–3):

> If, however, *mens rea* can be shown to have been displaced, it does not follow that the court should leap to the opposite extreme of absolute liability. Rather the presumption, if *mens rea* is displaced, should be of strict liability unless the words of a statute are so clear and unambiguous as to admit of no other construction.

Gibbs CJ in *Teh's* case considered four matters in assessing whether the presumption of *mens rea* was displaced (at (CLR) 528–30), namely:

1. The language of the section creating the offence;
2. The subject matter of the statute;
3. The consequences for the community of an offence;
4. Potential consequences for an accused, if convicted.

Similarly, Brennan J approached the issue of *mens rea* thus (at (CLR) 576):

> Principally, by reference to the language of the statute and its subject-matter. From those sources, the mischief at which the statute is aimed is derived, and the purpose of the statute is perceived. *The purpose of the statute is the surest guide of the legislature's intention as to the mental state to be implied.* [Emphasis added]

In *Teh's* case, it was considered by the majority that the severe penal provisions under the Customs Act enforced the presumption that *mens rea* was required and should not be displaced. In the instant case the parties have conceded that *mens rea* is not an essential element, the issue is whether reasonable precaution offers a defence, and to that extent the High Court's reasoning is pertinent. This is because the defence springs from the concept of offering an explanation for the offence based on an honest and reasonable belief in a state of facts, which if true, would be exculpatory.

Thus I am guided by the criteria for *mens rea* set out in *Teh's* case, in ascertaining whether a defence of reasonable precaution is available under the terms of this Act, or whether the legislation imposes absolute liability. Further assistance, and also from a court which binds me, is the Full Court decision of *Welsh v Donnelly* [1983] 2 VR 173. A provision of the *Motor Car Act 1958* (s 35(5)) made it an offence to overload a trailer above axle weights of stated levels. The court unanimously held that the provision imposed strict liability, although that term was used synonymously with absolute liability, which is to be understood in view of the fact it was decided prior to *Teh's* case. The language and intendment of the Act made it plain that an honest and reasonable belief in a state of facts which if true, did not provide a defence to a prosecution. The court thoroughly and extensively considered the authorities and academic writings concerning *mens rea* and reasonable mistake but concluded the defence was excluded by the terms of the Act. The court gave particular attention to *Proudman v Dayman* (1941) 67 CLR 536 at 540 per Dixon J; *Kain & Shelton Pty Ltd v McDonald* [1971] 1 SASR 39; *Iannella v French* (1968) 119 CLR 84; *Sweet v Parsley* [1970] AC 132 and 'Strict Liability in the High Court of Australia' by Professor C Howard (1960) 76 *LQR* 546. The Chief Justice (at 178) in the *Welsh* case said:

> I have ultimately come to the conclusion that the putting of the defendant under strict liability is necessary for the enforcement of the statute. In such a case the

exclusion of the defence of honest and reasonable mistake inevitably means that individuals are called upon so to conduct their affairs that the general welfare is not prejudiced and to that extent the rights of the individual are subjected to the common good. I think that the class of person included in s 35(5) shows that the legislature regards the legislation as being of that character and therefore intends that the defence of honest and reasonable mistake should be excluded.

McInerney J (at 186–7) said:

In the present case the condition of liability under s 35 is that 'a motor car is used on a highway in contravention of any … condition or provision contained in a permit'. The section does not contain the words 'knowingly' or 'wilfully'. The liability arises upon user in contravention of the conditions of the permit, and the courts have been stricter in their construction eg as to imposing criminal vicarious liability in cases where the prohibited conduct is 'user' unaccompanied by any express reference to the 'user' having been 'permitted' or 'allowed' or to the defendant having 'knowingly' or 'wilfully' used the article or property in question: see Glanville Williams, *The Criminal Law — The General Part*, 2nd ed, p 234, para 81, pp 280–1, para 96.

It may in this case be said that the legislation contained in Pt IV of the *Motor Car Act 1958* is legislation concerned with matters in which public safety is at stake. The object of the prescriptions provided in Pt IV is clearly to ensure that motor cars used on a highway are as safe as the legislation can make them.

Southwell J (at 199), expressly adopted a South Australian Full Court decision *Franklin v Stacey* (1981) 27 SASR 490.

This Act recites 'any person shall not cause' pollution. It would be difficult to frame language in more absolute and embracive terms. The phrase echoes commandments given elsewhere and is just as explicit. I find the terms of the Act impose absolute liability. I now turn to some supplementary reasons for this conclusion.

In s 39 of the Act, the severity of the penalty is one *indicium* which can be used to assess whether the offence is one of strict or absolute liability. Section 39(5) of the Act provides for a maximum penalty of not more than 100 penalty units ($10,000), and in the case of a continuing offence, a daily penalty of not more than 40 penalty units each day the offence continues after conviction. At first blush, this may be viewed as quite a severe financial penalty and thus suggest a categorisation of strict liability is appropriate. But as Gibbs J indicated, the potential penalty needs to be assessed in the context of the consequence for the community of the offence. That observation, which I find compelling, brings me to reflect upon the potential damage that may be incurred by the release of pollutants into waters, the potential hazard to health that may result, and the social costs which may be incurred by failing to dispose of pollutants in a safe manner. Viewed from that perspective the penalties are not oppressive.

I turn for assistance to the Parliamentary Debates where the Honourable E H Walker, Minister for Planning and Environment, in presenting the bill to the Legislative Council in his second reading speech on 4 April 1984, indicated the purpose and intent of the bill as follows:

> The bill is an essential element in the Government's program to establish effective and enforceable controls for the purpose of protecting and enhancing the quality of the environment.

Examining the Act as a whole and the purpose it is designed to serve, I conclude it is directed at penalising all those persons in control of potential pollutants who allow, whether by design, neglect or sheer inadvertence, the escape of those pollutants into the environment which then cause damage. The legislature has deliberately used the word 'cause' and has avoided using language such as 'knowingly cause' or 'negligently cause' (pollution) which would have been expected, if the intention had been to create an offence of merely strict and not absolute liability. This is a strong indication that absolute liability was intended.

I am further drawn to this conclusion after considering the subject matter of the Act. It is primarily concerned with pollution of the air or water, both are in the nature of common property, as distinct from property held in private hands. The usual constraints which prevent persons from intruding upon the property rights of others (eg actions in trespass or nuisance) are not effective in creating a regime which protects the general environment. The Act is social regulatory legislation designed to protect the environment. Pollution of the environment usually results in a burden and cost to the community. The Act penalises those who have 'caused' pollution and thereby brought a detriment to the community as a whole.

Based on these conclusions, the magistrate erred in law in finding that RL had a defence under the Act, in that it took reasonable precautions to prevent the pollution. Section 39 creates offences of absolute liability. I should add, if it is found RL took reasonable precautions to prevent pollution, it may be a relevant consideration as to penalty.

I now turn to the remaining grounds of the order *nisi* with respect to RL. Ground 3 is encapsulated in ground 2. The issue is whether RL is vicariously liable for the actions of its independent contractor, Mr Davis.

It was submitted by Mr McArdle for the applicant that as the legislation is regulatory in character, a person cannot delegate his/her duties and obligations. It was conceded that Davis was not a servant or agent of RL at common law, but was an independent contractor. It was contended, however, that the civil law principle of the vicarious liability should be extended beyond responsibility for a servant or agent, to encompass liability to a principal for any person doing any act in pursuit of that principal's business enterprise. Thus, it was contended, an accused person should be liable for the acts of its delegate.

The delegation concept is more apposite than the concept of a master's responsibility for a servant/agent in the civil jurisdiction. This is particularly so in view of my finding that this legislation is regulatory in character and imposes absolute liability. It is incompatible with these findings to subvert the intention of the Act by qualifying that principle.

Therefore, as a matter of law, RL is responsible for any infringement by Davis for any of his actions done in furtherance of his business relationship with it. *Goodes v General Motors Holden's Pty Ltd* [1972] VR 386 is authority for this proposition. The defendant was charged with an offence under s 6 of the *Navigable Waters (Oil Pollution) Act 1960,* which provided that the occupier of land shall be guilty of an offence if any discharge of oil occurs from such land into any waters within the jurisdiction. It was found as a matter of fact that the discharge was caused by a careless act of a servant of an independent contractor engaged by the defendant. Adam J held that the defendant's responsibility extended to its independent contractor engaged by it to perform operations in connection with oil on its land. Adam J said (at 389):

> ... where there is an attempt to delegate the entire performance of such duty [under the Act] to another person — that other person becoming, as it were, the alter ego for the purpose of the legislation imposing the offence — but I see no reason at all, and the cases support this, why it should not apply where the delegation is of any matter which is connected with the commission of such an offence. The person subject to the absolute and strict duty must bear the responsibility for its performance and does not relieve himself by delegation.

His Honour cited in support of this proposition *Linnett v Commissioner of Metropolitan Police* [1946] KB 290; *Quality Dairies (York) Ltd v Pedley* [1952] 1 KB 275; *Brentnall & Cleland Ltd v London County Council* [1945] KB 115; *United States v Parfait Powder Puff Inc* (1947) 163 F 2d 1008 and *Series v Poole* [1969] 1 QB 676.

I therefore find that grounds 2 and 3 of the order *nisi* with respect to RL are made out. I turn now to the order *nisi* with respect to UCM, and firstly to the second ground of this order, namely, that the deeming provision applied to it.

It is of assistance in considering the import of the deeming provision to examine its predecessor, introduced in 1972 by Act No 8277. That provision read:

> Where any offence against this Act with respect to the discharge or emission of waste or pollutants occurs in upon or from any premises in the course of any trade carried on in those premises the owner or occupier of the premises (as the case requires) shall be deemed to be guilty of the offence.

The section was central to the judgment of Murphy J in *Window v Phosphate Co-operative Co of Australia Ltd* [1983] 2 VR 287. Phosphate Co-operative carried on the trade of manufacturing superphosphate. Stored on its premises were quantities of sulphur required for the treatment of the phosphate rock. A fire commenced in the pit where the sulphur was stored, it gave off sulphur dioxide which polluted the atmosphere. The company was charged under the Act, the informant relying upon the then deeming provision. The cause of the fire in the sulphur pit could not be ascertained or proven. It was agreed that it was not part of the defendant's trade to ignite or burn sulphur. It was held the deeming provision did not apply where the informant was unable to establish how the fire started, or, whether the fire was caused by an employee of the company or some other unknown persons. In this respect, his Honour said (at 294):

> In my opinion, if it is desired to rely upon s 63(2) of the Act, it is not sufficient to prove only that certain factual elements of an offence occurred, such as the

> discharge of pollutants into the atmosphere from premises in the occupation of the defendant. It must also be proved, as the first link, and depending upon what charge is laid under s 41(1) of the Act, either that some person actually polluted the atmosphere, or caused the atmosphere to be polluted, or permitted the atmosphere to be polluted.

In that case the prosecution had not discharged its onus negating the suggestion that the fire could have been caused by a trespasser or by an act of God. It was noted, there was no obvious explanation how this fire could have occurred in the company's normal course of trade. Murphy J referred to *Alphacell's* case, where in the course of their judgments, Lords Wilberforce, Pearson and Salmon recognised it would be a defence under similar legislation, if the pollution was caused by the 'intervening act of a trespasser' or by an 'act of God' ([1972] AC 824 at 834, 845 and 847). His Honour also referred to *Impress (Worcester) Ltd v Rees* [1971] 2 All ER 357 at 358. As a further ground in finding that s 63(2) as it then was did not apply in *Window's* case, Murphy J noted that the discharge was required to occur in the course of any trade carried on in the premises. Such element was not established.

As a result of *Window's* case, the deeming provision in s 63(2) was amended by the legislature, in the terms in which it now stands.

I now return to the Minister's second reading speech on 4 April 1984 with respect to the amendment of s 63(2). Under the heading 'Removal of Enforcement Barriers', he said:

> Clause 26 amends s 63(2) and deals with prosecutorial proofs where a polluting discharge occurs from trade premises. The section is amended to provide that where it can be established that pollution has been caused by a discharge from any commercial or industrial premises then the occupier of those premises is deemed to have caused the pollution to occur unless he can establish that the discharge was unrelated to any commercial or industrial undertaking. This represents a significant change as perhaps the most serious difficulty confronting the authority in enforcing the Act is to prove that the defendant caused the polluting discharge which emanated from his premises. In most cases the discharge has ceased by the time an inspector has arrived. If the occupier of the premises does not cooperate and provide the authority with sufficient admissible evidence then it is often impossible to establish the precise cause of the discharge. *The amendment of s 63(2) reverses the onus of proof in cases where the Environment Protection Authority can prove that a particular discharge caused pollution and that the discharge emanated from certain premises, but where it cannot be proved that the occupier of the premises caused or permitted the polluting discharge to occur.* [Emphasis added]

The present deeming provision removes any reference to the emission having to occur 'in the course of trade' and clearly sets out the elements to be established by an informant, namely:

(i) The environment was polluted.
(ii) Such pollution was a result of a discharge from the premises.
(iii) The premises were used for a commercial or business undertaking.

If these elements are established, the onus shifts to the occupier to establish that the cause of the discharge was unrelated to any commercial or industrial undertaking. The initial onus is no longer on the informant to establish that the cause of the discharge was related to the commercial or industrial undertaking of the occupier and was not because of a trespasser or an act of God.

Returning to the fact situation before me, it is clear the informant established the three elements required to shift the burden to the occupier of the premises, ie UCM.

Mr Hammond for UCM, submitted that Davis by hosing down the tanker caused the pollution. It was an intervening act, severing any causal connection between the discharge of pollution and UCM's commercial and industrial undertaking. He submitted that the concept of intervening acts of a trespasser as enunciated in *Alphacell's* case was akin to the role of Davis in this case. Davis, although not a trespasser, was in effect an unknown third party. Neither he nor his tanker were under UCM's control. Despite the fact that these submissions were capably and forcefully put by Mr Hammond, I do not find them persuasive.

The delivery of latex to UCM was an integral part of its commercial undertaking, namely, the production of carpets. It was clearly within UCM's contemplation that Davis or some other such person would come on to its premises and deliver latex. In fact, their whole operation relied on such deliveries. Davis was not a trespasser, or an innocent passer-by, he was in the nature of an invitee.

The legislature has seen fit by the enactment of the deeming provision, to vest commercial occupiers such as UCM with liability for any acts done by persons such as Davis, coming on to their premises for purposes connected with their commercial and industrial undertakings.

I recognise the established principle of law that a court will decline to adopt the effect of a deeming provision if in any particular circumstances, it would result in injustice and absurdity. Relying upon this proposition, Mr Hammond submitted the deeming provision should only be applied when the facts do not reveal the actual polluter. As Davis was known and had already pleaded guilty to the offence, it was contended it would be unjust to also convict UCM. I am not attracted by this argument. The deeming provision is embedded in the section which creates offences of absolute liability. I find it was within the contemplation of the Act, that an occupier is to be responsible for persons coming on to the premises in connection with its commercial or industrial undertakings. I see no injustice or absurdity in Davis and UCM both being convicted of offences arising from the discharge of pollution, although their respective culpabilities and penalties may differ. Ground 2 of the order *nisi* with respect to UCM is sustained.

[Orders absolute.]

[See also *Kearon v Grant* [1991] 1 VR 321; and *Australian Iron and Steel Pty Ltd v Environment Protection Authority* (1992) 29 NSWLR 497.]

STRICT LIABILITY RECONSIDERED

The case for strict liability

13.42 At base, there are two reasons to support a conclusion that a statute imposes strict, or even absolute, liability:

(1) the absence of any reference to knowledge or intention in the statute; and

(2) the needs of public policy.

The first of these two reasons is that of the Mikado in Gilbert and Sullivan's light opera, quoted by Dixon J in *Thomas v R* (1937) 59 CLR 279 at 303–4:

> That's the pathetic part of it. Unfortunately the fool of an Act says 'compassing the death of the heir apparent'. There's not a word about mistake, or not knowing, or having no notion, or not being there. There should be of course; but there isn't. That's the slovenly way in which these Acts are drawn.

Students of the law may be permitted to wonder why the courts ever embarked on this line of reasoning; and it may be that the answer lies in the failure of the judges ever to develop an adequate theory of statutory interpretation. However that may be, it is clear that, on occasion, the judges have pushed the application of the literal rule of interpretation to the point of absurdity: 'The statute does not say anything about not knowing, or not intending'. One may rather ask why the judges should ever have supposed that the statute should make such references. If a judge drives his or her car along a road and comes to an intersection marked with the sign 'STOP', it may be assumed that, as a law-abiding citizen, the car is brought to a halt; but the judge does not either stay in the same spot forever, or turn back, merely because the sign fails to say when to go on. (Of course, the judge will know that the Road Traffic Regulations direct a driver to proceed when he or she can do so with safety; but it is hoped that the judge would do this, even if driving in a jurisdiction other than in which he or she sits and was unaware of the terms of the relevant legislation.) What the judge does is to use his or her common sense. To spell the matter out, he or she reads into the notice words which are actually not there. Why should the judge abandon common sense when acting as a judge?

13.43 Two answers to the latter question have, from time to time, been given. One is that modern statutes are so precisely drafted that it would be improper for the judge to suppose that parliament has failed to say fully and precisely what it intended. This answer, it may be observed, is given only when the occasion is suitable; on other occasions, judges are not hesitant in criticising parliamentary drafting. It might also be added that this answer would have been more appropriate in a much earlier age, when many statutes were lengthy and prolix. If anything, the tendency of modern drafting is to cut down the language to a minimum and to strive for simplicity and clarity. Plain English drafting is now accepted as the standard in Australian jurisdictions. In any event, *CTM v R* (at **13.3C**) is illustrative of the fact that, nonetheless, parliament, on occasion, clearly fails to indicate the intention of an Act in relation to issues of fault.

The second answer is that many statutes contain references to knowledge or intent, so that when such references are omitted, the omission should be regarded as significant. This is a variant of the old maxim of statutory interpretation, *expressio unius est exclusio alterius* (meaning that the mention of one thing in a statute is the exclusion of another) — a maxim which, in other contexts, has found little favour with the courts. It is strange that it should have been invoked in this context. For it makes an unwise assumption about a complete consistency of drafting. Many statutes are merely consolidations of a series of provisions enacted at different points in time; and it cannot be assumed that there has been consistency of drafting in such statutes. When the argument is made that references to intent or knowledge appear in other statutes but not in this one and that, therefore, the omission is significant, the situation is even worse, for this argument assumes consistency over the whole or a large part of the statute book. It would thus seem that the only case in which the omission of 'intent-words' is significant is that which arises in regard to a statute drafted as a single whole and containing some sections including such words and other sections omitting them. Even in such a case, the inference is but a slender one, and it would seem unsafe to rely on it without some further indication of what parliament actually intended.

13.44 Public policy provides stronger arguments for concluding that a statute was intended to impose strict liability. The courts, apart from relying on the omission of words, have also argued that the object of the legislature could not be achieved if the defence of mistake of fact and similar defences were permitted, and that, therefore, the legislature has excluded them. To some extent, the argument appears to be circular. However, putting this on one side, are judges making assessments of public policy accurately? They do now consult the parliamentary debates and sources outside the statute itself, and statutes do now set out their objects. The judges have, however, differed among themselves as to the conclusions which public policy requires, even in dealing with the very same subject matter: compare, for example, *Cundy v Le Cocq* (1884) 13 QBD 207 (at 13.28, note 1) with *Sherras v De Rutzen* [1895] 1 QB 918 (at 13.28, note 2). What is the public policy which requires the conviction of Cundy while permitting the acquittal of Sherras?

13.45 On this point, it may be noted that there are two aspects of public policy which are not often considered by judges who take this line of argument. The first is that if the innocent and the guilty are punished alike, the result may well be that a person may refrain from taking as much care to avoid transgressing as he or she otherwise might. The second is that it is questionable public policy to attribute to the legislature the intention to act with deliberate harshness. Can public policy truly justify the conviction of an accused who did not intend to commit a forbidden act, was not reckless as to its possibility and was not even negligent?

13.46 The development of strict criminal responsibility is however a reality. Most regulatory offences — for example, about food safety and traffic matters — and a number of more serious statutory offences make no reference to mens rea.

Among the text writers, Professor F B Sayre is perhaps the best known of those who have regarded the doctrine without distaste. His views are set out in a classic article, 'Public Welfare Offences' (1933) 33 *Colum L Rev* 55, which is still worth attention. In this article, Sayre traces the history, development, and modern status of the doctrine. He classifies the cases in which it has been applied as follows:

(1) illegal sales of intoxicating liquor;
(2) sales of impure or adulterated food or drugs;
(3) sales of misbranded articles;
(4) violations of anti-narcotic Acts (and this at a time when today's United States [and international] drug scene was outside the imagination of most people);
(5) criminal nuisances;
(6) violations of traffic regulations;
(7) violations of motor vehicle laws; and
(8) violations of general police regulations, passed for the safety, health or well-being of the community.

Sayre noted that the doctrine had also been applied to sex offences committed against those below a statutory age. He observed that this was anomalous, but regarded it as necessary since, in his view, the protection which the law wishes to afford to young persons could not be otherwise achieved.

13.47 As regards the public welfare offences, Sayre thought that the doctrine of strict liability could not be avoided if the law were to be effectively enforced:

> [S]wamped with such appalling inundations of cases of petty violations, the lower criminal courts would be physically unable to examine the subjective intent of each defendant, even were such determination desirable.

The matter of 'administrative convenience' for the courts is even more pressing today, with the lower courts hearing 523,168 individual matters (in the 2011–2012 year: ABS statistics), around 97% of all criminal matters.

It is important to note, however, that questions relating to the accused's culpability are not avoided by the imposition of strict liability. Such matters must still be investigated after conviction for the purposes of sentencing.

Seeking a middle ground

13.48 In Australia, the judgments of Dixon J in *Thomas v R* (1937) 59 CLR 279 and *Proudman v Dayman* (1941) 67 CLR 536; [1944] ALR 64 (at **13.29C**) pointed the way towards an intermediate approach which has the effect both of protecting the public and enabling the totally blameless accused to escape conviction. The stature of Sir Owen Dixon, who became Chief Justice of Australia in 1952, has helped to focus not only attention but also special regard for this analysis of the law and his enunciation of principle in those landmark decisions. His approach involves interpreting statutes imposing strict liability as imposing it only in respect of the constituent elements of the particular crime. It thus remains open to the accused to rely on any of the general defences, and in cases where the accused lacked mens rea, the defence the accused will rely on is that of honest and reasonable mistake. As with all the general defences, the accused bears the evidential burden of showing that mistake was both honest and reasonable. Any remaining uncertainty about the imposition of the legal burden has now been removed by the decisions of the High Court of Australia in *He Kaw Teh v R* (at **13.34**) and *CTM v R* (at **13.3C**). The legal burden of disproving the defence is upon the prosecution, and the prosecution must discharge this burden to the beyond reasonable doubt standard. This is further explored at **13.55–13.57**.

13.49 The effect of this approach is that crimes of strict liability become, in substance, crimes of negligence although with one significant difference. Were negligence to be regarded as a defining element of the crime, the prosecution would have both the evidential and the legal burden of establishing negligence. Since the issue of the reasonableness of the accused's belief arises by way of a general defence, however, the evidential burden of showing he or she acted without negligence rests on the accused.

13.50 This intermediate approach has been adopted in a number of subsequent cases; for example, *Mayer v Marchant* (1973) 5 SASR 567 (at **13.31C**). It is the view of the present writers that this approach constitutes a proper resolution of the competing requirements of convenience and justice. It relieves the prosecution of the task of proving mens rea in the ordinary case, yet allows the accused the opportunity of asserting that he or she was totally without blame where there is evidence to suggest this may have been the case. Any argument that such a relaxation of strict liability might open the floodgates to bogus defences is quite misconceived. Since the evidential burden of proof is on the accused, the defence of honest and reasonable mistake will not be left to the jury unless the accused is able to produce sufficient evidence to raise the existence of such a mistake as a real possibility.

13.51 The decision of the majority of the High Court of Australia in *He Kaw Teh v R* (at **13.33**), underscores this approach firmly, even though these justices concluded that the offences in s 233B of the Customs Act 1901 (Cth) are crimes of intention. That conclusion, drawn despite the language in the provision whereby possession of prohibited imports 'without reasonable excuse (proof whereof shall lie upon him)' (that is, the defendant), accompanied the finding that, were offences characterised as ones of strict liability, then the *Proudman v Dayman* defence would be almost universally available. Wilson J, the only dissentient, concluded that the offences were those of strict liability, but went on to say that if there was some evidence that the accused believed on reasonable grounds that the act was innocent 'then he is entitled to be acquitted unless the jury is satisfied beyond reasonable doubt that this was not so'. This approach has been further affirmed by the decision of the High Court in *CTM v R* (at **13.3C**). Nonetheless, the *He Kaw Teh* decision has not resulted in the complete demise of strict or absolute liability. Courts in New South Wales and Victoria have decided that specific enactments clearly and unequivocally exclude both the requirement to prove mens rea and the defence of honest and reasonable mistake (or 'due diligence' as it is now sometimes entitled): see *Allen v United Carpet Mills* (at **13.41C**).

13.52 The outcome of these developments has been the broad acceptance of a tripartite classification of statutory crimes. They can be categorised as (a) crimes requiring proof of intention (or knowledge); (b) crimes characterised as strict liability offences (for which a defence of mistake will be available); and (c) crimes characterised as absolute liability offences (for which the defence of mistake is not available). This tripartite classification is clearly manifested in the *United Carpet Mills* case (at **13.41C**).

The Criminal Code Act 1995 (Cth) has incorporated this classification into its general provisions on criminal responsibility. Section 6.1(1) of the Code states that: 'If a law that creates an offence provides that the offence is an offence of strict liability ... the defence of mistake of fact under section 9.2 is available'. Section 6.2(1) states that: 'If a law that creates an offence provides that the offence is an offence of absolute liability ... the defence of mistake of fact under section 9.2 is unavailable'. This clearly enunciates the conclusions of Sir Owen Dixon in *Proudman v Dayman* (at **13.29C**). Section 9.2(1), entitled 'Mistake of fact (strict liability)', provides that the defence entails that the defendant considered whether or not the critical facts in the case existed, and acted 'under a mistaken but reasonable belief about those facts; and had those facts existed, the conduct would not have constituted an offence'. Both ss 6.1 and 6.2 provide clearly that other general defences are available to defendants in both these categories.

13.53 The language of the Code excludes ignorance of the facts. It postulates advertence to, and a mistaken view or assessment of, the facts or circumstances. The legal burden of proof in relation to the defence of mistaken belief is upon the prosecution, though the defendant has the evidential burden: ss 13.1(2) and 13.3(1). See the final report, *Model Criminal Code — Chapters 1 and 2 — General Principles of Criminal Responsibility*, prepared by the Criminal Law Officers Committee of the Standing Committee of Attorneys-General (December 1992), pp 54–7.

13.54 The analysis of a statutory provision to ascertain the type of mental element (if any) which applies, it can be shown diagrammatically as follows:

Diagram 13.1: Statutory interpretation of the required mental element

1. There is a common law presumption that all offences require proof of mens rea (*He Kaw Teh*).

↓

2. This presumption can be rebutted upon analysis of (i) the words of the provision; (ii) the subject matter of the provision; and (iii) the policy implications of interpreting the provision as requiring, or not requiring, proof of mens rea (*He Kaw Teh*).

↓

3. There is then a presumption that all offences that do not require proof of mens rea are 'strict liability' offences to which the defence of 'honest and reasonable mistake of fact' applies.

↓

a. This defence requires proof (the defendant having the evidential burden) that (i) the defendant made a mistake which was honest and reasonable; (ii) which was a mistake of fact and not a mistake of law; and (iii) which involved a belief in facts which if true, would have made the act innocent.

↓

4. The presumption that the offence is one of 'strict liability' can be rebutted, if required upon considering the 'words, context, subject matter [and] general nature of the enactment' (*Proudman v Dayman*). If the presumption is found to be rebutted the offence is one of absolute liability.

Burden of proof and the defence of mistake

13.55 It has been stated above that the evidential burden of proving honest and reasonable mistake rests upon the accused. This is no more than an application of the ordinary principles relating to burden of proof discussed at 1.71–1.85. It has, however, been argued that the legal burden of proving honest and reasonable mistake of fact also rests on the accused. In other words, this defence constitutes an additional common law exception to the principle laid down in *Woolmington v Director of Public Prosecutions* [1935] AC 462 (at 1.82). The standard of proof which the accused must meet is that of the balance of probabilities. The most influential proponent of this view has been Professor C Howard: see 'Strict Responsibility in the High Court of Australia' (1960) 76 *LQR* 567; *Strict Responsibility*, Sweet & Maxwell, London, 1963, p 1059; *Criminal Law*, 4th ed, Law Book Co, Sydney, 1982, pp 376–7. See also, P Brett, 'Strict Responsibility: Possible Solutions' (1974) 37 *Mod LR* 417.

13.56 The view of Professor Howard was, it is submitted, never correct as a matter of principle and it has now been rejected by the High Court unanimously in both *He Kaw Teh v R* (at 13.33) and *CTM v R* (at 13.3C). The key case relied upon as supporting the view that the legal burden is upon the accused is *Proudman v Dayman* (1941) 67 CLR 536; [1944] ALR 64 (at 13.29C). In the course of his judgment, Dixon J stated:

> The burden of establishing honest and reasonable mistake is in the first place upon the defendant and he must make it appear that he had reasonable grounds for believing in the existence of a state of facts, which, if true, would take his act outside the operation of the enactment and that on those grounds he did so believe. The burden possibly may not finally rest upon him of satisfying the tribunal in case of doubt.

Although this passage is ambiguous, it would seem that, in the first sentence, Dixon J was referring to the evidential burden only. If this is so, then the correct interpretation of the second sentence would appear to be that he was leaving open the question of where the legal burden lies in respect of honest and reasonable mistake of fact.

13.57 The High Court has now settled the matter. It has decided that while the accused bears the evidential burden of proving honest and reasonable mistake, the legal burden rests upon the prosecution. The principle of *Woolmington v Director of Public Prosecutions* is properly regarded as central to our concept of a fair trial, and exceptions to that principle should be accepted only if sanctioned by clear authority or compelling reasons. The authorities are now conclusive. It was always difficult to find compelling reasons in support of the view that if the jury is of the opinion that it is as likely as not that the accused held an honest and reasonable belief in a state of facts which, if true, would have rendered the conduct innocent, it should nonetheless convict that person. It is argued that the burden should be placed upon the accused because, in most cases, the true facts are peculiarly within his or her knowledge. This, however, is a point equally true of other general defences such as automatism. In any event, leaving the evidential burden upon the accused would appear to be sufficient to meet this point. Since the decisions in *He Kaw Teh v R* and *CTM v R*, honest and reasonable mistake is, in Australia, on the same footing as other general defences. The congruent provisions of the Criminal Code Act 1995 (Cth) are mentioned at 13.52.

Mental Impairment and Related Defences

CHAPTER 14

INTRODUCTION

14.1 In all Australian jurisdictions, mentally impaired persons have a defence to a criminal charge brought against them. The name of this defence now varies in different jurisdictions: in Victoria, it is known as 'mental impairment', while in New South Wales the term 'mental illness' is more usually preferred. If found not guilty by reason of mental impairment, the defendant may be subject to various types of supervision orders, including custodial supervision orders. These orders are distinct from punishment as they do not follow a conviction that has resulted from a normal trial. These orders are referred to collectively as disposal or disposition orders. The modern statutory provisions in New South Wales and Victoria relating to the disposition of mentally impaired offenders are dealt with at 14.26–14.28.

14.2 Despite the significant changes to the law incorporated in the modern statutory regimes, and despite the modern preference to reject the stigmatising label of insanity, the modern law relating to mental impairment is very much a development of the old common law defence of insanity which developed in England and Wales in the nineteenth century. It follows from this that a great deal of the old common law of insanity is still relevant to the modern defence.

14.3 The notion that an insane person who commits what would, in other respects, be an offence should be exculpated by reason of his or her insanity appears to have first emerged in Islamic and Christian thought at about the eighth century of our present era. In England, the practice grew out of extending a Royal pardon to a 'lunatic' who had been convicted of a criminal charge, although the informal practice of excusing insane individuals pre-dates the use of Royal pardons. There are records of this informal practice running back at least as far as the second half of the thirteenth century. Gradually, the practice formalised into a rule and it came to be recognised that a person who was insane at the time when he or she committed a criminal act ought not to be convicted. The rule is recognised by Lord Coke in his *Third Institute* and by Hale in his *Pleas of the Crown*. Hale, in particular, gives a detailed account of the defence. Discussions of the matter are also to be found in Hawkins' *Pleas of the Crown* and Blackstone's *Commentaries*.

14.4 The foundations of the modern law on insanity are to be found, however, in two nineteenth century cases. The first is the *Trial of James Hadfield* (1800) 27 St Tr 1282. Hadfield attempted to kill King George III by shooting at him. At his trial it appeared that Hadfield had acted under a delusion, possibly brought on by an injury to the brain sustained while a soldier, that he was to be the saviour of the world and that this was to be accomplished by his being executed after commission of a spectacular crime. Lord Kenyon CJ stopped the trial and, at his direction, the jury returned a verdict of not guilty, stating that Hadfield was under the influence of insanity when he committed the act. Uncertainty about whether it was possible to detain Hadfield under the criminal law prompted Parliament to pass the Criminal Lunatics Act 1800 (39 & 40 Geo 3 c 94) (England and Wales). It provided that in cases where it appeared at a trial that the accused was insane and he was acquitted on this ground, the accused should not be released but should be ordered to be detained at the pleasure of the Sovereign. Although Hadfield had been ordered into custody before the passage of the statute, the statute was nonetheless used as authority for his continued detention. The provision in the 1800 Act that a defendant found 'not guilty on account of insanity' would be detained 'in strict custody … until His Majesty's pleasure be known' came to be known as indefinite detention, and carried over from England and Wales to the Australian states and territories.

14.5 The second, and probably the most famous, case in which the plea of insanity was raised was *M'Naghten's Case* (1843) 10 Cl & Fin 200; [1843–60] All ER Rep 229. Daniel McNaughtan shot and killed Edward Drummond, who was secretary to Sir Robert Peel, the then Prime Minister of England. At his trial for murder, before Tindal CJ and two other judges, it appeared that for some years McNaughtan had suffered from the delusion that he was being followed and persecuted by his enemies. McNaughtan also believed that these persecutors were 'the Tories', and he made several unsuccessful attempts to air his grievances, but without result. Ultimately, he seems to have decided that the only way he could end what he perceived as persecution was by killing Peel, who was the leader of the Tory Party, and it seems that he killed Drummond in mistake. At his trial, various lay witnesses testified to his delusions and five eminent doctors of the day also gave evidence in support of the view that he was insane. Tindal CJ, in effect, stopped the trial by advising the jury that they could, if they wished, return a verdict of not guilty without hearing further evidence. He added that, if they wished to take this course, the question they would have to decide was whether McNaughtan was able to distinguish right from wrong. The jury returned a verdict of acquittal on the ground of insanity, and McNaughtan was ordered to be detained.

The case created a great public uproar. Some people appear to have believed that McNaughtan's insanity was feigned and, reflecting the anxieties of the time, that he was part of a political plot. A detailed debate took place in the House of Lords on the question of whether the rules of law governing the defence of insanity were satisfactory. This was in effect a criticism of the decision of the Queen's Bench decision in McNaughtan's trial. It was decided that the judges should be consulted to ascertain exactly the present state of the law. For this purpose they were summoned to the House in June 1843 and asked five questions. The answers given by the judges to these questions are the foundation of the modern common law of the defence of insanity (now called mental impairment) and a sub-set of these answers came to be known as the *M'Naghten Rules*. They are set out at **14.7C**.

It is well recognised that the *M'Naughten Rules*-influenced insanity defence is hard to raise successfully. In addition, since the effect of a successful insanity plea may be long-term confinement subject to a supervision order, if the accused is regarded as dangerous, it follows that the defence is generally raised by an accused in the most serious cases such as murder.

14.6 A defence related to the defence of mental impairment is that of automatism (which is also referred to as non-insane automatism). This defence developed as a discrete entity in the 1950s in England and Wales. While there is no generally accepted definition of automatism, it may broadly be defined as a state in which the accused's mind or will does not accompany his or her bodily actions. In the New Zealand case of *R v Cottle* [1958] NZLR 999 at 1007, Gresson P defined automatism in the following terms:

> Automatism which strictly means action without conscious volition, has been adopted in criminal law as a term to denote conduct of which the doer is not conscious — in short doing something without knowledge of it, and without memory afterwards of having done it — a temporary eclipse of consciousness that nevertheless leaves the person so affected able to exercise bodily movements. In such a case, the action is one which the mind in its normal functioning does not control.

Automatism is a tightly circumscribed defence. It is available only to those individuals who are unconscious or acting involuntarily, and their loss of voluntary control must be total (albeit temporary). In addition, automatism must arise from an 'external' factor, rather than an 'internal' factor. It is on this basis that automatism is thought to mark out an individual who is less dangerous (or not dangerous at all) when compared with an insane individual. Due to the absence of dangerousness, a plea of automatism, if successful, results in a complete acquittal.

The distinction between mental impairment and automatism is thus of great significance to an accused, and has been the subject of considerable judicial discussion. Cases on automatism and its relationship with mental impairment are set out below. Not uncommonly, states of automatism (where the term is used in a non-technical way to describe a state of unconsciousness or involuntariness) are brought on by the consumption of alcohol or other drugs. Where this is the case, an accused will be dealt with under the law of intoxication. Although these matters are touched on in the present chapter, detailed consideration of the problem of the accused who commits criminal acts under the influence of alcohol or other drugs will be postponed until **Chapter 15**.

An additional defence dependent on the accused's mental state is the defence of substantial impairment by abnormality of mind (also known as diminished responsibility), available in New South Wales, but not in Victoria.

In addition, it is necessary to briefly mention unfitness to plead. Unfitness to plead is a procedural provision (rather than a defence) that exempts an accused from an ordinary trial (at least temporarily) on the basis that he or she cannot understand or participate in it. If a defendant is found unfit to plead, he or she is also subject to the disposal regime that follows a successful mental impairment defence.

Substantial impairment and unfitness to plead will be considered at **14.28**ff. A number of further issues raised by mental impairment will also be considered there. Issues relating to severe personality disorder will be canvassed at **14.50**ff.

CASES ON MENTAL IMPAIRMENT AND AUTOMATISM

14.7C M'Naghten's Case

(1843) 10 Cl & Fin 200; [1843–60] All ER Rep 229
House of Lords

Tindal CJ: My Lords, Her Majesty's Judges (with the exception of Mr Justice Maule, who has stated his opinion to your Lordships), in answering the questions proposed to them by your Lordship's House, think it right in the first place, to state that they have forborne entering into any particular discussion upon these questions, from the extreme and almost insuperable difficulty of applying those answers to cases in which the facts are not brought judicially before them. The facts of each particular case must of necessity present themselves with endless variety, and with every shade of difference in each case; and as it is their duty to declare the law upon each particular case, on facts proved before them, and after hearing argument of counsel thereon, they deem it at once impracticable, and at the same time dangerous to the administration of justice, if it were practicable, to attempt to make minute applications of the principles involved in the answers given by them to your Lordships' questions.

They have therefore confined their answers to the statements of that which they hold to be the law upon the abstract questions proposed by your Lordships; and as they deem it unnecessary, in this peculiar case, to deliver their opinions *seriatim*, and as all concur in the same opinion, they desire me to express such their unanimous opinion to your Lordships.

The first question proposed by your Lordships is this:

> What is the law respecting alleged crimes committed by persons afflicted with insane delusion in respect of one or more particular subjects or persons: as, for instance, where at the time of the commission of the alleged crime the accused knew he was acting contrary to law, but did the act complained of with a view, under the influence of insane delusion, of redressing or revenging some supposed grievance or injury, or of producing some supposed public benefit?

In answer to which question, assuming that your Lordships' inquiries are confined to those persons who labour under such partial delusions only and are not in other respects insane, we are of opinion that, notwithstanding the party accused did the act complained of with a view, under the influence of insane delusion, of redressing or revenging some supposed grievance or injury, or of producing some public benefit, he is nevertheless punishable according to the nature of the crime committed, if he knew at the time of committing such crime that he was acting contrary to law; by which expression we understand your Lordships to mean the law of the land. Your Lordships are pleased to inquire of us, secondly:

> What are the proper questions to be submitted to the jury, where a person alleged to be afflicted with insane delusion respecting one or more particular subjects or persons, is charged with the commission of a crime (murder, for example), and insanity is set up as a defence?
>
> And, thirdly:
>
> In what terms ought the question to be left to the jury as to the prisoner's state of mind at the time when the act was committed?

And as these two questions appear to us to be more conveniently answered together, we have to submit our opinion to be, that the jurors ought to be told in all cases that every man is to be presumed to be sane, and to possess a sufficient degree of reason to be responsible for his crimes, until the contrary be proved to their satisfaction; and that to establish a defence on the ground of insanity, it must be clearly proved that, at the time of the committing of the act, the party accused was labouring under such a defect of reason, from disease of the mind, as not to know the nature and quality of the act he was doing; or, if he did know it, that he did not know he was doing what was wrong. The mode of putting the latter part of the question to the jury is not, as we conceive, so accurate when put generally and in the abstract, as when put with reference to the party's knowledge of right and wrong in respect to the very act with which he is charged. If the question were to be put as to the knowledge of the accused solely and exclusively with reference to the law of the land, it might tend to confound the jury, by inducing them to believe that an actual knowledge of the law of the land was essential in order to lead to a conviction; whereas the law is administered upon the principle that everyone must be taken conclusively to know it, without proof that he does know it. If the accused was conscious that the act was one which he ought not to do, and if that act was at the same time contrary to the law of the land, he is punishable; and the usual course therefore has been to leave the question to the jury, whether the party accused had a sufficient degree of reason to know that he was doing an act that was wrong: and this course we think is correct, accompanied with such observations and explanations as the circumstances of each particular case may require.

The fourth question which your Lordships have proposed to us is this:

> If a person under an insane delusion as to existing facts, commits an offence in consequence thereof, is he thereby excused?

To which question the answer must of course depend on the nature of the delusion: but, making the same assumption as we did before, namely, that he labours under such partial delusion only, and is not in other respects insane, we think he must be considered in the same situation as to responsibility as if the facts with respect to which the delusion exists were real. For example, if under the influence of his delusion he supposed another man to be in the act of attempting to take away his life, and he kills that man, as he supposes, in self-defence, he would be exempt from punishment. If his delusion was that the deceased had inflicted serious injury to his character and fortune, and he killed him in revenge for such supposed injury, he would be liable to punishment.

The question lastly proposed by your Lordships is:

> Can a medical man conversant with the disease of insanity, who never saw the prisoner previously to the trial, but who was present during the whole trial and the examination of all the witnesses, be asked his opinion as to the state of the prisoner's mind at the same time of the commission of the alleged crime, or his opinion whether the prisoner was conscious at the time of doing the act that he was acting contrary to law, or whether he was labouring under any and what delusion at the time?

In answer thereto, we state to your Lordships, that we think the medical man, under the circumstances supposed, cannot in strictness be asked his opinion in the terms above stated, because each of those questions involves the determination of the truth of the facts deposed to, which it is for the jury to decide, and the questions are not mere questions upon a matter of science, in which case such evidence is admissible. But where the facts are admitted or not disputed, and the question becomes substantially one of science only, it may be convenient to allow the question to be put in that general form, though the same cannot be insisted on as a matter of right.

14.8C R v Porter

(1933) 55 CLR 182

High Court of Australia

[On 31 January and 1 February 1933 (before the passing of the Seat of Government Supreme Court Act 1933 (Cth)), Bertram Edward Porter was tried on indictment for murder at Canberra before Dixon J sitting in the original jurisdiction of the High Court under s 30B of the Judiciary Act 1903–32 (Cth).

It appeared that the prisoner had administered strychnine to his infant son aged 11 months and had then attempted to take strychnine himself but had been interrupted by the entry of the police. The child died, and this was the murder with which he was charged. His defence was that he was insane at the time he committed the act.

The facts set up in support of the defence were briefly as follows. After a period of separation from his wife during which he looked after the child, he made desperate but unsuccessful efforts to effect a reconciliation. He became extremely emotional and showed symptoms of a nervous breakdown. He was sleepless and took quantities of aspirin, phenacetin and caffeine. He then travelled with the child from Canberra to Sydney in circumstances which made it probable that he was without sleep for three nights. On his return, he had a final interview with his wife in which he appeared to have lost all control of his emotions. On her refusing to have anything to do with him or the child, he told her he would poison himself and the child and hastened away to obtain the strychnine. She informed the police, who found him shut in his house, sobbing. He had just given the strychnine to the child and was about to take it himself.]

Dixon J [summing up]: The accused stands charged under the name of Bertram Edward Porter, for the murder of his child, Charles Robert Porter, committed on 29 November 1932. The crime of murder is committed when, without any lawful justification, without any excuse, without any provocation, a person of sufficient soundness of mind to be criminally responsible for his acts intentionally kills another. To begin with, every person is presumed to be of sufficient soundness of mind to be criminally responsible for his actions until the contrary is made to appear upon his trial. It is not for the Crown to prove that any man is of sound mind; it is for the defence to establish inferentially that he was not of sufficient soundness of mind, at the time that he did the actions charged, to be criminally responsible. On the other hand, every person is to be presumed to be innocent of the actions charged against him until it is proved to the satisfaction of the jury beyond any reasonable doubt that he committed them.

You will see, gentlemen, that the presumptions are not of equal strength. The criminal law requires that, when a crime is charged, the things which constitute that crime shall be proved to the complete satisfaction of the jury; that they shall be so satisfied that those things were done that they have no reasonable doubt about it. On the other hand, when that is proved, and the jury turn from the consideration of the question whether the things which constitute the crime were done to the question whether the man who did them was criminally responsible for his actions or was not, because of unsoundness of mind at the moment, it is necessary for the accused person to make out positively, upon a balance of probability, that he was not criminally responsible, and that he was not of such a mental condition at that time as to be criminally responsible. He has not got to remove all doubt from your minds. He, or rather his counsel, has merely to make it appear to you as more probable on the whole that that was the state of his mind, at the time he did the things charged than otherwise ...

[His Honour referred to the facts material to the commission of the acts constituting the crime and proceeded:]

The facts, as I have said, appear to me to be clear, but if you disagree with that, you should give effect to your disagreement by finding the prisoner not guilty. The responsibility is yours, and not mine. If, on the contrary you are satisfied beyond reasonable doubt, to the exclusion of all doubt, of these three matters — (1) that he did administer strychnine to the child; (2) that he did so with the intention of killing it; and (3) that the child's death did result from that administration — then you will turn and proceed to consider whether, at that particular time when he did those things, his state of mind was such as to make him criminally responsible for his act. That means, has it been made out to your reasonable satisfaction that, at the time, the prisoner's faculties were so disordered that he is not in law criminally responsible for what he did. If you form the opinion that his faculties were so disordered that he is not criminally responsible you will find a verdict of not guilty on the ground that the prisoner was insane at the time the offence was committed. You do not find him guilty but insane, as they do in some British countries. According to the law in this country the technical verdict in such a case is: Not guilty on the grounds of insanity at the time of the commission of the offence charged. It is your function specifically to state that ground for your verdict of not guilty, because the legal consequences are quite different from those which follow a plain verdict of not guilty on the ground that the prisoner did not do the things charged. If you think it is not proved that the prisoner poisoned his child and brought about his death, your verdict, of course, will be simply not guilty, and he will be completely free. If, however, you think that he did the things charged against him, but that, at the time, his mind was so disordered that he could not be held responsible, then you will find him not guilty on the ground of insanity at the time of the offence charged.

There is a legal standard of disorder of mind which is sufficient to afford a ground of irresponsibility for crime, and a ground for your finding such a verdict as I have indicated. It is my duty to attempt to explain that standard to you. It is plain from what passed in the witness-box this morning, when Dr Henry was giving evidence, that the legal standard is a matter which he himself wished to discuss, but I prevented him, and kept him to his medical function. In my judgment, from remarks which have been made at the bar in the course of speeches, it appears that some difference of opinion between learned counsel exists as to what that legal standard is. You will take my explanation of it, and disregard the attempts which have been made elsewhere to explain it, because mine is the responsibility of laying down what the law is. Yours is the responsibility of applying it to the facts.

Before explaining what that standard actually is, I wish to draw your attention to some general considerations affecting the question of insanity in the criminal law in the hope that by so doing you may be helped to grasp what the law prescribes. The purpose of the law in punishing people is to prevent others from committing a like crime or crimes. Its prime purpose is to deter people from committing offences. It may be that there is an element of retribution in criminal law, so that when people have committed offences the law considers that they merit punishment, but its prime purpose is to preserve society from the depredations of dangerous and vicious people. Now, it is perfectly useless for the law to attempt, by threatening punishment, to deter people from committing crimes if their mental condition is such that they cannot be in the least influenced by the possibility or probability of subsequent punishment; if they cannot understand what they are doing or cannot understand the ground upon which the law proceeds. The law is not directed, as medical science is, to curing mental infirmities. The criminal law is not directed, as the civil law of lunacy is, to the care and custody of people of weak mind whose personal property may be in jeopardy through someone else taking a hand in the conduct of their affairs and their lives. This is quite a different thing from the question, what utility there is in the punishment of people who, at the moment, would commit acts which, if done when they were in sane minds, would be crimes. What is the utility of punishing people if they be beyond the control of the law for reasons of mental health? In considering that, it will not perhaps, if you have ever reflected upon the matter, have escaped your attention that a great number of people who come into a Criminal Court are abnormal. They would not be there if they were the normal type of average everyday people. Many of them are very peculiar in their dispositions and peculiarly tempered. That is markedly the case in sexual offences. Nevertheless, they are mentally quite able to appreciate what they are doing and quite able to appreciate the threatened punishment of the law and the wrongness of their acts, and they are held in check by the prospect of punishment. It would be very absurd if the law were to withdraw that check on the ground that they were somewhat different from their fellow creatures in mental make-up or texture at the very moment when the check is most needed. You will therefore see that the law, in laying down a standard of mental disorder sufficient to justify a jury in finding a prisoner not guilty on the ground of insanity at the moment of the offence, is addressing itself to a somewhat difficult task. It is attempting to define what are the classes of people who should not be punished although they have done actual things which in others would amount to crime. It is quite a different object to that which the medical profession has in view or other departments of the law have in view in defining insanity for the purpose of the custody of a person's property, capacity to make a will and the like. With that explanation I shall tell you what that standard is.

The first thing which I want you to notice is that you are only concerned with the condition of the mind at the time the act complained of was done. That is the critical time when the law applies to the man. You are not concerned, except for the purpose of finding out how he stood at that moment, what his subsequent condition was or what his previous condition was. He may have been sane before and he may have been sane after, but if his mind were disordered at the time to the required extent, then he should be acquitted on the ground of insanity at the time he committed the offence. It is helpful in finding out how he was at the time to find out how he was before and after. It is merely because it is helpful that we go into it in this case, not because it is decisive.

The next thing which I wish to emphasise is that his state of mind must have been one of disease, disorder or disturbance. Mere excitability of a normal man, passion, even stupidity, obtuseness, lack of self-control, and impulsiveness, are quite different things from what I have attempted to describe as a state of disease or disorder or mental disturbance arising from some infirmity, temporary or of long standing. If that existed it must then have been of such a character as to prevent him from knowing the physical nature of the act he was doing or of knowing that what he was doing was wrong. You will see that I have mentioned two quite different things. One state of mind is that in which he is prevented by mental disorder from knowing the physical nature of the act he is doing; the other is that he was prevented from knowing that what he was doing was wrong. The first relates to a class of case to which so far as I am concerned I do not think this case belongs. But again, that is my opinion of a matter of fact and it is for you to form your opinion upon it. In a case where a man intentionally destroys life he may have so little capacity for understanding the nature of life and the destruction of life, that to him it is no more than breaking a twig or destroying an inanimate object. In such a case he would not know the physical nature of what he was doing. He would not know the implications and what it really amounted to. In this case, except for the prisoner's own statement from the dock that after a certain time he remembered nothing of what he did, there seems to be nothing to support the view that this man was in such a condition that he could not appreciate what death amounted to or that he was bringing it about or that he was destroying life and all that is involved in the destruction of life. It is for you to form a conclusion upon that matter, but I suggest to you that the evidence of what he said to the police when he was found after he had given the poison to the child and was about, apparently, to administer it to himself, shows that he understood the nature of life and death and the nature of the act he was doing in bringing it about. But you are at liberty to take into account that he said he knows nothing of what he did at the time. If you form the conclusion that notwithstanding the evidence which I have mentioned the mental disorder of this man was such that he could not appreciate the physical thing he was doing and its consequences, you will acquit him on the ground of insanity at the time he did the thing charged.

The other head is of quite a different character, namely, that his disease or disorder or disturbance of mind was of such a character that he was unable to appreciate that the act he was doing was wrong. It is supposed that he knew he was killing, knew how he was killing and knew why he was killing, but that he was quite incapable of appreciating the wrongness of the act. That is the issue, the real question in this case. Was his state of mind of that character? I have used simple expressions, but when you are dealing with the unseen workings of the mind you have to come to close quarters with what you are speaking about, and it is very difficult to be quite clear as to what is meant in describing mental conditions. I have used the expression 'disease, disorder or disturbance of mind'. That does not mean (as you heard from the doctor's replies this morning to certain questions I asked him) that there must be some physical deterioration of the cells of the brain, some actual change in the material, physical constitution of the mind, as disease ordinarily means when you are dealing with other organs of the body where you can see and feel and appreciate structural changes in fibre, tissue and the like. You are dealing with a very different thing — with the understanding. It does mean that the functions of the understanding are through some cause whether understandable or not, thrown into derangement or disorder. Then I have used the expression 'know', 'knew that what he was doing was wrong'. We are dealing with one particular thing, the act of killing, the act of killing at a particular time a particular individual. We are not dealing with right or wrong in the abstract. The question is whether he was able to appreciate the wrongness of the particular act he was doing at the particular time. Could this man be said to know in this sense whether his act was wrong if through a disease or defect or disorder of the mind he could not think rationally of the reasons which to ordinary people make that act right or wrong? If through the disordered condition of the mind he could not reason about the matter with a moderate degree of sense and composure it may be said that he could not know that what he was doing was wrong. What is meant by 'wrong'? What is meant by wrong is wrong having regard to the everyday standards of reasonable people. If you think that at the time when he administered the poison to the child he had such a mental disorder or disturbance or derangement that he was incapable of reasoning about the right or wrongness, according to ordinary standards, of the thing which he was doing, not that he reasoned wrongly, or that being a responsible person he had queer or unsound ideas, but that he was quite incapable of taking into account the considerations which go to make right or wrong, then you should find him not guilty upon the ground that he was insane at the time he committed the acts charged. In considering these matters from the point of view of fact you must be guided by his outward actions to a very large extent. The only other matter which can help you really is the medical opinion. I think the evidence may be described as his outward conduct and the medical opinion. It is upon this you must act. The medical opinion included explanations of the course of mental conditions in human beings generally.

[His Honour reviewed the circumstances affecting the question of the prisoner's state of mind at the time of the commission of the acts charged and the medical evidence, and proceeded:]

In conclusion I go back to what I consider the main question of the case and it is whether you are of the opinion that at the stage of administering the poison to the child the man whom you are trying had such a mental disorder or diseased intelligence at that moment that he was disabled from knowing that it was a wrong act to commit in the sense that ordinary reasonable men understand right and wrong and that he was disabled from considering with some degree of composure and reason what he was doing and its wrongness. If you answer that question in his favour you will find him not guilty on the ground of insanity at the time of the commission of the offence charged.

[The jury returned the following verdict: not guilty on the ground of insanity at the time of commission of the act charged.]

[See also *R v Pangallo* (1989) 51 SASR 254; *R v Weeks* (1993) 66 A Crim R 466.]

14.9C

Willgoss v R

(1960) 105 CLR 295

High Court of Australia

[At the trial of the accused upon a charge of murder, a defence of insanity was raised. Evidence was given by two psychiatrists that the accused was a gross psychopath. They distinguished a psychopath by his gross lack of self-control and his gross lack or diminution of emotional feeling, which involved gross diminution of conscience. The accused was convicted and appealed to the High Court on the ground that, in instructing the jury, the trial judge did not adequately distinguish between an intellectual understanding of wrongfulness and an emotional appreciation of it.]

Dixon CJ, **McTiernan**, **Fullagar**, **Menzies** and **Windeyer JJ**: It seems evident even from the very brief account of the case given above that, whatever disease or disorder of the mind it might be thought proper to attribute to the prisoner, it would not be easy to conclude that he laboured under such a defect of reason from that cause as not to know the nature and quality of the act he was doing. That refers to the physical character of the act, in this case a capacity to know or understand the significance of the act of killing and of the shooting by which it was done. The weight of the defence of insanity was wisely placed by counsel for the prisoner upon the second branch of the well known formula defining the elements in a plea of insanity to a charge of crime. What was urged was that through disease or disorder of the mind the prisoner when he shot Gillett had not a capacity to know that he was doing what was wrong. His psychopathic condition as defined by the two psychiatrists was relied upon as showing that he could not 'know' that the act he did was wrong because, so it was said, to make up knowledge of right and wrong the capacity to appreciate or 'feel' the effect of his actions upon others and perhaps himself must exist in some degree and this, according to the psychiatrists, was deficient in a gross psychopath. Dr Sinclair clearly distinguished between what in his terminology is the intellectual process which contributes to knowing, that is to say the application of intelligence, and what he called the appropriate feeling about an act. Without the latter he would say that the man was incapable of knowing that what he was doing was wrong. It is upon some such view of what amounts to knowledge of wrongness that the grounds of this application ultimately rested. Dr Sinclair was asked to suppose that a gross psychopath did an act which the law and ordinary people would regard as very wrong and to say whether such a man would be capable of knowing that it was wrong. The witness answered: 'He would be capable of understanding, assessing intellectually what he was doing was wrong. I believe he would not have the appropriate feeling to have a full appreciation of knowing what he was doing was wrong.' In his charge to the jury O'Bryan J did not draw the distinction between the two ingredients of knowledge of wrong put forward by Dr Sinclair. His Honour gave a very full and clear exposition of the elements involved in a plea of insanity to a criminal charge. When he came to what amounted to knowledge of the wrongness of the act the learned judge went beyond what the facts of the case seem really to have demanded. For his Honour said: 'Now if he could not really reason about the matter with a moderate degree of composure it may be said he could not know that what he was doing was wrong.' Such a direction well may be called for in cases where the acts which but for insanity would form the crime charged are committed in a state of frenzy, uncontrolled emotion or suspended reason, the product of mental disease or disorder. No doubt O'Bryan J took the words from *R v Porter* (1933) 55 CLR 182 at 189–90 and perhaps *Sodeman v R* (1936) 55 CLR 192 at 215 and *Stapleton v R* (1952) 86 CLR 358 at 367. In *Porter's* case (1933) 55 CLR 182 the discussion of the facts of the case is not included in the report, but the point of the prisoner's defence was that in a condition of uncontrolled emotionalism characteristic of a nervous breakdown to which many factors had contributed he attempted to poison himself and his child succeeding only in the case of the latter. In *Sodeman's* case (1936) 55 CLR 192 it is unnecessary to say that the whole point was the possibility of his sexual frenzy accounting for the homicide and being attributed to mental disease. In *Stapleton's* case (1952) 86 CLR 358 it was perhaps not so much a case of frenzied condition but of a fixed state of unreason although perhaps temporary. In the case before us the alleged incapacity of the prisoner to comprehend the wrongness of the act seems to have depended on other considerations than a capacity to reason about the matter with a moderate degree of sense and composure. But if O'Bryan J went further in this respect than the facts of the case demanded, the tendency of it was all in the prisoner's favour.

The complaint, however, on behalf of the prisoner is that his Honour did not direct the jury that a mere intellectual apprehension on the prisoner's part of the wrongness of the act would not or might not amount to knowledge unless it was accompanied by some sufficient appreciation of, or feeling about, the effect of his act upon other people; perhaps some moral appreciation. The law provides no foundation for such a complaint. It is enough to say that it is an attempt to refine upon what amounts to knowledge of the wrongness of the act which is not countenanced by the law. The explanation made by O'Bryan J of what amounts to the wrongness of the act was adequate and as clear as can be desired for the purpose of submitting to a jury the issue as the law defines it.

[Appeal dismissed.]

14.10C Attorney-General for South Australia v Brown

[1960] AC 432
Privy Council

[At the trial of the accused on a charge of murder by shooting, in which the only defence was insanity, the medical evidence for the respondent was, inter alia, that he was a schizoid personality and that, at the moment of shooting, he knew the nature and quality of his act but did not know that what he was doing was wrong. In the course of his summing-up, the trial judge had directed the jury that 'uncontrollable impulse' was no defence in law. The accused was found guilty and sentenced to death. His first appeal having been dismissed, he appealed further to the High Court of Australia, who quashed the conviction and ordered a new trial. In the course of their judgment, the High Court stated:

> To treat his domination by an uncontrollable impulse as reason for a conclusion against his defence of insanity is quite erroneous. On the contrary it may afford strong ground for the inference that a prisoner was labouring under such a defect of reason from disease of the mind as not to know that he was doing what was wrong … the fact that the subject

was mentioned would make it necessary to put before the jury the true operation of uncontrollable impulse as a possible symptom of insanity of a required kind and degree.

The Crown appealed to the Privy Council.]

Lord Tucker [delivering the judgment of their Lordships]: The only real issue in the case was whether the defence had discharged the onus of proving on balance of probability that the respondent was legally insane when he shot Lord. The issue was further narrowed since the medical witnesses for the defence and for the prosecution agreed that the respondent was (1) what psychiatrists refer to as a schizoid personality, (2) that neither before nor after the shooting was the respondent suffering from any disease or disorder of the mind, and (3) that at the moment of shooting he knew the nature and quality of his act. Where they differed was that Dr Forgan, for the defence, testified that in his opinion at the time of the shooting the respondent had lapsed into a temporary state of simple schizophrenia in which he did not know that what he was doing was wrong.

Dr Shea, on the other hand, was of the opinion that the respondent never at any time had schizophrenia, and that even if he did he not only knew the nature and quality of his act but also that it is wrong, as the respondent had told him when he examined him in prison.

[His Lordship then referred to passages from the trial judge's summing-up and from the decision of the High Court, and continued:]

It is the concluding lines of the penultimate paragraph beginning with the words 'on the contrary' which in their Lordships' view give rise to questions of great importance and far-reaching consequences in the administration of the criminal law. They would naturally be read by the judge who presides over the new trial and by all judges in similar cases in States where the English common law prevails as requiring them to tell the jury *as a matter of law* and in the absence of any medical evidence to that effect that irresistible impulse is a symptom of some disease or disorder of the mind which, although not preventing the patient from knowing the nature and quality of his act, yet does prevent him from knowing that it is wrong.

The words 'the true operation of uncontrollable impulse as a possible symptom of insanity of a required kind and degree' must imply that the law knows and recognises uncontrollable impulse as a symptom of legal insanity within the meaning of the rule in *M'Naghten's* case 1 C & K 130 and in conjunction with the language used at the beginning of the passage in question, that it is the judge's duty to instruct the jury that it may afford strong ground for the inference that the prisoner was labouring under such a defect of reason from disease of the mind as not to know that he was doing what was wrong. Furthermore, this direction is required not only in a case where there may have been no medical evidence, but even in a case, such as the present, where the medical evidence for the defence was to the effect that the prisoner when he committed the act was suffering from a specific disease or disorder of the mind known as schizophrenia which, although not preventing him knowing the nature and quality of his act, did prevent him from knowing it was wrong, but of which it was never suggested that irresistible impulse was a symptom or that it played any part in helping the medical witness for the defence to arrive at his diagnosis. So much so that counsel for the respondent on the present appeal, far from relying on irresistible impulse, contended that the trial judge should never have mentioned the subject in his charge to the jury as it formed no part of the case for the defence.

Their Lordships can find no support for the view that this accurately represents the criminal law.

At various times in the past attempts have been made to temper the supposed harshness or unscientific nature of the M'Naghten Rules. These attempts were supported by the high authority of Sir James Fitzjames Stephen, but in the end the rules remain in full force and their harshness has in this country been to some extent alleviated by the recent legislative enactment affording the defence of diminished responsibility. While the High Court, of course, fully recognises the binding force of the M'Naghten Rules, their Lordships think that the directions which they have indicated as appropriate for use by trial judges would in effect make a very considerable inroad into those rules as hitherto interpreted. Moreover, unless the law is presumed to take cognisance of irresistible impulse as a symptom of legal insanity, whence does the judge derive his knowledge of these matters, it not being permissible for him to make use of what he may have learned from evidence given in other cases?

Their Lordships must not, of course, be understood to suggest that in a case where evidence has been given (and it is difficult to imagine a case where such evidence would be other than medical evidence) that irresistible impulse is a symptom of the particular disease of the mind from which a prisoner is said to be suffering and as to its effect on his ability to know the nature and quality of his act or that his act is wrong it would not be the duty of the judge to deal with the matter in the same way as any other relevant evidence given at the trial.

Sodeman v R (1936) 55 CLR 192, affirmed [1936] WN 190; [1936] 2 All ER 1138, PC is an Australian example of such a case. The actual decision in that case related to the burden of proof in cases where the defence of insanity is raised and to the sufficiency of the trial judge's direction thereon, but in the course of the judgments references were made to 'irresistible impulse' and its possible bearing on the defence raised by the medical evidence in that case to the effect that if a man has an obsession and if he gives way to that obsession and does the thing which is always before his mind as the thing he wants to do, then in doing it he does not know the quality of his act, he does not know what he is doing, and does not know whether it is right or wrong. (Vide the judgment of Latham CJ 55 CLR 192 at 203.) The learned Chief Justice used these words: ibid, 205.

> But on the other hand, it should be remembered that, as already stated, the law recognises that mental disease manifested in, for example, what is called 'uncontrollable impulse', may also be manifested in lack of knowledge, or incapacity to have knowledge, of the nature and quality of an act or of its character as a wrong act. Such an impulse may be evidence of this very lack or incapacity. *Indeed, that was the effect of the medical opinions given in evidence in this case, and this aspect of the case was definitely put to the jury by the judge.*

This passage must be read in the light of the concluding sentence now italicised. So read, their Lordships would not question it. But if the word 'recognises' in the first sentence is construed to mean that the words which follow are matters of law which must or may be accepted and acted upon by juries without evidence it would not in their Lordships' opinion be an accurate statement of the law. The word 'recognises' would seem to have been used in contrast to the rejection of irresistible impulse per se and means no more than that the law will not refuse to listen to evidence to the effect stated whereas it will refuse to listen to evidence of irresistible impulse per se.

The presumption that the law takes note of such matters without evidence is implicit in the language of the High Court's judgment in the present case. It is this that their Lordships with great respect feel unable to accept.

It may be observed in passing that in the case of *R v Porter* (1933) 55 CLR 182 the charge to the jury by Dixon J (as he then was) in which he dealt with the workings of the human mind appears to have been based upon the medical evidence given in that case. (Vide at 189, line 18, and at 190, line 18, 'the medical evidence included explanations of the course of mental conditions in human beings generally'.)

This distinction between what the law presumes and what the law will listen to is of the first importance in the present case since counsel for the respondent has disclaimed any reliance on irresistible impulse either per se or as an element in the particular kind of mental disease relied upon to support the defence that the respondent, although aware of the nature and quality of his act, did not know that it was wrong, and submitted that the trial judge should never have referred to it in his charge to the jury.

Their Lordships do not derive much assistance from the interlocutory observations of Greer J during the argument in the case of *R v True* (1922) 16 Cr App R 164 at 167. He was speaking from recollection of his summing up in a case which he had tried two years earlier and in which no medical evidence had been given. No reference was made to his observations by the other members of the court and no authority has been cited in which the Court of Criminal Appeal has given its approval to such a direction. In none of the leading cases in recent years such as *R v Kopsch* (1925) 19 Cr App R 50, CCA and *R v Rivett* (1950) 34 Cr App R 87, CCA where the defence of insanity was raised has there been any suggestion that although irresistible impulse affords no defence per se the law will recognise it as a symptom from which the jury may without evidence infer insanity within the M'Naghten Rules. In the latter of these cases the defence of insanity was based on evidence almost identical with the medical evidence in the present case: ibid, 92. It may, perhaps, be observed in passing that if such matters were left to a jury without the assistance of medical evidence there would seem to be two possible views which a layman might take as to the relevance of irresistible impulse to the M'Naghten tests. Some might think that before an impulse becomes irresistible there must have been some attempt to resist it and that the attempted resistance might well be due to knowledge of the wrongness of the act to which the prisoner felt himself impelled. Others might think that the irresistible impulse might impair the reasoning power to such a degree that it would no longer be able to appreciate the wrongness of the act. Why should the law prescribe that one of these views must be presumed to be correct rather than the other without medical evidence as to which is to be preferred with reference to the particular form of mental disease or disorder from which a prisoner is said to have been suffering?

Their Lordships are not, of course, suggesting that legal insanity cannot be sufficiently proved without medical evidence. The previous and contemporaneous acts of the accused may often be preferred to medical theory. But where the whole case for the defence is based upon the accused having a particular form of mental disease — such as schizophrenia, the nature and symptoms of which are known to psychiatrists but knowledge of which cannot be attributed to a jury — the law will not step in to instruct a jury in the absence of medical evidence as to the 'true operation of uncontrollable impulse as a possible symptom of insanity of a required kind and degree'.

[Appeal allowed. Judgment of the High Court set aside and the verdict and judgment of the trial court restored.]

14.11 Notes and illustrations

1. The word 'wrong' in the *M'Naghten Rules* contains a potential ambiguity. It may require showing that the accused did not appreciate the wrongfulness of the conduct from a moral point of view, or it may require showing that he or she did not realise that conduct was prohibited by law. In England and Wales, the *Rules* have been interpreted to convey the latter more strict requirement: *R v Codere* (1916) 12 Cr App R 21; *R v Windle* [1952] 2 QB 826. In Australia, the High Court has interpreted the *Rules* to convey the former, less strict requirement. In *Sodeman v R* (1936) 55 CLR 192, the court treated 'wrong' as meaning morally wrong, and the matter was fully debated in *Stapleton v R* (1952) 86 CLR 358. In *Stapleton*, the High Court considered and declined to follow the decision in *R v Windle*, and held that 'wrong' means wrong according to the reasons which govern the conduct of ordinary people. Its decision, which is carefully reasoned, seems to these authors to be more faithful to the *M'Naughten Rules* themselves than that of the English courts. In reality, the difference between the two approaches may not be of great practical significance. In *Stapleton v R*, the court stated (at 375):

> The truth perhaps is that, from a practical point of view, it cannot often matter a great deal whether the capacity of the accused person is measured by his ability to understand the difference between right and wrong according to reasonable standards, or to understand what is punishable by law, because in serious things the two ideas are not easily separable.

2. *Taylor v R* (1978) 22 ALR 599 concerned an appeal from D, who was charged with murder and raised the defence of insanity. Crown and defence evidence all pointed in the direction that, at the time of the killing, D had not known that what he was doing was wrong. In an unsworn statement, corroborated by testimony from relatives, D recounted problems of disassociation from reality and his family history. No doubt was cast by the Crown upon the reliability of the material upon which the medical evidence was based. In summing up to the jury, the trial judge said that, while the medical evidence all pointed one way, the jury was not bound to accept it. D was convicted. On appeal to the Federal Court of Australia, the conviction was quashed. The basic duty of the jury is to find a verdict according to the evidence. The jury cannot reject unanimous medical evidence unless there is other evidence which can displace or throw doubt on that evidence: *Taylor v R* (1978) 22 ALR 599. It seems possible that the jury can reject medical evidence that is not unanimous: *R v Byrne* [1960] 2 QB 396 at 403.

14.12C **R v Falconer**

(1990) 171 CLR 30
High Court of Australia

[The accused was convicted in the Supreme Court of Western Australia of the wilful murder of her husband by shooting. She gave evidence of the deceased's violence to her during their marriage, of her discovery that he had sexually interfered with her daughters, and of their separation. She said that on the day of his death, the deceased had entered her house unexpectedly, had sexually assaulted her and had reached out as if to grab her by the hair. From that point, she remembered nothing until she found herself on the floor with the gun beside her and the deceased dead on the floor. The trial judge rejected the evidence of two psychiatrists, received on voir dire, by which the accused sought to support a defence under s 23 of the Criminal Code (WA). Both expressed the view that she was sane at the time of the shooting. One said that the accused may have panicked and that that could have triggered a dissociative state in which she acted without awareness of what she was doing. The other said that the accused was in a setting of psychological conflict in which she was capable of acting in an automatic way. The Full Court of the Supreme Court allowed the accused's appeal and ordered a retrial. On appeal by the Crown.]

Mason CJ, **Brennan** and **McHugh JJ**: From the time when Sir Owen Dixon delivered his paper 'A Legacy of Hadfield, M'Naghten and Maclean', *Australian Law Journal*, vol 31, 1957, 255, the relationship between involuntariness and insanity has awaited consideration by this court. In the meantime, the problem has received extensive consideration in other courts and in learned writings.

The present case arises under the Code which is identical in its relevant provisions with the original form in which the Queensland Criminal Code was enacted. The author of those Codes, Sir Samuel Griffith, was not conscious of any divergence between the provisions he had drafted and the common law, except in respect of incapacity to control actions in s 27. Of course, that is not conclusive of the meaning of any particular provision in the Codes, but it is an indication that the problem which arises now in a statutory context may be answered in a way which answers the corresponding problems under the common law. Though special leave is granted to the Crown only in exceptional cases, this case raises exceptionally important questions and special leave should be granted to consider them …

When an act is done by an apparently conscious actor, an inference that the act is willed must be drawn — not as a matter of law but as a matter of fact — unless it be shown that the actor, being of sound mind, has been deprived of the capacity to control his actions by some extraordinary event or unless the actor, being of unsound mind, has thereby lost the capacity to control his actions. The accused bears no ultimate onus of proving that his act was not willed, but he bears the evidential onus of rebutting the inference that his act was willed, and there is no occasion for the jury to consider the possibility of an unwilled act unless that evidential onus is discharged. The inference that an act is willed is thus supported by the presumption that all persons have the capacity to control their actions unless they be of unsound mind, and an accused bears an ultimate onus of proving that he was of unsound mind if he chooses to raise that issue. The cause of any alleged loss of capacity is important, for the verdict of acquittal must be qualified if it is reached 'on account of' the accused's unsoundness of mind at the time. Section 653 of the Code, in its relevant parts, provides:

> … if on the trial of a person charged with any indictable offence, it is alleged or appears that he was not of sound mind at the time when the act or omission alleged to constitute the offence occurred, the jury are to be required to find specially if they find that he is not guilty, whether he was of unsound mind at the time when such act or omission took place, and to say whether he is acquitted by them on account of such unsoundness of mind; and if they find that he was of unsound mind, at the time when such act or omission took place, and say that he is acquitted by them on account of such unsoundness of mind, the Court is required to order him to be kept in strict custody in such place and in such manner as the Court thinks fit, until Her Majesty's pleasure is known.

Corresponding provisions have been enacted in jurisdictions where the common law governs criminal responsibility since 1800, when the Criminal Lunatics Act (UK) (39 & 40 Geo III c 94) was introduced.

The placing of an onus of proof on an accused to prove unsoundness of mind as a reason for rejecting the inference of a willed act raises the question: what is the position if the accused chooses to raise an issue of automatism — that is, of an act done independently of the exercise of his will — under the first limb of s 23 but fails or refuses to prove the cause of the automatism? It might be argued that, if it be not proved that unsoundness of mind caused or contributed to the automatism alleged, the verdict should be an outright acquittal. If this argument be valid, automatism caused or contributed to by unsoundness of mind entitles an accused to an outright acquittal provided the accused abstains from proving unsoundness of mind. If that were the position, procedural tactics would work substantive error. The solution lies in giving to s 26 its full effect: until unsoundness of mind be proved, it must be presumed for all purposes, including the finding of facts, that the accused was of sound mind when the act was done. In determining whether the prosecution has discharged an onus by proving any issue, the tribunal of fact must act upon the presumption that the accused is of sound mind unless and until the contrary is proved. Treating the accused as being of sound mind precludes the existence of automatism where the automatism could have been caused only by reason of unsoundness of mind or could not have existed but for unsoundness of mind. Thus s 26 precludes the hypothesis of automatism except for an automatism which, on the evidence, might have been caused exclusively by circumstances outside the operation of s 26. By operation of s 26, the jury is precluded from returning a verdict of acquittal under s 23 if the accused raises an issue of automatism which depends to some extent on unsoundness of mind. And, if an accused proves on the balance of probabilities that his alleged automatism was caused or contributed to by unsoundness of mind, a qualified verdict under s 653 must be returned.

A similar view seems to have been taken by Viscount Kilmuir LC in *Bratty* [1963] AC 386 at 403–4:

> ... The jury might not accept the evidence of a defect of reason from disease of the mind, but at the same time accept the evidence that the prisoner did not know what he was doing. If the jury should take that view of the facts they would find him not guilty. But it should be noted that the defence would only have succeeded because the necessary foundation had been laid by positive evidence which, properly considered, was *evidence of something other than a defect of reason from disease of the mind.* In my opinion, this analysis of the two defences (insanity and automatism) shows that where *the only cause alleged* for the unconsciousness is a defect of reason from disease of the mind, and that cause is rejected by the jury, there can be no room for the alternative defence of automatism ... I cannot therefore accept the submission that the whole of the evidence directed to the issue of insanity should have been left to the jury to consider whether there was automatism due to another cause. It was conceded ... that there was nothing to show or suggest that there was any other pathological cause for automatism (emphasis added).

However, if the reason for alleged automatism is not 'something other than a defect of reason from disease of the mind', the jury must not return an unqualified verdict of acquittal. In *Bratty* [1963] AC at 410, Lord Denning said:

> ... if the involuntary act proceeds from a disease of the mind, it gives rise to a defence of insanity, but not to a defence of automatism. Suppose a crime is

> committed by a man in a state of automatism or clouded consciousness due to a recurrent disease of the mind. Such an act is no doubt involuntary, but it does not give rise to an unqualified acquittal, for that would mean that he would be let at large to do it again. The only proper verdict is one which ensures that the person who suffers from the disease is kept secure in a hospital so as not to be a danger to himself or others.

The references to 'disease of the mind' in these speeches come, of course, from the definition of insanity in the Rules in *M'Naghten's* case (1843) 10 Cl & F 200 at 210; 8 ER 718 at 722; 4 St Tr (NS) 847 at 931:

> ... the jurors ought to be told in all cases that every man is to be presumed to be sane, and to possess *a sufficient degree of reason to be responsible for his crimes*, until the contrary be proved to their satisfaction; and that to establish a defence on the ground of insanity, it must be clearly proved that, at the time of the committing of the act, the party accused was labouring under such a defect of reason, from disease of the mind, as not to know the nature and quality of the act he was doing; or, if he did know it, that he did not know he was doing what was wrong. (Emphasis added.)

The emphasised words ensure that, under the common law, an accused who relies on a defect of reason from disease of the mind must establish that 'defence' just as, under the Code, an accused who relies on any ground of defence under s 27 or s 28 must, by force of s 26, establish that ground. The presumption that all persons have the capacity to control their actions unless they be of unsound mind and the presumption of soundness of mind combine to apply to cases under the Code the common law presumption 'that every man has sufficient mental capacity to be responsible for his crimes'. Whether under the Code or the common law, an accused raising automatism must prove unsoundness of mind or must raise on the evidence a reasonable hypothesis of some other cause sufficient *by itself* to have deprived the accused of his capacity to control his actions.

However, there are significant differences between the terms of the M'Naghten Rules and the terms employed by the Code relating to the defence of 'insanity' in ss 26, 27 and 28. Section 26 is quoted above. The first paragraph of s 27 reads:

> A person is not criminally responsible for an act or omission if at the time of doing the act or making the omission he is in such a state of mental disease or natural mental infirmity as to deprive him of capacity to understand what he is doing, or of capacity to control his actions, or of capacity to know that he ought not to do the act or make the omission.

Section 28 applies the provisions of s 27 to a mind 'disordered by intoxication or stupefaction caused without intention on [the accused's] part by drugs or intoxicating liquor, or by any other means'. For present purposes, the differences between the M'Naghten Rules and the Code are to be found in the terms used to describe the relevant condition of the mind and the effects which that condition produces.

There are two aspects of apparent difference between the M'Naghten Rules and the Code. The first relates to the cause of the insanity or unsoundness of mind. The M'Naghten Rules speak only of a 'disease of the mind' while the Code's umbrella term of 'unsound mind' comprehends mental disease, natural mental infirmity (s 27) and a mind disordered by intoxication or stupefaction (s 28). The second, and more significant difference, relates to the effects of these respective causes. The incapacities to which s 27 refers include the incapacity to control actions whereas the M'Naghten Rules speak only of such a defect of reason 'as not to know the nature and quality of the act he was doing; or, if he did know it, that he did not know he was doing what was wrong'. The explanation for the inclusion of the incapacity to control actions in s 27 is that it mirrors the provisions of s 23, as Sir Samuel Griffith explained in his notes to the Draft Code (1897), p 14:

> An act to involve criminal responsibility must be voluntary, as distinguished from involuntary [s 23] — that is to say, it must be accompanied by volition. In order that an action may be accompanied by volition there must be in the first place perception, more or less accurate, of the facts, then a determination or choice of the action to be taken upon those facts, and finally the action. If the person in question is incapable from mental disorder of rightly perceiving the facts, he should be treated on the same footing as a man who in good faith misapprehends the facts [s 24]. If he is for the same cause incapable of exercising the power of determination or choice, he should be treated on the same footing as a man who does an act independently of the exercise of his will [s 23].

(The section numbers are altered to reflect the numbering of the draft sections as enacted.) Under the Code, the practical difference in the operation of s 23 on the one hand and ss 26, 27 and 28 on the other depends on the aetiology of the condition which deprives the accused of the capacity to control his actions: if mental disease or natural mental infirmity (under s 27) or a disorder of the mind (under s 28) are proved to have deprived the accused of the capacity to control his actions, the verdict of acquittal must be qualified under s 653; if it be a reasonable hypothesis on the evidence that some other cause, by itself, deprived the accused of that capacity, the verdict is an absolute acquittal. The dichotomy between automatism caused by unsoundness of mind and automatism otherwise caused is reflected in the verdict to be returned.

At common law, although the defence of insanity was not expressed to cover an incapacity to control actions caused by a disease of the mind, yet the cases have held that, once disease of the mind appears to be a cause of an incapacity to control actions, an accused who relies on automatism must be acquitted, if at all, on the grounds of insanity: see, for example, *R v Tsigos* [1964–5] NSWR 1607 at 1629. The rationale of that approach was stated by Devlin J in *Hill v Baxter* [1958] 1 QB 277 at 285–6:

> For the purposes of the criminal law there are two categories of mental irresponsibility, one where the disorder is due to disease and the other where it is not. The distinction is not an arbitrary one. If disease is not the cause, if there is some temporary loss of consciousness arising accidentally, it is reasonable to hope

> that it will not be repeated and that it is safe to let an acquitted man go entirely free. But if disease is present, the same thing may happen again, and therefore, since 1800 [see The Criminal Lunatics Act 1800], the law has provided that persons acquitted on this ground should be subject to restraint.

A person in either category is not criminally responsible for his actions, but the law divides mental irresponsibility into two categories distinguished by the aetiology of that condition: is the mind diseased or is it not? Similarly, under ss 23 and 27 of the Code: an act may be unwilled, but the question is whether the aetiology of that condition is or is not mental disease or natural mental infirmity. In *R v Joyce* [1970] SASR 184 at 194, the Full Court of the Supreme Court of South Australia said:

> In our view there was no case to go to the jury on the issue of automatism apart from insanity, no evidence that is on which any reasonable jury could have had a reasonable doubt as to whether the appellant's acts in stabbing the girl were in the relevant sense involuntary or unconscious.
>
> We accept the authorities which have held that where the alleged automatism is said to be caused by some disease of the mind the relevant law to be applied is the law of insanity, and it is not open to the accused to escape the onus of proof of insanity by requiring the prosecution to negative automatism (*Cottle's* case [1958] NZLR 999; *Bratty's* case [1963] AC 386).

The position at common law was summed up by King CJ in *Radford* (1985) 42 SASR 266 at 273:

> If the conduct which would otherwise be criminal is involuntary, the accused is entitled to acquittal unless the involuntariness results from disease of the mind. If it results from disease of the mind, the accused is guilty unless the evidence proves on the balance of probabilities that the conduct resulted from a defect of reason caused by the disease of the mind in consequence of which the accused did not understand the nature and quality of his actions or did not know that they were wrong.

It seems incongruous for the common law to hold that an accused who is deprived by mental disease of his capacity to control his actions cannot be acquitted outright on the ground that his actions were involuntary, nor is he entitled to a qualified acquittal on the grounds of insanity unless he proves not only that he was deprived of his capacity to control his actions but also that he did not know the nature and quality of his act or that it was wrong. Perhaps the incongruity does not often arise in practice for, as King CJ observes (1985) 42 SASR at 275:

> Although possible in theory, it is from a practical point of view extremely difficult to conceive of a state of things in which a person acting automatically and without any exercise of the will would nevertheless know what he was doing and that it was wrong.

(Cf *Sodeman v R* (1936) 55 CLR 192 at 205; *Attorney-General (SA) v Brown* [1960] AC 432.)

Under the Code, as well as under the common law, it is necessary for the trial judge to determine what is meant by the terms used to describe the mental condition of a person who is of unsound mind or insane. The meaning of those terms is a question of law, not a question to be answered by medical witnesses. Although there is some divergence in the leading judgments, generally speaking a distinction has been drawn between an underlying mental infirmity which is productive of one of the prescribed effects and a transient nonrecurrent mental malfunction caused by external forces which produces an incapacity to control actions. The former is treated as unsoundness of mind or insanity; the latter is no more than a variation within the norm. Cases under the Code, as we shall see, have been decided by reference to concepts drawn from the common law despite some variations in terminology and there is no reason to hold that the term 'disease of the mind' in the M'Naghten Rules and the terms 'mental disease or natural mental infirmity' in s 27 of the Code connote different mental conditions.

In *R v Foy* [1960] Qd R 225, Philp J held that unsoundess of mind comprehended every condition which Hale (*Pleas of the Crown*) had called 'dementia', whether the dementia were complete or partial, permanent or temporary or intermittent and whether it was 'natural' or caused by physical disease, concussion, labour or any other cause. It comprehended any disorder or derangement of the understanding and any destruction of the will [1960] Qd R at 241–3. In his Honour's view, the limitation imported by 'a defect of reason … from disease of the mind' in the M'Naghten Rules did no more than exclude 'drunkenness, conditions of intense passion and other transient states attributable either to the fault or to the nature of man', those being the words of Sir Owen Dixon in the paper earlier mentioned adopted judicially by Owen J in *R v Connolly* (1959) 76 WN (NSW) 184 at 185. The same broad view of unsoundness of mind was taken by Wanstall J in dissent in *Cooper v McKenna; Ex parte Cooper* [1960] Qd R 406 at 412, to cover a case of concussion from a physical blow, but Stable J (for the majority) refused to accept the proposition that any lapse of consciousness by reason of an accident amounted to insanity [1960] Qd R at 419. In *R v Kemp* [1957] 1 QB 399, Devlin J took a broad view of the meaning of 'a defect of reason from disease of the mind'. Holding that temporary insanity whether incurable or not was sufficient to satisfy the M'Naghten Rules, he said [1957] 1 QB at 408:

> The primary thing that has to be looked for is the defect of reason. 'Disease of the mind' is there for some purpose, obviously, but the prime thing is to determine what is admitted here, namely, whether or not there is a defect of reason. In my judgment, the words 'from disease of the mind' are not to be construed as if they were put in for the purpose of distinguishing between diseases which have a mental origin and diseases which have a physical origin, a distinction which in 1843 was probably little considered. They were put in for the purpose of limiting the effect of the words 'defect of reason'. A defect of reason is by itself enough to make the act irrational and therefore normally to exclude responsibility in law …

> The words ensure that unless the defect is due to a diseased mind and not simply to an untrained one there is insanity within the meaning of the Rule.

His Lordship's view was approved by Lord Diplock in *R v Sullivan* [1984] AC 156 at 172:

> I agree with what was said by Devlin J in *R v Kemp* [1957] 1 QB at 407, that 'mind' in the M'Naghten Rules is used in the ordinary sense of the mental faculties of reason, memory and understanding. If the effect of a disease is to impair these faculties so severely as to have either of the consequences referred to in the latter part of the rules, it matters not whether the aetiology of the impairment is organic, as in epilepsy, or functional, or whether the impairment itself is permanent or is transient and intermittent, provided that it subsisted at the time of commission of the act. The purpose of the legislation relating to the defence of insanity, ever since its origin in 1800, has been to protect society against recurrence of the dangerous conduct. The duration of a temporary suspension of the mental faculties of reason, memory and understanding, particularly if, as in Mr Sullivan's case, it is recurrent, cannot on any rational ground be relevant to the application by the courts of the M'Naghten Rules, though it may be relevant to the course adopted by the Secretary of State, to whom the responsibility for how the defendant is to be dealt with passes after the return of the special verdict of 'not guilty by reason of insanity.
>
> To avoid misunderstanding I ought perhaps to add that in expressing my agreement with what was said by Devlin J in *Kemp*, where the disease that caused the temporary and intermittent impairment of the mental faculties was arterio-sclerosis, I do not regard that learned judge as excluding the possibility of non-insane automatism (for which the proper verdict would be a verdict of 'not guilty') in cases where temporary impairment (not being self-induced by consuming drink or drugs) results from some external physical factor such as a blow on the head causing concussion or the administration of an anaesthetic for therapeutic purposes.

His Lordship's exclusion of self-induced impairment by drink or drugs mirrors the exclusion of intentional intoxication or stupefaction from the disorders of the mind covered by s 28. Cases of automatism caused in these ways do not fall for present consideration.

In Canada a broad view was taken of the meaning of insanity in s 16(2) of the Criminal Code which provided that a person is insane 'when he is in a state of natural imbecility or had disease of the mind to an extent that renders him incapable of appreciating the nature and quality of an act or omission or of knowing that an act or omission is wrong'. In *Rabey v R* [1980] 2 SCR 513 at 519; (1980) 54 CCC (2d) 1 at 6–7 Ritchie J pointed out that the question whether a particular mental state amounts to 'a disease of the mind' is a question of law for the judge' adopting the statement of principle by Martin JA in the Ontario Court of Appeal who said (1977) 79 DLR (3d) 414 at 430; 37 CCC (2d) 461 at 477– 8:

> In general, the distinction to be drawn is between a malfunctioning of the mind arising from some cause that is primarily internal to the accused, having its source in his psychological or emotional make-up, or in some organic pathology, as opposed to a malfunctioning of the mind which is the transient effect produced by some specific external factor such as, for example, concussion. Any malfunctioning of the mind, or mental disorder having its source primarily in some subjective condition or weakness internal to the accused (whether fully understood or not), may be a 'disease of the mind' if it prevents the accused from knowing what he is doing, but transient disturbances of consciousness due to certain specific external factors do not fall within the concept of disease of the mind.

In that case a young man had battered a young woman, with whom he was infatuated, after he had been slighted. Martin JA concluded (1977) 79 DLR (3d) at 435; 37 CCC (2d) at 482–3 and his conclusion was upheld by a majority of the Supreme Court [1980] SCR at 520; 54 CCC (2d) at 7:

> ... that, in the circumstances of this case, the dissociative state in which the respondent was said to be, constituted a 'disease of the mind'. I leave aside until it becomes necessary to decide them, cases where a dissociative state has resulted from emotional shock without physical injury, resulting from such causes, for example, as being involved in a serious accident although no physical injury has resulted; being the victim of a murderous attack with an uplifted knife, notwithstanding the victim has managed to escape physical injury; seeing a loved one murdered or seriously assaulted, and the like situations. Such extraordinary external events might reasonably be presumed to affect the average normal person without reference to the subjective make-up of the person exposed to such experience.

In *R v Quick* [1973] QB 910 a distinction was drawn between a malfunction of the mind caused by an external factor and a malfunction caused by a bodily disorder in the nature of a disease which disturbed the working of the mind, the former type of malfunction not amounting to insanity. The view of Stable J in *Cooper* [1960] Qd R 406 was preferred to the broader view of unsoundness of mind espoused by Philp J in *Foy* [1960] Qd R 225.

Sholl J in *R v Carter* [1959] VR 105 and in *R v Meddings* [1966] VR 306 excluded from insanity some mental disturbances of a transient non-recurrent kind which are the consequence of external trauma. (That was the view which Stable J formed of concussion in *Cooper*.) In *Carter* [1959] VR at 110, Sholl J said that it is 'quite outside the policy of the law to extend the practice of [a qualified verdict resulting in indeterminate detention] to cases where there is no reason to fear any repetition of the crime and no evidence of any brain damage or disease which is likely to give rise to any such repetition'. Accepting that some words used by Dixon J in *R v Porter* (1933) 55 CLR 182 and by Devlin J in *Kemp* were wide enough to cover any temporary malfunction or disorder of the mind, he did not think he ought to take the words 'disease of the mind' so far. He adhered to these views in *Meddings*. Sholl J's comments, to the extent that they refer to the prospect of recurrence as a discrimen for determining sanity or insanity, echo the speech of Lord Denning in *Bratty* [1963] AC at 412, where his Lordship said:

> It seems to me that any mental disorder which has manifested itself in violence and is prone to recur is a disease of the mind. At any rate it is the sort of disease for which a person should be detained in hospital rather than be given an unqualified acquittal.

In his judgment in *Radford* (1985) 42 SASR at 274, 275, King CJ stated in summary form the effect of the authorities. In our respectful opinion, his Honour's judgment substantially states the common law and we quote the passage at length:

> if a jury is called upon to decide whether a state of automatism is due to disease of the mind, upon conflicting evidence or conflicting interpretations of the evidence, it must be told what the law understands by that phrase and it should be told that in language which a jury of laymen is likely to grasp. The expression 'disease of the mind' is synonymous, in my opinion, with 'mental illness'. In his charge to the jury in *R v Porter* (1933) 55 CLR at 188 Dixon J used the expression 'disease disorder or disturbance'. But the words 'disorder' and 'disturbance' must take their colour from the word 'disease' and refer to disorder and disturbance of the mental faculties which can be characterised as mental illness. In one sense automatism must always involve some disorder or disturbance of the mental faculties, but I do not think that a temporary disorder or disturbance of an otherwise healthy mind caused by external factors can properly be regarded as disease of the mind as that expression is held in the M'Naghten rules. As Lord Denning pointed out in *Bratty v Attorney-General (Northern Ireland)*, the major mental diseases or psychoses such as schizophrenia are clearly diseases of the mind. Moreover, physical diseases, such as psychomotor epilepsy, (*Bratty v Attorney-General (Northern Ireland)*) and arteriosclerosis (*R v Kemp*), when they affect the soundness of the mental faculties should be regarded as diseases of the mind. Lord Denning considered that any 'mental disorder which has manifested itself in violence and is prone to recur is a disease of the mind': *Bratty's* case. Disease of the mind is to be distinguished from 'mere excitability of a normal man, passion, even stupidity, obtuseness, lack of self control, and impulsiveness': *R v Porter*. The essential notion appears to be that in order to constitute insanity in the eyes of the law the malfunction of the mental faculties called 'defect of reason' in the M'Naghten rules, must result from an underlying pathological infirmity of the mind, be it of long or short duration and be it permanent or temporary, which can be properly termed mental illness, as distinct from the reaction of a healthy mind to extraordinary external stimuli. In my opinion the notion of 'disease of the mind' should be explained to the jury in some such terms.

One may cavil at the description of a mere physical condition such as arteriosclerosis, albeit one which produces a 'mental illness', as itself a disease of the mind. But the dichotomy between mental illness and a healthy mind is correctly drawn. However, we would think it necessary that a temporary mental disorder or disturbance must not be prone to recur if it is to avoid classification as a disease of the mind. That is because a malfunction of the mind which is prone to recur reveals an underlying pathological infirmity. Subject to that qualification, the law is as stated by King CJ in the passage cited. So stated, the law in Australia may not correspond precisely with the speech of Lord Diplock in *Sullivan*.

Particular difficulties are raised when a temporary mental disorder or disturbance is precipitated by psychological trauma. Psychological trauma and the strength of the individual mind to withstand it are reciprocal factors, on the balancing of which mental malfunction depends. It may be difficult for an accused who raises automatism to show that psychological trauma has not acted upon some underlying infirmity of mind to produce the automatism. In *R v Hennessy* [1989] 1 WLR 287 at 294; [1989] 2 All ER 9 at 14, Lord Lane CJ for the Court of Appeal said:

> In our judgment, stress, anxiety and depression can no doubt be the result of the operation of external factors, but they are not, it seems to us, in themselves separately or together external factors of the kind capable in law of causing or contributing to a state of automatism. They constitute a state of mind which is prone to recur. They lack the feature of novelty or accident, which is the basis of the distinction drawn by Lord Diplock in *R v Sullivan*: [1984] AC at 172.

However that may be, there seems to be no reason in principle why psychological trauma which produces a transient non-recurrent malfunction of an otherwise sound mind should be distinguished from a physical trauma which produces a like effect. That was the view of the minority in *Rabey*.

In *Rabey* [1980] 2 SCR at 549; (1980) 54 CCC (2d) at 29, Dickson J for the minority emphasised the externality of the precipitating 'psychological blow' which caused 'a loss of consciousness'. His Lordship agreed that there should be a shock precipitating the state of automatism and that: 'Dissociation caused by a low stress threshold and surrender to anxiety cannot fairly be said to result from a psychological blow.' To determine whether in a particular case automatism is to be judged sane or insane, his Lordship treated the likelihood of repetition of the action as a material indication. He added [1980] 2 SCR at 552; (1980) 54 CC (2d) at 31:

> In principle, the defence of automatism should be available whenever there is evidence of unconsciousness throughout the commission of the crime, that cannot be attributed to fault or negligence of his part. Such evidence should be supported by expert medical opinion that the accused did not feign memory loss and that there is no underlying pathological condition which points to a disease requiring detention and treatment.

The problem of classification in a case of a transient malfunction of the mind precipitated by psychological trauma lies in the difficulty in choosing between the reciprocal factors — the trauma and the natural susceptibility of the mind to affection by psychological trauma — as the cause of the malfunction. Is one factor or the other the cause or are both to be treated as causes? To answer this problem, the law must postulate a standard of mental strength which, in the face of a given level of psychological trauma, is capable of protecting the mind from malfunction to the extent prescribed in the respective definitions of insanity. That standard must be the standard of the ordinary person: if the mind's strength is below that standard, the mind is infirm; if it is of or above that standard, the mind is sound or sane. This is an objective standard which corresponds with the objective standard imported for the purpose of determining provocation: as to which, see *Radford* (1985) 42 SASR at 269; *R v Hill* [1986] 1 SCR 313 at 343–4; (1986) 25 CCC (3d) 322 at 345; *Johnson v R* (1976) 136 CLR 619 at 636.

In a given case, if the psychological trauma causes a sound mind, possessed of the requisite standard of strength, to malfunction only transiently so as to produce the effects mentioned in the M'Naghten Rules or in s 27 of the Code, the malfunction cannot be attributed to mental infirmity but to 'the nature of man': that is to say, a malfunction which is transient and not prone to recur and to which the mind of an ordinary person would be subject if exposed to the same psychological trauma is neither a mental disease nor a natural mental infirmity. It is neither an instance of unsoundness of mind under the Code nor an instance of insanity at common law. Having regard to the reason for distinguishing between sane and insane mental responsibility in *Hill v Baxter* [1958] 1 QB 277, there is no reason to require such a malfunction of the mind to attract a qualified verdict of acquittal.

If this be the substantive law, how does the shifting onus of proof work upon it? When an accused raises automatism and assigns some malfunction of the mind as its cause, he raises a defence of unsoundness of mind or insanity unless the malfunction of his mind was (1) transient (2) caused by trauma, whether physical or psychological, which the mind of an ordinary person would be likely not to have withstood and (3) not prone to recur. A malfunction of the mind other than a malfunction which satisfies those exempting qualifications amounts to a disease of the mind, or a mental disease or natural mental infirmity. As an accused bears no ultimate onus of proving that his act was not willed, in theory an accused may raise the issue of non-insane automatism on the evidence and claim to be acquitted outright unless the prosecution disproves the issue. But in practice an accused does not raise non-insane automatism by raising automatism based merely on mental malfunction. Prima facie, mental malfunction is the consequence of mental infirmity and, until it be proved that a particular instance of mental malfunction satisfies the exempting qualifications, mental malfunction must be treated as a consequence of mental infirmity.

It follows that, unless and until the automatism on which an accused relies is proved to be merely a transient mental malfunction of his otherwise sound mind caused by trauma and that the malfunction is not likely to recur, both s 26 of the Code and the common law preclude consideration of automatism for the purpose of determining whether the incriminated act was willed or voluntary. If an accused proves on the balance of probabilities that he was acting as an automaton when the act was done by reason of mental malfunction but fails to prove that his mental malfunction satisfied the exempting qualifications, he is entitled to be acquitted on account of unsoundness of mind or on the ground of insanity. However, if he proves that his mental malfunction satisfied the exempting qualifications, he is entitled to an outright acquittal. (To cast this onus on the accused does no violence to the principle in *Woolmington v Director of Public Prosecutions* [1935] AC 462, for the issue is not one of criminal responsibility but the cause of the condition which deprived the accused of criminal responsibility.) In some instances (eg concussion caused by physical trauma), the accused may be able to prove on the balance of probabilties at the outset that, if there were any malfunction of the mind which deprived him of the capacity to know the nature and quality of his act or to control his actions, the malfunction satisfied the exempting qualifications and therefore did not flow from an underlying mental infirmity. In such a case, the onus shifts to the prosecution to prove beyond reasonable doubt that there was no malfunction or that it did not affect the accused's control of his actions. But in cases where the accused, claiming to have acted as an automaton by reason of a transient malfunction precipitated by psychological trauma, seeks to take the malfunction out of the prima facie classification of unsoundness of mind or insanity, the onus of proving the exempting qualifications can hardly be discharged before the malfunction itself is proved. Where the accused succeeds in proving that the relevant act was done in a state of automatism by reason of a malfunction of his mind, he is at risk of a qualified verdict of acquittal (under s 653 or a provision corresponding with that section) unless and until he succeeds in discharging the onus of proving the exempting qualifications on the balance of probabilities.

A mental malfunction which deprives an accused of the capacity to control his actions (or to know the nature and quality of his act) and which does not fulfil the exempting qualifications amounts to unsoundness of mind (under the Code) or insanity (at common law). (As the terms 'unsoundness of mind' and 'insanity', like the terms 'willed' and 'voluntary', are interchangeable we shall follow the Code terminology.) That being so, an accused cannot rely on a mental malfunction to deny that an act done by him was willed unless it be proved that the qualifying conditions are fulfilled or that the accused was labouring at the time under an unsoundness of mind. If neither fulfilment of the exempting qualifications nor unsoundness of mind be proved on the balance of probabilities to account for a supposed absence of will, the jury cannot find that there may have been a mental malfunction which might have produced that result.

According to the state of the evidence as to the cause of an alleged mental malfunction, a trial judge may or may not leave the possibility of an unwilled act for the jury's consideration. In deciding whether the evidence is such that the issue of an unwilled act should be left for the jury's consideration and in directing the jury on that issue, the judge must distinguish between the evidence relevant to the question whether the proscribed act was in fact accompanied by an exercise of the will and the evidence relevant to the question whether the cause of the alleged mental malfunction is of the severity which would cause the mind of an ordinary person to lose the capacity to control an action of the kind charged. The personality and the state of mind of the accused before being subjected to the physical or psychological trauma which caused the alleged mental malfunction is relevant to the first question but not to the second. If the judge does allow the issue of an unwilled act to go to the jury, the jury will be directed that they should not acquit on account of a possible absence of will attributable to a mental malfunction unless they are satisfied on the balance of probabilities that the mental malfunction either fulfils the exempting qualifications or amounts to unsoundness of mind. To that direction the judge will add that, if they are satisfied that the mental malfunction falls within one or other category but are not satisfied on the balance of probabilities that the exempting qualifications are fulfilled, they should return a verdict of not guilty on the ground of unsoundness of mind.

When these principles are applied to the present case, they lead to the conclusion that the learned Commissioner erred in rejecting the evidence proposed to be given by Dr Schioldann-Nielsen and Dr Finlay-Jones. That evidence was admissible for the purpose of proving that at the time of the killing Mrs Falconer was in a state of non-insane automatism. It is, of course, another question whether the evidence of those doctors in combination with the rest of the evidence would have satisfied the exempting qualifications to which we have referred.

In determining whether the mind of an ordinary person would have malfunctioned in the face of the physical or psychological trauma to which the accused was subjected, the psychotic, neurotic or emotional state of the accused at that time is immaterial. The ordinary person is assumed to be a person of normal temperament and self-control. Consequently, evidence that, in the week preceding the shooting, Mrs Falconer had demonstrated fear, depression, emotional disturbance and an apparently changed personality would not have been relevant in determining the reaction of an ordinary person. Likewise, evidence of the stress that she suffered on discovering that her husband had sexually assaulted their two daughters would not have been relevant in determining the reaction of the ordinary person to the incidents which took place on the day of the shooting. But evidence of the objective circumstances of the relationship between the parties would have been relevant to that issue, for only by considering the pertinent circumstances of that relationship could the jury determine whether an ordinary person would have succumbed to a state of dissociation similar to that which Mrs Falconer claims overtook her on that day. Speaking generally, the issue for the jury on this aspect of the case would be whether an ordinary woman of Mrs Falconer's age and circumstances, who had been subjected to the history of violence which she alleged, who had recently discovered that her husband had sexually assaulted their daughters, who knew that criminal charges had been laid against her husband in respect of these matters and who was separated from her husband as the result of his relationship with another woman, would have entered a state of dissociation as the result of the incidents which occurred on the day of the shooting.

If the trial judge had considered the evidence given on the voir dire by the two doctors in the light of the relationship between Mrs Falconer and her husband, he might have held that that evidence was insufficient to establish that the mind of an ordinary person would have reacted in the way that Mrs Falconer alleges that her mind reacted. But that issue was not addressed and it is not a question that should be answered in this application. Much depends upon the impact of the evidence in the context of the trial. Evidence which was prima facie relevant and essential to the defence of non-insane automatism was improperly rejected. Indeed, Mrs Falconer was not allowed to tender any evidence in support of that defence. In that respect the trial miscarried. In the circumstances, it is neither appropriate nor proper to examine the evidence of the doctors, given on the voir dire, for the purpose of determining whether, if admitted, it would have established a case of non-insane automatism for consideration by the jury.

Had Mrs Falconer, having raised the issue of automatism caused by a mental malfunction, discharged the onus of proving that the malfunction satisfied the exempting qualification, she would have been entitled to be acquitted under s 23. Accordingly, the evidence was admissible as relevant to an issue arising under s 23 and the Court of Criminal Appeal was correct in allowing the appeal and ordering a new trial. However if, on the retrial, Mrs Falconer were to prove no more than the dissociated state occasioning an incapacity to control her action in discharging the gun, she would be entitled merely to a qualified verdict of acquittal under s 653. If the accused were not to prove any of the facts referred to in this paragraph, she would not be entitled to be acquitted under either s 23 or s 653.

We would grant special leave to appeal but dismiss the appeal.

Deane and **Dawson JJ**: Where an accused's acts are alleged to be involuntary by reason of mental disease or natural mental infirmity, no distinction can be drawn between the defence of automatism — the absence of will accompanying the relevant acts of the accused — and the defence of insanity under s 27 of the Code. This is necessarily so because s 27 relieves a person of criminal responsibility for an act done in 'such a state of mental disease or natural mental infirmity as to deprive him of capacity to understand what he is doing, or of capacity to control his actions …'.

The definition of what constitutes a mental disease or natural mental infirmity is a matter of law. Whether an accused suffered from such a disease or infirmity at the relevant time is a question of fact. Where the voluntariness of an accused's acts are to be determined by reference to a condition which, if it existed at all, must on the evidence have amounted to a state of mental disease or natural mental infirmity, the question whether the accused's acts were voluntary will be subsumed in the question whether the accused did in fact suffer from a state of insanity envisaged by the section such that it deprived him of the capacity to understand what he was doing or the capacity to control his actions. Section 27 also applies where a person is by reason of mental disease or natural mental infirmity deprived of the capacity to know that he ought not to have acted as he did. That would seem to raise a question distinct from that of voluntariness.

Where s 27 applies to relieve an accused of criminal responsibility, he is entitled to an acquittal but, under s 653 of the Code, the jury is required to find that he was of unsound mind at the relevant time and to say whether he was acquitted by them for that reason. The consequence of that is that an order is made that the accused be kept in custody at the Governor's pleasure.

If the evidence raises the question whether an accused's acts were involuntary, not because of mental disease or natural mental infirmity, but because of the operation of events upon a sound mind, it is s 23 rather than s 27 which applies. Section 23 provides that 'a person is not criminally responsible for an act or omission which occurs independently of the exercise of his will'.

Under s 26 of the Code (and for that matter at common law) there is a presumption of law that every person is of sound mind. That means that, in order to establish mental disease or natural mental infirmity under s 27, it is necessary to rebut the presumption. That can only be done by proving the existence of one or other of those conditions on the balance of probabilities. At common law the same considerations are reflected in the exceptions to the general rule that the burden of proving guilt beyond reasonable doubt remains throughout upon the prosecution. Those exceptions are the defence of insanity and any statutory exception: *Woolmington v Director of Public Prosecutions* [1935] AC 462 at 481.

However, there is no such presumption to be overcome in the application of s 23. The onus of proving guilt remains with the prosecution and that onus is not discharged if an accused is able to raise a reasonable doubt. Of course, common experience teaches us that a person's will ordinarily accompanies his actions and evidence will be required to establish the extraordinary circumstance that an accused's acts occurred independently of the exercise of his will or to raise a doubt whether that was so. It is sometimes said in that situation that the accused is required to rebut an evidentiary presumption or to discharge an evidentiary burden of proof, but it is merely a requirement that there be evidence to displace ordinary human experience. And it will not be enough for an accused merely to assert that his acts were involuntary or that he suffered a loss of memory. Evidence of his condition at the time of the alleged offence supported by some expert medical opinion will be required before an issue of sane automatism can realistically be said to be raised. Moreover, those conditions which will admit of involuntariness that is not the product of disease or natural mental infirmity will be quite confined. The few suggested instances would seem to include: sleepwalking in some circumstances, some cases of epilepsy, concussion, hypoglycaemia and dissociative states. Nevertheless, given these constraints, an accused in setting up a defence under s 23 does not have to prove his condition on the balance of probabilities in order to succeed; he merely has to raise a reasonable doubt that his actions were the result of an involuntary reaction of a sane mind.

In this case, the evidence did not pose any question under s 27. It was not suggested at the trial that the accused suffered from any mental disease or natural mental infirmity. Conversely, in cases where the question of mental disease or of natural mental infirmity under s 27 is raised, there will often be no question — on the evidence — of involuntariness other than as the product of mental disease or natural mental infirmity. That is to say, no question will arise under s 23. But there may be cases, perhaps rare, in which the evidence allows alternative contentions, namely, that an accused's acts were involuntary either by reason of mental disease or natural mental infirmity or by reason of the operation of events upon a normal mind.

Where that occurs, there is the apparent incongruity identified by Sir Owen Dixon in his paper entitled 'A Legacy of Hadfield, M'Naghten and Maclean', *Australian Law Journal*, vol 31, 1957, 255. The incongruity appears to arise because of the different burdens of proof affecting, on the one hand, insanity (and, hence, involuntariness arising from insanity) and, on the other, involuntariness arising from the operation of events upon a normal mind: insane automatism and sane automatism.

The problem is complicated by the consideration that it is no longer entirely appropriate to speak of insanity as a defence, having regard to the fact that the consequences of successfully raising the plea go beyond negativing volition or intent. True it is that insanity operates to produce an acquittal, but it is seldom raised by an accused now that there are no capital offences, because incarceration at the Governor's pleasure may be a harsher penalty than conviction and sentence. Indeed, nowadays it is often in the interests of the prosecution (or, at all events, the community) to raise the question of insanity, rather than in the interests of the accused. It used to be said that it was for the defence to raise a plea of insanity and not for the prosecution. That is probably still the case, but we think that the position has now been reached where it is only realistic to recognise that, if there is evidence of insanity, the prosecution is entitled to rely upon it even if it is resisted by the defence. In that regard, it is relevant to note that s 653 of the Code refers to the case where 'it is alleged or *appears*' (emphasis added) that the accused was not of sound mind. It may be anomalous for the prosecution to raise the matter initially because the prosecution should not commence proceedings if it is seeking an acquittal, even on the grounds of insanity. The responsibility for the protection of the community in those circumstances lies elsewhere than in the criminal law. But we can see no reason why, if there is evidence which would support a verdict on the grounds of insanity, the prosecution should not be able to rely upon it in asking for a qualified acquittal as an alternative to conviction.

The important thing is, however, that an accused is entitled to an acquittal if the prosecution fails to prove that his acts were voluntary. When, on the evidence, an accused's acts can only have been involuntary if he was suffering from a mental disease or natural mental infirmity, the prosecution is entitled to rely upon the presumption that every person is of sound mind. That means that a defence of insane automatism can only succeed if it is established on the balance of probabilities. But if on the evidence an accused's acts may have been involuntary as a result of the operation of events upon a sound mind — as a result of sane automatism — then a reasonable doubt about the voluntariness of those acts will be sufficient to entitle him to acquittal. In such a case, there will be a reasonable hypothesis consistent with both innocence and a sane mind and we do not conceive it to be the policy of the law that in that event there should be either a conviction or indefinite committal to an institution for the criminally insane. The law is possibly open to the criticism that it envisages the release of a person who may, on the balance of probabilities, be violently insane. That is, however, a matter to be dealt with by the means otherwise available for protecting the community from such persons and, if those means are thought to be inadequate, by legislative intervention.

It follows that, in a case where an issue of sane automatism is raised by positive evidence (including expert medical opinion), an accused will be entitled to an acquittal if the prosecution fails to disprove sane automatism beyond reasonable doubt. In that event, the jury will need to go no further. If, however, the prosecution disproves sane automatism and the evidence raises the question of insane automatism, the jury will have to ask themselves whether, on the balance of probabilities, the evidence establishes insanity under s 27. That will, as we have said, embrace insane automatism. If the evidence does establish insanity, an accused will be entitled to an acquittal, but the jury will be required to say that the acquittal is on account of unsoundness of mind. If the prosecution does disprove sane automatism and if insanity is not established on the balance of probabilities, in the absence of any other defence the jury should convict.

As Toohey J and Gaudron J demonstrate, there was evidence of sane automatism to be left to the jury in the present case. Special leave should be granted and the appeal should be dismissed.

[**Toohey J** and **Gaudron J** delivered separate judgments agreeing the appeal should be dismissed. Appeal dismissed.]

[See also *R v Youssef* (1990) 50 A Crim R 1; *R v Burgess* [1991] 2 WLR 1206; *Attorney-General's Reference (No 2 of 1992)* [1993] 3 WLR 982; *Hawkins v R* (1994) 179 CLR 500.]

14.13C Question of Law Reserved (No 1 of 1997)

(1997) 70 SASR 251

Full Court of the Supreme Court of South Australia

[A judge of the Supreme Court reserved certain questions of law for the Full Court. The case stated involved a person charged with murder. The accused person had a history of psychiatric illness and evidence of his inability to control himself at the time of the offence was available. The case also raised issues of self-defence. The questions reserved arose out of changes to the Criminal Law Consolidation Act 1935 (SA) which effectively established a code for dealing with issues of mental competence to commit an offence and mental fitness to stand trial.]

Duggan J: Section 269B provides as follows.

(1) An investigation under this Part by the Supreme Court or the District Court into —

(a) a defendant's mental competence to commit an offence or a defendant's mental fitness to stand trial; or

(b) whether elements of the offence have been established, is to be conducted before a jury unless the defendant has elected to have the matter dealt with by a judge sitting alone.

(2) The same jury may deal with issues arising under this Part about a defendant's mental competence to commit an offence, or fitness to stand trial, and the issues on which the defendant is to be tried, unless the trial judge thinks there are special reasons to have separate juries.

(3) Any other powers or functions conferred on a court by this Part are to be exercised by the court constituted of a judge sitting alone.

The procedure which the Act provides for dealing with these issues represents a significant departure from the common law procedure whereby, in a case where insanity was raised, all issues were dealt with at the same trial. The new procedure for dealing with mental competence to commit an offence identifies three issues which may call for determination, namely, the objective elements of the offence, the subjective elements of the offence and the accused's mental competence to commit the offence.

A 'subjective element' of an offence is defined as 'voluntariness, intention, knowledge or some other mental state that is an element of the offence'.

An 'objective element' of an offence is defined as 'an element of an offence that is not a subjective element'.

The issue of mental competence may be raised by the defendant or the court may direct an investigation into the issue on its own initiative or on application by the prosecution: s 269E(1). Once raised it must be separated from the remainder of the trial. The trial judge has a discretion to proceed first with the trial of the objective elements of the offence or with the trial of the mental competence of the accused: s 269E(2).

If the trial judge decides to proceed first with the trial of the accused's mental competence to commit the offence the procedure in s 269F must be followed. The court must hear 'relevant evidence and representations'. Then, if the court is not satisfied on the balance of probabilities that the accused was at the time of the alleged offence mentally incompetent to commit the offence, it must 'proceed with the trial of the offence in the normal way': s 269FA(3). If the court is satisfied on the balance of probabilities that the accused was at the time of the alleged offence mentally incompetent to commit the offence, it must record a finding to that effect: s 269FA(4). In the latter event the court must then hear evidence and representations relevant to the question whether it should find that the objective elements of the offence are established: s 269FB(1). If the court is satisfied that the objective elements of the offence are established beyond reasonable doubt the court must record a finding to that effect (s 269FB(2)) and find the accused not guilty of the offence but declare him or her to be liable to supervision under this part of the Act. If the objective elements are not established the court must find the accused not guilty of the offence and discharge the accused: s 269FB(3).

If, on the other hand, the trial judge decides to proceed first with the trial of the objective elements of the offence it must first hear evidence and representations on that issue and, if satisfied that the objective elements are established beyond reasonable doubt, it must record a finding to that effect: s 269GA(2). If not so satisfied it must record a finding that the accused is not guilty of the offence and discharge the accused.

If the court records a finding that the objective elements are satisfied it must then hear evidence on the question of the accused's mental competence to commit the offence. If satisfied on the balance of probabilities that the accused was at the time of the alleged offence mentally incompetent to commit the offence it must record a finding that the accused is not guilty of the offence and declare the accused to be liable to supervision under this part of the Act: s 269GB(3). If the court is not so satisfied it must proceed to consider whether the evidence establishes the subjective elements of the offence beyond reasonable doubt. If the subjective elements are established beyond reasonable doubt the court must record a finding of guilty of the offence 'and proceed to deal with the accused as if a finding of guilt had been made in the normal way'. If not so satisfied it must record a finding that the accused is not guilty of the offence: s 269GB(4). ...

The interpretation of the relevant provisions in the Act cannot be divorced entirely from the common law as it had developed up until the passing of the Act. The test for mental incompetence draws heavily on common law concepts and expressions, and although the procedures introduced by the legislation represent a marked departure from that which was in existence before the Act was passed, the previous law is of some assistance in determining the legislative intention in introducing some of the new procedures.

The legislation is clear in one respect: in whatever order the issues are tried a finding of mental incompetence, coupled with a finding that the objective elements have been proved beyond reasonable doubt, will result in a verdict of not guilty and a declaration that the accused is liable to supervision under the Act. There is no need for the subjective elements to be proved in order to achieve this result.

The exclusion of those matters referred to in the Act as subjective elements from the matters to be proved before making an order for supervision is based on a policy decision made by the legislature. In this respect the legislation addresses a difficulty which was encountered at common law, particularly in relation to the issue of voluntariness. In *R v Radford* (1985) 42 SASR 266 at 272 King CJ said:

> The problem in the present case is but another instance of a problem which has troubled the courts increasingly over the past 35 years, namely the relationship between involuntariness and insanity and the manner in which that relationship is to be worked out in the practical administration of justice. It is a problem which has arisen only in the last 35 years. Until the English case of *R v Harrison-Owen* [1951] 2 All ER 726, the question of involuntary act as a ground for escaping criminal liability does not appear to have arisen apart from insanity. The authorities since that time, however, leave no room for doubt that involuntary action, whether resulting from insanity or the effect on a sane mind of external factors, excludes criminal liability. Involuntariness is not to be confused with irresistible impulse where the act is willed although the mind is unable to control it *(R v Harm* (1975) 13 SASR 84); but if the act is performed involuntarily, in the sense of without the exercise of the will, there is no criminal liability whether or not the cause is insanity. Since 1951 the courts have had many opportunities to consider the issue of involuntariness and to explore its relationship to the defence of insanity.

Certain points which are pertinent to the present case have been settled by authority. If evidence is called by the defence to raise the issue of involuntariness, or automatism as it is often called, and that evidence is such that a jury could properly find insanity, the issue of insanity must be left to the jury: *R v Joyce* [1970] SASR 184. Similarly the fact that the evidence is open to an interpretation which would amount to insanity does not relieve the judge of the obligation of leaving automatism to the jury if the evidence is also reasonably capable of leading to that conclusion: *Bedelph v R* [1980] Tas R 23 at 27–8, per Green CJ. Where the evidence is capable of leading to either conclusion both should be left to the jury: *R v Cottle* [1958] NZLR 999.

A further point which is conclusively, if perhaps somewhat illogically and inconveniently, established by authority is that if the involuntary character of the conduct in question is referable exclusively to disease of the mind, the applicable law is that relating to insanity: *R v Cottle; Bratty v Attorney-General (Northern Ireland)* [1963] AC 386; *R v Joyce* especially per Bray CJ at 194. The rule produces an incongruity arising from the special verdict required by s 292 of the Criminal Law Consolidation Act where an acquittal is by reason of insanity.

The incongruity was pointed out as long ago as 1957 in a paper delivered by Sir Owen Dixon to the Tenth Legal Convention of the Law Council of Australia (O Dixon, 'A Legacy of Hadfield, M'Naghten and Maclean' (1957) 31 *ALJ* 255) and has since frequently been referred to in the various cases. If the conduct which would otherwise be criminal is involuntary, the accused is entitled to acquittal unless the involuntariness results from disease of the mind. If it results from disease of the mind, the accused is guilty unless the evidence proves on the balance of probabilities that the conduct resulted from a defect of reason caused by the disease of the mind in consequence of which the accused did not understand the nature and quality of his actions or did not know that they were wrong. The incongruity is intensified by the differing burdens of proof.

This incongruity produces real problems in the conduct of a trial in which there is evidence fit for the consideration of the jury as to both insanity and non-insane automatism. The two principal problems relate to the definition of disease of the mind, and to the directions to be given as to onus of proof and as to the manner in which the jury is to approach its task.

The policy considerations which flow from the dilemma referred to by King CJ were commented upon by Lord Denning in *Bratty v Attorney-General (Northern Ireland)* at 410:

> Again, if the involuntary act proceeds from a disease of the mind, it gives rise to a defence of insanity, but not to a defence of automatism. Suppose a crime is committed by a man in a state of automatism or clouded consciousness due to a recurrent disease of the mind. Such an act is no doubt involuntary, but it does not give rise to an unqualified acquittal, for that would mean that he would be let at

large to do it again. The only proper verdict is one which ensures that the person who suffers from the disease is kept secure in a hospital so as not to be a danger to himself or others. That is, a verdict of guilty but insane.

This reasoning, however, did not apply to every mental state. In *Hawkins v R* (1994) 179 CLR 500 the High Court held that, although evidence of mental disease was properly rejected in relation to the issue of voluntariness, its relevance could not be denied to the further issue of specific intent. The accused was charged with murder under the Criminal Code (Tas). Insanity was not raised by the defence and the trial judge ruled inadmissible medical evidence to the effect that the accused was suffering from a mental disease which may have affected his capacity to form an intention to kill or cause bodily harm. After referring to the insanity provisions under the Code the joint judgment of the High Court continued (at 512):

> Although the evidentiary presumption of sound mind is of general application, there is a reason why rebuttal of that presumption by evidence of mental disease, which is necessarily admissible on the issue of insanity, cannot be taken into account in determining whether an act is voluntary and intentional. Mental disease, by itself, is no excuse for the doing of an incriminated act but s 16 [the insanity provisions] provides an excuse ('not criminally responsible') when, and only when, the consequence and measure of the mental disease are as prescribed by paras (a) and (b) of s 16(1). It would destroy that limitation on the defence to allow evidence of mental disease to destroy the inference that an act is willed when it is done by a person of sound mind: *R v Falconer* (1990) 171 CLR 30 at 43. If it were otherwise, the practical consequence of destroying that inference would be the outright acquittal of an offender although that offender, if he was suffering to any extent from a mental disease, was not suffering to the extent prescribed by paras (a) and (b) of s 16(1). That is a sound enough reason to reject evidence of mental disease in determining the issue of the voluntariness of an act done by a person presumed to be of sound mind. But there is no such reason for excluding evidence of mental disease in determining whether an act done by a person who is criminally responsible for the act was done with a specific intent. In such a case, the actor is liable in any event to conviction for an offence constituted by the doing of the act but is liable to conviction for a more serious offence only if the prosecution establishes the intent which is the additional element in the more serious offence. The presumption of sound mind is not the equivalent of a presumption that a person intends the natural, or natural and probable, consequences of his act: *Smyth v R* (1957) 98 CLR 163. The reference in s 17(3) to the 'presumption that a person intends the natural and probable consequences of his acts' was not advanced by counsel for the respondent as a presumption of general application. In *Snow v R* [1962] Tas SR 271 at 288, that presumption was said to be a 'presumption of fact capable of rebuttal by an advanced degree of drunkenness'. It does not affect the general question whether an inference of specific intent should be drawn from the circumstances of the case, though it may

> restrict the effect of a lesser degree of drunkenness on the drawing of an inference of intent. What a person who is criminally responsible for his act intended when he did the act is an issue which must be determined by the jury as an inference from all the evidence which is relevant to that issue and no presumption of law exists to relieve the jury of that duty: *Thomas v R* (1960) 102 CLR 584 at 596, per Kitto J. The prosecution is entitled to invoke the presumption of sound mind but not to exclude any evidence which is relevant to rebut it.

These cases explain the inspiration for excluding the consideration of some elements, including voluntariness, from certain stages of the procedures set up under the new legislation, although if the word 'intention' in the definition of 'subjective element' is to be given a wide meaning, the amendments take the matter further than *Hawkins'* case would allow.

If the issue of mental competence is tried first pursuant to s 269FA(1) and the court is satisfied that mental incompetence is established, there is no room for the accused to contest the subjective issues referred to in the legislation. The court proceeds directly to determine whether the objective elements of the offence are established and, if they are, there must be a declaration that the accused is liable to supervision. A similar situation occurs if the objective elements are tried first pursuant to s 269A(1). If the objective elements are established, the issue of mental competence is the next issue to be tried. If mental incompetence is established the court must declare the accused liable to supervision. But the crucial question for the purposes of this part of the case stated is what is included in the categories of subjective and objective elements respectively. In particular it is necessary to decide whether the issue of self-defence is an element of the offence for the purposes of the legislation and, if so, into what category it is to be placed.

In my view there is good reason for rejecting Mr Millsteed's argument that self-defence has no place in either category. If the court embarks on the trial of mental competence first and is not satisfied that mental incompetence has been established, 'the court must proceed with the trial in the usual way': s 269FA(3). This would involve proof by the prosecution of the definitional elements of the offence and the consideration of any defence (including self-defence) raised by the accused. If, on the other hand, the objective elements are tried first and established and if mental incompetence is not established in the second stage of that inquiry, the court must then go on to consider the subjective elements. If they are established then the accused is to be found guilty of the offence: s 269GB(4). In other words if this alternative is adopted guilt can be established by proving the subjective and objective elements of the offence. If the Crown argument is correct, self-defence could not be raised at any stage of this particular procedure. I do not think that this anomaly can be explained by reason of the fact that the procedure could be conducted in an alternative manner which would avoid this result. The choice of the order of events is not left to the accused; the trial judge is given a discretion in the matter. In my view parliament did not intend that a person could be found guilty of an offence without being given the opportunity to raise recognised defences. I appreciate that the phrase 'an element of an offence' is more often than not used to describe an element in the definition of an offence, but in my opinion the concept of 'element' is wider. In the joint judgment of Wilson, Dawson and Toohey JJ in *Zecevic v Director of Public Prosecutions (Vic)* (1987) 162 CLR 645 at 657 there is a reference to 'the definitional and defence elements of the crime'.

It follows from this reasoning that self-defence must be regarded as being either a subjective or an objective element for the purposes of the legislation. The next question concerns the category into which self-defence should be placed. The definitions provided by the Act are not particularly helpful in this regard. However the use of the terms 'objective' and 'subjective' and the inclusion of 'voluntariness, intention, knowledge or some other mental state' as subjective elements suggest a distinction between actions and state of mind. And when regard is had to s 15 of the Criminal Law Consolidation Act, as it was at the time of the alleged offence, it is clear that the core of the defence, whether in relation to a charge of murder or some lesser offence, is the accused's genuine belief in the matter. It is true that some objective considerations are imported into the tests, but the primary focus is on the mental state of the accused.

The proper categorisation of self-defence in the general law was discussed in *Zecevic's* case. Counsel for the appellant in that case argued that it was sufficient for an accused person to hold an actual belief that self-defence was necessary, whether that belief was reasonable or not. The argument was supported by the submission that the defence 'is a negative condition of the offence and is therefore an integral part of it', a proposition argued by Professor Glanville Williams in *Textbook of Criminal Law* (2nd ed, 1983), pp 137–8. The argument was rejected, but that is not to say that self-defence is not concerned in large part with the accused's mental state.

The definition of subjective elements encompasses every mental state which qualifies as an element of the offence. It would seem that the rationale for excluding them from consideration after mental incompetence has been established rests on the assumption that the cause of any involuntariness, lack of intention or other similar exculpatory factor is likely to be the result of the mental incompetence. This causal connection may or may not exist as a matter of fact; involuntariness may have been due to other causes unconnected with mental incompetence as is recognised in cases such as *R v Cottle*. However, given the intent of the legislation that such mental states are not to be relied upon to support a complete acquittal if mental incompetence is established, it is not difficult to appreciate that the same policy reasons can be applied to self-defence. In the present case, for example, it would appear that the accused might want to rely for a defence on a delusional belief which was due to mental impairment as defined by the Act. In that event the policy of the legislation would require that evidence which supports a finding of mental incompetence (and in this case succeeds in establishing it) is not to be used to support a defence which would lead to a complete acquittal or a reduction of the offence from murder to manslaughter. If self-defence was an objective element for the purposes of the legislation the pursuit of such a result could not be prevented.

Finally, there is another provision in the legislation which throws some light on the content of the definition of 'objective element'. I have pointed out that Pt 8A also deals with the issue of mental fitness to stand trial. An order for supervision under the

Act cannot be made under this heading unless the court is satisfied on the balance of probabilities that the accused is mentally unfit to stand trial in accordance with the test which is set out in the legislation. However it is a further precondition to the making of such an order that:

(a) the objective elements of the offence are established beyond reasonable doubt; and
(b) there is, on the evidence before the court, no defence to the charge that could be established on the assumption that the defendant's mental faculties were not impaired at the time of the alleged offence: ss 269MB(2), 269NA(2).

The content of subpara (b) is a clear indication that defences such as self-defence are not included in the phrase 'the objective elements of the offence'. It follows that the state of mind which would attract the defence of self-defence is a subjective element of the offence for the purposes of Pt 8A.

[**Matheson** and **Nyland JJ** concurred.]

[Note also *R v WB* (1999) 73 SASR 45.]

SOME COMMENTS ON MENTAL IMPAIRMENT AND RELATED DEFENCES

Scope of the mental impairment defence

14.14 Many lawyers and psychiatrists have argued that the *M'Naghten Rules* (set out at **14.7C**), even as modified and explained in the more recent cases, are too restrictive in that they fail to extend to various forms of mental disorder. The scope of the *M'Naghten Rules* has been restricted to cognitive defects (defects of reason or rationality), excluding defects of conation, the psychological processes of desire and volition. Thus, the rules do not extend to cover the case of the psychopathy (*Willgoss v R* (at **14.9C**)), and are not readily applicable to the person who is aware both of the nature and wrongfulness of the acts he or she is performing but is yet unable to restrain herself or himself from so acting, that is, the person suffering from uncontrollable impulse: *Attorney-General for South Australia v Brown* (at **14.10C**).

14.15 A wider formulation of the mental impairment defence is contained in the American Law Institute's Model Penal Code, where it is provided as follows:

[4.01]

(1) A person is not responsible for criminal conduct if at the time of such conduct as a result of mental disease or defect he lacks substantial capacity either to appreciate the criminality [wrongfulness] of his conduct or to conform his conduct to the requirements of law.

(2) As used in this Article, the terms 'mental disease or defect' do not include an abnormality manifested only by repeated criminal or otherwise anti-social conduct.

14.16 In England, the Report of the Butler Committee, *Mentally Abnormal Offenders* (1975), Cmnd 6244 (the Butler Report), recommended that the defence of insanity be replaced by a new defence of mental disorder. The Butler Committee proposed a new special verdict, 'not guilty on evidence of mental disorder'. Aiming to 'avoid the use of medical terms about which there may be disputed interpretations or whose meaning may change with the years' (1975, [18.17]), the reformulated defence would have been comprised of two parts: (a) did the defendant know what he or she was doing?; or (b) was he or she suffering from 'severe mental illness or severe subnormality' at the time of the act? Severe subnormality is defined in s 4(2) of the Mental Health Act 1959 (UK) as:

> … a state of arrested or incomplete development of mind which includes subnormality of intelligence and is of such a nature or degree that the patient is incapable of living an independent life or of guarding himself against serious exploitation, or will be so incapable when of an age to do so.

Note that this legislation has since been repealed and replaced by the Mental Health Act 1983 (UK) which has also been reformed in recent years.

The Butler proposals were not implemented.

14.17 In Australia, the Commonwealth Criminal Code Act 1995 widens the common law defence of insanity. Section 7.3 provides:

(1) A person is not criminally responsible for an offence if, at the time of carrying out the conduct constituting the offence, the person was suffering from a mental impairment that had the effect that:
  (a) the person did not know the nature and quality of the conduct; or
  (b) the person did not know that the conduct was wrong (that is, the person could not reason with a moderate degree of sense and composure about whether the conduct, as perceived by reasonable people, was wrong); or
  (c) the person was unable to control the conduct.

'Mental impairment' is defined in subsections (8) and (9) as follows:

(8) In this section: ***mental impairment*** includes senility, intellectual disability, mental illness, brain damage and severe personality disorder.

(9) The reference in subsection (8) to mental illness is a reference to an underlying pathological infirmity of the mind, whether of long or short duration and whether permanent or temporary, but does not include a condition that results from the reaction of a healthy mind to extraordinary external stimuli. However, such a condition may be evidence of a mental illness if it involves some abnormality and is prone to recur.

These provisions depart from the common law most notably in including uncontrollable impulse and severe personality disorder (psychopathy) within the definition of mental impairment. The extension to include uncontrollable impulse has now been adopted in a number of Australian states and territories. Historically, it has been regarded as difficult to distinguish between a desire or an impulse that is uncontrollable and one that is simply not controlled by the defendant, and this is perhaps one reason why this limb of the mental impairment defence has been less popular than the 'nature and quality' and 'wrongness' limbs.

The inclusion of severe personality disorder has been more controversial. To include psychopathy as a form of mental illness is contrary to the view adopted by psychiatrists: see **14.50**. It involves opening the defence to persons aware of the nature and significance of their acts whose claim to be suffering from a mental illness is based solely on the fact that they have repeatedly and consistently behaved in an anti-social fashion. Although personality disorders are included within the scope of the Commonwealth Criminal Code defence, they have been excluded in a number of Australian jurisdictions on the basis of similar concerns (Criminal Law Consolidation Act 1935 (SA) Pt 8, discussed in Sentencing Advisory Council, Attorney-General's Department, South Australia, 2013).

14.18 In Victoria, the Crimes (Mental Impairment and Unfitness to be Tried) Act 1997 abolished the defence of insanity (s 25), replacing it with a defence of mental impairment. The defence of mental impairment is in generally similar terms to the *M'Naghten* formulation of insanity. Section 20 of the Act provides:

(1) The defence of mental impairment is established for a person charged with an offence if, at the time of engaging in conduct constituting the offence the person was suffering from a mental impairment that had the effect that —
  (a) he or she did not know the nature and quality of the conduct; or
  (b) he or she did not know that the conduct was wrong (that is, he or she could not reason with a moderate degree of sense and composure about whether the conduct, as perceived by reasonable people, was wrong).

(2) If the defence of mental impairment is established, the person must be found not guilty because of mental impairment.

In Victoria, the defence of mental impairment does not extend to personality disorder. In relation to irresistible impulse the words in brackets in para (b) would appear to do no more than adopt the approach taken by the High Court in *Sodeman v R* (1936) 55 CLR 192, approved by the Privy Council in *Attorney-General for South Australia v Brown* [1960] AC 432 (at 14.10C), that an incapacity to control conduct may be evidence that the accused did not know that what he or she was doing was wrong.

14.19 In New South Wales, the defence of mental impairment continues to be governed by the common law *M'Naghten Rules*, but a procedural framework for the defence has been included in the Mental Health (Forensic Provisions) Act 1990 (NSW). Section 38(1) provides that, if the person tried 'did the act or made the omission charged, but was mentally ill at the time', the jury should return a 'special verdict'— 'that the accused person is not guilty by reason of mental illness' ('NGMI'). For the purposes of the defence, mental illness is defined by reference to the Mental Health Act 2007. Section 4 provides:

> 'mental illness' means a condition that seriously impairs, either temporarily or permanently, the mental functioning of a person and is characterised by the presence in the person of any one or more of the following symptoms:
>
> (a) delusions,
> (b) hallucinations,
> (c) serious disorder of thought form,
> (d) a severe disturbance of mood,
> (e) sustained or repeated irrational behaviour indicating the presence of any one or more of the symptoms referred to in paragraphs (a)–(d).

14.20 Recently, the defence of mental illness has been reviewed in New South Wales (New South Wales Law Reform Commission (NSWLRC) Report No 138, 2013). The NSWLRC proposed a revised defence.

The proposal put forward in the commission's report is based on the Commonwealth Criminal Code provision on mental impairment (cl 7.2). As such, the proposed version of the defence includes volitional incapacity within the scope of the defence ('the person was unable to control the conduct') (rec 3.2). This inclusion would take into account the global way in which some mental disorders may affect individuals (see Yannoulidis, 2012 for discussion). It would also go some way to ameliorating the well-recognised narrowness of *M'Naghten* insanity (see NSWLRC, 2010, CP 6, [3.22]–[3.48] for discussion; see also Mackay, 1995, p 100). While it might cause some 'challenges', as the commission acknowledges (2013, [3.119]), the inclusion of volitional incapacity is a progressive development, and would bring the law into line with some of the Australian Code jurisdictions (see further Yannoulidis, 2012).

The revised defence would rest on statutory definitions of 'mental health impairment' and 'cognitive impairment'. 'Mental health impairment' is defined broadly as a 'temporary or continuing disturbance of thought, mood, volition, perception, or memory that impairs emotional wellbeing, judgment or behaviour, so as to affect functioning in daily life to a material extent'. Cognitive impairment is also defined broadly as an 'ongoing impairment in comprehension, reason, adaptive functioning, judgement, learning or memory that is the result of any damage to, dysfunction, developmental delay, or deterioration of the brain or mind'. The definitions of mental health and cognitive impairments exclude personality disorders, which, as the commission notes, have long been the subject of significant community concern (2013, [3.79]) and which, if included, would, in the commission's view, 'throw the net too wide' (2013, [3.78]).

In relation to the procedural practices relating to the mental illness defence, the NSWLRC recommended two changes that are relevant here. The first proposed change to procedural practices surrounding the defence relates to the conditions under which the court may accept the defence. According to rec 3.4, if the prosecution and defence agree that the evidence establishes the defence, the judge may review the evidence and, if he or she is satisfied, must enter a verdict that the defence has been successful. This means that the defence need not be left to the jury when it is not contested.

The second proposed change relevant here is the wording of the 'special verdict': the verdict that results from a successful insanity plea. The NSWLRC recommends that the special verdict be reformulated, with the reference to 'not guilty' replaced with a reference to 'not criminally responsible' (rec 3.6). This is a laudatory reform proposal, as the reformulated defence more accurately conveys the distinctive nature of the plea of mental illness.

The burden of proof

14.21 In *M'Naghten's Case* the legal burden of proof on the issue of insanity was clearly placed on the accused. Delivering the opinion of the judges (other than Maule J), Tindal CJ stated that 'the jurors ought to be told in all cases that every man is to be presumed to be sane, and to possess a sufficient degree of reason to be responsible for his crimes, until the contrary be proved to their satisfaction'. As this indicates, at common law, the insanity defence has to be left to the jury. The 'presumption of sanity' means that the accused bears the burden of proving that he or she was mentally impaired at the time of the offence. The standard of proof is on the balance of probabilities. Insanity is the only common law defence which imposes a legal (as opposed to evidentiary) burden on the accused, and it is referred to as the 'reverse burden of proof' on that basis.

14.22 In *Woolmington v Director of Public Prosecutions* [1935] AC 462 the House of Lords accepted insanity as an exception to the 'golden thread', and this view has been accepted in numerous Australian cases: see **1.82**. It has also been held that the burden of proof on substantial impairment by abnormality of mind and unfitness to plead, considered at **14.28**ff and **14.36**ff respectively, rests on the accused: *R v Dunbar* [1958] 1 QB 1; *R v Podola* [1960] 1 QB 325; *R v Robertson* [1968] 3 All ER 557. By contrast, the prosecution bears the legal burden of disproving automatism: *R v Joyce*

[1970] SASR 184; *R v Quick; R v Paddison* [1973] 1 QB 910; *R v Falconer* (1990) 171 CLR 30 (at 14.12C).

In Victoria, the rule regarding burden of proof is embodied in statute: Crimes (Mental Impairment and Unfitness to be Tried) Act 1997 (Vic) s 21. This section states that a person is presumed not to have been suffering from a mental impairment until the contrary is proved (s 21(1)). The question is one of fact, and to be determined by the jury on the balance of probabilities. The section explicitly provides for the possibility that the issue of mental impairment may in fact be raised by the prosecution, in which case it is the prosecution that bears the burden of proving that the defendant was suffering from a mental impairment. This possibility (which reflects the reality that a defendant may strenuously deny suffering from a mental impairment) was not provided for by the common law originally, but, in England and Wales in the mid-twentieth century, the rule was reinterpreted retrospectively (see *Bratty v Attorney-General for Northern Ireland* [1963] AC 386 at 411–12).

14.23 The placing of the legal burden on the accused in the defence of mental impairment may necessitate difficult directions to the jury. For instance, unlike mental impairment, the defence need only raise evidence of automatism, rather than prove it to a legal standard. Thus, if sufficient evidence of automatism is raised by the defence, the prosecution bears the burden of proving beyond reasonable doubt that the accused was not acting in an automatistic state. This means that if an accused raised both mental impairment and automatism, different directions regarding burdens will be required. This instance was considered by the High Court in *Falconer* (see 14.12C).

14.24 It is arguable that any difficulties faced by the prosecution in rebutting a defence of mental impairment would be adequately met by leaving the accused with the evidential burden, as is the case with the other general defences, while transferring the legal burden to the prosecution. This course was recommended by the English Criminal Law Revision Committee in their Eleventh Report, *Evidence (General)* (1972), Cmnd 4991, p 90.

14.25 The reverse burden is just one of the unusual procedural and evidentiary features of the insanity defence. See Loughnan, 2012 for discussion of these features of insanity in the law of England and Wales.

Disposition of mentally ill offenders

14.26 Over the last few decades, jurisdictions within Australia came to recognise that indeterminate detention for individuals found not guilty on the basis of mental impairment was no longer consistent with developments in expert medical knowledge of mental illness, or necessarily respectful of the human rights of those mentally ill individuals who are in the criminal justice system. As a result, laws in some jurisdictions were amended to provide alternatives to indefinite detention. The underlying rationale of current disposition rules is that an individual found not guilty by reason of mental illness should be subject to a regime that is the least restrictive of his or her freedom and autonomy as is consistent with the safety of the community.

In New South Wales, s 39 of the Mental Health (Criminal Procedure) Act 1990 provides that, on a finding of not guilty by reason of mental illness, the court may order that the person be detained in such place and in such manner as the court thinks fit until released by due process of law, or may make such other order (including an order releasing the person from custody, either unconditionally or subject to conditions) as the court considers appropriate. Subsection (2) provides that the court is not to make an order under this section for the release of a person from custody unless it is satisfied, on the balance of probabilities, that the safety of the person or any member of the public will not be seriously endangered by the person's release. This provision reflects an abiding concern with the dangerousness of the accused.

As this indicates, for individuals found 'not guilty by reason of mental illness' (NGMI), no limiting term exists. This means that the constraints imposed by the court apply indefinitely to NGMI individuals. In its recent report, the NSWLRC recommended introducing 'limiting terms' for those individuals who fall under s 39 (See NSWLRC, Report No 138, 2013). 'Limiting terms' are in use in Victoria (where they are known as 'nominal terms'), and are discussed below.

14.27 In Victoria, a new system of disposition was introduced by the Crimes (Mental Impairment and Unfitness to be Tried) Act 1997. A special hearing may be held under Pt 3 of the Act to determine whether the accused is not guilty of the offence, not guilty of the offence because of mental impairment, or committed the offence charged or an offence available as an alternative: s 15. A special hearing is to be conducted as nearly as possible as if it were a criminal trial. Section 17 provides:

> The following findings are available to the jury at a special hearing —
>
> (f) not guilty of the offence charged;
> (g) not guilty of the offence because of mental impairment;
> (h) the defendant committed the offence charged or an offence available as an alternative.

Alternatively, the question of mental impairment may be raised during a trial by the defence or, with the leave of the trial judge, by the prosecution: s 22. Where, either as a result of a special hearing or a trial, an accused is found not guilty because of mental impairment, the court must declare the accused is liable to supervision under Pt 5 of the Act or order the accused be released unconditionally: ss 18, 23. Part 5 entitles the court to impose one of two types of supervision order: a 'custodial supervision order' or a 'noncustodial supervision order'. By the former type of order, the court may commit a person to custody 'in an appropriate place' or 'in a prison', provided that a supervision order committing a person to prison may only be made if the court is satisfied 'that there is no practicable alternative in the circumstances': s 26. By the latter type of order, the court may 'release the person on conditions decided by the court and specified in the order': s 26(2)(b).

Whether the court makes a custodial or a non-custodial supervision order, it must set a 'nominal term' of supervision which is graded by reference to the maximum term of imprisonment which applies to the offence which has been committed: s 28. The nominal term fixed for murder is 25 years. By s 31, the person who is subject to the order may apply to the court in the case of a custodial supervision order for a variation of the order, and, in the case of a non-custodial supervision order, for a variation or revocation of the order. A person subject to a custodial supervision order cannot apply for a revocation of the order during the nominal term, but can apply to have the order varied to a noncustodial supervision order if the court is satisfied on the evidence available that the 'safety of the person subject to the order or members of the public will not be seriously endangered as a result of the release of the person on a non-custodial supervision order': s 32(2). A custodial supervision order can only be varied to a non-custodial order where the person has completed at least 12 months' 'extended leave' granted by the court under s 57 of the Act. The scheme of the Act is thus to provide for the release of persons found not guilty because of mental impairment in accordance with a graduated process supervised by the courts. A person in respect of whom a custodial supervision order has been made must first be granted at least 12 months' extended leave by the court and then be converted to a non-custodial supervision order before applying for revocation. For discussion of these provisions see *RDM v Director of Public Prosecutions* [1999] 2 VR 270.

The defence of substantial impairment by abnormality of mind

14.28 The defence that has come to be known as 'diminished responsibility' or 'substantial impairment by abnormality of mind' originated in Scotland in the nineteenth century. The Homicide Act 1957 (England and Wales) introduced the defence of diminished responsibility into English law as a partial defence to murder, reducing murder to manslaughter. The defence was amended by the Coroners and Justice Act 2009 (England and Wales), and s 2 of the 1957 Act now provides:

> (1) In section 2 of the Homicide Act 1957 (c. 11) (persons suffering from diminished responsibility), for subsection (1) substitute —
>
> (1) A person ('D') who kills or is a party to the killing of another is not to be convicted of murder if D was suffering from an abnormality of mental functioning which — (a) arose from a recognised medical condition, (b) substantially impaired D's ability to do one or more of the things mentioned in subsection (1A), and (c) provides an explanation for D's acts and omissions in doing or being a party to the killing.
>
> (1A) Those things are — (a) to understand the nature of D's conduct; (b) to form a rational judgment; (c) to exercise self control.
>
> (1B) For the purposes of subsection (1)(c), an abnormality of mental functioning provides an explanation for D's conduct if it causes, or is a significant contributory factor in causing, D to carry out that conduct.

(2) In section 6 of the Criminal Procedure (Insanity) Act 1964 (c. 84) (evidence by prosecution of insanity or diminished responsibility), in paragraph (b) for 'mind' substitute 'mental functioning'.

In its original form, the 1957 Act had provided that a defendant charged with murder would be liable for manslaughter instead if he or she suffered from an 'abnormality of mind' that 'substantially' impaired his or her 'mental responsibility' for the killing. The section stipulated that the requisite 'abnormality of mind' had to arise from 'arrested or retarded development of mind' or 'any inherent causes' or be 'induced by disease or injury'. The change in the law was the outcome of the Law Commission for England and Wales's review of the law of homicide. The commission proposed modernising the definition of diminished responsibility to ensure that it better accommodated expert medical knowledge of incapacity. A key feature of the new law of diminished responsibility is that the defence now includes an express requirement that a quasi-causal relationship exist between the abnormal mental state and the prohibited act of killing.

14.29 In 1974 the defence of diminished responsibility was introduced in New South Wales via s 23A of the Crimes Act 1900. The Crimes Amendment (Diminished Responsibility) Act 1997 (NSW) replaced that provision with a new s 23A and renamed the defence substantial impairment by abnormality of mind. Section 23A of the Crimes Act 1900 (NSW) now provides:

(1) A person who would otherwise be guilty of murder is not to be convicted of murder if:
   (a) it the time of the acts or omissions causing the death concerned, the person's capacity to understand events, or to judge whether the person's actions were right or wrong, or to control himself or herself, was substantially impaired by an abnormality of mind arising from an underlying condition, and
   (b) the impairment was so substantial as to warrant liability for murder being reduced to manslaughter.

(2) For the purposes of subsection (1)(b), evidence of an opinion that an impairment was so substantial as to warrant liability for murder being reduced to manslaughter is not admissible.

(3) If a person was intoxicated at the time of the acts or omissions causing the death concerned, and the intoxication was self-induced intoxication (within the meaning of section 428A), the effects of that self-induced intoxication are to be disregarded for the purpose of determining whether the person is not liable to be convicted of murder by virtue of this section.

(4) The onus is on the person accused to prove that he or she is not liable to be convicted of murder by virtue of this section.

(5) A person who but for this section would be liable, whether as principal or accessory, to be convicted of murder is to be convicted of manslaughter instead.

(6) The fact that a person is not liable to be convicted of murder in respect of a death by virtue of this section does not affect the question of whether any other person is liable to be convicted of murder in respect of that death.

(7) If, on the trial of a person for murder, the person contends:

(a) that the person is entitled to be acquitted on the ground that the person was mentally ill at the time of the acts or omissions causing the death concerned, or

(b) that the person is not liable to be convicted of murder by virtue of this section,

evidence may be offered by the prosecution tending to prove the other of those contentions, and the court may give directions as to the stage of the proceedings at which that evidence may be offered.

(8) In this section:

'Underlying condition' means a pre-existing mental or physiological condition, other than a condition of a transitory kind.

14.30 As the name 'substantial impairment' implies, this defence may be raised by individuals who can provide evidence that they were suffering from a relevant kind of 'impairment' at the time of the killing. The phrase 'abnormality of mind' has been drawn widely: it covers the mind's activities in all its aspects, not only perception of physical acts and matters and the ability to form a rational judgment as to whether an act is right or wrong, but also the ability to exercise will-power to control physical acts in accordance with that rational judgment (*R v Byrne* [1960] 2 QB 396 at 404). 'Underlying condition' has been defined more narrowly, as a 'pre-existing mental or physiological condition' (s 23A(8) of the Crimes Act 1900 (NSW)). Problems with the clarity of these phrases have led the NSWLRC to recommend that the words 'abnormality of mind arising from an underlying condition' be replaced by 'mental health or cognitive impairment' (rec 4.1) (see NSWLRC, Report No 138, 2013).

14.31 In New South Wales, the defence does not and has never specified that a causal or quasi-causal connection exist between an individual's 'abnormality of mind' and his or her 'acts or omissions causing the death concerned'. Rather, the 'abnormality of mind' must have been operative, or in some way pertained at the time of the killing (a temporal connection), but this does not (necessarily) mean that it precipitated the killing (the stricter requirement) (a quasi-causal component of the defence has been introduced into the law in England and Wales, as discussed above). The authors suggest that this is a strength of the New South Wales law. A temporal connection leaves open the question of precisely how a defendant's 'abnormality of mind' impairs his or her criminal responsibility. But this openness does not affect what is now a long-standing common law principle that certain conditions affecting a defendant's mental capacity are legitimately regarded as relevant to conviction, not just to sentence (although they do not give rise to a full defence of mental illness). Further, with its express requirement that the jury find that the impairment was 'so substantial as to warrant liability being reduced to manslaughter', the current law in New South Wales now clearly captures the moral-evaluative dimension of (partial) exculpation on the basis of mental incapacity, and usefully safeguards the role of the fact-finder (typically, the jury) in determining whether substantial impairment will succeed.

14.32 No diminished responsibility or substantial impairment defence has been introduced in Victoria. The Law Reform Commission of Victoria considered and rejected introduction of the defence of diminished responsibility in its Report No 40, *Homicide* (1991).

14.33 Diminished responsibility/substantial impairment continues to be a controversial defence, not least because it pathologises individuals relying on it (such as women who have been subject to prolonged domestic abuse, and subsequently kill their abusers). In addition, some commentators suggest that there are considerable conceptual difficulties involved with the concept of diminished responsibility or substantial impairment by abnormality of mind. The idea of being partially but not wholly responsible for one's actions raises profound philosophical difficulties. It has been difficult to pin down what role incapacity plays in substantial impairment, and this has left substantial impairment vulnerable to the charge that it is little more than enhanced mitigation, leading some to think that it could be abolished without major consequence. According to this line of argument, commentators suggest that the arguments in favour of diminished responsibility or substantial impairment by abnormality of mind as a defence reducing murder to manslaughter may be satisfied by the conferment upon judges of the power to impose sentences of less than life imprisonment for murder.

This has now been realised in Victoria, where the life sentence is now a maximum: Crimes Act 1958 (Vic), as amended by the Crimes (Amendment) Act 1986 (Vic) s 3. In New South Wales, also, the life sentence is a maximum, with the judge having power to pass a lesser sentence: Crimes Act 1900 (NSW) s 19A.

14.34 The introduction of the diminished responsibility defence in 1957 in England and Wales highlighted a problem that had long been inherent in the *M'Naghten Rules*. It has already been noted that, for the purposes of the *M'Naghten Rules*, mental incapacity was restricted to cognitive defects, or defects in reasoning. *M'Naghten* insanity does not encompass psychopathy, or what has been called 'irresistible impulse' or 'uncontrollable impulse' (*R v Heatley* [2006] NSWSC 1199) (although 'irresistible impulse' is accommodated by the criminal law in Code jurisdictions: see, for example, Criminal Code (Cth) 7.3, Mental Impairment). By contrast, the defence of diminished responsibility in England and Wales, and substantial impairment in New South Wales, has been held to be sufficiently wide to encompass psychopathy (*R v Byrne* [1960] 2 QB 396). The contrast may be explained in part by the later formalisation of the diminished responsibility/substantial impairment defence in the law of England and Wales, by which point advances in expert medical knowledge had exposed the *M'Naghten Rules* as highly restricted. In addition, because a successful plea of diminished responsibility/substantial impairment by abnormality of mind does not result in a complete acquittal, the consequences of widening the defence and accommodating psychopathy here are more circumscribed than if it was a part of the law of mental impairment. Psychopathy (also known as personality disorder) is discussed at 14.50ff.

An additional issue is raised by the contrast between the mental impairment defence and the defence of substantial impairment by abnormality of mind. Since the result of acquittal on the ground of mental impairment may be an indefinite detention (although subject to a limiting term in Victoria), the plea is in practice rarely raised except in defence to a murder charge and, in murder cases, the accused will commonly prefer to rely on some other defence, such as provocation or automatism.

14.35 This situation has, on occasions, led prosecutors to attempt to adduce evidence of *M'Naghten Rules* insanity, in order to safeguard the public interest by securing the detention of a dangerous person until the medical authorities are satisfied that he or she has recovered. This has been controversial. In *R v Joyce* [1970] SASR 184, the Supreme Court of South Australia stated that the Crown cannot raise the defence of insanity when it has not been raised by the accused. If, however, the accused raises the issue of his or her state of mind, by, for example, setting up a defence of automatism, then the trial judge may properly leave the issue of insanity to the jury. Similar views were expressed by the Full Court of the Victorian Supreme Court in *R v Jeffrey* [1967] VR 467.

In both England and New South Wales, it is provided by statute that if the accused raises a plea of one form of mental defect (insanity or diminished responsibility/substantial impairment by abnormality of mind), the prosecution may counter it by adducing evidence of the other form: Criminal Procedure (Insanity) Act 1964 (Eng) s 6; Crimes Act 1900 (NSW) s 23A(7).

It is clear now that, in Victoria, the issue of mental impairment may be raised by the prosecution, with the leave of the trial judge (Crimes (Mental Impairment and Unfitness to be Tried) Act 1997 s 22). In addition, the NSWLRC recently proposed that it be open to the court, and the prosecution (with leave of the court), to raise the defence at any time during the trial (rec 3.3) (NSWLRC, Report No 138, 2013). This proposal is positive in that it recognises the shared interests of all parties in ensuring that an insane individual is not dealt with via the usual trial process.

Unfitness to stand trial

14.36 It is a long-standing rule of the common law that an accused person cannot be put to his or her trial if, at the time of arraignment before the court, he or she is, by reason of a mental disorder or for some other reason, unable to enter a plea to the charge, or, at the time of the trial, unable to participate in the trial. It is important to note that the relevant point in time is the time of the arraignment or the time of the trial, not the time of the alleged offence. If it appears that an accused person is unfit, the jury or judge (acting as fact-finder) have to determine whether the person is unfit to plead/unfit to stand trial; and if they determine that the accused is unfit, then that person cannot stand trial, and an ordinary trial will not follow: see *R v Judge Martin; Ex parte Attorney-General* [1973] VR 339. The historical origins of the law on unfitness lie in the functional significance of an accused's plea to the medieval trial, although, in the current era, the rationale typically offered for the law is the principle of fair trial and the significance of due process.

14.37 As this brief overview suggests, unfitness to plead is not a defence. Unfitness to plead is a procedural provision exempting an individual from an ordinary trial, at least temporarily, on the basis that, at the time of the trial, he or she cannot understand or participate in it. In criminal law textbooks, unfitness to plead is usually included alongside exculpatory mental incapacity doctrines where it is usually, if implicitly, analysed as a procedural cognate of substantive criminal law doctrines such as insanity. Through a long process of formalisation of the common law, unfitness to plead is now a discrete procedural issue. Unfitness to plead provisions protect the accused and also safeguard the trial from the abuse of process entailed in trying an unfit individual.

14.38 Each accused coming before a criminal court is presumed to be fit to plead (*Eastman v The Queen* (2000) 203 CLR 1). Reflecting the close relationship between unfitness provisions and the integrity of the trial process, the question of unfitness to be tried may be raised by the prosecution, the accused or the judge. If the accused subsequently recovers from his or her unfitness, then, in certain circumstance, the trial may take place.

14.39 The common law provision for unfitness is substantially re-enacted by statute in New South Wales and Victoria: Crimes (Mental Impairment and Unfitness to be Tried) Act 1997 (Vic) Pt 2; Mental Health (Forensic Provisions) Act 1990 (NSW) Pt 2.

14.40 The issue of unfitness to stand trial is not confined to the accused's condition on arraignment or at the commencement of the trial. This is because an accused may become unfit during the course of a trial. Where a question as to the accused's unfitness to stand trial arises during the course of the trial, the issue should then be submitted to the judge or jury's determination. In considering the issue at the commencement of the trial, regard should be had not just to the accused's mental state at that time, but consideration should also be given to the nature of the trial and to what that condition will, or is likely to be, during the trial: *Kesavarajah v R* (1994) 181 CLR 230; 123 ALR 463.

14.41 At common law, the test to be applied in determining whether an accused is unfit to stand trial was stated by Smith J in *R v Presser* [1958] VR 45 at 48 to be 'whether the accused, because of mental defect, fails to come up to certain minimum standards which he needs to equal before he can be tried without unfairness or injustice to him' (see also *R v Pritchard* (1836) 7 C & P 303). In *Presser*, Smith J elaborated this test, stating:

> He needs, I think, to be able to understand what it is that he is charged with. He needs to be able to plead to the charge and to exercise his right of challenge.

> He needs to understand generally the nature of the proceeding, namely, that it is an inquiry as to whether he did what he is charged with. He needs to be able to follow the course of the proceedings so as to understand what is going on in court in a general sense, though he need not, of course, understand the purpose of all the various court formalities. He needs to be able to understand, I think, the substantial effect of any evidence that may be given against him; and he needs to be able to make his defence or answer to the charge. Where he has counsel he needs to be able to do this through his counsel by giving any necessary instructions and by letting his counsel know what his version of the facts is and, if necessary, telling the court what it is. He need not, of course, be conversant with court procedure and he need not have the mental capacity to make an able defence; but he must, I think, have sufficient capacity to be able to decide what defence he will rely upon and to make his defence and his version of the facts known to the court and to his counsel, if any.

Smith J's exposition was approved by the High Court in *Kesavarajah v R*, above.

Broadly, the *Presser* criteria provide that an accused should be able to understand the alleged offence, understand and follow the proceedings, and participate as required in the trial and in his or her defence.

14.42 As is the case for the defence of mental impairment, while clinical diagnoses of mental illness and other conditions are relevant to the court, the *Presser* criteria revolve around the *effect* or impact of those conditions on the accused. Intellectual disability (*R v Burles* [1970] 2 WLR 597; *R v Grant* [2002] QB 1030; *R v Martin* [2003] 2 Cr App R 322), mental illness (*R v Antoine* [2001] 1 AC 340) and situations where the defendant is 'deaf and dumb' (*R v Berry; Rex v Dyson* (1831) 7 C & P 305; *R v Roberts* [1954] 2 QB 329) have given rise to findings of unfitness. Inability to remember the offence is not a basis for unfitness. Thus, in *R v Podola* [1960] 1 QB 325 it was held that the fact that the accused was suffering from amnesia did not render him unfit to stand trial.

14.43 As was also the case for the defence of mental impairment, historically, a finding of unfitness to plead/unfitness to stand trial resulted in indefinite detention. The prospect of indefinite detention meant that, unless the defendant was charged with a serious offence, defence counsel had little incentive to initiate an inquiry into unfitness. As is the case with individuals found not guilty by reason of mental impairment, most jurisdictions now include a range of options for the disposition of unfit accused.

14.44 Unfitness provisions create a high threshold for a finding of unfitness (that is, it is not easy for an accused to be found to be unfit). It has long been clear that the legal question of a defendant's fitness to plead does not correspond to his or her ability to act in his or her own best interests (*R v Robertson* [1968] 1 WLR 1767; *R v M* [2003] EWCA Crim 3452). Similarly, in *Ngatayi v R* (1980) 147 CLR 1; 30 ALR 27 it was held that the fact that the accused, a tribal Aboriginal person, did not understand the legal concepts applicable to his defence did not render him unfit to stand trial.

14.45 In New South Wales and Victoria, the issue of unfitness to stand trial is now dealt with by statute, although the criteria for a finding of unfitness continue to be governed by the common law (the *Presser* criteria) in New South Wales.

14.46 In New South Wales, the Mental Health (Forensic Procedures) Act 1990 Pt 2 establishes a statutory regime for the determination of questions of unfitness to plead. In many ways the statute enunciates established common law rules; see *Mantell v Molyneux* (2006) 68 NSWLR 46.

A judge tries the issue of unfitness (s 11), unless there is an election for the matter to be heard by a jury: s 21A. An inquiry into unfitness is not to be conducted in an adversary manner, and the onus of proof does not rest on any particular party: s 12. If a person is found to be fit, a normal trial commences or continues: s 13. If a person is found unfit, the court must refer them to the Mental Health Review Tribunal, and may adjourn the proceedings, grant bail, remand the person or make any other order: s 14. After receiving advice from the Office of the Director of Public Prosecutions (ODPP), the court may hold a special hearing, which determines that the person can be acquitted unless it can be proved to the requisite criminal standard of proof that, on the limited evidence available, the person committed the offence charged or any other offence available as an alternative to the offence charged: s 19. At a 'special hearing' the verdicts available to the jury or the judge are: not guilty of the offence charged; not guilty on the ground of mental illness; that on the limited evidence available, the accused person committed the offence charged; or that on the limited evidence available, the accused person committed an offence available as an alternative to the offence charged: s 22. Depending on the outcome of a 'special hearing' into the alleged offence, which may follow a finding of unfitness, an unfit accused may be detained. His or her detention is then reviewed periodically by the Mental Health Review Tribunal.

14.47 Recently, the criteria for a finding of unfitness, and the procedures surrounding the law on unfitness, were examined by the NSWLRC. In its report, the commission recommended a statutory test for fitness. The commission recommends that the *Presser* standards be updated and incorporated into statute (rec 2.1), and that an overarching principle of a fair trial be incorporated into the test as a 'touchstone' for the determination of unfitness (2013, [2.66]) (see NSWLRC, Report No 138, 2013). This proposal maintains the common law approach of focusing on the individual capacities that an accused requires to participate in a criminal trial, and is oriented around understanding and using information that is relevant to the decisions he or she will need to make. According to the commission's earlier discussion paper, this option was not intended to raise or lower the standard for a finding of unfitness but rather to tidy up the law (NSWLRC, 2012, DP 1, [5]).

14.48 In Victoria, s 6 of the Crimes (Mental Impairment and Unfitness to be Tried Act) 1997 provides:

(1) A person is unfit to stand trial for an offence if, because the person's mental processes are disordered or impaired, the person is or, at some time during the trial, will be —
  (a) unable to understand the nature of the charge; or
  (b) unable to enter a plea to the charge and to exercise the right to challenge jurors or the jury; or
  (c) unable to understand the nature of the trial (namely that it is an inquiry as to whether the person committed the offence); or
  (d) unable to follow the course of the trial; or
  (e) unable to understand the substantial effect of any evidence that may be given in support of the prosecution; or
  (f) unable to give instructions to his or her legal practitioner.

(2) A person is not unfit to stand trial only because he or she is suffering from mental loss.

Unfitness to stand trial is determined by a jury empanelled for that purpose: s 7(3)(b). If the jury finds that the accused is unfit to stand trial, the judge must determine on the balance of probabilities whether or not the accused is likely to become fit to stand trial within the next 12 months and, if so, the period by the end of which the accused is likely to be fit to stand trial: s 11(4). The matter must then be adjourned for that period and the accused granted bail or remanded in custody: s 12. If the jury finds that the accused is unfit to stand trial and the judge determines that the accused is not likely to become fit within the next 12 months, the court must proceed to hold a special hearing under Pt 3 of the Act within three months: s 12(5). If at the end of the adjournment period, or the end of such further adjournment period as may be granted but not beyond a total period of 12 months, a real and substantial question of unfitness is raised again, the judge must proceed to hold a special hearing under Pt 3 of the Act: s 14(2). Special hearings under Pt 3 of the Act are dealt with at **14.46**, and result in a finding of (a) not guilty of the offence charged, (b) not guilty of the offence because of mental impairment, or (c) the accused committed the offence charged or an offence available as an alternative.

14.49 Further reading

Butler Committee (UK), *Report of the Committee on Mentally Abnormal Offenders* (1975), Cmnd 6244

Community Development Committee of the Victorian Parliament, *Inquiry Into Persons Detained at the Governor's Pleasure* (1995)

O Dixon, 'A Legacy of Hadfield, McNaughton and Maclean' (1957) 31 *ALJ* 255

J Ellard, 'Some Notes on Non-insane Automatism and the Will' (1995) 69 *ALJ* 833

A Loughnan, *Manifest Madness: Mental Incapacity in Criminal Law*, Oxford University Press, Oxford, 2012

—, 'Reforming the Law on Mental Incapacity' (2013) 25(2) *Current Issues in Criminal Justice*

R D Mackay, *Mental Condition Defences in the Criminal Law*, Oxford University Press, Oxford, 1995

B McSherry, 'Defining What is a "Disease of the Mind": The Untenability of Current Legal Interpretations' (1993) 1 *JLM* 76

—, 'Mental Impairment and Criminal Responsibility: Recent Australian Legislative Reforms' (1999) 23 *CLJ* 135

—, 'Revising the M'Naghten Rules' (1990) 64 *LIJ* 725

D J West and A Walk (eds), *Daniel McNaughton: His Trial and the Aftermath*, Gaskell Books, Ashford, 1977

C R Williams, 'Development and Change in Insanity and Related Defences' (2000) 24 *MULR* 711

S Yannoulidis, *Mental State Defences in Criminal Law*, Ashgate Publishing, London, 2012

PSYCHOPATHY, MENTAL ILLNESS AND PREVENTIVE DETENTION

14.50 The difficult issues raised by mentally impaired accused extend beyond the trial context. The purpose of this section is to briefly consider the issue of one type of mental condition — psychopathy or personality disorder — and preventive detention.

14.51 Understood broadly, preventive detention is a practice that detains individuals on the basis of the need to protect the community. In the common law world, the origins of what are now formal rules and procedures governing preventive detention lie in informal and discretionary detention practices. Preventive detention regimes grew up around a population of suspect individuals — vagrants, inebriates and habitual criminals, as well as the mentally ill. As a result, a discussion of preventive detention in the context of mental impairment is apposite.

14.52 There are a number of fundamental questions to be asked about preventive detention. What are the legal foundations of regimes of preventive detention, which have proliferated in recent years? Are existing risk assessment techniques sufficiently sophisticated to ground confidence that detention dispositions are warranted when ordered? What are the remedies available to people who seek to challenge these regimes? How do these regimes challenge fundamental principles, such as human rights? And, further, are regimes of preventive detention effective in protecting people from harm? The case of preventive detention of the mentally ill illustrates some of these difficult issues.

The development of preventive detention regimes in Australia

14.53 In the 1990s, the case of Gary David (otherwise known as Gary Webb) became a focus for discussion of the preventive detention of the mentally ill. His case, and that of Gregory Wayne Kable (considered below), provides a useful focus for our discussion.

Prior to his death in 1993 at the age of 38, Gary David spent almost all of his adolescent and adult life in institutions. As a child, his background was one of brutality and deprivation. He mutilated his body more than 70 times, threatened to kill public figures, cause a police bloodbath and commit a massacre that would make Melbourne's mass murders in Queen and Hoddle Streets 'look like a picnic'. He was sentenced to 14 years' gaol after a 1980 gun battle. Newly released from prison at the time, he had shot a woman in a pizza shop, leaving her a quadriplegic, and shot two policemen who came to her rescue. In prison, he assaulted more than 15 inmates and guards, but his main victim was himself, as he engaged in extensive and repeated self-mutilation. He was diagnosed as suffering from borderline personality disorder and antisocial personality disorder.

14.54 David was due for release in February 1990. His imminent release led to a public outcry and produced a flurry of administrative and ultimately legislative activity. David was charged with threatening to kill a former fellow prisoner (under the Crimes Act 1958 (Vic) s 20), and remanded in custody. He was then certified insane and transferred to J-Ward, Ararat, the state's maximum security psychiatric unit. He lodged an appeal to the Mental Health Review Board against that certification. In April, the Victorian Parliament passed the Community Protection Act 1990 (Vic), an extraordinary and unprecedented piece of legislation giving the Supreme Court power to continue David's detention beyond the expiration of his sentence. Later that month, David pleaded guilty in the Magistrates' Court to the charge of threatening to kill and was remanded in custody. In May, the Mental Health Review Board upheld David's appeal and ordered that he be returned to prison. The Attorney-General then successfully lodged an interim application for David's detention under the Community Protection Act 1990 (Vic).

14.55 In July 1990, David was sentenced to 12 months' imprisonment (with six months suspended) on the charge of threatening to kill. David then remained in custody pursuant to the Community Protection Act 1990 (Vic). A hearing under that Act was held before Mr Justice Fullagar: *Kennan v David* (18 September 1990, unreported). His Honour ordered that David remain in preventive detention for a period of six months. A further application was made at the expiration of that order before Mr Justice Hedigan, with the result that David was ordered to remain in preventive detention in Pentridge prison until November 1992: *Attorney-General v David* [1992] 2 VR 46. David then successfully applied to the court for an order that he be transferred to Mont Park Psychiatric Hospital. On the day of admission, a spectacular outburst of self-mutilation and threats to staff led to him being transferred, first to hospital for surgery and recuperation, and then back to Pentridge. Ultimately,

David's self-inflicted injuries proved too much for his body to bear, and, in June 1993, while a patient in the security wing of St Vincent's Hospital, he died of cardiac arrest.

14.56 The certification of David as insane in 1989 and his transfer to Ararat was, at the time, thought to present a solution to the problem posed by his imminent release. The law relating to the transfer of prisoners to psychiatric hospitals and to the civil commitment of mentally ill persons in Victoria was contained in the Mental Health Act 1986 (Vic). As a matter of terminology, a person serving a sentence who is transferred from prison to a mental hospital under s 16 of the Act is known as a security patient, and a person civilly committed under s 8 of the Act is known as an involuntary patient. These provisions set out a number of criteria which must be satisfied, the key ones being that the person appears to be suffering from a mental illness and that treatment for that illness can be obtained by admission and detention in a psychiatric hospital. The Act sets up a Mental Health Review Board, comprising a lawyer (chair), a psychiatrist and a community member, to review certifications and hear appeals from persons certified as security patients and involuntary patients. Had David's certification as a security patient been upheld, then, although at the expiration of his sentence he could no longer be held as a security patient, he could have been lawfully committed and held as an involuntary patient.

14.57 The flaw in this process, however, is that the evidence suggested that David was not mentally ill. A person with a personality disorder is not, for that reason, regarded as being mentally ill within the discipline of psychiatry. The word 'personality' refers to an individual's characteristic way of functioning psychologically. Some persons have traits of character that are abnormal or socially undesirable. At an extreme level such persons are described as having a personality disorder. The position of such persons is, however, different from that of a person suffering from a disturbance of mental functioning. The fact that a person's behaviour is deviant, maladapted or non-conformist does not necessarily mean that the behaviour is the product of any disturbance in mental functioning.

14.58 Gary David's status as a security patient was considered by the Mental Health Review Board in a detailed hearing over 16 days. The board found that David satisfied the diagnostic criteria for both borderline personality disorder and antisocial personality disorder. The board held that these personality disorders did not constitute a mental illness. The board went on to hold that, even were David suffering from a mental illness, no treatment for that mental illness within the meaning of the Act could be obtained.

14.59 The Community Protection Act 1990 (Vic) was unique in Australian legal history as being the first occasion on which an Act of Parliament was passed for the expressly stated purpose of enabling the detention of a named individual. Notwithstanding the general title of the Act, s 1 stated its purpose as being (a) to provide for the safety of members of the public and the care or treatment and the management of Gary David, and (b) to provide for proceedings to be instituted in the Supreme Court for an Order for the detention of Gary David.

The Act empowered the Minister to apply to the Supreme Court for an Order that David be placed in preventive detention. The test to be applied by the court in determining whether to order preventive detention for David was set out in s 8(1) as being whether the court was satisfied on the balance of probabilities, that Gary David (a) was a serious risk to the safety of any member of the public; and (b) was likely to commit any act of personal violence to another person. With the death of David, the Act ceased, of course, to have any operation and was repealed.

14.60 This one-person piece of legislation offended basic common law principles. In particular, it offended against the principle of the rule of law. The rule of law requires that laws be of general application; that is, that all members of the community be equally subject to the law. Yet this Act, penal in its effect, specifically applied only to a named individual. At the time of the introduction of the bill, the then shadow Attorney-General described it as creating 'a process that must be compared with the historical Bills of Attainder', and characterised it as 'one of the most obnoxious bills that has ever been introduced into Parliament'. Few persons, however, would deny the proposition that, in the case of a person suffering from a personality disorder of an extreme form and representing a grave threat to the physical safety of members of the public, society must be able to protect its members, if necessary, by depriving that person of their liberty. It is likely that such a view would be held by the overwhelming majority of members of the community, and a government that failed to respond to it would be widely and properly perceived as failing in its duty to protect its citizens.

14.61 A similar case arose in New South Wales around the same time. Gregory Wayne Kable stabbed his wife to death in 1990, following a bitter custody dispute. He was charged with murder and convicted of manslaughter when a plea of diminished responsibility based on acute depression was accepted by the Crown. Kable was sentenced to five years and four months' imprisonment. While in prison, Kable wrote a number of threatening letters. Although appearing far less spectacularly dangerous than David, Kable's pending release in 1994 provoked a political storm. The government responded with the Community Protection Act 1994 (NSW). The Act was similar in operation to the Victorian legislation, providing for Kable to be detained in prison for successive periods of up to six months. In February 1995, an order under the Act was made by the Supreme Court of New South Wales. An appeal to the New South Wales Court of Appeal was dismissed in May 1995. In August 1995, the Supreme Court declined to make a further order and Kable was released.

14.62 Notwithstanding his release, Kable pursued an appeal to the High Court against the original order for his detention on the basis that he remained liable to the risk that further orders for his detention could be applied for under the Community Protection Act 1994 (NSW). In *Kable v DPP for NSW* (1996) 189 CLR 51; 138 ALR 577, the High Court allowed Kable's appeal and declared the Community Protection Act 1994 (NSW) unconstitutional. The decision of the court was by a majority of four to two; Toohey, Gaudron, McHugh and Gummow JJ, Brennan CJ and Dawson J dissenting. The view of the majority was that the involvement of the courts in what was, in essence, an executive decision to detain Kable beyond the length of his term of imprisonment was unconstitutional as infringing the doctrine of separation of powers. Gaudron J stated (at 615):

> [W]hen regard is had to the precise nature of the function purportedly conferred by s 5(1) [of the Community Protection Act 1994 (NSW)], the matters to be taken into account in its exercise and its contrariety to what is ordinarily involved in the judicial process, the effect of s 5(1) is, in my view, to compromise the integrity of the Supreme Court of New South Wales and, because that court is not simply a state court but a court which also exists to exercise the judicial power of the Commonwealth, it also has the effect of compromising the integrity of the judicial system brought into existence by Ch 111 of the Constitution.
>
> The integrity of the courts depends on their acting in accordance with the judicial process and, in no small measure, on the maintenance of public confidence in that process. Particularly is that so in relation to criminal proceedings which involve the most important of all judicial functions, namely, the determination of the guilt or innocence of persons accused of criminal offences. Public confidence cannot be maintained in the courts and their criminal processes if, as postulated by s 5(1), the courts are required to deprive persons of their liberty, not on the basis that they have breached any law, but on the basis that an opinion is formed, by reference to material which may or may not be admissible in legal proceedings, that on the balance of probabilities, they may do so.

While the implications and scope of the decision in *Kable v DPP for NSW* have been significant, the decision has not meant that more general systems of preventive detention cannot be enacted by state parliaments, or that the courts may not have some involvement in such systems. McHugh J stated (at 626–7):

> The Parliament of New South Wales has the constitutional power to pass legislation providing for the imprisonment of a particular individual. And that is so whether the machinery for the imprisonment be the legislation itself or the order of a Minister, public servant or tribunal. Moreover, there is no reason to doubt the authority of the state to make general laws for preventive detention when those laws operate in accordance with the ordinary judicial processes of the state courts. However, whatever else the Parliament of New South Wales may be able to do in respect of the preventive detention of individuals who are perceived to be dangerous, it cannot, consistently with Ch 111 of the Constitution, invoke the authority of the Supreme Court to make the orders against the appellant by the methods which the Act authorises. This is because the Act and its procedures compromise the institutional impartiality of the Supreme Court.

14.63 The cases of Gary David and Gregory Wayne Kable raise the question of whether a more general form of legislation be enacted, designed to establish a system of preventive detention for persons in respect of whom there is substantial evidence to suggest they pose a major threat to the community at the expiration of their sentences? Such a system runs counter to traditional legal thinking, which views punishment as essentially retributive in nature. On this view, a person should only be punished for crimes he or she has committed, and should only be incarcerated for a period of time warranted by the severity of the crime committed and that person's moral culpability. For an excellent statement of the common law view of punishment and sentencing, see *Veen v R (No 1)* (1979) 143 CLR 458 and *Veen v R (No 2)* (1988) 164 CLR 465 and note R Fox, 'The Killings of Bobby Veen: The High Court on Proportion in Sentencing' (1988) 12 *Crim LJ* 339.

Recent developments in preventive detention

14.64 In the years since these decisions, preventive detention has gained wider acceptability and preventive detention regimes have been created in several jurisdictions. As a result of widespread public concern with sexual violence (particularly with offences committed against children), sex offenders now comprise the highest profile of those subject to preventive detention (alongside suspected terrorists). Laws enacted in the United States, which have been copied by jurisdictions around the world, permit the civil commitment of sexually violent predators and uphold the constitutionality of mandating a system of registration and selective community notification of convicted sex offenders. Several regimes applying to sex offenders are premised on the provision of treatment to those detained, but it is not clear that this is the sole rationale.

14.65 The creation of preventive detention regimes received a significant boost in the wake of the 9/11 attacks on the United States. In Australia, at Federal level, a raft of anti-terrorism legislation was passed in the first-half of 2002. More recently, the Commonwealth Government enacted the Anti-Terrorism Act (No 2) 2005, which was designed to strengthen existing anti-terrorism laws, and which encompasses a preventive detention scheme. According to this scheme, persons suspected of involvement with terrorism can be detained for up to 48 hours where there is insufficient evidence to support a formal charge (Criminal Code s 105.9 (Cth)). Several states have also amended their anti-terrorism legislation to encompass preventive detention in the years since 9/11. For instance, s 2A of the Terrorism (Police Powers) Act 2002 (NSW) provides for preventive detention (s 26D), but as the Ombudsman noted in his review of that Act, such powers have not been used since the commencement of the Act (New South Wales Ombudsman, Review of Parts 2A and 3 of the Terrorism (Police Powers) Act 2002, August 2011, Recommendation 13, p 33).

14.66 Beginning with the decision in *Kable*, Australian appellate courts have critically reviewed preventive detention regimes, giving careful consideration to the precise conditions under which the preventive detention of offenders will be acceptable. The main issues are the rule of law, proportionality, the principle against double punishment, and fairness to those subject to preventive detention. In addition, changes to the rules of evidence, use of the civil standard of proof, and the availability of review of decision-making, and, increasingly, concerns with compatibility with constitutional protections and human rights norms, are prominent. The most significant court decisions include *Fardon v Attorney-General for Qld* (2004) 210 ALR 50; *Attorney-*

General (Qld) v Francis (2005) QSC 381; *Attorney-General v Fardon* (SC(Qld), No 416, September 2003, unreported); *Attorney-General (NSW) v Gallagher* (2006) NSWSC 340; *Attorney-General (NSW) v Tillman* (2007) NSWSC 605; *Attorney-General (NSW) v Quinn* (2007) NSWSC 87; *Attorney-General (NSW) v Winters* (2007) NSWSC 1071; *Cornwall v Attorney-General (NSW)* [2007] NSWSC 374; *Director of Public Prosecutions (WA) v GTR* [2008] (unreported); *Director of Public Prosecutions (WA) v Mangolamara* (2007) WASC (27 March 2007); *TSL v Secretary to the Department of Justice* (2006) VSCA 199.

14.67 Predicting dangerousness is, of course, notoriously difficult, and the knowledge and practice around it is controversial. Some commentators have argued that it is possible to isolate a group of offenders of which a majority will commit further violence. Preventive detention should, it is submitted, be reserved only for the most extreme cases.

14.68 Further reading

P Fairall and W Lacey, 'Preventative Detention and Control Orders under Federal Law: The Case for a Bill of Rights' 31(3) *Melbourne University Law Review* 1072–98

Law Reform Commission of Victoria, *The Concept of Mental Illness in the Mental Health Act 1986* (1990)

A Loughnan and S Selchow, 'Preventive Detention Beyond the Law: The Need to Ask Socio-Political Questions' in P Keyser (ed), *Preventive Detention: Asking the Fundamental Questions*, Intersentia, 2013, pp 261–85

NSWLRC, *People with Cognitive and Mental Health Impairments in the Criminal Justice System: Criminal Responsibility and Consequences,* Report No 138, 2013

D Ruschena, 'Determining Dangerousness: Whatever Happened to the Rules of Evidence' (2003) 10 *Psychiatry, Psychology and Law* 122

Social Development Committee of the Victorian Parliament, Final Report, *Inquiry into Mental Disturbance and Community Safety* (1992)

C R Williams, 'Coping with the Highly Dangerous: Issues of Principle Raised by Preventive Detention', paper presented to the Australian Institute of Criminology Conference, *Serious Violent Offenders: Sentencing, Psychiatry and Law Reform* (Melbourne, 1991)

—, 'Psychopathy, Mental Illness and Preventive Detention: Issues Arising from the David Case' (1990) 16 *Mon LR* 161

D Wood, 'A One-Man Dangerous Offenders Statute — The Victorian Community Protection Act 1990' (1990) 17 *MULR* 497

Intoxication

CHAPTER 15

INTRODUCTION

15.1 Intoxication, whether as a result of the consumption of alcohol or of other drugs, is not a defence as such. Intoxication is *evidence* that may go to the issue of whether the prosecution has proved that the accused performed the requisite actus reus with the mens rea. Thus, the law on intoxication relates to the admissibility of evidence, rather than substantive law. Intoxication does not of itself excuse or exculpate an accused. As a result, it is not correct to refer to intoxication as a defence, and this chapter refers to the law on intoxication or intoxicated offending.

15.2 In criminal law, rules about intoxication cover intoxication by alcohol or illicit drugs. The law developed by reference to intoxication by alcohol, which was, historically, the most common intoxicant. Intoxication by prescription drugs is treated differently in a still emergent line of case law, and is discussed further below.

15.3 The relevance of evidence of an accused's state of intoxication at the time of committing the offence may be twofold. First, in extreme cases it may mean that the accused's conduct was involuntary; that is, that the acts were committed in an automatistic state in which the accused's physical actions were not directed by her or his will. Alternatively, intoxication may be relevant in showing that, although the accused's actions were performed voluntarily, the prosecution has not proved (beyond reasonable doubt) that the accused had the mens rea required to constitute the particular crime charged.

15.4 Thus, on a charge of murder committed by shooting, evidence of intoxication may be adduced to show the accused did not realise that he or she was handling a gun at all (that the conduct was involuntary) or that, although the accused's conduct was voluntary, he or she did not intend to cause death or grievous bodily harm, or realise that such a result was a likely or probable outcome of his or her actions (that is, that the accused lacked the mens rea required for murder).

15.5 Intoxication as a consequence of alcohol or drugs voluntarily consumed, and falling short of rendering the accused's conduct involuntary, cannot, however, give rise to a defence to a crime of absolute liability. This is because such crimes require no mens rea. Nor can such intoxication form the basis for a defence to a charge of negligent manslaughter, in relation to which neither intention nor foresight is required. Intoxication rendering the accused's conduct involuntary can, however, give rise to a defence in these cases. For an accused to be guilty even of a crime of negligence or of absolute liability, the accused must at least possess an awareness of the acts he or she is performing.

15.6 These basic common law principles apply in Australia in relation to crimes committed by persons under the influence of alcohol or illicit drugs. In both New South Wales and Victoria, however, the common law position has been significantly modified by statute. In New South Wales, the statutory modifications reflect an approach to the relevance of intoxication to criminal liability derived from the law of England and Wales, an approach which culminated in the decision of the House of Lords in *Director of Public Prosecutions v Majewski* [1977] AC 443 (at **15.15**). In the important case of *R v O'Connor* (1980) 146 CLR 64; 29 ALR 449 (at **15.23C**), the High Court of Australia rejected that decision. In Victoria, the *O'Connor* principles continue to apply in relation to non-homicide offences, but have been modified in statute in relation to homicide (at **15.31**).

15.7 An appreciation both of the decision in *R v O'Connor* and the New South Wales legislation requires an understanding of the background to *Director of Public Prosecutions v Majewski* and of that decision. The remainder of this section provides that background.

15.8 A convenient point from which to trace the development of the law in England is the decision of the House of Lords in *Director of Public Prosecutions v Beard* [1920] AC 479. The accused was charged with the murder of a girl whom he suffocated while raping her. His defence was that he was drunk and that he had not intended to cause either death or grievous bodily harm to the girl. He was convicted of murder and appealed to the Court of Criminal Appeal where a verdict of manslaughter was substituted. The Crown appealed to the House of Lords, where the conviction of murder was restored. The House of Lords based its decision on the ground that the accused, although drunk, had intended to rape the girl (this was not denied by the accused) and he was, therefore, necessarily guilty of murder by virtue of the felony-murder rule. Lord Birkenhead LC, with whom the other members of the House of Lords agreed, stated (at 499–500):

> [W]here a specific intent is an essential element in the offence, evidence of a state of drunkenness rendering the accused incapable of forming such an intent should be taken into consideration in order to determine whether he had in fact formed the intent necessary to constitute the particular crime … In a charge of murder based upon intention to kill or to do grievous bodily harm, if the jury are satisfied that the

> accused was, by reason of his drunken condition, incapable of forming the intent to kill or to do grievous bodily harm, unlawful homicide with malice aforethought is not established and he cannot be convicted of murder. But nevertheless unlawful homicide has been committed by the accused, and consequently he is guilty of unlawful homicide with out malice aforethought, and that is manslaughter ... [T]he law is plain beyond all question that in cases falling short of insanity a condition of drunkenness at the time of committing an offence causing death can only, when it is available at all, have the effect of reducing the crime from murder to manslaughter.

15.9 Over a long period of time, intoxication cases have made it clear that the question to be asked is not whether the accused was 'incapable' of forming the intent required, but rather whether the accused in fact formed the intent required. With this qualification, the *Beard* passage, quoted above, came to be treated as establishing a principle that in relation to crimes of 'specific intent', intoxication could be adduced to cast doubt on whether the Crown had proved the elements of the offence, but that in relation to crimes of 'basic intent', self-induced intoxication could not be adduced as evidence to cast doubt on the Crown case. The meanings attributed to these terms are considered below.

15.10 It may be noted that whether intoxication can ever give rise to a defence to a charge of manslaughter (a crime of basic intent) was not in issue in *Beard's* case. This is because that decision rested on a 'general rule' (which is now defunct) that juries are to presume a man to do what is the natural consequence of his act (in that case, strangling the victim in the course of a rape). It was conceded by counsel that the accused was guilty of manslaughter, and the only argument put was that the accused should not be guilty of murder because he had acted without intent to cause death or grievous bodily harm.

15.11 The *Beard* approach to intoxication, fault and 'specific intent' was adopted in subsequent appellate judgments. In *Bratty v Attorney-General for Northern Ireland* [1963] AC 386, Lord Denning stated in obiter that if a 'drunken man is so drunk that he does not know what he is doing, he has a defence to any charge ... in which a specific intent is essential' (at 410). Similarly, in *Attorney-General for Northern Ireland v Gallagher* [1963] AC 349, Lord Denning stated that 'if a man is charged with an offence in which a specific intention is essential ... then evidence of drunkenness which renders him incapable of forming that intention, is an answer' (at 381).

15.12 Over the twentieth century, the relationship between intoxication and liability further developed via the notion of specific intent. The term had first developed in the nineteenth century, but no definition of specific intention was provided by the courts and, although the term 'specific intent' was used, it was not used in all cases of intoxication, nor was it used consistently. By the twentieth century, through cases such as *Beard*, specific intent was invested with a distinct, technical meaning, and came to denote the intent required for an offence, over and above the intent to do the particular physical act that forms the external component of the offence (see *R v Heard* [2007]

3 WLR 475; *R v Hatton* [2006] 1 Cr App R 16). For this reason, specific intent is sometimes referred to as ulterior intent.

15.13 In any case, the New South Wales approach to the question of when evidence of intoxication can be introduced is determined by two factors: how the accused became intoxicated; and the kind of offence they are alleged to have committed. In relation to the way in which the person became intoxicated, a distinction is drawn between self-induced, voluntary, or advertent intoxication, on the one hand, and involuntary or inadvertent intoxication on the other. Involuntary intoxication is admissible as evidence across the spectrum of criminal offences. By contrast, the legal approach to voluntary intoxication — the type of intoxication at issue in the majority of cases — varies according to the type of offence with which an accused is charged, with evidence of it admissible only in relation to some offences. The offences for which it is possible to admit evidence of voluntary intoxication are known as offences of specific intent. The residual category of other offences — those for which evidence of voluntary intoxication may not be adduced — are known as offences of basic (or general) intent.

15.14 Before turning to *Director of Public Prosecutions v Majewski*, it may be useful to refer to one particularly vivid example of the importance of the distinction between crimes of specific intent and crimes of basic intent, and the rule prevailing in New South Wales that self-induced intoxication cannot be adduced as evidence in relation to crimes of the latter class. The case is *R v Lipman* [1970] 1 QB 152. The accused and the deceased, his girlfriend, took a quantity of the drug LSD. In the course of the hallucinatory experience which followed, the accused, believing he was being attacked by snakes and had to fight for his life, suffocated the deceased, his girlfriend, by cramming eight inches of sheet into her mouth. The accused was convicted of manslaughter on the basis both of the negligent manslaughter doctrine and the unlawful act manslaughter doctrine. He appealed to the Court of Appeal. The court upheld the accused's conviction on the basis of the unlawful act manslaughter doctrine. The court held that manslaughter was a crime of basic intent and that, therefore, evidence of self-induced intoxication could not be adduced to cast doubt on whether the Crown has discharged its burden of proof. Thus the accused was held guilty of unlawful act manslaughter notwithstanding that, at the time of causing death, he was totally unaware of the acts he was performing. The Court of Appeal noted that, had the defendant's girlfriend survived the attack, the defendant would have had to be acquitted, because the offences with which he would have been charged — causing grievous bodily harm with intent, or assault occasioning actual bodily harm — were specific intent offences, and evidence of voluntary intoxication would have been admissible to cast doubt on whether the Crown had proved the elements of those offences beyond reasonable doubt.

15.15 In *Director of Public Prosecutions v Majewski* [1977] AC 443, the accused was involved in a brawl at a public house in which he attacked the landlord and customers. He also attacked the police officer who arrested him, and another police officer while he was being driven to the police station and, the following morning, he attacked a police inspector in a cell at the police station. He was charged on a number of counts of assault occasioning actual bodily harm and assault on a police officer in the execution of his duty. The accused's defence was that the offences had been committed while he was suffering from the effects of alcohol and drugs, and that he had not intended to commit the assaults. The trial judge directed the jury that, as assault was not a specific intent crime, self-induced or voluntary intoxication by drink and drugs could not be adduced as evidence and was to be ignored by the jury in reaching their verdict. The accused was convicted and appealed unsuccessfully to the Court of Appeal. The court gave leave to appeal to the House of Lords, certifying that the following point of law of general public importance was involved:

> Whether a defendant may properly be convicted of assault notwithstanding that, by reason of his self-induced intoxication, he did not intend to do the act alleged to constitute the assault.

15.16 The appeal was heard by seven members of the House of Lords, who although they unanimously answered the question certified in the affirmative and dismissed the accused's appeal, gave separate judgments. In general, their Lordships took the view that considerations of public policy necessitated rejection of the accused's appeal. Lord Simon stated (at 476):

> One of the prime purposes of the criminal law, with its penal sanctions, is the protection from certain proscribed conduct of persons who are pursuing their lawful lives. Unprovoked violence has, from time immemorial, been a significant part of such proscribed conduct. To accede to the argument on behalf of the appellant would leave the citizen legally unprotected from unprovoked violence, where such violence was the consequence of drink or drugs having obliterated the capacity of the perpetrator to know what he was doing or what were its consequences.

15.17 Their Lordships accepted as crucial the distinction between crimes of specific intent on the one hand, and crimes of basic intent on the other. In relation to the former, intoxication voluntarily induced will be admissible to cast doubt on whether the Crown had proved the elements of the offence, or, put another way, to assist the defence to suggest that the accused's acts were involuntary or prevented her or him from forming the mens rea of the crime charged. In relation to crimes of basic intent, such as assault and manslaughter, however, voluntary intoxication cannot be adduced as evidence and may not be considered by the jury in determining whether the Crown has proved the elements of the offence. *R v Lipman* was referred to and approved.

15.18 What then is the distinction between crimes of specific intent on the one hand and crimes of basic intent on the other? The Law Lords gave different explanations. Possibly the clearest articulation of the distinction is contained in the judgment of Lord Simon in *Director of Public Prosecutions v Morgan* [1976] AC 182 (at 432). His Lordship there stated at (216–17):

> By 'crimes of basic intent' [crimes of general intent] I mean those crimes whose definition expresses (or, more often, implies) a *mens rea* which does not go beyond the *actus reus*. The *actus reus* generally consists of an act and some consequence. The consequence may be very closely connected with the act or more remotely connected with it; but with a crime of basic intent the *mens rea* does not extend beyond the act and its consequence, however remote, as defined in the *actus reus*. I take assault as an example of a crime of basic intent where the consequence is very closely connected with the act. The *actus reus* of assault is an act which causes another person to apprehend immediate and unlawful violence. The *mens rea* corresponds exactly …
>
> On the other hand there are crimes of ulterior intent [crimes of specific intent] — 'ulterior' because the *mens rea* goes beyond contemplation of the *actus reus*. For example, in the crime of wounding with intent to cause grievous bodily harm, the *actus reus* is the wounding. The prosecution must prove a corresponding *mens rea* (as with unlawful wounding), but the prosecution must go further: it must show that the accused foresaw that serious physical injury would probably be a consequence of his act, or would possibly be so, that being a purpose of his act.

15.19 The distinction drawn by his Lordship may be understood readily enough, but it is difficult to perceive its utility. If it were applied logically, it would lead to results which clearly do not represent the law in England, Wales or Australia. Logically, murder is a crime of basic intent. The actus reus of murder is causing death, and the mens rea, intent to cause death or foresight of its likelihood, does not go beyond the actus reus. Indeed, the mens rea of murder includes intent to cause grievous bodily harm or foresight of its likelihood which is less than the actus reus. Yet it was clearly established by *Beard's* case, and was accepted in *Majewski's* case, that self-induced intoxication can be a defence to a charge of murder.

15.20 The decision as to which crimes are of specific intent, and which are of basic intent, is quite clearly one of public policy rather than logic or principle. As the English case law has developed, it has become possible to draw up a partial list of crimes falling with in each category. Thus it is established that murder, wounding or causing grievous bodily harm with intent to cause grievous bodily harm, and theft are all crimes of specific intent. On the other hand, manslaughter, maliciously wounding or inflicting grievous bodily harm, assault occasioning actual bodily harm and, *a fortiori*, common assault are all crimes of general intent. The status of rape was uncertain but it was resolved in *R v Eatch* ([1980] Crim LR 650) that rape is a basic intent offence. The effect of the developments in case law has been such that it is now generally clear whether any given offence is one of specific intent or not. As a result, in New South Wales, s 428B of the Crimes Act 1900 contains a table setting out those crimes that are offences of specific intent.

15.21 The baseline reality of the distinction appears roughly to be that in respect of a particular type of criminal activity — the more serious offences associated with that activity are to be classified as crimes of specific intent, while the less serious offences associated with that activity are to be classified as crimes of basic intent. This means that, if an accused is charged with a specific intent offence, and he or she raises evidence of voluntary intoxication, there may well be a 'back up' basic intent offence with which they can be charged (for example, murder and manslaughter). The illogicality involved in distinguishing offences in such a fashion was appreciated by the House of Lords in *Majewski*, but their Lordships were in no real sense troubled by it. Lord Salmon stated (at 483–4):

> I accepted that there is a degree of illogicality in the rule that intoxication may excuse or expunge one type of intention and not another. This illogicality is, however, acceptable to me because the benevolent part of the rule removes undue harshness with out imperilling safety and the stricter part of the rule works with out imperilling justice … Absolute logic in human affairs is an uncertain guide and a very dangerous master.

15.22 Even if we accept the public policy motivations of the Law Lords decision of *Director of Public Prosecutions v Majewski*, we might still be concerned about the effect of this approach to intoxicated offending. Indeed, controversy surrounds the criminal law on intoxicated offending. The controversy arises because, at the point of intersection of voluntary intoxication and 'basic intent', the law derogates from standard principles of criminal liability. As it excludes an ingredient of the fact scenario — self-induced intoxication — from the adjudication process, the *Majewski* approach excludes certain intoxicated offenders from the standard subjectivist conception of criminal liability. This subjectivist conception holds that the cardinal mental state or fault element in the criminal law of the current era is subjective fault, where an individual is judged according to what they knew, perceived or intended at the time of the offence. This derogation from principle in the law on intoxication is thought to be justified on public policy grounds: to permit intoxication to be adduced as evidence across the spectrum of criminal offences is said to provide a 'drunkard's charter', running the risk that juries will acquit large numbers of intoxicated accused. But is this a real risk? The High Court thought not.

THE DECISION IN R V O'CONNOR

15.23C R v O'Connor

(1980) 146 CLR 64; 29 ALR 449
High Court of Australia

Barwick CJ: The respondent to this application by the Attorney-General of the State of Victoria for special leave to appeal was indicted before the Supreme Court of that State on two counts: one of stealing (s 72, *Crimes Act 1958* as amended (Vic)), the other, under s 17 of that Act, of wounding with intent to resist arrest. He was acquitted of these charges by the jury but found guilty of an alternative charge made available by s 423 of that Act...

The circumstances of the case were that the respondent was observed by a neighbour pilfering a car owned by an officer of the Victorian Police. The car was standing outside the block of flats in which the officer resided. The neighbour alerted the officer to what was going on. By the time the officer reached his car, the respondent had removed from it a map-holder and a knife. The officer, having identified himself to the respondent, asked the respondent why he took from the car the map-holder. The respondent apparently made no response and ran away. The officer caught up with him to arrest him. During the course of his arrest, the respondent opened the blade of the knife he had taken from the car and, seemingly in an endeavour to resist arrest, stabbed the constable. At this time, the respondent said: 'I don't know anything, I wasn't there.'

At his trial the respondent gave evidence that he had been taking a particular drug and also drinking alcohol during a substantial part of the day of the occurrence and that he had no recollection of what had occurred that day with the officer or with the officer's car. His only recollection was of placing his foot in an open door of a white car.

According to medical evidence called on behalf of the respondent, the drug he claimed to have been taking was hallucinatory and in association with alcohol could have rendered the respondent incapable of reasoning and of forming an intent to steal or wound. The acts attributed to the respondent were consistent with the effects of the hallucinogenic drug.

The learned trial judge instructed the jury that they could take into account the evidence as to the respondent's intoxicated condition when considering the charges of theft and of wounding to resist arrest, but that they could not take that evidence into consideration when considering the alternative charge of unlawful wounding. The judge founded this direction on the reasons given by their Lordships in *DPP v Majewski* [1977] AC 443; [1976] 2 All ER 142 (*Majewski's* case).

As I have indicated, the jury thus directed, acquitted the respondent on the two charges on which he had been indicted but convicted him of the alternative charge of unlawful wounding. He appealed to the Court of Criminal Appeal of Victoria. That court was not prepared to accept the views expressed by the House of Lords in *Majewski's* case. Basing themselves largely on views expressed by myself in *Ryan v R* [1967] ALR 577; 121 CLR 205 (*Ryan's* case), their Honours allowed the respondent's appeal and entered a verdict of acquittal on the alternative charge. Accordingly, the respondent was discharged.

The Solicitor-General for Victoria, appearing in support of the application for special leave, pressed on the court the views of their Lordships in *Majewski's* case. He submitted that the respondent's evidence of self-induced intoxication was irrelevant to the consideration by the jury of the charge of unlawful wounding. He claimed that such evidence was inadmissible on the trial of a charge of a crime which does not require that the act charged should have been done to achieve a particular purpose, that is to say, where the charge is not of a crime, as he said, of 'specific intent'.

The Solicitor-General explained the submission that voluntary intoxication whether by alcohol or by another drug or by a combination of drugs (which intoxication I shall hereafter throughout refer to simply as self-induced intoxication) is irrelevant in the case of a crime described as a crime of only 'basic intent' on the basis that the voluntary ingestion of the alcohol or self-administration of another drug by an accused precludes him asserting or endeavouring to establish that the acts performed whilst so intoxicated were involuntary acts, ie unaccompanied by an exercise of his will, or that he had not had an intent to do the act charged. The Solicitor-General said that the voluntary nature of the ingestion or administration of the alcohol or other drug renders all the acts of a criminal nature done during the resulting intoxicated state voluntary acts for relevant purposes; and that the intention to do the criminal act whilst so intoxicated must be unchallengeably presumed. Thus, the voluntary taking of the alcohol and drugs to the point of intoxication satisfied the requirements of the relevant *mens rea*.

An alternative explanation of the submission given by the Solicitor-General is that whilst criminal responsibility does not ordinarily attach to an involuntary act or to an act done with out the requisite intent, self-induced intoxication constitutes an exception from the general rule, an exception based on 'public policy'. Perhaps it was not quite clear what that public policy was said to be. But the Solicitor-General relied on the views expressed in this connection in *Majewski's* case.

The Crown also submits that whatever the reason for the rule, it is well established that self-induced intoxication is not a defence to or excuse for the commission of a crime which is not a crime of 'specific intent', and that the rule is one which ought not now to be disturbed.

The respondent's counsel submitted that this court ought not to adopt the reasoning and conclusion of the House of Lords; that it should declare the common law in accordance with now firmly recognised principles, namely, that no person can be convicted of doing a criminal act which that person had not voluntarily done and that no person can be convicted of any crime unless the proscribed act was done by that person with the actual intent appropriate to the commission of the particular crime. He submitted that there was no basis in the common law for presuming an act to be voluntary beyond challenge or for presuming unchallengeably that an accused had the actual intent necessary to constitute the crime.

The application for special leave thus raises a fundamental question of grave import.

Before entering upon a consideration of the very important question raised, I would like to reiterate the view I have already expressed as to the proper approach which this court ought now to take to the declaration of the principles of the common law: see *Cullen v Trappell* (1980) 29 ALR 1. The court now not being bound by any decision of the courts of the United Kingdom or of Her Majesty in Council has become the final arbiter of what is the common law in Australia until it is altered by a competent legislature. All State courts are bound by its decision: see *Viro v R* (1978) 18 ALR 257. Accordingly, the court has a very heavy responsibility. It would be easy simply to accept the declarations of common law which have heretofore been made by any of the courts of the United Kingdom, particularly if they are of long standing. The court will, of course, have regard to these declarations and, in particular, will pay the highest respect to the decisions of the House of Lords. But it seems to me quite inadequate in the performance of its high obligation to accept with out its own close, critical and independent examination those declarations of the common law which heretofore have been made. Whilst the common law itself may be said to be the same wherever it is operative, it may be differently declared in one juristic unit as compared with another: see *Australian Consolidated Press Ltd v Uren* [1969] 1 AC 590; (1968) 117 CLR 221; [1968] ALR 3. The court must, in my opinion, decide for itself upon principle what is the common law. It must take its declaration of principle in the sense of the common law as it understands it to be and to have been.

With these views in mind I have approached the question whether evidence of self-induced intoxication may be relevant on the trial of an accused for an offence which does not require that the act charged should have been done in order to attain a specific purpose or to attempt to attain a specific purpose where the only reason for introduction of such evidence is to raise a doubt as to the voluntary or the intentional quality of the accused's relevant conduct.

In days before the common law fundamentals of criminal liability with which we are now familiar had been educed and declared, it was said that drunkenness was no defence to or excuse for the commission of crime; indeed, it might be an exacerbation of the offence. This formulation still retains some currency. The use of the words 'defence' and 'excuse' suggests that the saying is based on the idea that drunkenness might furnish a defence to or excuse for an offence otherwise established. But proof of a state of intoxication, whether self-induced or not, so far from constituting itself a matter of defence or excuse, is at most merely part of the totality of the evidence which may raise a reasonable doubt as to the existence of essential elements of criminal responsibility. Such a doubt, if not removed by the Crown to the satisfaction of the tribunal of fact, will warrant an acquittal, not because the accused was intoxicated but because the charge will not have been proved beyond reasonable doubt. The onus made clear by the decision in *Woolmington v DPP* [1935] AC 462 (*Woolmington*'s case) will not have been discharged. Thus, the question raised in this case is really one as to the relevance of evidence as to the accused's state of body and mind in relation to the essentials of criminal responsibility if due to his own acts.

Before proceeding further, I should briefly discuss the need for some precision in the use of such terms as 'drunkenness' and 'intoxication'.

The state of drunkenness or intoxication can vary very greatly in degree. A person may be intoxicated in the sense that his personality is changed, his will is warped, his disposition altered, or his self-control weakened, so that whilst intoxicated to this degree he does acts voluntarily and intentionally which in a sober state he would or might not have done. His intoxication to this degree, though conducive to and perhaps explanatory of his actions, has not destroyed his will or precluded the formation of any relevant intent. Indeed, intoxication to this degree might well explain how an accused, otherwise of good character, came to commit an offence with which he is charged.

Intoxication to the stated degree might have rendered an accused less aware of what he was doing, or of its quality, significance or consequence. But, if voluntary, his acts remain his; and he intends to perform them. So long as will and intent are related at least to the physical act involved in the crime charged, and saving for the moment the case of a crime of so-called specific intent, the fact that the state of intoxication has prevented the accused from knowing or appreciating the nature and quality of the act which he is doing will not be relevant to the determination of guilt or innocence. Apart from provisions as to diminished responsibility where such provisions are available, it is only where the lack of appreciation of the nature and quality of what is voluntarily and intentionally done is due to a disease of the mind that such lack of appreciation bears on guilt; and then only for historical reasons on the nature of the verdict to be returned.

If the degree of intoxication produces only those results which I have so far described, that state of intoxication is clearly irrelevant to a consideration of the accused's criminal culpability, certainly if the offence charged does not require that the act charged be done to achieve or to attempt to achieve some specified result. There may remain a question whether, if a purpose to achieve such a result is required, his state of intoxication, whilst allowing the formation of an intent to do the physical act charged, may possibly be such as to preclude the formation of the relevant purpose. Whether it does so or not may need to be dealt with as a specific problem related to the particular degree of intoxication and to the nature of the relevant crime; and I do not pursue that question here. But the inclination of my mind is to think that no differentiation need be made in this respect.

What I have thus far written is, in my opinion, applicable, whether the state of intoxication is self-induced or the result of the activity of another. The concurrence of will and physical act and the concurrence of intent and physical act suffices to attract criminal liability.

But the state of intoxication may, though perhaps only rarely, divorce the will from the movements of the body so that they are truly involuntary. Or, again, and perhaps more frequently, the state of intoxication, whilst not being so complete as to preclude the exercise of the will, is sufficient to prevent the formation of an intent to do the physical act involved in the crime charged. It is in connection with these states of intoxication that the problem raised in this case arises.

It is proper here to remark that lack of recollection, attributable to a past state of intoxication, is not necessarily indicative of either of these states of intoxication. If no more is proved than a credible assertion of a lack of recollection, it is my opinion that an onus to establish the voluntary or intentional quality of what the accused is alleged to have done does not for that reason pass to the Crown. But probably such an assertion of amnesia will rarely stand alone; evidence of the actual state of the accused in relation to sobriety and the manner in which that state has been induced will be forthcoming.

Now, there can be little doubt that as of this time an accused in the state of intoxication which has rendered his acts involuntary or precluded the formation of a relevant intent and which has been brought about by the act of another could not be found guilty of any common law offence. What his body had done, he had not done, or what he had done had not been done with intent to do it. Nothing in the speeches in *Majewski's* case suggests the contrary.

It is the fact that the state of intoxication results from the accused's own acts which is said to warrant the exclusion of evidence as to his physical and mental condition. It is this exclusion which gives rise to the fundamental question in this case. As will appear, the decision in *Majewski's* case in reality is that the accused is to be denied the opportunity of proving or attempting to prove what was his physical and mental state vis à vis voluntariness or relevant intent at the time he is said to have committed the physical act charged, simply because he has contributed by his own act to that physical and mental state.

This may be an appropriate place to say something of the concept of self-induced intoxication. Of course, there can be the case of deliberate self-intoxication as a means of performing an intended act. The facts in *A-G for Northern Ireland v Gallagher* [1963] AC 349 (*Gallagher's* case) illustrate how an intent formed before intoxication to do an act whilst intoxicated may make the act when done in an intoxicated state a voluntary act: see also the instance suggested by Madden CJ in *R v Mary Egan* (1897) 23 VLR 159. The formation before intoxication of the requisite intent and the deliberate induction of a state of intoxication for the performance of the charged act understandably makes that act when done in a desired state of intoxication both a voluntary act and an act done with the requisite intent. But where the intent to do the proscribed act was not formed before intoxication or at all, these cases have, in my opinion, no relevance.

However, quite apart from circumstances of the kind illustrated by *Gallagher's* case, there are doubtless cases where a human sets out to become intoxicated, perhaps more likely in the administration of hallucinatory drugs than in the case of alcohol. But, I apprehend, many humans become intoxicated, certainly by alcohol, with out any intention of so becoming. Of course, they voluntarily imbibe the liquor or take the drug but with no thought of the ultimate state they may reach, more particularly in the case of alcohol. The addictive quality of alcohol or other drug for some of them may possibly reduce the voluntary nature of their consumption of alcohol or other drug in the final stages of their intoxication. Their resultant state, however, may fairly be described as self-induced because of the deliberation with which they have commenced the course of drinking or drug taking.

But the state of intoxication may be reached by inadvertence, even though the drug, whether alcoholic or other, may be taken voluntarily. Perhaps this is less likely in the case of some drugs than in the case of alcohol itself; but the rule proposed in *Majewski's* case is universal and not discriminatory as between intoxication by alcohol or by other drugs. An example which comes to mind is that of the person who at dinner does not observe the frequency with which the waiter tops up his glass. If in the result that person becomes intoxicated, is the opprobrium present in the description 'self-induced intoxication' as used in relation to criminal responsibility really warranted? Is the wickedness of mind which is thought to satisfy *mens rea* present in instances of this kind? Yet in the universality of the rule as to admissibility of evidence of self-induced intoxication, such an instance is included. It is no answer to the situation, in my view, to leave it to the judicial discretion in punishment to palliate the conviction for what is done by such a person.

Examples of wanton drinking of alcohol and perhaps more so of administration of other drugs are all too frequent. If the voluntary taking of the alcohol or other drug is to be a basis of criminal responsibility, it might well be thought that a distinction ought to be made between a deliberate or what I have called a wanton taking of alcohol or other drug with a view to becoming intoxicated or a taking with an indifference to becoming thereby intoxicated and instances of intoxication where these elements of deliberation, wantonness or indifference are absent. It seems to me unsatisfactory to place all instances of intoxication as the result of a voluntary imbibing of alcohol or a voluntary administration of another drug in one undifferentiated classification as self-induced.

Because it is basic to the Crown's submissions in this application, it is now necessary to examine the decision in *Majewski's* case and at least some of its implications.

[His Honour outlined the facts of *Majewski's* case, and continued:]

It is now appropriate to return to express the result of the decision of their Lordships in *Majewski's* case.

The House in substance decided that on the trial of an accused for a criminal offence which does not require that the proscribed act should be done to attain or to attempt to attain a specified result beyond the immediate consequence of the physical act involved, evidence as to the effect which self-induced intoxication has produced on the relationship of the accused's will or intent to the activity of his body is irrelevant and therefore inadmissible, if tendered solely to raise a doubt as to the voluntariness of, or as to the presence of intention to do, the physical act involved in the crime charged. Although, as I have said, not formally involved in the question certified by the Court of Appeal, in my opinion, the reasoning favoured by their Lordships extends to all the consequences of the self-induced intoxication by any means and is not limited to those which affect only the presence of an intent to do the physical act involved in the charge. The effect of intoxication, as I have said, may be so extensive as to render the acts of the accused involuntary or it may preclude the formation of an intent to do that physical act. In substance, therefore the decision in *Majewski's* case is that in the case of such a charge the act of the accused is to be incontestably presumed to have been voluntary and to have been done with an intent to do the physical act involved in the crime charged. Evidence to call in question either position is irrelevant and inadmissible if the accused's condition resulted from his own acts.

The decision was in part built upon acceptance of the dichotomy of crimes into crimes of 'specific' intent and crimes of 'basic' intent. Although all of their Lordships did not specifically define the former, I think that they used the notion of a crime of specific intent in the sense in which I have used it in my summary of the substance of their decision. The purposive nature of the proscribed act is the indication of a crime of specific intent:

hence the description I have used of what is involved in a crime of specific intent and by contrast what is not involved in a crime of so-called basic intent. My description is in line, I think, with Lord Simon's definition of specific intent. Having made this distinction, ie between crimes of basic intent and crimes of specific intent, their Lordships sought, as it seems to me, to bring their decision with in the symmetry of the basic principles of criminal responsibility by treating the wantonness of becoming intoxicated as a form of recklessness or of wickedness of mind which satisfied the requirement of *mens rea*: see [1977] AC 443, per the Lord Chancellor at 474 and 475 of the report and Lord Simon at 479 of the report.

Along with this attempt to accommodate the decision to the fundamentals of the common law as they have come to be understood, their Lordships appear to have based themselves on public policy, the policy of safeguarding the citizen and of maintaining social order. Indeed, such a policy was treated as paramount, even in the case of crimes of 'basic intent' to the point of conclusively presuming voluntariness and the presence of intent.

A distrust of jurors and an anxiety that they may too readily be persuaded to an acquittal if evidence of the result of self-induced intoxication, particularly by drugs other than alcohol, were allowed, may have formed some part of the public policy on which the decision rests. I may say at once that I have, of course, no experience of English juries; but I have of juries in New South Wales. Starke J, a most experienced judge in the hearing of criminal charges in Victoria, having had as well a long and distinguished career as an advocate, expressed himself in the present case in relation to the impact of evidence of intoxication upon Victorian jurors. He said:

> I, of course, have no knowledge of how English juries react. But over nearly 40 years' experience in this State I have found juries to be very slow to accept a defence based on intoxication. I do not share the fear held by many in England that if intoxication is accepted as a defence as far as general intent is concerned the floodgates will open and hordes of guilty men will descend on the community.

I share his views, as if they had been expressed about jurors in New South Wales. In my opinion, properly instructed jurors would be scrupulous and not indulgent in deciding an issue of voluntariness or of intention. Indeed, I am inclined to think that they may tend to think that an accused who had taken alcohol and particularly other drugs to the point of extreme intoxication had brought on himself what flowed from that state of intoxication.

But I do not doubt that admission of evidence of intoxication, including as most likely it will expert evidence, would call for careful direction by the presiding judge, a matter to which I shall later refer. But whatever the risks in a trial by jury, they do not justify, in my opinion, such a departure from fundamental principles of criminal responsibility as to my mind is involved in the decision of *Majewski's* case.

It is clear, I think, that no common law offence is made out by proof of the *actus reus* alone. In the case of all such crimes, at least an actual intent to do the physical act involved in the crime charged must be established. In so phrasing this principle, I have laid on one side recklessness of the kind which is at times accounted as a substitute for, if not indeed, a satisfaction of the need for, an actual intent. It is not necessary, in my opinion, for the purposes of resolving the question raised in this case to explore the area in which recklessness may suffice; or to examine the parameters of the concept of recklessness in this connection. In *Pemble v R* (1971) 124 CLR 107 at 119, I discussed the sense in which recklessness is used in this area of discourse and indicated what is involved in it. In putting recklessness on one side, I am not unmindful of the use of recklessness by their Lordships in *Majewski's* case, a use which, it seems to me, is outside the concept of recklessness as it is usually employed in relation to criminal responsibility. I shall say something later as to their Lordship's use of recklessness in that case. But I have confined my statement of principle for present purposes to the need for actual intent.

Stephen J, in *R v Tolson* (1889) 23 QBD 168 at 187, makes it clear that, whilst the requirement is not that the mental element in *mens rea* must always be of a like nature in all crimes, there must be in every case an intent appropriate to the definition of the crime. I would prefer to avoid the use of *mens rea* in these reasons because of the sense of moral turpitude vestigial from an earlier time which the expression tends to carry: but it is a convenient expression to convey the indispensable need for actual intent in criminal responsibility. But, where possible, I will use intent rather than *mens rea*.

In *Ryan's* case I attempted a summary statement of the principle that in all crime, including statutory offences, the act charged must have been done voluntarily, ie accompanied by the will to do it. I find no need to qualify what I then wrote. I stated the principle as with out qualification. *Gallagher's* case and *R v Mary Egan* are not instances of responsibility for involuntary acts for the reason I have already given and are not exceptions from the rule I expressed. The decision in *Majewski's* case would in substance engraft a qualification on that principle. The question in the present case is to determine both if and why that should be so, conformably to the understanding of the common law as to criminal responsibility which has resulted from the work of the courts in the last 50 years or so. I set that time because of the influence of *Woolmington's* case and more recent cases, and because of the influence *DPP v Beard* [1920] AC 479 ought, in my opinion, to have had and which in some areas it has had: cf *Kamipeli's* case.

In *Ryan's* case, which involved a charge of murder — oddly enough, a crime accounted to be a crime of specific intent — I had no need to consider the case of a voluntary act done with out the requisite intent. Consequently, my summary was confined to a lack of voluntariness. Of course, if the act be involuntary, there can be no question as to the intent with which it was done. But even where there is a conjunction of will and deed, there remains, as I think, in every case of common law crime, and indeed in many cases of 'statutory crime', the need for actual intent, at least an actual intent to do the physical act involved in the crime charged.

The intent to do the physical act which is required as part of an *actus reus* of a non-purposive kind has been called a 'basic intent' (per Lord Simon in *Morgan's* case, supra, at 216): although, as I have mentioned, his Lordship included in the necessary intent an intent to produce a result of the physical act. Such an intent is, of course, basic in the sense that it must always be present as one of the foundations of criminal responsibility.

But, as I think, so is the intent to do the act required where the *actus reus* is of a purposive kind. Discussions such as have taken place in *Hyam v DPP* [1975] AC 55; [1974] 2 All ER 41, and other cases have emphasised that the intent must be actual and not constructive: see also the judgment of Dixon CJ in *Parker v R* (1963) 111 CLR 610 at 632, which so strongly emphasises this feature of criminal culpability.

But the description 'basic intent' has been used to distinguish the intent required in a crime in which the *actus reus* does not require the physical act involved in the charge to have been done to achieve a stated purpose from the intent required in crimes which do so require. The latter are then styled crimes of 'specific intent'.

With great respect to those who have favoured this terminology in a classification of crimes, it is to my mind not only inappropriate but it obscures more than it reveals. The purpose with which a proscribed act must be done in order to be relevantly criminal is, in my opinion, part of the description of the *actus reus*: cf Lord Simon in *Morgan's* case at 216. Assault to resist arrest specifies, in my opinion, the *actus reus*. Although described in terms of intent it connotes the purposive quality of the proscribed act. It does not refer, in my opinion, to the *mens rea*, or intention to commit the act in question, though of course if, for example, an accused intends to assault a constable in order to resist arrest, it can scarcely be said that he did not intend the physical act necessary to carry out that purpose. None the less, the purpose of resisting arrest is, in my opinion, part of the *actus reus*. In other words, the suggested basis for classification of crimes is not, in my opinion, on the footing of a distinction based on the nature and extent of the relevant *mens rea* but, rather, it is a distinction founded on the description of the *actus reus*.

The description 'specific intent' gained its currency from Stephen J's judgment in *Tolson's* case. As an expression calling attention to the elements of the *actus reus* it has no doubt its uses. As the intent or *mens rea* is related to the content of the *actus reus*, the transference of the purpose of the *actus reus* to the *mens rea* is tempting, but it is preferable, in my opinion, not to effect that transference. In my respectful opinion, the distinction between basic and specific intent is unhelpful as a basis for distinction of crimes by reference to *mens rea*.

If I might for a moment turn to the requirements of a charge of wounding, the *mens rea* is at least an intent to do the physical act involved in the wounding. But if, conformably with Lord Simon's analysis in *Morgan's* case at 216 of the report, the requisite intent is to wound, ie it is an intent to produce a result, not merely to do a physical act, that result is, in my opinion, part of the description of the *actus reus*. The blow must have a purpose to wound. If the *mens rea* is to include an intent to produce the result if would seem to me to be difficult to distinguish in relation to the need for *mens rea* between such an offence and another offence which in prescribing the *actus reus* required the attempted attainment of a further result. Yet the one is sought to be distinguished from the other in the dichotomy of basic and specific intent.

[His Honour discussed *Director of Public Prosecutions v Beard* (at **15.8**), and continued:]

It is to my mind exceedingly strange that a person incapable of forming any intent may be found guilty of an offence which requires only an intent to do the physical act involved but may not be found guilty of doing an act to attain a specific result. If the cases to which Lord Birkenhead referred represented a movement in the common law, an amelioration in favour of the accused, there is no reason, it seems to me, why the movement had to stop at the point reached by these cases. That, it seems to me, is how the matter struck Lord Birkenhead and those who agreed with him: and, in my view, that is precisely the sense in which he expressed himself. Such cases were not exceptions from but examples of fundamental rules.

Thus, if the evidence of intoxication is sufficient to raise a doubt as to voluntariness or as to the presence of requisite intent, I can see no logical ground for determining its admissibility upon a distinction between a crime which specifies only the immediate result of the proscribed act and a crime which in addition requires a further result dependent on purpose.

But it is in substance held that the voluntary taking or administration of alcohol or other drugs producing an intoxicated state so infects that situation that what is done in that state must incontestably be accounted to be voluntary or, at the lowest, as having been done with the requisite intent. The view, that of Lord Elwyn-Jones to which their Lordships subscribed, is that to become intoxicated by your own act, is to supply an element of recklessness to the performance of any criminally proscribed act performed during that state: and thus to satisfy the requirement of *mens rea*. But this, in my respectful opinion, is a novel use of the word 'reckless' and, in my opinion, a use heretofore not thought acceptable. If to take alcohol or drugs with at least the risk of becoming intoxicated is in one sense a reckless thing to do, yet that variety of recklessness can scarce be carried forward and attributed as a substitute for actual intent to do the proscribed act. The recklessness which may on occasion satisfy the requirement of *mens rea* involves an awareness of possible consequences of doing the act, ie the proscribed act charged, and at least a decision to disregard them and to act with out caring for appreciated consequences. The recklessness or wantonness of the person taking alcohol or other drug with at least the chance of becoming intoxicated is surely of a quite different order. Further, it is, in my opinion, in a legal sense remote from the performance of the act charged. It is quite unlike the intent formed in *Gallagher's* case which was not remote from the act charged but in truth directly connected to it because of the intent formed before intoxication. To find an analogy in the field of recklessness to what occurred in *Gallagher's* case, it would be necessary to find an appreciation before intoxication of the risks of acts of a criminal kind during intoxication and a decision before intoxication to take those risks or at least a conceived indifference to the possibility of their turning into reality. For my part, I am unable to accept that the voluntary nature of the taking of the alcohol or other drug, whether or not it be an act of a wanton or reckless kind, supplies the *mens rea* for the commission of a crime which in the case supposed may have been done involuntarily or with out the requisite intent.

It is proper at this point to acknowledge that the reduction of murder to manslaughter by reason of a state of intoxication is so far an entrenched anomaly. In the first place, murder does not fit the definition of a crime of specific intent: but yet it is consistently so treated. Secondly, manslaughter for its part is very much affected by its definition as unjustifiable homicide. The anomaly has not been the subject of critical judicial examination. The wide discretion available in the punishment of manslaughter has no doubt contributed to its acceptability as an alternative to murder where the crime for any reason is not made out. In what I wrote in *Viro's* case, I discussed the use of manslaughter as an alternative to murder when self-defence is set up. The anomalous position of manslaughter ought not, in my opinion, to provide any justification for any further departure from fundamental principle where voluntariness or requisite intent is absent.

Then it is said that the protection of the community from violence, being a purpose of the criminal law, requires the conclusion to which the House came in *Majewski's* case. It may readily be granted that the frequency with which intoxicated persons act violently poses a distinct threat to our social order and, indeed at times to personal safety. Further, the use of drugs to produce intoxicated situations has become rife. It has added a new dimension to the possibility of violent and unsocial conduct on the part of those who have become intoxicated. That the society needs protection against violence by such persons can readily be conceded. But so it does in relation to armed robbery and, indeed, to housebreaking which is not infrequently accompanied by violence to the person. So it does in relation to many crimes of so-called specific intent. The question, it seems to me, which is posed for this court is whether it is consonant with the common law to make such an exception in the case of self-induced intoxication as has been held to be the case by the House of Lords. Does the situation created by the use of drugs arising or which may arise from what I might call intoxicated violence warrant a radical departure from those principles of the common law evolved over a period of time, but particularly elucidated in the last 50 or so years? These principles have been established bearing in mind and not disregarding the need of the society for protection from violent and unsocial behaviour. These principles, on the one hand, provide the society with a protection against violent and unsocial conduct, whilst on the other hand, maintain a just balance between the Crown and the citizen who is charged with having broken the criminal law. That *Majewski's* case is a departure from such principles can scarce be gainsaid. It seems to me to be completely inconsistent with the principles of the common law that a man should be conclusively presumed to have an intent which, in fact, he does not have, or to have done an act which, in truth, he did not do.

I can readily understand that a person who has taken alcohol or another drug to such an extent that he is intoxicated thereby to the point where he has no will to act or no capacity to form an intent to do an act is blameworthy and that his act of having ingested or administered the alcohol or other drug ought to be visited with severe consequences. The offence of being drunk and disorderly is not maintained these days in all systems of the common law. In any case it has not carried a sufficient penalty properly to express the public opprobrium which should attach to one who, by the taking of alcohol or the use of drugs, has become intoxicated to the point where he is the vehicle for unsocial or violent behaviour. But, though blameworthy for becoming intoxicated, I can see no ground for presuming his acts to be voluntary and relevantly intentional. For what is blameworthy there should be an appropriate criminal offence. But it is not for the judges to create an offence appropriate in the circumstances: cf *Knuller (Publishing, Printing & Promotions) Ltd v DPP* [1973] AC 435 at 457–8, 464–5 and 490. It must be for the Parliament.

There would be good sense, it seems to me, in a statutory provision which gave to a jury who were driven to the conclusion that an accused, due to the result of self-induced intoxication, was not culpable of the crime with which he is charged to be able to bring in an alternative verdict that he, by his own conduct, had brought himself to a state where he was not responsible for his acts. There should be a substantial penalty provided for his conviction of this alternative charge, a penalty of confinement which would include both an element of punishment and provide an opportunity for treatment for the tendency to take alcohol or drugs. It would, it seems to me, be quite just to make the accused responsible for his act of having taken alcohol or other drug to the point I have described.

In my opinion, evidence of the state of the body and mind of an accused tendered to assist in raising a doubt as to the voluntary character of the physical act involved in the crime charged is admissible on the trial of an accused for any criminal offence, whether an offence at common law or by statute. Further, in my opinion, such evidence tendered to raise a doubt as to the actual intention with which the physical act involved in the crime charged, if done, was done is admissible on the trial of an accused for any offence, whether at common law or by statute, with the exception of such statutory offences as do not require the existence of an actual intent, the so-called absolute offences.

As I earlier indicated, however, the jury needs careful and special instruction. If the evidence, if accepted, is not such as to be capable of raising a doubt as to either of the basic elements, voluntariness or actual intent, there being no other material to suggest a lack of voluntariness or actual intent, that evidence can be with drawn from the jury's consideration. It will have had no more than a tendency to establish that though the accused acted voluntarily and with the requisite intent, he was influenced in what he did by a state of insobriety. They should be told that if the evidence does not raise in their minds a doubt as to voluntariness or actual intent they may put that evidence out of their minds in considering the accused's guilt or innocence. But if the evidence is capable of raising a doubt either as to voluntariness or the existence of an actual intent, the jury should be told that if that evidence raises in their minds a reasonable doubt as to voluntariness or actual intent, it is for the Crown to remove that doubt from their minds and to satisfy them beyond reasonable doubt that the accused voluntarily did the act with which he is charged and that he did so with the actual intent appropriate to the crime charged. They should be instructed as to the meaning and scope of voluntariness and as to the precise intent which the crime charged requires. It would be proper in these cases to tell a jury that the fact that a man does not later remember what he did does not necessarily indicate that his will did not go with what he did do or that he did not have the necessary intent.

In my opinion, the Court of Criminal Appeal was justified in not accepting *Majewski's* case. It does not appear from their reasons that they attempted a detailed analysis of the evidence as to voluntariness or as to actual intent. But it is evident that they took the view that the jury in acquitting of the charges in the indictment could be taken under the trial judge's direction to have had a doubt at least as to intent, if not as to voluntariness. Consequently, there is no ground for disturbing the court's conclusion that the respondent should be acquitted of the alternative offence.

I would grant special leave to appeal and, for the reasons I have expressed, dismiss the appeal.

Stephen J [His Honour discussed the decision in *Majewski's* case, and continued]: These short extracts of course do far less than justice to their Lordships' expression of their views which, if I may say so with unfeigned respect, are of great persuasiveness and have the support of much English precedent and long practice. Nevertheless, after anxious consideration and free of the constraints which the unvaried practice of many years in England must necessarily impose upon any English tribunal, I find myself unpersuaded that for Australia the criminal law should be as their Lordships state it.

Considerations turning upon a concern for public order, coupled with forecasts of public outcry are, for me, answered by the experience of my own community in Victoria, which has, for some time now, lived with precisely that view of the law which is denied by *Majewski*. Since at least some time prior to 1964 some, perhaps many, Victorian judges have acted as did Monahan J in *R v Keogh* [1964] VR 400. There his Honour, founding himself upon what was, in fact, his own long experience as counsel in criminal cases in Victoria, upon his own experience on the bench and upon his knowledge of the practice of other judges of his court, said that he held 'firmly to the view that a state of automatism, even that which has been brought about by drunkenness, precludes the forming of the guilty intent which is the fundamental concept in criminal wrong-doing'.

To this may be added references to *R v Haywood* [1971] VR 755, to *R v Bugg* [1978] VR 251, especially to its addendum at 252, and to what was said by Starke and by Gray JJ in their judgments delivered in the Full Court in the case now under appeal. Starke J said: 'In this State in my own experience, until *Majewski's* case, intoxication has always been left to juries as evidence relevant to the issues of both general and specific intent', and Gray J was 'satisfied that for many years self-induced intoxication has been left for the jury's consideration in relation to all questions of intent'.

I am aware of no evidence suggesting that the incidence of crime committed under the influence of intoxication has been affected by this long-standing approach of Victorian judges, that Victoria stands in this respect in any worse position than do those jurisdictions where the *Majewski* principle prevails, including, as I understand it, most jurisdictions in the United States. Neither am I aware of any public outcry on the question.

The view that intoxication in itself furnishes the necessary element of a guilty mind, whether by way of recklessness or otherwise, thereby satisfying not only basic principles of law but also more generalised notions of abstract justice, in my view presents considerable difficulties. Recent academic writings on the topic abound with criticism of it and those interested in the topic will therefore already be familiar with the nature of the debate, upon which I have no occasion to enter in any detail. It is enough that I should state, quite shortly, my reasons for this view which I have formed.

To convict an accused, who was at the time intoxicated, of such serious crimes as manslaughter, rape, malicious wounding or assaults of varying degrees of gravity, none of which are, it seems, crimes of 'specific intent', may in some cases offend no general notions of what is fair and just. What may be called the 'Dutch courage' cases provide instances. So too, no doubt, do those cases in which an accused, while not contemplating any particular crime or, for that matter, any particular victim, well knows from past experience that when he takes drugs or alcohol or both he may under their influence commit a crime. But these by no means comprise all cases to which *Majewski* is applicable. Whether or not they represent more or less than a majority in any particular community is probably unknown, in the absence of statistical research.

Many and varied instances may be supposed (and one is necessarily very much in areas of supposition in this whole topic) in which ordinary notions of what is fair and just would be offended by such a conviction. Two instances will suffice: the young man or woman who under peer-group pressures, perhaps in the armed forces, perhaps after a sporting success, or at some reunion or initiation ceremony, for the first time drinks grossly to excess: again, the person who, under like pressures, is persuaded for the first time to sample an hallucinogenic drug or, perhaps, although no newcomer to so-called 'soft' drugs, knowingly takes what he believes to be such a drug but which in fact proves to be one of great potency. In such instances, not, I think farfetched, I would regard it as unfair and unjust that an accused, robbed of his faculties by resultant intoxication, should be deprived of the opportunity of having the evidence of the absence of the mental elements of the crime with which he is charged left to the jury.

So much for general notions of fairness and justice. That principle of the criminal law, that *mens rea* should accompany the *actus reus*, appears to me to be no less affronted by any rule which subtracts from the general requirement of a mental element in crime those cases which owe their origin to intoxication. No doubt even principles of the common law as fundamental as the insistence upon proof of mental element are subject to exceptions and criticism founded upon a lack of logic may readily enough be met by a principled exception. But a suggested exception which operates by means of uncertain criteria, in a manner not always rational and which serves an end which I regard as doubtful of attainment is one which I view with suspicion.

I regard the *Majewski* principle as suffering from just such defects. Of the uncertainty of the criterion by which it operates, the distinction between crimes of specific intent and all other crimes, I will say more later. Its lack of wholly rational operation seems to me to arise from the fact that it fails to ensure, as it might be hoped that it would, that the drunken criminal, although spared conviction of a major offence because of lack of specific intent, will nevertheless not go free but will instead suffer conviction of some lesser offence which does not call for proof of a specific intent. For it to operate in that way, providing a suitable gradation of offence and punishment, would at least be rational; it could then always be said of it that while the drunken criminal may escape conviction on the more serious charge 'there will be a lesser crime to which the intoxication — however mind stealing — will be no defence' (per Lord Russell in *Majewski* [1977] AC at 498–9). His Lordship of course appreciated that it did not always so operate, hence the qualifying word 'commonly' which precedes the passage which I have quoted. In some instances it will do so, especially so long as murder continues to be classified for this purpose as a crime of specific intent, despite the difficulties of definition which that appears to involve. But in a number of cases it will operate quite eccentrically, because of the particular category to which crimes are consigned by applying to them the test of specific intent. All attempts are apparently crimes of specific intent, yet if the actual crime be committed and not merely attempted it may very well not be; again, wounding or causing grievous bodily harm with intent requires specific intent, not so manslaughter or rape; theft involves a specific intent but not assault or malicious wounding. These are instances where the facts of a particular criminal incident might seem to call for some gradation, but the graduation which in fact results may run the wrong way. In many other cases *Majewski* will result in no gradation at all; for example, rape, and indecent assault are crimes of the same 'grade', neither requiring a specific intent.

This is all, no doubt, attributable to the particular criterion, 'specific intent', which has been adopted as determinative of the operation of the principle. Since the seriousness of the crime or its social consequences does not play any part in determining whether or not a crime is one of specific intent, it is hardly surprising that the operation of the principle may seem haphazard.

So far as the end sought to be attained is concerned this appears, in substance, to be that of the protection of the public from violence and the preservation of order. For that purpose the deterrent effect of the criminal law is invoked. Yet by the very nature of the case, concerned as it is with the grossly intoxicated, deterrence, if it operates at all, will only do so not at the time of the offence but at the earlier time when the drugs or alcohol are taken in excess. It would, in my view, require convincing evidence before one might conclude that, as a matter of human behaviour, the person who both becomes grossly intoxicated and also commits a crime while in that condition will be in any way discouraged from his initial act of becoming intoxicated by the knowledge that the fact of his intoxication will not be available for use in evidence at his trial to deny the presence of any mental element involved in his crime. Cases of 'Dutch courage' and of a known tendency to be violent when intoxicated aside, the possibility of the commission of any crime will not normally be contemplated when the drink or drugs are taken. For this reason, if for no other, the particular state of the criminal law seems to me to be unlikely to be capable of either encouraging or deterring the eventual offence.

There may be a strong case for the creation of a new offence such as that suggested in recommendation 56 of the Butler Committee Report, a new offence which might indeed operate as some deterrent, but that is quite a different question.

It is for these reasons that I see no sufficient reason for distinguishing, as the *Majewski* principle does, between the self-induced and other states of intoxication. I have already twice referred to those cases which involve 'Dutch courage', of which the facts of *Attorney-General for Northern Ireland v Gallagher* [1963] AC 349; [1961] 3 All ER 299, provide an instance, or in which there is knowledge on the accused's part, when he takes excessive quantities of alcohol or drugs, that he is prone to violence when intoxicated. They are, no doubt, prime instances in which an accused should not be able to gain any advantage from his intoxication; nor does he seem likely to in a jurisdiction where the *Majewski* principle has no operation. In the case of the former the necessary *mens rea* would seem to be supplied by the act of consciously becoming intoxicated so as to be better fitted for the contemplated crime. In the latter case there is surely recklessness. An accused's tendency to violent crime when intoxicated, known to him when he takes the fatal drink or drugs, would be evidence of recklessness sufficient on conventional principles to involve *mens rea*. If lack of contemporaneity is thought to be a difficulty, the analogy of the innocent agent, represented by the drunken state, as the mere instrument of the guilty mind, represented by the previously sober state may, as is suggested by Smith & Hogan: *Criminal Law* (4th ed) at 190, be thought to overcome it.

What I earlier described as the second notable feature of *Majewski*, the division of all crimes into two classes, those which do involve a specific intent and the rest, has probably occasioned as much controversy in journal articles and texts as any other feature of the case. That in itself supplies a reason for not adding to the volume of what has already been said about the various meanings which in the authorities, and notably in *Majewski* itself, have been proffered as definitive of 'specific intent'. I have also already remarked upon the consequences of adopting as the discrimen for the operation of *Majewski* this notion of 'specific intent', not elsewhere encountered as a term of art in the law. To this I would only add that if the development of the criminal law is seen as moving from early emphasis upon the *actus reus* to an increasing concern with the mental element in crime — *Majewski* at 480, 481 and 488–9 — the point in that gradual process which *Majewski* selects at which to call a halt, the frontier between crimes of specific intent and other crimes, seems, with all due respect, to be unfortunate. It is a point neither clearly defined nor easily recognisable, the selection of which does not reflect or give effect to any coherent attitude either as to the relative wrongfulness of particular conduct or the degree of social mischief which that conduct is thought to involve; it seems an inappropriate response to natural concern lest intoxication be used as a device to escape punishment for crime.

In the court below, Young CJ was assisted to his conclusion by *Thomas v R* (1937) 59 CLR 279. The passage from the judgment of Dixon J, at 309, which Young CJ cited in his judgment, merits repetition as particularly apposite:

> The truth appears to be that a reluctance on the part of courts has repeatedly appeared to allow a prisoner to avail himself of a defence depending simply on his own state of knowledge and belief. The reluctance is due in great measure, if not entirely, to a mistrust of the tribunal of fact — the jury. Through a feeling that, if the law allows such a defence to be submitted to the jury, prisoners may too readily escape by deposing to conditions of mind and describing sources of information, matters upon which their evidence cannot be adequately tested and contradicted, judges have been misled into a failure steadily to adhere to principle. It is not difficult to understand such tendencies, but a lack of confidence in the ability of a tribunal correctly to estimate evidence of states of mind and the like can never be sufficient ground for excluding from inquiry the most fundamental element in a rational and humane criminal code.

Unless reliance be placed upon juries, properly instructed, to 'estimate evidence of states of mind' relevant to that 'most fundamental element in a rational and humane criminal code', the state of mind of the accused, the consequence will be that described by Lord Hailsham in *Director of Public Prosecutions v Morgan* [1976] AC 182 at 213, juries will 'in effect be told to find an intent where none existed or where none was proved to have existed'. His Lordship, in the different circumstances of the case then before him said that he could not in conscience bring himself to sanction such a view of the law. The conclusion arrived at by the Full Court of the Victorian Supreme Court in the present case avoids such a view and should be upheld.

In the present case evidence of intoxication should, in my view, have been allowed to go to the jury. It, together with any other evidence, such as acts and words spoken by the accused, will form the material upon which a jury will then perform 'its proper function of deciding on all the evidence, including that of intoxication, whether the Crown has in fact discharged its onus' — *R v Kamipeli* [1975] 2 NZLR 610 at 614. It is upon the properly instructed jury that reliance should be placed to ensure that only when intoxication has truly deprived the accused of the mental element which the law has prescribed as requisite for commission of the particular crime will it avail the accused.

I would grant special leave and dismiss the appeal.

Wilson J *[dissenting]*: It seems to me that the proper starting point for a consideration of the present question is to recognise that the House of Lords' decision in *Majewski* is not a revolutionary decision. It does not break new ground. In essence, it confirms the common law as it has been understood and applied for at least the past century (cf *R v Doherty* (1887) 16 Cox CC 306). It may be open to criticism on the grounds that changing circumstances now call for a different decision as an expression of the capacity of the common law to respond to the needs of changing times. But if that be so, it is for those who advocate such a change to carry the burden of persuasion. Apart from some present uncertainty in New Zealand, where the matter has expressly been left open by the Court of Appeal (*R v Roulston* [1976] 2 NZLR 644 at 654, but cf *R v Kamipeli* [1975] 2 NZLR 610), Victoria would seem to be the only jurisdiction in the common law world to have departed from the traditional view on the relevance of self-induced intoxication; cf England: *Majewski*; NSW: *R v Menniss* [1973] 2 NSWLR 113; South Australia: *R v Fahey* (1978) 19 SASR 577; Canada: *Leary v R* (1977) 33 Can CC (2d) 473; South Africa: *S v Tsotsotso* [1976] 1 SALR 364; see also American Law Institute Model Penal Code s 2.08; Indian Penal Code s 86, as applied in *Basdev v State of Pepsu* [1956] SCR 363.

The only decisions to the contrary are two decisions of judges at first instance in Victoria: *R v Keogh* [1964] VR 400; *R v Haywood* [1971] VR 755.

It may also be remarked that hitherto no distinction has been drawn between the element of voluntariness and the basic intent attending the commission of the act. Evidence of self-induced intoxication has been held to be irrelevant in either case: cf *Bratty v Attorney-General for Northern Ireland* [1963] AC 386 at 410; *R v Lipman* [1970] 1 QB 152; [1969] 3 All ER 410.

The respondent advances several arguments against the maintenance of the old rule. These include the unreality of the distinction between offences of basic and special intent, the illogicality of holding that intoxication is relevant to some criminal intents but not others, the ethics of requiring a jury to convict a person of an offence notwithstanding that it may be evident that his mind did not go with the act, and the problem that may arise of directing a jury that it may take evidence of intoxication into account in relation to some charges but must ignore it in relation to others.

It was argued that, rightly understood, the judgment of Lord Birkenhead LC in *DPP v Beard* [1920] AC 479, drew no distinction between offences of basic intent and offences of specific intent and that the case is authority for the proposition that, when raised, evidence of intoxication should be taken into account in relation to all offences. In this submission the respondent drew some support from the judgments of Young CJ and Gray J in the Court of Criminal Appeal.

There are passages in Lord Birkenhead's judgment that are difficult to reconcile with one another. The apparent inconsistency between what appears at 499–500 and the passage at 504 has been the subject of much debate. However, with all respect to the learned justices in the Court of Criminal Appeal, I think, having regard to the historical survey made by the Lord Chancellor before coming to the passage at 499–500, that it is clear that he intended to draw a distinction between offences requiring a specific intent and those where no specific intent need be shown. I am fortified in this conclusion by the discussion of *Beard* in the speech of the Lord Chancellor in *Majewski* ([1977] AC at 473–5) and by the analysis made by Lord Russell of Killowen in the same case, at 499–500. After citing a passage from the judgment of Lord Denning in *Attorney-General for Northern Ireland v Gallagher* [1963] AC 349 at 380, and two passages from Lord Denning's judgment in *Bratty v Attorney-General for Northern Ireland* at 409 and 410, the Lord Chancellor concluded (at 474):

> The seal of approval is clearly set on the passage at 499 of the *Beard* decision. In no case has the general principle of English law as described by Lord Denning in *Gallagher's* case and exposed again in *Bratty's* case been overruled in this House and the question now to be determined is whether it should be.

In my respectful opinion, the difficulty of distinguishing between the two categories of offences has been exaggerated. In *Viro* (18 ALR at 273; 52 ALJR at 426) Gibbs J drew the distinction in words which I have already cited, namely:

> … when an intention to cause a particular result (a 'special intent') is an element of the crime — as in a charge of murder based upon an intention to kill or to inflict grievous bodily harm — the fact that the accused was intoxicated may have an important bearing on the question whether he had the necessary intent …

I find this statement acceptable. It identifies an offence which requires in addition to proof of a voluntary act attended with foresight of consequences, proof of an additional element related to the purpose with which the impugned conduct took place. In so doing, it corresponds to the phrase appearing in s 28 of the Criminal Code of Queensland and Western Australia to which I have already referred. In my opinion, these Codes accurately reflect the common law as it was understood at the time of their enactment (cf *Stephen's, Digest of the Criminal Law*, (5th ed, 1894) art 30: *R v Doherty*, supra).

It was also argued before us on behalf of the respondent, as it was argued before their Lordships in *Majewski*, that it is illogical to take evidence of intoxication into consideration in relation to some offences but not in relation to others, and that it is unethical to attach penal consequences to conduct in respect of which a defendant may have had no *mens rea* because of self-induced intoxication. These arguments were fully canvassed in *Majewski* and, in my opinion, having regard to the social issues involved, were answered satisfactorily in the course of the speeches in that case. I cite in particular the following passages of Lord Simon of Glaisdale ([1977] AC at 479–80):

> ... there is nothing unreasonable or illogical in the law holding that a mind rendered selfinducedly insensible ... through drink or drugs, to the nature of a prohibited act or to its probable consequences is as wrongful a mind as one which consciously contemplates the prohibited act and foresees its probable consequences (or is reckless as to whether they ensue). The latter is all that is required by way of *mens rea* in a crime of basic intent. But a crime of specific intent requires something more than contemplation of the prohibited act and foresight of its probable consequences. The *mens rea* in a crime of specific intent requires proof of a purposive element. This purposive element either exists or not; it cannot be supplied by saying that the impairment of mental powers by self-induced intoxication is its equivalent, for it is not. So that the nineteenth century development of the law as to the effect of self-induced intoxication on criminal responsibility is juristically entirely acceptable; and it need be a matter of no surprise that Stephen stated it with out demur or question.

In any event, it is relevant to recall the historical explanation for the so-called anomaly that evidence of intoxication is relevant to some offences but not to others. Before the nineteenth century evidence of intoxication was totally disregarded. The law was strict, perhaps harsh, but not illogical. Then, as is explained in the speech of the Lord Chancellor in *Majewski* (at 471–2), from 1819 onwards the courts began to mitigate the severity of the common law in cases such as murder and serious violent crime, where the penalty was death or transportation, and cases such as attempted suicide, where there was likely to be sympathy for the accused. The result was that evidence of drunkenness was admissible in some cases, where a specific intention was alleged on the part of the accused, but was generally inadmissible. It would be a strange result, however, if the merciful relaxation of a strict rule of law to allow an exception in some cases had the effect of denying any logical merit to the substance of the rule. If anything it is the exception, and not the basic rule, which disturbs the logical symmetry.

[His Honour discussed the reasons given by the Victorian Court of Criminal Appeal in allowing the appeal, and continued:]

Counsel for the respondent pressed us with the submission that the *Majewski* doctrine is one which could present great difficulty to a trial judge charging a jury, particularly in a case where there are a number of alternative verdicts open to the jury, some of which involve proof of a specific intent and some of which do not. I do not disregard the complexity which such a case may present to a trial judge, but, in the end, it must come down to an evaluation of competing principles. The desire for simplicity in the law cannot override the primary principle that the law must meet the needs and demands of the community. In my opinion, the community requires protection from the sometimes violent conduct of intoxicated individuals. Furthermore, the *Majewski* doctrine is comparable to the law contained in the Criminal Code of Queensland and Western Australia for virtually the whole of this century, and in Tasmania since 1924 (s 17 of the Tasmanian Criminal Code). It has not been shown to me that the task of directing juries has produced undue difficulties for trial judges in those States.

After anxious consideration, and in the light of the matters to which I have referred, I have come to the conclusion that *Majewski* should be followed in Australia.

I recognise the force of the arguments based on logic and principle, but what confirms me in my opinion is the conviction that such considerations, even if they have merit, should not necessarily determine the result.

We are not deciding this question in a vacuum, where there is no status quo. In effect, we are being asked to change the existing law.

Whilst this kind of judicial legislation may be acceptable in many cases, the court must consider the impact on the community of the proposed change. If that impact is likely to be substantial, and if there are political considerations which may be controversial, then I believe the court should refrain from innovation. Such a task should be left to the legislature.

In the present case, I believe that the impact on the community and the processes of law enforcement of a decision not to follow *Majewski* would be unfortunate. It is not a question of trusting juries to 'do the right thing'; they should not be asked to carry the burden of reconciling the felt needs of the community with the law. It would often be the case when an honest and conscientious jury, properly directed, will be left with a reasonable doubt as to the criminal responsibility of an accused, notwithstanding that great injury or disturbance may have been caused by the action of a person under the influence of drink or drugs.

I must acknowledge that a different view of the law has been applied from time to time in Victoria, apparently without attracting the consequences which I would have anticipated. Nevertheless, I remain unpersuaded. To my mind, it is sufficient answer to the critics of *Majewski* to cite the facts of the present case. A law which excuses from criminal responsibility a wounding in the circumstances that obtained here is, in my respectful opinion, seriously deficient. If it is then said that it is for the legislature to remedy the deficiencies of the law in this area, my answer is simply that I prefer to see the courts assert and maintain the traditional approach to intoxication so as to adequately preserve the Queen's peace pending any legislative action that may be considered appropriate.

Finally, I cannot close my mind to the very strong persuasive force that proceeds from the unanimous decisions of the Court of Appeal (Criminal Division) and the House of Lords in *Majewski*, and the six to three majority decision of the Supreme Court of Canada in *Leary*. I cannot accept that this court should be the first court of final appeal in the common law world to break new ground in this area.

I would therefore grant special leave, allow the appeal and restore the verdict and sentence.

[**Murphy** and **Aickin JJ** each delivered separate judgments dismissing the appeal. **Gibbs** and **Mason JJ** each delivered separate dissenting judgments. Appeal dismissed.]

[Note *R v Murray; R v Manton* [1980] 2 NSWLR 526; *R v Tucker* (1984) 36 SASR 135; *R v Perks* (1986) 41 SASR 335; *R v Coleman* (1990) 19 NSWLR 467; *R v Conlon* (1993) 69 A Crim R 92; *Cutter v R* (1997) 143 ALR 498.]

15.24 Notes

1. It is important to appreciate the limits of the decision of the majority in *R v O'Connor*. Intoxication will assist the accused to cast doubt on whether the prosecution have proved the elements of the offence only in the exceptional case where it is such as to have rendered the accused's conduct involuntary, that is, to have produced a condition in which the accused was not aware of the nature of the physical acts he or she was performing, or to have prevented the accused from forming the mens rea required to constitute the particular crime charged. In an evidentiary sense, it will be for the accused to adduce evidence fit for the consideration of the jury that the consumption of alcohol or drugs in fact produced this condition: note *R v Stokes and Difford* (1990) 51 A Crim R 25. For this purpose, the mere fact that the accused is unable to remember the incident constituting the crime charged (amnesia) may not of itself be sufficient to raise the suggestion that he or she did not act voluntarily and with the requisite intent. Where the accused satisfies the evidentiary burden, however, the ultimate burden of proving beyond reasonable doubt that the accused's acts were voluntary, and that the accused possessed the intent required to constitute the crime charged, will rest on the prosecution.
2. The fact that the accused would not have committed the acts which constitute the crime charged but for the disinhibiting effects of the alcohol or other drugs is not a relevant consideration for the jury, because this kind of effect does not go to the issue of whether the accused was not aware of the nature of the physical acts he or she was performing, or was prevented from forming the mens rea. This is so both where the drugs were voluntarily taken and where they were consumed unwittingly; for example, where the accused underestimated the effects of a particular drug or alcohol.
3. It continues to be the law in Australia that a person who, at a particular point in time, forms the intent to commit a crime, then takes drink or drugs in order to acquire what is sometimes termed 'Dutch courage' and commits the crime cannot avail himself or herself of any argument based on intoxication, whatever the state of that person's mind at the time of the commission of the crime. In *Attorney-General for Northern Ireland v Gallagher* [1963] AC 349 Lord Denning stated (at 382):

   > My Lords, I think the law on this point should take a clear stand. If a man, whilst sane and sober, forms an intention to kill and makes preparation for it knowing it is a wrong thing to do, and then gets himself drunk so as to

> give himself Dutch courage to do the killing, and whilst drunk carries out his intention, he cannot rely on this self-induced drunkenness as a defence to a charge of murder, nor even as reducing it to manslaughter. He cannot say he got himself into such a stupid state that he was incapable of an intent to kill. So also, when he is a psychopath, he cannot by drinking rely on his self-induced defect of reason as a defence of insanity. The wickedness of his mind before he got drunk is enough to condemn him, coupled with the act which he intended to do and did so.

The principle of *Gallagher's* case was expressly approved by the High Court in *R v O'Connor*.

4. Both *R v O'Connor* and *Director of Public Prosecutions v Majewski* were assault cases. It was, therefore, possible to argue that *R v O'Connor* did not directly affect the principle that self-induced intoxication could be used to cast doubt on whether the prosecution had proved the offence of murder but not the offence of manslaughter. In *R v Martin* (1984) 58 ALJR 217, the High Court rejected such an argument, holding that the decision in *R v O'Connor* applied in relation to homicide cases. In *R v Martin*, the accused and another man were charged with murder and convicted of manslaughter. They had been involved in a fight in the course of which a man had been fatally stabbed. At the time, the three men were considerably affected by liquor. The Court of Criminal Appeal of South Australia allowed an appeal by the accused on the ground that the jury had not been adequately directed with respect to the mental state necessary for manslaughter, and the possible effect of intoxication upon that mental state. The Crown appealed, arguing that *R v O'Connor* does not require the Crown to prove any mental state in order to establish manslaughter when, by reason of the intoxication of the accused, it fails to prove an intention to kill or do grievous bodily harm and consequently fails to prove murder.

   In a joint judgment, the court, comprising Gibbs CJ, Murphy, Brennan, Deane and Dawson JJ, rejected the Crown argument. The court stated (at 218):

   > The decision in *O'Connor's* case, however, establishes clearly that evidence of intoxication may be relevant whenever it is necessary to prove the mental element of a crime. And there can be no doubt that the Crown is required to prove in manslaughter, no less than in other crimes, that the actions of the accused upon which it relies were at least voluntary, since manslaughter is not only the unlawful, but also the voluntary, killing of another with out malice.

5. In cases of homicide, as in other cases, intoxication having the effect of rendering the accused's conduct involuntary will, prima facie, mean that the prosecution cannot prove the actus reus and result in a complete acquittal. This is so whether the alcohol or drugs were consumed voluntarily or unwittingly by the accused. Thus *R v Lipman* does not represent the

common law in Australia (and manslaughter is not included in the table listing offences of specific intent in the Crimes Act 1900 (NSW)).

6. In some cases, however, the prosecution may be able to obtain a conviction of manslaughter by arguing that the act of consuming the drugs was, of itself, an act involving a sufficient degree of negligence to render the accused responsible for the resulting death. This may be so in cases where the accused takes a drug which commonly causes violent conduct on the part of the taker. It will be so where the accused knows from prior experience that the particular drug produces violent conduct on his or her part. It is submitted that, on this basis, the result in *R v Lipman*, though not the reasons given by the Court of Appeal in upholding the conviction, may be justified. For two people to take a hallucinogenic drug together, without the precaution of having a third person present to prevent harm being done by the parties to themselves or to each other, may, it would seem, properly be described as an act of negligence of sufficiently high a degree to justify a conviction for manslaughter.

7. The importance of a proper direction on intoxication in homicide cases is illustrated by *R v Faure* [1999] 2 VR 537. The accused shot his female companion dead and was convicted of murder. The defence was that he and the victim were playing Russian roulette after they had both been drinking. There was evidence that the blood alcohol level of the accused within four hours of the shooting was 0.154%. The accused sought a verdict of manslaughter. The prosecution case was that the Russian roulette was a fabrication, but, in the alternative, the prosecution sought a verdict of murder with a mens rea of recklessness. The trial judge did not direct the jury on the use they might make of the intoxication of the accused for the purposes of determining liability. The Court of Appeal allowed an appeal by the accused and ordered a retrial. The Court of Appeal held that the jury should have been directed that, if satisfied Russian roulette was not being played, then, in considering whether to draw an inference of intent to kill, they should consider the evidence that the man who put the revolver to the woman's head and pulled the trigger was not sober but much affected by alcohol. Similarly, the jury should have been told that, in considering whether the man who pulled the trigger in the game of Russian roulette knew that the likely consequence was death or really serious injury, they should take into account the evidence of intoxication.

8. It is a well-known adage that, in criminal law, the reasonable person is always sober. This means that, in cases of negligence liability, intoxicated mistakes are likely to be regarded as unreasonable as a matter of law. So, in cases of homicide where the accused's acts were voluntarily performed, and where the facts are that the accused would be guilty of murder but for the fact that, because of intoxication, he or she lacked the intent to cause death or

grievous bodily harm, the accused will inevitably be liable for a manslaughter conviction. This is not because there exists a specific rule to this effect but, rather, because of the ordinary operation of the rules relating to involuntary manslaughter. If the accused possessed the intent to perform an unlawful and dangerous act, he or she will clearly be liable for a manslaughter conviction by virtue of the ordinary operation of the rules relating to manslaughter by an unlawful and dangerous act. If the accused's conduct was voluntary but, because of intoxication, he or she lacked the intent to commit any unlawful act, but the facts are such that a non-intoxicated person in the accused's position performing the very acts which the accused performed would inevitably have realised the likelihood of death or grievous bodily harm, then the accused will necessarily be guilty of manslaughter by criminal negligence. This is because negligent manslaughter is an objective form of liability and, in applying the objective ordinary man test, no account is taken of intoxication brought about by the voluntary consumption of alcohol or other drugs.

9. The arguments put above in respect of manslaughter by criminal negligence obviously apply equally to the negligent infliction of harm not resulting in death. In cases of serious assault, where the accused's acts were performed voluntarily the accused will, in Victoria and New South Wales, inevitably be guilty of the statutory offence of negligently causing grievous bodily harm: Crimes Act 1958 (Vic) s 24; Crimes Act 1900 (NSW) s 54.

INVOLUNTARY INTOXICATION

15.25 The law is different so far as involuntary or non-voluntary intoxication is concerned. Involuntary or non-voluntary intoxication is defined narrowly to encompass circumstances in which the accused is tricked or forced into consuming alcohol or other drugs. Consuming a seemingly non-alcoholic drink that has been laced with alcohol will be considered involuntary intoxication (*R v Allen* [1988] Crim LR 698), but underestimating the effect of alcoholic substances will not (*R v Eatch* [1980] Crim LR 650). Under the *Director of Public Prosecutions v Majewski* approach to intoxicated offending, evidence of involuntary intoxication may be adduced in relation to both 'specific intent' and 'basic intent' offences. Similarly, in *R v O'Connor*, Barwick CJ suggested that the principles to be applied are the same in cases of both voluntary and involuntary intoxication.

15.26 The narrowness of involuntary intoxication extends further than the definition of what constitutes involuntary. Even if intoxication is involuntary, it will not assist the accused unless the intoxication negatived mens rea. If the accused acts with the mental state required to constitute the crime charged, the fact that the accused was affected by drugs involuntarily consumed so as to perform acts he or she would not otherwise have performed would seem a matter to be taken account of in sentencing rather than to give rise to a complete defence. As Lane LJ stated in *R v Sheehan*; *R v Moore* [1975] 1 WLR 739 at 744, a 'drunken intent is nevertheless an intent'. See also *R v Bree* [2008] QB 131.

15.27 The precise way in which involuntary intoxication affects liability has been thoroughly explained by the House of Lords in *R v Kingston* [1994] 3 All ER 353. The accused, who had paedophiliac homosexual tendencies, was blackmailed by former business associates who arranged for another man, P, who had similar paedophiliac tendencies, to photograph and audiotape the accused in a compromising situation with a boy. P lured a boy to his flat, where he gave him what seemed an innocuous drink and some cannabis. The boy fell asleep on the bed and, while he was unconscious, P invited the accused to abuse the boy sexually. The accused did so, and was photographed and taped doing it. The accused and P were charged with indecent assault, and the accused raised evidence that P had laced his drink. The trial judge directed the jury that they should acquit the accused if they found that, because he was so affected by drugs, he did not intend or may not have intended to commit an indecent assault on the boy, but that if they were sure that, despite the effect of any drugs, he still intended to commit an indecent assault the case was proved because a drugged intent was still an intent. The accused was convicted and appealed successfully to the Court of Appeal.

The prosecution appealed to the House of Lords where the appeal was allowed and the accused's conviction restored. The Law Lords affirmed the trial judge's direction that Kingston could be acquitted only if his involuntary intoxication meant that he did not or might not have formed the intention to assault the boy. Their Lordships held that involuntary intoxication or disinhibition is of no assistance in defending a criminal charge if it is proved that the accused had the necessary intent when the necessary act was done by her or him, notwithstanding that the intent arose out of circumstances for which the accused was not to blame. If Kingston had formed the requisite mens rea, which the jury found he had, the fact that his behaviour was affected by a drug administered without his knowledge was no defence. Their Lordships also stated that a loss of self-control through the acts of a third party does not, in general, assist an accused, although it might be a matter for mitigation of the penalty imposed after conviction of the offence.

15.28 A different approach is adopted in the Criminal Code Act 1995 (Cth). A distinction is drawn between self-induced intoxication and intoxication which is not self-induced. Section 8.1 provides:

> For the purposes of this Division, intoxication is self-induced unless it came about:
>
> (a) involuntarily; or
> (b) as a result of fraud, sudden or extraordinary emergency, accident, reasonable mistake, duress or force.

In the case of crimes of negligence, s 8.3(2) provides that, if intoxication is not self-induced, regard must be had to the standard of a reasonable person intoxicated to the same extent as the person concerned.

Likewise, in the case of defences an element of which depends on whether a reasonable belief exists, s 8.4(3) provides if a person's intoxication is not self-induced, regard must be had to the standard of a reasonable person intoxicated to the same extent as the person concerned.

Section 8.5 provides:

> A person is not criminally responsible for an offence if the person's conduct constituting the offence was as a result of intoxication that was not self-induced.

The New South Wales legislation, below, likewise distinguishes between self-induced intoxication and intoxication which is not self-induced. The Victorian provisions (which apply only to 'relevant offences') also distinguish between these two types of intoxication.

STATUTORY PROVISIONS — NEW SOUTH WALES AND VICTORIA

15.29 In each jurisdiction the defence of intoxication has been placed on a statutory footing. The New South Wales provisions follow the *Majewski* approach, while the Victorian statute substantially reproduces the common law.

15.30 Section 428C of the Crimes Act 1900 (NSW) provides that self-induced intoxication may be a defence in the case of offences of specific intent. That section states:

> **428C Intoxication in relation to offences of specific intent**
>
> (1) Evidence that a person was intoxicated (whether by reason of self-induced intoxication or otherwise) at the time of the relevant conduct may be taken into account in determining whether the person had the intention to cause the specific result necessary for an offence of specific intent.
>
> (2) However, such evidence cannot be taken into account if the person:
>
> (a) had resolved before becoming intoxicated to do the relevant conduct, or
>
> (b) became intoxicated in order to strengthen his or her resolve to do the relevant conduct.

Section 428B lists numerous offences as offences of specific intent, and a further set of offences as offences of specific intent to the extent that an element of the offence requires a person to intend to cause the specific result necessary for the offence. Crimes listed as offences of specific intent include murder, acts done with intent to murder, attempts to murder, various forms of aggravated assault, abduction and kidnapping, various offences against property including burglary, false pretences and perjury and other offences against the administration of justice. In *R v Grant* (2002) 55 NSWLR 80, the Court of Criminal Appeal held that murder in all forms, including cases of murder by recklessness and of felony-murder, is to be regarded as a crime of specific intent.

Self-induced intoxication may not assist the accused in casting doubt on the prosecution case in the case of crimes other than those of specific intent, although intoxication that was not self-induced may be adduced as evidence. Section 428D provides:

428D Intoxication in relation to other offences

In determining whether a person had the mens rea for an offence other than an offence of specific intent, evidence that a person was intoxicated at the time of the relevant conduct:

(a) if the intoxication was self-induced cannot be taken into account, or
(b) if the intoxication was not self-induced may be taken into account.

Section 428E deals specifically with the situation in respect of murder and manslaughter, and provides:

428E Intoxication in relation to murder and manslaughter

If evidence of intoxication at the time of the relevant conduct results in a person being acquitted of murder:

(a) in the case of intoxication that was self-induced — evidence of that intoxication cannot be taken into account in determining whether the person had the requisite mens rea for manslaughter, or
(b) in the case of intoxication that was not self-induced — evidence of that intoxication may be taken into account in determining whether the person had the requisite mens rea for manslaughter.

Section 428F provides:

428F Intoxication in relation to the reasonable person test

If, for the purposes of determining whether a person is guilty of an offence, it is necessary to compare the state of mind of the person with that of a reasonable person, the comparison is to be made between the conduct or state of mind of the person and that of a reasonable person who is not intoxicated.

Section 428G provides:

428G Intoxication and the actus reus of an offence

(1) In determining whether a person has committed an offence, evidence of self-induced intoxication cannot be taken into account in determining whether the relevant conduct was voluntary.
(2) However, a person is not criminally responsible for an offence if the relevant conduct resulted from intoxication that was not self-induced.

15.31 Sections 9AB and 9AJ of the Crimes Act 1958 (Vic) are limited in application to homicide, and would appear to restate the common law. In relation to non-homicidal offences, the common law as stated in *O'Connor* continues to apply. Those sections provide:

9AB Definitions and application of Subdivision

(1) In this Subdivision —
intoxication means intoxication because of the influence of alcohol, a drug or any other substance;
relevant offence means murder, manslaughter or defensive homicide.

(2) With out taking away from the law relating to any other offences and except as otherwise expressly provided by this Subdivision, this Subdivision applies only to relevant offences.

9AJ Intoxication

(1) If any part of an element of a relevant offence, or of a defence to a relevant offence, relies on reasonable belief, in determining whether that reasonable belief existed, regard must be had to the standard of a reasonable person who is not intoxicated.

(2) If any part of an element of a relevant offence, or of a defence to a relevant offence, relies on a person having reasonable grounds for a belief, in determining whether those reasonable grounds existed, regard must be had to the standard of a reasonable person who is not intoxicated.

(3) If any part of an element of a relevant offence, or of a defence to a relevant offence, relies on reasonable response, in determining whether that response was reasonable, regard must be had to the standard of a reasonable person who is not intoxicated.

(4) If a person's intoxication is not self-induced, in determining whether any part of an element of a relevant offence, or of a defence to a relevant offence, relying on reasonable belief, having reasonable grounds for a belief or reasonable response exists, regard must be had to the standard of a reasonable person intoxicated to the same extent as the person concerned.

(5) For the purposes of this section, intoxication is self-induced unless it came about —

(a) involuntarily; or

(b) because of fraud, sudden or extraordinary emergency, accident, reasonable mistake, duress or force; or

(c) from the use of a drug for which a prescription is required and that was used in accordance with the directions of the person who prescribed it; or

(d) from the use of a drug for which no prescription is required and that was used for a purpose, and in accordance with the dosage level, recommended by the manufacturer.

(6) Despite subsection (5), intoxication is self-induced in the circumstances, referred to in subsection (5)(c) or (d) if the person using the drug knew, or had reason to believe, when the person took the drug that the drug would significantly impair the person's judgment or control.

THE FUTURE OF THE LAW ON INTOXICATED OFFENDING

15.32 Does the common law, as outlined in *O'Connor*, constitute a satisfactory state of affairs? Does the problem of intoxicated offending require substantial modification of the general principles of criminal liability along the lines of *Majewski*? Even if modification is deemed necessary, the adoption of the *Majewski* approach in New South Wales may be thought to be an unsatisfactory method of achieving reform, being based upon a distinction that is neither logical nor founded in sound principle. If the common law is to be changed in this area, then the adoption of a specific statutory offence of, perhaps, 'criminal intoxication' or 'dangerous intoxication' might be a more satisfactory approach. In *R v O'Connor* Barwick CJ stated (at 467):

> There would be good sense, it seems to me, in a statutory provision which gave to a jury who were driven to the conclusion that an accused, due to the result of self-induced intoxication, was not culpable of the crime with which he is charged to be able to bring in an alternative verdict that he, by his own conduct, had brought himself to a state where he was not responsible for his acts. There should be a substantial penalty provided for his conviction of this alternative charge, a penalty of confinement which would include both an element of punishment and provide an opportunity for treatment for the tendency to take alcohol or drugs. It would, it seems to me, be quite just to make the accused responsible for his act of having taken alcohol or other drugs to the point I have described.

Mason, Murphy and Aickin JJ each also referred to the possibility of such legislation without, however, indicating their view as to whether it should be enacted.

15.33 The model clearly present in the mind of Barwick CJ, and the others comprising the majority, was provided by the recommendations contained in the Report of the Butler Committee on Mentally Abnormal Offenders (1975), Cmnd 6244, [18.51]–[18.59]. The Butler Committee recommended the creation of a new offence of dangerous intoxication. The committee stated that the object of such an offence would 'not necessarily' be to punish offenders, but to ensure protection for the community from those who will not consent to treatment and who cannot otherwise be controlled.

The committee summarised the operation of its proposed offence as follows:

> We propose that it should be an offence for a person while voluntarily intoxicated to do an act (or make an omission) that would amount to a dangerous offence if it were done or made with the requisite state of mind for such offence. The prosecution would not charge this offence in the first instance, but would charge an offence under the ordinary law. If evidence of intoxication were given at the trial for the purpose of negativing the intention or other mental element required for the offence, the jury would be directed that they may return a verdict of not guilty of that offence but guilty of the offence of dangerous intoxication if they find that the

> defendant did the act (or made the omission) charged but by reason of the evidence of intoxication they are not sure that at the time he had the state of mind required for the offence, and they are sure that his intoxication was voluntary.

A 'dangerous offence' was defined by the committee as 'one involving injury to the person (actual bodily harm) or death or consisting of a sexual attack on another, or involving the destruction of or causing damage to property so as to endanger life'. The committee recommended a maximum penalty of one year's imprisonment for a first offence and three years for a second or subsequent offence.

15.34 Building on the unimplemented Butler proposal, in 1993 the Law Commission for England and Wales canvassed the introduction of an offence that it called 'criminal intoxication'. This offence would have applied where an intoxicated defendant caused the harm proscribed by a number of enumerated offences (most involving personal violence or property damage). According to this offence, a person would be 'intoxicated' when he or she had taken anything that caused his or her awareness or control to be 'substantially impaired'. It would be immaterial that the defendant lacked the mens rea for the offence or was in a state of automatism at the time he or she performed the actus reus (see Law Commission for England and Wales, Intoxication and Criminal Liability (No 127, 1993)). Neither of these reform proposals have been incorporated into legislation in England and Wales.

15.35 Should such an offence be enacted in Victoria? In 1999, the Law Reform Committee of the Victorian Parliament recommended that the law of criminal liability for self-induced intoxication in Victoria continue to be governed by the principles laid down in *O'Connor* (Victorian Law Reform Commission, *Criminal Liability for Self-induced Intoxication*, May 1999), and that view has been adopted.

15.36 It must be noted that intoxication may result in a complete acquittal only in extremely rare cases. For intoxication to assist an accused in casting doubt on whether the prosecution has proved the elements of the offence, he or she has to be very intoxicated indeed. It is true also that, in these cases, the accused cannot be said to have acted wrongfully in any sense other than (perhaps) becoming intoxicated in the first instance. Nonetheless, community protection and community expectations remain a consideration which must be taken into account. A person who voluntarily consumes alcohol or other drugs and commits 'an offence' shows herself or himself to be a danger to the community at large. The way in which the criminal law accommodates these potentially competing demands — via the *O'Connor* approach as in Victoria or via the *Majewski* approach as in New South Wales — continues to provoke debate and controversy.

15.37 Further reading

M Goode, 'Some Thoughts on the Present State of the 'Defence' of Intoxication' (1984) 8 *Crim LJ* 104

J Horder, 'Sobering Up? The Law Commission on Criminal Intoxication' (1995) 58(4) *Modern Law Review* 534–46

Law Commission for England and Wales, 'Legislating the Criminal Code: Intoxication and Criminal Liability', London (1995)

I Leader-Elliott, 'Voluntariness, Intoxication and Fault' (1991) 15 *CLJ* 112

P Robinson 'Imputed Criminal Liability' (1984) 93(4) *Yale Law Journal* 609–76

A P Simester 'Intoxication is Never a Defence' [2009] *Criminal Law Review* 3–14

J Tolmie, 'Alcoholism and Criminal Liability' (2001) 64(5) *Modern Law Review* 688–709

Victorian Law Reform Commission, Report No 6, *Criminal Responsibility: Intention and Gross Intoxication* (1986)

Bibliography

A

American Law Institute, *Model Penal Code* (1962)

American Psychiatric Association, *Diagnostic and Statistical Manual of Mental Disorders*, 4th ed, American Psychiatric Publishing, Arlington, 2000 [DSM 4]

T Anthony, *Indigenous People, Crime and Punishment*, Routledge, Abdingdon, 2013

K Arenson, '*The Queen v Getachew*: Rethinking *DPP v Morgan*' (2013) 77 *JCL* 151

A Ashworth, 'The Fourteenth Report of the Criminal Law Revision Committee: (4) Intoxication and General Defences' [1980] *Crim LR* 556

Andrew Ashworth, *Principles of Criminal Law*, 6th ed, Oxford University Press, United Kingdom, 2009

H Askola, 'Cut-off Point: Regulating Male Circumcision in Finland' (2011) 25(1) *Int J Law Policy Family* 100

J Austin, *The Province of Jurisprudence Determined*, Weidenfeld and Nicolson, London, 1954 (first published 1832)

Australian Institute of Health and Welfare, *Australian Young People — Their Health and Wellbeing 1999*, report prepared by L Moon, P Meyer, J Grau, Canberra, 1999

Australian Institute of Health and Welfare, *National Drug Strategy Household Survey Report*, 2010

—, *Statistics on Drug Use in Australia 2006*, Canberra, April 2007

Australian Law Reform Commission, Report No 7, *Human Tissue Transplants* (1977)

—, Report No 114, *Family Violence — A National Legal Response* (2010)

B

V Bailey and S Blackburn, 'The Punishment of Incest Act 1908: A Case Study of Law Creation' [1979] *Crim LR* 708

J Bentham, *An Introduction to the Principles of Morals and Legislation*, J H Burns and H L A Hart (eds), Athlone Press, London, 1970 (first published 1789)

H Biggs, 'Euthanasia and Death with Dignity: Still Poised on the Fulcrum of Homicide' [1996] *Crim LR* 878

W Blackstone, *Commentaries on the Laws of England*, Clarendon Press, Oxford, 1768

P Brett, 'Strict Responsibility: Possible Solutions' (1974) 37 *Mod LR* 417

A W Brian Simpson, *Cannibalism and the Common Law*, Penguin Books, Harmondsworth, 1986

S Bronitt, 'Criminal Liability for the Transmission of HIV/AIDS' (1992) 16 *Crim LJ* 85

—, 'The Right to Sexual Privacy, Sado-Masochism and the Human Rights (Sexual Conduct) Act 1994 (Cth)' (1995) 2 *AJHR* 59

Butler Committee on Mentally Abnormal Offenders, *Report of the Committee on Mentally Abnormal Offenders*, (1975) Cmnd 6244 (Butler Report)

C

E M Campbell, 'Reliance on Official Representations and Criminal Liability' (1994) 1 *Canb LR* 15

T Carney, *Drug Users and the Law in Australia*, Law Book Co, Sydney, 1987

J Clough and C Mulhern, *The Prosecution of Corporations*, Oxford University Press, Melbourne, 2002

M R Cohen, 'Moral Aspects of the Criminal Law' (1940) 49 *Yale LJ* 987

Sir Edward Coke CJ, *Coke's Institutes of the Lawes of England*, reprinted by Law Book Exchange, Union N J (USA), 2002 (first published 1628)

D Collins and H Lapsley, *The Costs of Tobacco, Alcohol and Illicit Drug Abuse to Australian Society in 2004/5*, National Drug Strategy Monograph Series No 66, 2009

—, Department of Human Services and Health (Cth), *The Social Costs of Drug Abuse in Australia in 1988 and 1992*, Report No 30 (February 2006)

E Colvin, 'Theory of the Intoxication Defence' (1981) 59 *Can Bar Rev* 750

Community Development Committee of the Victorian Parliament, *Inquiry Into Persons Detained at the Governor's Pleasure* (1995)

C Corns, 'Retrial of Acquitted Persons: Time for Reform of the Double Jeopardy Rule?' (2003) 27 *Crim LJ* 80

I G Coss, 'Provocative Reforms: A Comparative Critique' (2006) 30 *Crim LJ* 138

Criminal Law and Penal Methods Reform Committee of South Australia, *The Substantive Criminal Law*, Fourth Report, 1977 (the Mitchell Report)

Criminal Law Revision Committee (UK), Report 8, *Theft and Related Offences*, London, 1966 [(1966) Cmnd 2977]

—, Report 11, *Evidence (General)*, London, 1972 [(1972) Cmnd 4991]

—, Report 13, *Section 16 of the Theft Act 1968*, London, 1977 [(1977) Cmnd 6733]

—, Report 14, *Offences Against the Person*, London, 1980 [(1980) Cmnd 7844]

Ken Crispin, *The Quest for Justice*, Scribe, Victoria, 2010

P Crofts, *Wickedness and Crime*, Routledge, 2013

T Crofts, *The Criminal Responsibility of Children and Young Person: A Comparison of English and German Law*, Ashgate, United Kingdom, 2002

T Crofts and A Loughnan, 'Provocation: The Good, the Bad and the Ugly' (2013) 37 *CLJ* 23–37

R Cross, 'Necessity Knows No Law' (1968) 3 *Univ Tas LR* 1

I Cunliffe, 'Consent and Sexual Offences Law Reform in New South Wales' (1984) 8 *Crim LJ* 271

D

J Debeljak, 'Who is Sovereign Now? The *Momcilovic* Court Hands Back Power Over Human Rights that Parliament Intended It to Have' (2011) 22 *PLR* 15

S De Pasquale, 'Provocation and the Homosexual Advance Defence: The Deployment of Culture as a Defence Strategy' (2002) 26 *MULR* 110

Department of Community Services and Health (Cth), *Alcohol in Australia — A Summary of Related Statistics*, 4th ed, Canberra, 1988

Department of Health (Vic), *The Victorian Drug Statistics Handbook: Patterns of Drug Use and Related Harm in Victoria for the Period July 2009 to June 2010*, Report No 13 (2012)

Department of Health and Ageing (Cth), *Trends in Estimated Alcohol-Attributable Deaths and Hospitalisations in Australia*, National Alcohol Indicators Project (2009)

R Descartes, *Les Passions De L'âme* (*The Passions of the Soul*), J Martin and J Ridley, London, 1650

M J Detmold, 'Provocation to Murder: Sovereignty and Multiculture' (1997) 18 *Syd LR* 5

Lord Devlin, *The Enforcement of Morals*, Oxford University Press, London, 1965

J Dine, 'Company Controllers, Company Cheques and Theft: Another View' [1984] *Crim LR* 397

O Dixon, 'A Legacy of Hadfield, McNaughton and Maclean' (1957) 31 *ALJ* 255

R C Doeger, 'Strict Liability in Criminal Law, and *Larsonneur* Reassessed' [1998] *Crim LR* 791

Drug Policy Expert Committee, *Heroin: Facing the Issues*, Melbourne, February 2000

R A Duff, *Answering for Crime: Responsibility and Liability in the Criminal Law*, Hart Publishing, Oxford, 2007

—, *Trials and Punishments*, Cambridge University Press, New York, 1986

E

Sir Edward Hyde East, *A Treatise of the Pleas of the Crown*, J Butterworth and J Cooke, London, 1803

G Edwards, J Strang and J Jaffe (eds), *Drugs, Alcohol and Tobacco: Making the Science and Policy Connections*, Oxford University Press, Oxford, 1993

J Ellard, 'Some Notes on Non-insane Automatism and the Will' (1995) 69 *ALJ* 833

D W Elliott, 'Necessity, Duress and Self-Defence' [1989] *Crim LR* 611

M Ewing and R H Fullagar, 'The Lore and Law of Tissue Homotransplantation' 10 *Proc Med-Leg Soc Vic* 161

F

P A Fairall, 'Imprisonment Without Conviction in New South Wales: *Kable v Director of Public Prosecutions*' (1995) 17 *Syd LR* 573

J Faulkner, 'Mens Rea in Rape: Morgan and the Inadequacy of Subjectivism' (1991) 18 *MULR* 60

R Fileborn, 'Sexual Assault Laws in Australia', *Australian Centre for the Study of Sexual Assault Resource Sheet*, February 2011

J Finnis, 'Bland: Crossing the Rubicon?' (1993) 109 *LQR* 329

G Fletcher, *Rethinking Criminal Law*, Little, Brown and Co, Boston, 1978

Sir Michael Foster, *Crown Cases and Discourse on A Few Branches of the Crown Law*, 3rd ed, M Dodson (ed), 1792 (reprinted 1809)

R Fox, 'The Killings of Bobby Veen: The High Court on Proportion in Sentencing' (1988) 12 *Crim LJ* 339

R Fox and A Freiberg, *Sentencing: State and Federal Law in Victoria*, 2nd ed, Oxford University Press, Melbourne, 1999

R Fox and I Mathews, *Drugs Policy Fact, Fiction and the Future*, Federation Press, Sydney, 1992

R G Fox, *Victorian Criminal Procedure: State and Federal Law*, 12th ed, Monash Law Book Co-operative, Melbourne, 2005

I Freckelton, 'Contemporary Comment: When Plight Makes Right — The Forensic Abuse Syndrome' (1994) 18 *Crim LJ* 29

—, 'Masochism, Self-mutilation and the Limits of Consent' (1994) 2 *JLM* 48

—, 'Withdrawal of Life Support: The Persistent Vegetative State Conundrum' (1993) 1(1) *JLM* 35

L Fuller, 'The Case of the Speluncean Explorers' (1949) 62 *Harv LR* 616

G

H Gamble, 'Manslaughter by Neglect' (1977) 1 *Crim LJ* 247

E Geraghty, 'What Price Uncertainty? The Persistent Vegetative State in New South Wales' (2002) 2 *Macquarie LJ* 185

M Goode, 'Some Thoughts on the Present State of the "Defence" of Intoxication' (1984) 8 *Crim LJ* 104.

—, 'The Mental Element of Rape, the Naffin Report and Other Questions: A Defence of the Common Law' (1985) 9 *Crim LJ* 17

—, 'The Politics of Child Sexual Abuse and the Role of the Criminal Law' (1989) 13 *Crim LJ* 31

F Goodyear-Smith, 'Re Battered Woman's Syndrome [1997] *NZLJ* 436–8; [1998] *NZLJ* 39

S Gray and J Blokland, *Criminal Laws Northern Territory*, Federation Press, Sydney, 2012

E Griew, *The Theft Acts*, Sweet & Maxwell, London, 1995

A Grubb, 'The New Law of Abortion' [1991] *Crim LR* 659

H

L Haberfield, 'The Law and Male Circumcision in Australia: Medical, Legal and Cultural Issues' (1997) 23(1) *Mon LR* 92

Sir Mathew Hale, *Pleas of the Crown*, Sollom Emlyn (ed), reprinted by Law Book Exchange, Union N J (USA) 2003 (first published 1736)

J Hall, *General Principles of Criminal Law*, 2nd ed, Bobbs-Merrill Co, Indianapolis, 1960

—, *Theft, Law and Society*, 2nd ed, Bobbs-Merrill Co, Indianapolis, 1952

J I Clark Hare, *American Constitutional Law*, Little, Brown & Co, Boston, 1889

H L A Hart, *Law, Liberty and Morality*, Oxford University Press, London, 1963

—, *Punishment and Responsibility*, Oxford University Press, 1968

W Hawkins, *A Treatise of the Pleas of the Crown*, printed by E Nutt for J Walthoe, London, 1716–1721

J D Heydon, *Cross on Evidence*, 9th Aust ed, LexisNexis Butterworths, Sydney, 2013
T Hobbes, *Leviathan*, A Crooke, London, 1651
Oliver Wendell Holmes Jr, *The Common Law*, Belknap Press, Harvard, 2009 (first published 1881)
A Hopkins, H Easson and J Harrison, 'The Legal Response to Work-related Fatalities in NSW in 1984' (1992) *Aust and NZ Journal of Criminology* 135
A Houlihan, 'When "No" Means "Yes" and "Yes" Means Harm: HIV Risk, Consent and Sadomasochism Case Law' (2011) 20 *Law and Sexuality* 31
C Howard, *Criminal Law*, 4th ed, Law Book Co, Sydney, 1982
—, *Strict Responsibility*, Sweet & Maxwell, London, 1963
—, 'Strict Responsibility in the High Court of Australia' (1960) 76 *LQR* 567
G Hubble, 'Rape by Innocent Agent' (1997) 21 *Crim LJ* 204

J

J Joudo Larsen, *Responding to Substance Abuse and Offending in Indigenous Communities: Review of Diversion Programs*, Australian Institute of Criminology, Canberra, 2008
J Joudo Larsen et al, *Trafficking in Persons Monitoring Report: January 2009–June 2011*, Australian Institute of Criminology, Canberra, June 2012

K

D Kell, 'Social Disutility and the Law of Consent' (1994) 14 *OJLS* 121
C S Kenny, *Outlines of Criminal Law*, 15th ed, Cambridge: At the University Press, Cambridge, 1936
J Keown, 'The Scope of the Offence of Child Destruction' (1988) 104 *LQR* 120

L

N Lacey, 'Responsibility and Modernity in Criminal Law' (2001) 9(3) *J Polit Philos* 249
D Lanham, 'Accomplices and Withdrawal' (1981) 97 *LQR* 575
—, '*Larsonneur* Revisited' [1976] *Crim LR* 276
—, 'Obtaining a Financial Advantage by Deception in Victoria — The Meaning of Financial Advantage' (1977) 1 *Crim LJ* 188
—, 'Three Cases of Accessorial Absurdity?' (1990) 53 *MLR* 75
W Larcombe, '*Worsnop v The Queen*: Subjective Belief in Consent Prevails (Again) in Victoria's Rape Law (2011) 35 *MULR* 697
Law Commission for England and Wales, *Murder, Manslaughter and Infanticide*, 2006
I Leader-Elliott, 'Battered but not Beaten: Women Who Kill in Self Defence' (1993) 15 *Syd LR* 403
—, 'Prohibitions Against Heroin Use: Can They Be Justified?' (1986) 19 *Aust and NZ Journal of Criminology* 225
—, 'Sex, Race and Provocation: In Defence of *Stingel*' (1996) 20 *Crim LJ* 72
—, 'Voluntariness, Intoxication and Fault' (1991) 15 *CLJ* 112
L H Leigh, 'Some Remarks on Appropriation in the Law of Theft after *Morris*' (1985) 48 *Mod LR* 167

J E Lessenger and G F Roper (eds), *Drugs Court: A New Approach to Treatment and Rehabilitation*, Springer, 2007

A Loughnan, *Manifest Madness: Mental Incapacity in Criminal Law*, Oxford University Press, Oxford, 2012

M

R D Mackay, 'Fact and Fiction about the Insanity Defence' [1990] *Crim LR* 247

T Makkai and J Payne, *Drugs and Crime: A Study of Incarcerated Male Offenders*, Australian Institute of Criminology, Canberra, 2003

S Martin, 'Obtaining Bank Credits and Debits by Deception' (1992) 16 *Crim LJ* 77

I McKay, 'The Sleepwalker is Not Insane' (1992) 55 *MLR* 714

B McSherry, 'Defining What is a "Disease of the Mind": The Untenability of Current Legal Interpretations' (1993) 1 *JLM* 76

—, 'Mental Impairment and Criminal Responsibility: Recent Australian Legislative Reforms' (1999) 23 *CLJ* 135

—, 'Revising the *M'Naghten* Rules' (1990) 64 *LIJ* 725

—, 'The Return of the Raging Hormones Theory: Premenstrual Syndrome, Postpartum Disorders and Criminal Responsibility' (1993) 15 *Syd LR* 292

B McSherry and B Naylor, *Australian Criminal Laws: Critical Perspectives*, Oxford University Press, Melbourne, 2004

D Mendelson and M Ashby, 'The Medical Provision of Hydration and Nutrition: Two Very Different Outcomes in Victoria and Florida' (2004) 11(3) *JLM* 282

John Stuart Mill, *On Liberty*, reprinted by Penguin Books, Baltimore, 1974 (first published 1869)

—, *Utilitarianism, Liberty and Representative Government*, Everyman's Library, J M Dent and Sons, London, 1910 (reprinted 1962)

Model Criminal Code Officers' Committee, *Issue Estoppel, Double Jeopardy and Prosecution Appeals Against Acquittals* (November 2003)

Model Criminal Code Officers' Committee (then the Criminal Law Officers' Committee), *Model Criminal Code — Chapters 1 and 2 — General Principles of Criminal Responsibility, Report* (December 1992)

J Morgan, 'Provocation Law and Facts: Dead Women Tell No Tales, Tales Are Told About Them' (1997) 21 *MULR* 237

—, 'Rape in Medical Treatment: The Patient as Victim' (1991) 18 *MULR* 403

G O W Mueller, 'How To Increase Traffic Fatalities' (1960) 60 *Colum L Rev* 944

N

N Naffine, 'Possession: Erotic Love in the Law of Rape' (1994) 57 *Mod LR* 10

G Nash and M Bagaric, *Bourke's Criminal Law Victoria* (looseleaf), LexisNexis, Australia

B Naylor and B Saunders, 'Parental Discipline, Criminal Laws and Responsive Regulation' in M Freeman (ed), *Law and Childhood Studies: Current Legal Issues*, Vol 14, Oxford University Press, 2012

New South Wales Bureau of Crime Statistics and Research, *Illicit Drug Use and Property Offending Among Police Detainees* (2012)

A Norrie, *Crime, Reason and History: A Critical Introduction to Criminal Law*, 2nd ed, Cambridge University Press, 2001

NSWLRC, *People with Cognitive and Mental Health Impairments in the Criminal Justice System: Criminal Responsibility and Consequences*, Consultation Paper 6, 2010

—, *Young People and Consent to Health Care* (2008), Report No 119

New South Wales Parliamentary Select Committee on the Partial Defence of Provocation, *The Partial Defence of Provocation*, Final Report, 2013

O

K Oates, 'The Effects of Child Sexual Abuse' (1992) 66 *ALJ* 186

K O'Donovan, 'Law's Knowledge: The Judge, the Expert, the Battered Woman and Her Syndrome' (1993) 29 *Jo of Law and Society* 427

D Ormerod and D Williams (eds), *Smith's Law of Theft*, 9th ed, Oxford University Press, 2007

P

Parliamentary Joint Committee on the National Crime Authority, *Drugs Crime and Society*, Australian Government Publishing Service, Canberra, 1989

M Pathe, R Mackenzie and P Mullen, 'Stalking by Law: Damaging Victims and Rewarding Offenders' (2004) 12 *JLM* 103

J Payne, S Macgregor and H McDonald, *Prevalence and Issues Relating to Cannabis Use Among Prison Inmates: Key Findings from Australian Research Since 2001*, National Cannabis Prevention and Information Centre, Australia (2013)

R Perkins, *Cases and Materials on Criminal Law and Procedure*, The Foundation Press Inc, Brooklyn, 1952

F Pollock and R S Wright, *An Essay on Possession in the Common Law*, Clarendon Press, Oxford, 1888

Q

T Quigley, 'Reform of the Intoxication Defence' (1987) 33 *McGill LJ* 1

R

L Radzinowicz and J W C Turner, 'The Mental Element in Crimes at Common Law' in *The Modern Approach to Criminal Law*, Macmillan and Co, London, 1945

F Rinaldi, *Drug Offences in Australia: Sentencing*, Law Book Co, Sydney, 1986

F Rinaldi and P Gillies, *Narcotic Offences*, Law Book Co, Sydney, 1991

L Roth and L Blayden, *Provocation and Self-defence in Intimate Partner and Sexual Advance Homicides*, Briefing Paper 5/2012, New South Wales Parliamentary Research Service, 2012

A Rothschild, '*Gardner; Re BWV*: Resolved and Unresolved Issues at End of Life' (2004) 11 *JLM* 292

Royal Commission on Capital Punishment 1949–1953, Report, London [(1953) Cmnd 8932]

D Ruschena, 'Determining Dangerousness: Whatever Happened to the Rules of Evidence' (2003) 10 *Psychiat Psychol Law* 122

Lord Russell of Liverpool, *The Trial of Adolf Eichmann*, Heinemann, London, 1962

G Ryle, *The Concept of Mind*, Hutchinson's University Library, London, 1949

S

F B Sayre, 'Public Welfare Offences' (1933) 33 *Colum L Rev* 55

A Simester, 'The Mental Element in Complicity' (2006) 122 *LQR* 578

P Skegg, 'A Justification for Medical Procedures Performed Without Consent' (1974) 90 *LQR* 512

—, 'Irreversible Comatose Individuals: "Alive" or "Dead"?' [1974] *Camb LJ* 130

D Smith, 'Reckless Rape in Victoria' (2008) 32 *MULR* 1007

J C Smith, 'Obtaining Cheques by Deception or Theft' [1997] *Crim LR* 396

—, 'Proving Conspiracy' [1996] *Crim LR* 386

—, '*R v Larsonneur*' [1999] *Crim LR* 100

—, *The Law of Theft*, 8th ed, Butterworths, London, 1997

K J M Smith, 'Must Heroes Behave Heroically?' [1989] *Crim LR* 622

Social Development Committee of the Victorian Parliament, Final Report, *Inquiry into Mental Disturbance and Community Safety* (1992)

J R Spencer, 'The Metamorphosis of Section 6 of the Theft Act' [1977] *Crim LR* 653

A Steel, 'Taking Possession: The Defining Element of Theft?' (2008) 32 *MULR* 1030

—, 'The Harms and Wrongs of Stealing: The Harm Principle and Dishonesty in Theft' (2008) 31 *Univ of NSWLJ* 712

—, 'Problematic and Unnecessary? Issues with the Use of the Theft Offence to Protect Intangible Property (2008) *30 Sydney LR* 575

Sir James Fitzjames Stephen, *Digest of the Criminal Law*, Macmillan and Co, London, 1877

—, *The History of the Criminal Law of England*, Macmillan and Co, London, 1883

D A Stroud, *Mens Rea*, Sweet & Maxwell, London, 1914

G R Sullivan, 'Company Controllers, Company Cheques and Theft' [1983] *Crim LR* 512

T

V Tadros, *Criminal Responsibility*, Oxford University Press, 2005

Tasmania Law Reform Institute, *Non-Therapeutic Male Circumcision* (2012), Report No 17

J Temkin, *Rape and the Legal Process*, Sweet & Maxwell, London, 1987

—, 'The Limits of Reckless Rape' [1983] *Crim LR* 5

J B Thayer, *A Preliminary Treatise on the Law of Evidence*, Little, Brown & Co, Boston, 1898

D A Thomas, *Principles of Sentencing*, 2nd ed, Heinemann, London, 1979

The Drug Offensive, *Statistics on Drug Abuse in Australia 1989*, Australian Government Publishing Service, Canberra, 1990

S Tomsen and T Crofts, 'Social and Cultural Meanings of Legal Responses to Homicide Among Men: Masculine Honour, Sexual Advances and Accidents' (2012) 45(3) *Aust and NZ Journal of Criminology* 423

L Townsley and I Dobinson, 'Sexual Assault Law Reform in New South Wales: Issues of Consent and Objective Fault' (2008) 32(3) *CLJ* 152

J W C Turner (ed), *Kenny's Outlines of Criminal Law*, 18th ed, Cambridge University Press, Cambridge, 1962

D Tyson, *Sex, Culpability and the Defence of Provocation*, Routledge, Oxford, 2013

V

Victorian Law Reform Commission, *Criminal Liability for Self-induced Intoxication* (May 1999)

—, *Defences to Homicide: Final Report* (2004)

—, Final Report No 15, *Law of Abortion* (2008)

—, Report No 6, *Criminal Responsibility: Intention and Gross Intoxication* (1986)

—, Report No 34, *Mental Malfunction and Criminal Responsibility* (1990)

—, Report No 40, *Homicide* (1991)

—, Report No 43, *Rape: Reform of Law and Procedure* (1991)

—, *Sexual Offences: Law and Procedure — Final Report* (2004)

—, *The Concept of Mental Illness in the Mental Health Act 1986* (1990)

Victorian Law Reform Commissioner, Report No 3, *Criminal Liability of Married Persons* (1975)

—, Report No 9, *Duress, Necessity and Coercion* (1980)

Victorian Law Reform Commissioner, Working Paper No 8, *Murder: Mental Element and Punishment* (1984)

[Victorian] Premier's Drug Advisory Council, *Drugs and our Community: Report of the Premier's Drug Advisory Council*, Victorian Government, Melbourne, March 1996

P von Nessen, 'Company Controllers, Company Cheques and Theft — An Australian Perspective' [1986] *Crim LR* 154

W

P K Waight and C R Williams, *Evidence Commentary and Materials*, 7th ed, Law Book Co, 2002

N Walker, 'Unscientific, Unwise, Unprofitable or Unjust?' (1982) 22 *Brit J Criminol* 276

L Waller, 'Any Reasonable Creature in Being' (1987) 13 *Mon LR* 37

—, 'Intoxication and Criminal Responsibility', Fifteenth Leonard Ball Oration (May 1983)

—, 'Tracey Maund Lecture' (2002) 28 *Mon LR* 150

K Warner, 'The Mental Element and Consent Under the New "Rape" Laws' (1983) 7 *Crim LJ* 245

V Waye, 'Rape and the Unconscionable Bargain' (1992) 16 *Crim LJ* 94

D Weatherburn, *The NSW Drug Court: A Re-evaluation of its Effectiveness*, New South Wales Bureau of Crime Statistics and Research, RMIT Publishing, 2008

M Weinberg, 'Moral Blameworthiness — The "Objective Test" Dilemma' (2003) 24 *Aust Bar Rev* 173

D J West and A Walk (eds), *Daniel McNaughton: His Trial and the Aftermath*, Gaskell Books, 1977

J H Wigmore, *Treatise on the Anglo-American System of Evidence in Trials at Common Law*, 3rd ed, Little, Brown & Co, Boston, 1940

C R Williams, 'Coping with the Highly Dangerous: Issues of Principle Raised by Preventive Detention', paper presented to the Australian Institute of Criminology Conference, *Serious Violent Offenders: Sentencing, Psychiatry and Law Reform* (Melbourne, 1991).

C R Williams, 'Development and Change in Insanity and Related Defences' (2000) 24 *MULR* 711

—, 'Placing the Burden of Proof' in E Campbell and L Waller (eds), *Well and Truly Tried: Essays on Evidence in Honour of Sir Richard Eggleston*, Law Book Co, Sydney, 1982

—, *Property Offences*, 3rd ed, Law Book Co, Sydney, 1999

—, 'Psychopathy, Mental Illness and Preventive Detention: Issues Arising from the *David* Case' (1990) 16 *Mon LR* 161

—, 'Reining in the Concept of Appropriation in Theft' (2003) 29 *Mon LR* 261

E S Williams, *Australian Royal Commission of Inquiry into Drugs: Report*, Australian Government Publishing Service, Canberra, 1980

G Williams, 'Wrong Turnings in the Law of Attempt' [1991] *Crim LR* 416

G L Williams, 'Appropriation: A Single or Continuous Act?' [1978] *Crim LR* 69

—, *Criminal Law — The General Part*, 2nd ed, Stevens & Sons Ltd, London, 1961

—, 'Temporary Appropriation Should be Theft' [1981] *Crim LR* 129

—, *Textbook of Criminal Law*, 2nd ed, Stevens & Sons, London, 1983

J Willis, 'Manslaughter by the Intentional Infliction of Some Harm: A Category that Should be Closed' (1985) 9 *Crim LJ* 109

J Wilson, M Moore and I D Wheat Jr, 'The Problem of Heroin' (1972) 29 *The Public Interest* 3

D Wood, 'A One Man Dangerous Offenders Statute — The Victorian Community Protection Act 1990' (1990) 17 *MULR* 497

Y

G Yaffe, *Attempts in the Philosophy of Action and the Criminal Law*, Oxford University Press, 2010

S Yannoulidis, *Mental State Defences in Criminal Law*, Ashgate Publishing, London, 2012

S Yeo, 'Power of Self-Control in Provocation and Automatism' (1992) *14 Syd LR* 3

Index

References are to paragraph numbers

C

M

N